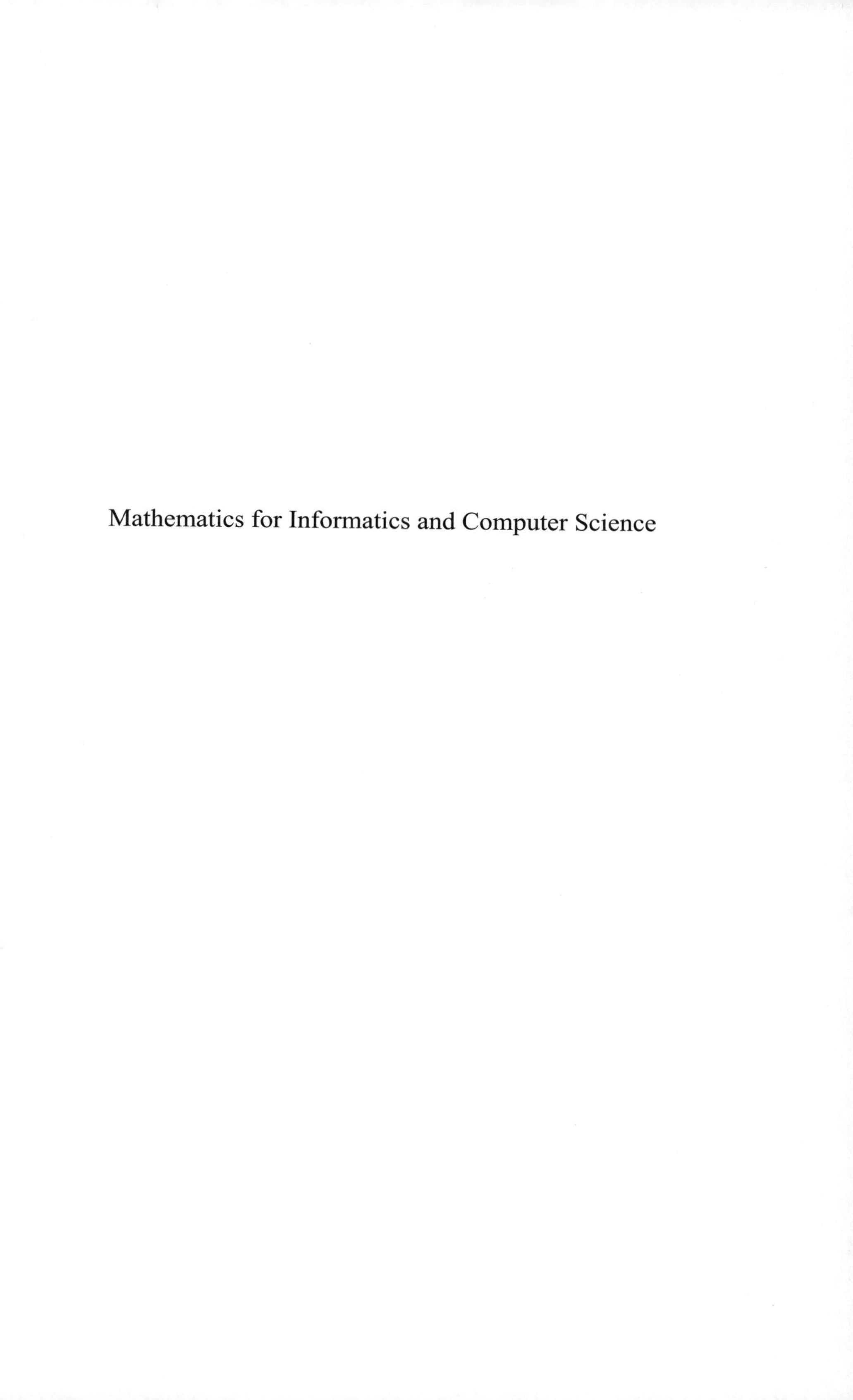

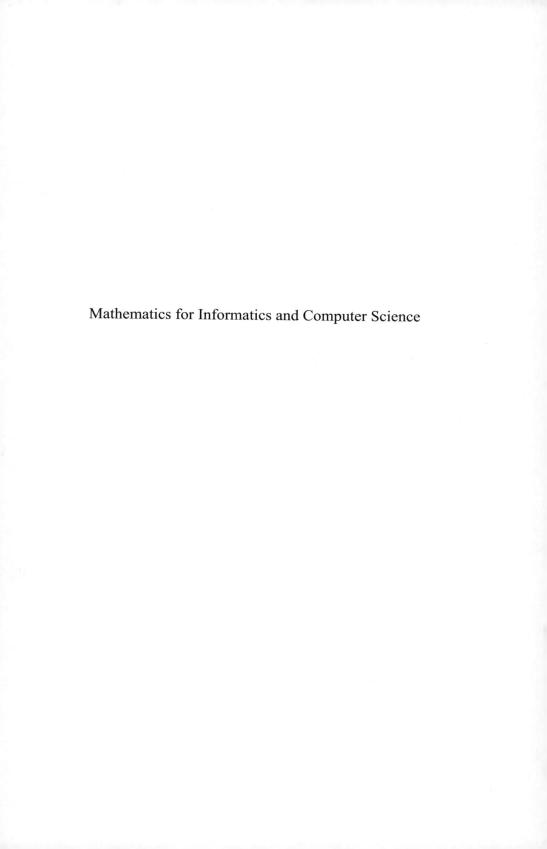

Mathematics for Informatics and Computer Science

Mathematics for Informatics and Computer Science

Pierre Audibert

First published 2010 in Great Britain and the United States by ISTE Ltd and John Wiley & Sons, Inc. Adapted and updated from three volumes *Combien ? Mathématiques appliquées à l'informatique 1, 2, 3* published 2008 in France by Hermes Science/Lavoisier © LAVOISIER 2008

ISTE Ltd
27-37 St George's Road
London SW19 4EU
UK

www.iste.co.uk

John Wiley & Sons, Inc.
111 River Street
Hoboken, NJ 07030
USA

www.wiley.com

Library of Congress Cataloging-in-Publication Data

Audibert, Pierre, 1941-
Mathematics for informatics and computer science / Pierre Audibert.
p. cm.
Includes bibliographical references and index.
ISBN 978-1-84821-196-4
1. Computer science--Mathematics. I. Title.
QA76.9.M35A83 2010
004.01'51--dc22

2010028591

British Library Cataloguing-in-Publication Data
A CIP record for this book is available from the British Library
ISBN 978-1-84821-196-4

Printed and bound in Great Britain by CPI Antony Rowe, Chippenham and Eastbourne.

Table of Contents

General Introduction xxiii

Chapter 1. Some Historical Elements 1

1.1. Yi King 1
1.2. Flavor combinations in India 2
1.3. Sand drawings in Africa 3
1.4. Galileo's problem 4
1.5. Pascal's triangle 7
1.6. The combinatorial explosion: Abu Kamil's problem, the palm grove problem and the Sudoku grid 9
1.6.1. Solution to Abu Kamil's problem 11
1.6.2. Palm Grove problem, where $N = 4$. 12
1.6.3. Complete Sudoku grids 14

PART 1. COMBINATORICS 17

Part 1. Introduction 19

Chapter 2. Arrangements and Combinations 21

2.1. The three formulae 21
2.2. Calculation of C_n^p, Pascal's triangle and binomial formula. 25
2.3. Exercises 27
2.3.1. Demonstrating formulae 27
2.3.2. Placing rooks on a chessboard 28
2.3.3. Placing pieces on a chessboard 29
2.3.4. Pascal's triangle modulo k. 30
2.3.5. Words classified based on their blocks of letters 31
2.3.6. Diagonals of a polygon 33

2.3.7. Number of times a number is present in a list of numbers 35
2.3.8. Words of length n based on 0 and 1 without any block of 1s repeated 37
2.3.9. Programming: classification of applications of a set with n elements
in itself following the form of their graph 39
2.3.10. Individuals grouped 2×2 42

Chapter 3. Enumerations in Alphabetical Order 43

3.1. Principle of enumeration of words in alphabetical order 43
3.2. Permutations 44
3.3. Writing binary numbers 46
3.3.1. Programming 46
3.3.2. Generalization to expression in some base B 46
3.4. Words in which each letter is less than or equal to the position 47
3.4.1. Number of these words 47
3.4.2. Program 47
3.5. Enumeration of combinations 47
3.6. Combinations with repetitions 49
3.7. Purchase of P objects out of N types of objects 49
3.8. Another enumeration of permutations 50
3.9. Complementary exercises 52
3.9.1. Exercise 1: words with different successive letters 52
3.9.2. Exercise 2: repeated purchases with a given sum of money 56
3.10. Return to permutations 58
3.11. Gray code 60

Chapter 4. Enumeration by Tree Structures 63

4.1. Words of length n, based on N letters 1, 2, 3, …, N, where each letter is followed by a higher or equal letter 63
4.2. Permutations enumeration 66
4.3. Derangements 67
4.4. The queens problem 69
4.5. Filling up containers 72
4.6. Stack of coins 76
4.7. Domino tiling a chessboard 79

Chapter 5. Languages, Generating Functions and Recurrences 85

5.1. The language of words based on two letters 85
5.2. Domino tiling a 2×n chessboard 88
5.3. Generating function associated with a sequence 89

5.4. Rational generating function and linear recurrence 91
5.5. Example: routes in a square grid with rising shapes without entanglement. 92
5.6. Exercises on recurrences 94
5.6.1. Three types of purchases each day with a sum of *N* dollars 94
5.6.2. Word building 96
5.7. Examples of languages 98
5.7.1. Language of parts of an element set $\{a, b, c, d, \ldots\}$ 98
5.7.2. Language of parts of a multi-set based on n elements *a*, *b*, *c*, etc., where these elements can be repeated as much as we want 99
5.7.3. Language of words made from arrangements taken from *n* distinct and non-repeated letters *a*, *b*, *c*, etc., where these words are shorter than or equal to *n* 99
5.7.4. Language of words based on an alphabet of *n* letters 100
5.8. The exponential generating function 101
5.8.1. Exercise 1: words based on three letters *a*, *b* and *c*, with the letter *a* at least twice. 101
5.8.2. Exercise 2: sending *n* people to three countries, with at least one person per country 103

Chapter 6. Routes in a Square Grid 105

6.1. Shortest paths from one point to another. 105
6.2. *n*-length paths using two (perpendicular) directions of the square grid 108
6.3. Paths from *O* to *B* (*n*, *x*) neither touching nor crossing the horizontal axis and located above it 109
6.4. Number of *n*-length paths that neither touch nor cross the axis of the adscissae until and including the final point 110
6.5. Number of *n*-length paths above the horizontal axis that can touch but not cross the horizontal axis 111
6.6. Exercises 112
6.6.1. Exercise 1: show that $C_{2n}^{n} = \sum_{k=0}^{n} (C_n^k)^2$ 112
6.6.2. Exercise 2: show that $\sum_{k=0}^{P} C_{N\text{-}1+k}^{k} = C_{N+P}^{P}$ 113
6.6.3. Exercise 3: show that $\sum_{k=1}^{n'} 2k\, C_{2n'}^{n'+k} = n' C_{2n'}^{n'}$ 113
6.6.4. Exercise 4: a geometrico-linguistic method 114
6.6.5. Exercise 5: paths of a given length that never intersect each other and where the four directions are allowed in the square grid 115

Chapter 7. Arrangements and Combinations with Repetitions 119

7.1. Anagrams 119
7.2. Combinations with repetitions. 121
7.2.1. Routes in a square grid. 121
7.2.2. Distributing (indiscernible) circulars in personalized letter boxes . 121
7.2.3. Choosing I objects out of N categories of object 121
7.2.4. Number of positive or nul integer solutions to the equation $x0 + x1 + ... + xn\text{-}1 = P$ 122
7.3. Exercises 125
7.3.1. Exercise 1: number of ways of choosing six objects out of three categories, with the corresponding prices 125
7.3.2. Exercise 2: word counting. 125
7.3.3. Exercise 3: number of words of P characters based on an alphabet of N letters and subject to order constraints 127
7.3.4. Exercise 4: choice of objects out of several categories taking at least one object from each category 128
7.3.5. Exercise 5: choice of P objects out of N categories when the stock is limited 128
7.3.6. Exercise 6: generating functions associated with the number of integer solutions to an equation with n unknowns. 129
7.3.7. Exercise 7: number of solutions to the equation $x + y + z = k$, where k is a given natural integer and $0 \leq x \leq y \leq z$. 130
7.3.8. Exercise 8: other applications of the method using generating functions 131
7.3.9. Exercise 9: integer-sided triangles 132
7.3.10. Revision exercise: sending postcards 133
7.4. Algorithms and programs 135
7.4.1. Anagram program 135
7.4.2. Combinations with repetition program 136

Chapter 8. Sieve Formula 137

8.1. Sieve formula on sets 138
8.2. Sieve formula in combinatorics 142
8.3. Examples 142
8.3.1. Example 1: filling up boxes with objects, with at least one box remaining empty 142
8.3.2. Example 2: derangements 144
8.3.3. Example 3: formula giving the Euler number $\varphi(n)$ 145
8.3.4. Example 4: houses to be painted 146
8.3.5. Example 5: multiletter words 148
8.3.6. Example 6: coloring the vertices of a graph 150

8.4. Exercises 153
8.4.1. Exercise 1: sending nine diplomats, 1, 2, 3, ..., 9, to three countries *A*, *B*, *C* 153
8.4.2. Exercise 2: painting a room 153
8.4.3. Exercise 3: rooks on a chessboard 155
8.5. Extension of sieve formula. 158
8.5.1. Permutations that have *k* fixed points 159
8.5.2. Permutations with *q* disjoint cycles that are *k* long 160
8.5.3. Terminal nodes of trees with *n* numbered nodes. 161
8.5.4. Revision exercise about a word: intelligent. 163

Chapter 9. Mountain Ranges or Parenthesis Words: Catalan Numbers . . 165

9.1. Number *c*(*n*) of mountain ranges 2*n* long 166
9.2. Mountains or primitive words 167
9.3. Enumeration of mountain ranges 168
9.4. The language of mountain ranges. 169
9.5. Generating function of the C_{2n}^{n} and Catalan numbers 171
9.6. Left factors of mountain ranges 173
9.6.1. Algorithm for obtaining the numbers of these left factors *a*(*N*, *X*) . 175
9.6.2. Calculation following the lines of Catalan's triangle 176
9.6.3. Calculations based on the columns of the Catalan triangle 177
9.6.4. Average value of the height reached by left factors. 178
9.6.5. Calculations based on the second bisector of the Catalan triangle . 180
9.6.6. Average number of mountains for mountain ranges 183
9.7. Number of peaks of mountain ranges 184
9.8. The Catalan mountain range, its area and height 187
9.8.1. Number of mountain ranges 2*n* long passing through a given point on the square grid. 187
9.8.2. Sum of the elements of lines in triangle *OO'B* of mountain ranges 2*n* long. 188
9.8.3. Sum of numbers in triangle *OO'B* 189
9.8.4. Average area of a mountain 2*n* long. 190
9.8.5. Shape of the average mountain range 192
9.8.6. Height of the Catalan mountain range. 194

Chapter 10. Other Mountain Ranges 197

10.1. Mountain ranges based on three lines ↗ ↘ → 197

10.2. Words based on three lines ↗ ↘ → with as many rising lines as falling lines. 198

10.2.1. Explicit formula $v(n)$ 199
10.2.2. Return to $u(n)$ number of mountain ranges based on three letters a, b, c and a link with $v(n)$ 200
10.3. Example 1: domino tiling of an enlarged Aztec diamond 200
10.4. Example 2: domino tiling of half an Aztec diamond 204
10.4.1. Link between Schröder numbers and Catalan numbers 207
10.4.2. Link with Narayana numbers 207
10.4.3. Another way of programming three-line mountain ranges 208
10.5. Mountain ranges based on three types of lines ↗ ↘ → . 210
10.6. Example 3: movement of the king on a chessboard 213

Chapter 11. Some Applications of Catalan Numbers and Parenthesis Words 215

11.1. The number of ways of placing n chords not intersecting each other on a circle with an even number $2n$ of points. 215
11.2. Murasaki diagrams and partitions 216
11.3. Path couples with the same ends in a square grid 218
11.4. Path couples with same starting point and length 220
11.5. Decomposition of words based on two letters as a product of words linked to mountain ranges 222

Chapter 12. Burnside's Formula 227

12.1. Example 1: context in which we obtain the formula 227
12.2. Burnside's formula. 231
12.2.1. Complementary exercise: rotation-type colorings of the vertices of a square 232
12.2.2. Example 2: pawns on a chessboard 232
12.2.3. Example 3: pearl necklaces 237
12.2.4. Example 4: coloring of a stick 239
12.3. Exercises. 239
12.3.1. Coloring the vertices of a square 239
12.3.2. Necklaces with stones in several colors 241
12.3.3. Identical balls in identical boxes 244
12.3.4. Tiling an Aztec diamond using l-squares 244
12.3.5. The 4×4 Sudoku: search for fundamentally different symmetry-type girls 246

Chapter 13. Matrices and Circulation on a Graph 253

13.1. Number of paths of a given length on a complete or a regular graph . 254
13.2. Number of paths and matrix powers 255

13.2.1. Example 1: *n*-length words in an alphabet of three letters 1, 2, 3, with prohibition of blocks 11 and 23 . . . 257
13.2.2. Simplification of the calculation . . . 259
13.2.3. Example 2: *n*-length words based on three letters 1, 2, 3 with blocks 11, 22 and 33 prohibited . . . 261
13.3. Link between cyclic words and closed paths in an oriented graph . . . 262
13.4. Examples . . . 263
13.4.1. Dominos on a chessboard . . . 263
13.4.2. Words with a dependency link between two successive letters of words . . . 265
13.4.3. Routes on a graded segment . . . 266
13.4.4. Molecular chain . . . 270

Chapter 14. Parts and Partitions of a Set . . . 275

14.1. Parts of a set. . . . 275
14.1.1. Program getting all parts of a set . . . 275
14.1.2. Exercises . . . 277
14.2. Partitions of a *n*-object set . . . 281
14.2.1. Definition. . . . 281
14.2.2. A second kind of Stirling numbers, and partitions of a n-element set in k parts . . . 281
14.2.3. Number of partitions of a set and Bell numbers . . . 283
14.2.4. Enumeration algorithm for all partitions of a set. . . . 285
14.2.5. Exercise: Sterling numbers modulo 2 . . . 286

Chapter 15. Partitions of a Number . . . 289

15.1. Enumeration algorithm . . . 289
15.2. Euler formula . . . 290
15.3. Exercises. . . . 292
15.3.1. Exercise 1: partitions of a number *n* in *k* distinct elements . . . 292
15.3.2. Exercise 2: ordered partitions . . . 296
15.3.3. Exercise 3: sum of the products of all the ordered partitions of a number . . . 297
15.3.4. Exercise 4: partitions of a number in completely distinct parts . . . 298
15.3.5. Exercise 5: partitions and routes in a square grid . . . 299
15.3.6. Exercise 6: Ferrers graphs . . . 302

Chapter 16. Flags . . . 305

16.1. Checkered flags . . . 305
16.2. Flags with vertical stripes. . . . 306

Chapter 17. Walls and Stacks 315

17.1. Brick walls 315
17.2. Walls of bricks made from continuous horizontal rows 316
17.2.1. Algorithm for classifying various types of walls. 317
17.2.2. Possible positions of one row above another 317
17.2.3. Coordinates of bricks 318
17.3. Heaps. 319
17.4. Stacks of disks 322
17.5. Stacks of disks with continuous rows. 324
17.6. Horizontally connected polyominos 326

Chapter 18. Tiling of Rectangular Surfaces using Simple Shapes 331

18.1. Tiling of a 2×n chessboard using dominos. 331
18.1.1. First algorithm for constructing tilings 332
18.1.2. Second construction algorithm 333
18.2. Other tilings of a chessboard 2×n squares long 334
18.2.1. With squares and horizontal dominos 334
18.2.2. With squares and horizontal or vertical dominos 335
18.2.3. With dominos and l-squares we can turn and reflect 335
18.2.4. With squares, l-squares and dominos 336
18.3. Tilings of a 3×n chessboard using dominos 337
18.4. Tilings of a 4×n chessboard with dominos. 339
18.5. Domino tilings of a rectangle 340

Chapter 19. Permutations 345

19.1. Definition and properties 345
19.2. Decomposition of a permutation as a product of disjoint cycles 347
19.2.1. Particular cases of permutations defined by their decomposition in cycles 349
19.2.2. Number of permutations of n elements with k cycles: Stirling numbers of the first kind 352
19.2.3. Type of permutation 353
19.3. Inversions in a permutation. 354
19.3.1. Generating function of the number of inversions 356
19.3.2. Signature of a permutation: odd and even permutations 357
19.4. Conjugated permutations 359
19.5. Generation of permutations. 360
19.5.1. The symmetrical group S_n is generated by the transpositions $(i\,j)$. 361
19.5.2. S_n is generated by transpositions of adjacent elements of the form $(i, i+1)$ 362
19.5.3. S_n is generated by transpositions (0 1) (0 2) ... (0 $n-1$) 362

19.5.4. S_n is generated by cycles (0 1) and (0 1 2 3 ... $n-1$) 363
19.6. Properties of the alternating group A_n. 363
19.6.1. A_n is generated by cycles three units long: ($i\,j\,k$). 363
19.6.2. A_n is generated by $n-2$ cycles (0 1 k) 363
19.6.3. For $n > 3$, A_n is generated by the cycle chain three units long, of the form (0 1 2) (2 3 4) (4 5 6) … ($n-3$ $n-2$ $n-1$) 364
19.7. Applications of these properties 365
19.7.1. Card shuffling 365
19.7.2. Taquin game in a n by p (n and $p > 1$) rectangle 368
19.7.3. Cyclic shifts in a rectangle. 371
19.7.4. Exchanges of lines and columns in a square 375
19.8. Exercises on permutations 376
19.8.1. Creating a permutation at random 376
19.8.2. Number of permutations $\begin{pmatrix} 0 & 1 & 2 & \ldots & n\text{-}1 \\ a(0) & a(1) & a(2) & \ldots & a(n\text{-}1) \end{pmatrix}$ with n elements 0, 1, 2, …, $n-1$, such that $|a(i)-i| = 0$ or 1 377
19.8.3. Permutations with $a(i) - i = \pm1$ or ±2 379
19.8.4. Permutations with n elements 0, 1, 2, …, $n-1$ without two consecutive elements 379
19.8.5. Permutations with n elements 0, 1, 2, …, $n-1$, made up of a single cycle in which no two consecutive elements modulo n are found . 381
19.8.6. Involute permutations 383
19.8.7. Increasing subsequences in a permutation 384
19.8.8. Riffle shuffling of type O and I for N cards when N is a power of 2 386

PART 2. PROBABILITY 387

Part 2. Introduction 389

Chapter 20. Reminders about Discrete Probabilities 395

20.1. And/or in probability theory 396
20.2. Examples 398
20.2.1. The Chevalier de Mere problem 398
20.2.2. From combinatorics to probabilities 399
20.2.3. From combinatorics of weighted words to probabilities 400
20.2.4. Drawing a parcel of objects from a box 401
20.2.5. Hypergeometric law 401
20.2.6. Draws with replacement in a box. 402
20.2.7. Numbered balls in a box and the smallest number obtained during draws 403

20.2.8. Wait for the first double heads in a repeated game of heads or tails 404
20.2.9. Succession of random cuts made in a game of cards 405
20.2.10. Waiting time for initial success 407
20.2.11. Smallest number obtained during successive draws 409
20.2.12. The pool problem 411
20.3. Total probability formula 412
20.3.1. Classic example 412
20.3.2. The formula 413
20.3.3. Examples 413
20.4. Random variable X, law of X, expectation and variance 418
20.4.1. Average value of X 418
20.4.2. Variance and standard deviation 418
20.4.3. Example. 419
20.5. Some classic laws 420
20.5.1. Bernoulli's law 420
20.5.2. Geometric law 420
20.5.3. Binomial law 421
20.6. Exercises. 422
20.6.1. Exercise 1: throwing balls in boxes 422
20.6.2. Exercise 2: series of repetitive tries 423
20.6.3. Exercise 3: filling two boxes 425

Chapter 21. Chance and the Computer 427

21.1. Random number generators 428
21.2. Dice throwing and the law of large numbers 429
21.3. Monte Carlo methods for getting the approximate value of the number π 430
21.4. Average value of a random variable X, variance and standard deviation 432
21.5. Computer calculation of probabilities, as well as expectation and variance, in the binomial law example 433
21.6. Limits of the computer 437
21.7. Exercises. 439
21.7.1. Exercise 1: throwing balls in boxes 439
21.7.2. Exercise 2: boys and girls 439
21.7.3. Exercise 3: conditional probability 441
21.8. Appendix: chi-squared law 443
21.8.1. Examples of the test for uniform distribution. 443
21.8.2. Chi-squared law and its link with Poisson distribution 445

Chapter 22. Discrete and Continuous 447

22.1. Uniform law. 448
22.1.1. Programming. 448
22.1.2. Example 1 449
22.1.3. Example 2: two people meeting 450
22.2. Density function for a continuous random variable and distribution function. 451
22.3. Normal law 452
22.4. Exponential law and its link with uniform law 454
22.4.1. An application: geometric law using exponential law. 456
22.4.2. Program for getting the geometric law with parameter p 457
22.5. Normal law as an approximation of binomial law 458
22.6. Central limit theorem: from uniform law to normal law. 460
22.7. Appendix: the distribution function and its inversion – application to binomial law $B(n, p)$. 465
22.7.1. Program. 465
22.7.2. The inverse function 467
22.7.3. Program causing us to move from distribution function to probability law. 468

Chapter 23. Generating Function Associated with a Discrete Random Variable in a Game 469

23.1. Generating function: definition and properties 469
23.2. Generating functions of some classic laws. 470
23.2.1. Bernoulli's law 470
23.2.2. Geometric law 470
23.2.3. Binomial law. 473
23.2.4. Poisson distribution. 475
23.3. Exercises. 476
23.3.1. Exercise 1: waiting time for double heads in a game of heads or tails 476
23.3.2. Exercise 2: in a repeated game of heads or tails, what is the parity of the number of heads?. 481
23.3.3. Exercise 3: draws until a certain threshold is exceeded. 482
23.3.4. Exercise 4: Pascal's law 487
23.3.5. Exercise 5: balls of two colors in a box 488
23.3.6. Exercise 6: throws of N dice until each gives the number 1 492

Chapter 24. Graphs and Matrices for Dealing with Probability Problems. 497

24.1. First example: counting of words based on three letters. 497
24.2. Generating functions and determinants. 499

24.3. Examples 500
24.3.1. Exercise 1: waiting time for double heads in a game of heads or tails 500
24.3.2. Draws from three boxes 503
24.3.3. Alternate draws from two boxes 505
24.3.4. Successive draws from one box to the next 506

Chapter 25. Repeated Games of Heads or Tails 509

25.1. Paths on a square grid 509
25.2. Probability of getting a certain number of wins after n equiprobable tosses 511
25.2.1. Probability $p(n, x)$ of getting winnings of x at the end of n moves 512
25.2.2. Standard deviation in relation to a starting point 512
25.2.3. Probability $\rho(2n')$ of a return to the origin at stage $n = 2n'$ 513
25.3. Probabilities of certain routes over n moves 514
25.4. Complementary exercises 516
25.4.1. Last visit to the origin 516
25.4.2. Number of winnings sign changes throughout the game 517
25.4.3. Probability of staying on the positive winnings side for a certain amount of time during the $N = 2n$ equiprobable tosses 519
25.4.4. Longest range of winnings with constant sign 520
25.5. The gambler's ruin problem 521
25.5.1. Probability of ruin 522
25.5.2. Average duration of the game 524
25.5.3. Results and program 525
25.5.4. Exercises 526
25.5.5. Temperature equilibrium and random walk 530

Chapter 26. Random Routes on a Graph 535

26.1. Movement of a particle on a polygon or graduated segment 535
26.1.1. Average duration of routes between two points 535
26.1.2. Paths of a given length on a polygon 542
26.1.3. Particle circulating on a pentagon: time required using one side or the other to get to the end 546
26.2. Movement on a polyhedron 547
26.2.1. Case of the regular polyhedron 547
26.2.2. Circulation on a cube with any dimensions 550
26.3. The robot and the human being 555
26.4. Exercises 559
26.4.1. Movement of a particle on a square-based pyramid 559
26.4.2. Movement of two particles on a square-based pyramid 561
26.4.3. Movement of two particles on a graph with five vertices 563

Chapter 27. Repetitive Draws until the Outcome of a Certain Pattern . . . 565

27.1. Patterns are arrangements of K out of N letters 566
27.1.1. Wait for a given arrangement of the K letters in the form of a block 566
27.1.2. Wait for a given cyclic arrangement of K letters in the form of a block 568
27.1.3. The pattern is a given arrangement of K out of N letters in scattered form 570
27.2. Patterns are combinations of K letters drawn from N letters 571
27.2.1. Wait for the outcome of a part made of K numbers in the form of a block 571
27.2.2. Wait for the outcome of any part of K numbers in the form of a block, out of N. 574
27.2.3. Wait for the outcome of a part with K given numbers out of N in scattered form 577
27.2.4. Wait for the outcome of any part of K numbers out of N, in scattered form 577
27.2.5. Some examples of comparative results for waiting times 579
27.3. Wait for patterns with eventual repetitions of identical letters 580
27.3.1. For an alphabet of N letters, we wait for a given pattern in the form of a n-length block 580
27.3.2. Wait for one of two patterns of the same length L 581
27.4. Programming exercises 586
27.4.1. Wait for completely different letters 586
27.4.2. Waiting time for a certain pattern. 588
27.4.3. Number of words without two-sided factors 589

Chapter 28. Probability Exercises 597

28.1. The elevator. 597
28.1.1. Deal with the case where $P = 2$ floors and the number of people N is at least equal to 2 597
28.1.2. Determine the law of X, i.e. the probability associated with each value of X. 598
28.1.3. Average value $E(X)$. 599
28.1.4. Direct calculation of $S(K+1, K)$. 600
28.1.5. Another way of dealing with the previous question 601
28.2. Matches 601
28.3. The tunnel. 602
28.3.1. Dealing with the specific case where $N = 3$. 606
28.3.2. Variation with an absorbing boundary and another method 608
28.3.3. Complementary exercise: drunken man's walk on a straight line, with resting time 610

28.4. Repetitive draws from a box 613
28.4.1. Probability law for the number of draws 615
28.4.2. Extra questions 616
28.4.3. Probability of getting ball number k during the game 617
28.4.4. Probability law associated with the number of balls drawn 617
28.4.5. Complementary exercise: variation of the previous problem 618
28.5. The sect 620
28.5.1. Can the group last forever? 620
28.5.2. Probability law of the size of the tree 621
28.5.3. Average tree size 622
28.5.4. Variance of the variable size 624
28.5.5. Algorithm giving the probability law of the organization's lifespan 625
28.6. Surfing the web (or how Google works) 627

PART 3. GRAPHS 637

Part 3. Introduction 639

Chapter 29. Graphs and Routes 643

29.1. First notions on graphs 643
29.1.1. A few properties of graphs 645
29.1.2. Constructing graphs from points 646
29.2. Representing a graph in a program 647
29.2.1. From vertices to edges 649
29.2.2. From edges to vertices 649
29.3. The tree as a specific graph 649
29.3.1. Definitions and properties 649
29.3.2. Programming exercise: network converging on a point 652
29.4. Paths from one point to another in a graph 654
29.4.1. Dealing with an example 654
29.4.2. Exercise: paths on a complete graph, from one vertex to another . 656

Chapter 30. Explorations in Graphs 661

30.1. The two ways of visiting all the vertices of a connected graph 661
30.2. Visit to all graph nodes from one node, following depth-first traversal 662
30.3. The pedestrian's route 665
30.4. Depth-first exploration to determine connected components of the graph 669
30.5. Breadth-first traversal 671
30.5.1. Program 671

30.5.2. Example: traversal in a square grid. 673
30.6. Exercises. 676
30.6.1. Searching in a maze. 676
30.6.2. Routes in a square grid, with rising shapes without entangling . . 680
30.6.3. Route of a fluid in a graph 683
30.6.4. Connected graphs with n vertices. 683
30.6.5. Bipartite graphs 685
30.7. Returning to a depth-first exploration tree 686
30.7.1. Returning edges in an undirected graph 687
30.7.2. Isthmuses in an undirected graph. 688
30.8. Case of directed graphs 690
30.8.1. Strongly connected components in a directed graph. 690
30.8.2. Transitive closure of a directed graph 693
30.8.3. Orientation of a connected undirected graph to become strongly connected 696
30.8.4. The best orientations on a graph 696
30.9. Appendix: constructing the maze (simplified version). 700

Chapter 31. Trees with Numbered Nodes, Cayley's Theorem and Prüfer Code 705

31.1. Cayley's theorem. 705
31.2. Prüfer code 706
31.2.1. Passage from a tree to its Prüfer code 707
31.2.2. Reverse process 707
31.2.3. Program. 709
31.3. Randomly constructed spanning tree 715
31.3.1. Wilson's algorithm 715
31.3.2. Maze and domino tiling 718

Chapter 32. Binary Trees 723

32.1. Number of binary trees with n nodes 725
32.2. The language of binary trees 725
32.3. Algorithm for creation of words from the binary tree language 728
32.4. Triangulation of polygons with numbered vertices and binary trees. . 729
32.5. Binary tree sort or quicksort 733

Chapter 33. Weighted Graphs: Shortest Paths and Minimum Spanning Tree 737

33.1. Shortest paths in a graph 737
33.1.1. Dijkstra's algorithm. 738
33.1.2. Floyd's algorithm 741
33.2. Minimum spanning tree. 746

33.2.1. Prim's algorithm. 747
33.2.2. Kruskal's algorithm. 749
33.2.3. Comparison of the two algorithms 754
33.2.4. Exercises 754

Chapter 34. Eulerian Paths and Cycles, Spanning Trees of a Graph 759

34.1. Definition of Eulerian cycles and paths 759
34.2. Euler and Königsberg bridges 761
34.2.1. Returning to Königsberg bridges 763
34.2.2. Examples 764
34.2.3. Constructing Eulerian cycles by fusing cycles 767
34.3. Number of Eulerian cycles in a directed graph, link with directed spanning trees 768
34.3.1. Number of directed spanning trees 771
34.3.2. Examples 774
34.4. Spanning trees of an undirected graph 776
34.4.1. Example 1: complete graph with p vertices 777
34.4.2. Example 2: tetrahedron. 778

Chapter 35. Enumeration of Spanning Trees of an Undirected Graph . . . 779

35.1. Spanning trees of the fan graph 779
35.2. The ladder graph and its spanning trees 782
35.3. Spanning trees in a square network in the form of a grid 784
35.3.1. Experimental enumeration of spanning trees of the square network 785
35.3.2. Spanning trees program in the case of the square network 786
35.3.3. Passage to the undirected graph, its dual and formula giving the number of spanning trees 788
35.4. The two essential types of (undirected) graphs based on squares . . . 789
35.5. The cyclic square graph. 791
35.6. Examples of regular graphs. 792
35.6.1. Example 1 792
35.6.2. Example 2: hypercube with n dimensions. 793
35.6.3. Example 3: the ladder graph and its variations 793

Chapter 36. Enumeration of Eulerian Paths in Undirected Graphs 799

36.1. Polygon graph with n vertices with double edges. 799
36.2. Eulerian paths in graph made up of a frieze of triangles. 801
36.3. Algorithm for Eulerian paths and cycles on an undirected graph . . . 804
36.3.1. The arborescence for the paths 804
36.3.2. Program for enumerating Eulerian cycles. 805

36.3.3. Enumeration in the case of multiple edges between vertices. . . . 807
36.3.4. Another example: square with double diagonals. 810
36.4. The game of dominos 813
36.4.1. Number of domino chains 813
36.4.2. Algorithms 816
36.5. Congo graphs 820
36.5.1. A simple case: graphs $P(2n, 5)$ 822
36.5.2. The first type of Congolese drawings, on $P(n + 1, n)$ graphs, with their Eulerian paths 826
36.5.3. The second type of Congolese drawings, on $P(2N, N)$ graphs . . . 826
36.5.4. Case of Eulerian cycles on $P(2N + 1, 2N - 1)$ graphs 830
36.5.5. Case of $I(2N + 1, 2N + 1)$ graphs with their Eulerian cycles 832

Chapter 37. Hamiltonian Paths and Circuits 835

37.1. Presence or absence of Hamiltonian circuits. 836
37.1.1. First examples 836
37.1.2. Hamiltonian circuits on a cube 837
37.1.3. Complete graph and Hamiltonian circuits. 839
37.2. Hamiltonian circuits covering a complete graph 840
37.2.1. Case where the number of vertices is a prime number other than two. 840
37.2.2. General case 841
37.3. Complete and antisymmetric directed graph. 843
37.3.1. A few theoretical considerations 843
37.3.2. Experimental verification and algorithms. 848
37.3.3. Complete treatment of case $N = 4$ 851
37.4. Bipartite graph and Hamiltonian paths 854
37.5. Knights tour graph on the $N \times N$ chessboard 855
37.5.1. Case where N is odd 855
37.5.2. Coordinates of the neighbors of a vertex 855
37.5.3. Hamiltonian cycles program. 856
37.5.4. Another algorithm. 857
37.6. de Bruijn sequences 859
37.6.1. Preparatory example 859
37.6.2. Definition. 860
37.6.3. de Bruijn graph 862
37.6.4. Number of Eulerian and Hamiltonian cycles of Gn 865

APPENDICES 867

Appendix 1. Matrices 869

A1.1. Notion of linear application 869

A1.2. Bijective linear application 872
A1.3. Base change 873
A1.4. Product of two matrices 874
A1.5. Inverse matrix 875
A1.6. Eigenvalues and eigenvectors 877
A1.7. Similar matrices 879
A1.8. Exercise 881
A1.9. Eigenvalues of circulant matrices and circular graphs. 882

Appendix 2. Determinants and Route Combinatorics 885

A2.1. Recalling determinants 885
A2.2. Determinants and tilings 887
A2.3. Path sets and determinant 892
A2.3.1. First example: paths without intersection in a square network . . 892
A2.3.2. Second example: mountain ranges without intersection, based on two diagonal lines. 895
A2.3.3. Third example: mountain ranges without intersection based on diagonal lines and plateaus. Link with Aztec diamond tilings 896
A2.3.4. Diamond tilings. 899
A2.4. The hamburger graph: disjoint cycles 901
A2.4.1. First example: domino tiling of a rectangular checkerboard *N* long, 2 wide. 902
A2.4.2. Second example: domino tilings of the Aztec diamond 904

Bibliography 907

Index 911

General Introduction

Combinatorics and all the fields deriving from it – the probabilities and graph theories – are no longer peripheral phenomena, at the edge of pure mathematics. We can even consider combinatorics as bringing a breath of fresh air into the universe of theory. Indeed it has its own style of demonstrations, which often require more tricks and common sense than the systematic application of the mainstream mathematical theories. It is also an introduction in a concrete manner of some abstract algebraic tools such as matrices and determinants. The recent development of combinatorics also results from the worldwide emergence of informatics, which offers unlimited possibilities of practice and experimentation, i.e. either to check or anticipate theoretical results, or to solve problems that theory cannot solve. Combinatorics associated with counting and enumerating allows us to encode events in words, made of numbers or letters, which brings the field closer to linguistics. The word dictionaries obtained can in turn be illustrated on computer screen through complex shapes and patterns, such as the new hieroglyphs, which are able to strike the imagination and stimulate the artistic interpretation.

Combinatorics is first studied in science classes at high school, where it is associated with the calculation of probabilities, and recently, with graphs theory. The calculation of the probabilities and its algorithms is also a favorite field used in the entrance examination for major business schools. On the other side of the coin, the number of high-level publications has multiplied in specialized journals, which are only accessible to a few. This book falls between the two camps. It gradually moves from basic introductory sections to the latest theoretical developments in the field, illustrated by numerous examples.[1]

1. In this respect, we used the work by Graham, Knuth and Patashnik, *Concrete Mathematics* [GRA 90] as a source of inspiration and a model.

This book targets students and researchers, and more broadly knowledgeable amateurs. High school and preparatory school teachers will find here many useful examples and exercises. Depending on the theoretical level of the audience, some readers will prefer to focus on the algorithms, or even the graphic visuals, others will concentrate on the algebraic or combinatorial implementations. The aim of this book is to achieve a global overview of the state of the art in the field.

About the algorithms and programs

One of the specific aspects of this book is to provide a large number of algorithms and programs, all explained in full detail. The programs are designed in abridged versions using C language, and they are easily adaptable to other similar languages such as *Pascal* or *Basic*. Mathematics enthusiasts will need to convert these programs directly into a scientific language such as *Mathematica* if they want to benefit from the graphic functions. In order to learn C programming and SDL graphics, I recommend that readers visit my website, created within the framework of LIASD (Laboratoire d'informatique avancée de Saint-Denis, Paris 8 University): www.ai.univ-paris-8.fr/~audibert/. Under the heading "Book Programs", we give many programs present in this book. They are in full programs, written in C with SDL graphical help, with their codes as well as their executable files.[2]

Structure of the book

The book is divided into three parts:

– Part 1: *Combinatorics*;

– Part 2: *Probability*;

– Part 3: *Graphs*.

2. In order to learn *C* programming and *SDL* graphics, the "happy few" who read French will find a brief introduction about their use, in my web pages. Under the rubric "Education", where IT and mathematics (level 1, L1) and algorithmics (Level 2, L2) courses are listed, in chapter entitled "Graphics SDL: second layer", two functions of basic graphics are listed: *putpixel* and *getpixel* (formerly called *peek* and *poke*), as well as the functions making it possible to draw lines and circles. Readers will also learn the way to draw a segment with arrows, which is highly necessary for drawing graphs. Should the need arise, the chapters dealing with recursivity and linked lists will enable easy comprehension of these more complex concepts. In "Complementary Works", some mathematical games, among others, are explained (such as Marienbad, Instant Insanity, Planarity) with their complete programmings. For algorithmic enthusiasts in general, see the following books for further detail: [AHO 87], [BER 91], [COR 02], [SED 91].

Although these three parts can be read separately, they are connected by counting and enumerating algorithms, following the same reading line, i.e. the concept of generating functions[3]. Despite the large number of subjects studied, this book does not claim to be exhaustive. Interested readers will find more details in [TUC 02], notably on games based on graphs, in [LEN 03] on mathematical linguistics, and in [STA 01] or [LOT 97] for a deeper theoretical vision. Let us not forget to mention [SLO 95], the global reference in the field of integer sequences, or the pioneering book by [COM 70].

Acknowledgements

I want to thanks my colleagues and friends, particularly F. Belhadj, P. Chibaudel, S. El Baz, C. Fer, P. Greussay, C. Lenormand, I. Saleh, H. Wertz, who helped me a lot. I also wish to thank the hundred or so students who wrote their MD or PhD theses under my supervision. They have allowed me to work on a diversity of subjects, but always on an algorithmic basis: ranging from my first student R. Abdoul (on sand avalanches) to my latest I. Mazouzi (about the Chinese theorem), to the other students who explored combinatorial problems and whose works are mentioned in this book: H. Arfa, A. Fathi, N. Grassa, N. Rifaai, Y. Naciri.

---

3. For a full understanding of generating functions refer to [WIL 94].

Chapter 1

Some Historical Elements

If numbers are the essence of things, as Archimedes said about natural whole numbers, combinatorics could be the essence of mutations, changes, combinations and the principle source of algorithms.

How? This is the first question that combinatorics answers. But if it boiled down to a simple counting of eventualities, it would only be a by-product of number theory. The implementation of shufflings and their exhaustive enumeration, with a succession order that leaves nothing to chance, makes up the background of combinatorics. If combination science is immemorial, like cooking recipes, which in turn become algorithms, its theoretical tools are affiliated with time. Some historical groundwork will enable us to extract its foundations, through its first known appearances, as fluid as this sometimes is.

1.1. Yi King

Discovered over 3,000 years ago, before being the subject of the *Book of Changes*, a Chinese literature classic, *Yi King* is, above all, a method of divination that is supposed to explain the influences that act on vital behaviors. In a more prosaic way, the *Yi King* system uses two symbols, *Yang* is represented by a long line and *Yin* by two short lines. It can also be called a two-letter alphabet. The combinations formed from three of these letters, placed one below the other, produce eight trigrams (see Figure 1.1).

In turn, the eight core trigrams, associated in pairs, enable us to form 64 hexagrams. The number of trigrams and hexagrams comes from an essential combinatorics formula: n^p is the number of ways to make words of length p from an alphabet of n letters. If we replace the *Yin* symbol with a 0 and the *Yang* with a 1, we get all the numbers, from 0 to 63, written in binary. But, originally, hexagrams were not written in ascending order, which is also alphabetical order, i.e. 000000, then 000001, 000010, 000100, etc. Hexagrams written in this order appeared later, in the 11th century, when what would become the binary system was in its preparation stage. This system would be elaborated by Leibniz in about 1700, before becoming a basis of current day computer science.

Furthermore, Leibniz attributes the discovery of binary arithmetics to the Chinese, from the most ancient times, even if there is no clear indication that the Chinese had this interpretation in mind. But if we consider Chinese writing itself to be organized using keys, themselves classified according to their number of lines, a counting process appears in the very interior of the writing system. This is where a sort of original *raison d'être* for combinatorics is formed [BIG 79].

Figure 1.1. *The eight Yi King trigrams*

1.2. Flavor combinations in India

It is in India that we find the first references to notions of permutations and combinations. In a medical text by sage Sushruta, going back 2,600 years, the mixes of six gustatory flavors, namely sweet, sour, salty, spicy, bitter and astringent, are discussed. It contains a systematic enumeration of the 63 possible combinations, six based on one single flavor, 15 on two, 20 on three, 15 with four, six with five, and one with all together.

Other examples of the same style, mixtures of various ingredients, re-appear in later eras. Notably, in the 500s, the mathematician Varahamihira indicated that in choosing four out of 16 ingredients to create perfumes, he finds 1,820 possibilities. It is likely that the formula related to the number of combinations, which we express as C_n^p, was known then, as it happens here $C_{16}^4 = 1{,}820$. Later, in 1150, the renowned mathematician, Bhaskara, explicitly gave the $n!$ formula related to the number of permutations of n objects [JOS 91].

1.3. Sand drawings in Africa

In Pharaonic Egypt, more than 3,000 years ago, engraved on scarab-form seals, ornamental patterns made from continuous lines that run through an underlying square grid already existed (see Figure 1.2). Many variations also developed in Mesopotamia, then later in India, notably on doorsteps, or on Native American tapestries. But it is in Central Africa that the tradition of such designs, drawn in the sand or embroidered, took root over a long period of time, and was transmitted from generation to generation, notably in the Congo (see Figure 1.3).

At the beginning of the 20th century an explorer named Emil Torday, who settled in the Bakuba (or Bushongo) population in the Congo, observed a group of young children sitting in a circle. They were playing in the sand and drawing simple diagrams with their fingers, using a single continuous line, without any hesitation or interruption and without ever passing over the same line twice:

> *"They invited me to join them, and one of them removed his loin cloth and offered it to me as a seat. This gesture was even more respectable than that of St. Martin offering half his coat, as the child was wearing nothing other than this loin cloth. The children were in the process of drawing and I was asked to accomplish impossible tasks. Great was their joy to see the white man fail at it."*

Sometimes, before drawing these pictograms, the artists use their fingertips to mark an orthogonal network of equidistant dots, using lines and columns more or less placed in a global rectangular shape. These dots mark the centers of squares stuck to one another. Then all the dots are run through once and only once with a single continuous line. This is what is now called Eulerian cycles or paths, well before Leonhard Euler (1750) dealt with this problem providing two theorems, which are considered as the starting point of graph theory.

Everything indicates that these African artists knew perfectly well how to run through all the points of a graph once and only once when the vertices of the graph had an even number of edges, and finally return to the starting point. They also knew that it was possible to run through a graph from one of its vertices to another specific vertex when the two vertices had an odd number of edges, provided that all the other vertices had an even number. These are precisely the two theorems attributed to Euler. For aesthetic reasons, the African artists were not satisfied with finding one single route, even if they preferred the one that had more symmetries. They introduced all sorts of variations, breaking up some symmetries, exercising clever methods of braiding, by breaking or combining several cycles [GER 95].

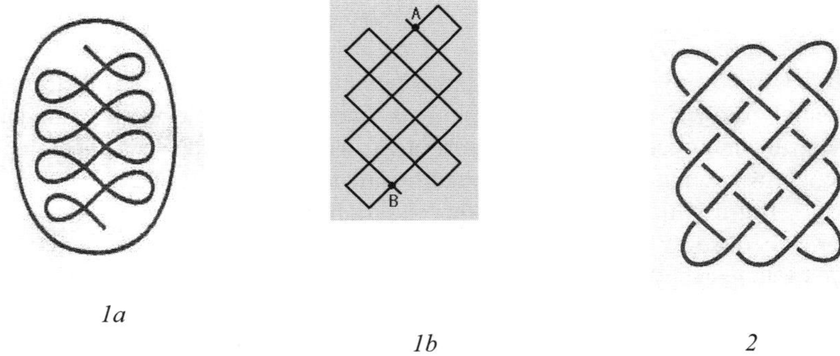

Figure 1.2. *Two designs engraved on scarab seals coming from ancient Egypt, as can be seen in the Cairo Egyptian Museum. Diagram 1b shows the underlying square grid of 1a; it is a Eulerian path from A to B, namely the only two vertices with an odd number of edges*

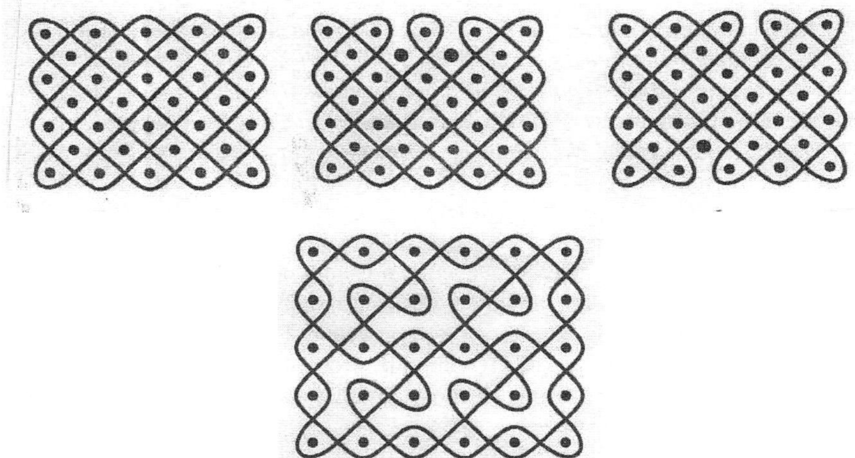

Figure 1.3. *Some sand drawing styles coming from Central Africa, with variations in their symmetries (from [GER 95])*

1.4. Galileo's problem

Probability theory is a part of combinatorics. The notion of probability is itself fundamentally linked to games of chance. Archaeologists exhumed ossicles or tali from prehistoric times that could be used for games. In Pharaonic Egypt, 4,500 years ago, paintings indicated use of these bones to determine movements on game tables.

Later, in Ancient Greece as well as in the Roman world, games played with dice or ossicles were very widespread, at the same time as games of chance but also like the divinatory processes used by fortunetellers. Nothing indicates that such an attempt at a rational explanation was made about these phenomena, considered as purely accidental or divine. We had to wait for the years 1300-1650 in Italy, then in France, for some paradoxes stemming from games of chance to produce the first known great breakthroughs of probability theory.

For example, let us imagine a box with 10 white balls and 20 black balls, from which one ball is drawn at random. Let us assume that the problem is formalized in the following way, noting that there are two possible events: getting one white ball or getting one black ball, and concluding that there is a one in two chance of having a white ball. How can this theoretical reasoning be false? The logical reason is that these two events do not have the same chances of occurring.[1] Simple common sense or minimal game intuition leads us to assume that we have 10 out of 30 chances of getting a white ball. And that must have been known for a very long time.

In more complex contexts, things are less evident. Notably, it is what we call Galileo's problem, posed around 1630 and found in a simplified form about a century before in Gerolamo Cardano's book on games of chance. This book remained in manuscript state until Cardano died in 1576 and was published only in 1667. Galileo's problem is also found in a Latin poem entitled *De Vitula*, dating from the 1300s. The notion of equiprobability finds itself faced with partitions of whole numbers in this book.

Here is the problem. The prince of Tuscany asked Galileo one day: "Why, when three dice are thrown, is the sum 10 obtained more often than the sum 9, even if each one of these sums is obtained in six different ways?". Indeed, we notice that 10 is obtained by $6+3+1$, $6+2+2$, $5+4+1$, $5+3+2$, $4+4+2$ and $4+3+3$. It is six partitions of the number 10 in three parts, noting that order does not come into play. $5+4+1$ for example, is considered as identical to $4+5+1$. Similarly, 9 comes from six partitions of 9 in three parts: $6+2+1$, $5+3+1$, $5+2+2$, $4+4+1$, $4+3+2$ and $3+3+3$.

This way of seeing things can be misleading, as the events corresponding to these partitions are not equiprobable. To have events with the same probability, we

1. The correct method consists of numbering the 30 balls from 1 to 30, which does not change anything about the problem. In these conditions, drawing ball number 1 has a one out of 30 chances of occurring and it is the same for each ball. All draws are equiprobable, there are 10 favorable cases, corresponding to the drawing of one white ball and 30 possible draws, hence the probability 10/30, corresponding to the number of favorable cases divided by the number of possible cases, when all these elementary events are equiprobable.

should take order into consideration, differentiating for example: 5 + 4 + 1 and 4 + 5 + 1.[2] We therefore check that the partitioning of 10 into three parts occurs in 27 cases and the partitioning of 9 into three parts in 25 cases, all these cases having the same probability. It is normal for a player who is accustomed to this game to notice that the sum of 10 appears more often than the sum of 9 by virtue of the law of large numbers. That is now theoretically explained.

In the poem *De Vitula*, an exhaustive breakdown of all the possible ways of drawing three die, and the corresponding partitions, can be found. There are six partitions in three equal parts, such as 1 + 1 + 1 or 2 + 2 + 2, with 30 partitions in three parts, exactly two of which are equal, such as 4 + 1 + 1 (as there are six ways of choosing the number repeated twice and five ways of choosing the third number each time). There are 20 partitions in three different parts, corresponding to C_6^3. The six partitions in three equal parts can only occur in one way; the 30 partitions with two equal parts can occur in three ways (for example 1 1 4 or 1 4 1 or 4 1 1), and the 20 partitions in different parts can occur in six different ways, which give a total of $6 \times 1 + 30 \times 3 + 20 \times 6 = 216$ completely equiprobable cases. The 27 output cases with a sum of 10 for the three die, and the 25 output cases with a sum of 9, come from this type of reasoning.

Later, whereas probability theory is affirmed even more clearly in Pascal's work around 1650, partition theory of numbers followed its own course, thanks to Leibniz around 1700, then Euler around 1740, with the appearance of generating functions, which became an essential tool of combinatorics.

---

2. To understand this, we should consider die as different objects, giving them for example a different color or even throwing them one after the other, which refers to giving them the numbers 1, 2 and 3. This does not modify the game in any way but now we are distinguishing the output order or the color. For example, the fact of having 6 3 1 is not the same event as the output 3 6 1. The number of possible cases is $6^3 = 216$, and they are all equiprobable. For a sum of 10, the favorable cases are:

- 6 3 1, which we can get from 3! = 6 ways, since it is a matter of permutations of three objects;
- 6 2 2 can be obtained in three ways only, depending on the place of the 6, with the two 2s taking the two remaining positions;
- 5 4 1 is obtained in six ways, just like 5 3 2;
- 4 4 2 and 4 3 3 are each obtained in three different ways.

This makes a total of 27 favorable cases, hence the probability 27 / 216. For a sum of nine, we have 6 2 1, 5 3 1 and 4 3 2 in six ways each, 5 2 2 and 4 4 1 in three ways, and 3 3 3 in a single way, hence a total of 25 favorable cases and a probability of 25 / 216.

1.5. Pascal's triangle

Pascal's book on the triangle that carries his name appeared in 1654. This triangle is made up of numbers, each of which is obtained by adding two numbers that are just above it. This gives the form shown in Figure 1.4.

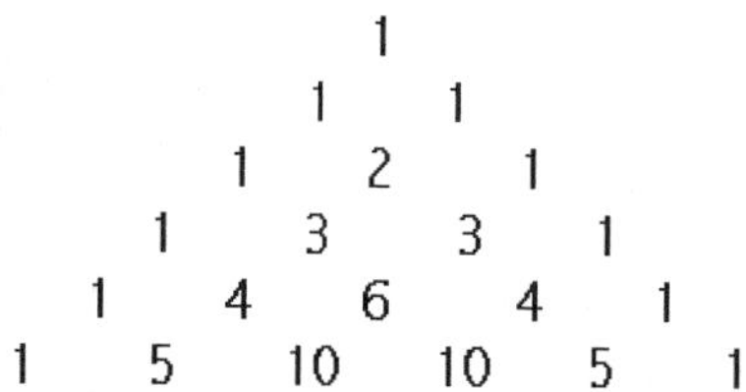

Figure 1.4. *The first lines of Pascal's triangle*

Pascal is clearly making the link between the two ways of seeing these numbers, which are on the one hand numbers of combinations C_n^p (the number of ways of taking p out of n objects) and on the other hand the binomial coefficients obtained when $(a+b)^n$ is developed, for example:

$$(a + b)^5 = a^5 + 5a^4b + 10a^3b^2 + 10a^2b^3 + 5ab^4 + b^5$$

and he gives several applications of them, notably in the domain of probabilities. Whereas Pascal notably contributed to the development of the art of combinatorics, the triangle attributed to him existed well before him, and elsewhere. This is present in the work of Tartaglia during the Italian Renaissance, and it kept appearing in the writings of Arab mathematicians, whether it is Al-Kashi's *Key to Arithmetic* (around 1400) or in Nasir ad Din at-Tusi's collection *Arithmetic with an Iron and Dust* (1255).

Before this, around 1100, As-Samawal dealt with the problem of binomial coefficients in his *Luminous Book on Arithmetic* and specified that he took the formula from Al-Karagi (beginning of the 1000s). In all these literary works, the triangle is not only drawn but its construction explained. For lack of really being used as a way of counting combinations, it is considered as an essential tool of algebraic calculus, notably for calculating values approaching n^{th} roots of numbers.

In China also, the famous triangle appears in Zhu Shi Jie's *The Precious Mirror of the Four Elements*, around 1300, as well as in more ancient texts (see Figure 1.5).

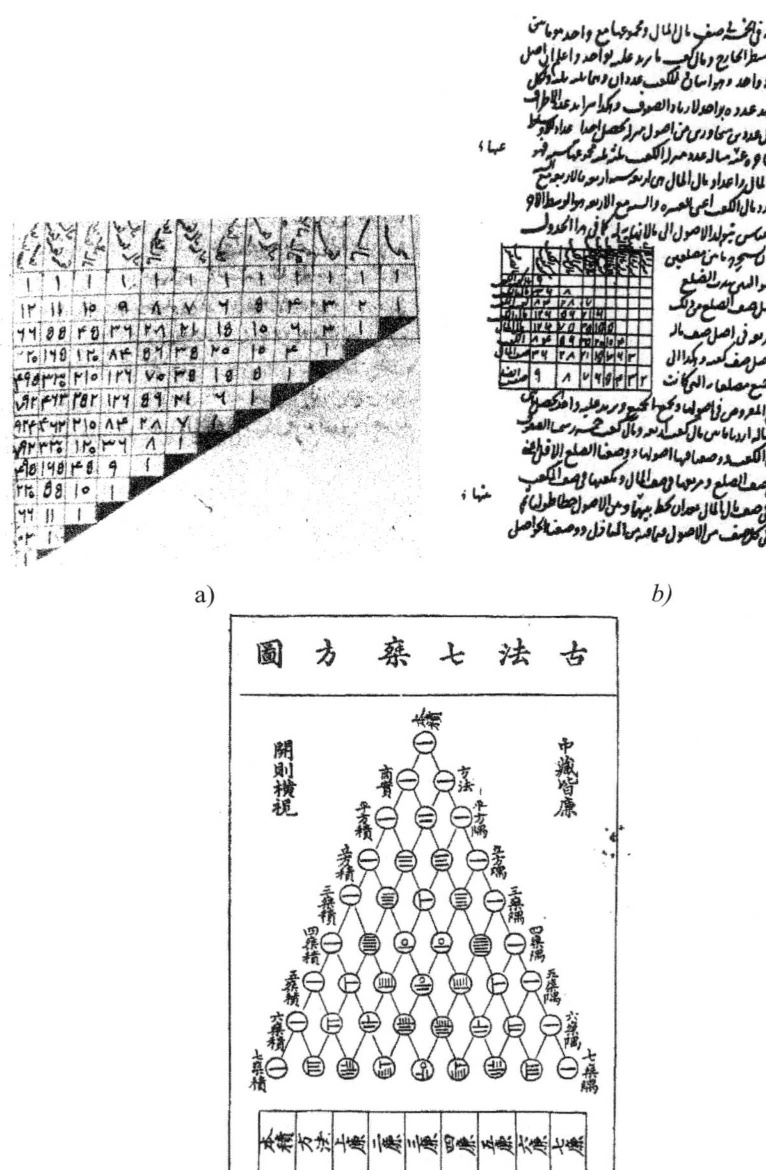

c)

Figure 1.5. *The triangle in Arab (a, b) and Chinese (c) manuscripts*

1.6. The combinatorial explosion: Abu Kamil's problem, the palm grove problem and the Sudoku grid

Many introductory problems in the domain of mathematics refer to farmer and farmyard problems. The art of the mathematician consisted above all of ensuring that there is only one solution to the problem posed. It was a long time before problems with multiple solutions, where the wider number of solutions became the most fascinating aspect of the problem, appeared. A pioneer in the subject was Abu Kamil, an Egyptian mathematician, in the 900s [YOU 76].

In his *Book of Rare Things in Arithmetic* he deals with a problem related to five types of fowl, totaling 100 and the price of 100 with the unit price 2, 1 / 2, 1 / 3, 1 / 4 and 1, respectively. He finds 2,676 solutions to this problem thanks to an algorithm that avoids trying all cases on an *ad hoc* basis (see its solution in section 1.6.1 below). Later another problem discovered, also stemming from Arab tradition, is that of the Palm Grove. In this case, whereas we guess that the problem has a certain number of solutions, above all we want to find one solution, which is not yet immediate.

Here is how the problem is originally posed: an agriculturist wants to bequeath the 81 palm trees in his Palm Grove to his nine children, sharing fairly. The palm trees are numbered 0 to 80, and that also constitutes their annual production of dates, in number of crates produced if you wish. Each child must receive a plot of nine palm trees, in such a way that each plot produces the same amount of dates – 360 crates, as it happens. If we generalize this problem, we take N^2 integers from 0 to $N^2 - 1$. We want to put them in N groups made up of N numbers each, in such a way that the sum of the numbers of each group is the same, namely $N\left(N^2 - 1\right)/2$. We have to find all the solutions. In the original problem, with $N = 9$, it was already difficult to find a solution by trial and error. The author of the problem gives one solution, a clever one. He suggests writing the successive numbers from 0 to $N^2 - 1$ in a square, line after line (see Figure 1.6). The reading of each diagonal modulo the dimensions of the square gives a sum equal to $N (N^2 - 1) / 2$. Actually, the main diagonal gives the following as a sum:

$$0 + (N + 1) + 2(N + 1) + 3(N + 1) + (N - 1)(N + 1)$$

$$= (N - 1)\, N(N + 1) / 2 = N(N^2 - 1) / 2$$

When we take the following diagonal, of the same length but extended modulo N, each number increases by 1 in relation to the preceding diagonal except for the last one, which is $N - 1$ less, which gives the same final sum. It is the same when moving from one diagonal to the next. Hence one solution to the problem.

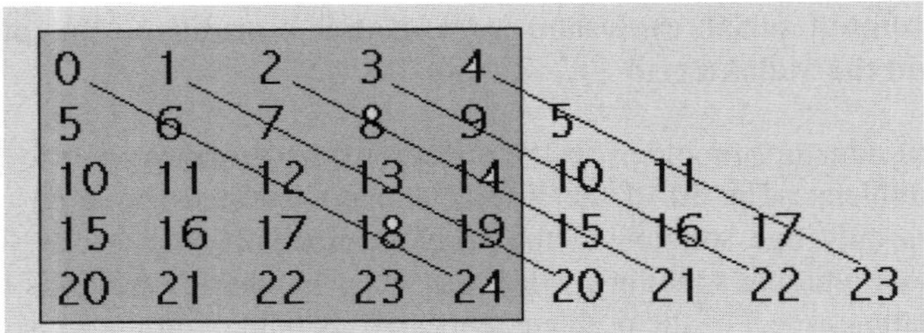

Figure 1.6. *Example with $N = 5$. Each oblique line of gradient 1 gives a sum of 60*

In the example where $N = 5$, the fair plots of palm trees are the following:

(0, 6, 12, 18, 24), (1, 7, 13, 19, 20), (2, 8, 14, 15, 21), (3, 9, 10, 16, 22), (4, 5, 11, 17, 23).[3]

It is only nowadays that an exhaustive search is possible, within certain limits, thanks to computers. That is where the surprise occurs. For $N = 5$ for example, we find that the problem has 3,245,664 solutions, whereas despite some tips it is laborious to find some solutions manually.[4] This combinatorial explosion is nothing exceptional and it continues to astonish us.

An example is that of Sudoku. Let us leave aside the problem of the player who has to complete a grid to find the only solution to this game. First, we have to create complete grids, in a big 9 by 9 square, i.e. place all the numbers from 1 to 9 in each one of the 9 lines, in each one of the 9 columns, as well as in each of the 9 square blocks of 3 by 3 which tile the big square. It was shown that the number of these grids completely filled in with the constraints indicated, is of order $6{,}671 \times 10^{21}$, which makes the game almost never ending.[5]

Below, we give the processing of the three problems that we evoked: Abu Kamil's problem, the Palm Grove problem and the Sudoku grid. The uninformed

---

3. This method gives the idea of finding other solutions by taking lines of gradient $1 / K$, just as we did with diagonals of gradient 1. If K is first with N, we effectively find other solutions. For example for $N = 5$, diagonals of gradient $1 / 2$ give the solution (0 7 14 16 23)(2 9 11 18 20)(3 5 12 19 21)(4 6 13 15 22).

4. Here is the number of solutions $S(N)$ as a function of N:

$S(2) = 1$, $S(3) = 2$, $S(4) = 392$, $S(5) = 3{,}245{,}664$. In turn, the computer is quickly passed.

5. See section 1.6.3 below for details with the method of calculation used by B. Felgenhauer, F. Jarvis and E. Russell ([FEI 06] and [RUS 06]).

reader will find it useful to read the chapters that follow to be able to better assimilate these algorithms.

1.6.1. *Solution to Abu Kamil's problem*

Here 2,678 solutions (and not 2,676 as proposed by Abu Kamil) can be found. To work this out, the two-equation system must be solved with positive integers:

$$\begin{cases} x+y+z+t+u=100 \\ 2x+y/2+z/3+t/4+u=100 \end{cases}$$

The second equation is also written:

$$24x + 6y + 4z + 3t + 12u = 1{,}200$$

We can easily verify that z must be a multiple of 3 and t must be even, i.e. $z = 3z'$, $t = 2t'$. The equation becomes:

$$4x + y + 2z' + t' + 2u = 200$$

From this we deduce that y and t' must have the same parity. We therefore distinguish two cases, as did Abu Kamil:

a) y and t' are even, i.e. $y = 2y'$ *and* $t' = 2t''$.

The second equation becomes $2x + y' + z' + t'' + u = 100$.

By eliminating x with the first equation, $3y' + 5z' + 7t'' + u = 100$ is left, which comes back to processing $3y' + 5z' + 7t'' < 100$.

The maximum possible value of y' is obtained for $z' = 1$ and $t'' = 1$, which gives $y' \leq 29$ or $y \leq 58$. Similarly, we find $z \leq 51$ and $t \leq 52$.

And today we have a computer to end the calculation, which gives 1,233 solutions.

b) y and t' odd, or $y = 2y' - 1$ *and* $t' = 2t'' - 1$.

Operating as before, we arrive at $3y' + 5z' + 7t'' < 105$. This imposes the conditions $y \leq 59$, $z \leq 54$ and $t \leq 50$. In this case we get 1,445 solutions.

The program can be written in the following way:

```
counter 1=0;  counter 2=0;  /* in the end we will have counter 1 = 1233 and
                                counter 2 = 1445 */
for(y=2; y<=58; y+=2)
for(z=3; z<=51; z+=3)
for(t=4; t<=52; t+=4)
if (3*y/2+5*z/3+7*t/4<100) counter 1++;
for(y=1; y<=59; y+=2)
for(z=3; z<=54; z+=3)
for(t=2; t<=50; t+=4)
if ((6*y+7*t)/4+5*z/3<100)  counter 2++;
```

1.6.2. *Palm Grove problem, where N = 4*

Let 16 palm trees be numbered 0 to 15. These palm trees are to be placed in four parcels, each with a value of 30. In each parcel, the numbers will be placed in ascending order. The parcels are classified in ascending order from their first number.

The variable *counter*, set to 0 at the beginning, will give the number of solutions at the end. The first parcel contains 0 and three other numbers *j*, *k* and *l* the sum of which is 30.

We will simply consider *j* between 1 and 9 (because for 10, it would be followed by 11 and 12 minimum, and that exceeds 30).

We will take all possible cases (first *for* loop). Each time, we mark the four numbers of this first parcel as being taken (*done*1[] = 1). Then we take four numbers *ii*, *jj*, *kk*, *ll* out of those that were not yet taken and the sum of which is 30. This gives the second *for* loop. Each time, we mark these numbers as being taken (*done*2[] = 1). Then in a third *for* loop, we choose numbers from the third parcel out of those that were not taken (either in the first or second parcel), on the condition that the smallest of them *iii* is bigger than the smallest *ii* of the second parcel. Then we mark the numbers obtained, the sum of which is 30, by *done*3[] = 1.

The remaining numbers automatically form the fourth parcel, but we only take them if the smallest among them is greater than the smallest *iii* of the third parcel. Each time we get a solution, the *counter* variable increases by 1.

The program continues:

```
counter=0;
first1=0;
for(j=1;j<=13;j++) for(k=j+1;k<=14;k++) for(l=k+1;l<=15;l++)
if (first1+j+k+l==30)
  { for(n=0;n<16;n++) done1[n]=0;
    done1[first1]=1;done1[j]=1;done1[k]=1;done1[l]=1;
    for(n=0;n<16;n++) if (done1[n]==0) { first2=n; break; }
    for(jj=first2+1;jj<=13;jj++)  if (done1[jj]==0)
    for(kk=jj+1;kk<=14;kk++)  if (done1[kk]==0)
    for(ll=kk+1;ll<=15;ll++)  if (done1[ll]==0)
    if (first2+jj+kk+ll==30)
      { for(n=0;n<16;n++) done2[n]=0;
        done2[first2]=1;done2[jj]=1;done2[kk]=1;done2[ll]=1;
        for(n=0;n<16;n++) if (done1[n]==0 && done2[n]==0)
           { first3=n; break; }
        for(jjj=first3+1;jjj<=13;jjj++)  if (done1[jjj]==0 && done2[jjj]==0)
        for(kkk=jjj+1;kkk<=14;kkk++)  if (done1[kkk]==0 &&
                                              done2[kkk]==0)
        for(lll=kkk+1;lll<=15;lll++)  if (done1[lll]==0 && done2[lll]==0)
        if (first3+jjj+kkk+lll==30)
          { for(n=0;n<16;n++) done3[n]=0;
            done3[first3]=1;done3[jjj]=1;done3[kkk]=1;done3[lll]=1;
            counter++;
            count=0;
            for(n=0;n<16;n++) if (done1[n]==1) { a[count++]=n;}
            for(n=0;n<16;n++) if (done2[n]==1) {a[count++]=n;}
            for(n=0;n<16;n++) if (done3[n]==1) {a[count++]=n;}
            for(n=0;n<16;n++)
            if (done1[n]==0 && done2[n]==0 && done3[n]==0)
               {  a[count++]=n;}
            for(count=0;count<16;count++)
                      { if (count>0 && count%4==0) printf(")  (");
                printf("%d ",a[count]);
              }
            printf(")\n");
          }
      }
  }
printf("\nNumber of solutions: %d ", counter);
```

1.6.3. *Complete Sudoku grids*

A calculation that leads to a number of solutions exceeding 10^{21} can only be done with the help of a computer. Even with a computer the final result is so big that it is not possible to imagine obtaining the exhaustive list of results in this way. The waiting time would be too long. We should first perform simplifications.

The idea is to group the solutions into a limited number of classes and count the number of these classes, as well as how many elements they have. We will indicate the beginning of this process. We begin by counting the number of ways of filling in the first band of 9×3 made up of three square blocks B_1, B_2 and B_3 (see Figure 1.7).

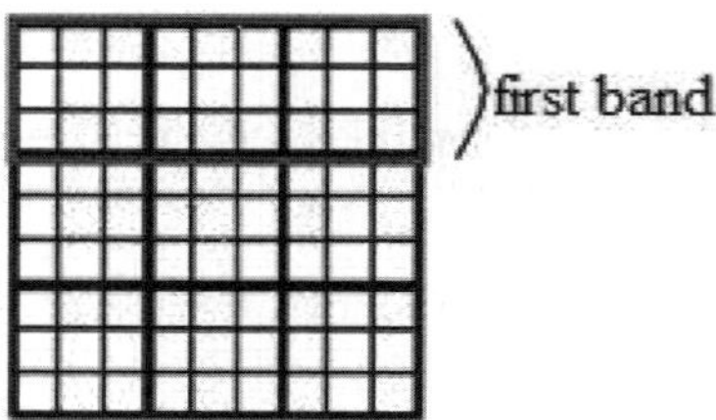

Figure 1.7. *The Sudoku grid and its first horizontal band*

First we fill in block B_1 in the simplest way, with the numbers in natural order (Figure 1.8).

1	2	3
4	5	6
7	8	9

Figure 1.8. *The first block B_1 filled in in natural order*

In fact there are 9! = 9.8.7. …3.2.1 ways to fill in this first block; as many permutations as there are of the 9 numbers. They all boil down to this standard filling: for this, it is sufficient to renumber the complete grid using the permutation that enables it to reduce to the natural order in block B_1. The number of solutions with this standard filling is 9! times smaller than the total number of solutions. Having filled in block B_1 in this way, let us finish filling in the first line of the band. In the first line of block B_2, we should choose three out of six figures, if we are not yet taking into consideration the order in which we place them, i.e. $C_6^3 = 20$ cases.

The first line of block B_3 therefore takes the three remaining numbers, in order-type. Out of these 20 cases, two cases exist where we find the three lines of block B_1 in B_2 (and B_3), but not at the same height:

1	2	3	4	5	6	7	8	9
4	5	6	7	8	9	1	2	3
7	8	9	1	2	3	4	5	6

1	2	3	7	8	9	4	5	6
4	5	6	1	2	3	7	8	9
7	8	9	4	5	6	1	2	3

Each time the first band is completely filled, in order-type of parts of lines of length 3 in each one of blocks B_2 and B_3. Now, let us take order into consideration. In block B_2 we can change the order of the first line, hence $3! = 6$ cases. We can also do this in the two other lines, or 6^3 cases, and similarly in block B_3. These two cases produce 2×6^6 different options.

The other 18 cases remain, such as, for example:

1	2	3	4	5	7	6	8	9
4	5	6	a	8	9	b	c	7
7	8	9	b	c	6	a	4	5

Still in order-type in each of the parts of lines of blocks B_2 and B_3. We notice that three numbers remain (*a*, *b* and *c*, here 1 2 and 3) to choose from, one in the second line of B_2 and two in the last, which gives three different cases. Each time, if we take into consideration the order in the lines, there are still 6^6 cases. It is this way for each of the 18 cases.

Finally the number of ways of filling in the first band, with natural order in block B_1 is $2\times6^6 + 18\times3\times6^6 = 2{,}612{,}736$. Taking all the possible fillings of B_1, that makes $2{,}612{,}736\times9! = 948{,}109{,}639{,}680$ cases for the first band.

Let us now arrange the filled in Sudoku grids in equivalence classes based on their first band. As a representative of each class, we take the grid where block B_1 is in natural order, with the first line of B_2, as well as the first line of B_3, in ascending order and with the first element of the line of B_2 being less than the first element of that of B_3, as for example a grid whose first row is:

1	2	3	4	5	7	6	8	9
4	5	6	1	8	9	2	3	7
7	8	9	3	2	6	1	4	5

From this grid, we can reverse the order of columns 4, 5, 6 or even columns 7, 8, 9, which gives $6\times6 = 36$ valid grids. Each time we can also reverse the order of the two vertical rows formed with block B_2 above in one and with block B_3 in the other, which doubles the valid grids. Taking all the possible B_1 blocks, and renumbering the grid, we again have 9! times more grids. Therefore, instead of having to take the 2,612,736 bands (with B_1 in natural order), we have 72 times less, or 36,288.

We can still improve the situation. A grid remains valid if we do a permutation of the three vertical rows with B_1, B_2 and B_3, respectively, as the first block. Evidently, as soon as block B_1 is concerned, it loses its natural order, but we can return its natural order by renumbering. In addition to the permutations of columns 4, 5, 6 and 7, 8, 9, we can also permutate columns 1, 2, 3. Again we renumber them to return the natural order. Note (by processing on a computer) that there are no longer only 2,051 different first bands with these equivalence-types, i.e. from blocks B_2 and B_3 with B_1 in natural order. We can also permutate the three lines of the first band, then renumber to return to natural order again in B_1. There are no longer 416 possibilities for the first band with B_1 in natural order.

Some extra tips enable us to further reduce the number of classes to 171, then to 71 and even to 44. Therefore for each class we have to search (using a computer) for the number of first bands coming from it, as well as the number of complete fillings of the Sudoku grid from any one of the first bands. Multiplying these two numbers for each one of the classes gives the total number of grids.

In this way the number of grids is found, i.e. $6{,}671 \times 10^{21}$. By dividing by 9! renumbering-types, then by 72 to get the first lines of B_1 and B_2 in the correct order, as well as by 72 so that it is the same on the first columns of B_4 and B_7, we obtain $2^7 \times 27{,}704{,}267{,}971$ as a result.

PART 1

Combinatorics

Part 1

Introduction

On first analysis, combinatorics can be summarized in three formulae, and this is the aim of Chapter 2. Notably, we will see that the number of combinations of p objects taken out of n objects, without taking into consideration the order in which they are taken, is deduced from the number of arrangements where order comes into play. This is a method that applies in quite a few other circumstances. Other theoretical elements – sieve formula and Burnside's formula – are presented in Chapters 8 and 11, respectively. The first formula enables us to select, from a set of objects, those that present certain characteristics and count them. The second enables us to group objects that present symmetries by counting only the groups of those that remain identical through these symmetries.

The practical aspect will be added to this theoretical aspect. How can the results obtained be enumerated without forgetting any of them or giving the same result several times in a row? There are two types of algorithms on this subject: namely, an enumeration of results in alphabetical order, created by searching for how to go from one word to the next; and an enumeration by tree structure, where words gradually get longer and longer, becoming the descending branches of the final tree. These two algorithms, developed in Chapters 3 and 4, answer practically all combinatorics problems when programmed on a computer. They will be implemented from the beginning to the end of this book.

Next, the tools necessary for problem-solving are implemented – the concepts of generating functions and recurrence relations that enable us to obtain counting formulae from the results. As we will see in Chapter 5, these concepts are the immediate result of formal series, i.e. they boil down to the syntax of languages. This is nothing other than combinatorics on words, which is nothing other than mathematical linguistics. These methods will be applied in several contexts. First, they will be applied in routes on a square grid (Chapter 6), also called taxicab geometry. This geometric view will then enable us to deal, in a simple way, with what is called arrangements and combinations with repetition, where arrangements with repetition of the same letters are nothing other than anagrams (Chapter 7). Still with this geometric background, we will bring it all together with the notion of mountain ranges, more officially called parenthesis words. This will provide the opportunity to define Catalan numbers, which appear in many circumstances and which, like Fibonacci numbers, are the basic numbers of combinatorics. The versatility of these numbers will be seen in its entirety in Chapters 9, 10 and 11. Finally, even before the part devoted to graphs, the link between word-making and circulation on a graph is evoked in Chapter 13, where a new tool – matrix calculation – appears.

The last chapters apply to specific contexts. Chapter 14 is devoted to set partition, Chapter 15 to number partition. Chapters 16, 17 and 18 deal with concrete examples linked to the idea of flags, stacking and tiling. Finally, Chapter 19 makes use of and develops the notion of permutations.

Chapter 2

Arrangements and Combinations

Combinatorics is essentially just three formulae, which are very few, but still we must succeed in applying them correctly, which requires some training. In this context, what we call combinations plays a major role. We call C_n^p the number of ways of choosing a parcel of p objects from a group of n objects. Let us indicate that this number, which we write as C_n^p, is also written in recent and originally American mathematical literature as:

$$\binom{n}{p}$$

2.1. The three formulae

Let us begin with a small problem: how many six-digit binary numbers are there? The answer is $2^6 = 64$. Actually, the first of the six digits is either 0 or 1. Each time when this first figure is chosen, there are two ways of taking the second figure: either 0 or 1. Each time the first and second figures are chosen, there are two ways of choosing the third figure. And so on and so forth. In the end, that makes $2 \,.\, 2 \,.\, 2 \,.\, 2 \,.\, 2 \,.\, 2 = 2^6$ cases. One of these binary numbers, namely 011011, can be visualized as indicated in Figure 2.1. This diagram corresponds to what is called an application of set {1, 2, 3, 4, 5, 6} in set {0, 1}.

By definition, an application of a p-element set in a n-element set causes a unique element in the final set to correspond to each element in the initial set. In other words, an arrow leaves each initial element and lands in the final set.

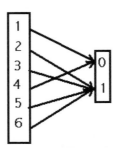

Figure 2.1. *Application of a six-element set in a two-element set. This can be seen as a binary number whose first digit is 0, the second 1, the third 1, etc.*

In the binary numbers example, there are exactly as many six-digit numbers as applications of a six-element set in a two-element set. Hence the property:

PROPERTY 2.1.– The number of applications of a p-element set in a n-element set is n^{p}.

This property can be demonstrated as above. From the first element at the start, we can draw n arrows towards the final set, one towards each element of this set. Each time an arrow is drawn from this first element, we can also draw n arrows from the second element. And so on and so forth. Hence $n \,.\, n \,.\, n \,....n = n^{\mathrm{p}}$ applications.

This property has an immediate consequence: the number of parts of a n-element set is 2^{p}.

Actually each part can be coded using a binary number. Let us take the part $\{a\ c\ d\}$ from the set $\{a\ b\ c\ d\ e\}$ as an example. This part can be coded using the number 0 1 0 0 1, or even: $\begin{pmatrix} a & b & c & d & e \\ 0 & 1 & 0 & 0 & 1 \end{pmatrix}$.

Computer scientists will recognize this as a table, with 0 that means "we take" and 1 that means "we do not take"; hence the reading: we take a, we do not take b, we take c and also d, and we do not take e. There are as many parts of a n-element set as binary numbers of length n, or 2^{n}. This can also be seen in the form of applications. There are as many parts of a n-element set as applications of a n-element set in a two-element set. This is shown, for example, in Figure 2.2.

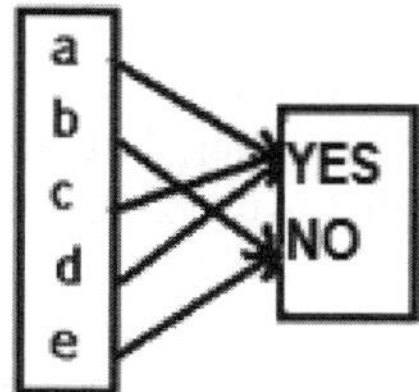

Figure 2.2. *This application corresponds to part {a c d}*

Now let us take a second problem: how many possible trifectas are there in a five-horse race? Let us call the horses *a*, *b*, *c*, *d* and *e*. Let us begin with the enumeration of these trifectas: *abc, abd, abe, acb, acd, ace, adb, adc, ade, aeb, aec, aed, bac, bad, bae, bca, bcd, bce, bda, bdc, bde, bea, bec, bed, cab,…* Note that we have written these successive trifectas in alphabetical order in such a way that we do not forget any of them. Now let us count them. For first place, there are five possible cases (each of the five horses). Each time the first has been chosen, there are four horses remaining that can be second to arrive. Each time the first and second have been chosen, there are three horses remaining for arrival in third place. Finally, the number of trifectas in order is 5 . 4 . 3 = 60. Let us call the arrangement of p out of n a certain way of taking these p objects in a certain order. In the example above, the objects are the horses: $n = 5$ and $p = 3$. The result obtained is generalized to give the following property:

PROPERTY 2.2.– The number of arrangements of p objects taken out of n is:

$$A_n^p = n(n-1)(n-2)\ldots(n-p+1)$$

Note that the number of factors in the formula above is p. To demonstrate the property, we do as above. As the first object, we have the choice from the n objects. Each time this first object has been chosen, there are $n-1$ objects to choose to be the second object. Each time the two first objects have been chosen there are $n-2$ objects to choose to be the third, and so on and so forth until the pth object to be chosen.

One particular case is the one where $n = p$. We call permutation a certain way of arranging n objects in a certain order. Applying the formula above:

– the number of permutations of n objects is $n!$

As a third problem, let us now take combination trifectas. How many are there in a five-horse race?

Let us begin by enumerating them: *abc, abd, abe, acd, ace, ade, bcd, bce, bde, cde*. We have just found 10 combination trifectas. Let us take the case *abc* for example. This trifecta is in random order, but note that among all the ways of writing it we have chosen the one that is the lowest in alphabetical order.

To be more precise, there are six ways of writing *abc* in all possible orders: *abc, acb, bac, bca, cab* and *cba*. We choose the one where the letters are placed in ascending alphabetical order. For each combination trifecta, we find six straight trifectas. We found 60 straight trifectas, so there are $60 / 6 = 10$ combination trifectas. Let us call the combination of p out of n objects a certain way of taking a parcel of p objects out of n. This implies that the order in which we take these p objects does not come into play. By analogy with the above, we arrive at the following property:

PROPERTY 2.3.– The number of combinations of p objects taken from n objects, or even the number of ways of taking p out of n objects without taking order into consideration, is:

$$C_n^p = \frac{n(n-1)(n-2)...(n-p+1)}{p!}$$

Note again that in the numerator exactly p factors are present. Another way of expressing this formula is:

$$C_n^p = \frac{n!}{p!(n-p)!}$$

but this introduces repetitions and this formula only applies in some theoretical cases – those that necessitate the exclusive presence of permutations (notably to apply Stirling's formula, which gives an approximate value of $n!$). To demonstrate the combinations formula, it is enough to note that one way of taking p objects in random order corresponds to $p!$ ways of taking p objects in order, where $p!$ is exactly the number of permutations of these p objects.

What is the real meaning of the number C_n^p? It is the number of ways of taking p out of n objects (parceled), so it is also the number of p-element parts of a n-element set. Let us now imagine that we have a set of pigeonholes with n empty pigeonholes in front of us. The number of ways of placing p objects considered as identical in these n pigeonholes, holding one object at most per case, is also the number of ways of choosing p out of n pigeonholes to be filled, i.e. C_n^p (see Figure 2.3).

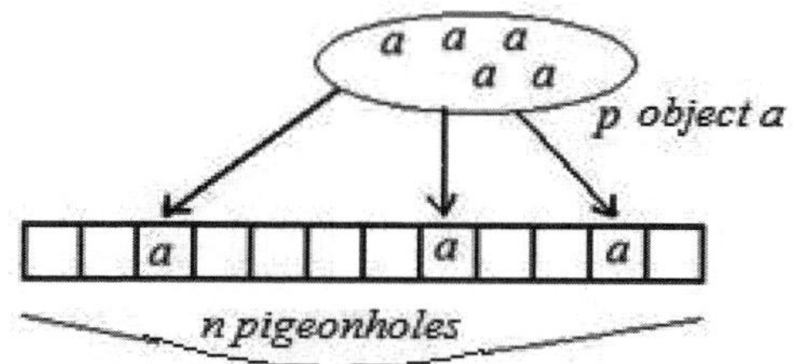

Figure 2.3. *C_n^p is the number of ways of placing p object a in n pigeon holes, holding at most one in each case*

2.2. Calculation of C_n^p, Pascal's triangle and binomial formula

There are two essential formulae for combinations:

– *The first formula is:*

$$C_n^p = C_n^{n-p}$$

because the number of ways of taking p out of n objects is also the number of ways of leaving (or eliminating) $n - p$ of them out of n. This formula enables us to simplify the calculations. Rather than calculating C_8^6, we will do $C_8^2 = 8.7 / 2 = 28$. As soon as p is greater than $n / 2$, we replace p with $n - p$.

– *The second formula is:*

$$C_n^p = C_{n-1}^{p-1} + C_{n-1}^p$$

To show this, let us imagine that out of the n objects we prefer one, called X for example. The combinations of p out of the n objects is divided into two categories: those that contain object X and those that do not contain it.

To get the combinations in the first category, containing X, $p - 1$ out of $n - 1$ objects are left to be taken, hence C_{n-1}^{p-1} ways.

To get those not containing X, this refers to taking p out of $n - 1$ objects, hence C_{n-1}^p ways.

By placing the combinations C_n^p in a benchmark n, p, we get what is called Pascal's triangle (see Figure 2.4).

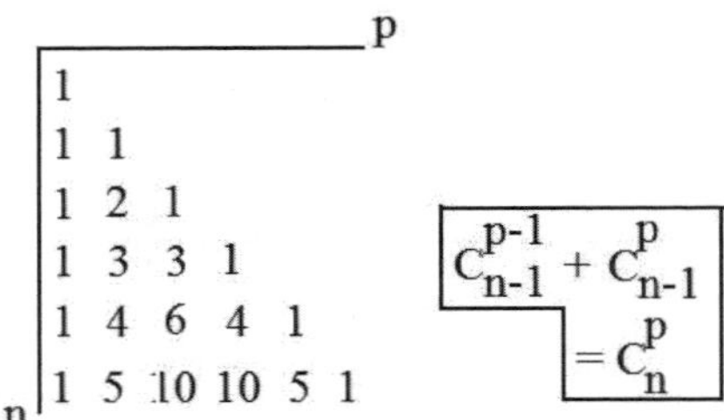

Figure 2.4. *Pascal's triangle and its construction*

An element of a line is obtained by adding the element that is in the line above it in the same column with the one that is in the preceding column. The algorithm that enables us to calculate C_n^p for a given n and p is deduced from it. We take line 0, as well as column 0 made up only of 1s. Each line, starting from line 0, is placed alternately in a table $c[p + 1]$. A line k of the triangle, located between lines 0 and n, has the occupied length $k + 1$, with everything following being set to 0. Knowing one line enables us to know the next line, on the condition that element 1 is added in the initial position. The new value of $c[i]$ is obtained by adding the old value of $c[i-1]$ to the old value of $c[i]$, hence the need to go from right to left (going from left to right we would get the new value of $c[i-1]$). We get the following program:

```
– c[0]=1;  for(i=1; i <= p; i++) c[i]=0;
– for(line=1; line <=n; line++) for(i= p; i >=1; i--)  c[i]+=c[i-1].
```

Pascal's triangle notably enables us to develop the polynomial $(a+b)^n$. For example, $(a+b)^4 = a^4 + 4a^3b + 6a^2b^2 + 4ab^3 + b^4$, where we find the elements of line 4 of Pascal's triangle as coefficients. This is called Newton's binomial formula, which is expressed in its general form:

$$(a+b)^n = \sum_{k=0}^{n} C_n^k a^k b^{n-k}$$

To show this formula, it is enough to see where the coefficient of the term in $a^k b^{n-k}$ is coming from. In the product $(a+b)(a+b)...(a+b)$, a term in $a^k b^{n-k}$ comes from the a terms taken in k parentheses (with b being taken in the $n - k$ other parentheses). There are as many $a^k b^{n-k}$ terms as ways of choosing k out of the n parentheses, or C_n^k ways, which gives the coefficient of the term in $a^k b^{n-k}$.

2.3. Exercises

2.3.1. *Demonstrating formulae*

a) Show that: $\sum_{k=0}^{n} C_n^k = 2^n$.

The number of parts of a n-element set is 2^n. These parts can be classified according to their number of elements. There are C_n^k k-element parts. By making k vary from 0 to n, and by adding the number of parts classified in this way according to their number of elements, we get the formula sought.

b) Show that: $C_n^0 - C_n^1 + C_n^2 - C_n^3 + \ldots + (-1)^n C_n^n = 0$

All we have to do is to develop $(1 + x)^n$ following binomial formula, then make $x = -1$.

c) Show that: $\sum_{k=0}^{q} C_n^k C_p^{q-k} = C_{n+p}^q$.

Let us consider a set with $n + p$ elements made up of n red balls and p green balls, for example. The number of ways of taking q objects out of these $n + p$ balls is C_{n+p}^q. These parts made up of q balls can be classified following the number k of red balls, where k is between 0 and q, at least when the total number n of red balls is at least equal to q. To get the parts with k red balls and $q - k$ green balls, we begin by choosing k red balls from the n balls, i.e. C_n^k ways, then each time $q - k$ balls are left to be taken from p, i.e. C_p^{q-k} ways. Hence the formula requested. This formula remains true when the total number n of red balls is less than q, as the additional terms C_n^k of the formula $k > n$ are all null.

d) Find two summation formulae using that of Pascal's triangle: $C_n^p = C_{n-1}^p + C_{n-1}^{p-1}$, *by repeatedly expanding the last term* C_{n-1}^{p-1}, *then the term* C_{n-1}^p.

Let us repeatedly expand the last term:

$$C_n^p = C_{n-1}^p + C_{n-1}^{p-1}$$

$$= C_{n-1}^p + C_{n-2}^{p-1} + C_{n-2}^{p-2}$$

$$= C_{n-1}^p + C_{n-2}^{p-1} + C_{n-3}^{p-2} + C_{n-3}^{p-3}$$

....

$$= C_{n-1}^{p} + C_{n-2}^{p-1} + C_{n-3}^{p-2} + C_{n-4}^{p-3} + \ldots + C_{n-k-1}^{p-k} + C_{n-k-1}^{p-k-1}$$

....

$$= C_{n-1}^{p} + C_{n-2}^{p-1} + C_{n-3}^{p-2} + C_{n-4}^{p-3} + \ldots + C_{n-k-1}^{p-k} + \ldots + C_{n-p}^{0}$$

$$= \sum_{k=0}^{p} C_{n-k-1}^{p-k}$$

For example: $C_6^3 = C_5^3 + C_4^2 + C_3^1 + C_2^0$.

Let us repeatedly expand the first term of the right member:

$$C_n^p = C_{n-1}^p + C_{n-1}^{p-1}$$

$$= C_{n-2}^p + C_{n-2}^{p-1} + C_{n-1}^{p-1}$$

$$= C_{n-3}^p + C_{n-3}^{p-1} + C_{n-2}^{p-1} + C_{n-1}^{p-1}$$

....

$$= C_{n-k}^p + C_{n-k}^{p-1} + C_{n-k+1}^{p-1} + \ldots + C_{n-3}^{p-1} + C_{n-2}^{p-1} + C_{n-1}^{p-1}$$

....

$$= C_{p-1}^p + C_{p-1}^{p-1} + C_p^{p-1} + C_{p+1}^{p-1} + C_{p+2}^{p-1} :+ .. + C_{p+k}^{p-1} + \ldots + C_{n-1}^{p-1}$$

$$= \sum_{k=0}^{n-p} C_{p-1+k}^{p-1}$$

For example: $C_6^3 = C_2^2 + C_3^2 + C_4^2 + C_5^2$.

2.3.2. *Placing rooks on a chessboard*

p rooks are placed on a $n \times n$ chessboard in such a way that no rook can be taken by another. This means that there are never two rooks in the same line or in the same column. This constraint means that *p* must be less than or equal to *n*. How many ways are there of placing these *p* rooks?

First, let us assume that the *p* rooks are placed on the *p* first columns of the chessboard (one per column). In the first column there are *n* ways of placing a rook. Once this first rook has been placed, there are $n - 1$ ways of placing a rook in the second column. And so on and so forth until column number *p*. This already gives a total of $n(n-1)(n-2)...(n-p+1) = A_n^p$ ways. What we have just done by taking the first p columns can be re-done with any other way of choosing p out of the n columns, which gives C_n^p cases. Finally, there are $C_n^p A_n^p$ ways of placing p rooks on the chessboard. Note that if $p = n$, we find the number of permutations. Placing n rooks in non-attack positions on a $n \times n$ chessboard visualizes a permutation of $n!$ possible permutations.

2.3.3. *Placing pieces on a chessboard*

Four pieces are placed on a chessboard with 4×4 = 16 squares.

a) How many possible placings are there?

$C_{16}^4 = 1{,}820$.

b) How many ways are there, where no column remains empty?

This requires us to place one piece per column, i.e. $4^4 = 256$ cases.

c) How many ways are there, where one and only one column remains empty?

We begin by choosing the column that remains empty, i.e. four cases. Once this column has been chosen, we are left with placing the four pieces on the three remaining columns without any of the columns remaining empty, which means we must place two pieces in one column, and one piece on each of the two remaining columns. There are three ways of choosing one of the three columns, the one where we are going to put two pieces, and each time there are $C_4^2 = 6$ ways of placing the two pieces there. Each time this is done, there are four ways of placing a piece on a remaining column, and still four ways of putting one of them in the last column. Hence a total of: 4×3×6×4×4 = 1,152 cases.

c) again: For the question above, someone suggests the following solution: we begin by choosing the column that is going to remain empty, which makes four cases. Each time, the four pieces need to be placed on the three remaining columns, without any of them remaining empty. To do this, we begin by placing three pieces, each one in a column, i.e. 4^3 cases. Then we place the last piece in one of the nine remaining squares. We get $4 \times 4^3 \times 9 = 2{,}304$ cases in total. But this calculation is incorrect. Correct it.

The error comes from the order taken for placing three pieces (written x) first, then the forth (written $*$). By doing this, the same placing is counted twice. For example, the two layouts in Figure 2.5 in fact only count as one.

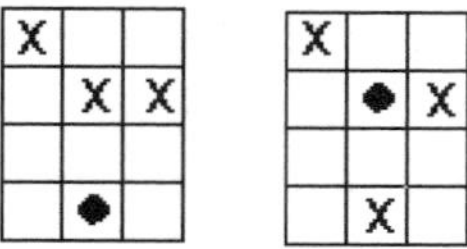

Figure 2.5. *Two identical layouts*

We deduce the exact result from it, obtained by dividing the preceding result by 2, i.e. 2,304 / 2 = 1,152 cases.

d) How many ways are there of placing the four pieces with exactly two empty columns?

We begin by choosing the two columns that remain empty, i.e. $C_4^2 = 6$ cases. Each time we are left with placing the four pieces in the two remaining columns. We therefore distinguish two cases:

– either we put three pieces in one column and one piece in the other: there are two ways of choosing the column where the three pieces are being placed, then $C_4^3 = 4$ ways of putting the three pieces there. Having done this, there are four ways of placing a piece in the remaining column left, hence a total of 2×4×4 = 32 cases; or

– we put two pieces in one column and two pieces in the other: there are $C_4^2 = 6$ ways of putting two pieces in one column, and as many ways of putting two of them in the other. Hence 6×6 = 36 cases in total.

Finally, we find: 6 (32 + 36) = 408 cases.

e) How many ways are there where three columns remain empty?

There are four ways of choosing the column in which to put the four pieces, hence four cases.

Therefore we can check that we have found all the ways of placing four pieces on the chessboard by adding all the cases according to the number of empty columns:

$$256 + 1{,}152 + 408 + 4 = 1{,}820$$

2.3.4. *Pascal's triangle modulo k*

Thanks to a program, we draw Pascal's triangle by coloring each point n, p with the color corresponding to the number C_n^p brought back modulo k, i.e. between 0 and $k - 1$, which needs k different colors (when C_n^p exceeds k, we take away the number k from the number C_n^p as many times as necessary to fall between 0 and $k-1$). The results for various modulos are shown in Figure 2.6.[1]

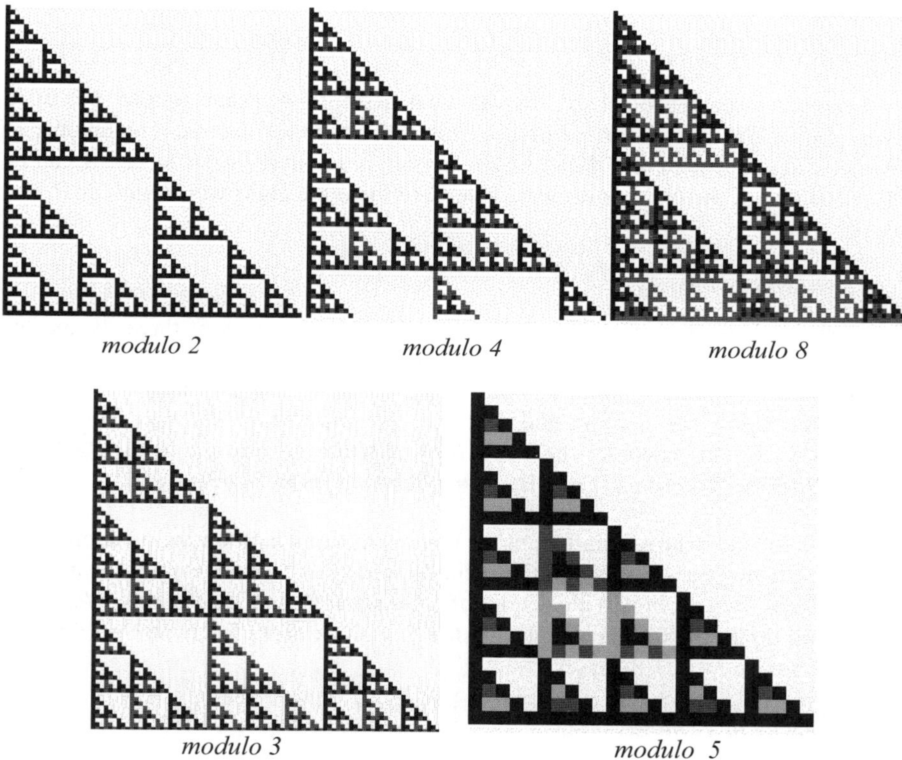

Figure 2.6. *Pascal's triangle modulo for a given number*

2.3.5. *Words classified based on their blocks of letters*

Here we will consider all 11-letter words made up of four letter *A*s and seven letter *B*s. We will then classify them according to their number of *A* blocks. A block of *A*s can be of length one, as in *BAB*..., of length two as in *BAAB*... or *AAB*..., of length three as in *BAAAB*..., or of length four as in *AAAAB*... We want to know how many words there are where the four letter *A*s make up a single block, then how many with two blocks, with three blocks, and with four blocks.

1. For theoretical specifications, see [AUD 95, LEN 98, PEI 04].

To find out how many of these words there are, we begin by placing the four *A*s, which will occupy four out of 11 places, i.e. $C_{11}^{4} = 330$ ways. Let us classify them now according to their number of blocks of *A*.

a) Words with one block of As.

Let us replace the block of four-*A*s with a single ***A***. For example, the word *BAAAABBBBBB* becomes *B**A**BBBBBB*. This conversion is bijective. The number of words of length 8 with one ***A*** and seven *B*s is eight (as many ways as one ***A*** can be placed in one of the eight positions). Therefore there are eight words with an *AAAA* block.

b) Words with two blocks of A.

Here we distinguish three cases: the first block is made up of three *A*s and the second of one single *A*, or the first block is composed of two *A*s as is the second, or the first block has one single *A* and the second three *A*s. Let us imagine any one of these three cases, for example the first. Let us replace the first four-letter block *AAAB* with ***A***. For example, the word *BBBAAABBBBA* becomes *BBB**A**BBBA*, or *AAABABBBBBB* becomes ***A**ABBBBBB*, and this conversion is bijective.

In this second expression, there is no longer any constraint on the position of the letter ***A***. The number of words of the second category is C_{8}^{2}, as many ways as there are of placing two ***A***s in two blocks out of eight squares, hence 28 words. We do the same in all three cases, always replacing the first block of ***A***s followed by a *B* with a single ***A***. Hence 3×28 = 84 cases.

c) Words with three blocks of A.

There are three cases here: 2-1-1, 1-2-1 and 1-2-2 according to the length of successive blocks of *A*. Let us replace the first two blocks of *A*, to which a *B* is added each time, with a single ***A***. For example, the word *BAABABBBABB* becomes *B**A**ABBABB*. There are $C_{8}^{3} = 56$ of these last words of length 8. Hence, finally, 3×56 = 168 words.

d) Words with four blocks of A.

Here we replace each one of the first three blocks of *A*, each of which is followed by a *B* with a single ***A***. For example, the word *BABABBABBBA* is transformed into *B**AA**B**A**BBA*. This makes $C_{8}^{4} = 70$ words.

2.3.6. *Diagonals of a polygon*

Let us consider a polygon with N sides and N vertices. Let us assume that three diagonals never intersect each other at the same point (see Figure 2.7).

a) What is the number of diagonals?

Starting from each vertex, we have $N - 3$ diagonals. With all the vertices, that makes $N(N - 3)$, but these diagonals are counted twice. The number of diagonals is therefore $N(N - 3) / 2$. Let us state another method: we take all the pairs of vertices, namely C_N^2 cases, but by doing this we count not only the diagonals but the N sides. The number of diagonals is $C_N^2 - N = N(N - 3) / 2$.

b) What is the number of intersection points of the diagonals, considered here as interior segments of the polygon?

Each pair of non-successive sides of the polygon forms a quadrilateral. This quadrilateral has four sides and two diagonals, i.e. six segments. If we remove the two sides of the original polygon, four segments remain: two are diagonals or sides of the polygon that do not intersect each other (as segments); and two are two diagonals of the polygon that intersect each other at a point within the polygon. For each pair of sides of the polygon, we have two diagonals that intersect each other at a point within the polygon. This association is bijective. The number of intersection points of the diagonals is C_N^4.

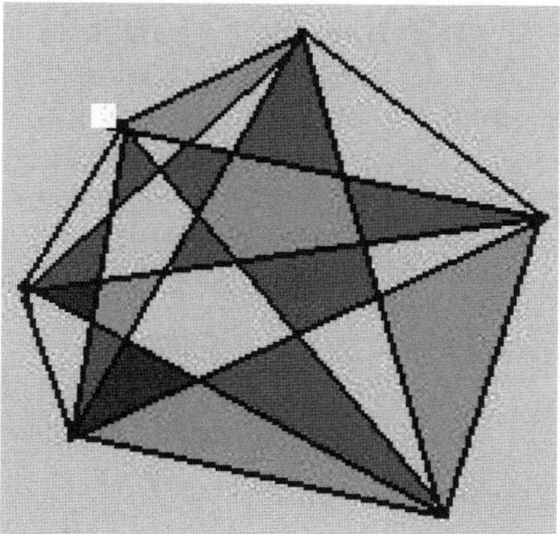

Figure 2.7. *Polygon with $N = 6$ vertices, with 9 diagonals, 15 intersection points between diagonals within the polygon, 39 segments cut on the diagonals, and 25 interior regions of the polygon*

c) How many segments do we get on the diagonals (as segments) of the polygon, delimited by the intersection points and the vertices?

There are $C_N^{\,2} - N$ diagonals. Each intersection point of two diagonals gives one more segment on each one of the two diagonals concerned, hence two more. The number of segments on the diagonals is:

$$C_N^{\,2} - N + 2C_N^{\,4} = N(N-3)(N^2 - 3N + 8) / 12$$

Let us state another method: starting from a vertex, we can trace $N - 3$ diagonals. The first of these diagonals leaves one vertex of the polygon on one side and $N - 3$ vertices on the other. This diagonal is intersected by $1(N-3)$ diagonals, which gives $1(N - 3) + 1$ segments on this diagonal. The second diagonal leaves two vertices on one side and $N - 4$ on the other, it is intersected by $2(N - 4)$ diagonals, which makes $2(N - 4) + 1$ segments. And so on and so forth. All the diagonals stemming from a vertex give:

$$1(N-3) + 2(N-4) + 3(N-5) + \ldots + (N-3)1 + N - 3 \text{ segments}$$

We do the same for each vertex, which multiplies the result above by N. With each diagonal being counted twice, however, we divide the whole thing by two. Finally the number of segments is:

$$(1(N-3) + 2(N-4) + \ldots + (N-3)1) \ + (N-3)\, N / 2$$

Furthermore the quantity $1N + 2(N-1) + \ldots + N1$ is the coefficient of X^{N-1} in the product: $(1 + 2X + 3X^2 + \ldots)^2 = 1 / (1 - X)^4$, and we know that the coefficient is equal to $C_{N+2}^{\,3}$. Now taking the term:

$$1(N-3) + 2(N-2) + \ldots + (N-3).1$$

this one is equal to $C_{N-1}^{\,3}$. The number of segments is therefore:

$$(C_{N-1}^{\,3} + N - 3)\, N / 2 = N(N-3)(N^2 - 3N + 8) / 12$$

d) What is the number of regions delimited by the diagonals and sides within the polygon?

The graph that concerns us is made up of $N + C_N^{\,4}$ vertices and:

$$N + C_N^{\,2} - N + 2C_N^{\,4} \text{ edges} = C_N^{\,2} + 2C_N^{\,4} \text{ edges.}$$

As this graph is connected and planar, we can apply Euler's formula, linking the number of regions R, the number of edges A and the number of vertices S (see Chapter 29), i.e.:

$$R = A - S + 2 = C_N^{\ 2} + 2C_N^{\ 4} - N - C_N^{\ 4} + 2 = C_N^{\ 2} + C_N^{\ 4} - N + 2$$

If we do not count the (infinite) region surrounding the polygon, the number of interior regions is:

$$C_N^{\ 2} + C_N^{\ 4} - N + 1$$

Here is an application of this result in a different context: we place N points on a circle and we draw all the chords joining these points 2×2, assuming that three chords never intersect each other at the same point. The inside of the circle is thus intersected in a certain number of regions. What is the number?

The chords give all the sides of a polygon with N vertices, as well as its diagonals. The number of regions inside this polygon is that of the formula obtained above. To get all the regions inside of the circle, all we have to do is to add the N regions situated between the circle and the sides of the polygon, hence the number sought, equal to $C_N^{\ 2} + C_N^{\ 4} + 1$.

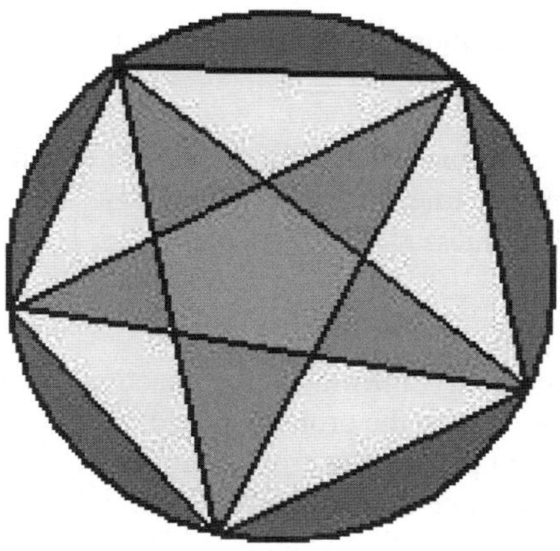

Figure 2.8. *A circle with N = 5 points and the corresponding chords, delimiting 16 regions*

2.3.7. *Number of times a number is present in a list of numbers*

Here we consider all the numbers from 0 to 999…999 made up of n number 9s. When we write all these numbers, how many times is the number 5 present? Deal notably with the case where $n = 5$.

2.3.7.1. *Method 1*

For $n = 1$, from 0 to 9 the number 5 is written once.

For $n = 2$, from 0 to 99 the number 5 is written 10 times as a figure in the tens, from 50 to 59, and 10 times as a figure of units, for each one of the ten blocks of tens, i.e. 20 times in all.

For $n = 3$, from 0 to 999 the number 5 is written 100 times as a figure in the hundreds, and 20 times for each block of hundreds, i.e. $20\times10 = 200$ times as a digit in the tens or units, hence 300 times in total.

For $n = 4$, from 0 to 9,999 the number 5 is written 1,000 times as a figure in the thousands, and elsewhere $300\times10 = 3{,}000$ times, i.e. 4,000 times in total.

For $n = 5$, from 0 to 99,999 the number 4 is written 10,000 times as a figure in the tens of thousands, and elsewhere $4{,}000\times10 = 40{,}000$ times, i.e. 50,000 times in total.

By immediate generalization, for some n, from 0 to $10^n - 1$, the number 5 is written: $n\times10^n - 1$ times.

This is shown by recurrence. It is true for $n = 1$. When it is true for a certain value of n, this remains true for $n + 1$ because the number 5 is written $10^n + n\times10^n = (n + 1)\ 10^n$ times.

2.3.7.2. *Method 2*

Method 1 above perfectly illustrates the reaction of a mathematician, with conventional arsenal, faced with the problem posed. At the same time it masks some aspects of the situation and prevents us from seeing the best solution to the problem. To find the solution, let us take all the words of N length, 10^N of them. Let us begin by considering the unit figure of these numbers. This number is as many times 0 as it is 1, 2, 3, …, 9. The number of times 5 is present is therefore $10^N / 10 = 10^{N-1}$. Next, let us take the tens figure. The number 5 is as present there as the other figures, hence there are 10^{N-1} number 5s as a figure in the tens. We continue in this way for the figure in the hundreds, thousands, etc. The number of 5s is therefore $N\times10^{N-1}$. This method is interesting as it shows that the number 5 is present the same number of times as a figure in the units, tens, etc., which the method above could not see.

2.3.8. *Words of length n based on 0 and 1 without any block of 1s repeated*

a) Determine the number $u(N)$ of words of length N, based on an alphabet of two letters 0 and 1, and not having any 11 blocks

For example, words of length 4 are 0000, 0001, 000, 0101, 1000, 1001 and 1010, numbering $u(4) = 8$ of them. Such words can be divided into two categories:

– those that end in 0. Words of length $N - 1$ that precede this 0 have no block 11, and they number $u(N - 1)$;

– those that end in 1, and therefore also in 01. Words of length $N - 2$, which precede this 01 block do not have any 11 blocks and number $u(N - 2)$.

Finally $u(N)$ obeys the recurrence relation: $u(N) = u(N - 1) + u(N - 2)$ with $u(1) = 2$, for words 0 and 1, and $u(2) = 3$ for words 00, 01, 10. We would also have $u(0) = 1$. As we will see later in a repeated way, a classic sequence called the Fibonacci sequence, generally written as $F(N)$, obeys the same recurrence relation: $F(N) = F(N - 1) + F(N - 2)$ with $F(0) = 0$ and $F(1) = 1$ to start. We deduce from this that:

$$F(2) = 1, F(3) = 2, \ldots$$

The sequence $u(N)$ is nothing other than Fibonacci's sequence with a difference, more precisely: $u(N) = F(N + 2)$.

b) We call the number of such words of length N with the presence of K letter 1s u(N, K). Determine u(N, K).

Method 1

The isolated letter 1s must be inserted between the $N - K$ letter 0s or at the ends of words. What we have to do is place K letters in $N - K + 1$ possible positions, which is valid even for $K = N$, i.e. $u(N, K) = C_{N-K+1}^{K}$. Notably, $u(N, K) = 0$ when $N - K + 1 < K$, i.e. $N < 2K - 1$.

Method 2

We separate these words into two categories: those that end in 0 and those that end in 1. In the case where the word ends in 0, all the 1s are followed by a 0, and we can group the 10 blocks by expressing them as A. We therefore have words of length $N - K$, based on 0 and A, where the letter A is present K times, i.e. C_{N-K}^{K} words. In the case where the word ends in 1, one word of length $N - 1$ remains, with the letter 1 present $K - 1$ times, and always followed by a 0. If we replace the 10 block in this word with A, we will get a word of length $N - 1 - (K - 1) = N - K$, with letter A present $K - 1$ times, i.e. C_{N-K}^{K-1} cases. Finally the number of these words is:

$$C_{N-K}^{K} + C_{N-K}^{K-1} = C_{N-K+1}^{K}$$

c) Deduce a relationship between the Fibonacci numbers and binomial coefficients from it.

Thanks to the above, $\sum_{K=0}^{[\frac{N+1}{2}]} u(N,K) = F(N+2)$, i.e. $\sum_{K=0}^{[\frac{N+1}{2}]} C_{N-K+1}^{K} = F(N+2)$ and assuming $n = N + 2$:

$$\sum_{K=0}^{[\frac{n-1}{2}]} C_{n-1-K}^{K} = F(n)$$

d) The words defined above are each written in the form $a_1\ a_2\ \ldots\ a_N$. Let us now place them on a circle where the graduations 1, 2, 3, ..., N are marked, forbidding the presence of 11 blocks from it, which comes back to adding a condition: block $a_N a_1$ must be different to 11. How many circular words are there?

What we have to do is to remove words corresponding to those beginning and ending in 1 from the number of words found before. These new forbidden words begin with 10 and end in 1.

This refers to placing $K - 2$ letter 10s or A out of: $(N - 3) - (K - 2) = N - K - 1$ letters, i.e. C_{N-K-1}^{K-2} cases. The number of circular words is $C_{N-K+1}^{K} - C_{N-K-1}^{K-2}$. Having done all these calculations, we find:

$$\frac{N}{N - K} C_{N-K}^{K} \text{ words.}$$

Another way of doing this consists of separating the circular words into two categories: those where the letter a_1 is 0, in this case we are left with $u(N - 1, K)$ words to be created; and those where the letter a_1 is equal to 1, which imposes $a_2 = 0$ and also $a_N = 0$, we are left with $u(N - 3, K - 1)$ words to be constructed. The number of words on the circle is:

$$C_{N-K}^{K} + C_{N-K-1}^{K-1} = (N / (N - K))\ C_{N-K}^{K}$$

having carried out all calculations.

This number can also be seen as the number of ways of choosing K non-consecutive points out of N points placed on a circle.

2.3.9. *Programming: classification of applications of a set with n elements in itself following the form of their graph*

Let us call 0, 1, 2, 3, ..., $N-1$ the elements of the initial set, like those of the final set. The number of applications of the set with N elements in itself is N^N because for each initial element we have the choice between the N elements of the final set.

a) Make the program that enumerates all these applications

Let us take a table $a[N]$ of length N where the indices from 0 to $N-1$ designate the elements of the initial set. The boxes contain the elements from the final set corresponding to the initial indices. Each filling of the table gives one of the applications sought.

As each case contains a number included between 0 and $N-1$, the table can be considered as a number of length N written in base N. Writing all these numbers one after the other in table $a[N]$, we get all the applications. The program consists of taking all the numbers (in base 10) from 0 to N^N-1, and converting them into base N with a length N. In this way all the applications are enumerated.

How do we go from a number to its expression in base N? To simplify things, let us take $N-2$. For example, the number 13 is written 1101 in binary, which means $1.2^3+1.2^2+0.2^1+1.2^0=13$ going from most significant to least significant, or if you prefer 1011, i.e. $1.2^0+0.2^1+1.2^2+1.2^3=13$ going from least significant to most significant. We can in this case add as many 0s as we want.

For example, 13 is written in base 2 with a length of six in the form 101100, going from least significant to most significant. To get this number, we begin by dividing 13 by 2. With $13=1.2^0+2.(0.2^0+1.2^1+1.2^2)$, the division gives 6 as quotient and 1 as remainder, which makes up the coefficient of the term in 2^0, i.e. the first digit of the binary expression going from least significant to most significant. Then we can start again with the quotient $6=0.2^0+1.2^1+1.2^2$. We divide it by 2, hence the new quotient is 3 and the remainder 0, which is the second digit of the binary expression of 13.

The successive remainders of the divisions by 2 give the binary expression. This method is generalized to the expression of a number in some base N. If we want to get the expression of a number in base *N* with a length *N*, all we have to do is make *N* successive divisions by *N*, noting the remainders obtained. Hence the program:

```
NN=(long int) pow((double)N, (double)N);        /* it is N^N */
for(number=0; number<NN; number++)
{ q=number;    /* q contains the successive quotients, with number at the start */
  for(i=0;i<N;i++)  {  r=q%N; q= q/N ; a[N-1-i]= r ; }  /* the remainders r are
                                                          placed in a[N] */
  display table a[N] giving the number in base N from most significant to least
  significant
}
```

b) Each time an application is found, and placed in array a[N], we construct a new array b[N] where we put in box number i the number of times the number i is touched in the final set by arrows coming from the initial set.

For example the application that is written 011 in a[] for N = 3 becomes 120 in b[]. Then we reorganize array b[] in such a way that it is sorted according to descending values of its contents. We need to develop a program to get b[] array.

All we have to do is to add back these few lines within the *for* loop made in the preceding question.

```
for(i=0; i<N; i++) b[i]=0;          /* set to zero array b[ ] */
for(i=0; i<N; i++)  b[a[i]]++;  /* we increase the number of times a[i] is present
                                   by 1 */
for(i=0; i<N-1; i++)  for(j=i+1; j<N; j++)     /* sort by selection-exchange  */
if (b[i]<b[j])  { aux=b[i];b[i]=b[j];b[j]=aux;}
display b[N]
```

c) For each application, if we take away its 0s at the end table b[N] contains what we call a partition of number N, i.e. a succession of positive numbers placed in descending order whose sum is worth N

The applications can now be grouped according to the partition of the number *N* they make up. This constitutes a way of classifying applications according to the form of their graph to make the program that gives all partitions of number *N*, with the number of corresponding applications each time.

Recall that for each application table *b*[*N*] contains a partition of number *N*, with extra 0s at the end, eventually. When a new application is found in the *for*() loop of the program, we perform a test to find out whether the corresponding partition has already been obtained for the preceding applications. If yes, we increase counter *c*[] by one unit that in the end will give the number of applications with this same partition. If not, we record the new partition in table *partition*[*i*][*j*], where each partition is numbered by *i*, and we set its counter *c*[*i*] at 1. Here is the complete program with the preliminary declarations:

```
#include <stdio.h>
#include <math.h>
#define N 6
long int NN, number, q ,c[100];   int a[N], b[N], nbpartitions, partition[100][N];
int same(int k);
main()
{ int i,j,aux,r,k,flag; long int cumul;float gf,ggff;
  NN=(long int)pow((double)N,(double)N); nbpartitions=0;
 for(number=0; number<NN; number++)
   { q=number;  for(i=0;i<N;i++) {r=q%N;q=q/N; a[N-1-i]=r;}
     for(i=0; i<N; i++) b[i]=0;  for(i=0; i<N; i++)  b[a[i]]++;
     for(i=0; i<N-1; i++)  for(j=i+1;j<N;j++)
     if (b[i]<b[j])  { aux=b[i];b[i]=b[j];b[j]=aux;}
     flag=0;
     for(j=0; j<nbpartitions; j++)  if (same(j)==1) {c[j]++; flag=1; break;}
     if (flag==0)
       { for(i=0; i<N; i++) partition[nbpartitions][i]=b[i];
         c[nbpartitions]=1; nbpartitions++;
       }
   }
 printf("\nNumber of partitions %d\n",nbpartitions);
 for(i=0; i<nbpartitions; i++)
    { for(j=0;j<N;j++) printf("%d ",partition[i][j]);    printf("    %ld \n", c[i]); }
}

int same(int k)          /* this function tests if the partition in b[] is the same
                            as partition number k already found  */
 { int q;
   for (q=0; q<N; q++)  if (b[q]!=partition[k][q]) return 0;
   return 1;
 }
```

2.3.10. *Individuals grouped 2×2*

We have eight people. How many ways are there of placing them in groups of two?

2.3.10.1. *Method 1*

As the sentence implies, the order in which the groups are formed does not come into play. Neither does the order in which we place the individuals in each group. Expressing people 1 to 8, the situation (13)(24)(57)(68) can also be written (75)(24)(31)(68) or in quite a few other ways.

As we have the choice, we decide to take as the expression the one in which the two individuals in each group are in ascending order, and in which the groups are classified in ascending order from the first (the smallest) of the group. Therefore, in the example above we choose (12)(24)(57)(68). To find out the number of ways of pairing up the individuals, we begin by making up the first group. It necessarily contains 1 in first place and one of the 7 remaining individuals as second place. Each time this first group is formed, we take the smallest number among those remaining as the first member of the second group, and one of the five remaining individuals as the second member. Each time, we take the member that has the smallest number among those remaining as the first member of the third group, and one of the three remaining people as the second member. Each time, there is only one way of taking the forth group. Hence the total: 7×5×3 = 105 ways of grouping individuals 2×2.

2.3.10.2. *Method 2*

We are first going to form groups of two in succession, one after the other, making order come into play even if this is not what is asked. For the first group, we choose two out of the eight individuals without taking order into consideration, i.e. $C_8^{\,2} = 8.7/2$ cases. Each time the first group is chosen, we obtain $C_6^{\,2} = 6 \times 5/2$ ways of choosing the second group. Each time, there are $C_4^{\,2} = 4 \times 3/2$ ways of choosing the third group, then one single way $\left(C_2^{\,2}\right)$ of choosing the last group, i.e. $8!/2^4$ cases in total. In fact the order in which the groups are constituted must not come into play. One case in random order corresponds to 4! cases in order – as many ways as there are of permutating the four groups. Hence $8!/\left(2^4 \times 4!\right)$ cases in the end, i.e.:

$$\frac{8.7.6.5.4.3.2.1}{4.3.2.1.2^4} = \frac{8.7}{4.2}\,\frac{6.5}{3.2}\,\frac{4.3}{2.2}\,\frac{2.1}{2.1} = 7 \times 5 \times 3 = 105$$

Chapter 3

Enumerations in Alphabetical Order

Let us take a dictionary. How do we know if one word comes before or after another? We begin by comparing the first letter of these two words. If they are different, we know how to classify the two words. If they are identical, we compare the second letter of the two words. If they are different, we know which word comes before the other. We continue in the same way as long as the two words have an identical initial block, until we find two different letters. It is this classic procedure that makes up the foundation of the enumeration algorithm we are going to develop.

3.1. Principle of enumeration of words in alphabetical order

When we have to build a set of words, we often have an interest in writing them one after the other in alphabetical order (also called lexicographical order). We begin by making the first word the smallest in alphabetical order. Then we have to find the game rule that enables us to go from one word to the next in alphabetical order. Finally, we define the stop test that marks the end of the enumeration.

How can we get the game rule that enables us to go from one word to its successor in alphabetical order? In the word concerned, we are seeking to keep the beginning of the word unchanged (a left factor), which is as long as possible, in such a way that we do not lose intermediate words when going from one word to the next. Behind this unchanged beginning comes the first letter we must change, by replacing it with a bigger letter, or more precisely the smallest possible among the largest letters possible.

We call this letter, which plays the key role of the pivot. Finally, to the right of this pivot letter we place the rest of the word in such a way that it is the smallest possible.

The classic example is permutation enumeration. Let us take an example: that of permutations of eight letters, written 1, 2, 3, …, 8. Let us consider the permutation 4 8 6 5 7 3 2 1, and let us look for the one that will come next. The longest left block that is not to be changed is 4 8 6. On the other hand, if we took 4 8 6 5 we would need to change the following letter 7 into a higher letter, and we would need to take this letter on its right (because on the left it remains unchanged). Furthermore there are none. This works in the same manner with even longer left blocks. With the unchanged block 4 8 6, the pivot letter is 5. We are going to replace it with a higher letter, the smallest possible, and located on its right. The letter is 7. The remaining letters are 3 2 1 as well as 5, which is the pivot letter. We write them in ascending order to get the smallest possible word: 1 2 3 5. Finally, the permutation that follows is: 4 8 6 7 1 2 3 5.

The method for passing is summarized as indicated in Figure 3.1.

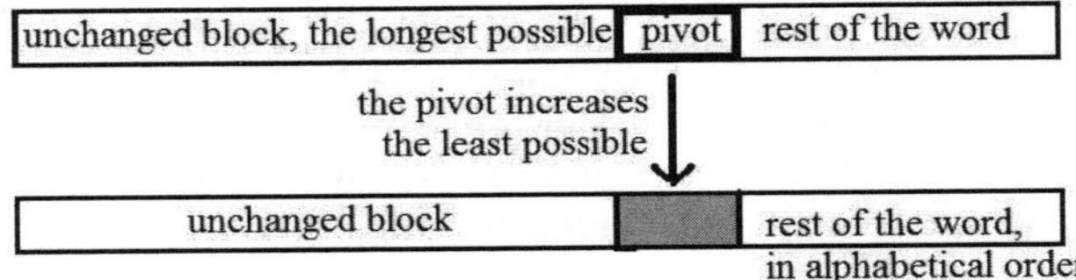

Figure 3.1. *Method enabling us to go from one word to the next*

Below we deal with several examples, starting with permutations.

3.2. Permutations

Let us consider permutations of the N elements written 0, 1, 2, …, $N-1$. The first permutation is exactly 0, 1, 2, …, $N-1$, which we put in a table a[]. To go from one permutation to the next, we look for the pivot element, leaving a fixed block of the longest possible length to its left. To do this, we start from the right and go left, searching for the first element that has a larger number than the one on its right. In other words, we go from right to left, as long as it is increasing, waiting for the first descent, because as long as increases are produced there is no letter that can be replaced by another bigger one located to its right. It is at the first descent that the pivot is found. The number that is going to replace the pivot is the smallest of the numbers located to its right, and greater than it. To get this number, all we have to do is to go from right to left, where the numbers are in ascending order, waiting to get the first number greater than the pivot. We therefore proceed to exchange the pivot and this number. After that, the right part is still in increasing direction from right to left. All we have to do is to reverse it to get the smallest word in alphabetical order. For example, for $N = 10$ let us take the permutation:

6 0 8 2 5 9 7 4 3 1

We proceed as indicated:

6 0 8 2 5 9 7 4 3 1 → 6 0 8 2 7 9 5 4 3 1 → 6 0 8 2 7 1 3 4 5 9

which is the next permutation.

Let us move on to the programming:

We give ourselves N *to get all the permutations of elements from 0 to* N – 1

```
for(i=0 ; i<N ;i++) a[i]=i;  /* the first permutation */
for(;;)
 { display array a[] where each permutation is found
   /* Searching for the pivot from right to left.
```

*Note that in the while loop we must make i > 0 to prevent index i – 1 in a[i – 1] from becoming negative, which would produce a fatal error. At the same time, when we got the last permutation with all its letters in descending order, the while loop stops for the first time with i which takes the value 0 the position of the pivot becomes -1. We therefore stop the for loop (;;) with a break */:*

```
   i=N−1; while (i>0 && a[i]<a[i-1]) i - -;
   pospivot= i-1;   if (pospivot == -1) break;

   /* Searching for the element that is going to replace the pivot */
   i=N−1; while (a[i]<a[pospivot]) i- -;  posreplacement= i;

   /* Exchange of pivot elements and its replacement */
   aux=a[pospivot]; a[pospivot]=a[posreplacement]; a[posreplacement]=aux;

   /* Reversing the right part */
   left=pospivot+1 ; right=N−1;
   while(left<right)
       { aux=a[left]; a[left]=a[right]; a[right]=aux;}
 }
```

Note that in this program, all the permutations are alternately placed in the same *a*[] table. Even if there are billions of billions of permutations, they will all be displayed on the screen. Let us indicate that 20!, the number of permutations of 20 objects, is around two billions of billions ($2.10^9.10^9$).

3.3. Writing binary numbers

We want to enumerate all the binary numbers with N digits. For $N = 4$, for example, this gives 0000, 0001, 0010, 0011, 0100, 0101, 0110, 0111, 1000, etc. In value, these numbers are in ascending order. They are also in alphabetical order when we treat them as words.

3.3.1. *Programming*

These numbers will be placed successively in array $a[N]$ indexed from 0 to $N - 1$. Initially we put 0s in this table, which gives the first number. Then a repetitive loop enables us to go from one number to the next.

What is the rule of passage? The pivot can only be a 0 and it is the number that is the furthest possible. All we have to do is to look for the first 0 starting from the right. It is this 0 that is the pivot. The longest possible unchanged block remains on its left. We are going to change the pivot from 0 to 1. All the digits after it are set to 0. The process is stopped when the pivot is in position -1.

Hence the program:

```
set a[N] to 0
for(; ;)
  { i = N−1;
    while(i >= 0 && a[i] ==1  ) i--;
    if (i== -1) break;
    a[i]=1;
    for(j= i+1; j<N; j++) a[j]=0;
  }
```

3.3.2. *Generalization to expression in some base B*

In the program above, all we have to do in the *while* loop is replace a[i] == 1 with $a[i]$ == $B - 1$, and do it for the pivot $a[i]$++.

3.4. Words in which each letter is less than or equal to the position

We consider words of length *N*, whose letters a_i (where *i* is between 0 and $N-1$) are taken from the alphabet of *N* letters 0, 1, 2, …, $N-1$, and such that the letter in position *i* in the word is less than or equal to *i*. For example, for $N = 3$, the words concerned are 000, 001, 002, 010, 011 and 012.

3.4.1. *Number of these words*

For the letter in position 0 there is only one possibility: 0. For the letter in position 1, there are two cases (0, 1). For the letter in position 2, there are three cases (0, 1, 2). The same goes for each time until the letter in position is $N-1$, for which there are *N* possibilities. The number of words is *N*!

3.4.2. *Program*

What we have to do is make all of these words for some given *N*. In initial conditions, we take the word 000…0. We are left with defining the rule of passage from one word to the next. To find out the pivot letter of the word concerned, we start from the right and go back as long as we fall on a letter equal to its index. As soon as we find the first letter a_i such that $a_i < i$, it is this letter that is the pivot, and we increase a_i by 1, then we set all the following letters to 0. We have therefore obtained the following word. We stop when the position of the pivot leaves the word, with the index -1. The program in section 3.8(c) results from it.

3.5. Enumeration of combinations

Starting with a set of *N* objects numbered from 0 to $N-1$, we take *P* out of these *N*, not taking into consideration the order in which we take them. We get a combination of *P* out of *N* objects, as we saw in Chapter 2. For example 3, 5 and 8 is a combination of three objects and is the same as 5, 8 and 3 or 8, 5 and 3. Out of all the ways of writing this combination, we have the right – and it is in our interest – to choose the one that seems the simplest. This is 3, 5 and 8, where the numbers are in ascending order. Out of all the words that represent a similar combination, it also comes back to taking the smallest word in alphabetical order. What we want is to enumerate all the combinations of *P* out of *N* objects, making use of the expression of each one of the combinations with its letters placed in ascending alphabetical order. For example, the combinations of two out of four objects are 0 1, 0 2, 0 3, 1 2, 1 3 and 2 3. This can be seen in another way. Taking two out of four objects placed in boxes means, if you prefer, setting two cases to 0, and leaving the others at 1. For example, for the combination 1 3, we set boxes 1 and 3 to 0, and the two others to 1, which gives 1010. Therefore the preceding combinations can be written 0011, 0101, 0110, 1001, 1010 and 1100. In this way we get words of length *N*, written in binary, with the presence of *P* zeros.

The first word is 00..011..1, made up of *P* zeros followed by $N - P$ ones. The rule of passage from one word to the next remains to be determined. The pivot is the first 0 from the right, which we can transform into 1. This implies that this 0 has at least one 1 to its right. This 0 cannot be followed by other 0s before falling on the 1 because if not we would have chosen the last of these 0s as the pivot. Therefore, all we have to do is to look for the first 01 block from the right. We are going to transform it into 10. Everything to its left remains fixed. In what is to its right, there is no 01 block. This means that the right part is made up of a block of 1s followed by a block of 0s, with one of these blocks able to be empty. All we have to do is to put this right part in reverse order to get the smallest word in alphabetical order. For example, the combination 001**01**1100 is followed by 001**10**0011. The process of passage from one combination to the next ends when the pivot we find is in position -1. Hence the program:

```
for(i=0; i<N-P; i++) a[N-1-i]=1;

                  /* we place the 1s at the end, the remainder already being at 0*/
counterc=1;   /* this variable will count the number of combinations */
for(;;)
  { display the combination : run through array a[] , if a[i] is worth 0 display i
    counterc++; i =N−1;
    while (i>0 && a[i]!=1 || a[i-1]!=0)  i --;
                  /* or if you wish   while (i>0 && !(a[i]==1 && a[i-1]==0) */
    pospivot = i−1;
    if (pospivot==-1) break;
    a[pospivot]=1; a[pospivot+1]=0;
    left=pospivot+2; right=N−1 ;
    while(left<right)
        { aux=a[left]; a[left]=a[right]; a[right]=aux; left++; right--; }
  }
```

3.6. Combinations with repetitions

Here we take *P* objects out of *N* types of objects in all possible ways. What we have to do is list the C_{N+P-1}^{P} cases obtained, thanks to a formula that we will see in Chapter 7. Let us call each type of object *A*, *B*, *C*, …, which constitutes our alphabet. What we have to do is make all the words of length *P* from this alphabet. Unlike the combinations in the section above, the same letters can be repeated several times. As order does not come into play, such a combination with repetitions can be written in several ways. For example *AABC* is also *ABAC* or *CABA*. It is up to us to choose the word that will represent it. We decide to put the *A*s before the *B*s, the *B*s before the *C*s, etc. In other words, the letters of each word are placed one after the other in alphabetical order. For example, the combinations obtained for $P = 4$ and $N = 3$ are:

AAAA, *AAAB*, *AAAC*, *AABB*, *AABC*, *AACC*, *ABBB*, *ABBC*, *ABCC*, *ACCC*, *BBBB*, *BBBC*, *BBCC*, *BCCC*, *CCCC*,

i.e. 15 possibilities.

How do we go from one word to the next? We are looking to start on the right of the first letter that is not the greatest. This letter is the pivot. We increase it by 1. To its right we repeat this process until the end. The program that results from it is:

```
for(i=0; i<P; i++) a[i]=0;  /* the letters are called 0, 1, 2, …, N-1 */
for(;;)
 { counter++;
   printf(« \n%3.d : » ,counter);   /* displaying the number of cases  */
   for(i=0; i<P; i++) printf("%d",a[i]);  /* displaying the word */
   i=P−1;
   while (i>=0 && a[i]==N-1) i--;
   pospivot=i;
   if (pospivot==-1) break;
   a[pospivot]++;
   for(i=pospivot+1; i<P; i++) a[i]=a[pospivot];
 }
```

3.7. Purchase of *P* objects out of *N* types of objects

This is the same problem as the one above, but we are going to treat it differently.

A person buys for example $P = 6$ shirts from $N = 3$ types of shirts. We want to enumerate all the ways of doing so.

By arranging the six shirts according to their category A, B, or C we get the words:

$$006, 015, 024, 033, 042, 051, 060, 105, 114, \ldots, 600$$

For example, the word 105 means that we take one shirt of type A, none of type B and 5 of type C. The pivot is the letter that precedes the first letter from the right that is not a 0. Actually, if we have a letter other than 0, which is only followed by 0, we cannot increase it because we can only increase this letter with what is behind it. When we come to the first letter other than 0, the pivot is the letter that precedes it because it will be able to increase this by taking a unit from the non-null letter that follows it. Once the pivot has been obtained, we increase it by 1 and put 0s behind it, except in the last case where we put everything that is left, i.e. what there was in the box following the pivot, reduced by 1. For example, for $N = 4$ and $P = 6$, the word 1500 has 1 as the pivot letter, which will become 2, then we put 0s behind until the last box that will contain $5 - 1 = 4$, hence the following word 2004.

We deduce the program from it:

```
a[N-1]=P;       /* the first word: we put P in the last box, and we leave
                   0s in all the other boxes */
for(;;)
 { counter++; printf("\n%3.d: ",counter);
   for(i=0;i<N;i++) printf("%d",a[i]);
   i=N−1;
   while(a[i]== 0) i--;  /* searching for pivot */
   pospivot=i−1;   if (pospivot== -1) break;  /*stop test */
   a[N-1]=a[i]−1;  a[pospivot]++;
   for(i=pospivot+1; i<N-1; i++) a[i]=0;
 }
```

3.8. Another enumeration of permutations

We consider a permutation of N numbers $0, 1, 2, \ldots, N-1$. It is placed in a table $b[N]$ with boxes numbered from 0 to $N-1$. With each number $b[i]$, we associate the number $a[i]$ of elements of $b[N]$ situated to the left of $b[i]$ and which are less than it.

For example, from the permutation *b*[10]: 2756019834, we get table *a*[10]: 0112016634.

Knowing table *b*[*N*], the following program enables us to get table *a*[*N*]:

```
for(i=0; i<N; i++)
  { a[i]=0;
    for(j=0; j<i; j++) if b[j]<b[i] )  a[j]++;

  }
```

Conversely, from table *a*[*N*], we can reconstitute table *b*[*N*] giving the corresponding permutation:

For example, $a[5]:00203$ will give the permutation $b[5]:21403$.

To do this, we run through *a*[*N*] step by step, and we fill in *b*[*N*] progressively: we put *a*[*i*] in *b*[*i*] and we increase by 1 the elements of *b*[*N*] situated to the left of *b*[*i*] which are greater than or equal to *b*[*i*]. For example:

0 0 2 0 3	which is *a*[*N*].
0	We progressively fill in table *b*[*N*], until
1 0	the final permutation.
1 0 2	
2 1 3 0	
2 1 4 0 3	

The validity of this method is easily explained, and the program is simple:

```
for(i=0; i<N; i++)

  { b[i]=a[i];
    for(j=0;j<i;j++) if (b[j]>= b[i])
    b[j]++;
  }
```

We have just found a bijection between two types of words of the same length, namely those contained in tables *b*[*N*] and *a*[*N*]. It is now from words in *a*[*N*] that we are going to construct the permutations.

Actually, the words from $a[N]$ are easier to enumerate than the permutations. By their very definition, they are words whose letters are less than or equal to their position, as already encountered in section 3.4.

All we have to do is convert them into permutations, thanks to the process in (*b*), hence the program:

```
main()
 {
   for(i=0; i<N; i++) a[i]=0;      /* first word */
   counter=1; conversion();
   for(;;)                          /* passage from one word to the next */
     { i=N−1;
       while(a[i]==i && i>=0) i--;
       if (i==-1) break;
       a[i]++;
       for(j=i+1;j<N;j++) a[j]=0;  counter++;  conversion();
     }
 }
void conversion(void)       /* we go from one word in a[] to a permutation b[]*/
 { for(i=0;i<N;i++)
     { b[i]=a[i];
       for(j=0; j<i; j++)  if (b[j] >= b[i])
       b[j]++;
     }
   printf("%3.d: ",counter);  for(i=0; i<N; i++) printf("%d ",a[i]);
   printf("    ");
   for(i=0;i<N;i++) printf("%d ",b[i]+1);     printf("\n");
 }
```

3.9. Complementary exercises

3.9.1. *Exercise 1: words with different successive letters*

Let us consider words of given length N, based on three letters 0, 1 and 2 (this could also be *a*, *b* and *c*), such that two successive letters of these words are never identical. These words are, in alphabetical order:

– for $N = 1$: 0, 1, 2;

– for $N = 2$: 01, 02, 10, 12, 20, 21;

– for $N = 3$: 010, 012, 020, 021, 101, 102, 120, 121, 201, 202, 210, 212; and

– for $N = 4$: 010$\underline{1}$, 01$\underline{0}$2, 012$\underline{0}$, 0$\underline{1}$21, 020$\underline{1}$, 02$\underline{0}$2, 021$\underline{0}$, $\underline{0}$212, 101$\underline{0}$, 10$\underline{1}$2, 102$\underline{0}$, 1$\underline{0}$21, 120$\underline{1}$, 12$\underline{0}$2, 121$\underline{0}$, $\underline{1}$212, 2010, etc. (we have underlined the pivot, which will be used in what follows).

a) From a word of length K, how many words of length K + 1 obtained by adding one letter at the end are there? Deduce from it the formula that gives the number of words of length N.

Behind the last letter of a word of length K, we have the choice between two letters forming a word of length $K + 1$. The number of words doubles during this passage. If the number of words of length K are called u(K), we have the recurrence relation $u(K + 1) = 2u(K)$ with $u(1) = 3$ at the beginning, hence:

$$u(N) = 3.\ 2^{N-1}$$

b) The pivot is the furthest letter possible behind a fixed block that must change in order to go from one word to the next. Indicate how to obtain the pivot, starting from the right.

The pivot cannot be the digit 2. It can either be digit 0 or digit 1, provided that this 1 is preceded by a 0 because were it is preceded by 2 we would not be able to make the pivot move on to 2.

c) What letter must we replace the pivot with?

If the pivot is 0, and in front of it a 2 is found, it changes to 1. If a 1 is found in front of it, it changes to 2. If the pivot is 1 (it is therefore preceded by 0) it changes to 2.

d) What is the first word of given length N?

It is the word 0101…

e) Create the program that gives all the words of length N.

/* *We make the first word, which we place in table a[N] where all the words will be found in turn* */

```
for(i=0; i<N; i++)
if (i%2==0) a[i]=0;
else a[i]=1;
counter=0;    /* each word is numbered using this counter variable */
for(;;)  /*  loop from the program which enables us to go from one word to the
             next */
 {
   displaying a word
   counter++;  printf("\n%d: ",counter);
   for(i=0; i<N; i++) printf("%d ",a[i]);
        /* Searching for the position of the pivot from the right */
   i=N−1;
   while(i>=1 &&  a[i]==2 || (a[i]==1 && a[i-1]==2))  i - -;
   pospivot=i;
        /* If the position of the pivot falls to 0, and the letter in position 0 is 2,
           we have obtained the last word, and the loop is stopped */
   if (pospivot==0 && a[i]==2)  break;
        /* We increase the pivot, distinguishing several cases, notably the one
           where the position of the pivot fell to 0 */
   if (pospivot==0) a[pospivot]++;
   else if (a[pospivot]==0 && a[pospivot-1]==1 ) a[pospivot]=2;
   else if (a[pospivot]==0 && a[pospivot-1]==2) a[pospivot]=1;
   else if (a[pospivot]==1) a[pospivot]=2;
        /* Behind the pivot, we place an alternation from 0 and from 1 */
   k=0;
   for(i=pospivot+1; i<N; i++)  {a[i]=k%2; k++; }
 }
```

3.9.1.1. *Exercise 1, part 2: another programming method*

In what follows, we are going to give another method of programming in order to get used to linked lists instead of tables.

Now let us use a doubly linked circular list.

We begin with the list of words of length $L = 1$. From there we make the list of words of length $L = 2$, and so on and so forth until we get the final list of words of length N.

Each cell contains one word placed in a table $a[N]$, of which only one part of length L (from box 0 to box $L - 1$) is used at each stage. This gives the evolution introduced in Figure 3.2.

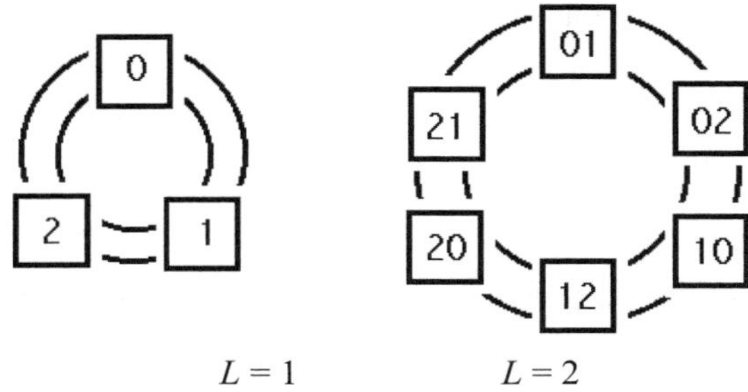

Figure 3.2. *First developments of the linked circular list of words*

We notice that to go from one step to the next, one word is replaced by two words and one cell is replaced by two cells. To do this, the contents of a cell will need to be modified by adding the last letter (distinguishing several cases), inserting a new cell after it, taking back the contents of the one before until a certain box, and adding a letter:

```
struct word { int a[N];  struct word * s;  struct word * p;  };
main()
{
L=1;     /* making of the embryo of the list */
start = (struct word *) (malloc(sizeof(struct word)));
cell1 = (struct word *)(malloc( sizeof (struct word)));
cell2 = (struct word *)(malloc( sizeof (struct word)));
start->a[0]=0; start->s=cell1; start->p=cell2;
cell1->a[0]=1; cell1->s=cell2; cell1->p=start;
cell2->a[0]=2; cell2->s=start; cell2->p=cell1;
for(L=2; L<=N; L++)
 {
 ptr=start;
 do
  {
  ptra=ptr->s;
  newcell= (struct word *)(malloc( sizeof (struct word)));
```

```
        for(i=0;i<L-1;i++) newcell->a[i]=ptr->a[i];
        if (ptr->a[L-2]==0) { ptr->a[L-1]=1; newcell->a[L-1]=2;}
        else if (ptr->a[L-2]==1) { ptr->a[L-1]=0; newcell->a[L-1]=2;}
        else if (ptr->a[L-2]==2) { ptr->a[L-1]=0; newcell->a[L-1]=1;}
        newcell->s=ptra; newcell->p=ptr; ptr->s=newcell;ptra->p=newcell;
        ptr=ptra;
        }
      while (ptr!=start);
      }
    pptr=start; n=0;
    do  { n++; printf("\n%d: ",n);  for(i=0;i<L;i++) printf ("%d ",pptr->a[i]);
pptr=pptr->s; }
    while (pptr!=start);
    getch();
    }
```

3.9.2. *Exercise 2: repeated purchases with a given sum of money*

A person has a sum of money made up of N bills of the same value. With this money, every day he buys one and only one object out of two products. The first product is worth one bill and the other is worth two bills. This happens day after day, until he has spent all the money.

We call a_N the number of ways to make this succession of daily purchases. The a_N words that correspond to these possible successions of purchases are based on 1 and 2, and the sum of their digits is worth N.

a) Give the words obtained for $N = 5$ in alphabetical order.

These words are: 11111, 1112, 1121, 1211, 122, 2111, 212 and 221. We find: [1]

$$a_5 = 8.$$

1. Let us separate the a_N words into two categories according to their last number. If this number is 1, the words that come before it number a_{N-1}; if it is a 2, the words in front of it number a_{N-2}. Hence the recurrence relation $a_N = a_{N-1} + a_{N-2}$, with $a_0 = 1$ and $a_1 = 1$. We recognize the Fibonacci series shifted by one notch.

b) In the general case we want to find out the rule of passage from one word to the next in alphabetical order. For example, for N = 12 the word 11212221 is followed by 1122111111. Here the questions to answer are:

– how can the pivot be determined, i.e. the first letter that changes behind the longest possible fixed block?

As usual we will search for it starting from the right, but beginning not with the last box but the one before this;

– once the pivot has been found and consequently modified, what must we place behind it?

Deduce from it the program that enables the enumeration of all the words of length N. Note that you will need to use a variable L to manage the length of each word.

The pivot is the first 1 found going from right to left starting from the one before the last box. Behind the pivot, which moves to 2, we only put 1s. When we leave this to search for the pivot, we will add a counter that will later give us the number of 1s to put behind the pivot. We deduce the following program from it:

```
for(i=0 ; i<N ; i++) a[i]=1;

L=N ; display a[]
for(;;)
  { i=L-2;   cumul=a[L-1];
    while (i>=0 && a[i]==2)
        { cumul+=a[i]; i- -; }
    pospivot=i; if (pospivot== -1) break;

    numberof1=cumul-1;
    a[pospivot]=2;
    for(i=0; i<numberof1; i++) a[pospivot+1+i]=1;
    L=pospivot+1+numberof1;    display a[]
  }
```

c) The person still has all his N bills. Now everyday he buys one and only one object out of three products A, B and C worth one bill for the first, two bills for the second and two bills for the third.

Calling the three types of purchases 1, 2 and 2', for $N = 4$, for example, we get: 1111, 112, 112', 121, 12'1, 211, 2'11, 22, 22', 2'2, 2'2' to create the program that enables us to enumerate all possible successions of purchases.

We are going to use the program above. This gives us, for example, word 21121 for $N = 7$.

Instead of displaying this result as before, we will expand it to get 21121, 2112'1, 2'1121 and 2'112'1 in this case. To do this we need to count the number k of number 2s in each word obtained in the program above. To this program we should add the piece of program that enables us to have all the words with 2s and 2's starting from words with only 2s.

To do this, we count the number of 2s in each word obtained in the program above. If there are k letter 2s, the word produces 2^k words. We will use binary numbers of length k: if we have a 0 in the binary word we will put 2 in the corresponding box of the word. If we have a 1, we will put 2' (or more likely 3) in the corresponding box. Hence the addition of this piece of program at the end of the one above (more precisely in the *for* loop (;;) just before *display*):

```
number2=0;

for(i=0; i<L; i++)  if (a[i]==2)
     {two[number2]=i; number2++ ;}
/* we recorded the number of the box where there is 2 in two[] */
for(i=0 ; i<pow(2,number2) ; i++)
    { q=i;
      for(j=0; j<number2; j++)
          { r=q%2;  if (r==0) a[two[j]]=2;  else a[two[j]]=3;   q=q/2; }
      display, replacing 3 with 2'
    }
```

3.10. *Return to permutations*

We are going to simplify the method seen in section 3.8. Let us begin with permutations of $n = 2$ elements, i.e. 01 and 10. To move on to permutations of $n = 3$ elements, all we have to do is insert the new element 2, first from right to left in 01, then from left to right in 10. This gives: 012, 021, 201, 210, 120 and 102. Then we move on to $n = 4$ by inserting element 3 alternatively from right to left and from left to right in the preceding permutations.

Here we get: 0123, 0132, 0312, 3012, 3021, 0321, 0231, 0213, 2013, 2031, 2301, 3201, 3210, 2310, 2130, 2103, 1203, 1230, 1320, 3120, 3102, 1302, 1032 and 1023.

We notice that the permutations are no longer given in alphabetical order, but following a simple rule of passage, where only two consecutive elements are exchanged at each step. Alphabetical order is, however, underlying to the extent that we are going to use the bijection between permutations and words whose figures are less than or equal to their position, i.e. for n = 4: 0000, 0001, 0002, 0003, 0010, 0011, 0012, 0013, 0020, 0021, 0022, 0023, 0100, etc.

On reading these words where the pivot letter is underlined, we notice that the position of this letter is 3, 3, 3, 2, 3, 3, 3, 2, 3, 3, 3, 1, 3, etc. A sort of rhythmics is established in the evolution of this position. We therefore realize that this position of the pivot is also, if we return to enumeration of permutations, the number (and not its position) that we cause to move in the permutation, exchanging it with its right or left neighbor. For example, when moving from the word 0000 to 0001, with the pivot in position 3, we move from the permutation 0123 to 0132, where it is the 3 that is moved to the left.

At another time, when we go from the word 0023 to 0100, with the pivot in position 1, we go from permutation 3201 to 3210, where it is digit 1 that is moved to the left. Then we go from 0100 to 0101 with the pivot in position 3 – hence the passage of permutation 3210 to 2310, where the number three is moved one notch to the right. The only thing that remains unknown is whether the movement is from right to left or from left to right.

Initially, we know that all the elements will move from right to left. It is therefore enough to notice that each time we cause a number to move, by exchanging it with its left or right neighbor, we must change the direction of movement for all the numbers that are greater than it. Hence the program that follows.

Words whose letters are less than or equal to their position are placed in array *a*[*N*], and the permutations are put in table *b*[*N*]. Table *sign*[*N*] contains +1 or -1. If *sign*[*i*] is worth 1, this means that the number *i* (and not its position) in the permutation will have to be moved to the right, if need be.

If table *b*[] enables us to go from position *i* to the corresponding number *b*[*i*] in the ongoing permutation, we also need the "reverse" array *position*[], where, starting from number *j* we find out its position *position*[*j*] in the permutation:

```
counter=0;
for(i=0; i<N; i++) a[i]=0;          /* initial conditions */
for(i=0; i<N; i++)
   {b[i]=i;sign[i]= - 1; position[i]=i;}
for(;;)  /* passage from one word to the next */
  { counter++;printf("\n%3.d: ",counter);
   for(i=0;i<N;i++printf("%d",b[i]);
   i=N−1;
   while (i>=0 && a[i]==i) i--;
   pospivot=i;   if (pospivot==-1) break;
   a[pospivot]++;
   for(i=pospivot+1;i<N;i++) a[i]=0;
  numbertomove=pospivot;       /* it is this number that is going to be exchanged
                                  with its neighbor */
   for(j=number+1; j<N; j++) sign[j]=-sign[j];
   position[numbertomove]+=sign[numbertomove];
   numberexchanged=b[position[numbertomove]];
                 /* the neighbor exchanged with the number */
   position[numberexchanged] - =sign[numbertomove];
   b[position[numbertomove]]= numbertomove;
   b[position[numberexchanged]]= numberexchanged;
  }
```

3.11. Gray code

The gray code is a sort of counter example, as alphabetical order cannot be used. Enumeration according to the so-called Gray code consists, in the simplest case, of enumerating numbers in binary code of given length n, following a simple procedure where each time only one single digit is modified when we go from one word to the next.

For numbers of length $n = 4$, for example, using a game of successive mirror effects gives what we see in Figure 3.3. We start from the two numbers 0 and 1. They are followed by symmetry of 1 and 0 to which we add a 1 in front. This gives the four numbers 10, 11, 01 and 00 that we change to be preceded by a 1.

In this way we end up with eight numbers, and we continue in the same way.

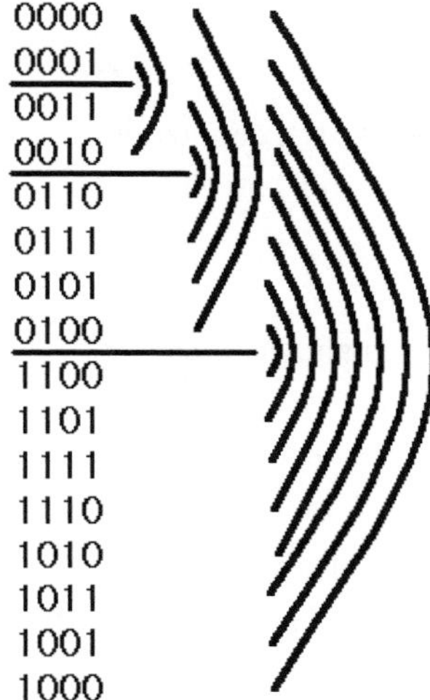

Figure 3.3. *Making of successive binary numbers using mirror effect games*

As before, let us call the pivot the unique letter that we causes the change from 0 to 1 or from 1 to 0, to go from one word to the next where the letters do not change.

Successive mirror effects mean that the pivot is the last digit every other go, the one before the last every four goes, the penultimate one every eight goes, the one before that every 16 goes etc. This is from words numbered 0, 1, 3, 7, … respectively.

For example, going from right to left, the pivot is in position 3 if the number of the word (called *counter* in the program) is of the form $7 + 16k$, or even of the form 7 modulo 16, i.e. *remainder* = *step* / 2 − 1 for one *step* = 16 (*remainder* is the remainder after dividing the *counter* by the *step*).

For each number of the word, we begin by taking *step* = 2. If we come to *remainder* = 0 we stop and the pivot is in position 0.

If not, we double the step: *step* = 4. IF we come to *remainder* = 1, we stop and the pivot is in position 1 going to the left.

If not we double the step: *step* = 8, and we come to *remainder* = 3, the pivot is in position 2 starting from the right (with *step* = 2^{i+1}, the position is *i*), etc. Hence the program:

```
for(i=0; i<N; i++)
    {a[i]=0; printf("%d",a[i]);}
display word number 0
for(counter=0; counter < pow(2,N); counter++)
  { step=2;
    for(i=0; i<N; i++)
      { remainder=step/2-1;
        if (counter%step == remainder) break;
        step=2*step;
      }
    pospivot=i;
    a[pospivot]=(a[pospivot]+1)%2;
   printf("\n%3.d:  ",counter+1);  for(i=N-1; i>=0; i--) printf("%d",a[i]);
  }
```

Chapter 4

Enumeration by Tree Structures

When we have to construct words obeying certain constraints, one method consists of making them letter after letter, each time asking ourselves what the possible successors are. By doing this, we are led to make a tree. The tree starts from a root placed at the top, corresponding to the first letter of the word, with its successors below, then the successors' successors, etc. Finally, vertical reading of the branches of the tree from top to bottom will give us all the words. We will begin with a particularly simple example, where the successors of a letter only depend on this letter, and not on those that come before it. Then the algorithm will be specified, enabling us to process all sorts of problems. Some of these problems can also be processed using the method explained in Chapter 3, others are more specifically adapted to the tree method.

4.1. Words of length n, based on N letters 1, 2, 3, …, N, where each letter is followed by a higher or equal letter

Let us take for example $N = 3$ and $n = 4$. The words obeying the constraint indicated are 1111, 1112, 1113, 1122, 1123, 1133, 1222, 1223, 1233, 1333, 2222, 2223, 2233, 2333 and 3333 (numbering 15). From the first letter of the word, which can be 1, 2 or 3, we take its possible successors, and so on and so forth, which produces three trees (see Figure 4.1).

The corresponding programming is typically recursive. The main program is simply called a *tree* function, starting from each of the letters from 1 to N, which make up the roots of the N trees.

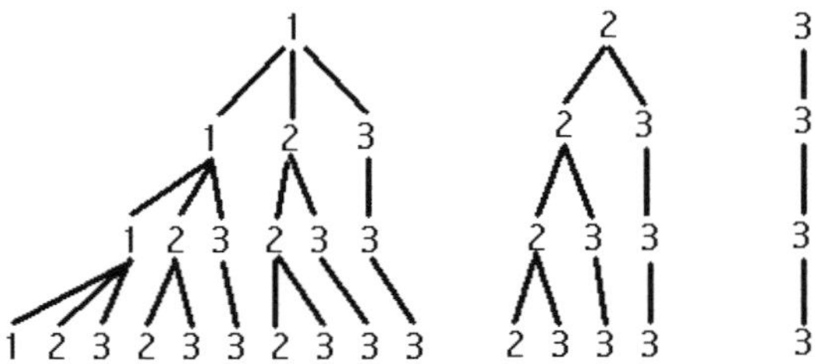

Figure 4.1. *Each tree branch, read from top to bottom, gives a word*

The *tree* function takes two arguments. On the one hand the letter considered, and on the other, the level where we are in the tree, with the succession of levels from top to bottom going from 1 to n – the final length of the word. In the main program, this function is called *tree*(i, 1), with i going from 1 to N. Now the *tree*(i, *level*) function remains to be constructed. This function is recalled each time on all the successors j of i, with the level that increases by 1.

This procedure produces a construction of trees by depth: the first branch, which is on the far left, is made first, going down to level n, then the second branch is made, etc. The stop test happens when we arrive at level n. We are therefore left with displaying the words, which necessitates reading each branch from level 1 to level n. This forces us to keep the predecessor of each letter of the word in reserve when going down the tree. To do this we will manage a table placed overall, giving the level's (and not the letter's) predecessor. In the example above, for the first tree the predecessor of level 2 will always be letter 1; the predecessor of level 3 will always be 1 first, then 2, then 3. Thanks to the recursive construction of the deep tree, where each branch is completely made before moving on to the next, from left to right, we will always have the right predecessor of each level, and of each letter of the words concerned. Finally we obtain the following program, including its preliminary declarations:

```
#define N  7   /* the alphabet has N letters */
#define n  9   /* the words have length n  */
void tree(int i,int level);
int predecessor[n+1];
int number; /* this variable, set here to 0, will count the words one by one */
main()    { int i;        for(i=1; i<=N; i++) tree(i,1); }

void  tree(int i,  int level)
```

```
{ int j,k;
  if (level==n)  /* stop test, when the word, read vertically, has length n */
    { number++; printf("%4.0d: ", number);  /* numbering of each one of
                                               the words */
     for (k=2;k<=n;k++) printf("%d", predecessor[k]); /* from the first to the
                                                         penultimate letter */
     printf("%d ",i);   /* the last letter of the word */
    }
  else  /* recall of the tree function on the successors at the level below */
    { for(j=1; j<=N; j++)  if (j>=i)
        { predecessor[level+1]=i;  tree(j, level+1); }
    }
}
```

Notice that the number of such words is C_{N+n-1}^{n}. Actually, a bijection exists between each one of these words and each path in a square grid going from point $O(0,0)$ to point $(n, N-1)$. All we have to do is read the height of each horizontal plateau of length 1 of the path to find a word (see Figure 4.2). For the formula giving the number of paths in a square grid, we will refer to Chapter 6.

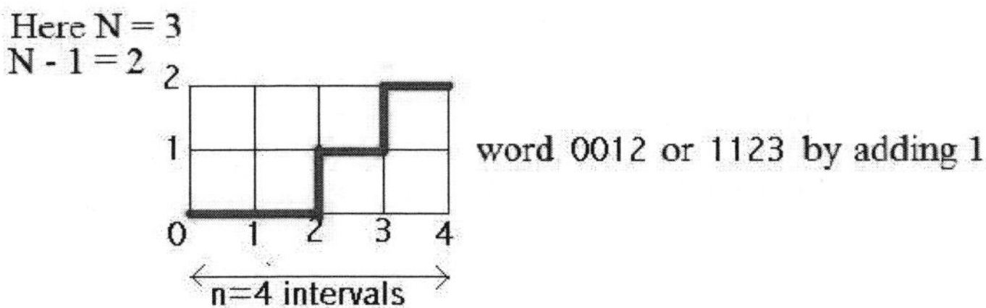

Figure 4.2. *Design of a word in a square grid*

We are now going to move on to the general case, where the successors of the letter of a word no longer only depend on this letter, but also on the preceding letters in the word. We begin with the simplest example, enabling us to obtain the permutations of n elements, then we will develop more complex examples. To do this we keep the notion of level predecessor, as before, but we must add a function that enables us to know what letters belong to the list of predecessors of a letter.

4.2. Permutations enumeration

Let us consider the permutations of N numbers 1, 2, 3, …, N, for example for $N = 4$. We begin by searching for all the permutations beginning with 1. This number 1 is the root of a tree we are going to develop level by level. Once this 1 has been placed at level 1 of the tree, the possible successors at level 2 of the tree being made are 2, 3 or 4. In turn, the successors of 2 are 3 or 4 at level 3, i.e. the numbers different to 2 and its predecessors in the tree. In turn, the only successor of 3 is 4 at the final level 4. We continue in the same way until the complete construction of the tree from root 1. Then we start again with root 2, etc. The tree with root 1 is represented in Figure 4.3.

The main program is simply called the *tree*(*i, l*) function on each number *i* between 1 and *N*, placed at level 1: *for(i=1; i<=N; i++) tree(i,1).*

This *tree*() function remains to be manufactured.

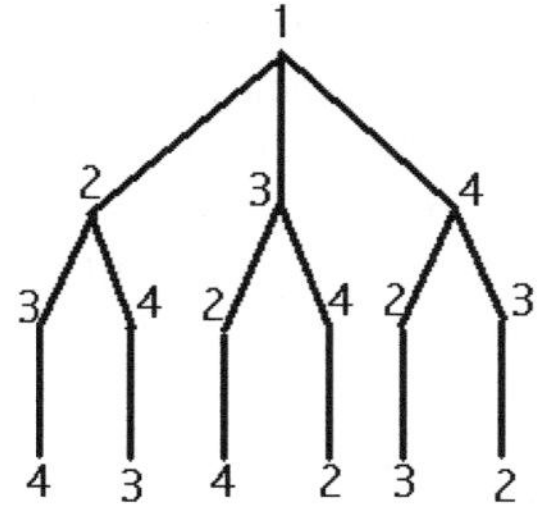

Figure 4.3. *Permutation tree beginning with 1*

```
void tree(int i, int level)
{  if (level==N)  { number++; printf("%4.0ld: ",number);
                    for (k=2; k<=N; k++) printf("%d",predecessor[k]);
                    printf("%d ",i);
                  }
   else  for(j=1; j<=N; j++)
            if (j!=i &&  belongstothelistofpredecessors(j,level)==NO)
                  { predecessor[level+1]=i ; tree(j,level+1); }
}
int belongstothelistofpredecessors(int j, int level)
{  for(k=level; k>=2; k--)  if (j= =predecessor[k]) return YES;
   return NO;
}
```

Thanks to the variable *level*, we place a stop test when the level becomes equal to N, and we display the corresponding branch of the tree going from root to terminal node.

As long as we are not there, the *tree*(i, *level*) function is recalled on the successors j of i using *tree*(j, *level* + 1). The j successors of node i must be different to i as well as the predecessors of i in the tree. To do this, we run a table *predecessor* [*level*], which is declared globally.

Even if in the tree several nodes in the same level have different predecessors, this has no importance because of the in-depth construction of the tree: as long as we have not descended to the leaf of a branch, we have the correct values of its predecessors. Moving to another branch keeps those predecessors of levels which do not change, and modifies those that do change.

This enables us to define a function *belongstolistofpredecessors* (j, *level*) that tests (yes or no) whether the number j is among the predecessors located in the tree above the level indicated.

4.3. Derangements

Out of the permutations, written in the form of an indexed table, such as for example:

$$\begin{pmatrix} 1 & 2 & 3 & 4 \\ 2 & 3 & 1 & 4 \end{pmatrix}$$

let us consider only those where each number is different to its index.

These are called derangements. Therefore, the derangements of length $N = 4$ are:

2143, 2341, 2413, 3142, 3412, 3421, 4123, 4312, 4321

To enumerate them, we construct trees as in Figure 4.4.

The program results from it. We start at level 1, from which $N - 1$ trees are going to be constructed.

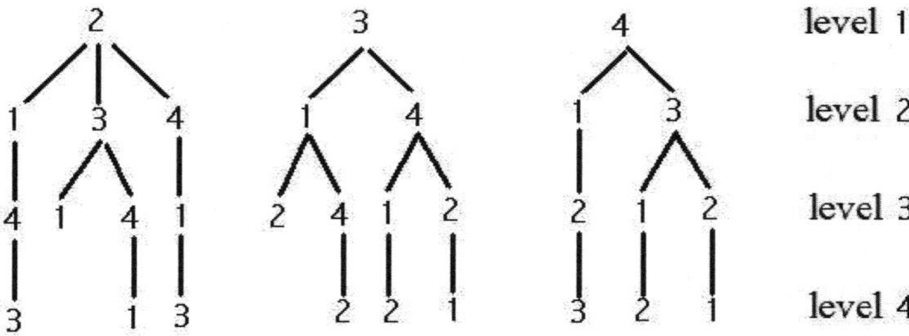

Figure 4.4. *Derangements of length 4*

For $N = 4$, we start from roots of three trees: 2, 3 and 4. At each descent from a level, we take numbers from the new level that are different from the list of predecessors obtained by going back up the tree, and also different from the number of their level. The program that results from it is very close to that of permutations, and we present it here *in extenso* (with the preliminary declarations):

```
#include <stdio.h>
#define N 7
#define YES 1
#define NO 0
void tree(int i,int level);
int belongstolistofpredecessors(int j, int level);
int predecessor[N+1]; long int number;

main()
{ int i; long int u,v,w;
  for(i=2; i<=N; i++) tree( i ,1);
  u=0; v=1;  /* theoretical calculation of the number of derangements for
                  verification. See Chapter 8 for this formula */
  for(i=3; i<=N; i++)  { w=(i-1)*(v+u); u=v; v=w;}
  printf("\nnumber=%ld",w);
}

void tree(int i, int level)
{ int j,k;
```

```
  if (level==N)
    { number++; printf("%4.0ld: ",number);
      for (k=2; k<=N; k++) printf("%d",predecessor[k]);
      printf("%d ",i);
    }
  else
    { for(j=1; j<=N; j++)
     if (j!=i && j!=level+1 && belongstolistofpredecessors(j,level)==NO)
        { predecessor[level+1]=i; tree(j,level+1); }
    }
}

int belongstolistofpredecessors(int j, int level)
{ int k;
  for(k=level; k>=2; k- -) if (j==predecessor[k]) return YES;
  return NO;
}
```

4.4. The queens problem

What we have to do is to place N queens on a chessboard with dimensions $N \times N$ without any of them being taken over by another, and to find all the possible ways this can be done. We immediately realize that there is no possibility for a 2×2 or 3×3 chessboard, and that there are two solutions for a 4×4 chessboard. Then the bigger the chessboard gets, the more the number of solutions rapidly increases. To this day, there is no known theoretical formula for this problem. Only an experimental study enables us to find the number of solutions. The method implemented to find the correct placements for the queens is done manually, using the progressive drawing of a tree. This is a typically recursive processing, which it will then be easy to program.

Here is the method. Let us begin by numbering the lines, as well as the columns, from 0 to $N - 1$. In this way we have coordinates of each square of the chessboard. Let us take for example a chessboard of $N = 5$ (see Figure 4.5). Let us begin by placing a queen on line 0. We will have to envisage each one of the five possibilities. Let us choose, for example, column 1. Let us now move on to line 1. Taking into consideration the positions forbidden by the queen in line 0, columns 3 or 4 are the only remaining possibilities.

Let us begin by choosing column 3, then let us move on to line 2. As a function of the squares forbidden by the two first queens, one single possibility is left in column 0. We continue in this way, from line to line. When we manage to place a queen on the last line, we have a solution to the problem. The process is done in a tree structure, going down along one branch. When a branch is finished, we start again from a node we had left in waiting. For the 5×5 chessboard, starting from the queen in position 1 on line 0, this gives the tree structure in Figure 4.6, with two solutions to the problem. Let us insist on the fact that this tree is created by a deep route. It is only when we have finished exploring case 1, 3 (the positions on the two first lines) of placement of the first two queens, going down to the lowest, that we can go back up in the tree to re-launch the exploration in case 1, 4. It is a classic recursive process, from which the program is easily deduced.

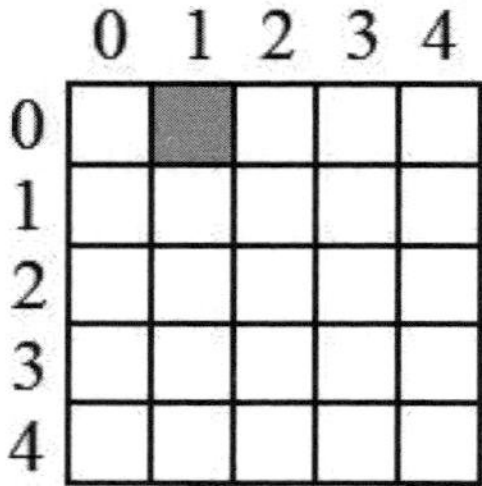

Figure 4.5. *Chessboard with numbered lines and columns*

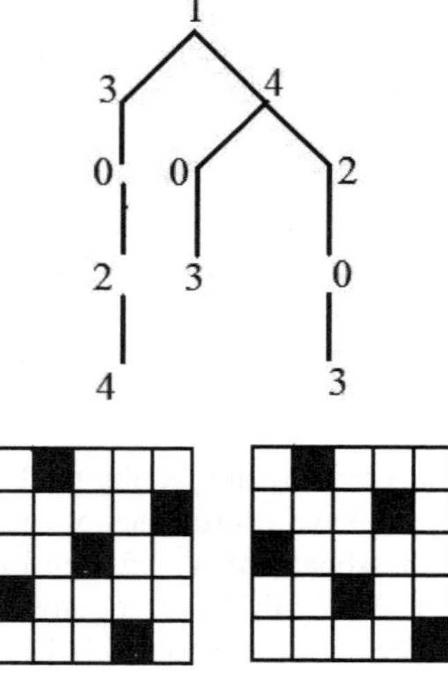

Figure 4.6. *Two solutions to the queen problem*

```
main()  { counter=0;
          for(column=0; column<N; column++)  queen(column,0);
        }

void queen(int c, int l)
{
x[l]=c; y[l]=l;
if (l ==N−1)
   { counter++; printf("\n%4.ld :",counter);
     for(ll=0;ll<N;ll++) printf("%d ",x[ll]);
   }
else
   { line=l+1;
     for(col=0;col<N;col++)
       { flag=0;
       for(ll=0; ll<=l; ll++) if (x[ll]= =col || abs(col-x[ll])==abs(line-y[ll]))
            { flag=1; break;}
       if (flag==0) queen(col,line);
       }
   }
}
```

Here are the first results obtained during the execution of the program:

N:	2	3	4	5	6	7	8	9	10	11	12	13
Number of ways:	0	0	2	10	4	40	92	352	724	2,680	14,200	73,712

In Figure 4.7 we will find an example of the movements of queens. Once this is obtained, the study could continue with the search for different solutions to the symmetry-types of the square. There are eight symmetries of the square that leaves it globally unchanged: the four rotations with an angle multiple of 90° (in particular the identity), as well as four reflections around the two diagonal axes, and vertical and horizontal axes.

When we take, for example, the first drawing obtained in Figure 4.7, exercising the eight symmetries of the square gives eight different ways of placing the seven queens, which is evidently found among the 40 ways.

It can happen that a drawing of the placement of queens remains globally unchanged by one of the symmetries of the square, notably by a rotation of 180° in this case. Whatever the case may be, the number of solutions to symmetry types is clearly smaller, even if it is not in the maximum ratio 8. In the case where $N = 7$, there are only six of the 40 ways that are different to symmetry types.

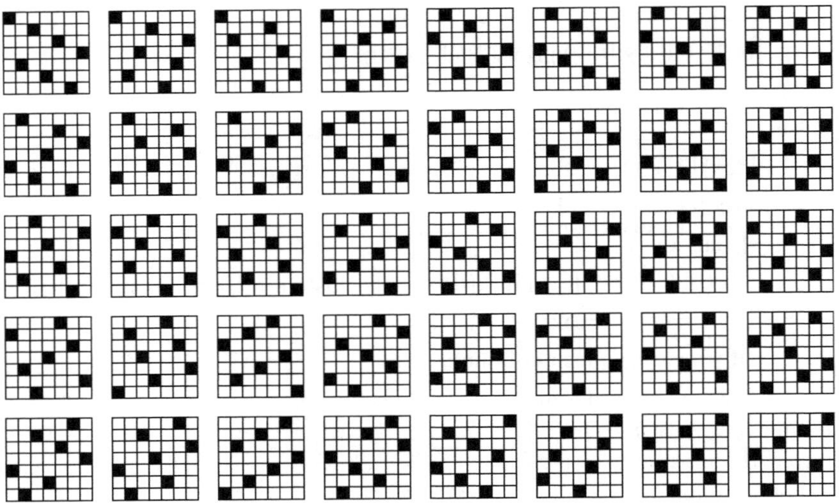

Figure 4.7. *The 40 ways of placing seven queens on a 7×7 chessboard*

4.5. Filling up containers

We are given three containers of varying capacities, where the first is full at the start. In the example that follows, these containers hold 10, 5 and 3 liters. By pouring the contents of one container into the other, according to rules that will be specified, we want to arrive at a certain final situation, for example that the last container containing exactly two liters. The rules for decanting are the following: either we completely fill a container by pouring part of the contents of another into it, or we completely empty a container into another, without causing the second to overflow.

In the example chosen, searching for solutions leads us to develop a tree whose first levels are shown in Figure 4.8.

The complete development of the tree leads to 14 solutions to this problem, the quickest requiring four steps. Clearly, when searching for a solution we must avoid any closing, i.e. returning to a situation already obtained before.

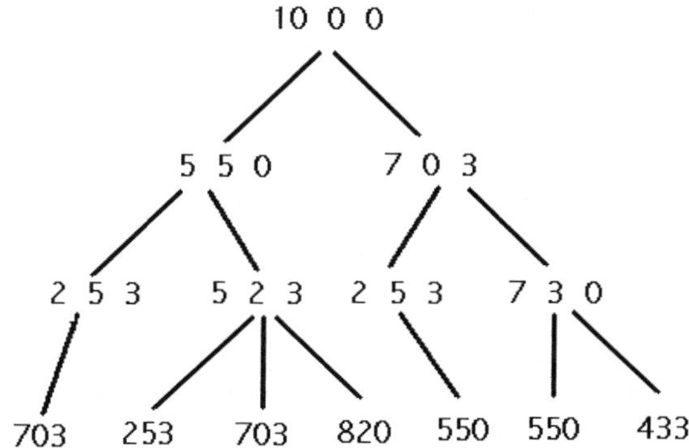

Figure 4.8. *First steps in the evolution of filling containers*

Figure 4.9 gives the first four solutions to the problem, the forth being the quickest of all.

Let us move on to the program: the three containers called 0, 1 and 2 have a maximum capacity *max*[]. Their content during pouring out is *c*[], and the difference between the maximum content and the current content is the remainder *r*[]. Each situation is numbered by a number in base 100, i.e.: $10000c[0]+100c[1]+c[2]$. For example, the configuration 451 is numbered 040501.

At the start we have the situation 100, which is numbered 10000.max[0] = 10000.10 = 100000. The *tree*(*number*, *level*) function searches for the following possible configurations, which are numbered *ni*:

```
main()  {  tree(10000*max[0], 1);  }

void tree(long int i, int level)

{
c[0]=(int)(i/10000); r[0]=max[0]-c[0];
c[1]=(int)(i/100)%100; r[1]=max[1]-c[1];
c[2]=(int)(i%100); r[2]=max[2]-c[2];
if (c[2]==2)  /* stop test */
```

```
{ number++; printf("\n%4.d: ",number);
  for (k=2;k<=level;k++)
  printf("(%d%d%d)",(int)(predecessor[k]/10000),
          (int)(predecessor[k]/100)%100,(int)(predecessor[k]%100));
  printf(" (%d %d %d) ",(int)(i/10000),(int) (i/100)%100,(int)(i%100));
}
else for(j=0;j<N;j++)  for(k=0;k<N;k++)  if (k!=j)
  if (c[j]>0 && c[j]<=r[k])  /* we empty the contents of container j in k */
   {nc[j]=0; nr[j]=max[j];   nr[k]=r[k]-c[j]; nc[k]=c[k]+c[j];
   for(ii=0;ii<N;ii++) if (ii!=j && ii!=k)
        { nc[ii]=c[ii]; nr[ii]=r[ii];}
   ni= (long)nc[0]*10000+(long)nc[1]*100+(long)nc[2];
      /* the new number */
   if (belongstolistofpredecessors(ni,level)==NO)
        { predecessor[level+1]=i; tree(ni,level+1);}
   }
  else if (r[k]>0 && c[j]>=r[k])
      /* we fill k with part of the contents of i  */
   { nc[j]=c[j]-r[k]; nr[j]=r[j]+r[k];
    nr[k]=0; nc[k]=max[k];
    for(ii=0;ii<N;ii++) if (ii!=j && ii!=k)
        { nc[ii]=c[ii]; nr[ii]=r[ii];}
    ni= (long)nc[0]*10000+(long)nc[1]*100+(long)nc[2];
    if (belongstolistofpredecessors(ni,level)==NO)
        { predecessor[level+1]=i; tree(ni,level+1);}
   }
}
int belongstolistofpredecessors(long int j, int level)
{  for(k=level;k>=2;k--)  if (j==predecessor[k]) return YES;
   return NO;
}
```

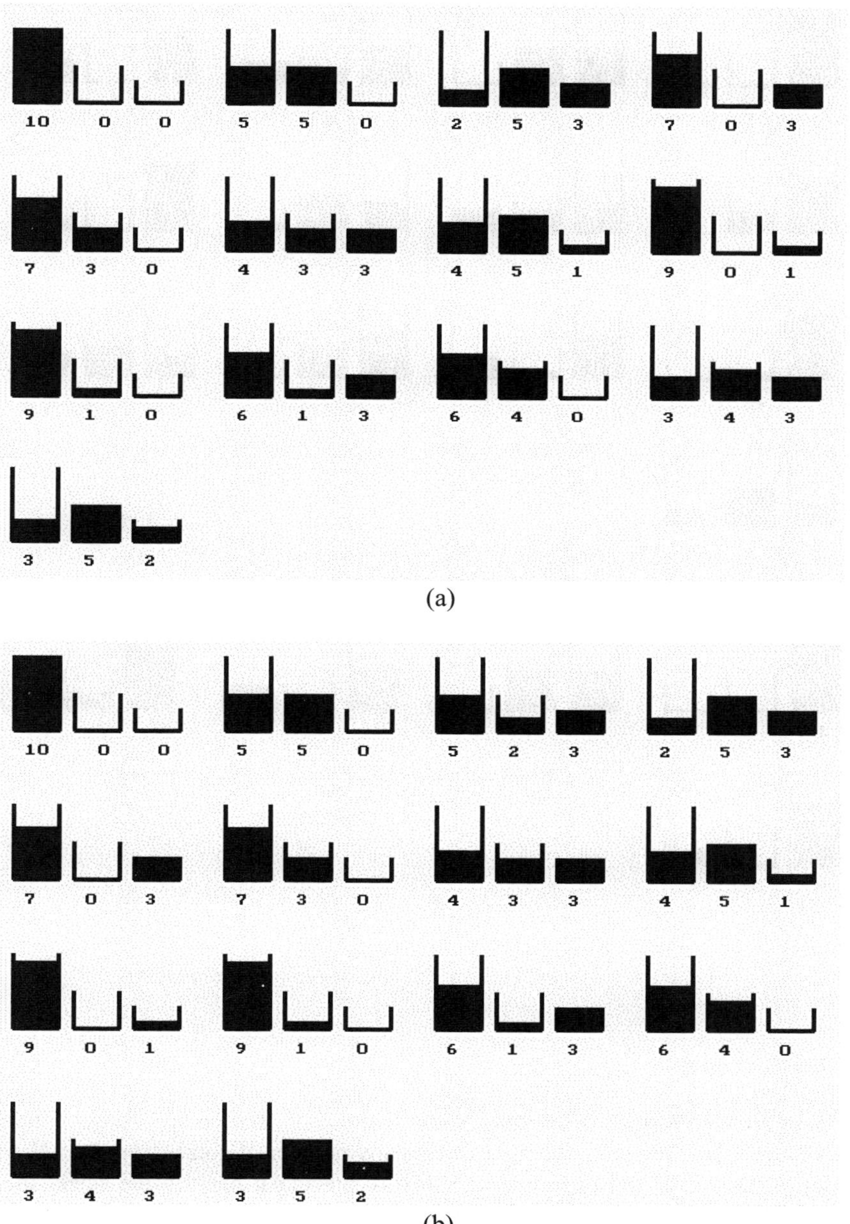

Figure 4.9. *a) and b) – first solutions to filling the containers*

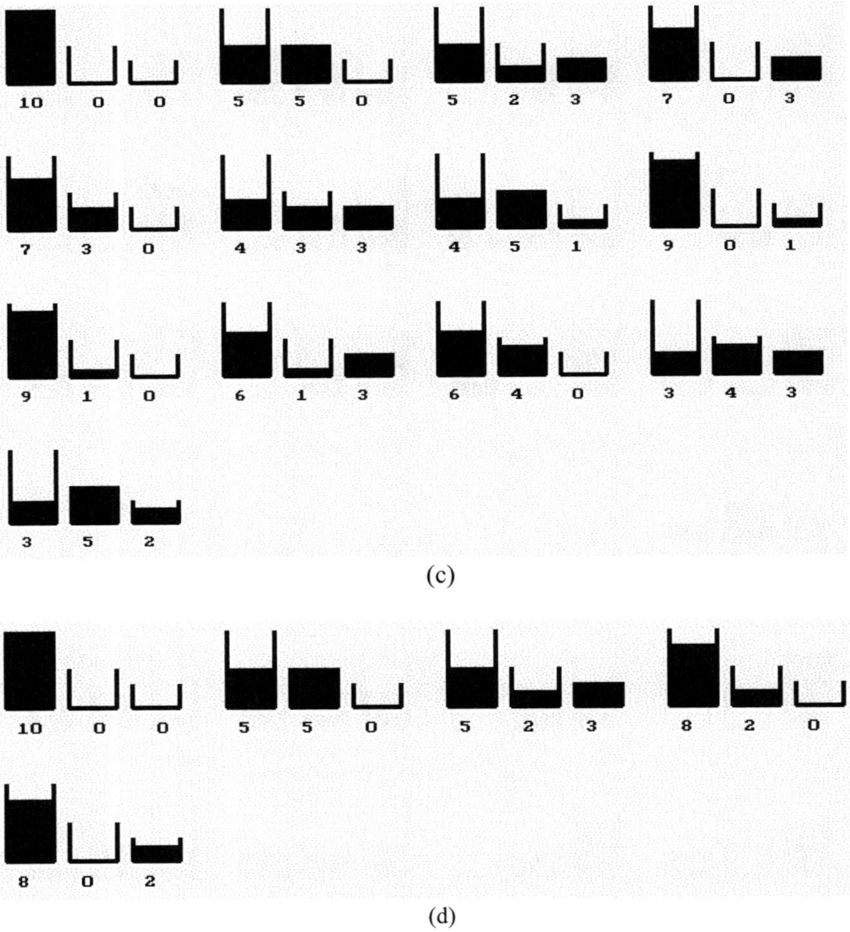

Figure 4.9. *c) and d) – first solutions to filling the containers*

4.6. Stack of coins

We start with a stack of N coins, some with heads face up and others with tails (see Figure 4.10). We have the right to take any number of coins, from 1 to N, from the top of the stack and to turn it over before placing it back in the stack. In this way, the heads in the reversed block become tails and *vice versa*. The object is to exercise these reversals in such a way that in the end all the coins have their heads face-side up.

The stack can be considered as a word based on 0 and 1, where the top of the stack becomes the beginning of the word; the letter 0 signifies heads and 1 tails. For example, the stack designed in Figure 4.10 is written 01100011. A simple strategy also exists for ending up with a word made up only of 0s.

Figure 4.10. *Stack of coins oriented heads or tails*

All we have to do is to separate the blocks of 0 and the blocks of 1, exercising reversals at each separation of blocks. This is done from left to right (including just after the last letter when it is a 1). For example:

0|11|000|11| → 111|00011 → 000000|11→ 111111111|→ 00000000

where we exercise successive moves 1, 3, 6 and 8. This the quickest way to arrive at the result, even if it is not the only one. By taking all the stacks of height *N* each time, we can easily find out the minimum number of moves to carry out. This is what the short program that follows does:

```
for(i=0; i<pow(2,N); i++)  /* all the numbers of length N in decimal  */
  { q=i; for(k=0;k<N;k++) {r[k]=q%2;q=q/2;}  /* we convert them into binary*/
    display the number in binary in r[]
    counter=0;          /* we are going to count the separations between blocks */
    for(k=0;k<N−1;k++) if (r[k]!=r[k+1]) counter++;
    if (r[N−1]==1) counter++;
    display the counter which gives the number of moves to carry out at
    minimum
  }
```

In more general terms, we now want to obtain all the possible solutions.

We start with a certain stack, coded in decimal by the number *i*, and we want to find out all the ways of ending up with the stack coded 0, where all the pieces have their heads face up. In doing this we want to avoid, in each case, falling back twice in a row on the same configuration. To do this, we develop a tree diagram. When we are at a certain level with a number *i*, we try all the following configurations obtained by making moves from length 1 to length *N*.

Each time we check whether this configuration has already been obtained (if it is equal to *i* or to one of the predecessors of *i* in the tree). If this is not the case, we take the configuration and re-launch the development of the tree from it, the level having increased by 1.

The number of nodes in the branches of the final tree, starting from the root, is at most equal to 2^N because it is the maximum number of configurations and we are avoiding finding the same one twice in a branch. All we have to do is carry out a stop test when the node becomes 0. Figure 4.11 shows the development of the tree starting from the stack of height 3 and coded 2, i.e. in ascending binary 010:

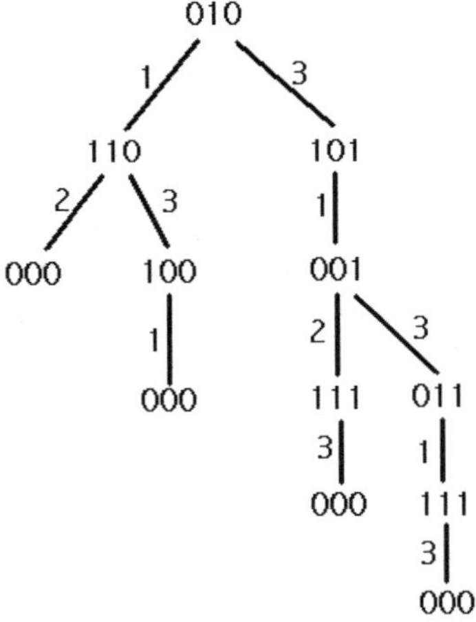

Figure 4.11. *Tree of configurations of a three-coin stack*

We find four solutions corresponding to the succession of moves:

12, 131, 3123 and 31313

We deduce the program from it:

main() { *we are given the number* i *in decimal, from which we start;* tree(i,1); }

void tree(int i,int level)
{ q=i; for(k=0;k<N;k++) {r[k]=q%2;q=q/2;} /* *conversion in binary* */

```
    if (i= =0)      /* stop test, when we fall on the number 0 */
      { number++;    for(k=1;k<level;k++) printf("%d ",cut[k]);  }
    else
      {  for(j=1;j<=N;j++)  /* cuts of length 1 ... N  */
        { for k=0;k<N;k++) rr[k]=r[k];
          /* the binary word rr[]will make up the new configuration after
             reversal, and will become  n after conversion in decimal */
          left=0;right=j−1;
          while (left<right)
             {aux=rr[left];rr[left]=rr[right];rr[right]=aux; left++;right--;}
          for(k=0;k<j;k++) rr[k]=(rr[k]+1)%2;
          then2=1; n=0;    for(k=0;k<N;k++) {n+=then2*rr[k]; then2=2*then2;}
          if (n!=i &&  belongstolistofpredecessors(n,level)==NO)
              {cut[level]=j;  predecessor[level+1]=i; tree(n,level+1);}
        }
      }
  }
  int belongstolistofpredecessors(int j, int level)
    { for(k=level;k>=2;k--) if (j==predecessor[k]) returnYES;  return NO; }
```

For this problem to become a real game, we can start with a stack where all of the coins are tails up ($i = 2^N - 1$) and make the maximum number of operations (without falling on the same configuration twice) to end up with a stack with all its coins heads up. As soon as $N > 2$, we can check that this maximum reaches the value $2^N - 1$, meaning that we pass through all possible configurations. In the program above, all we have to do is to modify the stop test by doing: *if (i==0 and level==2^N)*. With the number of routes of length $2^N - 1$ called $u(N)$, we find:

$u(2) = 0$, $u(3) = 1$, $u(4) = 4$, $u(5) = 183485$

4.7. Domino tiling a chessboard

Let us take a chessboard to be a rectangle marked out in squares of length M and width N. We want to tile it using dominoes that each occupy two adjacent squares (a white and a black), horizontally or vertically. We assume that M or N are even, because if M and N were both odd, the number of squares would be odd, whereas domino tiling requires an even number of squares. Let us number the squares of the rectangle from 0 to $M.N - 1$, successively running through the lines from left to right.

The position of a domino in the rectangle is expressed by two numbers x_1 and x_2, corresponding to the squares it occupies, read from left to right or from top to bottom, where $x_2 = x_1 + 1$ if it is horizontal, and $x_2 = x_1 + M$ if it is vertical.

To simplify the programming, we replace these two numbers x_1 and x_2 with a single *X*, taking the number *X* as being written with the two digits x_1 x_2 in base *M.N*, i.e.:

$$X = x_1 MN + x_2 \text{, and in reverse } x_1 = X / (MN),\ x_2 = X\%(MN)$$

We place the dominoes one after the other. For each part configuration obtained, with its last domino *A* put in place, we look for which domino to put after it, in all possible ways, starting from the following square. There is either zero, one or two possibilities, which we call the successors of *A*.

Taking the example of $M = 4$ and $N = 3$ (see Figure 4.12), we start from the horizontal domino 01 or from the vertical domino 04 (in more general terms 0M), which will give rise to two trees. Starting from 01, we can place the second domino either in 23 or 26. We fill in the first empty square first, reading from left to right and then from top to bottom. We continue in this way, taking the successors of each domino placed and making sure that it does not take a place already occupied by the dominoes placed before. These configurations are read on the vertical branches of trees. We stop when the last domino is placed on level $MN/2$, expressing the first level of the tree (that of its root) as 1. The number of vertical branches of the two trees, read from root to final leaf, is the number of all the possible tilings. In the example where $M = 4$ and $N = 3$, we find 11 solutions (see Figure 4.12). The following program results from it:

```
#define M 4
#define N 3        /* MN even */
#define MN (M*N)

main()
{ counter=0;
  explore(1,1); explore(M,1);
  printf(" %ld", counter);
}
```

The function *explore*() will take as arguments the number X associated with the last of the dominoes placed, as well as the level of the tree where it is found. Starting from X, we look for positions $x1$ and $x2$ of this domino. Then we look to place the following domino or dominos. To do this, we look for the first free square from left to right and top to bottom, expressed as $newx1$. Then we try to place a horizontal domino starting from there. This is possible except for when square $newx2 = newx1 + 1$ is already occupied or $newx1$ is found on the right border. If it is feasible, the number of successors moves from 0 to 1.

Finally, we envisage the second possibility: with the implementation of a vertical domino starting from $newx1$, where $newx2 = newx1 + M$. If we are not on the last line, this is always possible. Actually, thanks to our journey from left to right before going from top to bottom, and the horizontal filling before going down vertically, we are assured that this vertical domino can be placed. In this case, the number of successors moves to two. We are only left with recalling the function *explore*() on each one of the successors (possible horizontal before possible vertical) on the next level.

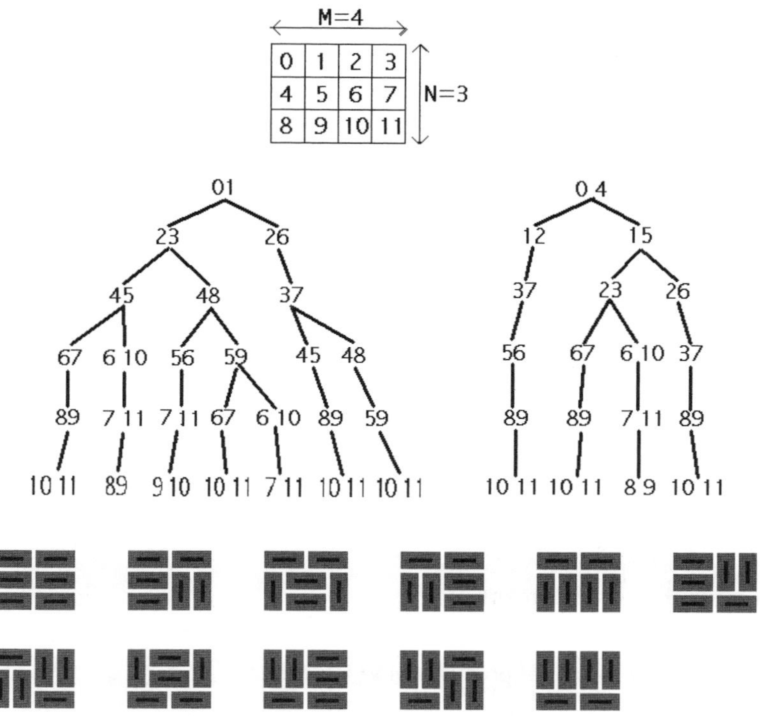

Figure 4.12. *The 11 tilings of the 4 by 3 rectangle*

```
void explore(int X, int level)
{
 if (level= =MN/2)
   { counter++; to eventually add the design of the tiling
   }
 else
   { nbsuccessors=0; x1=X/MN;x2=X%MN;
     newx1=x1+1; if (newx1==x2) newx1++;
     while(belongstolistofpredecessors(newx1,X,level)==1) newx1++;
     newx2=newx1+1;
     if (newx2%M!=0 && belongstolistofpredecessors(newx2,X,level)==0)
       { successor[nbsuccessors]=newx1*MN+newx2;
         pred[level+1]=X;
         nbsuccessors++;
       }
     if (newx1<MN−M)
       { newx2=newx1+M ;
        successor[nbsuccessors]=newx1*MN+newx2;pred[level+1]=X;
        nbsuccessors++;
       }
     if (nbsuccessors>0)
     for(i=0; i<nbsuccessors; i++)
     explore(successor[i],level+1);
   }
}
int belongstolistofpredecessors(int x,int xx, int level)
{
int xx1,xx2,k;
xx1=xx/MN; xx2=xx%MN;
if ( x==xx1 || x==xx2) return 1;
for(k=level; k>1; k--)
if (x==pred[k]/MN || x==pred[k]%MN) return 1;
return 0;
}
```

NOTE 4.1.– There is a formula giving the number of tilings of a $M{\times}N$ rectangle with 2×1 dominos, namely:

$$2^{\frac{MN}{2}} \prod_{\substack{1 \le j \le M \\ 1 \le k \le N}} \left(\cos^2 \frac{j\pi}{M+1} + \cos^2 \frac{k\pi}{N+1}\right)^{\frac{1}{4}}$$

which we will see later (in Chapter 18).

When $M = N$ (see Figure 4.13), we find:

– two tilings for $M = N = 2$;

– 36 tilings for $M = N = 4$;

– 6,728 tilings for $M = \mathrm{N} = 6$; and

– 12,988,816 for $M = N = 8$.

Figure 4.13. *The 36 tilings for M = N = 4*

Chapter 5

Languages, Generating Functions and Recurrences

What we have done so far shows that combinatorics essentially boils down to the enumeration of words, which are themselves codings representing diverse configurations or situations. In each problem, these words are based on an alphabet with several letters, and their set forms a language.

The specific study of these languages, with the formal series or generating functions that come from it, will enable us to deduce quantitative results with regards to the counting of these words.

A language based on two letters (*a* or *b*, 0 or 1, yes or no) is already enough to deal with many problems.

5.1. The language of words based on two letters

Let us begin with the simplest example: that of words of n characters based on two letters, x and y.

Calling these letters 0 and 1, this gives binary numbers of n characters, from 0 to $2^n - 1$. If we want to draw these words, we can also write the two letters in the form of diagonal lines ↗ and ↘ (see Figure 5.1). The set of all these words makes up the language L_n, which we write in the following way, for example, for $n = 3$:

$$L_3 = xxx + xxy + xyx + xyy + yxx + yxy + yyx + yyy$$

Two operations are present in this expression: the sign + signifies "or", considering words as sets themselves. The link between two successive letters of a word is the concatenation, which is written as if it were a (non-commutative) multiplication. By analogy with the distributivity of multiplication compared to addition, we also get:

$$(x + y)^3 = (x + y)(x + y)(x + y) = xxx + xxy + xyx + xyy + yxx + yxy + yyx + yyy$$

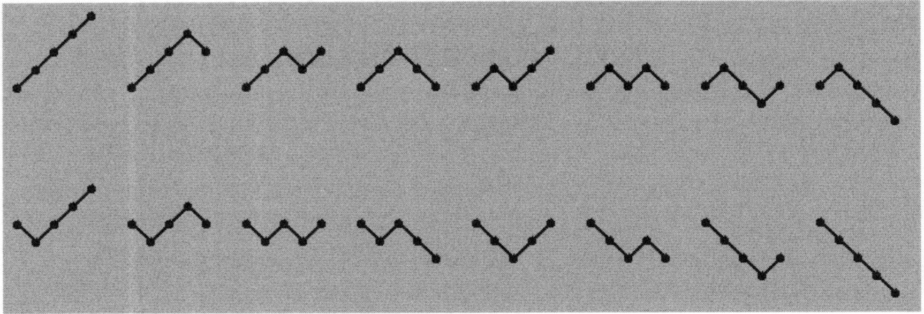

Figure 5.1. *The 16 words of 4 characters, from xxxx to yyyy, making up language L_4 where the two base letters are drawn in the form ↗ and ↘*

Therefore language L_n boils down to $L_n = (x + y)^n$.

The properties associated with these words will result from the formula above. Let us make the following simple conversion, which makes the concatenation-multiplication communicative. Each word can be written by putting the *x*s in front of the *y*s, keeping in alphabetical order. The language is transformed into:

$$L_3(x,y) = xxx + xxy + xxy + xxy + xyy + xxy + xyy + xyy + \text{yyy}$$

$$= xxx + 3xyy \ + 3xyy + yyy$$

This also comes back to developing $(x + y)^3 = x^3 + 3x^2y + 3xy^2 + y^3$, applying binomial formula. In the general case:

$$L_n(x,y) = (x+y)^n = \sum_{p=0}^{n} C_n^p x^p y^{n-p}$$

The polynomial obtained is called the generating function associated with the number of words that have the number of *x*s (or *y*s), because the coefficient of the term in $x^p y^{n-p}$ is exactly the number of words with the letter *x* *p* times.

Again we find that this number is C_n^p. By now making $x = y = 1$, each word of the language becomes 1, and adding them gives the total number of words of n characters. This goes back to replacing $(x + y)^n$ with $(1 + 1)^n$, which gives 2^n. Let us insist on the fact that these formulae have all been found again from the single initial definition of the language:

$$L_n = (x + y)^n$$

Let us extend what we have just done to all the words based on two letters. We obtain the language:

$$L = e + x + y + xx + xy + yx + yy + xxx + xxy + \dots$$

where the word e, which we will also call 1, signifies the empty word. Grouping the words according to length, this gives:

$$L = 1 + (x+y) + (x+y)^2 + (x+y)^3 + (x+y)^4 + \dots = \sum_{k \geq 0} L_k$$

By analogy with the infinite sum of the terms in a geometric progression, which is written $1 + X + X^2 + X^3 + \dots = 1 / (1 - X)$ in the case of convergence $(|X| < 1)$, language L takes the concentrated form:

$$L = 1 / (1 - x - y)$$

We can also classify the words of language L according to their beginning x or y by adding the empty word, which gives:

$$L = 1 + x\,(1 + x + y + xx + \dots) + y\,(1 + x + y + xx + \dots) = 1 + (x+y)\,L$$

Again we find the equation in $L : L(1 - x - y) = 1$ or $L = 1/(1 - x - y)$.

Now if we take $x = y$, with the empty word becoming unit number 1, this gives what is called the commutative image of L.

The language $L = e + x + y + xx + xy + yx + yy + xxx + \dots$ becomes the function:

$$L(x) = 1 + x + x + x^2 + x^2 + x^2 + x^2 + x^3 + \dots = 1 + 2x + 4x^2 + \dots$$

We get a series of powers of x, where the term in x^n has the number of words of n characters as its coefficient. This is called the generating function associated with the number of words of n characters. By making $x = y$ in the language L equation, we obtain this new generating function $L(x) = 1/(1 - 2x)$. This function is associated with the number of words of n characters, the development of which gives:

$$L(x) = 1 + 2x + 4x^2 + 8x^3 + \ldots$$

and we find again that the number of words of n characters is 2^n.

Let us now call $L_{\leq n}$ the number of words shorter than or equal to n. We have:

$$L_{\leq n} = e + (x+y) + (x+y)^2 + \ldots + (x+y)^n$$

corresponding to the recurrence relation $L_{\leq n} = L_{\leq n\text{-}1} + (x + y)^n$ with $L_{\leq 0} = e$. Now let us replace y with 1, and we get the function:

$$L_{\leq n}(x) = 1 + (x + 1) + (x + 1)^2 + \ldots + (x+1)^n = \frac{(1+x)^{n+1} - 1}{x} = \sum_{k \geq 1} C_{n+1}^{k} x^{k\text{-}1}$$

The fact of having replaced y with 1 gives the number of words with letter x k times as the coefficient of the term in x^k. Therefore the number of words shorter than or equal to n with letter x k times is C_{n+1}^{k+1}.

Let us now take another simple example, that of a tiling.

5.2. Domino tiling a 2×*n* chessboard

Let us consider the simple case where the chessboard has a width of 2 and an infinite length.

Each domino occupies two squares vertically or horizontally. The tiling seen lengthwise is formed by repeated blocks made either of a vertical domino ⊟ or of two horizontal dominos stuck one on top of the other ⊞. We find ourselves faced with a chain of characters based on two letters; hence the language of these tilings:

$$L = 1 + x + y + xx + xy + yx + yy + xxx + \ldots = 1 / (1 - x - y)$$

Replacing y with x^2, and giving back commutative multiplication, language L becomes the generating function:

$$L(x) = 1 + x + x^2 + x^2 + x^3 + x^3 + x^4 + x^3 + \ldots = 1 + x + 2x^2 + 3x^3 + 5x^4 + \ldots$$

Words are now classed according to their number of dominoes, or even according to the length occupied by the tiling. The generating function is associated with the number $u(n)$ of tilings on a given length n of the chessboard. It is also expressed:

$$L(x) = 1 / (1 - x - x^2)$$

The development of this fraction gives a series generally termed $u(n)\, x^n$. As we will see later, we recognize the generating function associated with the gap-type Fibonacci sequence.

These examples show that generating functions are deduced from the original language, and they are associated with number sequences. We are going to develop this last aspect linking generating functions to sequences.

5.3. Generating function associated with a sequence

Let us consider a number sequence: $u(0), u(1), u(2), u(3), \ldots$ generally termed $u(n)$. By definition the generating function associated with this sequence is the series:

$$F(x) = u(0) + u(1)x + u(2)\, x^2 + u(3)x^3 + \ldots$$

Here x designates an indeterminate. It is its exponent above all that interests us, because the coefficient of the term in x^n is precisely $u(n)$.

Interest in the generating function appears in the following context. Let us assume that we have a sequence, defined by its recurrence relation and its initial conditions. A generating function corresponds to it. If we manage to develop this generating function, the term in x^n will have $u(n)$ as its coefficient. Therefore we will have the general term of the sequence in its explicit form. Let us look at this using the Fibonacci series example.

By definition, the Fibonacci sequence obeys the recurrence relation:

$$u(n + 2) = u(n + 1) + u(n), \text{ with } u(0) = 0 \text{ and } u(1) = 1 \text{ at the beginning}$$

These data enable us to construct the successive terms of the series, which is quite unique. We would, however, like to find the term $u(n)$ in its explicit form, i.e. as a function of n only. Let us proceed in this way:

$$\begin{aligned}
F(x) &= u(0) + u(1)x + u(2)x^2 + u(3)x^3 + \ldots + u(n)x^n + \ldots \\
xF(x) &= \phantom{u(0) + {}} u(0)x + u(1)x^2 + u(2)x^3 + \ldots + u(n-1)x^n + \ldots \\
x^2F(x) &= \phantom{u(0) + u(1)x + {}} u(0)x^2 + u(1)x^3 + \ldots + u(n-2)x^n + \ldots
\end{aligned}$$

Subtracting the last two equalities from the first, and taking into account the recurrence relation $u(n) = u(n-1) + u(n-2)$, what remains is:

$$F(x) - xF(x) - x^2F(x) = u(0) + u(1)x - u(0)x, \text{ i.e. } F(x)\,(1 - x - x^2) = x$$

Hence the generating function:

$$F(x) = x / (1 - x - x^2)$$

Notice that the recurrence relation $u(n) - u(n-1) - u(n-2) = 0$ leads directly to the denominator of $F(x)$, which has the same coefficients, i.e. $1 - x - x^2$. The only thing left is to develop $F(x)$, and that is where the calculations begin!

Let us take the equation $X^2 - X - 1 = 0$, which assumes the numbers φ and φ', called golden numbers, as solutions. Using the sum and the product of the roots, it is easy to check that the denominator of $F(x)$ is expressed as $1 - x - x^2 = (1 - \varphi x)(1 - \varphi' x)$. $F(x)$ remains to be expressed in the form of simple fractions:

$$F(x) = x / (1 - x - x^2) = A / (1 - \varphi x) + B / (1 - \varphi' x)$$

By identification, we find:

$$F(x) = \frac{1}{\sqrt{5}}\left(\frac{1}{1-\varphi x} - \frac{1}{1-\varphi' x}\right) \text{ with } \varphi = \frac{1+\sqrt{5}}{2} \text{ and } \varphi' = \frac{1-\sqrt{5}}{2}$$

We can now progress, because:

$$1 / (1 - \varphi x) = 1 + \varphi x + \varphi^2 x^2 + \varphi^3 x^3 + \ldots$$

The coefficient of the term in x^n is:

$$u(n) = \frac{1}{\sqrt{5}}(\varphi^n - \varphi'^n)$$

which is the explicit form of $u(n)$.

The inconvenience of this method is that it forces the development of the generating function, notably the decomposition of a rational fraction in simple elements, as a phase of calculation. It also has advantages. For example, the generating function associated with the number of tilings of a 2×n chessboard with dominoes was $1/\left(1-x-x^2\right)$. By analogy with the generating function of the Fibonacci sequence, the number of tilings $p(n)$ is nothing other than the Fibonacci number shifted by one notch, i.e.:

$$p(n) = u(n+1)$$

5.4. Rational generating function and linear recurrence

There is a direct link between the generating function $F(x)$ of a sequence $u(n)$ when $F(x)$ is a rational function, i.e. a quotient with two polynomials, and the recurrence relation of this sequence when this relation is linear thanks to the following property: the generating function F of the sequence $u(n)$ is of the form:

$$F(x) = P(x) \,/\, Q(x)$$

with $Q(x) = 1 + a_1 x + a_2 x^2 + \ldots + a_d x^d$ (polynomial to the dth degree) and $P(x)$ polynomial to a degree less than d, if $u(n)$ verifies the recurrence relation of the form:

$$u(n+d) + a_1 u(n+d-1) + a_2 u(n+d-2) + \ldots + a_d u(n) = 0 \text{ for } n \geq d$$

Actually, if $F(x) = P(x) / Q(x)$ with $P(x) = b_0 + b_1 x + \ldots + b_{d-1} x^{d-1}$, we also have:

$Q(x)\, F(x) = P(x)$, i.e.:

$$(1 + a_1 x + a_2 x^2 + \ldots + a_d x^d)(u(0) + u(1)x + u(2)x^2 + \ldots)$$

$$= b_0 + b_1 x + \ldots + b_{d-1} x^{d-1}$$

Proceeding by identification, for the first terms of the sequence we get:

$$u(0) = b_0$$

$$u(1) + a_1 u(0) = b_1$$

$$\ldots$$

$$u(d-1) + a_1 u(d-2) + \ldots + a_{d-1} u(0) = b_{d-1}$$

then beyond that:

$$u(n+d) + a_1 u(n+d-1) + a_2 u(n+d-2) + \ldots + a_d u(n) = 0 \text{ for } n \geq d$$

which determines the $u(n)$ sequence in a unique way.

Conversely, if we are given the $u(n)$ sequence using its first terms $u(0)$ to $u(d-1)$, as well as by the linear recurrence relation of the order d:

$$u(n+d) + a_1 u(n+d-1) + a_2 u(n+d-2) + \ldots + a_d u(n) = 0$$

the system above linking the first terms of the sequence to the coefficients of the polynomial $P(x)$ assumes a unique solution b_0, b_1, …, b_{d-1} thanks to its triangular shape, and again we find it through identification of $Q(x)F(x) = P(x)$.

5.5. Example: routes in a square grid with rising shapes without entanglement

We consider routes based on a succession of three types of lines ($\leftarrow \uparrow \rightarrow$) oriented towards the west, east or north, all with the same unit length, without any of them passing over the other during the route. This notably forbids the succession west-east. We call $u(n)$ the number of these paths with n as length. We have to find the explicit form $u(n)$. To do this let us see how we move from paths of length $n-1$ to those of length n. We are led to distinguish paths of length n ending with a horizontal line numbering $H(n)$, and those ending with a line towards the north numbering $N(n)$. We have $u(n) = H(n) + N(n)$ for all $n > 0$, where $u(1) = 3$. We also have the recurrence relation:

$$H(n) = H(n-1) + 2N(n-1) \qquad [5.1a]$$

Actually, any path of length n ending with a horizontal line comes from a path of length $n-1$, ending either with a horizontal line (in which case we add a horizontal line in the same direction [west or east]), or with a vertical line (in which case we add a horizontal line towards west or east).

$$N(n) = H(n-1) + N(n-1) = u(n-1) \qquad [5.1b]$$

because each path of length n ending in a vertical line comes from a path of length $n-1$, ending with either a horizontal or a vertical line. We deduce from this that:

$$u(n) = 2H(n-1) + 3N(n-1) = 2u(n-1) + N(n-1) = 2u(n-1) + u(n-2)$$

We have just found the recurrence relation giving $u(n)$, i.e.:

$$u(n) - 2u(n-1) - u(n-2) = 0$$

to which we add the initial conditions $u(1) = 3$ and $u(2) = 7$, or even better $u(0) = 1$ and $u(1) = 3$.

Thanks to the results of the section above, we find the following is the generating function:

$$F(x) = \frac{1+x}{1-2x-x^2} = \frac{1+x}{(1-ax)(1-a'x)}$$

where a and a' are the roots of the polynomial reciprocal to that of the denominator, i.e. $X^2 - 2X - 1$, i.e. $a = 1+\sqrt{2}$ and $a' = 1-\sqrt{2}$. Then by breaking up the fraction into simple elements, we get:

$$F(x) = \frac{a}{2(1-ax)} + \frac{a'}{2(1-a'x)}$$

The development of the two fractions leads to the explicit form of $u(n)$, i.e.:

$$u(n) = 0.5\ (a^{n+1} + a'^{n+1})$$

The program constructing such forms leads to this genre of results (see Figure 5.2).

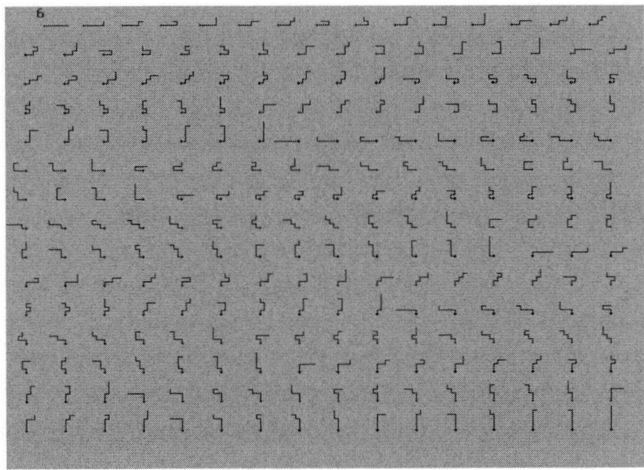

Figure 5.2. *All the shapes of length 6*

5.6. Exercises on recurrences

5.6.1. *Three types of purchases each day with a sum of N dollars*

A person has N dollars. With this money, everyday he buys one and only one of three products: either a cake for one dollar, a can of food for two dollars, or a magazine for two dollars. This happens day after day until he has spent all the money exactly. a_N is the number of ways of making this succession of daily purchases.

a) Show that $a_N = a_{N-1} + 2a_{N-2}$ with $a_0 = 1$ and $a_1 = 1$.

To distinguish the two types of purchases for two bills, we call them 2 and 2'.

Let us take a_N ways of spending his money. We can separate them into three parts:

– those where 1 dollar was spent on the last day. There are a_{N-1} ways of spending money on the days before. This makes a total of a_{N-1} ways;

– those where 2 dollars were spent on the last day. There are a_{N-2} ways of spending on the rest of the days before that. This makes a_{N-2} ways;

– those where 2' dollars were spent on the last day. This also makes a_{N-2} ways.

Hence: $a_N = a_{N-1} + 2a_{N-2}$.

On the other hand, $a_1 = 1$ and $a_0 = 1$ (in this case there is one way, the one where nothing is spent). We can also note that $a_2 = 3$, which confirms that $a_0 = 1$ is valid.

b) Deduce from it the explicit form of a_N, i.e. a_N as a function of N.

Let us turn our interest to the solutions of the recurrence relation, of which there is an infinite number. Let us first look for solutions in the form $a_n = r^n$. Referring to the recurrence relation, this imposes that $r^2 - r - 2 = 0$, what we call the characteristic equation. Its two solutions are $r_1 = 2$ and $r_2 = -1$, so the sequences with the general term $a_n = k\, r_1^{\,n} + k'\, r_2^{\,n}$, where k and k' are constants and also solutions to the recurrence relation. Among them let us look for the one that concerns us, where $u_0 = 1$ and $u_1 = 1$. This imposes that $k + k' = 1$, and $2k - k' = 1$, hence $k = 2/3$ and $k' = 1/3$.

Finally: $a_N = (2 / 3)\, 2^N + (1 / 3)(-1)^N$.

Let us note that a_N is also the closest integer to $(2 / 3)2^N$.

c) Program the counting of a_N solutions using two methods.

The first method uses the recurrence relation and initial conditions. The second takes the explicit form of a_N:

```
main()
{ a=1; b=1; printf("1 1 "); pow2=4;
  for(i=2; i<31; i++)
   {
     c=b+2*a; a=b; b=c; printf("%2.0f",c);
     aa=2./3.*pow2+0.5; printf("(%d) ",aa);
     pow2=2*pow2;

   }
}
```

d) Program to obtain the enumeration of all the solutions for a given number N.

The program will be recursive here.[1] The function $s(a,k,n)$ has three variables: a takes the values 1, 2 and 3 corresponding to each type of object (3 corresponds to 2'), k is the sum of money, with $k = N$ at the beginning, and which moves from k to $k-1$ when an object is bought for 1 dollar, or from k to $k-2$ in the two other cases, and n is the number of purchases, which is worth $n = 0$ at the beginning. At each step n of the process, the function is recalled three times in each of the possible cases, as long as the sum of money remaining k is ≥ 0. When $k = 0$, the result is displayed with the various purchases a having been recorded at each step in a table $b[n]$, declared globally:

```
main() { counter=0; cumul=0; s(0,N,0); }

void s(int a, int k, int n)

 { if (k==0)
    { b[n]=a; counter++; printf("%d : ",counter);
     for(i=1; i<=n; i++)
```

1. We already dealt with this problem in Chapter 3 following the classic method of enumeration.

```
        if (b[i]!=3) printf("%d ",b[i]);
        else printf("2' ");   printf("\n");
      }
    if (k>0)  { b[n]=a; s(1,k-1,n+1);  s(2,k−2,n+1);  s(3,k−2,n+1); }
}
```

Here are the results for $N = 5$:

1: 11111 2: 1112 3: 1112' 4: 1121 5: 112'1 6: 1211 7: 122
8: 122' 9: 12'11 10: 12'2 11: 12'2' 12: 2111 13: 212 14: 212'
15: 221 16: 22'1 17: 2'111 18: 2'12 19: 2'12' 20: 2'21 21: 2'2'1

5.6.2. *Word building*

From an alphabet with four letters a, b, c and d, how many words of n characters can we form such that letters a and b are not adjacent?

Let z_n be the number of words of n characters, made from the four letters a, b, c and d, and not having present blocks of two letters ab or ba. The number of those words that begin with a or b is called x_n and those beginning with c or d are called y_n.

a) Calculate z_0, z_1 and z_2.

$z_0 = 1$ (is the empty word), $z_1 = 4$, and for $n = 2$, $z_2 = 14$. Actually there are 2^4 ways of making words of 2 characters from a four-letter alphabet, but in this case we have to remove the two forbidden words *ab* and *ba*.

b) Starting with x_{n-1} words that have neither ab nor ba, and adding a letter to the front of them, how many words starting with c or d do we get, that have neither ab nor ba?

Do the same thing starting with y_{n-1} words. Deduce two recurrence relations between x_n, y_n and x_{n-1}, y_{n-1} from it.

Let us proceed by recurrence. Let us consider words of $n - 1$ characters that have no *ab* or *ba* blocks. Let the number of these words beginning with *a* or *b* be called x_{n-1}, and y_{n-1} the number of those beginning with *c* or *d*. This implies that $n > 1$. Similarly, the words of *n* characters with neither *ab* nor *ba* number x_n when they begin with *a* or *b*, and y_n when they begin with *c* or *d*.

How do we move from words of $n - 1$ characters to words of n characters by adding one letter in front of the words of $n - 1$ characters?

If the word of $n - 1$ characters begins with a or b, we can put as the first letter of the word of n characters either a but not b, or b but not a (respectively when the word of $n - 1$ characters begins with a or b), or c or even d. We get x_{n-1} words of n characters beginning with a or b, and $2x_{n-1}$ words beginning with c or d. If the word of $n - 1$ characters begins with c or d, we can put any one of the four letters in front of it. In this case we get $2y_{n-1}$ words of n characters beginning with a or b, and $2y_{n-1}$ words beginning with c or d.

We deduce following the recurrence relations from it:

$$x_n = x_{n-1} + 2y_{n-1}$$

$y_n = 2x_{n-1} + 2y_{n-1}$. This is true for $n > 1$.

c) Check that $y_n = 2\, z_{n-1}$. Also using $z_n = x_n + y_n$, find a recurrence relation linking z_n to z_{n-1} and z_{n-2}.

Let us return to $z_n = x_n + y_n$, the number of words of n characters with neither ab nor ba. We notice that $y_n = 2z_{n-1}$. By adding the two relations found above, we get:

$$z_n = 3x_{n-1} + 4y_{n-1} = 3z_{n-1} + y_{n-1} = 3z_{n-1} + 2z_{n-2}$$

The initial conditions are $z_0 = 1$ and $z_1 = 4$. We can check that we find $z_2 = 14$.

d) Deduce the explicit formula z_n.

Let us solve this recurrence relation: $z_n = 3z_{n-1} + 2z_{n-2}$.

The characteristic equation is $r^2 - 3r - 2 = 0$, whose roots are r_1 and r_2, i.e. $\left(3 \pm \sqrt{17}\right)/2$.

The general solution to the recurrence relation is $K_1\, r_1^{\,n} + K_2\, r_2^{\,n}$, where K_1 and K_2 are constants. Let us impose the initial conditions of our sequence z_n, for $n = 0$ and $n = 1$, which is written $K_1 + K_2 = 1$, and $K_1 r_1 + K_2 r_2 = 4$. From that we take:

$K_1 = (5 + \sqrt{17}\,)\ /\ (2\sqrt{17}\,)$ and $K_2 = (-5 + \sqrt{17}\,) / (2\ \sqrt{17}\,)$

Finally:

$$z_n = \frac{(5+\sqrt{17})}{2\sqrt{17}}\left(\frac{3+\sqrt{17}}{2}\right)^n + \frac{(-5+\sqrt{17})}{2\sqrt{17}}\left(\frac{3-\sqrt{17}}{2}\right)^n$$

The z_n sequence starting from z_0 is: 1, 4, 14, 50, 78, 634, ...

e) The solution above enables us to easily deal with an analogous exercise: how many words of n characters can we form from the alphabet with four letters a, b, c and d, in such a way that there is no ab, ba, cd or dc block?

We obtain the simple recurrence relation:

$$z_n = 3z_{n-1} \text{ for } n > 1 \text{ with } z_1 = 4$$

therefore:

$$z_n = 4\times 3^{n-1} \text{ for } n > 0$$

5.7. Examples of languages

5.7.1. *Language of parts of an element set {a, b, c, d, ...}*

Let us recall that in part the order of elements does not come into play. For example, part $\{a\ b\}$ is the same as $\{b\ a\}$, and because we have the choice we write this part $\{a\ b\}$ with its letters in ascending alphabetical order.

Therefore, for $n = 3$, the language of the parts of $\{a\ b\ c\}$ is:

$$L_3 = 1 + a + b + c + ab + ac + bc + abc$$

and is factorized by:

$$L_3 = (1 + a)(1 + b)(1 + c)$$

Converting each letter into x, we get:

$$L_3(x) = (1 + x)^3 = 1 + 3x + 3x^2 + x^3$$

Therefore the generating function associated with the number u_k of parts with k elements of an n-element set is:

$$L_n(x) = (1 + x)^n, \text{ hence } u_k = C_n^k$$

applying Newton's binomial formula.

5.7.2. *Language of parts of a multi-set based on n elements a, b, c, etc., where these elements can be repeated as much as we want*

As order does not come into play, these parts can be written as words with letters following each other in alphabetical order. For example, for $n = 3$ with letters a, b and c, the language is:

$$L_3 = 1 + a + b + c + aa + ab + ac + bb + bc + cc + aaa + aab + aac + abb$$
$$+ abc + acc + bbb + bbc + bcc + ccc + aaaa + \ldots$$
$$= (1 + a + aa + aaa + \ldots)\,(1 + b + bb + bbb + \ldots)\,(1 + c + cc + ccc + \ldots)$$
$$= (1 - a)^{-1}\,(1 - b)^{-1}\,(1 - c)^{-1} = ((1 - a)(1 - b)(1 - c))^{-1}$$

Converting each letter into x, this gives:

$$L_3(x) = 1 + 3x + 6x^2 + 10x^3 + \ldots = 1 / (1 - x)^3$$

In the general case, $L_n(x)$ is the generating function associated with the number u_k of ways of taking k objects out of n types of objects a, b and c, …, i.e.:

$$L_n(x) = 1 / (1 - x)^n\text{, hence } u_k = C_{n+k-1}^{\ k}$$

We will find this formula again for combinations with repetitions (see Chapter 7).

5.7.3. *Language of words made from arrangements taken from n distinct and non-repeated letters a, b, c, etc., where these words are shorter than or equal to n*

Now order comes into play. Let us begin with words of n characters, made from permutations of n letters. For example for $n = 3$, this permutations language is:

$$P_3 = abc + acb + bac + bca + cab + cba$$

It is the opportunity to introduce a new notion, that of the permanent (written *Per*) of a matrix. The permanent of a square matrix with dimensions $n \times n$ and coefficients a_{ij} for $n = 3$ is the sum of the permutations $a_{p(1)\,1}\ a_{p(2)\,2}\ a_{p(3)\,3}$ for all p permutations, i.e. $a_{11}a_{22}a_{33} + a_{11}a_{32}\,a_{23} + a_{21}a_{12}a_{33} + a_{21}a_{32}\,a_{13} + a_{31}a_{12}a_{23} + a_{31}a_{22}a_{13}$. Therefore the permutation language boils down to:

$$P_3 = Per\begin{pmatrix} a & a & a \\ b & b & b \\ c & c & c \end{pmatrix}$$

This permanent is developed as a determinant following its first column but all the signs are taken as positive here. Therefore by progressing following the first column:

$$Per\begin{pmatrix} a & a & a \\ b & b & b \\ c & c & c \end{pmatrix} = a\,Per\begin{pmatrix} b & b \\ c & c \end{pmatrix} + b\,Per\begin{pmatrix} a & a \\ c & c \end{pmatrix} + c\,Per\begin{pmatrix} a & a \\ b & b \end{pmatrix}$$

$$= abc + acb + bac + bca + cab + cba$$

In turn, language L_3 of arrangements of k out of n letters, here 3, for all values of k less than or equal to n, is written in the form of permanent:

$$L_3 = Per\begin{pmatrix} 1+a & a & a \\ b & 1+b & b \\ c & c & 1+c \end{pmatrix}$$

$$= (1 + a)((1 + b)(1 + c) + cb) + b(a(1 + c) + cb) + c(ab + (1 + b)a)$$

$$= 1 + a + b + c + ab + ac + ba + bc + ca + cb + abc + acb + bac + bca$$

$$+ cab + cba$$

The generating function associated with the sequence $u_k = A_3^k$ of arrangements of k out of n objects, here 3, is:

$$L_3(x) = Per\begin{pmatrix} 1+x & x & x \\ x & 1+x & x \\ x & x & 1+x \end{pmatrix}$$

5.7.4. *Language of words based on an alphabet of n letters*

For example for $n = 3$, with the three letters a, b and c as its alphabet, this gives the language:

$L_3 = 1 + a + b + c + aa + ab + ac + ba + bb + bc + ca + cb + cc + aaa + aab + ...$

In particular language $L_{3\,k}$ of these words that have length k is $(a + b + c)^k$. For example:

$$L_{3\,2} = aa + ab + ac + ba + bb + bc + ca + cb + cc$$

$$= (a + b + c)(a + b + c) = (a + b + c)^2$$

Consequently, the language of all the words is:

$$L_3 = L_{3\,0} + L_{3\,1} + L_{3\,2} + L_{3\,3} + L_{34} + \dots$$

$$= (a + b + c)^0 + (a + b + c)^1 + (a + b + c)^2 + (a + b + c)^3 + \dots$$

$$= (1 - (a + b + c))^{-1}$$

In the general case, $L_n = (1 - (a + b + c + \dots))^{-1}$. By conversion of each letter in x, we find the generating function of the number u_k of words of length k in an alphabet with n letters, i.e. $L_n(x) = 1 / (1 - nx)$. Hence $u_k = n^k$, as we could expect, because we find the number of applications of a k-element set in a n-element set.

5.8. The exponential generating function

By definition, the exponential generating function associated with a sequence $u(n)$ is of the form:

$$E(X) = u(0) + u(1)\frac{X}{1!} + u(2)\frac{X^2}{2!} + \dots + u(n)\frac{X^n}{n!} + \dots$$

This type of function is imposed in some contexts instead of the classic generating function, as the following examples, dealt with in the form of exercises, will show.

5.8.1. *Exercise 1: words based on three letters a, b and c, with the letter a at least twice*

a) Determine the number of words of four characters based on three letters a, b and c that have at least two, where the letters are in alphabetical order in each of these words. Give the generating function associated with the number of such words of some n characters.

Let us distinguish the words of four characters according to their number of *a*s. There is one single word with four *a*s: *aaaa*. Words with three *a*s are *aaab* and *aaac*. Those with two *a*s are *aabb*, *aabc*, *aacc*. In this way we get $u(4) = 6$. The language associated with this type of word, now of some length, is:

$$L = (aa + aaa + aaaa + \ldots)(1 + b + bb + bbb + \ldots)(1 + c + cc + ccc + \ldots)$$

Hence the generating function giving the number of these words according to their length, obtained by converting *a*, *b* and *c* into *X*:

$$F(X) = (X^2 + X^3 + X^4 + \ldots)(1 + X + X^2 + X^3 + \ldots)^2$$

$$= \frac{X^2 + X^3 + X^4 + \ldots}{(1 - X)^2} = (X^2 + X^3 + X^4 + \ldots)(1 + 2X + 3X^2 + 4X^3 + \ldots)$$

This notably enables us to find $u(4) = 1 + 2 + 3 = 6$.

b) Follow the same problem, except that the letters do not have to remain in alphabetical order in the words. Calling v(n) the number of such words, determine v(4). Then look for the associated exponential generating function.

Let us go back to the six words of the 1°. The word *aaaa* remains identical in this case. The words *aaab* and *aaac* each produce six words. Finally, the word *aabc*, produces 12 words (*aabc, aacb, abac, acab, abca, acba, baac, caab, baca, caba, bcaa, cbaa*). Hence $v(4) = 1 + 4 + 4 + 6 + 6 + 12 = 33$. We see that a generating function of the classic type cannot be sufficient. Let us make the analogous product using factorials:

$$E = (aa / 2! + aaa / 3! + aaaa / 4! + ..) \, (1 / 0! + b / 1! + bb / 2! + bbb / 3! + \ldots)$$

$$(1 / 0! + c / 1! + cc / 2! + ccc / 3! + \ldots)$$

During development, a word such as *aaabcc* has the coefficient: $1/(3!2!1!)$. Multiplying by 6!, this gives the number of anagrams formed with the letters *a, a, a, b, c, c*, and this is generalized. Let us move on to the corresponding function:

$$E(X) = \left(\frac{X^2}{2!} + \frac{X^3}{3!} + \frac{X^4}{4!} + \ldots\right)\left(\frac{1}{0!} + \frac{X}{1!} + \frac{X^2}{2!} + \ldots\right)^2$$

For example, the term in X^4 has the following coefficient:

$1/(2!\ 0!\ 2!) + 1/(2!\ 1!\ 1!) + 1/(2!\ 2!\ 0!) + 1/(3!\ 0!\ 1!) + 1/(3!\ 1! 0!) + 1/(4!\ 0!\ 0!)$

Multiplying by 4!, this gives all the anagrams of 4 characters formed from at least two letter *a*s, as well as *b*s and *c*s, i.e. the number $v(4)$ of words of 4 characters that concern us. We can verify that this does give $v(4) = 6 + 12 + 6 + 4 + 4 + 1 = 33$. From this, we deduce that $E(X)$ is the exponential generating function associated with the sequence (v_n):

$$E(X) = v(0) + v(1)X/1\,! + v(2)\,X^2/2! + v(3)X^3/3! + \ldots$$

$$= \left(\frac{X^2}{2!} + \frac{X^3}{3!} + \frac{X^4}{4!} + \ldots\right)\left(\frac{1}{0!} + \frac{X}{1!} + \frac{X^2}{2!} + \ldots\right)^2$$

$$= (e^X - X - 1)\,e^{2X} = e^{3X} - X\,e^{2X} - e^{2X}$$

thanks to the development of the exponential function.

This again enables us to find:

$$v(4) = 4!\,(3^4/4! - 2^3/3! - 2^4/4!) = 81 - 32 - 16 = 33$$

and to easily obtain $v(n)$ in the general case.

5.8.2. *Exercise 2: sending n people to three countries, with at least one person per country*

Each case can be coded using a word of n characters indexed using the numbers of people and containing the letters a, b and c corresponding to the three countries, with each of these letters present at least once in this table of n length. What is the exponential generating function associated with the number v(n) of ways of sending n people to these three countries?

By analogy with the example above, we take the following as the generating function:

$$E(X) = (X + X^2 / 2\,! + X^3 / 3! + \ldots)^3 = (e^X - 1)^3 = e^{3X} - 3e^{2X} + 3e^X - 1$$

From this we deduce that $v(n) = n!\,(3^n / n! - 3.2^n / n! + 3 / n!\,) = 3^n - 3.\,2^n + 3$.

This type of formula will be found again thanks to sieve formula (see Chapter 8).

Chapter 6

Routes in a Square Grid

Analogous to a big city, let us imagine an infinite square grid of evenly spaced streets. A square residential block between successive streets gives the unit of distance. At each intersection there are four possible directions in which a person can go, according to the four cardinal points, but in what follows we will generally prefer two of these directions. This type of circulation is called taxicab geometry, or *city block* geometry. It is also what happens on a computer screen, if screen size is not taken as a constraint.

6.1. Shortest paths from one point to another

A person wishes to go from point A to point B in the square grid, located at a distance of p blocks to the east and q blocks to the north. As the crow flies, there would be a single shortest path from A to B, but this is not allowed in this case. By walking the infinite square grid of streets, there is an infinite number of paths leading from A to B. If we are only interested in the shortest paths from A to B, it is easy to see that all these paths are of length $p + q$, whether they are all located in a rectangle with A and B as vertices, and whether the only acceptable directions are steps eastward or northward.

Using 0 to represent a step to the east, and 1 to represent a step to the north, a shortest path from A to B can be coded using a word based on 0 and 1, of length $p + q$, with the presence of the letter 0 p times and the letter 1 q times. For example, the path in the drawing (see Figure 6.1) with $p = 8$ and $q = 4$ is coded using the word 001100010001.

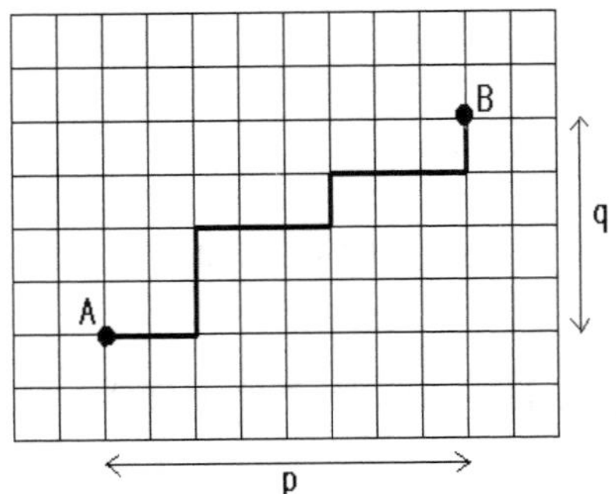

Figure 6.1. *One of the shortest paths from A to B*

There are as many shortest paths as words of length $p + q$, with 0 p times and 1 q times.

The number of these words is C_{p+q}^{p}, as we have to choose p out of $p + q$ boxes in order to place a 0, with the remaining boxes therefore being filled by 1. Hence the property:

– in a square network, the number of shortest paths from one point to another, located p steps in one direction and q steps in the other, is:

$$C_{p+q}^{p} = C_{p+q}^{q}$$

The enumeration algorithm of these paths is none other than that of the enumeration of combinations already dealt with (see Figure 6.2).

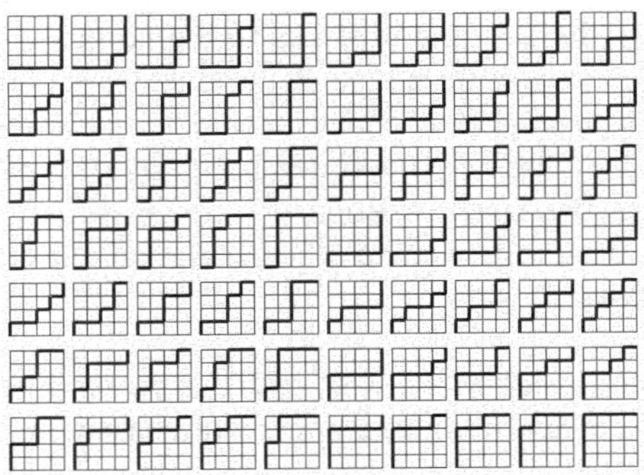

Figure 6.2. *The 70 (shortest) paths separating two points 4 steps horizontally and 4 steps vertically apart*

There is another way of seeing this problem. Let us imagine a repeated game of heads or tails with two players. If heads comes out, player *A* wins a counter and the other player loses one, and *vice versa* if tails comes up. After *n* goes, player *A*, who had no wins at the start now has a certain number of wins (or losses) *x*, and included between $-n$ and $+n$. This can be seen in the bench mark (*O, n, x*) using a route from point *O* to point *B*(*n, x*), as in Figure 6.3.

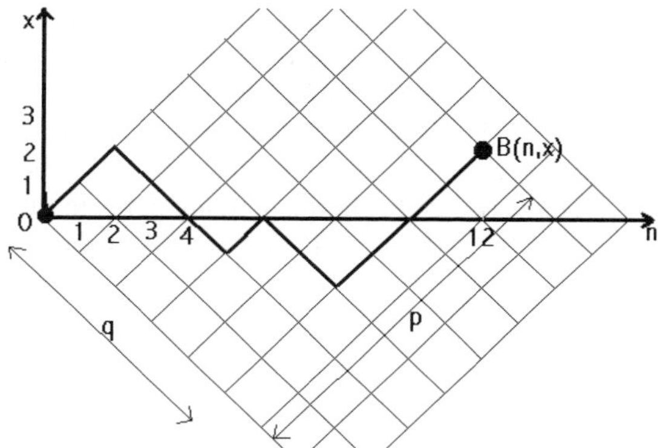

Figure 6.3. *Repeated game of heads or tails, with x number of wins after n goes*

Earning a counter corresponds to a diagonal line ↗ with coordinates (1, 1) and losing a counter corresponds to a diagonal line ↘ with coordinates (1, -1).

In the example in Figure 6.3, at the end player *A* has $x = 2$ counters at the end of $n = 12$ matches. As the diagram indicates, it is again a route in a square grid. Notice that *n* and *x* always have the same parity. Actually, when using the route starting from *O*(0,0), where *n* and *x* are even, the parity of *n* and *x* remains the same from one go to the next: if *n* and *x* are even, they both become odd on the following go, and the reverse happens if *n* and *x* are odd. In order to arrive at *B*(*n, x*), the player won *p* times and lost *q* times, with $p+q=n$ and $p-q=x$. This bijective link between *x*, *n* and *p*, *q* is also expressed as:

$$p = (n + x) / 2 \text{ and } q = (n - x) / 2$$

Let the number of such paths from *O* to $B(n,x)$ be $N(n,x)$. Thanks to the formula above, we have $N(n, x) = C_{p+q}^{\ p} = C_n^{\ (n+x)/2}$. The number of paths based on *n* (1 ,1) or (1, -1) lines of the form ↗ or ↘ with a horizontal length *n* and finishing with a vertical gap *x* compared to the start is:

$$N(n, x) = C_n^{\ (n+x)/2}$$

In particular, the number of $n = 2n'$-long paths that end at point $B(2n', 0)$, with 0 final winnings, is $C_{2n'}^{n'}$.

6.2. *n*-length paths using two (perpendicular) directions of the square grid

Let the two directions chosen, for example east and north, be 0 and 1. n-length paths are coded using words of n characters based on the two letters 0 and 1. The first letter of the word is either 0 or 1. Once the first letter is chosen, the second letter is either 0 or 1, and so on and so forth. The number of words and also paths concerned is 2^n. Now let us classify these words according to the number p of 0s. This number p is included between 0 and n. The number of words with the letter 0 p times is around C_n^p. Let us visualize the corresponding paths in the square grid, with the two perpendicular directions taken at 45° compared to the horizontal direction (see Figure 6.4).

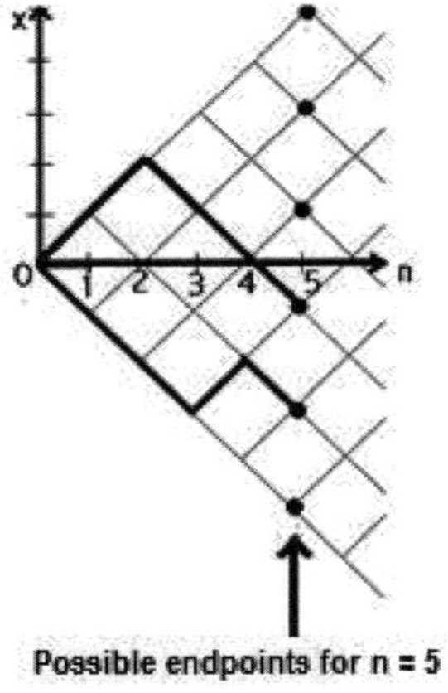

Figure 6.4. *Paths of length $n = 5$*

In this new benchmark O, n, x, paths of n length that have p ↗ steps and q ↘ steps with $p+q=n$, starting from origin O, all arrive at points with the same abscissa n, for example $n = 5$ in Figure 6.4 above. When n is odd, the endpoints of the paths have as ordinates $\pm 1, \pm 3, \ldots, \pm n$. When n is even, the endpoints have 0, $\pm 2, \pm 4, \pm n$ as ordinates. By adding the numbers of paths based on their endpoint, we find the formula:

$$\sum_{p=0}^{n} C_n^p = 2^n$$

6.3. Paths from O to $B(n, x)$ neither touching nor crossing the horizontal axis and located above it

Out of all the paths from O to $B(n,x)$, let us take those that neither touch nor cross the horizontal axis and are always located above it after leaving their starting point O, which means that $x > 0$ (see Figure 6.5). Let us call the number of these paths $P(n,x)$. As point $A(1,1)$ is an obligatory crossing point, $P(n,x)$ is also the number of paths from A to B that neither touch nor cross the horizontal axis, i.e. the total number of paths from A to B minus the number Q of paths from A to B that touch or cross the horizontal axis. As A and B are separated by a horizontal gap of $n - 1$ and a vertical gap of $x - 1$, the number of paths, whichever they may be, from A to B is $N(n - 1, x - 1)$, according to the formula seen above.

The number Q is left to be determined. To do this, let us take point A'(1,-1), which is symmetrical to A with respect to the horizontal axis. Let us consider one of the Q paths from A to B that touch or cross the horizontal axis, with C as its first point on the horizontal axis after O. Let us take the symmetrical reflection of this path between O and C, and conserve the remainder (see Figure 6.6).

We have just obtained a path from A to B. Conversely, from some path from A' to B that necessarily touches the horizontal axis and ends up crossing it, let us take the first meeting point with this axis C, and construct the symmetrical path between A' and C, while keeping the remainder. This gives a path from A to B that touches or crosses the horizontal axis. Thanks to the bijection between these two types of paths, there are as many paths from A to B that touch or cross the horizontal axis as paths from A' to B, with a horizontal gap of $n-1$ and a vertical gap of $x+1$, hence:

$$Q = N(n - 1, x + 1)$$

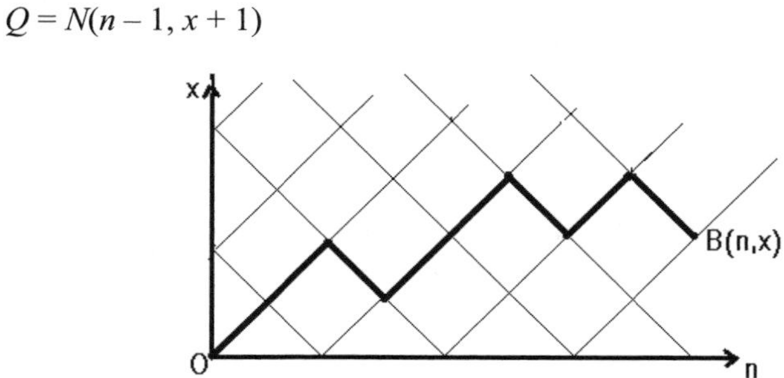

Figure 6.5. *Example of a path that neither touches nor crosses the horizontal axis*

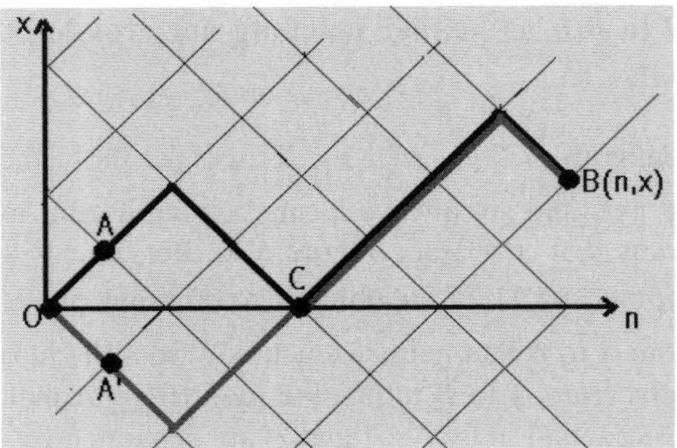

Figure 6.6. *There are as many paths from A' to B that touch or cross the horizontal axis as there are from A to B*

Finally $P(n,x) = N(n-1,x-1) - N(n-1,x+1)$. *A posteriori* we understand the interest in having used point *A* in order to apply the mirror effect that enabled us to calculate *Q*.

The number of paths from *O* to $B(n,x)$ with $x > 0$, which neither touch nor cross the horizontal axis after leaving *O* and remain above it, if we finish the calculation is:

$$P(n, x) = N(n-1, x-1) - N(n-1, x+1) = (x / n)\, N(n, x) = (x / n)\, C_n^{(n+x)/2}$$

Out of all the paths going from *O* to $B(n,x)$, the proportion of those that neither touch nor cross the axis of the abscissae is *x*/*n*. This is sometimes called ballot theorem: during the counting of a vote, the probability that a candidate always has more of a voice than his opponents is *x*/*n*, where *n* is the number of votes and *x* the number of additional voices the candidate has at the end of the count.

6.4. Number of *n*-length paths that neither touch nor cross the axis of the adscissae until and including the final point

First of all let us assume that *n* is even: $n = 2n'$. Such paths end up at points $B_2(2n',2), B_4(2n',4), \ldots B_{2n}(2n',2n)$, or at symmetrical points (with $x < 0$) with respect to the abscissae axis. There are as many paths above as below it. This gives in total:

$$2\,(P(2n', 2) + P(2n', 4) + \ldots + P(2n', 2n')),$$

and we saw that:

$$P(2n', 2k) = N(2n' - 1, 2k - 1) - N(2n' - 1, 2k + 1)$$

Chain simplifications are produced, and finally:

$$2\sum_{k=1}^{n'} P(2n',2k) = 2\sum_{k=1}^{n'} (N(2n'\text{-}1,2k\text{-}1) - N(2n'\text{-}1,2k+1))$$
$$= 2(N(2n'-1,1) - N(2n'\text{-}1,2n'+1))$$
$$= 2N(2n'-1,1) = 2C_{2n'\text{-}1}^{n'} = C_{2n'}^{n'}$$

The number of $n = 2n'$-length paths that neither touch nor cross the abscissae axis (being always above or below it) is equal to $C_{2n'}^{n'}$, which is also, let us recall, the number of paths from O to point $(2n',0)$. Those that always remain above the abscissa axis number $C_{2n'}^{n'}/ 2$. In the case where n is odd, i.e. $n = 2n'+1$, all we have to do is add a diagonal line to $2n'$-length paths, either to the top or bottom, which doubles the number of these paths.

The number of $2n' + 1$-length paths that neither touch nor cross the horizontal axis and are located above or below it is $2C_{2n'}^{n'}$. Those that remain above the axis number $C_{2n'}^{n'}$.

6.5. Number of *n*-length paths above the horizontal axis that can touch but not cross the horizontal axis

First of all let us assume that n is even: $n = 2n'$. We saw that the number of $2n'$-length paths that neither touch nor cross the axis of the abscissae is $C_{2n'}^{n'}/ 2$. It is also the number of $2n' - 1$-length paths from point $A(1, 1)$, that neither touch nor cross the axis of the abscissae by being above it, or even those that can touch but do not cross the horizontal axis stemming from A by being above it. Starting from each endpoint, we can add a diagonal step (to have a total length of $2n'$) either upwards or downwards, which doubles the number of paths. This does not produce a crossing of the horizontal axis stemming from A.

The number of $2n'$-length paths located above the horizontal axis that can touch but do not cross this axis is $C_{2n'}^{n'}$.

Now let us consider the case where the number n is odd: i.e. $n = 2n' + 1$. Paths $2n' + 1$ long that can touch but not cross the horizontal axis, and that are located above it, are also the paths that neither touch or cross the axis located at height -1, to which we can add an initial diagonal line in such a way as to start at height -1.

Therefore there are as many $2n' + 1$-length paths that can touch but not cross the horizontal axis by remaining above it, as there are $2n' + 1$-length paths that can neither touch nor cross the horizontal axis by remaining above. We saw that the number of these was $C_{2n'+2}^{n'+1} / 2$, and we can verify that it is also $C_{2n'+1}^{n'}$.

The number of $2n' + 1$-length paths that can touch but not cross the horizontal axis, and are located above, is $C_{2n'+1}^{n'}$. This also corresponds to the number of paths going from O to point B $(2n'+1, 1)$.

Let us elucidate another method: let us go back to $C_{2n'}^{n'}$ paths $2n'$ long and separate them into two categories:

– those that end up strictly above the axis: these number $C_{2n'}^{n'} - c(n')$, where $c(n')$ is the number of paths that end up at point $(2n', 0)$. To find the $2n' + 1$-length paths that obey the same constraints, we can add two diagonal lines to them, which makes $2(C_{2n'}^{n'} - c(n'))$ $2n' + 1$-length paths;

– those that end up at point $(2n', 0)$, numbering $c(n')$, and to which we add a single line at the top.

In all, we find $2C_{2n'}^{n'} - c(n')$ $2n' + 1$-length paths. As we will see later (in Chapter 9), $c(n')$ is the number of what we call mountain ranges $2n'$ long and we will see that $c(n') = C_{2n'}^{n'}/(n' + 1)$.

In these conditions:

$$2C_{2n'}^{n'} - c(n') = (2 - 1 / (n' + 1))\, C_{2n'}^{n'} = ((2n' + 1) / (n' + 1))C_{2n'}^{n'} = C_{2n'+1}^{n'}$$

6.6. Exercises

6.6.1. *Exercise 1: show that* $C_{2n}^{n} = \sum_{k=0}^{n} (C_n^k)^2$

The number of (shortest) paths from O to $A(n, n)$ is C_{2n}^{n}. Now let us classify these paths into several categories when obliged to pass through a point of the second diagonal of the square (see Figure 6.7).

One of these points is $B(k, n - k)$ with k between 0 and n. The number of paths from O to B is C_n^k, and from B to A is also C_n^k, hence $(C_n^k)^2$ paths from O to A passing through point B.

Next all we have to do is to take all the diagonal B points with their number of paths to obtain the formula requested.

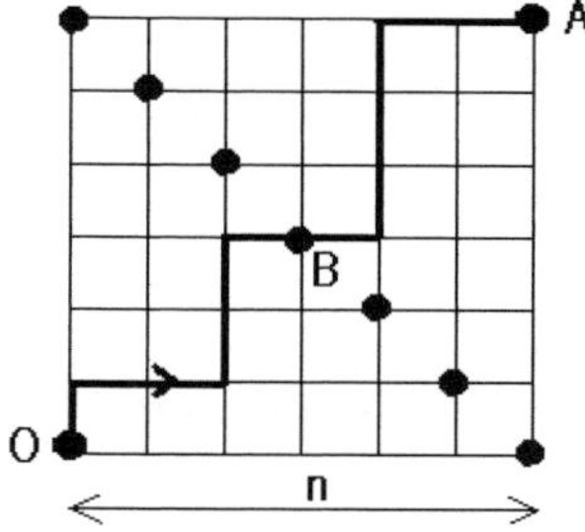

Figure 6.7. *Path with n horizontal steps and n vertical steps*

6.6.2. *Exercise 2: show that* $\sum_{k=0}^{P} C_{N-1+k}^{k} = C_{N+P}^{P}$

The number of paths from O to $A(N, P)$ is $C_{N+P}{}^{P}$. Each one of these paths borrows one of the horizontal steps joining points $(N-1, k)$ and (N, k). The paths from O to A can be classified according to their passage through one of these horizontal steps (see Figure 6.8). In addition $C_{N-1+k}{}^{k}$ paths ending up at point $(N-1, k)$ exist. Hence the formula requested.

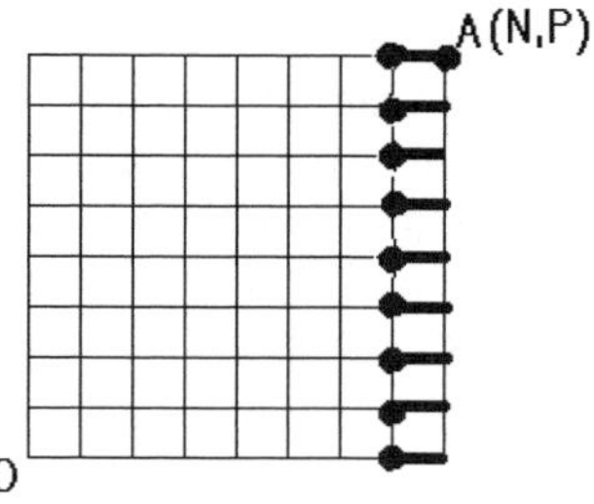

Figure 6.8. *Paths from O to A passing through one of the horizontal plateaus*

6.6.3. *Exercise 3: show that* $\sum_{k=1}^{n'} 2k\, C_{2n'}^{n'+k} = n' C_{2n'}^{n'}$

Section 6.4 explained that paths of length $2n'$ neither touching nor crossing the horizontal axis are $2\sum_{k=1}^{n'} P(2n',2k) = C_{2n'}{}^{n'}$.

We also know that $P(2n', 2k) = (2k / 2n')\, C_{2n'}{}^{n'+k}$.

The earlier formula becomes:

$$\frac{1}{n'}\sum_{k=1}^{n'} 2k\, C_{2n'}^{n'+k} = C_{2n'}^{n'}$$

6.6.4. *Exercise 4: a geometrico-linguistic method*

Using a geometrico-linguistic method, show that there are as many paths going from O to $B(2n, 0)$ as paths also of length $2n$, which can touch but not cross the horizontal axis.

To do this we will establish a bijective relation between each one of the two types of paths. Let us take a path from O to $B(2n, 0)$. Where it is located above the abscissae axis or touches without crossing it, it is associated with itself, like a path able to touch but not cross the abscissa axis. In the opposite case, it assumes a point with the lowest negative ordinate, and if there are several of them we choose the first from the left. Namely, this point is $K(k, m)$ (necessarily $m < 0$).

Let us take the piece of path between O and K, then make up its symmetrical reflection by rotating it with respect to a vertical axis (see Figure 6.9). Let us intertwine the piece of path thus obtained by placing its origin in B. This puts the end of if in C, which has the ordinate $-m$. Now let us consider the new path from K to C by taking a horizontal axis passing through K. Point C has as ordinate $-2m$, and this path can touch but not does not cross the horizontal axis. Therefore, we have gone from the first type of path to the second. Conversely, if we have a path that can touch but does not cross the horizontal axis, whose endpoint is C' $(2n, 2m)$, we take the first point K' from the right of the m ordinate, and we implement the reverse change of that above. Therefore we go from the second type to the first type of path. Hence their identical number.

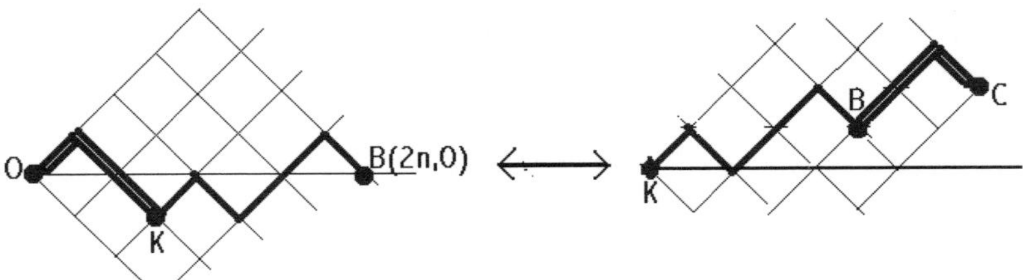

Figure 6.9. *Passage from one path to another*

6.6.5. *Exercise 5: paths of a given length that never intersect each other and where the four directions are allowed in the square grid*

In a square grid, where the sides are of its squares of equal length, we consider the N-length paths along the sides of the squares, all starting from a point O. Each 1 long step of the paths can be in one of the four directions, north, east, south and west, with sole condition that the path does not make a loop with itself. We assume, in addition, that the first step is to the north. Notice that for reasons of rotational symmetry, there are as many N-length paths going north as paths going in one of the other three directions, with these other three directions being deduced by rotating those found when we go north. Make the program that enables us to visualize all the N-length paths and determine their number $C(N)$.

This is circulation in a graph, here the square grid of N length, until the $N + 1^{\text{th}}$ point. Each point has four possible successors, but we must eliminate the point we are coming from as well as any future point we could already have passed. Therefore, exploring a point consists of exploring its four neighbors, under the conditions above. This recursive approach, which we are going to program, leads to an in-depth journey around the graph: we go to the end of a path, then we go backwards in search of a new opening, and we go until the end of this new path, etc. The stop test of the recursion is the Nth step, or the $N + 1^{\text{th}}$ point, with the points being numbered 0 to N.

To be able to draw a path, we are additionally led to keep the points that make it up in arrays $x[N+1], y[N+1]$ before the next path reupdates these arrays. Such arrays are declared globally. The main program boils down to:

```
main()
{
  x[0]=(y[0]=0); x[1]=0;y[1]=1;
  line(xo+zoom*x[0],yo-zoom*y[0],xo+zoom*x[1], yo-zoom*y[1]);
  counter=0; explore(0,1,3,1); display counter;
}
```

The four directions around a node are numbered in this way:

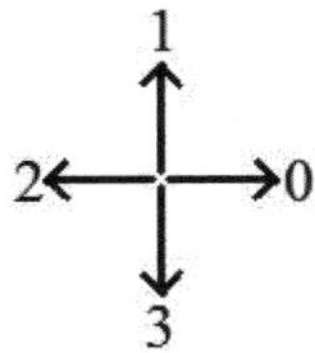

Initially, all we do is draw the first line (step) and call the function *explore*. This function takes the two co-ordinates from the point where we are (here 0,1) as variables, forbidding the direction from which we are coming (here 3) as a future direction, and lastly the number of the point. The exploration function remains to be written, which starts at point n and goes to point $n + 1$, recalling for each of the points $n + 1$, three at most. The process of deep runthrough finishes the path passing through the first of the $n + 1$ points before taking the path of the second point $n + 1$, etc. The path is finished, and drawn, when the function focuses on point $n = N$. We then erase it to move on to the design of the following path, hence the necessity to conserve the coordinates of the points (notably the common points in successive paths) in the arrays $x[]$ and $y[]$.

The explore function is as follows:

```
void explore (int xx, int yy, int forbid, int n)
{ if (n<N) for(i=0;i<4;i++) if (i!=forbid)
    { dx=((i+1)%2)*(1–i); dy=(i%2)*(2–i);
      newx=xx+dx; newy=yy+dy; alreadyfound=0;
      for(j=0;j<n;j++) if (newx==x[j] && newy==y[j]) {alreadyfound=1; break;}
      if (alreadyfound==0)
           {x[n+1]=newx;y[n+1]=newy; explore(newx,newy,(i+2)%4,n+1);}
    }

  else if (n==N)
    { for(j=0;j<N;j++)
      line(xo+zoom*x[j],yo-zoom*y[j],xo+zoom*x[j+1],yo-zoom*y[j+1]);
      counter++; erase;
    }
}
```

The results are shown in Figures 6.10 and 6.11.

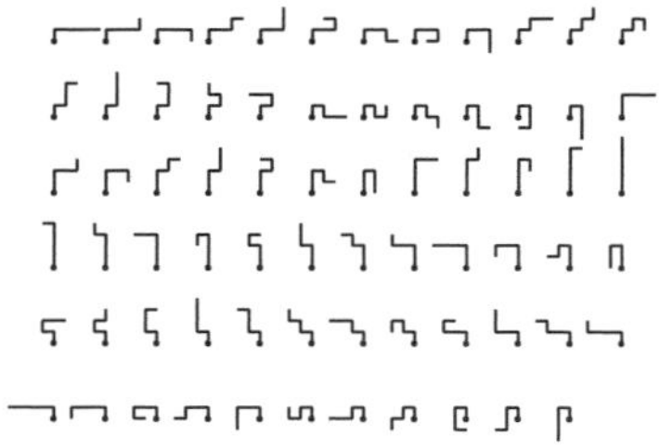

Figure 6.10. *The 71 paths of five steps*

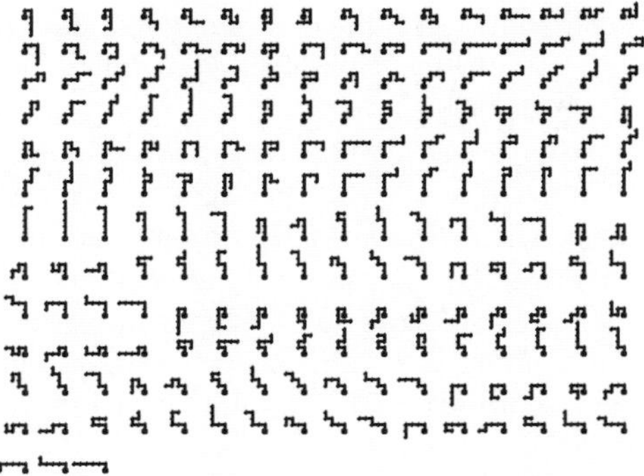

Figure 6.11. *The 195 paths of six steps, with a first step to the north*

By extension, we can choose the final point of each *N*–length path, then color in the points of the screen as a function of the number of times they are the final point of a path (see Figure 6.12).

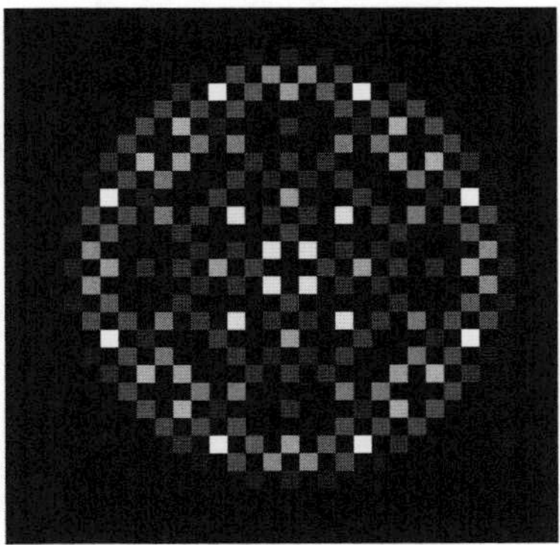

Figure 6.12. *Coloring of points based on the frequency with which they are reached as a final point of the paths, here 16 steps long*

Chapter 7

Arrangements and Combinations with Repetitions

In the previous chapters we have seen permutations, arrangements and combinations where it was assumed that all the objects concerned were distinct from each other. We are now going to work on collections of objects where some are undifferentiated, for example they carry the same number. Here again we distinguish the cases where order comes into play, and those where it does not.

7.1. Anagrams

Let us take the word *banana*, for example, made up of three *a*s, two *n*s and one *b*. We are interested in all six-letter words that, like *banana*, are made up of three *a*s, two *n*s and one *b*. Such words are called anagrams. They are arrangements or permutations of a group of letters, but with some letters repeated. How many such words are there? We find that there are 60 anagrams that can be deduced from the word *banana* (see Figure 7.1).

Here is a first method for finding the number of words, using the example above. We begin by placing the three letter *a*s in all possible ways, i.e. $C_6^{\,3} = 20$ ways (number of ways of placing three objects in three out of six boxes). Once the letter *a*s have been placed, the two letter *n*s are to be placed in the three remaining boxes, i.e. $C_3^{\,2} = 3$ ways. Finally we place the *b* in the only remaining box. In total we find 20. 3 = 60 anagrams:

1: aaabnn	2: aaanbn	3: aaannb	4: aabann	5: aabnan	6: aabnna
7: aanabn	8: aananb	9: aanban	10: aanbna	11: aannab	12: aannba
13: abaann	14: abanan	15: abanna	16: abnaan	17: abnana	18: abnnaa
19: anaabn	20: anaanb	21: anaban	22: anabna	23: ananab	24: ananba
25: anbaan	26: anbana	27: anbnaa	28: annaab	29: annaba	30: annbaa
31: baaann	32: baanan	33: baanna	34: banaan	35: banana	36: bannaa
37: bnaaan	38: bnaana	39: bnanaa	40: bnnaaa	41: naaabn	42: naaanb
43: naaban	44: naabna	45: naanab	46: naanba	47: nabaan	48: nabana
49: nabnaa	50: nanaab	51: nanaba	52: nanbaa	53: nbaaan	54: nbaana
55: nbanaa	56: nbnaaa	57: nnaaab	58: nnaaba	59: nnabaa	60: nnbaaa

Figure 7.1. *The 60 anagrams of the word banana*

This method can be generalized. We verify that the result found is also written $6!/(3!2!1!) = 60$. This formula corresponds to the following method, which we are going to apply in the general case.

We want to get all the words made from a_1 letter *A*s, a_2 letter *B*s, …, a_k letter *K*s. These words have the length $N = a_1 + a_2 + ... + a_k$. Their number will be written $Ana(a_1, a_2, ..., a_k)$. For example, $Ana(2,1) = 3$ because the words are *AAB*, *ABA*, *BAA*. To count this we begin by distinguishing each of the letters: the a_1 letter *A*s are written A_1, A_2, A_3, etc., each with its own number, and similarly for all the letters. With the *N* letters therefore all distinct, we create *N*! words in this way. These words can now be grouped in parcels of $a_1!$ words, with the same permutation-type positions of their numbers of the letter *A* in each parcel. If we no longer distinguish letter *A*s, $N!/a_1!$ words remain. Once this has been done, using parcels of $a_2!$ words we can group those that have the same permutation-type *B* positions of their numbers. We are left with $N!(a_1!a_2!)$ words where the letter *A*s, just like the letter *B*s, are no longer considered distinct. We continue in this way. Finally, the number of anagrams is:

$$Ana(a_1, a_2, ..., a_k) = (a_1 + a_2 + ... + a_k)! / (a_1!\ a_2! \ ...\ a_k!)$$

Note that anagrams of length *n* where all letters are distinct are permutations, and we find their number *n*!. Note also that anagrams of length *n*, based on two letters with *p* letter *A*s (or 0) and *n* – *p* letter *B*s (or 1) is C_n^p, as we have already seen.

7.2. Combinations with repetitions

7.2.1. *Routes in a square grid*

In a square grid, we go from point A to point B where these two points are separated, for example, by $N = 5$ horizontal steps and $P = 8$ vertical ones. The number of shortest paths from A to B is C_{13}^{5}. One of these paths is represented in the diagram in Figure 7.2. In the general case, the number of paths is C_{N+P}^{P} (see Chapter 6). This formula, with the corresponding design for the paths, will enable us to answer everything that follows.

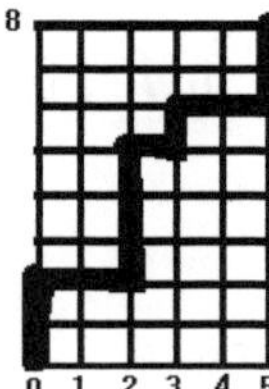

Figure 7.2. *Path in a square grid*

7.2.2. *Distributing (indiscernible) circulars in personalized letter boxes*

For example, if we have eight identical circulars and six letter boxes numbered 0 to 5, the path above gives one of the distributions: two circulars in box 0, three in box 2, one in box 3, two in box 5. All we have to do is to read the length of each vertical line in each abscissa. Each distribution is associated with a path in a bijective way. The number of possible distributions is therefore C_{13}^{5}. In the general case, if we have P circulars to distribute in N letter boxes, the number of distributions is C_{N+P-1}^{N-1}. Therefore, the number of ways of placing P indiscernible objects in N numbered boxes is:

$$C_{N+P-1}^{N-1} = C_{N+P-1}^{P}$$

7.2.3. *Choosing I objects out of N categories of object*

A shop has $N = 6$ categories of products, each one available without restrictions (for example packets of biscuits, canned foods, packs of drinks, etc., but to simplify things we number the products of each category 0, 1, 2, …, 5). A person buys $P = 8$ products out of these six categories, i.e. out of the products 0, 0, 0, ..., 1, 1, 1, …, 2,

2, 2, ..., 5, 5, 5. Linking this with the information above, the path in the diagram in Figure 7.2 indicates that the person buys the following products: 00222355, i.e. two objects of category 0, three objects of category 2, one of category 3, and two of category 5. In the parcel obtained, order does not come into play, but note that we have chosen to write the words with letters placed in ascending order. There is always bijection between each way of taking these eight products out of the six categories as well as paths with five steps to the east and eight steps to the north, i.e. $C_{13}^{\ 8}$ or $C_{13}^{\ 5}$. This is generalized. The number of ways of taking P products out of N categories of objects is $C_{N+P-1}^{\ P}$. We call this *combinations with repetitions*. Note that it is also the number of words of length P based on N letters, with the letters placed in alphabetical order in each word.

7.2.4. *Number of positive or null integer solutions to the equation $X_0 + X_1 + ... + X_{N-1} = P$*

7.2.4.1. *Method 1*

Here again, the diagram above for $P = 8$ and $N = 6$ gives a solution to the equation, with $x_0 = 2$, $x_1 = 0$, $x_2 = 3$, $x_3 = 1$, $x_4 = 0$, $x_5 = 2$. The number of solutions is again $C_{N+P-1}^{\ P}$ in the general case.

7.2.4.2. *Method 2*

Let us use the breakdown of a natural number P in an ordered sum of N natural numbers:

– Take an integer $P > 0$. We want to find how many ways it can be written in the form $P = a_1 + a_2 + ... + a_N$, with a_i all strictly positive, and order playing a role in this sum. For example, with $N = 3$, the number $P = 4$ can be written in three ways: 2 + 1 + 1, 1 + 2 + 1 and 1 + 1 + 2. In order to do this, let us write the number P in the form of P dots and place $N - 1$ vertical bars in the intervals separating the dots. We therefore split up the number P in N numbers > 0, with the bars always being inserted between two dots. For example, for $P = 4$, one of the layouts is: • | • • | •. There are $P - 1$ positions in which to place these $N - 1$ bars, hence $C_{P-1}^{\ N-1}$ ways, and each time we therefore get a certain splitting of the number P in N ordered pieces.

– Now, we no longer have the condition that the a_i numbers be strictly positive. We want to find out the number of ways $A(P, N)$ of writing $P = x_1 + x_2 + ... + x_N$, with $x_i \geq 0$, where this sum is ordered. This number $A(P, N)$ is also the number of solutions to the equation with N unknowns, $x_1 + x_2 + ... + x_N = P$, where the unknowns x_i are integers and P is a given natural number. Let us assume that $y_i = x_i + 1$, hence $y_i > 0$. The $A(P, N)$ sought is also the number of ways of writing the number $P + N$ as an ordered sum of N numbers y_i with $y_i > 0$, i.e. $C_{P+N-1}^{\ P}$, or even

C_{N+P-1}^{N-1}, thanks to the question above. In this new context, we find the combinations with repetition formula.

– Given a natural number P and a natural number N, how many ways are there of finding an ordered sum of N numbers $x_i \geq 0$ in such a way that:

$$x_1 + x_2 + \ldots + x_N \leq P?$$

Based on the above, the number of ways is:

$$C_{N+P-1}^{N-1} + C_{N+P-2}^{N-1} + \ldots + C_{N-1}^{N-1} = \Sigma C_{a+i}^{a}$$

Having done the summation on i from 0 to P, with $a = N-1$, this gives C_{N+P}^{N}. To verify this, all we have to do is to classify all of the paths ending at point (N, P), numbering C_{N+P}^{P}, according to their obligatory passage through one of the points $(N-1, i)$ with i from 0 to P.

7.2.4.3. *Method 3*

Now let us use the generating function associated with combinations with repetitions. Let us begin with an example: we have $N = 3$ types of objects written A, B and C. If we consider all the possible parcels we can make from these and write them according to their increasing size, i.e. the language, we get:

$$1 + A + B + C + AA + AB + AC + BB + BC + CC + AAA + AAB + AAC + ABB + ABC + ACC + BBB + BBC + BCC + CCC + AAAA + \ldots$$

Here digit 1 designates the empty word, the sign + signifies *or*, and each word is made up of the concatenation of letters (like multiplication). Each word is written, in itself, in alphabetical order – As before Bs, and Bs before Cs – but order does not come into play (we could use other orders). We notice that this infinite sequence of words is also written:

$$(1 + A + AA + AAA + \ldots)(1 + B + BB + BBB + \ldots)(1 + C + CC + CCC + \ldots)$$

where the distributive property of multiplication compared to addition is applied. Now, let us assume that we are only interested in the length of words obtained, and the number of words of each length.

We can assimilate the letters A, B and C to a single letter X. For example, the word $AABC$ becomes the X^4 where the length of the word appears in the exponent.

Each word of 4 characters becomes X^4. The number of X^4 terms is the number of words with 4 characters. The series above becomes:

$$(1 + X + X^2 + \dots)^3$$

Its development, having ordered the terms, gives $\Sigma a_k X^k$. The coefficient a_k of the term in X^k is exactly the number of words of k characters.

In the general case, let us consider the formal series with N variables x_i of the form:

$$(1 + x_1 + x_1^2 + \dots)(1 + x_2 + x_2^2 + \dots) \dots (1 + x_N + x_N^2 + \dots)$$

Its development gives terms of the form $x_1^{y1} x_2^{y2} \dots x_N^{yN}$, where the exponents are positive or null, corresponding to a combination with repetition of $y_1 + y_2 + \dots + y_N$ objects taken out of N categories of objects.

This series represents all the possible combinations of objects in some number taken out of N categories. By making $x_i = x$ for all the is, the coefficient of x^P is the number of combinations of P objects taken out of N categories; or it is the number of solutions to the equation with N unknowns $y_1 + y_2 + \dots + y_N = P$, where $y_i \geq 0$. It is the number $A(N, P)$. The generating function of $A(N, P)$ is:

$$F(x) = (1 + x + x^2 + \dots)^N = \Sigma A(P, N)\, x^P,$$

having done the summation on $P \geq 0$.

This generating function is also expressed as $F(x) = 1 / (1 - x)^N$.

From the development of $1 / (1 - x) = 1 + x + x^2 + \dots$, from which we derive N times, we get:

$$F(x) = \Sigma\, C_{N+P-1}^{\ N-1}\, x^P, \text{ hence } A(P, N) = C_{N+P-1}^{\ N-1}$$

In conclusion, let us summarize that: $C_{N+P-1}^{\ N-1}$ or even $C_{N+P-1}^{\ P}$ is:

– the number of ways of distributing P indiscernible objects (leaflet, balls, etc.) in N numbered boxes;

– the number of ways of taking P objects out of N categories of objects;

– the number of words of P characters based on N letters, where the letters are in alphabetical order within each word; and

– the number of solutions to the equation with N unknowns $x_1 + x_2 + ... + x_N = P$, where the unknowns are natural integers ($x_k \geq 0$).

7.3. Exercises

7.3.1. *Exercise 1: number of ways of choosing six objects out of three categories, with the corresponding prices*

A person buys six shirts out of three categories, with each shirt in its category costing 1, 2 and 3 units of silver. What is the number of possible choices, and what are the corresponding prices?

The number of ways of taking six objects from three types of products is $C_8^2 = 28$. Their enumeration gives the words: 006, 015, 024, 033, 042, 051, 060, 105, 114, ..., 600. The prices on the two extremes are 6 for the word 006 and 18 for the word 600.

When the word begins with 0, the prices range from 6 to 12, varying by one unit each time. When the word begins with 1, the prices range from 8 to 13, varying by one unit each time. When the word begins with 2, the prices range from 10 to 14, varying by one unit each time. And so on. Finally, the prices are 6, 7, 17, 18 one time, 8, 9, 15, 16 twice each, 10, 11, 13, 14 three times each, and 12 four times.

7.3.2. *Exercise 2: word counting*

We are interested in words of 14 characters that contain the five vowels *a*, *e*, *i*, *o* and *u*, one and only one time, and the letter *x* nine times.

a) How many such words are there?

What we have to do is count the anagrams. There are 14 ways of placing vowel *a*. Each time this letter is placed, there are 13 ways of placing vowel *e*. Each time, there are 12 ways of placing the *i*. There are then 11 ways of placing *o*, and 10 ways of placing *u*: i.e. a total of $14 \times 13 \times 12 \times 11 \times 10 = 240{,}240$ ways.

A second method involves assuming that the vowels are present in alphabetical order. Between them, and at the extremities of the words, six intervals are present (of eventually null length) containing the nine letter *x*s.

What we have to do is to count the number of distributions of nine identical objects in six intervals, i.e. $C_{14}^5 = 2{,}002$. We have just found 2,002 words. Each time, taking the vowels in some order, that makes $5! = 20$ cases.

In total, we find 240,240 words.

b) Out of these words, how many are there where the vowels are never consecutive?

Method 1

First, let us assume that the vowels are in alphabetical order. We distinguish four cases according to their positions:

– *none of the vowels is the first or last letter of the word.* Therefore we get six non-empty intervals where the nine letter *x*s can be placed. We have the equation:

$$x_1 + x_2 + ... + x_6 = 9$$

with $x_i \geq 1$ which are the lengths of each interval.

The number of solutions to this equation is, as we saw, $C_8^5 = 56$. Second, we begin by putting a letter in each one of the nine intervals. Then we are left with placing three letters in six boxes, i.e. C_8^3 ways:

– *A vowel is in first but not last position.* There are now five non-empty intervals where the nine letter *x*s can be placed, i.e. $C_8^4 = 70$ cases;

– *A vowel is in the last position, but not the first.* Again we find 70 cases;
two vowels are one in the first and second positions. Four non-empty intervals remain. This gives $C_8^3 = 56$ cases.

We have just found 252 cases. With the vowels put in some order, this gives $252 \times 120 = 30,240$ words. In terms of probability, if each one of the words has as many chances of being obtained as another, the probability of not having consecutive vowels in the word is $252 / 2,002$, or 12.5%.

Method 2

First let us assume that the vowels are placed in alphabetical order and that we carry out the following conversions:

– block *ax* is replaced with *A* ;

– block *ex* with *E*, block *ix* with *I* ;

– block *ox* with *O*.

For example, the word *axxxexixxoxxxu* becomes *AxxEIxOxxu*, and this conversion is bijective. We are brought back to counting the number of 10-letter words with the five vowels *AEIOu* in order and five *x*s:, i.e. C_{10}^5 ways. We are now only left with permutating the vowels to get all the words, i.e. C_{10}^5 5!.

7.3.3. *Exercise 3: number of words of P characters based on an alphabet of N letters and subject to order constraints*

a) How many words are there where successive letters are in strictly ascending order?

For example, for $P = 3$ and $N = 5$, where the letters used are 0, 1, 2, 3 and 4, the words are:

012, 013, 014, 023, 024, 034, 123, 124, 134, 234, numbering 10 of them.

Because of the strictly ascending order, the letters of each word are all different. To make up these words, we have to choose P out of N letters without taking order into consideration, i.e. C_N^P cases, then put them in ascending order. The number of these words is C_N^P.

b) How many words are there where successive letters are never all placed in strictly ascending or descending order?

Let us again take the example of $P = 3$ and $N = 5$. The words concerned are:

000, 001, 002, 003, 004, 010, 011, 020, 021, 022, 030, 031, 032, 033, 040, 041, 042, 043, 044, 100, 101, 102, 103, 104, 110, 111, 112, 113, 114, 120, 121, 122, 130, 131, 132, 133, 140, 141, 142, 143, 144, 200, etc.

To find out how many of them there are, all we have to do is remove the C_N^P strictly ascending words and the C_N^P strictly descending words totaling the number of words of length N that can be obtained from an alphabet with N letters. This gives:

$N^P - 2\ C_N^P$ words.

c) How many words are there where successive letters are in ascending order in the broad sense?

Let us take for example $P = 3$ and $N = 4$. The words are:

000, 001, 002, 003, 011, 012, 013, 022, 023, 033, 111, 112, 113, 122, 123, 133, 222, 223, 233, 333, etc. to number 20.

Repetitions of identical letters are now accepted and the number of these words is the number of combinations with repetitions of P letters chosen from N, i.e. C_{N+P-1}^P.

d) How many words where successive letters are neither in ascending or descending order in the broad sense?

In concrete terms, we are looking for words that undergo oscillations (at least one).

For $P = 3$ and $N = 4$, we find:

010, 020, 021, 030, 031, 032, 101, 102, 103, 120, 121, 130, 131, 132, 201, 202, 203, 212, 213, 230, 231, 232, 301, 302, 303, 312, 313, 323, i.e. 28 words.

To find out how many of them there are in the general case, we take the total number of words N^P and remove the $C_{N+P-1}{}^{P}$ ascending words and the same with the descending in the broad sense on the condition that we notice that we have removed the same words twice: those of the form *kkk*...*k*. The number of words concerned is:

$$N^P - C_{N+P-1}{}^{P} + N$$

7.3.4. *Exercise 4: choice of objects out of several categories taking at least one object from each category*

How many ways are there of taking P objects out of N categories, with at least one object from each category?

We begin by taking one object of each category, i.e. N in total. We are left with taking $P - N$ objects out of the N categories, i.e. $C_{N+P-N-1}{}^{N-1} = C_{P-1}{}^{N-1}$ ways. For example, if we take 12 products out of five categories with at least one product from each category, this gives $C_{11}{}^{4} = 330$ cases.

7.3.5. *Exercise 5: choice of P objects out of N categories when the stock is limited*

A person takes P = 10 objects out of N = 3 categories, but the first type of object is limited to five units. What is the number of possible choices?

We begin by assuming that stock is unlimited, which gives $C_{N+P-1}{}^{N-1} = C_{12}{}^{2} = 66$ cases. Then we remove all of the cases where the products of category one number at least six. To count these cases, we begin by taking the six objects from category 1, then we are left with taking four objects out of the three categories, i.e. $C_6{}^2 = 15$. The number sought is $66 - 15 = 51$.

7.3.6. *Exercise 6: generating functions associated with the number of integer solutions to an equation with n unknowns*

We will assume here that $n = 2$, given that it is easy to generalize to a number n. Let us recall that the use of generating functions in this type of problem is not necessarily the best method, as we have already noticed. The only aim of this exercise is to practice generating functions.

a) What is the number N(p) of integer solutions to $x + y = p$, with x and y positive or null, and p being a given natural integer?

Let us consider the power series:

$$F(X) = (1 + X + X^2 + X^3 + ...) (1 + X + X^2 + X^3 + ...)$$

When we develop this series, the term in X^p comes from adding all monomials of the form $X^x X^y$ with $x + y = p$, $x \geq 0$ and $y \geq 0$. The coefficient of X^p is the number $N(p)$ of whole solutions to the equation $x + y = p$ with $x \geq 0$ and $y \geq 0$. The generating function associated with the number $N(p)$ of solutions is:

$$F(X) = (1 + X + X^2 + X^3 + ...)^2$$

We also get $F(X) = 1 / (1 - X)^2 = 1 + 2X + 3X^2 + 4X^3 + ...$, as $1 / (1 - X)^2$ is the derivative of $1/ (1 - X)$. From this we deduce that $N(p) = p + 1$, as we could doubt it.

b) What is the number N(p) of whole solutions to $x + y = p$ with x and y positive (non null)?

For the same reasons as above, we have the following generating function:

$$F(X) = (X + X^2 + X^3 + X^4 + ...)^2 = X^2 / (1 - X)^2 = X^2 + 2X^3 + 3X^4 + ...$$

hence: $N(p) = p - 1$.

c) What is the number N(p) of integer solutions to $x + y = p$ with x and y between and including 0 and 3?

The generating function is now reduced to the polynomial:

$$F(X) = (1 + X + X^2 + X^3)^2$$

This is also written:

$$F(X) = ((1 - X^4) / (1 - X))^2 = (1 - X^4)^2 (1 + 2X + 3X^2 + ...)$$

$$= (1 - 2X^4 + X^8)(1 + 2X + 3X^2 + ...)$$

By developing it, we find that $N(p) = p + 1$ when $p < 4$, $N(p) = -p + 7$ when $4 \leq p < 8$, and $N(p) = 0$ for $p \geq 8$.

d) What is the number N(p) of whole solutions to the equation $x + 2y = p$, with x and y being positive or null?

The generating function is:

$$F(X) = (1 + X + X^2 + X^3 + ...)(1 + X^2 + X^4 + X^6 + ...) = 1 / ((1 - X)(1 - X^2))$$

The calculation, namely the breakdown of this rational fraction into simple elements, remains to be done:

$$F(X) = 1 / ((1 + X)(1 - X)^2) = a / (1 - X) + (b + cX) / (1 - X)^2$$

Proceeding by identification, we find:

$$F(X) = (1 / 4)(1 / (1 + X) + (3 - X) / (1 - X)^2)$$

Let us recall that:

$$1 / (1 + X) = 1 - X + X^2 - X^3 + \ldots, \text{ and } 1 / (1 - X)^2 = 1 + 2X + 3X^2 + 4X^3 + \ldots$$

After addition, we find that the coefficient of the term in X^p is:

$$N(p) = (1 / 4)(2p + 3 + (-1)^p)$$

If p is even, $N(p) = p / 2 + 1$; and if p is odd, $N(p) = (p + 1) / 2$, which boils down to:

$$N(p) = [p/2] + 1$$

7.3.7. *Exercise 7: number of solutions to the equation $x + y + z = k$, where k is a given natural integer and $0 \leq x \leq y \leq z$*

Let us change the unknowns by postulating $X = x$, $Y = y - x$ and $Z = z - y$, or inversely $x = X$, $y = X + Y$ and $z = X + Y + Z$. The equation above has as many integer solutions with $0 \leq x \leq y \leq z$ as the equation $3X + 2Y + Z = K$ with X, Y and Z

as integers ≥ 0. The generating function associated with the number of solutions to this equation is:

$$(1 + x + x^2 + \ldots)(1 + x^2 + x^4 + \ldots)(1 + x^3 + x^6 + \ldots) = \frac{1}{(1-x)(1-x^2)(1-x^3)}$$

The coefficient of the term in x^K in the development of this fraction gives the number of solutions to the initial problem.

7.3.8. *Exercise 8: other applications of the method using generating functions*

a) What is the number of ways of taking 16 objects out of categories, with at least two objects from each category?

This question can be dealt with directly: we begin by taking two objects from each category, i.e. 10 objects. We are left with taking six objects out of the five categories, in all possible ways, i.e. $C_{10}{}^6$ cases.

We can also use the generating function associated with the number of ways of taking k (with $k \geq 10$) objects out of five categories, i.e.:

$$(x^2 + x^3 + x^4 + \ldots)^5 = x^{10}(1 + x + x^2 + \ldots)^5 = x^{10} / (1 - x)^5$$

The coefficient of the term in x^{16} is also that of x^6 in the development of the quotient $1 / (1 - x)^5$, i.e. $C_{10}{}^6$.

b) How many ways are there of collecting 15 Euros from 20 people, given that a specified person gives 1 Euro or 5 Euros or nothing, and that all the others give 1 Euro or nothing?

The generating function associated with the number of ways of selecting k Euros in the conditions indicated is:

$$(1 + x)^{19}(1 + x + x^5) = (1 + C_{19}{}^1 x + C_{19}{}^2 x^2 + \ldots + C_{19}{}^{19} x^{19})(1 + x + x^5)$$

The coefficient of x^{15} is the number sought, i.e. $C_{19}{}^{15} + C_{19}{}^{14} + C_{19}{}^{10}$.

c) Twenty-five (identical) balls are thrown into seven numbered boxes, where the first box must receive 10 balls at most. How many possible distributions are there?

The associated generating function here is:

$$(1 + x + x^2 + \ldots + x^{10})\,(1 + x + x^2 + x^3 + \ldots)^6 = (1 - x^{11}) / (1 - x^7)$$

The term in x^{25} of $1 / (1 - x)^7$ is $C_{25+6}^{\ 6}$. That of x^{14} is $C_{14+6}^{\ 6}$. Hence the result:

$$C_{31}^{\ 5} - C_{20}^{\ 6}.$$

7.3.9. *Exercise 9: integer-sided triangles*

How many integer triangles with a given perimeter n are there, given that the three sides of these triangles are non null-positive integers?

Let us call the lengths of the three sides a, b and c, taking $a \geq b \geq c \geq 1$, and where these numbers have to obey the triangular inequality $a < b + c$, or even $b + c - a \geq 1$. Let us consider a triangle with a certain triplet (a, b, c) of integers obeying the conditions above.

Note that if c is equal to 1 then $a = b$ and we also have $b + c - a = 1$. Let us apply the following constructive process. If $b + c - a$ is greater than 1, then the triplet $(a - 1, b - 1, c - 1)$ also gives an integer-sided triangle, with $b + c - a$ that is reduced by 1. Let us continue to apply this as long as $b + c - a$ is greater than or equal to 1. Once we have arrived at $b + c - a = 1$, if we have achieved (1, 1, 1) we stop. If not, if we do not have the triplet $(a, a, 1)$ with $a > 1$, we are in the case where $a > b$ and we take $(a - 2, b - 1, c - 1)$ as a new triangle. This leaves $b + c - a = 1$, with the first side being greater than or equal to the second.

As long as this last condition is satisfied, we repeat the process $(a - 2, b - 1, c - 1)$. Therefore we arrive at $(a, a, 1)$. If $a = 1$ we stop, if not with $a > 1$ we take $(a - 1, b - 1, 1)$ as a new triangle, and we do this until we end up with (1,1,1).

Let us take the example of (16,13,6). Here we have the evolution:

$$(16,13,6) \rightarrow (15,12,5) \rightarrow (14,11,4) \rightarrow (12,10,3) \rightarrow (10,9,2) \rightarrow (8,8,1) \rightarrow (7,7,1) \rightarrow (6,6,1) \rightarrow (5,5,1) \rightarrow (4,4,1) \rightarrow (3,3,1) \rightarrow (2,2,1) \rightarrow (1,1,1)$$

We deduce from this that (16, 13, 6) = 3(1, 1, 1) + 3(2, 1, 1) + 7(1, 1, 0).

We have just proved that any integer-sided triangle (a, b, c) obeying initial conditions is such that $(a, b, c) = x\,(1, 1, 1) + y\,(2, 1, 1) + z\,(1, 1, 0)$ with x being strictly positive, and y and z positive or null, or more precisely:

$$a = x + 2y + z,\ b = x + y + z,\ c = x + y$$

On the other hand, any linear combination of (1, 1, 1), (2, 1, 1), (1, 1, 0) with integer coefficients x, y, z where $x > 0$, $y \geq 0$, $z \geq 0$, gives a triangle with

$a \geq b \geq c \geq 1$, with $a < b + c$ because $x = b + c - a > 0$, and we also have $y = a - b$, $z = b - c$.

Let us return to our problem, which consists of finding the number of solutions to the equation $a + b + c = n$ where n is an integer ≥ 3, and a, b and c are the integer sides of the triangles written in descending order. Thanks to the relations between a, b, c and x, y, z, this goes back to solving the equation $3x + 4y + 2z = n$ with x, y, z natural integers and $x > 0$.

We return to the problem of paying a sum of n units of money with 2-, 3- and 4-unit coins, using at least one 3-unit coin. The generating function associated with the number of solutions $u(n)$ is:

$$F(X) = \sum u(n)\, X^n = X^3\, (X^3 + X^6 + \ldots)\, (1 + X^4 + X^8 + \ldots)\ \ (1 + X^2 + X^4 + \ldots)$$

$$= X^3 / ((1 - X^2)\, (1 - X^3)\, (1 - X^4))$$

We will find the shapes of triangles of a given perimeter in Figure 7.3.

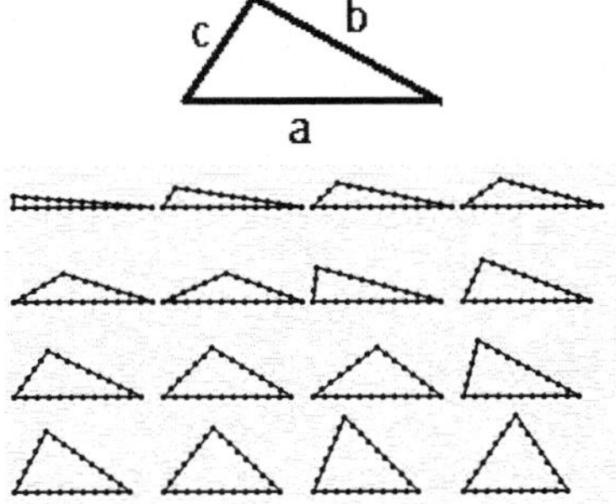

Figure 7.3. *The 16 integer triangles with a, b, c sides where $a \geq b \geq c$, with a perimeter of 25*

7.3.10. *Revision exercise: sending postcards*

a) A person buys six postcards from a shop with eight types of postcards to send to six people, one per person. How many ways of doing this are there?

Let us number the people from 1 to 6, and each type of post card from 1 to 8. For person 1, there are eight possibilities for postcards. For person 2, there are also eight cases, and similarly for each person, i.e. a total of 8^6 cases (this is the number of applications of the six-element set in an eight-element set).

b) Using the same situation as above, but where the person wants to send different cards to six friends, how many ways are there of doing this?

There are eight possible postcards that can be sent to person 1. There are seven possibilities for person 2. There are six possibilities left for person 3. And so on and so forth, i.e. a total of $A_8^{\ 6}$ = 8×7×6×5×4×3 cases. This is also the number of injections of a six-element set in an eight-element set.

c) Still in the same context, the person wants to send two different cards to each one of his six friends. How many ways of doing this are there?

There are $C_8^{\ 2} = 28$ ways of choosing two out of eight postcards. There are 28 possible choices for person 1. There are also 28 choices for person 2. And so on and so forth. In other words, there is a total of 28^6 possibilities.

d) A person has bought eight different postcards and wants to send them to six of his friends, given that the person can send several cards to the same person, or eventually no cards. How many ways of doing this are there?

Postcard number 1 can be addressed to any one of the six people, which makes six cases. Card number 2 can also be attributed to any one of the six people, and so on and so forth. We end up with a total of 6^8 cases.

e) In the same context as d), the person wants to send eight cards to his friends so each friend receives at least one card. How many ways are there of doing this?

We distinguish two cases:

– In the first case, the person sends three cards to one of his friends, and a single one to each of the others. There are $C_8^{\ 3} = 56$ ways of choosing three out of eight cards, and they can be sent to one out of the six people at random, which makes 56×6 cases. Each time, we are left with sending one of the five remaining cards to the five remaining people, i.e. 5! cases. This gives a total of 56×6×5! = 56×6! cases.

– In the second case, the person sends two cards each to two of his friends, and one to each of the others. There are $C_8^{\ 2} = 28$ ways of choosing two out of eight cards, and they can be sent to one of the six people at random, i.e. 28×6 cases. Each time we must still choose two out of the six remaining cards, i.e. $C_6^{\ 2} = 15$ cases, and send them to one of the five remaining people, i.e. 15×5 cases. Each time, we are left with sending one of the four remaining cards to each one of the four remaining people, i.e. 4! cases. Finally, this makes 28×6×15×5×4! = 28×15×6!. Taking into account the two cases, we find a total of (56 + 420)×6! = 476×6! cases.

f) The person now has eight identical postcards, which he is going to send to his six friends, given that each one can get one or several or none. How many ways of doing this are there?

We are in the combinations with repetitions context, which gives C_{13}^{5} cases (it is the number of paths in a square grid, from point O to point (5, 8)).

g) The person has eight types of postcards, with three of each type. He sends all of them to six friends. How many ways of doing this are there?

For the first type of postcard, there are $C_{6+3-1}^{3} = 56$ possible distributions. There are as many for the second type. And so on and so forth, with all having the same number of possible distributions, i.e. a total of $(56)^8$ cases.

7.4. Algorithms and programs

7.4.1. *Anagram program*

This program is very similar to that of permutations. In the case of the latter, to find the pivot we went from right to left, continuing to go backwards as long as there were rises, until the first descent (see Chapter 3). For anagrams we do almost the same thing, but by taking into consideration letters that can be identical. To have the pivot, we go from right to left as long as there are rises or plateaus, until the first real descent. Hence the program:

```
NB[0]=3;  NB[1]=2;  NB[2]=1; NB[3]=1;  /* Number of each of the 4 letters */
        */ calculation of N = length of anagrams */
N=0;  for(letter=0; letter<NBletters; letter++)  N+=NB[letter];
        /*making up of the first word, the smallest */
q=0;
for(letter=0; letter<NBletters; letter++)
for(i=0; i<NB[letter]; i++)     a[q++]=letter;
counter=0;
for(;;)
  { counter++; display();
    k=N–1;
    while (a[k]<=a[k–1] && k>=1) k--;
    pospivot=k–1;  if (pospivot==-1) break;
    k=N–1;  while(a[k]<=a[pospivot]) k--;   posreplacement=k;
```

```
    aux=a[pospivot];a[pospivot]=a[posreplacement];a[posreplacement]=aux;
    left=pospivot+1; right=N–1;
    while(left<right)
      { aux=a[left]; a[left]=a[right]; a[right]=aux; left++; right--;}
}
```

7.4.2. *Combinations with repetition program*

In Chapter 3 on enumeration algorithms, we have already seen two methods for getting combinations with repetitions. Now that we know the formula giving their number, using a route in a square grid we have a new method linked to combinations without repetition.

Let us assume that we have N types of objects, and that we take P in all possible ways. One way of doing this corresponds to a path from O to $B(N-1, P)$, i.e. to a word of $N+P-1$ characters with P vertical lines (and $N-1$ horizontal lines).

For example, for $N=6$ and $P=8$, one path is 1100111010011. This corresponds to the enumeration of combinations of P out of $N+P-1$ objects, which we know. This word is then converted by taking the abscissae of points touched by the path from point (0, 0), which gives a word of $N+P$ characters, 00012222334555 in this case, with the abscissae increasing by one unit each time the letter 0 is encountered in the path.

Then all we have to do is read the number of 0s, then of 1s, until the number of 5s, reducing these numbers by 1 to obtain the word 203102, which indicates that we have taken two objects of type 0, no objects of type 1, three objects of type 2, etc.

Chapter 8

Sieve Formula

As indicated by its name, the sieve formula consists of passing objects, essentially words or configurations for us, through a sieve and only keeping those that have certain characteristics. To see in what context this formula comes, let us begin by dealing with two simple examples.

First example: we want to find out how many words made up of two letter *A*s and four letter *B*s there are, where the two *A*s are isolated (i.e. without an *AA* block) in these words.

To do this, let us begin by counting all the words made up of two *A*s and 4 *B*s. The number of ways of putting two *A*s into six boxes is also the number of ways of choosing two out of six boxes, i.e. $C_6^2 = 15$ cases, with the *B*s therefore taking the remaining places. We get 15 words, but all the words with the *AA* block have to be removed. This goes back to counting words of five characters with a double *A* and four *B*s. There are five ways of placing the double *A*, hence five words. Finally, the number of words that have their two *A*s isolated is $15 - 5 = 10$, as summed up by the diagram in Figure 8.1, where removing the zone of words with double *A* from the words total, we find the colored zone containing the words sought. This is the core of sieve formula.

Figure 8.1. *Set (in black) of words without double A*

Second example: four people are going to three countries, with the characteristic that there is at least one person in each country. We want to find out how many ways there are of doing this.

To answer, let us begin by counting the number of ways of sending the four people to the three countries, without any constraints, which makes $3^4 = 81$ cases, i.e. the number of applications of a four-element set in a three-element set. Then we remove the cases where the four people are going to the same country, i.e. three cases. Finally we must remove all the cases where the four people go to exactly two of the three countries. Therefore we distinguish two cases. In the first case, three people go to the same country, and the forth to another; to do this, we begin by choosing three out of four people, hence four cases, and we send these people to one of the three countries, i.e. three cases again, and finally the last person is sent to one of the two remaining countries, which makes two cases, hence $4 \times 3 \times 2 = 24$ cases in total. In the second case, two people go to one country and the other two to another country, which leads us to choose two out of four people, i.e. $C_4^2 = 6$ cases. We then send these two people to one of the three countries, hence three cases. Then the two other people are sent to one of the two remaining countries, i.e. two cases. Hence there are $6 \times 3 \times 2 = 36$ cases in total. By doing this, however, the same cases are counted twice (for example persons 1 and 2 go to country A, then persons 3 and 4 to country B, and on the other hand persons 3 and 4 go to country B then persons 1 and 2 to country A). For this reason, only $36 / 2 = 18$ cases remain.

Finally, the number of ways of sending the four people to three countries, with at least one person in each country, is $81 - 3 - 24 - 18 = 36$. If we had been able to deal with this example using borders, it is clear that with a larger number of people in a larger number of countries, and at least one person in each country, the problem would quickly become inextricable.[1] It is in this context that the sieve formula is going to facilitate things for us.

8.1. Sieve formula on sets

Let us take two sets A_1 and A_2 whose numbers of elements, supposedly finite, are written $|A_1|$ and $|A_2|$. The union $A_1 \cup A_2$ of these two sets is made up, if you wish, of three disjoint sets $A_1 - (A_1 \cap A_2)$, $A_1 \cap A_2$, and $A_2 - (A_1 \cap A_2)$, shown in three colors in Figure 8.2, with numbers of elements: $|A_1| - |A_1 \cap A_2|$, $|A_1 \cap A_2|$, $|A_2| - |A_1 \cap A_2|$, respectively.

1. For this exercise, the use of sieve formula, which we will see, will enable us to write: $S_0 = 3^4$, $S_1 = 3 \times 2^4$, $S_2 = 3$, $S_3 = 0$, hence the number of cases: $S_0 - S_1 + S_2 - S_3 = 81 - 48 + 3 = 36$. We will also be able to see this later, in exercise 8.3.1.

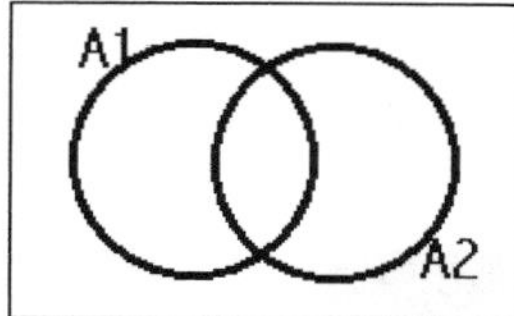

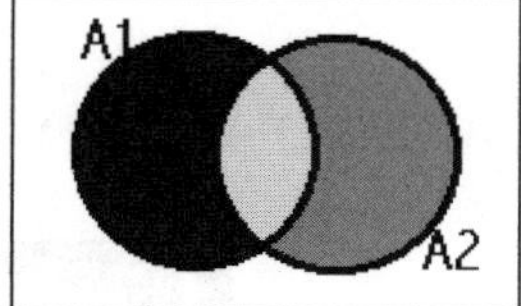

Figure 8.2. *Union of two sets*

By addition, we arrive at the classic formula, in terms of numbers of elements:

$$|A_1 \cup A_2| = |A_1| + |A_2| - |A_1 \cap A_2|$$

What goes for the two sets A_1 and A_2 is generalized to any number of sets, in the following form, which we call sieve formula. Given p parts $A_1, A_2,..., A_p$ of a set E we therefore get:

$$|A_1 \cup A_2 \cup ... \cup A_p| = S_1 - S_2 + ... + (-1)^{p-1} S_p \quad \text{with:}$$

S_1 = sum of the numbers of elements of each of the parts A_k;

S_2 = sum of the numbers of elements of all the pairs $A_i \cap A_j$ (with $i < j$);

S_3 = sum of the numbers of elements of all the parts $A_i \cap A_j \cap A_k$ ($i < j < k$), etc.

Let us insist on the fact that by counting the numbers S_k, the same objects can be counted several times.

This can be seen in another way. Let us go back to the two sets A_1 and A_2, both assumed to be included in a set E with S_0 elements. Therefore the number of elements not in A_1 or A_2, i.e. the number of elements being in the complement of $A_1 \cup A_2$, written $C(A_1 \cup A_2)$, is equal to:

$$|C(A_1 \cup A_2)| = S_0 - |A_1 \cup A_2| = S_0 - S_1 + S_2 \text{ with:}$$

$$S_1 = |A_1| + |A_2| \text{ and } S_2 = |A_1 \cap A_2|$$

This can be generalized. Take the complement of the set of unions above. By writing CA_i the complement of part A_i, i.e. the part of set E that contains all of the elements other than those of A_i, by assuming $S_0 = |E|$ the formula is also written:

$$S_0 - |C(A_1 \cup A_2 \cup ... \cup A_p)| = S_1 - S_2 + ... + (-1)^{p-1} S_p$$

or even:

$$|C(A_1 \cup A_2 \cup ... \cup A_p)| = S_0 - S_1 + S_2 - ... + (-1)^p S_p$$

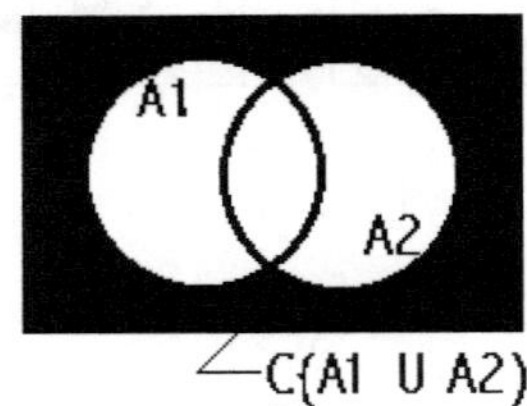

Figure 8.3. *Set of elements that are not in A_1 or A_2*

Let us note that $C(A_1 \cup A_2 \cup ... \cup A_p)$, complement of the set union, is also equal to $CA_1 \cap CA_2 \cap ... \cap CA_p$.[2]

Here is a first application of this sieve formula, with the following example concerning a group of foreign language students.

100 people can study three languages, which we will call 1, 2 and 3.

Among them, 40 study language 1, and eventually other languages; 40 study language 2, and maybe other languages; and 40 study language 3 at least. 20 people

---

2. How can the formula $|CA_1 \cap CA_2 \cap ... \cap CA_p| = S_0 - S_1 + S_2 - ... + (-1)^p S_p$ be demonstrated? We have to prove that there is the same number in the left member of $CA_1 \cap CA_2 \cap ... \cap CA_p|$ as in the right $S_0 - S_1 + S_2 - ... + (-1)^p S_p$. To do this let us take the elements of the global set E one by one, distinguishing two cases. First case: the element is not in any of the sets A_k, it is therefore counted once in $|CA_1 \cap CA_2 \cap ... \cap CA_p|$ and also once in $S_0 - S_1 + S_2 - ... + (-1)^p S_p$ because it is counted once in S_0 and zero times in S_1, S_2,... Second case: the element is not in $|CA_1 \cap CA_2 \cap ... \cap CA_p|$. It is therefore counted zero times. On the other hand, if this element is in set A_k and one single set, it is counted once in S_0, once in S_1 and zero times in the other sets S_2, S_3,..., therefore also zero times in $S_0 - S_1 + S_2 - ... + (-1)^p S_p$. If this element is exactly in two sets, for example A_1 and A_2, it is counted once in S_0, twice in S_1, once in S_2, and zero times elsewhere; hence zero times in $S_0 - S_1 + S_2 - ... + (-1)^p S_p$. More generally, if this element is found in k of the A_i sets, for example in A_1, A_2, ..., A_k, and not elsewhere, it is counted once in S_0, k times in S_1, C_k^2 times in S_2, C_k^3 times in S_3, ..., C_k^k times in S_k and zero times after, i.e. in total, $1 - C_k^1 + C_k^2 - ... + (-1)^k C_k^k$ in $S_0 - S_1 + S_2 - ... + (-1)^p S_p$. But this quantity is equal to zero. All we have to do for this is to develop the expression $(1 + x)^k$ according to binomial formula, then make $x = -1$. Finally, all the elements of the global set E are counted the same number of times in $|CA_1 \cap CA_2 \cap ... \cap CA_p|$ and $S_0 - S_1 + S_2 - ... + (-1)^p S_p$.

study at least languages 1 and 2; 20 study at least languages 1 and 3; and 20 study at least languages 2 and 3. Finally 10 people study all three languages.

We want to find out how many people study none of the three languages, namely: $|C(A_1 \cup A_2 \cup A) = |CA_1 \cap CA_2 \cap CA_3|$ based on the notations above (see Figure 8.4).

We have:

– $S_0 = 100$;

– $S_1 = |A_1| + |A_2| + |A_3| = 40 + 49 + 40 = 120$;

– $S_2 = |A_1 \cap A_2| + |A_1 \cap A_3| + |A_2 \cap A_3| = 20 + 20 + 20 = 60$; and

– $S_3 = |A_1 \cap A_2 \cap A_3| = 10$.

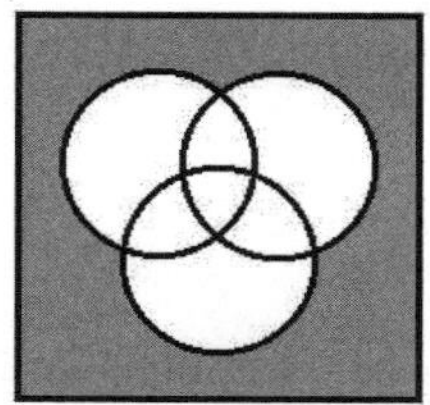

Figure 8.4. *Set (in gray) of students that study no languages*

Sieve formula states that the number of people that study none of the languages is: $100 - 120 + 60 - 10 = 30$.

Another method of calculation is indicated in Figure 8.5.

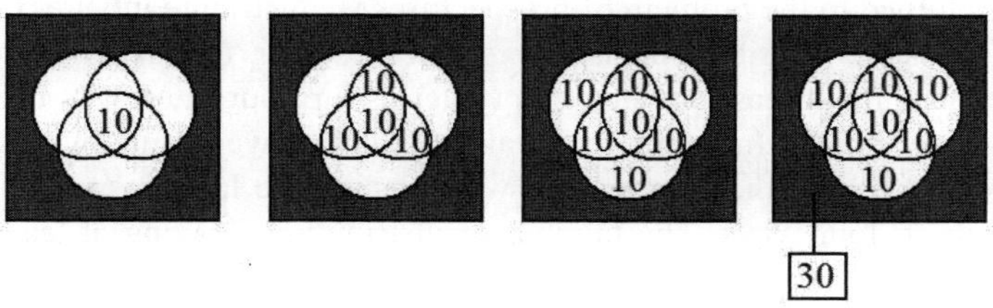

Figure 8.5. *Method for successive counts*

8.2. Sieve formula in combinatorics

Sieve formula can also be expressed in everyday language in the following way: we have S_0 objects and p properties numbered from 1 to p. Let S_1 be the number of objects that have at least property 1, plus the number of objects that have at least property 2, and so on and so forth for each of the p properties. Similarly, S_2 is the number of objects that have (at least) two of these properties, more precisely those that have at least properties 1 and 2, plus those that have properties 1 and 3, and so on and so forth. Similarly for S_3, etc.

Therefore the number of objects that have none of these p properties is equal to:

$$S_0 - S_1 + S_2 - \ldots + (-1)^{p} S_p$$

or even, the number of objects that have at least one of the properties is:

$$S_1 - S_2 + \ldots. + (1)^{p-1} S_p$$

8.3. Examples

8.3.1. *Example 1: filling up boxes with objects, with at least one box remaining empty*

We have five objects that we place in four boxes. We are interested in the number of ways of doing this when at least one of the boxes remains empty. We assume that the boxes are distinct and numbered from 1 to 4. For the objects, we distinguish two possibilities.

First case: the objects are identical, non-differentiated

We are returned to the problem of prospectuses we distribute in letter boxes. The number of possible distributions is $C_8^3 = 56$. In order to have the number of distributions leaving at least one box empty, let us turn our interest to distributions leaving no box empty. In order to obtain the latter, we begin by placing one prospectus in each box, then we are left with placing the last prospectus in a box, which is done in four ways. The number of distributions leaving at least one box empty is $56 - 4 = 52$.

We find this result by using the sieve method. We define four properties for the distributions. We say that a distribution has property k when box k remains empty, with k from 1 to 4. Let A_k be the set of distributions that have property k (at least). The number of distributions leaving at least one box empty is:

$S_1 - S_2 + S_3 - S_4$.

Let us say that $S_1 = |A_1| + |A_2| + |A_3| + |A_4|$. $|A_k|$ is the number of distributions leaving at least box k empty. We have to place the five prospectuses in the three other boxes, which gives $C_7^2 = 21$ cases. Hence $S_1 = 4 \times 21 = 84$ cases. In turn, S_2 is the sum of the $C_4^2 = 6$ terms $|A_i \cap A_j|$ with $i < j$, and $|A_i \cap A_j|$ is the number of distributions leaving (at least) the two boxes i and j empty, which goes back to distributing the five prospectuses in the two remaining boxes, i.e. $C_6^1 = 6$ ways. Here $S_2 = 6 \times 6 = 36$. For the same reasons, we find $S_3 = 4$ and $S_4 = 0$. The number of distributions leaving at least one box empty is: $84 - 36 + 4 = 52$.

Second case: the objects are differentiated and numbered from 1 to 5

There are $4^5 = 1{,}024$ ways of placing the five objects in the four boxes (object 1 has four boxes available, and each time object 2 also has four, etc.). Let us determine the number of cases where no box is empty. We begin by choosing four objects out of the five, i.e. five cases. Each time we place these four objects in the four boxes, which is done in $4! = 24$ ways. Then we place the last object in one of the four boxes, which is done in four ways. But by proceeding in this way, the distributions are counted twice (because we put an order in the placement of the two objects in a box). Finally this gives $5 \times 24 \times 4 / 2 = 240$ cases. The number of distributions leaving at least one box empty is $1{,}024 - 240 = 784$. Notice, however, that this method is only applied in the present case where we put n objects in $n - 1$ boxes.

Let us find this result using the sieve method: $S_1 = |A_1| + |A_2| + |A_3| + |A_4| = 4|A_1|$. As $|A_1|$ is the number of ways of placing the five numbered objects in boxes 2, 3 and 4, this makes $3^5 = 243$ cases. Hence:

$$S_1 = 4 \times 243 = 972$$

Similarly:

$$S_2 = C_4^2 \times 2^5 = 192$$

$$S_3 = 4$$

$$S_4 = 0$$

Finally, the number of distributions leaving at least one box empty is:

$$972 - 192 + 4 = 784$$

8.3.2. *Example 2: derangements*

This problem is practically posed in several forms. For example, it is the football victory problem: n supporters of the winning team throw their hats in the air, and when they get them back, none has his own. We want to find out how many ways this is possible. Or still, a person writes n personalized letters to n people, but when they put them in an envelope, none of the letters have the correct address. It is a matter of counting this number of derangements. In more abstract terms, a derangement is a permutation without a fixed point. For example, the permutation $\begin{pmatrix}1234\\4321\end{pmatrix}$ is a derangement.

This can be read in the following way: person 1's hat goes to person 4, that of person 2 goes to person 3, etc., and we have no fixed point (where person k's hat would go back to person k). In order to find the number of derangements, let us use sieve formula. Let us consider all the permutations of n objects, numbering $S_0 = n!$ of them. Then let us distinguish them according to their properties. In this case, property 1 is a fixed point, and more generally property k signifies that k is a fixed point, with k from 1 to n. The number of derangements $d(n)$ is the number of permutations that have none of these properties.

How many permutations are there with (at least) one fixed point? There are n ways of choosing this fixed point and each time all the possible permutations of the remaining $n - 1$ elements are left, i.e. $(n - 1)!$ cases, which makes a total of $n(n - 1)!$ possibilities. Similarly, there are $C_n^2\ (n - 2)!$ permutations with at least two fixed points because there are C_n^2 ways of choosing the two fixed points and each time there are all the permutations of the $n - 2$ remaining elements, etc. Let us apply sieve formula:

$$d(n) = n! - C_n^1 (n\text{-}1)! + C_n^2(n\text{-}2)! - ... + (\text{-}1)^n C_n^n$$

$$= n! - n!/1! + n!/2! - \ ...\ + (\text{-}1)^n n! \,/\, n!$$

thanks to the formula $C_n^k = n! \,/\, (k!\ (n - k)!)$

$$= \sum_{k=0}^{n} \frac{(-1)^k n!}{k!} = n!\ (1\ -1\ /\ 1!\ +\ 1\ /\ 2!\ -\ 1\ /\ 3!\ +\ ...\ +(-1)^n\ /\, n!)$$

We have just found the explicit formula:

$$d(n) = n!(1 - 1 / 1! + 1 / 2! - 1 / 3! + ... + (\text{-}1)^n / n!)$$

From this we deduce that when n tends to infinity, $d(n) / n!$ tends towards $1 / e$. In other words, the probability that none of the n supporters of the football team find their own hats, when they throw them and get back one of them in an equiprobable way, is approximately 0.37. The number of derangements obeys recurrence formula: $d(n) = n\, d(n-1) + (-1)^n$ for $n > 1$, with $d(1) = 0$.

To check this, for lack of a purely combinatoric demonstration, all we have to do is to note that the explicit formula $d(n)$ answers this recurrence relation, as well as the initial conditions.

8.3.3. *Example 3: formula giving the Euler number $\varphi(n)$*

The Euler number is an arithmetic application of sieve formula. Given a positive natural number $n > 1$, the Euler number $\varphi(n)$ is, by definition, the number of integers lower than or equal to n and which are prime with it.[3] For example $\varphi(18) = 6$ because the prime numbers lower than or equal to 18 are 1, 5, 7, 11, 13 and 17. Let us write the number n in the form of a product of k prime numbers: $n = p_1^{a1}\, p_2^{a2} \ldots p_k^{ak}$, and take the set of n numbers between 1 and n as set E, hence $S_0 = n$. Then let us define k properties of these numbers: property i, with i between 1 and k, means that the number concerned is divisible by the prime number p_i that intervenes in the decomposition of n. The objective is to find the numbers that have no properties: these are all the prime numbers that are lower than or equal to n.

Numbers with property 1 are $p_1, 2p_1, 3p_1, \ldots, n$. There are n / p_1 of them. Hence $|A_1| = n / p_1$, and more generally $|A_i| = n / p_i$, and:

$$S_1 = n(1 / p_1 + 1 / p_2 + \ldots + 1 / p_k)$$

Numbers with properties 1 and 2 are $p_1p_2, 2p_1p_2, \ldots , n$. There are $n / (p_1p_2)$, $|A_{12}| = n / (p_1p_2)$, of them and:

$$S_2 = n\,(1 / (p_1p_2) + 1 / (p_1p_3) + \ldots + 1 / (p_{k-1}\,p_k)),$$

the sum extending to all the pairs of integers.

3. The classic demonstration consists of showing first that $\varphi(p) = p - 1$ where p is prime (none of the numbers from 1 to $p - 1$ contain p as a factor), then $\varphi(p^a) = p^{a-1}\varphi(p)$ for all powers of prime numbers, and finally $\varphi(ab) = \varphi(a)\,\varphi(b)$ for a and b prime numbers between them, which necessitates using what is called "Chinese" isomorphism. Finally, with n breaking down in a unique way in a product of prime numbers: $n = p_1^{a1}\, p_2^{a2} \ldots p_k^{ak}$, we find that: $\varphi(n) = p_1^{a1-1}(p_1 - 1)\, p_2^{a2-1}(p_2 - 1) \ldots p_k^{ak-1}(p_k - 1) = n(1 - 1 / p_1)(1 - 1 / p_2) \ldots (1 - 1 / p_k)$.

We continue in the same way until $S_k = n / (p_1p_2...p_k)$. Thanks to sieve formula, the prime numbers less than or equal to n number:

$$\varphi(n) = S_0 - S_1 + S_2 \ldots +(-1)^k S_k$$

$$= n - n(1/p_1+1/p_2+ \ldots + 1/p_k) + n\,(1/(p_1p_2) +1/(p_1p_3) + \ldots +1/(p_{k-1}p_k))$$

$$- n(1/(p_1p_2p_3) + 1/(p_1p_2p_4) + \ldots) + \ldots + (-1)^k\, n/(p_1p_2\ldots p_k)$$

This result is nothing other than the development of the formula:

$$\varphi(n) = n(1 - 1 / p_1)(1 - 1 / p_2) \ldots(1 - 1 / p_k)$$

8.3.4. *Example 4: houses to be painted*

We consider a street where n houses are found, with the numbers of these houses going from 1 to n. We have k colors to paint them, each house having one unique color. These colors are called 1, 2, ..., k.

8.3.4.1. *Number of ways of painting this set of houses, not being obligated to use all the colors*

Any one of the k colors can be associated with each house. This gives k^n ways of painting them. It also concerns the number of applications of a n-object set (the houses) in a k-object set (the colors).

8.3.4.2. *Number of ways of painting houses where all colors are used*

Notice that out of all the above applications we now take only those we call *surjections*, where each element of the final set (the colors) is attained by at least one arrow coming from the initial set, or has at least one antecedent in the initial set (the houses). Let us take the $S_0 = k^n$ ways of painting them, without any conditions. Then let us distinguish these ways according to their characteristics. Property 1 means that color 1 is not present, and in more general terms property j means that color j is not present, with j between 1 and k. Out of all these possibilities, there are $|A_i|$ ways where no house has color 1. In more general terms, there are $|A_j|$ possibilities where no house has color j. Similarly, there are $|A_{ij}|$ possibilities where no house has colors i or j, and so on and so forth.

Out of the total number of possibilities, those we are interested in are those that have none of the k properties, i.e. those where all the colors are used (none of the colors are missing). It is this number X we are looking for.

We are able to apply sieve formula here. Begin by noting that, for example, $|A_1|$ is the number of ways where color 1 is not used. This corresponds to the number of applications of a n-object set in a $k-1$ object set, i.e. $(k-1)^n$. Let us also note that it is the same for each number $|A_i|$, which makes $C_k^1 = k$ cases. For the same reasons, with i and j given, we have $|A_{ij}| = (k-2)^n$. This goes for all the i and j couples, i.e. C_k^2 cases, etc. Hence:

$$X = S_0 - S_1 + S_2 - \ldots = k^n - C_k^1 (k-1)^n + C_k^2 (k-2)^n + \ldots + (-1)^k C_k^k 0^n$$

$$= \sum_{j=0}^{k} (-1)^j C_k^j (k-j)^n$$

8.3.4.3. *Consequence: number S(n, k) of partitions of a n-element set in k parts*

The number X found above corresponds to the number of surjections of a n-element set in a k-element set. By surjection, we understand that the whole final set is concerned – that is to say that each of its elements has at least one antecedent (see Figure 8.6). Each one of these surjections can be expressed by putting all the initial elements (the houses) that have the same final element 1 (color) in one first part, then all the final elements having color 2 in a second part, etc. This gives a partition of the initial set without any empty part, but where the parts are ordered.[4]

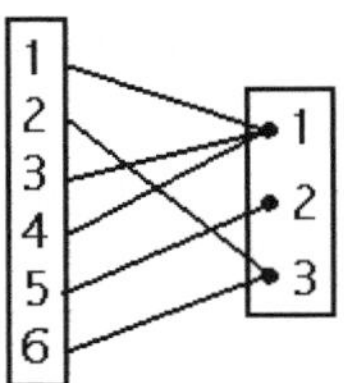

Figure 8.6. *An example of surjection*

In other words, one of the surjections giving the partition {1 3 4}, {5}, {2 6}, as in Figure 8.6, is distinct from the surjection giving {5},{2 6},{1 3 4}. Conversely, each partition in k parts with these parts taken in a certain order ends in a surjection.

4. In the strict sense, a partition of a set is a certain splitting up of this set into several parts that do not overlap and that cover the set completely where the order in which these parts are taken does not come into play, for example tiling, or the partition of a hard disk. In this case, where the order in which these parts are taken applies, we will keep this term partition, misusing language but to simplify things, and specifying that it is ordered partitioning (for more details, see Chapter 14 on set partitions).

There are as many partitions in k parts where the order of parts comes into play, as there are surjections. In a partition, in the classic sense of the term, the order in which the parts are taken does not come in. For each group of $k!$ surjections that have the same parts, we find a single partition of the n-element set in k parts, because order no longer comes into play. Finally $S(n, k) = X / k!$.

The number of partitions of a n-element set in k parts, which we call the Stirling number of the second kind, is:

$$S(n,k) = \frac{1}{k!}\sum_{j=0}^{k} (-1)^j \, C_k^j \, (k-j)^n$$

8.3.5. *Example 5: multiletter words*

We consider words of $2n$ number of characters, made up of two a_1 letters, two a_2 letters, etc. and two a_n letters, where the same two letters cannot follow each other in these words. We therefore have n different letters repeated twice to make up the word, but the same two letters never follow each other. How many such words are there?

8.3.5.1. *Processing of the case where $n = 3$*

Assume the letters are a, b and c. A multiletter word is *abcbca*, one which is not is *abaccb*. To deal with this question, we will proceed in the following way:

– Let us first determine the number of all the words of six characters with two *a*s, two *b*s and two *c*s, following each other or not. By distinguishing these six letters, which we put in the form $a_1\ a_2\ b_1\ b_2\ c_1\ c_2$, we would have 6! words. No longer distinguishing the two *a*s, this result is divided by two. Then, no longer distinguishing the two *b*s it is again divided by two. Similarly, no longer distinguishing the two *c*s the remaining result is divided by two. Namely $6! / 2^3 = 90$ in total. We have just found the anagram formula.

– Out of all these words, $|A_a|$ is the number of those that have an *aa* block; $|A_b|$ the number of those that have a *bb* block; and $|A_c|$ the number of those that have a *cc* block. Similarly, let $|A_{ab}|$ be the number of words with the *aa* block and *bb* block, and similarly for $|A_{ac}|$ and $|A_{bc}|$. Finally $|A_{abc}|$ is the number of words with the three blocks *aa*, *bb* and *cc*. This will enable us to deduce from it the number of multiletter words of six characters (see Figure 8.7).

In the present case, having property 1 means that the word has the *aa* block, having property 2 means having the *bb* block, and similarly for property 3 with *cc*. Clearly we have $|A_a| = |A_b| = |A_c|$, and we deduce $S_1 = 3\ |A_a|$ from it. Let us determine

$|A_a|$. To do this, let us consider the four letters b, b, c and c other than the aa block. They can be written in $4!/2^2$ way and then each time we insert block aa, which can be done in five ways. Hence $|A_a| = 5! / 2^2$, and $S_1 = 3{\times}5! / 4 = 90$. Similarly, $|A_{ab}| = |A_{ac}| = |A_{bc}|$ and $S_2 = 3\ |A_{ab}|$. Let us determine $|A_{ab}|$. To create words of this type, we start from the two letter ccs. We can insert block bb in three ways (before, between or after), then each time we can insert block aa in four ways. Hence $|A_{ab}| = 12$ and $S_2 = 36$. Finally $S_3 = |A_{abc}|$ is the number of words with the three blocks aa, bb and cc. S_3 is the number of permutations of these three blocks, so $S_3 = 6$.

Finally, the number of multiletter words (having none of the three properties) is $90 - 90 + 36 - 6 = 30$.

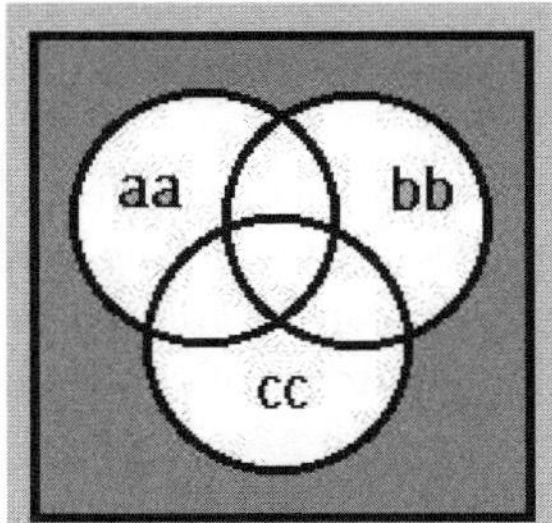

Figure 8.7. *Set (in gray) of multiletter words of six characters*

8.3.5.2. *Generalization to number n*

The number of words with two a_1 letters, two a_2 letters, etc. to two a_n letters is:

$$S_0 = (2n)! / 2^n$$

The number of words with block a_1a_1 is:

$$(2n - 1)(2n - 2)! / 2^{n-1} = (2n - 1)! / 2^{n-1}$$

as we can form $(2n - 2)! / 2^{n-1}$ words with the other letters, and because each time there are $2n - 1$ ways to place the a_1a_1 block. Hence:

$$S_1 = C_n^1\ (2n - 1)! / 2^{n-1}$$

Similarly, $S_2 = C_n^2\ (2n - 2)! / 2^{n-2}$ because in order to form, for example, words with a_1a_1 and a_2a_2 blocks, there are $(2n - 4)! / 2^{n-2}$ ways of placing the other letters, then each time there are $2n - 3$ ways of placing the a_2a_2 block, then each time $2n - 2$ ways of placing the a_1a_1 block.

Finally, the number of multiletter words is:

$$\sum_{k=0}^{n} (-1)^k \, C_n^k \, (2n - k)! \, / \, 2^{n-k}$$

For $n = 4$, we find 576 multiletter words.

8.3.6. *Example 6: coloring the vertices of a graph*

We have n colors. With them, we want to color the vertices of a graph in such a way that two vertices with one common edge are of different colors.

8.3.6.1. *Case of a complete graph*

For example, graph K_4 has four vertices and its edges join each vertex with all the others (see Figure 8.8). We begin by coloring a first vertex, i.e. n cases. Once this has been done, a second vertex can be colored in $n - 1$ ways. We continue in this way. Finally, for graph K_4 the number of colorings is:

$$n(n-1)(n-2)(n-3)$$

The polynomial in n that we have just found is called the chromatic polynomial of the graph. This is generalized to any complete graph K_N.

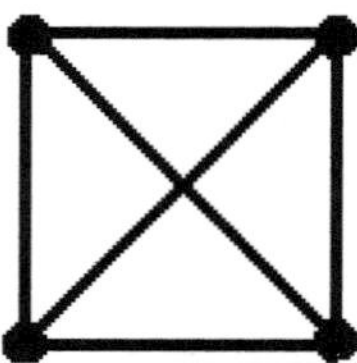

Figure 8.8. *The complete graph K_4*

8.3.6.2. *Case of a graph with four vertices and five edges*

The set that concerns us is made up of all possible colorings of the vertices of the graph in Figure 8.9. Its number of elements is n^4. Let us define five properties, one for each edge. Property k means that edge A_k has two vertices in the same color. We have:

– S_1 is the number of colorings where (at least) edge A_1 has its two vertices in the same color, in addition to the number of colorings where A_2 has its vertices in the same color, etc. The two vertices of edge A_1 have n possible colorings. Each time each one of the two remaining vertices has n possible colorings, i.e. n^3 colorings. It is the same for the other edges. So: $S_1 = 5\ n^3$.

– S_2 is the number of colorings where edges A_1 and A_2 each have the same colors for their two vertices, plus the number of colorings where edge A_1 and A_3 each have their vertices in the same color, plus etc. There are n colorings for edge A_i, and if edge A_j is adjacent, this always makes n colorings. Each time we are left with coloring in the remaining vertex, with n ways of doing so: i.e. n^2 cases. Even if stops A_i and A_j are not adjacent, we find the same number of cases. This is because there are n cases for edge A_i and n cases for A_j, and no remaining vertex, which makes n^2 cases. Finally:

$$S_2 = C_5^{\ 2}\ n^2$$

– S_3 is the number of ways in which each group of three edges has the same colors for the vertices of each of the edges. We must now distinguish two cases. Either the edges form a cycle – here a triangle – they have n colorings, and the remaining vertex is left to be colored in n ways or n^2 possibilities. There are two cycles of three edges. On the other hand, the three edges are successively adjacent. This happens on $C_5^{\ 3} - 2$ occasions, and in each one of these cases the three edges use all the vertices, which gives n colorings. Finally:

$$S_3 = 2n^2 + (C_5^{\ 3} - 2)n$$

More simply, we find that $S_4 = 5n$, and $S_5 = n$.

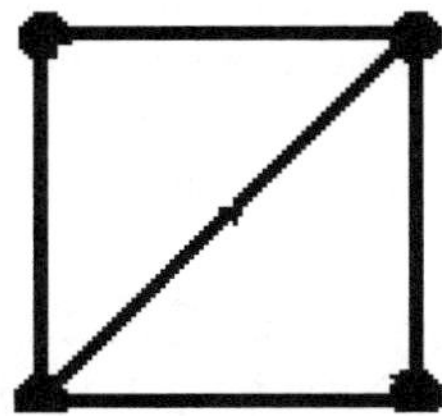

Figure 8.9. *Graph with four vertices and five edges*

Let us apply sieve formula to all the cases where none of the properties is carried out, which gives:

$$n^4 - 5n^3 + 10n^2 - 2n^2 - 8n + 5n - n$$

The chromatic polynomial is:

$$n^4 - 5n^3 + 8n^2 - 4n$$

8.3.6.3. *Case of a pentagon*

The number of possible colorings of vertices is $S_0 = n^5$. Next we find:

$$S_1 = 5n^4,\ S_2 = C_5^{\,2} n^3,\ S_3 = C_5^{\,3} n^2,\ S_4 = C_5^{\,4} n \text{ and } S_5 = n$$

The chromatic polynomial is:

$$n^5 - 5n^4 + 10n^3 - 10\,n^2 + 5n - n$$

For example, for $n = 3$, we find 30 colorings where two adjacent vertices do not have the same color. Calling the three colors a, b and c, we can enumerate the words corresponding to the colorings, in a reading order of successive vertices:

ababc, abacb, abcab, abcac, abcbc, acabc, acacb, acbab, acbac, acbcb

and similarly with b then c in first place. It involves all cyclic words of five characters, based on an a three-letter alphabet that does not have two identical consecutive letters.

8.3.6.4. *The Sudoku graph*

To simplify things, let us take the 4 by 4 Sudoku, divided into four square blocks size 2 by 2. We must place the four numbers 1, 2, 3 and 4 on each of the lines and on each of the columns, as well as in each of the square blocks. This goes back to searching for the value of a chromatic polynomial of the graph in Figure 8.10, for $n = 4$ colors. Because of the large number of edges, the calculation would be tedious, so we prefer to use another method (see Chapter 12).

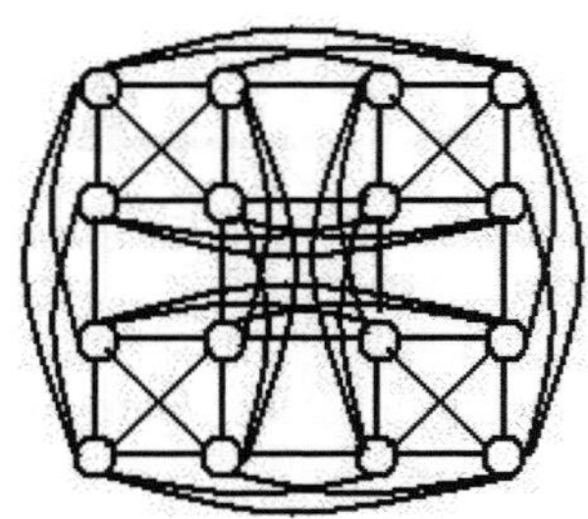

Figure 8.10. *The Sudoku graph with 4 by 4 dimensions*

8.4. Exercises

8.4.1. *Exercise 1: sending nine diplomats, 1, 2, 3, ..., 9, to three countries A, B, C*

a) How many ways are there of distributing the diplomats, all eventualities being possible, and a country can receive no diplomats?

Each way can be coded by one nine-letter word based on A, B and C, for example $\begin{pmatrix} 1 & 2 & 3 & 4 & 5 & 6 & 7 & 8 & 9 \\ B & A & A & C & A & C & B & C & C \end{pmatrix}$.

Diplomat 1 has three possibilities each time, as does diplomat 2, and so on, hence 3^9 ways, i.e. 19,683.

b) Each one of the three countries receives three diplomats. How many ways are there of doing this?

Using the coding above, this involves creating all the words that have three letter As, three Bs and three Cs. They are anagrams. The number of ways is $C_9^3\ C_6^3$, because we begin by placing the three As in three out of nine places, then each time we are left with placing three Bs in the six remaining places, and the letter C takes the last places. There are 1,680 possibilities.

c) Each one of the three countries receives at least one diplomat. How many ways are there of doing this?

Let us imagine the sieve formula context. We have 3^9 configurations, of which only some (at least one diplomat per country) concern us. We define three properties. Property 1 expresses that country A does not receive any diplomats, and similarly for the two other countries. We have to find the number of cases that have none of the three properties. $S_1 = 3\times 2^9$, $S_2 = 3\times 1$, hence the number sought is: $3^9 - 3\times 2^9 + 3 = 18{,}150$.

8.4.2. *Exercise 2: painting a room*

We have N colors to paint the ceiling (called 0) and the four vertical walls (called 1, 2, 3 and 4) of a room. Each one of these five surfaces is painted with one of the colors.

a) What is the number S_0 of possible colorings?

There are N ways of painting the ceiling, and each time also N ways of painting wall number 1, etc. Hence $S_0 = N^5$.

b) On the five surfaces we never have two with a side in common that have the same color. What is the number of ways the room can be painted?

In drawing the corresponding graph (see Figure 8.11) with five vertices representing the surface to be painted and eight junction edges, which we have numbered, we therefore do not want two neighboring vertices joined by an edge to have the same color. If $u(n)$ is the number of possible colorings in this context, we must determine $u(n)$ using the sieve formula.

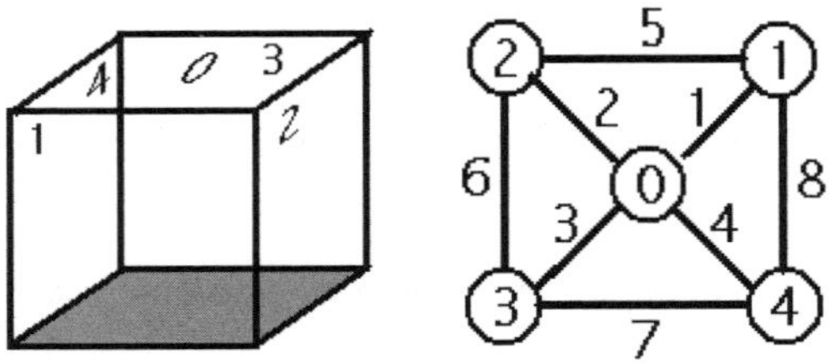

Figure 8.11. *The room with its four walls and ceiling. On the right, the corresponding graph*

We define eight properties. Property k means that the rooms joined by edge k have the same color. We must find the number of ways of painting when none of the properties applies. When property 1 is true, there are N ways of coloring in walls 0 and 1 with the same color, and each time N ways of coloring in wall 2, and similarly for the other walls, i.e. N^4 ways. When (at least) one of the eight properties is true, this makes $S_1 = 8N^4$. When properties 1 and 2 are true, the three walls 0, 1 and 2 have the same color, i.e. N cases, and each one of the two other walls can have any color, which gives N^3 cases. This is the same for all the other pairs of properties. Hence $S_2 = C_8^{\ 2} N^3 = 28\, N^3$.

Let us now move on to S_3. There are $C_8^{\ 3} = 56$ ways of choosing three out of the eight properties, but two eventualities occur: in most cases, like with edges 123 and the four walls concerned 0123, these latter have the same color, i.e. N ways, and a last wall remains with N possible colors, which makes N^2 ways. In four cases, those where the three edges form a triangle (125, 236, 347, 148), only three walls must have to have the same color, and two of them are left, which makes N^3 ways. Finally $S_3 = 52\, N^2 + 4\, N^3$.

Next let us look for S_4: if we take the three edges forming one of the four triangles previously obtained and we add back one edge, i.e. five eventualities like this one: 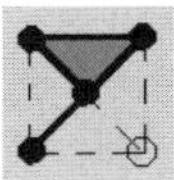 or this one:  we get four (or three) walls that must have the same color, and one (or two) walls are left to be painted independently of the rest, which makes N^2 ways, this is in 4×5 = 20 cases. The cases where four edges form a quadrilateral are added to this. This happens on the one hand for quadrilaterals with the form of a large triangle, i.e. four cases with vertices 0123, 0234, 0341 and 0412, like this one: as well as for the square with edges 5678, and in these five cases, one last vertex remains to be painted, hence there are N^2 ways of painting. Therefore there are 25 cases where the number of ways is N^2.

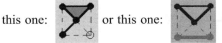

In all the other cases, i.e. $C_8^{\,4} - 25 = 70 - 25 = 45$ cases, the four properties correspond to four edges attached to the five vertices of the graph, with N ways of painting in each case. Finally: $S_4 = 45\,N + 25\,N^2$.

Let us move on to S_5: most often, the fact of taking five edges gives the same color to the five vertices, but the case of the four large triangles already obtained remains, this time with their height in addition, like this one: leaving a final vertex to be colored at will.

Therefore: $S_5 = 52N + 4N^2$.

For the remaining cases, we find $S_6 = 28\,N$, $S_7 = 8\,N$, $S_8 = N$. Sieve formula leads to the following result:

$$u(N) = N^5 - 8N^4 + 24N^3 - 31N^2 + 14N$$

We can verify that $u(1) = 0$, $u(2) = 0$ and $u(3) = 6$.

8.4.3. *Exercise 3: rooks on a chessboard*

8.4.3.1. *Visualization of a permutation*

Let us consider a $n \times n$ chessboard. Let us place n rooks on it in such a way that none is attacked by another. This means that each line and each column has only one rook. Each configuration obtained corresponds to a permutation. All we have to do is to read the numbers of the lines where the rooks are found, from the first to the last column. The correspondence is clearly bijective (see Figure 8.12).

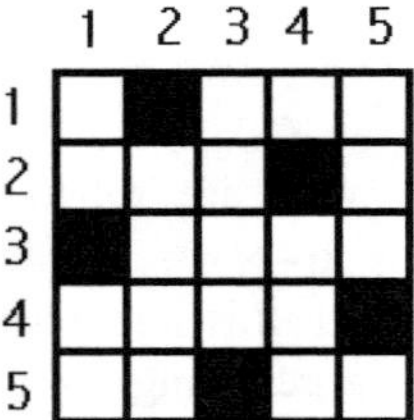

Figure 8.12. *Design of the permutation 3 1 5 2 4 (reading by columns)*

8.4.3.2. *Chessboard with forbidden positions*

Now let us add an extra constraint, forbidding the rooks from some squares on the chessboard, for example the black squares in Figure 8.13.

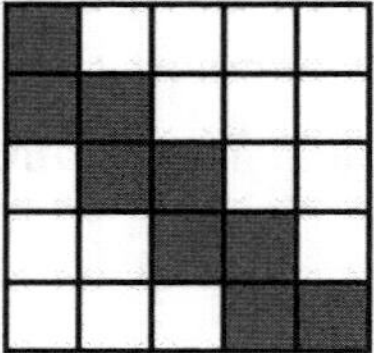

Figure 8.13. *Chessboard with forbidden positions in diagonal*

We want to find out the number of configurations of rooks (in mutual non-attack), where the n rooks are not in any of the black squares. To do this let us take the context of sieve formula. We begin by taking the set of all possible configurations for rooks on the chessboard, including forbidden positions. We know that there are $n!$ configurations – as many as there are of permutations of n objects. Now let us define n properties. Property 1 means that the rook located in column 1 is in a forbidden position. Property 2 means that the rook located in column 2 is in a forbidden position, and so on and so forth. The objective is to find the number of configurations outside the $n!$ that have none of the n properties.

In the example above, the number of cases with at least property 1 is 2×4!, as once the rook has been placed in one of the two forbidden positions of column 1, the four others remain to be placed anywhere in the four remaining columns. There are 2.4! cases with property 2, etc. Hence:

$$S_1 = (2 + 2 + 2 + 2 + 1) \times 4! = 9 \times 4!.$$

This is of the form $S_1 = r_1 \times 4!$ where r_1 is the number of ways of placing a rook in the forbidden positions.

The number of cases with at least properties 1 and 2 is $3\times3!$, as we begin by placing two rooks in the forbidden positions in columns 1 and 2, which gives three cases. Each time three rooks remain to be placed in the three remaining columns in all possible ways. The number of cases with properties 1 and 3 is $4\times3!$, etc. Finally:

$$S_2 = (3 + 4 + 4 + 2 + 3 + 4 + 2 + 3 + 2 + 1) \times 3! = 28\times3! = r_2\times3!$$

where r_2 is the number of ways of placing two rooks in non-attack position in two of the forbidden squares. We also have:

$$S_3 = (4 + 6 + 3 + 6 + 4 + 2 + 4 + 3 + 2 + 1)\ 2! = 35.\ 2!$$

with $r_3 = 35$, which is the number of ways of placing three rooks in mutual non-attack position in three of the forbidden squares. Next:

$$S_4 = (5 + 3 + 3 + 2 + 1)\ 1! = 14, \text{ with } r_4 = 14.$$

Finally:

$$S_5 = 1\times0!$$

with $r_5 = 1$. Thanks to sieve formula, the number of configurations of rooks avoiding the forbidden positions is:

$$5! - 9\times4! + 28\times3! - 35\times2! + 14\times1! - 1\times0! = 15$$

By generalizing, the number of ways of placing n rooks on a $n\times n$ chessboard in mutual non-attack position, while avoiding being placed in the forbidden squares we gave ourselves, is:

$$N = \sum_{k=0}^{n} (-1)^k r_k\, (n-k)!$$

where r_k is the number of ways of placing k rooks in mutual non-attack positions in the forbidden squares.

8.4.3.3. *The derangements example*

Because a derangement is a permutation without a fixed point, the forbidden positions on the chessboard are its diagonal (see Figure 8.14). For the

n-element permutations, we deduce from this that $r_k = C_n^k$, and by applying the formula above we again find the derangements formula:

$$d_n = \sum_{k=0}^{n} (-1)^k C_n^k (n-k)!$$

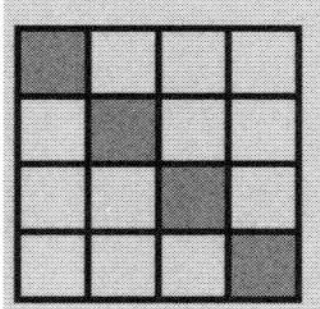

Figure 8.14. *Forbidden positions on the diagonal*

8.5. Extension of sieve formula

We have seen how to count the number E_0 of elements with none of the p properties, for example for $p = 3$ (the elements of the zone colored in gray in Figure 8.15) or even its complement (white on the drawing), i.e. the elements that have at least one property.

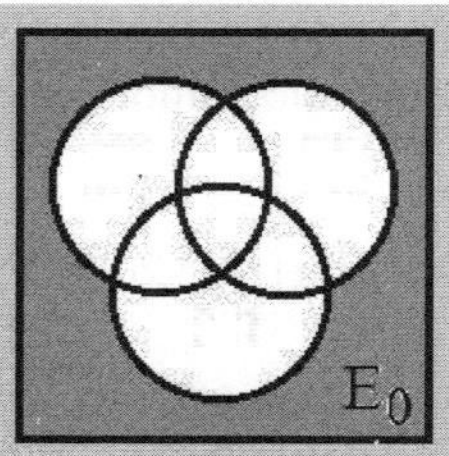

Figure 8.15. *Elements (in white) that have at least one out of the three properties*

Let us recall that the calculation is done using that of the S_k numbers, defined above. We now want to find out the number E_1 of elements that have exactly one property, the number E_2 of those that have exactly two properties, etc. These numbers are also associated with the S_k numbers. Therefore we have the following formulae:

– the number E_k of elements with the number of properties equal to k (out of p properties) is:

$$E_k = S_k - C_{k+1}^k S_{k+1} + C_{k+2}^k S_{k+2} - \ldots + (-1)^{p-k} C_p^k S_p$$

– if we call $S(x)$ the generating function of (S_k), i.e. $S(x) = \sum_{k=0}^{p} S_k x^k$ and $E(x)$ the generating function of (E_k), $E(x) = \sum_{k=0}^{p} E_k x^k$, then:

$$E(x) = S(x-1) = \sum_{k=0}^{p} S_k (x-1)^k$$

– on the other hand, the number of elements with a number of properties at least equal to k is:

$$S_k - C_k^{k-1} S_{k+1} + C_{k+1}^{k-1} S_{k+2} - \dots + (-1)^{p-k} C_{p-1}^{k-1} S_p$$

These formulae are demonstrated in the same way as the sieve formula. We will not demonstrate this here. Applying the formula that gives the generating function $E(x)$, we are able to find the average number of properties that have S_0 objects of the global set. Actually, the derivative of $E(x)$ is:

$$E'(x) = \sum_{k=1}^{p} k\, E_k\, x^{k-1}$$

hence:

$$E'(1) = \sum_{k=1}^{p} k\, E_k$$

By dividing the number $E'(1)$ by the total number S_0 of objects concerned, we have the sum of the numbers of each category of objects weighted by the number k of properties. The average number of properties that the objects possess is $E'(1) / S_0$.

8.5.1. *Permutations that have k fixed points*

Above we saw derangements and permutations with no fixed point. We can now find the number of permutations with exactly k fixed points (with k between 0 and n). The context is the same as for derangements, where we calculated $S_k = n! / k!$. Thanks to the formula above, the number of permutations with exactly k fixed points is:

$$E_k = n!\, \Sigma(-1)^k C_{k+q}^{k} / (k+q)!,$$

with the summation done on q from 0 to $n - k$.

The generating function associated with the sequence (E_k) is:

$$E(x) = \sum_{k=0}^{n} S_k \ (x-1)^k$$

the derivative of which is:

$$E'(x) = n! \sum_{k=1}^{n} (x-1)^{k-1} / (k-1)!$$

The average number of fixed points for n-element permutation is $E'(1)/n! = n!/n! = 1$. Permutations with a given number of elements have on average one fixed point.

8.5.2. *Permutations with q disjoint cycles that are k long*

The objects of the set are the permutations, numbering $S_0 = n!$. Now we consider all possible cycles of length k.[5] This refers to choosing k out of n objects, taking order into consideration – i.e. $n(n-1)\ldots(n-k+1)$ cases – then to considering the cycles, being at a gap-type, each end being repeated k times in the previous cases. The number of possible cycles with k elements is $n! / ((n-k)!\ k)$. We number all these cycles and say that a permutation has property number i if it has cycle number i.

Let us take $|A_1|$ as the number of permutations that have cycle $(1\ 2\ \ldots k)$. The other elements to be permutated are left, i.e. $(n-k)!$ possible permutations. We do the same with all cycles of length k, $n! / ((n-k)!\ k)$. Hence, $S_1 = n! / k$.

Now let us look for $|A_{ij}|$, that are the number of permutations with cycle numbers of at least i and j. If these two cycles are not disjoint, there is no permutation.

Now let us assume that the two cycles are disjoint. The remaining elements are left to be permutated in all ways, i.e. $(n-2k)!$ cases, on the condition that $2k$ is less than or equal to n. To get S_2, we must count how many cases there are where we have two disjoint cycles. We begin by choosing the first cycle, which is done in $n!/((n-k)!k)$ ways. Each time, k elements remain to be taken out of the $n-k$ remaining ones to form all of the possible cycles, i.e.

5. The notion of permutation cycles is explained in Chapter 19.

$(n-k)!/((n-2k)!k)$ possibilities. But having thus taken a first cycle then a second cycle, each pair of cycles is counted twice. Finally:

$$S_2 = (n-2k)!\ n!\ /\ ((n-k)!\ k)\ (n-k)!\ /\ ((n-2k)!\ k) = n!\ /\ (2k^2)$$

Similarly $S_3 = n!\ /\ (3!\ k^3)$, when $3k \leq n$, and 0 otherwise, etc.

Let us take an example with $n = 6$ and $k = 2$. We want to classify the $6! = 720$ permutations according to the number of their cycles of length 2. Using $S_0 = 6!$, $S_1 = 6!\ /\ 2$, $S_2 = 6!\ /\ 8$, $S_3 = 6!\ /\ 48$, we find the following results:

– the number of permutations with no cycles of length 2 is: $E_0 = S_0 - S_1 + S_2 - S_3 = 435$;

– the number of permutations with exactly one cycle of length 2 is: $E_1 = S_1 - 2S_2 + 3S_3 = 225$;

– the number of permutations with two cycles of length 2 is: $E_2 = S_2 - 3S_3 = 45$; and

– the number of permutations with three cycles of length 3 is $E_3 = S_3 = 15$.

8.5.3. *Terminal nodes of trees with n numbered nodes*

Let us take n points numbered 1 to n. We will assume (see Chapter 31 on trees) that there are n^{n-2} trees that have these points as numbered nodes. These trees can be classified according to the number of their terminal nodes, which are between 2 and $n - 1$. We want to find out the number E_k of these trees that have exactly k terminal nodes. Let us put ourselves in the context of sieve formula. Our objects are trees – $S_0 = n^{n-2}$ of them. Then let us define n properties. Property 1 means that node 1 is a terminal node, and more generally property k expresses that node k is a terminal node. The number of trees that have at least property 1 is $|A_1|$. To do this we begin by taking all the trees that have the points 2, 3, 4, …, n as numbered nodes, numbering $(n-1)^{n-3}$.

Next we link node 1 to any one of these points, which is done in $n - 1$ ways. We have just obtained all the trees that have at least point 1 as a terminal node. Hence $|A_1| = (n-1)^{n-2}$.

We do the same for each of the $|A_k|$. The number S_1 is the sum of these $|A_k|$, all equal, and of which there are n (or $C_n^{\ 1}$):

$$S_1 = C_n^{\ 1}\ (n-1)^{n-2}$$

This is generalized. Let us consider $|A_{123\ldots k}|$ to be the number of trees that have points 1, 2, 3, …, k as terminal nodes. We begin by taking all the other points, $n - k$ of them, and we get $(n - k)^{n-k-2}$ trees with these points as vertices. Then we link point 1 to each one of these trees, which is done in $n - k$ ways. It is the same for points 2, 3,…, k, hence $(n - k)^k$ cases, and $|A_{123\ldots k}| = (n - k)^{n-2}$.

We do the same for all the sets of k points obtained in C_n^k ways. Finally $S_k = C_n^k (n - k)^{n-2}$. From the generating function of S_k, i.e.:

$$S(x) = \Sigma\, S_k\, x^k = \Sigma\, C_n^k\, (n-k)^{n-2}\, x^k = \Sigma\, C_n^k\, k^{n-2}\, x^{n-k}$$

we deduce the generating function of the E_j:

$$E(x) = \sum_j E_j x^j = S(x-1) = \sum_k C_n^k\, k^{n-2}\, (x-1)^{n-k}$$

Developing this formula for the example $n = 5$, we get 60 trees that have two terminal nodes, 60 that have three, and five with four terminal nodes, for a total of $5^3 = 125$ trees (see Figure 8.16).

The algorithm enabling us to classify these trees in this way is an immediate consequence of Prüfer decoding (see Chapter 31 on trees). Still for $n = 5$, for example, each tree is coded by a word of three characters based on five numbers 1, 2, 3, 4 and 5.

Out of these 125 words: those that have exactly three numbers correspond to trees with two terminal nodes; those that have two numbers present give trees with three terminal nodes; and those with a single number present give trees with four terminal nodes.

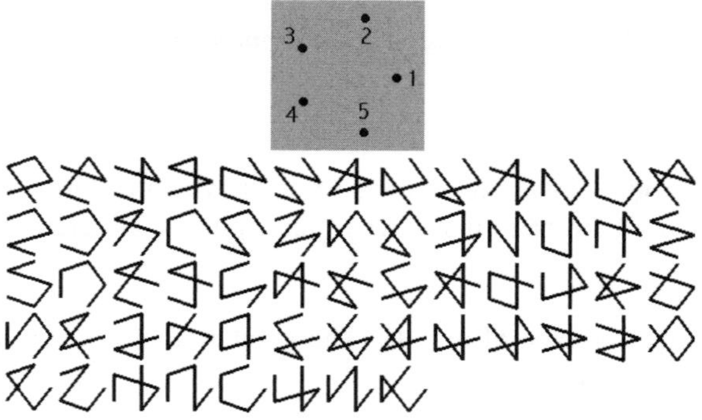

Figure 8.16a. *Out of the 125 trees with five vertices, 60 trees have two terminal nodes*

Figure 8.16b. *The 60 trees with three terminal nodes*

Figure 8.16c. *The five trees with four terminal nodes*

To find out the average number of terminal nodes for trees with n nodes, let us take the derivative of the generating function:

$$E'(x) = \Sigma\, C_n^{\ k}\, k^{n-2}\, (n - k)\, (x - 1)^{n-k-1},$$

from which we deduce:

$$E'(1) = C_n^{\ n-1}\, (n - 1)^{n-2} = n\, (n - 1)^{n-2}$$

The average number of terminal nodes is:

$$E'(1) / S_0 = n\, (n - 1)^{n-2} / n^{n-2} = n\, (1 - 1 / n)^{n-2}$$

which is of order n / e for large n. For example, trees with about 30 numbered nodes have on average about 10 terminal nodes.

8.5.4. *Revision exercise about a word: intelligent*

a) How many anagrams are there of this word?

The word has 11 characters. It has two *I*s, two *N*s, two *T*s, two *E*s, two *L*s and one *G*. The number of anagrams is $C_{11}^{\ 2}\, C_9^{\ 2}\, C_7^{\ 2}\, C_5^{\ 2}\, C_3^{\ 2} = 11! / 2^5 = 11! / 32$.

b) How many anagrams are there with no repeated block of two identical letters?

To answer, let us take the context of sieve formula and define five properties. Property 1 means that the word has block *II*. Property 2 indicates the presence of block *NN*, and this for each of the five blocks of two identical letters. The number of words with property 1 is $10 \times 9! / 2^4$. Actually, there are 10 ways to place the *II* block, and each time what is left is to take all the anagrams based on the nine remaining letters. Another method consists of taking all the anagrams based on one *I*, two *N*s, two *L*s, two *E*s, two *T*s and one *G* – i.e. $10! / 2^4$ words – and then all we have to do is double the *I*. From this we deduce that $S_1 = 5 \times 10! / 2^4$.

For the same reasons, the number of words with properties 1 and 2 (at least) is $9! / 2^3$, hence $S_2 = C_5^2\, 9! / 2^3$. We also find $S_3 = C_5^3\, 8! / 2^2$, etc. Finally, the number of words with no block of two identical letters is:

$$11! / 2^5 - 5 \times 10! / 2^4 + 10 \times 9! / 2^3 - 10 \times 8! / 2^2 + 5 \times 7! / 2 - 6!$$

c) How many words are there with at least two blocks, each made from two identical letters?

We apply the formula above on the number of elements that have at least two out of the five properties, i.e.:

$$S_2 - C_2^1 S_3 + C_3^1\, S_4 - C_4^1\, S_5 = 10 \times 9! / 2^3 - 2 \times 10 \times 8! / 2^2 + 3 \times 5 \times 7! / 2 - 4 \times 6!$$

Chapter 9

Mountain Ranges or Parenthesis Words: Catalan Numbers

Here we pursue the study of routes in a square grid, which began in Chapter 6. Out of paths based on two steps ↗ (1, 1) or ↘ (1, -1), we will now favor those that can touch but not cross the horizontal axis, remaining above, and that start from point $O(0, 0)$ and end at point $B(2n, 0)$. This notably imposes that there are as many ↗ as ↘. In the analogy with a repeated game of heads or tails, partial wins always remain positive or null, and end with a null win[1]. The shapes of these paths produce mountain ranges, hence their name. It is also a matter of words of $2n$ characters based on two letters a and b (for ↗ and ↘), with as many as as bs such that all the beginnings (or left factors) of these words have at least as many as as bs, which forbids us from going below the horizontal axis. Seen from another angle, in a square grid based on horizontal and vertical lines, these words are called over-diagonal words (see Figure 9.1)[2].

These words are also called *parenthesis words* as they correspond to a valid bracketing of an algebraic expression, with the letter a representing a left parenthesis and the letter b a right parenthesis. Actually, if we draw a mountain chain with its contour lines, all we have to do is to crop the higher and lower parts of these contours to get what we call a parenthesis word, which has as many left parentheses as right ones (see Figure 9.2).

---

1. This game has wins and losses. We consider a loss as a negative win.
2. We can consult G. Kreweras on the subject of these works (see notably [KRE 76]).

Parentheses written in this way correspond two by two, and the expression obtained is valid from the point of view of syntax. Finally we call them Dyck paths.

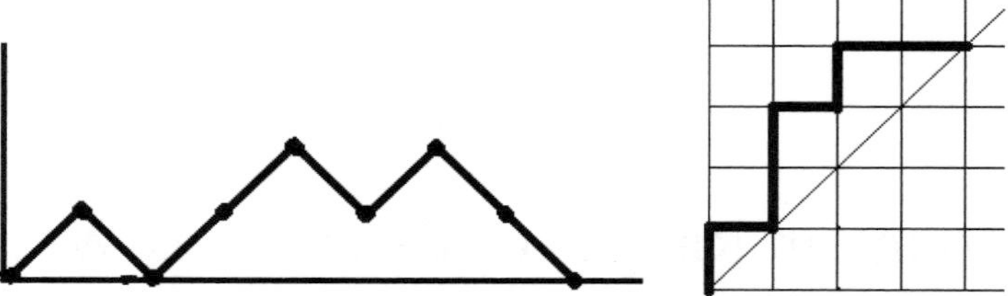

Figure 9.1. *A mountain range of eight steps (with four ↗ and four ↘), or even an over-diagonal word in a square network. The associated parenthesis word is written: ( ) (( ) ( ))*

Figure 9.2. *From mountain range to parenthesis word. The corresponding word is aaabbbaaabbabb and this range is made up of two mountains*

9.1. Number $c(n)$ of mountain ranges $2n$ long

Let us take paths $2n + 1$ long that beyond the origin O can neither touch nor cross the horizontal axis, and remain above, to finally arrive at point $B(2n+1,1)$. We saw in Chapter 6 that their number is:

$$P(2n + 1, 1) = (1 / n)\, C_{2n+1}^{\,n}$$

All these paths pass through point $A(1, 1)$. Let us trace the horizontal axis (AB). There are as many paths from O to B $2n + 1$ long, that neither touch nor cross the horizontal axis and pass through O, as there are paths from A to B, $2n$ long able to touch but not cross the (AB) axis, i.e. mountain ranges $2n$ long (see Figure 9.3).

Expressing this number, $c(n)$, we find:

$$c(n) = (1 / n)\, C_{2n+1}^{\,n}$$

which is also written:

$$c(n) = C_{2n}^{n} / (n + 1)$$

The number $c(n)$ of mountain ranges $2n$ long with n ↗ lines and n ↘ lines, is called the Catalan number, from the name of the Belgian mathematician Eugene Catalan (1814–1894). Nevertheless, let us point out that these numbers had already appeared in China in the works of Ming An-tu towards the 1730s.

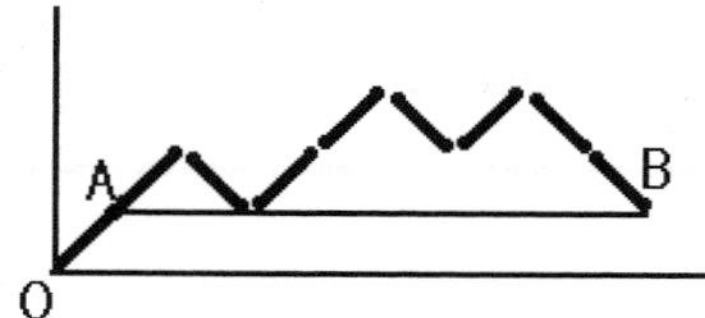

Figure 9.3. *Mountain range from A to B*

9.2. Mountains or primitive words

All mountain ranges can be divided into mountains. All we have to do is to take the points with null ordinates of a mountain range, i.e. O, A_1, A_2, …, B $(2n, 0)$. Between two of these successive points a mountain is found (see Figure 9.4). In other words, a mountain is a word based on two letters a and b, with as many as as bs, and of which all beginnings less than $2n$ long have more as than bs. As the mountains are the atoms that constitute a mountain range, they are designated by the term *primitive word.* There is a bijective link between mountain ranges $2n - 2$ long and mountains $2n$ long.

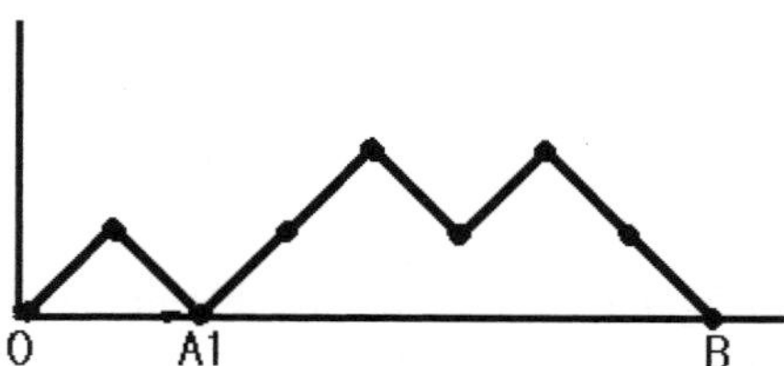

Figure 9.4. *A mountain range made up of two mountains*

To move from one to the other, all we have to do is to add or subtract two lines, a ↗ at the start and a ↘ at the end (see Figure 9.5). There are as many mountains that are $2n$ long as mountain ranges $2(n - 1)$ long. The number of mountains that are $2n$ long is the Catalan number $c(n - 1)$.

Note that outside the $c(n)$ mountain ranges $2n$ long, the proportion of those made up of a single mountain is:

$$c(n-1) \,/\, c(n) = (n+1) \,/\, (2(2n-1))$$

This proportion leans towards 1 / 4 when n increases to infinity.

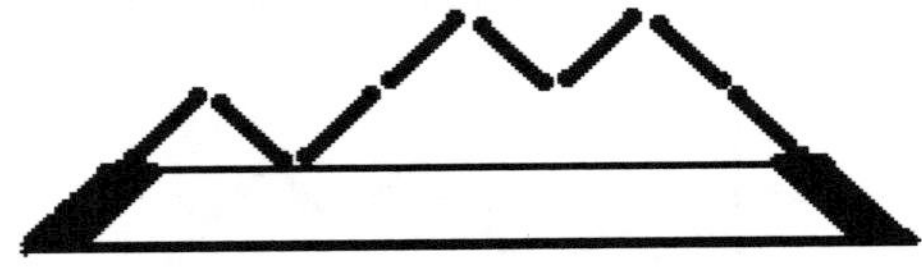

Figure 9.5. *Passage from one mountain to a mountain range*

9.3. Enumeration of mountain ranges

For computer requirements, an ascent is 0 and a descent is 1, instead of a and b. A mountain range $2N$ long has as many 0s as 1s, in such a way that by starting from ground level we finally come back to ground level without ever going below.

For each value of N, we have to write the words corresponding to the mountain ranges in alphabetical order. For example, for $N = 3$ we successively get the five ranges: 000111, 001011, 001101, 010011 and 010101. The first range is the one where all the 0s precede the 1s.

How do we move from one range to the next? Knowing that we are leaving the longest possible fixed block to the left, the first letter to change, namely the pivot, is a 0 that will become a 1. More precisely, we have to transform a $\nearrow\searrow$ peak into $\searrow\nearrow$, avoiding falling below ground level, which forces us to have a configuration in the form $\nearrow\searrow\searrow$.

We seek such a configuration as far as possible in the word. In order to find the pivot, we therefore run through the word from right to left until we first encounter a 011 block, the pivot being this 0.

The pivot is transformed into 1 and the first 1 that follows it is transformed into 0. Beyond this, we put all that remains in alphabetical order, i.e. with the 0s before the 1s. Hence the program:

```
for(i=0; i<2*N; i++)  if (i<N) a[i]=0; else a[i]=1;   /* the first chain */
```

```
for(;;)    /* passage from one range to the next */
{ display of table a[] or drawing of the chain
  counter0=0; /* we will count the 0s from the end */
  i=2*N-1;
  while (i>=2 && !(a[i]==1 && a[i–1]==1 && a[i–2]==0) )
     { if (a[i]==0) counter0++;  i--; }
  pospivot = i–2;  if (pospivot= = -1) break; /* stop test */
  a[pospivot]=1; a[pospivot+1]=0;  /*  01 becomes 10  */
  k=0;     /* we will modify what remains on the right */
  for(j=pospivot+2;j<2*N; j++)
    { if (k<counter0) a[j]=0;
      else a[j]=1;
      k++;
    }
}
```

We will see the results obtained thanks to this program in Figure 9.6.

9.4. The language of mountain ranges

Let us call the mountain range language C and the mountain language M. Thanks to what we saw in section 9.2, $M = a\ C\ \ b$. On the other hand, by definition:

$$C = 1 + ab + aabb + abab + aaabbb + aababb + aabbab + abaabb + ababab + aaaabbbb + \ldots$$

where 1 designates the empty mountain range. In the enumeration above, the first ranges indicated are classified according to their length. We can also classify them according to the first mountain that makes up their beginning.

$$\begin{aligned} C &= 1 + ab(1 + ab + aabb + \ldots) + aabb(1 + ab + aabb + \ldots) \\ &\quad + aaabbb(1 + ab + aabb + \ldots) + aababb\,(1 + ab + aabb + \ldots) + \ldots \\ &= 1 + M\,C \end{aligned}$$

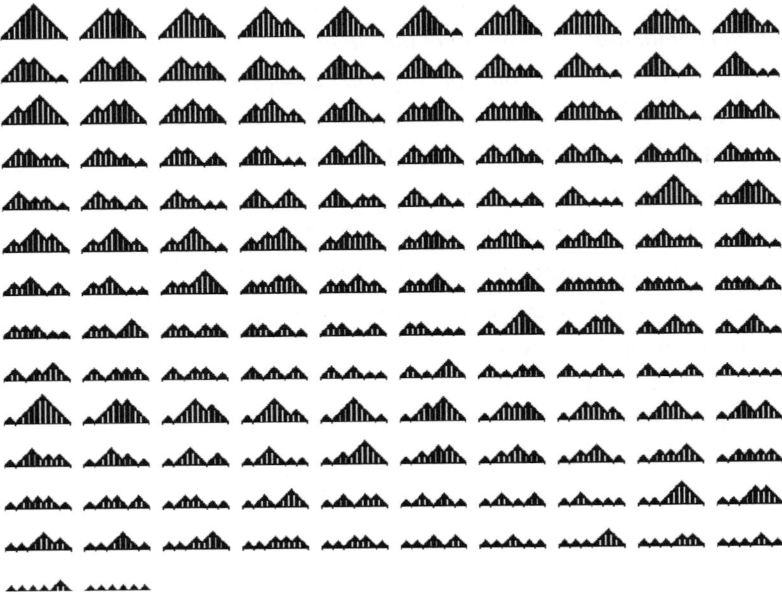

Figure 9.6. *The 132 mountain ranges for $N = 6$*

A mountain range is either the empty word or a mountain joined to a mountain range. Finally:

$$C = 1 + a\,C\,b\,C$$

Now, let us return all commutatives and let us replace *ab* (or *ba*) with *X*. Language $C = e + ab + aabb + abab + aaabbb + aababb + \ldots$. becomes the generating function:

$$C(X) = 1 + X + X^2 + X^2 + X^3 + X^3 + \ldots = 1 + X + 2X^2 + 5\,X^3 + \ldots$$

We get a series of powers of X whose coefficient of the term in X^n is the number of mountain ranges with the letter a n times and the letter b n times, i.e. $c(n)$. The generating function $C(X)$ associated with the Catalan numbers verifies $C(X) = 1 + X\,C(X)^2$.

The solution to this equation of the second degree in C gives:

$$C(X) = \frac{1 \pm \sqrt{1 - 4X}}{2X}$$

The limited development of $\sqrt{1-4X}$ beginning with $1 - 2X$ obliges us to choose the minus sign, hence:

$$C(X) = \frac{1-\sqrt{1-4X}}{2X} \quad ^{3}$$

As for the generating function, $M(X)$ associated with the number of mountains $2n$ long is:

$$M(X) = X\,C(X)$$

The equation $C(X) = 1 + X\,C(X)$ also gives us other information. The term in X^n of $C(X)$ is the Catalan number $c(n)$. The coefficient of the term in X^n of $1 + XC(X)^2$ is $c(0)$ for $n = 0$ and if not it is the coefficient of the term in X^{n-1} of $C(X)^2$, i.e. $c(0)c(n-1) + c(1)c(n-2) + \ldots + c(n-2)c(1) + c(n-1)c(0)$. Hence, the recurrence relation that Catalan numbers obey:

$$c(n) = c(0)c(n-1) + c(1)c(n-2) + \ldots + c(n-1)c(0)$$

for $n > 0$, with the initial condition $c(0) = 1$.[4]

9.5. Generating function of the $C_{2n}^{\,n}$ and Catalan numbers

Now we are interested in words $2n$ long based on the two letters ↗ and ↘, with as many ↗ as ↘, which means that we are talking about paths from (0, 0) to $(2n, 0)$ in a square network (see Figure 9.7).

---

3. If we want to get the generating function associated with the number of ranges $N = 2n$ long, we replace a with z and b with z, hence $C(z) = \frac{1-\sqrt{1-4z^2}}{2z^2}$ where the coefficient of the term in z^{2n} is $c(n)$.

4. This can also be found directly. Let us classify the $c(n)$ mountain ranges $2n$ long according to their first mountain (the one on the left). There are those whose first mountain is 2 long, numbering $c(0)$, and which is followed by mountain ranges $2(n - 1)$ long numbering $c(n - 1)$. There are $c(0)\,c(n - 1)$ of them. Then there are those whose first mountain is 4 long, followed by mountain ranges $2(n - 2)$ long, numbering $c(1)\,c(n - 2)$, and so on and so forth until the mountain ranges are made up of a single mountain $2n$ long numbering $c(n - 1)c(0)$, hence: $c(n) = c(0)\,c(n-1) + c(1)\,c(n-2) + \ldots + c(n-1)\,c(0)$.

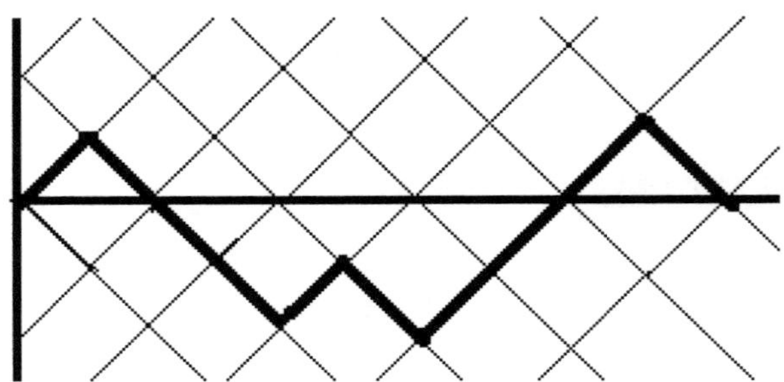

Figure 9.7. *Word with as many ascents as descents*

We know that there are C_{2n}^{n} paths. Let us consider the generating function $F(X)$ associated with the sequence (u_n) with $u_n = C_{2n}^{n}$, i.e.:

$$F(X) = \Sigma\, C_{2n}^{n}\, X^n$$

Let us specify that coefficient X^n is the number of words with n pairs of ↗ and ↘, and that the corresponding words are $2n$ letters long. We want to show that:

$$F(X) = 1 / \sqrt{1-4X}$$

With the direct calculation being laborious, we now provide another way to arrive at this result. Let us go back to the words of any length defined above. They form a language F.

Let us classify the words according to the primitive word that they start at. Let us recall here that a primitive word is a word that goes from altitude 0 to the first return to altitude 0. This primitive word is either a mountain ↗ ^{C}↘ or an inverted mountain ↘ $\underline{C}$↗ (with valleys beneath 0 level), C designating the language of mountain ranges, and $\underline{C}$ being this same language but with its two letters inverted.

Language F obeys the relation:

$$F = 1 + \searrow \underline{C} \nearrow F + \nearrow^{C} \searrow F, \text{ with } C = 1 + \nearrow^{C} \searrow C$$

As we are only interested in counting these words, let us return all commutatives and replace each ↗↘ (or ↘↗) pair with X, which enables us to assimilate C and $\underline{C}$. We get:

$$F(X) = 1 + 2X\, C(X)\, F(X),$$

from which we remove:

$$F(X) = 1 / (1 - 2X\,C(X)) \text{ with } C(X) = (1 - \sqrt{1-4X}\,) / 2X,$$

hence:

$$F(X) = 1 / \sqrt{1-4X}\ ^{5}$$

9.6. Left factors of mountain ranges

Let us limit ourselves to routes located in the final plan delimited by the horizontal axis and the first bisector of the benchmark, starting from O and arriving at a point $B(N, X)$, and able to touch but not cross the horizontal axis. We get what can be considered as left factors (or beginnings) of mountain ranges (see Figure 9.8).

They are also words, all the beginnings of which have at least as many *a*s as *b*s. Let $a(N, X)$ be the number of these paths from O to $B(N, X)$ with $X \geq 0$ that can touch but not cross the horizontal axis passing through O. Let us add a diagonal line $O'O$ in front of them, with $O'(-1, -1)$.

There are as many paths from O to $B(N, X)$ able to touch but not cross the axis passing through O as there are paths from O' to B unable to touch or cross the horizontal axis, passing through O'.

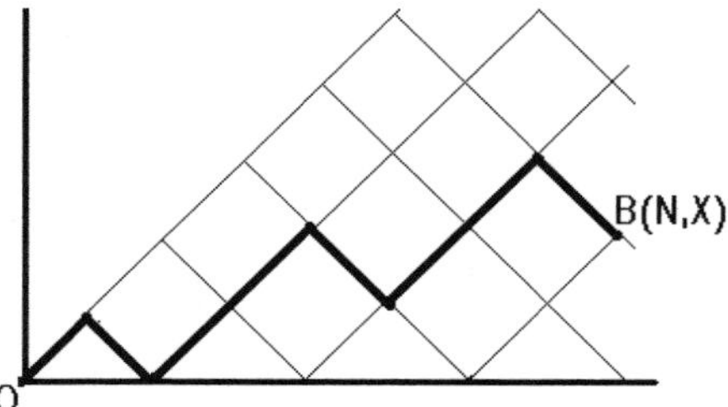

Figure 9.8. *A mountain chain left factor*

---

5. This formula enables us to find, once again, the explicit form of Catalan numbers. Actually, the formula is also expressed as: $-2 / \sqrt{1-4X} = -2\,(C_0^{\,0} + C_2^{\,1}X + C_4^{\,2}X^2 + \ldots)$. By integration, $\sqrt{1-4X} = 1 - 2\,(C_0^{\,0}X + C_2^{\,1}X^2 / 2 + C_4^{\,2}X^3 / 3 + \ldots)$. This result in the generating function of Catalan numbers is: $C(X) = (1 - \sqrt{1-4X}\,) / 2X$, hence $C(X) = C_0^{\,0} + (C_2^{\,1} / 2)\,X + (C_4^{\,2} / 3)\,X^2 + \ldots$ From this we deduce the explicit form of the Catalan number $c(n) = C_{2n}^{\,n} / (n + 1)$.

Furthermore, point B has $(N + 1, X + 1)$ coordinates in relation to point O'. Thanks to the formula obtained above (see ballot theorem, Chapter 6), we deduce the number of these paths, i.e.:

$$a(N, X) = \frac{X+1}{N+1} N(N+1, X+1) = \frac{X+1}{N+1} C_{N+1}^{\frac{N+X}{2}+1}$$

Let us turn to the language of these mountain range left factors. We can group them by categories according to the height of their end point B. Those that end at height 0 are the mountain ranges, and they have C as their language. Those that end at height 1 are of the form CaC. Those that end at height 2: $CaCaC$, etc.

Language G of these left factors is:

$$G = C + CaC + CaCaC + CaCaCaC + \ldots$$

$$= C(e + aC + aCaC + aCaCaC + \ldots)$$

$$= C(e + aC + (aC)^2 + (aC)^3 + \ldots)$$

$$= C / (1 - aC)$$

When we move on to the generating function $G(z)$ associated with the number of left factors that are N long, we get $G(z) = C(z) / (1 - z\, C(z))$ where we find the generating function $C(z)$ associated with the number of mountain ranges that are N long:

$$C(z) = \frac{1-\sqrt{1-4z^2}}{2z^2} = c(0) + c(1)z^2 + c(2)z^4 + c(3)z^6 + \ldots$$

The calculation gives:

$$G(z) = C(z) / (1 - zC(z)) = \frac{\sqrt{1+2z} - \sqrt{1-2z}}{2z\sqrt{1-2z}}$$

Aside from that, the generating functions associated with the number $a(N, X)$ of left factors N long ending at height X (with X and N of the same parity) are, for $X = 0$: $C(z)$, for $X = 1$: $z\, C(z)^2$, for $X = 2$: $z^2\, C(z)^3$, etc.

9.6.1. *Algorithm for obtaining the numbers of these left factors a(N, X)*

We take the final plan with the corresponding square grid. To have the number of paths (the shortest or even those that only use north-east and south-east directions) from O to a point B in the square grid, we proceed step by step, starting from O, taking that there is one path from O to O, then moving on to the neighboring point, and so on and so forth. Knowing the numbers on a vertical enables us to determine those on the following vertical. In the general case, the number of paths that arrive at a point is the sum of the numbers of paths coming from the two points on the vertical before (see Figure 9.9). Notably, when moving from an odd column to an even one:

$$a(2n, 2i) = a(2n-1, 2i-1) + a(2n-1, 2i+1) \text{ with } i \text{ non-null.}$$

In particular cases of points with only one neighbor, there are those of the first bisector of the benchmark where the 1s are passed down throughout, and on the other hand the points of the horizontal axis take the same values as the points of the line above, with a gap of one unit.

This diagonal square grid in the final plan is called a Catalan triangle.

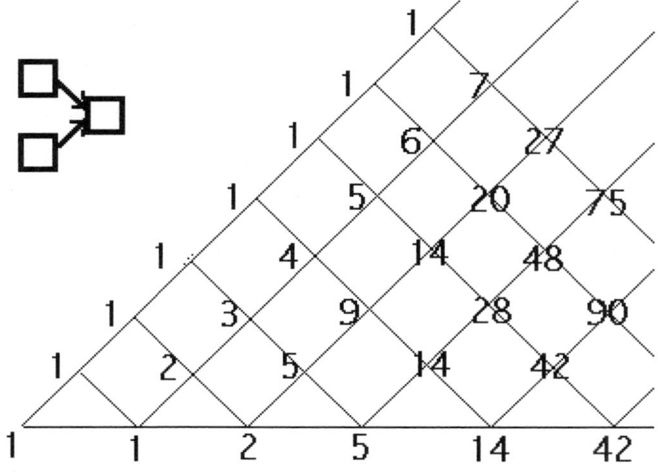

Figure 9.9. *Number of mountain range left factors, calculated step by step, from left to right*

9.6.2. *Calculation following the lines of Catalan's triangle*

We saw that the horizontal line 0 carries the numbers $a(N, 0)$, with N even, the generating function that is $C(z) = c(0) + c(1)z^2 + c(2)z^4 + \ldots$, i.e. $a(N, 0) = c(N / 2)$. In turn, line 1 corresponds to the generating function:[6]

$$zC(z)^2 = (C(z) - 1) / z = c(1)z + c(2)z^3 + c(3)z^5 + \ldots,$$

where the term in z^k corresponds to the abscissa k on line 1.

In the general case, line n corresponds to the generating function:

$$z^n C(z)^{n+1} = z^n C(z)^{n-1} C^2(z) = z^n C(z)^{n-1} (C(z) - 1) / z^2 = z^{n-1} C(z)^n / z - z^{n-2} C(z)^{n-1}.$$

This means that the numbers of line n are obtained by taking the terms of line $n - 1$ and subtracting the terms of line $n - 2$ from them with a gap of one notch:

on line 0: 1

on line 1: 1

on line 2: 1 -1 $c(1) - c(0) = 0$, then $c(2) - c(1) = 1$, then $c(3) - c(2)$, etc.

on line 3: 1 -2 $c(2) - 2c(1) = 0$, $c(3) - 2c(2) = 1$, $c(4) - 2c(3)$, etc.

on line 4: 1 -3 1 $c(3) - 3c(2) + c(1) = 0$, $c(4) - 3c(3) + c(2) = 1$, etc.

on line 5: 1 -4 3 $c(4) - 4c(3) + 3c(2) = 0$, $c(5) - 4c(4) + 3c(3) = 1$, etc.

on line 6: 1 -5 6 -1 $c(5) - 5c(4)+6c(3) - c(2)= 0$, $c(6) - 5c(5)+6c(4) - c(3)= 1$

The rule of passage is the following: to get the coefficients of line n, we take those of line $n - 1$ and minus those of line $n - 2$ shifted one notch to the right. For example, the coefficients of line 7 are obtained by:

```
   1 -5  6 -1
     -1  4 -3
 = 1 -6 10 -4
```

If we simply take the sequence of terms in line n starting from the 1 on the side at 45° of Catalan's triangle, the generating function is simply C^{n+1}. The generating functions of successive lines are therefore C, C^2, C^3, etc., as indicated in Figure 9.10.

6. Let us recall that the generating function $C(z)$ verifies the equation $C(z) = 1 + z^2C(z)^2$.

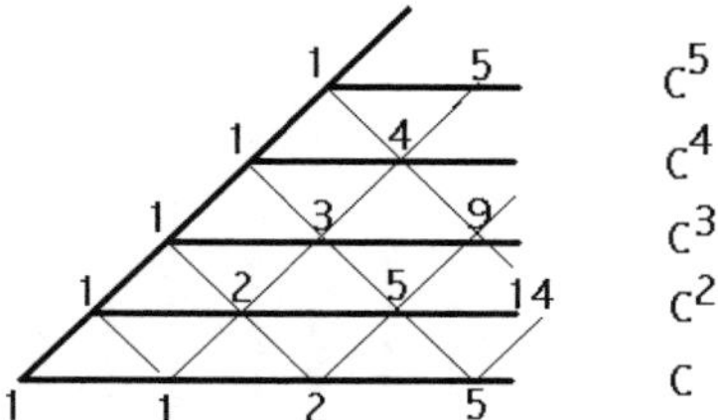

Figure 9.10. *Generating functions of lines*

9.6.3. *Calculations based on the columns of the Catalan triangle*

Each vertical of Catalan's triangle is characterized by its abscissa N (see Figure 9.11). The sum of the numbers in each column is equal to the number of routes in the final plan that can touch but not cross the horizontal axis, and that are of length N. It is the sum of the numbers $a(N, X)$ for a given N, where the values of X vary two by two between 0 and N. This can also be seen as the number of mountain chain left factors that are N long. From column 0, we find successively:

1, 1, 2, 3, 6, 10, 20, 35, 70, …

Above we have shown that this sum is C_{2n}^{n} for the even columns of abscissa $2n$, and $\frac{1}{2}C_{2n}^{n}$ for the odd columns of abscissa $2n - 1$.[7]

---

7. This can be found directly. When we move from an odd column (odd N) to the following even one, the sum doubles. Actually, each element $a(N, X)$ of an odd column is found twice in the following even column, at heights $X + 1$ and $X - 1$. It is almost the same when moving from an even column to an odd one, except for the element at height 0 (and which is equal to $c(N/2)$) which is only found once at height 1 in the following column. Therefore the sum doubles, on the condition that it is reduced by $c(N / 2)$. Let s_n be the sum of the $a(2n, X)$ for column $2n$. When moving from one even column to the following even one, we get the recurrence relation $s_{n+1} = 4s_n - 2c_n$, with $s_0 = 1$. The generating function $S(x)$ associated with this sequence (s) verifies $4xS(x) - S(x) = -1 + 2xC(x)$, where C is the generating function of the Catalan numbers. From it, we deduce that $S(x) = 1/\sqrt{1-4x}$, which is the generating function of the C_{2n}^{n} sequence. Finally $\sum_{i=0}^{n} a(2n,2i) = C_{2n}^{n}$. As the sum doubles when going from an odd column to an even one, we get $(1/2)\, C_{2n}^{n}$ for column $2n - 1$.

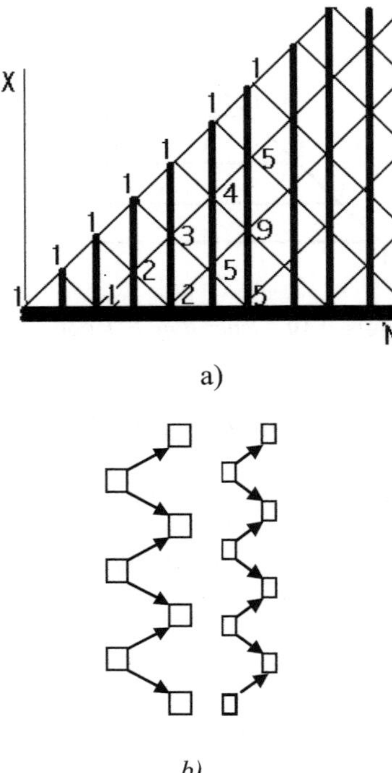

a)

b)

Figure 9.11. *a) Columns of the Catalan triangle; and b) passage from an odd column to an even one (left), and from an even column to an odd one (right)*

Another result is the following: *the sum of the squares of elements of column N is* $c(N)$. Actually, let us consider the $c(N)$ mountain ranges that are $2N$ long, and let us divide them up according to their left factor from 0 to N, and their right factor from N to $2N$. In each point $B(N, X)$ of the middle column N, there are $a(N, X)$ left factors that end up at B. For reasons of evident symmetry, there are as many right factors. There are hence $a(N, X)^2$ ranges passing through point B. Therefore:

$$\sum_X a(N,X)^2 = c(N)$$

9.6.4. *Average value of the height reached by left factors*

Let us take the column of abscissa $N = 2n$. The sum of the heights reached by all the left factors of the mountain ranges on this column is:

$$h(n) = \sum_{i=1}^{n} 2i\ a(2n, 2i)$$

To get the average height corresponding to this column $2n$, we will divide $h(n)$ by the number of paths $C_{2n}{}^{n}$.

We verify that when moving from an odd column to an even column the weighted sum doubles,[8] and in moving from an even column to an odd column the weighted sum doubles, on the condition that $c(n)$ is added. From it we deduce the recurrence formula:

$$h(n + 1) = 4h(n) + 2c_n, \text{ with } h(0) = 0$$

The generating function $H(x)$ associated with sequence (h) verifies:

$$H(x)\,(1 - 4x) = 2xC(x) = 1 - \sqrt{1-4x}$$

and:

$$H(x) = \frac{1}{1-4x} - \frac{1}{\sqrt{1-4x}}$$

which leads to:

$$h(n) = 2^{2n} - C_{2n}{}^{n}$$

The average height is: $h(n) / C_{2n}{}^{n} = 2^{2n} / C_{2n}{}^{n} - 1$.

When n tends to infinity, it tends to infinity as $\sqrt{n}$.

NOTE 9.1.– Now let us consider the paths in the background that do not touch the horizontal axis after leaving O. All we have to do for this is to add a diagonal path above the left factors of length $2n$, hence the height weighted by the altitudes:

---

8. Curiously, just as the number of paths doubled from an odd column to an even column, the number of paths weighted by the heights attained also doubles. If the successive numbers on an odd column starting from the bottom are $u_1, u_3, u_5, \ldots$, hence the weighted sum $1u_1 + 3u_3 + 5u_5 + \ldots$, on the following even column we get: $0u_1 + 2(u_1 + u_3) + 4(u_3 + u_5) + 6(u_5 + u_7) + \ldots = 2u_1 + 6u_3 + 10u_5 + \ldots$, which is double what there was in the odd column.

$$h'(n) = \sum_{i=0}^{n} (2i+1)\, a(2n, 2i)$$

We check that in this case this sum doubles when moving from an even column to an odd one as well as from an odd column to an even one. Hence:

$$h'(n) = 2^{2n}$$

The corresponding paths are $2n+1$ long and the average height attained is $2^{2n} / C_{2n}^{\ n}$.

9.6.5. *Calculations based on the second bisector of the Catalan triangle*

Still in the final plan, on the gridline with gradient -1 passing through point $(2n,0)$, the sum of elements $a(N,X)$ is equal to $c(n+1)$. Each element of this line makes the deduction of mountain ranges $2(n+1)$ long, including a precise number of mountains where:

$a(2n, 0)$ is the number of ranges with one mountain;

$a(2n-1, 1)$ the number of ranges with two mountains;

$a(2n-2, 2)$ that of ranges with three mountains;

...

$a(n, n)$ that of ranges with $n+1$ mountains.

Therefore $a(N,X)$ includes the number of mountain ranges that are $N+X+2$ long with $X+1$ mountains.

First, let us show that the sum of elements of a 45° line, numbered $n+1$ and ending at point $(2n,0)$ is equal to $c(n+1)$, notably:

$a(0, 0) = c(1)$ on line 1, then

$a(1, 1) + a(2, 0) = c(2)$ on line 2, then

$a(2, 2) + a(3, 1) + a(4, 0) = c(3)$ on line 3, etc.

To do this, let us take point (n,n) above line $n+1$, with $a(n,n)=1$. From there let us take the sum of the $j+1$ first elements of this line, i.e.:

$$s(j) = a(n, n) + a(n+1, n-1) + \ldots + a(n+j, n-j),$$

and let us show that:

$$s(j) = a(n + j + 1, n - j + 1),$$

for all j included between 0 and $n-1-1$ (see Figure 9.12).

This is done by recurrence. It is true for $s(0)=1$ and if we assume that it is true for a certain row j, it remains true at row $j+1$ because:

$$\begin{aligned} s(j+1) &= s(j) + a(n + j + 1, n - j - 1) \\ &= a(n + j + 1, n - j + 1) + a(n + j + 1, n - j - 1) \\ &= a(n + j + 2, n - j) \end{aligned}$$

Figure 9.12. *Calculation of sum* $s(j)$

Applying this formula for j = n, we get the number $a(2n+1,1) = a(2n+2,0) = c(n+1)$ as the sum of the elements of line $n+1$ at 45°. This creates the generating function associated with the sum of the elements of lines at 45°, numbered starting from 1 (see Figure 9.13), to be:

$$C(X) - 1 = XC^2 = c(1)X + c(2)X^2 + c(3)X^3 + \ldots$$ [9]

9. We also have another property associated with the weighted sum on a diagonal line. Again, let us take line $n + 1$, and let us make the sum: $s(0)+s(1)+s(2)+\ldots+s(n)= a(n+1,n+1)+a(n+2,n)+\ldots+a(2n+1,1)$, as we saw, i.e. the sum of the elements of the following line $\boldsymbol{n} + 2$, except the last one $a(2n+2,0)$. But we also get, by definition of partial sums, $s(j)$: $s(0) + s(1) + s(2) + \ldots + s(n) = (n + 1)\, a(n, n) + n\, a(n + 1, n - 1) + (n - 1)\, a(n + 2, n - 2) + \ldots + 1\, a(2n, 0)$. Finally the sum of the terms of a line, weighted by their altitude increased by 1, is equal to the sum of the terms of the following line up to the one before last. We will use this property below.

Now, let us show more specifically that the elements of line number n at 45° classify mountain ranges $2n$ long according to their number of mountains. This property is shown by recurrence. It is true at the start. Next let us assume that on a certain line, the $a(N,X)$ in each of the points (N,X) of this line exhaustively include mountain ranges based on their number of mountains, with the total sum being the corresponding Catalan number. Let us move on to the following line, by applying the rule of passage in a constructive way .

We start from the highest and leftmost point of the new line and add an elementary mountain ∧ to the corresponding range of the previous line. We go, for example, from ∧∧∧ to ∧∧∧∧ (see Figure 9.14 when moving from line 3 to line 4).

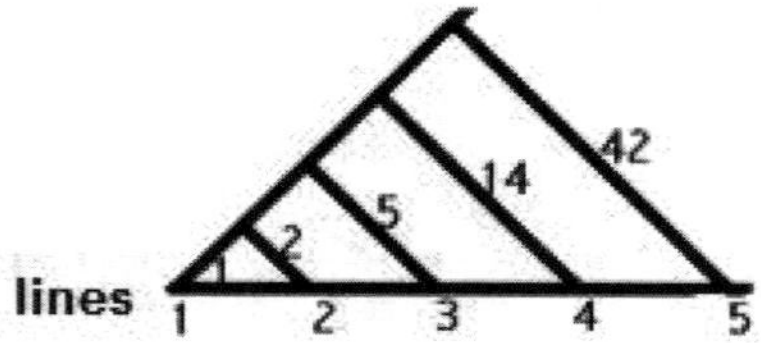

Figure 9.13. *The generating function of the sum of the elements of lines at 45° starting from line 1 is* $C - 1 = XC^2$

There is always a single range at this highest point of the line. We exercise the same rule for each passage from a point of a line to a point of the next, adding ∧ on the right. For now, the new line number $n + 1$ has as many mountain ranges as the one before. Note that the lowest point of the new line has no ranges in the current state. Then, when we move from one element of the new line to the next by going down on this same line, we construct new ranges. To do this, we take the mountain ranges drawn at a point, and proceed in the following way: we suppress a mountain by taking the first valley at ground level starting from the right, and we replace it with which refers to raising the right part of the mountain ranges by one notch. This gives a new range on the following point to the bottom right of the previous one. From one point to the next of the same diagonal line, mountain ranges are converted into as many new mountains with the same length. The total of the mountain ranges thus obtained at a point corresponds exactly to the rule of passage of numbers $a(N,X)$. These ranges are all distinct – each one in its category – as they do not end the same way (some end in ∧ and others do not). We continue in this way until the last element of the new line, knowing that this last element is only constructed from the one before last. All the mountains obtained are different, and we get them all because the total is $c(n+1)$.

The procedure is illustrated in Figure 9.14, with the passage from line 3 to line 4, and the results of the preceding algorithm are given in Figure 9.15 for mountain ranges that are $2n = 10$ long.

9.6.6. *Average number of mountains for mountain ranges*

We will see that the average number of mountains (or primitive blocks) included in mountain ranges $2n$ long is $3n/(n+2)$.

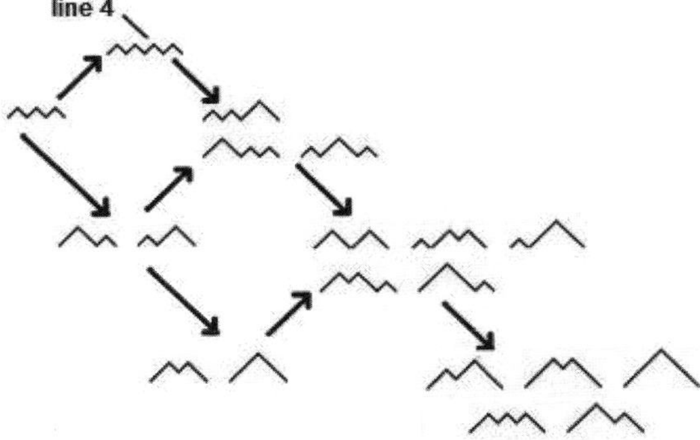

Figure 9.14. *Construction procedure for obtaining mountain ranges from one line at 45° to the next*

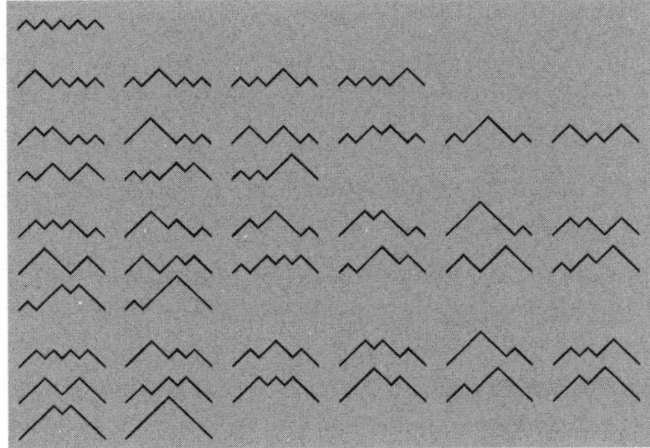

Figure 9.15. *Mountain ranges 2n = 10 long, classified based on the number of mountains, from five to one*

To do this, let us take line $n + 1$, the sum of whose terms includes the number of mountain ranges $2(n+1)$ long. We see that its initial term $a(n, n) = 1$ includes the number of ranges with $n+1$ mountains, that the next term $a(n+1, n-1)$ includes the number of ranges with n mountains, and so on and so forth until the final term $a(2n, 0)$ including the number of ranges with only one mountain.

The quantity $(n+1)a(n,n)+n\ a(n+1,n-1)+...1+a(2n,0)$ therefore includes exactly the number of mountains in all the mountain ranges $(2n+1)$ long. But we saw earlier that this weighted sum was equal to the sum of terms of the following line, except the last, i.e.: $a(n+1,n+1)+a(n+2,n)+...+a(2n+1,1)$. We also know that this sum of terms is equal to $(2n+2,2)$. Finally, we know that on the horizontal line at height 2 we have $a(2n+2,2)=c(n+2)-c(n+1)$. We have just obtained the cumulation of the number of mountains that all chains $2(n+1)$ long have. Finally, the average number of mountains for ranges $2n$ long is:

$$(\mathrm{c}(n + 1) - \mathrm{c}(n)) / \mathrm{c}(n) = \mathrm{c}(n + 1) / \mathrm{c}(n) - 1$$

$$= (2n + 2)(2n + 2) / ((n + 2)(n + 1)) -1$$

$$= 3n / (n + 2)$$

For example, the 42 mountain ranges that are 10 long have on average $15/7=2.1$ mountains. When n increases indefinitely, a mountain range tends to have three mountains on average.

9.7. Number of peaks of mountain ranges

Let us take the $c(n)$ mountain ranges $2n$ long and classify them according to their number of peaks, i.e. patterns of the form ↗↘, with $N(n,k)$ being the number of mountain ranges $2n$ long with k peaks, and P_k being the language of ranges with k peaks.

For example, going back to the notations in section 9.4:

$$P_1 = ab + aabb + aaabbb + \ldots$$

$$P_2 = abab + aababb + aabbab + abaabb + \ldots$$

and we agree that $P_0 = 1$ (the empty word). Let us go back to the decomposition of mountains as a function of their initial mountain, which already gave us $C = 1 + aCbC$. We now find:

$$P_k = abP_{k-1} + aP_1bP_{k-1} + \ldots + aP_kbP_0$$

$$= abP_{k-1} + \sum_{j=1}^{k} aP_jbP_{k-j}$$

for $k \geq 1$ and $P_0 = 1$.

Giving up all commutatives and converting *ab* into *x*, this gives the generating functions of $N(n+k)$ for fixed *k*, for example:

$$P_1(x) = x + x^2 + x^3 + \ldots$$

$$P_2(x) = x^2 + 3x^3 + \ldots$$

In the general case:

$$P_k(x) = N(0, k) + N(1, k)\mathrm{x} + N(2, k)\, x^2 + N(3, k)x^3 + \ldots$$

$$= \sum_{n \geq 0} N(n,k)x^n$$

The relation above becomes:

$$P_k(x) = xP_{k-1}(x) + \sum_{j=1}^{k} xP_j(x)P_{k-j}(x)$$

This enables us to get generating functions step by step, using $P_0(x) = 1$, notably:

$$P_1(x) = x + x\,P_1(x), \text{ i.e. } P_1(x) = x\,/\,(1 - x) = \sum_{n \geq 1} x^n \text{ and } N(n, 1) = 1$$

then:

$$P_2(x) = xP_1(x) + xP_1^{\,2}(x) + xP_2(x),$$
i.e.: $P_2(x) = x^2 / (1\text{-}x)^3$ and $N(n, 2) = C_n^{\,2}$,

and:

$$P_3(x) = xP_2(x) + xP_1(x)P_2(x) + xP_2(x)P_1(x) + xP_3(x),$$

hence:

$$P_3(x) = x^3 (1 + x) / (1 - x)^5 \text{ and } N(n,3) = C_n^{\ 4} + C_{n+1}^{\ 4}$$

We verify that we also have:

$$N(n, 3) = C_n^{\ 3} C_n^{\ 2} / n$$

In the general case, T.V. Narayana showed in 1955 that:

$$N(n, k) = C_n^{\ k} C_n^{\ k-1} / n$$

We also call $N(n,k)$ Narayana numbers.

Now let us introduce the generating function with two variables $F(x,t)$ associated with the numbers $N(n,k)$, where the coefficient of the term in $x^n t^k$ is exactly $N(n, k)$.

By definition:

$$F(t,x) = P_0(x) + P_1(x)\, t + P_2(x)\, t^2 + P_3(x)\, t^3 + \ldots$$

To find the equation verified by F, let us calculate:

$$F^2(x,t) = \sum_{k\geq 0} t^k \sum_{j=0}^{k} P_j(x)P_{k-j}(x) = \sum_{k\geq 0} P_k(x)t^k + \sum_{k\geq 1} t^k \sum_{j=1}^{k} P_j(x)P_{k-j}(x)$$

Using the recurrence relation on P_k, i.e.:

$$x\sum_{j=1}^{k} P_j(x)P_{k-j}(x) = P_k(x) - xP_{k-1}(x),$$

we find:

$$x\, F^2(x, t) = x\, F(x, t) + x\, (F(x, t) - 1) - x\, t\, F(x, t),$$

hence the equation:

$$xF^2 + (xt - x - 1)F + 1 = 0,$$

with the following as the only valid solution:

$$F(x, t) = \frac{-(xt - x - 1) - \sqrt{(xt - x - 1)^2 - 4x}}{2x}$$

Note that by making $t = 1$, we find $F(x,1) = C(x)$ because it is the generating function associated with the number of mountain ranges classified according to their length.

9.8. The Catalan mountain range, its area and height

9.8.1. *Number of mountain ranges 2n long passing through a given point on the square grid*

From counting routes in the final plan, we can find out the number of mountain ranges of a given length passing through the points concerned on the square grid.

Let us consider all mountain ranges of the same length ($2n$). They are all located in an isosceles rectangular triangle in the square grid, $OO'B$ (see Figure 9.16).

Let us take a point $M(k,x)$ inside this triangle, with $k \leq 2$ where k and x have the same parity. The number of left parts of mountains between O and M is $a(k,x)$. The number of right parts between M and O' is also, by symmetry, the number of paths from O to M', with M' being symmetrical to M in relation to the vertical axis passing through B, i.e. $a(2n-k,x)$. The number of mountain ranges $2n$ long passing through $M(k,x)$ or through $M'(2n-k,x)$ is: $a(k,x)a(2n-k,x)$. Figure 9.17 gives the results obtained for $2n = 8$.

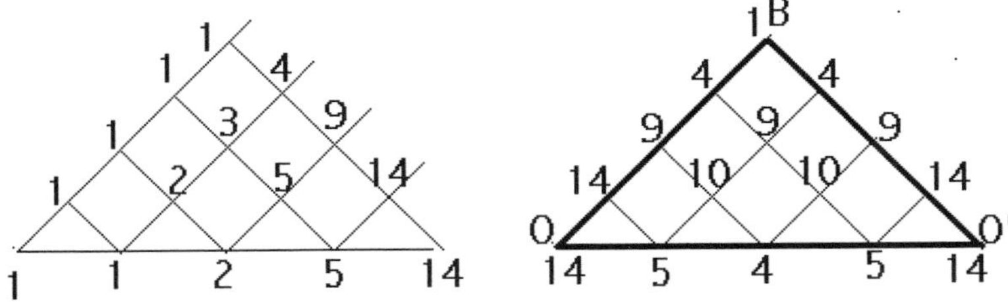

Figure 9.16. *Passage from routes in the final plan, on the left, to mountain ranges that are 2n long passing through the points of triangle OO'B on the right. Here 2n=8*

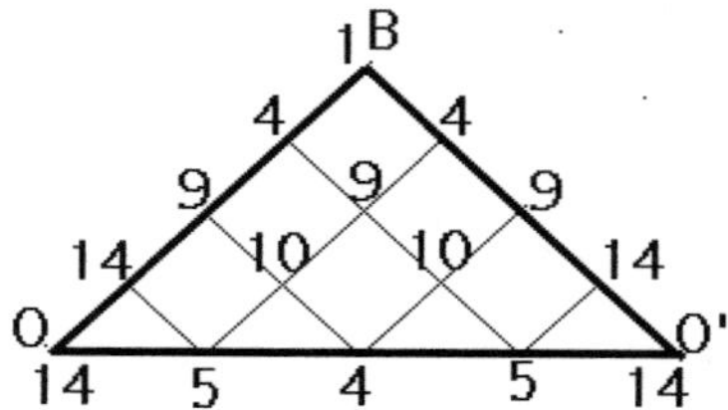

Figure 9.17. *Number of ranges that are 8 long passing through each point of triangle OO'B*

Taking the sum of these numbers multiplied by their height, column by column in triangle *OO'B*, we get the sum of all mountain ranges $2n$ long based on their height. For example, for $2n = 8$ (see Figure 9.17) we find:

0 14 18 22 22 22 18 14 0

namely, the altitudes of the mountain that is the sum of the 14 mountain ranges that are 8 long. By dividing this sum by the number of ranges, we will get the average mountain range, which we call the Catalan mountain range (see Figure 9.18).

Figure 9.18. *The average mountain (8 long) with maximum height 22 / 14 = 1.571*

9.8.2. *Sum of the elements of lines in triangle OO'B of mountain ranges 2n long*

Let us begin with the lowest line, *OO'*. We know that the numbers of the corresponding line for paths in the final plan, namely 1, 1, 2, 5, 14, …, have the generating function $C(X) = c(0) + c(1)X + c(2)X^2 + \ldots$ associated with Catalan numbers. On the other hand, the sum of the numbers:

$$s(n) = \sum_{i=0}^{n} a(2i, 0)\, a(2n - i, 0)$$

from line OO' $2n$ long has the generating function C^2, so that:

$C^2(X) = s(0) + s(1)X + s(2)X^2 + \ldots$, with $C^2 = (C - 1)/z$,

hence: $s(n) = c(n + 1)$

Therefore, in the example above:

$$s(4) = c(5) = 42,$$

and we have 14 + 5 + 4 + 5 + 14 = 42.

We do the same for each line. Let us recall that generating functions of successive lines are $C, C^2, C^3, C^4, \ldots$ starting from the side at 45° of the Catalan triangle. On line x, terms of the form $u(n,x) = \sum_{i=x}^{n} a(2i,x)\,a(2n-1,x)$ have the square of the preceding generating functions as a generating function:

$$C(X)^{2x+2} = u(x,x) + u(x+1,x)X + u(x+2,x)X^2 + \ldots,\ \text{or if you prefer:}$$

$$X^x\, C(X)^{2x+2} = u(x,x)X^x + u(x+1,x)X^{x+1} + u(x+2,x)X^{x+2} + \ldots$$

where the term X^k has the sum of elements of line x in triangle $OO'B$ with $OO' = 2k$ as the coefficient.

Line by line, starting from line 0, this gives:

$$C^2, XC^4, X^2C^6, X^3C^8, X^4C^{10}, \ldots$$

9.8.3. *Sum of numbers in triangle OO'B*

The sum $S(n)$ of all the preceding numbers taken in triangle $OO'B$, with $OO' = 2n$, has the sum of the preceding generating functions:

$$C^2 + XC^4 + X^2C^6 + X^3C^8 + \ldots = C^2(1 + XC^2 + X^2C^4 + \ldots) = \frac{C^2}{1 - XC^2} = \frac{C}{\sqrt{1-4X}}$$

as the generating function. To do this we used the fact that $C\sqrt{1-4X} = 1 - XC^2$ and that;

$$\frac{C}{\sqrt{1-4X}} = C + 2XC'.$$ [10]

10. Demonstration of these formulae: we know that $C = (1 - \sqrt{1-4X}\,) / (2X)$, hence: $\sqrt{1-4X} = 1 - 2XC$, and $C\sqrt{1-4X} = C - 2XC^2 = 1 - XC^2$ because $C = 1 + XC^2$. On the other hand, by deriving $C = 1 + XC^2$, $C' = C^2 + 2XCC'$, $C'(1 - 2XC) = C^2$, $C'\sqrt{1-4X} = C^2$, $C/\sqrt{1-4X} = C'/C = C + 2XC'$.

$$C^2 + XC^4 + X^2C^6 + X^3C^8 + \ldots = \sum_{k\geq 0} (2k+1)\,c(k)\,X^k$$

$$= 1 + 3X + 10X^2 + 35X^3 + 126\,X^4 + \ldots$$

We can check that in triangle *OO'B* drawn above with $n=4$ (see Figure 9.17), the sum of the numbers, taken line by line, is:

$$14 + 5 + 4 + 5 + 14 + 14 + 10 + 10 + 14 + 9 + 9 + 9 + 4 + 4 + 1 = 126$$

9.8.4. *Average area of a mountain 2n long*

The area of a mountain range is equal to the sum of the heights of each point with the integer coordinates of the range (see Figure 9.19). If we consider all the mountains or mountain ranges that have the same length, this leads the sum of their areas to be equal to the sum of the numbers of triangle *OO'B* multiplied by their height.

For mountain ranges $2n$ long, the generating function giving the sum of their areas $A(n)$ is:

$$XC^4 + 2X^2C^6 + 3X^3C^8 + 4X^4C^{10} + \ldots = XC^4(1 + 2XC^2 + 3X^2C^4 + 4X^3C^6 + \ldots)$$

$$= \frac{XC^4}{(1-XC^2)^2} = \frac{XC^2}{1-4X} = \frac{C-1}{1-4X}$$

$$= (X + 2X^2 + 5X^3 + 14X^4 + \ldots)(1 + 4X + 16X^2 + 64X^3 + \ldots)$$

$$= X + 6X^2 + 29X^3 + 130X^4 + 562X^5 + \ldots$$

but we also have:

$$\frac{C-1}{1-4X} = \frac{1}{1-4X} - \frac{2-C}{1-4X}$$

and

$$\frac{2-C}{1-4X} = \frac{C}{\sqrt{1-4X}} = \frac{C}{1-2XC} = C + 2XC'.$$

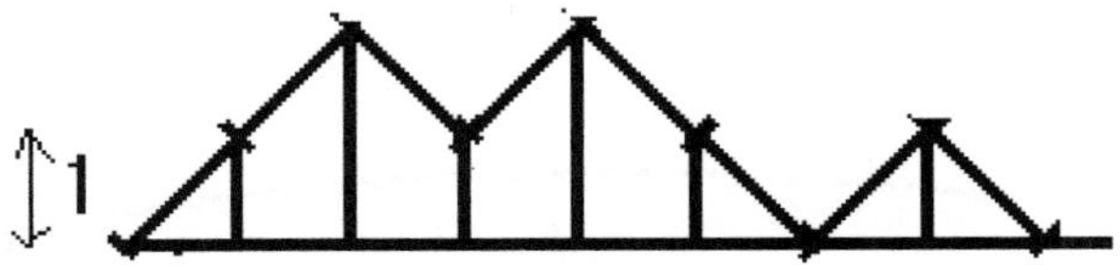

Figure 9.19. *Calculation of the area of a mountain range by adding up the vertical bars, here 1 + 2 + 1 + 2 + 1 + 1 = 8*

We deduce from this that the sum of the areas for mountain ranges $2n$ long is:

$A(n) = 4^n - (2n + 1)\, c(n)$ [11]

Their average area is:

$A(n) / c(n) = 4^n / c(n) - 2n - 1$

Thanks to Stirling formula we verify that for a large n, we have $c(n) \approx \dfrac{4^n}{\sqrt{\pi}\, n\sqrt{n}}$.

Therefore for a large n, the average area is of order $n^{3/2}$. If we return to a basic unit length ($2n$) of the mountain ranges, we divide the previous result by $4n^2$. The average area returned to a basic unit length is $n^{-1/2}$, and tends towards 0 for infinite n.

Hence this surprising result: the Catalan mountain range, average of all mountain ranges $2n$ long, returned to a unit length, tends to become flat when n increases

---

11. Instead of mountain ranges, let us take mountains of the same ($2n$). Line OO' is now at altitude 1, and OO' measures $2n' = 2(n-1)$. When we take successive lines of triangle $OO'B$, line OO' is at height 1, and the sum of numbers of $OO'B$ multiplied by their height has the generating function: $C^2 + 2zC^4 + 3z^2C^6 + 4z^3C^8 + \ldots = C^2(1 + 2zC^2 + 3z^2C^4 + 4z^3C^6 + \ldots) = \dfrac{C^2}{(1-zC^2)^2} = \dfrac{1}{1-4z} = \sum_{n\geq 0} 4^n z^n$ using the fact that $1 - zC^2 = C\sqrt{1-4z}$. The sum of the areas of mountains $2n$ long is equal to $4^{n'}$, i.e. 4^{n-1}. This result is simpler than that of mountain ranges. Now if we take mountain ranges $2n$ long and we raise them one notch we get mountains $2(n+1)$ long, the average area of which is $4^n / c(n)$. By removing the area at the base of height 1, the average area of mountain ranges is therefore $4^n / c(n) - (2n + 1)$ and we find we have already obtained the formula.

towards infinity (see Figure 9.20). The average of mountain ranges bristling with peaks is only a "dismal plain".

Figure 9.20. *Catalan mountain range for $2n = 34$, average of mountain ranges 34 long, maximum height therefore reaching 11% of the length*

9.8.5. *Shape of the average mountain range*

We are going to check that the curve associated with the sum of all mountain ranges $2n$ long corresponds to an increasing and concave function from 0 to n. Let us take the length $2n$. When we have a column with abscissa k (with k between 1 and n, and $x \leq k$), the terms $a(k,x)$ are the numbers of left factors of mountain ranges, and they come from splitting up the $a(k-1,x)$ of the preceding column (with $x \leq k+1$). This enables us to carry out the countdown in each point of column k for rising and falling lines that end up at point (k,x).

Similarly, as we have seen, the $a(2n-k,x)$ with $x \leq k$ of column $2n-k$ gives the numbers of right factors of the mountain ranges and comes from splitting the $a(2n-k-1,x)$ of the preceding column (with $x \leq k+1$), which by symmetry enables the countdown of rising or falling lines to the right of each point (k,x).

The junction of the ends of left factors and the beginnings of right factors gives four types of designs: the rising, the falling, the valleys, and the peaks.

The knowledge of the number of each one of these patterns at each point of the column of abscissa k enables us to obtain the variation in height of the sum of mountain ranges, on one hand between $k-1$ and k, as well as between k and $k+1$.

We will call these variations on either side of column k Δg and Δd. For example, for a rising line we have $\Delta g = 1$ and $\Delta d = 1$, and for a valley $\Delta g = -1$ and $\Delta d = 1$.

9.8.5.1. *Cases of even column k*

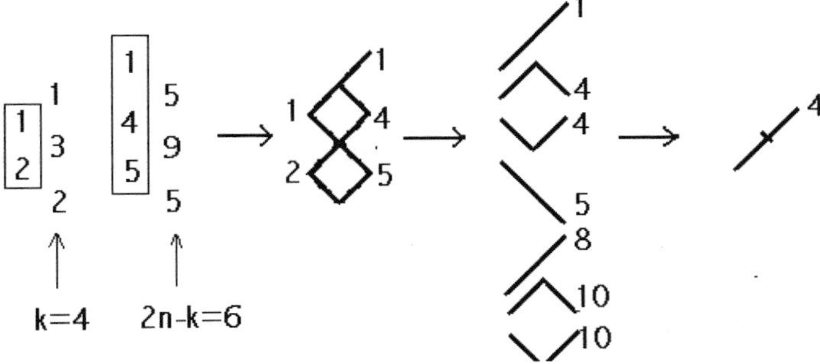

Figure 9.21. *Example: n = 5 and k = 4*

As the example in Figure 9.21 indicates, we get one segment with $\Delta g = \Delta d = 4$ on either side of abscissa k. It is the same in the general case, since each valley is offset by a peak due to the fact that ordinate x is greater than or equal to 1 for the odd columns $k - 1$ and $k + 1$. Only diagonal lines are left, hence $\Delta g = \Delta d$. For $k = 0$, the initial gradient of the sum of ranges is $c(n)$.

Then, each point of the even abscissa has a line between $k - 1$ and $k + 1$.

Finally, if n is even the central point $k = n$ assumes a horizontal plateau, because of the symmetry around this point (furthermore we can check it by taking column $k - 1$ twice).

9.8.5.2. *Case of odd columns*

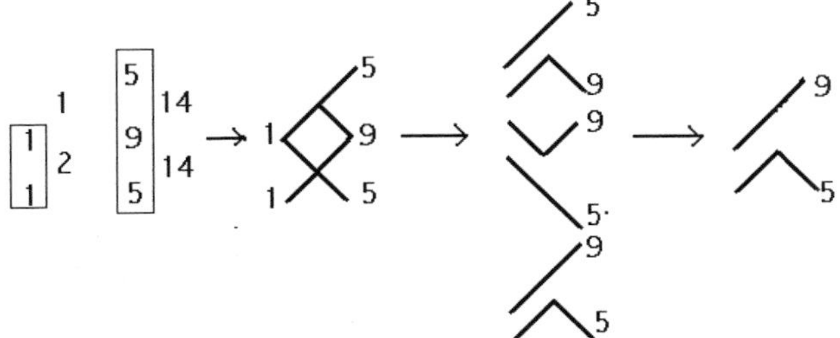

Figure 9.22. *Example: n=5 and k=3*

In the example in Figure 9.22, with $n = 5$ and $k = 3$, we end up with $\Delta g = 14$ and $\Delta d = 4$, i.e. $\Delta d - \Delta g = -10$.

In the general case, there is no longer offsetting of valleys and peaks. In addition to the diagonal lines, $c((k-1)/2)c((2n-k-1)/2)$ peaks are left, because of the presence of numbers in $x=0$. This proves that there is a negative gradient variation: $\Delta d - \Delta g = -2c((k-1)/2)c((2n-k-1)/2)$. Notably, for $k = n$, when n is odd, only $c((n-1)/2)^2$ peaks are left, which makes up the final gradient in n.

Therefore, in all cases, the gradient starts at $c(n)$ in order to arrive at the central point either with a null gradient or with a $c((n-1)/2))^2$ gradient, which is an insignificant value compared to $c(n)$. In the meantime it undergoes successive decreases. This proves that the corresponding function is increasing from 0 to n, while turning its concavity downwards. It is the same for the average mountain range, obtained by dividing the preceding result by the number $c(n)$. Its gradient continues to decrease from 1 to 0 or to $c((n-1)/2)^2/c(n)$ up to its central vertex.

9.8.6. *Height of the Catalan mountain range*

The results above enable us to determine the altitudes of the sum of the mountain ranges step by step, up to the maximum height. Let us take the example of ranges $2n=8$ long. We start at altitude 0, where the gradient on the right is $c(4)=14$. At the point of abscissa 1, the altitude is 14. We know that around this point there is a gradient variation of -2c(0) c(3) = -10. The gradient to the right of 1 is $14-10=4$, hence an altitude of 18 at the point of abscissa 2, then 22 at the point of abscissa 3, because we have a plateau around the points of the even abscissa.

Around point 3, the gradient variation is $-2c(1)c(2)=-4$, hence a gradient of 0 until the middle point of abscissa 4, and of altitude 22. This height $h_4=22$ is obtained by doing:

$$c(4) + 2(c(4) - 2c(0)\ c(3)) = 14 + 2 . 4$$

For mountain ranges $2n$ long, the sum of their heights at the middle n gives the maximum height h_n of the Catalan mountain $2n$ long. Using the preceding formulae on gradient changes, for even values of $n(n=2p)$ we find:

$$h_2 = c(0)c(1)$$

$$h_4 = 2(c(0)c(3) + 3c(1)c(2))$$

$$h_6 = 2(c(0)c(5) + 3c(1)c(4) + 5c(2)c(3))$$

$$h_8 = 2(c(0)c(7) + 3c(1)c(6) + 5c(2)c(5) + 7c(3)c(4))$$

and in the general case:

$$h_{2p} = 2\,(c(0)\,c(2p-1) + 3\,c(1)\,c(2p-2) + 5\,c(2)\,c(2p-3) + \ldots$$
$$+ (2k+1)\,c(k)\,c(2p-k-1) + \ldots + (2p-1)\,c(p-1)\,c(p))$$ [12]

If we plot the heights of mountain ranges in relation to level -1, which leads us to add 1 to the heights of each range and therefore $c(2p)$ to h_{2p}, this gives the heights:

$$h'_{2p} = 4(c(0)c(2p-1) + 2\,c(1)c(2p-2) + 3\,c(2)c(2p-3) + k\,c(k-1)c(2p-k)$$
$$+ \ldots + p\,c(p-1)c(p))$$

a simpler formula than the one above.

The formula changes slightly for odd values of $n\,(n = 2p+1)$ because in this case the summit of the Catalan mountain is a peak and not a plateau, like in the even n case, which adds an extra term:

$$h_{2p+1} = 3\,c(0)\,c(2p) + 7\,c(1)\,c(2p-1) + 11\,c(2)\,c(2p-2) + \ldots$$
$$+ (4k-1)\,c(k-1)\,c(2p-k+1) + \ldots$$
$$+ (4p-1)\,c(p-1)\,c(p+1) + (p+1)\,c(p)^2/2)$$

$$h'_{2p+1} = 4\,(c(0)\,c(2p) + 2\,c(1)\,c(2p-1) + 3\,c(2)\,c(2p-2) + \ldots$$
$$+ k\,c(k-1)\,c(2p-k+1) + \ldots + p\,c(p-1)\,c(p+1) + (p+1)\,c(p)^2/2)$$

---

12. Demonstration: for $n = 2p$, the rising line is $c(2p)$ for the first step. Next, we make the gradient variations intervene for each one of the odd ones, which gives:

$$h_{2p} = c(2p) + 2\,(c(2p) - 2c(0)c(2p\text{-}1)) + 2(\,c(2p) - 2c(0)c(2p\text{-}1) - 2c(1)c(2p\text{-}2)) + 2(c(2p)$$
$$- 2c(0)c(2p-1) - 2c(1)c(2p\text{-}2) - 2c(2)c(2p-3)) + \ldots + 2(c(2p) - 2c(0)c(2p-1)$$
$$- 2c(1)c(2p-2) - 2c(2)c(2p\text{-}3) - \ldots - 2c(p-2)c(p+1))$$
$$= (2p-1)c(2p) - 4\,(p-1)c(0)c(2p-1) + (p-2)c(1)c(2p-2) + (p-3)c(2)c(2p-3) + \ldots$$
$$+ 1c(p-2)c(p+1)).$$

By replacing $c(2p)$ with $2\big(c(0)c(2p-1) + c(1)c(2p-2) + \ldots + c(p-1)c(p)\big)$, what finally remains is:

$$h_{2p} = 2\,(\,c(0)c(2p-1) + 3c(1)c(2p-2) + 5c(2)c(2p-3) + \ldots + (2k+1)c(k)c(2p-k-1) + \ldots$$
$$+ (2p-1)c(p-1)c(p)\,).$$

The first terms of the sequence (h) from h_0 are:

0, 1, 2, 7, 22, 268, 971, 3470, ...

and those of the sequence (h'):

1, 2, 4, 12, 36, 120, 400, 1,400, 4,900, 17,640, ...

Chapter 10

Other Mountain Ranges

We have seen routes as well as mountain ranges based on two types of diagonal lines. We will now introduce variations, adding a third possibility: that of horizontal plateaus of 2 or 1 steps long.

10.1. Mountain ranges based on three lines 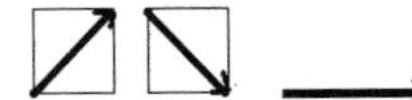

Let us denote the rising diagonal line $(1,1)$ by a, the falling diagonal line $(1,-1)$ by b and the horizontal line $(2,0)$ 2 steps long by c. The language of these mountain ranges is M. It verifies:

$$M = 1 + aMbM + cM$$

In this way we express that every mountain range is either the empty word, a mountain (aMb) joined to a mountain range or a horizontal line joined to a mountain range (cM). The ranges are therefore classified according to their initial primitive block. In a more restrictive way, we have a recurrence relation on the number $u(n)$ of these mountain ranges $2n$ long, classifying them according to their initial primitive block. It is either block ab that is 2 steps long, hence $u(n-1)$ mountain ranges behind this unique block, or it is the block 4 steps long starting with a and ending with b, hence $u(1)$ blocks, followed by $u(n-2)$ ranges $2n-4$ long, etc. The primitive block can also be reduced to line c, hence $u(n-1)$ ranges behind it. Finally:

$$u(n) = u(0)\,u(n-1) + u(1)\,u(n-2) + u(2)\,u(n-3) + \ldots + u(n-1)\,u(0) + u(n-1)$$
$$= u(n-1) + \sum_{k=0}^{n-1} u(k)u(n-1-k), \text{ with } u(0) = 1$$

Let us return to language M with all commutativity and replace ab or c with X. In the series $M(X)$ that we get, the coefficient of term X^n in the development of $M(X)$ is the number $u(n)$ of mountain ranges $2n$ long. We get:

$$M(X) = 1 + XM^2(X) + XM(X),$$

hence the equation:

$$XM^2 + (X-1)M + 1 = 0$$

The solution to this equation of the second degree is:

$$M(X) = (1 - X - \sqrt{1 - 6X + X^2}\,) / (2X)$$

The first terms of the sequence $u(n)$ are: 1, 2, 6, 22, 90, 394, …

We call them Schröder numbers.[1]

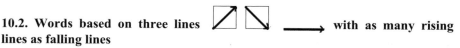

10.2. Words based on three lines 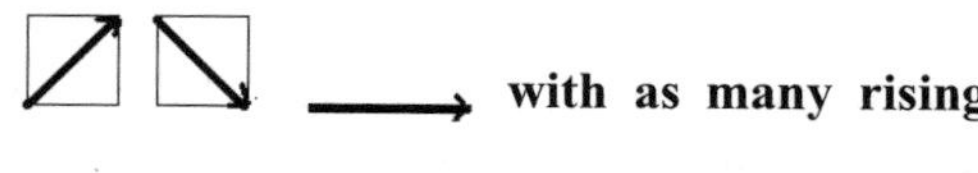 with as many rising lines as falling lines

Words of $2n$ characters start at $(0,0)$ and end at $(2n,0)$, but compared to the previous case they can now cross the horizontal axis and go below as well as above the axis (we are no longer talking about mountain ranges in the strict sense).

---

1. Let us indicate a restrictive variation where horizontal plateaus are forbidden at level 0. The corresponding language L follows the equation $L + 1 + aMbL$, hence the generating function $L(X)$, which in turn obeys $L(X) = 1 + XL(X)M(X)$, i.e. $L(X) = 1/(1 - XM(X))$. Returning to function $M(X)$ that generates Schröder numbers, verifying $XM^2 + (X-1) + M + 1 = 0$, we notice that it also verifies: $(1 - XM)(1 + M) = 2$, hence $L(X) = (1 + M(X))/2$. The first terms of this sequence are 1, 1, 3, 11, 45… The number of mountain ranges without horizontal plateaus at level 0 is twice as small as that of mountain ranges with horizontal plateaus at any level, as soon as $n > 0$.

Line $(1,1)$ is a, line $(1,-1)$ is b and line $(2,0)$ is c. The language made from these words is T. Each word is either empty or a primitive block of the form aMb or $b\underline{M}a$ or c, followed by a word from T, where M is the mountain range language defined above and $\underline{M}$ that obtained by inverting a and b starting from M. Hence:

$$T = 1 + aMbT + b\underline{M}aT + cT$$

Giving up all commutatives and replacing ab as well as c with X, we get the generating function associated with the number of words with $2n$ characters:

$$T = 1 + 2XMT + XT$$

$$T = 1 / (1 - X - 2XM),$$

which, using the formula that gives M, gives:

$$T(X) = 1 / \sqrt{1 - 6X + X^2}$$

A recurrence relation on the number $v(n)$ of words of $2n$ characters in which the sequence $u(n)$ of corresponding mountain ranges intervenes is deduced from the equation $T = 1 + aMbT + b\underline{M}aT + cT$. The recurrence relation is:

$$v(n) = 2\sum_{k=0}^{n-1} u(k)\, v(n-k-1) + v(n-1)$$

The first terms of sequence $v(n)$ are: 1, 3, 13, 63, 321, 1683, 8,689,.... We call them central Delaunay numbers.

10.2.1. *Explicit formula* $v(n)$

Consider $w(n,k)$ words with k letter as, and k letter bs, hence $n - k$ letter cs. These words are anagrams $n + k$ long. We begin by placing the k letter as in C_{n+k}^{k} possible ways, then each time the k letter bs in C_n^k ways, hence $w(n,k) = C_{n+k}^{k}\, C_n^{k}$. Now taking all possible values of number k of letters a or b, we get:

$$v(n) = \sum_{k=0}^{n} C_{n+k}^{k}\, C_n^{k}$$

10.2.2. *Return to u(n) number of mountain ranges based on three letters a, b, c and a link with v(n)*

Using the derivation formula:

$$(\sqrt{1-6x+x^2})' = \frac{x-3}{\sqrt{1-6x+x^2}} = (x-3)\sum_n v(n)x^n = -3v(0) + \sum_{n\geq 1}(v(n-1)-3v(n))x^n$$

by integration we get:

$$\sqrt{1-6x+x^2} = 1 - 3v(0)x + \frac{v(0)-3v(1)}{2}x^2 + \frac{v(1)-3v(2)}{3}x^3 + \ldots$$

We deduce from it the development of the generating function of $u(n)$, namely:

$M(x) = (1 - x - \sqrt{1-6x+x^2}) / (2x)$, hence:

$$u(n) = \frac{3v(n)-v(n-1)}{2(n+1)}$$

10.3. Example 1: domino tiling of an enlarged Aztec diamond

The type of diagonal square, as drawn in Figure 10.1 (left), is called the Aztec diamond. Unlike this shape that has two horizontal central rows, as well as the symmetries of the square, we will use the so-called enlarged Aztec diamond which, itself, has three horizontal central rows.

The drawing in Figure 10.1 (right) represents the enlarged diamond of $n = 6$ order and horizontal length of 12. The objective is to tile this checkerboard in all possible ways with horizontal or vertical dominos, each occupying two adjacent squares.

Let us turn our interest to the central ribbon made up of the succession of dominos from left to right, starting from the central square on the extreme left. This strip is made up of three types of dominos – horizontal ⟹, vertical going upwards ↗, and vertical going downwards ↘ – whose arrows are linked one after the other. This central ribbon of dominos, thus defined, is unique.

Figure 10.1. *Left, the classic Aztec diamond; right, the enlarged Aztec diamond with its central ribbon*

Here we show the following facts:

– Starting from the central left square, the ribbon ends up on the central right side. Actually, this means that there are as many upward vertical dominos as downward ones. If there was one more upward rather than downward domino, the length of the ribbon would be odd, and the ribbon should end up at the square directly above the central square, which corresponds to an even length. Similarly, if there were two more upward rather than downward dominos, the ribbon would have an even length, but should end up on the right in a position that corresponds to an odd length. As soon as the number of upward dominos is different to the downward one, we get a contradiction.

– Once the ribbon has been placed, the enlarged Aztec diamond is filled by dominos in a unique way, and all the dominos above as well as below the central ribbon are horizontal. When we place the dominoes of the central ribbon one after the other, this imposes constraints on the dominos above and below the ribbon. When a horizontal domino is placed, we are forced to place horizontal dominos above and below it, up to the top or bottom. When it is an upward vertical domino, we are forced to place horizontal dominos under it to the bottom. When it is a downward vertical domino, it is the same up to the top.

Therefore, there are as many tilings as central ribbons of dominos. These ribbons are exactly analogous to the paths based on three lines, with as many rising lines as falling ones, which we saw above. The number of tilings is therefore:

$$v(n) = \sum_{k=0}^{n} C_{n+k}^{k}\, C_{n}^{k}$$

and the number of tilings with k pairs of vertical dominos is:

$$w(n, k) = C_{n+k}^{\ k}\ C_n^{\ k}$$

For example, for $n = 5$, which gives a horizontal maximum length of 10 squares for the central rows, we have 1,683 tilings, one of which has no vertical dominoes, 30 of which have one pair of vertical dominos, 210 with two pairs, 560 with three pairs, 630 with four pairs, and 252 with five pairs.

Now let us move on to the program that enables us to compute the tilings. This program is an extension of the anagrams one: those $n + k$ long, with the presence of k letter 0s (vertical dominos with upward arrows), k letter 1s (downward vertical dominos), and $n - k$ letter 2s (horizontal dominos). This is for all values of k, from 0 to n, where n is in the order of an Aztec diamond, i.e. its horizontal half-length. Hence the function *anagrams*(k), which reproduces the program seen in Chapter 7. The main novelty is the design of the dominos. One result of this program is given in Figure 10.2. The program itself is:

```
main()
{ k=1; counter=0; xo=10; yo= 40;
  for(k=0; k<=N; k++)  anagrams(k);
}

void anagrams (int k)
{ NB[0]=k; NB[1]=k; NB[2]=N-k; q=0;
  for(letter=0;letter<3;letter++) for(i=0;i<NB[letter];i++) a[q++]=letter;
  for(;;)
    { LB=N;LH=N; design(k,xo,yo); xo+=2*N*pas +20;
      if (xo>600) {yo+=65; xo=10;}
      if (yo>450) {erase screen; xo=10;yo=50;}
      j=N+k-1; while (j>=1 && a[j]<=a[j-1]) j--;
      pospivot=j–1; if (pospivot== -1) break;
      j=N+k–1; while(a[j]<=a[pospivot]) j--; posreplacement=j;
     aux=a[pospivot]; a[pospivot]=a[posreplacement]; a[posreplacement]=aux;
     left=pospivot+1; right=N+k-1; while(left<right)
         { aux=a[left]; a[left]=a[right]; a[right]=aux; left++; right--;}
    }
}
void design(int k,int xo,int yo)
```

```
{x=xo,y=yo;
 for(i=0; i<N+k; i++)   if (a[i]==2)
   { rectangle(x-step/2,y- step/2,x+ step+ step/2,y+ step/2);
    xx=x;yy=y- step;
    for(j=0; j<LH; j++)
      { rectangle(xx-step/2,yy-step/2,xx+step+step/2,yy+step/2);
        xx+=step; yy-=step;
      }
    xx=x;yy=y+step;
    for(j=0; j<LB; j++)
     { rectangle(xx-step/2,yy-step/2,xx+step+step/2,yy+step/2);
       xx+=step;yy+=step;
     }
    LB--;LH--;  x=x+2*step;
   }
 else if (a[i]==0)
  { rectangle(x-step/2,y+step/2,x+step/2,y-step-step/2);  xx=x;yy=y+step;
    for(j=0;j<LB;j++)
      { rectangle(xx-step/2,yy-step/2,xx+step+step/2,yy+step/2);
        xx+=step;yy+=step;
      }
    LH--;  x=x+step;y=y-step;
   }
 else if (a[i]==1)
  { rectangle(x-step/2,y-step/2,x+step/2,y+step+step/2); xx=x;yy=y-step;
    for(j=0;j<LH;j++)
      { rectangle(xx-step/2,yy-step/2,xx+step+step/2,yy+step/2);
        xx+=step;yy-=step;
      }
   LB--;  x=x+step;y=y+step;
   }
}
```

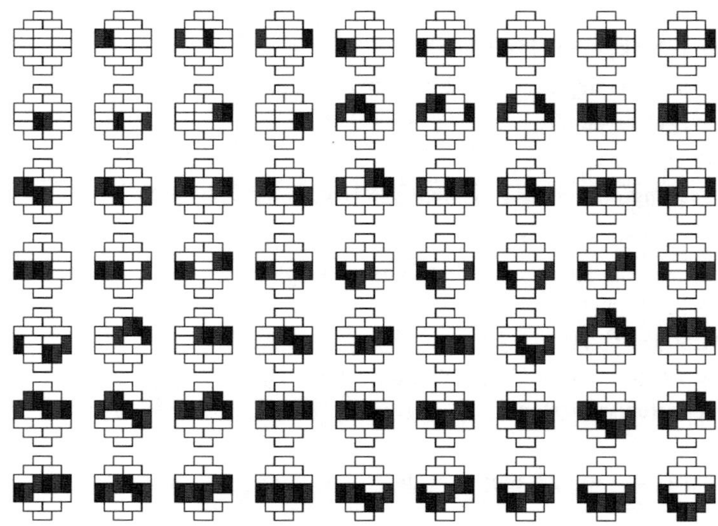

Figure 10.2. *All the tilings of the enlarged Aztec diamond of third order*

10.4. Example 2: domino tiling of half an Aztec diamond

Domino tiling of an Aztec half-diamond is represented in Figure 10.3. As before, we create the domino ribbon that starts from the lowest left square. It ends up in the lowest right-hand square. Placing dominos in succession on the central ribbon produces constraints that force the implementation of exclusively horizontal dominoes above and below the ribbon. In this case, the central ribbon is analogous to a mountain range based on three lines. The generating function, as we have seen, is:

$$M(X) = (1 - X - \sqrt{1 - 6X + X^2}\ ) / (2X)$$

Its development gives the number $u(n)$ of tilings of an Aztec half-diamond of order n (the length of the bottom row is $2n$).

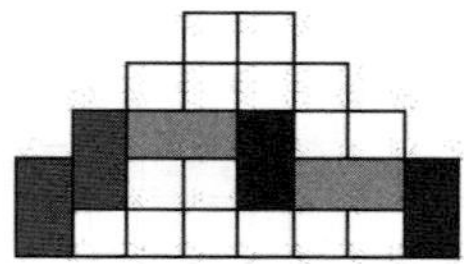

Figure 10.3. *Aztec half-diamond and its domino ribbon*

The program that enables us to get all the domino tilings of the Aztec half-diamond goes back to enumerating the three-line mountain ranges.

We begin by enumerating all the words n characters long based on 0 and 1, without 11 blocks. For example, for $n = 5$, we have the words 00000, 00001, 00010, 00100, 00101, 01000, 01001, 01010, 10000, 10001, 10010, 10100 and 10101. These words will first be placed, each in turn, in a table *aa*[] that is $n+1$ long, in boxes from 1 to n, and box 0 is set to 0. How can such words be obtained? Thanks to this initial dummy 0, when going from one word to the next the pivot is the first 0 preceded by a 0 that is found by moving from right to left. Behind the pivot, which moves from 0 to 1, we put only 0s.

The words above from table *aa*[] are transferred to table *a*[] by shifting them one notch to the left in order to fill in the boxes from 0 to $n - 1$, with the initial dummy 0 of table *aa*[] therefore being deleted. Then we place a 0 in box n of table *a*[]. In this way we get words of $n + 1$ characters based on 0 and 1, without any 11 blocks, and ending in 0.

Let us assume that $n + 1$ is an even number, i.e. $2N = n+1$, with table *a*[] occupying a length of 2*N*. Therefore, all we have to do is to replace the isolated 1s by a 2, also putting 2 in place of the 0 that follows. In this way we get words based on 0 and 22 blocks 2*N* long. The 22 blocks represent horizontal lines that are 2 units long. For $n = 5$, i.e. $N = 3$, this gives the words: 000000, 0000 —, 000 — 0, 00 — 00, 00 — —, 0 — 000, 0 — 0 —, 0 — — 0, — 0000, — 00 —, — 0 — 0, — — 00, — — —.

What is left to do is replace the 0s in each word above, which are an even number, with all the words from mountain ranges of the same length based on two diagonal lines. This is done to get mountain ranges based on three lines 2*N* long, which corresponds to the strip of preceding dominos. These words are placed in array *m*[]. Hence the program:

```
for(i=0; i<2*N; i++) aa[i]=0;
for(;;)
  { for(i=0;i<2*N-1;i++)  a[i]=aa[i+1];  a[2*N–1]=0;
    for(i=0;i<2*N-1;i++) if (a[i]==1) { a[i]=2; a[i+1]=2;}
    nb0=0; for(i=0;i<2*N;i++) if (a[i]==0) nb0++;
    if (nb0==0)    {for(i=0;i<2*N;i++) m[i]=a[i];   display table m[] }
    else mountain(nb0/2);
    i=2*N–1;  while( i>=1 && !(aa[i]==0 && aa[i-1]==0)) i--;
    pospivot=i;  if (pospivot==0) break;
   aa[pospivot]=1;  for(i=pospivot+1;i<2*N;i++) aa[i]=0;
  }
```

```
void mountain(int P)       /* two-line mountain ranges of length 2P with
                              P>0 */
{  for(i=0;i<2*P;i++) if (i<P) b[i]=0; else b[i]=1;
   for(;;)
    { k=0;  for(i=0;i<2*N;i++) if(a[i]===0) m[i]=b[k++]; else m[i]=2
      display table m[]
      i=2*P-3; counter0=0;
      while(i>=0 && !(b[i]==0 && b[i+1]==1 && b[i+2]==1))
          { if (b[i+2]==0) counter0++;  i--; }
      pospivot=i; if (pospivot==-1) break;
      b[pospivot]=1; b[pospivot+1]=0;  k=0;
      for(i=pospivot+2;i<2*P;i++)
          { if (k<counter0) b[i]=0; else b[i]=1;  k++; }
    }
}
```

Figure 10.4 gives a result of this program.

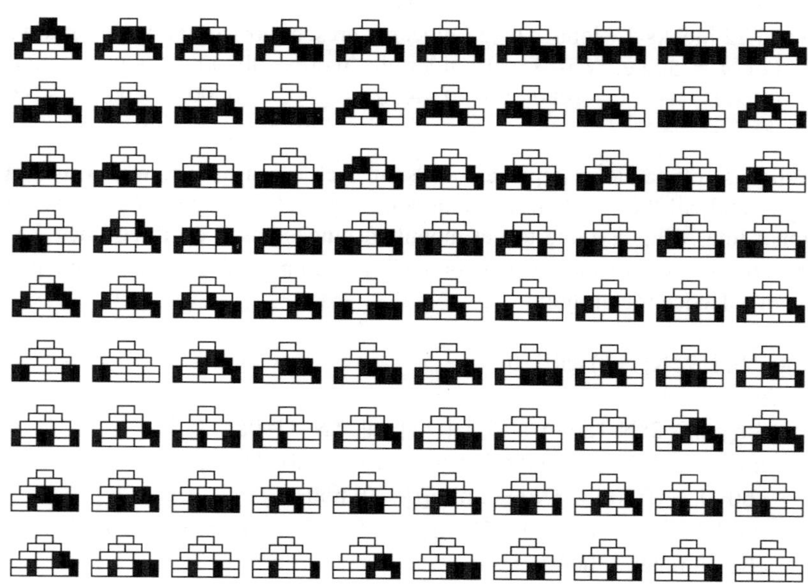

Figure 10.4. *The 90 tilings of the Aztec half-diamond 2N=8 long*

10.4.1. *Link between Schröder numbers and Catalan numbers*

Due to the algorithm above, we find a new formula for obtaining Schröder numbers, linked with Catalan numbers.

In order to do this, let us return to the example above, with $N = 3$. The 22 words obtained can be split into four groups, according to the number of their horizontal lines. Those that have no horizontal lines number $c(3)$, the Catalan number that counts the number of mountain ranges 6 units long.

Now let us take those that have a horizontal line: we have to place the four remaining 0s to the left or right of the horizontal line, which refers to distributing four identical objects in two boxes, i.e. C_5^4 ways, then each time we replace these 0s with $c(2)$ mountain ranges. Next we take words that have two horizontal lines: we place the two remaining 0s in the three possible places (the extreme left, extreme right or between the two lines), i.e. C_4^2 ways, with $c(1) = 1$ mountain ranges each time. Finally there is one single word that has three horizontal lines.

We deduce from it that the Schröder number $S(3)$ is expressed:

$$S(3) = C_6^6\, c(3) + C_5^4\, c(2) + C_4^2\, c(1) + C_3^0\, c(0),$$

and we have:

$$5 + 5.2 + 6.1 + 1 = 22$$

This formula is easily generalized, which gives:

$$S(n) = \sum_{k=0}^{n} C_{n+k}^{2k}\, c(k)$$

10.4.2. *Link with Narayana numbers*

Let us recall that these numbers $N(n,k)$ give the number of mountain ranges based on diagonal lines $2n$ long with k peaks (see Chapter 9). In this case, with the possible presence of plateaus, each $\nearrow\searrow$ peak can either be conserved or replaced by a plateau. If a two-line mountain range has k peaks, it produces 2^k three-line mountain ranges. Hence the formula:

$$S(n) = \sum_{k=1}^{n} 2^k\, N(n,k) = \frac{1}{n} \sum_{k=1}^{n} C_n^k\, C_n^{k-1}$$

10.4.3. *Another way of programming three-line mountain ranges*

Now let us designate a horizontal plateau by the 00 block, a rising line by 1 and a falling line by 2. Words classified in alphabetical order are, for example for $N = 3$:

000000, 000012, 001002, 001122, 001200, 001212, 100002, 100122, 100200, 100212, 110022, 111222, 112002, 112122, 112200, 112212, 120000, 120012, 121002, 121122, 121200, 121212

where we have underlined the pivot letter.

To find the pivot, we start from the right searching either for the first 00 block, in which case the first of the two 0s is the pivot which becomes 1, or from the first 122 block where 1 is the pivot, the block therefore being transformed into 200. What do we do behind the pivot?

When we come across the 00 block, we calculate the altitude where we are, i.e. the number 2 reduced by the number 1 behind the pivot, i.e. $nb2-nb1$, and as the pivot moves from 0 to 1, we will have to place a number 2 equal to $nb2-nb1+1$ to the right of the pivot.

When moving on to the next word, we place the smallest possible word end behind the pivot. Therefore we put the 2s at the end of the word and insert a block of 0s between the pivot and this block of 2s.

The procedure is analogous when we come across the 122 block.

We end up with the following program:

```
for(i=0; i<twoN; i++) a[i]=0;  /* the initial word */
for(;;)
  { display table a[2N]
    flag=0;  for(i=0;i<twoN;i+=2) if (! (a[i]==1 && a[i+1]==2))
          { flag=1; break;}
    if (flag==0) break;   /* final stop test when we come across 121212...12  */

    i=twoN–1;   while (! ( (a[i]==0 && a[i-1]==0 && i>=1)
                        || (a[i]==2 && a[i-1]==2 && a[i-2]==1 && i>=2))) i--;
    if (a[i]==0 && a[i-1]==0)   /* if we come across 00  */
      { pospivot=i–1;  a[pospivot]=1;   nb1=0; nb2=0;
```

```
        /* counting 1s and 2s behind the pivot */
      for(j=twoN–1;j>pospivot;j--)
        { if (a[j]==1) nb1++ ;  if (a[j]==2) nb2++; }
      if (nb1==0)  for(j=pospivot+1;j<twoN;j++) a[j]=2;
      else
        {for(j=twoN–1; j>twoN–1–(nb2–nb1+1); j--) a[j]=2;
         for (k=pospivot+1; k<=j; k++) a[k]=0;
        }
    }
  else     /* if we come across 122  */
    { pospivot=i–2;  a[pospivot]=2;   nb1=0; nb2=0;
      for(j=twoN–1; j>pospivot; j--)
        { if (a[j]==1) nb1++ ;  if (a[j]==2) nb2++; }
      for(j=pospivot+1; j<twoN; j++) a[j]=0;
      for(j=twoN–1; j>twoN–1–(nb2-nb1–2); j--) a[j]=2;
    }
}
```

Figure 10.5 results from the execution of this program.

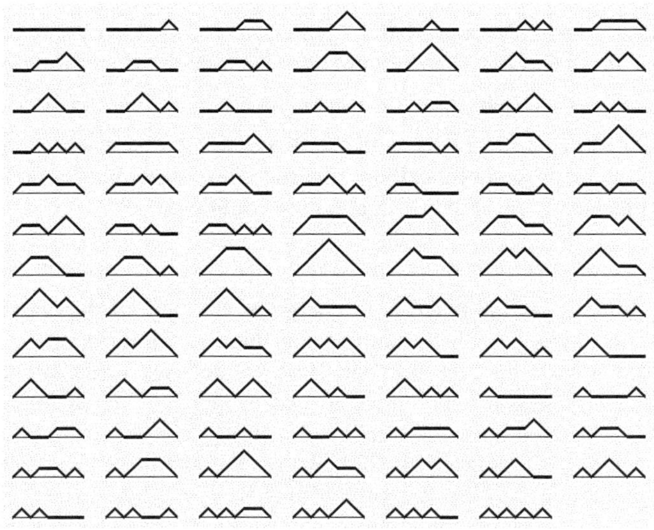

Figure 10.5. *The 90 mountain ranges based on three lines 8 units long*

10.5. Mountain ranges based on three types of lines

Unlike above, the horizontal line is now half as long (1 unit). The coordinates of the lines are now (1, 1), (1, -1), (1, 0). The language M of these words is the same as above, with:

$$M = 1 + aMbM + cM$$

Things change when we give up all commutativity in order to have the generating function associated with the number $v(n)$ of words of n characters. We replace a, b and c with x: $M(x) = 1 + x^2M^2 + xM$, hence after solving:

$$M(x) = (1 - x - \sqrt{1 - 2x - 3x^2}\,) / (2x^2)$$

the power series expansion of $M(x)$ gives its first terms of sequence $v(n)$ from $n = 0$:

1, 1, 2, 4, 9, 21, 51,127, ...

They are called Motzkin numbers.

To carry out the corresponding algorithm and program, we label two oblique lines 0 and 1, and the horizontal line 2. Mountain ranges are words of a given length N, based on the letters 0, 1 and 2. The main program is in charge of calling a function *combi*(k) where k is the number of horizontal plateaus for all possible values of k. If N is even k takes all even values from 0 to N, and if k is odd it takes all odd values from 1 to N. For each value of p, the function *combi*(p) writes all words based on 0 and 2 that have letter 2 p times. We find the classic combinations program seen in Chapter 3. These words are alternately placed in table $aa[N]$, copied in table $a[N]$ each time the other function, *mountain*(p), is used. The function *combi*(p) deals separately with the two extreme cases, where the number p of horizontal plateaus is null, calling the function *mountain*(0), and where the number p of plateaus is equal to N, which gives a single range.

For each word of combinations in $aa[N]$, $a[N]$ with its p letter 2s, and $N - p$ letter 0s, the function *mountain*(p) is in charge of creating all the classic mountain ranges based on 0 and 1, with as many rising lines as falling ones, on a length of $N - p$, which is always an even number. Here we go back to the program seen in Chapter 9. These ranges are alternately placed in table $b[]$. Each time table $b[]$ is decanted into all of the 0 boxes of combinations in table $a[]$. A word based on 0 and 2 created by *combi*(p) is replaced by all the words based on 0, 1 and 2 corresponding to three-line mountain ranges that we can now design. These words are found in table $a[N]$. When a new combination is created, all we have to do is to place it in table $aa[n]$ rather than $a[n]$, to avoid interferences.

```
main()
{ N=4;   rangecounter=0;
  if (N%2==0)  for(k=0; k<=N; k+=2)  combi(k);
  else if (N%2==1)  for(k=1; k<=N; k+=2)  combi(k);
 printf("%d ",rangecounter);  getch();
}
void combi(int p)
{  if (p==0)  mountain(0);
   else if (p==N) { for(i=0; i<N; i++) a[i]=2;  design; rangecounter++; }
   else
      { for(i=0; i<p; i++)  aa[N–1–i]=2;
        for(i=0; i<N–p; i++)  aa[i]=0;   /* the first */
        for(;;)
          { for(i=0; i<N; i++) a[i]=aa[i];      mountain(p);
            i=N-1;  while (aa[i]!=2 || aa[i-1]!=0 && i>0)  i--;
            ppospivot=i–1;   if (ppospivot==-1) break;
            aa[ppospivot]=2; aa[ppospivot+1]=0;
            g=ppospivot+2;d=N–1;
           while(g<d) { aux=aa[g]; aa[g]=aa[d]; aa[d]=aux; g++;d--;}
          }
      }
}
void mountain(int p)   /* mountain ranges in an even length N–p  */
{  for(i=0; i<N–p; i++) if (i<(N–p)/2) b[i]=0; else b[i]=1;  /* first range */
   for(;;)
     { q=0;   for(i=0;i<N;i++) if (a[i]!=2) a[i]=b[q++];
       design; rangecounter++;
       i=N–p–3; c0=0; if (b[i+1]==0) c0=1;
      while (i>=0 && (b[i]!=0 || b[i+1]!=1 || b[i+2]!=1))
          { if (b[i]==0) c0++;    i--;}
       pospivot=i;   if (pospivot==-1) break;    b[pospivot]=1; b[pospivot+1]=0;
      k=0;  for(j=pospivot+2;j<N–p;j++)
          { if (k<c0) b[j]=0; else b[j]=1; k++; }
     }
}
```

The results of this program are presented in Figures 10.6a and 10.6b.

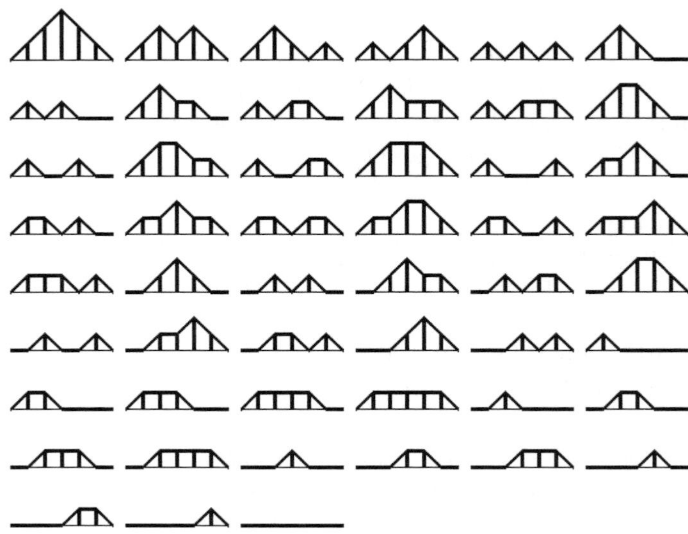

Figure 10.6a. *The 51 mountain ranges six units long*

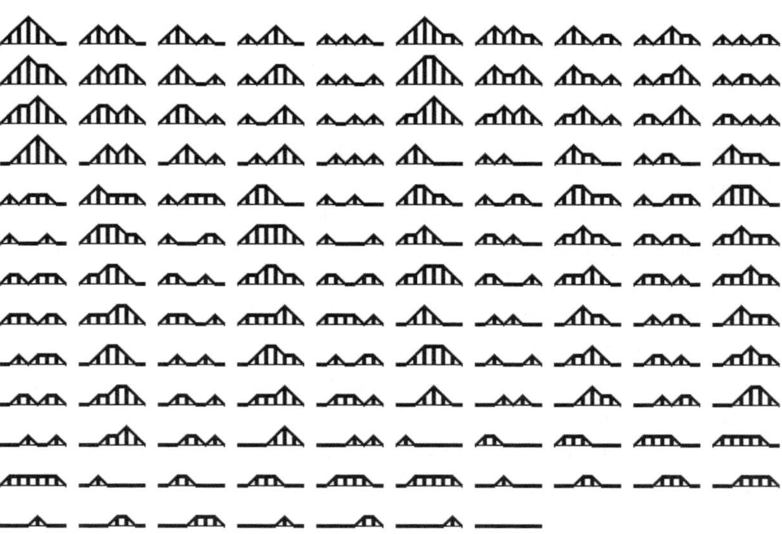

Figure 10.6b. *The 127 mountain ranges seven units long*

10.6. Example 3: movement of the king on a chessboard

Let us consider an infinite chessboard. The king moves from point $(0,0)$ to point $(n,0)$ located on the same row as the initial point. But it can go below as well as above this row (it is no longer a mountain range in the strict sense). We are interested in the number $u(n)$ of shortest paths taken by the king, which forces it to use the three types of steps: ↗ ↘ → that we call *a*, *b* and *c*.

Each path can be coded by a word *n* characters long based on three letters *a*, *b* and *c*, with as many rising lines *a* as falling ones *b*. The language formed by these words is *R*. We get the equation:

$$R = 1 + aMbR + cR$$

where *M* is the corresponding mountain range language. Moving on to generating functions, we find:

$$R(x) = 1 / \sqrt{1 - 2x - 3x^2}$$

The first terms of the sequence $u(n)$ are:

1, 1, 3, 7, 19, …

To calculate $u(n)$, let us consider words of *n* characters with *k* letter *a*s, *k* letter *b*s, and $n - 2k$ letter *c*s, with *k* included between 0 and $[n/2]$. There are $C_n^k\, C_{n-k}^k$ of them.

Finally, we get:

$$u(n) = \sum_{k=0}^{[n/2]} C_n^k\, C_{n-k}^k = \sum_{k=0}^{[n/2]} \frac{n!}{k!k!(n-2k)!}$$

Chapter 11

Some Applications of Catalan Numbers and Parenthesis Words

Let us recall that parenthesis words based on two letters *a*s and *b*s (or a left parenthesis and a right parenthesis) have letter *a* as many times as letter *b*, and they are such that by replacing *a* with 1 and *b* with -1, the partial sums obtained from the beginning are always greater than or equal to 0. This means that we never go below level 0, ground level. Drawing these words in the shape of mountain ranges, these partial sums are nothing other than the altitudes at each step. For example, the word ()(()()) is also written 1 -1 1 1 -1 1 -1 -1, hence the successive altitudes 010121210. The number of these words of $2n$ characters is the Catalan number $c(n)$. This style of word is found in numerous contexts, as shown by the following examples.

11.1. The number of ways of placing *n* chords not intersecting each other on a circle with an even number 2*n* of points

From the $2n$ points numbered from 1 to $2n$ by moving around the circle, consider a configuration of n chords, each with two of these points as extremities not intersecting each other (see Figure 11.1). Let us start from a point of the circle between 1 and $2n$ and move in the direction of increasing point numbers. Each time we come across a point where we meet a chord for the first time we add 1, and each time we encounter the chord for the second time we subtract 1. We get one parenthesis word, where the ends of the same chord play the role of two parentheses, one left and the other right, which correspond with each other. The relation between configurations of chords and parenthesis words is bijective. The number of ways of placing the n chords is $c(n)$.

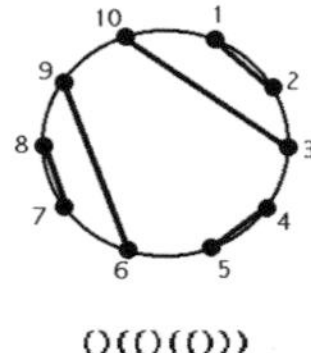

()(()(()))

Figure 11.1. *Configuration of five chords that do not intersect each other*

11.2. Murasaki diagrams and partitions

In 1600-1700, these diagrams appeared in the illustrated editions of Murasaki Shikibu's *Tale of Genji*. They represent the 52 partitions of a five-element set. Each of the elements of this set, called 1 to 5, is drawn in the shape of a vertical bar. To represent a part of a partition, the bars are joined by a horizontal line.

For example, the partition {124}{35} becomes .

Now, out of these partitions let us consider those whose diagrams have no criss-crossing between horizontal and vertical bars.

For example, the partition above is no longer accepted, but the partition {125}{34}, i.e. , is valid.

An example of such partitions is given in Figure 11.2.

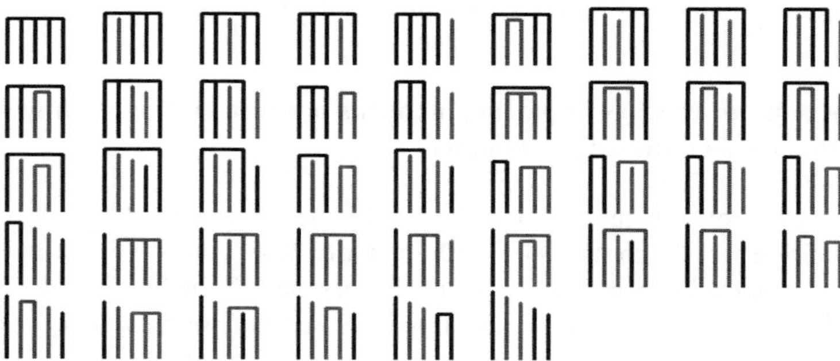

Figure 11.2. *The 42 partitions without criss-crossing of a five-element set*

The number of partitions of a n-element set without criss-crossing is no other than the Catalan number $c(n)$. To show this all we have to do is establish a bijection between such partitions and the mountain ranges, as indicated in the example in Figure 11.3. In this case we notice the presence of three blocks of rising lines. Each successive block of rising lines will constitute part of the partition. We will read these blocks one after the other by going from top to bottom, and numbering the corresponding lines of the blocks in ascending order, with the following nuance: each rising line of the bock where we are is associated with a descending line, if we come across a line of a following block that is inserted between the two, we number this one first. In the case in Figure 11.3, we begin by numbering the highest line of the first block 1. Then we go down one notch and we notice that between this rising line and its corresponding descending line, the top line of the second block is inserted. It is this one that is numbered 2. Then we come back to the block with the second line numbered 3, etc.

After the partitions of a five-element set of Figure 11.2, we will find those of a six-element set, still without criss-crossing, in Figure 11.4. The corresponding program is a consequence of the constructive algorithm above.

Figure 11.3. *Numbering of blocks of rising lines of a mountain range to get a partition without entangling*

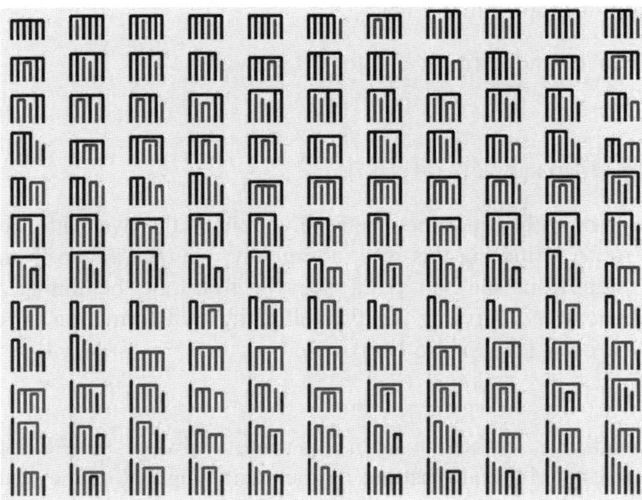

Figure 11.4. *Partitions without criss-crossing of a six-element set*

11.3. Path couples with the same ends in a square grid

Let us consider path couples n long with the same starting point and the same ending point, without the two paths meeting in between. We will show that the number of these couples is $c(n - 1)$. In order to do this, let us distinguish the bottom path and top path (for example Figure 11.5). They have the same number of horizontal lines $\rightarrow$ and vertical lines $\uparrow$. Let us run through these two paths synchronously from the common starting point, step by step. At the start, we always have $\uparrow\!\!\rightarrow$. Then at each new stage, the cumulation of the $\rightarrow$ of the bottom path is always strictly greater than that of the $\rightarrow$ of the top path, except at the last stage which again gives an inequality with a $\rightarrow\!\!\uparrow$ (if it was not this way, the two paths would meet before the end). Similarly there are strictly less $\uparrow$ accumulated in the bottom path than in the top path, except in the last step.

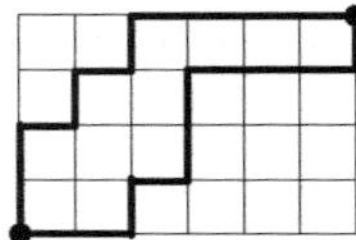

Figure 11.5. *Example of a path couple*

Let $hB(i)$ be the number of horizontal lines of the bottom path up to stage I; $vB(i)$ the number of vertical lines; and $hH(i)$ and $vH(i)$ the number of horizontal and vertical lines for the top path. We have:

$$hB(i) > hH(i) \text{ and } vB(i) < vH(i) \text{ for } 0 < i < n,$$

as well as:

$$hB(n) = hH(n) \text{ and } vB(n) = vH(n)$$

Let us carry out a bijection between the couple of the two paths above, each n long and the route defined in this way: alternately, we take a step from the bottom path then a step from the top path, starting from the beginning to the end, concatenating them and carrying out the following transformation on each step of the top path: $\rightarrow \leftrightarrow \uparrow$ (see Figure 11.6).

In these conditions the beginning of this route is always $\rightarrow\rightarrow$ and its end $\uparrow\uparrow$. The path is $2n$ long with ends that are on the same diagonal of the square grid. On the other hand, thanks to the property of the couple above, we have:

$$hB(i) + vH(i) > hH(i) + vB(i) \text{ for } 0 < i < n$$

i.e. more → than ↑ throughout the route, with equality only at stage n. This characterizes a sub-diagonal route without touching the diagonal axis except at the beginning and the end.

It is what we called a mountain (a primitive word for mountain ranges). The number of such routes is therefore $c(n - 1)$, and it is also the number of path couples n long.

Figure 11.7 shows all the path couples obtained for $n = 7$.

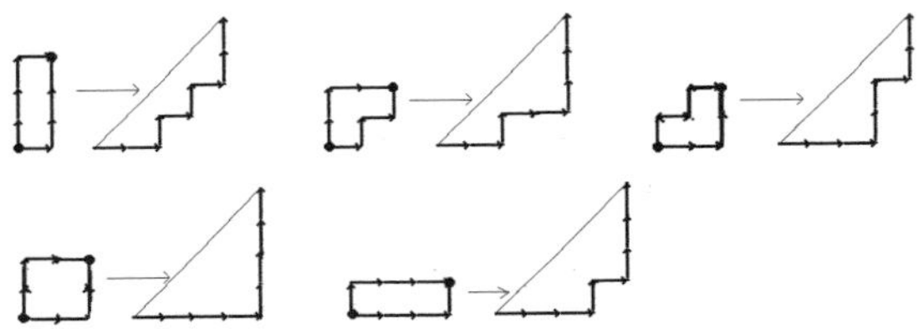

Figure 11.6. *Bijection between the two types of routes, in the case where $n = 4$, with $c(3) = 5$ cases*

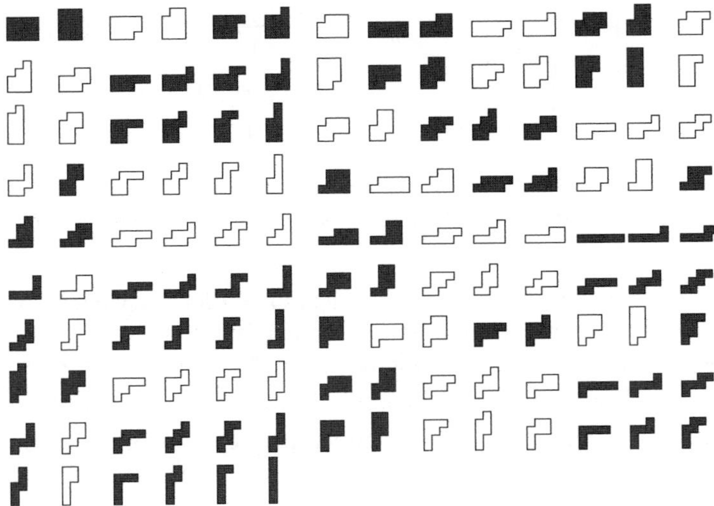

Figure 11.7. *Path couples $n = 7$ long, numbering $c(7) = 132$, with the area they delimit in grey when the area is even and in white when it is odd*

11.4. Path couples with same starting point and length

Now let us consider the more general case where path couples have a common starting point, a same length n, with no meeting point except eventually at the end, and their two final ends not necessarily mixed up (see Figure 11.8). These two ends are on a 45° angle. Let k be the distance that separates them, measured in number of diagonal steps. The case where $k = 0$ was studied above. Let us call $b(n,K)$ the number of path couples n long, separated by k units in the end. These numbers track the following relations:

$$b(n + 1, k) = 2b(n, k) + b(n, k + 1) + b(n, k - 1) \text{ for } k > 1$$

$$b(n, 0) = c(n - 1)$$

$$b(n, 1) = c(n) \text{ for } n \geq 1, \text{ and } b(0, 1) = 0$$

(we also have $b(k, k) = 1$ and $b(n, k) = 0$ if $n < k$).

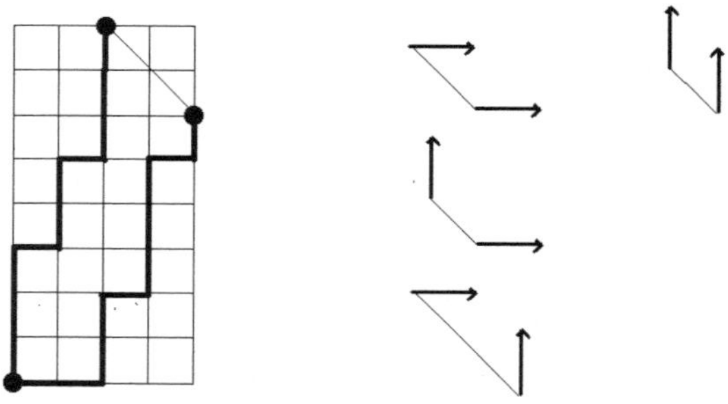

Figure 11.8. *A path couple for n = 10 and k = 2 (left); and passage from a path couple n long to a couple n + 1 long (right)*

In order to verify this, let us take path couples $n + 1$ long separated from k at the end. They either come from paths n long separated from k at the end and completed in two possible ways, or from paths n long separated from $k - 1$ that we complete in one single way. Hence the formula for $k > 1$. We also know that $b(n,0) = c(n-1)$. On the other hand, there is bijection between path couples of length $n + 1$ with $k = 0$, and those n long with $k = 1$ (obtained by removing the final steps), hence $b(n,1) = c(n)$.

We find that: $b(n,k) = \frac{k}{n} C_{2n}^{n-k}$.

This can be proved by recurrence using the formulae above. We can also use generating functions F_k of the $b(n, k)$ for each value of k, i.e.:

$$F_k(z) = b(0, k) + b(1, k)z + b(2, k)z^2 + b(3, k)z^3 + \ldots$$

This gives the successive coefficients:

– for F_1: 0, 1, 2, 5, 14, 42, 132, 429, …;

– for F_2: 0, 0, 1, 4, 14, 48, 165, 572, …; and

– for F_3: 0, 0, 0, 1, 6, 27, 110, 429, ….

For $k = 1$, $b(n, 1) = c(n)$ with $b(0, 1) = 0$, the generating function is $C - 1 = zC^2$, where C is the generating function of Catalan numbers.

For $k = 2$, let us consider the successive distances when running through two paths n long, the final distance being 2. When we reach a certain point, we are at the last time the distance between the two paths is equal to 1 – after a certain length the run through in common is k' ($1 \le k' < n$). Thanks to this split in k', for all the corresponding path couples the number of paths up to k' is $b(k', 1)$, and beyond this number of paths it is $b(n - k', 1)$. All we have to do for this is to translate one of the two paths one unit distance towards the other. In total this makes:

$b(k', 1)\, b(n - k', 1)$ paths

Then we do the sum for all possible values of k' (from 1 to $n - 1$, or even from 0 to n because we get 0 for 0 and n). This corresponds to the generating function:

$$(C - 1)^2 = (zC^2)^2 = z^2 C^4$$

This is generalized to some value of k, cutting the paths up to the last time the distance is 1, then up to the last time the distance is 2, etc. The generating function F_k of the $b(n, k)$ is $(zC^2)^k$.

We can also establish a bijective link between these path couples and routes in a background.

Let us take $k = 1$ for example. This means that the bottom path has one $\rightarrow$ more than the top path (and therefore one $\uparrow$ less).

Let us complete each one of the two paths using an extra line ($\uparrow$ for the bottom path and $\rightarrow$ for the top path) so that they have the same end point. Again, we come across our previous study (putting each line of the two paths end to end with the second ones reversed, and removing the two lines at both ends), which gives a mountain range. We deduce from this that $b(n, 1) = c_n$. Removing the last vertical line that had been added, the final point is at a height 1/2 the diagonal (taking the diagonal of a square of the square grid as the unit of length).

Now let us take the half-diagonal of a square as the unit, and the benchmark (O, N, X). The final height is $X = 1$ and the abscissa is $2n-1$. Therefore $b(n,1)$ is the number of paths in final plan up to point $(N = 2n-1, X = 1)$. This is generalized to some k: $b(n,k)$ is the number of paths in the final plan up to point $(2n-1, 2k-1)$, taking those in N,X from the start as the benchmark (see Figure 11.9). Effectively, we are verifying that:

$$b(n, k) = a(2n-1, 2k-1) = (k / n)\, C_{2n}^{\,n-k}$$

(see section 9.6 for the definition of $a(N, X)$).

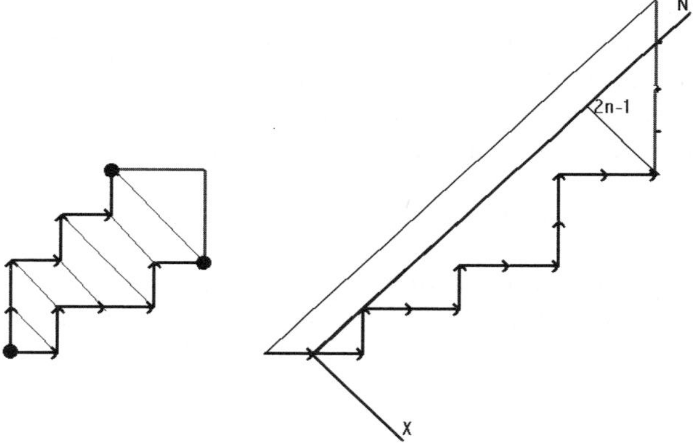

Figure 11.9. *Bijective link between the two types of paths for n = 6 and k = 2*

11.5. Decomposition of words based on two letters as a product of words linked to mountain ranges

Let us consider words N characters based on two letters – binary numbers if you prefer – which we can draw using upward or downward diagonal lines. This property is shown in Figure 11.9.

All words made up of two letters can be broken up, in a unique way, into three factors *dcg*, with these three factors defined in the following way:

– g is a route which, after starting at level 0, neither touches nor crosses the horizontal axis while remaining on the positive side, and it can be empty. When it is not empty, it can be considered as a left mountain factor but is not a mountain. On the other hand, all its beginnings, up to the complete word, can have more letter *a*s than letter *b*s. The language of these words is:

$$G_1 = e + aC + aCaC + aCaCaC + \ldots$$

This language is obtained by classifying words according to their final height reached, and C designates the mountain range language:[1]

– c is a mountain range;

– d is the empty word, i.e. a right mountain factor that is not a mountain. The corresponding path ends on the negative side, and the end of the word is not a mountain range. Its language is:

$$D_1 = e + Cb + CbCb + CbCbCb + \ldots$$

To show this property, let us take the minimum altitude reached by the word designed in the shape of a route. It is negative or null. This minimum value can be reached several times. Let us call the first and last positions of the minimum *first* and *last*. In the case where the minimum is negative and *first* is different from *last*, the word is broken up into a right mountain range factor between O and the first minimum, then into a mountain range between the first and last minimums, and finally into a left mountain range factor between the last minimum and end of the word. In the case where the minimum is negative, but the minimum is reached only once (*first* = *last*), the word is broken up into dg or even dgc, with the empty mountain range for c. The case where the minimum is at altitude 0 remains. If we have a single minimum, therefore in O, the word is reduced to g (with d and c being empty). If we have several minimums, we either have a last minimum in N, and the word is reduced to c, or the last minimum is before N, and the word is reduced to cg. There is no other case. All words are of the form dcg, that eventually have empty factors. We deduce the algorithm and the program enabling us to cut up a word into three factors dcg:[2]

```
a[0]=0;  /* word created at random, of given length N, based on two letters,
            here 1 and -1  */
for(i=1; i<=N; i++)
     { accident=random(2);if (accident==0) a[i]=1; else a[i]=-1;}
```

1. We saw that the language corresponding to left mountain range factors was $G = e + C + CaC + CaCaC + \ldots$. There is a simple link with left mountain factor language G_1, $G_1 = e + aG$.

2. For more details, see [LEN 98a].

```
cumul=0;
for(i=0; i<=N; i++)
        {cumul+=a[i];s[i]=cumul;}   /* s[] is the altitude at each point */
min=10000;
for(i=0; i<=N; i++)   /* search for the first and last minimums */
if (s[i]==min)
        {exaequo++; last=i;}
else if (s[i]<min)
        {min=s[i]; exaequo=1; first=i; last=i;}
if (first==0 && last==0)
    for(i=1; i<=N; i++)  color[i]=COLORG;
else if (first==0 && last==N)
    for(i=1; i<=N; i++)  color[i]=COLORC;
else if (first==0)
    { for(i=0; i<=last; i++) color[i]=COLORC;
      for(i=last+1; i<=N; i++) color[i]=COLORG;
    }

else if (first==last && first==N)
    for(i=1; i<=N; i++)  color[i]=COLORD;
else if (first==last)
    { for(i=1; i<=first; i++) color[i]=COLORD;
      for(i=first+1; i<=N; i++) COLOR[i]=COLORG; }
else

    { for(i=0; i<=first; i++) color[i]=COLORD;
     for(i=first+1; i<=last; i++) color[i]=COLORC;
     for(i=last+1; i<=N; i++) color[i]=COLORG; }
for(i=1; i<N; i++)       /* design with the three colors */
  { setcolor(color[i]);
    line(zoom*(i–1),yo-zoom*s[i–1],zoom*i,yo-zoom*s[i]);
  }
```

An example of a word cut up in this way in three factors by this program is shown in Figure 11.10. The generating function $G_1(x)$ associated with the number of words g of the same length is: $G_1(x) = 1 / (1 - xC(x))$. We find that:

$$G_1(x) = \frac{\sqrt{1+2x}+\sqrt{1-2x}}{2\sqrt{1-2x}}.$$

Thanks to commutativity and assimilation of *a* and *b*, the generating function associated with the number of words *d* of the same length is also $G_1(x)$. We can verify that $G_1(x) = 1 + x\,G(x)$ (see section 11.5, note 1) and we also have:

$$C\,G_1(x)^2 = 1 / (1 - 2x)$$

which is the generating function associated with the number of words based on two letters of a given length, because all words are expressed *dcg*. Out of all these words, let us turn our interest to those which, when written in *dcg* form, have the non-empty mountain range factor *c*. The associated generating function is:

$$G_1(x)\,C(x)\,D_1(x) - G_1(x)\,D_1(x) = G_1(x)^2\,C - G_1(x)^2 = G_1(x)^2\,(C(x) - 1)$$

$$= G_1(x)^2\,C(x)\,(C(x) - 1) / C(x)$$

With $C(x) = 1 + x^2C(x)^2$, we find $x^2\,C(x) / (1 - 2x)$ as the generating function.

The number of words *n* long with a non-null factor *c* is the coefficient of x^n or even that of x^{n-2} in:

$$C(x) / (1 - 2x) = 1+ (c(1)x^2 + c(2)x^4 + c(3)x^6 + \ldots)\,(1 + 2x + 4x^2 + 8x^3 + \ldots)$$

i.e.: $\sum_{k=0}^{\left[\frac{n-2}{2}\right]} 2^{n-2-2k}\,c(k)$

For example, out of the 16 words of four characters, there are five presenting a non-empty factor, *c*. The proportion of these words with non-empty *c* out of those *n* long is:

$$\sum_{k=0}^{\left[\frac{n-2}{2}\right]} \frac{c(k)}{2^{2(k+1)}}$$

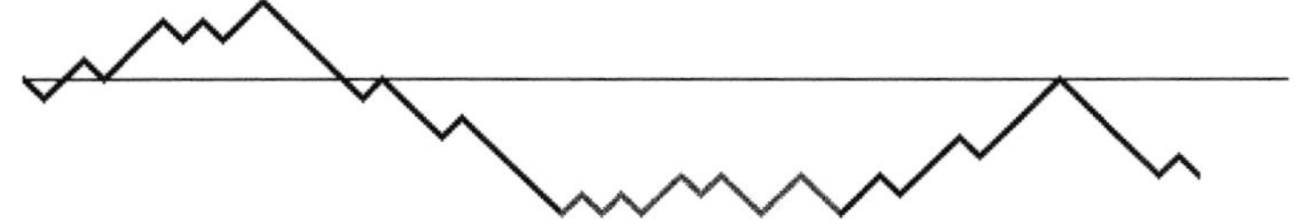

Figure 11.10. *A word 60 characters long and its decomposition into three factors dc*

Chapter 12

Burnside's Formula

When we do an enumeration of shapes or patterns, we are often confronted with a large number of possible cases, although there are many resemblances between some of these shapes. We are therefore led to consider equivalent shapes that result from one another by reflecting or rotating. Using these symmetries, namely rotations or reflections (in two dimensions) which cause us to move from some shapes to others, we only keep the shapes that are not equivalent, and the inventory ends up being greatly reduced by this. It is in this context that Burnside's formula will come in to use.[1]

12.1. Example 1: context in which we obtain the formula

Let us consider a group of permutations G acting on a set E. To understand the situation, we will immediately take an example where a group G of permutations and a set E intervene in a concrete way.

Let us take a square whose four vertices $ABCD$ are painted with one of two colors. Therefore, we find $2^4 = 16$ different possible configurations, one example being $A_1B_2C_2D_1$, written by indexing each vertex with its color. It is these 16 colored squares that form set E. On the other hand, we know that a square remains globally invariant under the effect of four rotations and four reflections. These eight transformations form what is called the symmetry group of the square.

1. Polya enumeration formula is found in the extension of Burnside's formula. For more details on this subject, see [POL 87, TUC 02].

Each one of these symmetries produces a certain permutation of the four *ABCD* vertices. For example, the 90° rotation transforms *ABCD* into *BCDA*, or even (considering that it is the colors that turn and not the points) $A_1B_2C_2D_1$ will become $A_1B_1C_2D_2$ for example.

These eight symmetries make up the group of permutations *G*.[2] They act on set *E* since each one of these permutations transforms a colored square of set *E* into a colored square of set *E*. In fact, what we want to find is the number of distinct symmetry-type configurations of the square. Out of the 16 configurations indicated above some are equivalent, in the sense that they result from one another through one or more symmetries of the square. How many distinct configurations are there? We will group the identical symmetry-type configurations into classes, and the number of equivalence classes will give the number sought. This leads us to the following definition.

DEFINITION 12.1.– Let *x* be an element of set *E*. When an element, *y*, of *E* is such that $y = g(x)$, where *g* is a permutation of *G* (the group of permutations) we say that *y* is equivalent to *x*. Thanks to this equivalence relation, we can define the equivalence class of *x*, and all the classes thus obtained (also called orbits) form a partition of set *E*. In our example, with the vertices of the square numbered in this way: $\begin{bmatrix} D & C \\ A & B \end{bmatrix}$, we find the following classes:

– $\{A_1B_1C_1D_1\}$. This element *x* is invariant under the effect of the eight symmetries. Its class is reduced to itself.

– $\{A_2B_2C_2D_1, A_2B_2C_1D_2, A_2B_1C_2D_2, A_1B_2C_2D_2\}$. We go, for example, from the first element to the second either by a rotation of -90° or by reflection on the vertical axis. Notice that there are always two symmetries that let us go from one of the elements of this class to another. Observe that this number (2) is the relationship of the total number of symmetries (8) through the number of elements of this class.

– $\{A_1B_2C_2D_1, A_2B_2C_1D_1, A_2B_1C_1D_2, A_1B_1C_2D_2\}$. Here also we go, for example, from the first to the second either by rotation of -90° or by reflection through the *AC* axis.

– $\{A_2B_1C_2D_1, A_1B_2C_1D_2\}$. We go from the first element to the other through four of the symmetries (rotations of ± 90°, or horizontal and vertical reflections), and this

2. It is essentially one group because the product of two symmetries (which consists of changing them one after the other) is still in symmetry, since the product of two transformations leaving one shape invariant leaves this next shape invariant. Furthermore, we know that permutations are reversible.

number is still the relationship of the total number of symmetries through the number of elements of this class.

– $\{A_1B_1C_1D_2, A_1B_1C_2D_1, A_1B_2C_1D_1, A_2B_1C_1D_1\}$.

– $\{A_2B_2C_2D_2\}$, as in the first case.

Through this exhaustive breakdown, we find six colorings of square vertices that are different symmetry-types of the square (see Figure 12.1).

How can the search for these six configurations be programmed? The 16 configurations are considered as words of four characters based on 0 and 1 depending on the color of the *ABCD* vertices. These colorings are converted into decimal numbers, from 0 to 15, to simplify things. They become the indices of a table called *do*[] with 16 elements, the contents of whose squares is first set to 0, to indicate that nothing is done yet. Then we run through this table.

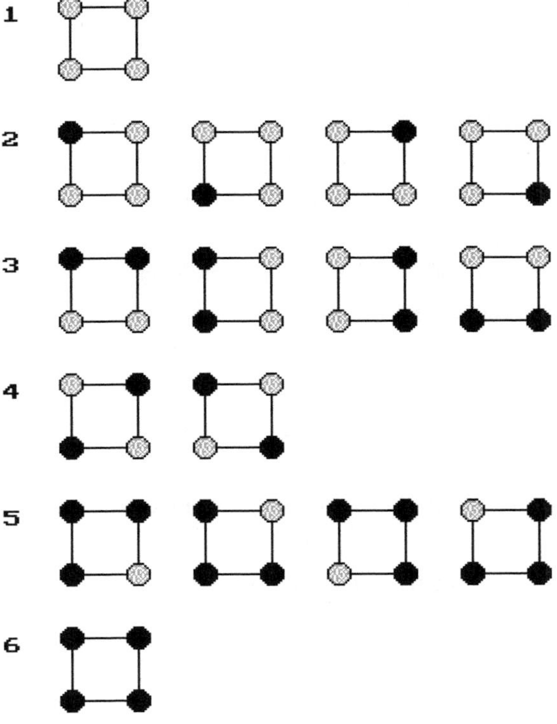

Figure 12.1. *The six ways of coloring the vertices of the symmetry-types of the square*

When we come across a box indexed by *number* and whose content is 0, we set it at 1 to indicate that it is now processed, and we determine the numbers of the seven other configurations deduced by symmetries. Then the boxes corresponding to these numbers are also set at 1 to indicate that we no longer have to worry about them.

In order to determine the numbers of configurations that result from one of the symmetries starting from a certain *number*, we are led to convert this number into a binary word of four characters, then to place it in a square matrix *m*[][] with two lines and two columns, which gives the colors 0 or 1 of each vertex.

From there we carry out each symmetry, which we then reconvert into a decimal number called *newnumber*. For example, *number* = 13 gives table $m[\ ]=1011$ in ascending binary, the +90° rotation transforms it into 1101, i.e. *newnumber* = 11, etc. Hence the program:

```
for(number=0; number<16; number++)  if (do[number]==0)
          { q=number;  do[number]=1; counter++;
  for(L=0;L<2;L++)  for(C=0;C<2;C++)    { m[L][C]=q%2; q=q/2; }
  k=0; square(xo,yo); k++;
  rotationp(); if (do[newnumber]==0)
          { nsquare(xo+60*(k++),yo); do[newnumber]=1;  }
  rotationm(); if (do[newnumber]==0)
          { nsquare(xo+60*(k++),yo); do[newnumber]=1;  }
  rotationd(); if (do[newnumber]==0)
          { nsquare(xo+60*(k++),yo); do[newnumber]=1;  }
  reflecth();   if (do[newnumber]==0)
          { nsquare(xo+60*(k++),yo); do[newnumber]=1;  }
  reflectv();   if (do[newnumber]==0)
          { nsquare(xo+60*(k++),yo); do[newnumber]=1;  }
  reflectd();  if (do[newnumber]==0)
          { nsquare(xo+60*(k++),yo); do[newnumber]=1;  }
  reflectdd();  if (do[newnumber]==0)
          { nsquare(xo+60*(k++),yo); do[newnumber]=1;  }
  yo+=60;   /* we go down on the screen to prepare the new row */
 }
```

The functions *square*(*xo*, *yo*) and *nsquare*(*xo*, *yo*) draw the square (one vertex of which is in *xo*, *yo*) with its four colored vertices based on the colors in *m*[*L*][*C*] or *newm*[*L*][*C*]. The rotation and reflection functions are given later, in the pawns on a chessboard example (see section 12.2.2).

This example put us in the context where Burnside's theorem will come in. As soon as the situation becomes complicated compared to the example above, we can no longer do an exhaustive breakdown, as we just did for the squares, and we need to use the following theorem.

12.2. Burnside's formula

Let us consider a set E and a group G of permutations acting on this set. The number of orbits (or equivalence classes) is equal to:

$$\frac{1}{|G|}\sum_{g \in G}|S_g|$$

where S_g associated with permutation g is the set x of elements of E that are stable through g, i.e. $g(x) = x$.[3] We will now use this formula in several examples.

First, let us return to our initial example of colorings of the vertices of a square, with four rotations called *Id* (identity), r_1, r_2, r_3 and the four reflections of the diagonal axes *BD* and *AC*, the vertical *V* or horizontal *H*, let us apply the formula:

– $|S_{Id}| = 16$, as each configuration is stable through identity;

– $|S_{r1}| = |S_{r3}| = 2$, as only configurations with one color, 1 or 2, remain stable under the effect of rotations of ±90° angles. To see it, we give one of the two colors to *A*. The +90° rotation forces *B* to be of the same color. Then this rotation forces *C* to be the same color. Then it forces *D* to be of this color;

– $|S_{r2}| = 4$, as under the effect of the rotation of a 180° angle, we have the stable configurations $A_1B_1C_1D_1$, $A_2B_2C_2D_2$, $A_2B_1C_2D_1$ and $A_1B_2C_1D_2$;

---

3. The two bars around a set indicate that it is the number of elements of this set. We will not show Burnside's theory here. We will simply give the following indications:

– with x belonging to set E, let us call its orbit (or class) O_x, i.e. the set of elements gx with g describing the group of permutations G. For an element x of E, we call the set G_x of g permutations, such that $gx = x$ is the stabilizing sub-group of x. Therefore we show that $|O_x| = |G| / |G_x|$.

– when two elements are in the same orbit, we show that they have conjugacy stabilizing sub-groups, i.e. if x and y are two elements of E such that g is in G with $gx = y$, then $gG_xg^{-1} = G_y$, G_x and G_y being the stabilizing sub-groups of x and y.

– $|S_{BD}| = |S_{AC}| = 8$;

– $|S_V| = |S_H| = 4$.

Finally, the number sought is:

$$(1 / 8)(16 + 2 + 2 + 4 + 8 + 8 + 4 + 4) = 6$$

12.2.1. *Complementary exercise: rotation-type colorings of the vertices of a square*

Still with the vertices of a square colored with a choice of one of two colors, how many different rotation-type only configurations are there, where these rotations leave the square invariant?

This is the context of Burnside's formula. The four rotations actually form a group of permutations, the product of two rotations being one rotation. Let us indicate that it is not the same for the four reflections, the product of two reflections never being one reflection.

The same problem could be posed in the following way: four chairs are placed around a square table. These chairs are of two possible colors. How many different arrangements of chairs are there, considering arrangements that result from rotations around the table are identical?

We find $|S_{Id}| = 16$, $|S_{r1}| = |S_{r3}| = 2$, $|S_{r2}| = 4$, hence by Burnside's formula:

$$(1 / 4)(16 + 2 + 2 + 4) = 6 \text{ solutions}$$

Furthermore they are the same as those obtained previously. In this case, we could have also easily found this result without Burnside's formula.

12.2.2. *Example 2: pawns on a chessboard*

On a 4×4 square chessboard, how many square symmetry-type ways are there of placing eight pawns?

As before, rotations are called Id, r_1, r_2, r_3 in order of increasing angles 0, 90, 180 and 270°, and the reflections are called H, V, AD and BC, according to their axes. For this group G, we have $|G| = 8$.

On the other hand:

– $|S_{Id}| = C_{16}^{8} = 12\ 870$, as they are all the possible configurations;

– $|S_{r1}| = |S_{r3}| = C_4^2 = 6$, as we must take two out of four squares from a quarter of the square in the top left (see Figure 12.2), then take their reflections through successive quarter turns, which finally makes eight occupied boxes remaining globally invariant by rotation r_1;

– $|S_{r2}| = C_8^4 = 70$, because we take four out of the eight boxes of the half-square and we reproduce them by rotation, which gives eight boxes globally invariant through half-turn rotation;

– $|S_{AC}| = |S_{BD}| = C_6^4 + C_4^2 C_6^3 + C_6^2 = 150$. We actually begin by taking the case where no pawn is found on the diagonal (see Figure 12.3), we are left with occupying four out of six boxes of the half-square bordered by AC, i.e. C_6^4 cases, and we take the four symmetrical cases, which gives a globally invariant configuration each time.

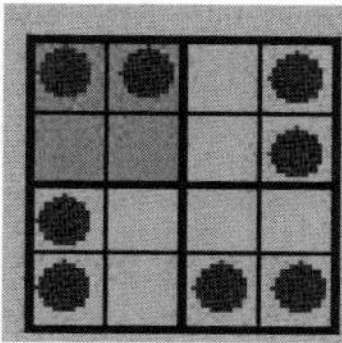

Figure 12.2. *Configuration invariant through +90° rotation*

Then we have the case where two boxes of the diagonal are occupied (i.e. C_4^2 cases), and each time we need to take three out of six boxes of the half-square, i.e. C_6^3, which we reproduce by reflection.

Finally, the case where the four diagonal squares are taken remains, and we take two out of six boxes from the half-square, i.e. C_6^2 cases, which we reproduce by reflection. Note that it is impossible to have an odd number of squares occupied on the diagonal.

$$|S_H| = |S_V| = C_8^4 = 70$$

as we are taking four out of eight boxes from the half-square, and we are reproducing them by reflection.

The total number of configurations is:

$$(1 / 8)(12870 + 6 + 6 + 70 + 2\times150 + 2\times70) = 1{,}674$$

Now, let us deal with some complementary questions.

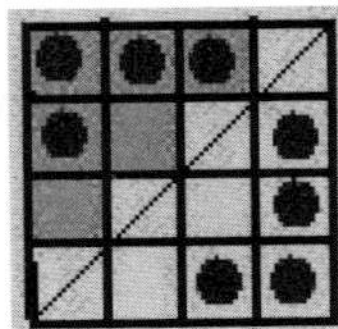

Figure 12.3. *Configuration invariant through diagonal symmetry*

12.2.2.1. *Programming for the creation of all these configurations*

For lack of a better way, we begin by creating all possible configurations of the eight pawns on the chessboard, i.e. 12,870. As a configuration can be read as a 16-letter word with eight 0s (empty squares) and eight 1s (occupied squares), which gives a binary number that can be converted into a decimal. Each configuration therefore carries a number. The 12,870 configurations, with their number, are recorded in an array *a*[12870]. Then we run through the table using a method similar to the sieve of Eratosthenes.

We start from the first configuration and take its seven symmetries, eliminating them when they carry a number different from that of this first configuration. Elimination consists of setting the contents of the box where they are found in table *a*[] to 0. We run through the table in this way.

Each time we come across a square *i* that is not at 0, we display the corresponding configuration. Then we eliminate (by setting to 0) all those with a different number that are obtained by symmetries and located in squares with numbers greater than *i*.

Some configurations out of the 1,674 are given in Figure 12.4.

We deduce from it the following program:

N is the number of squares on the chessboard, here 16, with length 4 and NP is the number of pawns, here 8.

```
k=0;

for(number=0; number<pow(2.,N); number++)
  { q=number; counter1=0;
    for(j=0; j<N; j++)   {r[j] = q%2; q = q/2;  if (r[j]= =1) counter1 ++; }
    if (counter1==NP) a[k++]=number;
  } /* array a[] , of length k=12870, contains all  the configurations */
```

```
for ( i =0; i<k; i++)  if (a[i]!=0)
  { q=a[i];
   /* starting from number a[i], we reconstitute the matrix using 0 and 1
      m[L][C] */
    for(L=0; L<length; L++)  for(C=0; C<length; C++)

      { m[L][C]=q%2; q=q/2; }
     rotationp();   for(j=i+1;j<k;j++) if (newn==a[j]) {a[j]=0; break;}
     rotationm();   for(j=i+1;j<k;j++) if (newn==a[j]) {a[j]=0; break;}
     rotationd();   for(j=i+1;j<k;j++) if (newn==a[j]) {a[j]=0;break;}
     reflecth();    for(j=i+1;j<k;j++) if (newn==a[j]) {a[j]=0;break;}
     reflectv();    for(j=i+1;j<k;j++) if (newn==a[j]) {a[j]=0;break;}
     reflectd();    for(j=i+1;j<k;j++) if (newn==a[j]) {a[j]=0;break;}
     reflectdd();   for(j=i+1;j<k;j++) if (newn==a[j]) {a[j]=0;break;}
  }
```

Then counting the boxes of table a[] *which are not at 0, with drawings of corresponding chessboards.*

```
void rotationp(void)     /* rotation of 90° */
{ newn=0; f =1;
  for(L=0; L<length; L++)  for(C=0; C<length; C++)
     { newm[L][C]=m[C][length-1-L]; newn+=newm[L][C]*f; f=2*f; }
}
```

For other symmetries we give only the associated formula:

rotationm() of 270°: newm[L][C]=m[length-1-C][L];

rotationd () of 180°: newm[L][C]=m[length-1-L][length-1-C];

reflecth() , reflection of horizontal axis: newm[L][C]=m[length-1-L][C];

reflectv() of vertical axis : newm[L][C]=m[L][length-1-C];

reflectd() of the axis of the first diagonal: newm[L][C]=m[C][L];

reflectdd() of the axis of the second diagonal:
newm[L][C]=m[length-1-C][length-1-L];

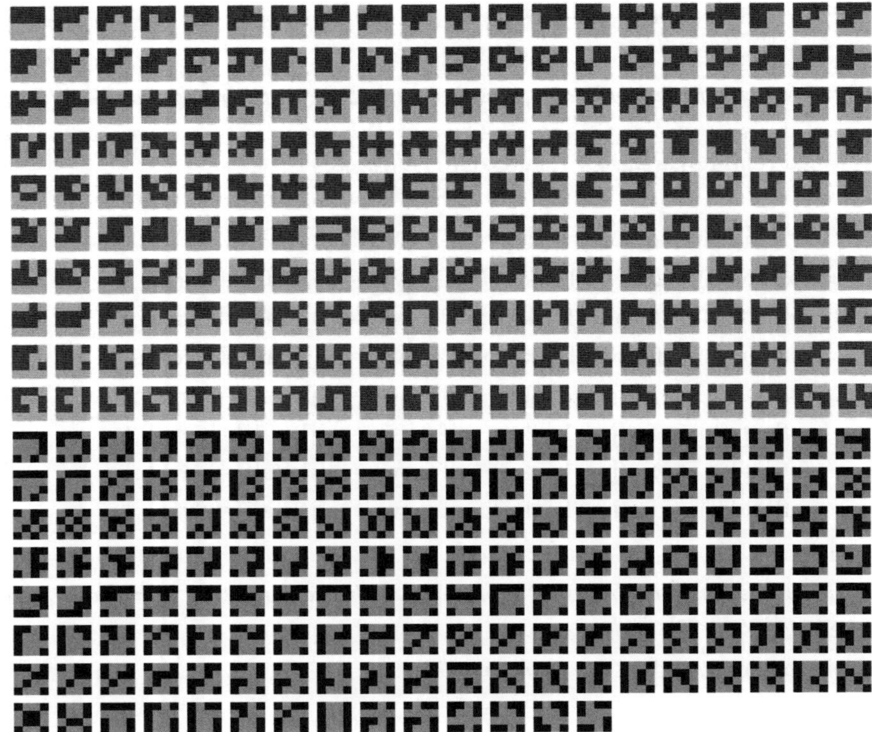

Figure 12.4. *First and last symmetry-type configurations of the square of the eight pawns on the 16-square chessboard*

On the subject of results, we can vary the number of pawns. For a 16-square chessboard, with the number of pawns varying from one to eight (or from 15 to 8), the number of configurations is:

3, 21, 77, 252, 567, 1,951, 1,465, 1,674

12.2.2.2. *Connected configurations*

Now, out of the 1,674 configurations obtained we only want those where the zone occupied by the pawns is connected, i.e. such that the squares corresponding to the occupied squares are all stuck to each other on one of their sides.

In order to carry out this pruning, we devote ourselves on each one of the 1,674 configurations to a graphical exploration (see Chapter 29 on graphical exploration).

We start from a square occupied by a pawn and do an in-depth exploration of adjacent occupied squares.

If, at the end of the exploration, we have fallen exactly on the eight occupied squares, this configuration is kept and answers our problem. Therefore we find 195 connected configurations (see Figure 12.5).

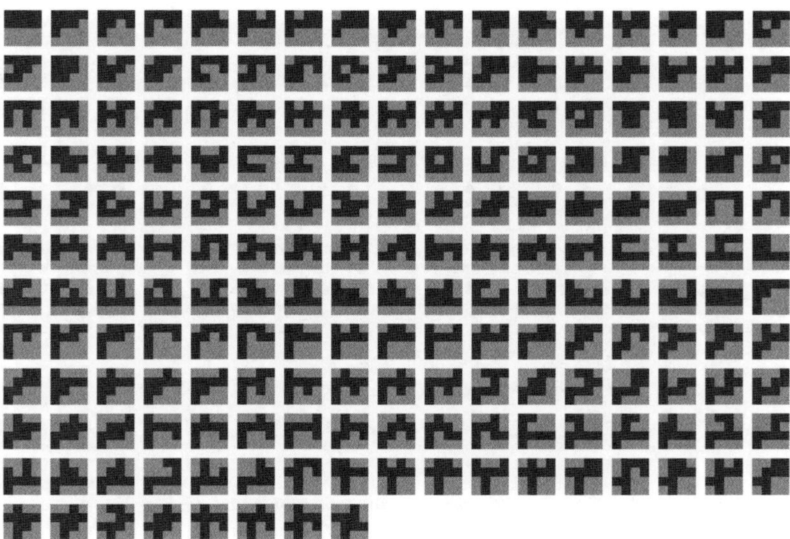

Figure 12.5. *All the connected shapes of surfaces occupied by the eight pawns on the 4×4 chessboard, numbering 195*

12.2.3. *Example 3: pearl necklaces*

12.2.3.1. *We have 10 pearl necklaces with five pearls in one color and five in another. How many rotation-type necklaces are there (those of the corresponding regular decagon)?*

There are 10 rotations: $|G| = 10$. Let us number the angle rotation k: $k \,.\, 2\pi / 10$.

$|S_{\text{Id}}| = C_{10}^{\,5} = 252$, because all the possible configurations remain invariant by identity.

$|S_1| = |S_3| = |S_5| = |S_7| = |S_9| = 0$, as any rotation of an odd number is opposite to the presence of five pearls of the same color. Therefore, when we give a color to a pearl the repetition of the rotation r_1 produces the same coloring for all the pearls.

$|S_2| = |S_4| = |S_6| = |S_8| = 2$, because in the case of rotation 2 there are two ways of placing two pearls with different colors on a 1/5 turn. This is reproduced five times by rotations to make a full turn, which gives five pearls in one color and five in the other. It is the same for multiple rotations of 2. The number of necklaces (see Figure 12.6) is:

$$(252 + 2 + 2 + 2 + 2) / 10 = 26$$

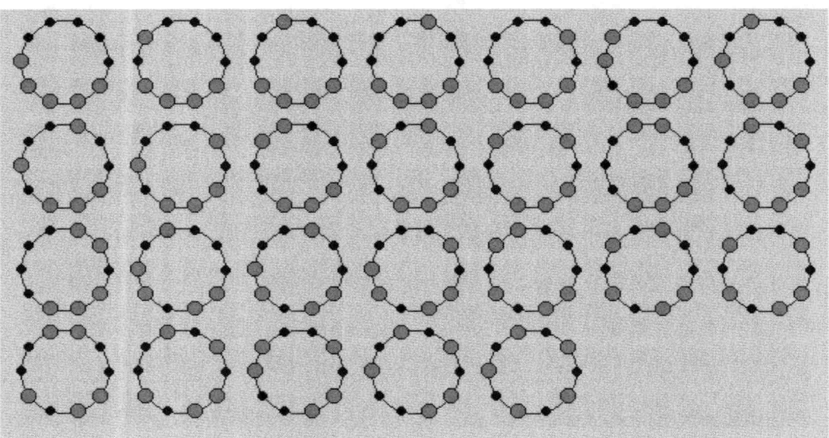

Figure 12.6. *The 26 different rotation-types for pearl necklaces with five pearls in one color and five in another*

12.2.3.2. *How many rotation and reflection-type necklaces made up of 10 pearls, with five pearls in one color and five in another, are there?*

Now $|G| = 20$. The two types of reflections are added to the rotations seen above:

– for reflections of intermediate axes between two vertices, we need an even number of pearls of the same color, and this does not happen;

– for reflections passing through two opposite vertices, it is necessary for a pearl of one color to be on one of the two vertices, and a pearl of the other color on the other vertex, which makes two possibilities.

Each time, two pearls of the same color remain to be placed in four positions located on one side of the axis, i.e. $C_4^{\,2} = 6$ cases. We then reproduce the drawing by reflection, which gives five pearls of the same color. We do this for the five axes concerned.

The number of necklaces is $(260 + 5 \,.\, 12) / 20 = 16$.

12.2.3.3. *Case where the necklace has N different pearls. How many different rotation-type configurations are there?*

There are $N!$ ways of placing the N objects in the circle. Now, if we make the rotations act, each orbit (equivalent class) has N of these configurations. The number of orbits is $N! / N = (N-1)!$.

Burnsides's formula enables us to obtain the same result, because $(1 / N) \Sigma |S_a|$, with $|S_{Id}| = N!$ and all the others are $|S_a| = 0$, giving $(N-1)!$.

12.2.4. *Example 4: coloring of a stick*

A cylindrical stick is divided into five stripes with the same dimensions. We have N colors to paint each one of the stripes. How many symmetry-type colorings of the stick, namely identity, and 180° rotations that reverse it, are there?

The number of possible colorings is N^5, if we do not take into consideration the symmetries. A configuration where the colors are the same by symmetry around the center of the stick gives an orbit (a class of equivalent configurations) to an element. This case is presented N^3 times. We are left with $N^5 - N^3$ remaining configurations, whose classes include both elements.

Finally the number of orbits is:

$$N^3 + (N^5 - N^3) / 2 = (N^5 + N^3) / 2$$

Using Burnside's theorem, this makes:

$$(1 / 2) \Sigma |S_a|, \text{ with } |S_{Id}| = N^5,$$

and: $|S_{Rotation}| = N^3$

hence the same result.

12.3. Exercises

12.3.1. Coloring the vertices of a square

a) We consider words of n characters based on three letters a, b and c where two successive letters of the word are always different, in other words there are no aa, bb or cc blocks. How many such words are there?

Let us begin with a word that starts with *a*. The second letter is *b* or *c*. Each time after that, the third letter has two possibilities. And so on and so forth. There are 2^{n-1} words beginning with *a*, because there is a single word of length 1, and the number of words doubles when the length increases by 1. We do the same with words starting with *b* then *c*, i.e. a total of $3 \,.\, 2^{n-1}$ words.

b) We add the extra constraint that the last letter of the word must be different from the first and call the number of these words u(n). Show that $u(n) = 3 \,.\, 2^{n-1} - u(n-1)$ *for* $n > 1$, *and* $u(1) = 0$.

To show this, we construct a tree where words are read going down the branches, starting from *a*, and similarly starting from *b* and *c* (see Figure 12.7). We take words beginning with *a*, obtained at 1°, of which there are 2^{n-1}, and remove all those that end in *a*. Furthermore this last letter *a* comes from words $n-1$ long not ending with *a*, and number $u(n-1)$ that should be divided by three because we only took words beginning with *a*. Hence, $u(n) = 3 \,.\, 2^{n-1} - u(n-1)$. Pursuing the calculation, the following explicit formula results: $u(n) = 2^n + 2(-1)^n$.

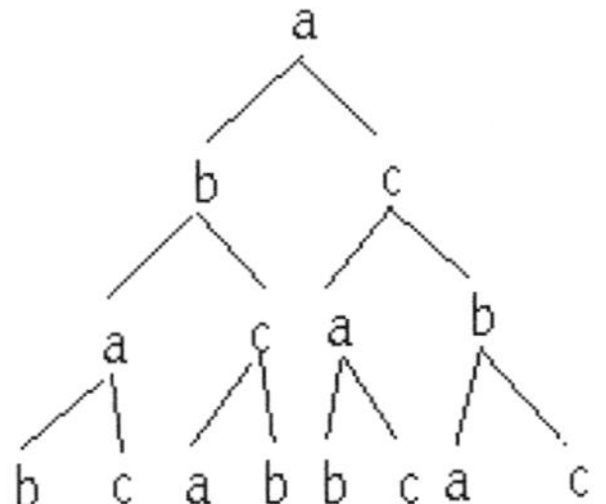

Figure 12.7. *Tree structure of words*

c) Consider a square ABCD whose vertices can be colored using three colors, without being forced to use all of them, where two neighboring vertices never have the same color. How many possible colorings are there?

The colorings can be coded using cyclical words of four characters, based on three letters, without two successive letters being identical. The number of colorings was found in the previous question, i.e. $u(4) = 18$.

d) How many possible symmetry-type colorings of the square are there?

In order to do this, we take the conditions of Burnside's theorem. Among the colorings found in part c) we only keep those that are different after the rotation- and reflection-type of the square. We have $|S_{id}| = 18$, $|S_{r1}| = |S_{r3}| = 0$ and $|S_{r2}| = 6$ (two opposite vertices have three possible colors, and each time the two remaining have two possible colors), $|S_H| = |S_V| = 0$ and $|S_{diag1}| = |S_{diag2}| = 12$ (the two opposite vertices that are not on the diagonal have one of the three colors, and each time one of the two remaining has two possible colors). The number of symmetry-type colorings of the square is: (18 + 6 + 12 + 12) / 8 = 6.

12.3.2. *Necklaces with stones in several colors*

A regular heptagon – a regular polygon with seven vertices numbered *ABCDEFG* – has two vertices colored in blue, four in green and one in red.

a) How many ways are there of placing these colors at the seven vertices ABCDEFG ?

This is an anagram problem. Coding the blue using 0, green using 1 and red using 2, we have to form all the words of seven characters with letter 0 twice, letter 1 four times and letter 2 once, i.e. $C_7^2\ C_5^4 = 105$ ways.

b) Consider the heptagon as a necklace that can be flipped using rotations. How many different necklaces are there based on the rotation-type colors of the heptagon?

The regular heptagon has seven rotations. With the notations associated with Burnside's formula, this gives $|S_{Id}| = 105$ and $|S_{r1}| = |S_{r2}| = \ldots = |S_{r6}| = 0$, because no configuration can remain stable by rotation of a non-null angle. Finally, the number of different rotation-type necklaces is 105 / 7 = 15.

c) The necklaces can now be not only flipped (rotations) but turned (reflections). How many different symmetry-type necklaces of the heptagon are there?

When we do the axis reflection passing through vertex *A* and look for the configurations that remain stable, vertex *A* must be red. Then we symmetrically place the two vertices with blue, which is done in three ways. Hence $|S_{sA}|=3$. It is this way for the seven reflections. Hence the number of symmetry-type necklaces is: (105 + 7×3) / 14 = 9.

d) Set up a program to find these results, and out of the nine symmetry-type necklaces, extract those that are auto-symmetrical (which assumes one reflection axis).

```
NB[0]=1;NB[1]=4;NB[2]=2;  /* the seven given colors */
N=0;for(letter=0;letter<NBletters;letter++)N+=NB[letter]; /*here N=7 */
q=0;
```

```
for(letter=0;letter<NBletters;letter++) for(i=0;i<NB[letter];i++)  a[q++]=letter;
counter=0; /* the first word, here 0111122, in table a[] */
for(;;)
 { display the word in table a[]
   pow3=1;nbd=0;    /* conversion of the word into a decimal number nbd */
   for(k=0;k<N;k++) {nbd+=a[k]*pow3; pow*=3;}
   b[counter]=nbd;
              /* the number-configurations are placed in table b[]*/
             /* anagram programs  */
   k=N–1;   while (a[k]<=a[k-1] && k>=1) k--;
   pospivot=k–1;  if (pospivot==-1) break;
   k=N–1;  while(a[k]<=a[pospivot]) k--;   posreplacement=k;
   aux=a[pospivot];a[pospivot]=a[posreplacement];a[posreplacement]=aux;
   g=pospivot+1;d=N–1;   while(g<d){ aux=a[g]; a[g]=a[d]; a[d]=aux;g++; d--;}
   counter++;  /* in our example the counter will reach 105 */
 }
for(n=0; n<counter;n++)  done[n]=NO;
for(n=0;n<counter;n++)  if(done[n]==NO)
  { q=b[n];      for(k=0;k<N;k++) {r[k]=q%3; q=q/3;}
   for(head=1;head<N;head++)  /* we carry out the six rotations */
     { nbd=0;pow3=1;   /* calculation of the number nbd corresponding to one
                          rotation */
       for(k=0;k<N;k++) {nbd+=r[(head+k)%N]*pow3; pow3*=3;}
       for(k=n+1;k<counter;k++) if (b[k]==nbd) {done[k]=YES; break;}
              /* search for the number corresponding to a rotation in array
                 b[], set to YES in do[] */
     }
   for(head=0;head<N;head++)     /* we carry out the seven reflections */
    { nbd=0;pow3=1;
       for(k=0;k<N;k++) {nbd+=r[(head+N–k)%N]*pow3; pow3*=3;}
      for(k=n+1;k<nombre;k++) if (b[k]==nbd) {done[k]=YES; break;}
     }
  }
for(k=0;k<number;k++) if (done[k]==NO) printf("%d ",b[k]);
```

```
            /* here we have the nine symmetry-type necklaces in the form of
numbers.
                What is left to do is to draw them */
          /* search for auto-symmetrical necklaces */
   for(k=0;k<number;k++) if (done[k]==NO)  for(head=0;head<N;head++)
     { flag=YES;
       q=b[k]; for(i=0;i<N;i++)  {r[i]=q%3; q=q/3;}
      for(i=0;i<N;i++) if (r[(head+N-i)%N]!=r[(head+i)%N]) {flag=NO; break;}
      if (flag==YES)  draw the necklace
     }
```

The results are shown in Figures 12.8a, b and c.

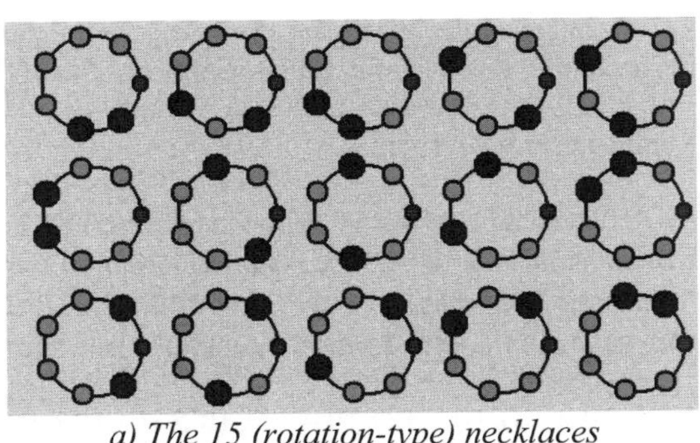

a) The 15 (rotation-type) necklaces

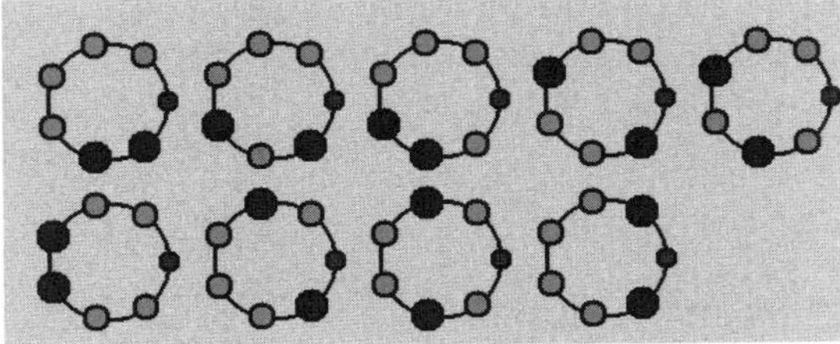

b) The nine (symmetry-type) necklaces

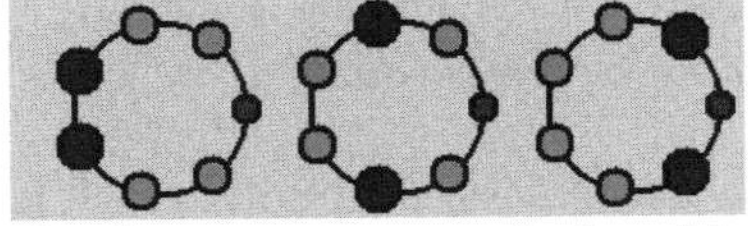

c) The three auto-symmetrical necklaces

Figure 12.8. *Necklaces made up of seven pearls, with four pearls in one color, two in another color and one in a third color*

12.3.3. *Identical balls in identical boxes*

How many ways are there to distribute 15 identical balls in three identical boxes?

Let us begin by assuming different boxes. The number of ways of placing the 15 identical balls in these three boxes is $C_{17}^{2} = 136$. Then let us now consider the boxes to be identical. We have to determine the different permutation-type configurations of the three boxes considered to be different. Furthermore, six permutations act on the three boxes. We are in the context of Burnside's formula. We have three fixed points on the six permutations – the identity permutation, three with one fixed point, and two (the derangements) have no fixed point. When the permutation has its three fixed points, $|S_{\text{Id}}| = 136$. When a permutation p_1 has a fixed point, $|S_{\text{p1}}| = 8$ because the stable configurations under the effect of p_1 are such that two of the boxes must contain the same number of balls, i.e. 0 or 1 or 2 … or 7. Finally, in case of derangement d, $|S_{\text{d}}| = 1$ because the three boxes must contain the same number of balls, i.e. five in this case, and there is only one possibility. The number of ways is:

$$(136 + 3 \,.\, 8 + 2 \,.\, 1) / 6 = 27$$

For the program, all we have to do is split the number 15 into three numbers (positive or null) whose sum is equal to 15, with the order in which we take these three numbers not coming into play. We can therefore choose to write the three numbers in ascending order in the broad sense. We get the configurations:

(0 0 15), (0 1 14), (0 2 13), (0 3 12), (0 4 11), (0 5 10), (0 6 9), (0 7 8), (1 1 13),

(1 2 12), …., (5 5 5)

Hence the program:

```
for(i=0; i<=5; i++)  for(j=i; j<=7; j++)  if (15–i–j >= j)

{ k=15–i–j;  printf("(%d %d %d)",i,j,k); }
```

12.3.4. *Tiling an Aztec diamond using l-squares*

We consider an Aztec diamond of third order (see Figure 12.9 on the left) and tile it in all possible ways with patterns in the shape of l-squares (three squares stuck along their side at right angle), i.e. ⊾. We want to find all the non-equivalent tilings (different with a symmetry-type Aztec diamond).

Just like the square, the Aztec diamond has four rotations and four reflections that leave it invariant. Thanks to a program analogous to the one used for the domino tilings of a rectangle, experimentally we find 18 tilings for this Aztec diamond using l-squares. We also notice that only four subsist are different to symmetry-types (see Figure 12.9).

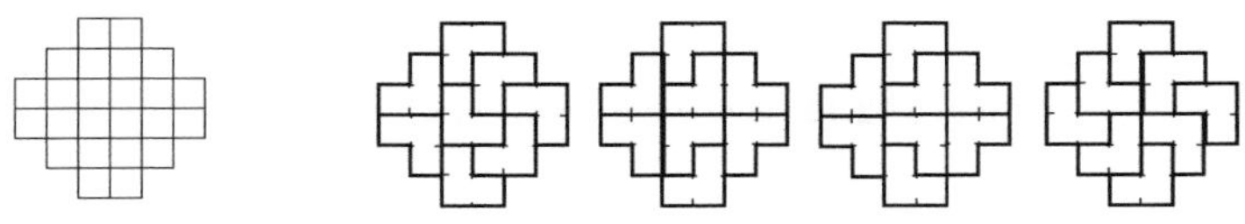

Figure 12.9. *Aztec diamond of third order (left), and the four tilings using different symmetry-type l-squares (right)*

The first equivalence class is made up of eight tilings. The second is made up of four tilings, just like the third. Finally the fourth class has two tilings. Note that the first has no internal symmetry, the second and third have one (a rotation of 180° for one, a horizontal reflection axis for the other), and that the forth has the four symmetries of rotation.

We can find this result using Burnside's formula. The number of invariant tilings by identity is 18. The number of invariant tilings through 90° rotation is two, this is similar for a -90° rotation (see Figure 12.10).

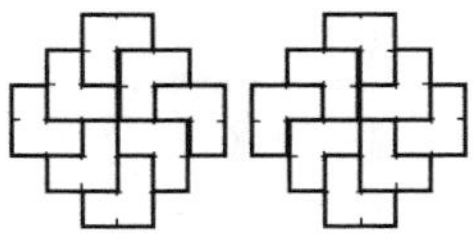

Figure 12.10. *Two invariant tilings through a rotation of 90°*

The number of those unchanged by half-turn is six: the two that are already stable through 90° rotation plus four others (see Figure 12.11).

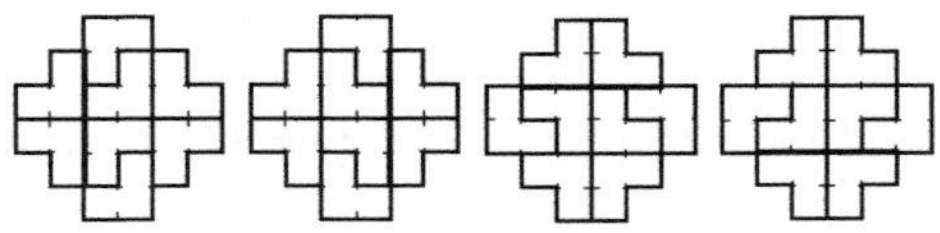

Figure 12.11. *Four invariant tilings by half-turn*

None remain invariant by reflection in the diagonal axis, and two remain stable by reflection around a vertical axis (see Figure 12.12), similarly by reflection around a horizontal axis.

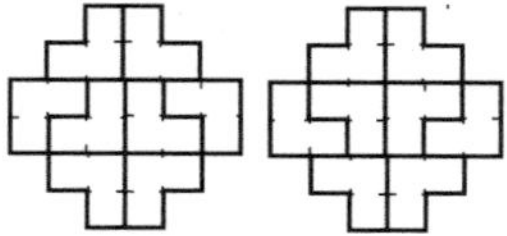

Figure 12.12. *Two invariant tilings by vertical reflection*

The number of different tilings is $(18 + 2 + 6 + 2 + 2 + 2) / 8 = 4$.

12.3.5. *The 4×4 Sudoku: search for fundamentally different symmetry-type grids*

Let us recall the principle of the game. The 4×4 square is in turn divided into four square blocks of 2×2, called B_1, B_2, B_3 and B_4 (see Figure 12.13). We have the four numbers 1, 2, 3 and 4. These four numbers must be found in the squares of each one of the four squares. All four must also be found in each one of the four columns and in each of the four lines.

We want to find out the number of possible fillings in keeping with these constraints, i.e. the number of valid complete grids (see [FEI 06, RUS 06]).

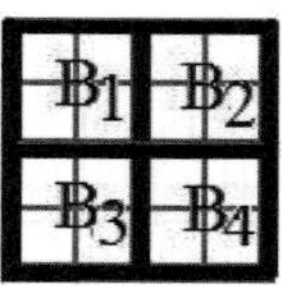

Figure 12.13. *4×4 Sudoku grid*

Let us begin by filling the small square in the top left-hand corner. There are as many ways of filling as there are permutations of the four numbers, i.e. $4! = 24$. Let us choose the permutation in natural order (see Figure 12.14 on the left). Using renumbering-type permutations, there is only one way of filling the grid.

Actually, if we have block B_1 filled as in Figure 12.14 on the right, for example, all we have to do is to add the permutation that exchanges 1 and 4 to find block B_1 in natural order, and we do the same permutation on all the numbers present in the grid: with this renumbering, the grid remains valid.

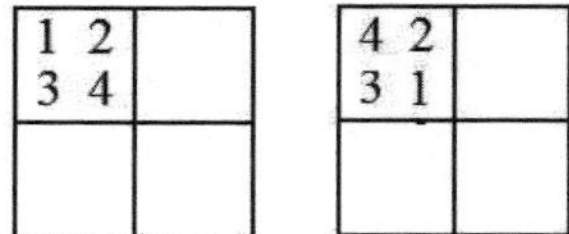

Figure 12.14. *Two valid ways of filling block B1*

Let us complete the first line that already contains 1 2: we can add 3 4 or 4 3 to the right. As a grid remains valid if we exchange the final two columns, there are as many cases with 3 4 as there are 4 3. Let us take 3 4 and finish filling the first row made up of blocks B_1 and B_2. We have two possibilities, indicated in Figure 12.15.

1 2	3 4		
3 4	1 2		

1 2	3 4		
3 4	2 1		

Figure 12.15. *The two ways the first band can be filled*

Now let us fill the first column of B_3 by choosing 2 4 or 4 2. If we take 2 4, we notice that for the first band found above there are two ways to finish filling square B_3 then B_4, and one single way for the second band. Hence three cases (see Figure 12.16).

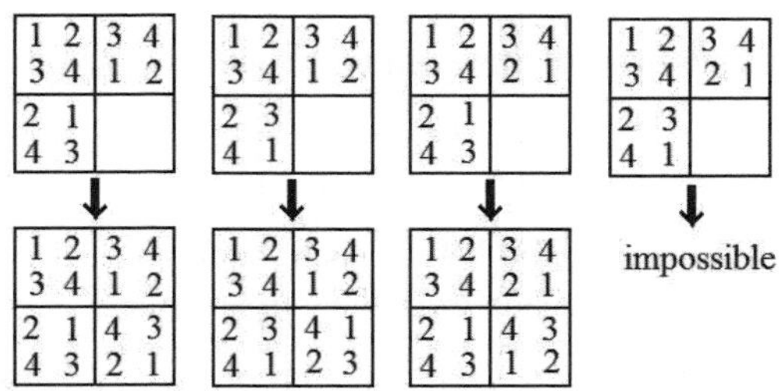

Figure 12.16. *End of filling*

Then we exchange the last two lines, the grid remaining valid. The first column of B_3 becomes 4 2, which gives three more possibilities. Hence a total of six possibilities, and as many more by exchanging the last two columns. Finally, with block B_1 in natural order, there are 12 valid grids (see Figure 12.17). With the 24 possible block B_1 permutations, the total number of ways of filling the Sudoku 4×4 grids is $24 \times 12 = 288$.

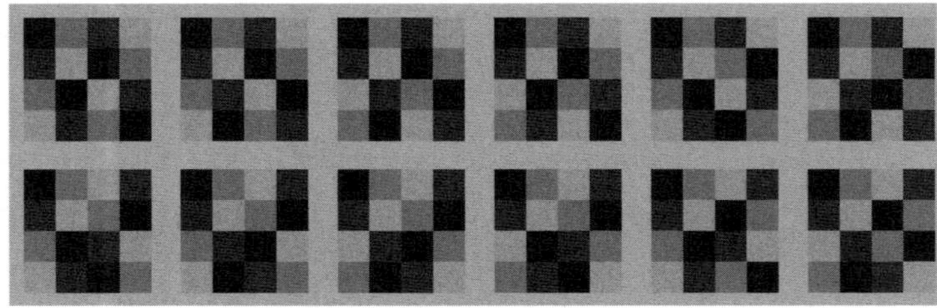

Figure 12.17. *The 12 renumbering-type grids of squares. Here block B_1 is always filled in natural order. Numbers 1,2,3,4 are replaced by four colors (black, light gray, mid gray and dark gray)*

Now let us turn our interest to symmetries of the grid. How many fundamentally different fillings are there?

By this we mean complete grids that are different "symmetry"-types, with these symmetries being the permutations that leave a grid valid. In fact there are two types of symmetries:

– renumberings by permutations of four numbers;

– symmetries belonging to the grid.

We find 12 valid renumeration-type configurations. We are simply going to work on the cases where block B_1 is in natural order. Therefore what are the symmetries of the grid? There are:

– the exchanges of the first column with the second, or the third column with the forth;

– the exchanges of lines one and two, or three and four;

– the exchange of two horizontal bands, each made up of two lines: those made from the two first lines, and that made from the two last lines;

– the exchange of vertical rows, each made up of two columns: the first and the second, or the third with the fourth;

– the "symmetries" of the large square: 90°, 180° and 270° rotations, reflections around a vertical axis or a horizontal axis, as well as around one of the two diagonal axes.

Not all of these symmetries are independent. Some are deduced from others. Notably, reflection of the vertical axis refers to first exchanging the two large vertical rows, then exchanging columns 1 and 2, then exchanging columns 3 and 4, with the order in which these three transformations are done having no importance.

It is the same for a reflection along the horizontal axis. In turn, a 90° rotation refers to a reflection in the vertical axis followed by a reflection in the diagonal axis ↘. This reflection in the diagonal axis refers to transposing the grid. Finally, the eight symmetries of the square (identity, 90°, 180° and 270° rotations, and the four reflections) are all deduced from two symmetries: identity and transposition (diagonal symmetry), as well as exchanges of lines or columns.

Finally, the symmetries of the grid are generated by:

– the two exchanges of successive columns, called $c12$ and $c34$;

– the two exchanges of successive lines, $l12$ and $l34$;

– the exchange of the two vertical rows, C;

– the exchange of the two horizontal bands, L;

– the transposition T.

They produce a group of $2^7 = 128$ permutations (all different). To construct them, we begin by numbering the 16 squares of the grid as in Figure 12.18.

0	1	2	3
4	5	6	7
8	9	10	11
12	13	14	15

Figure 12.18. *Numbering the squares in the Sudoku grid*

The identity, called 0, is defined by the permutation 0 1 2 3 4 5 … 15. Second, the exchange of the first two columns, written 1, is the permutation 1 0 2 3 5 4 6 7 9 8 10 11 13 12 14 15. Next we make up these two permutations by exchanging the last two columns, hence the permutations written 2 and 3.

The four permutations obtained are in turn made up by the exchange of the first two lines, hence the new permutations numbered from 4 to 7. The eight permutations obtained are each made up with the exchange of the last two lines. We arrive at a total of 16 permutations. By exchanging the two vertical rows, we arrive at 32 permutations, then at 64 by exchanging the two horizontal bands, and finally 128 including the permutations obtained with transposition.[4]

These 128 permutations of the squares of the grid can be created using a program, thanks to successive permutation products, and they each carry a number. For example, the 90° rotation is obtained by making up the exchange $c12$ (number 1), the exchange $c34$ (number 2), which gives the number 2 + 1 = 3, then the exchange C of the two vertical rows, hence the number 16 + 3 = 9, then the transposition T, hence the final number 64 + 19 = 83.

Now let us bring out the necessarily different symmetry-type grids.

– *First method:* we found 12 renumbering-type grids. These are reduced to six with the exchange of the last two column-types. These six grids reduced to three with the exchange of the last two line-types (see Figure 12.19a). But are these three grids different, all having different symmetry-types?

No, because we notice that the second becomes the third if we transpose (diagonal reflection) then renumber it (23) in order to return natural order to block B_1 (see Figure 12.19b). Finally, only two necessarily different grids remain (see Figures 12.19c and 12.20).

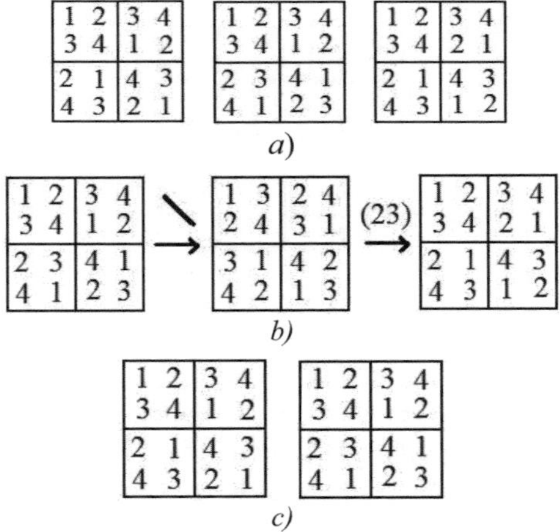

Figure 12.19. *The three grids boil down to two necessarily different grids*

4. We did the succession of permutations that generate the group in a certain order. Do we therefore get all the elements of the group? The answer is yes, but all we have to do is check that all the products in reverse order have already been found: for example C followed by c_{12} is equal to c_{34} followed by C, or even $T c_{12} = l_{12} T$, …, etc.

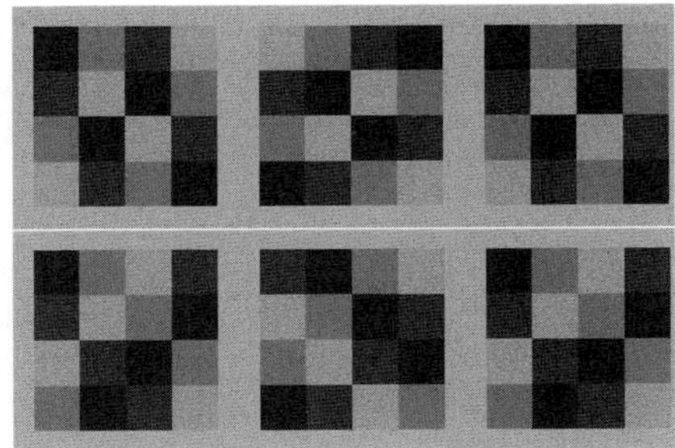

Figure 12.20. *The two grids that remain fixed through 90° rotation, after renumbering. The grid located on the left is turned 90° to the center, then this grid is renumbered on the right, and we end up with the initial grid*

– *Second method:* here we use Burnside's formula. The number of valid renumbering-type grids is 12. The group of permutations acting on the grids is made up of 128 elements. To apply Burnside's formula, all we have to do for each one of the 128 permutations is look for grids outside the 12 that remain fixed. Clearly, when the permutation modifies the natural order of block B_1, we carry out the renumbering that returns it to natural order. For example, the +90° rotation is permutation number 83. Applied to the 12 configurations, we find that only two remain fixed, as seen in Figure 12.20. First we placed the initial grid, then we rotated it 90°, and finally we renumbered the boxes to return block B_1 to natural order, which gives the initial grid in these two cases.

Using a program, by adding the number of configurations that remain fixed under the effect of each one of the 128 symmetries, we arrive at a sum of 128 numbers:

$$12 + 0 + 0 + 8 + 0 + 0 + 0 + 4 + 0 + 0 + 0 + 4 + 8 + 4 + 4 + 4 + 6 + 4 + 4 + 6 + 2 + 0 + \ldots. + 2 + 0 + 0 + 2 = 256$$

Due to Burnside's formula, we find $256/128 = 2$ necessarily different configurations.

Finally, let us move on to groupings in conjugacy classes. As indicated by the calculation above, we have to find 128 numbers corresponding to the invariant configurations through each symmetry. Fortunately, we come across 0 a large number of times. We can simplify the calculations further by grouping the 128 symmetries in classes that we call conjugacy classes. To do this we take a symmetry f then we construct all the symmetries $f' = g^{-1} f g$ where g is a symmetry. We say that f and f' are conjugates. All symmetries of the form f' make up conjugacy class C

of *f*. Then we take a symmetry *h* which is not in *C*. In turn this symmetry assumes a conjugacy class *C'*. The two classes *C* and *C'* are distinct.[5] Continuing in this way, we end up distributing the set of 128 symmetries into a limited number of conjugacy classes.

The interest in these groupings hangs on the fact that elements of the same class have exactly the same number of configurations. In other words, instead of calculating the 128 symmetries as before, it is enough to calculating them on a representative of each conjugacy class.[6] In the case of the 4×4 Sudoku, we find 20 conjugacy classes thanks to a short program that gives us a representative of each class as well as the number of elements of the class, i.e.:

(0 1)(1 4)(3 2)(5 4)(7 4)(15 1)(16 2)(17 4)(20 8)(21 8)(28 4)(29 4)(48 4)
(49 8)(53 4)(64 8)(65 16)(67 8)(80 16)(81 16)

For example, we check that permutation class number 80, with its 16 elements, notably contains rotation 83 (of 90°) of which we found two configurations. For this class we therefore find 2×16 = 32 fixed configurations. We do the same for each class. Instead of having 128 cases to deal with, this is reduced to only 20 cases, which simplifies the calculations.

---

5. If the class of *f* and that of *h* had a common element, we would have two symmetries *p* and *p'* such that $p^{-1} fp = p'^{-1} hp'$. Hence by multiplying the two members, on the left by *p'* and on the right by p'^{-1}, this gives $p' p^{-1} fpp'^{-1} = h$, or $(p\, p'^{-1})^{-1} f\, (p\, p'^{-1}) = h$, h and *f* would be conjugates, which is contrary to the hypothesis.

6. Let us take two symmetries (permutations) *g* and *g'* in the same conjugacy class, i.e. that there is a symmetry *h* such that $g' = h^{-1} gh$. Let us assume that *g* sets exactly *n* Sudoku grids, and notably a renumbering-type grid *X* (which is also a permutation, i.e. *p* in this case). This means that *p*(*X*) is *X* of this permutation type, i.e. *pg*(*X*) = *X*). As $g = h\, g'\, h^{-1}$, this makes $p\, h\, g'\, h^{-1}(X) = X$. By multiplying on the two sides by p^{-1} then by h^{-1}, $g' h^{-1}(X) = h^{-1}\, p^{-1}(X)$ remains. Therefore we use the fact that some symmetry of the grid can commute with a renumbering: therefore renumbering p^{-1} then the symmetry h^{-1} involves applying h^{-1} followed by p^{-1}: $g'(h^{-1}(X)) = p^{-1}(h^{-1}\,(X))$. We have just proved that *g'* sets the configuration $h^{-1}(X)$. Therefore, if *g* sets *n* different grids like *X*, *g'* sets at least as many – all those of the form $h^{-1}(X)$, as well as all the different ones. By starting again on the reverse, with grids set by *g'*, we would find that *g* sets at least as many grids. Therefore *g* and *g'* set exactly the same number of grids.

Chapter 13

Matrices and Circulation on a Graph

In this chapter we will see the direct link that exists between combinatorics on words, routes on a graph, and matrix theory.[1]

To begin with we need to find the number of paths of a given length on a graph. A path from vertex i to vertex j consists of a succession of arches, the first starting at I and the last finishing at j, where the end of one is the beginning of the next, its length being the number of arches that have been run through.

If the graph is not oriented, each edge can be replaced by two arches with opposite directions, and we return to an oriented graph. In this case, a path can contain the same edge that was run through in two directions. With the vertices of the graph marked by letters or numbers, a path becomes a succession of letters or numbers, i.e. a word.

An immediate link exists between reading paths on a graph and word enumeration.

We will begin by studying some simple cases, such as those concerning complete graphs, where counting paths is easy. Then we will see how to carry out calculations using the adjacency matrix of the graphs.

1. In Appendices 1 and 2, we call to mind matrices and determinants.

13.1. Number of paths of a given length on a complete or a regular graph

A complete graph K_n with n numbered vertices is such that each vertex is linked to all the others by a unique arch starting from it. This is like the complete graph K_5 in Figure 13.1, for example.

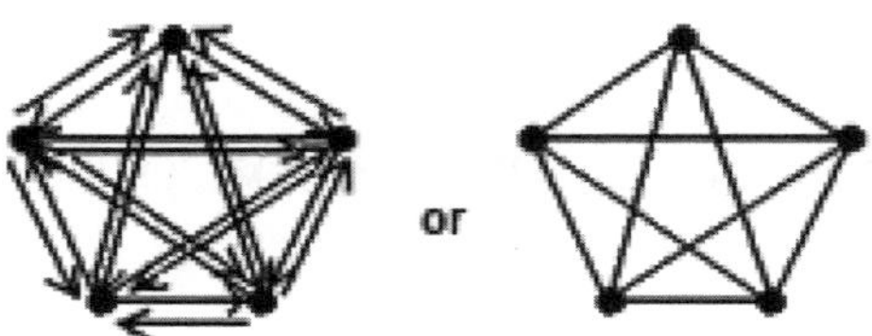

Figure 13.1. *The complete graph K_5*

We want to find the number of paths of a given length k on this graph. Let us choose a starting vertex. Starting from this, we have $n - 1$ arches leading to a neighboring vertex. Then from each one of these neighboring vertices, again we have $n - 1$ possibilities. And so on and so forth until the kth vertex. Starting from a given vertex, we therefore find $(n - 1)^k$ paths.

As each one of the n vertices can be taken as a stating point, the number of paths of length k is $n(n - 1)^k$. With each path thus obtained being constituted from the succession of $k + 1$ vertices, where two adjacent vertices are never identical we find the number of words of length K ($K = k + 1 > 0$) based on n letters with no block of identical letters is $n(n - 1)^{K-1}$.

This is generalized to any so-called (non-oriented) graph, where each vertex has the same degree, which means that each vertex of the non-oriented graph has the same number d of edges attached to it. Starting from a given vertex, there are d^k paths of length k. Starting from a vertex, this makes a total of nd^k paths k long. The generating function associated with this number of paths of a given length is:

$$F(X) = \sum_k nd^k X^k = \frac{n}{1 - dX}$$

Finally let us take the complete bipartite graph $K_{m,n}$. This means that the set of vertices is divided into two parts, having m and n vertices, respectively, and each vertex of one part is linked by an edge to each vertex of the other, as for example graph $K_{3,4}$ in Figure 13.2.

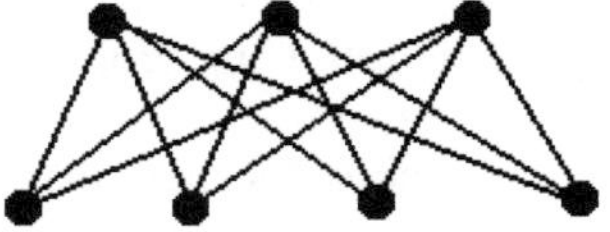

Figure 13.2. *The bipartite complete graph $K_{3,4}$*

First assume that the length k of the paths is even. Alternately taking the m vertices as starting points, there are $mn\ mn...mn = (mn)^{k/2}$ paths, and similarly starting from one of the n vertices, i.e. in total:

$$(m+n)\ (mn)^{k/2} \text{ paths}$$

If the length k of paths is odd, we find $n(mn)^{(k-1)/2}$ paths from each of the m vertices, and $m(mn)^{(k-1)/2}$ paths from each of the n vertices, i.e. in total:

$$(mn + nm)(mn)^{(k-1)/2} = 2(mn)^{(k+1)/2} \text{ paths}$$

We can easily check that the generating function associated with the number of paths of a given length is:

$$F(X) = \frac{m+n+2mnX}{1-mnX^2}$$ [2]

Now let us move on to the general case of a graph where matrix theory comes in.

13.2. Number of paths and matrix powers

We have an oriented graph D with p vertices and take its adjacency matrix A. By definition, the term A_{ij} in line i and column j of this pxp square matrix, is equal to 1 or 0 depending on whether or not there is an arch joining vertex i to vertex j (we will assume that there are not several arches from i to j, but this could be generalized in this case).

Let us express A_{ij} in the form $A_{ij}(1)$ to indicate that it is also the number of paths of length 1 going from vertex i to vertex j. If we remove matrix A to the power n, A^n

2. Actually, the even part of the generating function is: $(m + n) + (m + n)mnX^2 + (m + n)(mn)^2X^4 + \ldots = (m + n) / (1 - mnX^2)$, and the odd part of the function is: $2mnX + 2(mn)^2X^3 + 2(mn)^3X^5 + \ldots = 2mnX(1 + mnX^2 + (mn)^2X^4 + \ldots) = 2mnX / (1 - mnX^2)$.

has as entrance terms that have the interesting characteristic of answering the number of paths problem, due to the following property.

PROPERTY 13.1.– When A is the adjacency matrix of an oriented graph, A^n has coefficient $A_{ij}(n)$ in line i and column j, i.e. the number of n-length paths starting from vertex i and ending up at vertex j. The number of all the n-length paths is equal to the sum of all of the terms in matrix A^n.

To show this property, let us make an argument using recurrence. The property is true in row 1. It is the definition of the adjacency matrix.

Now assume that the property is true for a certain row n: the coefficients of matrix A^n are $A_{ij}(n)$, the number of paths from i to j of length n. Let us show that the property remains true for the following row. The term in line i and column j of matrix $A^{n+1} = A^n A$ is, by definition of the multiplication of matrices:

$$\sum_k A_{ik}(n) A_{kj}(1)$$

i.e. the number of n-length paths from i to k multiplied by those of all the 1-length paths from k to j, with this being done for each intermediate vertex k. We find that it is $A_{ij}(n + 1)$, which is the number of n + 1-length paths going from i to j.

Therefore in order to count all the n-length paths from any vertex, all we have to do is to add up all the coefficients of matrix A^n. We are brought back to a calculation of matrix power.

But how can such a calculation be carried out without doing the multiplications leading to matrix A^n one by one? There is a classic procedure that makes use of the diagonalization of adjacency matrix A (for reminders about matrices see Appendix 1). We are going to see another, often more advantageous, procedure that uses generating functions.

PROPERTY 13.2.– Given $F_{ij}(x)$ the generating function associated with sequence $A_{ij}(n)$ giving the number of n-length paths from i to j:

$$F_{ij}(x) = \sum A_{ij}(n)\, x^n$$

Therefore $F_{ij}(x)$ is the coefficient in line i and column j of matrix $(I - xA)^{-1}$, I being the identity matrix or even, thanks to the matrix inversion formula:

$$F_{ij}(x) = (-1)^{i+j} \frac{\text{determinant of } (I - xA) \text{ where line } j \text{ and column } i \text{ were removed}}{\text{determinant of } (I - xA)}$$

The generating function of all n-length paths is:

$$\sum_{i,j} F_{ij}(x) = \text{sum of all the terms of matrix } (I - xA)^{-1}$$

Actually, by definition: $F_{ij}(x) = A_{ij}(0) + A_{ij}(1)x + A_{ij}(2)x^2 + \ldots$. Therefore, $F_{ij}(x)$ is the entrance of line i and column j of matrix $I + xA + x^2A^2 + \ldots = (I - xA)^{-1}$. All we have to do then is to apply the formula giving the terms of an inverse matrix and using the co-factors, to get the result indicated.

13.2.1. *Example 1: n-length words in an alphabet of three letters 1, 2, 3, with prohibition of blocks 11 and 23*

Oriented graph D creating such words is represented in Figure 13.3. Its adjacency matrix is:

$$A = \begin{pmatrix} 0 & 1 & 1 \\ 1 & 1 & 0 \\ 1 & 1 & 1 \end{pmatrix} \text{ where all paths of length 1 are included:}$$

$$A_{11}(1) = 0, A_{12}(1) = 1, A_{13}(1) = 1, \text{ etc.}$$

In turn $A^2 = \begin{pmatrix} 2 & 2 & 1 \\ 1 & 2 & 1 \\ 2 & 3 & 2 \end{pmatrix}$ gives all paths of length 2:

Where $A_{11}(2) = 2$, there are paths 121 and 131 to $A_{12}(2) = 2$, i.e. 122 and 132, $A_{13}(2) = 1$, i.e. 133, etc.

Note that a n-length path (with n arches) corresponds to a $n + 1$-length word (i.e. $n + 1$ vertices). To get all the n-length paths from any vertex, we carry out $\sum A_{ij}(n)$, where the summation is done on i and j. If we sum all of the generating functions $F_{ij}(x)$ for each value of i and j, the term in x^n of $\sum_{i,j} F_{ij}(x)$ also has $\sum_{i,j} A_{ij}(n)$ for its coefficient.

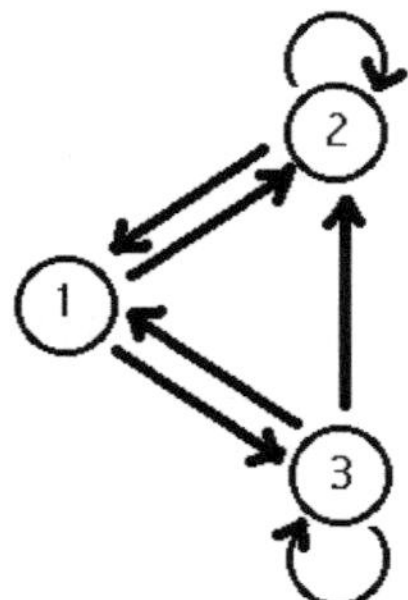

Figure 13.3. *The graph that makes words with neither 11 nor 23 characters*

The generating function $\sum_{i,j} F_{ij}(x)$ is associated with the sequence that gives the number of n-length paths. On the other hand, as we saw: $\sum_{i,j} F_{ij}(x)$ is the sum of terms of matrix $(I - xA)^{-1}$. In this example, the determinant of matrix $I - xA$ is:

$$|I - xA| = \begin{vmatrix} 1 & -x & -x \\ -x & 1-x & 0 \\ -x & -x & 1-x \end{vmatrix} = 1 - 2x - x^2 + x^3$$

The inverse matrix is:

$$(I - xA)^{-1} = \frac{1}{|I - xA|} \begin{pmatrix} (1-x)^2 & x & x(1-x) \\ x(1-x) & 1-x-x^2 & x^2 \\ x & x(1+x) & 1-x-x^2 \end{pmatrix}$$

By adding the terms in the matrix, we find:

$$\sum_{i,j} F_{ij}(x) = (3 + x - x^2) / (1 - 2x - x^2 + x^3)$$

The term in x^n is the number of n-length paths, or even the number of $n + 1$-length words, which we express as $m(n + 1)$:

$$\sum_{i,j} F_{ij}(x) = m_1 + m_2 x + m_3 x^2 + \ldots$$

By adding $m_0 = 1$, the generating function associated with series $m(n)$ is:

$$\sum m(n)x^n = 1 + x \sum_{i,j} F_{i\,j}(x) = (1 + x) / (1 - 2x - x^2 + x^3)$$

and we find $m(1) = 3$, $m(2) = 7$, $m(3) = 16$, $m(4) = 36$, etc.

13.2.2. *Simplification of the calculation*

When calculating the generating function that gives the total number of n-length paths n, for an n, namely $\sum_{i,j} F_{i\,j}(x)$, we get a quotient of polynomials P and Q:

$$\sum_{i,j} F_{ij}(x) = \frac{P(x)}{Q(x)} = \frac{\sum_{q=0}^{e} \beta_q x^q}{\sum_{q=0}^{d} \alpha_q x^q}$$

where e and d are degrees of polynomials P and Q.

More precisely $Q(x)$ is the determinant of matrix $I - xA$. This determinant is linked to the characteristic polynomial of matrix A. By definition, this characteristic polynomial, whose roots are the eigenvalues of matrix A, is the determinant:

$$|A - XI| = (-1)^p (X^p + \alpha_1 X^{p-1} + \alpha_2 X^{p-2} + \ldots + \alpha_{p-r} X^r)$$

where p is the number of lines or columns of matrix A, and r is the degree of multiplicity of the eigenvalue 0. In turn:

$$Q(x) = |I - xA| = |-xI\,(A - (1/x)\,I)|$$

$$= (-1)^p x^p\, |A - (1/x)\,I|$$

$$= (-1)^p x^p (-1)^p ((1/x)^p + \alpha_1 (1/x)^{p-1} + \ldots + \alpha_{p-r} (1/x)^r)$$

$$= 1 + \alpha_1 x + \alpha_2 x^2 + \ldots + \alpha_{p-r} x^{p-r}$$

We find the same coefficients for $Q(x)$ as for the characteristic polynomial of A, and the degree of polynomial Q is $d = p - r \le p$. If matrix A does not have a null eigenvalue, the degree of Q is p.

On the other hand, the polynomial P comes from developing the determinant of matrix $I - xA$ from which we removed one line and one column, as we have seen.

Its degree e is therefore less than or equal to $p - 1$. The difference $e - d$ of the degrees of P and Q is less than the multiciplicity of eigenvalue 0. In particular, if 0 is not the eigenvalue, the difference in degrees is less than 0. We know that in this case (see Chapter 5) the sequence associated with the number $c(n)$ of n-length paths obeys a linear recurrence relation corresponding to the polynomial $Q(x)$, i.e.:

$$\alpha_0\, c(n) + \alpha_1\, c(n-1) + \alpha_2\, c(n-2) + \ldots + \alpha_p\, c(n-p) = 0, \text{ and with } \alpha_0 = 1:$$

$$c(n) = -\alpha_1\, c(n-1) - \alpha_2\, c(n-2) - \ldots - \alpha_p\, c(n-p)$$

Knowing the first terms $c(0)$, $c(1)$, …, $c(p-1)$ therefore enables us to determine the coefficients β_0, β_1, …, β_e of polynomial P. It is the same for the generating function associated with the number $m(n)$ of words corresponding to paths ($n - 1$ long), where only the polynomial of the numerator is modified, becoming $Q(x) + x\,P(x)$, and its degree becoming less than or equal to p. Notably, the sequence $(m(n))$ obeys the same recurrence relation as the sequence $(c(n))$. The method remains analogous in the general case (when 0 is the eigenvalue of A), at the price of some corrections.

Let us apply this method to the example above, where we had $p = 3$. Once $Q(x) = |\, I - xA \,| = 1 - 2x - x^2 + x^3$ has been calculated, we get the recurrence relation on the number of paths $c(n)$, which is written:

$$c(n) = 2\, c(n-1) + c(n-2) - c(n-3)$$

β_0, β_1, β_2 remains to be calculated, from $c(0) = 3$, $c(1) = 7$ (they are the words 12, 13, 21, 22, 31, 32, 33) and $c(2) = 16$ (the corresponding words are 121, 122, 131, 132, 133, 212, 213, 221, 222, 312, 313, 321, 322, 331, 332 and 333). With:

$$P(x) = Q(x)\, (c(0) + c(1)x + c(2)x^2 + \ldots)$$

by identification we deduce from it that:

$$c(0) = \beta_0 \text{ hence } \beta_0 = 3,\ c(1) - 2c(0) = \beta_1,$$

hence $\beta_1 = 1$, $c(2) - 2c(1) - c(0) = \beta_2$ and therefore $\beta_2 = -1$.

The generating function of $c(n)$ is:

$$(3 + x - x^2) \,/\, (1 - 2x - x^2 + x^3)$$

This method enables us to avoid calculating the cofactor matrix leading to $P(x)$.

13.2.3. *Example 2: n-length words based on three letters 1, 2, 3 with blocks 11, 22 and 33 prohibited*

The corresponding graph is nothing other than the complete K_3 graph. The adjacency matrix of this oriented graph is $A = \begin{pmatrix} 0 & 1 & 1 \\ 1 & 0 & 1 \\ 1 & 1 & 0 \end{pmatrix}$.

$$Q(x) = |I - xA| = \begin{vmatrix} 1 & -x & -x \\ -x & 1 & -x \\ -x & -x & 1 \end{vmatrix} = 1 - 3x^2 - 2x^3$$

The number $c(n)$ of n-length paths obeys the recurrence relation:

$$c(n) = 3\ c(n-2) + 2\ c(n-3) \text{ for } n \geq 3$$

Let us determine the initial conditions. We find that:

$$c(0) = 3,\ c(1) = 6 \text{ and } c(2) = 12$$

Assuming that $P(x)= \beta_0 + \beta_1 x + \beta_2 x^2$, and proceeding by identification on the first terms of $P(x) = Q(x)\ (c(0) + c(1)x + c(2)x^2 + \ldots)$, we find:

$$\beta_0 = c(0) = 3,\ \beta_1 = c(1) = 6 \text{ and } \beta_2 = c(2) - 9 = 3$$

The generating function of $(c(n))$ is: $\sum_{i,j} F_{ij}(x) = (3 + 6x + 3x^2) / (1 - 3x^2 - 2x^3)$, which, after simplification by $(1 + x)^2$ is reduced to $3 / (1 - 2x)$.

Calling the number of n-length words $m(n)$, we have: $3 / (1 - 2x) = m(1) + m(2)x + m(3)x^2 + \ldots$, hence the generating function:

$$\sum_{n \geq 0} m(n)x^n = m(0) + m(1)x + m(2)\,x^2 + \ldots = 1 + 3 / (1 - 2x) = (1 + x) / (1 - 2x)$$

We deduce from it that $m(n) = 3\ .\ 2^{n-1}$ for $n \geq 1$ and $m(0) = 1$.[3]

---

3. The calculation that was just done using matrices is principally a school exercise here. To find the number $m(n)$ of such words, the direct calculation is immediate because when moving from a n-length word to words $n + 1$ long obtained by adding a letter at the end, there are always two possibilities. Hence, with $m(1) = 3$, $m(n) = 3 \times 2^{n-1}$.

13.3. Link between cyclic words and closed paths in an oriented graph

In the two examples above, the words were submitted to the constraints of neighboring between letters. Now let us return to these cyclic words, imposing the same constraints between the last letter a_n and the first letter a_1 of each word. A word $a_1a_2...a_n$ can also be expressed as $a_1a_2...a_na_1$. It is therefore bijectively associated with the closed n-length path on the oriented graph. Let $f(n)$ be the number of cyclic n-length words, or even that of closed paths with n arches. Notably, in example 1 of section 13.2.1, where blocks 11 and 23 were forbidden, closed paths two units long are 121, 131, 212, 222, 313 and 333. Cyclic words of two characters long are obtained by dropping the last letter of the paths, i.e. 12, 13, 21, 22, 31 and 33. Therefore $f(2) = 6$. Paths three units long are: 1221, 1331, 1321, 2122, 2132, 2212, 2222, 3133, 3213, 3313, 3333, and $f(3) = 11$.

The number of closed n-length paths from any starting point is obtained by getting the sum of $A_{ii}(n)$ terms in the diagonal of matrix A^n, which we call the *trace* of A^n. We know that the matrix trace is invariant by changing the base. If we know the eigenvalues λ_k (with k from 0 to $p-1$) of matrix A, those of matrix A^n are λ_k^n. Returning to the diagonal matrix by changing the base, the matrix trace A^n is the sum of the n powers of the eigenvalues, hence $f(n) = \sum_{k=0}^{p-1} \lambda_k^n$.

A method for determining the generating function of the $f(n)$ series of closed paths results from this. This function is a polynomial quotient of the form $P(x) / Q(x)$, where $Q(x) = | I - xA |$, as above. $P(x)$, and its coefficients β_k, remain to be found. We can do this using the recurrence formula given by $Q(x)$ and initial conditions. We can also express the generating function:

$$\sum f(n)\, x^n = f(1)x + f(2)x^2 + f(3)\, x^3 + \ldots$$

$$= \sum_{n>0} \operatorname{trace}\left(A^n\right) x^n$$

$$= \sum_{n>0} \Big(\sum_{k=0}^{q} \lambda_k^n\Big) x^n = \sum_{k=0}^{q} \lambda_k x(1 + \lambda_k x + \lambda_k x^2 + \ldots)$$

Where the λ_k designate the non-null eigenvalues (k between 0 and $q \leq p$-1):

$$= \sum_k \frac{\lambda_k x}{1-\lambda_k x} = \frac{-x\,Q'(x)}{Q(x)}$$

because $Q(x) = (1 - \lambda_0 x)(1 - \lambda_1 x)\ldots (1 - \lambda_q x)$, and because by reducing the fractions above to the same denominator $Q(x)$, the numerator becomes $-x\,Q'(x)$.

We end up with the following property.

PROPERTY 13.3.– The number of closed *n*-length paths on a graph of adjacency matrix *A* is equal to the trace of matrix A^n, or even to the coefficient of x^n in the development of:

$$\frac{-xQ'(x)}{Q(x)} \text{ with } Q(x) = \text{determinant of } (I - xA)$$

Let us apply this to example 1 above: we found $Q(x) = 1 - 2x - x^2 + x^3$. After derivation, we get the following generating function of closed paths:

$$\sum f(n)\, x^n = (2x + 2x^2 + 3x^3) \,/\, (1 - 2x - x^2 + x^3)$$

hence $f(1) = 2$, $f(2) = 6$ and $f(3) = 11$, then $f(n + 3) = 2f(n + 2) + f(n + 1) - f(n)$ for $n > 0$.

Let us also apply this method to example 2: with $Q(x) = 1 - 3x^2 - 2x^3$, which we had found before simplification, we get:

$$\sum f(n)x^n = (6x^2 + 6x^3) \,/\, (1 - 3x^2 - 2x^3) = 6x^2 \,/\, (1 - x - 2x^2)$$

hence $f(1) = 0$, $f(2) = 6$, $f(3) = 6$, $f(4) = 18$, and $f(n + 2) = f(n + 1) + 2f(n)$ for $n > 0$.[4]

13.4. Examples

13.4.1. *Dominos on a chessboard*

To count the number of chessboard tilings using 2×1 dominos, we use a vertical line code of the chessboard for each tiling, with one number per line. We put the number 1 if the domino concerned crosses the vertical line – therefore it is a horizontal domino – and 0 if not (see Figure 13.4).

4. Another method consists of using the fact that the adjacency matrix of the graph is circulant (see Appendix 1, section A1.9). The eigenvalues are $\lambda_k = j^k + j^{2k}$ for *k* from 0 to 2, hence $\lambda_0 = 2$, $\lambda_1 = -1$ and $\lambda_2 = -1$. Therefore $f(n) = \text{trace}(A^n) = 2^n + 2\,(-1)^n$.

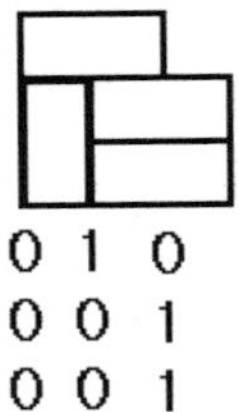

Figure 13.4. *Vertical line code*

13.4.1.1. *2×n chessboard*

From one column to the next, we have passage rules:

$$(0, 0) \to (0, 0) \text{ or } (0, 0)\to(1, 1), \text{ and } (1, 1)\to(0, 0)$$

hence oriented graph D and its adjacency matrix $A=\begin{pmatrix}1 & 1\\ 1 & 0\end{pmatrix}$, which gives:

$$I - xA = \begin{bmatrix}1-x & -x\\ -x & 1\end{bmatrix} \text{ and } |I - xA| = 1 - x - x^2$$

Domino tiling on length n corresponds to a code using a word $n + 1$ long, or even a n-length path on the graph, with a starting point and end point in (0, 0), see Figure 13.5. To find the generating function $F_{00}(x)$ of the number of these paths, we need the determinant of matrix $I - xA$ stripped of its first line and column, i.e. 1, hence:

$$F_{00}(x) = 1 / (1 - x - x^2)$$

We recognize the gap-type generating function of the Fibonacci sequence $(F(n))$. The number of tilings on the chessboard of length n is therefore $F(n + 1)$.

Figure 13.5. *Code for a domino tiling (left), graph for passing from one word to the next (right)*

13.4.1.2. *3×n chessboard*

Let column 0 be (0, 0, 0), 1 be (1, 0, 0), 2 be (0, 0, 1), 3 be (0, 1, 1), 4 be (1, 1, 0) and 5 be (1, 1, 1). These are the only possible configurations. The rules for passage from one column to the next give the oriented graph D in Figure 13.6.

As we are only interested in counting words, we can compare vertices 1 and 2 of graph D, and construct the new simpler graph with four D' vertices of the adjacency matrix:

$$A = \begin{pmatrix} 0 & 2 & 0 & 1 \\ 1 & 0 & 1 & 0 \\ 0 & 1 & 0 & 0 \\ 1 & 0 & 0 & 0 \end{pmatrix} \quad \text{and} \quad |I - xA| = \begin{vmatrix} 1 & -2x & 0 & -x \\ -x & 1 & -x & 0 \\ 0 & -x & 1 & 0 \\ -x & 0 & 0 & 1 \end{vmatrix} = 1 - 4x^2 + x^4$$

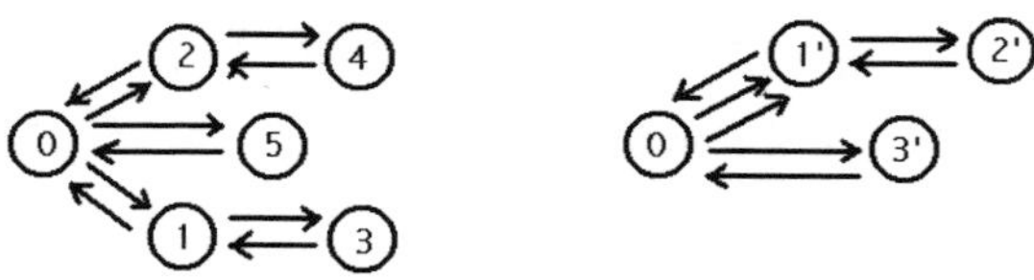

Figure 13.6. *Graph D (left); and graph D' (right)*

The n-length paths with which we are concerned all begin at vertex 0 corresponding to column (0, 0, 0) and also end at vertex 0. To get their generating function $F_{00}(x)$, we need the determinant of matrix $I - xA$, from which we have removed the first line and first column, i.e.:

$$\begin{vmatrix} 1 & -x & 0 \\ -x & 1 & 0 \\ 0 & 0 & 1 \end{vmatrix} = 1 - x^2$$

Therefore, $F_{00}(x) = (1 - x^2) / (1 - 4x^2 + x^4)$. It is also the generating function of the number of tilings on length n.

13.4.2. *Words with a dependency link between two successive letters of words*

We are interested in n-length words that are written $a_1 a_2 \ldots a_n$, with the following conditions: each letter a_i belongs to the alphabet of k letters 0, 1, 2, …., $k - 1$, and each letter a_i of the word (with i from 1 to $n - 1$) is followed by letter a_{i+1}

equal to a_i or $a_i + 1$ or $a_i - 1$ returned to modulo k. We want to find out the number $u(n)$ of these words for a given k.

For example, for $k = 4$, words $n = 3$ long beginning with 0 are: 000, 001, 003, 010, 011, 012, 030, 031 and 033, numbering nine, hence $u(3) = 4 \times 9 = 36$.

In the general case it is easy to check that $u(1) = k$, and that we move from $u(n)$ to $u(n + 1)$ through multiplication by three because to each n-length word we can add a choice of one letter out of three. Hence $u(n) = k.3^{n-1}$.

The same result could be found using the adjacency matrix A of the graph, but would be much more laborious to achieve.

Now let us take the particular case where modulo k is equal to 4, and return to cyclic words, further imposing that a_1 be equal to a_n, $a_n + 1$ or $a_n - 1$ modulo k. The number $f(n)$ of these cyclic n-length words is $trace(A^n)$, thanks to property 13.3. As matrix A is circulant, we get the following as eigenvalues:

$$\lambda_k = 1 + i^k + i^{3k}, \text{ with } k \text{ from 0 to 3}$$

hence $\lambda_0 = 3$, $\lambda_1 = 1$, $\lambda_2 = -1$, $\lambda_3 = 1$, and $f(n) = 3^n + 2 + (-1)^n$ [5]

13.4.3. *Routes on a graded segment*

Let us consider the graph made up of n i vertices (with i from 1 to n), joined from one to the next by edges in two directions of unit length $(i, i + 1)$, as, for example in the graph in Figure 13.7 for $n = 5$.

13.4.3.1. *First problem*

An object leaves a particular vertex and circulates from one vertex to a neighboring one. We want to find out the number of paths that are K long.

---

5. If we keep $k = 4$, we can find the results directly. For each value of n, there are as many words beginning with 0, 1, 2 or 3. Let us take, for example, words beginning with 1. By creating words in a tree structure from one stage to the next from 1 to stage 1, we find that for even stage n the number of 0s is equal to the number of 1s and also the number of 2s, i.e.: $nb_0 = nb_1$, $nb_2 = (3^{n-1} - 3)/4 + 1$, and that the number of 3s is: $nb_3 = (3^{n-1} - 3)/4$. We find that for odd n: $nb_0 = nb_2 = nb_3 = (3^{n-1} - 1)/4$, and $nb_1 = (3^{n-1} - 1)/4 + 1$. The demonstration of these formulae is done using recurrence. The total number of words at stage 1 is obtained by calculating $4(nb_0 + nb_1 + nb_2 + nb_3)$. We find for even as well as odd n that $u(n) = 4.3^{n-1}$. If we simply take cyclic words, we get: $f(n) = 4\,(nb_0 + nb_1 + nb_2) = 3^n + 3$ for even n, and 3n + 1 for odd n.

This can be seen in another way: it appears to be diagonal paths from left to right (with steps (1, 1) or (1, -1)) in a rectangle with dimensions K by $(n - 1)$, starting from one of the n point on the left vertical and moving as far as the end on the right vertical, with K steps done (see Figure 13.7 on the right).

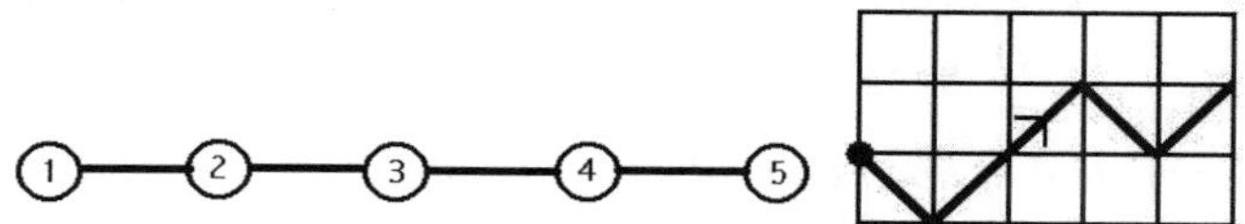

Figure 13.7. *A graded graph segment with five vertices (left); and a path K=5 long on a segment with n = 4 vertices, traced in the 5×3 rectangle*

Let us deal with this problem as an exercise using matrix diagonalization.

a) Write the adjacency matrix of the graph.

It is $A = \begin{pmatrix} 0 & 1 & 0 & 0 \\ 1 & 0 & 1 & 0 \\ 0 & 1 & 0 & 1 \\ 0 & 0 & 1 & 0 \end{pmatrix}$ in the case $n = 4$.

b) Show that the eigenvectors are written (in the form of column vectors): $V_q = (\sin(q\pi / (n + 1)), \sin(2q\pi / (n + 1)), \ldots, \sin(nq\pi / (n + 1)))$. Deduce that the eigenvalues are: $\lambda_q = 2 \cos (q\, \pi / (n + 1))$.

All we have to do is check that $AV_q = \lambda_q V_q$ for each component of these vectors.

c) Give the unit length to the eigenvectors. Calculate the length L of the vectors found in part b).

$$L^2 = \sin^2(q\pi / (n+1)) + \sin^2(2q\pi / (n+1)) + \ldots + \sin^2(nq\pi / (n+1))$$

$$= (1/2)(1 - \cos(2q\pi / (n+1)) + (1/2)(1 - \cos(4q\pi / (n+1)) + \ldots + (1/2)(1 - \cos(2nq\pi / (n+1))$$

$$= n/2 - (1/2)(\cos(2q\pi / (n+1)) + \cos(4q\pi / (n+1)) + \ldots + \cos(2nq\pi / (n+1)))$$

$$= n/2 + 1/2 = (n+1)/2. \text{ Hence } L = \sqrt{\frac{2}{n+1}}$$

d) Calling the matrix with normalized eigenvectors (of unit length) such as column vectors Q, and the diagonal matrix of eigenvalues D, check that $A = Q D Q^T$ where Q^T is the transpose of matrix Q.

As for all non-oriented graphs, matrix A is symmetrical. It assumes distinct eigenvalues, and normalized eigenvectors make up an orthonormal base, hence $Q^{-1} = Q^{\mathrm{T}}$, and $A = QDQ^{\mathrm{T}}$ by changing the base.

e) v_{ij} is the coefficient in line i and column j of matrix Q with eigenvectors of length 1. Check that the number of n-length paths with a starting point on the graph is:

$$\sum_{q=1}^{n} C_q \lambda_q^n \text{ with: } C_q = \left(\sum_{i=1}^{n} v_{iq} \right)^2$$

The number of n-length paths is the sum of all the terms of matrix A^n, or even of matrix QD^nQ^{T}. The coefficient in line i and column j of this matrix is $\Sigma v_{iq}\, v_{jq}\, \lambda_q^{n}$, and the sum of all these terms is:

$$\sum_{i\,j}\sum_{q} v_{iq}\, v_{jq}\, \lambda_q^n = \sum_{q} \lambda_q^n \sum_{i\,j} v_{iq}\, v_{jq} = \sum_{q=1}^{n}\left(\sum_{i=1}^{n} v_{iq} \right)^2 \lambda_q^n$$

f) Show that in this case $C_q = (2 / (n + 1)) \operatorname{cotan}(\frac{q\pi}{2(n+1)})$ for odd q and 0 for even q.

$C_q = (2 / (n + 1))\, B^2$ with $B = \sin(q\pi / (n + 1)) + \sin(2q\pi / (n + 1)) + \ldots + \sin(nq\pi / (n + 1))$

$C_q = \dfrac{2}{n+1} \operatorname{cotan}(\dfrac{q\pi}{n+1})$ when q is odd, and 0 if not, having done all of the calculations.

g) Deduce the formula giving the number of paths $N_{n,K}$.

$$N_{n,K} = C_1 \lambda_1^n + C_3 \lambda_3^n + \ldots = \frac{2^{n+1}}{n+1} \sum_{p=1}^{\left\lceil \frac{n+1}{2} \right\rceil} \operatorname{cotan}^2 \frac{(2p-1)\pi}{2(n+1)} \cos^n \frac{(2p-1)\pi}{n+1}$$

For example, for $n = 5$ we the number of paths, for successive values of K from 1 are: 8, 14, 24, 42, 72, 126, 216, 378, ...

13.4.3.2. *Second problem*

The moving object leaves vertex 1 and circulates the graded segment with n vertices to finally return to vertex 1. We want to find out the number of paths of length $K = 2p$ (the length run through to be even). It is, if you prefer, the number of mountain ranges $2p$ long and of $n - 1$ maximum height.

– *First method:* let us form the determinant $D_n(x) = | I - xA |$, which gives a tridiagonal matrix whose three central diagonals are made up with -xs, of 1s and -xs respectively. The development of this determinant gives the following recurrence relation at the start:

$$D_n(x) = D_{n-1}(x) - x^2 D_{n-2}(x), \text{ with } D_0(x) = D_1(x) = 1$$

The generating function giving the number of paths from vertex 1 returning to vertex 1 is:

$$F_{11}(x) = D_{n-1}(x) / \mathrm{D_n}(x)$$

Let us take the particular case where $n = 3$. The generating function is:

$$F_{11}(x) = D_2(x) / D_3(x) = (1 - x^2) / (1 - 2x^2)$$

Developing it gives:

$$F_{11}(x) = 1 + x^2 + 2x^4 + 4x^6 + 8x^8 + \ldots.$$

The number of mountain ranges $2p$ long and 2 high maximum is 2^{p-1}.

– *Second method:* using eigenvalues $\lambda_q = 2\cos(q\pi / 4)$ and eigenvectors previously calculated, with $v_{1q}^2 = (1 / 2) \sin^2(q\pi / 4)$, the number of paths from vertex 1 to vertex 1 is:

$$v_{11}^2 \lambda_1^{2p} + v_{12}^2 \lambda_2^{2p} + v_{13}^2 \lambda_3^{2p} = v_{11}^2 \lambda_1^{2p} + v_{13}^2 \lambda_3^{2p} = 2v_{11}^2 \lambda_1^{2p} = 2(1 / 4)2^p = 2^{p-1}$$

– *Third method:* we establish a bijection between mountain ranges of length $2p$ and maximum height 2 and binary numbers of length $p - 1$. All we have to do is take the even abscissae included between 2 and $2p - 2$ and put a 1 if we have a peak of height 2, and 0 if not, as in the example in Figure 13.8 where $2p = 6$.

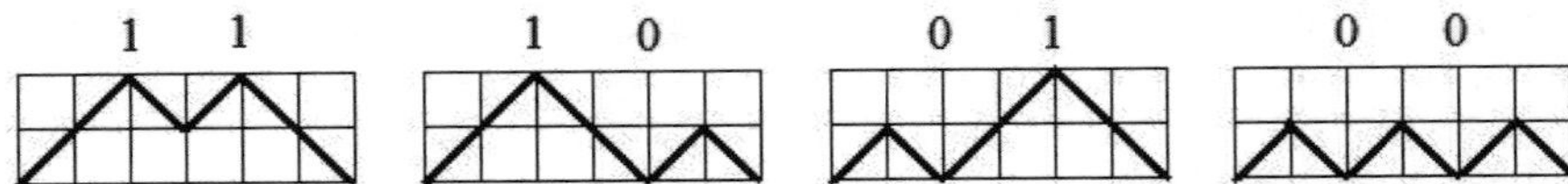

Figure 13.8. *Configurations code*

13.4.4. *Molecular chain*

Consider regular polygons with an even number of sides. By concatenating them in a chain – with one edge in common between two successive polygons, and in such a way that the two edges a polygon has in common with its neighbors has no vertex in common – we get a bipartite graph, with the image of a classic chessboard (see [CVE 80]). This means that each vertex can be colored in white or black in such a way that it exclusively has vertices of the other color to its neighbors (see Figure 13.9). It is to return to such possible coloring that we take polygons with an even number of sides. We can therefore tile this graph using dominos covering each one of the two neighboring boxes in a different color, which we also call a perfect coupling of the bipartite graph. The objective is to count the number $p(n)$ of such tilings possible for a chain of n polygons $C_1, C_2, \ldots, C_n$.

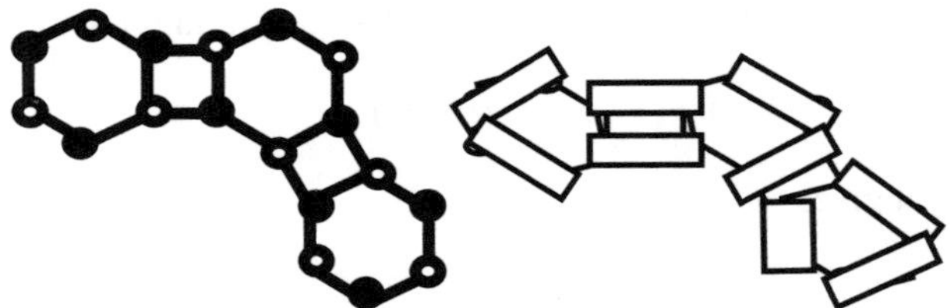

Figure 13.9. *A molecular chain that is also a bipartite graph (left); and one of the tilings of the chain (the associated word is a b a a a) (right)*

If we take a polygon in isolation, there are always two ways to be tiled. We can already affirm that $p(1) = 2$. But what is it when we juxtapose several in a chain? To simplify, we will first assume that the chain is a horizontal alignment of hexagons and squares, the junction edges all being vertical (see Figure 13.10).

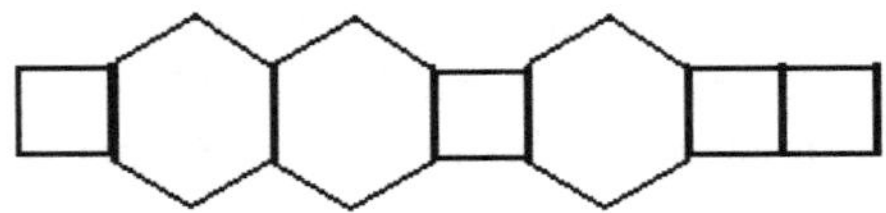

Figure 13.10. *A linear chain*

Now let us code the tiling of each polygon C_i with dominos.

Either the junction edge located on the right (with polygon C_{i+1}) has its two vertices occupied by the ends of the two dominos, with the edge itself being unoccupied. We will therefore code this tiling with letter *b*, and in turn the following polygon will only have one possible tiling, at least without counting the following junction edge. If not, it will be coded using letter *a*. In this last case, there will be two ways of tiling the following polygon C_{i+1}, either by recovering the junction edge with a domino, or with both vertices of the junction edge occupied by the beginnings of two dominos in C_{i+1}.

This shows that any letter *a* will be followed by *a* or *b*. For the last polygon in the chain, which has no neighbor to its right, if needed we should give an artificial vertical junction edge as with all the other polygons. Each tiling is thus coded by a *n*-length word based on two letter *a*s and *b*s.

As the designs in Figure 13.11 show, when a polygon is coded *b*, its successor is coded either by *a* or *b* depending on its own configuration. To do this, we distinguish the two types of polygons in the following way. Each hexagon, with its two junction edges at the left and right antipodes, is said to be even (type *E*), because the edges inserted in one side or the other of the junction edges number two, i.e. an even number. Contrarily, each square is said to be odd (type *O*) because a single edge fits on one or the other side of the junction edges. This characteristic, *E* or *O*, is valuable for our aligned hexagons and squares, except for the first in our chain (which does not have a junction to its left). It can then be generalized to any type of polygon.

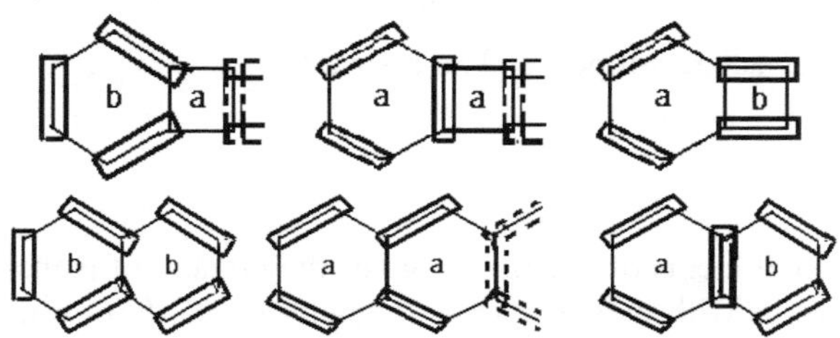

Figure 13.11. *Code for tiling configurations*

In the case where a polygon is followed by an even polygon, we therefore have rules of succession: $a \to a$ $a \to b$ $b \to b$ (see the top of Figure 13.12). In the case where it is followed by an odd polygon: $a \to a$ $a \to b$ $b \to a$ (see the bottom of Figure 13.12).

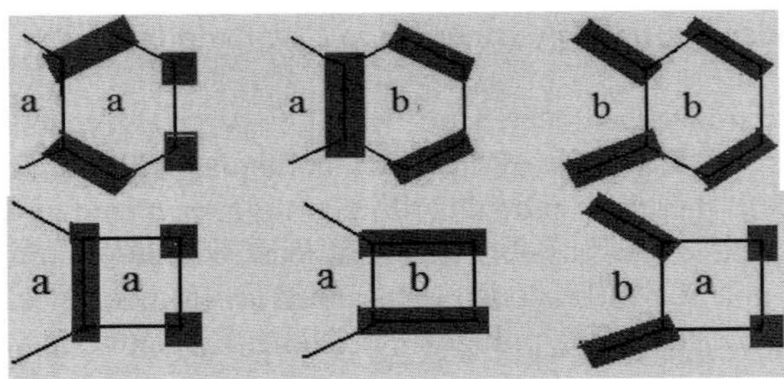

Figure 13.12. *Case where a polygon is followed by an even polygon (above); and case where it is followed by an odd polygon (below)*

A n-length word based on two letters a and b, ends up being associated in a bijective way with each tiling of the chain of n polygons, obeying the rules of succession above. All we have to do is to count the number of these words in order to get the number of tilings. This can be generalized to all sorts of polygons. Our even hexagon with its two junction edges at the antipodes, can be replaced by any even polygon.

Similarly, our odd square can be replaced by any odd polygon, for example by a hexagon whose two junction edges are separated by an odd number of edges on each side: $\equiv$. This does not modify the number of tilings.

Let us assume that we have one chain of even polygons, from the second to the last (the shape of the first having no importance), for example hexagons with their two junction edges at the antipodes. The associated graph a $\longrightarrow$ b has matrix $P = \begin{pmatrix} 1 & 1 \\ 0 & 1 \end{pmatrix}$.

The sum of coefficients of this matrix gives the number of paths 1 unit long, i.e. the number of words with two characters (namely *aa*, *ab*, *bb*), or number of tilings for two polygons. If we have a chain of N juxtaposed polygons, even starting from the second polygon the sum of coefficients of matrix P^{N-1} (N>1) gives the number of tilings. Such a calculation of matrix powers can be avoided in this case. It is easy to check that the number of words obeying the constraints of even polygons is $p(n) = n + 1$.

Similarly, if we have a chain of odd polygons starting from the second polygon, the associated graph (a) ⇄ (b) has matrix $I = \begin{pmatrix} 1 & 1 \\ 1 & 0 \end{pmatrix}$, and the number of tilings of N juxtaposed odd polygons starting from the second, is equal to the sum of coefficients of matrix I^{N-1}. In this case it is also easy to check that the number of tilings, or corresponding words, verifies:

$$p(n) = p(n-1) + p(n-2), \text{ with } p(1) = 2 \text{ and } p(3) = 3, \text{ hence } p(n) = F_{n+1}$$

where we find Fibonacci series (F_n), or even the tilings of a $2 \times n$ chessboard using dominos.

Now let us imagine that we have one polygon C_1 followed by an odd and then an even polygon. The associated matrix is $O\,E = \begin{pmatrix} 1 & 2 \\ 1 & 1 \end{pmatrix}$. We find that there are five possible tilings for this three-polygon chain, with the corresponding words *aaa*, *aab*, *abb*, *bab* and *bba*.

More generally, let us assume that the first polygon is followed by repeated blocks formed by an odd and then even polygon, for example $C_1OEOEOEOEOE$. The number of tilings is the sum of the coefficients of matrix $(OE)^5$. The characteristic determinant is:

$$|Od - x(OE)| = 1 - 2x - x^2$$

The generating function associated with the number $U(n)$ of tilings of n OE blocks, corresponding to the number of tilings $p(2n+1)$ of a chain with $2n+1$ polygons, is of the form:

$$F(x) = U(0) + U(1)x + U(2)x^2 + \ldots = (b_0 + b_1x) / (1 - 2x - x^2)$$

Thanks to $U(0) = p(1) = 2$, which corresponds to the initial polygon C_1, and $U(1) = p(3) = 5$ for C_1OE, we find:

$$F(x) = (2 + x) / (1 - 2x - x^2)$$

Series $U(n)$ obeys the recurrence relation $U(n) = 2U(n-1) + U(n-2)$ with $U(0) = 2$ and $U(1) = 5$. Its first terms are:

2, 5, 12, 29, 70, …

If we have a succession $C_1EO\ EO\ EO\ EO \ldots$, with n EO blocks, the EO matrix is worth:

$$\begin{pmatrix} 2 & 1 \\ 1 & 0 \end{pmatrix}$$

Notably, for the three polygons C_1EO, we have four tilings corresponding to the words *aaa*, *aab*, *aba* and *bba*. The characteristic determinant is:

$$|Od - x(EO)| = 1 - 2x - x^2$$

The generating function associated with the number of tilings $V(n)$ for a number n of EO blocks is of the form $F(x) = (b_0 + b_1 x) / (1 - 2x + x^2)$. Thanks to $V(0) = 2$, which corresponds to the initial polygon C_1, and $V(1) = 4$ for $C_1\ EO$, we find:

$$F(x) = 2 / (1 - 2x - x^2)$$

Sequence $V(n)$ begins with 2, 4, 16, 24, 58, … and obeys the recurrence:

$$V(n) = 2V(n-1) + V(n-2),$$

starting from $V(0) = 2$ and $V(1) = 4$

As we have just seen, the interest in matrices appears as soon as the molecular chain is formed from repeating identical blocks.

Chapter 14

Parts and Partitions of a Set

14.1. Parts of a set

The parts of a set can be numbered from the smallest, the empty part – written ∅ or {} – to the biggest, the whole part – i.e. the set itself. For example, the set {1, 2, 3, 4} with four elements has the following parts:

> ∅, {1}, {2}, {3}, {4}, {1, 2}, {1, 3}, {1, 4}, {2, 3}, {2, 4}, {3, 4}, {1, 2, 3}, {1, 2, 4}, {1, 3, 4}, {2, 3, 4}, {1, 2, 3, 4}

In this case we find 16 parts.

This is generalized, and we have already shown the formula giving the number of parts, as well as their number based on the number of elements (see Chapter 2). Let us recall this result: the number of parts of a n-element set is 2^n, and the number of k-element parts is C_n^k.

14.1.1. *Program getting all parts of a set*

All we have to do is use the method associated with the demonstration of the property, each part being linked in a bijective way to a n-length word based on 0 and 1, for example for $n = 4$: {1, 3, 4) ↔ 1011 or $\begin{pmatrix} 1 & 2 & 3 & 4 \\ 1 & 0 & 1 & 1 \end{pmatrix}$ in the form of an array, which means we take the 1, we do not take the 2, we take the 3 as well as the 4.

We return to creating all the n-length binary numbers, placing them in table r[], and attaching the indices of the cases where the 1s are found to them. Let us recall that converting the binary number through successive divisions by two, taking the remainders obtained each time, gives the ordered binary number from the least to the most significant.

```
for(n=0; n<(long int)pow(2.,(float)N); n++)
  { q=n;
    for(j=0; j<N; j++)
      { r[j]=q%2; q=q/2; }
    printf("%d:{ ",n+1);
    for(j=0; j<N; j++) if (r[j]!=0) printf("%d ",j+1);   printf("} ");
    }
```

As a training exercise, we give a second version by constructing a tree structure, represented in Figure 14.1.

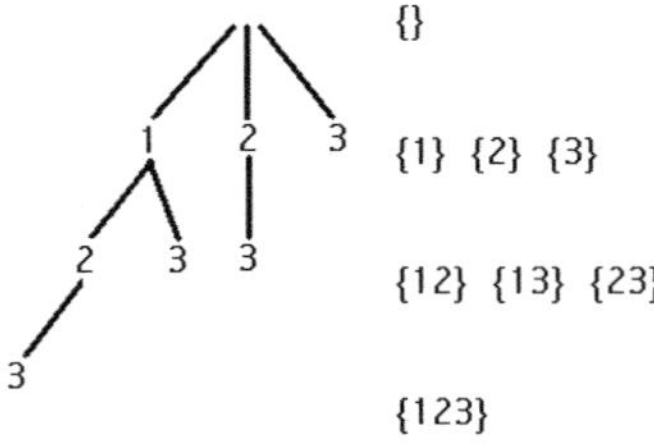

Figure 14.1. *The parts of a three-element set, in the form of a tree structure*

Each node of the tree carries the number of an element of the set, except at level 0, where the root node carrys the number 0 and corresponds to the empty set that has successive nodes carrying numbers greater than it. That is as long as some exist, as in the diagram for $n = 3$ (Figure 14.1). When constructing the tree node after node, we display each node that has reached i plus its predecessors up to the root not included. From this we deduce the program:

```
main()
    {number=0; tree(0,0);}
        /* node 0 corresponds to the root; the variable number numbers the parts
           found each time a node is obtained */
```

```
void tree(int i, int level)
 { int j;
   number++; printf("%d:",number);
   if (level==0) printf("{} ");
   else
      { printf("{"); displaypredlist(level); printf("%d} ",i);}
  for(j= i+1; j<=N; j++)
      { pred[level+1]=i; tree(j, level+1); }
 }
void displaypredlist(int level)
      {int j;   for(j=2; j<=level; j++) printf("%d ", pred[j]); }
```

14.1.2. *Exercises*

14.1.2.1. *Generating functions associated with the number of k-element parts of a n-element set {1, 2, …, n}*

Let $u(n, k)$ be the number of k-element parts of the n-element set $\{1, 2, \ldots, n\}$, and let us introduce the three generating functions associated with it:

$$G(x, y) = \sum u(n, k)\, x^k\, y^n$$

$$F_n(x) = \sum u(n, k)\, x^k$$

$$H_k(x) = \sum u(n, k)\, y^n$$

We have to determine these functions as well as their links.

The k-element parts of a n-element set $\{1, 2, \ldots, n\}$ are split into two categories: those that contain 1, numbering $u(n-1, k-1)$, and those that do not contain 1, numbering $u(n-1, k)$. Hence we have the recurrence formula: $u(n, k) = u(n-1, k) + u(n-1, k-1)$, which is none other than Pascal triangle relations. Let us take $F_n(x)$, the generating function of $u(n, k)$ for a given n, i.e.:

$$F_n(x) = \sum_{k \geq 0} u(n,k)\, x^k$$

Thanks to the recurrence formula, we find that:

$$F_n(x) - 1 = F_{n-1}(x) - 1 + xF_{n-1}(x), \text{ i.e. } F_n(x) = (1 + x)\, F_{n-1}(x)$$

which should correspond to a geometric series $(1 + x)$, hence:

$F_n(x) = (1 + x)^n$ because $F_0(x) = 1$.

Therefore we find that $u(n, k) = C_n^k$

The fact that $u(n, k)$ depends on two variables invites us to take the generating function associated with two variables:

$$G(x,y) = \sum_{n\geq 0,k\geq 0} u(n,k)x^k y^n = \sum_{n\geq 0} y^n \sum_{k\geq 0} u(n,k)x^k = \sum_{n\geq 0} (1+x)^n y^n = \sum_{n\geq 0} ((1+x)y)^n$$
$$= \frac{1}{1-(1+x)y}$$

Now let us introduce the generating function $H_k(x)$ of $u(n, k)$ for a given k:

$$H_k(y) = \sum_{n\geq 0} u(n,k)y^n$$

Because $G(x,y) = \sum_{n\geq 0,k\geq 0} u(n,k)x^k y^n = \sum_{k\geq 0} H_k(y)x^k$, $H_k(y)$ is the coefficient of the term x^k in the development of $G(x, y)$:

$$G(x,y) = \frac{1}{1-(1+x)y} = \frac{1}{1-y-xy} = \frac{1}{1-y}\frac{1}{1-\frac{y}{1-y}x} = \frac{1}{1-y}\sum_{k\geq 0}\frac{y^k}{(1-y)^k}x^k$$

hence:

$$H_k(y) = y^k / (1-y)^{k+1} \text{ and } \sum_{n\geq 0} C_n^k y^n = \frac{y^k}{(1-y)^{k+1}}$$

14.1.2.2. *Number of parts of the set {1, 2, 3, ..., N} not including consecutive elements*

a) Determine the number f(N) of parts of the N-element set numbered from 1 to N, without consecutive elements, i.e. not having numbers that follow each other when we write the part with its elements in ascending order.

Each part is represented by a word N characters long, based on 0 and 1, of the form $a_1a_2\ldots a_i \ldots a_N$, where $a_i = 1$ indicates that we take element i, and 0 when we do not. We have to determine the number $f(N)$ of these N-length words, in the alphabet with two letters 0, 1 that do not have consecutive 1s. We check as soon as $f(0) = 1$ (the empty word), and $f(1) = 2$, with words 0 and 1.

Now take $N > 1$. Let us split the words of N characters into two categories, those beginning with 0 and those beginning with 1. Those beginning with 0 are made up, if we remove the initial 0, of words of length $N - 1$ without consecutive 1s, hence $f(N - 1)$ words.

Those that begin with 1 also begin with 10, and are followed by words $N - 2$ long without consecutive 1s, i.e. $f(N - 2)$ words. Hence the recurrence relation in Fibonacci style:

$$f(N) = f(N - 1) + f(N - 2)$$

With the initial conditions where $f(0) = F_2$ and $f(1) = F_3$, this gives $f(N) = F_{N+2}$, the numbers F_N being those of the Fibonacci series.

From this we deduce that F_{N+2} parts of $\{1, 2, \ldots, N\}$ exist, not including consecutive elements.

b) Still starting from the set {1, 2, ..., N}, let f(N, K) be the number of its K-element parts that do not have two consecutive elements. Determine f(N, 0), f(N, 1), then a recurrence relation on f(N, K) for K > 1. Find the generating function associated with a given number K.

– for $K = 0$, $f(N, 0) = 1$, because we get the empty part each time. Hence the generating function for $K = 0$:

$$F_0(x) = 1 + x + x^2 + \ldots = 1 / (1 - x)$$

– for $K = 1$, we have $f(N, 1) = N$ when $N > 0$ and $f(0, 1) = 0$. From this we deduce the generating function:

$$F_1(x) = x + 2x^2 + 3x^3 + 4x^4 + \ldots = x(1 + 2x + 3x^2 + 4x^3 + \ldots) = x / (1 - x)^2$$

– now take $K > 1$. Let us choose element N. The $f(N, K)$ parts are divided into two categories: those that do not contain element N, and those that do. In the first case, each part contains K elements taken out of $N - 1$, i.e. $f(N - 1, K)$ possibilities. In the second case, each part contains element N but not $N - 1$, and we are left with choosing $K - 1$ numbers out of $N - 2$ numbers, element N already being taken, and elements N and $N - 1$ being excluded from the choice. This gives $f(N - 2, K - 1)$ possibilities. Hence the recurrence relation:

$$f(N, K) = f(N - 1, K) + f(N - 2, K - 1)$$

The generating function associated with $f(N, K)$ for given $K > 1$ is, by definition:

$$F_K(x) = f(0, K) + f(1, K)x + f(2, K)x^2 + \ldots + f(N, K)\, x^N + \ldots$$

Note that for sets with less than $2K - 1$ elements, there are no K-element parts without consecutive elements: $f(n, K) = 0$ when $0 \leq n < 2K - 1$.

Using the recurrence above, we arrive at the relation:

$$x\, F_K(x) + x^2\, F_{K-1}(x) = F_K(x),$$

i.e. $F_K(x) = (x^2 / (1 - x))\, F_{K-1}(x)$, which using $F_1(x)$ gives us:

$$F_K(x) = x^{2K-1} / (1 - x)^{K+1} \quad (K > 0)$$

c) Deduce from this the explicit form of f(N, K).

$F_K(x) = x^{2K-1} / (1 - x)^{K+1} = x^{2K-1}(C_K^{\ K} + C_{K+1}^{\ K}\, x + C_{K+2}^{\ K}\, x^2 + \ldots + C_{K+N}^{\ K}\, x^N + \ldots)$, due to a well-known formula, i.e. for $K > 0$:

$$F_K(x) = C_K^{\ K}\, x^{2K-1} + C_{K+1}^{\ K}\, x^{2K} + C_{K+2}^{\ K}\, x^{2K+1} + \ldots + C_{K+N}^{\ K}\, x^{2K-1+N} + \ldots$$

From this we deduce that $f(N, K) = C_{N+1-K}^{\ K}$. Note that this formula remains valid for $K = 0$.

Now keeping N fixed and making K vary, we obtain:

$$\Sigma\, f(N, K) = F(N + 2),$$

namely, the Fibonacci number we found in the first part of the question. Hence the formula:

$$\sum_K C_{N+1-K}^{K} = F(N+2)$$

All we have to do is take the terms so that $K \geq 0$ and $2K \leq N + 1$. For example, for $N = 4$, $C_5^{\ 0} + C_4^{\ 1} + C_3^{\ 2} = F(6)$, which gives 8.

14.1.2.3. *Cyclic words without identical blocks of letters*

a) Consider n-length words in an alphabet with two letters, 0 and 1, without consecutive 1s, and unable to have 1 at the beginning and end at the same time. Determine how many of words there are.

Let us call the number of words $g(n)$. We must remove the words beginning and ending with 1 from $f(n)$, defined in the exercise above. Furthermore, such words begin with 10 and end in 01. The rest is made up of words $n-4$ characters long that do not have consecutive 1s, i.e. $f(n-4)$ words of this type. Finally:

$$g(n) = f(n) - f(n-4) = F_{n+2} - F_{n-2} = F_{n+1} + F_n - F_{n-2} = F_{n+1} + F_{n-1} + F_{n-2} - F_{n-2}$$

$$= F_{n+1} + F_{n-1}.$$

b) The integers 1, 2, 3,..., n are placed in consecutive order in a circle. How many ways are there of choosing parts of this set of numbers without two numbers following each other?

This is the same problem as above, hence $F_{n+1} + F_{n-1}$ parts.

14.2. Partitions of a *n*-object set

14.2.1. *Definition*

When we break up a n-element set into several non-empty parts that do not overlap and whose union forms the set, this is called a *set partition*. For example, the $n = 4$ element set {1, 2, 3, 4} notably assumes as partition in three parts: {1} {2, 3} {4}. Let us specify that the order in which the parts are written does not come into play. Our objective is to count the number of partitions of a set and number them. Let us first turn our interest to the number of partitions in k parts of a n-element set.

14.2.2. *A second kind of Stirling numbers, and partitions of a n-element set in k parts*

Let $S(n, k)$ be the number of partitions in k parts of a n-element set ($n>0$), whose study was initiated by mathematician James Stirling, and that are called Stirling numbers of the second kind (those of the first kind include permutations with a certain number of cycles). We easily verify that $S(n, k) = 0$ as soon as $k > n$. We also have $S(n, n) = 1$, and $S(n, 1) = 1$.

14.2.2.1. *Some particular cases*

Let us show that $S(n, n-1) = C_n^2$. Such partitions have all their parts reduced to one element, except one that has two elements. There are as many partitions as there are ways of taking one part with two elements in a n-element set, i.e. C_n^2.

Let us show that $S(n, 2) = 2^{n-1} - 1$. It is all the partitions in two parts. The number of parts of the set is 2^n. If we take each one of these parts of these partitions, avoiding the first or second part being empty, this makes $2^n - 2$ partitions, but these are counted twice when the second part finds itself back in first place. Finally we have $2^{n-1} - 1$ partitions.

14.2.2.2. *Recurrence formula on S(n, k)*

We want to find out the number $S(n + 1, k)$ in relation to the Stirling numbers that precede it. The partitions of the set $\{1, 2, \ldots, n, n + 1\}$ with $n + 1$ elements in k parts can be separated into two categories:

– element $n + 1$ is a separate band, forming its own part alone; it is therefore added to the partitions with $k - 1$ parts of set $\{1, 2, \ldots, n\}$ of the n other elements, hence $S(n, k - 1)$ possibilities;

– or element $n + 1$ is integrated in one parts of the partitions with k parts of the n-element set $\{1, 2, \ldots, n\}$, which can be done in k different ways in each partition. Because there are $S(n, k)$ partitions, there are $k\ S(n, k)$ possibilities. There are no other cases. Finally:

$$S(n + 1, k) = k\ S(n, k) + S(n, k - 1)$$

with as initial conditions: $S(n, 1) = 1$ and $S(1, k) = 0$ for $k > 1$, and $S(1, 1) = 1$ respectively.

14.2.2.3. *Exponential generating function of S(n, k) numbers*

By applying the sieve formula (Chapter 8), we calculated the number X of surjections of a n-element set in a k-element set, i.e.:

$$X = k^n - C_k^1 (k - 1)^n + C_k^2 (k - 2)^n - C_k^3 (k - 3)^n + \ldots\ldots + (-1)^k C_k^k 0^n$$

This is also the number of ordered partitions of a n-element set in k parts. No longer taking order into consideration, $k!$ ordered partitions give a single partition in the strict sense of the term. Therefore $S(n, k) = X / k!$

The exponential generating function of $S(n, k)$ for a given k is:

$$E_k(z) = \sum_{n=k}^{\infty} S(n,k)\frac{z^n}{n!} = \sum_{n=0}^{\infty} S(n,k)\frac{z^n}{n!}$$

with the summation done for n from k to infinity and from 0 to infinity able to be included by adding back 0, because $S(n, k) = 0$ for $n < k$:

$$E_k(z) = \frac{1}{k!}\sum_{n\geq 0}(C_k^0 k^n - C_k^1(k-1)^n + C_k^2(k-1)^n - ... + (-1)^k C_k^k (k-k)^n)\frac{z^n}{n!}$$

$$= \frac{1}{k!}(\sum_{n\geq 0} C_k^0 \frac{(kz)^n}{n!} - \sum_{n\geq 0} C_k^1 \frac{((k-1)z)^n}{n!} + \sum_{n\geq 0} C_k^2 \frac{((k-2)z)^n}{n!} - ... + (-1)^k \sum_{n\geq 0} C_k^k \frac{(0z)^n}{n!}$$

$$= \frac{1}{k!}(e^z - 1)^k$$

applying binomial formula.

14.2.3. *Number of partitions of a set and Bell numbers*

Let b_n be the number of ways of carrying out a set partition of n objects. The b_n numbers are called Bell numbers. Let us number the objects of the set from 1 to n. Therefore $b_1 = 1$ with partition {1}; $b_2 = 2$ with two partitions {1 2} and {1}{2}; and $b_3 = 5$ with partitions {1 2 3}, {12}{3}, {13}{2}, {1}{2 3}, {1}{2}{3}.

14.2.3.1. *Recurrence of Bell numbers*

We are going to show that $b_{n+1} = \sum_{k=0}^{n} C_n^k b_{n-k}$, by acknowledging that $b_0 = 1$.

To do this, let us consider, as above, the object numbered $n + 1$ of set $\{1, 2, ..., n, n + 1\}$. It is found in one of the parts of each partition, where this part has between 1 and $n + 1$ elements. The partitions of the $n + 1$ element set according to the number $k + 1$ of elements of the part where object $n + 1$ is found, with k between 0 and n. For this part with $k + 1$ elements, there are C_n^k ways of choosing k out of n objects. Each time such a part is chosen, the other parts correspond to a partition of the $n - k$ remaining objects.

There are b_{n-k} ways of making such partitions. This gives $C_n^k\ b_{n-k}$ partitions, where the part that contains object $n + 1$ has $k + 1$ objects. In turn, the number k takes all values between 0 and n. In particular, for $k = n$ there is a single partition, and we are led to take $b_0 = 1$. Hence, in total:

$$b_{n+1} = C_n^0 b_n + C_n^1\ b_{n-1} + C_n^2\ b_{n-2} + ... + C_n^{n-1}\ b_1 + C_n^n\ b_0, \text{ with } b_0 = 1$$

$$= \sum_{k=0}^{n} C_n^k b_{n-k}$$

14.2.3.2. *Exponential generating function B(x) of Bell numbers*

Let us recall that the exponential generating function of a sequence (b_n) is the series $B(x) = \sum_{n\geq 0} b_n \frac{x^n}{n!}$. The term exponential is due to the fact that the constant sequence of terms 1, 1, 1, … has the series $E(x) = \sum_{n\geq 0} \frac{x^n}{n!} = e^x$ as an exponential generating function.

We notably have the following two properties:

1) $B'(x) = b_1 + b_2 \frac{x}{1!} + b_3 \frac{x^2}{2!} + \ldots = \sum_{n\geq 0} b_{n+1} \frac{x^n}{n!}$, therefore the derivation corresponds to a gap;

2) The product of two exponential generating functions $F(x)$ and $G(x)$ of the sequences (f_n) and (g_n) is an exponential generating function $H(x) = F(x)\ G(x)$ associated with a sequence (h_n) where $h_n = \sum_{n\geq 0} C_n^k f_k g_{n-k}$.[1]

In this case, sequence (b_n) of Bell numbers has the exponential generating function $B(x)$, which verifies:

$$B(x)\ e^x = B(x)\ E(x) = H(x)$$

in general terms:

$$h_n = \sum_{n\geq 0} C_n^k\, 1 b_{n-k} = b_{n+1}$$

$$= \sum_{n\geq 0} b_{n+1} \frac{x^n}{n!} = B'(x)$$

We get the differential equation:

$$B'(x) = B(x)\ e^x, \text{ thus } B'(x) / B(x) = e^x$$

$$\ln B(x) = e^x + K.$$

With $B(0) = b_0 = 1$, this imposes $K = -1$. Finally: $B(x) = e^{e^x - 1}$.

---

1 Actually $F(x)G(x)$ gives a term in x^n with coefficient $f_0\ g_n/n! + f_1\ g_{n-1}\ /(1!\ (n-1)!) + f_2\ g_{n-2}\ /(2!\ (n-2)!) + \ldots + f_n\ g_0\ /n! = h_n\ /\ n!$, hence by dividing by $n!$ the result presented for h_n.

14.2.4. *Enumeration algorithm for all partitions of a set*

Consider all the partitions of a n-element set. Let us add back an $n + 1^{\text{th}}$ element. Either it forms its own part alone, or is integrated in parts of a partition of the set with $n + 1$ elements. Envisaging all these eventualities, we will find all the partitions of a set with $n + 1$ elements.

The method of reasoning that enabled us to count all the partitions of a n-element set will now enable us to enumerate step-by-step all the partitions of a set.

We take $n = 1$, as the initial conditions, the only partition being {1}. Then we move on to $n = 2$, which gives two partitions, i.e. {1}{2} (in other words {12}). Then for $n = 3$ we get {1}{2}{3} or {12}{3} or {13}{2} or {1}{23} or {123}. And so on and so forth.

From this we deduce the program:

```
/* We use two arrays a[][] and aa[][], the first containing partitions already
known for N elements (at the start N=1), and aa[][] containing the new partitions or
n+1. When we find the new ones, we put them in the place of the old ones, from
aa[][] in a[][], and we start again.   */
int a[1000][15];

int aa[1000][15]

main()
{
 a[0][0]=1; nblocks[0]=1; numberofpartitions=1; cardinal=1;
 printf("Number of elements of the set=%d\n",cardinal); printf("1: 1");
 for(N=2; N<=7; N++)
  { k=0; newcardinal=cardinal+1;
   for(numberpartition=0;numberpartition<numberofpartitions;
       numberpartition++)
    {
     for(j=0;j<nblocks[numberpartition]+cardinal; j++)
         aa[k][j]=a[numberpartition][j];
     aa[k][nblocks[numberpartition]+cardinal]= newcardinal;
     newnblocks[k]=nblocks[numberpartition]+1;
     k++;
    }
   for(numberpartition=0;numberpartition<numberpartitions;numberpartition++)
   for(i=0;i<nblocks[numberpartition]+cardinal; i++)
```

```
        { if (a[numberpartition][i]==0)
           { for(j=0;j<i;j++)    aa[k][j]=a[numberpartition][j];
             aa[k][i]=newcardinal;
             for(j=nblocks[numberpartition]+cardinal-2; j>i ; j--)
                aa[k][j+1]=a[numberpartition][j];
             newnblocks[k]=nblocks[numberpartition];
             k++;
           }
        }
      numberofpartitions=k;    cardinal=newcardinal;
     for(numberpartition=0;numberpartition<numberofpartitions;numberpartition++)
       { for(j=0;j<=newnblocks[numberpartition]+cardinal;j++)
            a[numberpartition][j]=aa[numberpartition][j];
         nblocks[numberpartition]=newnblocks[numberpartition];
       }
     printf("\n\nNumber of elements of the set: %d\n",cardinal);
     for(numberpartition=0;numberpartition<numberofpartitions;numberpartition++)
       { printf("\n%d: {",numberpartition+1);
         for(j=0;j<nblocks[numberpartition]+cardinal;j++)
         if (a[numberpartition][j]!=0) printf(" %d ",a[numberpartition][j]);
         else if (j<nblocks[numberpartition]+cardinal-1) printf("} {");
         else if (j==nblocks[numberpartition]+cardinal-1) printf("}");
       }
    }
  }
```

14.2.5. *Exercise: Sterling numbers modulo 2*

The triangle formed by Stirling numbers brought back modulo 2, is presented as indicated in the table in Figure 14.2 and the diagram in Figure 14.3. Let us recall that Stirling numbers (of the second kind) verify the recurrence relation:

$$S(n, p) = S(n-1, p-1) + p\,S(n-1, p)$$

By boiling down to modulo 2, when p is even, we deduce from it that:

$$S(n, p) = S(n-1, p-1) \text{ modulo } 2$$

It follows that the even columns are identical to the odd columns that precede them, and are deduced from them using a simple vertical interval.

n \ p	1	2	3	4	5	6	7	8	9	10
1	1									
2	1	1								
3	1	1	1							
4	1	1	0	1						
5	1	1	1	0	1					
6	1	1	0	1	1	1				
7	1	1	1	0	0	1	1			
8	1	1	0	1	0	0	0	1		
9	1	1	1	0	1	0	0	0	1	
10	1	1	0	1	1	1	0	0	1	1

Figure 14.2. *Stirling triangle, modulo 2*

On the other hand, for odd p, we have:

$$S(n, p) = S(n-1, p-1) + S(n-1, p) \text{ modulo } 2$$

How do we go directly from an even column to the following odd column? With even p, $S(n, p) = S(n - 1, p - 1) = S(n - 2, p - 2) + S(n - 2, p - 1)$ with $S(n-1, p) = S(n-2, p-1)$. Hence:

$$S(n, p) = S(n-2, p-2) + S(n-1, p) \text{ modulo } 2$$

Nevertheless, let us assume that p is even and make a benchmark change with $x = n - p$ and $y = p / 2$: $S(n, p) = S(x + 2y, 2y)$ become a function of x and of y. By postulating that $S(n, p) = R(x, y)$, we get a new recurrence relation:

$$R(x, y) = R(x, y-1) + R(x-1, y) \text{ modulo } 2.$$

In the benchmark x, y, this gives:

x \ y								
	1	1	1	1	1	1	1	1
	1	0	1	0	1	0	1	0
	1	1	0	0	1	1	0	0
	1	0	0	0	1	0	0	0
	1	1	1	1	0	1	0	0

The recurrence relation is that of combinations C_{x+y}^{x}, but the starting conditions create a horizontal gap of one unit, i.e. $R(x, y) = C_{x+y-1}^{x}$, and finally:

$$S(n, p) = C_{n-p/2-1}^{n-p} \text{ modulo } 2.$$

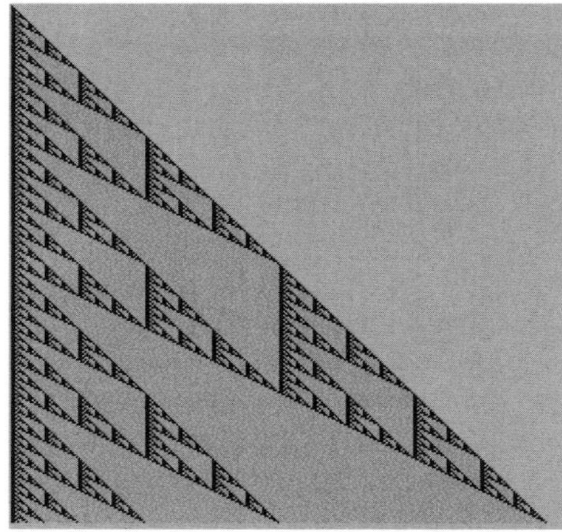

Figure 14.3. *Strirling triangle, modulo 2 with 256 lines*

Chapter 15

Partitions of a Number

Partition of a positive integer N is a way of cutting it up into pieces, with these pieces being positive integers (> 0) whose sum is N, assuming that the order in which these numbers are taken does not come into play. For example, partition of the number 8 is 4, 3, 1 because $4 + 3 + 1 = 8$, and this partition can also be written 3, 1, 4 or 1, 4, 3 if you prefer. As order does not come into play, we choose to write the partition in ascending order, or more so in descending order in this case, of the numbers that make it up. Let us begin by enumerating the partitions of a number N.

15.1. Enumeration algorithm

Let us take for example $N = 7$. The partitions of seven are:

7, 6 1, 5 2, 5 1 1, 4 3, 4 2 1, 4 1 1 1, 3 3 1, 3 2 2, 3 2 1 1, 3 1 1 1 1,

2 2 2 1, 2 2 1 1 1, 2 1 1 1 1 1, 1 1 1 1 1 1 1

They are written one after the other in descending alphabetical order and each one has its letters (digits in this case) written in descending order. We have underlined the pivot, i.e. the furthest element to the right that is the first letter to modify, more precisely reduce by 1, when we move from one partition to the next. This pivot is easy to obtain. All we have to do is start from the right going left, searching for the first element that is not a 1. Once this element has been reduced by 1, we need to make the changes behind it. When we are looking for the pivot, we calculate the sum r of the elements that are behind it at the same time.

After reducing the pivot by 1, the sum of elements behind it takes the new value r = $r + 1$. Because we have to place the longest possible word in alphabetical order behind the pivot, and because the first letter behind the pivot has to be the greatest possible without exceeding the pivot, we have to distinguish two cases. Either r is less than or equal to the pivot (after changing), and we simply put the number r alone behind the pivot. Or r is strictly greater than the pivot, and we repeat this pivot letter behind the pivot as many times as possible, i.e. as many times as the pivot number is found in r, as we would do for the quotient in a division. If this does not give exactly r, we add back what remains as the last element. Hence the program below.

Partitions of the number N are placed in an array a[N] whose length L must be managed, as the length is variable. The variable counter will give the number of partitions.

```
counter=0;  a[0]=N;  L=1;   /* the first partition  */
for(; ;)
  { counter++;  display table a[] by its length L
    i=L–1;  r=0;   while(i>=0 && a[i]= =1) {i--; r++; }
    pospivot=i;   if (pospivot= = -1) break;
    a[pospivot]= = a[pospivot]–1;    pivot= a[pospivot];   r= r+1;
    if (r<=pivot) { a[pospivot+1]= r; L= pospivot+2; }
    else  {  j=pospivot+1;
               while (r>=pivot)  { a[j]=pivot;  r = r- pivot; j++;}
               L=j;   if (r != 0)  {a[j]= r; L= j+1;}
            }
  }
```

15.2. Euler formula

Let $p(N)$ be the number of partitions of the number N, and $p_{\leq M}(N)$ the number of partitions of N with numbers less than or equal to M. Leonardt Euler found the formula that gives $p(N)$, using that of $p_{\leq M}(N)$, which we will use here.

Euler's formula:

$$p(N) = p(N-1) + p(N-2) - p(N-5) - p(N-7) + p(N-12) + p(N-15) - \ldots$$

is as long as the argument of function p is positive or null, with the convention $p(0) = 1$.

This is more precisely expressed as:

$$p(N)=\sum_{k>0}(-1)^{k+1}\,(p(N-\frac{1}{2}(3k^2-k)+p(N-\frac{1}{2}(3k^2+k)$$

The first values of $p(N)$ are given in Table 15.1.

N	0	1	2	3	4	5	6	7	8
p(N)	1	1	2	3	5	7	11	15	22

Table 15.1. *First values of p(N)*

Here we simply give some indications about demonstrating this formula, in the form of an exercise:

a) Show that the generating function of $p_{\leq M}(N)$ for a given M is:

$$\prod_{N=1}^{M}\frac{1}{1-x^N}$$

Let us recall that $p_{\leq M}(N)$ is the number of partitions of N with the greater part less than or equal to M. Consider the formal series:

$$\prod_{n=1}^{M}\frac{1}{1-x^n}=\frac{1}{1-x}\frac{1}{1-x^2}\cdots\frac{1}{1-x^M}$$
$$=(1+x+x^2+x^3+\ldots)(1+x^2+x^4+x^6+\ldots)\ldots.(1+x^M+x^{2M}+x^{3M}+\ldots)$$
$$=c_0+c_1x+c_2x^2+\ldots+c_Nx^N+\ldots.$$

The term in x^N is obtained by taking x^{k1} in the first parenthesis, x^{2k2} in the second parenthesis, and so and so forth until x^{Mk_M} in the last, which imposes:

$$k_1+2k_2+\ \ldots\ +j\,k_j+\ \ldots+M\,k_M=N$$

with k_j being positive or null all possible ways. Furthermore, the number of ways of writing N in the form above corresponds exactly to the number of partitions of N with the greater part being less than or equal to M. Hence $c_N=p_{\leq M}(N)$. We get:

$$\prod_{n=1}^{M}\frac{1}{1-x^n}=\sum_{N\geq 0}p_{\leq M}(N)x^N$$

b) Show that the generating function of p(N) is $\prod_{n=1}^{\infty}\frac{1}{1-x^n}$

Because $p(N) = p_{\leq M}(N)$ when $M \geq N$, all we have to do is tend M towards infinity in the generating function of $p_{\leq M}(N)$ to get that of $p(N)$, hence the formula presented.

We will assume the following formula:

$$\prod_{n=1}^{\infty}(1-x^n) = 1+\sum_{j=1}^{\infty}(-1)^j(x^{(3j^2+j)/2} + x^{(3j^2-j)/2})$$

and will then deduce the formula giving $p(n)$ from it.

We know that $\prod_{n=1}^{\infty}\frac{1}{(1-x^n)} = \sum_{k=0}^{\infty}p(k)x^k$. With the formula given in the statement, this gives:

$$\left(1+\sum_{j=1}^{\infty}(-1)^j(x^{(3j^2+j)/2})+x^{(3j^2-j)/2})\right)\sum_{k=0}^{\infty}p(k)x^k = 1$$

and by identification, we notice that the term in x^n is:

$$p(n) - p(n-1) - p(n-2) + p(n-5) + p(n-7) - p(n-12) - p(n-15) + \ldots = 0$$

15.3. Exercises

15.3.1. *Exercise 1: partitions of a number n in k distinct elements*

Using a positive integer N we want to express the distinct positive integers as a sum of K, in all possible ways without order coming into play. As we are free to take the order we wish, we choose to express each partition with its digits in ascending order. Then we number them one after the other in alphabetical order. For example for $N = 22$ and $K = 5$, we find:

1 2 3 4 12, 1 2 3 5 11, 1 2 3 6 10, 1 2 3 7 9, 1 2 4 5 10, 1 2 4 6 9, 1 2 4 7 8, 1 2 5 6 8, 1 3 4 5 9, 1 3 4 6 8, 1 3 5 6 7, 2 3 4 5 8, 2 3 4 6 7,

i.e. 13 partitions.

Note that the first partition, the smallest, is obtained by starting from 1 and placing it behind consecutive integers, and this is done until the penultimate number. This gives a sum equal to $S = K(K - 1) / 2$, with the last number having to be $N - S$. This imposes itself as a condition of existence of partitions with a given N and K:

$$N \geq K(K+1)/2$$

To count the number of these partitions from a number N in K distinct parts, let $p(N, K, v)$ be the number of partitions when the smallest part, i.e. the number placed in first place, is at least equal to a given number v. Returning to the example above with $N = 22$ and $K = 5$, we notice that $p(22, 5, 1) = 13$, $p(22, 5, 2) = 2$ and $p(22, 5, 3) = 0$. The $p(N, K, v)$ partitions are split into two categories: those that begin with the number v; and those that begin with a number at least equal to $v + 1$.

In the first case, all we have to do is count what the number behind v is, i.e. the partitions of number $N - v$ in $K - 1$ parts with a first number at least equal to $v + 1$, i.e. $p(N - v, K - 1, v + 1)$ partitions. In the second case, the number of partitions is $p(N, K, v + 1)$. We end up with the recurrence relation:

$$p(N, K, v) = p(N - v, K - 1, v + 1) + p(N, K, v + 1)$$

with $p(N, 1, v) = 1$ being initial conditions, which also assume $N \geq v$:

$$p(N, K, v) = 0 \text{ if } v + (v+1) + (v+2) + \ldots + (v + K - 1) \leq N$$

because, no partition is possible otherwise. This condition is also expressed:

$$N \geq Kv + K(K-1)/2$$

From this we deduce the program for counting partitions. The main program simply calls the function $p(N, K, 1)$, N and K, given, and displays counter c that gives the number of partitions. Function $p()$ is written:

```
void p(int n, int k ,int v)

{ if (k==1) c++;
  /* the condition n≥v is produced by the condition n>=k*v+k*(k-1)/2 */
  else if (n>=k*v+k*(k–1)/2)
    { p(n–v,k–1,v+1);
```

```
            p(n,k,v+1);
        }
    }
```

Let us take this further to insist on the methods of programming by proceeding to a recursive enumeration of partitions. An adjustment to the counting algorithm above also enables us to enumerate the partitions. Now let $P(N, K, v)$ be the set of partitions of N in K distinct parts whose smallest part is at least equal to v. Among them we find those that are expressed as $P(N - v, K - 1, v + 1)\ v$, where v is concatenated to partitions of the number $N - v$ in $K - 1$ distinct parts, the smallest part of which is at least equal to $v + 1$.

In this case, the parts are taken in descending order. On the other hand we find partitions that make up $P(N, K, v + 1)$, the smallest term of which is at least equal to $v + 1$. From this we deduce the program:

```
Take N and K, then declare: int counter= 0;  int a[K];
main()
{ p(N, K, 1); }


void p(int n, int k , int v)
{ a[k–1]= v;
  if (k= =1)
      { counter++;  a[0] = n;  printf("%4.d: ", counter);
        for(j=0; j<k; j++) printf("%3.d ",a[j]) ; printf("\n");
                  /*displaying a partition */
                }
  else if ( n>=k*v + k*(k-1)/2 )   { p( n–v, k–1, v+1);  p( n, k, v+1);  }
}
```

Each partition is in turn recorded in an array $a[K]$. Let us take an example in order to understand how this program works. Here $N = 10$ and $K = 3$ (see Figure 15.1). Therefore we find the four partitions: 7 2 1, 6 3 1, 5 4 1 and 5 3 2, displayed each time we reach the stop condition $k = 1$.

An iterative algorithm may be preferred. In this case, each partition will be placed alternately in table $a[K]$, with boxes numbered from 0 to $K - 1$. The first partition is obtained by taking the successive integers 1 2 3 ... up to $K - 1$, with their sum totaling S. The last integer in the table is number $K - 1$, with $N - S$. Using this first partition, we will develop an algorithm enabling us to go from one partition to the next. To do this we have to look for the pivot element each time, namely the first number we will increase by one behind a fixed block of the longest possible length. To do this we start from the right, searching for the closest number that we will increase by 1. As long as we have two successive terms with a difference of 1, we must continue to move left.

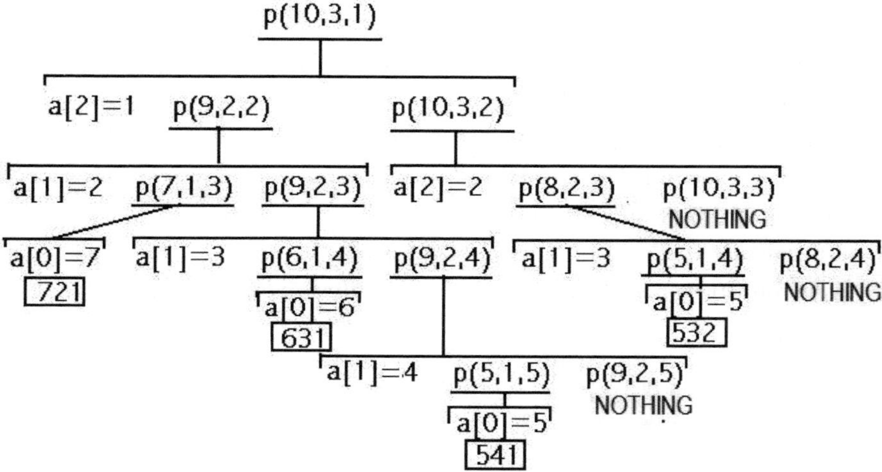

Figure 15.1. *Functioning of the recursive algorithm*

Even if we get a difference of 2 once and only once, we continue to move left. Actually, increasing the pivot element by one forces us to reduce a term located to its right by one, at least once, without causing equality between two neighboring terms.

Let us check this by going back to the example $N = 22$ and $K = 5$, with the pivot element underlined at each step:

1 2 3 **4** 12, 1 2 3 **5** 11, 1 2 3 **6** 10 , 1 2 **3** 7 9, 1 2 4 **5** 10, 1 2 4 **6** 9, 1 2 **4** 7 8, 1 **2** 5 6 8, 1 3 4 **5** 9, 1 3 **4** 6 8, **1** 3 5 6 7, 2 3 4 **5** 8, 2 3 4 6 7

The process stops when the pivot is found in -1 position. At each stage, once the pivot element has been found and increased by one, we move to its right from box to box, placing numbers that increase by one each time until the penultimate box, with the last box taking the only possible number remaining. Hence the program:

```
if (N<K*(K+1)/2) { printf("Take K smaller"); exit(0);}
S=0;  counter=0;
for(i=0;i<K–1;i++) {a[i]=i+1; S+=a[i];}
a[K–1]=N–S;
for(;;)
 {
 counter++; display the contents of array a[K]
 i=K–2;              /* searching for the position of the pivot */
 while(i>=0 && a[i+1]-a[i]==1) i--;
 if (i>=0 && a[i+1]–a[i]==2) i--;
 while(i>=0 && a[i+1]-a[i]==1) i--;
 pospivot=i;  if (pospivot==-1) break;
 a[pospivot]++;
 S=0; for(i=0;i<=pospivot;i++) S+=a[i];   /* filling in behind the pivot */
 for(i=pospivot+1; i<K–1;i++)
    { a[i]=a[i–1]+1; S+=a[i];}
 a[K–1]=N–S;
 }
```

15.3.2. *Exercise 2: ordered partitions*

Now what we have to do is split a given positive number *N* into several positive numbers whose sum totals *N*, taking into consideration the order in which these numbers are taken. We want to count and enumerate the number of such ordered partitions of *N*. For example, the ordered partitions of five are:

> 5, 4 1, 3 2, 3 1 1, 2 3, 2 2 1, 2 1 2, 2 1 1 1, 1 4, 1 3 1, 1 2 2, 1 2 1 1, 1 1 3, 1 1 2 1, 1 1 1 3, 1 1 1 1 1

totaling 16.

As order comes into play here, the ordered partition 1 1 3 is not the same as 1 3 1 or 3 1 1. We will show that the number of ordered partitions of the number n is 2^{n-1}. To do this, let us draw the number n using n vertical bars. Then let us insert k points in all possible ways between these bars, i.e. C_{n-1}^{k} ways. This gives all the ordered partitions of the number n in k parts. The number of ordered partitions is:[1]

$$\sum_{k=0}^{n-1} C_{n-1}^{k} = 2^{n-1}$$

15.3.3. *Exercise 3: sum of the products of all the ordered partitions of a number*

Recall that an ordered partition of a number n is made up of numbers a_i so that $n = a_1 + a_2 + \ldots + a_k$, with $k \geq 1$ and $a_i \geq 1$, where these numbers are chosen in a precise order. In other words, the ordered partition (1, 1, 2) of the number 4 is not the same as the ordered partition (1, 2, 1). The ordered partitions of $n = 4$ are (1111), (112), (121), (13), (211), (22), (31) and (4), i.e. eight.

We want to find the sum of the products of elements of each ordered partition, i.e. $\Sigma(a_1a_2\ldots a_k)$. For example, for $n = 4$ we get: $1 + 2 + 2 + 3 + 2 + 4 + 3 + 4 = 21$. We find the Fibonacci number $F(8)$.

What we have to do is prove that in general, for a number n:

$$\Sigma(a_1a_2\ldots a_k) = F(2n)$$

Let us consider the generating function $(x + 2x^2 + 3x^3 + 4x^4 + \ldots.)^k$. The coefficient of the term in x^q is none other than $\Sigma(a_1a_2\ldots a_k)$, where the numbers a_i form an ordered partition of the number q, with this partition of a given length k. To get all the possible lengths, we take the following as the generating function:

$$F(x) = \sum_{k\geq 1} (x + 2x^2 + 3x^3 + 4x^4 + \ldots.)^k$$

The coefficient of the term in x^q is $\Sigma(a_1a_2\ldots a_k)$, where the numbers a_i form an ordered partition of q. This is the case for all partitions k units long. It is the generating function that concerns us:

---

1. This result can also be obtained in the following way. Imagine that each number j of a partition is represented by a pile of j bricks placed one on top of the other. A partition corresponds to a juxtaposition of piles of bricks, and we find the brick wall problem (see Chapter 16). As we will see, we code each brick wall using a series of N numbers 0 or 1, with the bricks placed on the ground being 1, and the others being 0. The bricks are read from bottom to top, then from left to right. Such words all begin with 1, the rest being made up of a choice of 0 or 1, hence 2^{N-1} words. The number of ordered partitions is therefore 2^{N-1}.

$$F(x) = \sum_{k\geq 1} x^k (1+2x+3x^2+4x^3+...)^k = \sum_{k\geq 1} \frac{x^k}{(1-x)^{2k}} = \frac{x}{(1-x)^2} \sum_{k\geq 0} \left(\frac{x}{(1-x)^2} \right)^k$$

$$= \frac{x}{(1-x)^2} \frac{1}{1-\frac{x}{(1-x)^2}} = \frac{x}{x^2-3x+1}$$

We have just found the generating function of the Fibonacci series $F(2n)$. Actually:

$$F(2n) = F(2n-1) + F(2n-2) = 2F(2n-2) + F(2n-3)$$

$$= 2F(2n-2) + F(2n-2) - F(2n-4)$$

$$= 3F(2n-2) - F(2n-4)$$

Furthermore, the sequence $u(n)$ characterized by the recurrence relation $u(n) = 3u(n-1) - u(n-2)$ with $u(0) = 0$ and $u(1) = 1$ at the start has the generating function: $G(x) = x / (1 - 3x + x^2)$. This sequence is none other than $(F(2n))$.

15.3.4. *Exercise 4: partitions of a number in completely distinct parts*

a) With what number sequence is the following generating function:

$$F_{12}(x) = (1+x)(1+x^2)(1+x^3)\ ...(1+x^{12})\ ?$$

Each one of the terms in x^k obtained when developing $F_{12}(x)$ has an exponent of the form $\sum_{i=1}^{12} \delta_i i$, where δ_i is equal to 0 or 1. The number of these terms in x^k is the number of ways of writing the number k in the form $\sum_{i=1}^{12} \delta_i i$, i.e. the number of partitions of the number k in completely distinct parts less than or equal to 12.

b) If $p_{\neq}(n)$ is the number of partitions of n in completely distinct parts, give its generating function.

By analogy with the previous question, we get:

$$\sum_{k=0}^{\infty} p_{\neq}(k) x^k = \prod_{n=1}^{\infty} (1+x^n)$$

15.3.5. *Exercise 5: partitions and routes in a square grid*

We are placed in a square grid, with benchmark $O\ x\ y$, and have paths going from point O to point A with coordinates (L, h), based on unit steps east or north where the last step is directed eastwards (see Figure 15.2).

a) Determine the number of possible paths. Deduce the generating function $G_L(y)$ associated with the number of paths of given horizontal length L, i.e. with L steps eastwards, from it.

Because the last step is imposed, the number of paths is also that of the paths leading from point O to point $(L - 1, h)$, i.e. the number of combinations C_{L-1+h}^{L-1} (the formula seen in Chapter 6).

The associated generating function is:

$$G_L(y) = \frac{1}{(1-y)^L}$$

To get this we used the well-known formula:[2]

$$\sum_{n\geq 0} C_{a+n}^{a} x^n = \frac{1}{(1-x)^{a+1}}$$

2. Here is another demonstration. To get the terms in y^h in developing the following expression:

$$\frac{1}{(1-y)^L} = \frac{1}{(1-y)(1-y)...(1-y)},$$
$$= (1+y+y^2+y^3+...)(1+y+y^2+y^3+...)...(1+y+y^2+y^3+...)$$

we should take a term y^{a_k} in each L factor in such a way that the sum of their exponents gives n, i.e. $y^{a_0} y^{a_1}...y^{a_{L-1}} = y^h$, or even $a_0 + a_1 +... + a_{L-1} = h$ with numbers a_k all being positive or null, and k between 0 and $L - 1$. By doing this in all possible ways, we get the coefficient of the term in y^h.
Now let us take a path leading from O to point $A(L, h)$ with the last step towards the east where number of paths to the north for each abscissa k between 0 and $L - 1$, which imposes $a_0 + a_1 +... + a_{L-1}= h$, is a_k. (For example on the drawing above with $L = 6$ and $h = 5$, the list of a_k is 0, 0, 2, 2, 0, 1.) A bijection exists between the number of such paths and the list of these paths to the north, i.e. the number of solutions (a_k) to the equation $a_0 + a_1 +... + a_{L-1}= h$. The coefficient of y^h is therefore C_{L-1+h}^{L-1} (the formula seen in Chapter 7).

coming from successive derivations of the basic formula:

$$\sum_{n\geq 0} x^n = \frac{1}{1-x}$$

In developing the generating function $G_L(y)$, the coefficient of the term in y^h is the number of paths h high (and horizontal paths L long).

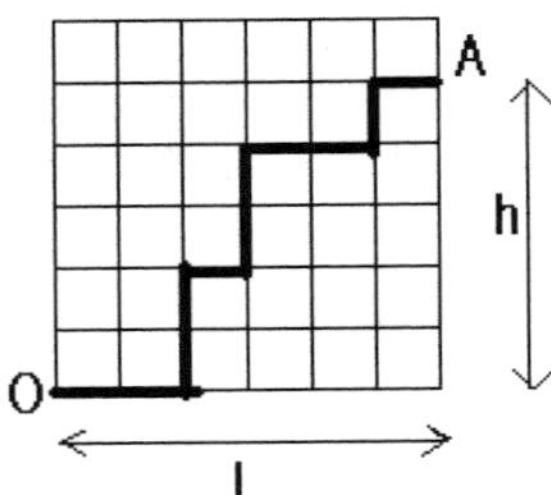

Figure 15.2. *A path with the last step eastward*

b) For each path, we now consider the area of the surface marked off by the path, the x-axis and the vertical border x = L. This area is the number of unit squares inscribed in the surface. Determine the generating function associated with the number u(k) of horizontal paths L long that have an area of k.

Let us take a path leading to point $A(L, h)$ of area k and divide the surface it delimits in h rows. The sum of the lengths of these rows gives the area k of the surface. By taking the rows from bottom to top, their lengths are decreasing, at most being equal to L, and at least equal to 1. Therefore, when L is given and we want to calculate an area k, the lengths of the rows form a partition of the number k in parts that are all less than or equal to L, with the number h of parts therefore being any number. There are as many horizontal paths that are L long with area k as there are partitions of the number k with parts less than or equal to L, i.e. $p_{\leq L}(k)$. Therefore $u(k) = p_{\leq L}(k)$. The generating function sought is:

$$\sum_{k\geq 0} p_{\leq L}(k) z^k = \prod_{i=1}^{L} \frac{1}{1-z^i}$$

as we saw above. For example, where $L = 3$ this generating function is:

$$1 + z + 2z^2 + 3z^3 + 4z^4 + 5z^5 + 7z^6 + 8z^7 + 10z^8 + \ldots$$

Taking for example an area equal to four with $L = 3$, we find four paths, corresponding to the partitions of four: $3 + 1$, $2 + 2$, $2 + 1 + 1$ and $1 + 1 + 1 + 1$, with their parts all being less than or equal to three (see Figure 15.3).

c) Deduce the generating function $G_L(y, z)$ of the sequence of elements $u(h, k)$ giving the number of paths of a given length L, with height h and area k.

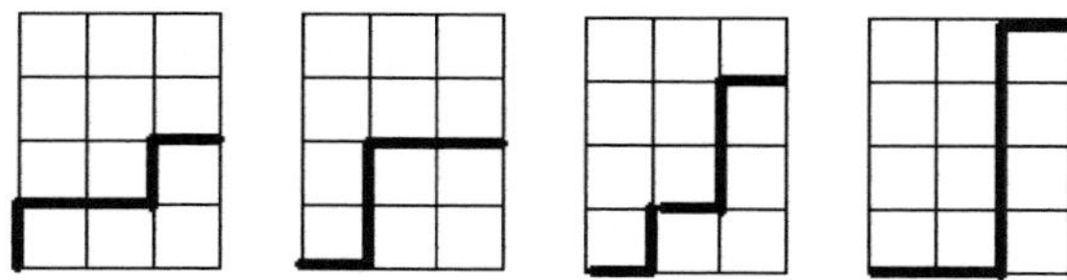

Figure 15.3. *Paths making $L = 3$ paths east and marking off an area equal to 4*

Above we saw two generating functions, both for given L: one $\dfrac{1}{(1-y)^L}$ for the height h, the other $\prod_{i=1}^{L}\dfrac{1}{1-z^i}$ for area k. The combination of these two results gives the generating function of $u(h, k)$:

$$G_L(y,z) = \frac{1}{\prod_{i=1}^{L}(1-yz^i)}$$

For example, its development gives, for $L = 3$:

$$G_3(y, z) = 1 + (z + z^2 + z^3)y + (z^2 + z^3 + 2z^4 + z^5 + z^6)y^2$$
$$+ (z^3 + z^4 + 2z^5 + 2z^6 + 2z^7 + z^8 + z^9)y^3 + \ldots$$ [3]

d) Determine the generating function $G_N(z)$ associated with the number $p_{=M}(N)$ of partitions of a given number n, with a greater part equal to M ($M \leq N$).

---

3. Mathematical software immediately gives this result. For example, with Mathematica all you have to do is program something of the style: Series[1/(1–y*z)(1–y*z^2)*(1–y*z^3)),{y,0,5},{z,0,15}].

All we have to do for this is to use the relation $p_{=M}(N) = p_{\le M}(N - M)$. From this we deduce the generating function:

$$G_N(z) = \sum_{N \ge M} p_{=M}(N) z^N = \sum_{N \ge M} p_{\le M}(N - M) z^N$$

$$= z^M \sum_{N \ge M} p_{\le M}(N - M) z^{N-M} = \frac{z^M}{\prod_{n=1}^{M} (1 - z^n)}$$

15.3.6. *Exercise 6: Ferrers graphs*

Ferrers graphs enable us to visualize partitions. Let us take a number N and a certain partition of this number, made up of strictly positive numbers a_k arranged in descending order. Each part of this partition is represented by a horizontal row of a_k points, and the successive parts are placed one below the other, as in Figure 15.4, with the number $N = 13$ and the partition $13 = 6 + 3 + 2 + 1 + 1$. Note that by reading the diagram following vertical columns we get another partition of the same number, called a *conjugated partition*, i.e. here it is $13 = 5 + 3 + 2 + 1 + 1 + 1$.

Figure 15.4. *Ferrers diagram of the partition of 13 = 5+3+2+1+1+1*

a) Show that the number of partitions of N in exactly K parts is also the number of partitions of N in parts, the largest of which is K.

The answer to this is an immediate consequence of what precedes it: the number K of rows in the Ferrers diagram is also the biggest part of the conjugated partition, corresponding to the first column of the diagram.

b) Program the passing of one partition to the conjugated partition.

Let us consider a partition of a number N. The parts of this partition are placed, in descending order, in an array $a[]$ whose squares are numbered starting from 0. The length La of the array is the number of parts of this partition. How do we obtain the conjugated partition? We use an array $c[]$ in which this partition is placed.

Thanks to the Ferrers graph of the initial partition, we notice that the first part of the conjugated partition is $c[0] = La$, and that the number of these parts is $Lc = a[0]$.

Returning to the example of the partition of $N = 13$ drawn in Figure 15.4, with $La = c[0] = 5$ and $Lb = a[0] = 6$, we notice that we go from $c[0] = 5$ to the following part $c[1]$ by removing 2, which is the number of parts of the initial partition that are equal to 1, hence $c[1] = 5 - 2 = 3$. Then we go from $c[1]$ to $c[2]$, by removing 1, which is exactly the number of parts equal to 2 in the initial partition, hence $c[2] = 3 - 1 = 2$. This can be generalized: to go from $c[i]$ to $c[i + 1]$, we remove the number of parts of the starting partition that are equal to I and continue until we reach the end. Hence the program:

```
main()
{ we are given array a[La] filled in with La parts in descending order.
  we put the array nbtimes[] at 0.
  c[0]=La; Lc=a[0];
  for(i=0; i<La; i++) nbtimes[a[i]]++;
      /* we make a run through array a[] containing the partition to find out
        the number of parts equal to 1, the number of those equal to 2, etc. */
  for(i=1; i<Lc; i++)  c[i]=c[i-1]-nbtimes[i];
      /* progressive filling in of array c[] */
  printf("\nc: "); for(i=0; i<Lc; i++) printf("%d ",c[i]);  /* display */
}
```

c) Determine the generating function $G_L(y)$ associated with the number $u(h)$ of Ferrers diagrams whose biggest part is a given positive number L, and the greatest number of rows is h.

Let us re-draw a reverse partition of the biggest part L with the benchmark $O\,x\,y$ (see Figure 15.5). Here we get a route in the gridline of the plan, based on steps eastward or northward from point O to point $A(L, h)$.

Such paths are obligatorily a first step northward and a last step eastward.

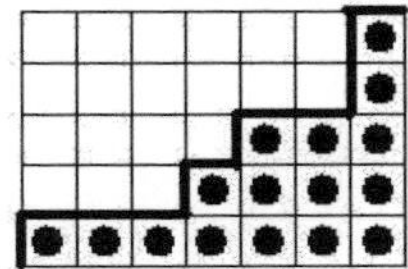

Figure 15.5. *Reverse Ferrers diagram and border path*

The number of these paths leading from O to A is also that of paths from $O'(0, 1)$ to A' $(L - 1, h)$, including $L - 1$ horizontal paths and $h - 1$ vertical paths, i.e. $u(h) = C_{L-1+h-1}^{L-1}$.

The generating function of $u(h)$ is:

$$G_L(y) = \sum_{h \geq 1} C_{L-1+h-1}^{L-1} y^h = y \sum_{h \geq 1} C_{L-1+h-1}^{L-1} y^{h-1}.$$ Let us positulate $h' = h - 1$

$$= y \sum_{h' \geq 0} C_{L-1+h'}^{L-1} y^{h'} = y \frac{1}{(1-y)^L}$$

Now let us take the number $u(L, h)$ of partitions whose biggest part is L and the number of parts h. Its generating function is by definition:

$$G(x, y) = \sum u(L, h) x^L y^h$$

and it is expressed:

$$G(x, y) = \sum_{L \geq 1} \frac{x^L y}{(1-y)^L}$$

Finally, let us take the number $u(L, h, N)$ of partitions of the number N, with L as its biggest part and h as the number of parts. Its generating function is:

$$G(x, y, z) = \sum_{L \geq 1} \frac{x^L y z^L}{\prod_{i \geq 0}^{L} (1 - yz^i)}$$

For this we used the results of the exercise above, with N being the area marked off by the path. In developing $G(x, y, z)$, the coefficient of the term in $x^L y^h z^N$ is exactly $u(L, h, N)$.

Chapter 16

Flags

This chapter, as well as those that follow in Part 1, are mostly application exercises in concrete domains.

16.1. Checkered flags

A flag is made up of two rows of n squares, each one having its own color. We have three colors (see Figure 16.1). We want to find out how many ways there are of coloring in this flag using these three colors, at most, and so that no two adjoining squares have the same color?

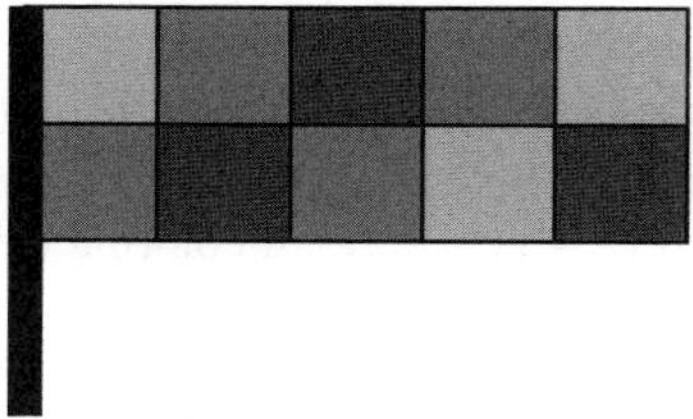

Figure 16.1. *A checkered flag n= 5 long*

Let three colors be 0, 1, 2 and $u(n)$ be the number of flags depending on their colors. We will start by determining $u(1)$. For $n = 1$, the two squares that make up the flag have a different color. Let us order the squares from top to bottom.

For example, couple (0, 1) indicates that the square above is color 0, and the one below is color 1. $u(1)$ is the number of ways of two out of three colors can be chosen taking order into consideration, i.e. $u(1) = A_3^2 = 6$. Now let us take the $u(n-1)$ colorings of flags $n - 1$ long. Their last column contains the two colors (A, B) where A is different to B. Let us add an nth column in all possible ways:

A ⟶ B   A ⟶ C
B ⟶ A, C   B ⟶ A

We find three possibilities. For each coloring $n - 1$ long there are three colorings on a flag n long, hence $u(n) = 3u(n - 1)$. With the initial condition $u(1) = 6$, this gives $u(n) = 6 \times 3^{n-1} = 2 \times 3^n$.

16.2. Flags with vertical stripes

A rectangular shaped flag is divided into N vertical stripes, numbered from 1 to N from the pole where the flag will be attached. We have P colors in order to color each stripe, in such a way that two successive stripes never have the same color. This constraint will remain valid in all the questions that follow.

The problem can be posed in another way: we want to construct a word N characters long from an alphabet of P letters, and this word must not have any two consecutive letters that are identical. We want to find out how many ways this can be done.

a) How many different flags $A(N, P)$ of N stripes do we get when we use a maximum of P colors?

There are P ways of coloring in the first stripe. Each time for the second stripe, there are $P - 1$ possible colors. This is the same for each one of the other stripes. In total, this makes $A(N, P) = P(P - 1)^{N-1}$ ways of coloring the flags (see Figure 16.2).

b) How many flags with N vertical stripes with a maximum of P colors, but that can be attached to a pole from one side or the other, do we get?

Let $v(N, P)$ be the number of such flags that are of a half-turn type, i.e. a reversal-type in relation to the vertical line in the center of the flag. We distinguish two cases based on whether N is odd or even:

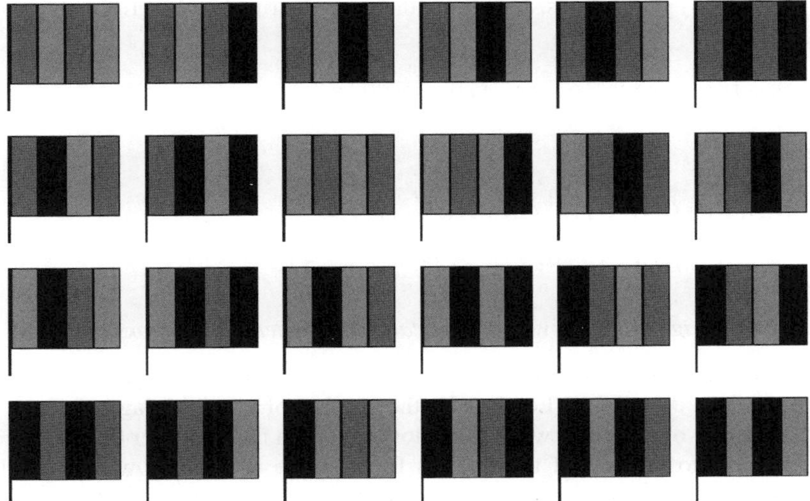

Figure 16.2. *The 24 flags with N = 4 stripes and P = 3 possible colors*

– *Case where N is even:* for example $v(4, 2) = 1$ because we had $A(4, 2) = 2$, and because now flag 0101 is also flag 1010 when we attach it from the other side. In relation to the central line, a flag is divided into two parts $N / 2$ long. The last stripe in the first half has to be the same color as its neighbor to the right, which is the first stripe of the second half. If we reverse the flag, we will have two different flags. We can divide the $A(N, P)$ flags in the previous question into two equal parts. If we place the pole on one side or the other, all we have to do is to take half of the flags to get all the possibilities:

$$v(N, P) = A(N, P) / 2 = P(P-1)^{N-1} / 2.$$

– *Case where N is odd:* let us divide a flag into two equal parts with $(N-1) / 2$ stripes each, and one stripe remaining in the center. For $A(N, P)$ flags, a number S remain identical after reversal, and a number $T = A(N, P) - S$ do not become different. For these T flags, half of them become identical to the other half after reversal. Depending on whether the pole is placed on one side or the other, this gives:

$$v(N, P) = S + T / 2 = S + (A(N, P) - S) / 2 = (A(N, P) + S) / 2$$

Let us determine S. For each autosymmetrical flag there are two parts equal in length on the left and right that are also symmetrical, and therefore the same direction-type. As each of the parts constitutes a flag $(N-1) / 2$ long, this makes

$A((N-1)/2, P)$ possibilities. Each time the central stripe has $P-1$ possible colors. Hence:

$$S = P(P-1)^{(N-3)/2}\,(P-1) = P(P-1)^{(N-1)/2}.$$

therefore:

$$v(N, P) = (P\,(P-1)^{N-1} / 2) + P\,(P-1)^{(N-1)/2}$$

$$= P\,(P-1)^{(N-1)/2}\,(\,(P-1)^{(N-1)/2} + 1) / 2$$ [1]

c) How many flags are there with N vertical stripes when the P colors are used?

Now we add this extra constraint, with all the P colors used. These colors are numbered from 0 to $P-1$. Let $D_{N,P}$ be the number of possible flag colorings, and $S_{N,P}$ the number of colorings when the colors appear in natural order 0, 1, 2, ... going from the pole to the end of the flag, as for example in the flag written 0101201 where the first 1 is only preceded by 0, and the first 2 is only preceded by 0 or 1, with this flag being one of the $S_{7,3}$ flags.

i) Give a relation between $D_{N,P}$ and $S_{N,P}$.

Let us take one of the $S_{N,P}$ flags where the colors appear alternately in natural order. Any change in this order corresponds to a permutation of the P colors. For each one of the $S_{N,P}$ flags, exercising all the permutations of the colors according to their natural order of appearance starting from the pole, we get $P!$ flags that are all different, out of the $D_{N,P}$ flags. Similarly, the $D_{N,P}$ flags can be split into groups of $P!$ to give a single flag of $S_{N,P}$. We end up with the relation:

$$D_{N,P} = P!\; S_{N,P}.$$

ii) Find a recurrence relation on the $D_{N,P}$.

As soon as $N < P$, it is certain that $D_{N,P} = 0$. Nevertheless let us take $N \geq P$. When $N = P$ there is only one possible coloring in natural order of the colors, hence $D_{P,P} = P!$. When $N > P$, we find $D_{N,1} = 0$ and $D_{N,2} = A(N, 2) = 2$, i.e. flags 010101... and 101010..., hence $S_{N,2} = 1$.

---

1. Evidently we get the same result using Burnside's formula with a group G of permutations formed using Id and the reflection of the vertical axis V leaving the rectangle invariant. We have $S_{Id} = A(N, P)$ and $S_V = S$, hence the result:

$$(A(N,P) + S) / 2 = (P\,(P-1)^{N-1} + P\,(P-1)^{(N-1)/2}) / 2.$$

Let us take $P = 3$. We know that there are $A(N, 3)$ ways (see section 16.2b) to color a flag with three colors at most. To have $D_{N,3}$, all we have to do is remove all the colorings using two of the three colors from $A(N, 3)$, i.e. $C_3^2 D_{N,2}$. Hence:

$$D_{N,3} = A_{N,3} - C_3^2 D_{N,2} = 3 \,.\, 2^{N-1} - 6 = 3\,(2^{N-1} - 2) = 6 \,.\, (2^{N-2} - 1)$$

therefore $S_{N,3} = 2^{N-2} - 1$.

For $P = 4$, we get:

$$D_{N,4} = A(N, 4) - C_4^3 D_{N,3} - C_4^2 D_{N,2} = 4 \,.\, 3^{N-1} - 4 \,.\, 3\,(2^{N-1} - 2) - 6 \,.\, 2$$

$$= 4 \,.\, 3^{N-1} - 3 \,.\, 2^{N+1} + 12$$

$$= 24\,((3^{N-2} + 1) / 2 - 2^{N-2})$$

$$S_{N,4} = (3^{N-2} + 1) / 2 - 2^{N-2}$$

For $P = 5$, we find:[2]

$$D_{N,5} = 5 \,.\, 4^{N-1} - 5\,(4 \,.\, 3^{N-1} - 3 \,.\, 2^{N+1} + 12) - 10 \,.\, 3\,(2^{N-1} - 2) - 10 \,.\, 2$$

$$= 5 \,.\, 4^{N-1} - 20 \,.\, 3^{N-1} + 30 \,.\, 2^{N-1} - 20 = 120\,((4^{N-2} - 3^{N-1} - 1) / 6 + 2^{N-3})$$

$$= 120\,(2^{2N-4} + 3 \,.\, 2^{N-2} - 3^{N-1} - 1) / 6$$

hence: $S_{N,5} = (2^{2N-4} + 3 \,.\, 2^{N-2} - 3^{N-1} - 1) / 6$.

In the general case the recurrence formula is written:

$$D_{N,P} = P\,(P-1)^{N-1} - C_P^{P-1} D_{N,P-1} - C_P^{P-2} D_{N,P-2} - \ldots - C_P^2 D_{N,2}$$

for the same reasons. This relation enables us, step by step, to obtain the values of $D_{N,P}$ and $S_{N,P}$.

iii) Find a recurrence relation between $S_{N,P}$, $S_{N-1,P}$ and $S_{N-1,P-1}$.

The $S_{N,P}$ flags can be separated into two categories. In the first category, the last color $P - 1$ only appears in the last stripe N, which makes $P - 1$ colors present in

2. These results would also be obtained using the sieve formula, starting from the set of configurations numbering $A_{N,5}$ in this case by introducing five properties, with property k meaning that color k is not present. $D_{N,5}$ is therefore the number of configurations that have none of the five properties.

natural order in the $N-1$ remaining stripes, which makes $S_{N-1,P-1}$ cases. In the second category, color $P-1$ appears before the last stripe, and for the $N-1$ remaining stripes there are $S_{N-1,P}$ colorings. For the last stripe, there are $P-1$ possibilities (all colors except that of stripe $N-1$). In total this makes $(P-1)\,S_{N-1,P}$ cases. Finally:

$$S_{N,P} = (P-1)\,S_{N-1,P} + S_{N-1,P-1}$$

where at the start we have $S_{1,1} = 0$ and $S_{1,P} = 0$ for $P > 1$, and $S_{N,1} = 0$ for $N > 1$.

This formula gives a quick method of calculating $S_{N,P}$. For the first values of P we find the results indicated in Figure 16.3.

N \ P	1	2	3	4	5	6	7	8
1	1	0	0	0	0	0	0	0
2	0	1	0	0	0	0	0	0
3	0	1	1	0	0	0	0	0
4	0	1	3	1	0	0	0	0
5	0	1	7	6	1	0	0	0
6	0	1	15	25	10	1	0	0
7	0	1	31	90	65	15	1	0
8	0	1	63	301	350	140	21	1

Figure 16.3. *Number of flags with N stripes and P numbered colors, these colors appearing in the natural order of their numbers*

iv) Create a program enabling us to enumerate, in the case of drawing, the $S_{N,P}$ flags with their P colors all present, and appearing alternately in natural order.

Here we are led to create a tree (see Figure 16.4). Each descent in the tree, from one level to the next level N, represents a flag.

At level 1 in the tree, corresponding to stripe number 1, the root of the tree with color 0 is found. At level 2, corresponding to stripe number 2, only one single node with color 1 is found. At level 3, two possible successors from the preceding node are found, with colors 0 or 2. And so on and so forth until level N. When we descend from one level of a node with its color, we take a different color.

For this new node, we choose either a color already present by going back up in the tree, or a color not yet used, which has to be the smallest number of the remaining colors. This leads us to manage an array *done*[*level*][*color*] for each node where the colors already used are indicated.

We stop at level N and should prune the descents where not all colors are present, which the array *done*[][] enables us to determine.

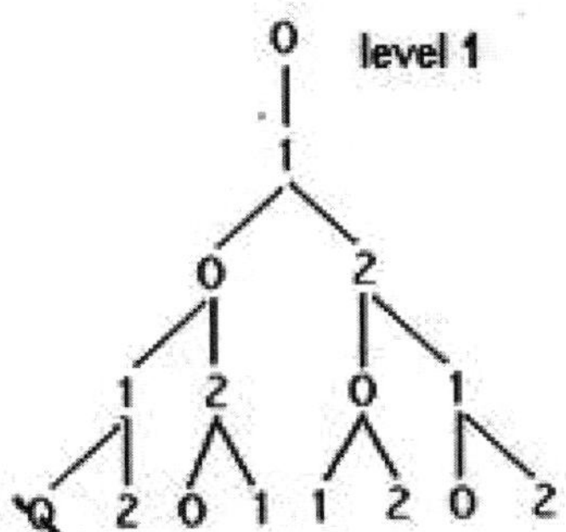

Figure 16.4. *Tree structure of flags for N = 5 and P = 3*

Here is the program (the results obtained are given in Figures 16.5 and 16.6):

```
#define P 3
#define N 5
int done[N+1][P],d[N],predecessor[N+1],counter=0;

main()    { done[1][0]=1;  tree(0,1);  display counter  }
void tree (int a, int level)

{  int smallest,i,j,flag;
   if (level ==N)   /* display of a descent, i.e. a flag  */
     {              /* the descent in the tree is placed in d[i]  */
       for(j=2; j<=N; j++)  d[j-2]=predecessor[j];
       d[N-1]=a;
       for(i=0; i<P; i++)  if(done[level][i]==0)
           {smallest=i; break;}
       if (i==P) smallest=-1;
       if(smallest==-1)
           { counter++; display table d[N] or draw the flag  }
     }

   else          /* creation of successors of a node  */
     {  for(i=0; i<P; i++)  if(done[level][i]==0)
           {smallest=i; break;}
        if (i==P) smallest=-1;
```

```
            /* this case indicates that the table done[][] is at 1 */
      for(i=0; i<P; i++)
      if (done[level][i]==1 && i!=a)   /* color already used */
          {
            predecessor[level+1]=a;
            for(j=0; j<P; j++) done[level+1][j]=done[level][j];
            done[level+1][i]=1;
            tree(i, level+1);
          }
      if (smallest ! = -1)   /* we take a color not yet used */
          {
            predecessor[level+1]=a;
            for(j=0; j<P; j++) done[level+1][j]=done[level][j];
            done[level+1][smallest]=1;
            tree(smallest , level+1);
          }
    }
}
```

Figure 16.5. *The 31 flags for N=7 stripes and P=3 colors, with the three colors used and appearing in order, with white (color 0) in first place, pale gray (1) next and dark gray (2) last*

Figure 16.6. *The 90 flags for N = 7 and P = 4, with the four colors used in order*

Chapter 17

Walls and Stacks

17.1. Brick walls

We make walls with neither holes nor overlaps from n rectangular shaped bricks. All these rectangles are displayed in the same vertical plane, either on the ground or on another rectangle, side-by-side without gaps. We want to find the number $u(n)$ of distinctly shaped walls that can be constructed with n bricks. For example, for $n = 5$ we find 16 walls (see Figure 17.1) and note the possibility of walls with battlements.

There is a simple method for determining $u(n)$. With the number n of bricks being given, we code each wall using a word with n letters based on 0 and 1. Each brick placed on the ground is called 1, and the others are called 0. In order from left to right, each brick on the ground is written 1, followed by the 0 bricks that are above it. For example, the five walls in the first line in Figure 17.1 are coded 10000 10001, 10010, 10011 and 10100. These n-letter words ($n > 0$) always begin with 1, and this is the only constraint imposed. There are as many walls of n bricks as words $n - 1$ characters long written in binary, i.e. $u(n) = 2^{n-1}$. The program enabling us to construct these walls is a simple consequence of writing numbers in binary.

Now let $v(n, k)$ be the number of walls with n bricks that have k bricks at the bottom. The coding above indicates that apart from the 1 wedged in first position, $k - 1$ letter 1s are left to be placed in $n - 1$ boxes; hence $v(n, k) = C_{n-1}^{k-1}$. We check that:

$$\sum_{k=1}^{n} v(n,k) = \sum_{k=1}^{n} C_{n-1}^{k-1} = 2^{n-1} = u(n)$$

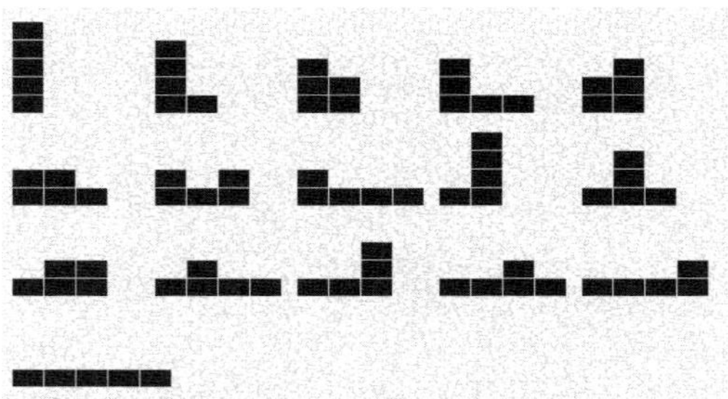

Figure 17.1. *Walls made up of five bricks*

17.2. Walls of bricks made from continuous horizontal rows

In this case we no longer accept the presence of battlement. Each horizontal row of bricks is connected, i.e. made up of a continuous block of bricks. Let $w(n, k)$ be the number of such walls of n bricks with k bricks on the ground. Let us take an example: how can we get $w(7, 4)$? Once the four bricks have been placed on the ground, we need to place walls of three bricks on top with a pedestal made of j bricks, where j goes from 3 to 1. But for each value of j, there are several ways to place the j bricks on the second level on top of the k bricks on the first, i.e. $k - j + 1$ ways of placing the second level over the first. In this case:

$$w(7, 4) = 4\, w(3, 1) + 3\, w(3, 2) + 2\, w(3, 3)$$

This formula is generalized for $n \geq 1$:

$$w(n, k) = 0 \text{ if } n < k$$

$$w(n, n) = 1$$

$$w(n,k) = \sum_{\substack{j=1 \\ j \leq n-k \\ j \leq k}} (k - j + 1)\, w(n-k, j)\text{, in particular } w(n, 1) = 1$$

All this enables us to calculate $w(n, k)$ little by little. On the other hand, if $u(n)$ designates the number of walls of n bricks with continuous rows, we get the relation $u(n) = \sum_{k=1}^{n} w(n,k)$. Using $n = 1$, the successive values of $u(n)$ are:

1, 2, 4, 8, 15, 27, 47, 79, 130, 209, 330, 512, 784, 1183, …

The algorithm and program enabling us to count and enumerate the $u(n)$ walls without battlement results from the method above.

17.2.1. *Algorithm for classifying various types of walls*

Let us begin by classifying the different types of walls according to the number of bricks by continuous row for a given n. For example, for $n = 5$ we want to get the following words, written in descending alphabetical order: 5, 41, 32, 311, 221, 2111 and 11111, where the number of bricks at each level starting from the ground ends up being indicated. They are partitions of the number n. These types of walls are recorded in an array $a[]$, and this results in the following program:

```
counter=1; a[0]=n; L=1 ; nbwalls=1; /* the first wall with one row */
for(;;)   /* passage from one word to the next */
  { counter++; k=L–1; cumul=0;
      /* we must manage the length L of words */
    while (a[k]==1 && k>=0) {k--; cumul+=1;}
    pospivot=k;  if (pospivot== -1) break;
    a[pospivot]- =1; remainder=cumul+1; L=pospivot+1;
    if (remainder<=a[pospivot]) { a[pospivot+1]=remainder; L+=1; }
    else { r=remainder; k=pospivot+1;
           while(r>=a[pospivot])
              { a[k]=a[pospivot];r-=a[pospivot];L+=1;k+=1; }
           if (r!=0) { a[k]=r; L+=1;}
         }
  }
```

17.2.2. *Possible positions of one row above another*

With $n = 5$, for example, we found seven types of wall. Now we have to count how many walls each one of these categories has. To do this we have to make all the rows slide in all possible positions along those under them. Let us place the number of possible positions of row number i in $b[i]$. This number is equal to $a[i - 1] - a[i] + 1$. For example, for the word 631 obtained with $n = 10$, we find $b[0] = 0$, $b[1] = 4$ because we can make the row three bricks long slide four bricks over the row with six bricks and $b[2] = 3$, which will give $4 \,.\, 3 = 12$ walls. This result is placed in variable *cumulb*. For the program, in the *for(;;)* loop started above, we add:

```
for(i=1; i<L; i++) b[i]= -a[i]+a[i–1]+1;
      /* add to initial conditions b[0]=0 */
cumulb=1;
for(i=1; i<L; i++) cumulb*=b[i];
nbmurs+=cumulb;
```

17.2.3. *Coordinates of bricks*

We have to determine the coordinates of the bricks, notably those located at the start of each row, in order to enable the walls to be drawn. Still in the big *for(;;)* loop above, we create a series of words placed in $c[L]$ where the corresponding gaps are found in table $b[]$. For example, for the category with 631 walls, $L = 3$ long, where we had got $b[1] = 4$ and $b[2] = 3$, we create the words 000, 001, 002, 010, 011, 012, 020, 021, 022, 030, 031 and 032, which correspond to the abscissae of the beginning of the three rows of the 12 walls, with the first remaining number at 0, the second going from 0 to 3 (because $b[1] = 4$), and the third from 0 to 2 (because $b[2] = 3$). We now have the coordinates of the start of each wall's row. This enables us to complete the program above.

```
for(i=0; i<L; i++) c[i]=0;
for(;;)
  { cumulx=0; x[0]=0;
   for(i=1; i<L; i++)
     { x[i]=c[i]+cumulx; cumulx+=c[i]; }
   for(i=0; i<a[0]; i++) brick(i,0);
        /* the function brick() is in charge of drawing a brick given a corner
         of the corresponding rectangle */
   for(level=1; level<L; level++)
   for(i=0; i<a[level]; i++)
     { brick(x[level]+i,level); }
   i=L–1;
   while(c[i]==b[i]–1) i--;
   ppospivot=i; if (ppospivot==0) break;
   c[ppospivot]++;
   for(i=ppospivot+1; i<L; i++) c[i]=0;
  }
```

The complete program, obtained by placing the pieces of the program already done end-to-end, results in the final answer, shown in Figure 17.2.

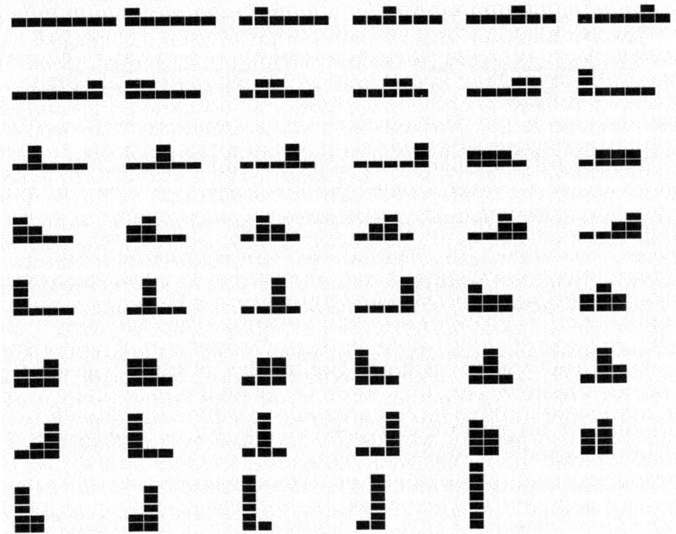

Figure 17.2. *The 47 walls with continuous rows made up of seven bricks*

17.3. Heaps

Let us imagine a unit step square grid with a surface whose base is a horizontal segment and whose upper border includes a succession of horizontal and vertical steps, in such a way that we have the shape of a heap. This means that this border has an increasing altitude to begin with, which is at least equal to one at the start, then decreasing after that the plateau to at least equal to one at the end. This heap has a "peak" made up of a horizontal plateau of a length equal to or more than one (see Figure 17.3 on the left). The objective is to find all the heaps that have a length of $L \geq 1$ and a height of $H \geq 1$.

Let us take the upper border of a heap. The path formed by it starts off with a vertical step *OI*, then rises by horizontal plateaus until a final vertical step upwards, *BA*, followed by a horizontal step, *AC*. Starting from this point *C*, the path is made up of plateaus of decreasing altitude up to a final vertical step downwards, *JO'*. Let us specify that to the right of point *C*, at altitude *H*, there can still be one or more horizontal steps (see Figure 17.3 on the right).

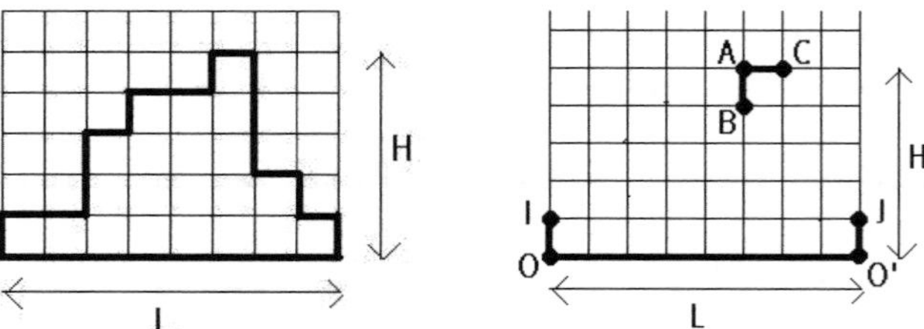

Figure 17.3. *Example of a heap (left); and the constraints imposed at the beginning, end and top of the heap (right)*

Let us choose point A with abscissa X. We are led to count the number of paths from I to B based on eastward and northward steps, of X long horizontally and $H-2$ high, then the number of paths from C to J based on eastward and southward steps of $L-X-1$ long and $H-1$ high. The number of these paths is C_{X+H-2}^{H-2} and $C_{L-X-1-H-1}^{H-1}$ respectively. The number $T(L, H)$ of piles is the product of these two numbers of paths for all positions of point A, i.e. for X included between 0 and $L-1$:

$$T(L,H)=\sum_{X=0}^{L-1} C_{L+H-2-X}^{H-1}\, C_{H-2+X}^{H-2} = C_{L+2H-3}^{2H-2}$$

To do this we used the well-known formula: $\sum\limits_{0\le k\le l} C_{l-k}^{m}\, C_{q+k}^{n} = C_{l+q+1}^{m+n-1}$.

For example for $L = 5$ and $H = 3$, the number of heaps is $C_8^4 = 70$ (see Figure 17.4).

To program the design of these heaps, knowing their length and height, all we have to do is to adapt the program enabling us to trace the shortest paths from one point to another. Now let us take H high heaps and search for the generating function G_H associated with the number $u(L)$ of heaps L long:

$$G_H(x)=\sum_{L\ge1} C_{2H-3+L}^{2H-2}x^L = x\sum_{L\ge1} C_{2H-2+L-1}^{2H-2}x^{L-1}$$

$$=\frac{x}{(1-x)^{2H-1}}$$

thanks to the formula: $\sum\limits_{k} C_{c-1+k}^{c-1}x^k = \dfrac{1}{(1-x)^c}$.

For example:

$$G_1(x) = x / (1 - x) = x + x^2 + x^3 + \ldots,$$

$$G_2(x) = x / (1 - x)^3 = x + 3x^2 + 6x^3 + \ldots$$

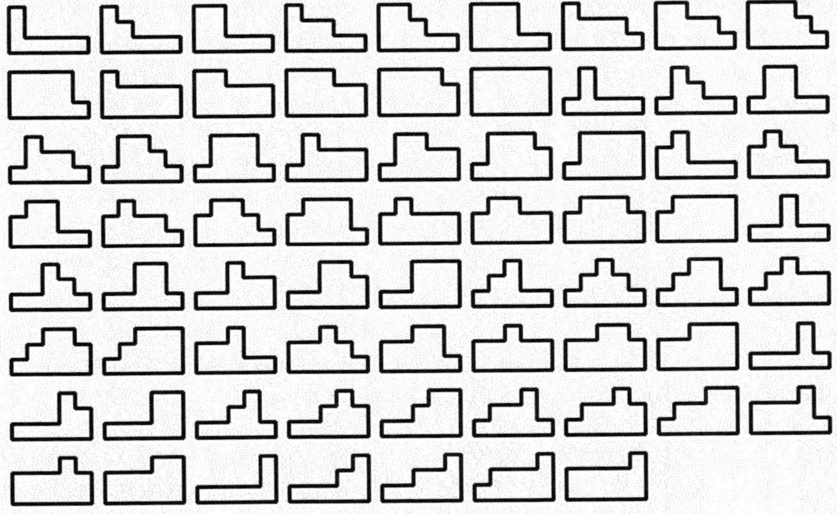

Figure 17.4. *The 70 heaps with a base five units long and three units high*

Finally let us take the generating function G associated with the sequence $(u(L,\ H))$ of the number of heaps L long and H high, with L and H greater than or equal to one:

$$G(x,y) = \sum_{L\geq 1, H\geq 1} C_{2H-3+L}^{2H-2} x^L y^H = \sum_{H\geq 1} \frac{x}{(1-x)^{2H-1}} y^H$$

$$= x(1-x)\sum_{H\geq 1}\left(\frac{y}{(1-x)^2}\right)^H = x(1-x)\left(\frac{1}{1-\dfrac{y}{(1-x)^2}} - 1\right) = \frac{x(1-x)^3}{(1-x)^2 - y} - x(1-x)$$

$$= \frac{xy(1-x)}{1-2x+x^2-y}$$

In developing this function, the term in $x^L y^H$ has as coefficient the number of heaps L long and H high.

Therefore:

$$G(x, y) = (x + x^2 + x^3 + \ldots)y + (x + 2x^2 + 6x^3 + \ldots)y^2 + (x + 5x^2 + 15x^3 + \ldots)y^3$$

$$+ (x + 7x^2 + 28x^3 + \ldots)y^4 + \ldots$$

or even:

$$G(x, y) = (y + y^2 + y^3 + \ldots)x + (y + 3y^2 + 5y^3 + \ldots)x^2 + (y + 6y^2 + 15y^3 + \ldots)x^3$$

$$+ (y + 10y^2 + 35y^3 + \ldots)x^4 + \ldots$$

17.4. Stacks of disks

Now we have disks that fit one upon another to form a stack. The base is made up of a continuous row, but several mounds can form.

Figure 17.5 shows that by drawing squares over the disks we get a mountain range shape. If $u(k)$ is the number of stacks that have k disks as a base, we find that $u(k)$ is the Catalan number of the order k, i.e. $u(k) = C_{2k}^{\ k} / (k + 1)$.

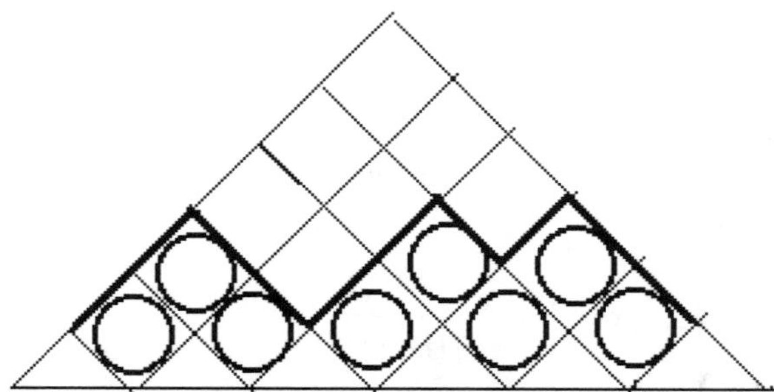

Figure 17.5. *Link between a stack of disks and a mountain range*

All we have to do is adapt the corresponding program to get the results presented in Figures 17.6a and 17.6b.

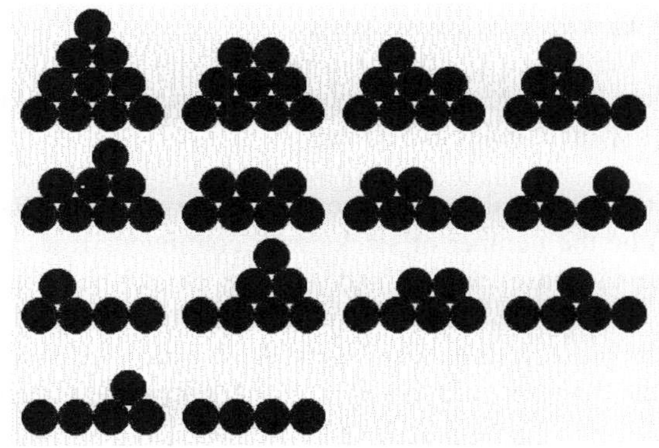

Figure 17.6a. *The 14 stacks for k = 4 disks on the ground*

Figure 17.6b. *The 42 stacks for k = 5 disks on the ground*

17.5. Stacks of disks with continuous rows

As we did before for brick walls, we now impose that stacks of disks are formed in continuous rows without holes in between.

We notice first of all that above a row of length j, we can only have a row shorter than j. Let $v(n, k)$ be the number of stacks with continuous rows that have n disks with k of them at the base, with n and k being greater than 0. We notice that $v(n, n) = 1$ and $v(n, k) = 0$ when $k > n$, and also that $v(n, k) = 0$ as soon as $k(k + 1) / 2 < n$, because with a base k long there cannot be more disks than that corresponding to the triangular number $k(k + 1) / 2$, giving the maximum stack.

When k is greater than 1, we get $v(n, k) = \sum_{j \geq 1} j\,v(n-k, k-j)$, with the summation being done as long as j verifies $(k - j)(k - j + 1) / 2 \geq n - k$.

Actually, above the socle of k disks, we can put a row of length $k - 1, k - 2, \ldots, k - j$ in general, and $n - k$ disks are left to be placed with $k - j$ disks at the base, hence $v(n - k, n - j)$ ways. In turn, a row $k - j$ long can be placed in j ways by making it slide on the socle k disks long.

The formula obtained gives, for example: $v(12, 6) = v(6, 5) + 2v(6, 4) + 3v(6, 3)$, or even $v(13, 6) = v(7, 5) + 2v(7, 4)$. These relations enable us to calculate $v(n, k)$ little by little.

We can also take $f(k)$ as being the number of stacks of disks with k disks at the base, where the number n of disks goes from k to $k(k + 1)/2$.[1] We agree that $f(0) = 1$, verify that $f(1) = 1$, and for $k > 1$:

$$f(k) = f(k-1) + 2\,f(k-2) + 3\,f(k-3) + \ldots + (k-1)\,f(1) + 1$$

Actually, the stacks whose socle is k disks long are divided into several categories depending on the length of the row above. This row is $k - 1$ long or $k - 2, \ldots$, or 1, or 0, in which case the stack is reduced to its socle, hence the term 1 at the end of the formula above. This is also written:

$$f(k) = \sum_{j=1}^{k-1} j\,f(k-j) + 1 = \sum_{j=1}^{k-1} (k-j)\,f(j) + 1$$

1. It would not have been possible to do the same with brick walls, the number n of bricks being able to become infinite for a given socle k.

Let $F(X)$ be the generating function associated with the sequence $(f(k))$:

$$F(X) = f(0) + f(1)\,X + f(2)\,X^2 + f(3)\,X^3 \ldots$$

Using the formula above:

$$F(X) = 1 + X + (f(1) + 1)X^2 + (f(2) + 2f(1) + 1)X^3$$

$$+ (f(3) + 2f(2) + 3f(1) + 1)X^4 + \ldots$$

$$= (1 + X + X^2 + X^3 + \ldots) + f(1)X^2\,(1 + 2X + 3X^2 + \ldots)$$

$$+ f(2)X^3\,(1 + 2X + 3X^2 + \ldots) + \ldots$$

$$= 1 / (1 - X) + X(1 + 2X + 3\,X^2 + \ldots)\,(f(1)X + f(2)X^2 + f(3)X^3 + \ldots)\;^2$$

$$= 1 / (1 - X) + X\,(F(X) - 1) / (1 - X)^2$$

After calculation we find: $F(X) = (1 - 2X) / (1 - 3X + X^2)$.

The first experimental results indicate that the sequence $(f(n))$ is formed, using $f(1)$, from odd terms of the Fibonacci sequence. Let us verify this.

Given $G(x) = a(0) + a(1)x + a(2)x^2 + \ldots$, the generating function of the Fibonacci sequence is written $(a(n))$ here. We know that:

$$G(x) = x / (1 - x - x^2) = x / ((1 - \varphi x)(1 - \varphi' x)),$$

where φ and φ' are the golden numbers.

Let us form the odd function $(G(x) - G(-x)) / 2$ and multiply it by x:

$$x\,(G(x) - G(-x)) / 2 = a(1)\,x^2 + a(3)\,x^4 + a(5)\,x^6 + \ldots$$

2. In the general case we form $f(k)\;X^k = \sum_{j=1}^{k-1}(k-j)X^{k-j}f(j)X^j + X^k$, and verify that $\sum_{j=1}^{k-1}(k-j)X^{k-j}\,f(j)X^j$ is the general term from the development of:

$(f(1)X + f(2)\,X^2 + f(3)\,X^3 + \ldots)\,(X + 2X^2 + 3X^3 + \ldots) = (F(X) - 1)\,X / (1 - X)^2$.

On the other hand:

$$x\,(G(x) - G(-x)) / 2 = (x / 2)\,(x / (1 - x - x^2) + x / (1 + x - x^2))$$

$$= x^2(1 - x^2) / ((1 - x - x^2)\,(1 + x - x^2))$$

$$= x^2(1 - x^2) / (1 - 3x^2 + x^4)\,.$$

Let us assume $X = x^2$:

$$= X(1 - X) / (1 - 3X + X^2)$$

Finally:

$$X(1 - X) / (1 - 3X + X^2) = a(1)X + a(3)X^2 + a(5)X^3 + \ldots$$

and by adding 1:

$$1 + X(1 - X) / (1 - 3X + X^2) = (1 - 2X) / (1 - 3X + X^2)$$

This is the generating function of the sequence $(f(n))$ above:

$$f(n) = a(2n - 1) \text{ for } n > 0 \text{ and } f(0) = 1$$

17.6. Horizontally connected polyominos

By definition, a *polyomino* is a collection of identical squares stuck to each other by at least one common side. It is called horizontally connected when each horizontal line of squares of a polyomino is one single block. We want to find out the number of these polyominos made up of n square cells, with its row of squares stuck to each other. To do this we also introduce two other variables: the number k of lines of the polyomino, and the number L of squares on the line above (see Figure 17.7).

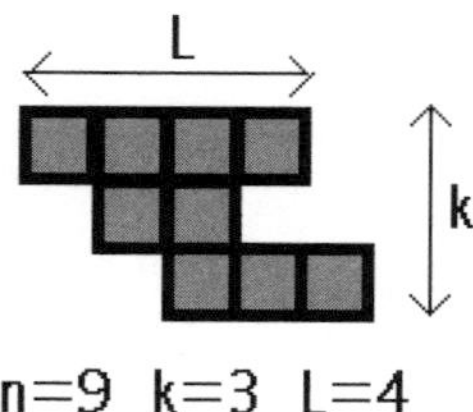

Figure 17.7. *An example of a horizontally connected polyomino*

Let $u(n, k, L)$ be the number of horizontally connected polyominos characterized by the values of n, k and L.

All we have to do is consider the top line L long as being placed above a $n-L$ cell polyomino with $k-1$ lines, with j cells on its own top line. The line L long can slide over the line j long below it, and this can be done in $L+j-1$ ways. Hence the recurrence relation:

$$u(n,k,L) = \sum_{j \geq 1} (j+L-1)u(n-L,k-1,j)$$

with $k > 1$ and $u(n, k, L) = 0$ whenever $L + k - 1 > n$, and at the start $u(n, 1, L) = 0$ if $L \neq n$ and $u(n, 1, n) = 1$.

This is enough to find out the number of polyominos step by step, for example:

$$u(4, 2, 2) = 3\, u(2, 1, 2) = 3,$$

or even:

$$u(5, 3, 2) = 2u(3, 2, 1) + 3u(3, 2, 2) = 2\,(2\, u(2, 1, 2)) + 3(2\, u(1, 1, 1))$$

$$= 4 + 6 = 10$$

To go a bit further, let us introduce the generating function:

$$F_{k,L}(x) = u(1, k, L)x + u(2, k, L)\mathbf{x}^2 + \ldots + u(n, k, L)x^n + \ldots$$

with $F_{1L}(x) = x^L$ in particular.

Thanks to the recurrence relation:

$$\begin{aligned}
F_{k,L}(x) &= \sum_{n}\sum_{j\geq 1}(j+L-1)u(n-L,k-1,j)x^n = \sum_{j\geq 1}(j+L-1)x^L\sum_{n}u(n-L,k-1,j)x^{n\text{-}L} \\
&= x^L\sum_{j\geq 1}(j+L-1)\,F_{k\text{-}1,j}(x) \\
&= x^L\sum_{j\geq 1}(L-1)\,F_{k\text{-}1,j}(x) + x^L\sum_{j\geq 1}j\,F_{k\text{-}1,j}(x) \\
&= (L-1)\,x^L\sum_{j\geq 1}F_{k\text{-}1,j}(x) + x^L\sum_{j\geq 1}j\,F_{k\text{-}1,j}(x) \\
&= (L-1)\,x^L U_{k\text{-}1} + x^L V_{k\text{-}1}
\end{aligned}$$

where we postulate:

$$U_k = \sum_{j\geq 1} F_{k,j} \text{ and } V_k = \sum_{j\geq 1} j\,F_{k,j}$$

we therefore get:

$$U_k = F_{k1} + F_{k2} + F_{k3} + \ldots = xV_{k-1} + x^2(V_{k-1}+U_{k-1}) + x^3(V_{k-1}+2U_{k-1}) + \ldots$$

from which we deduce:

$$U_k = \frac{x}{1-x}V_{k-1} + \frac{x^2}{(1-x)^2}U_{k-1}$$

and similarly,

$$V_k = \frac{x}{(1-x)^2}V_{k-1} + \frac{2x^2}{(1-x)^3}U_{k-1}$$

The elimination of V_k leads to a recurrence relation on U_k, i.e.:

$$\frac{1-x}{x}U_{k+1} - \frac{1+x}{1-x}U_k - \frac{x^2}{(1-x)^3}U_{k-1} = 0$$

with:

$$U_0(x) = \sum_{j\geq 1} F_{0j}(x) = F_{01}(x) + F_{02}x) + F_{03}(x) + \ldots + 0$$

at the start, and:

$$U_1(x) = F_{11}(x) + F_{22}(x) + \ldots = x + x^2 + x^3 + \ldots = \frac{x}{1-x}$$

Let us deal with this linear recurrence of the form $aU_k + bU_{k-1} + cU_{k-2} = 0$ using a generating function $G(y)$ so that $G(y) = U_0 + U_1 y + U_2\, y^2 + U_3\, y^3 + \ldots$. Forming byG and cy^2G, we get the relation:

$$a(G - U_1 y) = byG + cy^2G$$

and, all calculations done, we find:

$$G(y) = \frac{x(1-x)^3 y}{(1-x)^4 - xy(1-x-x^2+x^3+x^2y)}$$

In $G(y) = \sum_{j\geq 1} F_{1j}(x).y + \sum_{j\geq 1} F_{2j}(x).y^2 + \sum_{j\geq 1} F_{3j}(x).y^3 + \ldots$, the term in $x^n y^k$ comes from the term in x^n in $F_{k1} + F_{k2} + F_{k3} + \ldots$, and its coefficient is $u(n, k, 1) + u(n, k, 2) + u(n, k, 3) + \ldots$

Let us assume that $g(n, k) = u(n, k, 1) + u(n, k, 2) + u(n, k, 3) + \ldots$. This number is none other than the number of polyominos with n cells and k lines (independently of the length of its top line), and $G(y)$, which is also a function of x, is the generating function associated with $g(n, k)$.

By taking $y = 1$, function G becomes the generating function associated with the number of polyominos with n cells, i.e.:

$$\frac{x(1-x)^3}{(1-x)^4 - x(1-x+x^3)} = \frac{x(1-x)^3}{1-5x+7x^2-4x^3}$$

The first terms of its development are $x + 2x^2 + 6x^3 + 19x^4 + 61x^5 + \ldots$. For example, we find six polyominos with three cells, but among them only two different rotation and reflection-types remain (see Figure 17.8).

Figure 17.8. *The six polyominos with three cells (left); and the two symmetry-types that remain (right)*

Similarly, for the 19 polyominos with four cells, only five rotation and reflection-types of them remain (see Figure 17.9).

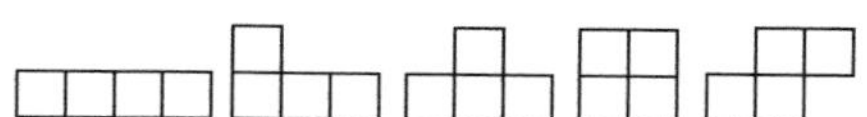

Figure 17.9. *The five different rotation and reflection-type polyominos with four cells*

Chapter 18

Tiling of Rectangular Surfaces using Simple Shapes

We begin this chapter by recalling the most classic example – that of tiling a rectangle two dominos high (see Chapter 5). Then we will develop more complex examples.[1]

18.1. Tiling of a 2×n chessboard using dominos

The chessboard is n squares long and two dominos high. We have to tile it using dominos occupying each one of the two squares. These dominos are either horizontal or vertical. We want to find out the number $u(n)$ of possible tilings.

Let us recall that language T for all possible tilings, in order of increasing size, is written:

$$T = 1 + \quad + \quad + \quad + \quad + \quad + \quad + \cdots$$

All tilings are made up using two primitive blocks: or . By calling the vertical domino x and the block of two horizontal dominos y^2, we get:

$$T(x, y) = 1 + x + x^2 + y^2 + x^3 + xy^2 + y^2x + \ldots$$

---

1. For more details on these tilings consult [NAC 05] and [NAC 06].

where multiplication indicates non-commutative concatenation. The sum of exponents of each term is the number of dominos of the tiling concerned. Let us arrange the tilings according to their beginning:

$$T(x, y) = 1 + x\,(1 + x + x^2 + y^2 + \ldots) + y^2\,(1 + x + x^2 + y^2 + \ldots)$$

$$= 1 + x\,T(x, y) + y^2\,T(x, y)$$

From this we deduce: $T(x, y) = (1 - x - y^2)^{-1} = 1 + (x + y^2) + (x + y^2)^2 + \ldots$, by re-developing the formula.

Now let us return to commutative variables. For example, $x^2y^2 + xy^2x + y^2xx$ becomes $3x^2y^2$. The function $T(x, y)$ is made up of monomials of the form Ax^iy^j where A is the number of tilings with i vertical dominos and j horizontal dominos. More specifically:

$$T(x, y) = 1 + x + y^2 + (x + y^2)^2 + \ldots$$

$$= \sum_{k\geq 0}(x+y^2)^k = \sum_{k\geq 0}\sum_{0\leq j\leq k} C_k^j\,x^j\,y^{2(k-j)} = \sum_{j,m\geq 0} C_{m+j}^j\,x^j\,y^{2m}$$

From this we deduce that $C_{m+j}^{\ j}$ is the number of ways of tiling a chessboard of $2m + j$ long with j vertical dominos and m blocks of horizontal dominos. For a tiling n long we get: $2m + j = n$, hence we deduce that j and n have the same parity. Because $m = (n - j) / 2$, the number of tilings on a board n long with j vertical dominos is: $C_{(n+j)/2}^{\ j}$ or even $C_{(n+j)/2}^{\ (n-j)/2}$.

Finally, if we make $x = y$ we find the generating function corresponding to the series $u(n)$ giving the number of tilings on a board n long, i.e.:

$$G(x) = 1 / (1 - x - x^2).$$

18.1.1. *First algorithm for constructing tilings*

One way of programming the enumeration of tilings consists of writing them in the form of words n characters long based on 0 and 1, where 0 designates a vertical domino and two successive 1s designate a block of two horizontal dominos. For example, for $n = 5$ we find these eight words in alphabetical order: 000<u>0</u>0, 00<u>0</u>11, 0<u>0</u>110, 011<u>0</u>0, <u>0</u>1111, 110<u>0</u>0, 11<u>0</u>11 and 11110. The pivot (underlined in the above) is found by starting from the right and searching for the first 0, followed either by a 0 or a 1. We replace this 0 with a 1 and put 1 behind it. Everything that follows it is set to 0.

18.1.2. *Second construction algorithm*

Let us designate a vertical domino with the letter *a* and a block of two horizontal dominos with the letter *b*. Each tiling is a word based on *a* and *b*, but its length is variable. We should distinguish two cases:

– *n* is an even number: $n = 2p$. A tiling has $2k$ letter *a*s and $p - k$ letter *b*s, where k is between 0 and p. For a given k, the number of these words is C_{p+k}^{2k}. Taking all the values of k, we find the number of tilings is:

$$\sum_{k=0}^{p} C_{p+k}^{2k} = F(2p+1) = F(n+1)$$

where $F(n)$ is row n's Fibonacci number.

– *n* is an odd number: $n = 2p + 1$. In the same way we find:

$$\sum_{k=0}^{p} C_{p+1+k}^{2k+1} = F(2p+2) = F(n+1)$$

This gives another way of enumerating all the tilings because it refers to an anagram problem (see Figure 18.1).

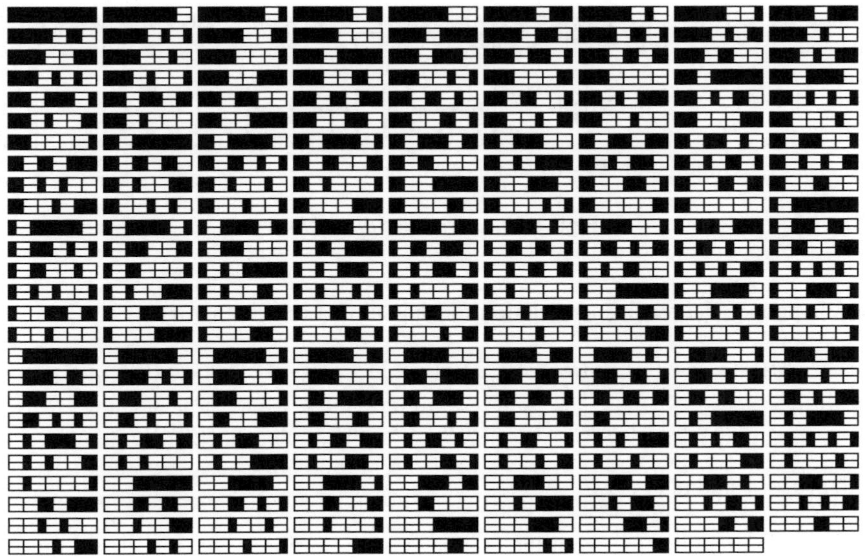

Figure 18.1. *All of the tilings on a board 12 squares long*

18.2. Other tilings of a chessboard 2×*n* squares long

18.2.1. *With squares and horizontal dominos*

Here the squares are 1×1 and the dominos are 2×1 (horizontal length × height, where they are all horizontal). The two lines of the chessboard are therefore tiled independently. We know that on one line n squares long the number of tilings using dominos of 1×2 is $F(n + 1)$, the Fibonacci number from row $n + 1$. When we take the two lines, the number of tilings is $F(n + 1)^2$.

18.2.1.1. *Associated generating function*

Let us consider primitive tiling blocks, i.e. the minimum number of blocks that are delimited by vertical lines and that we cannot split up again. All tilings can be resolved in this way. The blocks that appear are made up of a mixture of squares and dominos. Such primitive blocks can be classified according to their length (see Figure 18.2). Using a length of three, we find two cases each time.

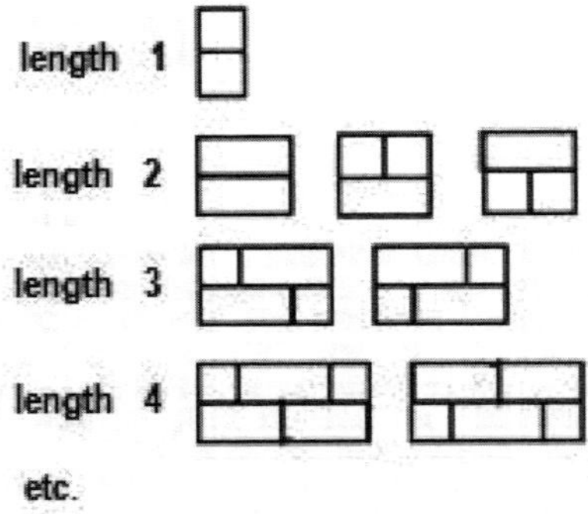

Figure 18.2. *Primitive tiling blocks*

We deduce the recurrence relation for the number of tilings $u(n)$:

$$\begin{aligned} u(n) &= u(n-1) + 3u(n-2) + 2\,(\,u(n-3) + u(n-4) + \ldots + u(0)) \\ &= u(n-1) + u(n-2) + 2\,(u(n-2) + u(n-3) + \ldots + u(0)) \end{aligned}$$

with $u(0) = 1$ and $u(1) = 1$.

If you prefer, starting from the language of these tilings the generating function $G(x)$ associated with the number of tilings n long verifies:

$$G(x) = 1 + xG(x) + 3x^2G(x) + 2(x^3 + x^4 + x^5 + \ldots)G(x)$$

$$= 1 + xG(x) + 3x^2G(x) + 2x^3G(x)/(1 - x)$$

hence: $G(x) = \dfrac{1-x}{1-2x-2x^2+x^3}$

18.2.1.2. *Construction algorithm*

Dividing the n long chessboard into primitive blocks constitutes an ordered partition of n. We know that the number of ordered partitions of n is 2^{n-1}. For each term of an ordered partition, we have the number of primitive blocks, as we have just seen. For example, for $n = 4$, taking the lengths of successive primitive blocks we have the ordered partitions 1 1 1 1, i.e. a tiling, then 1 1 2, with three corresponding tilings, 1 2 1 with three tilings, 2 1 1 (three tilings), 2 2 (3×3 = 9 tilings), 3 1 (two tilings), 1 3 (two tilings), and 4 (two tilings). The sum gives $F(5)^2 = 25$ tilings.

18.2.2. *With squares and horizontal or vertical dominos*

These tilings present the same primitive blocks as before, with a single block more 1 unit long made up of a vertical domino ▯. Classifying the tilings according to their initial primitive block, we deduce the recurrence relation:

$$u(n) = 2\,u(n-1) + 3\,u(n-2) + 2\,(u(n-3) + u(n-4) + \ldots + u(0))$$

$$= u(n-2) + 2\,(u(n-1) + u(n-2) + \ldots + u(0)),$$

with $u(0) = 1$ and $u(1) = 2$.

The generating function is:

$$G(x) = \frac{1-x}{1-3x-x^2+x^3} = 1 + 2x + 7x^2 + 22x^3 + \ldots$$

18.2.3. *With dominos and l-squares we can turn and reflect*

Primitive blocks are indicated in Figure 18.3. Their recurrence relation is:

$$u(n) = u(n-1) + u(n-2) + 2\,(u(n-3) + u(n-4) + \ldots + u(0))$$

with $u(0) = 1$ and $u(1) = 1$, and the generating function is:

$$G(x) = \frac{1-x}{1-2x-x^3} = 1 + x + 2x^2 + 5x^3 + 11x^4 + \dots$$

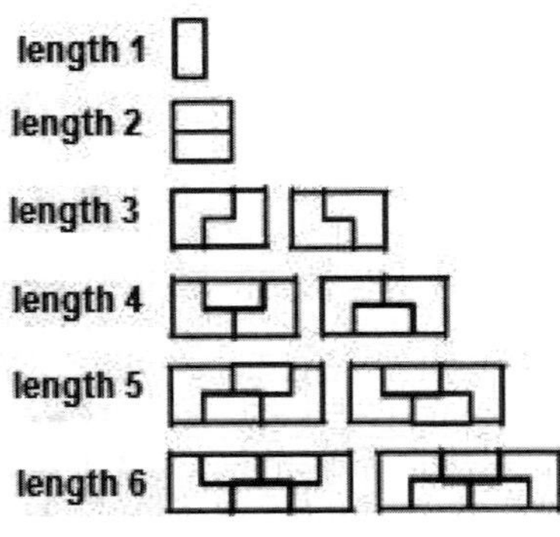

Figure 18.3. *Primitive blocks*

18.2.4. *With squares, l-squares and dominos*

Let us construct the first primitive blocks (see Figure 18.4). From length 3 rectangle and beyond, we always find eight blocks. Considering this, we begin by taking a pattern that has two l-squares at the two ends, separated by horizontal dominos in staggered rows, then we cut each one of the two l-squares with a horizontal line, and then the two l-squares, which gives a total of four cases. Finally we reflect the square along the middle horizontal axis. Hence we get a total of eight cases (see the bottom of Figure 18.4).

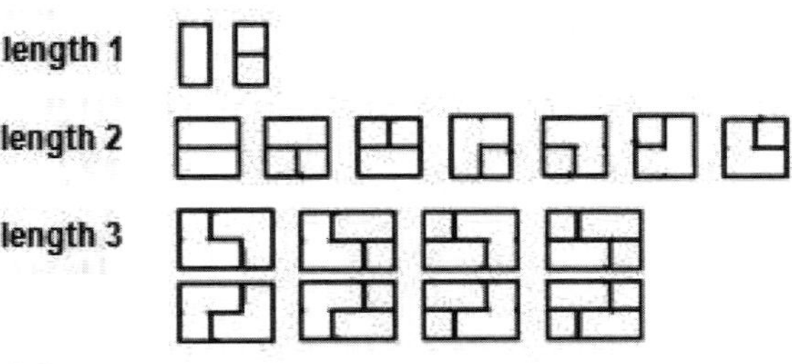

Figure 18.4. *Primitive blocks*

The number of tilings $u(n)$ obeys the recurrence relation:

$$u(n) = 2u(n-1) + 7u(n-2) + 8(u(n-3) + u(n-4) + \ldots + u(0))$$

for $n \geq 3$, with $u(0) = 1$ and $u(1) = 2$.

The generating function is:

$$G(x) = \frac{1-x}{1-3x-5x^2-x^3} = 1 + 2x + 11x^2 + 44x^3 + \ldots$$

18.3. Tilings of a 3×*n* chessboard using dominos

For the same reasons as for primitive blocks four units long, we find two blocks six units long, then two of eight units long, etc. (see Figure 18.5).

Let us consider the language whose words are tilings. We can classify the tilings according to their initial primitive word, i.e. the blocks in Figure 18.5. Taking the generating function G associated with the sequence giving the number of tilings as a function of word length, i.e. the length n of the chessboard, we get:

$$G(x) = 1 + 3x^2G(x) + 2x^4G(x) + 2x^6G(x) + \ldots$$

hence:

$$G(x) = (1 - x^2) / (1 - 4x^2 + x^4).$$

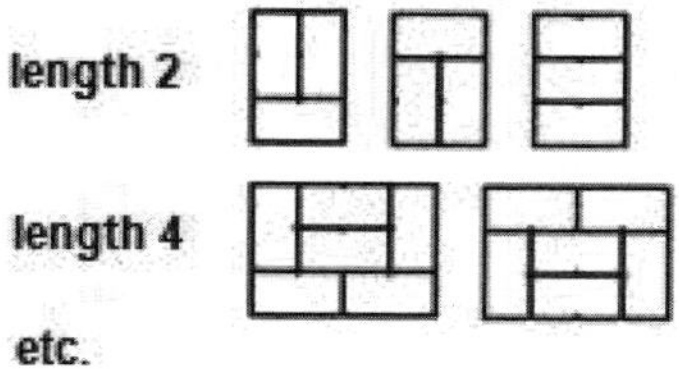

length 2

length 4

etc.

Figure 18.5. *Primitive blocks of height 3*

There is another method obtained by considering the start of a tiling. Three shapes are possible (see Figure 18.6). Note that we are no longer talking about primitive blocks.

or or

Figure 18.6. *The start of a tiling*

Considering language U of tiling words, we can write:

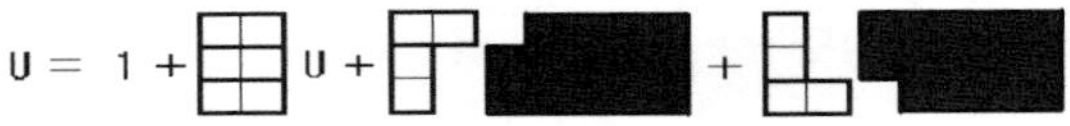

U = 1 + U + +

with:

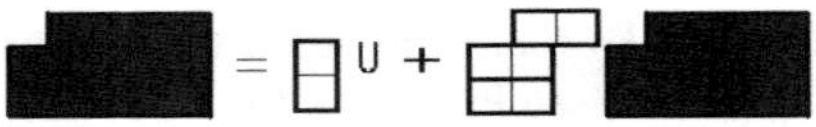

= U +

and:

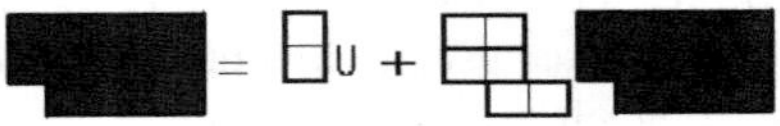

= U +

The two colored shapes are chessboard tilings with one corner removed. From all of this we can deduce U. To simplify things let us move on to commutativity and replace a horizontal domino with an X and a vertical domino with a Y. This will enable us to find out the number of tilings that can follow the number of horizontal dominos and vertical dominos. B is the language of tilings of chessboards with a corner removed. Here we get the system of equations:

$$U(X, Y) = 1 + X^3\, U(X, Y) + 2XY\, B(X, Y) \text{ and:}$$

$$B(X, Y) = Y\, U(X,Y) + X^3\, B(X, Y),$$

hence:

$$U(X, Y) = \frac{1}{1 - \dfrac{2XY^2}{1-X^3} - X^3} = \frac{1-X^3}{(1-X^3)^2 - 2XY^2}$$

If we are satisfied with finding out the number of tilings based on the number of dominos, all we have to do is make $X = Y$, i.e.:

$$U(X) = \frac{1-X^3}{1-4X^3+X^6}$$

and if we want to get the number of tilings according to the length of the rectangle, all we have to do is replace X^3 with Z^2, i.e.:

$$U(Z) = \frac{1 - Z^2}{1 - 4Z^2 + Z^4} = 1 + 3Z^2 + 11Z^4 + 41Z^6 + 153Z^8 + \ldots$$

18.4. Tilings of a 4×*n* chessboard with dominos

Let us take the abscissa columns 0, 1, 2, 3, … of the chessboard, and on each column, line by line, write 0 when the column does not go through a domino and 1 when it does. We have already encountered this type of coding in a previous chapter (see section 13.4.1). The configurations in columns are:

$$A\begin{pmatrix}0\\0\\0\\0\end{pmatrix}\; B\begin{pmatrix}0\\0\\1\\1\end{pmatrix}\; B'\begin{pmatrix}1\\1\\0\\0\end{pmatrix}\; C\begin{pmatrix}1\\0\\0\\1\end{pmatrix}\; C'\begin{pmatrix}0\\1\\1\\0\end{pmatrix}\; D\begin{pmatrix}1\\1\\1\\1\end{pmatrix}$$

and their links lead to a transition graph that can be simplified (see Figure 18.7).

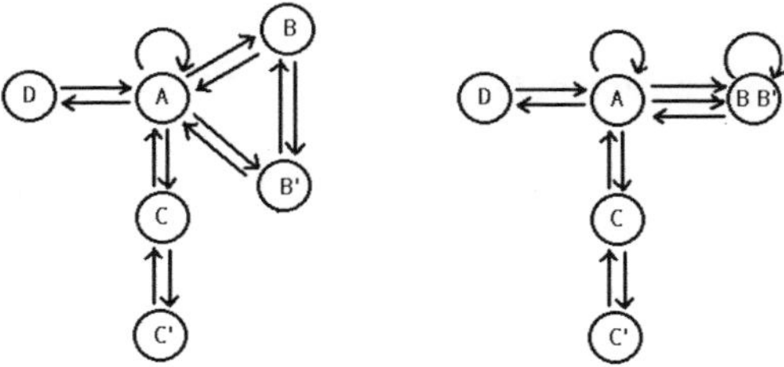

Figure 18.7. *Transition graph between configurations (left); and the simplified graph (right)*

The adjacency matrix of the simplified graph is:

$$M = \begin{bmatrix} 1 & 2 & 1 & 0 & 1 \\ 1 & 1 & 0 & 0 & 0 \\ 1 & 0 & 0 & 1 & 0 \\ 0 & 0 & 1 & 0 & 0 \\ 1 & 0 & 0 & 0 & 0 \end{bmatrix}$$

with lines and columns in the order $A\ B\ B'\ C\ C'\ D$. From which we deduce the determinant:

$$|I - xM| = \begin{vmatrix} 1-x & -2x & -x & 0 & -x \\ -x & 1-x & 0 & 0 & 0 \\ -x & 0 & 1 & -x & 0 \\ 0 & 0 & -x & 1 & 0 \\ -x & 0 & 0 & 0 & 1 \end{vmatrix} = (1-x)(1-x-5x^2-x^3+x^4)$$

For the tilings, the initial configuration is A, and the final configuration as well.

Thanks to the determinant obtained by removing the first line and column $|I - xM, 0, 0| = (1 - x)(1 - x^2)$, the generating function $F_{AA}(x)$ associated with the number of paths of given length on the simplified graph is:

$$F_{AA}(x) = (1 - x^2) / (1 - x - 5x^2 - x^3 + x^4)$$

$$= 1 + x + 5x^2 + 11x^3 + 36x^4 + 95x^5 + 281x^6 + \ldots$$

The number of tilings along a length n is the coefficient of the term in x^n. For example, there are 36 tilings on chessboard four squares long.

18.5. Domino tilings of a rectangle

Let us consider a chessboard in the shape of a rectangle with sides M and N that are both even. A domino is either vertical or horizontal and it always covers a white square and a black square.

We want to find out the number of ways of covering such a rectangle with dominos. The corresponding graph is a square grid whose vertices are alternatively black and white squares. It is a bipartite graph, obtained by grouping the black squares on one side and the white squares on another, with the edges always touching a black vertex and a white vertex. The connections joining each black vertex to each white vertex correspond to a domino tiling.

Numbering the black vertices first and then the white vertices, the adjacency matrix is of the form:

$$A = \begin{pmatrix} 0 & B \\ B^T & 0 \end{pmatrix}$$

For example, for $M = 4$ and $N = 2$, with the numbering of the squares as indicated in Figure 18.8, this gives:

$$A = \begin{pmatrix} 0 & 0 & 0 & 0 & 1 & 0 & 1 & 0 \\ 0 & 0 & 0 & 0 & 1 & 1 & 0 & 1 \\ 0 & 0 & 0 & 0 & 1 & 0 & 1 & 1 \\ 0 & 0 & 0 & 0 & 0 & 1 & 0 & 1 \\ 1 & 1 & 1 & 0 & 0 & 0 & 0 & 0 \\ 0 & 1 & 0 & 1 & 0 & 0 & 0 & 0 \\ 1 & 0 & 1 & 0 & 0 & 0 & 0 & 0 \\ 0 & 1 & 1 & 1 & 0 & 0 & 0 & 0 \end{pmatrix} \quad \text{and } B = \begin{pmatrix} 1 & 0 & 1 & 0 \\ 1 & 1 & 0 & 1 \\ 1 & 0 & 1 & 1 \\ 0 & 1 & 0 & 1 \end{pmatrix}$$

Figure 18.8. *Numbering of squares in the 4×2 chessboard*

We recall that the permanent of B is obtained by taking an element in each line and column without one element being taken over another, by taking their product (in all possible ways), then by adding these products. Only the presence of elements that are all equal to 1 gives a product equal to 1, with the others being null. By taking a 1 in each line and column, we get a connection of the bipartite graph.

For example, the choice of this permutation:

$$\begin{pmatrix} \mathit{1} & 0 & 1 & 0 \\ 1 & 1 & 0 & \mathit{1} \\ 1 & 0 & \mathit{1} & 1 \\ 0 & \mathit{1} & 0 & 1 \end{pmatrix}$$

gives the connection (1 1')(2 4')(3 3')(4 2'), and the tiling . Therefore the number of possible tilings is equal to the permanent of B. On the other hand $Per\ A = (Per\ B)^2$. The number of tilings is also the square root of the permanent of A. But how can we get this permanent? The trick is to simplify things to a calculation of a determinant. Therefore we verify that $Per\ A = Det\ \underline{A}$ where matrix $\underline{A}$ is deduced from A by putting the complex number i in the place of 1 for each vertical line, i.e.:

$$\underline{A}=\begin{pmatrix} 0 & \underline{B} \\ \underline{B}^T & 0 \end{pmatrix}^2$$

As the initial graph of matrix A is the sum of two path graphs M and N long,[3] the eigenvalues of A are:

$$2\cos(\pi j / (M+1)) + 2\cos(\pi k / (N+1))$$

for all j between 1 and M, and all k between 1 and N.

In turn, matrix $\underline{A}$ is that associated with the sum of the path graph M long, and the path graph N long, where the latter has its edges weighted by i. The eigenvalues of $\underline{A}$ are:

$$2\cos(\pi j / (M+1)) + i\, 2\cos(\pi k / (N+1))$$

by grouping the factors in k and $N+1-k$, because N is even:

$$Det\,\underline{A} = \prod_{j=1}^{M}\prod_{k=1}^{N}(2\cos\frac{\pi j}{M+1} + i2\cos\frac{\pi k}{N+1}) = \prod_{j=1}^{M}\prod_{k=1}^{N/2}(4\cos^2\frac{\pi j}{M+1} + 4\cos^2\frac{\pi k}{N+1})$$

Then by grouping the factors in j and $M+1-j$:

---

2. We saw that the number of tilings is equal to the permanent of B. We also get $Per\, B = Det\, \underline{B}$. This determinant can be calculated. In the example of the 2x4 tiling, it equals:

$$\begin{vmatrix} 1 & 0 & i & 0 \\ 1 & 1 & 0 & i \\ i & 0 & 1 & 1 \\ 0 & i & 0 & 1 \end{vmatrix} = 1 - 3i^2 + i^4 = 5$$

In this case there are five tilings. The result obtained even specifies that there is one completely horizontal tiling, three tilings with two vertical dominos, and one tiling with four vertical ones. In this way we can calculate the number of tilings of all sorts of rectangular shapes with eventual battlements alongside. To get the formula of the $M \times N$ rectangle in the general case, however, we prefer to use the square root of the determinant of $\underline{A}$, because the determinant corresponds to the rectangular network, which we know is the sum of two graph segments. Knowing the eigenvalues of a graph segment, we know that the eigenvalues of the total graph are obtained by adding each eigenvalue of one graph segment to each one of the other graph segments. This enables us to obtain the general formula for tiling a rectangle.

3. See Chapter 35 for more details.

$$Det\,\underline{A} = \prod_{j=1}^{M/2}\prod_{k=1}^{N/2}(4\cos^2\frac{j\pi}{M+1}+4\cos^2\frac{k\pi}{N+1})^2$$

Finally, the number of tilings, for even M and N, is:

$$\prod_{j=1}^{M/2}\prod_{k=1}^{N/2}(4\cos^2\frac{j\pi}{M+1}+4\cos^2\frac{k\pi}{N+1})$$

Chapter 19

Permutations

19.1. Definition and properties

Let us recall that a permutation of n objects called 0, 1, 2, …, $n-1$, is a word made up of these n letters 0, 1, 2, … all of which are different.

A permutation can also be seen as a transformation when placed in numbered boxes, looking like an array in a computer program. For example the permutation of six letters 350421 is more specifically written: $\begin{pmatrix} 0 & 1 & 2 & 3 & 4 & 5 \\ 3 & 5 & 0 & 4 & 2 & 1 \end{pmatrix}$ and is read: 0 becomes 3, 1 becomes 5, 2 becomes 0, etc.

The permutation becomes a bijection on the set with elements $\{0, 1, 2, \ldots, n-1\}$ (see Figure 19.1).

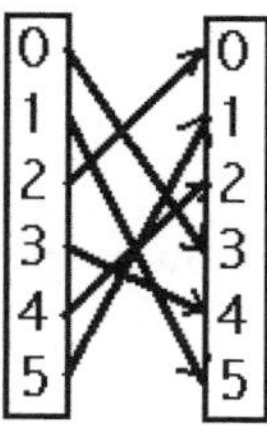

Figure 19.1. *Permutation seen as a bijection*

This ambivalence in the definition of permutations is concretely manifested in many problems. For example, if we have six cards in our hand, the permutation above expresses that they are the cards 3, 5, 0, 4, 2 and 1 in this order. In other words, the card in position 0 is the 3, the card in position 1 is 5, etc. If you prefer, it can express that we carried out a certain mix by putting the card that was in position 0 in position 3, that the card in position 1 moves to position 5, etc. By doing this, any objects can undergo this change: we can take the king of hearts, the 10 of spades, etc.

The product $_{\rightarrow}pp'$ of two permutations p and p', where the arrow ($_{\rightarrow}$) indicates that we calculate p first and p' second, is obtained by doing permutation p followed by permutation p', as in the following example (see Figure 19.2):

$$\begin{pmatrix} 0 & 1 & 2 & 3 & 4 & 5 \\ 3 & 5 & 0 & 4 & 2 & 1 \end{pmatrix} \begin{pmatrix} 0 & 1 & 2 & 3 & 4 & 5 \\ 5 & 1 & 4 & 2 & 0 & 3 \end{pmatrix} = \begin{pmatrix} 0 & 1 & 2 & 3 & 4 & 5 \\ 2 & 3 & 5 & 0 & 4 & 1 \end{pmatrix}$$

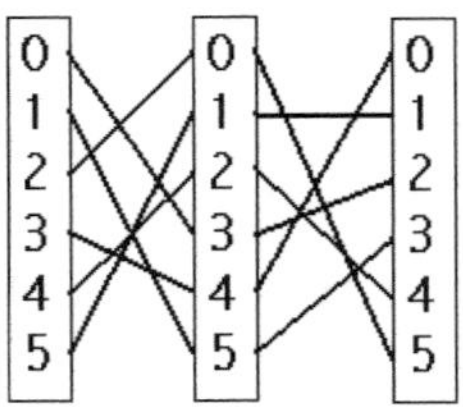

Figure 19.2. *Product of two permutations*

If permutation p is placed in array p[6] and permutation p' in array p' [6], permutation $_{\rightarrow}pp'$, where the arrow indicates the order in which we carry out the permutations, is obtained by carrying out the succession:

$$i \rightarrow i_1 = p(i) \rightarrow i' = p'(i_1) = p'(p(i))$$

hence the simple program that corresponds to it:

```
for(i=0; i<N; i++) display p'[p[i]]
```

Let us note that carrying out p followed by p' is expressed as $_{\leftarrow}p'p$, reading from right to left.[1]

---

1. We have $_{\rightarrow}pp'(i) = {}_{\leftarrow}p'p(i) = p'(p(i))$.

The fact that permutation p is a bijection also enables us to define permutation p^{-1}, the inverse of p, such that $pp' = p'p = I$, where I is the identical permutation preserving natural order. This refers to inverting the initial set and final set by changing the order of the junction arrows.

For example, the permutation:

$$\begin{pmatrix} 0 & 1 & 2 & 3 & 4 & 5 \\ 3 & 5 & 0 & 4 & 2 & 1 \end{pmatrix}$$

assumes as its inverse the permutation obtained by reading from bottom to top, i.e.:

$$\begin{pmatrix} 0 & 1 & 2 & 3 & 4 & 5 \\ 2 & 5 & 4 & 0 & 3 & 1 \end{pmatrix}$$

For the corresponding program, with permutation p placed in an array $p[n]$, the inverse permutation p' is obtained by filling in array p' $[n]$ that is empty to begin with, thanks to the loop:

for(i=0; i<n; i++) p'[p[i]] = i , where we find the fact that $\leftarrow pp' = I$.

The set of permutations with n elements, with the composition operation making the product of two permutations, has a group structure.[2] We call it the *symmetrical group* of order n, and we write it S_n.

19.2. Decomposition of a permutation as a product of disjoint cycles

Another way of obtaining a permutation consists of writing it in the form of cycles. For example the cycle (134) means that 1 is replaced by 3, that 3 is replaced by 4 and that 4 is replaced by 1:

All permutations are decomposed in a unique, order-type way, in disjoint cycles.

---

2. Actually the product of two permutations of S_n is a permutation of S_n, where this operation is associative. There is also a neutral element that is the identity I (or *Id*), and each permutation assumes an inverse permutation.

For example, the permutation $\begin{pmatrix} 0 & 1 & 2 & 3 & 4 & 5 \\ 3 & 5 & 0 & 4 & 2 & 1 \end{pmatrix}$ is expressed (0 3 4 2) (1 5), where the order in which we carry out the cycles is of no importance.

Conversely, the permutation that is expressed in the form of disjoint cycles (0 3) (1) (2 5 4) is the permutation $\begin{pmatrix} 0 & 1 & 2 & 3 & 4 & 5 \\ 3 & 1 & 5 & 0 & 2 & 4 \end{pmatrix}$.

Note that we also include those with a single element as cycles, such as (1) that indicates number 1 remains 1.

Let us show this property. To do this, we take an element a and make it undergo the repeated permutation p, hence the trajectory:

$$a \rightarrow p(a) \rightarrow p^2(a) \rightarrow p^3(a) \rightarrow \ldots$$

Because the permutation has a finite number of objects, the trajectory must necessarily end by returning to where it already passed, which gives a *rho* shape for this trajectory:

but we notice that the entrance point in the loop assumes two antecedents, which is impossible for the bijection that is a permutation. The only possible configuration is the looping of the starting point a, hence the formation of a cycle:

Having obtained the cycle of element a, two cases are presented: either all elements of the permutation are found in the cycle, and the property is shown, or not all of the elements are in the cycle. In this latter case, let us take one element, b, and create its cycle as before. This new cycle has no common element with a's cycle, otherwise b would be in a's cycle. If all the elements of the permutation are in the cycles of a and b, the property is shown. If not, we take an element c that is not present in the previous cycles and create its cycle.

Continuing in this way, we are sure that the process stops, because of the finite number of elements of the permutation, and we have decomposed the permutation as a product of disjoint cycles. Let us observe that all elements are placed in a cycle, and that if an element d is in b's cycle, d's cycle is the same as that of b. For example, the cycle (024) is also (240) or (402). Thus we are assured that decomposition in cycles is unique, in order-type of cycles, which is not awkward because operating a succession of disjoint cycles is commutative.

From this we deduce the cycle creation program using a given permutation:

– Place permutation p in array $p[N]$ and set an array $done[N]$ to 0 (NO), then do the loop:

```
for(i=0 ; i<N ; i++)  if (done[i]= =NO) cycle(i);
```

– Do the function that determines the cycle of an element a:

```
void cycle(int a)
{ display «(»; q=a;
  do {done[q]=YES; display q ; q=a[q];} while (q!=a) ;
  display « ) »;
}
```

19.2.1. *Particular cases of permutations defined by their decomposition in cycles*

19.2.1.1. *Number of permutations of n elements with a single cycle*

The permutation $\begin{pmatrix}1234\\3421\end{pmatrix}$ presents the unique cycle (1 3 2 4), for example. Let us consider a permutation presenting only a single cycle. This cycle is in turn expressed as a permutation of the n elements, one out of the $n!$ possible. But by cyclic gaps, we find the same permutation with the same cycle n times. Finally, the number of permutations with one cycle is $n! \;/\; n = (n - 1)!$. The probability of getting a permutation with a single cycle among all permutations is $1 / n$.[3]

---

3. The same problem is asked about the number of Hamilton circuits presented by a complete graph K_n in graph theory. By complete graph K_n, we mean a graph with n vertices numbered 1, 2, ..., n, where each vertex is linked to all the others (we say it has a degree of $n - 1$). A Hamilton circuit consists of following the edges of the graph in such a way that we pass all the vertices once and only once, where this circuit is closed. Such a circuit corresponds to a permutation of the n vertices and $n!$ permutations are possible. Considering that no circuit has a specific starting point, it is defined using a cyclic-type gap of the vertices, and for the same circuit we have n permutations by successive gaps. The total number of Hamilton circuits is $(n - 1)!$

19.2.1.2. *Number of permutations without a fixed point*

We have already dealt with this problem using sieve formula. Such permutations without a fixed point (without a cycle of one unit long) are called derangements, and there are $d(n)$ of them. Here we will provide another way of finding formulae for $d(n)$. To determine a recurrence relation, let us take $n-1$-length derangements using numbers from 1 to $n-1$.

To get some of these n-length derangements we begin by placing the number n in last position, which adds the cycle (n) to a $n-1$-length derangement, then we exchange n with any one of the number places in the $n-1$-length derangement, i.e. the number a placed in position k. Using $k \rightarrow a$ ($k \neq a$ because of the derangement) and $n \rightarrow n$, we arrive at $k \rightarrow n$ and $n \rightarrow a$ with $a \neq k$. For example, we go from the derangement four units long $\begin{pmatrix} 1234 \\ 2143 \end{pmatrix}$ to the derangement five units long $\begin{pmatrix} 12345 \\ 25431 \end{pmatrix}$, with links $2 \rightarrow 5$ and $5 \rightarrow 1$. Taking the $n-1$ possible positions of number a, we get derangements n long, numbering $(n-1)\ d(n-1)$.

There are other derangements. Now let us take permutations $n-1$ long with one and only one fixed point b. There are $(n-1)\ d(n-2)$ of these. Next, let us move on to length n, by exchanging number n for number b, which was the fixed point. Therefore we obtain a derangement with the presence of cycle $(n\ b)$ in addition to those coming from the $n-2$-length derangement. This makes a total of $(n-2)\ d(n-2)$ derangements – different from those found previously because here we have the presence of $b \rightarrow n$ and $n \rightarrow b$.

There are no derangements other than those we have just found. Actually, in a n-length derangement we have links $n \rightarrow c$ and $d \rightarrow n$, for example for $n = 5$: $5 \rightarrow 2$ $3 \rightarrow 5$ in permutation $\begin{pmatrix} 12345 \\ 34512 \end{pmatrix}$. When $c \neq d$, as in the example, we find the first category of derangements we had before: removing n and putting link $d \rightarrow c$ back returns us to a derangement $n-1$ long. When $c = d$, with links $n \rightarrow c$ and $c \rightarrow n$, removing them gives a derangement $n-2$ long, as we found in the second category of derangements. Finally, we get the recurrence relation:

$$d(n) = (n-1)\ (d(n-1) + d(n-2))$$

with the initial conditions $d(1) = 0$ and $d(2) = 1$.

From this we deduce the explicit formula giving the number of derangements:

$$d(n) = n!\ (1 - 1\ /\ 1! + 1\ /\ 2! - 1\ /\ 3! + ... + (-1)^n\ /\ n!)$$

We could show this formula by verifying that the value $d(n)$ that we just gave obeys the recurrence relation above, as well as the initial conditions.

But let us present another method here. It is the opportunity to use a formula, called the *inversion formula,* which turns out to be practical in certain circumstances. Inversion formula is:

$$\text{If } f_n = \sum_{k=0}^{n} C_n^k\, g_k\,, \text{ then } g_n = \sum_{k=0}^{n} (-1)^{n-k} C_n^k\, f_k \text{ or } g_n = \sum_{k=0}^{n} (-1)^k\, C_n^k\, f_{n-k}$$

Let us return to our problem. The number of permutations with exactly k fixed points is $C_n^k\, d(n-k)$ because there are C_n^k ways of choosing the fixed points. Each time the permutations are left to be taken from the $n-k$ remaining elements without a fixed point, i.e. $d(n-k)$. With the $n!$ permutations being thus classified according to their number of fixed points, we get:

$$n! = \sum_{k=0}^{n} C_n^k\, d(n-k) = \sum_{k=0}^{n} C_n^k\, d(k)$$

by exchanging k and $n-k$

Now let us apply inversion formula with $g_k = d(k)$ and $f_n = n!$. We find that $d(n) = \sum_{k=0}^{n} (-1)^k\, C_n^k\, (n-k)!$. By replacing C_n^k with $n! / (k!\,(n-k)!)$, this gives:

$$d(n) = \sum_{k=0}^{n} (-1)^k\, n!/k!$$

i.e.: $d(n) = n!\,(1 - 1/1! + 1/2! - 1/3! + ... + (-1)^n / n!)$.[4]

---

4. Let us recall that when n is big, $d(n)$ is equal to $n!\,/\,e$. The probability of getting a permutation that is a derangement is of the order $1\,/\,e$. We also have another recurrence formula: $d(n) = n\,d(n-1)+(-1)^n$. To show this formula, all we have to do is check that the explicit formula of $d(n)$ verifies this recurrence relation as well as the initial conditions, for lack of a combinatorics demonstration. Finally, the exponential generating function $G(z)$ associated with derangements is: $G(z) = e^{-z} / (1-z)$. Actually:

$G(z) = \sum_{n\geq 0} \frac{d(n)z^n}{n!} = 1 + (1 - 1/1!)z + (1 - 1/1! + 1/2!)z^2 - (1-1/1! + 1/2!-1/3!)z^3 + \ldots = (1 + z + z^2 + \ldots) - (1/1!)\,z\,(1 + z + z^2 + \ldots) + (1/2!)\,z^2\,(1 + z + z^2 + \ldots) - (1/3!)\,z^3\,(1 + z + z^2 + \ldots) = (1 - z/1! + z^2/2! - z^3/3! + ...)/(1-z) = e^{-z}/(1-z)$.

19.2.1.3. *Number of permutations of {1, 2, ..., n} where the cycle of element 1 is k long*

Let us consider the cycle of given length k containing 1. We can obtain this cycle by taking the $k-1$ remaining elements from the $n-1$ elements other than 1, taking order into consideration, i.e. the number of arrangements A_{n-1}^{k-1}. Each time the cycle of 1 is constituted. What remains to be done is to take elements out of this cycle in all possible orders, i.e. $(n-k)!$. The number of permutations sought is:

$$A_{n-1}^{k-1}\,(n-k)! = (n-1)\,!$$

In terms of probabilities, the probability that the cycle of 1 is k long is $(n-1)!\,/\,n\,! = 1\,/\,n$. Therefore the probability is the same no matter what the length k of the cycle containing 1.

19.2.2. *Number of permutations of n elements with k cycles: Stirling numbers of the first kind*

Let $c(n, k)$ be the number of permutations with k cycles belonging to the set S_n of permutations of n elements, with n and k given, and let us search for a recurrence relation verified by these numbers. To do this we need to separate the permutations being decomposed into k disjoint cycles following their categories:

– the permutations where element n is a fixed point, forming a cycle with itself alone. These permutations number $c(n-1, k-1)$ because $n-1$ elements are left to be placed in $k-1$ cycles. This assumes that n and k are greater than or equal to 1;

– those where element n is in a cycle with at least two elements. If we remove this element n, we get a permutation of $n-1$ elements with k cycles. When we add element n to these $c(n-1, k)$ permutations expressed in the form of cycles, we must place element n behind any one of the elements of the cycles numbering $n-1$. This is done in $n-1$ ways. The number of permutations obtained is $(n-1)\,c(n-1, k)$.

Finally, we obtain the recurrence relation:

$$c(n, k) = (n-1)\,c(n-1, k) + c(n-1, k-1)$$

for $n \geq 1$ and $k \geq 1$, with initial conditions: $c(n, 0) = 0$ for $n > 0$, $c(0, k) = 0$ for $k > 0$, and $c(0, 0) = 1$, in such a way that the recurrence formula functions notably for $c(1, 1) = c(0, 0) = 1$.

For given n, the generating function associated with $c(n, k)$ is:

$$F_n(x) = x\,(x+1)\,(x+2)\ \dots\ (x+n-1) \text{ for } n \geq 1$$

Let us verify this using our calculation. We already have:

$$F_1(x) = c(1, 0) + c(1, 1)x + c(1, 2)x^2 + \dots = x$$

However, let us assume $n > 1$. Thanks to the recurrence relation: $c(n, k) = (n-1)$ $c(n-1, k) + c(n-1, k-1)$ for $k > 0$, it results that:

$$F_n(x) - c(n, 0) = (n-1)(F_{n-1}(x) - c(n-1, 0)) + xF_{n-1}(x),$$

i.e.: $F_n(x) = (x + n - 1)F_{n-1}(x)$.

Finally we get:

$$F_n(x) = x\,(x+1)\,(x+2)\ \dots\ (x+n-1) \text{ for } n \geq 1.$$

19.2.3. *Type of permutation*

During decomposition in disjoint cycles, all permutations of n elements have a_1 cycles one unit long, a_2 cycles two units long, ..., a_n cycles n units long. This is therefore of the type $a_1, a_2, \dots, a_n$. Numbers $a_1, a_2, \dots, a_n$ are all positive or null, and they verify $a_1 + 2a_2 + \dots + na_n = n$. Our objective is to find out the number of permutations of a given type. To do this, let us begin by showing the following property: with numbers a and k being given, when we take ka elements from n elements and form a cycles all k long, the number of ways is $A_n^{ka} / (a!\, k^a)$.

Actually, the number of ways to take ka out of n objects, taking order into consideration, is $A_n^{ka} = n! / (n - ka)!$. Let us separate these ka objects ordered in a pieces, which corresponds to a cycles that are k long. We know that the layout of the cycles is commutative. The $a!$ permutations of the cycles form different arrangements, but only make one single configuration. The number of ways to get the a cycles is reduced to $A_n^{ka} / a!$. Finally, each cycle is defined using a cyclic permutation-type, and the same cycle is written in k different ways. With a cycles, this makes k^a arrangements that give only one configuration. The number of ways is therefore reduced to $A_n^{ka} / (a!\, k^a)$.

Now let us return to counting permutations of a given type problem.

We begin by forming the a_1 cycles one unit in length, which is done in $A_n^{1a1} / (a_1!\ 1^{a1})$ ways, or even $n! / ((n - 1a_1)!\ a_1!\ 1a_1)$ ways. For each of these, we take the $2a_2$ elements enabling us to have the a_2 cycles two units long from the $n - 1a_1$ remaining elements, which makes $(n - 1a_1)! / ((n - 1a_1 - 2a_2)!\ a_2!\ 2a_2)$.

Each time $n - 1a_1 - 2a_2$ elements remain. From these, we take the $3a_3$ elements, enabling us to have the a_3 cycles that are three units long. And so on and so forth. Hence the number $c(a_1, a_2, \ldots, a_n)$ of permutations of type $a_1, a_2, \ldots, a_n$ is:

$$c(a_1, a_2, \ldots, a_n) = \frac{n!}{(n-1a_1)!a_1!1^{a_1}} \frac{(n-1a_1)!}{(n-1a_1-2a_2)!a_2!2^{a_2}} \cdots$$
$$= \frac{n!}{a_1!a_2!\ldots a_n!1^{a_1}2^{a_2}\ldots n^{a_n}}$$

19.3. Inversions in a permutation

In a permutation p, the number of inversions is by definition the number of pairs of indices (i, j) with $i < j$ such that we have $p(i) > p(j)$. The comparisons carried out are of the form indicated in Figure 19.3.[5]

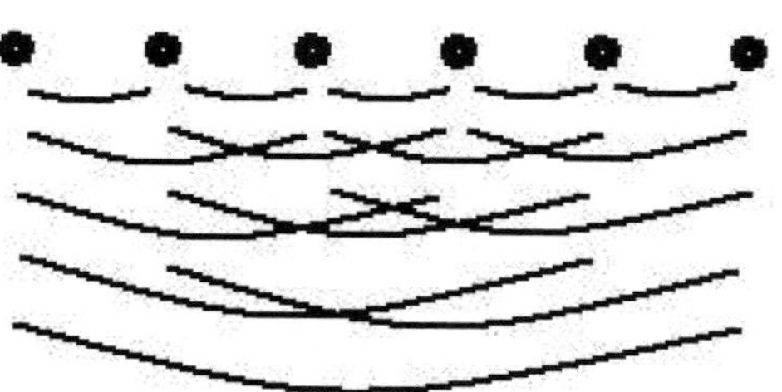

Figure 19.3. *Comparisons of terms two by two to determine inversions*

5. We can compare each element to those that come before it, as well as each element to those that follow it.

For example, the permutation $\begin{pmatrix} 0 & 1 & 2 & 3 \\ 2 & 0 & 3 & 1 \end{pmatrix}$ presents three inversions.

To count them, we take the elements of index k with k going from 0 to 3, and each time we compare $p(k)$ with all the elements that come before it, noting the cases of inversion. Here, for $k = 1$ we have the inversion (2 0), and for $k = 3$ we have inversions (2 1) and (3 1). From this we deduce what we call the inversion table for the permutation, where for each element j of the permutation we associate the number $ti[j]$ of elements located before it and which are greater than it.

The inversion table for the permutation above is:

$$\begin{bmatrix} 0 & 1 & 2 & 3 \\ 1 & 2 & 0 & 0 \end{bmatrix}$$

All permutations with n elements from 0 to $n - 1$ assume an inversion table, also made up of n numbers, where each one of these numbers $ti(j)$ is included between 0 and $n - 1 - j$. Actually element 0 of the permutation has a maximum of $n - 1$ elements in front that are greater than it, and a minimum of 0. Element 1 has a maximum of $n - 2$ elements in front that are greater than it, and a minimum of 0. And so on and so forth until the last element $n - 1$, which has no element in front that is greater than it: we always have $ti(n - 1) = 0$.

But the most important is that using a table $ti[]$ made up of numbers $ti(j)$ included between 0 and $n - 1 - j$, we always find one and only one permutation where numbers $ti(j)$ correspond to inversions of the permutation. Let us use a constructive method to show this, taking table $ti[]$ below as an example:

$$\begin{bmatrix} 0 & 1 & 2 & 3 & 4 & 5 & 6 & 7 & 8 & 9 \\ 5 & 2 & 4 & 6 & 2 & 1 & 3 & 0 & 1 & 0 \end{bmatrix}$$

We will run through this table from right to left, and construct the permutation element by element. Let us begin by writing 9, which we know thanks to the inversion table has no element greater than it. Next let us take the 8, which has an element in front that is greater than it: this element can only be 9, and we are therefore sure that these elements are in the order 9 8. Then let us take the 7, which has no element greater than it in front of it: 8 and 9 are necessarily behind it. The three elements will be in the order 7 9 8. In turn, the 6 must have three elements (which are necessarily 7, 8 and 9) in front of it that are greater than it. The four elements will be in the order 7 9 8 6. Then element 5 has to have one element (out of 6, 7, 8 and 9) in front of it that is greater than it. The five elements will be in order 7 5 9 8 6. And we continue in this way, which gives 7 5 4 9 8 6, then 7 5 4 9 8 6 3, then 7 5 4 9 2 8 6 3, followed by 7 5 1 4 9 2 8 6 3, and finally 7 5 1 4 9 0 2 8 6 3. This last order is the permutation with table *ti*[] as its inversion table.

From this we deduce the program enabling us to go from the inversion table to the permutation:

We are given the number of elements N and the inversion table *ti*[N].

```
for(i=0; i<N; i++) a[i]=0;    /* We set table a[] to 0. At the end it will contain the
                                 permutation */
a[N–1]=N–1; first=N-1;
      /* We place the last number in the last box and take a variable first
         that indicates the position of the first element of the permutation
         being created. At each stage in the process, the variable first will
         be reduced by 1, and will reach 0 when the entire permutation fills
         array a[] */
for(i=N–2; i>=0; i--)
   { first--;  for(j=first; j<first+ti[i]; j++) a[j]=a[j+1];
     a[first+ti[i]]=i; }
      /* We move all the elements one notch to the left, numbering ti[i]of them,
         that must precede element i, then we put i just after in the box that
         has become empty. The following elements remain in place. */
```

19.3.1. *Generating function of the number of inversions*

Having obtained a bijection between permutations with n elements and their n-long inversion table *ti*[], where $ti(j)$ is between 0 and $n - 1 - j$, this will enable us to find the generating function associated with the number $I(n, k)$ of permutations of n elements 0, 1, …, $n - 1$, presenting k inversions, for given n, i.e.:

$$F_n(x) = \sum_{0 \le k \le C_n^2} I(n,k)\, x^k$$

The number k of inversions of a permutation with n elements is actually between 0 and C_n^2, with this last number corresponding to the permutation in inverse order of natural order, and having the maximum number of inversions. We saw that each number $ti(j)$ of the inversion table is included between 0 and $n - 1 - j$, and by addition we find:

$$ti(0) + ti(1) + \ldots + ti(n-1) = k$$

We return to searching for natural integer solutions of this equation with n unknowns with the constraints $0 \leq ti(j) \leq n - 1 - j$. We encountered this type of problem in Chapter 7 on combinations with repetition. From this we deduce the generating function:

$$F_n(x) = (1 + x)\,(1 + x + x^2) \ldots (1 + x + x^2 + \ldots + x^{n-1})$$

For example for $n = 4$, we find:

$I(4, 0) = 1$, $I(4, 1) = 3$, $I(4, 2) = 5$, $I(4, 3) = 6$, $I(4, 4) = 5$, $I(4, 5) = 3$, $I(4, 6) = 1$.

19.3.2. *Signature of a permutation: odd and even permutations*

If the number of inversions is even, we say that the signature of the permutation is equal to +1, and if this number is odd, the signature is equal to -1.

Permutations of n elements are divided into two types of permutations: even permutations, whose signature is 1; and odd permutations, whose signature is -1. When we work out the product of several permutations, their signatures are multiplied. The product of two even permutations or two odd permutations is even; that of an even permutation and an odd permutation is odd.

There is a link between the number of inversions and the number of permutation cycles. For this, let us begin by showing the following property:

PROPERTY 19.1.– A transposition $(p(i)\ p(j))$, i.e. the exchange of two elements in a permutation (or even a cycle two units long) changes the parity of the number of inversions.

Let us take two indices i and j with $i < j$ and consider all the elements of the permutation located between $p(i)$ and $p(j)$, without taking these: of the m elements separating them, some (numbering a_1) are less than $p(i)$ and the others (numbering a_2) are greater than it; on the other hand a certain number b_1 of elements are less than $p(j)$ and b_2 are greater than it, with $a_1 + a_2 = b_1 + b_2 = m$. Before transposition, the number of inversions that concern m elements as well as $p(i)$ and $p(j)$ is $a_1 + b_2$. The number of inversions is therefore $a_2 + b_1$. The number of inversions changed by:

$$a_2 + b_1 - (a_1 + b_2) = a_2 - b_2 + b_1 - a_1 = 2(a_1 - b_2)\text{ , because } a_2 - b_2 = b_1 - a_1$$

The number obtained is even, but we must also cause the exchange of $p(i)$ with $p(j)$ to intervene, which produces one inversion more or less, with the rest not having moved. Finally we find an odd number of inversions. The transposition has changed the parity of the permutation.

Now let us take a cycle m long of a permutation ($m > 1$). Let us begin by showing that it is decomposed into $m - 1$ transpositions, i.e. s is cycle $(a_1\ a_2\ a_3\ \ldots\ a_q)$. We can verify that $s = {}_{\rightarrow}(a_{q-1}\ a_q)\ldots\ (a_2\ a_3)\ (a_1\ a_2)$ by working out the products successively from left to right.

For example $(0\ 1\ 2) = {}_{\rightarrow}(1\ 2)\ (0\ 1)$, i.e.:

$$\begin{pmatrix} 0 & 1 & 2 \\ 0 & 1 & 2 \end{pmatrix} \rightarrow \begin{pmatrix} 0 & 1 & 2 \\ 0 & 2 & 1 \end{pmatrix} \rightarrow \begin{pmatrix} 0 & 1 & 2 \\ 1 & 2 & 0 \end{pmatrix} = \text{cycle } (0\ 1\ 2)$$

The succession of $m - 1$ transpositions, all odd, gives an odd permutation if m is even and *vice versa.*

If we take decomposition in disjoint cycles of a permutation with n elements, the number of transpositions is $n - q$, where q is the number of cycles. Actually, if m_i is the length of cycle number i, with i from 1 to q, this cycle is decomposed into $m_i - 1$ transpositions, hence a total number of transpositions equal to:

$$\sum_{i=1}^{q}(m_i - 1) = (\sum_{i=1}^{q} m_i) - q = n - q$$

As the permutation is obtained by carrying out $n - q$ successive transpositions using natural order $0\ 1\ 2\ 3\ \ldots\ n$ the signature of which is +1, the signature of the permutation is therefore $(-1)^{n-q}$. We have just obtained the following results:

– a transposition (two cycle order) changes the parity of a permutation;

– a cycle of length m corresponds to an even permutation if and only if m is odd;

– the signature of a permutation is $(-1)^{n-q}$, with its number of elements being n, and its number of disjoint cycles being q.

Now let us show that the group S_n of permutations with n elements contains as many even as odd permutations. For this let us take the application of the set of even permutations in the set of odd permutations, which the permutation ${}_{\rightarrow}tp$, with t that is a given transposition, associates with each even permutation p of S_n. We therefore get tp which is odd.

On the other hand, it is a bijection, because $(tp)^{-1} = p^{-1}t^{-1} = p^{-1}t$. Therefore every odd permutation is the unique image of an even permutation. There are as many even as odd permutations. Alternate group A_n is the set of even permutations with the composition operation making the product of two permutations.[6] Alternate group A_n has $n!$ / 2 elements.

19.4. Conjugated permutations

In the set S_n of permutations with n elements, two permutations p and p' are said to be conjugated when there is a permutation q such that $p' =_{\rightarrow} q^{-1} pq$.

It is easy to verify that two conjugated permutations have the same period.[7] The period of a permutation is the minimum number of times this permutation must be repeated to fall back on the identity (natural order). Even better: two conjugated permutations are decomposed into disjoint cycles which each have the same length, respectively.

In other words, two conjugated permutations have the same type. Even more precisely, each cycle of the conjugated permutation p' is deduced from the corresponding cycle by carrying out permutation q on the cycle of p. Let us take an example: permutation p is expressed in the form of disjoint cycles (0 1 2 5)(3 6)(4) and q is expressed (0 2 4)(1 3 5)(6). Therefore $p' =_{\rightarrow} q^{-1}\ p\ q$ is expressed (2 3 4 1)(5 6)(0).[8]

We will now define what is called conjugacy classes in S_n and determine their number. In set S_n of permutations of n elements, let us take a permutation p and let us form all permutations of the form $g^{-1}pg$, where g is some permutation of S_n. We say that $g^{-1}pg$ is the conjugate of p through g, and the set of all these permutations $g^{-1}pg$ forms what is called the conjugacy class of p. These permutations $g^{-1}pg$ all have cycles exactly identical in length to those of p, and obtained from the decomposition of p into cycles by replacing each element i of these cycles by $g(i)$.

---

6. It is a group or a sub-group of S_n because the product of two even permutations is an even permutation.

7. If p' has as its period T', we have $p'^{T'} = Id$, hence $(q^{-1}\ p\ q)^{T'} = Id$, which is simplified into $q^{-1}\ p^{T'}\ q = Id$, then $p^{T'} = Id$, therefore period T of p divides T'. Conversely we start again with $p^T = Id$, which implies that $q\ p^T\ q^{-1} = Id$ and $p'^T = Id$, hence T' divides T. Finally $T' = T$.

8. To show this property, let us take an element i of a cycle of p and its successor $p(i)$. The images g of these two elements are $g(i)$ and $g(p(i))$. We have to verify that the second is in the image of the first through $p' = g^{-1}pg$. Actually: ${}_{\rightarrow}(g^{-1}pg)(g(i)) = {}_{\leftarrow}(g\ p\ g^{-1})(g(i)) = g(p(g^{-1}(g(i)))) = g(p(i))$. Finally all the conjugated permutations of p have as many cycles of the same length as those of p.

And conversely, any permutation p' with the same lengths of cycles as those of p is in the conjugacy class of p: all we have to do to verify it is to choose a permutation g so that g transforms an element of a cycle of p into the corresponding element in p'. This is the case for each element.

The permutations of a conjugacy class have the characteristic property of cycles that are identical in length. They are also characterized as having the same type (see section 19.2.3 for the definition of permutation type).[9]

These congugacy classes form a partition set S_n of permutations. For this, let us take the conjugacy class of a permutation p, characterized by the lengths of its cycles. Then let us take a permutation q that is not in this class, as well as its own conjugacy class, characterized by other lengths of cycles. Continuing in this way, we divide set S_n into disjoint conjugacy classes, and there are as many classes as there are ways of choosing lengths of cycles, i.e. ways of expressing n in the form of a sum of positive integers. The number of conjugacy classes of S_n is the number of partitions of number n.

19.5. Generation of permutations

Let S_n be the group of permutations of n objects, called 0, 1, 2, 3 , ... , $n-1$. Group S_n is made up of $n!$ permutations. We want to find out whether, among this multitude of permutations, we are capable of finding some that, multiplied with each other, will be able to give the $n!$ permutations. Therefore we say that these permutations generate group S_n, i.e. they are generators of the group. Let us specify that if we take k permutations and multiply them between themselves in all possible ways, we get a group of permutations that constitutes a sub-group of S_n.

---

9. Let us take for example $p = \begin{pmatrix} 1 & 2 & 3 & 4 \\ 2 & 4 & 3 & 1 \end{pmatrix} = (1\ 2\ 4)\ (3)$, with two cycles of length 3 and 1, and $g = \begin{pmatrix} 1 & 2 & 3 & 4 \\ 4 & 3 & 2 & 1 \end{pmatrix}$. Therefore we verify that $g^{-1}pg = (4\ 3\ 1)\ (2)$, with its two cycles of three and 1 units long. Conversely, if we take a permutation with two cycles that are three and one units, like $p' = (2\ 4\ 3)(1)$, it is also of the form $g^{-1}pg$, taking for example $g = \begin{pmatrix} 1 & 2 & 3 & 4 \\ 2 & 4 & 1 & 3 \end{pmatrix}$. As cycle (2 4 3) can be expressed in two other ways – (4 3 2) or (3 2 4) – we still have two other permutations g that fit. Let us take another example with two cycles of the same length: $p = (1\ 2)(3\ 4)$ and $p' = (1\ 4)(2\ 3)$. According to the order in which we divide these cycles, we find eight permutations g such that: $p' = g^{-1}pg$, notably $g = \begin{pmatrix} 1 & 2 & 3 & 4 \\ 1 & 4 & 2 & 3 \end{pmatrix}$ or $\begin{pmatrix} 1 & 2 & 3 & 4 \\ 2 & 3 & 1 & 4 \end{pmatrix}$.

The k permutations will form a system of generators of S_n when the group they generate is exactly S_n. We will now discuss some ways to generate group S_n of permutations.

19.5.1. *The symmetrical group S_n is generated by the transpositions $(i\,j)$*

We saw that all permutations decompose into disjoint cycles, and that each cycle can be replaced by a product of transpositions. This proves that all permutations decompose into the product of transpositions, and that S_n is generated by transpositions $(i\,j)$, numbering C_n^2. Note that there is another demonstration, clearly more attractive, and linked to sorting algorithms.

One sort is a permutation, which causes us to go from a permutation of unordered objects to that which corresponds to natural order. In this case, it is enough to note that sorting by selection-exchange, the simplest sort, is done by a succession of transpositions. Here is how this sort operates: we begin by comparing the first element (the one which is in box 0) with all the others. There is eventually an exchange if the two elements compared are not in ascending order, which places the smallest element in first place. Then we start again from the second element, etc. Let us take the permutation 214053 and carry out a selection-exchange sort (see Figure 19.4).

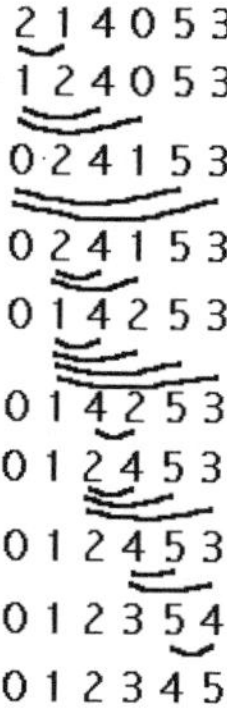

Figure 19.4. *Selection-exchange sort*

We go from permutation 214053 to the identity 01234 by the succession of transpositions, written according to the indices of the boxes where the exchange is carried out: $_{\rightarrow}$(01) (03) (13) (23) (35) (45).

by doing this in the opposite way, from right to left, we create the permutation 214053 from 012345. The permutation 214053 was generated by a succession of transpositions.

19.5.2. S_n *is generated by transpositions of adjacent elements of the form (i , i + 1)*

We verify that $(p, q) = (q - 1, q)\ (p, q - 1)\ (q - 1, q)$, where the middle transposition is not necessarily made up of adjacent elements. We proceed by recurrence, with the gap between p and $q - 1$ being one notch weaker than that between p and q. This comes back to re-starting the decomposition on $(p, q - 1)$, then on $(p, q - 2)$ until we get to $(p, p + 1)$.

All transpositions therefore decompose into the product of transpositions of successive elements, and all we have to do is apply the result in section 19.5.1 to achieve this. There is another simpler method, that of bubble sort, which consists of comparing two successive elements and exchanging them if need be to get them in ascending order.

We compare the first and second element. Then the second and third, etc. At the end of this process, the biggest element is found in the last box. Then we start again from the first to the one before the last element, and so on and so forth. For example:

$$\underline{21}4053 \rightarrow 1\underline{24}053 \rightarrow 12\underline{40}53 \rightarrow 120\underline{45}3 \rightarrow 1204\underline{53} \rightarrow 120435$$

$$\underline{12}0435 \rightarrow 1\underline{20}435 \rightarrow 10\underline{24}35 \rightarrow 102\underline{43}5 \rightarrow 102345$$

$$\underline{10}2345 \rightarrow 0\underline{12}345 \rightarrow 01\underline{23}45 \rightarrow 012345$$

$$\underline{01}2345 \rightarrow 0\underline{12}345 \rightarrow 012345$$

$$\underline{01}2345 \rightarrow 012345$$

We move from the permutation 214053 in natural order by carrying out, from left to right, the succession of transpositions of adjacent elements, expressed according to the indices of the boxes concerned: (01) (23) (45) (12) (34) (01). Conversely, we create this permutation by carrying out these same transpositions but from right to left.

19.5.3. S_n *is generated by transpositions (0 1) (0 2) ... (0 n – 1)*

Actually all transpositions other than those of the form $(0\ k)$ can be decomposed in the following way:

$$(i\,j) = {}_{\rightarrow}(0\ i)\ (0\ j)\ (0\ i) \quad \text{with } i \text{ and } j \text{ different from } 0.$$

19.5.4. S_n *is generated by cycles (0 1) and (0 1 2 3 ... n – 1)*

With c as the circular permutation:

$$(0\ 1\ 2\ \ldots\ n-1) = \begin{pmatrix} 0 & 1 & 2 & \ldots & n-1 \\ 1 & 2 & 3 & \ldots & 0 \end{pmatrix}$$

the succession c^{-k} (0 1) c^{k} gives the transposition of neighboring elements (k, k + 1) and the transpositions (k, k + 1) generate S_n.

19.6. Properties of the alternating group A_n

Let us recall that a permutation is even when the number of inversions is even, or even when the difference between the number n of elements and number of cycles m of the permutation is an even number. By definition, the alternating group A_n is made up of all the even permutations, numbering $n!$ / 2. More precisely, we discuss the properties from sections 19.6.1 to 19.6.3.

19.6.1. A_n *is generated by cycles three units long: (i j k)*

We know that an even permutation is the product of an even number of transpositions, because a transposition produces a change in parity. On the other hand we verify that ${}_{\rightarrow}(i\ j)\ (i\ k) = (i\ j\ k)$ and that $(i\ j)\ (k\ l) = {}_{\rightarrow}(i\ l\ j)\ (j\ k\ l)$. The pairs of transpositions, whether they are disjoint or not, are expressed in all cases in the form of third-order cycles. It is the same for every even permutation. The alternating group A_n is generated by cycles three units long.

19.6.2. A_n *is generated by n – 2 cycles (0 1 k)*

To show this, all we have to do is check that every cycle three units long decomposes following particular cycles of the form (0 1 k).

We check the formulas:

– $(i\ j\ k) = {}_{\rightarrow}(0\ 1\ i)\ (0\ 1\ k)\ (0\ 1\ j)\ (0\ 1\ i)\ (0\ 1\ k)$ assuming that i, j and k are all different from 0 and 1;

– $(0\ i\ 1) = (0\ 1\ i)\ (0\ 1\ i)$;

– $(0\ i\ j) = {}_{\rightarrow}(0\ 1\ i)\ (0\ 1\ i)\ (0\ 1\ j)$ with i and j different from 0 and 1; and

– $(1\ i\ j) = {}_{\rightarrow}(0\ 1\ i)\ (0\ 1\ j)\ (0\ 1\ j)$.

19.6.3. ***For $n > 3$, A_n is generated by the cycle chain three units long, of the form (0 1 2) (2 3 4) (4 5 6) … ($n-3$ $n-2$ $n-1$)***

Note that all these cycles have three elements that follow each other, and each one has one element in common with the cycle that follows it (except the one before the last, which has two elements in common with the last, if n is even). Let us begin by taking the example of A_5, with its 60 permutations. The 20 cycles three units in length of A_5 are:

(0 1 2) (0 1 3) (0 1 4) (0 2 1) (0 2 3) (0 2 4) (0 3 1) (0 3 2) (0 3 4) (0 4 1) (0 4 2) (0 4 3) (1 2 3) (1 2 4) (1 3 2) (1 3 4) (1 4 2) (1 4 3) (2 3 4) (2 4 3),

We saw that these cycles generate A_5. Next let us consider only cycles (0 1 2), (0 1 3) and (0 1 4). We also saw that these three cycles generate A_5.

Finally, thanks to the property above, if we take just the two cycles (0 1 2) and (2 3 4) in turn they generate A_5. *A fortiori* the three cycles of the form $(i, i+1, i+2)$ with i from 0 to 2 also generate A_5. This is equal to A_n in the general case. All we have to do is take the cycles three units in length with successive elements that have a single element in common, or eventually two at the end, of the form (0 1 2) (2 3 4) (4 5 6) etc., that number $(n-1) / 2$ for odd n, and $n / 2$ for even n.

Let us show the previous property. We saw that A_n was generated by cycles (0 1 k). All we have to do is check that each one of these cycles is the product of cycles of the chain (0 1 2) (2 3 4) (4 5 6) etc.

If $k = 2$, this is already done.

If $k = 3$, all we have to do is $_{\rightarrow}$(2 4 3) (0 1 2) (2 3 4) = (0 1 3).[10] Note in passing that (2 4 3) = $(2\ 3\ 4)^{-1} = (2\ 3\ 4)^2$.

If $k = 4$, then $_{\rightarrow}$(2 4 3) (0 1 3) (2 3 4) = $_{\rightarrow}$(2 4 3) (2 4 3) (0 1 2) (2 3 4) (2 3 4)

= (0 1 4).

If $k = 5$, then $_{\rightarrow}$(4 6 5) (0 1 4) (4 5 6)

= $_{\rightarrow}$(4 6 5) (2 4 3) (2 4 3) (0 1 2) (2 3 4) (2 3 4) (4 5 6)

= (0 1 5).

---

10. By doing this, we use the properties of the conjugated permutations seen above. Therefore $_{\rightarrow}$(2 4 3) (0 1 2) (2 3 4) is of the form $g^{-1}pg$, and cycle (0 1 2) is transformed into (0 1 3) by applying g.

This is easy to generalize to a value of k. This involves taking the conjugate of the cycle (0 1 2) by the succession (2 3 4) (2 3 4) (4 5 6) (4 5 6) (6 7 8) etc., with the presence of $k-2$ cycles, counting blocks of two repeated identical cycles as two.[11]

19.7. Applications of these properties

We are now going to apply these results to two types of problems: one where combinatorics rejoins arithmetics, namely some ways of shuffling cards;[12] the other being the *taquin game* that resembles it.

19.7.1. *Card shuffling*

19.7.1.1. *Card shuffling generated by both types of riffle shuffling, O and I, for an odd number of cards*

Let us take a pack of cards with a supposedly odd number N of cards. We carry out what we can call a riffle shuffle, i.e. we cut the pack in two and alternatively interleave the cards of the second pack with those of the first. Because of the odd number of cards, the preliminary cut is not in exactly two equal parts.

There are two ways of doing this, one consisting of keeping the first card in place, and the other where the first card moves second. Let us call these shuffles O and I (see Figure 19.5). For example, $N = 5$ gives the two permutations:

$$O: \begin{pmatrix} 0 & 1 & 2 & 3 & 4 \\ 0 & 3 & 1 & 4 & 2 \end{pmatrix}$$

Taking it that the card in position 0 stays in position 0, that the card in position 1 goes into position 2, that the card in position 2 moves into position 4, etc., we get the permutation $\begin{pmatrix} 0 & 1 & 2 & 3 & 4 \\ 0 & 2 & 4 & 1 & 3 \end{pmatrix}$ where the even numbers are placed, in order, before

11. Another method consists of using the fact that A_n is generated by whichever cycles are three units long of the form $(i\ j\ k)$, and showing that any cycles $(i\ j\ k)$ are the product of the cycles of the chain (0 1 2) (2 3 4) (4 5 6) etc. Without going into detail, because there are several cases, let us take an example showing how for $n = 7$, the cycle (1 2 5) is deduced from the three cycles (0 1 2), (2 3 4) and (4 5 6). For this purpose we use conjugacy permutations. We begin by noting that: $_{\rightarrow}$(2 3 4) (0 1 2) (2 4 3) = (0 1 4). In turn $_{\rightarrow}$(4 6 5) (0 1 4) (4 5 6) = (0 1 5). Finally $_{\rightarrow}$(0 2 1) (0 1 5) (0 1 2) = (1 2 5).

12. See [DIA 83] and [LEV 73] about card shuffling.

the odd ones, also in order. This permutation is the reverse of the previous one. It has the same period, which we will use.

I: $\begin{pmatrix} 0 & 1 & 2 & 3 & 4 \\ 2 & 0 & 3 & 1 & 4 \end{pmatrix}$ or even, taking the reverse $\begin{pmatrix} 0 & 1 & 2 & 3 & 4 \\ 1 & 3 & 0 & 2 & 4 \end{pmatrix}$, where the odd numbers are placed before the evens.

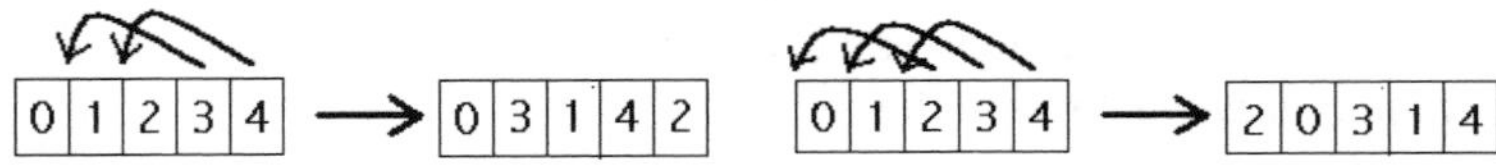

Figure 19.5. *Shuffle O (left); and shuffle I (right) for an odd number of cards*

Let us begin by taking shuffle *O*. Placing ourselves in set $\boldsymbol{Z}_N$ of modulo *N* numbers (which we will write [*N*]), the permutation causes us to go from one *x* element to an *x′* element through $x' = 2x$ [*N*]. Repeating this shuffle *k* times gives the final element $x^{(k)} = 2^k x$ [*N*]. Period *T* of this shuffle operation is the smallest value of *k*, for which we have $x = 2^k x$ [*N*] for all values of *x*. This is reduced to the smallest value of *k* so that $2^k = 1$ [*N*], i.e. the period of 2 (we say order of 2) in $\boldsymbol{Z}_N$. Therefore:

$T =$ order of 2 [*N*]

Permutation *O* generates a cyclic group with *T* elements.

Now let us take shuffle *I*. Placing ourselves in set $\boldsymbol{Z}_N$ of modulo *N* numbers, permutation causes us to go from *x* to *x′* with $x' = 2x + 1$ [*N*]. Repeating this shuffle *k* times gives $x' = 2^k x + 1 + 2 + 2^2 + \ldots + 2^{k-1}$, i.e. $x' = 2^k (x + 1) - 1$ [*N*]. From this we deduce that the period is still $T =$ order of 2 [*N*].

Finally, let us choose *O* or *I*. What we have to do is to find the group of permutations generated by *O* and *I*. First of all, notice that $I = Oc$, where *c* designates the circular permutation $(0\ 1\ 2\ \ldots\ N-1)$, causing us to go from *x* to *x′* through $x' = x + 1$ [*N*]. Since $I = Oc$ or conversely $c = O^{-1}I$, the group of permutations generated by *O* and *I* is the same as that generated by *O* and *c*. We therefore notice that $O\,c^2 = c\,O$. In both cases it is a matter of $x' = 2x + 2$ [*N*].

In any product of *O* or *c* type permutations, the replacement of *cO* by Oc^2 as many times as we can (as well as $O^{\text{order of 2}}$ through *Id* and c^N through *Id*) will always give a product of the form $O^j c^k$, with $0 \le j <$ order of 2 [*N*], and $0 \le k < N$. Such products are all different: they number *N* times the order of 2 [*N*]. Therefore, the group of permutations generated by O and I is made up of: $N \times$ order of 2 $[N]$ elements.

19.7.1.2. *Shufflings of N cards produced by a succession of cuts c or riffle shuffles of type O*

If the number of cards is odd, we have seen that the permutations generated by the circular permutation c and the riffle shuffle O number:

$$N \times \text{order of } 2\ [N]$$

What is left to do is to examine the case where the number N of cards is even. This will turn out to be very different from the odd case, since now it is the entire group of permutations S_N that will be obtained, i.e. $N!$ permutations.[13] Let us recall that shuffle O, after the pack is cut into two equal parts, places the even cards before the odd ones.

For example, for $N = 6$ permutation O is written $\begin{pmatrix} 0 & 1 & 2 & 3 & 4 & 5 \\ 0 & 2 & 4 & 1 & 3 & 5 \end{pmatrix}$ and cut c:

$$\begin{pmatrix} 0 & 1 & 2 & 3 & 4 & 5 \\ 1 & 2 & 3 & 4 & 5 & 0 \end{pmatrix}.$$

We know that group S_N of permutations is generated by the circular permutation c and the transposition (0 1) or any other transposition of successive elements. But how can a transposition of successive elements be obtained using O and c? For this, let us form $O^{-1}cO$, i.e. the conjugate of c through O. We know that the permutation thus obtained is split up into cycles with exactly the same length as those of c, which with $N = 6$ is written with a unique cycle (0 1 2 3 4 5). For $O^{-1}cO$ we obtain the unique cycle (0 2 4 1 3 5). Permutation $p = O^{-1}cO$ is always in the form $p(x) = x + 2$, for x between 0 and $N - 3$, and $p(N - 2) = 1$, $p(N - 1) = 0$. For example, for $N = 6$:

$$\begin{pmatrix} 0 & 1 & 2 & 3 & 4 & 5 \\ 2 & 3 & 4 & 5 & 1 & 0 \end{pmatrix}$$

13. Let us indicate that for even N, the group generated by the two types of riffle shuffle O and I is not S_N, because the link $I = Oc$ is no longer only valid for odd N.

therefore all we have to do is to carry out cut c^{N-2} on $O^{-1}cO$ to obtain the transposition $(N-2, N-1)$. Finally, the succession $O^{-1}cOc^{N-2}$ gives a transposition of successive elements.

The group of permutations generated by c and O is also that generated by the cyclic gap c and transposition $(N-2, N-1)$. It is S_N.

19.7.2. *Taquin game in a n by p (n and p > 1) rectangle*

We fill in the np boxes of a rectangle with numbers from 0 to $np - 2$, in any order, with one box remaining empty and placed on the bottom right. This empty box can be exchanged with any one of its neighbors that has a side in common with it. The empty box can therefore be moved throughout the rectangle, causing the movement of numbered boxes.

We want to find out whether, by starting from a permutation of numbers on the boxes, we can finally end up with natural order.[14] The answer is two fold:

– If we have an odd permutation of $np - 1$ numbers to begin with, and the empty box being on the bottom right, we will never be able to reach natural order if it remains in bottom right.

When the empty box makes a return journey on a path one unit long or more, there is finally no movement. Now let us assume that it does not make a return journey, because nothing is changed. It will therefore make a true cycle because it returns to the starting point. During this cycle, whatever it may be, the empty box makes an even number of horizontal movements and an even number of vertical movements because it has to return to the starting point.

When the cycle of the empty box does not intersect itself, it is therefore easy to check that this produces a cyclic shift of the numbered boxes through which the empty box moves on its path – the cycle is an odd length, hence an even permutation. If the cycle of the empty box does intersect itself, we can split it up into several cycles without intersections which, each one separately, also produce even permutations.

We notice that the journey of a cycle by the empty box causes the numbers placed on this cycle to shift by one notch in the reverse direction of the movement of the empty box (see Figure 19.6).

14. The creation of software for the taquin game (*jeu de taquin*) can be found in [RIF 06].

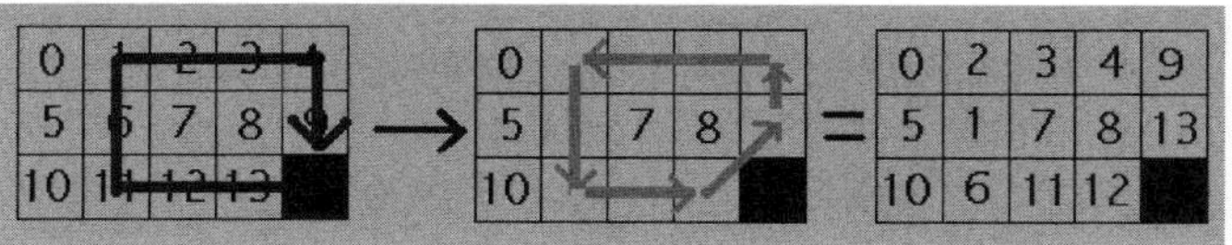

Figure 19.6. *Cycle completed by the empty box, and corresponding cycle of the numbered boxes*

Lastly, any movement of the empty box with return to its starting point creates even permutations. Therefore, in the case where we start from an initial odd permutation, we can never reach natural order.

On the other hand, one question remains shelved: if we start at a given permutation that does not produce any *a priori* impossibility, are we really going to reach natural order?

– If we start with an even permutation, whatever it may be, we can always end up with natural order. In other words, the movements of the empty box create permutations that enable us to generate the alternate group A_{np-1}. All we have to do for this is prove that any cycle in the chain (0 1 2) (2 3 4) (4 5 6) can be obtained by moving the empty box. We distinguish two cases, based on the cycle three units long and a same line or encroaching on two lines.

- *First case.* Let us designate the elements of a cycle of the form (0 1 2) or (2 3 4), which are displayed on the same line by *a*, *b* and *c*.

We begin by sending the empty box below the third element of the cycle (see Figure 19.7), and if this is not possible we place it above, which avoids crossing the cycle. Next we subject it to a 3×2 rectangular counterclockwise cycle. Then we make a square cycle in clockwise direction (focusing on the three elements of the cycle). Finally we re-run the rectangular cycle in the other direction. The only thing left to do is to return the empty box to its place on the bottom right using the same path as the outward journey. We have carried out the cycle (*a b c*). Note that it is sufficient to carry out a localized movement in a 3×2 rectangle, with the rest remaining stationary.

- *Second case.* The cycle, still belonging to the cycle chain, encroaches on two lines.

We have to work within a 2×*n* rectangle (see Figure 19.8). If *n* is odd, the first element of the cycle is on the right of a line, and the two following elements are on the following line on the left, as for example cycle (6 7 8) in Figure 19.8. We will only deal with this case here, the other one with even *n* being analogous. We begin by interlinking cycles on the first line, and henceforth we know how to carry out these cycles.

This enables us to put the last element first (6 in the drawing). Therefore we have the triangle that can be rotated one notch, then we re-run the cycle chain in the reverse direction.

6
7 8

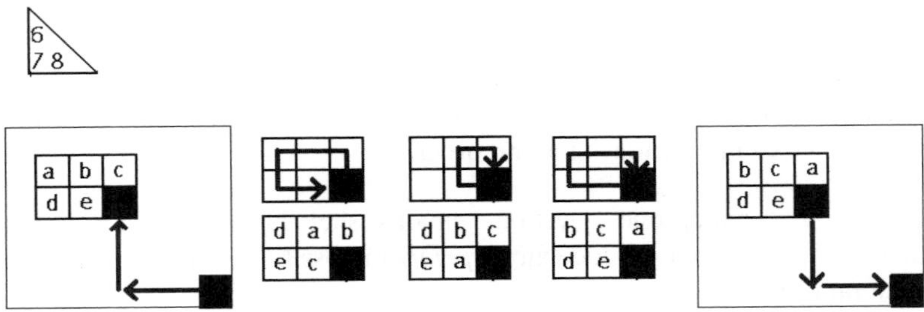

Figure 19.7. *Creation of cycle (a b c)*

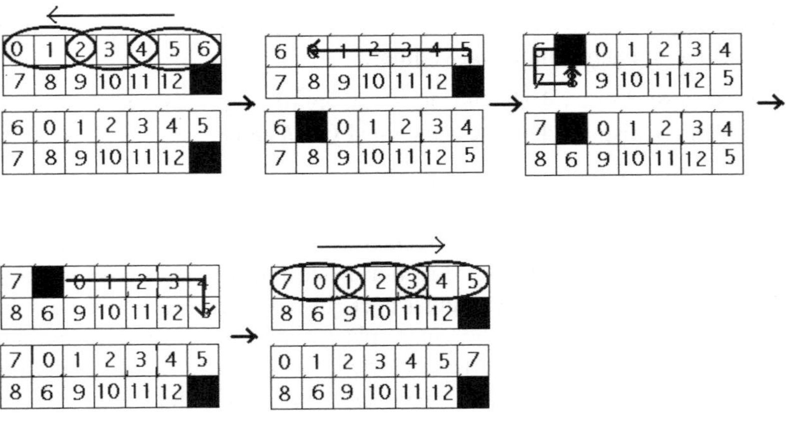

Figure 19.8. *Creation of cycle (6 7 8)*

Since we can create all the cycles of chain (0 1 2) (2 3 4) etc. thanks to moving the empty *taquin* case, and these cases generate the alternate group A_{np-1}, we deduce from it that we will be able to move from an even permutation to any other even permutation, notably the one in natural order. After this, the only thing left to do is find game strategies using the fewest movements possible, but this is another story.

19.7.3. *Cyclic shifts in a rectangle*

Let us consider a gridded triangle with p lines and n columns. We fill it in line after line using successive numbers 0 1 2 3 ...... $np - 1$. Let us assume that $N = np$. The only moves allowed in this game are cyclic shifts of one notch to the left on any line, or cyclic shifts of one notch upwards on the column.

We proceed in this way to a succession of horizontal or vertical cyclic shifts (see Figure 19.9). Let us number the lines 0, 1, 2, ... and the columns in the same way. Let L_i be a shift of one notch to the left on line number i, and C_i a shift of one notch upwards on column number i.

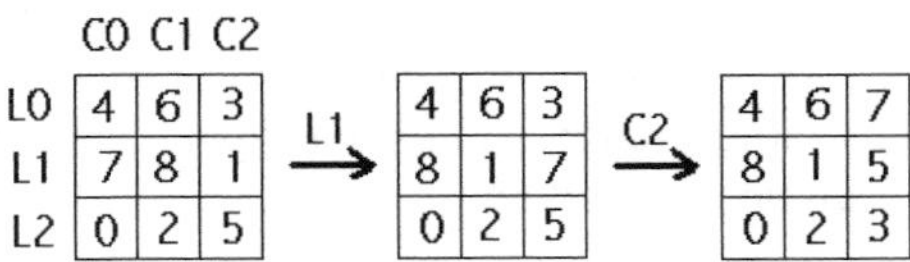

Figure 19.9. *Example where permutation 463781025 becomes, through L_1 463817025, then through C_2 467815023*

The question is to find out which are the permutations obtained in this way, starting from natural order. More precisely, does the set of these cyclic shifts generate the entire group S_n?

Conversely, starting from a permutation in the rectangle, i.e. displaying numbers 0 to $N - 1$ in an order on the rectangle, is it possible to find natural order 0, 1, 2, ..., $N - 1$, using a succession of cyclic shifts? And if yes, what is the succession of shifts to be done?

We already have a restriction in the case where the number of boxes $N = np$ of the rectangle is odd, with the following property:

– If the rectangle has an odd number of boxes, i.e. its two sides of length n and p are odd, only even permutations are obtained.

Let us demonstrate this property. A shift is a cycle of order n if it is horizontal, and of order p if it is vertical. We know that a cycle of even length gives an odd permutation, and that a cycle of odd length gives an even permutation. This imposes an irreparable constraint as soon as n and p are both odd. Shifts can only produce even permutations in this case.

If we start with an odd permutation, the shifts will never allow us to get an even permutation; notably we will never end up with the identity permutation.

Conversely, as soon as n or p are even, the cyclic shifts create odd or even permutations; even if n and p are both even, the odd permutations created by the shifts give even permutations as soon as they are composed of an even number of shifts.

We will now deal with the most simple cases, with boxes of short dimensions.[15]

19.7.3.1. *Case of the 2×2 square: the game generates the group S_4 of permutations*

To prove it, let us begin by placing the numbers 0 1 2 3 in the square, in this order. The shifts allowed correspond horizontally to the transpositions (0 1) (2 3) and vertically to the transpositions (0 2) (1 3). We know that S_4 is generated by the three transpositions (0 1), (0 2) and (0 3). The game already has (0 1) and (0 2). We check that $(0\ 3) = {}_{\rightarrow}(0\ 1)(1\ 3)(0\ 1)$. Using the four transpositions in the square, we can obtain the three generating transpositions. Our game generates S_4. The line shift (2 3) is superfluous. It can be replaced by:

$$(2\ 3) = {}_{\rightarrow}(2\ 0)\ (0\ 3)\ (2\ 0) = (2\ 0)\ (0\ 1)\ (1\ 3)\ (0\ 1)\ (2\ 0)$$

using the formula $(i\ j) = (i\ q)\ (q\ j)\ (i\ q)$.

What is left is to find out, starting from permutation 0 1 2 3 (which is even) is in how many goes we can obtain a given permutation. Through one of the four transpositions, we get an odd permutation. This therefore gives four odd permutations. They are 1 0 2 3, 0 1 3 2, 2 1 0 3 and 0 3 2 1. Let us carry out a new transposition on each of these four permutations, avoiding returning to the start (since $L_i^2 = Id$). This gives three possibilities for each permutation, i.e. 12 in total. But these permutations are not all different, because:

$$L_0 L_1 = L_1 L_0 \text{ and } C_0 C_1 = C_1 C_0$$

Finally 10 different permutations, all even, remain. They are:

$L_0 L_1 = 1\ 0\ 3\ 2$, $L_0 C_0 = 2\ 0\ 1\ 3$, $L_0 C_1 = 1\ 3\ 2\ 0$, $L_1 C_0 = 3\ 1\ 0\ 2$, $L_1 C_1 = 0\ 2\ 3\ 1$,
$C_0 L_0 = 1\ 2\ 0\ 3$, $C_0 L_1 = 2\ 1\ 3\ 0$, $C_0 C_1 = 2\ 3\ 0\ 1$, $C_1 L_0 = 3\ 0\ 2\ 1$, and
$C_1 L_1 = 0\ 3\ 1\ 2$

15. In fact we can show that the game generates all permutations of S_N when the number N of squares of the rectangle is even, and it generates A_N when the rectangle has an odd number of boxes. For the complete demonstration of the software for this game see [ARF 05].

Note that at this stage all the even permutations (12 of them) were obtained except one, namely 3 2 1 0. This one will be obtained in four goes. Here 3 2 1 0 = $L_0 L_1 C_0 C_1$ or $C_0 C_1 L_0 L_1$. Now let us consider odd permutations obtained in three goes, avoiding re-discovering those obtained before. This gives:

$$L_0 L_1 C_0 = 3\ 0\ 1\ 2,\ L_0 L_1 C_1 = 1\ 2\ 3\ 0,\ L_0 C_0 L_0 = 0\ 2\ 1\ 3,\ L_0 C_0 L_1 = 2\ 0\ 3\ 1$$

$$L_0 C_0 C_1 = 2\ 3\ 1\ 0,\ L_0 C_1 L_0 = 3\ 1\ 2\ 0,\ L_0 C_1 L_1 = 1\ 3\ 0\ 2,\ L_1 C_0 C_1 = 3\ 2\ 0\ 1$$

which exhausts all the remaining odd permutations, noting that there are four ways of obtaining these permutations.[16]

19.7.3.2. *Case of the 3×3 square: the game generates the alternate group A_9*

Let us consider the nine numbers 0 1 2 3 ... 8 displayed line after line in a square, in this order. The line shifts correspond to cycles (0 1 2), (3 4 5) and (6 7 8). The column shifts are (0 3 6), (1 4 7) and (2 5 8). We have to prove that these six cycles generate the alternate group A_9. For this, it is sufficient to prove that they enable us to obtain all the cycles of the form (0 1 k), with k between 2 and $N - 1 = 8$, depending on the property seen in group A_n. Actually, we verify that:

$(0\ 1\ 3) = L_0\, C_0\, L_0^2\, C_0^2$
$(0\ 1\ 4) = C_1\, L_0^2\, C_1^2\, L_0$
$(0\ 1\ 5) = C_2\, L_0\, C_2^2$
$(0\ 1\ 6) = L_0\, C_0^2\, L_0^2\, C_0$
$(0\ 1\ 7) = C_1^2\, L_0^2\, C_1\, L_0$
$(0\ 1\ 8) = C_2^2\, L_0\, C_2$

All these cycles are obtained in four or six goes, and in three or four goes if we accept shifts of one notch from one side or the other.

19.7.3.3. *Case of the 4×4 square: the game generates S_{16}*

First of all, we will show how to get transposition (0 1) through shifts in line 0 and column 0 (see Figure 19.10). Through the shift succession $L_0\ C_0\ L_0^2\ C_0^3$ we get transposition (0 1), but at the same time a cyclic shift (3 4 2) of odd length

16. If we draw the graph whose vertices are the 24 permutations of S_4, placing junction edges when a horizontal or vertical shift enable us to move from one permutation to another, we notice that we can go from any vertex to any other one in at most four goes. We therefore say that the diameter of the graph is equal to 4. The diameter is the maximum number of permutations it takes for us to go from one vertex to another.

happens. Repeating the succession $L_0\ C_0\ L_0^2\ C_0^3$ three times, all the numbers return to their initial place except 0 and 1. These numbers exchange places with each other.[17]

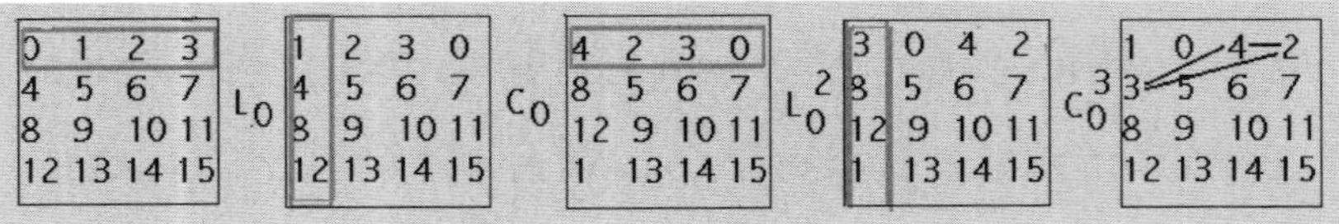

Figure 19.10. *Creation of transposition (0 1)*

What we have just done for transposition (0 1) goes for all transpositions of the form $(i, i + 1)$, provided that the number i is not placed on the right border, with $i + 1$ therefore being on the left border below. With i being different from 3 modulo 4, transposition $(i, i + 1)$ is obtained by $L_i\ C_i\ L_i^2\ C_i^3$.

What is left is to examine the remaining transpositions, here (3 4) (7 8) and (11 12). For (3 4), for example (see Figure 19.11), we begin by moving the 4 back up on line 0, through shift C_0. Next, on line 0, we carry out transposition (0 4) between the boxes numbered 0 and 4. Finally we bring the 3 back down through C_0^{-1}. We know that transposition (0 4) can be written (0 4) = (2 3) (0 2) (2 3), and in turn (0 2) = (1 2) (0 1) (1 2), i.e. (0 4) = (2 3) (1 2) (0 1) (1 2) (2 3), and saw how to do these transpositions of adjacent elements on the same line.

Since the game allows all transpositions of adjacent elements, it enables us to obtain all the permutations of S_{16}. In order to generalize the 4x4 square transpositions, we changed them to any nxp rectangle with even n.

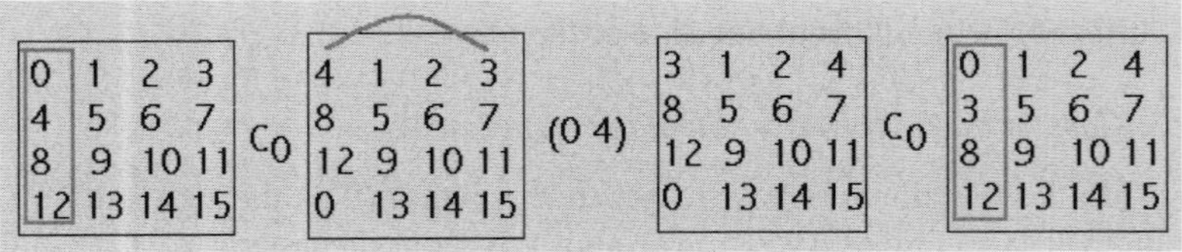

Figure 19.11. *Creation of transposition (3 4)*

---

17. The transposition (0 1) is only possible because cycle (3 4 2) has an odd length. On the other hand if n was odd we would have a cycle of even length and the (0 1) exchange is no longer possible, which is normal because the transposition (0 1) is odd, and we cannot obtain it.

19.7.4. *Exchanges of lines and columns in a square*

Let us consider a 3×3 square, the boxes of which are numbered from 0 to 8. Exercising exchanges of lines or columns, number permutations ensue (see Figure 19.12). We want to find the group of permutations thus generated.

Let the lines be L_0, L_1, L_2 and the columns be C_0, C_1, C_2. Permutations on lines only form one group of permutations. This group assumes two generators, called a and b, i.e. the exchanges (L_0, L_1) and (L_0, L_2). From them, we know that all the permutations of three objects can be obtained. More precisely, the two transpositions a and b generate six permutations on the lines, which are Id, a, ab, aba, b and ba, since the generators follow the relations:

$$a^2 = b^2 = Id \text{ and } (ab)^2 = ba$$

This group is comparable to symmetry group S_3. Similarly, the group generated by exchanges between columns is made up of six permutations and is generated by the two exchanges c and d, i.e. (C_0, C_1) and (C_0, C_2).

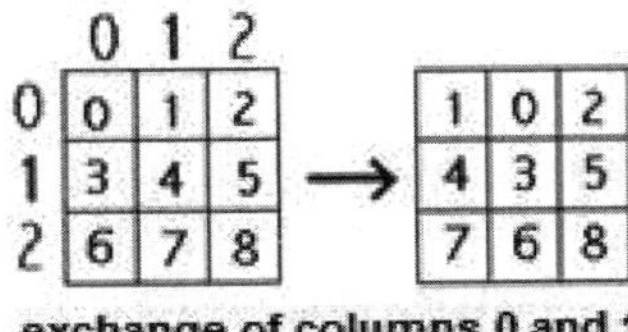

Figure 19.12. *Exchanges of lines or columns in a square*

But what happens when we exercise a mix of exchanges of lines and columns? We can easily see that the exchanges of lines a and b commute with the exchanges of columns c and d. In other words, any permutation in the square that is expressed as a product of the four generators a, b, c and d, can be reduced to a product of two blocks, with the first containing only a and b, and the second only c and d.

We deduce from this that the group of permutations sought is group $S_3{*}S_3$, containing 6×6 = 36 permutations. This group can be defined by relations between generators:

$$a^2 = b^2 = c^2 = c^2 = Id,$$

$$(ab)^2 = ba, \quad (cd)^2 = dc, \quad \text{and}$$

$$(ac)^2 = (ad)^2 = (bc)^2 = (bd)^2 = Id.$$

19.8. Exercises on permutations

19.8.1. *Creating a permutation at random*

If we consider all permutations of N elements to have the same chances of being obtained as each other, each one has as the probability $1 / N!$ of being obtained. How can we create a permutation at random? The simplest method consists of drawing a first number from N numbers, which gives the first element of the permutation, then drawing a second number from N, but avoiding finding the first again, then drawing a third number out of the N, avoiding taking one of the first two numbers again, and so on and so forth until the last number. The program results from it, taking elements of the permutations as numbers from 0 to $N-1$:

```
set an array done[N] to 0
for(i=0; i<N; i++)
{ do  a[i]=random(N);
  while (done[a[i]]==1);
  done[a[i]]=1;
}
```

The inconvenience of this method is that we have to carry out numerous superfluous random draws that return numbers that have already been drawn. There is a way of avoiding this, using the following method.

We begin by placing numbers 0 1 2 ... $N-1$ in an array also indexed from 0 to $N-1$. Then we proceed to modifications starting from the last box and going up to the first.

First of all we draw a number h at random between 0 and $N-1$, and exchange the contents of the boxes numbered h and $N-1$. We have just obtained the last element of the permutation, with equiprobability. Then we draw a number h at random between 0 and $N-2$, and we exchange the contents of boxes h and $N-2$. We have just obtained the penultimate element of the permutation, also with equiprobability. We continue in this way.

When we want to fill in box number i, all those located to its right having been filled definitively, we take a number h at random between 0 and i and exchange the contents of boxes h and i, which fills in box number i with a number that has as many chances of being obtained as any remaining number.

We stop after having filled box number 1, with box number 0 therefore also being filled.

Let us take an example where $N = 5$ with boxes numbered 01234:

i=4 *h*=2 01432;

i=3 *h*=3 01432;

i=2 *h*=0 41032;

i=1 *h*=0 14032.

The program for this example is:

```
fill table a[N] with a[i]=i
for(i=N–1; i>0; i--)
{ h=random(i); aux=a[i];a[i]=a[h];a[h]=aux; }
```

19.8.2. ***Number of permutations*** $\begin{pmatrix} \mathbf{0} & \mathbf{1} & \mathbf{2} & \ldots & \mathbf{n-1} \\ a(\mathbf{0}) & a(\mathbf{1}) & a(\mathbf{2}) & \ldots & a(\mathbf{n-1}) \end{pmatrix}$ ***with n elements 0, 1, 2, …, n – 1, such that*** $|a(i) - i| = 0$ ***or 1***

Let $u(n)$ be the number of these permutations. We notice that for $n = 1$ the only permutation is 0, $u(1) = 1$. For $n = 2$, we find $u(2) = 2$ permutations: 0 1 or 1 0. For $n = 3$ we find $u(3) = 3$ with permutations 0 1 2, 0 2 1 and 1 0 2. In the general case, when we split up the permutations into disjoint cycles, we notice that the only possible cycles are a fixed point or a cycle with two successive elements. There are two primitive blocks one or two units long (see Figure 19.13). To get the $u(n)$ permutations, we separate them into two categories: those beginning with cycle (0), hence $u(n - 1)$ cases for the remaining elements; and those beginning with cycle (0 1), hence $u(n - 2)$ cases.

Lastly $u(n) = u(n - 1) + u(n - 2)$. With the initial conditions $u(0) = 1$ and $u(1) = 1$, we have Fibonacci numbers shifted one notch, i.e.:

$$u(n) = F(n + 1).$$

The generating function is $1 / (1 - x - x^2)$.

Figure 19.13. *The two cycles making up primitive blocks*

For example, for $n = 5$ we get the permutations 1 2 3 4 5, 1 2 3 5 4, 1 2 4 3 5, 1 3 2 4 5, 1 3 2 5 4, 2 1 3 4 5, 2 1 3 5 4, 2 1 4 3 5 and $u(5) = 8$.[18]

Now let us return to these cyclic permutations, with $a(i) - i = 0$ or ± 1 modulo n, which adds two extra possibilities $a(0) = n - 1$ and $a(n - 1) = 0$. Let $v(n)$ be the number of these permutations. We check that $v(0) = 1$, $v(1) = 1$ and $v(2) = 2$ as before, but $v(3) = 6$ with the permutations 0 1 2, 0 2 1, 1 0 2, 1 2 0, 2 0 1 and 2 1 0. In addition to primitive blocks made up of one fixed point or one cycle of two successive elements, this now being done via modulo n: we get two new primitive n-length blocks, i.e. the cycles:

$$(0, 1, 2, 3, \ldots, n - 1) \text{ and } (0, n - 1, n - 2, \ldots, 1)$$

which are distinguished from the previous ones as soon as $n > 2$. We classify the $v(n)$ permutations based on their initial primitive block: either (0), hence $u(n - 1)$ cases for the remaining elements; or (0 1), hence $u(n - 2)$ cases; or $(0, n - 1)$ hence $u(n - 2)$ cases; or $(0, 1, 2,\ldots, n - 1)$ hence one case; and similarly with $(0, n - 1, n - 2, \ldots, 1)$. The recurrence formula is expressed:

$$v(n) = u(n - 1) + 2u(n - 2) + 2 \text{ for } n > 2$$

Let us determine the generating function $F(x)$ of the sequence $(v(n))$, calling $G(x)$ that of $(u(n))$:

$$F(x) - v(0) - v(1)x - v(2)x^2 = v(3)x^3 + v(4)x^4 + v(5)x^5 + \ldots$$

$$= (u(2) + 2u(1) + 2)x^3 + (u(3) + 2u(2) + 2)x^4 + \ldots$$

$$= (u(2)x^3 + u(3)x^4 + \ldots) + 2\,(u(1)x^3 + u(2)x^4 + \ldots) + 2\,(x^3 + x^4 + \ldots)$$

$$= xG(x) - u(0)x - u(1)x^2 + 2x^2G(x) - 2u(0)x^2 + 2x^3/(1 - x).$$

With $G(x) = 1 / (1 - x - x^2)$, we finally find that:

18. Another method for arriving at the result consists of re-writing these permutations replacing $a(k)$ with $a(k) - k$, which gives words n characters long based on the three letters 0,1 and -1. In these words, blocks of two characters can only be 00, 01, -10, -11, 10 or 1-1 with the blocks, 0-1, -1-1 and 11 being impossible. There is bijection between the permutations that concern us and the words n characters based on three letters 0, 1, -1 with no block 0-1, -1-1 or 11. This means that these words are all made up of 0 and blocks 1-1. This can be seen as words of n characters based on lines of one character (0s) and lines of two characters (i.e. blocks 1-1). Hence their number, $F(n + 1)$.

$$F(x) = 1 - x^2 + (x + 2x^2) / (1 - x - x^2) + 2x^3 / (1 - x).$$

19.8.3. *Permutations with a(i) – i = ±1 or ±2*

Here again, decomposition into disjoint cycles enables us to determine the primitive blocks. Only cycles or possible compositions of cycles are represented in Figure 19.14.

Figure 19.14. *The cycles making up the primitive blocks*

It is the same for cycles of greater length, for example if n is odd, we have two cycles of the form: and *vice versa*. Classifying the $u(n)$ permutations according to their initial primitive block, we find the recurrence relation: $u(n) = u(n - 2) + u(n - 4) + 2\,(u(n - 3) + u(n - 4) + \ldots + u(0))$ for $n > 3$.

The initial conditions are $u(0) = 1$, $u(1) = 0$ and $u(2) = 1$, either the permutation 1 0, $u(3) = 2$, or the permutations 1 2 0 and 2 0 1. The recurrence formula then gives $u(4) = 4$, which corresponds to the permutations 1 0 3 2, 1 3 0 2, 2 0 3 1 and 2 3 0 1. The associated generating function $F(x)$ verifiers are:

$$F(x) - u(0) - u(1)x - u(2)x^2 - u(3)x^3$$
$$= x^2F(x) - u(0)x^2 - u(1)x^3 + x^4F(x) + 2(x^3F(x) - u(0)x^3 + x^4F(x) + x^5F(x)$$
$$+ x^6F(x) + \ldots)$$

This gives:

$$F(x) - 1 - x^2 - 2x^3 = x^2F(x) - x^2 + x^4F(x) + 2x^3F(x) / (1 - x) - 2x^3$$

We deduce from it that:

$$F(x) = (1 - x) / (1 - x - x^2 - x^3 - x^4 + x^5).$$

19.8.4. *Permutations with n elements 0, 1, 2, …, n – 1 without two consecutive elements*

We are interested in permutations where no block $a(i)\, a(i + 1)$ is made up of two consecutive numbers. Let $u(n)$ be the number of such permutations. We have $u(0) = 1$, $u(1) = 1$ and $u(2) = 1$, i.e. the permutation 1 0, $u(3) = 3$, with the permutations 0 2 1, 1 0 2, 2 1 0 and $u(4) = 11$, with the permutations 0 2 1 3, 0 3 2 1, 1 0 3 2, 1 3 0 2, 1 3 2 0, 2 0 3 1, 2 1 0 3, 2 1 3 0, 3 0 2 1, 3 1 0 2 and 3 2 1 0.

To find $u(n)$, let us take the context of the sieve formula. The objects concerned are all permutations of n elements, i.e. $n!$. Let us define $n-1$ properties:

– property 1 means that the permutation has the block 01;

– property 2 expresses the presence of the block 12 in the permutation, …,

– property $n-1$ expresses the presence of block $n-2, n-1$.

We want to find out the number $u(n)$ of permutations with none of these properties. To get the number $|A_1|$ of permutations with at least block 01, we begin by placing this block, which is done in $n-1$ ways. Then we put the remaining elements in all possible orders, i.e. $(n-2)!$ ways. In total, this makes $(n-1)!$ cases. It is the same for $|A_2|$, etc. Finally:

$$S_1 = (n-1)(n-1)! = C_{n-1}^{\ 1}\,(n-1)!$$

To get the number $|A_{12}|$ of permutations with blocks 01 and 12, i.e. at least block 012, there are $n-2$ ways to place it, and the remaining elements can be placed in $(n-3)!$ ways, i.e. $(n-2)!$ ways in all.

To get the number $|A_{13}|$ of permutations with blocks 01 and 23, we notice that we get exactly the same result. Whether the blocks are stuck together or separated, we find $(n-2)!$ cases. The choice of two blocks is made in $C_{n-1}^{\ 2}$ ways, hence:

$$S_2 = C_{n-1}^{\ 2}\,(n-2)!$$

Similarly $S_3 = C_{n-1}^{\ 3}(n-3)!$. And so on and so forth. Finally:

$$u(n) = S_0 - S_1 + S_2 - \ldots + (-1)^{n-1} S_{n-1}$$

$$= \sum_{k=0}^{n-1} (-1)^k C_{n-1}^k (n-k)! = \sum_{k=0}^{n} (-1)^k \frac{n-k}{k!}(n-1)! = (n-1)! \sum_{k=0}^{n} (-1)^k \frac{n-k}{k!}$$

$$= n! \sum_{k=0}^{n} \frac{(-1)^k}{k!} + (n-1)! \sum_{k=1}^{n} \frac{(-1)^{k-1}}{(k-1)!} = n! \sum_{k=0}^{n} \frac{(-1)^k}{k!} + (n-1)! \sum_{k=0}^{n-1} \frac{(-1)^k}{k!}$$

$$= d(n) + d(n-1)$$

where $d(n)$ is the number of derangements of n elements.

From the first values of $d(n)$ starting at $d(0)$: 1, 0, 1, 2, 9, 44, 265, we find the first values of $u(n)$: 1, 1, 1, 3, 11, 53, 309.

19.8.5. *Permutations with n elements 0, 1, 2, …, n – 1, made up of a single cycle in which no two consecutive elements modulo n are found*

If it is reduced, modulo n indicates that we also refuse the succession of numbers $n - 1$, 0 in the cycle. With $v(n)$ being the number of these permutations, which we will write in the form of a cycle beginning with 0, we notice that $v(0) = 1$, $v(1) = 1$, $v(2) = 0$ and $v(3) = 1$, i.e. the permutations made up of the cycle (0 2 1), $v(4) = 1$, namely (0 3 2 1), $v(4) = 8$, with (0 2 1 4 3), (0 2 4 1 3), (0 2 4 3 1), (0 3 1 4 2), (0 3 2 4 1), (0 4 1 3 2), (0 4 2 1 3) and (0 4 3 2 1).

To find $v(n)$, we consider all the permutations to be written in the form of a unique cycle, and define properties analogous to those of the previous example, but there are n of them this time. Property 1 expresses that block 01 is present in the cycle. And so on up to property n indicating that the cycle contains block $n - 1$, 0. We want to find out the number $v(n)$ of permutations that have none of these properties. Let us recall that there are $(n - 1)!$ permutations written in the form of a unique cycle (we take all the permutations of n objects, i.e. $n!$, then group them in parcels of n resulting from cyclic shifts, which makes $(n - 1)!$ cyclic expressions).

As in the example above, we find:

$$S_0 = (n - 1)!$$

then $|A_1| = (n - 2)\,!$, $|A_2| = (n - 2)!$ also by starting the expression of the cycle at 12, hence $S_1 = n\,(n - 2)!$. Similarly $S_2 = C_n^{\,2}\,(n - 3)!$, … and $S_n = 1$. Finally:

$$v(n) = (n - 1)! - C_n^{\,1}\,(n - 2)! + C_n^{\,2}\,(n - 3)! - \ldots + (-1)^{n-1}\,C_n^{\,n-1}\,0! + (-1)^n\,C_n^{\,n}$$

Let us check that $v(n) + v(n + 1) = d(n)$, with $d(n)$ being the number of derangements. For this, we calculate:

$$v(n+1) + v(n) = n! - (C_{n+1}^{\,1} - C_n^{\,0})(n - 1)! + (C_{n+1}^{\,2} - C_n^{\,1})(n - 2)! - \ldots$$

$$+(-1)^n\,(C_{n+1}^{\,n} - C_n^{\,n-1})0\,! + (-1)^{n+1}\,(1 - 1)$$

Checking that $C_{n+1}^{\,k} - C_n^{\,k-1} = n!\,/\,k!$, what remains is:

$$v(n+1) + v(n) = (-1)^k\,n!\,/\,k\,! = d(n)$$

The first terms of the $v(n)$ sequence are 1, 1, 0, 1, 1, 8, 36, 229, 1,625, 13,208, 120,299.

To create the program that enumerates these permutations, we have to make a tree structure from root 0 located at level 1. Each time we take the successors of element i, which must be different from i, $i + 1$ and the predecessors going back up in the tree up to the root. We stop and display the result (the branch of the tree) when we arrive at level N, which is the length of the permutation, and when we do not have element $N - 1$ (for $N > 1$) at this level:

```
main()
  { ancestor[0]= -1; tree(0,1); }

void tree(int i,int level)
{int j,k,son[N];
 if (level==N && i!=N–1)      /* only works for N>1 */
   { number++; printf("%4.0ld: ",number); listiancestors(i,level);
    for(k=1;k<=N;k++) printf("%d ",d[k]); printf("\n");
   }
 else
   { k=0;
     for(j=0; j<N; j++)
     if (j!=i && j!=0 && j!=i+1 && belongstoantecedent(j,i)==NO)
          { son[k]=j; ancestor[son[k]]=i; tree(son[k],level+1);k++ ; }
   }
}
int belongstoantecedent(int j, int i)
  { if (j==i) return YES;
    if (j!=i && ancestor[i]==-1) return NO;
    if (ancestor[i]!=-1) belongstoantecedent(j,ancestor[i]);
  }

void listiancestors(int i,int level)
{ int k;
 if (i!=0)  { d[level]=i;  listiancestors(ancestor[i],level-1);}
}
```

19.8.6. *Involute permutations*

We say that a permutation p is an involution when its square – its repetition twice provides the identity. The objective is to determine all the permutations that are involutions, or even the square roots of the unit (identity *Id*). For this, we use the decomposition into disjoint cycles. The identity permutation *Id* boils down to n cycles of unit length: (1) (2) ... (n). We want to get $p^2 = Id$. If permutation p assumed cycles of an odd length greater than one unit, repeating the permutation to get p^2 would mean taking the elements of these cycles two by two. This would again give cycles of the same length, therefore greater than one, which is impossible if we want to obtain the identity.

The only acceptable cycles of odd length are those of length one unit. Cycles of even length remain. Taking elements two by two to get p^2 splits up each one of these cycles into two cycles of half length. As in the end we can only have cycles of length one unit, the only cycles of even length for p are two units long. Permutation p cannot only have cycles one or two units long. This necessary condition is also sufficient.

We now need to find the number of such permutations with n elements. For this, we distinguish them according to their number k of two-element cycles, with k between 0 and $[n / 2]$. Notably, there is only one single involute permutation with no two-element cycle, the identity *Id*.

Let us move on to the general case with k. Let us begin by taking a first two-element cycle. This means choosing two out of n elements, i.e. C_n^2 cases. Having done this, we take a second two-element cycle, which means choosing two elements out of the remaining $n - 2$, i.e. C_{n-2}^2 cases. Each time we do the same with the remaining elements, until we get the kth cycle. We therefore end up with $C_n^2\, C_{n-2}^2\, C_{n-4}^2 \dots C_{n-2k}^2$ cases.

By proceeding in this way, we have taken the cycles in a certain order, whereas order does not come into play for decomposing a permutation into disjoint cycles. The same permutation is thus repeated $k!$ times, i.e. as many times as there are ways of permuting the two-element cycles. Finally the number of permutations with k cycles two units long, with the rest being one unit long, is:

$$C_n^2\, C_{n-2}^2\, C_{n-4}^2 \dots C_{n-2k}^2 \,/\, k! = \frac{n!}{2^k\, k!\,(n-k)!}$$

The number of involute n-length permutations is:

$$\sum_{k=0}^{[n/2]} \frac{n!}{2^k\, k!\,(n-2k)!}$$

Starting from $n = 1$, and up to $n = 12$, we find the number of involutions:

1, 2, 4, 10, 26, 76, 232, 764, 2,620, 9,496, 35,696 and 140,152.

19.8.7. *Increasing subsequences in a permutation*

Any permutation can be split up into blocks, in each of which the elements follow each other in ascending order, with these blocks being separated by drops. We begin by taking care of the first increasing subsequence, i.e. the sequence of elements located at the beginning of the permutation that continue increasing from the first element, and this happens until the first drop. We are interested in its length L, which goes from 1 to n. For example, the permutation 1 5 6 8 9 7 2 4 3 of nine elements has the first increasing sub-sequence 1 5 6 8 9 where $L = 5$ units long.

a) Determine the number of permutations whose first increasing subsequence has a certain length L.

Let us turn our interest to permutations where the first increasing sub-sequence has a length L greater than or equal to a given number k. This means that the k first elements are in ascending order, and the $n - k$ other elements do not obey any constraints of the arrangement. There are C_n^k ways of taking k out of n elements. In each one of these cases, these k elements can be arranged in any way, which makes $(n - k)!$ ways. We have just obtained $C_n^k\,(n - k)!$ permutations so that $L \geq k$, i.e. $n!\,/\,k!$ out of the $n!$ possible permutations. The permutations where $L = k$ are obtained by removing those so $L \geq k + 1$ (except for $k = n$) from those with a length $L \geq k$. The number of these permutations is:

$$n!\,/\,k! - n!\,/\,(k+1)! = n!\,k\,/\,(k+1)! \text{ when } k < n$$

For $k = n$, there is only the *Id* permutation, all of whose elements are in ascending order. Taking L as random variable, we will deduce the law of L from it, i.e. the probability $p(L = k)$ that L has a certain length, as well as the average length of the first increasing subsequence in permutations with n elements. Using the result above:

$$p(L = k) = k\,/\,(k+1)! \text{ when } k \neq n, \text{ and } p(L = n) = 1\,/\,n!,$$

where the average length $E(L)$ of the first increasing subsequence is equal to:

$$E(L) = 1\,p(L = 1) + 2\,p(L = 2) + ... + n\,p(L = n)$$

$$= 1(p(L \geq 1) - p(L \geq 2)) + 2(p(L \geq 1) - p(L \geq 2)) + 3(p(L \geq 2) - p(L \geq 3)) + \dots + n\,p(L \geq n)$$

$$= p(L \geq 1) + p(L \geq 2) + ... + p(L \geq n)$$

$$= 1 / 1! + 1 / 2! + 1 / 3! + ... + 1 / n!$$

When n is large, $E(L)$ is approximately equal to $e - 1$.

b) Determine the average number of increasing subsequences in permutations with n elements.

Two successive increasing subsequences are separated by a drop. The last element a_i of the first subsequence is followed by the first element a_{i+1} of the next, and we have: $a_i > a_{i+1}$. Let N be the number of increasing subsequences in a permutation. N is between 1 and n, and the number of intermediate drops is equal to $N - 1$. As we cannot obtain the law of N in the general case, let us just search for its average value.

For this, let us introduce the random variables X_k, equal to 1 if $a_k > a_{k+1}$ and 0 if not, where k is between 0 to $n - 2$, and where the elements of the permutation go from a_0 to a_{n-1}. For each one of these values of k, there is a one in two chance that $a_k > a_{k+1}$ and a one in two chance that $a_k < a_{k+1}$.

Variables X_k all follow a Bernoulli law with parameter 1 / 2, and their average value is also equal to 1 / 2. These values are linked by N through $N = X_0 + X_1 + X_2 + ... + X_{n-2} + 1$. The average values are also added, and the average number of increasing subsequences is: $E(N) = (n + 1) / 2$.

19.8.8. *Riffle shuffling of type O and I for N cards when N is a power of 2*

Let us assume that $N = 2^k$. The cards are numbered from 0 to $N - 1$, and their numbers are expressed in binary in the form of words k characters long: $a_0\, a_1 \ldots a_{k-1}$. Under the effect of shuffle O (defined in section 19.7.2 for even N), these binary numbers undergo a shift of one notch:

$$a_0\, a_1 \ldots a_{k-1} \rightarrow a_1\, a_2 \ldots a_{k-1}\, a_0$$

The period of the shuffle is k, which corresponds to an order of 2 modulo $2^k - 1$. The group generated by O is cyclic, of order k.

Under the effect of *I*, binary numbers also undergo a shift with a slight modification:

$$a_0\, a_1 \ldots a_{k-1} \rightarrow a_1\, a_2 \ldots a_{k-1}\, \underline{a}_0$$

where $\underline{a}_0$ is equal to 1 if a_0 is 0 and *vice versa*.

At the end of *k* shuffles, the numbers are $\underline{a}_0\, \underline{a}_1 \ldots \underline{a}_{k-1}$. It is only at the end of 2*k* shuffles that we again come across the initial numbers. The period of the shuffle is 2*k*, which corresponds to second order modulo $2^k + 1$. The group generated by *I* is cyclic of the order 2*k*.

Under the effect of $_{\rightarrow}OI$, each number undergoes the transformation:

$$a_0\, a_1 \ldots a_{k-1} \rightarrow a_2\, a_3 \ldots a_{k-1}\, a_0\, \underline{a}_1$$

If *k* is even, at the end of *k* / 2 goes we end up with $a_0\, \underline{a}_1\, a_2\, \underline{a}_3 \ldots \underline{a}_{k-1}$. We need *k* / 2 more goes to find the initial numbers. The period of the shuffle is *k*. If *k* is odd, at the end of *k* goes we come across $\underline{a}_0\, \underline{a}_1 \ldots \underline{a}_{k-1}$ and *k* more goes are needed to find the initial numbers. The period of the shuffle is 2*k*. The group generated by *OI* is cyclic of *k* or 2*k* order, depending on whether *k* is odd or even.

Now let us take group *G* generated by *O* and *I*. This group already contains the subgroup generated by *O*, of *k* order. Now let us take the *k* shuffles M_j of the form $M_j = O^{j-1}\, I\, O^{-j}$, with *k* between 0 and $k-1$:

– for $j = 0$, this gives the passage: $a_0\, a_1 \ldots a_{k-1} \rightarrow a_0\, a_1 \ldots \underline{a}_{k-1}$;

– for $j = 1$, this makes: $a_0\, a_1 \ldots a_{k-1} \rightarrow \underline{a}_0\, a_1 \ldots a_{k-1}$; and

– for some *j*, it is $a_0\, a_1 \ldots a_{j-1} \ldots a_{k-1} \rightarrow a_0\, a_1 \ldots \underline{a}_{j-1} \ldots a_{k-1}$.

The only change comes from the number placed in position $j - 1$ [*k*]. The subgroup generated by M_j (*j* from 0 to $k - 1$) is such that for each number of cards, a_0 remains a_0 or is transformed into $\underline{a}_0$; a_1 remains a_1 or gives $\underline{a}_1$; and similarly for each binary number. It is therefore made up of 2^k elements.

On the other hand, as $I = O^{-j+1} M_j\, O_j$, the group generated by *O* and *I* is the same as the group generated by *O* and M_j. The subgroups generated by *O* and M_j have nothing else in common other than the identity. The number of elements generated by *O* and M_j is therefore $k\, 2^k$.

PART 2

Probability

Part 2

Introduction

Part 2 is not the same as typical probabilities course books. In this field, there is a legion of course books and exercise books, especially those aimed at preparatory classes in elite business schools, where probability is an important part of the program. These are reference books for introduction to probability (e.g. [HAR 79, MAL 02]).[1]

The characteristics of Part 2 are the following:

– *Priority for combinatorics on words*. On the basis of these, probability theory boils down to counting events. This gives an immediate and concrete view of probabilities. The theory part will also end up being simplified by this, for example we will not probabilistically reformulate sieve formula, which is already extensively dealt with in combinatorics in the previous part.

– *The importance of examples and application exercises is greater than the course itself.* Only concept manipulation enables examples and exercises to be assimilated. Dealing with examples and particular cases is indispensable before arriving at the general case. We too frequently see students mechanically applying formulae that have nothing to do with the question asked, and thus covered by the prestige of theory and nomenclature they arrive at absurd results, for example finding a probability greater than 1. The first thing to do is immerse ourselves in the problem. If we are talking about throwing balls into boxes, we should first put ourselves in the thrower's shoes. Thus returning to reality, we will notice that when all is said and done, a small number of formulae are to be used.

1. Let us also cite two classic works on the subject [CHU 74, FOA03], and for an initial introduction [JAC 00].

– *The importance of creating and using generating functions through transition graphs*. This all-powerful tool, at least in all problems where we expect a certain event to occur, will be constructed from graph drawings. This can be considered to be practical work, even a game. It is about translating a problem into a drawing, and this can require several drafts before arriving at the final one.

– *The fundamental role of experimenting using computers.* Most examples dealt with in this book produce programs.[2] There is always great satisfaction in finding experimental results that agree with theoretical results. When theory proves to be powerless, like in many problems close to reality, and therefore complex, computer processing is the only possible answer.[3]

– *The importance of discrete (discontinuous) probabilities.* These probabilities concern problems where there is a finite number of possible cases or an infinite number when they numbered by an integer. Every introduction to probability starts here. The path to probabilities is termed continuous where the infinite numbers of possible cases are, for example, the various positions of a point on a straight line. This opens new perspectives. It is, however, a passage that borders on discrete phenomena, and in any case computer processing requires a division into discretized cases.

Organization of Part 2

Initially, probability theory is the preferred field of application in combinatorics. It always involves adding a certain number of results. Let us take a simple example. Imagine a box contains four red balls and six black balls, and we draw one ball at random. Using common sense or intuition acquired over time, it is natural to say that there are four in 10 chances of getting a red ball. More specifically, let us give a number to each ball, from 1 to 10, with the red balls being 1 to 4. This does not change the problem in any way. When a ball is drawn, we are just as likely to get ball 1 as ball 2, etc. There are 10 possible cases. If we are now interested in drawing a red ball, there are four "favorable" cases corresponding to this event. The probability of getting a red ball is none other than the number of favorable cases divided by the number of possible cases. This argument applies to all sorts of problems, which amount to combinatorics on words – even weighted words – whose letters are represented by numbers. We will see this in Chapter 20.

---

2. Recall that our programs are written in *C* language. They are easily convertible into syntax-type similar languages, such as Pascal or Basic. In my webpages (ai.univ-paris8.fr/~audibert/) you can find some complementary works on probabilities, with complete programs included (in *C* language with *SDL*).

3. [KNU 73] or Chapter 35 of [SED 91] can also be consulted for an introduction to random number programming.

Nevertheless, let us indicate that intuition or common sense, and even the experience of an informed player, can prove to be inoperative.[4] As Borel said:

> "It is above all the habit of games of chance that renders some minds refractory to the notion of independence of successive events; as they observed, in a long series, that tossing heads or tails is almost equally numerous, they conclude from this that a long series of tosses having lead to tails must be followed by a heads toss: it is a debt that the game owed them. All we need to do is to think about it a bit to convince ourselves to what extent this anthropomorphism is perilous: the reasons for which chances of heads or tails are equal remain in each match and we cannot conceive any mechanism by which the results of previous matches could modify the equality of chances. This anthropomorphic belief in memory and conscience of the coin therefore does not have any positive basis." [BOR 38]

Certain probability results sometimes seem surprising and unexpected. A good example is what we call the birthday paradox.

The birthday paradox

Here is the problem: a box contains N balls numbered from 1 to N. We make P repeated draws of one ball taken at random, which we replace in the box each time. We want to find out the probability $p(N, P)$ that the same ball will be drawn at least twice during P draws. First let us search for the probability that during P draws all the balls drawn are different. The favorable cases correspond to choosing P different numbers out of N numbers, taking order into consideration,[5] i.e. A_N^P. As for the number of possible cases, there are N^P,[6] hence the probability is equal to A_N^P / N^P. The probability requested is deduced from this by complementarity:

$$p(N, P) = 1 - A_N^P / N^P$$

4. See Galileo's problem, found in Chapter 1 (section 1.4). This chapter gave a quick historical perspective. For more details, [BAR 04, BER 98, COU 08, RIC 07] can be referred to.

5. Let us recall that in order to do this, we begin by choosing the first out of the N numbers, i.e. N cases. Each time we do this, we choose the second number out of the $N - 1$ remaining, and so on and so forth, until the Pth number, chosen out of the $N - P + 1$ remaining. Hence the formula giving A_N^P, the number of arrangements of P out of N objects, seen in Chapter 2: $A_N^P = N(N-1)(N-2)\ldots(N-P+1)$.

6. Let us recall that we are dealing with the number of applications of a P-element set in a N-element set. The first ball drawn is one of the N balls. Because we put it back into the box, each time the second ball drawn it is one of the N balls. And so on and so forth until the Pth ball, hence N^P cases.

Now let us imagine that we have a group of 23 people chosen at random, in the sense that their birthdays are random numbers. The probability that two of these people are born on the same day of the year is exactly $p(365, 23)$. We get a result very slightly greater than 0.5. There is a little more than a one out of two chance that in a group of 23 people two were born on the same day. It is this surprising result that we call the birthday paradox. Even more surprising, this probability quickly increases when the number of people grows, for example for 30 people the probability moves to $p(365, 30) = 0.7$.[7]

Probabilities and computer science

Originating from combinatorics, probability formulae have a certain autonomy, especially when we are dealing with events that are not equiprobable. They are even more autonomous when we move from discrete probabilities to continuous probabilities.

Combinatorics counting is mainly adapted to discrete probabilities, when elementary events have a non-null probability, and are of a finite number, or even an infinite but countable number. If we consider continuous probabilities to be made by moving from summations to integrals, where bar diagrams are replaced by areas delimited by curves, however, discretization is always underlying. This phenomenon is that much more striking when dealing with probability problems on computers. There is therefore no escape: all problems must be discretized. Using experiments to deal with probabilities on a computer benefits from the capacity of machines to complete millions of tests in a just few moments. A player in the real world would not be able to complete this many tests a lifetime.

In Chapter 21 we will see how probability problems are dealt with on a computer, with results that follow theory well, at least when it gives an answer to the question asked. In Chapter 22 we will see the link between discrete and continuous phenomena, especially how to create discrete phenomena from the continuous ones.

Probabilities – the link between combinatorics and graphs

As we saw in Part 1, the use of generating functions is a key tool in problem solving. It is the same in probabilities. This method was notably promoted in

---

7. Generalizing this problem, the link between combinatorics and probability is again specified. We will see in Chapter 20 (section 20.2.6) that the probability of getting k different balls out of the P balls drawn with replacement in the box containing N balls is: $p(N, P, k) = S(P, k)\, A_N^k / N^P$ where $S(P, k)$ is the number of partitions of a P-element set in k parts, i.e. a Stirling number of the second kind, the formula for which we saw in Chapter 8.

Graham, Knuth, and Patashnik's book [GRA 94]. In dealing with problems, the generating function associated with probabilities constitutes a concentration of information. It enables us to extract all the results linked to an experiment. In order to find it, a good, easily comprehensible method involves using the drawing of a graph, with its nodes and junction arrows. Such graphs, called transition graphs, are types of machines for creating words weighted by their probabilities. These probabilities are obtained when we circulate on the graph, by moving from an initial node to a final node. The generating function will be deduced from the transition graph by solving a system of equations, or if you prefer by matrix processing, as we will see in Chapters 23 and 24.

After that, numerous examples can be dealt with. A game as simple as repeated tosses of heads or tails opens up many perspectives (Chapter 25). We are indebted Feller for his remarkable book on this subject [FEL 71]. Being placed in a binary universe notably enables us to deal with a classic problem – that of gambler's ruin or fortune. This is found again in the random movement of a particle – one step forward or one step backward – over various forms of networks (Chapter 26). This is also called the drunken man's walk [MLO 08]. The use of generating functions and transition graphs, whereas it does not enable us to solve all problems, is perfectly adapted to all waiting problems. In such problems, a game is repeated until a certain configuration is obtained. This is the aim of Chapter 27. As our aim is to concretely manipulate basic concepts, the final chapter (Chapter 28) deals with various examples, including the Google search engine.

Chapter 20

Reminders about Discrete Probabilities

In this chapter, we place ourselves in the framework of a game, also called a test or experiment. For example, the throwing of a die or playing heads or tails three times. This game leads to results called *elementary events*. The throwing of a die gives the six elementary events 1, 2, 3, 4, 5 and 6. Playing heads (written *H*) or tails (written *T*) three times gives eight elementary events, *HHH*, *HHT*, *HTH*, *HTT*, *THH*, *THT*, *TTH* and *TTT*. Playing heads or tails until heads is obtained for the first time gives an infinite number of elementary events: *H*, *TH*, *TTH*, *TTTH*, etc. The set of these elementary events is called the *space of possibles*. A number between 0 and 1, called probability, is attributed to each elementary event. We know that when throwing a die, provided that the die is not loaded, there is a one in six chance of getting the 3: the probability of this event is 1/6. The probability of getting *HHT*, when playing the game of heads or tails three times is 1/8, as there is a one in eight chance of this occurring, when heads has as many chances of coming out as tails. Thus we have a certain distribution of probabilities over elementary events. The events are weighted by these probabilities between 0 and 1, where the 1 corresponds to the sure event. For example, in throwing a die, the probability of getting the 1 or 2 or 3 or 4 or 5 or 6 is equal to 1. Note that this refers to adding back the six probabilities of 1/6.

In the context of the game, of which we know the possible results, we are interested in precisely one event. This is not necessarily reduced to an elementary event, but can be made up of several of these events. Its probability is obtained by adding the probabilities of the elementary events of which it is composed. For example, the probability of getting an even result when throwing the die is:

$$p(2 \text{ or } 4 \text{ or } 6) = 1/6 + 1/6 + 1/6 = 1/2$$

20.1 And/or in probability theory

Now let us take two events A and B that have nothing in common: we say that they are incompatible. Like elementary events, we therefore have the property with $p()$ that designates a probability: $p(A \text{ or } B) = p(A) + p(B)$.[1] It is enough to break down each one of the two events into its elementary events, and add the corresponding probabilities. For example, the probability of getting either an even number or the 1 when throwing the die is equal to $1 / 2 + 1 / 6 = 4 / 6$. But that of getting an even number or getting the 2 boils down to getting an even number, i.e. 1/2, where the initial events concerned are no longer incompatible, and where the 2 is part of the even numbers.

A formula results from the above. When the elementary events that make up an event are equiprobable, the probability of getting this event is equal to the number of favorable cases corresponding to the event concerned divided by the number of cases possible. For example, in a game of heads or tails repeated three times, the probability of finally getting heads twice is equal to:

$$p(HHT \text{ or } HTH \text{ or } HHT) = p(HHT) + p(HTH) + p(HHT)$$

$$= 1 / 8 + 1 / 8 + 1 / 8 = 3 / 8$$

and it is the number of favorable cases over the number of possible cases.

Another property of probabilities is attached to the notion of conditional probability where we are interested in one event, knowing that another has already happened: $p(A \mid B)$ means $p(A \text{ knowing } B)$, and we get the formula:

$$p(A \text{ and } B) = p(A)\, p(B \mid A) \text{ or even:}$$

$$= p(B)\, p(A \mid B)$$

Let us check this formula using an example: we pull one card from 52 cards, and we want to find out the probability of getting the king of hearts, using the formula above. We notice that $p(\text{king of hearts}) = 1 / 52$, $p(\text{king}) = 4 / 52$, $p(\text{heart}) = 13 / 52$, $p(\text{king} \mid \text{heart}) = 1 / 13$ and $p(\text{heart} \mid \text{king}) = 1 / 4$. The probability of getting the king of hearts is $p(\text{king and heart}) = p(\text{king})\, p(\text{heart} \mid \text{king})$, and again we find the same result in the two calculations:

1. The general formula is deduced from it with certain events, not necessarily incompatible ones: $p(A \text{ or } B) = p(A) + p(B) - p(A \text{ and } B)$. As the *or* is a synonym for the union of events, and the *and* signifies their intersection, again we find the formula already seen in the sieve formula (see Chapter 8).

$$p(\text{king and heart}) = 1 / 52 \text{ and } p(\text{king})\, p(\text{heart} \mid \text{king}) = (4 / 52)(1 / 4) = 1 / 52$$

and it is also equal to $p(\text{heart})\, p(\text{king} \mid \text{heart}) = (13 / 52)(1 / 13) = 1 / 52$.

The formula is simplified when events A and B have no influence on each other. They are said to be independent. In this case, we get:

$$p(A \mid B) = p(A),$$

and the formula amounts to:

$$p(A \text{ and } B) = p(A)\, p(B) \text{ with } A \text{ and } B \text{ being independent.}$$

In summary we have the two fundamental formulae, which are considered axioms in probability theory:

$$\text{proba(A or B)} = \text{proba(A)} + \text{proba(B)}$$

when the events are incompatible (they have nothing in common). We get:

$$\text{proba(A and B)} = \text{proba(A) proba(B)}$$

when the events are independent (no influence on each other).

In other words, under certain conditions, the *or* becomes an addition and the *and* becomes a multiplication when moving from events to probabilities.

Probabilities, which are numbers included between 0 and 1, are attributed to elementary events where there sum is equal to 1. This corresponds to the sure event, where everything can happen. In the case of the equiprobability of elementary events, the probability of an event is the relationship between the number of favorable elementary events belonging to the event concerned, over the number of possible events:

$$proba(\text{event}) = \frac{\text{number of favorable cases}}{\text{number of possible cases}}$$

when all possible cases are equiprobable.

The calculation of a probability as a relationship between the number of favorable cases over that of possible cases is particularly simple when we are doing it directly. This implies that all events concerned are equiprobable, and of a finite number. This is not always the case.

In the problems where events are not visibly equiprobable, a practical rule is necessary: when we have a probability problem where objects that look identical are present (for example balls or die or white balls), these objects are well and truly all different.

When dealing with a problem we should differentiate the objects, for example by giving them different colors or numbering them. And so we will find ourselves in the midst of equiprobable events.

It is exactly these probability questions that were the stumbling blocks for the first probability enthusiasts in the field of games of chance. Let us recall Galileo's problem, encountered in Chapter 1, where the question was asked why when throwing three die we get a sum of 10 more often than a sum of nine, although these two sums are both obtained in six different ways (notably we find nine by doing 1 + 2 + 6 or 1 + 3 + 5 or 1 + 4 + 4 or 2 + 2 + 5 or 2 + 3 + 4 or 3 + 3 + 3). The answer was held in the fact that these six ways did not all have the same probabilities, once we differentiated the three die. Some decades later, another paradox problem was posed by Chevalier de Mere. We will deal with it below, as well as other classic problems.

20.2. Examples

20.2.1. *The Chevalier de Mere problem*

In the 17th century Chevalier de Mere, a man of letters who increased his income by playing dice games, bet that with an ordinary die he was going to get at least one 1 in four throws.

a) Check that his strategy was good.

Writing down the numbers obtained during the four throws of the die, we get words of four characters based on six letters 1, 2, 3, 4, 5 and 6. This gives 6^4 possible cases, all of which are equiprobable. To find out the number of favorable cases corresponding to the outcome of a 1 at least once, let us take the complementary event: never getting the 1, which gives 5^4 cases. The probability of getting no number ones is $5^4 / 6^4$, and that of getting at least one number one is $1 - (5 / 6)^4$. This last probability, of 0.518 order, is greater than 1/2 as Chevalier de Mere experimentally noticed by repeatedly playing the game.

b) Carried away by his success, Chevalier de Mere began to bet that he would get at least one double 1 with two die in 24 moves, but he began to lose. Why?

Here, again, we should differentiate the two die. The number of possible cases corresponding to a throw of the two die is $6 \times 6 = 36$, all equiprobable. Out of these, the number of cases where the double 1 is not obtained is 35. The number of possible cases corresponding to throwing the two die 24 times is 36^{24}, all equiprobable. The number of favorable cases corresponding to getting no double 1s is 35^{24}. By complementarity, the probability of getting at least one double 1 is $1 - (35 / 36)^{24}$, of 0.4911 order, which is less than 1/2. It would have been enough for Chevalier de Mere to bet on the double 1 in 25 moves (rather than 24 moves) for him to win again.

20.2.2. *From combinatorics to probabilities*

An box contains w white balls and r red balls.

a) We draw one ball at random and then replace it in the box. We then draw a second ball. What is the probability we will get two red balls?

Let us number the balls from 1 to $n = w + r$, where n is the total number of balls. This enables us to differentiate the balls. To get the number of possible draws, there are n possible numbers for the first ball drawn and each time still n numbers for the second, i.e. n^2 possible cases. As for favorable cases corresponding to two red balls drawn, we have r choices for the first ball and r choices for the second each time, i.e. r^2 cases. The probability sought is r^2 / n^2. This result can be found again by using the probability formulae we have just seen. Where R is the chance of drawing a red ball, we get:

$$p(R \text{ then } R) = p(R)\, p(R),$$

where these two events are independent, i.e.:

$$p(R \text{ then } R) = (r / n)(r / n) = (r / n)^2.$$

b) A first ball is drawn at random followed by a second, this time without the first ball being replaced. What is the probability of getting two red balls?

To get the number of possible cases, we begin by picking one out of n numbers, i.e. n cases. Each time we pick a second ball it is out of the $n - 1$ remaining numbers, i.e. $n(n - 1)$ possible cases. For the favorable cases, for the first draw we have the choice between r numbers for the red balls, i.e. r cases, then $r - 1$ cases for the second red ball, i.e. a total of $r(r - 1)$ favorable cases. The probability sought is:

$$\frac{r(r-1)}{n(n-1)}$$

We can also write this directly in terms of probabilities:

$$p(R \text{ then } R) = p(R)\, p(R \mid R) = \frac{r}{n}\,\frac{r-1}{n-1}.$$

c) Two balls are drawn simultaneously at random. What is the probability of getting two red balls?

For the possible cases, we choose a parcel of two balls out of the n, i.e. $C_n^2 = n(n-1)/2$ cases. For the favorable cases, we choose two out of the r red balls, i.e. $C_r^2 = r(r-1)/2$ cases. The probability sought is $\frac{r(r-1)}{n(n-1)}$. This is the same result as above. The fact probability of drawing the two balls one after the other is the same as drawing two balls at the same time.

20.2.3. *From combinatorics of weighted words to probabilities*

We play heads or tails five times. The probability of getting heads is p, and that of getting tails is q, with $p + q = 1$. We want to determine the probability of getting heads three times.

a) Deal with the case where $p = q = 1 / 2$.

The possible cases correspond to all words based on H and T, of five characters, i.e. 2^5 cases. The favorable cases correspond to words containing three letter Hs and three letter Ts, i.e. C_5^3 cases, as many as there are of ways of placing three Hs in five possible positions. The probability sought is $C_5^3 / 2^5$. We can also say that an event which gives three Hs and two Ts, for example *HTHHT*, has a probability of $(1 / 2)^5$, as each toss of tails (or heads) has the probability 1/2, and the probabilities are multiplied because they are independent successive events. On the other hand, the events with three Hs and two Ts number C_5^3. Their probabilities are added because they are incompatible events, hence the probability sought is $C_5^3\,(1 / 2)^5$.

b) Deal with the case where $p = 2 / 3$ and $q = 1 / 3$.

Now the outcome of a head is twice as likely as a tail. Let us say that heads value is two and tails one. A favorable elementary event, such as *HHTHT*, value is $2^3 1^2$. It is the same for all elementary events numbering C_5^3, hence $C_5^3\, 2^3$ words thus weighted, which corresponds to the favorable cases. As for possible cases, their weighting depends on the number of heads. This gives:

$$C_5^0 + C_5^1\, 2 + C_5^2\, 2^2 + C_5^3\, 2^3 + C_5^4\, 2^4 + C_5^5\, 2^5$$

possible weighted words. Furthermore this sum is equal to $(2 + 1)^5 = 3^5$, in accordance with the binomial formula. The probability sought is: $\frac{C_5^3 2^3}{3^5}$ but now, an argument in purely probabilistic terms is simpler.

An elementary event such as *HHHTT* actually has a probability of $(2 / 3)^3 (1 / 3)^2$ because the probabilities are multiplied. All these elementary events with three *H*s and two *T*s have this same probability, and there are C_5^2 of them. Hence by adding their probabilities, the probability requested is again: $\frac{C_5^3 2^3}{3^5}$.

20.2.4. *Drawing a parcel of objects from a box*

A person has N objects in a box in front of him. By dipping his hand into the box, he takes out a certain number. Ultimately, he can take out no objects or all of them. The number k of objects taken out is between 0 and N. We assume that there is an equiprobability of draws: all the parcels have equal chances of being taken out, whether they are big or small.

We are given a number K, between 0 and N. What is the probability of getting a parcel with dimension K?

Let us call the objects 0, 1, 2, …, $N - 1$, and associate each one with the number 0, when the object concerned is not taken, or the number 1 when the object is taken. Each draw is therefore written in the form of a word N characters long based on 0 and 1. All of the draws give 2^N words that are equiprobable. This equiprobability also means that each object has equal chances of being taken or left. There are C_N^K draws of K objects, i.e. all the ways of placing K letter 1s in N positions. The probability of getting a parcel of K objects is: $C_N^K / 2^N$.

20.2.5. *Hypergeometric law*

A box contains a white balls and b black balls. We draw N balls at random in a single go. We want to find out the probability of getting K white balls out of the N balls.

Let us differentiate the $a + b$ balls, calling the white balls $A_1\ A_2\ \ldots\ A_a$ and the black balls $B_{a+1}\ B_{a+2}\ \ldots B_{a+b}$. Order does not come into play when drawing N balls. We can therefore choose to write the draw in the form of a word of N characters placed in ascending order, for example $A_1\ A_2\ A_4$ or $A_2\ B_{a+1}\ B_{a+2}$ for $N = 3$. All draws of N balls are equiprobable and there are C_{a+b}^{N} ways of taking N out of $a + b$. The number of favorable cases corresponds to words with K letter A_i with i between 1 and a, and $N - K$ letters N_j with j between $a + 1$ and $a + b$. This goes back to choosing K white balls out of a, i.e. C_a^K, ways. Each time this is done, $N - K$ balls remain to be chosen from b black balls, i.e. C_b^{N-K}, hence a total of $C_a^K C_b^{N-K}$ favorable cases. The probability sought is:

$$C_a^K C_b^{N-K} / C_{a+b}^N.$$

This law is called the hypergeometric law.

20.2.6. *Draws with replacement in a box*

A box contains N balls numbered from 1 to N. We perform M successive draws with replacement and note the numbers of the balls obtained. We want to find out the probability that there are exactly T different balls obtained during the M draws.

Because the draws take place following replacement, each time a ball is drawn is independent of those that precede it. These successive draws are equiprobable. The M successive draws can be written in the form of words M characters long based on N letters. These words give all possible and equiprobable cases. The number of possible cases is N^M: there are N possibilities for the first ball drawn, and N cases for the second ball, and so on and so forth until the Mth draw.

Now let us look at the favorable cases. We begin with an example with $N = 4$, $M = 5$ and $T = 3$. Favorable cases are for example 11213, or 12213 or 12333. Here the three different letters are 1, 2 and 3 and they have come out in this order. Let us begin by counting how many such cases we find. In order to do this, consider the partitions in $T = 3$ parts of the set with $M = 5$ elements, written $\{a, b, c, d, e\}$. A partition in $T = 3$ parts would for example be $\{a, b, d\}, \{c\}$ and $\{e\}$. As the order of the parts does not come into play, we choose to write the parts in ascending order from their smallest letter. This means that we get the favorable case 11213, or $\begin{pmatrix} a & b & c & d & e \\ 1 & 1 & 2 & 1 & 3 \end{pmatrix}$, by mapping the first part on 1, the second part on 2 and the third part on 3. More specifically, we decide to map letter a over 1, as well as all the other letters of the same part, then the first remaining letter (in alphabetical order) is mapped on 2, as well as the other letters of the same part, then the remaining letters are mapped on 3. Each one of the partitions is thus associated in a bijective way with words of five characters based on three letters 1, 2 and 3, where they appear in this order in the word. We find the specific favorable cases that concern us. For example:

$\{a\}\{b\}\{c\ d\ e\} \leftrightarrow 12333$, $\{a\}\{b\ d\ e\}\{c\} \leftrightarrow 12322$, $\{a\}\{b\ c\ e\}\{d\} \leftrightarrow 12232$, $\{a\}\{b\ c\ d\}\{e\} \leftrightarrow 12223$, $\{a\ d\ e\}\{b\}\{c\} \leftrightarrow 12311$, etc.

which gives 10 cases, then the other partitions:

$\{a\}\{b\ c\}\{d\ e\} \leftrightarrow 12233$, $\{a\}\{b\ d\}\{c\ e\} \leftrightarrow 12323$, $\{a\}\{b\ e\}\{c\ d\} \leftrightarrow 12233$, etc.

which gives 15 cases. We find 25 words in this way. There are as many partitions in three parts as there are such words, and we are dealing with a Stirling number of the second kind $S(5\ ,\ 3)$ in this case.

Then we start again, changing the order of the three letters 1, 2 and 3 to get other favorable cases, which gives $3! = 6$ times more words, i.e. $3!\ S(5, 3) = 150$ words.[2] Lastly, as we did with the combination 1, 2, 3, we take all possible combinations of three letters out of the $N = 4$ letters 1, 2, 3, 4, which multiplies the cases by $C_4^{\ 3} = 4$. Finally, the number of favorable cases is $S(5, 3)\ 3!\ C_4^{\ 3} = 600$. The probability sought is: 600 / 1,024.

This can be generalized. We begin by choosing T out of the N numbers. Next we take all the partitions in T parts of the M-element set, i.e. $S(M\ ,\ T)$ cases, with each part written in ascending order of its elements, and each partition written with these parts classified in order of their first element. Then we send their T parts over the T numbers previously chosen, in all possible orders, which gives $T!\ S(M, T)$ favorable cases. Lastly we start again with all the combinations of T taken out of N, i.e. a total of $C_N^{\ T}\ T!\ S(M, T)$, or even $S(M, T)\ A_N^{\ T}$ cases, with $A_N^{\ T}$ designating the number of arrangements of T out of N numbers.[3] The probability sought is:

$$S(M, T)\ A_N^{\ T} / N^M.$$

20.2.7. *Numbered balls in a box and the smallest number obtained during draws*

20.2.7.1. *The problem*

A box contains N balls numbered from 1 to N. We remove a handful of P balls from the box at random and call the smallest number obtained X. Determine the probabilities obtained for each value of X (called the *law of* X).

---

2. We could also have argued directly on ordered partitions (see Chapter 14 on set partitions, especially Stirling numbers of the second kind, $S(N, K)$, counting the number of partitions of a N-element set in K parts, and $K!\ S(N, K)$ counting the number of ordered partitions).

3. This is an extension of the birthday paradox.

The number of ways of taking a handful of P balls from the container is C_N^P, and all of these cases are equiprobable. Let us now turn our attention to the favorable cases where the smallest number obtained is k, i.e. $X = k$ (see section 20.4 below about the notion of random variable X).

k is the smallest number, so $P - k$ objects with a number greater than k remain to be taken out of the $N - k$ objects with a greater number in the box, i.e. C_{N-k}^{P-k} favorable cases. Thus, the probability that the smallest number X is equal to k is:

$$p(X = k) = C_{N-k}^{P-k} / C_N^P.$$

20.2.7.2. *Draws with replacement*

Now we take P balls in the container through successive draws, each time replacing the ball after being drawn. have want to determine the law of X corresponding to the smallest number drawn.

The number of possible cases, all equiprobable, is N^P because it concerns all the words of N characters based on an alphabet of P letters. For the favorable cases, events corresponding to $X \geq k$ are words of N characters based on the letters k, $k + 1$, …, N, numbering $(N - k + 1)^P$. The elementary events corresponding to $X = k$ are none other than those such as $X \geq k$, from which we remove those such as $X \geq k + 1$, numbering $(N - k + 1)^P - (N - k)^P$. Hence:

$$p(X = k) = \frac{(N-k+1)^P - (N-k)^P}{N^P}.$$

20.2.8. *Wait for the first double heads in a repeated game of heads or tails*

a) To start off, let us consider words n characters long based on two letters 0 and 1, where the 1s are always isolated, with no 11 block being present. How many such words are there?

Let $u(n)$ be the number of words. They end in 0 or 1. When they end in 0, they are preceded by words $n - 1$ long based on 0 and 1 without any blocks of 0s, which gives $u(n - 1)$ words. When they end in 1, they must also end in 01, and they are preceded by words based on 0 and 1 without the presence of 11 blocks, i.e. $u(n - 2)$ words. Therefore:

$$u(n) = u(n - 1) + u(n - 2), \text{ with } u(0) = 1 \text{ and } u(1) = 2$$

We find a gap-type Fibonacci sequence $F(n)$, i.e. $u(n) = F(n + 2)$.

b) In a game of heads or tails, a person plays heads or tails with equiprobability repeatedly until double heads are obtained for the first time. With random variable X corresponding to the number of moves, determine the law of X, i.e. the probabilities obtained for each value of X.

The event $X = N$ with $N > 1$ is made up of elementary events of the type *THTT...THTHH*. Such N-length words necessarily end in *THH*, as long as N is greater than two, and they are preceded by words based on two letters with *HH* blocks present. According to the question above, there are $u(N - 3) = F(N - 1)$ words. As each elementary event has the probability $(1/2)^N$ because of the succession of N independent tosses, we deduce from it that $p(X = N) = F(N - 1) / 2^N$. Because we also have $p(X = 2) = 1/4$ the formula is true for all N greater than or equal to two. Note that by adding all these probabilities, we find the formula:

$$\sum_{N \geq 2} \frac{F(N-1)}{2^N} = 1 \text{, i.e. } 1/4 + 1/8 + 2/16 + 3/32 + 5/64 + \ldots = 1$$

Later we will see other ways of dealing with this problem.

20.2.9. *Succession of random cuts made in a game of cards*

In a pack of N cards, the cut operation consists of cutting the pack in two parts, the second of which has q cards, and inverting the two packs obtained. We then repeat this operation, cutting in the same place, until we again find the initial order of the cards for the first time. The number of cuts is therefore what we call period T of the shuffle.

a) Determine T as a function of N and q.

Let us number the positions of cards from 0 to $N - 1$. During a cut, the card in position 0 moves to position q, and in the general case the card in position k moves to position $k + q$ brought back modulo N (which means that if number $k + q$ reaches N or passes it, we remove N from it). During successive cuts, the card in position 0 moves to position q, then $2q$ [N], then $3q$ [N], etc. The trajectory of card 0 is the additive sub-group generated by q in the modular group $\boldsymbol{Z}_N$. We know that this sub-group (q) is the same as the one generated by the gcd (greatest common divisor) g of q and of N: $(q) = (g)$.[4] This sub-group has N / g elements. The trajectory of a card in position k is deduced from that of 0 by adding k [N], and also has N / g elements.

4. Because g is the pgcd of N and q, we notably have $q = k\,g$. Every element of group (q) generated by q is also a multiple of g modulo N, hence $(q) \subseteq (g)$. On the other hand, we know that the pgcd g is a linear combination of N and q (even the smallest positive), hence $g = Kq + K'N = Kq$ [N]. Every multiple of g is also a multiple of q, hence $(g) \subseteq (q)$.

There are therefore g distinct trajectories, which are those of cards in position 0, 1, 2, ..., $g - 1$, where this results from the fact that two elements are on the same trajectory if and only if their difference is a multiple of q, and hence of g.

Finally, the permutation corresponding to cutting the cards is broken down into g disjoint cycles, all N / g long and with the trajectories of 0, 1, ..., $g - 1$. Period T sought is therefore N / g. For example, with $N = 32$ and $q = 12$, we have $g = 4$ and $T = 8$. We can verify that the permutation corresponding to this cut is broken up according to the four cycles:

(0 12 24 4 16 28 8 20) (1 13 25 5 17 29 9 21)
(2 14 26 6 18 30 10 22) (3 15 27 7 19 31 11 23).

b) Instead of repeating the same cut as above, which a human hand would have difficulty in carrying out, let us make random cuts. There are $N - 1$ possible cuts, with the length q of the second pack going from 1 to $N - 1$. In this way we avoid having an empty pack when cutting the cards. Each time, we make $N - 1$ random cuts, assuming that these cuts are equiprobable. We want to find out in how many cuts on average we get the initial layout of the cards.

Note that a cut corresponds to a cyclic shift of q notches. The succession of two cuts of q and q' notches equals one cut of $q + q'$ $[N]$. Let q be the cut corresponding to a shift of q notches. The succession of cuts boils down to a sum of numbers (between 1 and $N - 1$) that we expect to reach 0 $[N]$ for the first time. For example, for $N = 6$ we can have the succession 1, 3, 4, 1, 5, 3, 1 where $1 + 3 + 4 + 1 + 5 + 3 + 1 = 18 = 0$ [6], without having had 0[6] before. In this case the number of cuts is seven. This can also be expressed with accumulated partial sums: 1, 4, 8, 9, 14, 17, 18, or even by reducing modulo 6: 1, 4, 2, 3, 2, 5, 0, which indicates the situation obtained after each one of the seven cuts. Generalizing this, we get a succession of numbers taken at random, between 0 and $N - 1$, with equiprobability, where 0 can never be the first number and no two successive numbers are identical, because this means that we would be doing a cut with one empty hand (i.e. no cards).

Therefore we can see the problem in the following way: N numbered balls are placed in a box, with ball 0 colored red. We remove this red ball and draw out of the $N - 1$ balls. We do not replace the ball that we just pulled out, but we replace the red ball that was removed at the start. Then we draw from the new $N - 1$ balls present. We do not replace the ball that was just drawn, but we replace the one which was removed with the previous move. We continue in this way until the red ball is drawn for the first time. It is a draw with delayed replacement. X being the random variable corresponding to the number of draws carried out, where X goes from two to infinity we get:

– $p(X = 2) = p$ (to get the red on the second draw, with the first draw having no importance) = $1 / (N - 1)$;

– $p(X = 3) = p$ (we do not get the red on the second draw but get it on the third draw) = $\frac{N-2}{N-1}\frac{1}{N-1}$;

– in the general case: $p(X = k) = \left(\frac{N-2}{N-1}\right)^{k-2} \frac{1}{N-1}$, with $k > 1$.

For our card game, this probability is that of returning to the initial order for the first time at the end of k cuts. The average number of cuts is the expected value for $E(X)$ of X, i.e. the sum of the values of X weighted by their respective probabilities (see section 20.4). Assuming that $Q = (N - 2) / (N - 1)$:

$$E(X)=\frac{1}{N-1}(2+3Q+4Q^2+...)=\frac{1}{(N-1)Q}(\frac{1}{(1-Q)^2}-1)=\frac{1}{N-2}((N-1)^2-1)=N$$

Similarly we show that the standard deviation is:

$$\sigma=\sqrt{(N-1)(N-2)}$$

therefore the average number of cuts that return us to the initial layout of the game is N, and the standard deviation is close to N.

20.2.10. *Waiting time for initial success*

Q white balls and q red balls are placed in a box. We draw one ball at random from the box, with equiprobability, and repeat these draws (without replacement) until we draw a red ball for the first time. X being the random variable corresponding to the number of draws, we want to find out the law of X and its average value. Note that if we consider drawing a red ball as corresponding to success and that of a white ball as corresponding to failure, it is a matter of waiting for the first success, in the case where success and failure are influenced by the failures that precede them.

a) Determine the law of X when $q = 4$.

The number of draws X takes whole values included between 1 and $Q + 1$ (when the first red ball is drawn with the $Q + 1^{th}$ move, the three other red balls are remain in the box).

Using conditional probabilities, we notice that:

$$p(X=1)=\frac{4}{Q+4},\ p(X=2)=\frac{4}{Q+4},\ p(X=3)=\frac{4}{Q+4}$$

$$p(X=4)=\frac{Q}{Q+4}\,\frac{Q-1}{Q+3}\,\frac{Q-2}{Q+2}\,\frac{4}{Q+1}$$

$$p(X=5)=\frac{Q}{Q+4}\,\frac{Q-1}{Q+3}\,\frac{Q-2}{Q+2}\,\frac{Q-3}{Q+1}\,\frac{4}{Q}=\frac{Q-1}{Q+4}\,\frac{Q-2}{Q+3}\,\frac{Q-3}{Q+2}\,\frac{4}{Q+1}$$

$$p(X=6)=\frac{Q}{Q+4}\,\frac{Q-1}{Q+3}\,\frac{Q-2}{Q+2}\,\frac{Q-3}{Q+1}\,\frac{Q-4}{Q}\,\frac{4}{Q-1}=\frac{Q-2}{Q+4}\,\frac{Q-3}{Q+3}\,\frac{Q-4}{Q+2}\,\frac{4}{Q+1}$$

if $(Q\geq 5)$

...

$$p(X=K)=\frac{Q}{Q+4}\,\frac{Q-1}{Q+3}\,\frac{Q-2}{Q+2}\,\frac{Q-3}{Q+1}\cdots\frac{Q-K+4}{Q-K+6}\,\frac{4}{Q-K+5}$$
$$=\frac{Q-K+4}{Q+4}\,\frac{Q-K+3}{Q+3}\,\frac{Q-K+2}{Q+2}\,\frac{4}{Q+1}$$

We can check that this formula, with its four factors in the numerator as well as the denominator, remains valid for all values of K between 1 and $Q+1$.

b) Give the law of X in the general case.

The random variable X takes values between 1 and $Q+1$. By generalizing the above and proceeding with the same simplifications, we find a fraction with q factors in the numerator and as many in the denominator:

$$p(X=K)=\frac{(Q-K+q)(Q-K+q-1)\ldots(Q-K+3)(Q-K+2)\ q}{(Q+q)(Q+q-1)\ldots(Q+3)(Q+2)(Q+1)}$$

$$=A\ C_{Q+q-K}^{q-1}\quad \textit{with}\quad A=\frac{q!}{(Q+q)(Q+q-1)\ldots(Q+2)(Q+1)}=\frac{1}{C_{Q+q}^{q}}$$

c) Find the average value E(X) of X.

By definition: $E(X) = A\sum_{K=1}^{Q-1} K\,C_{Q-q-K}^{q-1}$.

Without going into the details of the calculations,[5] we show that:

$$\sum_{K=1}^{Q+1} K\,C_{M-K-1}^{M-N-1} = \frac{N}{M-N+1}C_M^{M-N}$$

All we have to do is to apply this formula for $M = Q + q + 1$ and $N = Q + 1$, and we get:

$$E(X) = A\,\frac{Q+1}{q+1}\,C_{Q+q+1}^{q} = \frac{Q+1}{q+1}\frac{C_{Q+q+1}^{q}}{C_{Q=q}^{q}} = \frac{Q+q+1}{q+1}.$$

20.2.11. *Smallest number obtained during successive draws*

20.2.11.1. *The problem*

A box contains n balls numbered from 1 to n. We take out a handful of p balls and note the smallest number obtained. The random variable X corresponds to this smallest number. Determine the law of X.

Let us begin with an example, with $n = 4$ and $p = 3$. The possible draws of the three balls are: 123, 124, 134 and 234. In three cases, the smallest number is 1 and in one case, it is 2. Hence:

$p(X = 1) = 3 / 4$ and $p(X = 2) = 1 / 4$

In the general case, the smallest number k obtained is included between 1 and $n - p + 1$. The number of possible draws, all equiprobable, is the number of ways we can choose p out of n balls, i.e. C_n^p. The number of draws where the smallest number obtained is k is also the number of ways of choosing $p - 1$ balls (other than k) out of $n - k$ balls, the number of which is greater than k, i.e. C_{n-k}^{p-1}. Hence:

$$p(X = k) = \frac{C_{n-k}^{p-1}}{C_n^p}$$

5. We will find the demonstration in [GRA 94], problem 2, pages 175-177.

If we check that the sum of these probabilities gives 1, i.e. $\sum_{k=1}^{n-p+1} p(X=k)=1$, we find the combinatorics summation formula:

$$C_{n-1}^{p-1} + C_{n-2}^{p-1} + C_{n-3}^{p-1} + \ldots + C_{p-1}^{p-1} = 1$$

20.2.11.2. *Draws with replacement*

The box still contains n balls numbered from 1 to n. Now we remove p balls, one after the other in the box, replacing them in the box each time before drawing the next. We take the smallest number obtained as random variable X. Determine the law of X.

We are in the context of equiprobable draws. The probabilities sought are obtained by dividing the number of favorable cases by the number of possible cases. The number of possible cases is n^P, because with each of the draws the n numbers can come out. The favorable cases remain to be counted, based the values taken by X, which go from 1 to n.

Let us return to the example where $n = 4$ and $p = 3$. The smallest number obtained is between 1 and 4. The number of possible draws of p balls is $4^3 = 64$, since the first ball drawn is a choice of one of the four balls, and each time the second ball is also one of the four balls, and similarly for the third, etc. Now let us take the simplest case – the one where the smallest number obtained is 4. There is only one single draw in this case, i.e. 444, hence $p(X = 4) = 1 / 64$. When the smallest number is 3, the corresponding draws are 333, 334, 343, 344, 433, 434 and 443, numbering seven, hence $p(X = 3) = 7 / 64$. Note that to get this result we can first search for the number of draws where the smallest number is either 3 or 4, i.e. we have the choice between two numbers during each of the three successive draws, i.e. $2^3 = 8$ cases. Then we remove the case already found where 4 is the smallest number. Here $8 - 1 = 7$ cases where the smallest number is 3 remain. To get the number of cases where the smallest number is 2, we begin by searching for the number of cases where the smallest number is either 2 or 4, which is a choice of three numbers for each of the three draws, i.e. $3^3 = 27$ cases. Next we remove the number of cases where the smallest number is 3 or 4, i.e. the eight cases already found, hence $p(X = 2) = 19 / 64$. We do the same to find $p(X = 1) = (64 - 27)/64 = 37 / 64$.

Let us generalize this: X is between 1 and n. The number of elementary events where the smallest number ball withdrawn is greater than k is also the number of p-length words, based on $n - k$ letters $k + 1, k + 2, \ldots, n$, hence:

$$p(X > k) = \frac{(n-k)^p}{n^p}$$

The number of draws where k is the smallest number drawn is obtained by subtracting the number of draws where the smallest number is greater than $k - 1$ and the one where the smallest number is greater than k:

$$p(X = k) = \frac{(n-k+1)^p - (n-k)^p}{n^p}.$$

20.2.12. *The pool problem*

Three players A, B and C repeatedly play heads or tails, two by two. A and B play the first match. The one who loses gives his place to player C. We continue in the same way: after a toss, the loser gives his pace to the third player, who is waiting. The game stops when one of the three players has won two consecutive games. It is this player who is declared the winner. We want to find out the probability each player has of winning.

Let us distinguish two cases based on the result of the first match:

– *It is A who wins the first match.* Let us write down the possible games in the form of successions of players winning a match, up to the final winner. What we have is words whose length indicates the number of times the game of heads or tails was repeated. Let us arrange these words in increasing length:

AA, ACC, ACBB, ACBAA, ACBACC, ACBACBB, etc.

Dropping the last repeated letter of these words, words that are successive left factors of the periodic sequence *<u>ACB</u>ACBACB...* remain. Each player wins in turn. This means that the same player is the winner in all three games:

– *It is B who wins the first match.* We have the following games:

BB, BCC, BCAA, BCABB, BCABCC, BCABCAA, etc.

where the same player is the winner in all three games.

With the probability of a heads or tails toss being 1 / 2, the probability of a repeated game corresponding to a L-length word is $(1/2)^L$ because the probabilities are multiplied, as successive tosses are independent. Let us take the case of player C: he wins after three tosses, after six tosses, after nine tosses, etc., when A wins with the first toss. His probability of being the winner, in this case, is obtained by adding the probabilities of games where he wins, where these events are incompatible, i.e.:

$$(1 / 2)3 + (1 / 2)6 + (1 / 2)9 + \ldots = (1 / 2)3\ (1 + (1 / 2)3 + (1 / 2)6 + \ldots)$$

$$= \frac{1}{8} \frac{1}{1 - \frac{1}{8}} = \frac{1}{8} \frac{8}{7} = 1 / 7$$

It is the same when *B* wins the first move. Finally, the probability that player *C* has of winning is 2 / 7. As *A* and *B* each have the same probabilities of winning, and because they share the remaining probability – i.e. 5 / 7 – this gives each one 5 / 14 probability of winning; slightly greater than that of *C*.

20.3. Total probability formula

After the two probability formulae associated with two events linked by *or* or *and*, which we have already made use of, the third important formula is that of total probabilities.

20.3.1. *Classic example*

A person is placed in front of two boxes U_1 and U_2, including the respective proportions p_1 and p_2 of white balls.[6] *The person chooses one of the two boxes at random. What is the probability of getting a white ball?*

When the choice of boxes is equiprobable, we intuitively think that the probability requested is the average of the two probabilities, i.e. $(p_1 + p_2)/2$. By analogy, if we have a two in three chance of choosing box U_1, and a one in three chance of taking box U_2, we are led to take the weighted average $2/3\ p_1 + 1/3\ p_2$. This needs to be theoretically specified. Let $p(W)$ be the probability of obtaining a white ball, and $p(U_1)$ the probability that the draw is in box U_1, and similarly for $p(U_2)$. We have:

$$p(W) = p((W \text{ and } U_1) \text{ or } (W \text{ and } U_2))$$

$$= p(W \text{ and } U_1) + p(W \text{ and } U_2)$$

6. Having a proportion p_1 of white balls in a box means that, during an equiprobable drawing, the probability of drawing a white ball is exactly p_1.

because these events are incompatible:

$$= p(W \mid U_1)\, p(U_1) + p(W \mid U_2)\, p(U_2) = p_1\, p(U_1) + p_2\, p(U_2)$$

Again we find this notion of average, of equilibrium point.

20.3.2. *The formula*

The above is easily generalized. Each time we have what we call a *complete system of events*, as in our example where there is no possibility other than to draw from box U_1 or U_2, with these two events having nothing in common. A complete system of events is by definition a partition of the space of possibles: the union of all these events is the space of possibles, and the events taken two by two have nothing in common. We deduce total probability formula from this.

Given a test with a complete system of N events, U_i with i from 1 to N, and B an event, we get:

$$P(B) = \sum_i p(B \mid U_i)\, p(U_i)\,.$$

20.3.3. *Examples*

20.3.3.1. *Example 1: transmitting messages*

A message is successfully transmitted N times. With each transmission it has a five out of six chance of remaining unchanged (identical to its initial form), and a one out of six chance of becoming false the time after. When it is false, it has a five out of six chance of remaining so the time after that, and a one out of six chance of becoming correct again. We want to find out its probability of remaining unchanged at the end of N transmissions.

Let p_k be the probability that the message remains unchanged at the end of k transmissions, with $k > 0$. Either it was unchanged the move before $k - 1$, with probability p_{k-1}, or it was falsified with probability $1 - p_{k-1}$, which constitutes a complete system of events. Thanks to total probability formula, we get $p_k = (5 / 6)\, p_{k-1} + (1 / 6)\,(1 - p_{k-1})$ and from this we deduce the recurrence relation:

$$p_k = (2 / 3)\, p_{k-1} + 1 / 6,$$

with the initial condition, $p_1 = 5 / 6$.

This is an arithmetico-geometric sequence, which we deal with using the classic method: we look for its fixed point P, which verifies $P = (2 / 3)P + 1 / 6$, i.e. $P = 1 / 2$, then by subtracting $P = (2 / 3)P + 1 / 6$ term-by-term from the previous recurrence relation, this gives:

$$p_k - P = (2 / 3)(p_{k-1} - P), \text{ i.e. } p_k - 1 / 2 = (2 / 3)(p_{k-1} - 1 / 2)$$

Let us assume: $u_k = p_k - 1 / 2$ this sequence is geometric, verifying $u_k = (2 / 3)\, u_{k-1}$

with, at the start, $u_1 = 5 / 6 - 1 / 2 = 1 / 3$, hence $u_k = (1 / 3)\,(2 / 3)^{k-1}$ and:

$$p_k = (1 / 3)\,(2 / 3)^{k-1} + 1 / 2$$

Finally we find:

$$p_N = (1 / 3)\,(2 / 3)^{N-1} + 1 / 2$$

Let us indicate a second method: during a transmission, either the message remains unchanged with a probability of 5 / 6, or it changes with a probability of 1 / 6.

The N transmissions leading to a final, unchanged message can be expressed in the form of a word of N characters, based on two letters U (unchanged) and C (changed), presenting an even number of Cs. The first C in the word means that the message moved from true to false, the second C means that the message moves from false to true, and so on and so forth. With an even number of Cs, and only in this case, the message ends up being correct at the end of N transmissions. We count the words obtained according to their number of Cs. If the words do not contain any Cs, they are written $UUU...U$. The probability of this is $(5 / 6)^N$. If they contain two Cs, there are C_N^2 words each with a probability of $(5 / 6)^{N-2}\,(1 / 6)^2$, hence the probability $C_N^2\,(5 / 6)^{N-2}\,(1 / 6)^2$, etc. Finally, we find:

$$p_N = (5 / 6)^N + C_N^2\,(5 / 6)^{N-2}\,(1 / 6)^2 + C_N^4\,(5 / 6)^{N-4}\,(1 / 6)^4 + \ldots$$

where the number of terms is finite. We notice, thanks to binomial formula, that:

$$(5 / 6 + 1 / 6)^N + (5 / 6 - 1 / 6)^N = 2\,p_N, \text{ hence } p_N = (1 / 2) + (1 / 2)(2 / 3)^N$$

Finally, we introduce a method that will be further explained in Chapter 24 on graphs and matrices. We draw the weighted oriented graph as indicated in Figure 20.1. Our problem consists of being interested in paths traversing N arches of the graph, starting from node U to return to node U. The adjacency matrix of the graph, weighted by probabilities, is:

$$A = \begin{bmatrix} 5/6 & 1/6 \\ 1/6 & 5/6 \end{bmatrix}$$

From it, we deduce the determinant:

$$|I - xA| = 1 - (5 / 3)x + (2 / 3)x^2$$

as well as the determinant obtained by removing line 0 and column 0:

$$(|I - xA|, 0, 0) = 1 - (5 / 6)x$$

The generating function associated with the probability p_n of having a transmission that is correct at the end of n transmissions is:

$$F(x) = \frac{1 - \frac{5}{6}x}{1 - \frac{5}{3}x + \frac{2}{3}x^2} = \frac{1 - \frac{5}{6}x}{(1 - x)(1 - \frac{2}{3}x)} = (1 - \frac{5}{6}x)(\frac{3}{1 - x} - \frac{2}{1 - \frac{2}{3}x})$$

Developing this, and taking the term in x^N, we find its coefficient, namely:

$$p_N = 3 - 2(2 / 3)^N - (5 / 6)\,(3 - 2(2 / 3)^{N-1}) = (1 / 2)\,(1 + (2 / 3)^N)$$

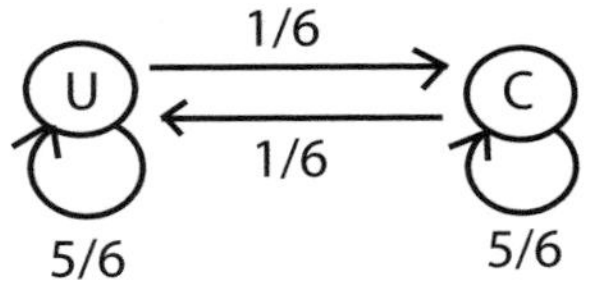

Figure 20.1. *Transition graph*

20.3.3.2. *Example 2: route on a square and its diagonals*

We consider a square whose vertices are numbered 1, 2, 3 and 4. The edges, as well as the two diagonals, are split up into arches in opposite directions. A particle moves in the following way. It starts at vertex 1. At each stage in time, it moves from the vertex where it is found to a neighboring vertice following one of the junction arches. Movement on an arch of the square has probability p, and movement on a diagonal arch has probability q, hence $q = 1 - 2p$. We take random variable X_n as the number of the vertex where we are at the end of n moves. We want to find out the probability law of X_n.

At the end of k moves (k stages of time), we express the probability of being located at vertex 1, i.e. event $X_k = 1$ compared to what happened previously, thanks to the total probability formula:

$$p(X_k = 1) = p(X_{k-1} = 2)\, p + p(X_{k-1} = 3)\, q + p(X_{k-1} = 4)\, p$$

and similarly for arriving at the other vertices.

Let us introduce the probability vectors P_k and P_{k-1}, where the column vector P_k is expressed $P_k = (p(X_k = 1), p(X_k = 2), p(X_k = 3), p(X_k = 4))^T$.[7] We get the relation:

$$P_k = A\, P_{k-1}$$

where A is the 4x4 circulant matrix whose first line is 0 p q p.

This matrix has 1, $-q$, $(q - 2p)$, $-q$ as eigenvalues, and the corresponding eigenvectors:

$$(1\ 1\ 1\ 1),\ (1\ {-i}\ {-1}\ i),\ (1\ {-1}\ 1\ {-1}),\ (1\ i\ {-1}\ {-i})$$

D being the diagonal matrix resembling matrix A in the eigenvectors base, that is to say the matrix with eigenvalues on its diagonal and 0s elsewhere, and Q the matrix of basis change whose column vectors are eigenvectors in the initial base, we have $A = Q\, D\, Q^{-1}$.

The recurrence relation enables us to end up with:

$$P_n = A^n\, P_0, \text{ or even } P_n = Q\, D^n\, Q^{-1}\, P_0, \text{ with } P_0 = (1\ 0\ 0\ 0)^T$$

The calculation gives:

$$P(X_n = 1) = (1 + 2\,(1 - 2p)^n + (1 - 4p)^n)\, /\, 4$$

$$P(X_n = 2) = P(X_n = 4) = (1 - (1 - 4p)^n)\, /\, 4$$

$$P(X_n = 3) = (1 - 2\,(1 - 2p)^n + (1 - 4p)^n)\, /\, 4$$

---

7. When transposed, the line vector (a, b, c, d) is expressed $(a, b, c, d)^T$. Transposition exchanges the lines and columns of a matrix. Vector $(a, b, c, d)^T$ is the corresponding column vector.

20.3.3.3. *Example 3: draws from boxes*

We have $R + 1$ boxes U_0, U_1, …, U_R, containing white balls and red balls, with the proportion of red balls in the box U_j being j / R. We choose one box at random, with equiprobability, and make N successive draws replacing the balls in this box. X being the random variable corresponding to the number of red balls obtained, we want to find out the law of X as well as its average value $E(X)$.

We are in the context of total probability formula, with $p(U_j) = 1 / (R + 1)$ being the probability of choosing box U_j. The probability of obtaining k red balls during N draws, knowing that this happens in box U_j, is:

$$p(X = k \mid U_j) = C_N^k \, (j / R)^k \, (1 - j / R)^{N-k}$$

because it is a binomial law. In the framework of the complete system of events obtained:

$$p(X = k) = \frac{1}{R+1} \sum_{j=0}^{R} C_N^k \left(\frac{j}{R}\right)^k \left(1 - \frac{j}{R}\right)^{N-k}$$

Now let us take expectation:

$$E(X) = \frac{1}{R+1} \sum_{k=0}^{N} k \sum_{j=0}^{R} C_N^k \left(\frac{j}{R}\right)^k \left(1 - \frac{j}{R}\right)^{N-k}$$

Let us reverse the Σ:

$$E(X) = \frac{1}{R+1} \sum_{j=0}^{R} \sum_{k=0}^{N} k C_N^k \left(\frac{j}{R}\right)^k \left(1 - \frac{j}{R}\right)^{N-k}$$

We recognize the expectation of binomial law $\boldsymbol{B}(N, j / R)$ in the second Σ:

$$E(X) = \frac{1}{R+1} \sum_{j=0}^{R} N \frac{j}{R} = \frac{N}{R(R+1)} \sum_{j=0}^{R} j = \frac{N}{R(R+1)} \frac{R(R+1)}{2} = \frac{N}{R}$$

(for reminders about binomial law, which deals with the number of successes obtained during N repeated experiments with success or failure, see section 20.5.3).

20.4. Random variable X, law of X, expectation and variance

In order to move forward in probability theory, it is useful to quantify events, hence the notion of the random variable. A number is associated with each elementary event, which for us will be an integer. In dice throwing, we can take the number that comes out as random variable X, the event corresponding to drawing the number 1 will be expressed $X = 1$, and the associated probability will be $p(X = 1) = 1 / 6$. In throwing two die, if we take the sum of the numbers obtained as random variable X, the values taken by the random variable are integers included between 2 and 12, and we have for example:

$$p(X = 2) = p((1 \text{ then } 1)) = 1 / 36, p(X = 3) = p((1 \text{ then } 2) \text{ or } (2 \text{ then } 1)) = 2 / 36$$

The probabilities associated with each value of the random variable X form what we call the law of X.

20.4.1. *Average value of X*

Taking each one of the values of X and weighting them by their respective probabilities – the sum of which we know is equal to 1 – we get the average value of X or the expected value or the expectation, expressed as $E(X)$. Hence the formula:

$$E(X) = \sum_k k\, p(X = k)$$

with the summation extending to all values k taken by X.

The average obeys the following properties, called *linearity*, when several random variables can be present:

$$E(X + Y) = E(X) + E(Y)$$

$$E(kX) = k\, E(X)$$

In particular:

$$E(aX + b) = aE(X) + b.$$

20.4.2. *Variance and standard deviation*

In addition to the average value of random variable X, we are interested in the average of the deviations around this average value. But because the deviations, which we express as $X - E(X)$, can be positive as well as negative and can also compensate for and cancel each other out, we use the square of the deviations. By definition, variance $V(X)$ is the average of the square of deviations compared to the average value $E(X)$, i.e.:

$$V(X) = E((X - E(X))^2$$

Note that variance is always a positive number, and to return to deviations rather than their squares we call the number $\sigma(X) = \sqrt{V(X)}$ the standard deviation. Variance, as well as standard deviation, indicates the degree to which the results spread, but because the squares are involved this notion is relatively abstract. It only becomes quantitatively significant when compared to several standard deviations: the greater the variance $V(X)$, the more the experiment results associated with variable X are spread around the average $E(X)$.

The variance obeys the following properties:

– if we have two random variables X and Y with $Y = aX + b$, then $V(Y) = a^2 V(X)$; and

– if X and Y are two independent variables, $V(X + Y) = V(X) + V(Y)$.

20.4.3. *Example*

A person plays heads or tails n times, where each time the probability of getting heads is equal to p and that of getting tails is equal to q. If heads comes out, the person wins a sum of A dollars, and if it is tails he loses B dollars. We want to find out the average final winnings at the end of n moves, as well as the variance.

Let us introduce the random variables X_k, where k is between 1 and n, corresponding to the winnings obtained at move number k: X_k is equal to A or $-B$ depending on whether the result is heads or tails – this is at the kth move. Let the final winnings be X, which can vary between $-nB$ and $+nA$. We have the relation: $X = X_1 + X_2 + X_3 + \ldots + X_n$. The average winnings at the kth move is $E(X_k) = pA - qB$. The final average winnings is obtained by adding the punctual average winnings: $E(X) = n\,(pA - qB)$. Note that the game will be fair, with $E(X) = 0$, if we take $pA - qB = 0$, i.e. $A / B = q / p$. On the other hand, by definition:

$$V(X_k) = p\,(A - E(X_k))^2 + q\,(-B - E(X_k))^2$$

$$= p\,(A - pA + qB)^2 + q\,(B + pA - qB)^2$$

$$= p\,(Aq + Bq)^2 + q\,(Bp + Ap)^2 = p\,q\,(A + B)^2$$

Because the variables X_k are independent, their variances are added up to give $V(X) = n\,p\,q\,(A + B)^2$.

20.5. Some classic laws

20.5.1. *Bernoulli's law*

This concerns the simplest game. It consists of playing heads or tails once, assuming that the coin can be loaded: the probability of getting heads is p and that of getting tails is q, with $p + q = 1$. We take the number of times heads is obtained as random variable X, hence the two events are $X = 0$ or $X = 1$. The law of X is therefore:

$$p(X = 1) = p, \text{ and } p(X = 0) = q.$$

From this we deduce the expected value and the variance:

$$E(X) = p(X = 0)\,.\,0 + p(X = 1)\,.\,1 = p$$

$$V(X) = p(X = 0)\,(0 - E(X))^2 + p(X = 1)\,(1 - E(X))^2$$

$$= qp^2 + pq^2 = pq(p + q) = pq$$

Let us indicate that in this binary game, heads or tails can also mean success or failure, win or lose, 1 or 0, the valid product or defective product in a business, etc.

All the phenomena where two things can happen, each one with its own probability, are called Bernoulli trials. For example, in dice if we take throwing a 6 as a success, and drawing another number as a failure, we are in the context of Bernoulli's law, with $p = 1 / 6$ and $q = 5 / 6$.

20.5.2. *Geometric law*

We repeatedly play heads or tails, written H and T, with p and q as their respective probabilities, and stop with the outcome of the first head. We are interested in the number of moves that were necessary, which constitutes random variable X of the game. This could also be called the waiting time. We want to find the law of X. The values taken by X are integers greater than or equal to 1. We find:

$$p(X = 1) = p(H) = p$$

$$p(X = 2) = p(TH) = p(\text{tails first and heads second}) = q\,p$$

where the events are independent. We easily generalize this to:

$$p(X = k) = p(TT...TF) = q^{k-1} p$$

From this we deduce the expectation and variance:

$$E(X) = \sum_{k\geq 1} k\, p(X = k) = p\sum_{k\geq 1} kq^{k-1} = p\frac{1}{(1-q)^2} = \frac{1}{p}$$

$$V(X) = \sum_{k\geq 1} pq^{k-1}(k - \frac{1}{p})^2 = p(\sum_{k\geq 1} k^2 q^{k-1} - \frac{2}{p}\sum_{k\geq 1} kq^{k-1} + \frac{1}{p^2}\sum_{k\geq 1} q^{k-1})$$
$$= p(q\sum_{k\geq 2} k(k-1)q^{k-2} + \sum_{k\geq 1} kq^{k-1} - \frac{2}{p}\sum_{k\geq 1} kq^{k-1} + \frac{1}{p^2}\sum_{k\geq 1} q^{k-1})$$

where we replaced k^2 with $k(k - 1) + k$ to use the formula:

$$\sum_{k\geq 2} k(k-1)q^{k-2} = \frac{2}{(1-q)^3}$$

$$= p(\frac{2q}{p^3} + \frac{1}{p^2} - \frac{2}{p^3} + \frac{1}{p^3}) = \frac{1-p}{p^2} = \frac{q}{p^2}$$

20.5.3. *Binomial law*

A person plays heads or tails n times. The probability of getting heads is p, and that of getting tails is q. We take the number of times we get heads during n draws as random variable X. The objective is to find the law of X. In this game, random variable X is between 0 and n. The elementary events are written in the form of words n characters long, based on two letters H and T.

Note that these elementary events are not equiprobable, except in the particular case where $p = q = 0.5$. Let us take an event where H is present k times. Its probability is $p^k q^{n-k}$, because the probabilities are multiplied. The n draws are independent. The number of elementary events where H is present k times is C_n^k, the number of words where H is present k times, and T present $n - k$ times, or even the number of ways to fill k of n boxes with Hs. All these events have the same probability and are incompatible. Their probabilities are added, hence:

$$p(X = k) = C_n^k p^k q^{n-k}$$

We have just obtained the law of X for the binomial with parameters n and p, which we write $\boldsymbol{B}(n, p)$. As the calculation of $E(X)$ and $V(X)$ is more laborious, we will wait for more effective calculation tools to carry it out (see Chapter 22). Here are the results:

$$E(X) = n\,p,\; V(X) = n\,p\,q.$$

20.6. Exercises

20.6.1. *Exercise 1: throwing balls in boxes*

We have B boxes, numbered from 1 to B.

a) We throw one ball at random into a box. It has as many chances of falling in one box as in the other. What is the probability that it falls in box number k?

This is a Bernoulli trial, where success – the ball falls in box number k – has a probability of $1 / B$ and failure has the probability $(B - 1) / B$.

b) We now throw the ball n times. What is the average number of balls in a given box k?

Intuitively, as each box receives on average as many balls as another, this average number must be n / B. Let us find this result again by taking the context of a succession of n Bernoulli trials.

Here we use the binomial formula $\boldsymbol{B}(n, 1 / B)$. Let X be the random variable corresponding to the number of balls that have fallen in box number k. Variable X is between 0 and n. We get:

$$p(X = j) = C_n^j\,(1 / B)^j\,((B - 1) / B)^{n-j},$$

and the average number is $E(X) = n / B$.

c) How many balls must we throw on average until a given box k contains one ball?

Let Y be the random variable corresponding to the number of throws required for the first ball to fall into box k. Variable Y is greater than or equal to 1 and obeys the geometric law with parameter $1 / B$:

$$p(X = j) = ((B - 1) / B)^{j-1}(1 / B)$$

with $j - 1$ failures followed by one success. The average number of throws is $E(Y) = B$.

d) How many throws on average must we make until each box contains at least one ball?

Let X be the number of throws until no box remains empty, which means that each box contains at least one ball. For example, with $B = 4$, we have an event with $X = 15$, where for each throw we note the number of the box the ball fell into, which gives this word of 15 characters: $\underline{2}$ 222$\underline{4}$ 4224$\underline{1}$ 2144$\underline{3}$. Let X_1 be the number of throws for a box to contain at least one ball. We always have $X_1 = 1$. Next let X_2 be the number of throws needed from the time a box contains one ball until a second box is no longer empty, i.e. $X_2 = 4$ in the example above. Similarly, let X_3 be the number of throws needed from the moment a second box contains one ball until a third box is no longer empty, i.e. $X_3 = 5$ in the example above. And so on and so forth until X_B.

We have the relation $X = X_1 + X_2 + X_3 + \ldots + X_B$. On the other hand, each random variable X_j follows a geometric law because it is about waiting for a certain success. Notably, X_2 follows a geometric law where the probability of success is $(B - 1) / B$, because when a first box has at least one ball, there is a $B - 1$ out of B chance of on the next ball landing in another box, hence $p(X_2 = q) = (1 / B)^{q-1}(B - 1) / B$.

Similarly: $p(X_3 = q) = (2 / B)^{q-1}(B - 2) / B$.

This is generalized, with:

$$p(X_j = q) = ((j - 1)/B)^{q-1}(B - j + 1) / B \text{ and } E(X_j) = B / (B - j + 1)$$

The average value of X is obtained by adding the average values of X_j:

$$E(X) = E(X_1) + E(X_2) + \ldots + E(X_B) = 1 + B / (B - 1) + B / (B - 2) + \ldots + B / 1$$

$$= B\,(1 / B + 1 / (B - 1) + 1 / (B - 2) + \ldots + 1 / 1)$$

This value is close to $B \ln B$ for big enough B.

20.6.2. *Exercise 2: series of repetitive tries*

a) A person makes n telephone calls to n correspondents, at the rate of one call per person. The probability of getting a correspondent is p, and that of not getting him is q (q = 1 – p). The calls are considered to be independent of one another. X is the random variable equal to the number of correspondents who answered the telephone. We want to find out the law of X.

Because the person makes n independent (Bernoulli) tries with the same probability of success p, we get the binomial law $\boldsymbol{B}(n, p)$ as the law of X.

b) After this first series of calls, the person makes a second series of calls to the correspondents they did not get the first time. Y is the random variable equal to the number of correspondents obtained the second time, and Z = X + Y the total number of correspondents obtained at the end of the two series of tries. We want to find the law of Z.

When k people have answered the first series of calls, random variable Y in turn follows a binomial law $\boldsymbol{B}(n-k, p)$.[8] Notice that variable Z takes values between 0 and n, and let us determine the probability $p(Z = s)$ with s between 0 and n:

$$p(Z=s)=\sum_{k=0}^{s} p(X=k \text{ and } Y=s-k)=\sum_{k=0}^{s} p(Y=s-k \mid X=k)\, p(X=k)$$

$$=\sum_{k=0}^{s} C_{n-k}^{s-k} p^{s-k} q^{n-s}\, C_n^k p^k q^{n-k}$$

$$=C_n^s p^s q^{2n-s} \sum_{k=0}^{s} C_s^k q^{-k} \text{ because } C_n^k C_{n-k}^{s-k}=C_n^s C_s^k$$

$$=C_n^s p^s q^{2n-s}(1+1/q)^s=C_n^s (p(1+q))^s (q^2)^{n-s}$$

We recognize the binomial law $\boldsymbol{B}(n, 1-q^2)$.

c) The person makes a third series of calls to the correspondents they could not get in touch with U is the number of people answering the telephone this third time and T the total number of correspondents answering at the end of three series of tries. What is the law of U?

We have:

$$T=X+Y+U=Z+U$$

$$p(T=u)=\sum_{s=0}^{u} p(Z=s \text{ and } U=u-s)$$

$$=\sum_{s=0}^{u} C_{n-s}^{u-s} p^{u-s} q^{n-u}\, C_n^s (p(1+q))^s (q^2)^{n-s}=\sum_{s=0}^{u} C_n^u C_u^s p^u q^{3n-2s-u}(1+q)^s$$

$$=C_n^u p^u q^{3n-u} \sum_{s=0}^{u} C_u^s \left(\frac{1+q}{q^2}\right)^s=C_n^u p^u q^{3n-u}\left(\frac{1+q+q^2}{q^2}\right)^u$$

$$=C_n^u p^u q^{3n-3u}(1+q+q^2)^u=C_n^u (p(1+q+q^2))^u (q^3)^{n-u}$$

---

8. As X and Y are no longer independent random variables, the generating functions formula related to the sum of two independent variables does not apply.

We find the binomial law $\boldsymbol{B}(n, 1 - q^3)$.

This is generalized: when the series of calls are repeated n times, the random variable equal to the number of correspondents having finally answered the telephone obeys the binomial law $\boldsymbol{B}(n, 1 - q^n)$. This is proved by recurrence.

20.6.3. *Exercise 3: filling two boxes*

We have two boxes. Box U_1 can contain M balls at most, and box U_2 can contain N balls. Initially these two boxes are empty. A person has an unlimited stock of balls. He takes one out and throws it at random into one of the boxes, with probability p it lands in box U_1 and probability $q = 1 - p$ it lands in box U_2. Next he takes a second ball and throws it into one of the two boxes, with the same probabilities as before. The person continues in this way until one of the boxes is full. There are therefore k balls in the box that is not full, with $0 \leq k < N$ if it is box U_1 that is full and $0 \leq k < M$ if U_2 is full. We take random variable X as the number of balls found in the box that is not full.

a) Write the succession of throws in the form of words based on two letters.

A succession of throws is an elementary event that can be expressed by a sequence of 1s and 2s. For example, the word 112 indicates that the first and second balls land in box U_1 and the third in U_2. The probability associated with this throw 112 is $p^2 q$ because the successive throws are independent.

b) Take the case where $M = 3$ and $N = 2$. Determine the law of X. For what values of p does box U_1 have more chances of filling up before box U_2?

– For $k = 0$ we have the two throws 111 or 22. For $k = 1$, the throws are 1121, 1211 and 2111 when it is U_1 that is full, and 122 and 212 if it is U_2;

– For $k = 2$, we have 1122, 1212 and 2112 and it is only box U_2 that is full.

From this we deduce the law of X in this case to be:

$$p(X = 0) = p^3 + q^2$$

$$p(X = 1) = 3p^3q + 2pq^2$$

$$p(X = 2) = 3p^2q^2$$

On the other hand:

$$p(U_1 \text{ is filled before } U_2) = p^3 + 3p^3q$$

and:

$$p(U_2 \text{ filled before } U_1) = q^2 + 2pq^2 + 3p^2q^2$$

Box U_1 will be the first to become full if $p^3 + 3p^3q > 0.5$, or even with $q = 1 - p$: $8p^3 - 6p^4 - 1 > 0$. A quick study of function $y = 8x^3 - 6x^4 - 1$ between 0 and 1 shows that this function is increasing, from -1 to 1. It is canceled one single time for $x_0 = 0.614$. As soon as probability p exceeds this value, box U_1 has more chances of being filled first.

c) Determine the law of X in the general case.

Let us take the case where box U_1 is full and the other box contains k balls, with $0 \leq k < N$. The corresponding elementary events are represented by words of $M + k$ characters made up of M letter 1s and k letter 2s, with the additional constraint of having a letter 1 in last place. The number of these words is the number of ways of placing $M - 1$ letter 1s in $M + k - 1$ boxes, i.e. C_{M+k-1}^{M-1}. The probability associated with each one of these elementary events is $p^M q^k$. Hence we have the probability $C_{M+k-1}^{M-1} p^M q^k$. We do the same when box U_2 is full.

$$p(X = k) = \underset{\substack{\text{if } 0 \leq k < N \\ \text{else } 0}}{C_{M+k-1}^{M-1} p^M q^k} + \underset{\substack{\text{if } 0 \leq k < M \\ \text{else } 0}}{C_{N+k-1}^{N-1} p^k q^N}$$

Chapter 21

Chance and the Computer

Every computer language is equipped with a random number generator that is supposed to supply a uniform distribution of probabilities. Each number must have almost as many chances of coming out as another at the end of a certain number of tries, given that these numbers belong to a number interval that has been set. But this is not enough for ensuring the truly random character of the succession of numbers produced by the generator. If we want to have a random sequence of 0s and 1s, and we want the generator to release all the 0s first then all the 1s, then as many 0s as 1s will have come out but the sequence can, with difficulty, be considered random. This is also the case if the generator alternately releases 0s and 1s. Even if the 0s and 1s outcome does not seem to be ordered, we cannot be satisfied with a sequence that will give exactly the same number of 0s and 1s over a certain sequence length than over a double or triple length sequence. The difficulty comes from the inherent contradiction in the problem: a sequence where only chance is involved must be created in the computer following a deterministic law which, itself, owes nothing to chance. This is why we often speak of pseudo-random numbers rather than random numbers. The other difficulty comes from the very notion of the random character of a sequence. We have no strict definition of the term random, and only some criteria can be preferred, for want of dreaming of obtaining all the properties we would be right to expect from a random sequence.

Initially, we will see how pseudo-random numbers are created, with the tests they are made to undergo to ensure their relative validity. The confidence in their accuracy will come above all from the use of the random number generator in many experimental contexts. We will note that in general the experimental results obtained on the computer are in correct accordance with the theoretical results, and this is enough to reassure us.

21.1. Random number generators

These are simple processes that issue random numbers produced by the generator. They are integers, modulo a certain number N, created by a recurrence relation using given initial conditions. By modulo, we mean that these numbers are always reduced between 0 and $N-1$. In the case of excess, we replace them with the remainder of their division by N, or we remove N from them as many times as necessary for them to be reduced to between 0 and $N-1$. It is the action of this modulo that provokes the expected disorder in the results. Here are some examples of recurrence relations used to create chance, all modulo to an integer N:

$u(n+1) = a\,u(n) + b$, or:

$u(n+1) = a\,u(n) + b\,u(n-1)$, or:

$u(n+1) = a\,u(n)^2 + b$,

where the correct choices of constants need to be made.

Changing the initial conditions enables us to modify the sequences of numbers obtained. This relaunch of the generator is done by the functions *randomize* () or *srand*(*time*(*NULL*)), which are dependent on the clock time of the machine. Without the clock time, the generator would imperturbably give the same number sequence. Note also that because of the modulo, the generators issue number sequences that are periodically repeated. It is useless to make the generator work on a succession of numbers where the period would find itself repeated several times, with the results not being more precise. It is better to repeat a limited succession of moves several times – some dozens of thousands – each time relaunching the random number generator.

Various tests can be carried out to check the accuracy of the generator. The most well-known and simplest is the chi-squared test. It enables us to verify whether the numbers obtained follow the rules of uniform distribution, not only in terms of equal proportions between numbers but also with variations between them compatible with this uniform distribution. We will give some explanations about the chi-squared law in section 21.8 at the end of this chapter (see also [SED 91]).

Evidently there are other complementary tests for testing the accuracy of a random generator, but we will not go any further into these. This is so that we can now take on the fundamental question: how can valid results be obtained as a matter of probabilities thanks to computer experiments? We will see this in a particularly simple case first.

21.2. Dice throwing and the law of large numbers

Here is the first example to process on a computer, where a die is thrown (a simple extension of the heads or tails game). We throw a die with six faces numbered from 1 to 6, where each number has as many chances of landing face up as another, i.e. a one in six chance. We make N throws. We want to find out the number of times the 1 lands face up, the number of times the 2 lands face up, etc., and represent what is called the frequency histogram. The program is simple.

We take the number N, and overall we declare the frequency array *freq*[7], which is thus set to 0. Then we launch the random number generator, thanks to the function *randomize*() or *srand*(), coupled with the internal clock of the machine, in such a way that with each new execution of the program, the generator releases a list of random numbers different to the one obtained before. Finally, the function *random*(K) gives a random number between 0 and $K-1$.[1]

```
srand(time(NULL));
for(throw=1; throw<=N; throw++)
  { number=random(6)+1;
  freq[number]++;
  }
for(number=1;number<=6;number++) /* drawing of the bars of the histogram */
  bar3d( xo+zoom*number, yo – freq[number]*6/(float)N*300,
       xo+zoom*number+0.7*zoom, yo, 15, 1);
```

What do we observe? When the number of tries is low, the bars in the frequency diagram have clearly different heights, but the higher the number of tries, the more the bars have the tendency to be the same height, which expresses that the probability of throwing the 1 for example, is 1 / 6 (see Figure 21.1). Therefore repeating experiments a large number of times, which a computer does easily, gives a value very close to that obtained theoretically.

The underlying reason is a consequence of what we call the *(weak) law of large numbers*, namely: the probability of an event is the limit of the percentage of the realization of this event in N experiments, when N increases to infinity.

---

1. If the programming language only has function *rand*(), which returns a random number between 0 and *RAND_MAX*, you can make your own functions:
float rand01(void) { return (float) rand() / ((float)RAND_MAX + 1.);} which returns a number in [0 1[, and:
int random(int n) { return rand01()*n;}

This law of large numbers is a statistical view of probabilities. We understand the interest in computer simulations, capable of doing thousands or millions of experiments in a short space of time. This enables us to verify the validity of a formula obtained theoretically. This sometimes enables us, in the absence of theoretical results, to obtain experimental results, even to extract from these the supposed existence of a certain law, which we will then be able to try and prove by calculation. Lastly, computer experiments are susceptible to giving approximate values of numbers, as shown in the following section.

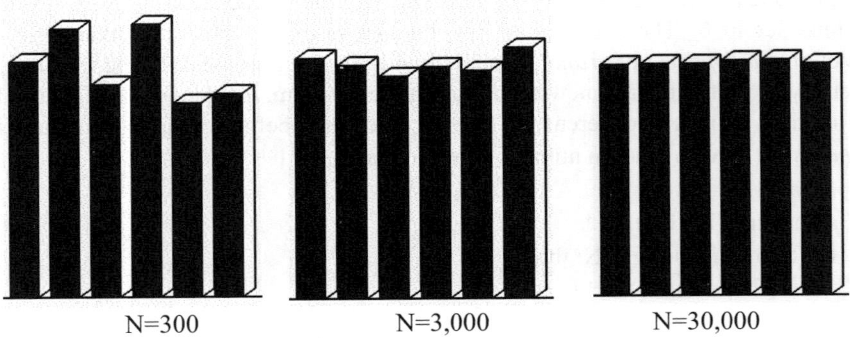

Figure 21.1. *Frequency histogram*

21.3. Monte Carlo methods for getting the approximate value of the number π

Monte Carlo method is used when we can obtain the approximate value of a specific number by chance. In the present case, the result to be obtained is the number π, an approximate value.

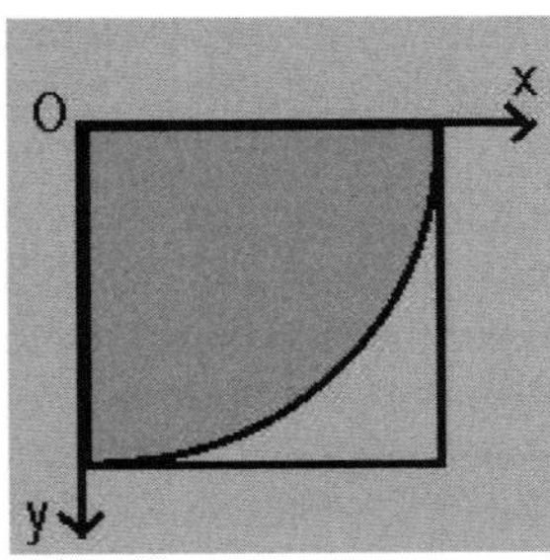

Figure 21.2. *Mechanism for getting π*

The *first method* consists of drawing a quarter circle of radius R in a square (see Figure 21.2). Next we make a shower of points (x, y) fall at random on the square, which a computer does easily. For this, it is sufficient to carry out $x = random(R + 1)$ and $y = random(R + 1)$ in the program. Out of the N points that have fallen in the square, n fall inside the quarter-circle, which we test by the inequality $x^2 + y^2 \leq R^2$. When N is large, the relationship n / N is generally equal to the relationship of the area of the quarter-circle over the area of the square, i.e. $n / N \approx \pi / 4$, hence $\pi \approx 4\, n / N$. Knowing n and N enables us to obtain an approximate value of π. But we can see that this experimental result is relatively vague, for example can get 3.12.

The *second method* is the *needle method*, thanks to Buffon (1707-1788) who carried out a theoretical and experimental study on this subject. It consists of accidentally dropping a needle on a floor made up of parallel boards. The needle is l long, the boards are all W wide, with $l < W$ (see Figure 21.3). We want to find the probability the needle has of touching a separating line between two boards. The experiment can be easily carried out on a computer.

The position of the needle is determined by the coordinates (x, y) of its location and by an angle a with the lines of the floor, between 0 and π. In actual fact, the y ordinate of the location of the needle is of no interest. It is enough to take the number x at random between 0 and W because one single board is enough, or even between 0 and $W / 2$, because it is the same on the other half of the board for reasons of symmetry.

The only angle that can be taken is between 0 and $\pi / 2$, still for reasons of symmetry. The needle cuts line 0 if $x \leq (l / 2) \sin a$. Repeating the experiment a large number of times, we find the proportion of cases where the needle touches a line on the floor, which corresponds to the probability sought. Modifying the values of l and W, we can check that this probability is of the form $k\, l / W$, notably it only depends on the relationship l / W, which is logical.

But what is the value of constant k? For this let us consider the elementary events associated with this experiment. They are defined by the two numbers, with x between 0 and $W / 2$ and a an angle between 0 and $\pi / 2$. Here we return to throwing points at random in a rectangle $L / 2$ long and $\pi / 2$ wide.

The favorable events – those where the needle touches a line – correspond to the constraint $x \leq (l / 2) \sin a$. The corresponding points are located on a surface delimited by an arch of the sine curve inside the rectangle (see Figure 21.3 on the right).

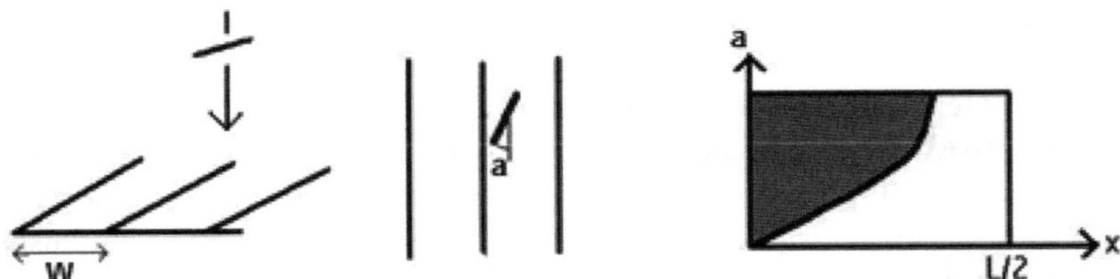

Figure 21.3. *Buffon's needle*

The probability sought is the relationship of the area of this surface to that of the rectangle. Hence the probability equal to $(l / 2) / (W \pi / 4) = (2 / \pi) (l / W)$.

Constant k is none other than $2 / \pi$. The experimental study on the computer enables us to get constant k and deduce an approximate value of π from it.[2]

21.4. Average value of a random variable X, variance and standard deviation

Beyond calculating the probability of certain events, the computer also enables us to find experimental values of the expectation and variance of a random variable. Let us begin with the expectation $E(X)$. Recall that taking each one of the values of X and weighting them by their respective probabilities (the sum of which we know is equal to 1), we get the average value of X, or the expected value or the expectation $E(X)$. We get the formula:

$$E(X)=\sum_k k\, p(X = k)$$

where the summation extends to all the values k taken by X. But if we are interested in possible results, namely elementary events e_i, with which is associated a value of X which we can write $X(e_i)$, we also get:

$$E(X) = \sum X(e_i)\, p(e_i)$$

where the probability $p(ei)$ is also the relationship between the number of times the event happens and the total number NE of experiences, i.e.:

$$E(X) = \frac{1}{NE} \sum X(e_i)(number\ of\ times\ e_i\ occurs)$$

2. For other examples of geometric probabilities, see [CUC 96].

Therefore, we have no need to calculate probabilities to get an approximate value of $E(X)$ on a computer. To get this average value, it is sufficient to carry out a large number of experiments, and accumulate the value of X found for each experiment each time. The only thing left to do is the final average, by dividing the accumulation of Xs by the number of experiments.

It is the same for calculating variance or standard deviation. By definition, variance $V(X)$ is the average of the square of deviations compared to the average value $E(X)$, i.e.:

$$V(X) = E((X - E(X))^2)$$

Returning to deviations rather than their squares, we also define the standard deviation: $\sigma(X) = \sqrt{V(X)}$.

For computer processing, the formula above for variance is not practical because it forces us to begin by calculating the average value, and then seek the average of the deviations, which would necessitate two calculation steps. Therefore we transform the formula for variance in the following way:

$$\begin{aligned} V(X) &= E((X - E(X)^2) \\ &= E(X^2 - 2X\,E(X) + E(X)^2) \\ &= E(X^2) - 2E(X)\,E(X) + E(X)^2 \\ &= E(X^2) - E(X)^2, \end{aligned}$$

all thanks to the linearity of expectation.

On a computer, at the same time that we determine the average $E(X)$ of X over a large number of experiments, we determine the average of X^2, i.e. $E(X^2)$, and the variance results from it.

We will see how these experimental procedures apply in a first classic example.

21.5. Computer calculation of probabilities, as well as expectation and variance, in the binomial law example

Let us take the context of binomial law (see section 20.5.3). A person plays heads or tails N times. The probability of getting heads is p, that of getting tails is q, with $p + q = 1$. We take random variable X as the number of times we get heads during N throws. We are interested in the probability of getting $X = k$, where k is a number between 0 and N. The theoretical calculation indicates that this probability is:

$$p(X = k) = C_N^{\ k}\, p^k\, q^{N\text{-}k}$$

as we saw in the previous chapter. Computer processing, itself, consists of carrying out this experiment a large number of times, and counting the number of times we get heads exactly k times. This occurs for each value of k.

Hence the program:

– we carry out *NE* experiments, for example *NE* = 30,000;

– each time we play heads or tails N times, for example $N = 20$ with a probability p of getting heads. To get this probability p, we will draw a number at random between 0 and 9,999 N times. If the number is less than *onsetp* = 10,000. p (which is equal to 6,000 for $p = 0.6$), we consider it to be heads that came out;

– for each one of the *NE* experiments, we count the number of times we get heads, and increase the frequency of this number of heads by 1. We end up with the result given in Figure 21.4.

```
onsetp=10000.*p;
for(expe=1; expe<=NE; expe++)
 { nbofheads=0;
  for(toss=1; toss<=N; toss++)
   { nbchance=random(10000);
    if (nbchance<onsetp) nboftimes++;
   }
  freq[nboftimes]++;
 }
```
display this frequency for each value included between 0 and N

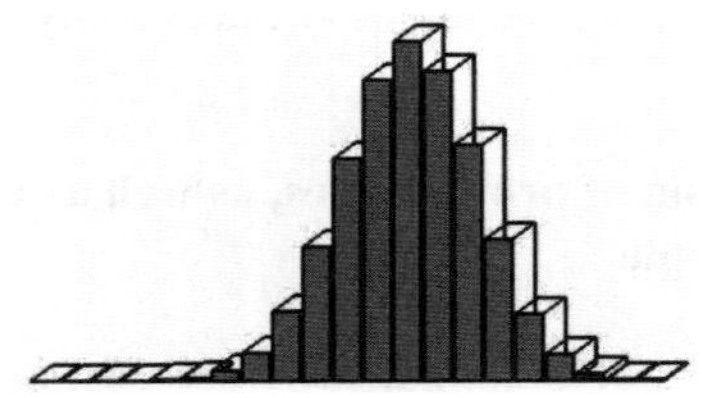

Figure 21.4. *Probability histogram p(X = k), with k from 0 to N = 20, and p = 0.6 for binomial law B(N, p)*

In turn, the expectation $E(X)$, which is the average number of times we get heads comes during N tosses of a coin with probability p, is experimentally obtained by accumulating the number of times we get heads for each one of the *NE* experiments, then dividing this accumulation by the number *NE* of experiments.

Variance $V(X)$ is obtained using the formula $V(X) = E(X^2) - (E(X))^2$, with $E(X^2)$ which is experimentally calculated by accumulating the number of times we get heads in each experiment, squared. Just as with probabilities, $p(X = k)$, we find a good adequacy between the theoretical and experimental results for the expectation and variance.

Here is the program:

```
cumul=0.; cumulV=0.;
for(expe=1;expe<=NE; expe++)
 { nboftimes=0;
  for(toss=1; toss<=N; toss++)
    { nbchance=random(10000);
     if (nbchance<onsetp) nboftimes++;
    }
  cumul+=nboftimes;  cumulV+=nboftimes*nboftimes;
 }
EX=cumul/(float)NE;  EX2=cumulV/(float)NE;  VX=EX2-EX*EX;
display the expectation E(X) and the variance V(X)
```

NOTE 21.1.– Even if this is not indicated in previous programs, it is advisable not just to do *NE* experiments, for example 30,000 experiments. It is recommended that we repeat this succession of *NE* experiments a certain number of times, for example 10 times, relaunching the random generator each time using the function *randomize*(). This is so we then calculate an average of the averages obtained.

We will therefore be able to see that for the blocks of *NE* experiments the results vary slightly each time, which is reassuring for the validity of the generator, and the final average will be more precise.

Let us extend this example by making the link with hypergeometric law (see Chapter 20). Recall that hypergeometric law $\boldsymbol{H}(n, a, b)$ consists of performing n draws without replacing the balls in a box containing a of white balls, and b balls of a different color, i.e. a total of $C = a + b$ balls, with as random variable X_C, which is the number of white balls obtained out of n balls when the total number of balls is C.

When we determine its probability law by taking an increasing C, but still keeping the same proportions of balls of each color, i.e. the same values of the a / C and b / C relationships, it can be shown that the sequence of these random variables X_C associated with hypergeometric law tends to be identified with random variable X of the binomial law $\boldsymbol{B}(n, a / C)$.[3] We can check this experimentally, for example in the case where $a / C = 4 / 10$ and $b / C = 6 / 10$ (see Figure 21.5).

Here is the corresponding program:

```
for(i=0; i<=n; i++) freqb[i]=0;  /* binomial law */
for(expe=1; expe<=NE; expe++)
 { nbwhites=0;
  for(drawing=1; drawing<=n; drawing++)
   { number=random(1000);
   if (number<(int)((1000.*a)/(float)C)) nbwhites++;
   }
  freqb[nbwhites]++;
 }
for(X=0; X<=n; X++) {proba=(float)freqb[X]/(float)NE); display }

for(expe=1; expe<=NE; expe++)  /* hypergeometric law */
 { nbwhites=0; for(i=0; i<C ; i++) done[i]=0;
  for(drawing=1; drawing<=n; drawing++)
   { do number=random(C);
    while (done[number]==1);   done[number]=1;
    if (number<a) nbwhites++;
   }
  freq[nbwhites]++;
 }
for(X=0; X<=n; X++) {proba= (float)freq[X]/(float)NE; display }
```

3. Therefore we say that there is convergence as a law of the sequence (X_n) to random variable X when the probability limit $p(X_n = k)$ for infinite n is equal to $p(X = k)$ for all values of k.

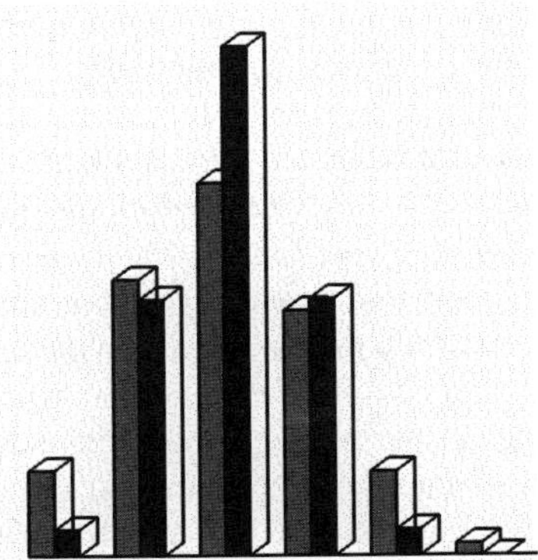

$a = 4$, $b = 6$, i.e. $C = a + b = 10$ and $n = 5$ drawings

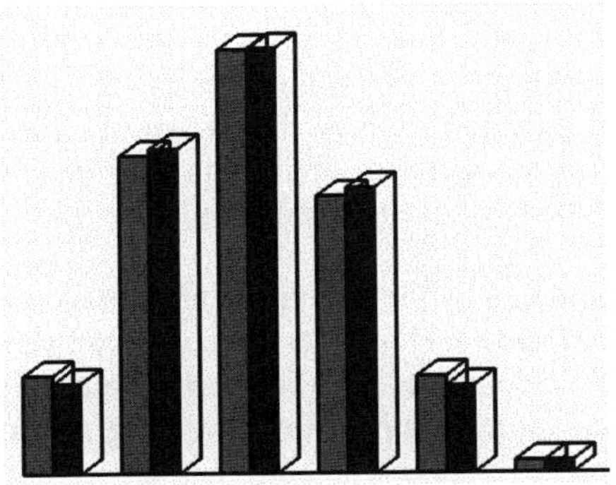

$a = 40$, $b = 60$, i.e. $C = 100$ and $n = 5$ drawings

Figure 21.5. *Comparison between hypergeometric law $H(5, a, b)$ (in black) and binomial law $B(5, 4 / 10)$ (in gray) for two values (a, b) which preserve the relation $a / (a + b) = 4 / 10$. There is a tendency towards harmonization when $C = a + b$ becomes larger*

21.6. Limits of the computer

While the computer gives convincing results in many contexts, there are nevertheless particular occasions where this is not the case, especially when the expectation $E(X)$ becomes infinite. We imagine that on this occasion the computer will give a large number and unstable results when several series of experiments are repeated, as if to warn us of the special case in which we find ourselves. This can happen, but surprises are to be expected. The classic example in this domain is what we call the *Saint Petersburg's paradox*, according to a problem posed by Bernoulli in the 18th century. Here is how it can be formulated.

A casino organizes a game of heads or tails that is repeated until the first head is thrown (H). The coin is fair so there are as many chances of getting tails as heads. If the first head is thrown before the tenth move, the player loses 10 chips. If the first head is thrown on the $(10 + k)^{th}$ *move, where k is a natural integer* ≥ 0*, the player wins* 2^k *chips. Is this game valuable for the player or the casino?*

Intuitively, we can imagine that no player will risk such a game! But if we seek the theoretical expectation of the player's winnings, the calculation shows that his expected winnings are infinite and the casino goes bankrupt. Actually, with $(1 / 2)^n$ probability of getting heads at the nth move, the expected winnings on average are:

$$-10(1/2+1/4+1/8+ \ldots +1/512) + (1/2)10+ 2(1/2)11+4(1/2)12+\ldots$$

$$= -9.98 + (1/2)10(1+1+1+\ldots) = +\infty$$

But what happens when we carry out the experiment on a computer? The program responds with great consistency that we must expect a loss of 9.95 chips. We are far from the theoretical result of infinite winnings, and the computer to a certain extent has the same response as a human player.

The expectation calculated by the formula is an average out of a large number of moves, and in the present case this number of moves can very much exceed human limits, and even those of a computer. The random generator, on releasing some tens of thousands of numbers, is not supposed to give long series of the number 0, in a binary universe of 0 and 1, because we could then criticize it for not being random enough. If the theoretical winnings are infinite, it is because of a very long series of the outcome of the number 0, with very weak probability, which is incompatible with the limited nature of the random generator.[4]

On the other hand, if instead of taking an onset of 10 moves (nine tails and one head) to start winning, we reduce this onset two or three, the results still remain false and even slightly negative instead of being positive and large, but such results are sufficiently unstable to incite caution.

---

4. Another striking phenomenon occurs. If we assume that the coin is slightly loaded, with the probability p of tossing heads being slightly greater than that of tossing tails, we find that the theoretical expectation is -9.94 for $p = 0.51$ and -5.1 for $p = 0.5001$.

21.7. Exercises

21.7.1. *Exercise 1: throwing balls in boxes*

Let us return to the exercise dealt with theoretically in section 20.6.1. We have N boxes, initially empty. We throw one ball at random into a box, repeating this type of throw until no box is empty. Random variable X is the number of throws carried out during this experiment. We want to experimentally find out, on a computer, the average number of moves E(X), and this is done for various values of N.

We take the number of boxes B and number of experiments carried out NE.

```
cumul =0.;
for (exp=1; exp<=NE ; exp++)
 { for (i=1; i<=B ; i++) filled[i]=NO ;
   nbmoves=0; nbnonemptyboxes=0;
   do { nbmoves++; number=1+random(B);
        if (filled[number]==NO)
          {filled[number]=YES; nbnonemptyboxes++;}
      }
   while (nbnonemptyboxes < B);
   cumul+=(float) nbthrows;
 }
EX = cumul/(float)NE;
```

21.7.2. *Exercise 2: boys and girls*

In a group made up of N boys and N girls, each boy likes one of the N girls, and each girl likes one of the N boys, in all equiprobability. What is the probability that the liking of one boy for one girl is reciprocated?

21.7.2.1. *Approximate probabilistic solution*

Let us begin by determining the number of possible cases. When a boy likes a girl, he has N possibilities. The number of ways for the boys to be linked to a girl is N^N. It is also the number of applications of a N-element set (boys) in a N-element set (girls). Similarly there are N^N ways for the girls to be linked with the boys. For each one of the N^N ways for the boys to be linked to the girls, there are N^N ways for the girls to be linked to the boys, hence N^{2N} supposedly equiprobable possible cases.

One method of solving the problem consists of creating all the applications (reciprocations of feelings) of boys to girls. For each one of these applications, we take all the applications of girls to boys in order to carry out the comparison on a case-by-case basis to see if there is a similar link (their feelings are reciprocated). In this way we get the exact number of favorable cases out of the N^{2N} possible cases. This exhaustive method demands a lot of time as soon as N increases (for $N = 10$, we would need to process 10^{20} cases one by one). It is therefore better to be satisfied with an approximate result using a Monte Carlo-style method. We make a large number of tries. Each time, we randomly create a boys-to-girls application, then a girls-to-boys application, and by comparison we determine whether or not it is a favorable case, with at least one reciprocal liking. From this we deduce the probability sought. Hence the program:

```
#define N 10
#define NE 30000   /* number of experiments */
main()
{ cumulproba=0.;
 for(block=0; block<20; block++) /* we do the NE experiments 20 times */
  { randomize(); c=0;
   for(exp=0; exp<NE; exp++)
    { for(b=0; b<N; b++) gg[b]=random(N)%N;
     for(g=0; g<N; g++)  bb[g]=random(N)%N;
     flag=0;
     for(b=0; b<N; b++) for(g=0; g<N; g++)
     if (gg[b]==g && bb[g]==b) { flag=1; g=N; b=N;}
     if (flag==1) c++;
    }
   proba=(float)(NE-c)/(float)NE; display;   cumulproba+=proba;
  }
 printf("\nFor N= %d, Probability= %3.3f ", N, cumulproba/20.);
}
```

In this way we go from a probability of order 0.717 for $N = 5$ to a probability of 0.636 for $N = 100$.

21.7.2.2. *Exact combinatorics method*

In Chapter 2 we saw how to create applications from an initial set – in section 21.7.2.1 the set of boys – to a final set – here the set of girls – and how to group them in parcels following the partition of the number N obtained on at the final set.

For example for $N = 3$, i.e. $3^3 = 27$ applications (and three partitions), we find three cases where the boys like the same girl (partition 3), 18 cases where two boys like the same girl, and the third another girl (partition 2 + 1), and six cases where each girl is liked by a boy (partition 1 + 1 + 1). We write each one of these partitions in a table with $N = 3$ elements, filling it in with 0s. In the example with partition 2 + 1, this means that a girl is liked by two boys, another is liked by one single boy, and the third girl not liked by any of the boys. In each one of these cases, we take the complement at $N = 3$ of each term in this table.

In this way, from partition 210, which happens 18 times, we form the table containing 123. By multiplying these three numbers, we find the number of cases where girls like the boys without the feelings being reciprocated. For each one of the 18 cases where two boys like the same girl, there are six possibilities without reciprocal liking. Actually, the girl who is liked by two boys can therefore only like the third boy; the girl who is liked by one single boy can only like the two others; and the one who is not liked by any has the choice between the three. Therefore we find $18 \times 6 = 108$ cases of absence of reciprocal love. We do the same for the other partitions.

It is enough to add this type of calculation to the applications program grouped in parcels to get the exact number of cases without reciprocal liking, then taking the complement in relation to the total number of cases N^{2N}, the one with at least one reciprocal liking. We find that the probability moves from 0.875 for $N = 2$ to 0.676 for $N = 9$. The results for the first values of N, with the probability of getting at least one reciprocal relationship, are given in Table 21.1. These calculations quickly become prohibitive as soon as N exceeds 10.

N	2	3	4	5	6	7	8	9
probability	0.875	0.785	0.742	0.717	0.701	0.690	0.682	0.676

Table 21.1.

21.7.3. *Exercise 3: conditional probability*

A business creates coins, 90% of which work well, the others being defective. When the coins are tested, those that work well are all accepted, but 1 / 11 of those that do not work well are also accepted. The others are placed in the garbage. We want to find the probability a coin that is tested and accepted as good is in fact defective.

We distinguish three types of coins: those that are good and also accepted, in the proportion 9 / 10; those that are bad but accepted at the time of the test, in the proportion $\frac{1}{11}\frac{1}{10}=\frac{1}{110}$; and those that are bad and refused, in the proportion $\frac{1}{11}\frac{1}{10}=\frac{1}{110}$. Let $p(GA)$ be the probability that a coin is good and accepted, and $p(BA)$ the probability that a coin is bad and accepted at the time of the test. The probability $p(A)$ that a coin is accepted is equal to:

$$p(GA \text{ or } BA) = \frac{9}{10}+\frac{1}{110}=\frac{100}{110}$$

The probability $p(B \mid A)$ that a coin is bad (knowing that it is part of those that were accepted) is such that $p(B \mid A)\, p(A) = p(BA)$ i.e.:

$$p(B \mid A) = \frac{p(BA)}{p(A)} = \frac{1}{110}\frac{110}{100} = \frac{1}{100}$$

There is one chance in 100 that a coin that accepted as good is defective.

Let us find this experimentally, thanks to the program that follows. For this, we carry out a large number of experiments, i.e. *NBEXP*. Each time, we draw a number h at random so that $0 \leq h < 11{,}000$. If h is such that $0 \leq h < 9{,}900$, we are in the 90% proportion, and we have a good and accepted coin. If h is such that $9{,}900 \leq h < 10{,}000$, with the proportion 100 / 11,000, we have a bad but accepted coin, with the other values of h corresponding to the bad and refused coins. It is enough to count the number *nbBA* of times we get a bad but accepted coin, as well as the number *nbGA* of times a coin is good (and accepted), and number *nbA* of times a coin is accepted, i.e. *nbA* = *nbGA* + *nbBA*. The probability sought is *nbBA* / *nbA*. Hence the program will give a value very close to 0.01:

```
randomize(); nbGA=0; nbBA=0;
for(i=0;i<NBEXP;i++)
  { h=random(11000);
    if (h<9900) nbGA++;  else if (h<10000) nbBA++;
  }
nbA = nbGA + nbBA; proba = (float)nbBA/(float)nbA; display proba
```

21.8. Appendix: chi-squared law

Here is the context in which chi-squared law is involved. Let us imagine that we have a box filled with balls with S colors c_1, c_2, …, c_S, where the balls of each color are in the same proportions, i.e. $1 / S$. We carry out N successive draws of one ball with replacement. X_i is the random variable equal to the number of color balls c_i that came out during the N draws. We are interested in the sum of the squares of deviations of the number of balls of each color in relation to their average number N / S, by introducing the random variable:

$$Y = \frac{\sum_{i=1}^{S} (X_i - \frac{N}{S})^2}{\frac{N}{S}}$$

In other words, we want to quantitatively find the spread of results in the case of a uniform distribution. We show that this spread obeys chi-squared law when N is sufficiently high. More specifically, the random variable Y with S types of balls follows the chi-squared law to $S - 1$ degrees of freedom – the law of distribution that we know perfectly. All we have to do is compare the numerical results it gives with the experimental results provided by the random number generator whose validity we want to test. Now let us take two examples.

21.8.1. *Examples of the test for uniform distribution*

A random number generator, including numbers between 1 and 4, creates 10,000 numbers, with the following, fairly spread-out, results: number 1 appears 2,611 times; number 2 appears 2,540 times; number 3 appears 2,458 times; and number 4 appears 2,391 times. We want to test the accuracy of this generator. Everything happens as if we had a box with balls in four colors in identical proportion $1 / 4$, where we make 10,000 draws. From this we deduce that random variable Y equals:

$$\frac{\sum_{i=1}^{4} (X_i - 2{,}500)^2}{2{,}500} \approx 11$$

Now taking what is given by the tables related to the distribution function F_3 of chi-squared law to three degrees of freedom, we notice that:

$$F_3(10) = p(Y < 10) \approx 0.97$$

The probability of getting $Y > 10$ is about 3%.

If there were uniform distribution, we would have a very low probability (less than 3%) of having the result obtained by the random number generator. From this we deduce that this generator is not valid, or at least it has very few chances of being so. This conclusion can be confirmed by re-starting the experiment several times.

Let us take a second example: out of a total of 10,000 numbers, with characters from 1 to 5, the random generator produces: number 1 2,020 times; number 2 1,982 times; the number 3 2,005 times; number 4 1,991 times; and number 5 2,002 times, with low spread. Variable Y is now equal to about 0.4, while chi-squared law to four degrees of freedom gives:

$$F_4(0.5) = p(Y < 0.5) \approx 0.04$$

With a uniform random distribution, the probability of getting the frequencies of previous outcomes is less than 5%. We may even consider the generator to be worthless.

The two preceding examples show that the spread of results must not be too strong or too weak, according to the norms of chi-squared law. On the other hand we take it that by placing ourselves between these two extremes, in the middle zone, conditions are favorable for getting a uniform distribution. We verify that this middle zone corresponds to a value of Y of order S. It is now possible to check that the random number generator integrated in our computer successfully passes the chi-squared test. It is sufficient to calculate the value of Y after a large number of tries. We begin by exercising this simplification in the calculation of Y:

$$Y = \frac{\sum_{i=1}^{S}(X_i - \frac{N}{S})^2}{\frac{N}{S}} = \frac{\sum_{i=1}^{S}(X_i^2 - 2\frac{N}{S}X_i + \frac{N^2}{S^2})}{\frac{N}{S}} = \frac{S}{N}(\sum_{i=1}^{S} X_i^2) - 2N + N = \frac{S}{N}(\sum_{i=1}^{S} X_i^2) - N$$

The following program results from it, here $N = 30{,}000$ and $S = 100$:

```
randomize(); /* we launch the random number  generator  */
for(i=0; i<100; i++)
   f[i]=0; /* the frequency table of the outcome of the 100 numbers is set to 0 */
for(exp=0; exp<30000; exp++)  /* we carry out the drawing of 30,000 random
                                  numbers */
  { h=random(100);  f[h]++; }
```

```
cumulf=0.;
for(i=0; i<100; i++) cumulf+=(double)f[i]*(double)f[i]/30000.;
Y= 100.*cumulf - 30000.;
printf("\n%3.2lf ", Y);
```

In this case we will have to obtain a number close to 100.

21.8.2. *Chi-squared law and its link with Poisson distribution*

By definition, a random variable Y_λ follows Poisson distribution $\boldsymbol{P}(\lambda)$ with parameter λ with $\lambda > 0$ when its probability law is:

$$p(Y_\lambda = k) = e^{-\lambda}\frac{\lambda^k}{k!}.$$

We can show (but will not do so here) that chi-squared law to $2n$ degrees of freedom, with random variable X_{2n}, is linked to Poisson distribution through the relation $p(X_{2n} > 2\lambda) = p(Y_\lambda < n)$. As the formulae associated with the definition of chi-squared law are more complex than those of Poisson distribution, we have a way of finding out the distribution function of chi-squared law to $2n$ degrees of freedom using Poisson distribution.

Let us recall that the distribution function $F_{2n}(x)$ of chi-squared law gives the probability $p(X_{2n} < x)$ as a function of x, where x is a real number (see Chapter 22 for reminders on the distribution function, i.e. $F_{2n}(x) = p(X_{2n} < x)$). The formula above can be expressed:

$$\begin{aligned} p(X_{2n} > x) &= p(Y_{x/2} < n) \\ &= e^{-x/2}\sum_{k=0}^{n-1}\frac{x^k}{2^k\,k!} \quad \text{for } x > 0 \end{aligned}$$

hence $F_{2n}(x) = 1 - p(Y_{x/2} < n)$ for $x > 0$, and $F_{2n}(x) = 0$ for $x \le 0$.

From this we deduce the program enabling us to trace the distribution function of chi-squared law with an even number of degrees of freedom (see Figure 21.6):

```
for(x=0.; x<100.; x+=0.001)
 { X=x/2.; cumul=1.; cumulX=1.; cumulk=1.;
  for(k=1;k<n;k++)
```

```
{ cumulX=X*cumulX;  /* calculation of (x/2)k */
  cumulk=k*cumulk;   /* calculation of k! */
  cumul+=cumulX/cumulk;
}
result=exp(-X)*cumul; y=1.-result;
draw point (x, y) on the screen, i.e. the point
xo+zoomx*x, yo-zoomy*y
}
```

This is the opportunity to indicate a better method of calculation, called Horner's method. By postulating that $X = x / 2$ we can write:

$$\sum_{k=0}^{n-1} \frac{X^k}{k!} = 1 + X/1! + X^2/2! + \ldots + X^{n-1}/(n-1)!$$

$$= 1 + X(1 + (X/2)(1 + (X/3)(1 + \ldots\ (1 + X/(n-1))\ldots)))$$

hence the program:

```
for(x=0.; x<100.; x+=0.001)
 { X=x/2.; cumul=1.;
  for(k=1; k<n; k++) cumul=cumul*X/(n-k)+1.;
  result=exp(-X)*cumul; y=1.-result;  draw the point }
```

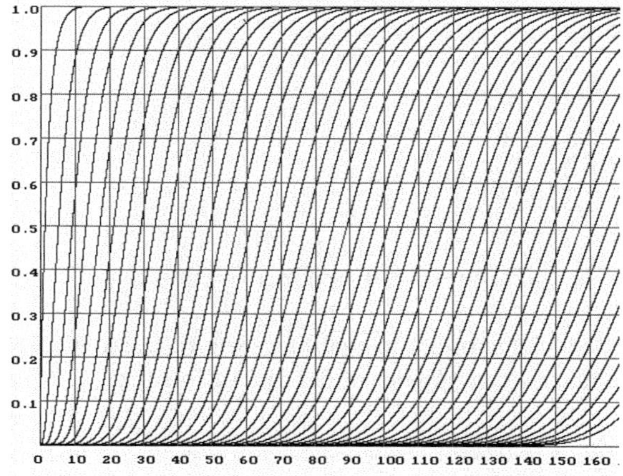

Figure 21.6. *Distribution functions F_2, F_6, F_{10}, ..., from 4 of 4 for the degrees of freedom*

Chapter 22

Discrete and Continuous

Probability theory, in its theoretical form, is not limited to the case of random variables taking a finite number of values, even an infinite number when dealing with the set of integers, as in the case of geometric law. It concerns discrete probabilities.

Now let us imagine that the random variable takes its values from an interval $[a\ b]$ of real numbers, for example [0 1]. The notion of elementary event loses all meaning, to the extent that the probability $p(X = a)$, with a that is a given real number, for example: $a = 1 / 3$, becomes null: there is no chance of falling directly on 1 / 3. Nevertheless the sum of the probabilities taken on all points, and which are all null, must give 1. Therefore we are led to divide the interval into small sub-divisions, where the probability is no longer null. Thus we return to discrete probabilities, but ultimately in passing, the size of the parts leaning towards 0, we end up at what is called *continuous probabilities*.

The probability distribution at each point x of an interval now becomes a density $d(x)$. For want of being able to take the sum of the densities at all the points, we take the integral of the density function on the interval $[a\ b]$ concerned, i.e.:

$$\int_a^b d(t)dt$$

and this integral is equal to 1. The weight of each isolated point is null, without its density being so, and the higher its density, the greater the chance of falling in the vicinity of this point.

For computer processing of this type of problem, we go no further than a fine discretization on the vicinities of points, which constitutes a good approximation of continuous phenomena.[1] Let us begin by taking the simplest example – the one where the random variable follows a uniform law.

22.1. Uniform law

In this case, the probability density is constant at interval [0, 1], more specifically $d(x) = 1$ over [0, 1] and $d(x) = 0$ elsewhere. The random variable X is a real number between $-\infty$ and $+\infty$. Let us put ourselves in the vicinity of a point x, on interval $[x, x + h]$, where h is a small real number, with $[x, x + h]$ included in [0, 1]. Let the probability of random variable X being on this interval, i.e. $p(x \leq X < x + h)$, which corresponds to a "weight", be equal to the probability density $d(x)$, here equal to 1, multiplied by the length h of the interval, i.e. $1 . h = h$.

For example let us divide interval [0, 1] into intervals of length 1 / 10. On each of these intervals $[k / 10, (k + 1) / 10]$ with k from 0 to 9, we get:

$$p(k / 10 \leq X < (k + 1) / 10) = 1 / 10, \text{ i.e. } 1 / 10 \,.\, d(k / 10)$$

The sum of all these probabilities forms the area delimited by the curve $d(x)$, and it is equal to 1.

22.1.1. *Programming*

On the computer, the drawing of a number following a uniform law is simple. This is what the random number generator does. If the function *rand*() returns a random integer between 0 and *RAND_MAX* – often the number 32767. All we have to do is drift, calling *rand*() / *RAND_MAX*, which returns a number between 0 and 1. By repeating this drawing a large number of times, i.e. *NBEXP* times, it is sufficient to count on how many ocassions we fall into each interval of type $[k / 10, (k + 1) / 10]$. Dividing these results by the number *NBEXP*, we find the probability $p(k / 10 \leq X < (k + 1) / 10)$.

1. This is what we do to get the approximate value of the integral of the function f between a and b. This integral is equal to the area included between the curve of f and the x-axis, and to obtain its value we cut it up into small rectangles in the form of vertical sticks whose area is easy to calculate. Continuous probabilities are also called *geometric probabilities*. These appeared in Chapter 21 in Buffon's needle method.

Lastly, it is sufficient to divide the probability by the length 1 / 10 of the interval (i.e. multiply it by 10) to get the density *d*(*x*) in discretized form (see Figure 22.1), hence the program below.

We are given the number *NBEXP*. In the main program, variable *u* is a number taken at random between 0 and 1 declared to be a floating-point number. Variable *ue* is declared to be an integer, the latter being the integer part of 10 *u*, since it becomes an index in the table *numberoftimes*[]. For example, if we get *u* = 0.8674, then *ue* = 8, with 8 corresponding to the interval [0.8 0.9[and *numberoftimes*[8] increases by 1.

```
for(expe=0; expe<NEXP; expe++)
  { u=uniform(); ue=10.*u; nbtimes[ue]++;}
for(i=0; i<10; i++)
 { proba=(float)nbtimes[i]/(float)NEXP;
   draw the probabilities multiplied by 10 in the shape of vertical bars
 }
float uniform(void)
{ float u;   u=(float)rand()/(float)RAND_MAX; return u; }
```

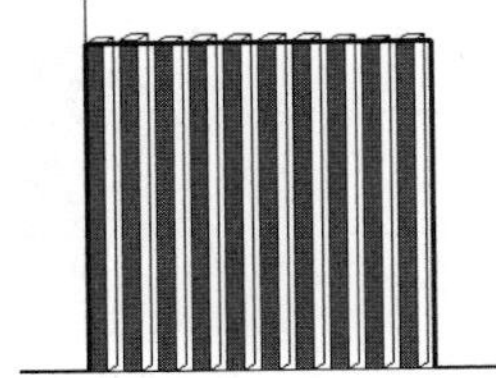

Figure 22.1. *The density function d(x) of uniform law from dividing interval [0 1] into 10 intervals*

22.1.2. *Example 1*

Taking traffic problems into consideration, a person is sure to arrive at a specific location between 7 and 7.30pm. It is implied that the person's probability of arrival is uniform in this time interval. He decides to wait exactly 10 minutes in that location. What is the person's probability of being there at exactly 7.15pm?

To be at the location at 7.15pm means that this person must arrive between 7.05 and 7.15pm. Taking an hour as the unit of time, and considering 7.00pm as time 0, the uniform density between 0 and 1 / 2 is equal to 2, and it is 0 elsewhere. The probability sought is obtained by dividing the length 1 / 6 of the interval corresponding to favorable cases by the length 1 / 2 of the interval corresponding to the possible cases, which gives a one in three chance, or even:

$$p(1 / 12 < X < 1 / 4) = 2 \,.\, 1 / 6 = 1 / 3$$

Experimental computer processing would consist of throwing a shower of particles (numbers) between 0 and 1 / 2, and counting the proportion of those that fall in interval [1 / 12, 1 / 4] (see Figure 22.2).

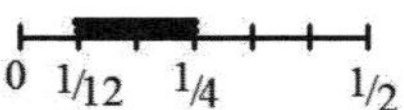

Figure 22.2. *Probability of falling in an interval*

22.1.3. *Example 2: two people meeting*

Two people A and B must meet at the same place between 12 and 12.30am with uniform probability during this time interval. Each one decides to wait exactly 10 minutes in that location. What is the probability that they meet?

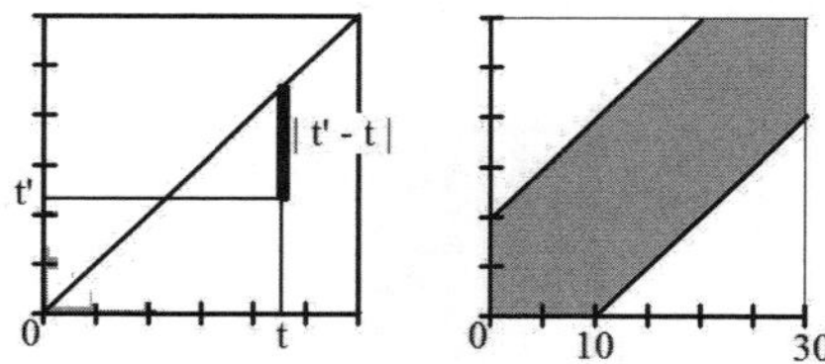

Figure 22.3. *The difference between the arrival times of the two people (left); and the diagonal strip corresponding to their meeting (right)*

Let us take a benchmark where the arrival time t of person A is placed on the horizontal axis and the arrival time t' of person B is placed on the vertical axis. This gives a point M (t, t') located in a square with side 1 / 2 (see Figure 22.3). The position of this point has a uniform probability inside this square. The time difference $| t' - t |$ is read on a vertical segment between point M and the diagonal of the square starting at O (see Figure 22.3, left). For there to be a meeting, this difference must be less than 10 minutes above or below this diagonal. The favorable cases are located in a strip around this diagonal (see Figure 22.3, right). The probability of meeting is obtained by dividing the area of this strip by the area of the square. We find (900 – 400) / 900 = 5 / 9. There again, experimental verification would consist of sending a shower of particles inside the square, as we have already seen for the approximate calculation of the number π in section 21.3.

22.2. Density function for a continuous random variable and distribution function

What we did for uniform law is generalized to every random variable X that takes its values out of a set of real numbers $\boldsymbol{R}$.

Let us begin with a discretized perspective. In the vicinity of point x in interval $[x, x + h[$, let us take the probability of random variable X being in this interval, i.e. $p(x \leq X < x + h)$. Next let us divide this "weight" by the length h of the interval, i.e. $p(x \leq X < x + h)) / h$. Making h lean towards 0, we get what is called the density $d(x)$ of the point:

$$d(x) = \lim_{h \to 0} \frac{p(x \leq X < x + h)}{h}$$

Thus defined, the density function is supposed to be continuous on R,[2] in such a way that we can calculate its integral. It is positive or null over R, and the area it delimits with the x-axis is equal to 1, since it is a sum of areas of small rectangles h wide and $p(x \leq X < x + h) / h$ high, which gives the sum of the probabilities on all successive intervals h long, i.e. 1, and is also the integral of the density taken between $-\infty$ and $+\infty$.

Finally, we can define a continuous random variable X using a density function d, provided that this density $d(x)$ is:

– continuous on $\boldsymbol{R}$ (except eventually in a finite number of discontinuous points);

– positive or null; and

– $\int_{-\infty}^{+\infty} d(t)dt = 1$.

We are therefore able to calculate the probability associated with every event of the form $X < x$, i.e.:

$$p(X < x) = \int_{-\infty}^{x} d(t)\, dt$$

We call distribution function F of random variable X the function of the real variable x such that:

2. We can even accept discontinuities at isolated points. Let us take one of these points x_k, and impose that it be the end of a subdivision. It is enough that over $[x_k, x_k + h[$ the function be continuous at x_k on the right side, because it must have a limit on the right side equal to $d(x_k)$.

$$F(x) = p(X < x) = \int_{-\infty}^{x} d(t)\, dt$$

For example, the uniform random variable defined above has the distribution function $F(X) = 0$ for $x < 0$, $F(x) = x$ on [0 1], and $F(x) = 1$ for $x > 1$. Its curve is drawn in Figure 22.4.

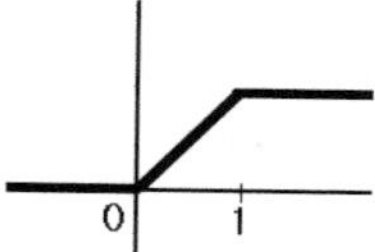

Figure 22.4. *Distribution function of uniform law*

22.3. Normal law

Another law that is just as classic on the subject of continuous probabilities is the so-called *normal law*. During statistical observation of many phenomena, the frequency diagram has the appearance of a bell-shaped curve, also called the Gauss curve or Gauss-Laplace's curve, and it is there that normal law was born (see Figure 22.5).

For example, if we measure the height of each individual in a large population, we notice that the stick diagram, with all sticks of constant width h, corresponding to the number of individuals with a height between T and $T+h$, i.e. a small neighborhood of size T, has this appearance of a bell curve: symmetrical around the vertical axis passing through its maximum. Two characteristic elements are released from the shape of this curve: the position of its peak, corresponding to the average value m of the results on the horizontal axis, and the relatively tightened shape of the curve around its maximum, indicating the degree of spreading of the results around the average value, and associated with the notion of standard deviation σ. This led to a mathematical definition of this type of law, no longer in discretized form but in continuous form.

We say that a continuous random variable X follows a normal law $N(m,\sigma)$ with parameters m and σ (average and standard deviation), when it has the density function:[3]

3. We check that d is a density: it is continuous on R; it is positive; its integral between $-\infty$ and $+\infty$ exists and is equal to 1.

$$d(x) = \frac{1}{\sigma\sqrt{2\pi}} e^{-\frac{(x-m)^2}{2\sigma^2}}$$

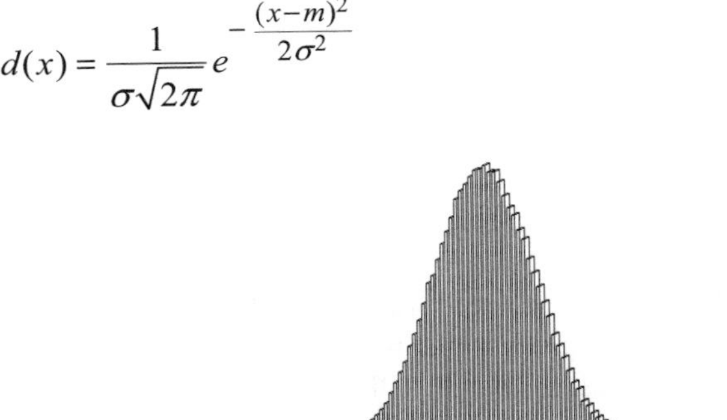

Figure 22.5. *Stick diagram giving the Gauss-Laplace bell curve*

The corresponding curve has a maximum at $x = m$, it is symmetrical with respect to the vertical straight line $x = m$, and the distance between m and the two points of inflection is equal to σ. Because of symmetry, m is the average value (the expectation). We can also check that σ is the standard deviation as defined theoretically. In particular, normal law $N(0, 1)$ with average 0 and standard deviation 1 corresponds to what is called the *reduced centered normal variable*, the distribution function of which is expressed $\Phi(x)$. Therefore every random variable X that follows a normal law with parameters m and σ is such that variable $\dfrac{X-m}{\sigma}$ follows the reduced centered normal law $N(0, 1)$.

It is here that the essential advantage of this definition of normal law in continuous form appears. For every statistical phenomenon that has the appearance of a bell-shaped curve, the calculations can be reduced to the distribution function $\Phi(x)$ of normal law $N(0, 1)$. The values at each point of $\Phi(x)$ have long been recorded in numerical tables.

Let us return to the example of the height of individuals in a population where we observe that the average height is 170 cm and the standard deviation 10 cm. The corresponding random variable X is the height of the individuals. We want to find the probability, within this population, of having a height greater than 180 cm, i.e. $p(X > 180)$. First of all we notice that $p(X > 180) = 1 - p(X < 180)$. Event $X < 180$ is also expressed $X - 170 < 10$, or:

$$\frac{X-170}{10} < 1 \text{, i.e. } \frac{X-m}{\sigma} < 1$$

Now the variable $\frac{X-170}{10}$ is reduced centered normal and $p(X < 180) = p(\frac{X-170}{10} < 1) = \Phi(1) \approx 0.84$ according to the numerical tables.

Finally, the probability of having a height greater than 180 cm is 16%.

We could believe that in this context the computer's only interest is to automatically calculate what can already be read in the numerical tables. It is nothing of the sort, however, because as we will see normal law as well as other laws involving continuous variables can be simulated on a computer using its random number generator, the one that obeys uniform law. Before returning to normal law, let us look at another case, that of exponential law.

22.4. Exponential law and its link with uniform law

By definition, the exponential random variable with parameter k (k positive real) has the density $d(x) = k\,e^{-kx}$ for $x \geq 0$ and $d(x) = 0$ for $x < 0$.[4] The distribution function is:

$$F(x) = \int_{-\infty}^{x} d(t)dt \text{, i.e. } F(x) = 0 \text{ for } x < 0$$

$$\text{and: } F(x) = \int_{0}^{x} ke^{-kt}dt = 1 - e^{-kx} \quad \text{for } x \geq 0$$

How can such a law be simulated on a computer, where the computer only has one random number generator following one uniform law? For this, we will establish a link between random variable X that follows an exponential law with parameter k, and random variable U that follows a uniform law on [0 1]. As it happens, we will show that for all x:

$$p(X < x) = p(-\frac{1}{k}\ln(1-U) < x)$$

4. Let us check that it is a matter of a density: $d(x)$ is continuous except in 0 where it is continuous on the right (and has a limit on the left), it is ≥ 0 everywhere, and $\int_{-\infty}^{+\infty} d(t)dt = -\left[e^{-kt}\right]_{0}^{+\infty} = 1$.

i.e. the distribution function of X is the same as that of $-\frac{1}{k}\ln(1-U)$ or even that these two random variables follow the same law.

Indeed, the event $-\frac{1}{k}\ln(1-U) < x$ is also expressed:

$$\ln(1-U) > -kx\,,\ 1-U > e^{-kx} \text{ or } U\ <\ 1-e^{-kx}$$

and: $p(-\frac{1}{k}\ln(1-U) < x) = p(U < 1-e^{-kx})$

For $x < 0$, $1 - e^{-kx}$ goes from 0 to $-\infty$, and $p(U < 1 - e^{-kx}) = 0$, while for $x > 0$, $1 - e^{-kx}$ goes from 0 to 1, and $p(U < 1 - e^{-kx}) = 1 - e^{-kx}$. We have just found the distribution function of the exponential random variable. Note that U and $1 - U$ follow the same uniform law, for reasons of evident symmetry.

Finally, the exponential random variable X, with parameter k, obeys the same law as $-\frac{1}{k}\ln U$. We will therefore be able to simulate exponential law on a computer using the uniform random generator. The following program results from it. Function *hexp*()returns a random number that obeys the exponential law with parameter k. Note that we forbid the number h from being null by adding a bit more to it, to avoid the eventuality of a fatal error when calculating the logarithm of h.

```
float hexp(void)
 { float h,he;
  h=(float)rand()/(float)RAND_MAX+0.0000000001;
  he=-log(h)/k;
  return he;
 }
```

As for the main program, it repeats the experiment a large number of times, and records the number of times the random number falls in an interval of length 1/10 (see Figure 22.6):

```
for(nbexpe=0; nbexpe<NBEXP; nbexpe++)
 {chanceexpo=hexp();
  hinteger = (int)(chanceexpo*10.);
```

```
    nbtimes[hinteger]+ +;
  }
  for(i=0; i<30; i++)
  { density=10.*(float)nbtimes[i]/(float)NBEXP;
    draw a vertical bar giving density d(x) on each interval
  }
```

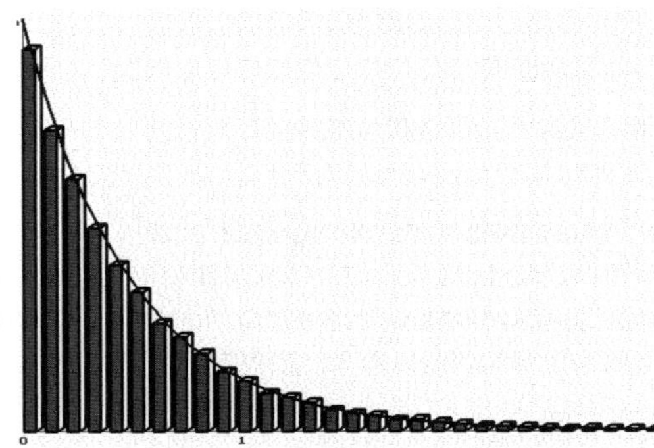

Figure 22.6. *Density d(x) corresponding to exponential law, here with parameter k = 2*

22.4.1. *An application: geometric law using exponential law*

We saw how to create a continuous random variable using discrete procedures and from uniform law. In turn, the exponential law thus obtained enables us to rediscover geometric law, in other words we will move from continuous to discrete variables. Let us recall that random variable Y that obeys geometric law with parameter p, i.e. the waiting time for the first success (with probability p) in a game of heads or tails, takes its values on $\boldsymbol{N}^*$ with the probability $p(X = i) = (1 - p)^{i-1} p$ for i integer > 0. On the other hand, the exponential random variable X is such that:

$$p(i - 1 \leq X < i) = p(X < \mathrm{i}) - p(X \leq i - 1) = 1 - e^{-k\,i} - 1 + e^{-k(i-1)} = e^{-k(i-1)}(1 - e^{-k})$$

The event $i - 1 \leq X < i$ is also expressed $[X] = i - 1$ or $[X] + 1 = i$, where $[X]$ designates the integer part of X. By choosing parameter k of the exponential law using parameter p of geometric law so that $p = 1 - e^{-k}$ with $k = -\ln(1 - p)$, we get probability $p([X] + 1 = i) = (1 - p)^{i-1} p$. Therefore, the random variable $[X] + 1$ follows the geometric law with parameter p.

By way of verification, we can use the program above to again find geometric law from exponential law.

22.4.2. *Program for getting the geometric law with parameter p*

We take p, from which we deduce parameter k of the associated exponential law. Function *geometr*() returns a random integer that obeys geometric law:

```
k= -log(1.-p);
for(nbexpe=0; nbexpe<NBEXP; nbexpe++)
  { chancegeo=geometr(); nbtimes[chancegeo]++; }
for(i=1; i<15; i++) { proba=nbtimes[i]/(float)NBEXP; draw }

int geometr(void)
 { float h,he; int ge;
  h=(float)rand()/(float)RAND_MAX+0.0000000001;
  he=-log(h)/a;
  ge=(int)he+1;  return ge;
 }
```

We can compare the results thus obtained with those given by the classic geometric law problem (see Figure 22.7), which we recall below:

```
onset = (int)(p*1000.);
for(nbexpe=0; nbexpe<NBEXP; nbexpe++)
  { X=0;  do { X++; h=random(1000);} while(h>=onset);   nbtimes[X]++; }
for(i=1; i<15; i++)  { proba=nbtimes[i]/(float)NBEXP; drawing }
```

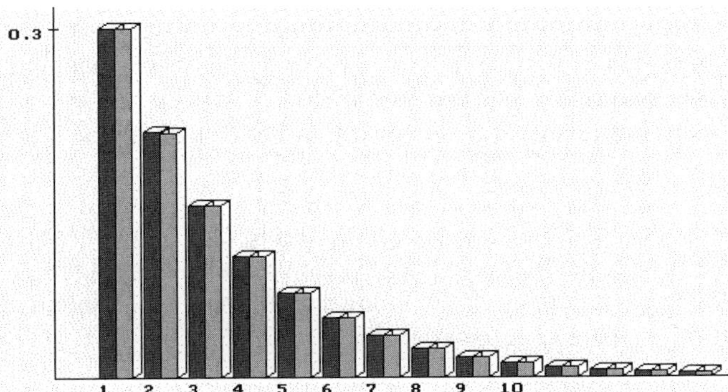

Figure 22.7. *Geometric law with parameter 0.3, obtained by the two methods*

22.5. Normal law as an approximation of binomial law

In the previous chapter we saw the notion of convergence of a probability law on another law. We thus dealt with the hypergeometric law example $\boldsymbol{H}(C, a, b)$ that converged with binomial law when the number of balls C tended towards infinity while respecting the proportion of the two types of balls. In more general terms, we say that a sequence of discrete random variables X_n (with values in N) converges, for infinite n, on a discrete variable X when the probabilities at each point become the same, i.e. every integer k: $p(X_n = k)$ tends towards $p(X = k)$.

When a discrete variable X_n converges on a continuous and no longer discrete variable it is no longer possible to say that the probabilities at each point are ultimately the same. We should take the vicinities of the points. Therefore we will say there is convergence when the distribution functions of the two variables tend to become the same.

In this context, let us take the case of binomial law $\boldsymbol{B}(n, p)$ with n (number of times coin is tossed) which tends towards infinity, p remaining fixed. For each value of n, random variable X_n follows this binomial law, with np being the average value and $\sigma = \sqrt{np(1-p)}$ standard deviation. In this way we get a sequence (X_n) of binomial random variables. Next, let us take the sequence (Y_n) of reduced centered binomial random variables associated with X_n, i.e.:

$$Y_n = \frac{X_n - np}{\sigma}$$

Therefore we have the following property: sequence (Y_n) converges on normal law $\boldsymbol{N}(0, 1)$, that is to say the distribution function of Y_n, for large n, is a good approximation of that of $\boldsymbol{N}(0, 1)$. In practice, we see that this is valid as soon as n is greater than or equal to 20, and that p is about 0.5 with np and $n(1 - p) \geq 10$. It is actually only for p around 0.5 that binomial law has a symmetrical appearance like normal law.

We are now left to create the program. Saying that (Y_n) converges on $\boldsymbol{N}(0, 1)$ comes back to saying that the sequence (X_n) converges on normal law $\boldsymbol{N}(np, \sigma)$. This is what we are beginning to do in the following program, with binomial law $\boldsymbol{B}(N, p)$ where we took $N = 30$ and $p = 0.6$ as example.

Using the property above, with Np and $N(1 - p) \geq 10$, we check that the binomial law stick diagram sticks to the normal law curve $\boldsymbol{N}(Np, sigma)$, with: $sigma^2 = N\,p\,(1 - p)$.

```
onset=1000.*p; /* we will repeat the N throws NBEXP times, for example
                  30,000 times */
for(expe=0; expe<NBEXP; expe++)
  {nbsuccess = binomial (N); nbtimes[nbsuccess]+ +;}
for(i=0; i<=N; i++)
  { proba=(float)nbtimes[i]/(float)NEXP;
    draw the bars of abscissa i and of height proba
  }
Normal ((float)N*p, sqrt ((float)N*p*(1.-p))); /* to compare with
                          the bell-shaped curve */
```

This program uses the two functions binomial(n) *and* Normal (average, standard deviation):

```
int binomial(int n)
     /* returns the number of successes on the n successive throws */
{ int i,h,succes=0;
  for(i=0; i<n; i++) { h=random(1000); if (h<onset) success++; }
 return success;
}
void Normal(float m, float s) /* normal law theoretical curve */
 { float k,kk,x,fx,oldfx;
   k=1./(s*sqrt(2.*M_PI)); kk=2*s*s;  oldfx=0.;
  for(x=-5.; x<30.; x+=0.01)
   { fx=k*exp(-(x-m)*(x-m)/kk);
    draw point x, fx,
    or join point x-0.01, oldfx to point x, fx
    oldfx=fx;
   }
 }
```

We can also take the reduced centered binomial variable Y_N and compare it with reduced centered normal variable $\boldsymbol{N}(0, 1)$, see Figure 22.8. We have the relation: $Y_N = X_N / sigma - Np / sigma$. This goes back to dividing the abscissae by *sigma* and carrying out a translation to the left of *Np / sigma*.

To respect the densities, we must also multiply the ordinates by *sigma*. Hence this addition to the previous program:

```
sigma=sqrt(N*p*(1.-p));
for(i=0; i<=N; i++)
 { proba=(float)nbtimes[i]/(float)NEXP;
 ordinate = proba*sigma; abscissa=(float)i/sigma-(float)N*p/sigma;
 draw the bar with abscissa abscissa and height ordinate
 }
Normal(0,1);
```

We will now find normal law again using a classic theorem.

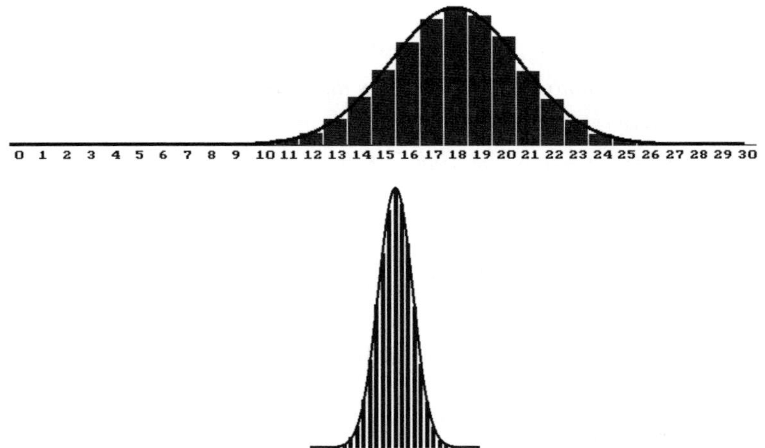

Figure 22.8. *The binomial law stick diagram B(30, 0.6) and the normal law bell-shaped curve N (30×0.6, 30×0.6×0.4) (top); and the reduced centered normal law N(0, 1) (below). This corresponds to the reduced centered binomial law, provided that the abscissa are divided by σ and the ordinates are multiplied by σ, while carrying out a horizontal translation of $-Np / \sigma$*

22.6. Central limit theorem: from uniform law to normal law

This theorem, which we give here without any demonstration, is stated in this way:

– when we have N random variables X_k, with k from 1 to N, where these variables are all independent and obey the same law, and therefore have the same expectation $E(X_k) = m$ and same standard deviation $\sigma_k = \sigma$, then the random variable:

$$Y_N = \frac{X_1 + X_2 + ... + X_N - Nm}{\sigma\sqrt{N}}$$

converges on reduced centered normal law $\boldsymbol{N}(0, 1)$, in the sense that it tends to have the same distribution function;

– note that variable Y_N has a null expectation because:

$$E(X_1 + X_2 + \ldots + X_N) = E(X_1) + E(X_2) + \ldots + E(X_N) = Nm$$

and that its standard deviation is equal to 1:

$$V(X_1 + X_2 + \ldots + X_N) = V(X_1) + V(X_2) + \ldots + V(X_N) = N\sigma^2$$

since the variables are independent. Hence:

$$V(Y_N) = \frac{1}{(\sigma\sqrt{N})^2} N\sigma^2 = 1$$

If we consider the N variables X_k as obeying the same Bernoulli's law, i.e. repeatedly getting heads or tails with the same probability p of success, the sum of these variables follows binomial law $\boldsymbol{B}(N, p)$, and variable Y_N is none other than the reduced centered binomial variable. Central limit theorem tells us that it converges on normal law $\boldsymbol{N}(0, 1)$, and this is what we used in the previous section.

We can, however, take other contexts. Let us take a dice with six faces, numbered for simplification from 0 to 5 (and not from 1 to 6). Let us throw it N times and add the numbers obtained.

The corresponding random variable is $U_N = X_1 + X_2 + ... + X_N$, where each variable X_k follows a uniform law: $p(X_k = 0) = 1 / 6$, $p(X_k = 1) = 1 / 6$, ..., $p(X_k = 5) = 1 / 6$.

Its average value is $m = 5 / 2 = 2.5$, and its standard deviation is equal to $\sigma = 1.708$. U_N takes its values from 0 to 5N, which makes 5N + 1 integer values going from 1 to 1.

Its average value is Nm, and its variance is $N\sigma^2$, hence its standard deviation is $\sigma\sqrt{N}$. Now let us take random variable $Z_N = U_N / N$ which goes from 0 to 5, always taking $5N + 1$ values going from $1 / N$ to $1 / N$. Its average value is m and its standard deviation is $\frac{\sigma\sqrt{N}}{N} = \frac{\sigma}{\sqrt{N}}$. Finally, let us take the random variable $Y_N = \frac{(Z_N - m)\sqrt{N}}{\sigma}$. Its average is now 0, and its standard deviation is equal to 1. It is a reduced centered variable that we know, thanks to the central limit theorem, which converges on normal law $\boldsymbol{N}(0, 1)$. Hence the program:

```
sigma=1.708;m=2.5;
for(expe=0;expe<NBEXP;expe++)
   { cumul=0; for(i=0;i<N;i++) { h=random(6); cumul+=h; }
     nbtimes[cumul]++; }
for(i=0; i<=N*5; i++)
   { proba=(float)nbtimes[i]/(float)NBEXP; ordinate=proba*sigma*sqrt(N);
     zn=(float)i/(float)N; yn=(zn-m)*sqrt(N)/sigma;
     draw a bar around abscissa yn, and height ordinate }
```

The results obtained for three values of N (see Figure 22.9), show rapid convergence on normal law. Thus, from a uniform distribution of probabilities that a random number generator delivers, we can arrive at a distribution that follows a bell-shaped curve, i.e. normal law.

What we have done with one six-faced dice, with the equiprobable chance of throwing a number between 0 and 5, can be generalized to any number, even a very large number. This will enable us to simplify the calculations, notably avoiding the heaviness of calculating σ. Therefore, we throw a number at random between 0 and H, for example with H = 1,000 or even H = RAND_MAX, the maximum number delivered by the generator (usually 32,767 or 65,535) and let us repeat this operation N times. Each time, we have a random variable X_k that takes its values between 0 and H, with a probability approximately equal to $1 / H$ of the output of each one of these numbers.

The expectation is: $E(X_k) = H / 2$ and the variance: $V(X_k) = \sum_{k=0}^{A} (k - H/2)^2 \frac{1}{H}$.

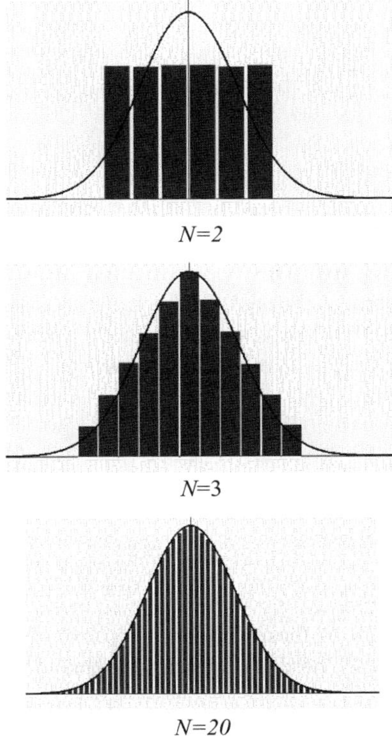

Figure 22.9. *Stick diagram for three values of N, with convergence on normal law*

To calculate this variance, us consider the curve of equation $y = (Hx - H/2)^2$ with x between 0 and 1. Taking $x = k / H$, $(k - H/2)^2/H$ is the area of a small core rectangle of $1 / H$ bordered by the curve. The sum of these areas can roughly be compared to the area included between the curve and horizontal axis on interval [0 1], i.e. an integral, hence:

$$V(X_k) \simeq \int_0^1 (Hx - H/2)^2 \, dx = H^2 \int_0^1 (x - 1/2)^2 \, dx = \frac{H^2}{12}$$

We deduce the standard deviation from this: $\sigma_k = H / (2\sqrt{3})$.

Let us take the framework of central limit theorem, taking the reduced centered random variable:

$$Y_N = \frac{\sum_{k=1}^{N} X_k - NH / 2}{\sqrt{N}\,\sigma_k}$$

This is of the form $a\sum_{k=1}^{N} X_k - b$ with $b = \sqrt{3N}$ and $a = \frac{2b}{NH}$. It roughly follows a reduced centered normal law. This approximation turns out to be good even for small N, as it is experimentally checked. In the program that follows, we simply take $N = 4$, with H = (float)RAND_MAX, from which we deduce a and b. The following function enables us to generate a number that follows normal law $\mathcal{N}(0, 1)$:

```
double nbgauss (void)
{ sum=0;
  for(i=0; i<N; i++) sum+=rand();
  return (a*sum-b);
}
```

The repeated production of these Gaussian numbers enables us to extract their frequencies on short intervals, here 0.1 long, and to deduce the Gaussian bell-shaped curve (see Figure 22.10):

```
N=4.;
H=(float)RAND_MAX;
b=sqrt(3.*N);
a=2.*b/(N*H);
randomize();
for(throw=0; throw<300000; throw++)
  { number=nbgauss();
   parcel=(int)(10.*(number+5.));
   freq[parcel]++;
  }
display the frequency bars
```

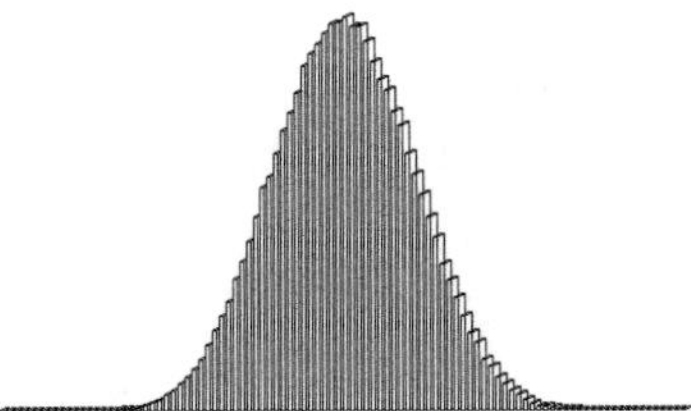

Figure 22.10. *Gaussian curve obtained thanks to the central limit theorem from the uniform generator of random numbers*

22.7. Appendix: the distribution function and its inversion – application to binomial law *B*(*n*, *p*)

We have seen how the distribution function F of a continuous variable was defined. This definition also applies to a discrete variable X. It is a function F of a variable x defined on the set of real numbers $\boldsymbol{R}$, such that $F(x) = p(X \leq x)$, i.e. the probability $p()$ that the random variable X is less than a given real number x.

Let us take the case of binomial law, with its probabilities $p(X = k)$ where k goes from 0 to N. When $x < 0$, $F(x) = 0$, then for x over $[0\ 1[$, $F(x) = p(X = 0)$, and more generally for x over $[k, k{+}1[$ with k from 0 to $N - 1$, $F(x) = p(X = 0) + p(X = 1) + \ldots + p(X = k)$. Finally, for $x \geq N$, $F(x) = 1$. The distribution function accumulates the probabilities. It is an increasing step function, which reaches a maximum equal to 1 once all the probabilities have been accumulated.

In the example that follows, with binomial law ***B***(6, 0.5), we see how we move from probability law to the distribution function (see Figure 22.11).

22.7.1. *Program*

First of all let us recall the experimental method that enables us to get binomial probability law. At the beginning of the program, we are given N and parameter p of binomial law ***B***(N, p), as well as the number of experiments *NBEXPE* carried out. During each experiment, we toss a coin N times and include the number of successes (heads) X obtained. Then during the *NBEXPE* experiments we count how many times we find $X = 0$, how many times $X = 1$, etc., thanks to the accumulation table *nbtimes*[*X*].

```
randomize(); onset=p*10000.;
for(expe=1;expe<=NBEXPE; expe++)
```

```
{ X=0;
  for(toss=1; toss<=N; toss++)
     { h=random(10000); if (h<onset) X++;}
  nbtimes[X]++;
}
for(X=0; X<=N; X++)
   {proba=(float)nbtimes[X]/(float)NBEXPE; display proba }
```

On the other hand, here is the theoretical method, using the formulae that give probability law, from which the distribution function *F*(*X*) is deduced by accumulating the probabilities.

```
for(i=0; i<=N; i++) F[i]=0.;
c[0]=1;  for(i=1; i<=N; i++) c[i]=0; /* calculation of the combinations C_N^i */
for (line=1; line<=N; line++) for(k=N; k>0; k--) c[k]+=c[k–1];
for(i=0; i<=N; i++)
  { proba=(float)c[i]*pow(p,(float)i)*pow(1.-p,(float)(N–i)); display

 if (i==0) F[0]=proba;  else F[i]=F[i–1]+proba;
  }
for(i=0; i<=N; i++) display F[i]);
```

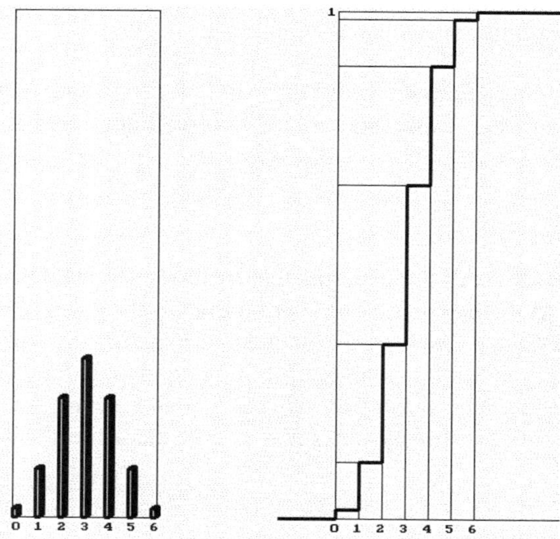

Figure 22.11. *The binomial law (left); and its distribution function (right)*

22.7.2. *The inverse function*

Now let us invert the distribution function, which involves inverting the two axes. This gives a new function $G(y)$, where y is the real number in [0 1]. This new step function has horizontal steps, the first between 0 and $F[0]$, the second between $F[0]$ and $F[1]$, etc. The length of these steps is probability $p(X = 0)$, then $p(X = 1)$, then $p(X = 2)$, etc. The height of every step is an integer between 0 and N.

This new function corresponds to one uniform probability law per piece. Let us take a random number y between 0 and 1. For example y is situated between $F[2]$ and $F[3]$. The probability of being on this interval is $p(X = 3)$ corresponding to the length of the interval concerned compared to the total length, which is 1. This also corresponds to the probability that $G(y)$ is equal to 3:

$$p(\mathrm{G}(y) = 3) = p(y \text{ between } F[2] \text{ and } F[3]) = p(X = 3)$$

In the general case:

$$p(G(y) = k) = p(X = k)$$

This gives a new way of getting the probability law of X, using the function $G(y)$, the inverse of the distribution function $F(X)$ of X, provided that we know the latter.

In the following example (see Figure 22.12), we will find the passage of the curve from G to the probability law of X, in the case of binomial law $\boldsymbol{B}(6, 0.5)$.

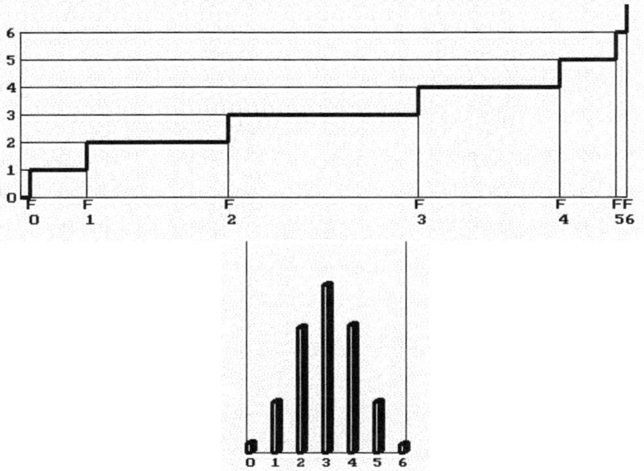

Figure 22.11. *The inverse distribution function (top), and binomial probability law rediscovered (bottom)*

22.7.3. *Program causing us to move from distribution function to probability law*

Knowing the distribution function F enables us to experimentally rediscover probability law, repeating *NBEXPE* experiments. With each experiment, we remove a random number y between 0 and 1 and search for the zone in which it is found, which gives a value of X:

```
for(i=0; i<=N; i++) nbtimes[i]=0;
for(expe=1; expe<=NBEXPE; expe++)
  { i=0; y=(float)rand()/32768.;
   while(F[i]<y) i++;
   X=i; nbtimes[X]++;
  }
for(X=0; X<=N; X++)
  { proba=(float)nbtimes[X]/(float)NBEXPE;  display proba  }
```

Chapter 23

Generating Function Associated with a Discrete Random Variable in a Game

Let us take the context of a game, where events are characterized by a random variable X that is a natural integer, as defined in Chapter 20. The objective is therefore to find the probabilities corresponding to each of the values of X concerned, which we call the law of X, and deduce from them the important numbers that can be associated with it, essentially its average value or expectation, and its variance. To facilitate these calculations, we will define a fundamental tool regarding probabilities: the generating function associated with X. Once this has been found, we will extract all the results of the game concerned and its variable X. First of all, we will apply this method to several classic laws, then we will do so for other problems.

23.1. Generating function: definition and properties

By definition, the generating function G associated with random variable X is the formal series of the form:

$$G(z) = p(X = 0) + p(X = 1)\, z + p(X = 2)\, z^2 + p(X = 3)\, z^3 + \ldots$$

This generating function corresponds to a game where we took a certain random variable X, taking its values from the set of natural integers $\boldsymbol{N}$. The coefficient of z^k is probability $p(X = k)$, such is the principal characteristic of the generating function.

Variable z is considered to be an indeterminate. It is mainly its exponent k that we are interested in, as it indicates that the coefficient of z^k is probability $p(X = k)$. The generating function obeys several properties, easily shown:

– $G(1) = 1$;

– $E(X) = G'(1)$, with G' being derived from G in relation to z;

– $V(X) = G''(1) + G'(1) - G'(1)^2$.

If $X = X_1 + X_2$ where X_1 and X_2 are independent random variables, the generating function G_X associated with X is the product of the generating functions associated with X_1 and X_2: $G_X(z) = G_{X1}(z)\, G_{X2}(z)$.

If, from the law of X, we were to simply deduce the generating function, this function would only have one interest of pure form, if not as a concentration of information. In fact we will develop ways of obtaining the generating function *a priori,* using graphs, and this will enable us to deduce the law of X from it, as well as its expected value and variance, i.e. the complete solution to a probabilities problem. Using classic examples, we will progressively indicate the method enabling us to find the generating function.

23.2. Generating functions of some classic laws

23.2.1. *Bernoulli's law*

Let us recall that this game consists of tossing a coin once, with the probability of getting heads being p, and that of getting tails q, with $p + q = 1$. Random variable X is the number of times we get heads, hence the two events $X = 0$ or $X = 1$, and the law of X: $p(X = 1) = p$ and $p(X = 0) = q$. The generating function associated with X is $G(z) = q + pz$. From this we deduce the average value of X as well as its variance:

$$E(X) = G'(1) = p \text{ and } V(X) = p(1 - p).$$

23.2.2. *Geometric law*

We repeatedly toss a coin, with the respective probabilities of getting heads and tales being p and q, until the first head outcome. Random variable X corresponds to the number of moves until the first success, for us getting a head. Geometric law can be expressed $\boldsymbol{G}(p)$ with parameter p being the probability of success and all results related to this law depending on p alone.

Let us look for the generating function associated with X. For this, let us draw what we call the transition graph associated with our problem (see Figure 23.1).

We start from the initial state, 0, and the objective is to reach the final state, 1. These two states make up the two vertices of the graph. From state 0, either we toss H and arrive at 1, or we toss T and stay at 0. This gives two junction arches, and the design of the graph.

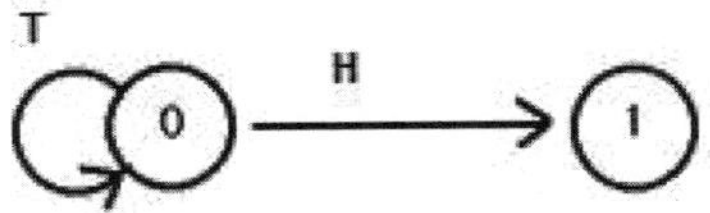

Figure 23.1. *Transition graph of geometric law*

Now we will circulate on this graph, a little as if we were on a railway. The paths leading from 0 to 1, of variable length, can be expressed in the form of words based on T and H depending on whether we take an arch marked T or one marked H. For example the word $TTTH$ indicates that we turned three times on loop T, staying at state 0, before taking arch H leading to state 1. Such words correspond exactly to the events that concern us and whose probability we want to calculate. Let S_1 be the language formed by all words going from 0 to 1. It is expressed: $S_1 = \{H\}$ or $\{TH\}$ or $\{TTH\}$ or …, but we will call it more simply:

$$S_1 = H + TH + TTH + TTTH + TTTTH + \dots$$

with two operations present: the operation + which means *or*, and the concatenation operation between the letters, written as a multiplication would be.

Now let us carry out the following conversion: let us replace T with qz and H with pz, with the *or* now really becoming + forever, and the concatenation becoming a multiplication. This gives a z series that we will also call S_1:

$$S_1(z) = pz + qpz^2 + q^2pz^3 + q^3pz^4 + \dots$$

Thanks to this conversion, we have just obtained the generating function associated with the number of moves X. For example, $TTTTH$ becomes q^4pz^5, the length of the word becomes the exponent of z, and the coefficient of z^5 is the probability $p(X = 5)$ since the probabilities of this independent series of events $TTTTH = T$ and T and T and P and H, linked up by *and*s, are multiplied. Finally:

$$S_1(z) = pz\,(1 + qz + q^2z^2 + q^3z^3 + \dots) = pz \,/\, (1 - qz)$$

In this simple problem, the generating function, in its final form of the polynomial quotient, causes us to concentrate on what we found in Chapter 20, namely $p(X = k) = p\, q^{k-1}$.

Even if this is not imposed in this case, let us return to this problem, applying to it the general method that we will then use in more complex cases. We will now start with the graph for deducing the generating function. Let S_0 be the language of words going from state 0 to state 0. We have:

$$S_0 = 1 + T + TT + TTT + \ldots$$

where 1 designates the empty word, which means we go from state 0 to state 0 without moving. We should never forget this empty word when we use language S_0. Separating the empty word and words ending in T, we find the S_0 equation:

$$S_0 = 1 + (1 + T + TT + TTT + \ldots)T = 1 + S_0T$$

Without calculation, this equation can be found directly from the graph. A single arrow, called T, falls on state 0. This means that, in addition to the 0-length empty word as usual, S_0 is made up of all the words going from 0 to 0, including the empty word, followed by T, with a length of at least one character, which gives S_0T. Hence:

$$S_0 = 1 + S_0T$$

Note that we would be wrong if we had forgotten the empty word in the S_0 of S_0T, corresponding to words of longer than 0, since we would lose word T.

Now let us take language S_1 together with words going from 0 to 1. According to the graph, with a single arrow called H falling on state 1 after having left state 0, we have all the words of S_0 (going from 0 to 0) followed by H; hence the equation $S_1 = S_0H$. The graph gives us the system of two equations with two unknowns:

$$S_0 = 1 + S_0T$$

$$S_1 = S_0H$$

Doing the conversion above ($T \rightarrow qz$, $H \rightarrow pz$), language S_1 will become the generating function $S_1(z)$ associated with the number of moves until the first head, and S_0 is replaced by $S_0(z) = 1 + qz + q^2z^{\,2} + q^3z^3 + \ldots$, which gives:

$$S_0(z) = 1 + q\, z\, S_0(z)$$

$$S_1(z) = p\, z\, S_0(z)$$

It is sufficient to solve this system in order to obtain the generating function $S_1(z)$:

$$S_0(1 - qz) = 1,\ S_0 = 1 / (1 - qz), \text{ hence } S_1(z) = pz / (1 - qz)$$

Developing:

$$S_1(z) = pz\,(1 + qz + q^2z^2 + \ldots) = pz + qpz^2 + q^2pz^3 + \ldots + q^{k-1}pz^k + \ldots$$

we deduce from it the law of X:

$$p(X = k) = q^{k-1}p, \text{ then: } E(X) = S_1'(1) = 1 / p,$$

$$\text{and: } V(X) = S_1''(1) + S_1'(1) - S_1'(1)^2 = 2q / p^2 + 1 / p - 1 / p^2 = q / p^2$$

It is possible to simplify the calculation of expectation. Indeed, with the generating function $F(z)$ being a z polynomial quotient, we can manage to express it as $F(z) = P(z) / Q(z)$ seeing to it that $Q(1) = 1$. Now let us derive $F\,Q = P$, which gives $F'Q + FQ' = p'$, and let us make $z = 1$, with $F(1) = Q(1) = 1$, $F'(1) + Q'(1) = P'(1)$ is left. Finally:

$$E(X) = P'(1) - Q'(1)$$

For example, with geometric law and its generating function $S_1(z)$, the latter can be expressed as $S_1(z) = z / ((1 - qz) / p)$, with $P(z) = z$ and $Q(z) = (1 - qz) / p$. We have $Q(1) = 1$, hence $E(X) = P'(1) - Q'(1) = 1 + q / p = 1 / p$.

23.2.3. *Binomial law*

Let us recall that binomial law consists of playing heads or tails n times. The probability of getting heads, corresponding to a success if you wish, is p; that of getting tails, or a failure, is q. The number of times heads comes out during n tosses, or even the number of successes during n tosses is random variable X. This law is expressed as $\boldsymbol{B}(n, p)$, with its two parameters n and p on which all the results depend. Random variable X can take all values between 0 and n.

We already found the law of X, i.e. $p(X = k) = C_n^k\, p^k\, q^{n-k}$. To find this result again, and also find the expectation that we left in waiting, let us now use the generating function method. The graph corresponding to binomial law, with initial state 0 and final state n, is represented in Figure 23.2.

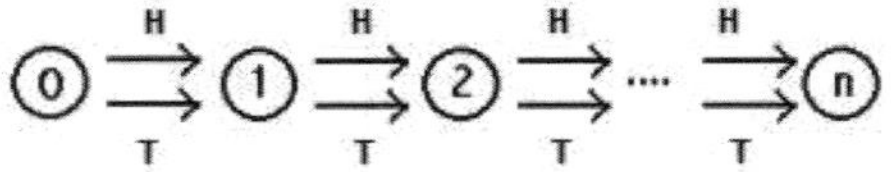

Figure 23.2. *Transition graph of binomial law*

The intermediary states correspond to the number of moves carried out along the way. Language S_n made from words obtained by going from state 0 to state n on the graph number 2^n. It is made up of all possible cases. Let us take $n = 3$, for example:

$$S_3 = HHH + HHT + HTH + HTT + THH + THT + TTH + TTT$$

Converting $H \to pz$ and $T \to q$, with the *or* becoming + and the concatenation (the *and*) becoming a multiplication, we obtain the z series, here the polynomial:

$$S_3(z) = p^3z^3 + p^2qz^2 + p^2qz^2 + pq^2z + p^2qz^2 + pq^2z + pq^2z + q^3$$

$$= p^3z^3 + 3\,p^2qz^2 + 3\,pq^2z + q^3,$$

since all is commutative.

In each term, the exponent of z is the number of times heads appears (because of $H \to pz$ and $T \to q$). The coefficient of a term in z^k is the number of times the event with k heads occurs, multiplied by its probability $p^k q^{n-k}$, i.e. $p(X = k)$. The polynomial $S_3(z)$ is the generating function associated with X.

But how do we obtain the generating function in the general case? For this, we proceed as above, with S_k being the language obtained by going from initial state 0 to state k. This gives the following system of equations, from simply reading the graph, looking at the arrows on each node and their origin:

$S_0 = 1$ (this 1 corresponds to the empty word)

$S_1 = S_0\mathrm{H} + S_0\mathrm{T}$

$S_2 = S_1\mathrm{H} + S_1\mathrm{T}$

...

$S_n = S_{n-1}\mathrm{H} + S_{n-1}\mathrm{T}$

For example, to find out S_2 we look at which arrows fall on state 2: here we have an H arrow coming from S_1, hence the term S_1H, as well as a T arrow coming from S_1, hence the term S_1T. Carrying out conversion $H \to pz$ and $T \to q$, this gives:

$$S_0(z) = 1$$

$$S_1(z) = (q + pz)S_0(z)$$

$$S_2(z) = (q + pz)S_1(z)$$

$$\ldots,$$

$$S_n(z) = (q + pz)S_{n-1}(z),$$

hence by immediate recurrence:

$$S_n(z) = (q + pz)^n$$

which is the generating function.

Developing this expression according to binomial formula, we deduce from it the probability law of X, i.e. $p(X = k) = C_n^k p^k q^{n-k}$. By derivation:

$E(X) = S_n'(1) = np$, then $V(X) = npq$.[1]

23.2.4. *Poisson distribution*

Let us recall the definition of Poisson distribution. A random variable X verifies Poisson distribution with parameter μ when $p(X = k) = e^{-\mu} \frac{\mu^k}{k!}$ with k being positive or null integer. The associated generating function is:

$$\begin{aligned} G(z) &= p(X = 0) + p(X = 1)z + p(X = 2)z^2 + \ldots \\ &= e^{-\mu}(1 + \frac{\mu}{1!}z + \frac{\mu^2}{2!}z^2 + \frac{\mu^3}{3!}z^3 + \ldots) = e^{-\mu}e^{\mu z} \\ &= e^{\mu(z-1)} \end{aligned}$$

1. We can find the generating function in another way. Let X_k be the random variable equal to 1 if we get H in the kth move, and 0 if we get T. We are therefore in the context of Bernoulli's law for random variable X_k, whose generating function is expressed: $G_{Xk}(z) = q + pz$. In turn, random variable X is equal to the number of Hs that we get during n tosses. It is linked with the Bernoulli variables above by: $X = X_1 + X_2 + \ldots + X_n$. As the variables X_k are independent, the generating function associated with X is obtained by working out the product of the generating functions of X_k, and we again find $G(z) = (q + pz)^n$.

By deriving this, we notice that $G'(z) = \mu G(z)$ and that the nth derivative is equal to: $G^{(n)}(z) = \mu^n G(z)$. We deduce from this that:

$$E(X) = G'(1) = \mu, \text{ and } V(X) = G''(1) + G'(1) - G'(1)^2 = \mu.$$

23.3. Exercises

23.3.1. *Exercise 1: waiting time for double heads in a game of heads or tails*

In a repeated game of heads or tails, with probability p for H (heads) and q for T (tails), we are interested in the waiting time for the outcome of a HH pattern for the first time, i.e. the number of moves necessary for HH to be obtained.

23.3.1.1. *Constructing the graph*

The random variable X associated with this game is the length of the word obtained, knowing that this word ends in *HH* without having had double *H* before, and that it is created out of the alphabet of the letters *H* and *T*, with the respective probabilities of appearing p and q. The transition graph is represented in Figure 23.3. The words corresponding to the game are created by circulating on the graph from state 0 to state 2. How do we get this transition graph? When it has been run through by all possible paths by following the arrows, between the initial state and final state, it must supply all the words corresponding to our game. When we circulate on it, it behaves like a sort of machine that creates the words involved in our problem. Here is how to proceed to get this graph: the shortest word is *HH*, which gives a first drawing (see Figure 23.4a), with the presence of an intermediate state called 1 between the initial state called 0 and the final state called 2.

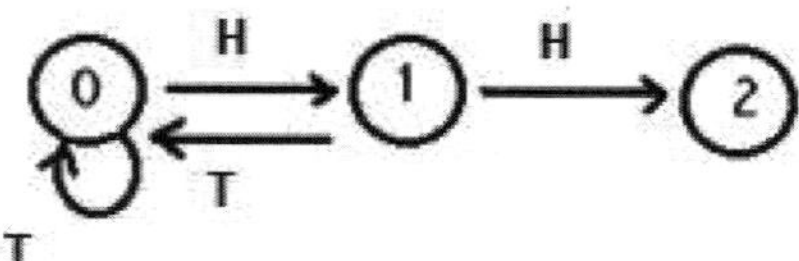

Figure 23.3. *Transition graph waiting for HH*

Next we know that at each stage either heads or tails can occur. Two arrows must start from each state of the graph, except the final state. First we must add an arrow T from state 0 (see Figure 23.4b). This arrow can only return to 0, or else we would obtain an invalid word. For example, if we sent it from 0 to 1, we would have created the word *TH*, which is not valid.

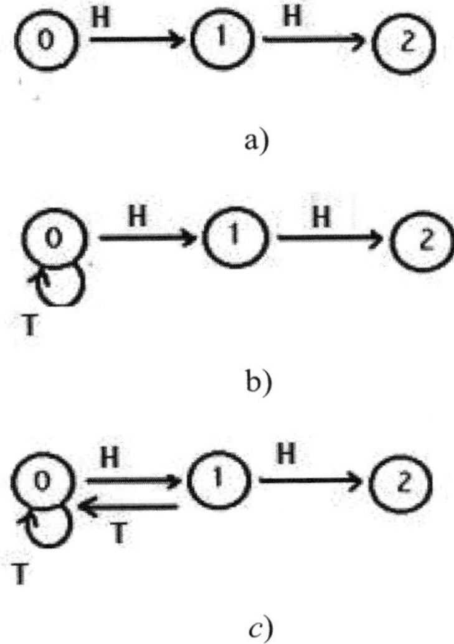

Figure 23.4. *Progressive construction of the transition graph*

We must also add an arrow T from state 1. This arrow can only go from 0 so that errors are not produced. If we sent it to 1, we would have created the word HTH, which is not valid. We then have the final graph (see Figure 23.4c).

We are interested in words obtained by going from initial state 0 to final state 2. Let this set of words be S_2. Let S_0 be the set of words formed by going from 0 to 0, and S_1 be words going from 0 to 1. Circulating on the graph, we notice:

$$S_0 = 1 + T + TT + HT + TTT + THT + HTT + TTTT + TTHT + \ldots,$$

where 1 designates the empty word e, the sign + means *or*, and where concatenation is written as a multiplication – all this before the sequence. In addition to the empty word, S_0 words end in T and are preceded by words containing only isolated Hs or no Hs at all. Similarly:

$$S_1 = H + TH + TTH + HTH + TTTH + THTH + HTHT + \ldots,$$

and:

$$S_2 = HH + THH + TTHH + HTHH + TTTHH + THTHH + HTTHH + \ldots$$

Relationships exist between these sets of words. Let us take a word from S_0: either it is the empty word or it is a word ending in T and preceded by a word from S_0 (itself either empty or ending in T), or it is a word ending in T preceded by a word from S_1 (ending in H):

$$S_0 = 1 + (1 + T + TT + HT + TTT + \ldots)\, T + (H + TH + TTH + HTH + \ldots)\, T$$

Hence the relation $S_0 = 1 + S_0\, T + S_1\, T$. It is easy to read this relationship directly on the transition graph. We notice that two arrows fall on state 0: one with T coming from 0, which gives words of S_0T; and the other with T coming from state 1, which gives words of S_1T, not forgetting the empty word obtained without moving. In this way we find the relation $S_0 = 1 + S_0\, T + S_1\, T$.

We do the same with S_1. Only one arrow called H falls on state 1 originating from 0, hence $S_1 = S_0\, H$, and we can check that:

$$S_1 = (1 + T + TT + HT + TTT + THT + HTT + TTTT + \ldots)\, H$$

Finally $S_2 = S_1H$ for the same reasons. This brings us to the system of three equations with three unknowns:

$$S_0 = 1 + S_0\, T + S_1\, T$$

$$S_1 = S_0\, H$$

$$S_2 = S_1\, H$$

Only S_2 truly concerns us, the other unknowns S_1 and S_0 being only secondary to the calculation.

Now let us carry out the next conversion: $H \rightarrow pz$, $T \rightarrow qz$, with the *or* becoming + and the concatenation becoming multiplication. We return all commutatives. A k-length word of S_2 (or S_0 or S_1) is transformed into a monomial αz^k, where α is the probability of obtaining such a word. Indeed, we know the formula: $p(A$ and $B) = p(A)\, p(B)$ for independent events. For example the word THH becomes $qz\ pz\ pz = p^2q\ z^3$ and p^2q is its probability. Now let us take the words of S_2 after conversion and group them according to their power. We obtain a series $S_2(z)$ where the term in z^k has the sum of coefficients of the terms in z^k coming from each k-length word as its coefficient. This coefficient obtained by addition is the probability of getting a k-length word, since it is in accordance with the addition rules $p(A$ or $B) = p(A) + p(B)$ when the events are incompatible. This coefficient is exactly $p(X = k)$.

In this way we move from the set of words S_2 to the power series of z that is expressed: $S_2(z) = p(x = 0) + p(x = 1)\, z + p(x = 2)\, z^2 + p(x = 3)\, z^3 + \ldots$. We note the language and series in an analogous manner, to simplify the notations, even if they are different concepts. The system of equations becomes:

$$S_0 = 1 + qz\, S_0 + qz\, S_1$$

$$S_1 = pz\, S_0$$

$$S_2 = pz\, S_1$$

Solving the system by substitution gives the S_0 equation:

$$S_0 = 1 + qz\, S_0 + pq\, z^2\, S_0,\text{ i.e. } S_0 = 1 / (1 - qz - pqz^2)$$

which finally leads to the generating function associated with X:

$$S_2(z) = p^2z^2 / (1 - qz - pqz^2)$$

We notably deduce $E(X) = (p + 1) / p^2$ from this.

23.3.1.2. *Generalization*

To move from the language to the series or generating function, we proceeded to a precise conversion so a term in z corresponds to each arrow. Running through k arrows therefore gave a term in z^k, which corresponded perfectly to the events that concerned us, with the random variable X being equal to the length of the words.

Other random variables can be taken into consideration. In order to take a more general context, let us convert $H \rightarrow px$ and $T \rightarrow qy$. In these conditions we obtain a series with two variables x and y, verifying the system:

$$S_0 = 1 + qy\, S_0 + qy\, S_1$$

$$S_1 = px\, S_0$$

$$S_2 = px\, S_1$$

hence: $S_2(x, y) = p^2x^2 / (\, 1 - qy - pqxy)$.

By making $x = y$, we evidently find the initial problem again. Let us assume that we take the number of times tails comes out in this game as random variable Y. This refers to converting $H \rightarrow p$ and $T \rightarrow qy$. The generating function associated with Y is obtained by making $x = 1$, i.e. $S_2(1, y) = p^2 / (1 - q(1 + p)y)$, and:

$p(Y = k) = p^2\ (q(1 + p))^k.$

23.3.1.3. *Complementary exercise 1: waiting time for pattern TH*

Still in the same game, we now wait for pattern TH for the first time. What should the values of p and q be for the average waiting time, in this case to be equal to the waiting time for HH in the previous problem?

Proceeding as indicated above, we get the transition graph in Figure 23.5.

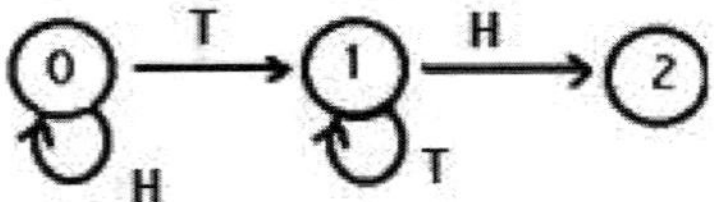

Figure 23.5. *Waiting time transition graph for TH*

By converting $H \to pz$ and $T \to qz$ directly, we find the following system of equations openly on the graph:

$S_0 = 1 + pz\ S_0$

$S_1 = qz\ S_0 + qz\ S_1$

$S_2 = pz\ S_1$

Proceeding by substitution, we find that the waiting time for *TH* is the generating function of this game:

$S_2(z) = pqz^2 / (1 - z + pqz^2),$

hence: $E(X) = 1 / pq$

This expectation is equal to that of the previous problem for $p = \varphi'$, namely the second golden number $(\sqrt{5} - 1) / 2 = 0.618$.

We note, by observing the transition graph, that S_0 corresponds to the empty word or all the words containing only *H*s, i.e.:

$S_0(z) = 1 / (1 - pz) = 1 + pz + p^2z^2 + \ldots$

We check that the probability of getting a *k*-length word from S_0 is p^k. In turn, S_1 corresponds to all the words made from a block of *H*s (or the empty word) followed by a block of Ts, with at least one T. The coefficient of the term in z^k in $S_1(z)$ is the probability of getting a block of Hs eventually followed by a non-empty block of Ts in k throws. This term $S_1(z)$ in z^k is also the term in z^k in the product:

$$(1 + pz + p^2z^2 + \ldots)\,(qz + q^2z^2 + \ldots) = (1 / (1 - pz))\,(qz / (1 - qz))$$

$$= (1 / (1 - pz))\,(qz / (1 - qz))$$

$$= qz / (1 - z + pqz^2),$$

as already indicated by the previous calculation.

23.3.1.4. *Complementary exercise 2: waiting time until the outcome of a second double H, as for example with the word TTHTHHHTTHTHTTTHH*

Here the random variable X is equal to the waiting time X_1 for the outcome of a first HH, plus the waiting time X_2 for the second HH after the first. Variables X_1 and X_2 are independent, and like $X = X_1 + X_2$ the generating function associated with X is the product of those associated with X_1 and X_2, i.e.:

$$G(z) = p^4z^4 / (1 - qz - pqz^2)^2 \text{ and } E(X) = 2(p + 1) / p^2.$$

23.3.2. *Exercise 2: in a repeated game of heads or tails, what is the parity of the number of heads?*

This game consists of tossing a heads or tails coin n times, where n is fixed. The probability of getting heads is p, and that of getting tails is q. We are interested in the parity of the number of times heads comes out.

a) What is the probability u_n of getting heads twice?

We are in the context of binomial law $\boldsymbol{B}(n, p)$ where the random variable X is the number of heads tossed. Its associated generating function is:

$$G(z) = (q + pz)^n = \sum_{k=0}^{n} C_n^k p^k q^{n-k} z^k$$

We know that $G(1) = 1$ is the sum of the probabilities of all the elementary events. These events are divided into those with an even number of heads, and those with an odd number, with respective probabilities u_n and $1 - u_n$. The probability u_n requested is the sum of the terms of $G(z)$ where k is even, where we then make $z = 1$, and its complementary $1 - u_n$ is the sum of terms with odd k and $z = 1$. The difference between the two is $u_n - 1 + u_n$, i.e. $2\,u_n - 1$. This is also obtained by taking $G(-1)$. Therefore:

$$2u_n - 1 = (q - p)^n = (1 - 2p)^n,$$

hence: $u_n = 0.5 + 0.5(1 - 2p)^n$

We notice two phenomena:

– for $p < 0.5$, probability u_n is greater than 1 / 2, whether n is even or odd;

– for even n, the probability is greater than or equal to 1 / 2 whatever p may be;

– for odd n, the probability is greater than 1 / 2 for $p < 0.5$ and less for $p > 0.5$.

b) *In a two-person game, when k heads came out during n tosses, the first player ends up with k counters when k is even, else he has nothing. A second player ends up with k counters when k is odd, else he has nothing. When p < 0.5, we have to show that the second player earns on average more counters than the first, even if we know that an even number of heads has more chances of occurring.*

For binomial law, the average number of heads that come out, i.e. the expectation of X, is obtained by taking $G'(1)$, with:

$$G'(z) = np(q+pz)^{n-1} = \sum_{k=1}^{n} k\, p(X = k) z^{k-1} \text{ and } p(X = k) = C_n^k p^k q^{n-k}$$

Let us form:

$$G'(-1) = -\sum_{k=1}^{n} (-1)^k kp(X = k) = -\Big(\sum_{k=2,k\ even}^{n} kp(X = k) - \sum_{k=1,k\,odd}^{n} kp(X = k)\Big)$$

$G'(-1)$ is the average number of counters won by the second player minus the number of counters of the first player, and we get $G'(-1) = np(1 - 2p)^{n-1}$. This number is effectively positive when $p < 0.5$. More specifically, for odd n, the second player wins more counters than the first. For even n, the second one wins more counters for $p < 0.5$ and less for $p > 0.5$.

23.3.3. *Exercise 3: draws until a certain threshold is exceeded*

We have a box with two balls; one numbered 1 and the other numbered 2. We are given a number $N \geq 0$. The game consists of equiprobable drawings with replacement of balls in the box, until the sum of the numbers obtained over the balls drawn exceeds N. X is the random variable corresponding to the number of draws made. We want to find out the average number of draws $E_N(X)$, as a function of N.

a) Deal with the cases where N = 0, 1 and 2.

Let us draw the transition graph associated with this game (see Figure 23.6). The initial state is 0 and the final state F. The intermediate states are 1, 2, …, N, which correspond to the sum of numbers obtained up to there. In these first examples, $S_F(z)$ constitutes the generating function associated with X.

For $N = 0$, we find:

$$S_0(z) = 1,\ S_F(z) = (1 / 2)\ zS_0 + (1 / 2)\ zS_0 = z$$

hence: $E_0(X) = S'_F(1) = 1$

For $N = 1$:

$$S_0(z) = 1\ ,\ S_1(z) = (1 / 2)\ zS_0 = (1 / 2)\ z$$

$$S_F(z) = (1 / 2)\ zS_0 + (1 / 2)\ zS_1 + (1 / 2)\ zS_1$$

with: $S_F(z) = (1 / 2)\ z^2 + (1 / 2)\ z$

$$E_1(X) = S'_F(1) = 3 / 2$$

The words obtained for $N = 2$ are 111, 112, 12, 21 and 22, their sum being equal to either 3 or 4. The system of equations is expressed:

$$S_0 = 1$$

$$S_1\ (z) = (1 / 2)\ zS_0 = (1 / 2)z$$

$$S_2(z) = (1 / 2)\ zS_0 + (1 / 2)\ zS_1 = (1 / 4)\ z^2 + (1 / 2)\ z$$

$$S_F(z) = (1 / 2)\ zS_1 + zS_2 = (3 / 4)\ z^2 + (1 / 4)\ z^3$$

hence: $E_2(X) = S'_F(1) = 9 / 4$

Note that the arrows arriving on state F come either from state 1 or state 2, and a single arrow produces a sum of numbers drawn equal to 4. Since $S_F(1) = 1$ corresponds to the sure event, and:

$$S_F(1) = (1 / 2)\ S_1(1) + (1 / 2)\ S_2(1) + (1 / 2)\ S_2(1)$$

the first two terms correspond to words of three characters exactly. When the sum of the numbers exceeds two, the probability of getting words whose sum is three (namely 111, 12 and 21), is equal to:

$$(1 / 2) S_1(1) + (1 / 2) S_2(1) = 1 / 4 + 3 / 8 = 5 / 8$$

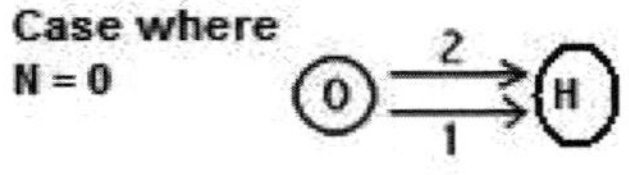

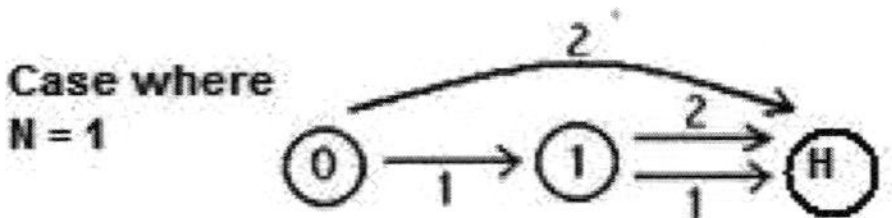

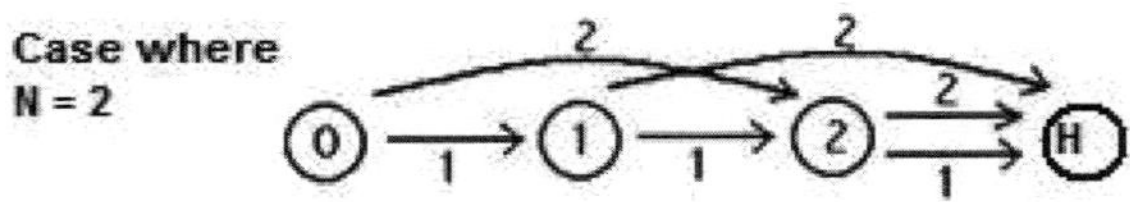

Figure 23.6. *Transition graphs for N = 0, 1 and 2*

b) In the case where N = 2, we now take Y as the random variable corresponding to the final sum obtained. Determine the average value E(Y) of the final sum.

Thanks to the preceding calculation, with a probability of 5 / 8 of getting a sum equal to 3 and then 3 / 8 of getting a sum equal to 4, we get:

$$E(Y) = 5/8 \,.\, 3 + 3/8 \,.\, 4 = 27 / 8 \approx 3.3$$

This can also be found thanks to the transition graph and generating function S_F associated with Y. Now an arrow carrying the number 1 is converted into $(1 / 2)\, z$, and an arrow carrying the number 2 is converted into $(1 / 2)\, z^2$, since it is in the sum of exponents that the final sum is found, hence the system of equations leading to the new generating function S_F:

$$S_0 = 1$$

$$S_1 (z) = (1 / 2)\, zS_0 = (1 / 2)\, z$$

$$S_2(z) = (1 / 2)z^2 S_0 + (1 / 2)\, zS_1 = (3 / 4)\, z^2$$

$S_F(z) = (1 / 2)\, z^2 S_1 + (1 / 2)\, z S_2 + (1 / 2)\, z^2 S_2 = (5 / 8)\, z^3 + (3 / 8)\, z^4$

therefore: $E_2(X) = S'_F(1) = 3 \,.\, 5 / 8 + 4 \,.\, 3 / 8 = 27 / 8$.

c) Determine the average duration of the game $E_N(X)$ and the final sum obtained on average, $E_N(Y)$, for any N.

The modified graph (see Figure 23.7) gives a simplified system of equations, of the form:

$S_0 = 1$

$S_1 = (1 / 2)\, z S_0 = (1 / 2)\, z$

$S_n = (1 / 2)\, z\, S_{n-1} + (1 / 2)\, z\, S_{n-2}$ for all $n > 1$

Now let us take the true transition graph of our game for a given number N, with $N \geq 2$. Only the last equation, with generating function $S_F(z)$ associated with X, differs from the case above:

$S_0 = 1$

$S_1 = (1 / 2)\, z S_0 = (1 / 2)\, z$

$S_n = (1 / 2)\, z S_{n-1} + (1 / 2)\, z S_{n-2}$ for $2 \leq n \leq N$

$S_F = (1 / 2)\, z S_N + (1 / 2)\, z S_N + (1 / 2)\, z S_{N-1}$

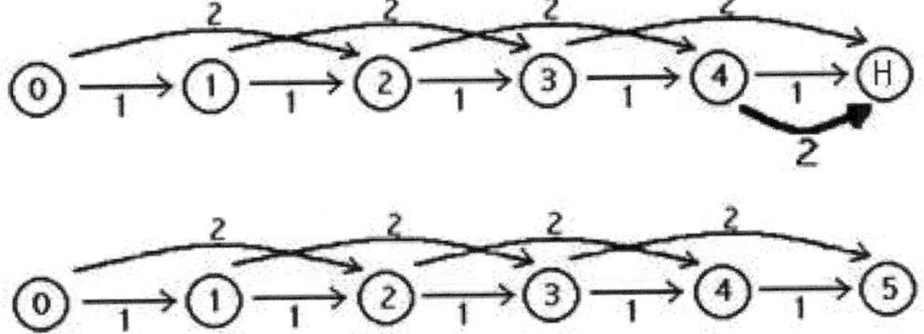

Figure 23.7. *The transition graph for N = 4 (top); and the modified graph, with one less final arrow (bottom)*

In turn, we can write $S_F = S_{N+1} + (1 / 2)\, z S_N$. By derivation, we find the average value $E_N(X) = S'_{N+1}(1) + (1 / 2)\, S'_N(1) + (1 / 2)\, S_N(1)$. We are returned to exclusively working on the $S_n(z)$ sequence, more specifically on sequences (s_n) and (s'_n) so that $s_n = S_N(1)$ and $s'_n = S'_N(1)$.

Thanks to the recurrence relation above:

$$S_n(z) = (1 / 2)\, z\, S_{n-1}(z) + (1 / 2)\, z\, S_{n-2}(z)$$

We also have $s_n = (1 / 2)\, s_{n-1} + (1 / 2)\, s_{n-2}$, with $s_0 = 1$ and $s_1 = 1 / 2$ at the start. The generating function associated with sequence (s_n) is:

$$F(z) = \frac{1}{1-(1/2)z-(1/2)z^2}$$

Now let us derive the recurrence relation:

$$S_n(z) = (1 / 2)\, z\, S_{n-1}(z) + (1 / 2)\, z\, S_{n-2}(z)$$

which gives:

$$S'_n(z) = (1 / 2)\, z\, S'_{n-1}(z) + (1 / 2)z\, S'_{n-2}(z) + (1 / 2)S_{n-1}(z) + (1 / 2)\, S_{n-2}(z)$$

hence:

$$s'_n = (1 / 2)\, s'_{n-1} + (1 / 2)\, s'_{n-2} + s_n\text{, with } s'_0 = 0 \text{ and } s'_1 = 1 / 2$$

Let G be the generating function associated with sequence (s'_n): It therefore verifies:

$$G - (1 / 2)\, z = (1 / 2)\, xG + (1 / 2)\, x^2G + F - 1 - (1 / 2)\, z\,,$$

$$\text{i.e.: } G = (F - 1) / (1 - (1 / 2)z - (1 / 2)z^2)$$

$$\text{or: } G(z) = \frac{0.5\, z(z+1)}{(1-0.5\, z-0.5\, z^2)^2}$$

The average value $E_N(X)$, as we have seen, verifies:

$$E_N(X) = s'_{N+1} + (1 / 2)\, s'_N + (1 / 2)\, s_N$$

Let $H(z)$ be the generating function associated with the sequence $(E_N(X))$. It gives:

$$H(z) = G(z) / z + (1 / 2)\, G(z) + (1 / 2)\, H(z)$$

$$= \frac{1}{(1-z)^2(1+(1/2)z)} = \frac{1}{1-(3/2)z+(1/2)z^3}$$

all calculations being done.

Sequence ($E_N(X)$) verifies the recurrence relation:

$$E_N(X) = 1.5\, E_{N-1}(X) - 0.5\, E_{N-2}(X) \text{ with } E_0(X) = 1 \text{ and } E_1(X) = 3 / 2$$

A classic calculation enables us to get the explicit form:

$$E_N(X) = \frac{6N+8}{9} + \frac{1}{9}(-\frac{1}{2})^N$$

Now let us move on to random variable Y. As we saw in the example where $N = 2$, when we waited for the sum of the numbers to exceed N, the probability of getting a sum equal to $N + 1$ is:

$$(1 / 2)\, S_{N-1}(1) + (1 / 2)\, S_N(1) = (1 / 2)\, s_{N-1} + (1 / 2)\, s_N = s_{N+1}$$

The probability of getting a sum equal to $N + 2$ is $1 - s_{N+1}$. This results in:

$$E_N(Y) = (N + 1)\, s_{N+1} + (N + 2)(1 - s_{N+1}) = N + 2 - s_{N+1}$$

The recurrence relation on sequence (s_N), $s_{N+1} = (1 / 2)\, s_{N-1} + (1 / 2)\, s_N$, leads to the sequence on ($E_N(Y)$):

$$E_N(Y) = (1 / 2)\, E_{N-1}(Y) + (1 / 2)\, E_{N-2}(Y) + 3 / 2,$$

with: $E_0(Y) = 3 / 2$ and $E_1(Y) = 9 / 4$

at the start. From this we deduce the explicit formula:

$$E_N(Y) = \frac{3N+4}{3} - \frac{1}{3}(-\frac{1}{2})^{N+1}.$$

23.3.4. *Exercise 4: Pascal's law*

A coin is tossed so the probability of getting heads is p and that of getting tails is q. Y_k is the number of moves necessary for heads to come out k times out of all tosses, provided that we stop the game when we get the kth head. We want to find the law of Y_k.

Let us introduce the random variables X_i with i between 1 and k. Variable X_1 corresponds to the number of moves until the first head outcome. In the general case, variable X_i, for $i \geq 2$ corresponds to the number of tosses after the $i - 1^{th}$ head outcome, until the ith head is obtained. Variables X_i are linked to Y_k by the relation: $X_1 + X_2 + \ldots + X_k = Y_k$.

Variables X_i all follow the same geometric law with parameter p, since it concerns the waiting time for a first success – here the outcome of a head. On the other hand, variables X_i are independent. Their generating function is $pz / (1 - qz)$, and that of Y_k is:

$$F(z) = (pz / (1 - qz))^k = p^k z^k (1 + qz + q^2z^2 + q^3z^3 + \ldots)^k$$

The probability $p(Y_k = Q)$, where Q is a number greater than or equal to k, is the coefficient of the term in z^Q in the development of the generating function. We have to find the term in z^{Q-k} in the development of $(1 + qz + q^2z^2 + \ldots)^k$. For k factors, this involves a term in z^{x1} in the first factor, then a term in z^{x2} in the second factor, … and a term in z^{xk} in the kth factor, in such a way that the sum $x_1 + x_2 + \ldots x_k = Q - k$, with x_i all positive or null integers. We know that the number of solutions to this equation is $C_{Q-1}{}^{Q-k}$ (see Chapter 7). Hence the probability law of Y_k:

$$p(Y_k = Q) = C_{Q-1}{}^{Q-k}\, p^k q^{Q-k}.$$

23.3.5. *Exercise 5: balls of two colors in a box*

A box contains white balls and black balls, the latter being in proportion p. We carry out a succession of draws replacing the ball drawn each time as follows: we note the color of the first ball drawn, then we continue to draw balls until a ball of the other color is obtained. Here we continue until we find a ball with the color of the first one drawn again. For example have the following succession of draws *WWWWBBBBBBW* or even *BBBBWWB*. X is the number of draws made.

a) Determine the law of X, as well as its expectation.

The first ball drawn is either white or black. Let us take the case where it is a white ball. After this drawing a white ball, X_1 is the number of draws until the first black ball is drawn: X_1 follows a geometric law with parameter $q = 1 - p$. After that, we wait for a first white ball to be drawn, and the number of moves X_2 also follows a geometric law, with parameter p. The total number of draws is $1 + X_1 + X_2$. The generating function associated with X_1 is:

$$G_{X_1}(Z) = \frac{pZ}{(1 - qZ)}$$

Similarly, generating function associated with X_2 is:

$$G_{X_2}(Z) = \frac{qZ}{(1-pZ)}$$

The product of these two generating functions gives the function associated with $X_1 + X_2$, i.e.:

$$G_{X_1+X_2}(Z) = \frac{pqZ^2}{(1-pZ)(1-qZ)}$$

and the function associated with $1 + X_1 + X_2$ is:

$$\frac{pq^2Z^3}{(1-pZ)(1-qZ)}$$

This result could just as well be found using the transition graph in Figure 23.8.

Let us do the same when the first ball drawn is black, hence the generating function $\frac{p^2qZ^3}{(1-pZ)(1-qZ)}$.

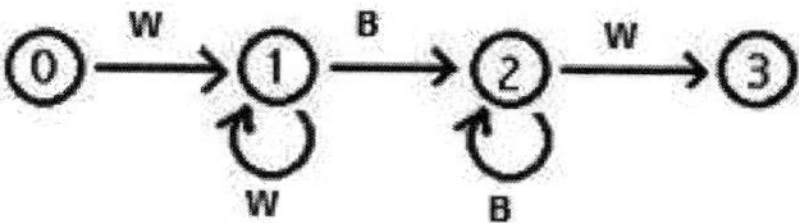

Figure 23.8. *Transition graph*

The generating function associated with X is the sum of the two generating functions that we have just obtained:

$$G_X(Z) = \frac{(pq^2 + p^2q)Z^3}{(1-pZ)(1-qZ)} = \frac{pqZ^3}{(1-pZ)(1-qZ)}$$

By developing this function, for $k \geq 3$ we obtain:

$$p(X = k) = pq(p^{k-3} + qp^{k-4} + q^2p^{k-5} + \ldots + q^{p-3}) = pq\frac{p^{k-2} - q^{k-2}}{p-q}$$

By introducing the function $f(Z)=\frac{1}{pq}(1-pZ)(1-qZ)$ so that $f(1) = 1$, the generating function is expressed:

$$G_X(Z)=\frac{Z^3}{f(Z)}$$

and we deduce from it the expectation:

$$E(X)=-f'(1)+3=-\frac{1}{pq}(-1+2pq)+3=\frac{1}{pq}+1.$$

b) A succession of drawings is split up into a first block of identical balls, then a second block of identical balls a different color to those of the first block, and ends with a ball in the same color as that of the first block. For example, the succession of draws WWWBBBBBW gives a first block of three white balls and a second one of five black balls. Determine the average length of each of these two blocks.

Now let us take a generating function with two variables, Z and Z' corresponding, respectively, to the output of balls with the color of the first block (i.e. those of the first block as well as the last block) or balls of the second block. From the transition graph (see Figure 23.9) we get:

$$S_0 = 1$$

$$S_1 = qZS_0 + qZS_1$$

$$S_2 = pZ'S_1 + pZ'S_2$$

hence: $S_2=\frac{pqZZ'}{(1-qZ)(1-pZ')}$

similarly: $S'_2=\frac{pqZZ'}{(1-pZ)(1-qZ')}$

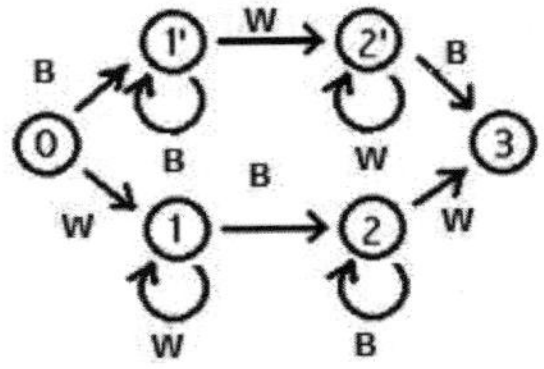

Figure 23.9. *Transition graph*

finally: $S_3 = \dfrac{pq^2Z^2Z'}{(1-qZ)(1-pZ')} + \dfrac{p^2qZ^2Z'}{(1-pZ)(1-qZ')}$

Note that by making $Z = Z'$, we again find the generating function associated with random variable X of the previous question.

Let us take $Z = 1$. We get the generating function associated with the length of the second block, i.e.:

$$G(Z') = \frac{pq^2Z'}{p(1-pZ')} + \frac{p^2qZ'}{q(1-qZ')} = \frac{q^2Z'}{1-pZ'} + \frac{p^2Z'}{1-qZ'}$$

Let us derive: $G'(Z') = \dfrac{q^2}{(1-pZ')^2} + \dfrac{p^2}{(1-qZ')^2}$. We deduce from this that: $G'(1) = 2$, which is the average length of the second block.

Now let us make $Z = 1$. We get the generating function associated with the length of the first block increased by 1, i.e.:

$$G(Z) = \frac{pq^2Z^2}{q(1-qZ)} + \frac{p^2qZ^2}{p(1-pZ)} = \frac{pqZ^2}{1-qZ} + \frac{pqZ^2}{1-pZ} = \frac{pq\,Z^2(2-Z)}{(1-pZ)(1-qZ)} = \frac{2Z^2 - Z^3}{f(Z)}$$

with: $f(Z) = \dfrac{1}{pq}(1-pZ)(1-qZ)$

such that $f(1) = 1$, hence:

$$G'(1) = -f'(1) + 4 - 3 = \frac{1}{pq} - 1$$

This is the average value of the length of the first block increased by 1, hence the average length of the first block:

$$\frac{1}{pq} - 2$$

Note that for $p = q = 1/2$, the average length of the first block is 2, just like that of the second block, and that otherwise the average length of the first block is greater than that of the second.

c) Devise the program giving the average length of each of the two blocks.

Here is the program (complete, even with declarations) giving the average length of each one of the two blocks:

```
#include <stdio.h>
#include <stdlib.h>
#include <time.h>
#define NBEXP 30000
int a[1000];
main()
{
float p,onset,cumul[2],block1t; int h,K,L[2],block,i,exp;
p=0.1;  onset=p*1000.;
srand(time(NULL)); cumul[0]=0.;cumul[1]=0.;
for(exp=0; exp<NBEXP; exp++)
  { h=random(1000);
  if (h<(int)onset) a[0]=1; else a[0]=0;
  K=a[0];
  for(expe=0; expe<=NE; expe++)
   { i=1;
   do { i++;  h=random(1000);if (h<(int)onset) a[i]=1; else a[i]=0; }
   while (a[i]==K);
   L[bloc]=i–1; cumul[block]+=L[block];    K=a[i];
   }
  }
for(block=0; block<2; block++)
printf("\nbloc(%d)=%3.3f",bloc+1,cumul[block]/(float)NBEXP);
}
```

23.3.6. *Exercise 6: throws of N dice until each gives the number 1*

We throw N dice. From the first throw, we take back the dice that did not return the number 1. We therefore proceed to a new throw with these dice, and so on and so forth until N number 1s have been obtained. X is the random variable equal to the number of throws necessary for getting N number 1s. We want to find the law of X.

a) Dealing with the case where N = 2.

When we throw two dic, we have 6×6 = 36 possible cases, one of which gives the two number 1s, 10 of which give one number 1, and the other 25 which do not give any number 1. We deduce from this the transition graph with three states corresponding to the number of dice thrown: state 2 then 1 then the final state 0 (see Figure 23.10).

The system of equations is expressed:

$$S_2 = 1 + (25 / 36)\, zS_2$$

$$S_1 = (10 / 36)\, zS_2 + (5 / 6)\, zS_1$$

$$S_0 = (1 / 36)\, zS_2 + (1 / 6)\, zS_1$$

Finally, the generating function is:

$$S_0 = \frac{6z + 5z^2}{(36 - 25z)(6 - 5z)}$$

Its development leads to:

$p(X = 1) = 1 / 36, p(X = 2) = 85 / 1{,}296$, etc.

With the derivative of the numerator $(6z + 5z^2) / 11$ being $6 + 10z$, and that of the denominator $(36 - 25z)(6 - 5z) / 11$ being $(-330 + 250z) / 11$, the expectation is equal to:

$$E(X) = 16 / 11 + 80 / 11 = 96 / 11$$

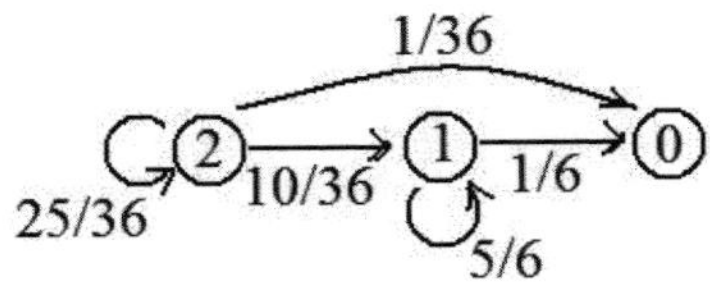

Figure 23.10. *Transition graph for N = 2*

This calculation could be generalized to any N, but there is another simpler, cleverer method, which we will look at now.

b) Calculate $p(X \leq k)$ for the geometric law.

Recall that geometric law corresponds to the waiting time for the first success in a succession of heads or tails tosses (or success-failure) with a probability of success equal to p. This gives the law: $p(X = k) = p\, q^{k-1}$. We deduce from it that:

$$\begin{aligned} p(X \leq k) &= p(X = 1) + p(X = 2) + \ldots\, p(X = k) \\ &= p(1 + q + q^2 + \ldots + q^{k-1}) \\ &= 1 - q^k \end{aligned}$$

This can be seen in another way. Let us imagine that we repeat k heads or tails tosses. The probability of getting no success is q^k. The probability of getting at least one success is $1 - q^k$.

Again we find the same result as for probability $p(X \leq k)$. This is normal since the probability of getting a first success in at most k tosses $p(X \leq k)$ is also the probability of getting at least one success in k tosses.

c) Application to the problem: instead of re-throwing only the dice that did not give number 1, we can also re-throw the N dice each time, waiting for each one of the dice to give number 1.

– the probability that die number i does not give any number 1s in k throws is: q^k with $q = 5 / 6$;

– the probability that it gives at least one number 1 in k throws is: $1 - q^k$; and

– the probability that the n dice each give at least one number 1 in k throws is: $(1 - q^k)^N$;

This corresponds exactly to probability $p(X \leq k)$, where:

$$p(X \leq k) = \left(1 - \left(\frac{5}{6}\right)^k\right)^N$$

and:

$$p(X = k) = p(X \leq k) - p(X \leq k\text{-}1) = p\left(1 - \left(\frac{5}{6}\right)^k\right)^N - \left(1 - \left(\frac{5}{6}\right)^{k-1}\right)^N$$

After calculation, the formula for expectation is:

$$E_N(X) = \sum_{K=1}^{N} \frac{(-1)^{K-1} C_N^K}{1-q^K}$$

Notably, $E_1(X) = 6$, $E_2(X) = 8.7$ and $E_3(X) = 10.5$.

d) Write the program for the dice game.

The program for N dice giving number 1 in k throws is:

```
#define N 50
#define NBE 30000

main()
{
q=5./6.; randomize();
cumul=0; /* for the expectation */
for(expe=1; expe<=NBE; expe++)
  { for(i=0; i<N; i++) finite[i]=NO;
    nbthrows=0; nbfinite=0;
    while(nbfinite<N)
    { nbthrows+ +;
      for(i=0;i<N;i++) if (finite[i]==NO)
        { h=random(6)+1;  if (h==1) {finite[i]=YES; nbfinite++;} }
    }
   counter[nbthrows]++; cumul+=nbthrows;
 }
cumulproba=0.;
for(i=1; i<200; i++)
  { proba=(float)counter[i]/(float)NBE;
   qi=pow(q, (float)i); qiminus1=pow(q, (float)i-1.);
   probath=pow(1.-qi, N) - pow(1.-qiminus1, N);
   cumulproba+=proba;
   if (proba!=0.) printf("%3.d %3.3f %3.3f  ", i, proba, probath);
  }
EX=(float)cumul/(float)NBE;  printf("\n\n%d E(X)= %3.3f",N,EX);
}
```

Chapter 24

Graphs and Matrices for Dealing with Probability Problems

In Chapter 13 we saw how the use of an oriented graph associated with a problem enabled us to enumerate words going from one node to another, using the adjacency matrix A of the graph. This method can be extended to probability theory with one novelty: the arches of the graph will now be weighted by probabilities. We will begin by recalling this method using a combinatorics example, before extending it to probability theory.

24.1. First example: counting of words based on three letters

We consider words based on the three letters 1, 2, 3 where letter 1 can only be followed by a 1, letter 2 can only be followed by 1 or by 2, and letter 3 being able to be followed by 1, 2 or 3. For example, words of three characters are 111, 211, 221, 222, 311, 321, 322, 331, 332 and 333. Let $u(n)$ be the number of n-length words. Notably, we have $u(0) = 1$, $u(1) = 3$, $u(2) = 6$ and $u(3) = 10$. We want to find the formula that gives $u(n)$.

Let us construct the graph that corresponds to our problem (see Figure 24.1). We always start at node 3, from which we can go to nodes 1, 2 or 3. Traversing one of these arches gives unit length words of 1, 2 or 3. Therefore, when we traverse the 3 to 1 arch, we write only the letter 1 corresponding to the end of this arch. We continue in the same way. Traversing n arches, the end number of which we write each time, gives a word of n letters. In this example:

– the adjacency matrix of the graph is: $A = \begin{bmatrix} 1 & 0 & 0 \\ 1 & 1 & 0 \\ 1 & 1 & 1 \end{bmatrix}$;

– from which we deduce matrix $I - xA = \begin{bmatrix} 1-x & 0 & 0 \\ -x & 1-x & 0 \\ -x & -x & 1-x \end{bmatrix}$; and

– the determinant $|I - xA| = (1 - x)^3$.

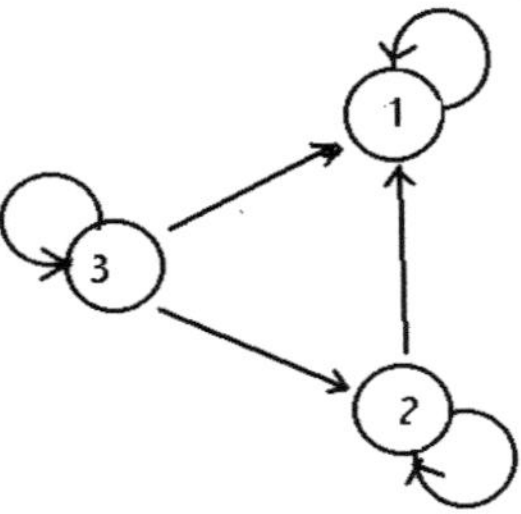

Figure 24.1. *Graph for creating words*

Let $F_{33}(x)$ be the generating function associated with the number $u_3(n)$ of n-length paths going from node 3 to 3, with $u_3(n)$ also being the number of n-length words of ending in the letter 3. Thanks to the formula seen in Chapter 13, we get:

$F_{33}(x) = det(I - xA$, where we removed line 3, and column 3) $/ / (1 - x)^3$

$= (1 - x)^2 / (1 - x)^3 = 1 / (1 - x)$

hence: $u_3(n) = 1$

Similarly, going from node 3 to node 2, we get the generating function:

$F_{32}(x) = \text{-det}(I - xA$, removing 2,3) $/ (1 - x)^3$

$= x(1 - x) / (1 - x)^3 = x / (1 - x)^2$

hence: $u_2(n) = n$

Finally, if we go from node 3 to node 1, we get:

$F_{31}(x) = x / (1 - x)^3$

hence: $u_1(n) = n(n + 1) / 2$

Finally the number of words is:

$$u(n) = u_1(n) + u_2(n) + u_3(n) = 1 + n + n(n + 1) / 2 = (n + 1)(n + 2) / 2$$

In this way we find the so-called triangular numbers. The associated generating function is $1 / (1 - x)^3$.[1] We will see below how this method applies to probabilities as well.

24.2. Generating functions and determinants

Let us take the framework of probability theory. We want to find the probability, starting from a certain node i of the graph, of ending up at a node j after having traversed n arches. Each arch ends up being affected by a certain probability. The graph is weighted by these probabilities and we obtain the weighted adjacency matrix A of the graph. Each 0 of this matrix indicates not only the absence of an arch from one point to the other, but also the null probability of going from this point to the other in one single step. Therefore we have the fundamental property:

PROPERTY 24.1.– Let A be the weighted adjacency matrix of an oriented graph. The coefficient in line i and column j, called $a_{ij}^{(n)}$ of matrix A^n, is the probability starting from node i of ending up at node j in n steps (or arch traversals).

Let us prove this property by recurrence. It is obviously true for $n = 1$, by definition of matrix A. It is even true for $n = 0$: actually, with the identity matrix, since $a_{ii} = 1$ and 0 if not, the fact of remaining on a node in zero moves is a sure event. Let us assume the property is true at a certain rank n and show that it remains so at rank $n + 1$. We use the fact that $A^{n+1} = A^n A$, hence by definition of the product of matrices the coefficient in line i and column j of matrix A^{n+1} is $a^{(n+1)}{}_{ij} = \sum a^{(n)}{}_{ik}\, a^{(1)}{}_{kj}$, with the summation focusing on all nodes called k.

With $a^{(n)}{}_{ik}$ being the probability of going from node i to node k in n moves, assuming recurrence, we get $a^{(n)}{}_{ik}\, a^{(1)}{}_{kj}$, which is the probability of going from i to j passing through k in $n + 1$ moves, where these events are independent, hence the multiplication of the probabilities. The summation on the k nodes corresponds

1. These results could evidently be obtained in other ways. It is a matter of words, each letter of which must be followed by a letter that is less than or equal to it. This can be generalized to a N-letter alphabet. We easily verify that the generating function is $1 / (1 - x)^N$. We know that $1 / (1 - x)^N = \sum_{n \geq 0} C_{N+n-1}^{N-1} x^n$, hence the number of words $u(n) = C_{N+n-1}^{N-1}$.

exactly to total probability formula. The property is shown in this way using recurrence.

Let us consider the generating function $F_{ij}(x)$ associated with the probabilities of going from node i to node j with X as the random variable, which is the number of stages. The generating function is:

$$F_{ij}(x) = a^{(0)}_{ij} + a^{(1)}_{ij}\, x + a^{(2)}_{ij}\, x^2 + a^{(3)}_{ij}\, x^3 + \ldots$$

which is the coefficient of indices i and j of the matrix:

$$I + xA + x^2A^2 + x^3A^3 + x^4A^4 + \ldots$$

i.e. of matrix $(I - xA)^{-1}$. Hence, thanks to the inverse of a matrix formula:

$$F_{ij}(x) = (-1)^{i+j}\,(\det(I - xA, j, i) / \det(I - xA))$$

or $\det(I - xA, j, \mathrm{i})$ is the determinant of matrix $I - xA$ from which we remove line j and column i. We deduce from this the following property:

PROPERTY 24.2.– The generating function $F_{ij}(x)$ associated with random variable X corresponding to the number of arches traversed on the graph to go from node i to node j is:

$$F_{ij}(x) = (-1)^{i+j}\,(\det(I - xA, j, i) / \det(I - xA))$$

In Chapter 23, we used a transition graph to find the generating function. At that time we had to solve a system of equations linked to this graph. Solving a system of linear equations also means inversing a matrix, even if this is not explicit in practice. The new method we have just presented is a variation on the same theme. It is up to us to choose between solving a system of equations by substitution and calculating determinants. Here some examples dealt with using the determinants method, and notably the one we have encountered above. This will enable us to carry out a comparison with the solving a system of equations method.

24.3. Examples

24.3.1. *Exercise 1: waiting time for double heads in a game of heads or tails*

In a repeated game of heads or tails, with probability p for H (heads) and q for T (tails), we are interested in the waiting time for the outcome of HH for the first time, i.e. the number of moves necessary for HH to be obtained.

The random variable X associated with this game is the length of the word obtained, knowing that this word ends in HH without having had double H before, and knowing that it is created out of the alphabet with the two letters H and T, with the respective probabilities of belonging p and q. Let us draw the transition graph (see Figure 24.2). The system of equations that corresponds to this graph is:

$$S_0 = 1 + qx\, S_0 + qx\, S_1$$

$$S_1 = px\, S_0$$

$$S_2 = px\, S_1$$

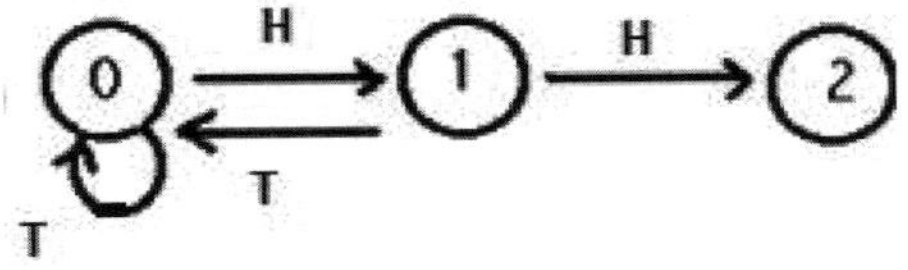

Figure 24.2. *Transition graph*

Solving the system finally leads to the generating function associated with X:

$$S_2(x) = p^2x^2 / (1 - qx - pqx^2)$$

We deduce $E(X) = (p + 1) / p^2$ from this equation. We have proceeded in this way up to this point.

Now we can use the purely matrix-related method. Knowing that H has p as its probability and T has q as its probability, the adjacency matrix of the weighted oriented graph is:

$$\mathrm{A} = \begin{bmatrix} q & p & 0 \\ q & 0 & p \\ 0 & 0 & 0 \end{bmatrix} \text{ and } |I - xA| = \begin{bmatrix} q & p & 0 \\ q & 0 & p \\ 0 & 0 & 0 \end{bmatrix} = 1 - qx - pqx^2$$

therefore: $\det(I - xA, 2, 0) = p^2x^2$.

We deduce from this that the generating function associated with random variable X corresponding to the number of moves until HH is obtained is:

$$F(x) = p^2x^2 / (1 - qx - pqx^2)$$

In fact, the two methods are practically the same. The system of equations of the first method has the transpose of matrix $I - xA$ as its matrix, which is the matrix used in the second method. If it is transposed, the coefficients in the system of equations correspond to the arrows that end up on a node, and not to those that start at it. Only the choice in exercising the solution remains: either we deal with a system of equations using classic substitution methods or use Cramer formulae linked to matrix inversion to obtain the generating function.

But what is the specific meaning of the other series, S_0 and S_1? S_0 corresponds to the empty word as well as to all words ending in T (of length at least equal to 1) and containing isolated Hs or no Hs at all. We find:

$$S_0(x) = 1 / (1 - qx - pqx^2)$$

if we take the series:

$$S_0(x) - 1 = (qx + pqx^2) / (1 - qx - pqx^2) = qx(1 + px) / (1 - qx - pqx^2)$$

This refers to removing the empty word. We obtain the series associated with all words ending in T and containing isolated Hs or no Hs. The language formed by these words is:

$$T + TT + HT + TTT + THT + HTT + TTTT + \ldots$$

Using this language, series $S_0(x) - 1$ is obtained by replacing H with px and T with qx, which comes back to weighting each word by its probability and grouping the words according to their length. This means that $S_0(x) = p_1 x + p_2 x^2 + p_3 x^3 + \ldots$, where p_k is the probability at the end of k tosses that we will get a word ending in T with isolated Hs or no Hs at all. $S_0(x) - 1$ has nothing to do with a generating function associated with a random variable, but it is the generating function of the sequence of probabilities p_k.

Moreover we find this generating function again by constructing the graph enabling us to create such words (see Figure 24.3). Going from state 0 to state 2 rightly corresponds to words ending in T and including isolated Hs or no Hs at all.

The weighted adjacency matrix of the graph is:

$$A = \begin{bmatrix} 0 & p & q \\ 0 & 0 & q \\ 0 & p & q \end{bmatrix}$$

from which we deduce: $|I - xA| = 1 - qx - pqx^2$.

The generating function $F_{02}(x)$ associated with paths from 0 to 2, with their probabilities being:

$$F_{02}(x) = \det(I - xA, 2, 0) / |I - xA| = (qx + pqx^2) / (1 - qx - pqx^2)$$

Its development leads to terms in x^k whose coefficient is the probability of getting a k-length word ending in T and with isolated or no Hs. We find the generating function $S_0(x) - 1$ above.

Similarly, series S_1 corresponds to words ending in H and containing only isolated Hs. As each of these words is obtained by concatenating a word from S_0 (including the empty word) with one H, this gives $S_1(x) = px / (1 - qx - pqx^2)$. This is found in the graph in Figure 23.4 by taking the paths leading to state 0 and state 1. Hence the generating function:

$$F_{01}(x) = -\det(I - xA, 1, 0) / |I - xA| = px / (1 - qx - pqx^2)$$

We do find $S_1(x)$ again. The term in x^k has the probability of getting, at the end of k tosses, a word ending in H and containing only isolated Hs as its coefficient.

Therefore, the solution to the initial problem enables us, in a secondary way, to deal with other problems linked to it.

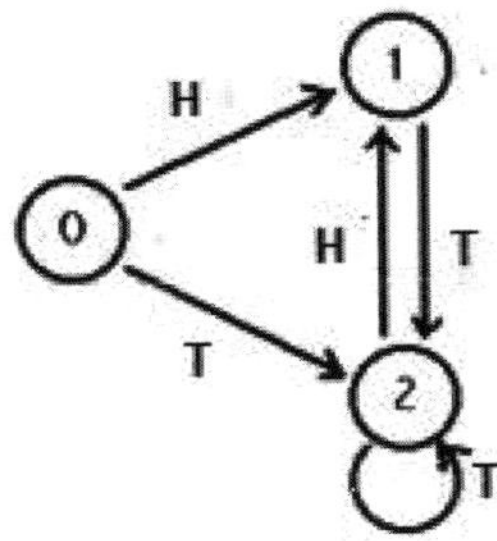

Figure 24.3. *Transition graph building words going from 0 to 2, or 0 to 1*

24.3.2. *Draws from three boxes*

We have three boxes. Box U_1 contains a ball numbered 1, box U_2 contains two balls numbered 1 and 2, and box U_3 contains three balls numbered 1, 2 and 3. We perform a sequence of draws, replacing balls at the rate of one ball per box, according to the following procedure: the first draw is always from box U_3, the one that contains the most balls. Each time a ball numbered i is drawn from a box, the next draw will take place in box number i. We want to find out, at the end of n draws, the probabilities $p_k(n)$ that the last ball drawn carries the number k, with k between 1 and 3.

The graph is the same as the one given in section 24.1 of this chapter on counting words based on three letters, but now each arch carries a weight (see Figure 24.4). Arch ij has the probability that ball j is drawn from box i as its weight. A path on the graph is weighted by the product of the weights of every arch that make it up. We want to count the number of n-length weighted paths leaving node 3 to arrive at node k, giving the probability $p_k(n)$ sought. The corresponding matrix is:

$$A = \begin{bmatrix} 1 & 0 & 0 \\ \frac{1}{2} & \frac{1}{2} & 0 \\ \frac{1}{3} & \frac{1}{3} & \frac{1}{3} \end{bmatrix} \text{ and } I - xA = \begin{bmatrix} 1-x & 0 & 0 \\ -1/2x & 1-1/2x & 0 \\ -1/3x & -1/3x & 1-1/3x \end{bmatrix}$$

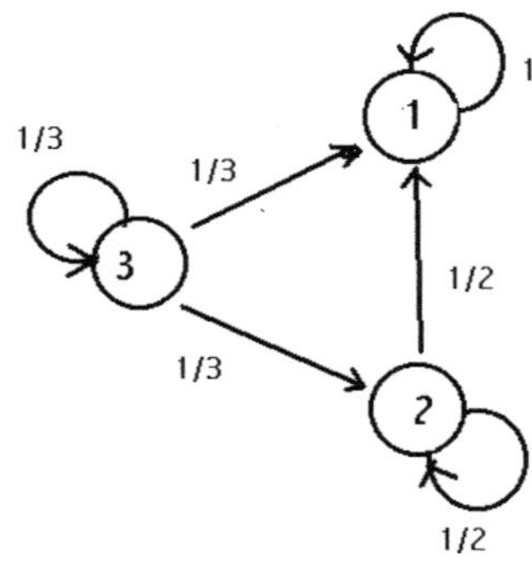

Figure 24.4. *Transition graph weighted by probabilities*

From this we deduce the generating functions associated with the probabilities:

$F_{33}(x) = 1 / (1 - (1 / 3)\, x)$ hence $p_3(n) = (1 / 3)^n$

$$F_{32}(x) = \frac{(1/3)\ x}{(1-(1/2)\ x)(1-(1/3)\ x)} = (1/3)\ x\ (\frac{3}{1-(1/2)x} - \frac{2}{1-(1/3)x})$$

which gives:

$p_2(n) = (1 / 2)^{n-1} - 2(1 / 3)^n$

and:

$$F_{31}(x) = \frac{(1/3)\ x}{(1-x)(1-(1/2)\ x)(1-(1/3)\ x)} = (1/3)\ x\ (\frac{3}{1-x} - \frac{3}{1-(1/2)x} + \frac{1}{1-(1/3)x})$$

therefore:

$$p_1(n) = 1 - (1\ /\ 2)^{n-1} + (1\ /\ 3)^n$$

We can check that the sum of the three probabilities obtained is 1.

24.3.3. *Alternate draws from two boxes*

We have two boxes U_1 and U_2. The first one contains a proportion p_1 of white balls and the second a proportion p_2 of white balls, the other balls being black. At first we make a random draw from box U_1 or U_2.

If we get a white ball we put it back in the box and we decide to make the second draw from the same box. If not we choose the other box. We continue in this way move after move, replacing the ball drawn in its box each time. We want to find the probability p_n of making the nth draw in box U_1.

The graph with three nodes corresponding to this game is given in Figure 24.5. Node 0 corresponds to the initial state, where we will choose to draw either in box U_1 or U_2. The first move therefore corresponds to traversing an arch. Nodes 1 and 2 correspond to boxes U_1 and U_2. At the end of traversing n arches, if we have arrived at U_1, this means that we will carry out the nth draw in box U_1. In our problem, we are interested in the number of n-length paths weighted by their probability, starting from node 0 and ending up at node 1.

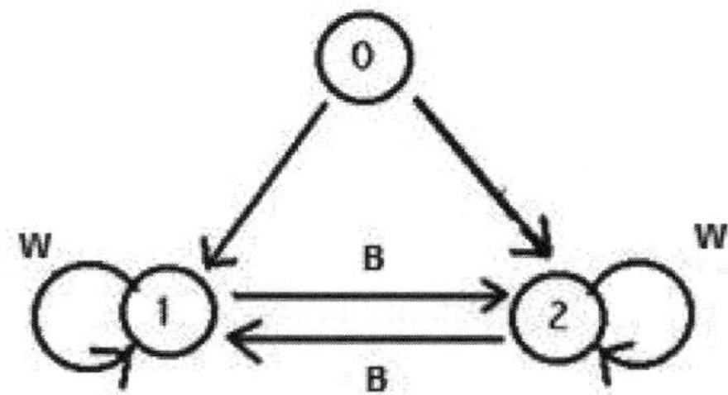

Figure 24.5. *Transition graph of alternate drawings. We are interested in paths from 0 to 1*

With the arches being weighted by their probability, we get the matrix of the weighted graph:

$$A = \begin{bmatrix} 0 & 0.5 & 0.5 \\ 0 & p_1 & 1-p_1 \\ 0 & 1-p_2 & p_2 \end{bmatrix}$$

We deduce from it that:

$$|I - xA| = \begin{vmatrix} 1 & -x/2 & -x/2 \\ 0 & 1-p_1 x & -(1-p_1)x \\ 0 & -(1-p_2)x & 1-p_2 x \end{vmatrix}$$

$$= (1 - p_1 x)(1 - p_2 x) - (1 - p_1)(1 - p_2)x^2$$

$$= 1 - (p_1 + p_2)x - (1 - p_1 - p_2)x^2$$

$$-|I\text{-}xA, 1, 0| = \begin{vmatrix} x/2 & x/2 \\ -(1-p_2)x & 1-p_2 x \end{vmatrix} = 0.5\, x\,(1 + (1 - 2p_2)x)$$

The generating function associated with the lengths of weighted paths starting at node 0 to arrive at node 1, i.e. the generating function associated with the probabilities (p_n) is:

$$F_{01}(x) = 0.5\, x\,(1 + (1 - 2p_2)x) \,/\, (1 - (p_1 + p_2)x - (1 - p_1 - p_2)x^2)$$

We deduce from it that $p_1 = 0.5$, $p_2 = 0.5(p_1 - p_2 + 1)$, $p_3 = 0.5(1 + p_1^2 - p_2^2)$. Thanks to the denominator, we have the recurrence relation:

$$p_n = (p_1 + p_2)\, p_{n-1} + (1 - p_1 - p_2)\, p_{n-2},$$

which is valid from $n = 3$.

24.3.4. *Successive draws from one box to the next*

We have N boxes. The first one contains a proportion p_1 of white balls; the others being black. All the other boxes contain a white balls and a black balls. We make one draw from the first box, place the ball obtained in the second box, then make a draw from this second box and we place the ball in the third box. We continue in this way drawing one ball from one box and placing it in the next, until drawing a ball from the last box. We are interested in the probability of getting a white ball in this last draw.

On the corresponding graph (see Figure 24.6), node 1 corresponds to drawing a ball from box 1. Node 2 corresponds to making a draw from another box when this box has received a white ball, and node 3 when it has received a black ball. The arches are weighted by their probability. The number of N-length paths starting at node 1 and ending at node 2 gives the probability sought, as the last draw is a white ball. Matrix A of the weighted graph is:

$$A = \begin{bmatrix} 0 & p_1 & 1-p_1 \\ 0 & \frac{a+1}{2a+1} & \frac{a}{2a+1} \\ 0 & \frac{a}{2a+1} & \frac{a+1}{2a+1} \end{bmatrix} \text{ then: } |I - xA| = 1 - 2\frac{a+1}{2a+1}x + \frac{1}{2a+1}x^2$$

and:

$$|I - xA, 2, 1| = p_1 x + (\frac{a}{2a+1} - p_1)x^2$$

The generating function associated with the number of weighted paths from 1 to 2 is:

$$F_{12}(x) = (\, p_1 x + (\frac{a}{2a+1} - p_1)x^2\,) \,/\, (\, p_1 x + (\frac{a}{2a+1} - p_1)x^2\,)$$

Using decomposition:

$$\frac{1}{1 - 2\frac{a+1}{2a+1}x + \frac{1}{2a+1}x^2} = \frac{1}{(1-x)(1 - \frac{x}{2a+1})} = \frac{1}{2a}(\frac{2a+1}{1-x} - \frac{1}{1 - \frac{1}{2a+1}x})$$

the calculation gives the coefficient of the term in x^N as the probability p_N of drawing a white ball from the Nth box:

$$p_N = 1/2 + (p_1 - 1/2)/(2a+1)^{N-1}$$

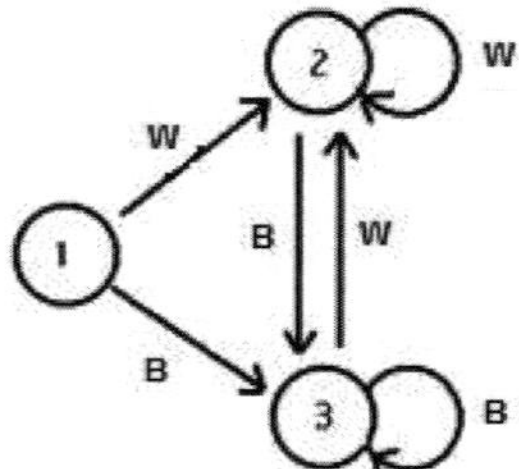

Figure 24.6. *Graph of successive drawings, where we want to go from 1 to 2*

Finally, let us give details of another method. It is a classic method, not making use of generating functions but using a recurrence on probabilities, backed up by matrices. p_k and q_k are the respective probabilities of drawing a white ball and a black ball from the kth box. We get the matrix recurrence relation:

$$\begin{pmatrix} p_{k+1} \\ q_{k+1} \end{pmatrix} = A \begin{pmatrix} p_k \\ q_k \end{pmatrix} \text{ with } A = \begin{bmatrix} \frac{a+1}{2a+1} & \frac{a}{2a+1} \\ \frac{a}{2a+1} & \frac{a+1}{2a+1} \end{bmatrix}$$

using total probability formula, hence:

$$\begin{pmatrix} p_N \\ q_N \end{pmatrix} = A^{N-1} \begin{pmatrix} p_1 \\ 1-p_1 \end{pmatrix}$$

The calculation of A^{N-1} is done by diagonalizing matrix A, which gives:

$$D = \begin{bmatrix} 1 & 0 \\ 0 & \frac{1}{a+1} \end{bmatrix}$$

and the matrix of passage $P = \begin{bmatrix} 1 & 1 \\ 1 & -1 \end{bmatrix}$ with $P^{-1} = (1/2)\,P$.

We deduce from it that $A^{N-1} = P\,D^{N-1}P^{-1}$, then p_N as before.

The two methods are of equal merit in this case, in terms of calculation. In the first method we must decompose a rational fraction; in the second method we need to find the eigenvalues and eigenvectors of a matrix.

Chapter 25

Repeated Games of Heads or Tails

A repetitive game of heads or tails can be shown by a route in a square grid following two directions – an upwards diagonal line in the case of heads, and a downwards diagonal line for tails (see Figure 25.1). We have already dealt with this problem in Chapter 6. We will now specify the probabilities, after recalling some results.

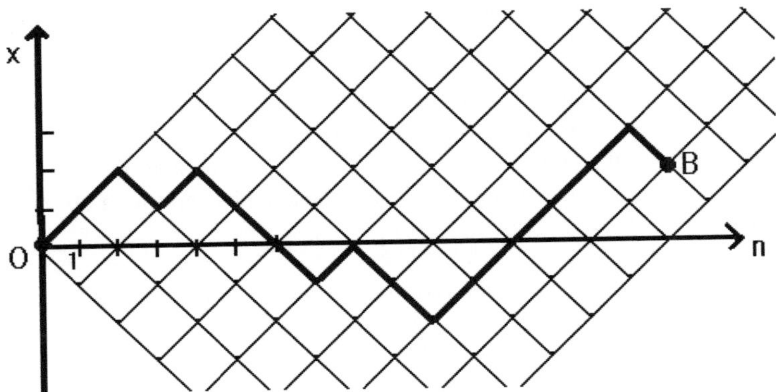

Figure 25.1. *Path from O to B representing a repeated game of heads or tails*

25.1. Paths on a square grid

Let $N(n, x)$ be the number of paths going from the origin O to point $B(n, x)$ making n steps in a choice of two directions $\nearrow$ $\searrow$. Out of these paths, $P(n, x)$ is the number of those that neither touch nor cross the horizontal axis originating at point O, which imposes $x > 0$ (or $x < 0$) as soon as we are no longer at O. We saw that:

$$N(n, x) = C_n^{(n+x)/2}$$

and: $P(n, x) = (x / n)\, N(n, x)$

a) Number of 2n'-length paths, which neither touch or cross the horizontal axis, and are located above = (1 / 2) $C_{2n'}^{n'}$.

Indeed it concerns $P(2n', 2) + P(2n', 4) + \ldots + P(2n', 2n')$, and we use the formula:

$$P(2n', 2k) = N(2n' - 1, 2k - 1) - N(2n' - 1, 2k + 1)$$

which produces a spate of simplifications, and leads to the result.[1]

b) Number of 2n' + 1-length paths that neither touch or cross the horizontal axis, and are located above = $C_{2n'}^{n'}$.

Indeed, from the $2n'$-length paths obtained above, we add a diagonal line either upwards or downwards at the end, which doubles the number of $2n' + 1$-length paths compared to those $2n'$ long.

c) Number of 2n'-length paths that can touch but not cross the horizontal axis, and are located above = $C_{2n'}^{n'}$.

We take $2n'$-length paths that neither touch or cross the axis and remain above it, numbering $(1 / 2)\, C_{2n'}^{n'}$. We then remove the first step, we take height 1 as the new horizontal axis. At the end of the paths we add a diagonal line downwards or upwards. This gives twice as many paths, and these paths can touch but not cross the axis. Hence the $C_{2n'}^{n'}$.

d) Number of 2n' + 1-length paths that can touch but not cross the horizontal axis, and are located above = $C_{2n'+1}^{n'}$ *(it is the same number as that of paths ending up at point (2n' + 1, 1)).*

---

1. This result: $\sum_{k=1}^{n'} P(2n',2k) = \frac{1}{2} C_{2n'}^{n'}$ is also expressed using the formula on $P(n,x)$: $\sum_{k=1}^{n'} \frac{k}{n'} C_{2n'}^{n'+k} = \frac{1}{2} C_{2n'}^{n'}$, hence $\sum_{k=1}^{n'} P(2n',2k) = \frac{1}{2} C_{2n'}^{n'}$. We will use this formula in section 25.2.2.

We take the $C_{2n'}^{n'}$ paths $2n'$ long that can touch but not cross the horizontal axis while remaining above it, and we separate them into two categories:

– *Those that end up above the axis*: there are $C_{2n'}^{n'} - c(n')$, where $c(n')$ is the number of mountain ranges $2n'$ long. By adding an upwards or downwards diagonal line to them at the end, this doubles the number of $2n' + 1$-length paths that can touch but not cross the axis.

– *Those that end up at 0*: there are $c(n')$, and we can only add an upwards diagonal line to them, which gives $c(n')$ paths $2n' + 1$ long that can touch but not cross the axis.

Finally we find:

$$2C_{2n'}^{n'} - c(n') \text{ paths } 2n' + 1 \text{ long,}$$

or even:

$$((2n' + 1)/(n' + 1))\, C_{2n'}^{n'} = C_{2n'+1}^{n'+1} \text{ paths.}^{2}$$

25.2. Probability of getting a certain number of wins after *n* equiprobable tosses

Let us consider the game of heads or tails, with equiprobable tosses, where we carry out n tosses. Visually, this gives a worn out line route on a square grid, with a diagonal rising line ↗ of 1 for a head being tossed, and a falling line ↘ of 1 for a tail being tossed, from point O to point $B(n, x)$.

If we associate a win of +1 with a head being tossed and a loss of -1 to a tail being tossed, the drawing (like the one in Figure 25.1) enables us to follow the evolution of a player's winnings throughout the stages, from an initial null up until his final winnings of x at the nth stage. More specifically, the winnings are $x_0 = 0$ at move 0, then x_1 at move 1, etc., until they reach $x_n = x$ at the nth move.

The winnings, if you prefer, are the difference between the number of heads obtained and the number of tails. There is also another way of seeing this game: as the drunken man's walk, where the man makes either one step forward, or one step

2. Another method: $2n' + 1$-length paths that can touch but not cross the horizontal axis, and are situated above it, end up at points of the form $(2n' + 1, 2q + 1)$ with q between 0 and n'. They are also paths that do not touch or cross the axis located at -1 height. The total number of paths from O to point $B(2n'+ 1, 2q + 1)$ is $N(2n'+ 1, 2q + 1)$. The number of paths from O to point $(2n' + 1, 2q + 1)$ that touch or cross the axis -1 high is $N(2n' + 1, 2q + 3)$. It is sufficient to apply the reflection principle (see Chapter 6) to see this. The number of paths that neither touch or cross axis -1 is therefore: $N(2n' + 1, 2q + 1) - N(2n' + 1, 2q + 3)$. Summing up all the values of q, $N(2n' + 1, 1)$ remains.

back on a straight line, starting from a point of origin O, and we are interested in his position x at the nth stage. This is the projection of the previous movement on the vertical x axis.

25.2.1. *Probability p(n, x) of getting winnings of x at the end of n moves*

When n is even, the final winnings can be 0, ±2, ±4,..., $\pm n$. When n is odd, the final winnings are equal to ±1, ±3, ±5, ..., $\pm n$. In all cases, there are $n + 1$ possible endpoints. The number of ways of making n tosses is 2^n. Let $p(n, x)$ be the probability, starting from O, of ending up at point $B(n, x)$. The number of paths leading to point $B(n, x)$ is $N(n, x)$. Hence:

$$p(n, x) = N(n, x) / 2^n$$

Taking the final winnings x at the end of n moves as random variable X, we have:

$$p(n, x) = p(X = x)$$

At the end of n moves, the final winnings are between $-n$ and n (and it goes 2 by 2). The average final winnings $E(X)$ is null because of the symmetry of the possible endpoints in n moves in relation to the horizontal axis.[3]

25.2.2. *Standard deviation in relation to a starting point*

Now we no longer reason in terms of winnings or losses, positive or negative, but work in absolute value. We want to find the deviation (from one side or the other) of the drunk man at the end of n steps, in relation to his starting point O. This deviation is between 0 and n:

– if n is even, it takes all the even values from 0 to n; and

– if n is odd, the deviation takes all the odd values from 1 to n.

---

3. Let $X_1, X_2, \ldots, X_n$ be the random variables associated with the winnings during successive tosses. For each one of these variables $E(X_k) = 0$ and $V(X_k) = 0.5\ (-1)^2 + 0.5\ (1)^2 = 1$. The expected value of each of these variables is 0. With $X = X_1 + X_2 + \ldots + X_n$, the expectations are added up, as are the variances since the random variables are independent. The expectation $E(X)$ of the winnings at the end of n moves is null, and the variance is n, hence a standard deviation of $\sqrt{n}$.

For even n, with $n = 2n'$, the average deviation is:

$$2\sum_{k=0}^{n'} 2k\; p(2n',2k) = \frac{1}{2^{n-1}}\sum_{k=0}^{n'} 2k\; N(2n',2k)$$

with the summation being done on k from 0 (or 1) to n'.

We saw that: $\sum_{k=1}^{n'} 2k\, C_{2n'}^{n'+k} = n' C_{2n'}^{n'}$. The average deviation at the end of $n = 2n'$ moves is equal to:

$$\frac{n'}{2^{n-1}} C_{2n'}^{n'} = \frac{n}{2^n} C_n^{n/2}$$

and for large n, it is of the order $\dfrac{2\sqrt{n}}{\sqrt{\pi}}$, close to the standard deviation.

In the case where n is odd, we check that the average deviation is the same as that obtained for the following even number, i.e. $n + 1$. To show this, it is enough to take the result found for even n and apply the combinations formula enabling us to construct Pascal's triangle:

$$C_n^p = C_{n-1}^{p-1} + C_{n-1}^p,$$

which enables us to move on to odd $n - 1$[4].

25.2.3. *Probability $\rho(2n')$ of a return to the origin at stage $n = 2n'$*

By return to the origin, we mean that we end up on a null ordinate or null winning after n moves. The number of paths from O to $B(2n', 0)$ is $C_{2n'}^{n'}$.

Hence the probability $\rho\,(2n')$ of return to the origin at the end of n moves, with the tosses of heads or tails being equiprobable:

$$\rho(2n') = C_{2n'}^{n'} / 2^{2n'}$$

---

4. Average deviation at the end of $n = 2n'$ moves
$= (2/2^n)\,(2(C_{2n'-1}^{n'} + C_{2n'-1}^{n'+1}) + 4(C_{2n'-1}^{n'+1} + C_{2n'-1}^{n'+2}) + (2n' - 1)\,(C_{2n'-1}^{n'} + C_{2n'-1}^{n'+1}))$
$= (2/2^n)\, 2\,(C_{2n'-1}^{n'} + 3C_{2n'-1}^{n'+1} + 5C_{2n'-1}^{n'+2} + \ldots + (2n' - 1)C_{2n'-1}^{n'})$
= average deviation at the end of $2n' - 1$ moves.

in particular $\rho(0) = 1$.

For large $2n'$, $\rho(2n')$ is approximately equal to $\frac{1}{\sqrt{\pi n'}}$, applying Stirling's formula: $n! \approx \sqrt{2\pi n}\left(\frac{n}{e}\right)^n$.

25.3. Probabilities of certain routes over *n* moves

Now let us impose certain constraints on the n-length routes in order to find out their probability. We know that the number of $2n'$-length even paths that neither touch nor cross the abscissa axis up to and including $2n'$ and remaining either above or below, is $C_{2n'}^{n'}$.

We deduce from this that the probability of neither touching or crossing the abscissa axis over a length of $2n'$ is equal to $C_{2n'}^{n'} / 2^{2n'} = \rho(2n')$, when rising or falling steps are equiprobable:

$$p(x_1 \neq 0, x_2 \neq 0, \ldots, x_{2n'} \neq 0) = \rho(2n'),$$

and therefore:

$$p(x_1 > 0, x_2 > 0, \ldots , x_{2n'} > 0) = \rho(2n') / 2$$

We also saw that the number of $2n'$-length paths located above the horizontal axis, which can touch but not cross this axis, is $C_{2n'}^{n'}$. Hence the corresponding probability:

$$p(x_1 \geq 0, x_2 \geq 0, \ldots, , x_{2n'} \geq 0) = \rho(2n')$$

Now let us turn our interest to the probability $f(2n')$ of a first return to the origin at move $n = 2n'$, i.e. event $x_1 \neq 0$, $x_2 \neq 0$, …, $x_{2n'-1} \neq 0$, and $x_{2n'} = 0$.

Either the routes are above the horizontal axis and correspond to mountains (or primitive blocks of parenthesis words), or they are below, which gives the same number as above. We know that the number of $2n'$-length mountains is the Catalan number $c(n' - 1)$. Hence the probability of the first return to 0 at the end of $2n'$ moves is:

$$f(2n') = 2\ c(n' - 1) / 2^{2n'} = 2\ C_{2'n-2}^{n'-1} / (n'\ 2^{2n'}) = C_{2n'}^{n'} / ((2n' - 1)\ 2^{2n'})$$

Finally[5]:

$$f(2n') = \rho(2n') / (2n' - 1)$$

We check that $f(2) + f(4) + ... + f(2n') = 1 - \rho(2n')$. Indeed, $f(2)$ for example, is the probability of a first return to the origin after two moves, and is also the probability that for a $2n'$-long route the first return to 0 takes place after two moves.

The left hand side of the equality is the probability a $2n'$-length path will touch the axis or cross it before or at stage $2n'$. It is also the complement at 1 of probability $p(x_1 \neq 0, x_2 \neq 0,..., x_{2n'} \neq 0) = \rho(2n')$.

This has an important consequence. As $\rho(2n')$ tends towards 0 for large n (or n'), the sum $f(2) + f(4) + f(6) +...$ tends towards 1, i.e. this event is sure. This indicates that every route starting at origin O is sure to pass 0 again sooner or later, and consequently an infinite number of times. When moving in a straight line, left or right in an equiprobable way, the drunk man is sure to always pass the point he has crossed before.

What is the average time (or average number of moves) until the first return to 0? It is:

$$2f(2) + 4f(4) + 6f(6) + ...$$

$= 2\,(\rho(0) - \rho(2)) + 4\,(\rho(2) - \rho(4)) + 6\,(\rho(4) - \rho(6)) + \ldots$ (see footnote 4, page 513)

$$= 2\,(\rho(0) + \rho(2) + \rho(6) + \ldots)$$

We saw that for a large n', $\rho(2n')$ is equivalent to: $\dfrac{1}{\sqrt{\pi n'}}$.

This type of series is divergent. We end up with an infinite result. Thus the probability of returning to the starting square is equal to 1, but the average time necessary to reach there is infinite.

---

5. Another method is as follows: we have seen that $p(x_1 \neq 0, x_2 \neq 0,..., x_{2n'} \neq 0) = \rho(2n')$. We also obtain the relationships between the probabilities:

$p(x_1 \neq 0, x_2 \neq 0,..., x_{2n'-2} \neq 0)$

$= p(x_1 \neq 0, x_2 \neq 0,..., x_{2n'-1} = 0) + p(x_1 \neq 0, x_2 \neq 0,..., x_{2n'-1} \neq 0, x_{2n'} \neq 0)$.

Hence:

$\rho(2n'-2) = f(2n') + \rho(2n')$, and $f(2n') = \rho(2n-2) - \rho(2n') = \rho(2n') / (2n'-1)$.

25.4. Complementary exercises

25.4.1. *Last visit to the origin*

Let us consider routes of even length ($n = 2n'$) where the last visit to the origin takes place at move $2k$, at point K (see Figure 25.2). This means that $x_{2k} = 0$, then that $x_{2k+1}, x_{2k+2},... x_{2n'}$ are all different to 0. The number of paths from O to K is $C_{2k}^{\ k}$, and from K to the final point is $C_{2(n'-k)}^{\ n'-k}$. Therefore, during $2n'$-length routes with equiprobability of steps landing to the left or right of the line, the probability that the last visit to the origin is at move $2k$ is: $\rho(2k)\ \rho(2n' - 2k)$. We could have believed that the routes looked like repeated oscillations around the abscissa axis, which would have implied that the last visit to 0 had a much greater chance of happening at the end of the initial traverse.

On the contrary the property we have just given indicates that there are as many chances that the last visit to the origin takes place at the beginning as at the end of the process, because of the symmetry of the formula. It also shows that the last visit has a greater chance of occurring at the beginning or end than in the middle of the route, which can also seem paradoxal (see Figure 25.2 below).

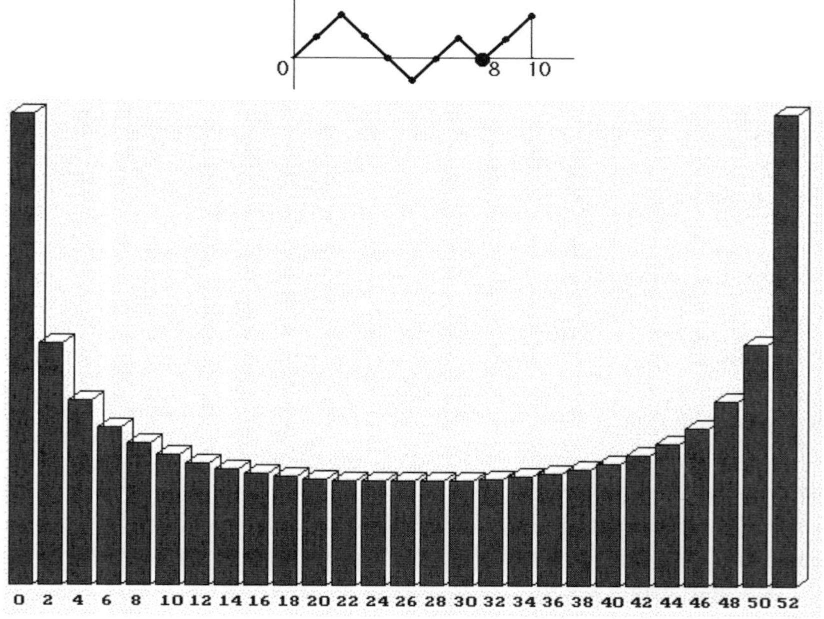

Figure 25.2. *Example of last passage to 0 at point 8 for n = 2n' = 10 (top); and probability histogram of the last passage to 0 for n = 2n' = 52 (bottom)*

To verify these results, let X be the random variable corresponding to the last passage from winnings to 0. X takes the even values 0, 2, 4, …, n with n supposedly being even. We have to experimentally determine the law of X, which the following program does:

We take n=2n'*, as well as the number of experiments* NE*, and set* nbtimes[n+1] *to 0*

```
for(expe=1; expe<=NE; expe++)
 { lastreturn=0; winnings=0;
  for(move=1; move<=n; move++)
   { h=random(2);
    if (h==1) winnings++; else winnings--;
    if (winnings==0) lastreturn=move;
   }
  nboftimes[lastreturn]++;
 }
for(i=0; i<=n; i+=2) printf("%3.d : %3.3lf\n",i,(float)nbtimes[i]/(float)NE);
```

25.4.2. *Number of winnings sign changes throughout the game*

A winnings sign change occurs when the horizontal axis is crossed. When we consider paths of odd length $N = 2n' + 1$, K sign changes occur, and K is between 0 and n' (see Figure 25.3).

We have the following property:[6] the number of $2n' + 1$-length paths subject to K sign changes ($0 \leq K \leq n'$) is $2C_{2n'+1}^{n'+K+1}$. In terms of probabilities, with X being the random variable corresponding to the number of sign changes, X takes all values between 0 and n'.

With equiprobable tosses, this gives the following result: the probability of having K sign changes during $2n' + 1$ moves (with winnings of +1 or -1) is:

$$p(X = K) = C_{2n'+1}^{n'+K+1} / 2^{2n}$$

The result is that for any value of n', even very large ones, the probability of having no sign change is greater than that of having one (and only one) sign change,

6. For a demonstration, see [FEL 71]. For $K = 0$, we again find the formula for $2n' + 1$-length number of paths being able to touch but not cross the horizontal axis, located above or below.

which is in turn greater than that of having two sign changes, etc. For example, the probability of having no sign change during 99 tosses is of the order 0.16.

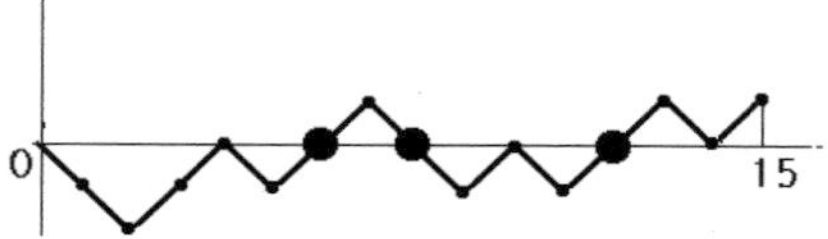

Figure 25.3. *Example for $N = 15$, with $K = 3$ sign changes*

The objective is now to make the corresponding program, in order to compare the experimental results with the theoretical results deduced from the previous formula.

We notice that any passage to 0 takes place during an even toss. The sign change test is done by comparing the signs of two successive odd tosses on either side of an even move. We call the winnings from an odd move *oldow*, which will be followed by winning *ew* for the even move, itself followed by winning *ow* from the following odd move. The sign change test is *oldow*ow* = -1.

At the start, at move 0, $ew = 0$. Then we launch the throws loop, doing them in twos (odd then even), i.e. throws 1, 2, then 3, 4, …, until N, $N + 1$, with this last throw being in excess, but as it corresponds to an even move, it has no influence. The test is done between *oldow*, which is the *ow* of the previous move, and the current *ow*. Before launching the loop, we should give a false value to *oldow*, for example 0 or 10 (only avoiding ±1) so that *oldow* is different from -1.

The program below follows, with an example of results in Figure 25.4:

We are given the number of throws odd N and n so that N=2n+1 as well as number of experiments NE

```
for(expe=1; expe<=NE; expe++)
 { ew=0; ow=0; nbchanges=0;
  for(move=1; move<=N; move+=2)
   { oldow=ow;   /* first odd throw */
    h=random(2); if (h==0) ow=ew+1; else ow=ew-1; /* odd throw */
    h=random(2); if (h==0) ew=ow+1; else ew=ow-1; /* even throw */
    if (oldow*ow==-1) nbchanges++;
```

```
  }
 nboftimes[nbchanges]++; /* frequency of the number of sign changes */
 }
for(i=0; i<=n; i++) printf(" (%d : %3.3f",i,(float)nboftimes[i]/(float)NE);
```

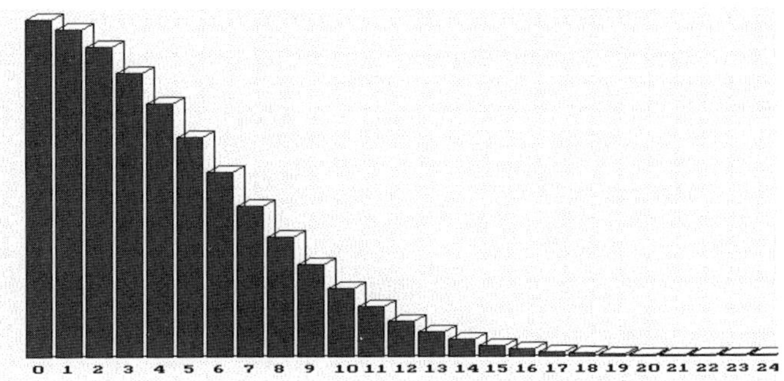

Figure 25.4. *Histogram of the number of sign changes for n = 139 tosses*

25.4.3. *Probability of staying on the positive winnings side for a certain amount of time during the N = 2n equiprobable tosses*

Let X be the number of units of time spent on the positive winnings side during $N = 2n$ tosses. We notice that this number is always even, of the form $2k$, with k taking 0, 1, 2, …, n as its values. It has been shown that the probability of spending $2k$ units of time on the positive side, and consequently $2n - 2k$ units of time on the negative side during the $N = 2n$ tosses, is: $p(X = 2k) = \rho(2k)\ \rho(2n - 2k)$.

Using the graphs in Figure 25.5, we notice that having a positive winning over a unit of time means that we are on the positive side between two successive moves, or that the line joining the two corresponding points is on the positive side. The objective is now to carry out the program enabling us to experimentally find the law of X.

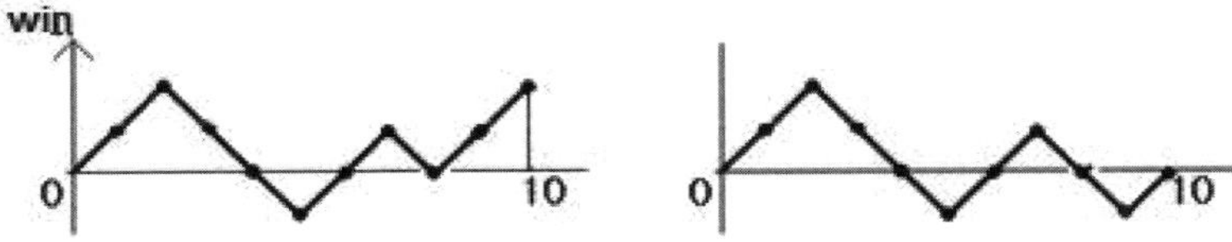

Figure 25.5. *Two examples, with N = 10 and 2k = 8 on the left, and 2k = 6 on the right*

During each toss, we note the winnings w and keep the winnings *oldw* obtained from the previous move. Being on the positive side means that we have either $w > 0$, or $w = 0$ and *oldw*> 0. Hence the program, which again gives the same probabilities histogram as in section 24.4.1:

```
We take even N, the number of experiments NE, and we set nboftimes[N+1] to 0
   for(expe=1 ;expe<=NE ; expe++)
    { nbtimespositive=0; w=0;
     for(move=1; move<=N; move++)
      { oldw=w; h=random(2);
       if (h==0) w++ ; else w--;
       if (w>0 || (w==0 && oldw>0)) nbtimespositive++;
      }
     nboftimes[nbtimespositive]++;
    }
   display probability nboftimes[i] / NE for i from 0 to N in twos
```

25.4.4. *Longest range of winnings with constant sign*

We repeatedly play heads or tails N times with even N. During these N equiprobable tosses, we remain on the positive or null winnings side during certain periods, and on the negative or null side during other periods. We want a program to find the longest period T, on average, during which we remain on one side – either positive or negative – over an experiment of N tosses (see Figure 25.6).

The program goes back to the one enabling us to extract the winnings sign changes (see section 25.4.2). During each experiment we record the moves where sign changes occur in a table *ch*[], adding 0 at the start in *ch*[0] and N at the end. Running through this table enables us to find the length of each range and the range with maximum length. $L(N)$ being the average length of the longest range where the winnings sign remains the same over the N tosses, experimentally we find:

$L(4) = 3.5$ (i.e. 87% of the total), $L(10) = 8.1$ (82%),

$L(100) = 69.6$ (70%), $L(1{,}000) = 650$ (65%).

Here is the program:

```
cumul =0.;
```

```
for(exp=0; exp<NE; exp++)
 { ew=0; ow=10; ch[0]=0; k=1;
  for(move=1; move <=N; move+=2)
  {oldow=ow;
   h=random(2)%2;if (h==0) ow=ew+1; else ow=ew-1;
   h=random(2)%2;if (h==0) ew=ow+1; else ew=ow-1;
   if (oldow*ow==-1) ch[k++]=move;
  }
  ch[k]=N; maxrange= -1;
  for(i=1; i<=k; i++)
       {range=ch[i]-ch[i–1]; if (range>maxrange) maxrange=range;}
  cumul+=(float)maxrange;
 }
averagerange=cumul/(float)NE; display
```

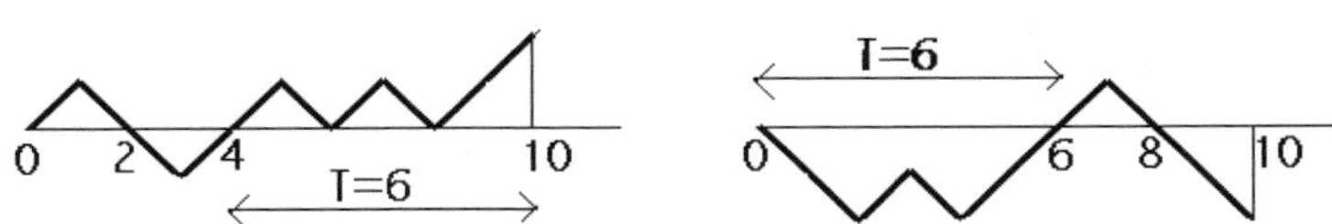

Figure 25.6. *Two examples of the longest range of winnings with either positive or negative signs*

25.5. The gambler's ruin problem

Making a step forward or back on a straight line constitutes what we can call a Brownian motion, or (in a colorful way) the drunken man's walk, as we have already seen. Let us take a graduated segment a long where, at each stage of time, the particle (or the individual) makes a step to the right with probability p or a step to the left with probability q ($p + q = 1$). It is initially found on graduation z. The extremities 0 and a of the segment are absorbing barriers, with the movement of the particle stopping as soon as it reaches one of these barriers (see Figure 25.7). We want to find the probability of reaching barrier 0 and that of reaching barrier a, as well as the average duration of the movement.

This can also be seen as the *gambler's ruin* problem. A player starts off with z capital and he plays against an opponent who has $a - z$ capital. Through a repeated game of heads or tails, at each move the player wins a chip or loses a chip, which he takes or gives to his opponent. Thus the sum of the capitals remains the same, i.e. a.

The player has probability p of winning a chip, and probability q of losing a chip. The game continues until the player is ruined, having lost all his z capital or made a fortune by attaining capital a and has therefore won $a - z$ chips while his opponent is at 0 (see Figure 25.7).

25.5.1. *Probability of ruin*

Let us call $Q(z)$ the players' probability of ruin, where his capital goes from z to 0, and $P(z)$ his probability of making a fortune, where his capital goes from z to a. We will check, especially, that $P(z) + Q(z) = 1$. In other words, there is no other possibility than to lose everything or win everything. An indefinite evolution between the two boundaries 0 and a can occur, there is even an infinite number of routes of this type, but their probability is null, they almost never happen.

We already know that $Q(0) = 1$ and $Q(a) = 0$. During the game, let us assume that at a certain moment, the player has a capital n strictly included between 0 and a. His probability of ruin is $Q(n)$. To move on to the next stage of the game, a heads or tails toss takes place. Either it is heads that comes out with probability p, the player will have capital $n + 1$, and the player's probability of ruin will be $Q(n + 1)$, or it is tails that comes out, with probability q, and the player's probability of ruin becomes $Q(n - 1)$. Thanks to total probability formula:

$$Q(n) = p\, Q(n + 1) + q\, Q(n - 1)$$

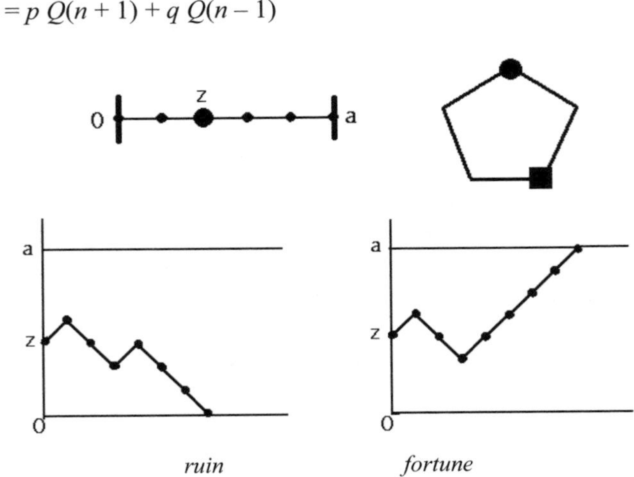

Figure 25.7. *Above on the left, the segment, here of a = 6 long on which the particle circulates between the two absorbing barriers, and on the right the equivalent in a closed circuit, below the same problem seen as the evolution of the player's winnings between ruin and fortune*

It is a linear and homogeneous recurrence relation (without a second member) of order two: $p\, Q(n+1) - Q(n) + q\, Q(n-1) = 0$ with as extreme conditions $Q(0) = 1$ and $Q(a) = 0$. This gives a unique solution:[7]

$$Q(n) = ((q / p)^{a} - (q / p)^{z}) / ((q / p)^{a} - 1)$$

when $q / p \neq 1$ and:

$$Q(n) = 1 - n / a \text{ for } p = q$$

Finally, postulating $\alpha = q / p$:

$$Q(z) = \frac{\alpha^{a} - \alpha^{z}}{\alpha^{a} - 1} \text{ if } p \neq q \text{, and } Q(z) = 1 - \frac{z}{a} \text{ if } p = q$$

Now let us take the point of view of our player's opponent, who has the initial capital $a - z$. His probability of ruin $Q'(a - z)$ is the player's probability of victory, i.e. $P(z)$. To obtain $Q'(a - z)$, it is sufficient to resume the formula obtained for $Q(z)$, exchanging p and q, and replacing z with $a - z$. After calculation, we find that:

$$Q'(a - z) = ((1 / \alpha)^{a} - (1 / \alpha)^{a-z}) / ((1 / \alpha)^{a} - 1) = (1 - \alpha^{z}) / (1 - \alpha^{a}) \text{, for } p \neq q$$

and:

$$Q'(a - z) = 1 - (a - z) / a \text{ for } p = q$$

We check that we have:

$$Q(z) + Q'(a - z) = 1 \text{, i.e.: } P(z) + Q(z) = 1 \text{, as announced.}$$

---

7. We begin by looking for sequences (u_n) of the form r^n that are solutions to the recurrence relation. We must have $p\, r^{n+1} - r^n + q\, r^{n-1} = 0$ for every integer n. The number r ($r \neq 0$) must verify the equation $r^2 - r + q = 0$, called the *characteristic equation* of the recurrence relation. When p is different from q, this equation assumes two distinct solutions: 1 and (q / p). In turn, sequences A (A being a constant) and $B(q / p)^n$ verify the recurrence relation, as well as their sum $A + B(q / p)^n$. We have just found an infinite number of solutions to the recurrence relation. Among them, let us look for the one that verifies the extreme conditions $u_0 = 1$ and $u_a = 0$. This imposes $A + B = 1$ and $A + B(q / p)^a = 0$. We find the unique solution: $A = (q / p)^a / ((q / p)^a - 1)$ and $B = -1 / ((q / p)^a - 1)$. Hence the formula indicated above. Note that, whatever extreme conditions we may take, we always find a unique solution (A, B) in the system of equations. This proves that there is no other solution to the recurrence relation than $A + B\, (q / p)^n$. The case where $p = q$ remains to be examined. The two particular solutions found before are no longer only 1, and this is not enough. We therefore look for a second particular solution to the recurrence relation, here $u_n = n$. The general solution to the recurrence relation is therefore $A + Bn$. Here, with the extreme conditions, we get $1 - n / a$.

At the end of the game, the player has won $a - z$ chips or has lost his z chips. From this we deduce the player's average winnings W, thanks to total probability formula:

$$W = (a - z)\,P(z) - z\,Q(z) = a\,P(z) - z$$

In the case where capital a becomes infinite, the player competes against an infinitely rich opponent. Making a lean towards infinity in the formulae above, we find that $Q(z) = 1$ when $p \leq q$, and $Q(z) = \alpha^z$ if $p > q$. Thus, the player is practically sure to be ruined as soon as $p \leq q$. Even a particle undergoing Brownian motion on a straight line (our previous example) has probability 1 of moving from position z to position 0 when $p \leq q$. In this case, a particle leaving a point is practically sure to reach another point, wherever it may be, or even to return to somewhere it has already passed.

25.5.2. *Average duration of the game*

Let $D(z)$ be the average duration of the game for the player with initial capital z. In extreme cases, $D(0) = 0$ and $D(a) = 0$. Otherwise, at a certain moment in the game the player has a capital n that is between 0 and a, and the average duration of the game from then on is $D(n)$. To move on to the next stage, a heads or tails toss occurs, and the duration of the game increases by 1.

If the coin lands heads up, with probability p, the player will have $n + 1$ capital, and the average duration of the game from then on will be $D(n + 1)$. If the coin lands tails up, with probability q, the average duration of the game will therefore be $D(n - 1)$. Thanks to total probability formula:

$$D(n) = 1 + p\,D(n+1) + q\,D(n - 1)$$

This gives a linear and non-homogeneous recurrence relation of second order because of the presence of a second member, $p\,D(n+1) - D(n) + q\,D(n-1) = -1$, with the extreme conditions $D(0) = D(a) = 0$. Finally we find:

$$D(z) = \frac{z}{q-p} - \frac{a}{q-p}\frac{1-\alpha^z}{1-\alpha^a} \text{ for } p \neq q, \text{ and } D(z) = z\,(a - z) \text{ for } p = q$$

Note that for $p = q = 0.5$, when a is infinitely large, the average duration of the game is infinite, whereas the player's ruin is sure.

25.5.3. *Results and program*

The program consists of determining, during each experiment, the number of moves until the winnings fall to 0 or increase to a, which will give the duration of the game, as well as the number of times we ended up at a. This will enable us to calculate the probability of winning.

```
We take z, a, p, and the number of experiments NE
randomize(); cumulduration=0.; cumulvictory=0; onsetp=1000.*p;
for(exp=1; exp<=NE; exp++)
 { winnings=z; nbmoves=0;
  while(winnings!=0 && winnings!=a)
    { h=random(1000)%1000; if (h<onsetp) winnings++; else winnings--;
      nbmoves++;}
  cumulduration+=(double)nbmoves;
  if (winnings==a) cumulvictory++;
 }
probawin=cumulvictory/(float)NE; display
averageduration=cumulduration/(float)NE; display
```

Some results are given in Tables 25.1 and 25.2.

z	a	Probability of ruin	Average duration
9	10	0.1	9
45	50	0.1	225
90	100	0.1	900
180	200	0.1	3,600
900	1,000	0.1	90,000

Table 25.1. *Results of the program for $p = q = 0.5$*

z	a	Probability of ruin	Average duration
9	10	0.21	11
90	100	0.86	766
95	100	0.64	583
99	100	0.18	172

Table 25.2. *Results of the program for $p = 0.45$, in case of a slightly unfavorable game for the player*

25.5.4. *Exercises*

25.5.4.1. *Exercise 1: summation formulae on Catalan numbers*

Show that $\sum_{k=0}^{\infty} \frac{c(k)}{2^{2k+1}} = 1$, *where the c(k) designate Catalan numbers.*

Let us consider only the ruin problem; therefore with infinite a, where the player has the initial capital $z = 1$, with the same probability 0.5 of winning or losing in each move. We know that the probability of ruin is equal to 1. All corresponding $2k + 1$-long routes with $k \geq 0$ correspond to mountain $2k$-long ranges, followed by a downward diagonal line. There are therefore as many routes as there are mountain ranges. On the other hand, each $2k + 1$-length path has the probability $1 / 2^{2k+1}$. To summarize: by summation we find the formula requested.

25.5.4.2. *Exercise 2: time to win a certain number of games more than an opponent*

Player A plays a repeated game, similar to heads or tails, against an opponent B. At each move, he has probability p of winning and probability q of losing ($p + q = 1$), and we will assume that p is different from q.

It is exactly the reverse for his opponent. The game stops when one of the players has won on k occasions more than his opponent, k being a number given beforehand.

For $k = 3$, for example, a game is:

HHTHTTTHTHHTHHTHH

with H when player A wins and T when he loses. In this example, he won 10 times, and lost seven times, and the game stopped as soon as he won three times more than his opponent (and without his opponent first winning three moves more than him). This resembles the gambler's ruin game.

We can consider player A to have a capital of k chips at the start, just like his opponent. The game stops when player A attains a capital of $2k$ chips – he won and his opponent lost – or when it falls to 0 and he has lost. We want to find out his probability of winning at the end of n moves. This involves finding the generating function $F_{k,2k}(x)$ where the coefficient of the x^n term is this probability of winning at the end of n moves.

The method used above gives player A's probability of winning. In this case, $p^k / (p^k + q^k)$. It also enables us to get the average duration of the game. But it does not enable us to find out the probability of winning at the end of n moves. This leads us to resume the graph and its weighted adjacency matrix method.

The graph has the shape of a chain, with $k + 1$ states. The initial state is called k, and the final states are called $2k$ when player A wins and 0 when he loses. The drawing in Figure 25.8 gives the graph obtained for $k = 3$.

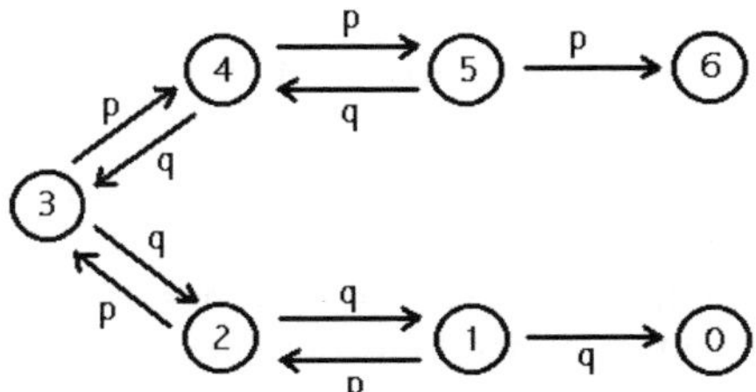

Figure 25.8. *Transition graph*

The weighted adjacency matrix of the graph is:

$$A = \begin{bmatrix} 0 & 0 & 0 & 0 & 0 & 0 & 0 \\ q & 0 & p & 0 & 0 & 0 & 0 \\ 0 & q & 0 & p & 0 & 0 & 0 \\ 0 & 0 & q & 0 & p & 0 & 0 \\ 0 & 0 & 0 & q & 0 & p & 0 \\ 0 & 0 & 0 & 0 & q & 0 & p \\ 0 & 0 & 0 & 0 & 0 & q & 0 \end{bmatrix}$$

and:

$$I - xA = \begin{bmatrix} 1 & 0 & 0 & 0 & 0 & 0 & 0 \\ -qx & 1 & -px & 0 & 0 & 0 & 0 \\ 0 & -qx & 1 & -px & 0 & 0 & 0 \\ 0 & 0 & -qx & 1 & -px & 0 & 0 \\ 0 & 0 & 0 & -qx & 1 & -px & 0 \\ 0 & 0 & 0 & 0 & -qx & 1 & -px \\ 0 & 0 & 0 & 0 & 0 & -qx & 1 \end{bmatrix}$$

for $k = 3$

To get the determinant $|I - xA|$, we can remove the border that surrounds the matrix, and:

$$|I - xA| = \begin{vmatrix} 1 & -px & 0 & 0 & 0 \\ -qx & 1 & -px & 0 & 0 \\ 0 & -qx & 1 & -px & 0 \\ 0 & 0 & -qx & 1 & -px \\ 0 & 0 & 0 & -qx & 1 \end{vmatrix}$$

This determinant is of fifth order when $k = 3$. Let us call it D_5. Generalizing, for any k we get a determinant D_{2k-1} of $2k - 1$ order, where this determinant has the same form as the previous one, with the presence of a tridiagonal matrix. By developing this determinant according to its first line, we find that:

$$D_{2k-1} = D_{2k-2} - p\,q\,x^2\, D_{2k-3}$$

This determinant obeys the recurrence relation:

$$D_n = D_{n-1} - p\,q\,x^2\, D_{n-2}$$

with the initial conditions: $D_0 = 1$ and $D_1 = 1$. Notably we find that: $D_2 = 1 - p\,q\,x^2$, and $D_3 = 1 - 2\,p\,q\,x^2$.

We also need the determinant of matrix $I - xA$ from which we remove the last line $2k$ and the middle column k, i.e. $|I - xA,\ 2k,\ k|$. By developing this determinant from the bottom right corner, we verify that:

$$|I - xA,\ 2k,\ k| = p^k\, x^k\, D_{k-1}$$

Finally the generating function sought, corresponding to paths from state k to state $2k$, is:

$$F_{k,2k}(x) = |I\text{-}xA,\ 2k,\ k| \;/\; |I\text{-}xA| = p^k\, x^k\, D_{k-1} \,/\, D_{2k-1}$$

The following will enable us to simplify the calculations.

a) Give the explicit form of determinant D_n, and simplify the generating function.

The sequence of determinants (D_n) obeys the recurrence relation:

$$D_n = D_{n-1} - pqx^2\, D_{n-2}$$

with the initial conditions $D_0 = 1$ and $D_1 = 1$.

The characteristic equation of the recurrence relation is $r^2 - r + a = 0$, where we posited $a = pqx^2$. As p is different from q, it assumes two distinct solutions:

$$\mathrm{r} = (1 + \sqrt{\Delta})/ 2$$

and:

$$r' = (1 - \sqrt{\Delta}) / 2,$$

with $\Delta = 1 - 4a$.

We deduce from it that D_n is a linear combination of the two particular solutions r^n and r'^n to the recurrence relation. Taking into consideration the initial conditions, we find:

$$D_n = \frac{1}{\sqrt{\Delta}} (r^{n+1} - r'^{n+1}) = r^n + r^{n-1} r' + r^{n-2} r'^2 + \ldots + r\, r'^{n-1} + r'^n$$

since $r - r' = \sqrt{\Delta}$. We deduce from it that:

$$F_{k,2k}(x) = p^k x^k D_{k-1} / D_{2k-1} = p^k x^k (r^k - r'^k) / (r^{2k} - r'^{2k}) = p^k x^k / (r^k + r'^k).$$

b) Show that: $D_{2n+1} = D_n (D_{n+1} - a D_{n-1})$ *with* $a = pqx^2$.

$$D_{n+1} - a\, D_{n-1} = \frac{1}{\sqrt{\Delta}} (r^{n+2} - r'^{n+2} - a\, r^n + a\, r'^n)$$

$$= \frac{1}{\sqrt{\Delta}} (r^n (r^2 - a) - r'^n (r'^2 - a)).$$

We check that: $r^2 - a = r - 2a = r\sqrt{\Delta}$, and that $r'^2 - a = -r'\sqrt{\Delta}$:

$$D_{n+1} - a\, D_{n-1} = r^{n+1} + r'^{n+1}$$

hence:

$$D_n (D_{n+1} - a\, D_{n-1}) = \frac{1}{\sqrt{\Delta}} (r^{n+1} - r'^{n+1})(r^{n+1} + r'^{n+1})$$

$$= \frac{1}{\sqrt{\Delta}} (r^{2n+2} - r'^{2n+2}) = D_{2n+1}$$

Finally:

$$F_{k,2k}(x) = p^k x^k D_{k-1} / D_{2k-1} = p^k x^k / (r^k + r'^k) = p^k x^k / (D_k - p\, q\, x^2 D_{k-2})$$

Notably we get:

$$F_{2,4}(x) = p^2 x^2 / (1 - 2\, p\, q\, x^2)$$

$$F_{3,6}(x) = p^3 x^3 / (1 - 3\, p\, q\, x^2)$$

$$F_{4,8}(x) = p^4 x^4 / (1 - 4\, p\, q\, x^2 + 2\, p^2 q^2 x^4)$$

$$F_{5,10}(x) = p^5 x^5 / (1 - 5\, p\, q\, x^2 + 5\, p^2 q^2 x^4)$$

$$F_{6,12}(x) = p^6 x^6 / (1 - 6\, p\, q\, x^2 + 9\, p^2 q^2 x^4 - 2\, p^3 q^3 x^6)$$

The probability of player A winning is none other than $F_{k,2k}(1) = p^k / (p^k + q^k)$ since for $x = 1$, r and r' become p and q. We find the formula obtained above.

25.5.5. *Temperature equilibrium and random walk*

25.5.5.1. *Temperature equilibrium*

Let us take a square grid of the plan and draw a closed curve on it, which delimits a surface. If you wish, this can represent a room surrounded by walls. Let us impose a certain temperature on every point of the boundary curve, as if we were putting radiators along the walls.

This temperature can vary from one point to the next of the curve but it remains fixed at each point in time, even if we add or take away energy using a thermostat, so that the temperature remains constant at each point considered. Over time, the temperature changes inside of the room and the heat of the radiators is diffused, until it creates an equilibrium for itself. In the end, the temperature $u(x, y)$ remains constant at each point on the surface.

For example, if the room is round and the temperature is fixed at 20°C everywhere along the walls, then whatever the initial temperature inside the room it will end up balancing out everywhere at 20°C. If we take a rectangular room where two of the opposing walls are at 10°C and 30°C, and the two others have a regular variation from 10°C to 30°C, the temperature inside will balance out, going regularly from 10°C to 30°C between the two corresponding walls.

At equilibrium, the temperature $u(x, y)$ obeys Laplace's equation:

$$\Delta u = 0$$

where the Δ designates the Laplacian, i.e. $\partial^2 u / \partial x^2 + \partial^2 u / \partial y^2 = 0$, causing two second derivatives to be involved.

The solution to this differential equation, to which the conditions at the borders are added, enables us to obtain the temperature $u(x, y)$ at each point $P(x, y)$. In discrete fashion, Laplace's equation becomes:[8]

$$u(P) = (u(vwP) + u(veP) + u(vsP) + u(vnP)) / 4$$

where *vwP*, *veP*, *vsP* and *vnP* designate the four neighbors of point *P* in each of the directions west, east, south and north (see Figure 25.9). The temperature at any point is the average of the neighboring temperatures.

If *N* designates the number of points on the surface square grid, we have an equation for the temperatures at each point. This gives a system of *N* equations with *N* unknowns. Solving this system can be done using the Gauss-Seidel method.[9] It enables us to get the temperature at each point, taking into consideration the conditions at the borders.

---

8 . Let us take a two-dimensional plane, like in the drawing in Figure 25.9. Laplace's equation $\Delta u = 0$, corresponding to the temperature equilibrium, is expressed $d^2u / dx^2 + d^2u / dy^2 = 0$, $u\ (x,y)$ being the temperature at any point $P(x,y)$. Let us move in a discrete fashion, with the surface gridded into small squares. A point *P* inside the surface has four neighbors: *veP*, *vnP*, *vwP* and *vsP*. Let us rewrite d^2u / dx^2 in this context. The first derivative du/dx in $P(x, y)$ is a small variation in temperature *du* compared to a small variation *dx* in *x*. Taking the step of the square grid as unit length, as small as it is, we deduce from it that with $dx = 1$, $du / dx \approx u(veP) - u(P)$ or $\approx u(P) - u(vwP)$, depending on whether we are placed to the right of *P* or to the left. More specifically, $u(veP) - u(P)$ represents the derivative du / dx at point *I* in the middle of [*P veP*], and $u(P) - u(vwP)$ that of point *J* in the middle of [*vwP P*], with $IJ = 1$. In turn $d^2u / dx^2 = d(du/dx) / dx$ is by definition the variation of derivative du/dx compared to a small variation *dx* in *x*. We can write $d^2u / dx^2 = (du / dx)$ at $I - du / dx$ at *J*, since the distance between *I* and *J* is equal to $dx = 1$. Finally: $d^2u / dx^2 \approx u(veP) - u(P) - u(P) + u(vwP) = u(veP) + u(vwP) - 2\ u(P)$. Doing the same vertically, we find that $\Delta u = 0$ is expressed $u(veP) + u(vwP) + u(vnP) + u(vsP) - 4\ u(P) = 0$, i.e. $u(P) = (1 / 4)\ (.u(veP) + U(vwP) + u(vnP) + u(vsP))$. There is temperature equilibrium when the temperature at each point *P* is equal to the average of the temperatures of its four neighbors.

9. It is an iterative method. Only the temperatures on the border are known. To start with, we take any temperature at each point inside of the surface, and using the temperature of its neighbors, we recalculate the temperature of the *P* points thanks to the equations of the system. Then we restart the process a certain number of times. We therefore get the phenomenon of convergence on the solutions to the system. In concrete terms, this means that using the only correct values on the boundary, these values are gradually diffused to the neighbors to give values of the temperature inside, which progressively get closer to exact values.

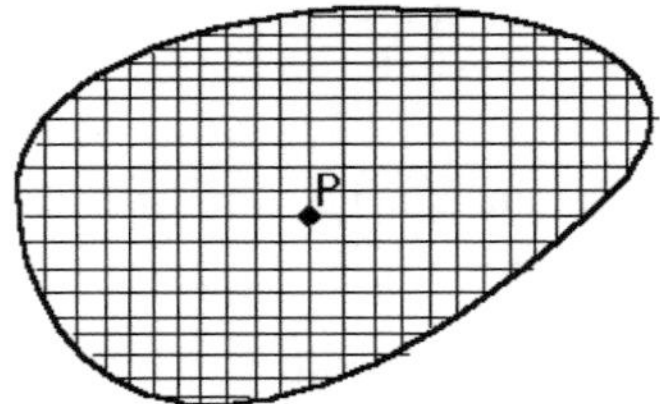

Figure 25.9. *The surface is cut up following a square grid. The temperature at each point, like point P, is the average of those of its four neighbors*

25.5.5.2. *A random walk*

Let us resume the same gridded surface as before, bordered by its boundary, and imagine that the temperatures on the boundary are now sums of money. A person is standing at a point P inside the surface. From there, step-by-step this person will move in a random manner in one of the four directions of the square grid, with each direction being equiprobable, until he reaches a point on the boundary. The person has therefore won the money that is found on this point of the boundary.

With each point P of the interior surface we can thus associate the sum of money that the person initially placed at P can win on average, depending on the random walk they take to the boundary.

In concrete terms, this refers to taking a large number of random paths to the boundary from P, and to taking the average of the sums of money obtained depending on the point at which the boundary was reached. This average sum of money $S(P)$ obtained is associated with each point P of the surface. Starting at point P, after the first step, we are sure to find ourselves at vwP, veP, vsP or vnP, the immediate neighbors of P on the square grid, and this is done in an equiprobable way. We can therefore affirm that:

$$S(P) = (S(vwP) + S(veP) + S(vsP) + S(vnP)) \,/\, 4$$

by taking an average of the averages. Therefore we again find exactly the same equations as for temperature equilibrium, with the same boundary conditions.

CONCLUSION 25.1.– Seeking the equilibrium temperature at a point on a surface is equivalent to knowing the average sum of money we would get by starting from this point and walking in a random manner to the boundary, provided that the sum of money is compared to the temperature at each point of the boundary.

What we have done so far is valid in a two-dimensional plane. But it is the same in a one-dimensional plane (on a straight line) or in space in three dimensions? We now know that to solve this probability problem we can use Laplace's equation, and *vice versa*.

25.5.5.3. *Random walk on a straight line*

In a one-dimensional plane let us consider a segment delimited by abscissa points 0 and a. Temperatures u_0 and u_a are given at these boundary points. Laplace's equation boils down to $d^2u / dx^2 = 0$. By solving this equation, and taking into consideration the two conditions at the boundaries, we find:

$$u(x) = ((u_a - u_0) / a)x + u_0$$

This evolution is linear, as we could expect. Let us take the particular case where $u_0 = 0$ and $u_a = a$. This gives $u(x) = x$. Now consider the identical problem, where a person starts off with a sum of money x, and repeatedly plays, winning or losing a counter each time, in an equiprobable way. This is done until he is ruined by ending up with 0 or until he makes a fortune and ending up with a. This is the gambler's ruin problem. Let $Q(x)$ be the probability of ruin starting with a sum x, and assume that its complement $1 - Q(x)$ is the probability of making a fortune. In these conditions the average sum obtained through this game is $a(1 - Q(x))$. Compared to the temperature problem, we must get $a(1 - Q(x)) = x$, hence $Q(x) = 1 - x / a$. We have just found the probability of ruin.

25.5.5.4. *Two-dimensional walk*

Let us consider a ring shape, i.e. the surface delimited by two concentric circles with center O, where the small circle has radius r and the large one radius R. On the small circle, the temperature is fixed at one unit, and on the big one it is equal to 0. Because of the circle symmetries, the equilibrium temperature at a point P on the surface is a function of $\rho = OP$. Laplace's equation, as well as the boundary conditions, give the solution:[10]

$$u(\rho) = (\ln R - \ln \rho) / (\ln R - \ln r)$$

Let r remain small and R lean towards infinity. Therefore the temperature $u(\rho)$ tends to become equal to 1 everywhere. Now let us make the analogy with a random walk in the surface square grid. The small circle with radius r resembles point O where the sum of money is 1. As the average sum obtained by starting from P tends to be equal to 1, as we saw for temperature, this means that the random walk from P always ends at O.

10. See for example [PIS 70].

In other words, starting from a point on the square grid, we are sure to pass another point of the same square grid sooner or later. Or still, starting from point P of the square grid we are sure to pass point P again. Laplace's equation enables us to conclude this.

25.5.5.5. *Three-dimensional walk*

Now let us consider the volume delimited by a small sphere with center O and radius r, and by a large sphere with the same center and radius R. On the small sphere the temperature is fixed at one unit, and on the large sphere it is null. The temperature at point P is a function of $OP = \rho$. The solution to Laplace's equation, with the boundary conditions, is:

$$u(\rho) = (1 / R - 1 / \rho) / (1 / R - 1 / r)$$

Let R tend lean towards infinity, keeping r small. We notice in this case that $u(\rho)$ leans towards r / ρ, and no longer towards 1 as before. By analogy, the random walk from point P does not necessarily lead to point O. In other words, in a three-dimensional plane starting from point P we are not sure to pass at another fixed point on the square grid. Or still, starting from point P we are not sure to pass P again. Curiously, the result is not the same in the three-dimensional plane as in the two- (or one-)dimensional plane. Laplace's equation warned us about this.

Chapter 26

Random Routes on a Graph

26.1. Movement of a particle on a polygon or graduated segment

26.1.1. *Average duration of routes between two points*

A particle is found on a vertex of an N-sided polygon. At each unit of time, it moves from one vertex to one of the two neighboring vertices in an equiprobable way. When it arrives on the vertex located opposite,[1] as far as possible from its starting point, it stops moving (see Figure 26.1). X is the random variable equal to the time it takes the particle to arrive at the point farthest from the start. If the polygon has regular sides, it is also the distance traversed. We want to find the law of X and the average time $E(X)$ taken to reach this point.

26.1.1.1. *Determining E(X)*

We can view this problem in another way. Consider a particle located on a graded straight line at the middle point $[N/2]$. By postulating $N = 2n$ if N is even, and $N = 2n + 1$ if N is odd, this starting point is at abscissa n. We place absorbing barriers at points 0 and N, i.e. the particle stops moving when it reaches one of its boundaries.

The particle moves on the segment, making a unit step at each time interval, and stops when it touches an absorbing barrier.

1. A point located exactly opposite only exists if N is even. When N is odd, there are two points situated furthest from the starting point.

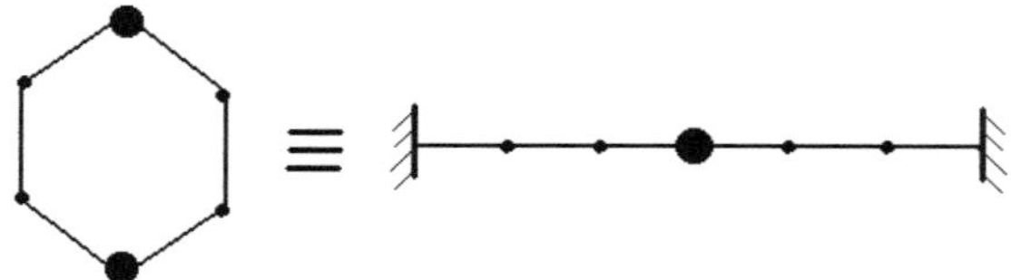

Figure 26.1. *Circulation from one point to another on a polygon, which is equivalent to circulating on a segment with two absorbing barriers*

At a certain moment, the particle is located at point k. Let D_k be the time it needs on average to arrive on an edge. Thanks to total probability formula, we have:

$$D_k = 0.5(1 + D_{k+1}) + 0.5(1 + D_{k-1}),$$

i.e. $D_{k+1} = 2D_k - D_{k-1} - 2$

Actually, the particle that is at point k at a certain instant will be located, one unit of time later, either at point $k + 1$ or point $k - 1$, and we should calculate the weighted average between the average times D_{k+1} and D_{k-1} to arrive at the edge, not forgetting the extra unit of time that has elapsed. The solution to the recurrence relation obtained is of the form $D_k = A + Bk - k^2$. Let us apply the initial conditions: $D_0 = 0$ and $D_N = 0$. $D_k = Nk - k^2$ is left. Hence, $D_n = Nn - n^2$:

– if N is even ($N = 2n$), $D_n = n^2 = N^2 / 4$; and

– if N is odd ($N = 2n + 1$), $D_n = n^2 + n = (N^2 - 1) / 4$.

From $N = 2$, the successive values of $E(X)$ are 1, 2 (for the triangle), 4 (for the square), 6 (for the pentagon), 9 (for the hexagon), 12, 16, 20, 25, etc.

26.1.1.2. *Generating function associated with X, for N = 2n (even)*

26.1.1.2.1. Example of the square, $n = 2$

For the transition graph, the states are numbered as being the minimum distances to the endpoint. The initial state corresponds to $n = 2$, the final state to 0, and the intermediate state is 1. The transition graph results from it (see Figure 26.2), as well as the system of equations where S_0 is the generating function:

$$S_2 = 1 + 0.5\, zS_1$$

$$S_1 = zS_2$$

$$S_0 = 0.5\, zS_1$$

We deduce from this that: $S_0 = z^2 / (2 - z^2)$.

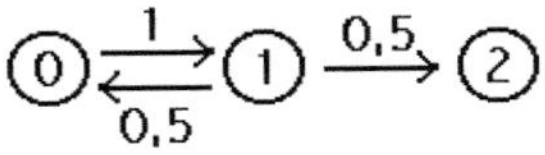

Figure 26.2. *Transition graph for the square*

26.1.1.2.2. Example of the hexagon, n = 3

The transition graph gives the following system of equations:

$S_3 = 1 + 0.5\ zS_2$

$S_2 = zS_3 + 0.5\ zS_2$

$S_1 = 0.5\ zS_2$

$S_0 = 0.5\ zS_1$

hence: $S_0 = z^3 / (4 - 3z^2)$.

26.1.1.2.3. General case, with n > 2.

To simplify, we postulate: $S_n = F_0$, $S_{n-1} = F_1$, ..., $S_0 = F_n$. We get the equation system:

$F_0 = 1 + 0.5\ zF_1$

$F_1 = zF_0 + 0.5\ zF_2$,

hence: $F_1 = (2z + zF_2) / (2 - z^2)$.

– If $n = 3$, we add $F_2 = 0.5\ zF_1$ and $F_3 = 0.5\ zF_2$ back, which gives:

$F_2 = z^2 / (2 - z^2) + z^2 / (4 - 2z^2)F_2$, $F_2(1 - z^2 / (4 - 2z^2)) = z^2 / (2 - z^2)$

$F_2 = 2z^2 / (4 - 3z^2)$,

and finally:

$F_3 = z^2 / (4 - 3z^2)$

– If $n > 3$, the next equation is:

$F_2 = 0.5\ zF_1 + 0,5\ zF_3$,

which gives:

$$F_2(1 - z^2 / 4 - 2z^2) = z^2 / (2 - z^2) + 0.5\, zF_3$$

(except for the last term, it is the same calculation as for $n = 3$), where:

$$F_2(4 - 3z^2) / (4 - 2z^2) = z^2 / (1 - z^2) + 0.5\, zF_3$$

$$F_2 = 2z^2 / (4 - 3z^2) + ((2 - z^2) / (4 - 3z^2))\, zF_3.$$

– If $n = 4$, we add $F_3 = 0.5\, zF_2$ and $F_4 = 0,\, 5zF_3$, which gives:

$$F_3(1 - 0.5\, z^2(2 - z^2) / (4 - 3z^2)) = z^3 / (4 - 3z^2)$$

$$F_3(4 - 3z^2 - z^2 + 0.5z^4) = z^3,\ F_3(4 - 4z^2 + 0.5\, z^4) = z^3$$

$$F_4 = z^4 / (8 - 8z^2 + z^4)$$

Postulating: $P_2 = 2 - z^2$ and $P_3 = 4 - 3z^2$, we notice that:

$F_4 = z^4 / P_4$ with $P_4 = 2P_3 - z^2P_2$.

– If $n > 4$, the next equation is:

$$F_3 = 0.5\, zF_2 + 0{,}5\, zF_4,$$

hence, making use of the above:

$$F_3(4 - 4z^2 + 0.5\, z^4) = z^3 + 0.5\, z(4 - 3z^2)F_4$$

$$F_3 = 2z^2 / (8 - 8z^2 + z^4) + (4 - 3z^2)\, zF_4 / (8 - 8z^2 + z^4)$$

or even:

$$F_3 = 2z^3 / P_4 + z\, F_4 P_3 / P_4.$$

– If $n = 5$, $F_4 = 0.5\, zF_3$ and $F_5 = 0.5\, zF_4$:

$$F_4(1 - 0.5\, z\, P_3 / P_4) = z^4 / P_4$$

$$F_4(0.5\, P_5 / P_4) = z^4 / P_3$$

postulating: $P_5 = 2P_4 - z^2P_3 = 16 - 20z^2 + 5z^4$:

$$F_4 = 2z^4 / P_5$$

$$F_5 = z^5 / P_5.$$

– If $n > 5$:

$$F_4 = 0.5\, z\, F_3 + 0.5\, z\, F_5.$$

Making use of the above:

$$F_4 = 2\, z^4 / P_5 + 0.5\, z\, F_5\, P_4 / P_5.$$

– If $n = 6$, we find:

$$F_6 = z^6 / P_6$$

with: $P_6 = 2P_5 - z^2 P_4 = 32 - 48z^2 + 18z^4 - z^6$.

– If $n > 6$, we continue as before and we notice by recurrence that:

$$F_n = z^n / P_n \text{ with } P_n = 2P_{n-1} - z^2 P_{n-2},$$

and at the start:

$$P_1(z) = 1 \text{ and } P_2(z) = 2 - z^2.$$

The polynomials P_n are the following:

n coefficients of the z^{2k} terms according to increasing powers of z:

1	1				
2	2	-1			
3	4	-3			
4	8	-8	1		
5	16	-20	5		
6	32	-48	18	-1	
7	64	-112	56	-7	
8	128	-256	160	-32	1
9	256	-576	432	-120	9

Return to the expectation $E_n(X)$, as:

$$P'_n(1) = 2P'_{n-1}(1) - P'_{n-2}(1) - 2$$

$$E_n(X) = n - P'_n(1) = n - 2P'_{n-1}(1) + P'_{n-2}(1) + 2$$

$$= n - 2(n - 1 - E_{n-1}(X)) + n - 2 - E_{n-2}(X) - 2$$

We obtain the recurrence relation:

$$E_n(X) = 2E_{n-1}(X) - E_{n-2}(X) + 2 \text{ with } E_1(X) = 1 \text{ and } E_2(X)=4$$

We find:

$$E_n(X) = n^2.$$

26.1.1.3. *Generating function for N = 2n + 1 (odd)*

Proceeding with the same type of argument as above, we again find that the generating function is of the form:

$$G_n(z) = z^n / Q_n(z)$$

with:

$$Q_n(z) = 2Q_{n-1}(z) - z^2Q_{n-2}(z)$$

and at the start:

$$Q_1(z) = 2 - z, \text{ and } Q_2(z) = 4 - 2z - z^2$$

Hence the coefficients of the terms of the Q_n polynomials:

n coefficients of the z^k terms according to increasing powers of *k*:

1	2	-1				
2	4	-2	-1			
3	8	-4	-4	1		
3	16	-8	-12	4	1	
4	32	-16	-32	12	6	-1

Return to $E(X)$. Here we also find the recurrence relation:

$$E_n(X) = 2E_{n-1}(X) - E_{n-2} + 2,$$

with:

$$E_1(X) = 2 \text{ and } E_2(X) = 6,$$

hence: $E_n(X) = n^2 + n$.

26.1.1.4. *Variation with additional resting time*

A particle circulates on interval $[-M, M]$, with M being a positive natural integer. At each stage in time, the particle makes a (unit) step to the right, a step to the left, or remains at rest. Each of these three events has a probability of 1 / 3. At the start, the particle is at origin O. The movement stops when the particle reaches M or $-M$

(the absorbing boundaries). The random variable X is the duration of the experiment and random variable Z corresponds to the resting time. We want to find $E(X)$ and $E(Z)$, that is to say the average duration of the game and the average resting time.

26.1.1.4.1. Dealing with the case where $M = 2$

The transition graph consists of three states corresponding to the distance of the particle in relation to point O. For random variable X, each arrow of the transition graph, with its associated probability p, intervenes through pz in the generating function. The system of equations results from the graph:

$$S_0 = 1 + (1/3)\, z\, S_0 + (1/3)\, z\, S_1$$

$$S_1 = (2/3)\, z\, S_0 + (1/3)\, zS_1$$

$$S_2 = (1/3)\, z\, S_1$$

We find the generating function associated with X is:

$$S_2(z) = \frac{z^2}{0.5\,(9 - 6z - z^2)}$$

Developing this, we get:

$$p(X = 2) = 2\,/\,9, p(X = 3) = 4\,/\,27, p(X = 4) = 10\,/\,81, \text{etc.}$$

and derive that:

$$E(X) = 6$$

For random variable Z, each arrow of the transition graph, with its associated probability p, intervenes through pz when the particle remains at rest and through p otherwise. The system of equations becomes:

$$S_0 = 1 + (1/3)\, z\, S_0 + (1/3)\, S_1$$

$$S_1 = (2/3)\, S_0 + (1/3)\, z\, S_1$$

$$S_2 = (1/3)\, S_1$$

We find the generating function associated with Z is:

$$S_2\,(z) = \frac{1}{0.5\,(7 - 6z + z^2)}$$

This gives: $p(Z = 0) = 2 / 7$, $p(Z = 1) = 12 / 49$, $p(Z = 2) = 29 / 49$, etc., and $E(Z) = 2$. This last result was predictable, since a third of the time on average is spent at rest, hence:

$$E(Z) = (1 / 3)\, E(X)$$

26.1.1.4.2. General case

– *Generating function associated with X*: we show that for any positive M, the generating function associated with X is of the form $S_M(z) = z^M / P_M(z)$, where $P_M(z)$ is a polynomial verifying the recurrence relation:

$$P_M(z) = 3\,(1 - (1 / 3)\, z)\, P_{M-1}(z) - z^2\, P_{M-2}(z),$$

with $P_1(z) = (3 / 2) - (1 / 2)\, z$ and $P_2(z) = 9 / 2 - 3z - (1 / 2)\, z^2$ at the start

– *Calculation of E(X)*: by derivation, $P'_M(z) = (3 - z)P'_{M-1}(z) - P_{M-1}(z) - 2zP_{M-2}(z) - z^2P'_{M-2}(z)$, hence:

$$P'_M(1) = -3 + 2P'_{M-1}(1) - P'_{M-2}(1)$$

$$E_M(X) = M - P'_M(1) = M + 3 - 2P'_{M-1}(1) + P'_{M-2}(1)$$

$$= M + 3 - 2(M - 1 - E_{M-1}(X)) + M - 2 - E_{M-2}(X)$$

$$= 3 + 2\, E_{M-1}(X) - E_{M-2}(X)$$

We get (a third order linear and non-homogeneous) recurrence relation:

$$E_M(X) = 2E_{M-1}(X) - E_{M-2}(X) + 3,$$

with, $E_1(X) = 3 / 2$ and $E_2(X) = 6$ at the start.

We verify that $E(X) = 3/2\, M^2$ is the solution. Finally:

$$E_M(X) = 3/2\, M^2 \text{ and } E_M(Z) = 1/2\, M^2.$$

26.1.2. *Paths of a given length on a polygon*

The polygon has p vertices numbered from 0 to $p - 1$. Its edges are replaced by bidirectional arches. A particle is found at the start, at moment 0 and at vertex 0. At each stage in time, it traverses an arch, going from one vertex to one of the two neighboring vertices, in an equiprobable way. At the end of n stages in time, it has traversed n arches. We will say that its path is n long and it has reached its end vertex k, with k between 0 and $p - 1$. We take the number of the end vertex after having traversed n arches as random variable X_n.

For example, for $p = 5$ and $k = 0$ we are interested in n-length paths where the particle starts at 0 and arrives at 0 (see Figure 26.3).

We notice that there are no paths 1 or 3 units long, and that there are two paths 2 units in length and six paths 4 units in length. Out of the 2^n paths that are n long, all equiprobable, only some arrive at 0. On the pentagon, the probability of returning to 0 after having traversed four arch lengths is $p(x_4 = 0) = 6 / 2^4 = 3 / 8$. We would also have:

$$p(X_4 = 1) = 1 / 16, p(X_4 = 2) = 4 / 16, p(X_4 = 3) = 4 / 16, \ p(X_4 = 4) = 1 / 16$$

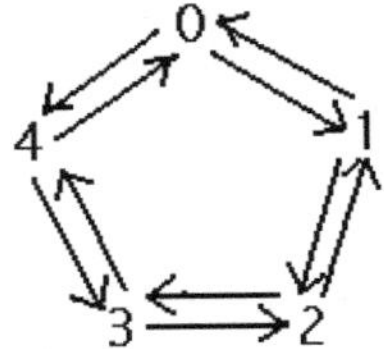

Figure 26.3. *Example of the pentagon where the particle starts at 0 and arrives at 0*

26.1.2.1. *First method of calculation*

We notice that every path on the polygon from point O is associated in a bijective way with a path of the same length based on ↗ ↘ on a square grid (see Figure 26.4). Let us apply this to some examples.

a) Case of the square p = 4, and n = 8 for the length of the paths

As n is even, the only possible endpoints from vertex 0 are the vertices 0 and 2. The number of possible paths is $2^8 = 256$. To go from 0 to 0 in eight steps means that on the square grid we end up at point (8, 0) by having made as many steps in one direction as in the other, or that we end up at point (8, 4) by having made one more complete round of the square, or we end up at point (8, 8) by having made two rounds of the square. We also have points (8, -4) and (8, -8) by turning in the other direction. The number of paths is therefore:

$$N(8, 0) + 2\,N(8, 4) + 2\,N(8, 8)$$

where $N(n, x) = C_n^{(n+x)/2}$ is the number of paths on the square grid going from the origin to point (n, x). The probability of returning to 0 is:

$$(C_8^4 + 2\, C_8^6 + 2C_8^8) / 256 = 128 / 256 = 1 / 2$$

That of ending up at point 2 is also 1 / 2.

b) Case of the hexagon $p = 6$, still with $n = 8$

The possible endpoints are 0, 2 or 4. To go from 0 to 0 in eight steps on the square grid means ending up on the square grid at point (8, 0) with as many steps in one direction as in the other, or ending up at points (8, 6) or (8, -6) by making one more round of the hexagon in one direction or the other. The number of paths is:

$$N(8, 0) + 2\, N(8, 6) = C_8^4 + 2\, C_8^7 = 72$$

Going from 0 to 2 means that we end up at points (8, 2) or (8, 8) or (8, -4), i.e.:

$$N(8, 2) + N(8, 8) + N(8, -4) = 85$$

(see Figure 26.4).

Going from 0 to 4 leads to $N(8, 4) + N(8, -2) = 85$ ways as well. We deduce from this that:

$$p(X = 0) = 86 / 256,$$

$$\text{and: } p(X = 2) = p(X = 4) = 85 / 256$$

This is generalized. To go from vertex 0 of any polygon with p vertices, to a vertex numbered a, with n-length paths we should take the paths of the square grid that end up at points included between $-n$ and $+n$ and which are equal to a when we reduce them by modulo p.

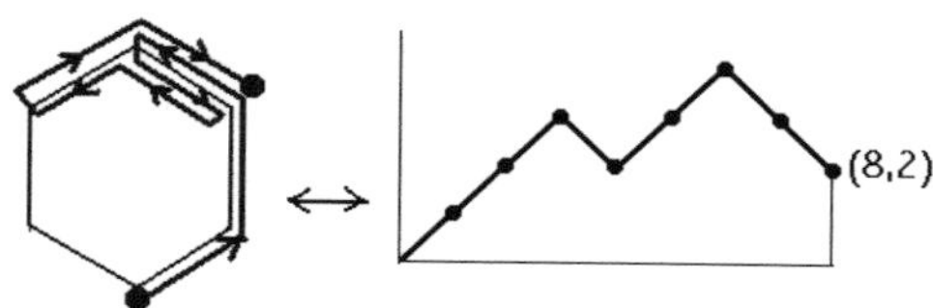

Figure 26.4. *Path on a hexagon, and its analogue in a square grid*

26.1.2.2. *Second method, using matrices and generating functions*

The adjacency matrix A of the polygon's graph is circulant: each line is cyclically shifted one notch in relation to the above. For example, for $p = 5$:

$$A = \begin{pmatrix} 0 & 1 & 0 & 0 & 1 \\ 1 & 0 & 1 & 0 & 0 \\ 0 & 1 & 0 & 1 & 0 \\ 0 & 0 & 1 & 0 & 1 \\ 1 & 0 & 0 & 1 & 0 \end{pmatrix}$$

We know that the eigenvectors are of the form $Vq = (a^0, a^q, a^{2q}, \ldots, a^{(p-1)q})$ with $a = \exp(i\, 2\pi / p)$, and the eigenvalues are $\omega_q = a^q + \bar{a}^q$, with q from 0 to $p - 1$. The formula giving the generating function associated with the number of paths from vertex 0 to vertex k is:

$$F_{0k}(x) = (-1)^k \det(I - Ax, k, 0) / \det(I - Ax)$$

The coefficient of the x^n term gives the number of n-length paths between vertices 0 and k. As the matrix is symmetrical, it is diagonalizable in $\boldsymbol{R}$, and the determinant is invariant by changing the base. In the base where matrix A becomes diagonal, i.e. D, matrix $I - Ax$ becomes $I - Dx$ and its determinant is $(1 - \omega_0 x)(1 - \omega_1 x) \ldots (1 - \omega_{p-1} x)$. Knowing the eigenvalues gives the determinant of $I - Ax$. Let us specify that we always have the eigenvalue 2. If p is an odd number, the other eigenvalues are all repeated twice.

If p is even there we have eigenvalue -2, and the other eigenvalues are double this. Specifically, the eigenvalues are $\omega_q = 2 \cos 2\pi q / n$ with q from 0 to $p - 1$.[2] Let us deal with some examples.

a) Case of the square $p = 4$.

The eigenvalues are ± 2, and 0 as a double root, i.e. the determinant $|I - Ax| = (1 - 2x)(1 + 2x) = 1 - 4x2$. Finishing the calculation, we find the generating functions:

---

2. The generating function F_{0k} is rational: $F_{0k}(x) = P(x) / Q(x)$, where $Q(x)$ is the determinant $|I - Ax|$. Let us recall that the degree of P reduced by the degree of Q is less than the multiplicity of eigenvalue 0. If 0 is not an eigenvalue, the degree of P is less than that of Q. On the other hand, if the degree of P is less than that of Q, the sequence $u(n)$ giving the number of paths from 0 to k obeys a recurrence relation that is immediately deduced from the form of $Q(x)$; it is sufficient to add the initial conditions. For any end vertex k, the recurrence relation is the same, only the initial conditions change and they enable us to calculate $P(x)$.

$$F_{00}(x)=\frac{1-2x^2}{1-4x^2}, F_{01}(x)=F_{03}(x)=\frac{x}{1-4x^2}, F_{02}(x)=\frac{2x^2}{1-4x^2}$$

By developing, for example, $F_{00}(x) = 1 + 2x^2 + 8x^4 + 32x^6 + 128x^8 + \ldots$, the coefficient of the x^n term is the number of n-length paths going from point 0 to point 0. Dividing by the number of possible paths, 2^n, we get the probability requested, for example $p(X_8 = 0) = 128 / 256$.

b) Case of the hexagon $p = 6$.

The eigenvalues are ±2 and the double values ±1, hence the determinant $|I - Ax| = (1 - 4x^2)(1 - x^2)^2$. The calculation notably gives:

$$F_{00}(x)=\frac{1-3x^2}{(1-4x^2)(1-x^2)}, \text{ and } F_{02}(x)=\frac{x^2}{(1-4x^2)(1-x^2)}$$

We deduce from this, for example, that $p(X_8 = 0)$ is coefficient of x^8 in $F_{00}(x)$, divided by 256 = 86 / 256.

26.1.3. *Particle circulating on a pentagon: time required using one side or the other to get to the end*

A particle is located on a vertex of a pentagon. At each stage in time, it moves towards a neighboring vertex. This is done until it reaches point *O* located at the furthest point from where it started, i.e. a distance of two edges from the starting point or three edges, depending on the direction of the traversal. The particle can end up at *O* when traveling from one side or the other. We want to find out the average time required to end up there using one side or the other, the right or the left on the drawing in Figure 26.5.

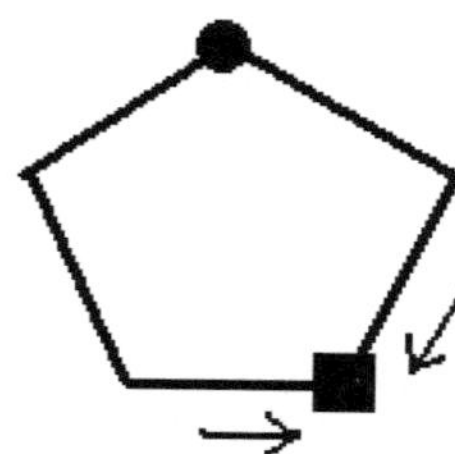

Figure 26.5. *Routes on a pentagon*

Let X be the random variable corresponding to the time required for the particle to go from its starting point to the endpoint. The generating function associated with random variable X is:

$$S_0(z) = z^2 / (4 - 2z - z^2)$$

and the average time required to get to the endpoint using one side or the other is:

$$E(X) = S'_0(1) = 6$$

The elementary events are expressed as words based on two letters. Depending on whether we end up at O from one side or the other, these words have an even or an odd length. To separate these two types of words, we write $S_0(z)$ as the sum of an even function S_E and that of an odd function S_O, with:

$$S_E(z) = (S_0(z) + S_0(-z)) / 2 = z^2 (4 - z^2) / (16 - 12 z^2 + z^4)$$

$$S_O(z) = (S_0(z) - S_0(-z)) / 2 = 2 z^2 / (16 - 12z^2 + z^4)$$

Making S_E (1) and $S_O(1)$, we obtain the probabilities of ending up at O using one side or the other, i.e.:

$$S_E(1) = 3 / 5 \text{ and } S_O(1) = 2 / 5$$

On the other hand, with $S'_E(z)$ derived from S_E (z), $S'_E(1)$ is the sum of the times of the elementary events corresponding to arrival from the right, weighted by their probabilities, but the sum of these probabilities is equal to 3 / 5. The average time required to arrive from the right is therefore $T_E = S'(1) / (3/5) = 16 / 3$, and the time to arrive from the left is $T_O = S'_O(1) / (2/5) = 7$. We can verify that the average time needed to arrive from one side or the other is the weighted average of the two times T_E and T_O: $3/5\ T_E + 2/5\ T_O = 6$.

26.2. Movement on a polyhedron

26.2.1. *Case of the regular polyhedron*

There are five regular polyhedrons, which we can draw by flattening them (see Figure 26.6). A particle circulates on this type of graph. It starts at one vertex and must reach a vertex located at the opposite side. At each stage in time, it traverses one edge, going from one vertex to one of the neighboring vertices, in an equiprobable way. X is the random variable corresponding to the number of stages. We want to find the average duration $E(X)$ of the movement.

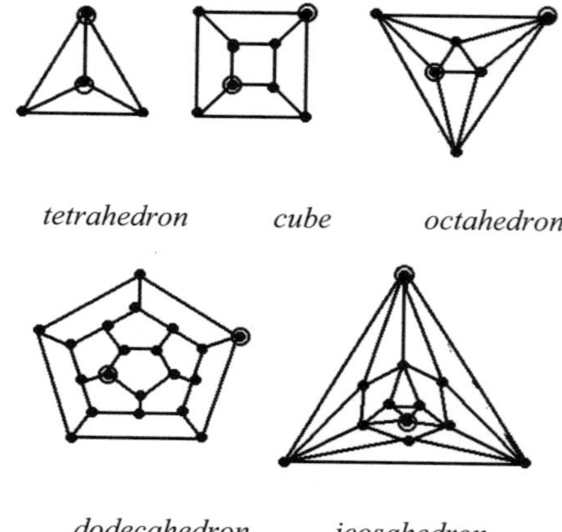

Figure 26.6. *Graphs of regular polyhedrons face down, with the start and end vertices*

For this, we construct the transition graph in each of the five cases, from which we deduce the generating function associated with X, then $E(X)$. These graphs are given in Figure 26.7:

– for the tetrahedron, the generating function is $F(z) = z / (3 - 2z)$, and $E(X) = 3$;

– for the cube, $F(z) = z^2 / (9 / 2 - (7/2) z^2)$, $E(X) = 10$;

– for the octahedron, $F(z) = z^2 /(4 - 2 z - z^2)$, $E(X) = 6$;

– for the icosahedron, $F(z) = 2 z^3 / (25 - 20 z - 5 z^2 + 2 z^3)$, $E(X) = 15$; and

– for the dodecahedron we have the system of equations:

$$S_5 = 1 + (1/3) z S_4$$

$$S_4 = z S_5 + (1/3) z S_3$$

$$S_3 = (2/3) z S_4 + (1/3) z S_3 + (1/3) z S_2$$

$$S_2 = (1/3) z S_3 + (1/3) z S_2 + (2/3) z S_1$$

$$S_1 = (1/3) z S_2$$

$$S_0 = (1/3) z S_1$$

Tetrahedron

Cube

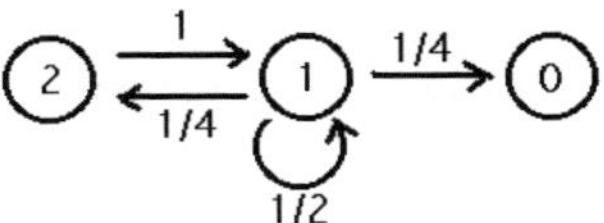

Octahedron

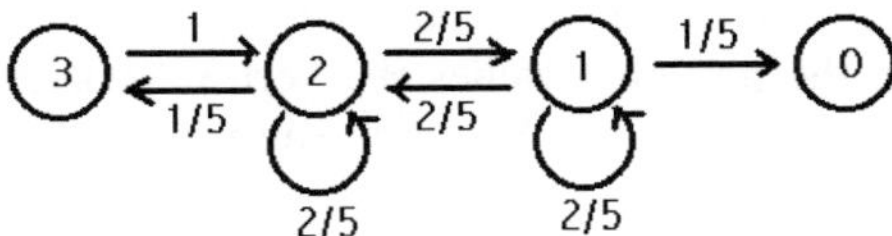

Icosahedron

Dodecahedron

Figure 26.7. *Transition graphs of the five polyhedrons*

At the end of the calculation, the generating function is:

$$S_0(z) = z^5 / (81 / 2 - 27\, z - (63 / 2)\, z^2 + 15\, z^3 + 5\, z^4 - z^5)$$

The average duration is:

$$E(X) = 35.$$

26.2.2. *Circulation on a cube with any dimensions*

With the number N designating the space dimension, we get N-cubes based on successive values of N from $N = 1$ (see Figure 26.8). The rule of passage, to go from N-cube to the $N + 1$ cube, consists of duplicating the N-cube once, then joining the corresponding vertices of the two N-cubes. Now let us turn to our problem.

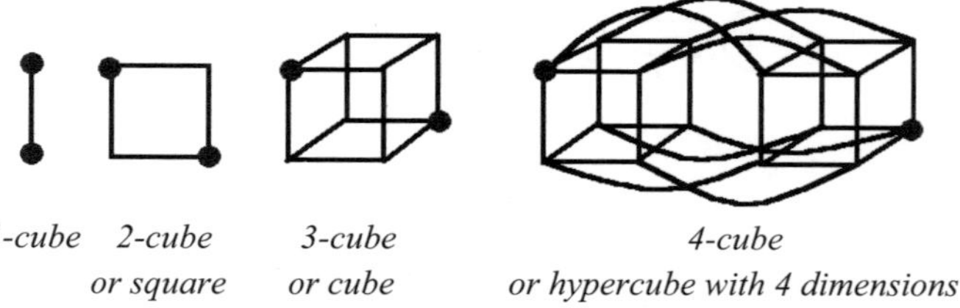

Figure 26.8. *Drawings of the first N-cubes, with the two start and end vertices*

To start with, a particle is placed at a vertex of the N-cube. At each stage in time, it goes from one vertex to one of the neighboring vertices, with equiprobability. The movement stops when the particle reaches the vertex located at the point opposite the starting vertex. Random variable X is the time required to go from the starting point to the end.

26.2.2.1. *Case of the square*

We consider states 2, 1 and 0, following the distance of the vertex where the particle is found in relation to the endpoint (see Figure 26.9). The initial state is 2 and the final state 0. We deduce the transition graph from these. We end up with the generating function:

$$S_0(z) = z^2 / (2 - z^2)$$

The expected value (average time) is:

$$E(X) = 4$$

and the variance:

$$V(X) = 8.$$

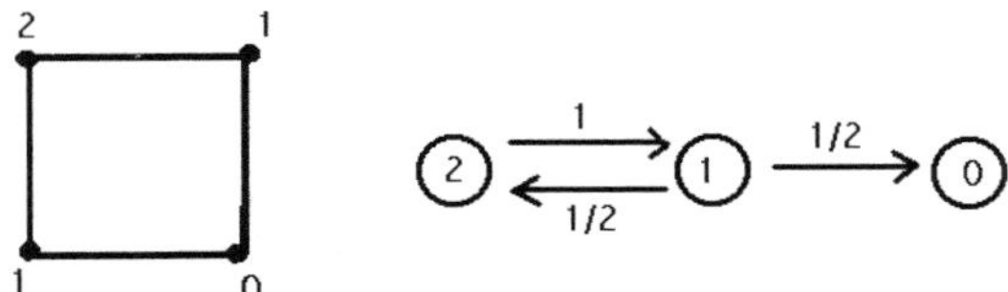

Figure 26.9. *Square and corresponding transition graph*

26.2.2.2. *Case of the cube*

The vertices are numbered according to their distance in relation to the end vertex, which gives the states 3, 2, 1 and 0 (see Figure 26.10). This gives the system of equations:

$$S_3 = 1 + (1/3)\, z\, S_2$$

$$S_2 = z\, S_3 + (2/3)\, z\, S_1$$

$$S_1 = (2/3)\, z\, S_2$$

$$S_0 = (1/3)\, z\, S_1$$

Solving the system leads to the generating function:

$$S_0(z) = z^3 / (9 / 2 - 7 / 2\, z^2)$$

hence the expectation 10 and variance 63.

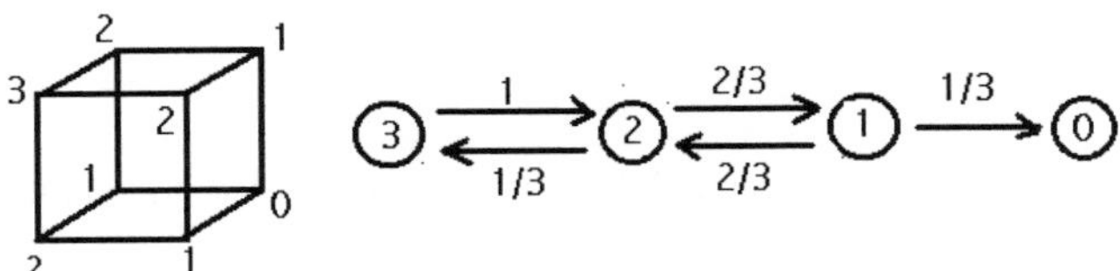

Figure 26.10. *Cube and corresponding the transition graph*

26.2.2.3. *General case*

From the transition graph (see Figure 26.11) we extract the system of equations:

$$S_n = 1 + (1 / n)\, zS_{n-1}$$

$S_{n-1} = z\, S_n + (2 / n)\, z\, S_{n-2}$

…

$S_k = ((k + 1) / n)\, z\, S_{k+1} + ((n + 1 - k) / n)\, z\, S_{k-1}$ for k between 2 and $n - 1$

…

$S_1 = (2 / n)\, z\, S_2$

$S_0 = (1 / n)\, z\, S_1$

Mixing the first two equations gives:

$S_{n-1}\, P_1 = z + (2 / n)\, z\, P_0\, S_{n-2}$ with $P_0 = 1$ and $P_1 = 1 - (1 / n)z^2$.

– If $n = 3$, that makes $S_2 P_1 = z + (2 / n)\, z\, S_1$, hence making use of the last two equations:

$S_2\, (1 - (1 / n)z^2 - (4 / 9)z^2 = z,\ S_2 = z / (1 - (7 / 9)z^2),$

and $S_0 = z^3 / (9/2 - 7/2\, z^2)$, hence:

$E(X) = 10.$

– If $n > 3$ we continue in the same way:

$S_{n-2} = ((n - 1) / n)\, z\, (z + (2 / n)\, z\, S_{n-2}) / P_1 + (3 / n)\, z\, S_{n-3}$

$S_{n-2}\, P_2 = ((n - 1) / n)\, z^2 + (3 / n)\, z\, P_1\, S_{n-3}$

with $P_2 = P_1 - ((n - 1) / n)(2 / n)z^2$.

– For $n = 4$, that makes $S_2\, P_2 = (3/4)z^2 + (3/4)\, z\, (1 - (1/4)z^2)\, S_1$, with:

$P_2 = 1 - (5 / 8)\, z^2$

$S_2\, (1 - z^2 + (3 / 32)z^2) = (3 / 4)\, z^2,$

hence $S_0 = z^4 / (32 / 3 - 32/3\, z^2 + z^4)$ and:

$E(X) = 64 / 3 = 21.33.$

– If $n > 4$, $S_{n-3}\, P_3 = ((n - 2) / n)((n - 1) / n)\, z^3 + (4 / n)\, z\, P_2\, S_{n-4}$, with:

$P_3 = P_2 - ((n - 2) / n)(3 / n)\, z^2\, P_1.$

– For $n = 5$, this gives: $S_2 P_3 = (3 / 5)(4 / 5) z^3 + (4 / 5) z P_2 S_1$ with:

$P_2 = 1 - (13 / 25) z^2$ and $P_3 = 1 - (22 / 25) z^2 + (9 / 125) z^4$

$S_2 (1 - (30 / 25) z^2 + (149 / 625) z^4) = (12 / 25) z^3$

hence:

$S_0 = z^5 / (625 / 4 - (125 / 4) z^2 + (149 / 24) z^4$

and:

$E(X) = 128 / 3 = 42{,}67$, $V(X) = 328$.

– In the general case:

$S_{n\text{-}1} P_1 = (n / n) z + (2 / n) z P_0 S_{n\text{-}2}$

$S_{n\text{-}2} P_2 = ((n - 1) / n) z^2 + (3 / n) z P_1 S_{n\text{-}3}$

$S_{n\text{-}3} P_3 = ((n - 1) / n)((n - 2) / n) z^3 + (4 / n) z P_2 S_{n\text{-}4}$

…

$S_{n\text{-}k} P_k = ((n - k + 1) / n) ((n - k + 2) / n) \dots ((n - k + k - 1) / n) z^n$

$+ ((k + 1) / n) z P_{k\text{-}1} S_{n\text{-}k\text{-}1}$

with:

$P_k = P_{k\text{-}1} - (k(n - k + 1) / n^2) z^2 P_{k\text{-}2}$:

…

$$S_2 P_{n\text{-}2} = \frac{n-1}{n}\frac{n-2}{n}\dots\frac{3}{n}z^{n-2} + \frac{n-1}{n} z P_{n-3} S_1$$

Having obtained S_2 as a function of S_1, the last two equations enable us to arrive at S_0:

$S_1 = (2 / n) z S_2$, then $S_0 = (1 / n) z S_1$

hence the generating function:

$$S_0(z) = \frac{(n-1)!}{n^{n-1}} \frac{z^n}{(P_{n-2}(z) - \frac{2}{n}\frac{n-1}{n} z^n P_{n-3}}$$

where the polynomials P_k obey the recurrence relation:

$$P_k = P_{k-1} - (k(n - k + 1) / n^2)\, z^2\, P_{k-2}$$

with $P_0 = 1$ and $P_1 = 1 - (1 / n)\, z$ at the start.

For $n = 6$, we find:

$$S_0 = z^6 / (324 / 5 - 90\, z^2 + (136 / 5)\, z^4 - z^6) \text{ and } E(X) = 83.2.$$

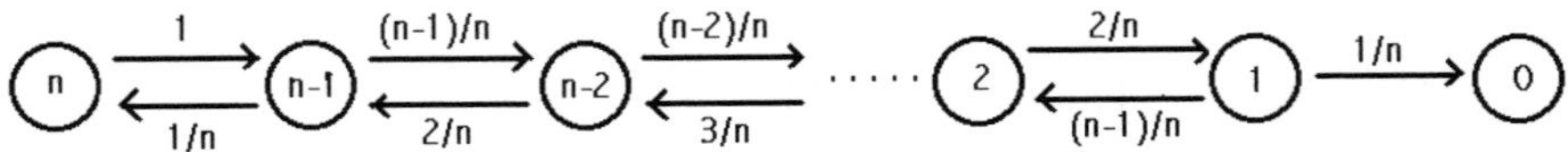

Figure 26.11. *Transition graph for the n-cube*

26.2.2.4. *Program*

We notice that each vertex of the N-cube has N neighbors. With each move of the particle, only one of its coordinates $x[N]$ changes, moving either from 0 to 1 or from 1 to 0, which is expressed, if it is the ith coordinate, as:

$$x[i] = (x[i]+1)\%2$$

This enables us to have the same program, no matter what the value of N:

```
randomize(); cumul=0.; cumulf=0.;
for(expe=1; expe<=NE; expe++)
 { finished=NO; nbmoves=0; for(i=0; i<N; i++) x[i]=0;
   do
    { nbmoves++;  i=random(N); x[i]=(x[i]+1)%2;
     finished=YES;
     for(j=0; j<N; j++) if (x[j]!=1)
       {finished=NO;break;}
    }
   while(finished==NO);
   cumul+=(float)nbmoves; cumulf+=(float)nbmoves*nbmoves;
 }
EX=cumul/(float)NE; VX=cumulf/(float)NE-EX*EX; display
```

Some results of this program are given in Table 26.1.

N	1	2	3	4	5	6	7	8
$E(X)$	1	4	10	21.3	42.7	83.3	161.2	312

Table 26.1.

26.3. The robot and the human being

A robot and a human being are placed in two adjacent boxes of a pentagonal circuit (see Figure 26.12). At each stage in time they each move towards one of the two neighboring boxes (vertices of the polygon), with the same probability. When they both end up in the same box, the game is finished: the robot kills the human being. We want to find out the average lifespan of the human being in this context. We assume that the robot and the human being see nothing of the neighboring boxes, so neither of them knows their relative position. They can cross each other without a problem. For this it is enough to imagine that they each circulate in different corridors. It is only meeting at a vertex that is fatal.

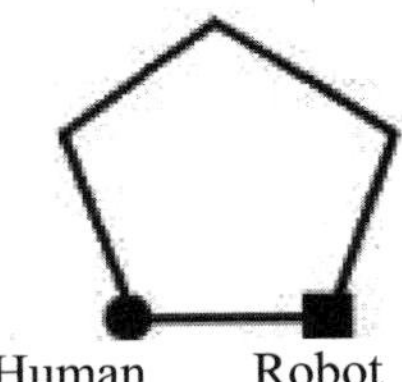

Figure 26.12. *Initial configuration of the game*

Immediately we notice that if the polygon has an even number of vertices, the robot and the human being never meet and man becomes eternal. Henceforth let us take the case where the polygon has an odd number of vertices. If k is the minimum distance in number of edges of the polygon separating the robot and the human being, the initial state with distance $(N-1)/2$ is state 0, the final state with distance 0 between the two is $P = (N-1)/2$, and all the intermediate states are expressed by whole numbers between 0 and P.

From each related location, the robot and the human being can make one of two moves. This produces four equiprobable situations, which we then arrange according to state. This enables us to draw the transition graph. We will now give some particular cases (see Figure 26.13) before moving on to the general case:

– Where $N = 3$:

$S_0 = 1 + (3 / 4)\, z\, S_0$

$S_1 = (1 / 4)\, z\, S_0$

We deduce from this the generating function $S_1(z) = z / (4 - 3z)$.

– Where $N = 5$:

$S_0 = 1 + (3 / 4)\, zS_0 + (1 / 4)\, zS_1$

$S_1 = (1 / 4)\, zS_0 + (1 / 2)\, zS_1$

$S_2 = (1 / 4)\, zS_1$

hence the generating function $S_2(z) = z^2 / (16 - 20\, z + 5\, z^2)$.

– General case:

$S_0 = 1 + (3 / 4)\, zS_0 + (1 / 4\,)\, zS_1$

$S_1 = (1 / 4)\, zS_0 + (1 / 2)\, zS_1 + (1/ z)\, S_2$

....

$S_k = (1 / 4)\, zS_{k-1} + (1 / 2)\, zS_k + (1 / z)\, S_{k+1}$ for k from 1 to $P - 2$

....

$S_{P-1} = (1 / 4)\, zS_{N-2} + (1 / 2)\, zS_{N-1}$

$S_P = (1 / 4)\, zS_1$ where $P = (N - 1) / 2$

Let us proceed by substitution, from the top down. The first equation gives:

$S_0\, (4 - 3z) = 4 + z\, S_1$

as soon as $P > 1$ (or $N > 3$).

Let us postulate: $Q_1 = 4 - 3z$. Therefore $S_0\, Q_1 = 4 + z\, S_1$.

– If $N = 5$, the last two equations become:

$$S_1 = (1 / 4)\, z\, (4 + z\, S_1) / Q_1 + (1 / 2)\, z\, Q_1\, S_1,$$

hence $S_1\, Q_2 = 4z$, with:

$$Q_2 = (4 - 2z)\, Q_1 - z^2 = 16 - 20\, z + 5\, z^2, \text{ then } S_2(z) = z^2 / Q_2(z).$$

– If $N > 5$, the second equation is expressed:

$$S_1 = (1 / 4)\, z\, (4 + z\, S_1) / Q_1 + (1 / 2)\, z\, S_1 + (1 / 4)\, z\, S_2$$

$$S_1\, (Q_1 - (1 / 4)\, z^2 - (1 / 2)\, z\, Q_1) = z + (1 / 4)\, z\, Q_1\, S_2, \text{ or } S_1\, Q_2 = 4z + z\, Q_1\, S_2.$$

– If $N = 7$, the last two equations give:

$$S_2 = (1 / 4)\, z\, (\,4z + z\, Q_1\, S_2) / Q_2 + (1 / 2)\, z\, S_2,$$

i.e. $S_2\, Q_3 = 4z$ and $S_3 = z^3 / Q_3$

with $Q_3 = (4 - 2\, z)\, Q_2 - z^2\, Q_1 = 64 - 112\, z + 56\, z^2 - 7\, z^3$.

– If $N > 7$, the third equation is expressed as before, and we get:

$$S_2\, Q_3 = 4\, z + z\, Q_2 S_3.$$

– If $N = 3$:

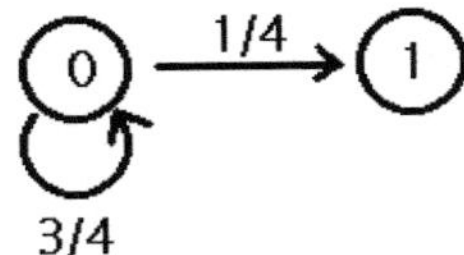

– If N = 5:

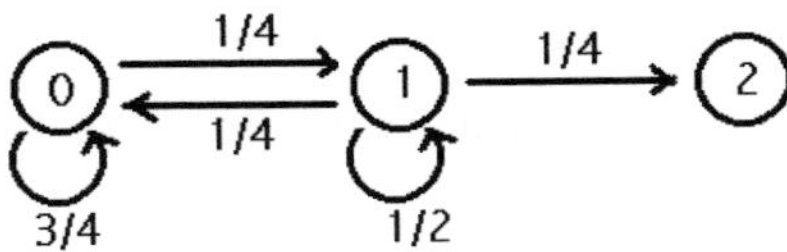

– with any odd N:

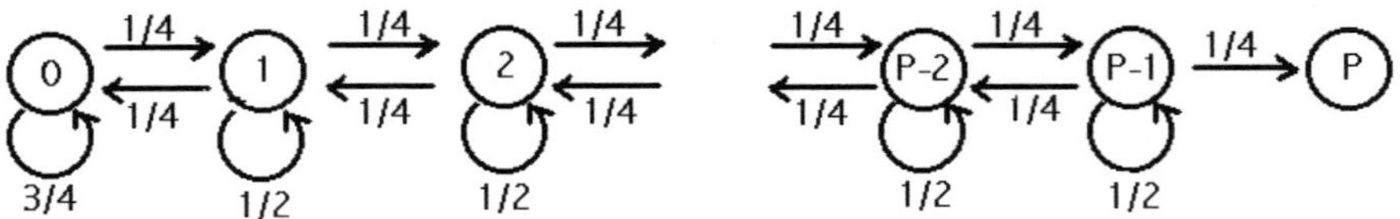

Figure 26.13. *Transition graphs, from which we deduce the generating functions*

This is generalized to the kth equation when $N > 2k + 1$. Polynomial Q_k obeys the recurrence relation:

$$Q_k = (4 - 2z)\, Q_{k-1} - z^2\, Q_{k-2}$$

with $Q_0 = 1$ and $Q_1 = 4 - 3z$ at the start.

The generating function for any $N = 2P + 1$ is:

$$S_P(z) = z^P / Q_P(z)$$

Let us move on to the average lifespan and the corresponding standard deviation. By deriving the recurrence relation on Q_k polynomials, we find that:

$$Q'_k(1) = 2\, Q'_{k-1}(1) - Q'_{k-2}(1) - 4$$

On the other hand, the average duration of the game is:

$$E_k(X) = k - Q'_k(1)$$

for a polygon with $2k + 1$ vertices. This gives the recurrence relation:

$$E_k(X) = 2\, E_{k-1}(X) - E_{k-2}(X) + 4,$$

with $E_1(X) = 4$ and $E_2(X) = 12$ at the start. We deduce from this that:

$$E_P(X) = 2P(P + 1), \text{ for } N = 2P + 1$$

Deriving a second time for the variance, we finally find:

$$V_N(X) = (2 / 3)\, P\, (P + 1)\, (2P + 1)^2$$

and the standard deviation is equal to:

$$\sigma_N = (2P+1)\sqrt{\frac{2}{3}P(P+1)}$$

The quotient $E_N(X) / \sigma_N$ is of order $2 / \sqrt{6} \approx 0.816$ for large N, and remains practically constant.

Some results are given in Table 26.2.

Number N of vertices of the polygon	**Expected value $E(X)$**	**Standard deviation σ**	**$E(X)/\sigma$**
3	4	3.5	0.86
5	12	10	0.83
7	24	20	0.83
9	40	33	0.82
11	60	48	0.82
13	84	68	0.82
15	113	92	0.82
17	144	117	0.82
19	180	148	0.82
21	219	179	0.82

Table 26.2.

26.4. Exercises

26.4.1. *Movement of a particle on a square-based pyramid*

We consider a square-based pyramid, the tip of which is P (see Figure 26.14). At the initial moment a particle is at point A, which is one of the vertices of the square base. At each stage in time, the particle moves from one vertex to one of the neighboring vertices, and this is done in an equiprobable way. We expect it to end up at the opposite vertex C. Random variable X corresponds to the time it takes the particle to go from A to C. Determine the average value E(X).

The minimum time to go from A to C is 2 units. The states of the transition graph are the minimum number of moves to end up at C from each vertex, i.e. 2, 1 and 0. Point P has four edges coming from it, while the four vertices of the base square only have three. As P is at one unit of time from C, just as two of the vertices of the square are, we must distinguish two states: 1 and 1′.

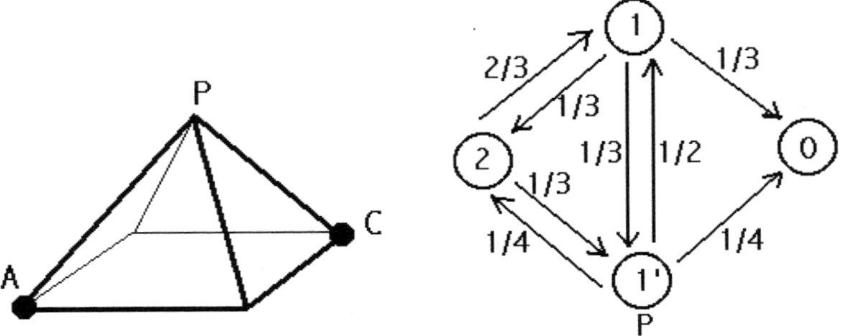

Figure 26.14. *The pyramid with start and end points A and C (left); and the corresponding transition graph (right)*

We deduce from this the transition graph (see Figure 26.14, right) and the system of equations that results from it:

$$S_2 = 1 + (1/3)\, z\, S_1 + (1/4)\, z\, S_1$$

$$S_1 = (2/3)\, z\, S_2 + (1/2)\, z\, S_1$$

$$S_{1'} = (1/3)\, z\, S_2 + (1/3)\, z\, S_1$$

$$S_0 = (1/3)\, z\, S_1 + (1/4)\, z\, S_1$$

After calculation, we find the generating function associated with X:

$$S_0(z) = \frac{11z^2 + 4z^3}{36 - 17z^2 - 4z^3}$$

hence $E(X) = 16 / 3$.

To create the program enabling us to experimentally obtain the average value of X, we re-draw the flattened pyramid to get the simple coordinates for each vertex (see Figure 26.15).

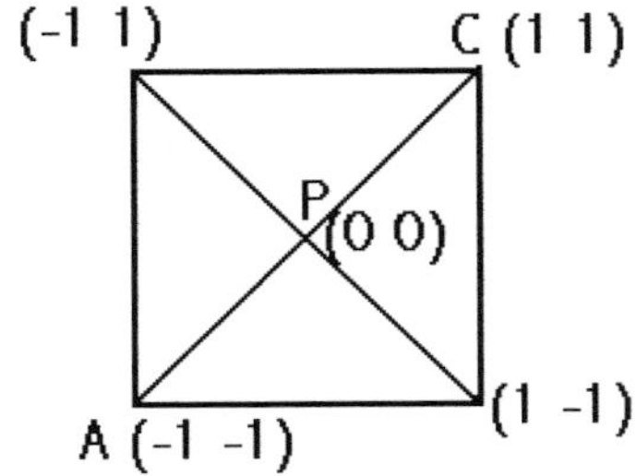

Figure 26.15. *Outline of the flattened pyramid*

Hence the program:

```
randomize(); cumul=0.;
 for(expe=1; expe<=NE; expe++)
   { nbmoves=0; x= -1; y =-1;
     do {  nbmoves++;
           if (x==0 && y==0)
              { x=2*random(2)-1; y=2*random(2)-1; }
          else { h=random(3);
                 if (h==0) {x=0;y=0;}
                 else if (h==1) x=-x; else y=-y;}
          }
      while( !(x==1 && y==1));
      cumul+=(float)nbmoves;
   }
      average=cumul/(float)NE;
      printf("\average nNumber of moves= %3.3f ",average);
```

26.4.2. *Movement of two particles on a square-based pyramid*

One particle is placed on the tip of the pyramid, another on a vertex of the square base. At each stage in time, each particle located at a vertex moves on to one of the neighboring vertices, each of which has the same chance of being reached. Random variable X corresponds to the time required for the two particles to be located for the first time at the same vertex.

a) Give the corresponding transition graph. It is advisable to distinguish four states according to the relative position of the two particles.

The four states are indicated in Figure 26.16. The transition graph results from it.

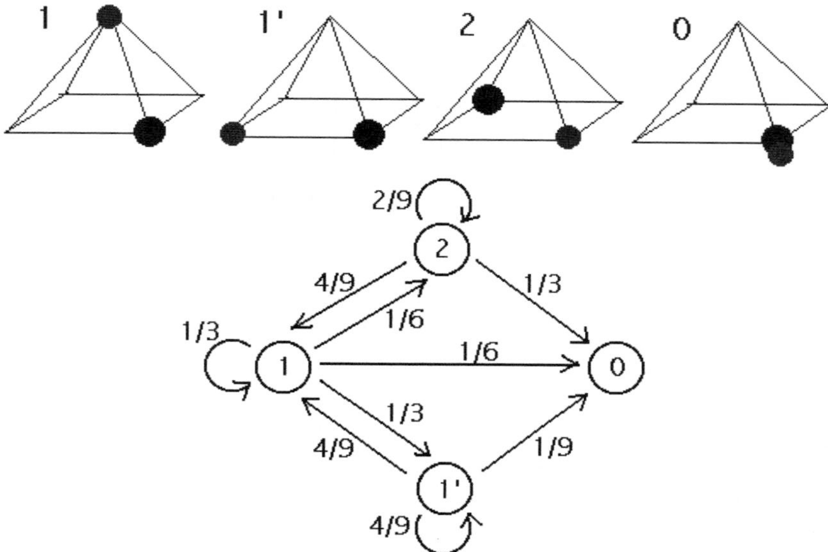

Figure 26.16. *The four possible states, with the initial state being 1 and the final state 0 (top); and the corresponding transition graph (bottom)*

b) Program in such a way as to obtain the average duration E(X).

```
cumulblock=0.;
for(block=1; block<=50; block++) /* 50 blocks of 60,000 experiments each */
  { randomize(); cumul=0.;
    for(expe=1; expe<=NB;expe++)
      { nbmoves=0; x1=0; y1=0; x2=1; y2= -1;
        do { nbmoves++;
              if (x1==0 && y1==0) { x1=2*random(2)-1; y1=2*random(2)-1; }
              else { h=random(3);
                     if (h==0) {x1=0;y1=0;}
                     else if (h==1) x1=-x1;
                     else y1=-y1;
                   }
```

```
            if (x2==0 && y2==0) { x2=2*random(2)-1; y2=2*random(2)-1; }
            else { h=random(3);
                   if (h==0) {x2=0;y2=0;}
                   else if (h==1) x2=-x2;
                   else y2=-y2;
                 }
          }
      while(!(x1==x2 && y1==y2));
      cumul+=(float)nbmoves;
    }
  average=cumul/(float)NB;
  printf("\average nNumber of moves= %3.3f ",average);
  cumulblock+=average;
}
maverage=cumulblock/50.; /* average of the averages of each block */
printf("\n*** Average of the averages: %3.3f ",maverage);
```

26.4.3. *Movement of two particles on a graph with five vertices*

We consider a graph with five vertices, as indicated in Figure 26.17, with two particles displayed at the top left and bottom right at the start.

At each stage in time, each particle moves from the vertex where it is found to a neighboring vertex. X is the random variable corresponding to the time put in until the particles are found together on the same vertex. Draw the transition graph and deduce from it the average value of X.

There are four states: the final state 0 where the two particles are on the same vertex; and the three other states (see Figure 26.17).

From state 2, which is also the initial location, there are four equiprobable locations for the next moment: state 2, with probability 1 / 4; state 1 with probability 1 / 2; state 0 with probability 1/4.

We do the same with state 1, which produces eight equiprobable cases for the next move, and with state 1′, which gives four equiprobable cases for the next move. We end up with the transition graph (see Figure 26.17).

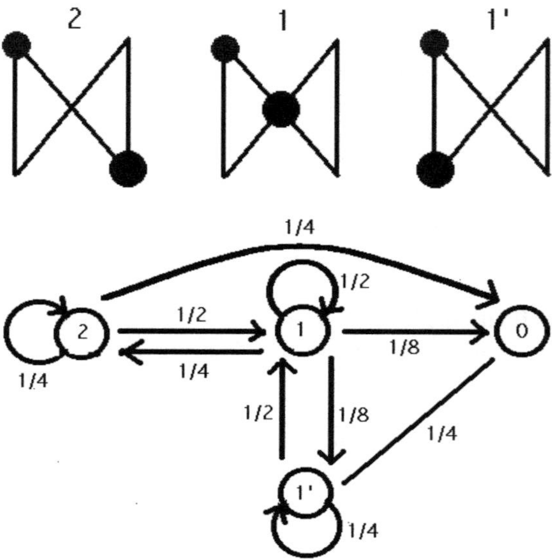

Figure 26.17. *The three states called 2, 1, and 1', with state 2 corresponding to the initial configuration (top); and the transition graph that results from it (bottom)*

This leads to the system of equations:

$$S_2 = 1 + (1 / 4)\, z\, S_2 + (1 / 4)\, z\, S_1$$

$$S_1 = (1 / 2)\, z\, S_2 + (1 / 2)\, z\, S_1 + (1 / 2)\, z\, S_1$$

$$S_{1'} = (1 / 8)\, z\, S_1 + (1 / 4)\, z\, S_1$$

$$S_0 = (1 / 4)\, z\, S_2 + (1 / 8)\, z\, S_1 + (1 / 4)\, z\, S_1$$

Solving it gives the generating function:

$$S_0(z) = \frac{\frac{1}{4}z - \frac{1}{8}z^2 + \frac{1}{64}z^3}{1 - z + \frac{1}{8}z^2 + \frac{1}{64}z^3}$$

from which we deduce the average duration of the game:

$$E(X) = 48 / 9.$$

Chapter 27

Repetitive Draws until the Outcome of a Certain Pattern

Many probability problems are linked to waiting times for a certain event. Here we give some results in this domain in such as way as to no longer lose time dealing with these problems on a case-by-case basis. The generic problem is the following: N balls numbered from 0 to $N-1$ are placed in a box. We draw balls and replace them until the outcome of a certain pattern that we were given beforehand. This pattern is a succession balls with certain numbers, either in the form of a block that we want to obtain by consecutive draws, or a scattered succession, without the corresponding draws necessarily being consecutive. The random variable X corresponding to this type of experiment is the number of draws required. We are interested in the generating function $G(z)$ that is associated with it. This function gives us the law of X, as well as the expectation $E(X)$, which is equal to $G'(1)$, and also the variance $V(X)$.

Another way of seeing the problem involves creating words randomly, from an alphabet of N letters, still written from 0 to $N-1$. These letters are just as likely to be obtained as each other. We draw one letter out of the N letters each time, which gives a word. We continue drawing letters until the given pattern appears for the first time. The random variable X corresponds to the length of the word obtained. It is also the waiting time for the outcome of the pattern given.

In all that follows, the drawing of letters is assumed to be equiprobable, except in the exceptional cases where it ends up being indicated.

We will be able to distinguish cases where we are waiting for a pattern in the form of a block – a factor of the word, or more specifically a word ending – or a pattern in a spread-out form, with other letters eventually between two successive elements of the pattern. We start with patterns where the letters are all different. We will then take certain patterns where the same letters can find themselves repeated.

27.1. Patterns are arrangements of *K* out of *N* letters

We consider a pattern with K letters from N possible letters, involving the order in which these letters are placed.

27.1.1. *Wait for a given arrangement of the K letters in the form of a block*

For example, for $K = 3$ and $N = 5$, with letters from 0 to 4, we wait for the outcome of the pattern 012 for the first time, such as in the word 30134420$\underline{012}$ corresponding to the successive draws made. Whether we choose this arrangement or another of the same length K, this does not change the result because of the equiprobability of each draw. We have the following property where the generating function is:

$$G(z) = \frac{z^K}{N^K - N^K z + z^K}$$

and $E(X) = N^K$.

To prove this formula on the generating function, let us draw the transition graph associated with the problem (see Figure 27.1). The system of equations is deduced from the graph:

$$S_0 = 1 + ((N-1)/N)\,z\,S_0 + ((N-2)/N)\,z\,(S_1 + S_2 + \ldots + S_{K-1})$$

$$S_1 = (1/N)\,z\,S_0 + (1/N)\,z\,(S_1 + S_2 + \ldots + S_{K-1})$$

$$S_i = (1/N)\,z\,S_{i-1}$$

for all i included between 2 and K.

Solving the system leads to:

$$S_0\,(1 - ((N-1)/N)\,z) = 1 + ((N-2)/N)\,z\,B\,S_1$$

$$S_1(1 - (1/N)\,z\,B) = (1/N)\,z\,S_0$$

with:

$$B = 1 + z / N + (z / N)^2 + \ldots + (z / N)^{K-2} = (1 - (z / N)^{K-1}) / (1 - z / N)$$

Eliminating S_0:

$$S_1[(1 - (1 / N) B z)(1 - ((N - 1) / N) z) - ((N - 2) / N^2) B z^2] = (1 / N) z$$

$$S_1[1 - ((N - 1) / N) z - (1 / N) B z (1 - z / N)] = (1 / N) z$$

$$S_1 = (1 / N) z / (1 - z - z^K / N^K)$$

hence we deduce S_K, which is the generating function sought.

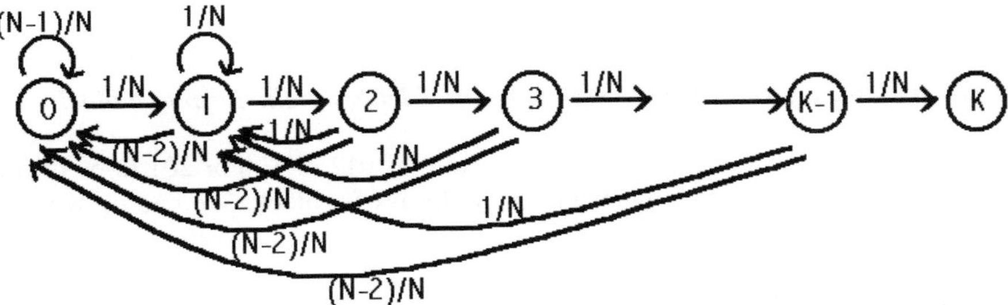

Figure 27.1. *Transition graph for the arrangements*

As a specific case, let us determine the waiting time for the outcome of a given permutation of N letters of the alphabet, from 0 to $N - 1$. We wait, for example, for the N-length pattern 012... $(N - 1)$ to be drawn, i.e. the outcome of N letters in this order by consecutive draws. Thanks to the above, the associated generating function is:

$$G(z) = z^N / (N^N - N^N z + z^N)$$

The expectation is N^N, which gives the following successive values of the expectation:

1, 4, 27, 256, ...

In the specific case where $N = 2$, the problem can be seen as a repeated game of heads (H) or tails (T) until we get block HT for the first time. The average number of moves is $2^2 = 4$. In this particularly simple case, we can also assume that the tosses are not equiprobable, with p being the probability of getting heads and q that of getting tails, with $p + q = 1$. We find the generating function:

$$G(z) = \frac{pqz^2}{(1-pz)(1-qz)}$$

hence:

$$E(X) = \frac{pqz^2}{(1-pz)(1-qz)}$$

We get the same result if we wait for block *HT* to be drawn, as p and q are interchangeable in the formulae.

27.1.2. *Wait for a given cyclic arrangement of K letters in the form of a block*

For example, for $K = 3$ we wait for the patterns 012 or 120 or 201 to be drawn, which makes K possible arrangements in the form of a block. We end up with the following result.

The generating function is:

$$G(z) = \frac{Kz^K(N-z)}{N^{K+1} - N^{K+1}z + N(K-1)z^K + (N-K)z^{K+1}}$$

and the expectation is:

$$E(X) = \frac{N(N^K - 1)}{K(N-1)}$$

To prove this generating function formula, let us construct the transition graph (see Figure 27.2). The system of equations follows:

$S_0 = 1$

$S_1 = (z + ((N-1) / N)\, z\, (S_1 + S_2 + \ldots + S_{k-1})$

$S_i = (1 / N)\, z\, S_{i-1}$ for all i between 2 and K

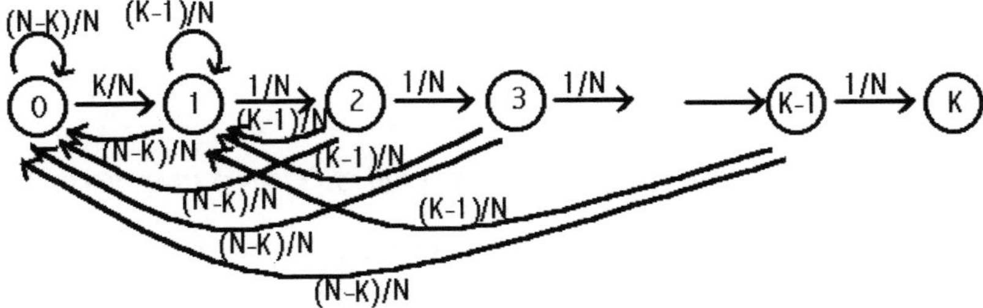

Figure 27.2. *Transition graph of cyclic arrangements*

We deduce from it the generating function:

$$S_K(z) = (K / N^{K+1})\, z^K (N - z) / (1 - z - ((K - 1) / N^K)\, z^K - ((N - K) / N^{K+1})\, z^{K+1})$$

In the specific case where we wait for a circular permutation of the N letters (i.e. a choice of N permutations obtained by cyclic shifts), the generating function is:

$$G(z) = z^N (N - z) / (N^N - N^N z + (N - 1)\, z^N$$

and the expectation:[1]

$$E(X) = (N^N - 1) / (N - 1) = N^{N-1} + N^{N-2} + ... + 1$$

For example, for $N = 2$, we are playing heads or tails again until the outcome *HT* or *TH* for the first time. The average number of moves is 3. This can be generalized to any probabilities: p for heads, and q for tails. The generating function is:

$$G(z) = \frac{pqz^2(2 - z)}{(1 - pz)(1 - qz)}$$

hence:[2]

---

1. Note that this result on the expected value $E(X)$ is N times smaller than the average time required during repeated heads or tails tosses, in an equiprobable way, until N consecutive heads are tossed.

2. This result can again be found directly. We either get H or T in the first throw. In the first case, we wait for the first tail (for example *HHHHHHT*), which corresponds to a geometric law from the second throw, with an average of $1 / q$, i.e. $1 / q + 1$ altogether. In the second case, where from the second throw we wait for the first head, the average time is $1 / p + 1$ for the same reasons. The only thing left to do is calculate the weighted average using the first move, H or T: $p(1 / q + 1) + q(1 / p + 1) = 1 / (pq) - 1$, after calculation.

$$E(X) = \frac{pqz^2(2-z)}{(1-pz)(1-qz)}$$

27.1.3. *The pattern is a given arrangement of K out of N letters in scattered form*

If we wait, for example, for the outcome of the scattered arrangement 0...1...2 with $K = 3$ and $N = 5$, a word that can be created, among other things, is $42132\underline{0}0232\underline{1}43410\underline{2}$. The results will be the same for any other arrangement of $K = 3$ letters. We find the following formulae:

– The generating function is:

$$S_K(z) = \frac{z^K}{(N-(N-1)z)^K}$$

and: $E(X) = K\,N$

Indeed, the system of equations results from the transition graph (see Figure 27.3):

$$S_0 = 1 + ((N-1)/N)\,zS_0$$

$$S_i = (1/N)\,zS_{i-1} + ((N-1)/N)\,zS_i \text{ for } i \text{ between } 1 \text{ and } K-1$$

$$S_K = (1/N)S_{K-1},$$

which gives $S_K(z)$ of the formula just above.

– In the specific case where $K = N$, we wait for a certain scattered permutation of the N letters. The expectation is therefore $E(X) = N^2$.

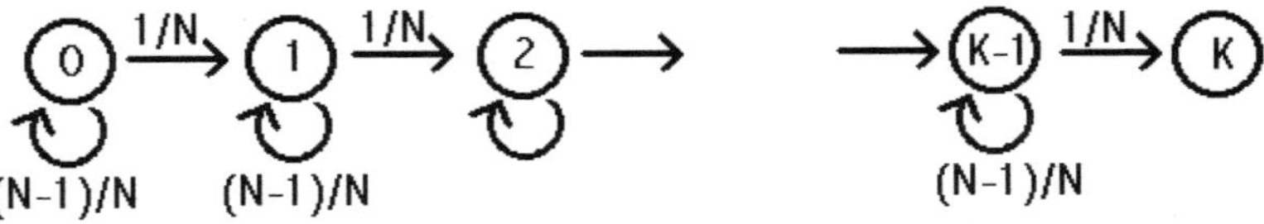

Figure 27.3. *Transition graph for scattered arrangements*

27.2. Patterns are combinations of K letters drawn from N letters

27.2.1. *Wait for the outcome of a part made of K numbers in the form of a block*

For example, for the part {0, 1, 2} of $K = 3$ letters out of $N = 5$ letters, namely 0, 1, 2, 3, 4, the pattern we are waiting for is 012 or any permutation of these three numbers 0, 1, 2, i.e. six possibilities in this case. We get, for example, the word 0342123104<u>201</u>. The result will be the same if we wait for the outcome of another part with K given elements. We find the formulae:

– the generating function is $G(z)$ where:

$$G(z) = \frac{K!\, z^K}{N^K - N^{K-1}(N-1)z - 1!N^{K-2}(N-2)z^2 - 2!N^{K-3}(N-3)z^3 - \ldots - (K-1)!(N-K)z^K};$$

– the expectation is:

$$E(X) = \frac{1}{K!} \sum_{q=0}^{K-1} q!N^{K-q};$$

– with $K = 2$, the generating function is:

$G(z) = 2z^2 / (N^2 - N(N-1)z - (N-2)z^2)$

and: $E(X) = (N^2 + N) / 2$;

– for $K = 3$, we find:

$G(z) = 6z^3 / (N^3 - N^2(N-1)z - N(N-2)z^2 - 2(N-3)z^3)$ and:

$E(X) = (N^3 + N^2 + 2N) / 6$;

– for $K = 4$:

$G(z) = 24z^4 / (N^4 - N^3(N-1)z - N^2(N-2)z^2 - 2N(N-3)z^3 - 6(N-4)\mathbf{z}^4)$

and: $E(X) = (N^4 + N^3 + 2N^2 + 6N) / 24$;

– for $K = N$, it is about waiting for the first permutation from N letters in a block. The generating function is therefore:

$G(z) = (N-1)!\, z^N / (N^{N-1} - N^{N-2}(N-1)z - 1!\, N^{N-3}(N-2)z^2$

$- 2!\, N^{N-4}(N-3)z^3 - \ldots - (N-2)!\, z^{N-1})$

and: $E(X) = \dfrac{1}{(N-1)!}\sum_{q=0}^{N-1} q!N^{N-q-1}$.

Proof of this formula

In the transition graph (see Figure 27.4), the initial state is K and the final state 0. The generating function is $S_0(z)$. At stage $K - j$, we have just drawn the jth number out of the K awaited. If we now draw the same number, we must return to stage $K - 1$. If we remove the number drawn at the $j - 1^{th}$ move, we return to stage $K - 2$, etc., and if we draw the first number obtained when moving from stage K to $K - 1$, we remain at stage K. We deduce from this the system of equations:

$S_0 = (1 / N)\, zS_1$

$S_1 = (2 / N)\, zS_2 + (1 / N)\, zS_1$

$S_2 = (3 / N)\, zS_3 + (1 / N)\, z\,(S_1 + S_2)$

....

$S_j = ((j + 1) / N)S_{j+1} + (1 / N)\, z(S_j + S_{j-1} + ... + S_1)$ for j from 1 to $K - 1$

...

$S_K = 1 + ((N - K) / N)(S_K + S_{K-1} + ... + S_1)$

By successive substitutions from the top down, we notice that:

$S_j = ((j + 1) / N)\, (B_{j-1} / B_j\,)\, z\, S_{j+1}$ for $K > j \geq 1$

with $B_0 = 1$, $B_1 = 1 - (1 / N)z$ and $B_2 = 1 - (2 / N)z - (1 / N^2)z^2$ when we make the first calculations of B_j polynomials with degree j.

More specifically, the calculation gives a recurrence relation on these polynomials:

$B_{j+1} = B_j + (jB_j - (j+1)B_{j-1})\, z / N$

We have to show the following formula on the B_j (as long as $j < K$):

$B_j = 1 - (j / N)z - 1!\, ((j - 1) / N^2)z^2 - 2!\, ((j - 2) / N^3)z^3$

$\quad - 3!\, ((j - 3) / N^4)z^4 - .. - (j - 1)! / N^j)z^j$

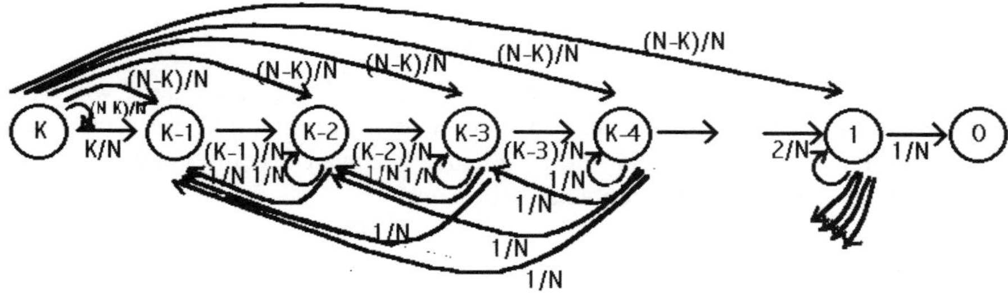

Figure 27.4. *Transition graph associated with combinations*

Let us proceed by recurrence, with the formula being true at the start. Assume that it is true up to row j, and it remains true to row $j + 1$. We notice that:

$$jB_j - (j + 1)B_{j-1} = -1 - (1 / N)z - 1!\ (2 / N^2)z^2 - 2!\ (3 / N^3)z^3 - \ldots$$

$$- (j - 2)!\ ((j - 1) / N^{j-1})z^{j-1} - (j - 1)!\ (j\ ./ N^j)z^j$$

Next we apply the previous relation $B_{j+1} = B_j + (jB_j - (j + 1)B_{j-1})\ z / N$, and we thus verify that the formula remains true at row $j + 1$. We know this is the case, as long as $j < K$, $S_j = ((j + 1) / N)\ (B_{j-1} / B_j)\ z\ S_{j+1}$.

We are led to use this formula with j from 1 to $K - 1$. Then we calculate S_K. We find that S_K is of the form $S_K = B_{K-1} / C_K$.

More specifically, we notice that a simple link between C_K and B_K exists. It is sufficient to replace terms of the form $K - q$ in B_K by $N - 1 - q$ to get C_K. Thus, from:

$$B_K = 1 - (K / N)\ z - 1!\ ((K - 1) / N^2)\ z^2 - 2!\ ((K - 2) / N^3)\ z^3 - 3!\ ((K - 3) / N^4)\ z^4$$

$$- \ldots - (K - 1)! / N^K)\ z^K$$

we get:

$$C_K = 1 - ((N - 1) / N)\ z - 1!\ ((N - 2) / N^2)\ z^2 - 2!\ ((N - 3) / N^3)\ z^3$$

$$- \ldots - (K - 1)!\ (N - K) / N^K)\ z^K$$

Starting from $S_K = B_{K-1} / C_K$ and going back up to S_0, we finally find that $S_0 = K!\ z^K / (N^K\ C_K)$, which is the formula announced on the generating function.

27.2.2. *Wait for the outcome of any part of K numbers in the form of a block, out of N*

In this case we wait for the outcome of a block of K different letters, whatever these letters may be, i.e. a combination of K letters. For example, for $K = 3$ and $N = 5$, a suitable word is 0334440<u>031</u>. Whether we wait for any combination or arrangement of K numbers, the problem is the same.

The generating function is:

$$G(z) = A(z) / B(z)$$

with: $A(z) = ((N - K + 1)(N - K + 2)) \dots ((N - 1) / N^{K-1})\, z^K$

and: $B(z) = (1 - (K - 1)\, z / N - (K - 2)\,(N - K + 1)\, z^2 / N^2$

$- (K - 3)\,(N - K + 1)(N - K + 2)\, z^3 / N^3 - \dots$

$- (N - K + 1)(N - K + 2) \dots (N - 2)\, z^{K-1} / N^{K-1})$

and: $E(X) = K + N^{K-1}\,((1 / N)(K - 1) + (2 / N^2)(K - 2)\,(N - K + 1)$

$+ (3 / N^3)(K - 3)\,(N - K + 1)\,(N - K + 2) + \dots$

$+ ((K - 1) / N^{K-1})\, 1\,(N - K + 1)(N - K + 2) \dots (N - 2))$

$/ ((N - K + 1)(N - K + 2) \dots (N - 1)).$

27.2.2.1. *Specific cases*

– for $K = 2$:

$G(z) = (N - 1)\, z^2 / (N - z)$ and $E(X) = 2 + 1 / (N - 1)$;

– for $K = 3$:

$G(z) = (N - 1)(N - 2)\, z^3 / (N^2 - 2Nz - (N - 2)z^2)$

and: $E(X) = (3N - 2) / (N - 2)$;

– for $K = 4$:

$G(z) = ((N - 1)(N - 2)(N - 3) / N^3)\, z^4 / (1 - (3 / N)z - 2(N - 3)z^2 / N^2$

$- (N - 2)(N - 3)z^3 / N^3)$

and: $E(X) = (4N^3 - 14N^2 + 17N - 6) / (N^3 - 6N^2 + 11N - 6)$;

– when N increases, $E(X)$ leans towards K, which is logical;

– when $K = N$, we wait for the first permutation coming from N letters in a block. We find the same formula as in section 27.2.1, and notably:

- for $N = 2$:

$G_2(z) = z^2 / (2 - z)$, hence the expectation $E(X) = 3$,

- for $N = 3$:

$G_3(z) = z^3 / (9/2 - 3z - (1/2)z^2)$ and $E(X) = 7$,

- for $N = 4$:

$G_4(z) = z^4 / (32/3 - 8z - (4/3)z^2 - (1/3)z^3)$ and: $E(X) = 47/3 = 15.67$,

- for $N = 5$:

$G_5(z) = z^5 / (625/24 - (500/24)z - (75/24)z^2 - (20/24) - (6/24)z^4)$

and $E(X) = 35.5$.

27.2.2.2. *Information about the demonstration of the preceding formula*

The transition graph has initial state K and final state 0 (see Figure 27.5). The generating function is S_0. The passage from initial state K to state $K - 1$ has a probability of 1.

The passage from state $K - 1$ to $K - 2$ corresponds to the outcome of a new number with the probability $(N - 1) / N$. If we fall back on the first number, we remain at stage $K - 1$. At stage $K - 2$, if we get a third number, the probability is $(N - 2) / N$ and we move on to the next stage $(K - 3)$. If we fall back on the second number, we return to stage $K - 1$ and if we return to first number, we remain at stage $K - 2$. And so on and so forth. The system of equations, where we postulated $Q = N - K$ results from the transition graph:

$$S_0 = ((Q + 1) / N)\, z\, S_1$$

$$S_1 = ((Q + 2) / N)\, z\, S_2 + (1 / N)\, z\, S_1$$

$$S_2 = ((Q + 3) / N)\, z\, S_3 + (1 / N)\, z\, (S_2 + S_1)$$

...

$S_j = ((Q + j + 1) / N)\, z\, S_{j+1} + (1 / N)\, z\, (S_j + S_{j-1} + ... + S_1)$ for j from 1 to $K - 1$

...

$S_{K-1} = z + (1 / N)\, z\, (S_{K-1} + S_{K-2} + ... + S_1)$ (with $S_K = 1$)

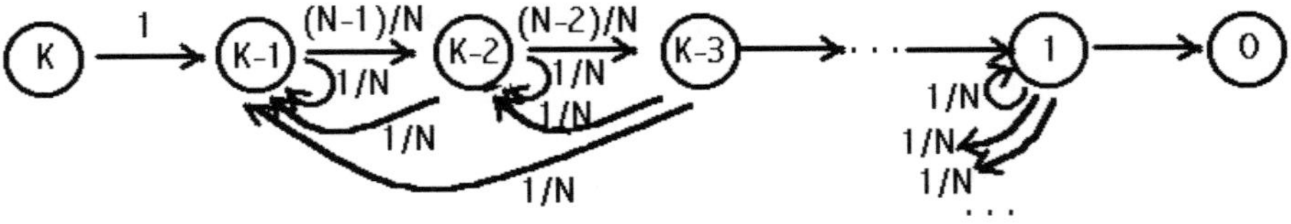

Figure 27.5. *Transition graph associated with parts*

We proceed to substitutions from the top down:

$S_1 = ((Q + 2) / N)\, (z / B_1)\, S_2$ with $B_1 = 1 - (1 / N)z$

– if $K = 2$, $S_0 = ((N - 1) / N)\, z^2 / B_1$, i.e.: $S_0 = ((N - 1) / N)\, z^2 / (1 - (1 / N)z)$, then:

$S_2 = ((Q + 3) / N)\, (z\, B_1 / B_2)\, S_3$

with:

$B_2 = 1 - (2 / N)\, z - (Q + 1)\, z^2 / N^2$;

– if $K = 3$, $S_0 = ((N - 2)(N - 1) / N^2)\, z^3 / B_2$, i.e.: $S_0 = ((N - 2)(N - 1) / N^2)\, z^3 / (1 - (2 / N)z - ((N - 2) / N^2)z^2)$, then:

$S_3 = ((Q + 4) / N)\, (z\, B_2 / B_3)\, S_4$

with:

$B_3 = 1 - (3 / N)z - 2\,(Q + 1)\, z^2 / N^2 - (Q + 1)(Q + 2)\, z^3 / N^3$;

– if $K = 4$, $S_0 = ((N - 3)(N - 2)(N - 1) / N^3))\, z^4 / B_3$, i.e.:

$$S_0 = ((N - 3)(N - 2)(N - 1) / N^3)\, z^4 / (1 - (3 / N)z - 2\,(N - 3))\, z^2 / N^2 - (N - 3)(N - 2)\, z^3 / N^3$$

By recurrence we show the formula indicated just above.

27.2.3. *Wait for the outcome of a part with K given numbers out of N in scattered form*

We wait for the outcome of $K = 3$ letters (0, 1 and 2), for example, without taking order into consideration, and in scattered form. For $N = 5$, a possible word is 334232214130, among other things. The generating function is:

$$S_K(z) = \frac{K!z^K}{(N-(N-K)z)(N-(N-K+1)z)...(N-(N-1)z)}$$

and:

$$E(X) = N(1 + 1/2 + 1/3 + ... + 1/K)$$

27.2.3.1. *Proof of the previous formula*

The transition graph (see Figure 27.6), with initial state 0 and final state K, leads to the system of equations:

$$S_0 = 1 + ((N-1)/N)\, z\, S_0$$

$$S_j = ((K-(j-1))/N)\, z\, S_{j-1} + ((N-(K-j))/N)\, z\, S_j \text{ for } j \text{ from 1 to } K-1$$

$$S_K = (1/N)\, z\, S_{K-1}$$

By successive substitutions from the bottom up, we find the generating function:

$$S_K(z) = (K!/N^K)\, z^K / ((1-((N-1)/N)\, z)\, (1-((N-2)/N)\, z) \ldots$$
$$(1-((N-K)/N)\, z)\,).$$

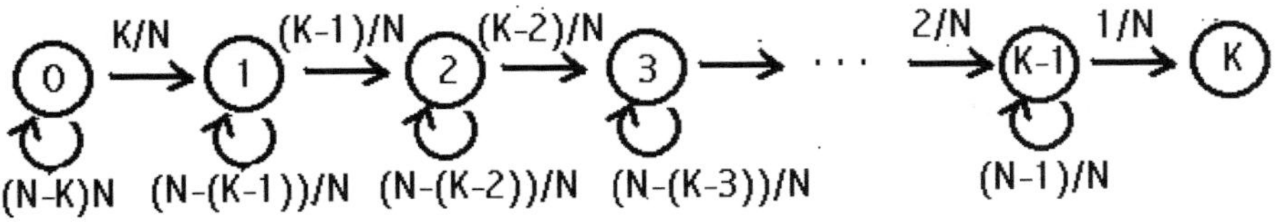

Figure 27.6. *Transition graph associated with scattered parts*

27.2.4. *Wait for the outcome of any part of K numbers out of N, in scattered form*

For example, for $N = 5$ and $K = 3$, we get the possible word 444040042.

The generating function is:

$$S_K(z) = \frac{z^K}{\frac{N-z}{N-1}\frac{N-2z}{N-2}\cdots\frac{N-(K-1)z}{N-(K-1)}}$$

and:

$$E(X) = K + 1 / (N - 1) + 2 / (N - 2) + 3 / (N - 3) + \ldots + (K - 1) / (N - (K - 1))$$

Note that for $K = N$, we find that:

$$E(X) = N(1 / 1 + 1 / 2 + 1 / 3 + \ldots + 1 / N)$$

just as in section 27.2.3.

We notice this with the formula:

$$N + H_1 + H_2 + \ldots + H_{N-1} = N H_N$$

where $H_j = 1 / 1 + 1 / 2 + 1 / 3 + \ldots + 1 / j$.

27.2.4.1. *Proof of the formula giving the generating function*

From the transition graph (see Figure 27.7) we get the following system of equations:

$$S_0 = 1$$

$$S_1 = z\, S_0 + (1 / N)\, z\, S_1$$

$S_i = ((N - (i - 1)) / N)\, z\, S_{i-1} + (i / N)\, z\, S_i$ for i included between 2 and $K - 1$

$$S_K = ((N - (K - 1)) / N)\, z\, S_{K-1}$$

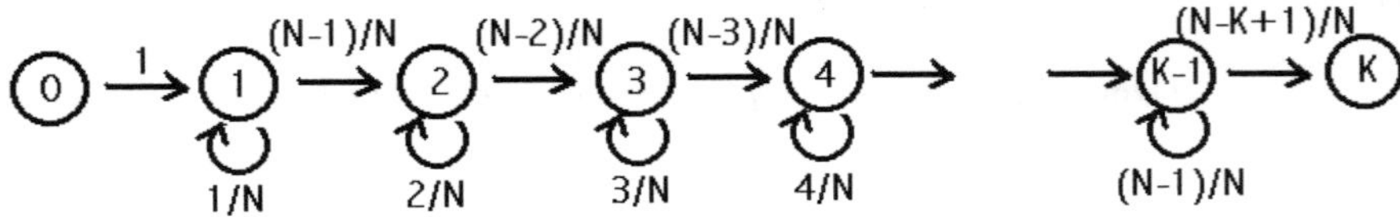

Figure 27.7. *Transition graph associated with any scattered part*

By substituting from the top down, we end up with the generating function:

$$S_K(z) = (N-1)(N-2)...(N-K+1)\, z^K \,/\, (N^{K-1}\, (1-(1\,/\,N)\,z)\,(1-(2\,/\,N)\,z) \ldots$$

$$(1-((K-1)\,/\,N)\,z)).$$

27.2.5. *Some examples of comparative results for waiting times*

27.2.5.1. *Example 1*

For $N = 6$ and $K = 2$:

– we wait for 01: $E(X) = 36$;

– we wait for 01 or 10: $E(X) = 21$;

– we wait for 0.....1: $E(X) = 12$;

– we wait for 0....1 or 1......0: $E(X) = 9$;

– we wait for the outcome of the first two different letters (or the first block of two distinct letters, such as $\underline{3}3333333\underline{5}$, which is also written $3333333\underline{35}$): $E(X) = 11 / 5$.

27.2.5.2. *Example 2*

For $N = 6$ and $K = 3$:

– we wait for 012: $E(X) = 216$;

– we wait for 012 or 120 or 201: $E(X) = 86$;

– we wait for 0...1...2: $E(X) = 18$;

– we wait for one of the six combinations from 0, 1, 2 in a block: $E(X) = 44$;

– we wait for any combination of three letters in a block: $E(X) = 4$;

– we wait for one of the six combinations from 0, 1, 2 in scattered form:

$E(X) = 11$;

– we wait for any combination of three letters in scattered form:

$E(X) = 3.7$.

27.3. Wait for patterns with eventual repetitions of identical letters

27.3.1. *For an alphabet of N letters, we wait for a given pattern in the form of a n-length block*

The pattern is now a block where letters that are the same can be found repeated. For example: possible patterns two characters long for $N = 2$ are 00, 01, 10 or 11. For a given length L, the number of such patterns is N^L.

In the case where $N = 2$, we have the following rule to get the average length of a word ending in a given pattern L characters long, with this pattern appearing for the first time.

Using the pattern given, we consider its beginnings and ends of the same and identical length k ($0 < k < L$), and take $a_k = 1$ or 0, depending on the presence or absence of such an identical k-length beginning and end. Thus we obtain a word $a_1a_2 \ldots a_{L-1}$ based on 0 and 1. The expectation is therefore:

$$E(X) = 2^L (1 + a_1 / 2^{L-1} + a_2 / 2^{L-2} + \ldots + a_{L-1} / 2)$$

$$= 2a_1 + 2^2 a_2 + 2^3 a_3 + \ldots + 2^{L-1} a_{L-1} + 2^L$$

For example, the waiting time for the pattern 00100100, which gives the word 1100100, is $E(X) = 2 + 4 + 32 + 256 = 295$.

27.3.1.1. *Proof of the previous rule*

Let S be the set of words (in the form of their union) ending in the given L-length pattern M, with the latter appearing there for the first time. S' is the set of words that do not contain pattern M anywhere. We find two relations linking S and S':

– $e + S'0 + S'1 = S + S'$ (the sign + corresponding to the union, with e being the empty word). Actually, $S'0$ and $S'1$ do not have any word in common and do not contain the neutral element e. If pattern M ends in 0, $S'0$ is made up of all the words of S as well as all the words of S' ending in 0, and $S'1$ is made up of all the words of S' ending in 1. This is the same if the pattern ends in 1.

Hence, this first relation does not depend on the pattern. In terms of formal series, and keeping the same notations, S and S' become $S(z)$ and $S'(z)$, and the formal series is translated by:

$$1 + z\, S' = S + S', \text{ i.e. } S = 1 + (z - 1)\, S'$$

– take a_k as the indicator, being equal to 1 if pattern M has an identical beginning and end of the same length k, and 0 otherwise. Let us form $S'M$, which will be formally translated by $S'z^L / 2^L$:

$$S'M = S + \sum_{k=1}^{L-1} a_k \, f_{L-k} \, S$$

where f_j designates the end of pattern M of length j. Or even:

$$S' \frac{z^L}{2^L} = S \, P(z)$$

with:

$$P(z) = 1 + \sum_{k=1}^{L-1} a_k \frac{z^{L-k}}{2^{L-k}} .$$

Finally the generating function is expressed:

$$S = z^L / (z^L - (z-1)\, 2^L) P(z)$$

and the expectation obtained by derivation is:

$$E = 2^L + \sum_{k=1}^{L-1} a_k \, 2^k$$

NOTE 27.1.– For given L the expectation is minimal and is equal to 2^L, when the pattern has neither an identical beginning or end.

27.3.1.2. *Generalization to any N*

The expectation formula, given just above for $N = 2$, can be generalized to any N:

$$E = N^L + \sum_{k=1}^{L-1} a_k \, N^k .$$

27.3.2. *Wait for one of two patterns of the same length L*

We begin by dealing with two examples where $N = 2$ and $L = 3$. This will be the opportunity to note that the probability of getting one pattern before the other in each of the two cases is not necessarily the same. Next let us move on to the general case.

27.3.2.1. *Wait for the pattern 001 or 011 for the first time*

The generating function results from the transition graph (see Figure 27.8a):

$$S_3(z) = z^3 (4 - z) / ((2 - z)^2(4 - z^2))$$

and the expectation is:

$$E(X) = 16 / 3$$

A variation of this problem consists of making two people play a game. Player *A* wins if block 001 appears before 011, and player *B* wins if 011 appears first. Do the two players have the same chance of winning?

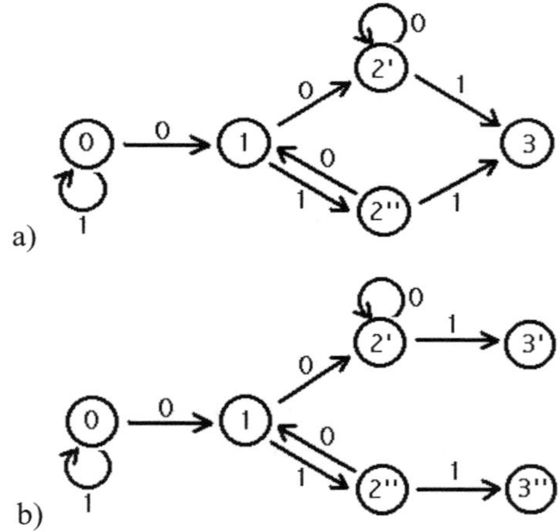

Figure 27.8. *a) Transition graph for the wait for 001 or 011; and b) variation with two players*

In view of the transition graph (see Figure 27.8b), where we now replace state 3 with two final states 3′ and 3″, we notice that we do not get the same result. We find that:

$$S_{3'}(z) = z^3/(2 - z)(4 - z^2)(1 - 0.5z)$$

and:

$$S_{3''}(z) = z^3/ (2 - z)(4 - z^2)$$

with:

$$S_{3'}(z) + S_{3''}(z) = S_3(z).$$

The probability of getting 001 before 011 is $S_{3'}(1) = 2 / 3$, and that of getting 011 first is $S_{3''}(1) = 1/3$. Similarly, the average time T_A needed to get 001 before 011 is not the same as the time T_B needed to get 011 before 001. These times are obtained by weighting of probabilities, the sum of which is equal to 1. To get T_A, we should therefore take the derivative at 1 of the function $(3 / 2)\ S_{3'}(z)$, which gives $T_A = 17 / 3$, and similarly for $T_B = (3\ S_{3''})'(1) = 14 / 3$. Moreover we check that:

$$2/3\ T_A + 1/3\ T_B = E(X).$$

27.3.2.2. *Wait for the patterns 001 or 100*

From the transition graph (see Figure 27.9) we find the generating function:

$$S_3(z) = z^3 / (8 - 4z) + 3z^3 / (16 - 8z - 4z^2)$$

and:

$$E(X) = 25 / 4$$

With two players *A* and *B*, one winning when pattern 001 is drawn before 100 and the other winning if 100 is drawn before 001, we divide the preceding final state 3 into two states – 3′ and 3″ – with:

$$S_{3'}(z) = z^3 / (8 - 4z) \text{ and } S_{3''}(z) = 3z^3 / (16 - 8z - 4z^2),$$

we find:

$$S_{3'}(1) = 1 / 4 \text{ and } S_{3''}(1) = 3 / 4$$

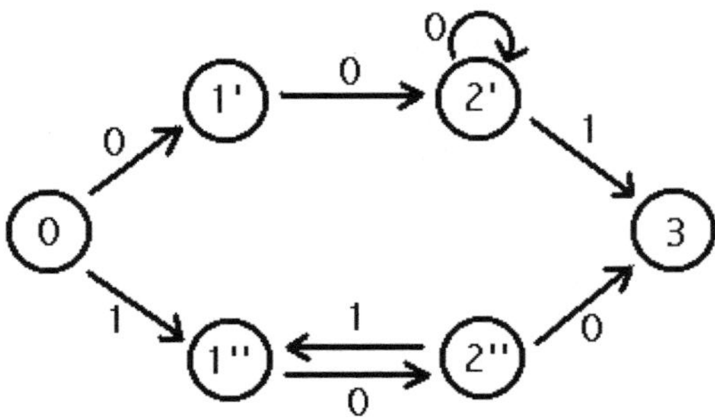

Figure 27.9. *Transition graph in waiting for 001 or 100*

The first player A has only a one in four chance of winning. The average time T_A needed to end up at 001 before 100 is obtained by calculating:

$$T_A = (4S_{3'})'(1) = 4$$

and similarly:

$$T_B = ((4/3)S_{3''})'(1) = 7$$

and we check that $(1/4)T_A + (3/4)T_B = E(X)$.

27.3.2.3. *General case*

We assume that two patterns A and B have the same length L. Let S' be the set of words that contain neither pattern A or pattern B; S_A the set of words ending in pattern A and not containing it before; and similarly S_B, with pattern B at the end. We have the equations:

$$1 + S'0 + S'1 = S' + S_A + S_B$$

$$S'A = S_A + S_A \sum a_k f_{L-k} + S_B \sum a'_k f'_{L-k}$$

$$S'B = S_B + S_B \sum b_k f'_{L-k} + S_A \sum b'_k f_{L-k}$$

with the following conventions:

– a_k is equal to 1 when the end of k-length word A is equal to its beginning, otherwise a_k is equal to 0, and similarly for b_k with word B;

– f_{L-k} is the end of word A over $L - k$ characters long, and similarly f'_{L-k} for word B;

– a'_k is equal to 1 when the end of k-length word B k is equal to the beginning of word A of the same length, and 0 otherwise;

– b'_k is equal to 1 when the end of word A is equal to that of the beginning of word B over length k, and 0 otherwise;

– the number k is between 1 and $L - 1$, and the summation Σ is extended to all these values of k.

An example with $A = 101$ and $B = 010$ gives:

$$1 + S'0 + S'1 = S + S_A + S_B$$

$$S'101 = S_A + S_A 01 + S_B 1$$

$$S'010 = S_B + S_B\,10 + S_A\,0$$

Let us move on to formal series where each k-length word is replaced by $(1 / 2^k)\,z^k$, which indicates that X, the length of the words, is the random variable with the total coefficient of the z^k term being the probability of $X = k$. Notably $\Sigma a_k f_{L-k}$ becomes $\Sigma a_k\, z^{L-k} / 2^{L-k}$.

Let us postulate:

– $\Sigma a_k f_{L-k} = sa$;

– $\Sigma b_k f_{L-k} = sb$;

– $\Sigma a'_k f_{L-k} = sba$; and

– $\Sigma b'_k f_{L-k} = sab$.

Finally let us take $F = S_A + S_B$. F is therefore the generating function associated with random variable X. The first equation becomes:

$$1 + zS' = S' + F, \text{ i.e. } S' = (F - 1) / (z - 1)$$

For the other two equations, having $S'_A = S'_B$ gives:

$$S_A\,(1 + sa - sab) = S_B(1 + sb - sba),$$

$$\text{or: } S_B = S_A(1 + sa - sab) / (1 + sb - sba)$$

We also have $S_A = \alpha\,(S_A + S_B) = \alpha F$ with:

$$\alpha = (1 + sb - sba) / (2 + sa + sb - sab - sba)$$

and we have $S_B = (1 - \alpha)(S_A + S_B) = (1 - \alpha)\,F$, with:

$$1 - \alpha = (1 + sa - sab)/(2 + sa + sb - sab - sba)$$

Taking the relation between S' and F of the first equation and transferring the results giving S_A and S_B as a function of F, the second equation will give F:

$$z^L / (2^L)\,(F - 1) / (z - 1) = \alpha\,F\,(1 + sa) + (1 - \alpha)\,F\,sba$$

$$= F\,(\alpha(1 + sa) + (1 - \alpha)\,sba)$$

$$= (Q / P)\,F$$

with:

$$Q = 1 + sa + sb + sa\ sb - sab\ sba \text{ and } P = 2 + sa + sb - sab - sba$$

Hence:

$$F\ (z^L - 2^L\ (z - 1)\ Q\ /\ P) = z^L$$

Finally:

$$F(z) = P\ z^L\ /\ (P\ z^L - 2^L\ Q\ z + 2^L\ Q)$$

We deduce from it the number of moves to obtain pattern A or pattern B for the first time:

$$E(X) = 2^L\ Q(1)\ /\ P(1)$$

Let us recall that:

$$Q = 1 + sa + sb + sa\ sb - sab\ sba$$

and:

$$P = 2 + sa + sb - sab - sba$$

with:

$$sa = \sum a_k\ z^{L-k}\ /\ 2^{L-k}$$

having done the summation from $k = 1$ to $k = L - 1$, with a_k being equal to 0 or 1 depending on whether or not pattern A has a beginning equal to the end over length k, and similarly for sb, sba and sab.

27.4. Programming exercises

27.4.1. *Wait for completely different letters*

We have N letters (or numbers) 0, 1, 2, …, $N - 1$. We keep drawing one letter at random, with equiprobability, until for the first time we draw K completely different letters successively, K being given ($K \leq N$). We have to create the program enabling us to calculate the average number of draws needed (see the formula in section 27.2.2).

During each experiment, we use a K-length array $a[]$ in which, with each new draw, the last K numbers drawn are already recorded. In initial conditions, we make the first K draws. If they are different, we stop. If not, we launch the drawing loop, where we keep drawing numbers until K different numbers are obtained in the table. Note that array $a[]$ is rendered cyclic, with a rotating variable *head*, that moves one notch forward with each draw, and returns to 0 after having reached the last box $K - 1$. With each draw, we suppress the contents of $a[head]$ in order to put therein the letter that has just been drawn: the last K draws are therefore found in table $a[]$, from the last one to the draw K moves before, in the boxes *head*, $head - 1$, …, 0, $K - 1$, $K - 2$, …, $head + 1$, respectively. With each stage, where *head* moves forward one notch, the new draw suppresses the oldest, which we no longer need to keep.

We are given N, K, and the number NE of experiments to be carried out.

```
cumul=0 ; /* this variable will accumulate the number of moves for each
        experiment */
for(expe=1; expe<=NE; expe++)
{
 for(j=0; j<N; j++) done[j]=0;  nbmoves=0; finished=YES;
 for(i=0; i<K; i++)  { a[i]=random(N); done[a[i]]++; nbmoves++;}
 for(i=0; i<K; i++) if (done[a[i]]>1) { finished=NO; break; }
 if (finished==YES) cumul+= nbmoves;
 else
  { head=0;
  while (finished==NO)
   { finished=YES; nbmoves++; done[a[head]]--;
    a[i]=random(N); done[a[head]]++;
    for(i=0; i<K; i++) if (done[a[i]]>1) { finished=0; break; }
    head++; if (head==K) head=0;
   }
  cumul+=nbmoves;
  }
 }
printf("E(X) = %3.3f", cumul/(float)NE);
```

The results obtained are very close to the theoretical values from the formula in section 27.2.2, for example for $N = 6$ we get the values in Table 27.1.

K	E(X)
2	2.2
3	4
4	7.6
5	18.4
6	83.2

Table 27.1. *Program results for N = 6*

27.4.2. *Waiting time for a certain pattern*

We are given the number of experiments *NE*, length *lpattern* of the pattern, and we begin by creating all the patterns based on 0 and on 1, numbering $2^{lpattern}$. These are placed in the table *pattern*[*lpattern*]. For each pattern, we launch *NE* experiments enabling us to extract the average time *EX*:

```
for(number=0; number<pow(2.,(float)lpattern); number++)
 { q=number;
  for(i=0; i<lpattern; i++) { pattern[i]=q%2; q=q/2;}    display the pattern
  cumul=0;
  for(exp=1; exp<=NE; exp++)
   { for(nbmoves=0; nbmoves<lpattern; nbmoves++) a[nbmoves]=random(2);
     head=lpattern-1;
     if (finished()==YES) cumul+=nbmoves;
     else
      { head=0;
        for(;;)
         { nbmoves++; a[head]=random(2);
           if (finished()==YES) {cumul+=nbmoves; break;}
           head=(head+1)%lpattern;
         }
      }
   }
  time=cumul/(float)nbtries;
 }
int finished(void)
{ int i,k,j;  k=0;  j=(head+1)%lpattern;
  for(i=0; i<lpattern; i++)
    { if (a[j]!=pattern[k]) return NO; j=(j+1)%lpattern; k++;}
  return YES;
}
```

27.4.3. *Number of words without two-sided factors*

Let $W(n)$ be the set of n-length words from an alphabet of two letters 0 and 1 without two-sided factors and starting with 0. Let there be $u(n)$ of them. By words without two-sided factors, we mean all words with no beginning equal to their end. The start s of a n-length word w is such that $w = sq$, with the length of s being between 1 and $n-1$, and similarly for the end e such that $w = q'e$, with the length of e being between 1 and $n-1$. It is understood that $n \geq 2$. If we took all the words without two-sided factors starting with 0 or with 1, there would be $2u(n)$ of them. Such words are linked to what we did previously, when we defined the a_k indicators (see section 27.3.1). In this case they are all null.

The results over $u(n)$ are:

n	1	2	3	4	5	6	7	8	9	10	11	12	13	14	15	16
$u(n)$	1	1	2	3	6	10	20	37	74	142	284	558	1116	2212	4424	8811.

The properties of sequence $u(n)$ are:

– $u(2n+1) = 2\,u(2n)$; and

– $u(2n) = 4\,u(2n-2) - u(n)$.

These two recurrence relations enable us to construct the sequence $u(n)$ from $u(1) = 1$ (by coherent convention) and $u(2) = 1$. Before showing these two properties, let us show the following lemma.

LEMMA 27.1.– given a word is of even length $2n$, if we find a start equal to an end $> n$ long, then there is also a start equal to an end $< n$ long.

PROOF OF LEMMA 27.1.– let $w = w_1 w_2$ with n-length w_1 and w_2. Let us assume that we have a $> n$-length start S and end E with $S = E$. We can write $S = w_1 e$ with e as the start of w_2 and $E = sw_2$, with s as the end of w_1, and the lengths of s and e are equal: $|s| = |e|$. We deduce that se is a factor of w, and like $S = E$, se is a beginning of w and also an end of w.

In the case where $|e| < n/2$ if n is even or $|e| \leq (n-1)/2$ if n is odd, $|se| < n$, and the property is verified. In the case where $|e| = n/2$ with even n, we have exactly $s = e$ which is a start and an end for w that is $n/2 < n$ long.

We have just dealt with the case where $|S| = |E| \leq [3n/2]$. Now let us take the case where $|S| = |E| > [3n/2]$. We can write $w = S\,q' = q\,E$ with $|q| = |q'| < [n/2]$. Like $S = E$, q start of S is also the start of E, hence qq is also the start of S, and the process is repeated, until we finally get $S = q^k\,e$. Similarly,

$E = s\ q'^{k}$. The remainders e and s are such that $0 \leq |\ s\ | = |\ e\ | < n / 2$. If there is no remainder after division, $|\ s\ | = 0$, we deduce from it that $q = q'$, and q is the start and end of w at the same time, with a length less than $n / 2$. If $|\ s\ | > 0$, e is an end of E and q', and s a start of S and q.

Next we check that s start of q is mixed up with e as the end of q'. With $s = e$, we have just found a beginning and an end of w less than $n / 2$ long.

The consequence of this is that given an even 2n-long word, if we do not find any start equal to any $\leq n$-length end, then the word belongs to $W(2n)$.

Actually, by hypothesis there is no n-length beginning equal to an end. There is no $< n$-length start equal to an end either. This leads to there no longer being a $> n$-length start equal to an end, according to the lemma. Finally, no start – regardless of its length – is equal to an end. It is a word of $W(2n)$.

27.4.3.1. *Showing property u(2n + 1) = 2 u(2n) using a constructive procedure*

Given a word $W(2n)$, let us cut it in two n-length parts and insert either 0 or 1 between them. We thus obtain two words and will show that they are in $W(2n + 1)$:

– with this word of $W(2n)$ being w, we have $w = w_1 w_2$ with $|\ w_1\ | = |\ w_2\ |$;

– let us form $w' = w_1 a\ w_2$ with a, which is either 0 or 1, and $|w'\ | = 2n + 1$;

– let us take the starts and ends of w' that are $\leq n$ long, these are also the starts and ends for w_1 and w_2, or they are w_1 and w_2. What we have are starts and ends for w. They cannot be equal, since w is in $W(2n)$.

Now given a start S and an end E of w' with $|\ S\ | = |\ E\ | > n$:

– If $|S| = n + 1$, $S = w_1 a$ and $E = a w_2$. If $S = E$, then $a = 0$ would be the start of w and $a = 1$ the end of w. This is impossible.

– If $|S| > n + 1$, $S = w_1 a s$ with s being a start of w_2, hence $w_2 = sq$, and $E = eaw_2$ with e end of w_1: $w_1 = q'e$. So $S = q'e\ a\ s$, $E = easq$. If we had $S = E$, eas would also be a start of S and end of E, with $|\ eas\ | < |\ w_1\ | + 1 + |\ w_2\ | < |\ w\ |$, $|\ eas\ | < 2n$. In the case where$|\ eas\ | \leq n$, eas would be a start of w_1 or w_1, and would also be an end of w_2 or w_2. Since w is in $W(2n)$ this is impossible. The case where $|\ eas\ | > n$ remains. With $w' = Se_1 = s_1 E$, s_1 would be a start of S and e_1 an end of E, of same length as s_1. With $S = E$, s_1 would also be the start of E, hence $e_1^{\ 2}$ would be the start of S, and continuing in this way, as for a Euclidean division, we would have $S = (s_1)^{k} e' = s'\ (e_1)^{k}$ with $0 \leq |\ e'\ | = |\ s'\ | < |\ s_1\ |$. We also necessarily have $k > 1$. If $|\ s'\ | = |\ e'\ | = 0$, we would have $s_1 = e_1$, with $|\ s_1\ | \leq n$. s_1 would be a start and an end of w, which is impossible. When $|\ s'\ | > 0$, $s_1 = s'\delta$ with s' being the start of s_1 and

$e_1 = \delta e'$, we have: $s_1\ s_1 = s'e_1\ \delta = s'\ \delta 'e'\delta$, hence $s_1 = \delta '\delta$. With $s_1 = s'\delta$, we deduce from it that $s' = e'$, s' would be a start and end of w, which is impossible.

By inserting 0 or 1 into the center of a word of $W(2n)$ long, we succeeded in constructing a word of $W(2n + 1)$ long. Now let us prove that there are no words other than those in $W(2n + 1)$ in length.

Given a word w' of $W(2n + 1)$ long, we can express it as $w' = w_1 a w_2$ with a being equal to 0 or 1, and $| w_1 | = | w_2 |$. We have to prove that $w = w_1 w_2$ is in $W(2n)$, thus the word w' will originate from the previous construction:

– let us assume that we found a start S of $w = w_1 w_2$ equal to an end E of w. If $| S | < n$, S is a start of w_1 and w', and similarly E is an end of w_2 and w'. With $S = E$, we get an impossibility;

– if $| S | = n$, $S = w_1$ and $E = w_2$, S is a start of w' and E an end of w'. Here again this is impossible;

– if $| S | > n$ with $S = E$ we know, according to the initial lemma, that there is also a beginning equal to an end, less than n long, which brings us back to an impossible previous case;

– finally, we find that word w is in $W(2n)$.

We have just found the constructive procedure for getting all the words of $W(2n + 1)$ long using those of $W(2n)$: we insert either a 0 or 1 at the center of each word of $W(2n)$.

27.4.3.2. *Showing property $u(2n) = 4\ u(2n - 2) - u(n)$ using a constructive procedure*

Here is the constructive procedure that will enable us to go from $W(2n - 2)$ to $W(2n)$. For each word of $W(2n - 2)$, we insert at the center the two letters 00 or 01 or 11, or 10 at the center in certain conditions only, which we will specify.

27.4.3.2.1. First case

In a word w of $W(2n - 2)$ characters, let us insert one of the three blocks $b = 00$ or 01 or 11 in its center. Using $w = w_1 w_2$ with $| w_1 | = n - 1$, we get the word $w' = w_1 b w_2$. Since w is in $W(2n - 2)$, no start of w_1 (nor w_1 itself) can be an end of w_2 (or w_2), i.e. no start of length less than or equal to $n - 1$ can be an end of w'.

Next let us consider the start $w_1 a$ of w', and its end $a' w_2$, with $b = a\ a'$, and assume that they are equal. If $b = 00$ or 01, w' should end in 0, which is impossible. If $b = 11$, word w' should start with 1, which is impossible. In the case where $b = 10$, the same type of argument prevents us coming to a conclusion.

27.4.3.2.2. Second case: $b = 10$

We are interested in words of $W(2n - 2)$ long that are not in $W(2n)$, when 10 is inserted in them, and will show that they number $u(n)$:

– Let us take a word w of $W(n)$ long. It can be expressed as $w = w_1 1$ or $w = 0w_2$. Now let us form the word w_1w_2. It is $2n - 2$ long. Let us show that it is in $W(2n - 2)$. As the starts of w are also the starts of w_1 or w_1 itself, and the ends of w are the ends of w_2 or w_2, and the starts and ends are never equal, it is the same for the starts and ends of w_1w_2 whose greatest length is $n - 1$. Thanks to the initial lemma, it is the same for all the starts and ends of greater length, and w_1w_2 is a word of $W(2n - 2)$ long. But when we create the $2n$-length word $w_1 10 w_2$, it has a start $w_1 1$ equal to an end $0w_2$, and is not in $W(2n)$. We have just found $u(n)$ words of $W(2n - 2)$, created from $W(n)$ by concatenating a word start of $W(n)$ that is $n - 1$ long with an end of the same length, which we cannot expand by adding 10 for them to become words of $W(2n)$. Lastly let us show that there are no others.

– Let us take a word of $W(2n - 2)$ long that we cannot transform into a word of $W(2n)$ long by adding 10 to the center. As the $< n$-length starts are not equal to the ends, and it is the same for those $> n$ long, this forces the n-length start to be equal to the corresponding end. Given such a word w from $W(2n - 2)$, with $w = w_1w_2$ and $| w_1 | = | w_2 | = n - 1$, w_1 and w_2 are the same length. It is therefore necessary for $w_1 1 = 0w_2$. We can write $w_1 = 0w'$ and $w_2 = w'1$. Whether word $0w'\,1$ belongs to $W(n)$ remains to be shown. Let us take the starts s of w that are $< n$ long. These are also the start of the word $w_1 1 = 0w'1$. Similarly the ends e of w that is $< n$ long are also the ends of the word $0w_2 = 0w'1$. As none of these starts is also an end, this proves that the word $0w'1$ is in $W(n)$.

We have proved the formula $u(2n) = 4u(2n - 2) - u(n)$. At the same time we have a constructive procedure that creates four or only three words of $W(2n)$ from a word of $W(2n - 2)$ long. To decide the disputed case where we add 10, it is enough to test whether $w_1 1 = 0w2$ or not. In the first case, we do not take this word.

We have found the rule enabling us to go from a word of $W(2n - 2)$ to three or four words of $W(2n)$: we cut the $2n - 2$-length word into two words w_1 and w_2 of the same length $(n - 1)$. We insert 00 or 01 or 11 between them. If we do not have $w_1 1 = 0\, w_2$, we also insert 10.

From there we deduce the program that enables us to obtain all the words with neither identical start nor end.

27.4.3.3. *Program*

From *L*-length words whose number we know (they are placed in arrays *w*[][]), we move on to words that are *L* + 2 long whose number we determine. We place them in arrays *ww*[][]. Then we put *ww* in *w* and we start over.

```
L=2; number=1; w[0][0]=0; w[0][1]=1; /* the only word 2 characters long */
for(length=4; length<=12; length+=2)
 { q=0;
  for(n=0; n<number; n++)
   {for(i=0; i<L/2; i++) for(j=0; j<4; j++)
      { ww[q+j][i]=w[n][i]; ww[q+j][L/2+i+2]=w[n][L/2+i];}
    ww[q][L/2]=0; ww[q][L/2+1]=0;
    ww[q+1][L/2]=0; ww[q+1][L/2+1]=1;
    ww[q+2][L/2]=1; ww[q+2][L/2+1]=1;
    ww[q+3][L/2]=1; ww[q+3][L/2+1]=0;
    valid=NO;
    for(i=0; i<L/2+1; i++)
    if (ww[q+3][i]!=ww[q+3][L/2+1+i]) { valid=YES; break; }
    if (valid==NO) q=q+3;  else q=q+4;
   }
  L=L+2; number=q;
  for(i=0; i<number; i++) for(j=0; j<L; j++)  w[i][j]=ww[i][j];
  display table w[][]
 }
```

27.4.3.4. *Some results from the program*

Where $L = 4$ and the number = 3:

1: 0 0 0 1

2: 0 0 1 1

3: 0 1 1 1

Where $L = 6$ and the number = 10:

1: 0 0 0 0 0 1

2: 0 0 0 1 0 1

3: 0 0 1 1 0 1

4: 0 0 0 0 1 1

5: 0 0 0 1 1 1

6: 0 0 1 1 1 1

7: 0 0 1 0 1 1

8: 0 1 0 0 1 1

9: 0 1 0 1 1 1

10: 0 1 1 1 1 1

Where $L = 8$ and the number = 37:

1: 0 0 0 0 0 0 0 1

2: 0 0 0 0 1 0 0 1

3: 0 0 0 1 1 0 0 1

4: 0 0 0 0 0 1 0 1

5: 0 0 0 0 1 1 0 1

6: 0 0 0 1 1 1 0 1

7: 0 0 0 1 0 1 0 1

8: 0 0 1 0 0 1 0 1

9: 0 0 1 0 1 1 0 1

10: 0 0 1 1 1 1 0 1

11: 0 0 1 1 0 1 0 1

12: 0 0 0 0 0 0 1 1

13: 0 0 0 0 1 0 1 1

14: 0 0 0 1 1 0 1 1

15: 0 0 0 1 0 0 1 1

16: 0 0 0 0 0 1 1 1

17: 0 0 0 0 1 1 1 1

18: 0 0 0 1 1 1 1 1

19: 0 0 0 1 0 1 1 1

20: 0 0 1 0 0 1 1 1

21: 0 0 1 0 1 1 1 1

22: 0 0 1 1 1 1 1 1

23: 0 0 1 1 0 1 1 1

24: 0 0 1 0 0 0 1 1

25: 0 0 1 0 1 0 1 1

26: 0 0 1 1 1 0 1 1

27: 0 1 0 0 0 0 1 1

28: 0 1 0 0 1 0 1 1

29: 0 1 0 1 1 0 1 1

30: 0 1 0 1 0 0 1 1

31: 0 1 0 0 0 1 1 1

32: 0 1 0 0 1 1 1 1

33: 0 1 0 1 1 1 1 1

34: 0 1 0 1 0 1 1 1

35: 0 1 1 0 0 1 1 1

36: 0 1 1 0 1 1 1 1

37: 0 1 1 1 1 1 1 1.

Chapter 28

Probability Exercises

28.1. The elevator

In a building with P floors, N people take the elevator on the ground floor. They each go to a floor chosen at random and this is done independently of the others. X is the random variable corresponding to the number of floors where the elevator stops.

28.1.1. *Deal with the case where $P = 2$ floors and the number of people N is at least equal to 2*

Everything happens as if, on the ground floor, each person pulled a number at random – either 1 or 2 – to find out on what floor they will get off. Numbering the people from 1 to N, and attributing the number of the floor that corresponds to them, we get N-length words based on two letters: 1 and 2. For example, for $N = 3$, the word 211 means that person 1 gets off on the 2nd floor, and persons 2 and 3 on the first. This produces 2^N configurations, all equiprobable, with the probability of each being $1 / 2^N$. Event $X = 1$ means that everyone gets off on the same floor, either floor 1 or floor 2. This corresponds to the words 111…1 or 222…2, i.e. two cases. From this we deduce the probability:

$$p(X = 1) = 2 / 2^N = 1 / 2^{N-1}$$

Event $X = 2$ corresponds to words where the two letters are present, i.e. $2^N - 2$ cases, and:

$$p(X = 2) = (2^N - 2) / 2^N = 1 - 1 / 2^{N-1}.$$

28.1.2. *Determine the law of X, i.e. the probability associated with each value of X*

We are dealing with N-length words out of an alphabet with P letters. The letter in position j designates the floor where person j gets off. We are in the presence of P^N possible situations, all of which are equiprobable. Random variable X can take all values between 1 and P. Event $X = K$ indicates that the elevator stopped at K different floors, where K is between 1 and the smaller of the two numbers P and N. There are C_P^K ways of choosing K out of P floors. Each time, the situations corresponding to $X = K$ are N-length words using exactly K letters, which is equivalent to $S(N, K)$ surjections of a N-element set in a K-element set. We deduce from it the law of X:

$$p(X = K) = C_P^K \, S(N, K) \,/\, P^N$$

As an exercise, let us find the surjections formula again. Consider the surjections of a N-element initial set in a K-element final set. A surjection is an application where all the elements of the final set are touched (they are called images). This forces N to be greater than or equal to K. To find the number $S(N, K)$ of surjections, let us isolate an element a of the initial set. So we separate the $S(N, K)$ surjections into two categories:

– Surjections where element a has a correspondent in the final set – an image, that no other element touches. There are K ways of picking this image, and each time there are $S(N-1, K-1)$ possible surjections for elements other than a. This makes a total of $K\,S(N-1, K-1)$ cases.

– Surjections where element a has an image that other elements also have. There are K ways of taking the image of a, and each time the other elements numbering $N - 1$ are in surjection with the K final elements, i.e. a total of $K\,S(N-1, K)$ cases.

We end up with the recurrence relation:

$$S(N, K) = K\,S(N-1, K-1) + K\,S(N-1, K)$$

where $K > 1$ (and $N \geq K$), with the initial conditions $S(N, 1) = 1$.

To find the explicit formula, let us introduce the generating functions indexed by K. Let us assume:

$$F_K(x) = S(K, K)\,x^K + S(K+1, K)\,x^{K+1} + \ldots + S(N, K)\,x^N + \ldots,$$

hence:

$$KxF_K(x) = K\,S(K,K)\,x^{K+1} + \ldots + K\,S(N-1, K)x^N + \ldots$$

$$KxF_{K-1}(x) = KS(K-1, K-1)x^K + KS(K, K-1)x^{K+1} + \ldots$$

$$+ KS(N-1, K-1)x^N + \ldots$$

The recurrence relation therefore gives:

$$F_K(x) = K\,x\,F_K(x) + K\,x\,F_{K-1}(x)$$

$$\text{i.e.: } F_K(x) = \frac{Kx}{1-Kx}F_{K-1}(x)$$

and at the start:

$$F_1(x) = x / (1-x)$$

Going down we deduce from it:

$$F_K(x) = \frac{Kx}{1-Kx}\frac{(K-1)x}{1-(K-1)x}\cdots\frac{2x}{1-2x}\frac{1}{1-x} = \frac{K!\,x^K}{(1-Kx)(1-(K-1)x)\ldots(1-2x)(1-x)}$$

We verify this by breaking down into simple elements:

$$\frac{1}{(1-x)(1-2x)\ldots(1-Kx)} = \sum_{j=1}^{K}\frac{(-1)^{K-j}\,j^{K-1}}{(j-1)!(K-j)!(1-jx)}$$

so:

$$F_K(x) = K!x^K\sum_{j=1}^{K}\frac{(-1)^{K-j}\,j^{K-1}}{(j-1)!(K-j)!}(1+jx+j^2x^2+\ldots+j^{N-K}x^{N-K}+\ldots)$$

finally:

$$S(N, K) = K!\sum_{j=1}^{K}\frac{(-1)^{K-j}\,j^N}{j!\,(K-j)!}$$

28.1.3. *Average value E(X)*

Without appealing to the law of X, we have to find the average value $E(X)$. For this, we will introduce the random variable X_{ij} taking the value 1 if person j gets off on floor i and the value 0 otherwise. We will also introduce the random variable X_i taking the value 1 if the elevator stops on the ith floor, and 0 otherwise:

$$p(X_{ij} = 1) = 1 / P \text{ and } p(X_{ij} = 0) = 1 - 1 / P$$

This is a Bernoulli's law.

In turn:

$$p(X_i = 0) = p(X_{i1} = 0 \text{ and } X_{i2} = 0 \text{ and } \ldots \text{ and } X_{iN} = 0) = (1 - 1 / P)^N$$

$$p(X_i = 1) = 1 - (1 - 1 / P)^N$$

X_i also follows a Bernoulli's law, hence:

$$E(X_i) = 1 - (1 - 1 / P)^N$$

and with $X = X_1 + X_2 + \ldots + X_P$:

$$E(X) = P\,(1 - (1 - 1 / P)^N) = (P^N - (P - 1)^N) / P^{N-1}.$$

28.1.4. *Direct calculation of S(K+1, K)*

Directly calculate S(K + 1, K) from recurrence formula, and deduce from it the probability that the elevator stops on each floor when there is one more person than floors, i.e.: N = P + 1.

From the recurrence formula on the $S(N, K)$, we deduce that:

$$S(K + 1, K) = K\,K! + K\,S(K, K - 1)$$

Then from $S(K, K - 1) = (K - 1)\,(K - 1)\,! + (K - 1)\,S(K - 1, K - 2)$:

$$K\,S(K, K - 1) = (K - 1)\,K! + K(K - 1)\,S(K - 1, K - 2)$$

and so on and so forth:

$$K(K - 1)\,S(K - 1, K - 2) = (K - 2)\,K! + K(K - 1)(K - 2)\,S(K - 2, K - 3)$$

$$\ldots$$

$$K(K - 1)\ldots 2\,S(2, 1) = K!$$

By adding member-by-member and a spate of simplification, what remains is:

$$S(K+1, K) = K\,!\,(K + (K-1) + (K-2) + 1)$$

$$= K!\,K(K+1) / 2 = (K+1)!\,K / 2$$

The probability requested is:

$$p(X = P) = S(P+1, P) / P^{P+1} = (P+1)! / (2\,P^P)$$

When $P = 2$, we again find a probability of 3 / 4. For $P = 3$, the probability is 12 / 27. For $P = 4$, it is no longer only 15 / 64.

28.1.5. *Another way of dealing with the previous question*

The situations concerned correspond to P + 1-length words based on P letters where all the letters are present. This means that one letter is present twice and the others once. There are $P + 1$ ways of choosing the double letter present. Each time, it can be placed in $C_{P+1}^{\ 2}$ ways. What is left to do is place all the other letters, i.e. $P!$ ways. The number of words is $P\ C_{P+1}^{\ 2}\ P! = P\ (P+1)! / 2$. With the number of possible cases being P^{P+1}, the probability sought is:

$$P\,(P+1)! / (2\,P^{P+1}).$$

28.2. Matches

A smoker has two boxes of matches, each containing N matches. He takes one match from one of the boxes at random, and continues in this way until one of the boxes is empty. There are therefore k matches remaining in the other box. With this number of matches remaining in a box being random variable X, determine the law of X, as well as the average value E(X).

The number of matches remaining in a box is between 1 and N. Where A is a match taken from one box, and B a match taken from the other, an elementary event corresponding to k matches remaining in the box B for example, the other box being empty, is a word of the form $BBABAA...BA$ that is $2N - k$ long with the letter A appearing N times and the letter B $N - k$ times, with an A being the last letter. With this succession of independent events, all with probability 1 / 2, the probability of this elementary event is $(1/2)^{2N-k}$. The number of such elementary events is also the number of ways of placing $N - 1$ letter As in a word $2N - k - 1$ long, i.e. $C_{2N-k-1}^{\ N-1}$. There are also as many elementary events where it is box B that is empty. With these events being incompatible, their probabilities are added up:

$$p(X = k) = 2\ C_{2N-k-1}^{\ N-1}\ (1/2)^{2N-k} = C_{2N-k-1}^{\ N-1}\ (1/2)^{2N-k-1}$$

To get $E(X)$, let us first of all look for a relation between $p(X = k)$ and $p(X = k - 1)$. Taking their quotient, we find after simplification that:

$$p(X = k) / p(X = k - 1) = 2\,(N - k + 1) / (2N - k)$$

$$(2N - k)\, p(X = k) = 2\,(N - k + 1)\, p(X = k - 1) \text{ for } k > 1$$

or even:

$$2N\, p(X = k) - k\, p(X = k) = 2N\, p(X = k - 1) - 2(k - 1)\, p(X = k - 1)$$

Next, let us add all these equalities for k going from 2 to N member-by-member. Taking into consideration the fact that $\sum_{k=1}^{n} p(X = k) = 1$ and $\sum_{k=1}^{n} k\, p(X = k) = E(X)$, there remains:

$$2N(1 - p(X = 1)) - (E(X) - p(X = 1))$$
$$= 2N\,(1 - p(X = N)) - 2\,(E(X) - Np(X = N))$$

i.e.:

$$E(X) = (2N - 1)\, p(X = 1)$$
$$= (2N - 1)\, C_{2(N-1)}^{N-1}\, (1 / 4)^{N-1}.$$

Applying Stirling's formula $n! \simeq \sqrt{2\pi n}(\frac{n}{e})^n$ valid for sufficiently large n, we get:

$$E(X) \simeq 2\sqrt{\frac{N}{\pi}}\,.$$

28.3. The tunnel

A mobile object – an automobile for example – drives through a tunnel at constant speed. At each stage in time it swerves to the left or to the right at random. The tunnel is $2N$ wide and at the start the car is in the middle, at a distance N from each wall of the tunnel (see Figure 28.1).

As the unit of length, we took the movement (horizontal or vertical) of the vehicle at each stage in time, with each swerve corresponding to a diagonal movement in the tunnel, on one side or the other.

We want to find what distance the mobile object traverses before crashing into a wall of the tunnel. The random variable X_N corresponds to the time (or the horizontal distance traversed) until the collision with one of the walls of the tunnel.

This problem can be posed in two other ways. A particle starts off located in the middle of a *2N*-long segment with unit gradations. At each stage in time, it traverses a gradation, with equiprobability, from one side or the other. The extremities of the segment are absorbing barriers, in the sense that the movement stops when one of the extremities is touched.

This movement is the projection on a vertical of the journey of the automobile in the tunnel.

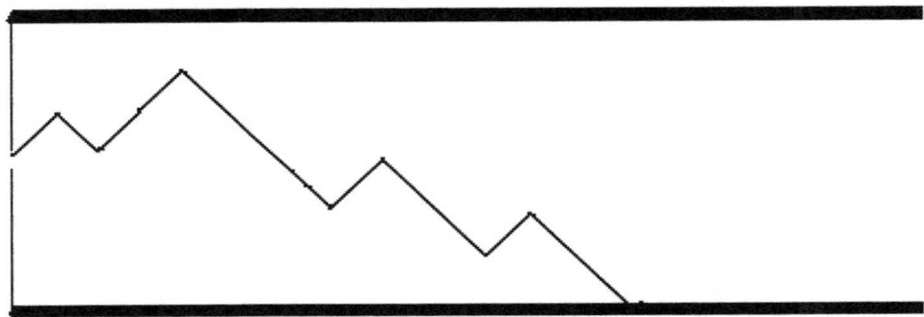

Figure 28.1. *Movement of the vehicle in a tunnel until crashing into one of its sides*

We can view the problem more simply still: a particle is located at extremity O of a segment with gradations 1, 2, 3, …N.

At each stage in time, the particle traverses a gradation to the right or left. Extremity O of the segment plays the role of reflecting barrier, whereas the other extremity N is an absorbing barrier where the particle's route ends (see Figure 28.2).

Let us write the system of equations associated with the corresponding transition graph (see Figure 28.2 below) for a N-length segment:

$$S_0 = 1 + (1 / 2)\, z\, S_1$$

$$S_1 = z\, S_0 + (1 / 2)\, z\, S_2$$

$$S_2 = (1 / 2)\, z\, S_1 + (1 / 2)\, z\, S_3$$

....

$$S_{N-2} = (1 / 2)\, z\, S_{N-2} + (1 / 2)\, z\, S_{N-1}$$

$$S_{N-1} = (1 / 2)\, z\, S_{N-1}$$

$$S_N = (1 / 2)\, z\, S_{N-1}$$

S_N being the generating function associated with X.

Between the first two equations and the last two, the others present the same shape, which will enable us to obtain a general formula.

Let us deal with the system going down, from the first equation, which gives S_0 in relation to S_1:

$$S_0 = 1 + (1 / 2)\, z\, S_1$$

–if $N = 2$, we also have $S_1 = zS_0$, and $S_2 = (1 / 2)\, z\, S_1$, hence:

$$S_2 = (1 / 2)\, z^2 / P_2 \text{ with } P_2 = 1 - (1 / 2)\, z^2$$

– if $N > 2$, the first two equations are always the same. The second one is expressed $S_1 = z\, S_0 + (1 / 2)\, z\, S_2$. Hence with the first equation:

$$S_1 = z\, (1 + (1/2)\, z\, S_1) + (1/2)\, z\, S_2$$

which is of the form:

$$S_1\, P_2 = z + (1/2)\, z\, P_1\, S_2$$

with:

$$P_1 = 1 \text{ and } P_2 = 1 - (1/2)\, z^2$$

– if $N = 3$, we deduce from it that:

$$s_3 = (1 / 4)\, z^3 / P_3, \text{ with } P_3 = 1 - (3 / 4)\, z^2$$

– if $N > 3$, the third equation is always:

$$S_2 = (1 / 2)\, z\, S_1 + (1 / 2)\, z\, S_3$$

hence with the preceding equation:

$$S_2 = z\, (z + (1 / 2)\, z\, P_1\, S_2) / P_2 + (1 / 2)\, z\, S_3$$

or even:

$$S_2\,P_3 = (1\,/\,2)\,z^2 + (1\,/\,2)\,z\,P_2\,S_3$$

with:

$$P_3 = P_2 - (1\,/\,4)\,z^2\,P_1 = 1 - (3\,/\,4)\,z^2$$

– when $N = 4$, we deduce from it that:

$$S_4 = (1\,/\,8)\,z^4\,/\,P_4$$

with:

$$P_4 = P_3 - (1\,/\,4)\,z^2\,P_2$$

i.e.: $S_4 = (1\,/\,8)\,z^4\,/\,(1 - z^2 + (1\,/\,8)\,z^4)$

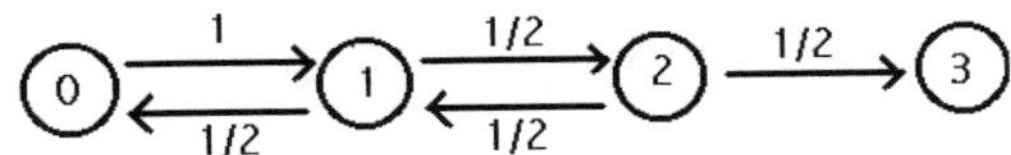

Figure 28.2. *The graded segment where the movement takes place, with origin O as the reflecting barrier (top); and the transition graph when N = 3 (bottom)*

This can be generalized. For $N > k$, we find:

$$S_{k-1}\,P_k = (1\,/\,2^{\,k-2})\,z^{k-1} + (1\,/\,2)\,z\,P_{k-1}\,S_k$$

and the generating function associated with X for a segment N long is:

$$S_N(z) = (1\,/\,2^{N-1})\,z^N\,/\,P_N$$

where polynomial P_k obeys the recurrence relation:

$$P_k = P_{k-1} - (1\,/\,4)\,z^2\,P_{k-2}$$

with $P_1 = 1$ and $P_2 = 1 - (1\,/\,2)\,z^2$ at the start.

The generating function associated with X for a N-length segment N is also expressed:

$$S_N(z) = z^N / Q_N(z), \text{ with } Q_N = 2^{N-1} P_N,$$

verifying that:

$$Q_N(1) = 1$$

In liaison with P_k, the polynomial Q_k obeys the recurrence relation:

$$Q_k = 2\, Q_{k-1} - z^2\, Q_{k-2}$$

with:

$$Q_1 = 1 \text{ and } Q_2 = 2 - z^2$$

By derivation:

$$Q'_k = 2\, Q'_{k-1} - z^2\, Q'_{k-2} - 2\, z\, Q_{k-2} \text{ and } Q'_k(1) = 2\, Q'_{k-1}(1) - Q'_{k-2}(1) - 2$$

The average duration $E_N(X)$ of the movement is:

$$E_N(X) = S'_N(1) = N + Q'_N(1)$$

This average value in turn obeys the recurrence relation:

$$E_N(X) = 2\, E_{N-1}(X) - E_{N-2}(X) + 2$$

with:

$$E_1(X) = 1 \text{ and } E_2(X) = 4$$

We deduce by immediate verification that:

$$E_N(X) = N^2$$

Results obtained on the computer are given in Figure 28.3, notably for $N = 3$, which we will now study in detail.

28.3.1. *Dealing with the specific case where $N = 3$*

In the case where $N = 3$, the previous method gives the generating function associated with random variable X_3, corresponding to the number of stages of time it takes to arrive at the endpoint of abscissa 3, namely:

$$S_3(z) = (1 / 4)\, z^3 / (1 - (3 / 4)\, z^2)$$

Stopping the process on graduation 3 corresponds to an odd number of moves. Developing the formula leads to the probability:

$$p(X_3 = 2k + 1) = (1 / 4)\,(3 / 4)^{k-1} = (1 / 3)\,(3 / 4)^k, \text{ with } k > 0, \text{ and } E(X_3) = 9$$

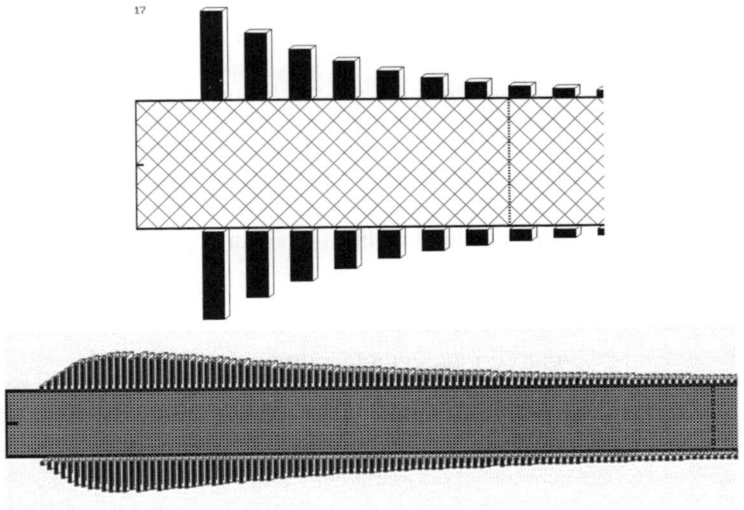

Figure 28.3. *A tunnel 2n = 6 long with vertical bars indicating the probabilities of collision with the sides. There is a 90% chance of collision when the length reaches 17 (vertical dotted line) (top). Where N = 10 in a tunnel 20 units wide with probabilities of collision and the rectangular zone units 206 long where the probability of collision reaches 90% (bottom)*

We end up with the same result by directly dealing with the weighted adjacency matrix of the transition graph, i.e.:

$$A = \begin{bmatrix} 0 & 1 & 0 & 0 \\ 1/2 & 0 & 1/2 & 0 \\ 0 & 1/2 & 0 & 1/2 \\ 0 & 0 & 0 & 0 \end{bmatrix}$$

Next we calculate the determinant $|I - xA| = 1 - (3 / 4)\,x^2$.

The generating function associated with the probabilities of going from 0 to 3 in a certain number of moves being:

$$det\,|I - xA, 3, 0| \,/\, |I - xA| = (1 / 4)\,x^3 / (1 - (3 / 4)\,x^2)$$

after all calculations, which again gives the result previously obtained.

We can also find the probabilities of going from 0 to 0, corresponding to the formal series:

$$det\,|I - xA, 0, 0| \,/\, |I - xA| = (1 - (1/4)\,x^2) \,/\, (1 - (3/4)\,x^2)$$

$$= (1 - (1/4)\,x^2)\,(1 + (3/4)\,x^2 + (3/4)^2\,x^4 + \ldots)$$

which is series S_0, obtained just above. We deduce from this that the probability of going from 0 to 0 in $2k$ moves, with this number of moves being even, is:

$$(3/4)^k - (1/4)\,(3/4)^{k-1} = (1/2)\,(3/4)^{k-1} \text{ for } k > 0 \text{ and } 1 \text{ for } k = 0$$

We could similarly obtain the probabilities of ending up at abscissa points 1 or 2 in a certain number of moves.

28.3.2. *Variation with an absorbing boundary and another method*

Still for $N = 3$, let us now consider the boundary of abscissa 3 to be absorbing in the sense where the particle, once it has arrived at 3, does not end up there again over time. This changes the transition graph, which becomes the one in Figure 28.4.

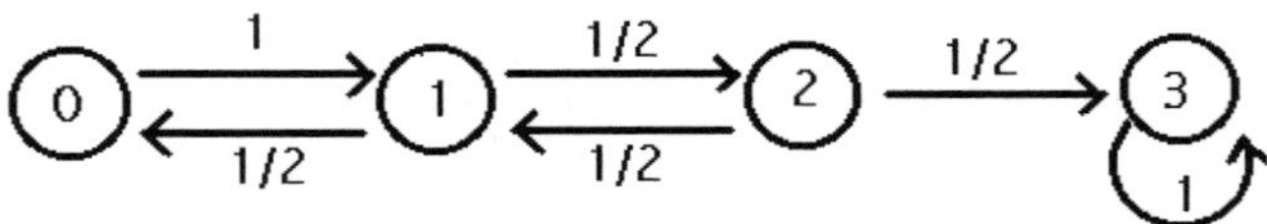

Figure 28.4. *Transition graph with absorbing boundary*

Let $p_i(n)$ be the probability, having started at O, of arriving at the point of abscissa i in n moves, with n taking values from 0 to $+\infty$.

The weighted adjacency matrix is:

$$B = \begin{bmatrix} 0 & 1 & 0 & 0 \\ 1/2 & 0 & 1/2 & 0 \\ 0 & 1/2 & 0 & 1/2 \\ 0 & 0 & 0 & 1 \end{bmatrix}$$

Let us introduce the probability vector: $\boldsymbol{U}_n = (p_0(n), p_1(n), p_2(n), p_3(n))^t$. This is in fact a column vector, and the sum of its four terms is equal to 1, whatever $n \geq 0$ may be. Total probability formula gives the recurrence relation:

$$\boldsymbol{U}_{n+1} = B' \, \boldsymbol{U}_n$$

where B' is the transpose of B, hence the explicit form:

$$\boldsymbol{U}_n = B'^n \boldsymbol{U}_0$$

with $\boldsymbol{U}_0$, the column vector with (1, 0, 0, 0) as its transpose.

The eigenvalues of B' are 1, 0, $\pm\sqrt{2}/2$, and the associated eigenvectors are:

$$(1, 0, -2, 1), (0, 0, 0, 1), (1, \sqrt{3}, 1, -2-\sqrt{3}), (1, -\sqrt{3}, 1, -2+\sqrt{3})$$

Passage matrix P assumes these eigenvectors are column vectors. We have $B' = P\ D\ P^{-1}$, hence $B'^n = P\ D^n\ P^{-1}$, with D being the diagonal matrix of the eigenvalues. This enables us to calculate the probability vector $\boldsymbol{U}_n$, which distinguishing two cases depending on the parity of n, finally gives:

$$p_0(2n') = (2 / 3)\ (3 / 4)^{n'} \text{ for } n' > 0 \text{ and } p_0(0) = 1$$

$$p_1(2n'+1) = (3 / 4)^{n'}$$

$$p_2(2n') = p_0(2n') \text{ with } n' > 0$$

$$p_3(2n') = 1 - (3 / 4)^{n'-1} \text{ for } n' > 1$$

and:

$$p_3(2n'+1) = 1 - (3 / 4)^{n'} \text{for } n' > 0$$

These results enable us to return to the previous case, where we waited for the first arrival at abscissa point 3. The probability arriving at 3 for the first time after $2K + 1$ moves is the probability of arriving at 3 in $2K + 1$ moves and having arrived at 2 in $2K$ moves, i.e.:

$$(1 / 2)\ p_2(2k) = (1 / 3)\ (3 / 4)^{k} = (1 / 4)\ (3 / 4)^{k-1}.$$

28.3.3. *Complementary exercise: drunken man's walk on a straight line, with resting time*

A particle – sometimes considered to be a drunken man – circulates on interval [-*N, N*], with *N* being a positive natural integer (see Figure 28.5). At each stage in time, the drunken man makes either a (unit) step to the right, or to the left, or remains at rest. Each of these three events has the probability of 1 / 3. At the start, the drunken man is at origin *O*. He stops when he reaches the boundaries *N* or -N (absorbing boundaries). Random variable *X* is the duration of the experiment, and random variable *Z* corresponds to the resting time. We want to find out *E*(*X*) and *E*(*Z*), that is to say the average duration of the game, and the average resting time.

This problem can also be seen as the movement of a vehicle in a tunnel, with three possibilities of movement at each stage of time – either diagonally upwards or downwards, or horizontally.

28.3.3.1. *Dealing with the case where N = 2*

The transition graph consists of three states corresponding to the distance of the particle in relation to point *O*. For random variable *X*, each arrow of the transition graph, with its associated probability *p*, intervenes through *pz* in the generating function. The system of equations that results from the graph (see Figure 28.5) is:

$$S_0 = 1 + (1 / 3)\, z\, S_0 + (1 / 3)\, z\, S_1$$

$$S_1 = (2 / 3)\, z\, S_0 + (1 / 3)\, zS_1$$

$$S_2 = (1 / 3)\, z\, S_1$$

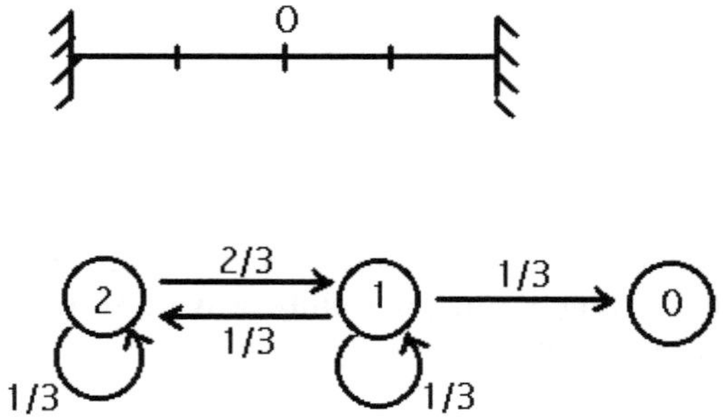

Figure 28.5. *The drunken man's walk between two boundaries in the case where N = 2 (top); and the corresponding transition graph (bottom)*

We find the generating function associated with X is:

$$S_2(z)= \frac{z^2}{0.5\,(9-6z-z^2)}$$

Developing this, we get:

$$p(X=2)=2/9, p(X=3)=4/27, p(X=4)=10/81, \text{etc.}$$

by deriving:

$$E(X)=6$$

For random variable Z, each arrow of the transition graph, with its associated probability p, intervenes through pz when the particle remains at rest, otherwise it is at p. The system of equations becomes:

$$S_0=1+(1/3)\,z\,S_0+(1/3)\,S_1$$

$$S_1=(2/3)\,S_0+(1/3)\,z\,S_1$$

$$S_2=(1/3)\,S_1$$

We find the generating function associated with Z is:

$$S_2(z)=\frac{1}{0.5\,(7-6z+z^2)}$$

This gives:

$$p(Z=0)=2/7, p(Z=1)=12/49, p(Z=2)=29/49, \text{etc.}$$

and:

$$E(Z)=2$$

This last result was predictable, since a third of the time on average is spent at rest, hence $E(Z)=(1/3)\,E(X)$.

28.3.3.2. *General case*

By the same procedure as the one used previously, we can show that for a positive N the generating function associated with X is:

$$S_N(z) = z^N / P_N(z)$$

where $P_N(z)$ is a polynomial verifying the recurrence relation:

$$P_N(z) = (3 - z)\, P_{N-1}(z) - z^2\, P_{N-2}(z)$$

with $P_0(z) = 1$ at the start and:

$$P_1(z) = 3 / 2 - (1 / 2)\, z$$

We can verify that:

$$P_2(z) = (9 / 2) - 3z - (1 / 2)\, z^2$$

$$P_3(z) = 27 / 2 - (27 / 2)\, z + z^3, \text{ etc.}$$

Now let us calculate the expectation $E(X)$. By derivation:

$$P'_N(z) = (3 - z)\, P'_{N-1}(z) - P_{N-1}(z) - 2\, z\, P_{N-2}(z) - z^2\, P'_{N-2}(z)$$

hence:

$$P'_n(1) = -3 + 2\, P'_{N-1}(1) - P'_{N-2}(1)$$

$$E_N(X) = N - P'_N(1) = N + 3 - 2\, P'_{N-1}(1) + P'_{N-2}(1)$$

$$= N + 3 - 2(N - 1 - E_{N-1}(X)) + N - 2 - E_{N-2}(X)$$

$$= 3 + 2\, E_{N-1}(X) - E_{N-2}(X)$$

We obtain the (third order linear and non-homogeneous) recurrence relation $E_N(X) = 2\, E_{N-1}(X) - E_{N-2}(X) + 3$, with $E_1(X) = 3 / 2$ and $E_2(X) = 6$ at the start. We verify that $E_N(X) = 3/2)\, N^2$ is the solution.

Finally:

$$E_N(X) = (3 / 2)\, N^2 \text{ and } E_N(Z) = (1 / 2)\, N^2$$

We experimentally verify (see Figure 28.6) that the length of the tunnel where the probability of collision reaches 90% is 28 for $N = 3$ (instead of 17 when the vehicle only swerves, without rectilinear movement, as was the case in section 28.3.1) and 308 for $N = 10$ (instead of 206).

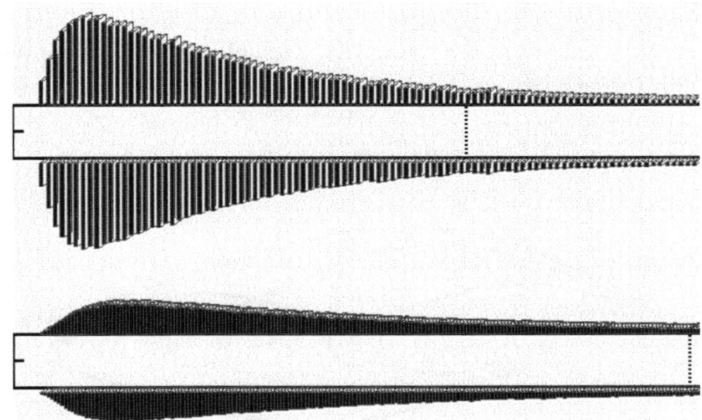

Figure 28.6. *Probabilities of collision in the case of diagonal movements (top); and with an extra horizontal movement (bottom)*

28.4. Repetitive draws from a box

Here n balls numbered from 1 to n are placed in a box. We draw one ball at random, with equiprobability, and repeatedly draw balls according to the rule of the following game: each time we draw a ball, with number k, in addition to ball number k we remove all of the balls with a number greater than k (we keep those whose number is between 1 and $k - 1$). We stop when ball 1 is drawn, i.e. when there are no longer any balls in the box. The random variable corresponds to the number of draws made (see also [LEN 98b]).

Another way of seeing the problem is the following: a tree trunk is placed horizontally, with n notches, where notch 1 is leftmost and notch n on the right. We split the tree trunk at random where a notch is found, each time suppressing the right hand part. Repeating the process, the remaining tree trunk becomes shorter and shorter, until we split it at notch number 1.

Returning to the example of balls in a box. The number of draws (splits) is n at most. The states of the transition graph are written from the initial state n to the final state 0, and they correspond to the number of balls remaining in the box. When we arrive at state k, we have just drawn ball $k + 1$. For $n = 4$, for example, we get the transition graph in Figure 28.7, where the arrows are indexed by the number of the ball drawn.

A drawing sequence can, for example, be 421 or even 31, with these words always ending in 1. We can read these words by following some of the arrows that lead from the initial state to the final state. Now let us involve the probabilities. The arrows originating from state i, except for $i = 0$, all have a probability of $1 / i$. In this context, for example for $n = 4$, the word 421 – which means that we passed through states 4310 – has the probability $1 / 4 . 1 / 3 . 1 / 1$, and the word 31 (or 420 for the states) has the probability $1 / 4 . 1 / 2$, which gives the respective probabilities for these words as $1 / 12$ and $1 / 8$, since the probabilities are multiplied.

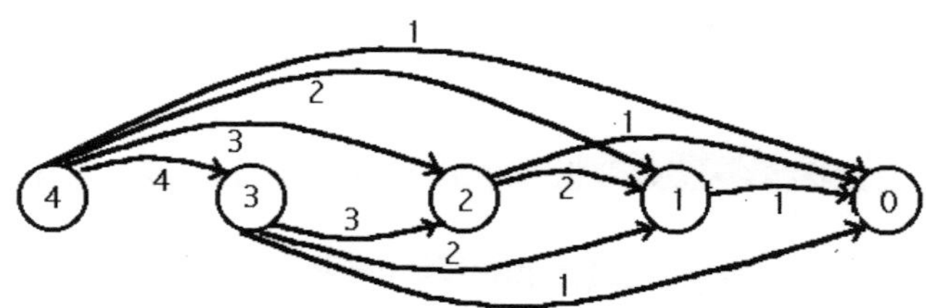

Figure 28.7. *Transition graph of successive draws*

More specifically, let us introduce variables $z_1, z_2, \ldots, z_n$, with each arrow going from state i to state j. Let us associate not only its probability $1 / i$ but also the product $(1 / i)\, z_{j+1}$, where $j + 1$ is the number of the ball drawn, since we get state j.

In these conditions, for $n = 4$, the word 321 is converted into the three-variable monomial $(1 / 4)\, z_3\, (1 / 2)\, z_2\, z_1 = (1 / 8)\, z_3 z_2 z_1$, where we find its probability is $1 / 8$, as well as the numbers of the balls successively drawn.

Therefore the transition graph gives the system of equations in the specific case where $n = 4$:

$$S_4 = 1$$

$$S_3 = (1 / 4)\, z_4\, S_4 = (1 / 4)\, z_4$$

$$S_2 = (1 / 4)\, z_3\, S_4 + (1 / 3)\, z_3\, S_3 = (1 / 4)\,(\,1 + (1 / 3)\, z_4)\, z_3$$

$$S_1 = (1 / 4)\, z_2\, S_4 + (1 / 3)\, z_2\, S_3 + (1 / 2)\, z_2\, S_2$$

$$= (1 / 4)\, z_2\,(1 + (1 / 3)\, z_4) + (1 / 2)\, z_2\,(1 / 4)\, z_3\,(1 + (1 / 3)\, z_4)$$

$$= (1 / 4)\,(1 + (1 / 3)\, z_4)\,(1 + (1 / 2)\, z_3)\, z_2$$

$$S_0 = (1 / 4)\, z_1\, S_4 + (1 / 3)\, z_1\, S_3 + (1 / 2)\, z_1\, S_2 + z_1\, S_1$$

$$= (1 / 4)\, z_1\,(1 + (1 / 3)\, z_4)\,(1 + (1 / 2)\, z_3) + z_1\, S_1$$

$$= (1 / 4)\,(1 + (1 / 3)\, z_4)\,(1 + (1 / 2)\, z_3)\,(1 + z_2)\, z_1$$

Note that to get S_0, which contains one more term than S_1, we take S_1 changing z_2 into z_1 and add the extra term z_1 S_1, which enables the final factorization. This also goes for any line, and works in the general case. Developing S_0 will give monomials, such as (1 / 4) (1 / 3) z_4 (1 / 2) z_3 z_1 for example, which correspond to drawing balls 431, where this event has a probability of 1 / 24. In the general case we have the system:

$$S_n = 1$$

$$S_{n-1} = (1 / n)\, z_n\, S_n = (1 / n)\, z_n$$

$$S_{n-2} = (1 / n)\, z_{n-1}\, S_n + (1 / (n-1))\, z_{n-1}\, S_{n-1} = (1 / n)\,(1 + (1 / (n-1))\, z_n)\, z_{n-1}$$

$$S_{n-3} = (1 / n)\, z_{n-2}\, S_n + (1 / (n-1))\, z_{n-2}\, S_{n-1} + (1 / (n-2))\, z_{n-2}\, S_{n-2}$$

$$= (1 / n)\,(1 + (1 / (n-1))\, z_n)(1 - (1 / (n-2))\, z_{n-1})\, z_{n-2}$$

...

$$S_0(z_1, z_2, \ldots, z_n) = (1 / n)\,(1 + (1 / (n-1))\, z_n)\,(1 + (1 / (n-2))\, z_{n-1})$$

$$(1 + (1 / (n-3))\, z_{n-2}) \ldots (1 + z_2)\, z_1$$

Developing this polynomial, $S_0(z_1, z_2, \ldots, z_n)$ gives monomials weighted by probabilities that represent all the words associated with balls being drawn. Each word is obtained by taking one of the two terms of each factor between parentheses, with the number 1 corresponding to the neutral element for multiplication-concatenation.

28.4.1. *Probability law for the number of draws*

Let X be the random variable equal to the number of draws made until ball 1 is drawn. X is between 1 and n. In the previous generating function this refers to replacing each variable z_i with z. Actually, when we develop the polynomial with one single variable z, thus obtained as a sum of the monomials with the concatenation becoming multiplication, exponent k of a z^k term will correspond exactly to the number of draws, and its coefficient will indicate the probability $p(X = k)$. From this we deduce the generating function associated with X:

$$F(z) = (1 + z / (n-1))\,(1 + z / (n-2)) \ldots (1 + z / 2)\,(1 + z)\, z / n$$

$$= \frac{1}{n!} z\,(z+1)(z+2)\ldots(z+n-1)$$

We deduce from it, by calculating the derivative $F'(1)$, that:

$$E(X) = \sum_{k=1}^{n} \frac{1}{k}$$

This average value is close to logarithm ln n, for large n.

28.4.2. *Extra questions*

a) A player bets that for $n = 6$ balls the game has more chances of stopping in $k = 2$ moves (or less) than continuing. Show that he is right.

It is enough to determine the terms of the first and second degree of z in $F(z)$. We find $(1 / 6) z + (1 / 6) z^2 (1 + 1 / 2 + 1 / 3 + 1 / 4 + 1 / 5)$. Making $z = 1$, this gives the probability that the game will stop in two moves at most, i.e. here 0.547, which considerably exceeds 1 / 2.

b) Next, the player bets that with $n = 16$ balls, the game has more chances of stopping in $k = 3$ turns at most than continuing. He also bets that with $n = 50$ balls, the game has more chances of stopping in $k = 4$ moves at most than continuing. Is he still correct? For write a program to perform an experimental check on a computer.

The program is written in the following way:

```
cumulS=0; randomize();
for(try=1; try<=NE; try++)
   /* We carry out a large number NE of experiments */
  { draw=N+1;
   for(i=1; i<=K; i++)   /* We carry out K draws and we have N balls */
     { draw=random(draw-1)+1;  if (draw==1) break;  }
   if (i<=K) cumulS++;
  }
probaS=(double) cumulS/(double) NE; printf("\n%3.10lf", probaS);
```

In this way we notice that the player was right in both cases.

28.4.3. *Probability of getting ball number k during the game*

Let Z_k be a random variable with k between 1 and n, with $Z_k = 1$ when ball number k is obtained during the draws, and $Z_k = 0$ when it is not. In function $S_0(z_1, z_2, \ldots, z_n)$ found previously, this refers to keeping only the words containing ball k, i.e. all of the words containing variable z_k. Moreover, z_k only appears in term $1 + (1 / (k-1))\, z_k$, except for $k = 1$ where we immediately have $p(Z_1 = 1) = 1$. We deduce from it that:

$$S_0 (z_1, z_2, \ldots, z_n)$$

$$= A\,(z_2, z_3, \ldots, z_{k-1}, z_{k+1}, \ldots, z_n) + A(z_2, z_3, \ldots z_{k-1}, z_{k+1}, \ldots, z_n)\, z_k / (k-1)$$

The probability sought $p(Z_k = 1)$ is none other than $A(1, 1,\ldots,1) / (k-1)$.

But we know that $S_0(1, 1, \ldots, 1) = 1$, hence:

$$A(1, 1, \ldots, 1) + A(1, 1, \ldots, 1) /(k-1) = 1$$

$$A(1, 1, \ldots, 1) = (k-1) / k$$

and:

$$p(Z_k = 1) = 1 / k$$

Note that this probability is independent of the initial number of balls n. This enables us to again find $E(X)$, where X corresponds to the number of draws.

Actually:

$$X = Z_1 + Z_2 + Z_3 + \ldots. + Z_n$$

since the sum of Z_k gives the number of balls drawn. We deduce from it that:

$$E(X) = E(Z_1) + E(Z_2) + \ldots + E(Z_n) = 1 + 1/2 + 1/3 + \ldots + 1/n.$$

28.4.4. *Probability law associated with the number of balls drawn*

Y is the random variable corresponding to numbers obtained in a succession of draws. The associated generating function $G(z)$ is obtained by replacing each variable z_k with z^k, in the generating function of weighted words, namely $S_0(z_1, z_2, \ldots, z_n)$:

$$G(z) = (1 / n)\,(1 + z^n / (n-1))\,(1 + z^{n-1} / (n-2))\ \ldots.\ (1 + z^3 / 2)\,(1 + z^2)\,z$$

The expectation $E(Y)$ is equal to $G'(1)$. We know that the derivative of a product is obtained by successively deriving each factor, such as in:

$$(u\,v\,w)' = u'\,v\,w + u\,v'\,w + u\,v\,w'$$

In this case, the derivative of factor $(1 + z^k / (k-1))$ is equal to $k / (k-1)$ when $z = 1$, i.e. the value of this same factor for $z = 1$. It is the same for the last factor z. Each one of the n terms of the derivation is equal to 1. Finally $E(Y) = n$.

28.4.5. *Complementary exercise: variation of the previous problem*

Here n balls numbered from 1 to n are placed in a box. We repeatedly draw balls according to the following conditions: if ball number k is drawn, we then replace it in the box but remove all the balls with a number greater than k. The game stops when ball number 1 is drawn for the first time.

The transition graph, for example for $n = 4$, is represented in Figure 28.8. The states correspond to the number of balls remaining. Let each arrow from state i to state j be associated with the product $(1 / i)\,z^j$, where $1 / i$ is the probability and j is the number of the ball drawn. We obtain a system of equations. For example for $n = 4$:

$$S_4 = 1 + (1 / 4)\,z_4\,S_4$$
$$= 1 / (1 - (1 / 4)\,z_4)$$

$$S_3 = (1 / 4)\,z_3\,S_4 + (1 / 3)\,z_3\,S_3$$
$$= (1 / 4)\,z_3 / ((1 - (1 / 4)\,z_4)\,(1 - (1 / 3)\,z_3))$$

$$S_2 = (1 / 4)\,z_2\,S_4 + (1 / 3)\,z_2\,S_3 + (1 / 2)\,z_2\,S_2$$
$$= (1 / 4)\,z_2 / ((1 - (1 / 4)\,z_4)\,(1 - (1 / 3)\,z_3)(1 - (1 / 2)\,z_2))$$

$$S_1 = (1 / 4)\,z_1\,S_4 + (1 / 3)\,z_1\,S_3 + (1 / 2)\,z_1\,S_2$$
$$= (1 / 4)\,z_1 / ((1 - (1 / 4)\,z_4)\,(1 - (1 / 3)\,z_3)(1 - (1 / 2)\,z_2))$$

The generating function of the weighted words is:

$$S_1(z_1, z_2, z_3, z_4) = \frac{z_1}{4(1 - (1/4)\,z_4)(1 - (1/3)\,z_3)(1 - (1/2)\,z_2)}$$

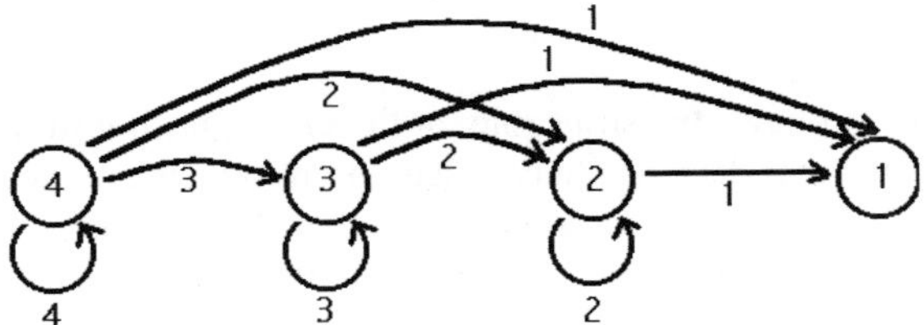

Figure 28.8. *Transition graph for a box with four balls*

In the general case, for the same reasons we find:

$$S_1(z_1,\ldots,z_n) = \frac{z_1}{n\,(1-\frac{1}{n}z_n)(1-\frac{1}{n-1}z_{n-1})\ \ldots\ (1-\frac{1}{2}z_2)}$$

$$= \frac{z_1}{\frac{1}{(n-1)!}(n-z_n)(n-1-z_{n-1})\ \ldots\ (2-z_2)}$$

Now let X be the random variable corresponding to the number of draws during the game. This variable takes all integers from 1 to infinity. Its generating function is:

$$F(z) = \frac{z}{\frac{1}{(n-1)!}(n-z)(n-1-z)\ \ldots\ (2-z)}$$

We deduce the average duration of the game from this:

$$E(X) = 1 + 1 + 1/2 + 1/3 + \ldots + 1/(n-1)$$

Taking random variable Y as the sum of numbers drawn during the game, we similarly find the generating function:

$$G(z) = \frac{z}{n(1-\frac{1}{n}z^n)(1-\frac{1}{n-1}z^{n-1})\ \ldots\ (1-\frac{1}{2}z^2)}$$

and:

$$E(Y) = 1 + 2/1 + 3/2 + 4/3 + \ldots + n/(n-1).$$

28.5. The sect

An organization obeys this strict rule: at the end of each unit of time (a year for example), if a member has not succeeded in introducing a new member he is excluded, and if he introduces a new member he remains. At the start, the organization has n members. We assume that the probability of finding a new member is p.[1]

For $n = 1$, the evolution of the group is represented using a binary tree, where we distinguish the non-terminal nodes associated with probability p, where two branches start, and the terminal nodes with probability $q = 1 - p$, which have no descendants. For $n > 1$ the evolution of the group is represented using a forest with n trees. Thanks to the independence of the evolution of these n trees, the average values obtained for $n > 1$ and $n = 1$ are the same, as well as the variances. Henceforth we will assume that $n = 1$ with a unique tree (see Figure 28.9).

Each node of the tree at one level corresponds to a unit of time. A non-terminal node, associated with one person at a certain moment in time, and having probability p, splits up: on the left, the same person continues to be a member of the organization, and on the right the new member appears. A terminal node (without descendants) with probability $q = 1 -$ p, corresponds to the last stage of time in which a person is found in the group, before having to leave.

Let S be the size of the tree – i.e. its number of nodes – and L the lifespan of the organization – i.e. the height of the tree increased by 1, or even the number of levels of the tree, starting at the top with level 1. The lifespan of an individual in the group is obtained by counting the number of nodes in a diagonal branch in the tree. The number of terminal nodes is also the number of people P having belonged to the group. As there is always one more terminal node than non-terminal node in this type of tree, $P = (S + 1) / 2$.

28.5.1. *Can the group last forever?*

Let Q be the probability of eventual disappearance of the group for lack of followers. Let us take the founder of the group, with the probability Q of future disappearance.

1. In another context this problem, in rudimentary form, can simulate the spread of an epidemic (see [LEN 98a]).

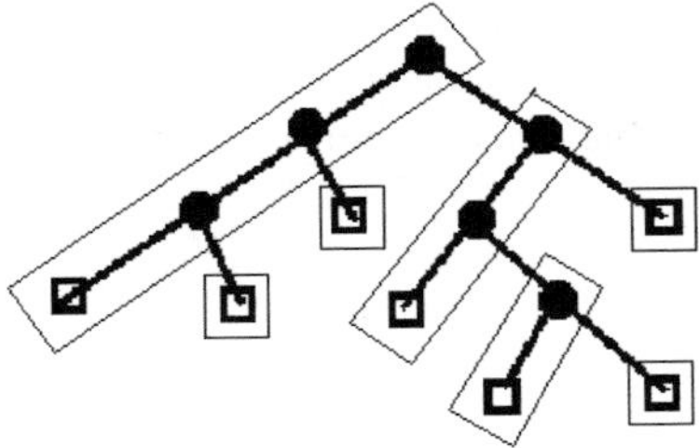

Figure 28.9. *An example of evolution of the group: the size of the tree is $S = 13$, its lifespan is $L = 5$. The group altogether had $P = 7$ people, having spent 4, 3, 2, 1, 1, 1, 1 years in the group respectively*

Either it does not find any followers (with probability q) and the probability of disappearance of the group is equal to 1, or it finds one follower (with probability p) and we have two people at the next stage in time. Each follower, with his potential sub-tree, has the probability Q of eventual disappearance from the group. Thanks to the total probability formula, we get the recurrence relation:

$$Q = q + p\,Q^2$$

This quadratic equation assumes two solutions: 1 or q / p. If $p \leq 1 / 2$, the only possible solution is 1, otherwise q / p exceeds 1. On the other hand, if $p > 1 / 2$ the other solution q / p prevails: when p is close to 1, the probability of the group disappearing is close to 0, and when p is close to 0.5 the probability of the group eventually disappearing is close to 1. For reasons of continuity, the probability of eventual disappearance of the group is q / p. Thus the group will have probability 1 of having a finite lifespan when $p \leq 1 / 2$, and this probability is q / p when $p > 1 / 2$.

In what follows, we will assume that the organization has a limited lifespan, i.e. $p \leq 1 / 2$ and even $p < 1 / 2$.

28.5.2. *Probability law of the size of the tree*

Let the size S of the organization's tree be the random variable. Each node has a probability associated with it. This probability is p in the case of a non-terminal node, and q for a terminal node. The probability we will have a certain tree with S nodes is that of all the independent elementary events, each having probabilities p and q, with the first numbering $P - 1$ and the second numbering P. Hence the result: the probability of having a tree of size S (with $P = (S + 1) / 2$) is $p^{P-1}\, q^P$.

Let us recall that the number of binary trees with $P-1$ non-terminal nodes is the Catalan number c_{P-1}. Trees of the same size all have the same probability. The sum of probabilities for all possible trees is 1 for $p \leq 1/2$. We must have:

$$\sum_{P>0} c_{P-1} p^{P-1} q^{P} = 1$$

Let us verify this:

$$\sum_{P>0} c_{P-1} p^{P-1} q^{P} = \sum_{k \geq 0} c_k p^k q^{k+1} = q \sum c_k x^k$$

by postulating $x = pq$

$$= q\,(1 - \sqrt{1-4pq}\,)\,/\,(2pq) = (1 - (1 - 2p))\,/\,(2p) = 1$$

knowing that the generating function of Catalan numbers is:

$$C(x) = (1 - \sqrt{1-4x}\,)\,/\,(2x).$$

28.5.3. *Average tree size*

Here is a first demonstration. Let S_a be the average size of the tree. Either the starting node does not split up, and the size of the tree remains 1, or it splits up and its average size is $1 + 2S_a$. We now need to weight these two events that form a complete system by their respective probabilities q and p, which thanks to total probability formula always give:

$$S_a = q + p\,(1 + 2S_a)$$

We draw from it that:

$$S_a = 1\,/\,(2q - 1)$$

Note that for $p = 1/2$ the average size of the tree is infinite, while the probability the tree will eventually stop growing is 1.

Thus, for $p < 1/2$, the average size S_m of the trees is $1 / (2q - 1)$.

Let us give a second demonstration. P_a is the average number of terminal nodes (or people having belonged to the group). The lifespan of each of these people in the group obeys a geometric law with parameter q. They have an average lifespan of $1 / q$. There are P_a people. Hence the relation:

$$P_a .\ 1 / q = S_a$$

and as $P_a = (S_a + 1) / 2$, the following results:

$$S_a = 1 / (2q - 1)$$

Finally, we have a third demonstration. The size S of the tree (the random variable) only takes odd values. We know that the number of size S trees with $P - 1 = (S - 1) / 2$ non-terminal nodes is c_{P-1}, which is the corresponding Catalan number, hence:

$$p(S = k) = c_{(k-1)/2}\, p^{(k-1)/2}\, q^{(k+1)/2}$$

using the previous results. Notably:

$$p(S = 1) = q,\ p(S = 3) = c_1 pq^2,\ p(S = 5) = c_2 p^2 q^3, \text{ etc.}$$

We deduce from it that the average size is:

$$S_a = q + 3c_1 pq^2 + 5c_2 p^2 q^3 + \ldots = q \sum (2k + 1)\, c_k\, (pq)^k$$

where the summation is taken for all $k \geq 0$. We are assured that the summation Σ converges for $p < 1 / 2$.

The average size is thus also:

$$S_a = q \sum_{k \geq 0} (2k+1)\, c_k\, (pq)^k$$

where c_k designates the Catalan number of k order. This will again enable us to find $S_a = 1 / (2q - 1)$.

Let us postulate: $x = pq = p(1 - p) = q(1 - q)$. When p describes the convergence interval [0, 1/2[, x describes [0, 1/4[, and we have the relation $q = 0.5(1 + \sqrt{1 - 4x})$. Therefore:

$$S_a / q = \sum_{k \geq 0} (2k+1)\, c_k\, x^k$$

Let us use the Catalan numbers generating function: $C(x) = (1 - \sqrt{1-4x}\,) / (2x)$. We can write:

$$S_a / q = \Sigma(2k+1)\, c_k x^k = C(x) + 2xC'(x)$$

We calculate that:

$$C'(x) = \frac{1-2x-\sqrt{1-4x}}{2x^2\sqrt{1-4x}}$$

All calculations complete, we find:

$$\sum_{k\geq 0}(2k+1)c_k\, x^k = \frac{1-\sqrt{1-4x}}{2x\sqrt{1-4x}}$$

This formula focusing on Catalan numbers is valid for $x \in [0, 1/4[$. Finally:

$$S_a / q = \frac{1-\sqrt{1-4x}}{2x\sqrt{1-4x}}$$

with $x = pq$ and $\sqrt{1-4x} = 2q - 1$.

By eliminating x, we again find:

$$S_a = q\frac{1-2q+1}{2pq(2q-1)} = \frac{1}{2q-1}.$$

28.5.4. *Variance of the variable size*

Let us calculate the expectation $E(S^2)$:

$$E(S^2) = \Sigma\,(2k+1)^2 c_k p^k q^{k+1} = q\,\Sigma\,(2k+1)^2 c_k x^k, \text{ with } x = pq$$

$$= q\,\Sigma(4k^2+4k+1)\, c_k x^k = 4q\,\Sigma\,(k+1)\,k\, c_k x^k + q\,\Sigma\, c_k x^k$$

$$= 4q\,(x^2 C'(x))' + q\,C(x) = 4q\,(x^2 C''(x) + 2x\,C'(x)) + q\,C(x)$$

$$= 4qx^2 C''(x) + 8qx\,C'(x) + q\,C(x)$$

On the one hand $q\ C(x) = 1$, because it is the sum of the probabilities associated with the size of each tree. On the other hand, according to the above:

$$2\ x\ C'(x) = 2p\ /\ (q\ (2q - 1)) \text{ and } 8qx\ C'(x) = 8p\ /\ (2q - 1)$$

therefore:

$$8qx\ C'(x) + qC(x) = (7 - 6q)\ /\ (2q - 1)$$

Let us calculate $C''(x)$ from $C'(x)$ found above. We find that:

$$C''(x) = (-24x^2 + 24x - 4 + 4\ (1 - 4x)\sqrt{1-4x}\ )\ /\ (4x^3\ (1 - 4x)\ \sqrt{1-4x}\ )$$

and:

$$4qx^2\ C''(x) = q\ (-24x^2 + 24x - 4 + 4\ (1 - 4x)\sqrt{1-4x}\ )\ /\ (x\ (1 - 4x)\sqrt{1-4x}\ )$$

$$= (-24q^4 + 80q^3 - 96q^2 + 48q - 8)\ /\ ((1 - q)(2q - 1)^3)$$

Finally:

$$E(S^2) = (4q^3 - 10q^2 + 7q - 1)\ /\ ((1 - q)(2q - 1)^3)$$

$$= (-\ 4q^2 + 6q - 1)\ /\ (2q - 1)^3$$

$$V(S) = E(S^2) - E(S)^2 = (-\ 4q^2 + 6q - 1)\ /\ (2q - 1)^3 - 1\ /\ (2q - 1)^2$$

$$= (-\ 4q^2 + 4q)\ /\ (2q - 1)^3$$

$$= 4q\ (1 - q)\ /\ (2q - 1)^3$$

The variance $V(S)$ associated with the size of the trees is equal to

$$V(S) = 4q\ (1 - q)\ /\ (2q - 1)^3.$$

28.5.5. *Algorithm giving the probability law of the organization's lifespan*

Let L be the lifespan of the organization, or height of the tree increased by 1. For each value of L, we partition the set of trees obtained according to their number of nodes located on the last level (this number is even) as well as their size (in what follows these two numbers will be put in parentheses behind the number of trees with both characteristics):

– for $L = 1$, we have a tree that is expressed 1 (1,1), and $p(L = 1) = q$;

– for $L = 2$, we expand the previous tree by taking 1 (1,1) as producing 1 (2,3), and $p(L = 2) = pq^2$;

– for $L = 3$, we expand the previous tree by taking 1 (2,3) as producing 2 (2,5) and 1 (4,7), and $p(L = 3) = 2p^2q^3 + p^3q^4$;

– more generally, during the passing from one value of L to the next, we get the following expansion rules:

$$1(2, n) \to 2(2, n + 2)\ 1(4, n + 4)$$

$$1(4, n) \to 4(2, n + 2)\ 6(4, n + 4)\ 4(6, n + 6)\ 1(8, n + 8)$$

$$1(6, n) \to 6(2, n + 2)\ 15(4, n + 4)\ 20(6, n + 6)\ 15(8, n + 8)\ 6(10, n + 10)$$
$$1(12, n + 12)$$

$$1(8, n) \to 8(2, n + 2)\ 28(4, n + 4)\ 56(6, n + 6)\ 70(8, n + 8)\ 56(10, n + 10)$$
$$28(12, n + 12)\ 8(14, n + 14)\ 1(16, n + 16)$$

i.e.: $1(2k, n) \to C_{2k}^{1}(2, n + 2)\ C_{2k}^{2}(4, n + 4)\ .....\ C_{2k}^{2k-1}(4k - 2, n + 4k - 2)$
$1(4k, n + 4k)$

When there are N trees in a category, we multiply the preceding by N:

$$N(2k, n) \to NC_{2k}^{1}(2, n + 2)\ NC_{2k}^{2}(4, n + 4)$$
$$NC_{2k}^{2k-1}(4k - 2, n + 4k - 2)\ N(4k, n + 4k)$$

It is the value of size that gives the probability associated with the tree, which leads us, at each new stage, to expand each one of the classes of trees previously being obtained by introducing shifts.

For example, let us look at the passage from $L = 3$ to $L = 4$. Event $L = 3$ is expressed as 2(2, 5) 1(4, 7). During the passage to $L = 4$ this gives:

$$2(2, 5) \to 4(2, 7)\ 2(4, 9)$$

$$1(4, 7) \to 4(2, 9)\ 6(4, 11)\ 4(6, 13)\ 1(8, 15)$$

$$p(L = 4) = 4p^3q^4 + 6p^4q^5 + 6\,p^5q^6 + 4p^6q^7 + p^7q^8$$

The passage to $L = 5$ consists of expanding all the previous parenthesis numbers, numbering six. We find:

8(2, 9) 4(4, 11)
8(2, 11) 12(4, 13) 8(6, 15) 2(8, 17)
8(2, 11) 4(4, 13)
24(2, 13) 36(4, 15) 24(6, 17) 6(8, 19)
24(2, 15) 60(4, 17) 80(6, 19) 60(8, 21) 24(10, 23)
4(12, 25) 8(2, 17) 28(4, 19) 56(6, 21) 70(8, 23)
56(10, 25) 28(12, 27) 8(14, 29) 1(16, 31)

$$p(L = 5) = 8p^4q^5 + 20p^5q^6 + 40p^6q^7 + 68p^7q^8 + 94p^8q^9 + 114p^9q^{10} +$$
$$116p^{10}q^{11} + 94p^{11}q^{12} + 60p^{12}q^{13} + 28p^{13}q^{14} + 8p^{14}q^{15} + p^{15}q^{16}$$

Note that:

– the first term of $p(L = k)$ is $2^{k-2}\, p^{k-1}\, q^k$;

– the second term is $2^{k-3}(2k - 5)p^kq^{k+1}$ for $k \geq 3$ (and 0 otherwise).

$$p(L = k) = p^{k-1}q^k\,(2^{k-2} + 2^{k-3}(2k\text{-}5)\,x + ... + x^{2^{k-1}-k})\text{ with } x = pq.$$

28.6. Surfing the web (or how Google works)

Let us take an oriented graph, like the one in Figure 28.10, and imagine a random surfer who circulates on the graph moving from one vertex to a neighboring vertex at each stage in time, using a junction arch chosen at random. At the end of a large number of stages of time, we want to find out his probability of being at a certain vertex.

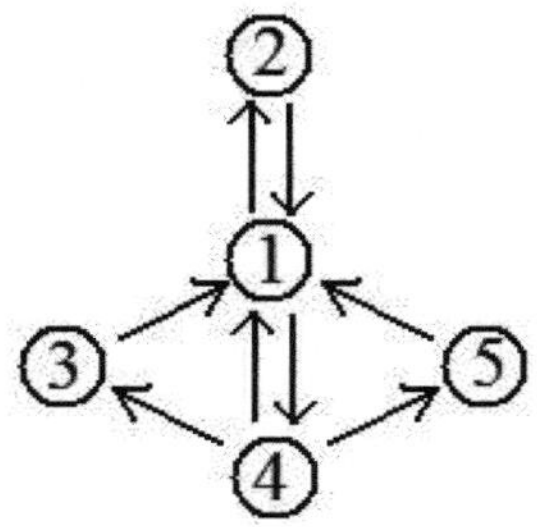

Figure 28.10. *Example of a graph*

Let us start by recording the graph and writing down the neighbors of each one of the vertices. In our example, vertex 1 has two neighbors: 2 and 4; vertex 2 has one unique neighbor 1, just like vertices 3 and 5; and vertex 4 has three neighbors: 1, 3 and 5. Let a_{ij} be the probability of going from vertex j to vertex i during a certain stage of time. This probability is null in the absence of a junction arch from j to i, and if vertex j has k neighbors, it is equal to $1 / k$ for each of these neighbors, notably $1 / k$ for neighbor i. Taking the a_{ij} as coefficients of a matrix A, in the chosen example we get:

$$A = \begin{pmatrix} 0 & 1 & 1 & 1/3 & 1 \\ 1/2 & 0 & 0 & 0 & 0 \\ 0 & 0 & 0 & 1/3 & 0 \\ 1/2 & 0 & 0 & 0 & 0 \\ 0 & 0 & 0 & 1/3 & 0 \end{pmatrix}$$

Note that each column j of this matrix has a sum of its coefficients that is equal to 1, since it is the sum of the probabilities of going from vertex j to its neighbors.

At 0 stage in time, the surfer chooses a starting vertex at random, which gives a probability of $1 / N$ at each vertex, i.e. 0.2 in our example. Now, how does the probability $p_t(i)$ evolve from being at i when we go from time t to $t + 1$? It is enough to apply total probability formula:

$$p_{t+1}(i) = \sum_{neighbors\ j} a_{i\,j}\, p_t(j)$$

Thus, in the chosen example, taking time 1 we have:

$$p_1(1) = 1\, p_0(2) + 1\, p_0(3) + (1 / 2)\, p_0(4) + 1\, p_0(5) = 0.2 + 0.2 + 0.1 + 0.2 = 0.6$$

and also:

$$p_1(2) = 0.1, p_1(3) = 0.067, p_1(4) = 0.167, p_1(5) = 0.066$$

Let us take the probability vector:

$$\boldsymbol{P}_t = \begin{pmatrix} p_t(1) \\ p_t(2) \\ p_t(3) \\ p_t(4) \\ p_t(5) \end{pmatrix}$$

notably initial vector:

$$P_0 = \begin{pmatrix} 0,2 \\ 0,2 \\ 0,2 \\ 0,2 \\ 0,2 \end{pmatrix}$$

We deduce the matrix relation $P_{t+1} = A\ P_t$ from it, hence by recurrence $P_t = A^n\ P_0$.

Over time, there is a diffusion of probabilities, and these probabilities have a tendency to stabilize, in some cases at least, as we see in Figure 28.11.

P being the probability vector, once equilibrium has been reached this vector verifies $P = A\ P$. This is another way of seeing the problem – as a system of equations to solve. Initially we have to find the unknown components of a vector P obeying the system of equations that is expressed $P = AP$. The surfer's journey is just the colorful version of a solution by successive approximations.

We start with any values for P_0: where we had chosen initial values of 0.2 to respect the random model, we could have taken other values of the components of P_0 by giving them a sum equal to 1, which will last throughout the process. Next, from these values in AP_0, we find P_1, then from the values of P_1 the calculation of AP_1 gives P_2, and so on and so forth until we finally arrive at the unique solution to the system, namely P.

This is a first draft of what a search engine does on the Internet. The user makes a request, and the search engine answers with a series of responses arranged in order of importance. In this case the graph is the spider web – the web, with webpages as vertices and the links between these pages as arches. The responses to a request are classified according to the notoriety of the pages concerned.

It is not simply a matter of the number of links that point to them, but the number of links are themselves weighted by the importance of the pages they come from. This is exactly what the calculation of vector P gives.

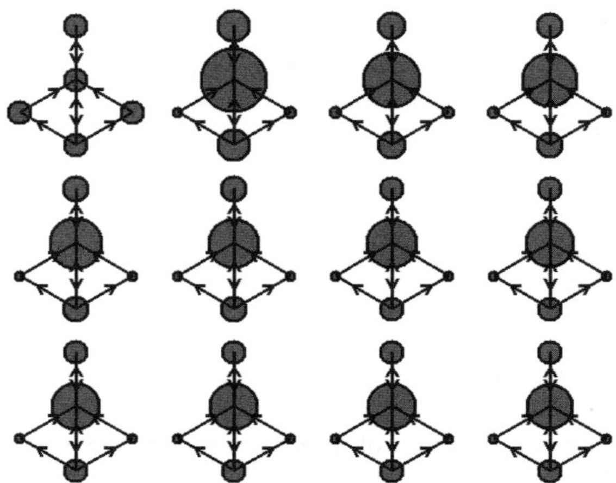

Figure 28.11. *Random journey of the Internet surfer. The probabilities of ending up on a website are represented by circles. There is a rapid equilibrium*

One problem remains, if we go to a page that has no arrow starting from it heading to other vertices, like vertex 6 in Figure 28.12, we end up adding an arch from the node to itself. It is easy to understand that in this case the random journey of the surfer always ends in being trapped on this vertex, which plays the role of a pit. The vertex concerned takes probability 1, leaving nothing to the others. Variations (see Figure 28.13) also exist where a blinking effect occurs, with two vertices – each in turn taking predominance – without any final equilibrium.

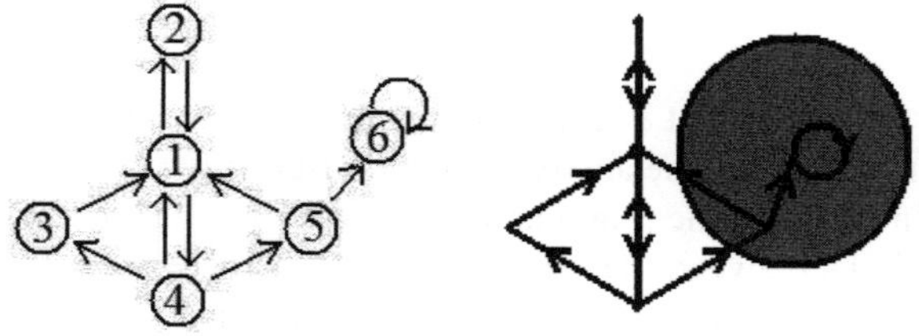

Figure 28.12. *Presence of an attracting pit of trajectories*

Figure 28.13. *Infinite blinking effect between two nodes, without convergence, on this three-node graph*

To compensate for these defects, we are lead to modify the surfer's journey. We will consider that at moment t he will continue his random journey with probability $1 - c$, and that with probability c he restarts his journey at 0 from a vertex taken at random. Thanks to total probability formula, we end up with:

$$P_{t+1} = c\,P_0 + (1-c)\,A\,P_t$$

Thanks to this correction, the surfer no longer remains a prisoner in a pit. We also end up with a stabilization of the probabilities in all contexts, and this stabilization respects the relative importance of the nodes (see Figure 28.14). As value of constant c, we agree to take $c = 0.15$. The fact that c is strictly bigger than 0 assures convergence of the process on the value of equilibrium P,[2] the only solution to the system of equations $P = A\,P$.

The formula above is the one used for Google's PageRank, which made Sergey Brin and Lawrence Page – the two founders of Google in 1998 – famous. It enabled us to arrange pages in response to requests in a more pertinent manner than had existed until then, according to the criterion that a page is much more important than important pages pointing to it.

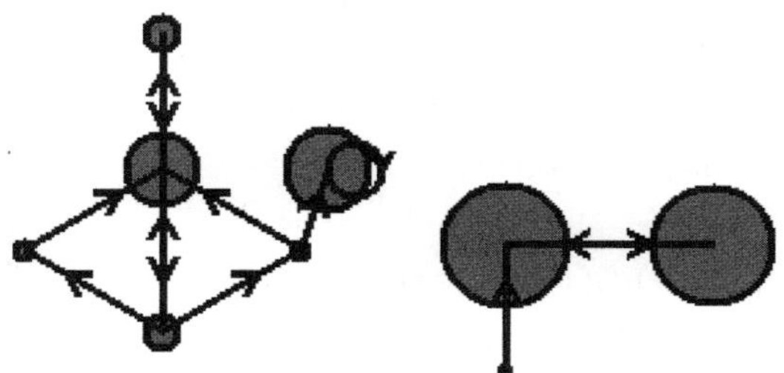

Figure 28.14. *Final equilibrium of the probabilities on the graphs in Figures 28.3 and 28.4*

If a pit no longer attracts all the trajectories, it retains some importance, in contradiction to reality, as we see in Figure 28.14. To compensate for this defect, we can decide to link up such a vertex to all vertices of the graph to produce a dispersal that is articulated with the surfer starting a new search from one time to the other. We therefore get the best classification of the nodes by order of importance (see Figure 28.15).

---

2. For a demonstration of this property, see [EIS 08] or the entrance competition mathematics exam at the ESSEC international business school in Europe in 2008.

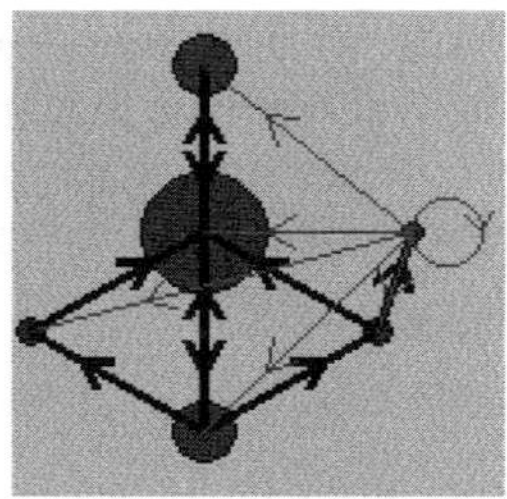

Figure 28.15. *Node classification, after dispersion from the vertex-pit to all the vertices. Equilibrium is reached in about 10 stages*

Here is the program enabling us to arrive at the result in Figure 28.15, and it can be generalized to any graph (see Figure 28.16):

```
/* entry of the list of the neighbors of the six nodes */
v[1][1]=2; v[1][2]=4;v[2][1]=1;v[3][1]=1;v[4][1]=1;v[4][2]=3;v[4][3]=5;
v[5][1]=1;v[5][2]=6;
for(i=1;i<=5;i++) v[6][i]=i; /* spread of node 6 */
nbv[1]=2;nbv[2]=1;nbv[3]=1;nbv[4]=3;nbv[5]=2;nbv[6]=5;
/* calculation of the coefficients aij of matrix A */
for(i=1;i<=6;i++) for(j=1;j<=6;j++)
{ flag=0;
for(ii=1;ii<=nbv[j];ii++) {if (v[j][ii]==i) flag=1; }
 if (flag==1) a[i][j]=1./(float)nbv[j];   else a[i][j]=0;
}
/* random walk over 10 stages, up until convergence */
for(i=1; i<=6; i++) p[i]=1/6.;  drawing
for(move=1; move<=10; move++)
{ for(i=1; i<=6;i++)
  { cumul=0.15/6.;
   for(j=1; j<=6; j++) cumul+=0.85*a[i][j]*p[j];
   p[i]=cumul;
  }
 drawing
}
```

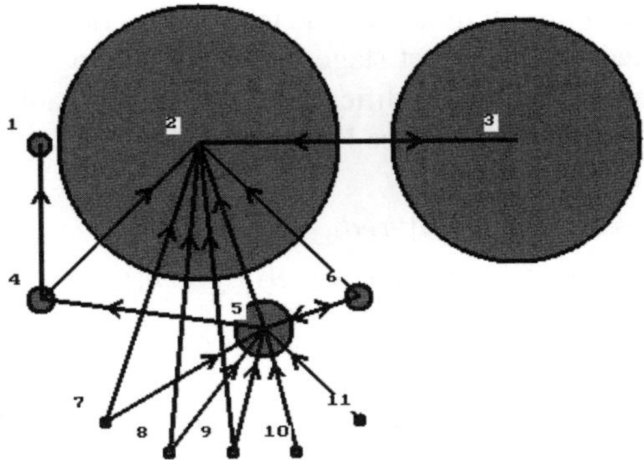

Figure 28.16. *PageRank of a graph (this graph is the one taken as an example in en.wikipedia.org/wiki/PageRank). We notice the importance of page 3, which only receives one single link, but this link coming from page 2 is heavily weighted*

Let us observe the end of the program. With each *move*, the new value of vector P is supposed to be calculated from the old one. This is not so. If the new value of $p(1)$ is calculated from the old values of $p(i)$ with i from 1 to 6, the new value of $p(2)$ is calculated from the new value of $p(1)$ and the old values of the others, and so on and so forth. We could believe that that is an error causing us to confuse a parallel algorithm and a sequential algorithm. This deserves some explanation.

To understand the difference between a sequential algorithm and a parallel algorithm, let us take the example of a forest. We have a row of trees numbered from 0 to $N-1$, with the following rule: at each stage of time, if one of the trees is on fire it transmits the fire to its right hand neighbor. Let us also assume that the first tree (tree 0) is on fire at the initial moment. Then the fire will spread from one tree to the next at each stage in time, until the last tree is on fire. At time N, all the trees will be on fire, after a steady spread in time.

Let us program this phenomenon using a table with N boxes, from 0 to $N-1$, with two possible contents: green (tree not on fire) or red (tree on fire). Therefore we have:

```
time=0 ; tree[0]=red; for(i=1 ; i<N ; i++) tree[i]=green;
do
  { time++;
  for(i=1 ;i<N ;i++) if (tree[i-1]==red) tree[i]=red;
  }
while (tree[N–1]=green); /* we expect the last tree to be on fire */
```

What will it happen? From time 1 all the trees are on fire (see Figure 28.17). The total spread happened from the first stage in time. Our program is obviously false. To correct it, we must store the modifications in a second table in such a way that we do not mix the old and the new (see Figure 28.18):

```
time=0; tree[0]=red ; newtree[0]=red;
for(i=1; i<N; i++) {tree[i]=green; newtree[i]=green;}
do
  { time++;
   for(i=1; i<N; i++) if (tree[i–1]==red) newtree[i]=red;
     /* above we go through table tree[], without modifying it, and we put
      the changes in the new table*/
   for(i=0; i<N; i++) tree[i]=newtree[i];
     /* after a complete traversal, we return newtree [], where the modifications
       were done, in tree [] */
  }
while (tree[N–1]=green);
```

The second program is correct, after certain complications. These are due to the fact that our computer works in sequence, while the first program behaved as if we were in parallel. With a computer in parallel, with each stroke of the clock the modifications would happen simultaneously throughout our table *tree*[], and the program would have worked. This is not the case with our computers.

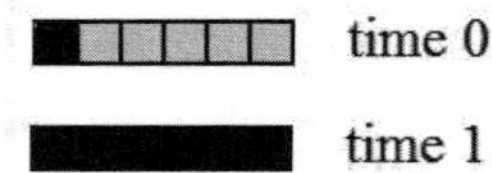

Figure 28.17. *Error in the spread*

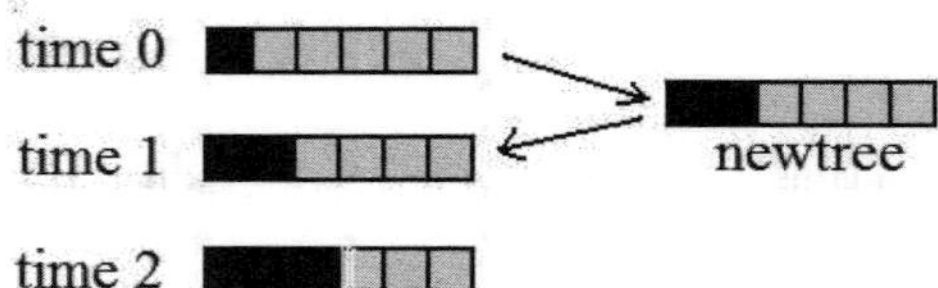

Figure 28.18. *Correcting the program with the use of an extra array*

The same problem is posed when we solve a system of equations by successive approximations. This method, also called the Jacobi-Richardson method, imposes that the new values are calculated from the old ones, as if we were in parallel, but the computer imposes a sequential treatment, hence the use of a second table that slows down the process. There is another method called Gauss-Seidel's method, which is typically sequential, calculating the value of the unknown $p(i)$ at each stage from the new values of the unknowns $p(k)$ for k from 1 to $i - 1$, and the old ones for k from i to the last one. This method also ensures convergence on the solution, often more quickly than with the classic iterative method, provided that the sum of the terms of each column in the matrix is strictly less than 1 [DEM 79]. This is exactly the case in our problem, the matrix concerned not being A, where the sum of the terms of the columns is equal to 1, but $(1 - c)A$. Our program is therefore valid.

PART 3

Graphs

Part 3

Introduction

In the 1950s, some Parisian subway stations proposed an interactive map. You only had to push the button corresponding to a destination to see the journey across the lines and stations of the network to light up. For every stranger arriving in Paris for the first time it was a fascinating subject, just like the Eiffel tower. Today, in the time of GPS, this can seem outdated. But it still remains quite marvelous when, faced with our computer screen, on a network created by our imagination, with a program we built up, we see paths take shape with implacable precision. It is in this perspective that this part is written, the third and last stage of our *combinatorics* journey.

It is the same on the theoretical plane. Some demonstrations on the subject of graphs have a certain charm, in the sense that they appeal more to common sense and cunning than to the heavy artillery of mathematics. This is the case especially for two theorems by Euler – one about planar graphs and the other about paths that carry his name. Of course, as soon as the explanation becomes more complex, classic algebra resumes its rights. This is the reason for which we added two appendices devoted to matrices and determinants, presented in a simplified form at the end of the book. This is done in such a way as to facilitate its comprehension, even for those who are not restricted by the framework of a university science course.

Lastly, individual creativity is to be mentioned. From the many programs we give, it is possible to elaborate, as many masters students I have supervised did, two of whose realizations I quote, among others, at the end of this chapter (see Figures 1 and 2). It is sometimes difficult to link theoretical constraint with artistic freedom. It is up to the individual to combine the two or prefer one to the other.

Organization of Part 3

Graph theory is an integral part of combinatorics. When we drew paths on a square grid in Part 1, we were already dealing with graphs. Similarly when we used transition graphs for probability theory in Part 2. At the start, a graph resembles a network of streets or paths between various sites. Either it is already constructed, and we have to circulate on it, or it is to be constructed and using points we have to trace the junction lines responding to certain constraints. If the graph is already present, the first problem consists of finding all the paths leading from one point to another, and that again is an enumeration problem, which is the subject of Chapter 29. But very quickly we come to problems of existence: does a path from one given point to another exist? For this, all we have to do is to learn to explore a graph, i.e. to find all the sites that can be reached from one of them.[1] We will see this in Chapter 30, and this will enable us to explore mazes. The age-old attraction of mazes is not about disappearing, even if this game is now safe because we leave it in the hands of the computer to find a way out.

When a graph is to be constructed, we often use optimization problems. For example, we can be led to look for a minimalist solution of junctions between sites, where the graph is reduced to an arborescence, i.e. a sort of burgeoning from a preferred point called the root. These arborescent structures, which we will call trees, are the focus of Chapter 31. Notably in Chapter 32 their simplest organized form, namely binary trees, will again cause us to return to the famous Catalan numbers, already encountered in several chapters of Part 1. Another optimization problem, for a given graph consists of searching for the shortest path between two points. This assumes that the graph is weighted, i.e. that its junctions each have a number associated with them, that is supposed to represent their length or another parameter in other contexts. Weighted graphs are studied in Chapter 33. It is also the opportunity to look for the minimum spanning tree, i.e. choosing part of the edges of the graph in such a way that they form a tree passing through all the vertices, the sum of the distances being minimal.

We are also interested in two particular types of paths – those where all the graph edges must be traversed once and only once, which we call Eulerian paths; and those where all the graph vertices must be reached once and only once, which we call Hamiltonian paths. Eulerian cycles and paths, taken up in Chapter 34, follow simple properties. Notably, the number of Eulerian cycles is linked to that of spanning trees of the graph when it is directed. The case of undirected graphs is

---

1. Exploration algorithms have played a big role since the end of the 1950s, especially in the field of artificial intelligence. One of the pioneers on the subject of algorithms is Tarjan [TAR 73, TAR 83]. For algorithmics on graphs in general, the chapters devoted to this in books that have become classics can be consulted [AHO 74, COR 02, SED 91].

dealt with in Chapters 35 and 36, with the enumeration of spanning trees, then that of Eulerian cycles and paths, which also underlie the game of dominos as well as the artistic patterns largely developed in Africa. Lastly, Chapter 37 is devoted to Hamiltonian paths, and ends with De Bruijn graphs.

Figure 1. *Random domino tiling of an Aztec diamond. The surface is a network of small squares, here 600 squares on the length of the central horizontal, and each domino occupies two boxes, horizontally or vertically. Here we have 90,300 dominos and we observe the phenomenon called the Arctic circle, with a sort of gelling of the dominos, in the sense that they are all horizontal or all vertical in the four corners of the Aztec diamond. A circular central zone where the dominos are in disorder remains (realization of Fathi [FAT 01])*

Figure 2. *Braiding in the image of a pattern that exists in central Africa corresponding to a Eulerian cycle on a square network (realization of Arfa [ARF 04])*

Chapter 29

Graphs and Routes

29.1. First notions on graphs

A graph is made up of points (nodes or vertices), some of which are linked in twos by lines (arcs or edges), like that of a subway plan. Either it is directed, and the arcs have an arrow that gives them a direction of traversal from one vertex to another, or it is undirected and the edges of the graph can be traversed in one or the other direction.

An undirected graph is, in simple cases, made up of a single connected component, in the sense that we can go from one point to another of this component by following the edges, like the subway network in a city. We therefore say that the graph is connected (see Figure 29.1). In more general terms, it can have several connected components that cannot be accessed by a path between them.[1] In an undirected graph, the number of edges that touch a vertex is called the *degree* of that vertex.

In a directed graph, for a vertex we distinguish the indegree, which is the number of arcs that end at this vertex, and the outdegree, which is the number of arcs that leave from it. On a graph, a path consists of a succession of nodes linked by edges or arcs. The length of the path is the number of edges traversed.

---

1. The problem is more delicate for a directed graph. We speak of strongly connected components when any two vertices of a strongly connected component can be reached one from the other and *vice versa*.

We say that a path is elementary if the path passes through each path vertex only once. In other words, no return journeys or detours (in the form of a loop) are made on the route.[2] In all that follows, the paths used will be assumed to be elementary, and they form a route from one vertex to another via other vertices. We speak of a *circuit* or *cycle* when the path closes in on itself.

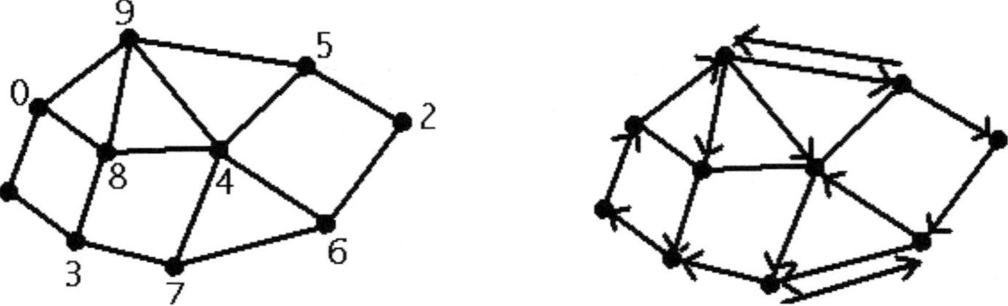

Figure 29.1. *Examples of graphs: a connected, directed graph with 10 numbered vertices and 16 edges (left); and a directed graph with 10 vertices and 18 arcs (right)*

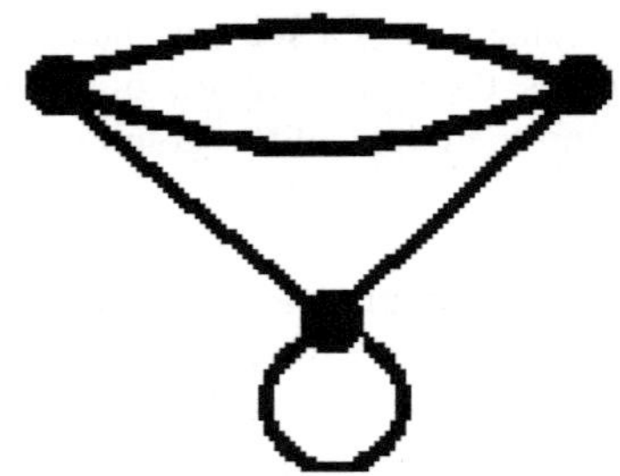

Figure 29.2. *An example of a multigraph with a double edge and a loop*

More complex configurations can exist, with loops linking a vertex to itself, or even several edges linking two vertices, instead of a single one in classic graphs (see Figure 29.2). We therefore speak more of multigraphs than graphs.

2. Sometimes we make a distinction between a simple path, where each edge on the path is traversed one single time, while the nodes can be crossed several times, and an elementary path, where each node is passed through only once.

29.1.1. *A few properties of graphs*

A few simple properties of undirected graphs exist:

– the sum of all the vertex degrees is equal to twice the number of edges. Hence it immediately results that the number of vertices with an odd degree is even;[3]

– a connected graph with n vertices has at least $n - 1$ edges;[4]

– a connected planar graph, with V vertices and E edges, splits the plane into R regions, with the relation: $R = E - V + 2$. This formula was discovered by Euler around 1750.

By planar graph, we mean a graph where none of the edges cuts another. In other words, the plane is divided into regions made by closed polygons delimited by edges, with the external region in addition.[5] For example, the undirected graph taken as an example in Figure 29.3 is connected and planar. It has 10 vertices and 16 edges. It therefore delimits $16 - 10 + 2 = 8$ regions, as can be verified below.

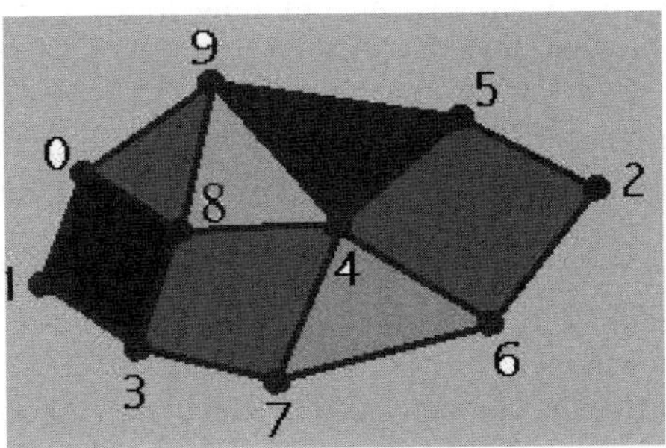

Figure 29.3. *Example of the planar graph with eight regions*

To show this property on a planar connected graph, it is sufficient to create this graph edge by edge, in the following way. We begin by tracing one edge. We therefore notice that we have two vertices, one edge, and one single region: the formula $R = E - V + 2$ is verified. Then we attach a new graph edge to the previous

3. The sum of the node degrees gives the number of edges touched by all the nodes. The edges are counted twice – once for each of its two extreme vertices. Hence the formula.

4. Thanks to the process of exploration of a connected graph, which we will see, the graph has a spanning tree passing through all its vertices and a part of its edges. We will also see that a tree with n vertices has $n - 1$ edges. A connected graph with n vertices therefore has at least $n - 1$ edges.

5. See the *Planarity game* created by Tantalo [TAN 05]. By moving the graph vertices, the graph may be untangled to make it planar.

one: we have one additional vertex, one additional edge and still one single region. The formula remains true. We continue in this way, attaching a new edge to the ones already placed. Such attaching is always possible as the final graph is connected. But two cases are presented:

– either the new edge, attached by a vertex to the old ones, has a second vertex that is not attached to it – in this case, there is one more vertex, one more edge, and still as many regions; or

– the new edge is attached by the two ends to the part of the graph already constructed, forming a new region, since the graph is planar. In this case, there are as many vertices as before, one more edge, and one more region: the formula is still verified. Therefore, until the final graph is obtained in its entirety, the formula is preserved.

29.1.2. *Constructing graphs from points*

We take n points. We want to find out how many undirected graphs can be obtained with n points for vertices.

Let E be the number of junction edges that can be constructed from the n vertices. There are as many possible edges as ways of taking two out of n points, i.e.:

$$E = C_n^2 = n(n-1)/2$$

A graph with n vertices is characterized by the choice of some of the edges from E possible edges, i.e. by a part of the set of E edges. There are as many graphs as parts of an E-element set, i.e.:

$$2^E = 2^{n(n-1)/2}$$

(see Figure 29.4). Now, how many directed graphs with n points for vertices can we obtain? In this context, any two vertices can be joined, either by no arcs or by an arc in one direction, or by one arc in the other direction. The number of possible arcs is the number of vertex couples, i.e. the number of arrangements:

$$A_n^2 = n(n-1)$$

The number of directed graphs with n given vertices is:

$$2^{n(n-1)}$$

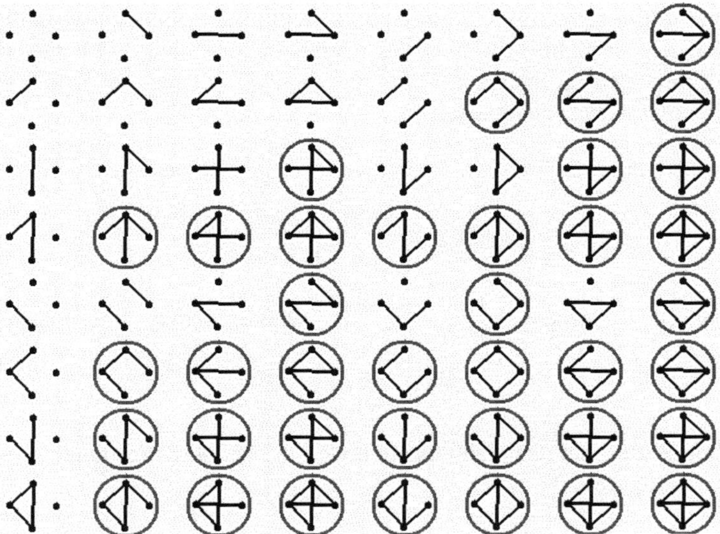

Figure 29.4. *The 64 graphs with four vertices. The connected graphs are surrounded by a circle*

29.2. Representing a graph in a program

There are two ways of representing a graph within a program, either by an adjacency matrix or by adjacency lists.

The adjacency matrix consists of a table with a double entry $M[i][j]$ of dimensions N by N, where N is the number of vertices. Box $M[i][j]$ of this square table is set to 1 if an arc from i to j exists for a directed graph or an edge between i and j for an undirected graph, else it is set to 0. In the case of an undirected graph, this matrix is symmetrical, since $M[i][j] = M[j][i]$.

The second way to represent a graph consists of giving the list of neighbors of each graph vertex. A chained list containing all the vertices adjacent to vertex i is therefore associated with each vertex i.

Naturally, adjacency lists occupy less memory space than the adjacency matrix because of the many 0s the latter can include, and they are recommended when the graph is sparse, i.e. it has relatively few edges, while a dense graph can have one representation as well as the other.

In what follows, for simplicity's sake, we will use adjacency lists in the form of an array where each line contains the neighbors of a node, with the number of neighbors indicated, even if this limits the eventual advantages of this method in terms of memory space occupied.

Let us take the example of the graph with five vertices and seven edges in Figure 29.5.

Its adjacency matrix is: $\begin{bmatrix} 0 & 1 & 1 & 0 & 1 \\ 1 & 0 & 1 & 0 & 0 \\ 1 & 1 & 0 & 1 & 1 \\ 0 & 0 & 1 & 0 & 1 \\ 1 & 0 & 1 & 1 & 0 \end{bmatrix}$ where, notably, line 0 corresponding to node 0 indicates that its neighbors are nodes 1, 2 and 4, corresponding to columns where the 1s are present.

To get the adjacency lists, we take the neighbors of each node, i.e.:

$$0 \rightarrow 1\ 2\ 4, \quad 1 \rightarrow 0\ 2, \quad 2 \rightarrow 0\ 1\ 3\ 4, \quad 3 \rightarrow 2\ 4, \quad 4 \rightarrow 0\ 2\ 3$$

For this we define a table of neighbors $n[N][N]$, where $n[i][j]$ is neighbor number j of node i, and we also indicate the number of neighbors $nbn[i]$ of node i. This gives:

$$n[0][0] = 1, \quad n[0][1] = 2, \quad n[0][2] = 4, \quad nbn[0] = 3$$

$$n[1][0] = 0, \quad n[1][1] = 2, \quad nbn[1] = 2$$

$$n[2][0] = 0, \quad n[2][1] = 1, \quad n[2][2] = 3, \quad n[2][3] = 4, \quad nbn[2] = 4$$

etc.

As a programming exercise, let us see how to move from vertices to edges, and *vice versa*.

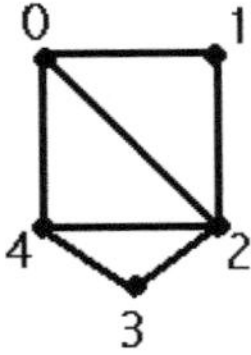

Figure 29.5. *An example of a graph*

29.2.1. *From vertices to edges*

An undirected graph, with *NV* vertices numbered from 0 to *NV* – 1, is recorded by the adjacency lists *n*[*i*][*j*] giving the neighbors of each vertex *i* and their number *nbn*[*i*].

We need the edges of this graph. We have to make the program that gives a number to each edge as well as its two extremities, the first e_1 being less than the second e_2. The program will also need to give the number *NE* of graph edges. Here is the program:

```
k=0;
for(i=0; i<NV; i++)  for(j=0; j<nbn[i]; j++)  if (i < n[i][j])
   {  e1[k]= i; e2[k]= n[i][j];  k++;}
NE= k;
```

29.2.2. *From edges to vertices*

A graph is given by its *NE* edges numbered from 0 to *NE* – 1 and we know the vertices extremities *e1*[*k*] and *e2*[*k*], with *e1*[*k*] < *e2*[*k*], of each edge *k*. The vertices are numbered 0, 1, 2, ... From there, let us write the program that gives the neighbors *n*[*i*][*j*] of each vertex *i* and their number *nbn*[*i*], as well as the number of vertices *NV*.

```
max= -1;
set table nbn[] to 0
for(i=0; i< NE; i++) if (e2[i] > max)  max= e2[i] ;
NV=max+1;      /* the number of vertices is the largest of the vertices e2[i]
                  increased by 1*/
for(i=0; i< NE; i++)
   { n[e1[i]] [nbn[e1[i]]] = e2[i];  nbn[e1[i]++];
     n[e2[i]] [nbn[e2[i]]] = e1[i];  nbn[e2[i]++];
   }
```

29.3. The tree as a specific graph

29.3.1. *Definitions and properties*

By definition, an undirected tree is an acyclic connected undirected graph. We distinguish the terminal nodes (or leaves) with 1 degree, a single edge being attached to them, and internal nodes with a greater degree. On the tree in Figure 29.6a, the terminal nodes are 2, 4, 5, 6 and 7. To find the classic form of a tree again, like the ones we meet in nature, even if we draw it in reverse in this case, we are led to choose one node, which we call a root, and draw the tree obtained with the root on top, making the levels of the tree stand out, with the non-terminal nodes having descendants under them, as for example in Figure 29.6c.

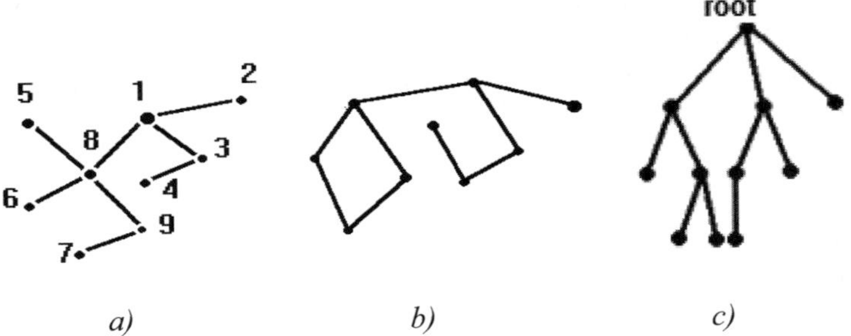

Figure 29.6. *a) A tree; b) a non-tree; and c) a rooted tree*

In the context where levels are used, a node can have successors (either sons or daughters) when nodes are attached to it and located just below it.

A node located above it is called a predecessor (either a father or mother).[6] The successors of a node, then the successors' successors, and so on, are called the descendants of the node. Similarly the predecessor, the predecessor's predecessors, and so on up to the root, form the ancestors of the node.

A simple link exists between an unrooted tree, which we sometimes specify as a free tree, and a rooted tree.

If we take an unrooted tree with n vertices, we can choose one of its nodes, in n different ways, and making this node play the role of the root we thus obtain a rooted tree, in n possible ways (see Figure 29.7).

Conversely, if we start with a rooted tree, it is sufficient to drop the role of the chosen one occupied by the root, to obtain one (and only one) unrooted tree, where

6. Let us recall that, in a graph, the neighbors of a vertex are those that are adjacent to it, and that their number is called the *vertex degree*. When the graph is a tree and we give it a root, the neighbors of a node are its successors located below and its predecessor above. The definition of node degree is therefore modified: for a rooted tree, it is only the number of successors of a node.

all the nodes are equal. This two-facedness of trees enables us to demonstrate their essential properties.

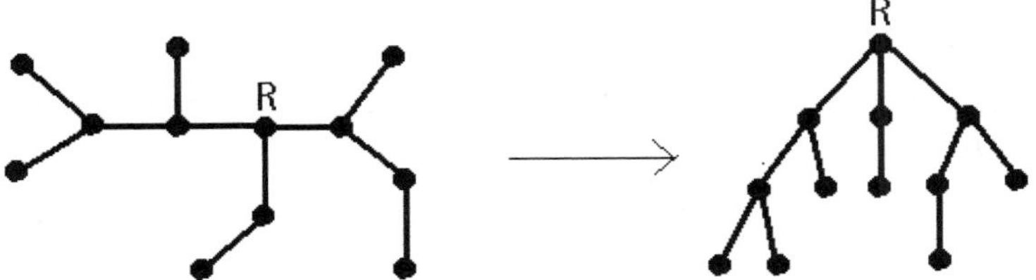

Figure 29.7. *Passage from a free tree to a rooted tree*

PROPERTY 29.1.– A tree (unrooted or rooted) is such that one and only one (elementary) path exists from one vertex to another.

Actually, let us take an unrooted tree and assume that we want to go from vertex A to vertex B. At least one path always exists since the tree graph is connected.

Now let B be the root, and let us construct the rooted tree associated with the previous one. A single path from A going back up to B exists because if there were two of them, we would get a cycle and we would no longer have a tree. Finally, one unique path from A to B exists.

It would be easy to check that this property is characteristic. In other words, a connected graph where a unique path from any vertex to another vertex is a tree, i.e. an acyclic connected graph. This has an essential consequence when the graph has node O as its root, and we want to go from O to vertex B of the graph. Instead of trying to go from O to B, by trying several descending paths to finally keep only one, we prefer to go from B to O because one single possibility is offered at each stage. It is sufficient to go back up the tree via each predecessor.

PROPERTY 29.2.– A tree with n vertices has $n - 1$ edges.

Let us replace the tree with n vertices with the one obtained by taking one of its vertices as the root. Henceforth each vertex, with the exception of the root, has one unique edge attached to it and located above it. There are no others. Hence a total of $n - 1$ edges.

Here are the characteristic properties of a tree:

– a tree is an acyclic, connected, undirected graph;

– a tree is a connected, undirected graph with a number of edges equal to the number of vertices minus 1;

– a tree is an undirected graph, any two vertices of which are connected by one unique elementary path;

– a tree is a connected, undirected graph such that if we drop any edge, it loses its connectivity;

– a tree is an acyclic, undirected graph, such that if we add an edge to it, it will contain a cycle.

As we can see, a tree is a sort of minimalist and unstable structure among the diversity of graphs, in the sense that it loses its tree nature as soon as we remove or add an edge to it. It is also the graph that has one unique path from one vertex to another, whereas in general for any graph several (elementary) paths from one vertex to another, or no paths exist, depending on the case.

29.3.2. *Programming exercise: network converging on a point*

Let us assume that we have a network of airlines all converging on the same city, which corresponds to a tree with N numbered nodes whose root is the city called O. We take any city, corresponding to a node numbered K, and we want to determine the unique path leading from O to K.

The tree is registered beforehand on the computer, indicating the successors $n[i][j]$ of each node i, as well as their number $nbn[i]$, with city O carrying the number 0. This enables us to immediately determine the unique predecessor $predec[i]$ of each of the nodes, except the root, by doing:

```
for(i=1; i<N; i++)  for(j=0; j<nbn[i]; j++)  predec[n[i][j]] = i;
```

Next we take the node corresponding to the endpoint and go back up to the root, moving from one node to its predecessor, and recording the nodes of the path obtained in a table $p[k]$. To go from O to K, it is enough to read this table in reverse. Hence the part of the program:

```
endpoint=K;  p[0]=endpoint;  k=0;
while(p[k] != 0)  {  k++; p[k]=predec[p[k-1]];  }
length=k+1;
for(i=length-1; i>=0; i--)  printf("%d ",p[i]);
and do the drawing of the path.
```

We now take any two cities *K* and *M* and have to use a program to determine the shortest path, in a number of steps from city to city, between these two agglomerations. To do this, it is sufficient to use the program above to get the path from *K* to root *O*, then the path from *M* to *O*. The only thing left to do is to drop the common part located at the end of these two paths. In Figure 29.8 we will find two examples of paths on a tree with 19 vertices.

What we now know how to do for a graph in the shape of a tree must be generalized to any graph.

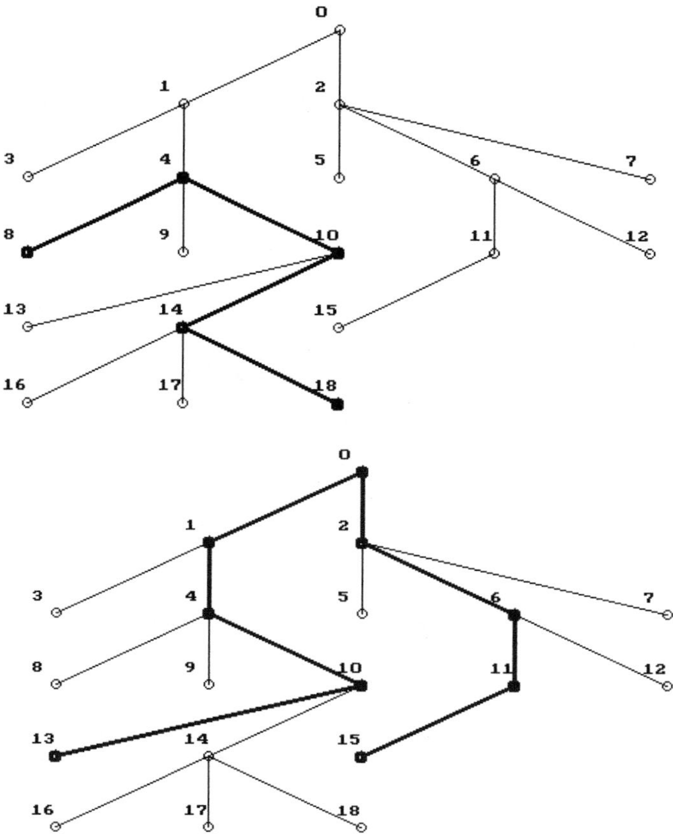

Figure 29.8. *Two paths on the tree, one from vertex 8 to vertex 18 (top) and the other from vertex 13 to vertex 15 (bottom)*

29.4. Paths from one point to another in a graph

The first problem that is posed in graphs is traveling from one point to another. Given two vertices of a directed or undirected graph, one making up the starting point and the other the endpoint, we have to find the paths leading from the first point to the other, avoiding every intermediate return path and every superfluous cycle on the route, i.e. what we call *elementary paths*. We begin here by looking for all the possible paths through a process of enumeration by arborescence, as we saw in Chapter 4.

29.4.1. *Dealing with an example*

Let us take the example of the undirected, connected graph in Figure 29.9 (on the left), and imagine that we want to go from vertex 0 to vertex 5.

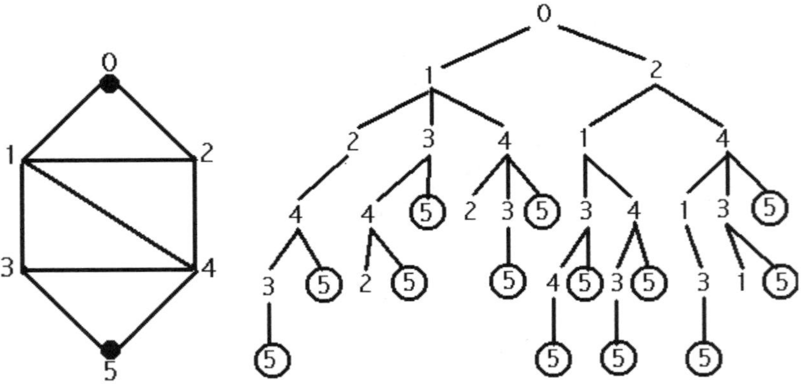

Figure 29.9. *The graph (left); and the arborescence enabling us to get all the paths from node 0 to node 5 (right)*

To do this we construct an arborescence from root 0 and associate each node with its successors, namely the neighbors of the node, avoiding resuming those that are among the ancestors of the node. We make the branches of the tree go down until they reach node 5, with the other branches stopping when the node reached has no more successors. In our example, this finally gives 13 paths from 0 to 5 (see Figure 29.9 on the right).

The program results from it, and we will see the results of it in Figure 29.10. We begin by taking the number of vertices N, here $N = 6$, placing all the variables overall (before the *main*()), and for each one of the vertices *i* from 0 to 5, we take its neighbors which we place in table *n*[*i*][], indicating their number in *nbn*[*i*].

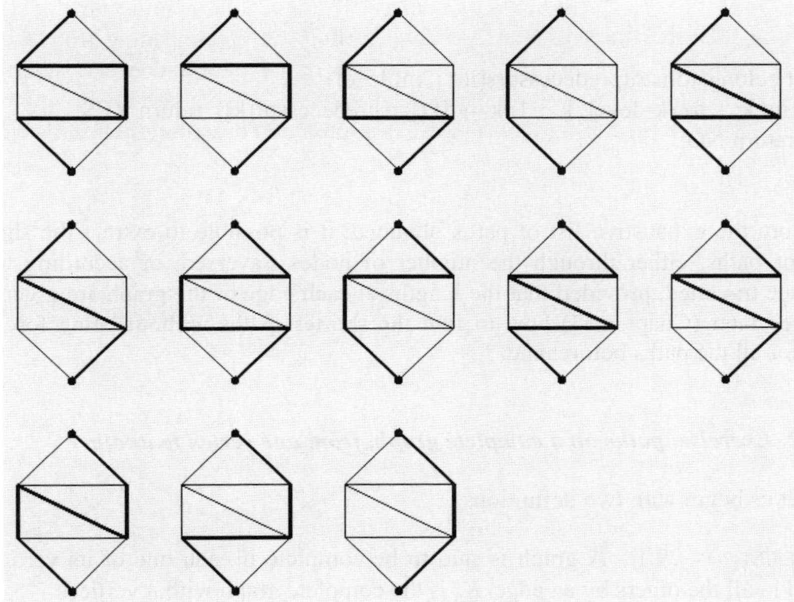

Figure 29.10. *The 13 paths obtained from the previous graph*

The main program simply takes the starting node *s*, the endnode *e*, the variable *count* giving the number of paths (having initially been set to 0), and we call the recursive function *path(s, 0)*, from the starting point *s* that is located at level 0. Let us recall that the table *predecessor*[*k*] has level *k* as the variable where the node is found at the time a branch is created, and not the node itself.

```
main()  { s=0;  e=5;  count=0;   path(s,0); }.

void path(int i, int level)
{  int j, k;
   if (i==e)
     { count++;   display number
       for (k=1; k<=level; k++) printf("%d ", predecessor[k]);
       printf("%d ",e);   draw the path obtained
     }
   else
     {  for(j=0; j<nbn[i]; j++)
```

```
            if ( belongstolistofpredecessors(n[i][j],level)==NO)
                     { predecessor[level+1]=i;  path(n[i][j],level+1); }
         }
   }

   int belongstolistofpredecessors(int j, int level)
   {  int k;    for(k=level; k>=1; k--)  if (j==predecessor[k])  return YES;
      return NO;
   }
```

From the exhaustive list of paths obtained, it is possible to extract the shortest path or paths, either through the number of nodes traversed, or according to the distance travelled, provided that the lengths at each edge of the graph are given. We will see later (Chapter 33) how to find the shortest paths without being forced to look for all the paths beforehand.

29.4.2. *Exercise: paths on a complete graph, from one vertex to another*

Let us begin with two definitions.

DEFINITION 29.1.– A graph is said to be complete if each one of its vertices is linked to all the others by an edge. K_n is the complete graph with n vertices.

DEFINITION 29.2.– Two graphs G and G' are isomorphic if we can establish a bijection between the vertices of one and those of the other in such a way that any two vertices from one are adjacent (joint by an edge) iff they are adjacent in the other.

An example of isomorphic graphs is given in Figure 29.11.

 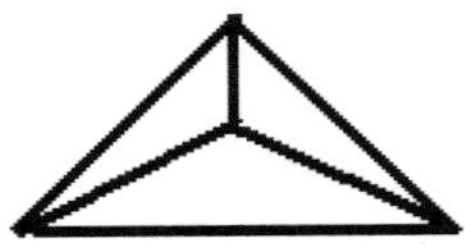

Figure 29.11. *Example of two isomorphic graphs, the second being planar*

a) Check that two complete graphs K_n and K'_n with the same number of vertices, but with the vertices numbered differently, are isomorphic.

Let us consider the bijection causing vertices to move from one to those of the other, with $0 \to 0'$, $1 \to 1'$, $2 \to 2'$, $3 \to 3'$, $4 \to 4'$, etc., which comes back to doing a permutation p on the vertices of the complete graph, i.e. in the example in Figure 29.12:

$$p = \begin{pmatrix} 0 & 1 & 2 & 3 & 4 \\ 0 & 2 & 1 & 3 & 4 \end{pmatrix}$$

This bijection transforms every edge (i, j) of one into edge (i', j') of the other, and *vice versa*, since we have a complete graph.

b) Deduce from this that on graph K_n there are as many paths from one vertex to another vertex.

Thanks to the isomorphism of graphs K_n and K'_n, every path on a graph is in bijective correspondence with a path on the other. In the example of the previous graphs K_5 and K'_5, path 0241 is linked to path $0'2'4'1'$, which is none other than path 0142, and we deduce from this that there are as many paths from 0 to 2 as paths from 0 to 1 in this example.

c) c(n) is the number of paths from a given vertex to another vertex, the choice of these vertices being arbitrary as we have just seen. The aim is to determine number c(n) as a function of n.

Without losing generality, let us choose vertex 0 as the starting vertex and vertex $[n / 2]$ located at the opposite side as the end vertex. First include all paths taking edge 01 at the start. Once we have arrived at 1, we have to take all paths from 1 to $[n / 2]$ that no longer pass through 0, i.e. all the paths on a graph of type K_{n-1}, i.e. $c(n-1)$ paths. It is the same if we take edge 02 at the start or any edge starting at 0, except the edge between 0 and $[n / 2]$ where we arrive directly at the endpoint.

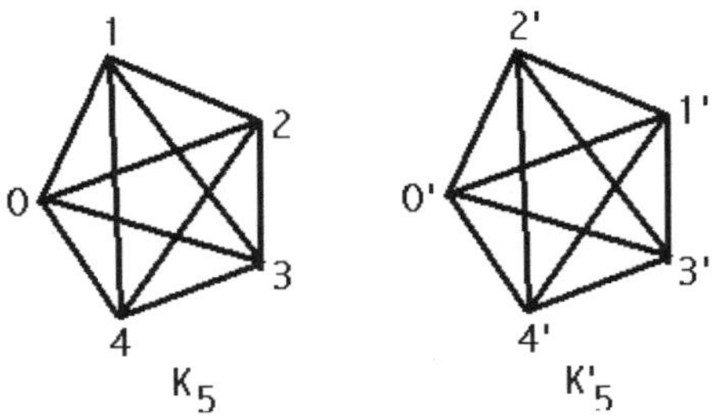

Figure 29.12. *Bijection between two graphs*

There are $n-2$ of these edges, which gives $(n-2)\ c(n-1)$ paths. It is enough to add the direct path from 0 to $[n/2]$. Finally, we obtain the recurrence relation:

$$c(n) = (n-2)\ c(n-1) + 1 \text{ for } n \geq 3$$

with $c(2) = 1$ at the start.

In this way we find:

$$c(2) = 1 \quad c(3) = 2 \quad c(4) = 5 \quad c(5) = 16 \quad c(6) = 65$$

$$c(7) = 326 \quad c(8) = 1{,}957 \quad c(9) = 13{,}700$$

and we end up with the explicit formula:

$$c(n) = 1 + (n-2) + (n-2)(n-3) + \ldots + (n-2)(n-3)\ldots 3.2$$

$$+ (n-2)(n-3)\ldots 3.\ 2.\ 1$$

$$= (n-2)!\ (1/(n-2)! + 1/(n-3)! + \ldots + 1/2! + 1/1! + 1/0\,!)$$

Finally $c(n)$ is of order $e.\ (n-2)!$.[7]

29.4.2.1. *Program*

```
main()
{
for(i=0; i<N; i++)     /* vertices of the regular polygon with N vertices */
      { x[i]=R*cos(2.*M_PI*i/(float)N); y[i]=R*sin(2.*M_PI*i/(float)N);}
start=0;  end=N/2;  xo=5+R;yo=5+R;  path(start,0);
}

void path(int i, int level)
{ if (i==end)
   { for(i=0; i<N; i++) for(j=0; j<N; j++) if (i!=j)
     line(xo+x[i],yo-y[i],xo+x[j],yo-y[j]);    /* drawing of the graph in gray  */
     for(k=1; k<level; k++)   /* drawing of the path in black */
```

7. Another method can be used to determine this: between vertices 0 and [n / 2], either no other vertex, one vertex, two vertices, …, or $n-2$ vertices are inserted. We get all the paths by taking these inserted vertices in all possible orders. We therefore get the arrangements of a certain number of vertices out of $n-2$ vertices. Hence: $c(n) = A_{n-2}^{0} + A_{n-2}^{1} + \ldots + A_{n-2}^{n-2} = 1 + (n-2) + (n-2)(n-3) + \ldots + (n-2)(n-3)\ldots 3.\ 2.\ 1$. We again find the previous formula, and at the same time find the number of paths of a certain length in the number of edges traversed.

```
    line(xo+x[predecessor[k]],yo−y[predecessor[k]],xo+x[predecessor[k+1]],
         yo−y[predecessor[k+1] ]);
   line(xo+x[predecessor[level]],yo-y[predecessor[level]],xo+x[end],yo-y[end]);
   xo+=5+2*R; if (xo>750)  {yo+=10+2*R; xo=5+R; }
                              /* new origin (xo, yo) for the next drawing */
  }
else
  { for(j=0; j<N; j++) if (j!=i) /* neighbors of node i */
    if (  belongstolistofpredecessors(j,level)==NO)
        { predecessor[level+1]=i; path(j,level+1); }
  }
}

int belongstolistofpredecessors(int j, int level)
{ for(k=level; k>=1; k--)  if (j==predecessor[k]) return YES;
  return NO;
}
```

The results for $N = 6$ are given in Figure 29.13.

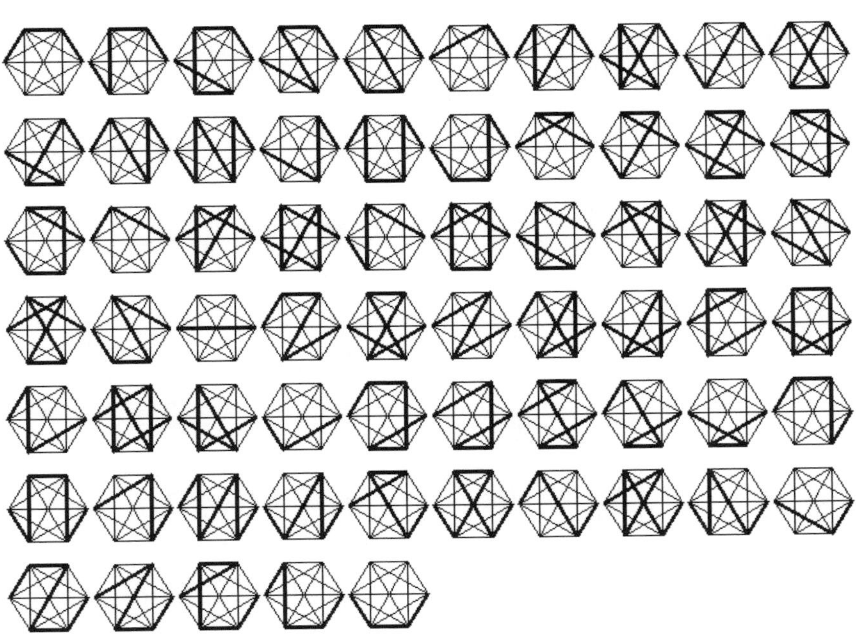

Figure 29.13. *The 65 paths from one point (the rightmost one) to the opposite point, on a complete graph with six vertices*

Chapter 30

Explorations in Graphs

Having made paths on a graph from one point to another, we are now interested in a global exploration of graphs, which will enable us to reach all its vertices, at least if the graph is connected, thanks to a process of finding a path in an arborescence. This will naturally lead us to the maze traversal problem.

30.1. The two ways of visiting all the vertices of a connected graph

There are two ways to circulate on a graph: either as a pedestrian moving forward along a route, choosing one path out of others at each crossroads – a node of the graph – who eventually turns back to take another route he had abandoned up until then; or like a fluid that circulates in pipes and that infiltrates all the paths that open in front of it at each node.

Evidently, the graph must be visualized on the computer screen and its traversal followed with our own eyes. In what follows, we will choose a node of the graph, that constitutes the starting point (or the source).

Exploring the graph consists of starting at this point and going to all the nodes that can be reached from it, without necessarily passing through all the arcs or edges, based on a mechanical and simple method that demands specification.

A graph can therefore be explored in two ways – depth or breadth first:

– *according to a depth-first traversal*, a bit like a pedestrian would do. Each time we arrive at a node with several routes open in front of us, i.e. edges going to nodes that have not yet been reached, we choose the first route that comes, eventually reserving taking another route for later. We thus pursue our path as far as possible, hence the name *depth-first traversal*. A path ends when we arrive at a node at a dead end or even at a node that has routes going to neighboring nodes that we have already passed through. Therefore we go back, hence the term *backtracking*, until we reach a node where open routes (to nodes not yet reached) are left. In the end, all nodes were reached, at least all those that can be reached from the starting point, i.e. the connected component to which the source node belongs. If the graph is connected, all the vertices are reached;

– *according to a breadth-first traversal*, a little like a liquid would do. Each time the fluid reaches a new node, with several routes open in front of it, it takes all these routes, except those that lead to nodes where the fluid has already passed. This will be specified later.

Regardless of the type of traversal, the edges traversed during exploration form a tree that partially covers the graph and that has the starting point as its root. It is a tree because the exploration as we make it forbids us from going round in circles and making a whole loop in the graph.

30.2. Visit to all graph nodes from one node, following depth-first traversal

Initially, the graph is defined by the coordinates $x[N]$, $y[N]$ of its N nodes. Associated with each node i is the list of its direct neighbors (either successors, sons or daughters) $n[i][N]$ linked to it by an edge or an arc.

The N lists of neighbors form a table $n[N][N]$ where we find the number of neighbors of each node *nbneighbors*$[i]$ (we could prefer chained lists). For the graph in Figure 30.1, in this undirected case, the adjacency lists are indicated in the table (on the left).

0	1 2 5 7	4
1	0 4 7	4
2	0	1
3	4 5 6	3
4	1 3 6 7	4
5	0 3 6	3
6	3 4 5	3
7	0 1 4	3

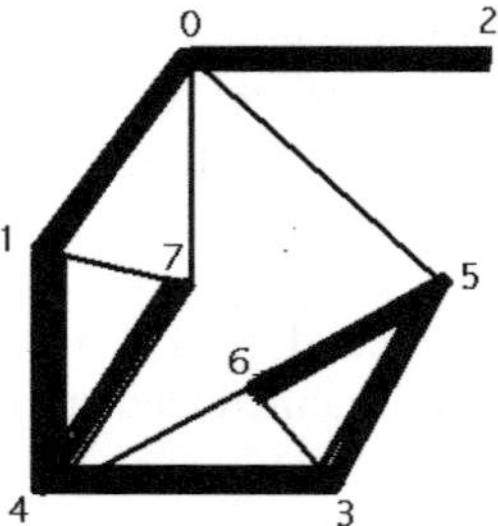

Figure 30.1. *Adjacency lists of graph vertices (left); and depth-first traversal tree from node 0 (right)*

In this example, exploration starts from 0 and gives the succession of nodes: 0 1 4 3 5 6 7 2. We get a tree with root 0. Evidently, as we choose the first neighbor that has come to a node, the tree of exploration changes if we modify the order of neighbors in the table *n*[*i*][].

For this depth-first exploration, the program is naturally recursive. The main program simply draws the graph and calls the function *visit*(*startingpt*), taking for example *startingpt* = 0. The function *visit*(*i*) takes a node *i* as its parameter. This function consists of taking all the neighbors of *i* (by following a *for* loop) and recalling itself on each one of these neighbors (in fact only those not yet reached). Due to the recursive recalls, the neighbors loop is not traversed in direct succession. First of all it is the first neighbor of the list that is recalled on its neighbors. Next the first of these neighbors is recalled on its own neighbors, etc. Hence the notion of depth-first traversal. But to what point?

Sequential traversal of a path ends when we get a node without a successor, either because it does not have any (for a directed graph) or because we have already passed through all its eventual neighbors. This leads us to run a global variable *alreadyseen*[*i*], which is set to *YES* as soon as we arrive at node *i* for the first time. For each node we are only interested in its neighbors that have not yet been "seen". Hence the program that draws the exploration tree:

```
visit (int i)
{ display i;  /* if we want to have the list of nodes in order of being visited */
  alreadyseen [i]=YES;
               /* this array is set to 0 (NO) at the time of its overall declaration */
  for(j=0; j < nbneighbors[i]; j+ +)
    { neighbor = n[i][j];  if ( alreadyseen[neighbor] == NO)
        { line (x[i],y[i],x[neighbor],y[neighbor]);  visit(neighbor); }
    }
}
```

It is notable that the visit function is only called once on each node. As soon as a node is reached for the first time, it is marked as *already seen*, and will never be visited again as a result. An improvement to the program consists of giving three states (three colors) to each node: yet unexplored, during exploration (as soon as *alreadyseen* moves to *YES*), and finishes exploring once all routes coming from it have been tried (when the *for* loop of the visit function ends). Hence the program:

```
void visit(int i)
{ alreadyseen[i]=YES;  color the node as being in the process of exploration
  for(j=0; j<nbn[i]; j++)
    { neighbor=n[i][j];
      if (alreadyseen[neighbor]==NO)
        { line(x[i],y[i],x[neighbor],y[neighbor]);  visit(neighbor);}
    }
  endseen[i]=YES;  color the node as exploring being finished}
```

This corresponds to a prefixed traversal of the exploration tree: we color a node as soon as it is reached for the first time, as well as a postfixed traversal when we color the node as exploring being finished.

As we can see, this type of exploration differs from a simple walk because of its traversal discontinuities. Actually, when the pedestrian arrives at a dead end (a leaf of the tree) and he makes a U-turn, the program is in charge of finding the first preceding node where routes still remain to be explored. This backtrack route is not concretely realized, however. Everything happens as if the pedestrian was taking the plane or coming out of the screen to regain a node not yet totally explored. Initially we can color the branches of the tree that are not linked in a continuous way during the traversal in a different way.

It is enough to run the moment of the U-turn (the arrival in a leaf of the tree) by producing a change in color for future path traces. For this all we have to do is to add a line to the previous program.

```
visit (int i)
{
alreadyseen[i]=YES;  counter=0;
for(j=0; j < nbneighbors[i]; j+ +)
   { neighbor = n[i][j];
     if ( alreadyseen[neighbor] == NO)
          { counter++;
            setcolor color[icolor]; line(x[i],y[i],x[neighbor],y[neighbor]);
            visit(neighbor);
          }
   }
if (counter== 0) icolor++;    /* node i has no unexplored neighbors */
}
```

In the example above, the routes effectively traversed take three colors (see Figure 30.2).

30.3. The pedestrian's route

What remains is to eliminate the previous discontinuities. We now want to see the continuous pedestrian's route.

In the example, after having traversed 014356, the pedestrian makes a U-turn. He returns to nodes 5 and 3 that have already been completely explored. Then having arrived at 4 he goes to 7 and comes back to 4, which has finished being explored. Then he goes back up to 1 and 0, which he finishes exploring by going to 2, before finally returning to 0.

Besides variable *alreadyseen*[*i*] for node *i*, which indicates whether or not we have passed through the node, we use the variable *finished*[*i*] to find out whether all the paths coming from the node were explored or not. In other words, whether the exploration of the node is finished.

Each time we encounter a node that we have finished exploring, we back track, and this needs to be visualized. To do this we have to find out the predecessor of the node, hence the addition of a table *pred*[] placed overall.

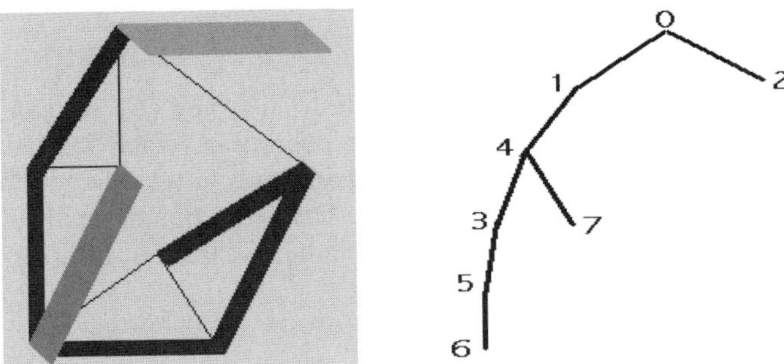

Figure 30.2. *Three paths separated by a discontinuity (corresponding to the graph in Figure 30.1) (left); and the depth-first exploration tree (right)*

```
visit (int i)      /* in the initial call of main(), we make visit(0) */
{ if (finishedi[i]==NO)
    { alreadyseen[i]= YES;
      for(j=0; j < nbneighbors [i]; j++ )
          { neighbor=n[i][j];
            if (alreadyseen[neighbor] == NO )
              { line (x[i],y[i],x[neighbor],y[neighbor]); add an arrow
                pred[neighbor]= i;  visit(neighbor);
              }
```

```
            }
            /* the for loop is finished */
            finished[i] = YES; line (x[i]+8,y[i]+8,x[pred[i]]+8,y[pred[i]]+8);
            add an arrow
        }
    }
```

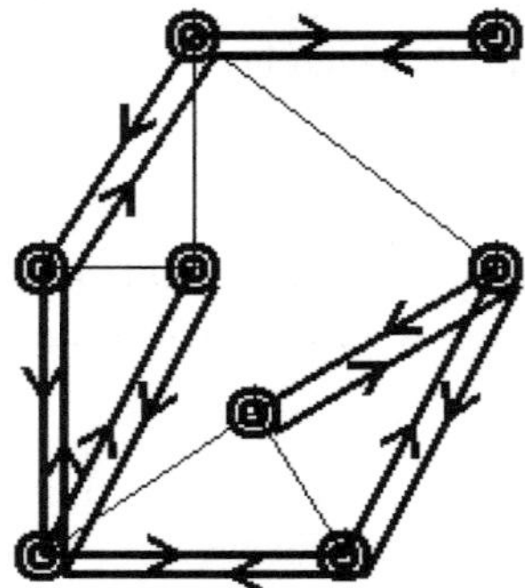

Figure 30.3. *The pedestrian's route with visibility from a distance*

We have just explored the graph as a pedestrian would. As we can see on the drawing in Figure 30.3, this implies that the pedestrian, when located at a node opposite a path, knows whether the place this path leads to was already found on his route, in which case he does not take this path. The pedestrian has a visibility, as if a reference point placed at a neighboring node indicated from a distance whether or not to traverse such a path towards this neighbor.

We are now going to take the most general case – the one where the pedestrian does not have any view from a distance. What will he do now?

When the pedestrian is at a crossroads, i.e. at a graph vertex, and he wants to move forward on his route, he has several paths in front of him. He eliminates the path from which he is coming (the one he has just traversed) as well as the paths where reference points indicate to him that he already passed there. He marks the remaining open paths and takes the first one that he comes to, for example the one that is rightmost, which he knows has not yet been traversed. He moves forward in this way node after node, remembering that he has passed through these nodes, with certain paths still waiting to be traversed for the first time.

In two situations he will need to return on these steps. In the first case, he ends up on a node that has not finished being explored, but taking an open route arrives at a node he already passed, in which case he makes a U-turn and returns to the node where he was. In the second case, he is on a node where all the paths were already explored, in which case he backtracks up to a node he is coming from, some of the paths having yet to be traversed. In the end, he finds himself back at the starting point. At the end of this route, all paths have been traversed twice in two directions. Therefore, if we consider the graph to be directed, with two bidirectional arcs everywhere, to enable bidirectional traveling, the pedestrian has just done what we call a *Eulerian cycle* on this graph.

During exploration, crossroads are either not yet reached (*alreadyseen = NO*), reached but have not yet finished being explored (*alreadyseen=YES*) or finished being explored (*finished=YES*). From a crossroads that we have just reached, and that is not finished, the first possible path (going from right to left) is taken. If the pedestrian comes to a crossroads that has never before been reached, he seeks to take a path from this new crossroads. If he comes to a crossroads that has already been reached, he makes a U-turn at the crossroads where he was, hence he will try to take a new path. The very principle of recursive depth-first traversal prevents us from traversing a path more than once in two directions. Once the pedestrian has finished exploring the crossroad, the only possibility is returning to its predecessor.

```
void visit(int i)
{if (finished[i]==NO)
   { alreadyseen[i]=YES;
     for(j=0; j<nbn[i]; j++) if (n[i][j]==pred[i]) {decal=j; break; }
              /* we choose the rightmost open route decal */
     for(j=0; j<nbn[i]; j++)
       {  neighbor=n[i][(j+decal)%nbn[i]];
          if (alreadyseen[neighbor]==NO)
            { draw the path between node i and the neighbor, in dark gray
              pred[neighbor]= i;  visit(neighbor);
            }
          else if (alreadyseen[neighbor]==YES && finished[neighbor]==NO
                   && pred[i]!= neighbor)
          {draw the path between i and its neighbor in light gray
           then draw the path between the neighbor and i in gray
          }
       }
     finished[i]=YES;
   }
  if (finished[i]==YES && pred[i] != -1)
      draw the path between i and its previous neighbor in black
}
```

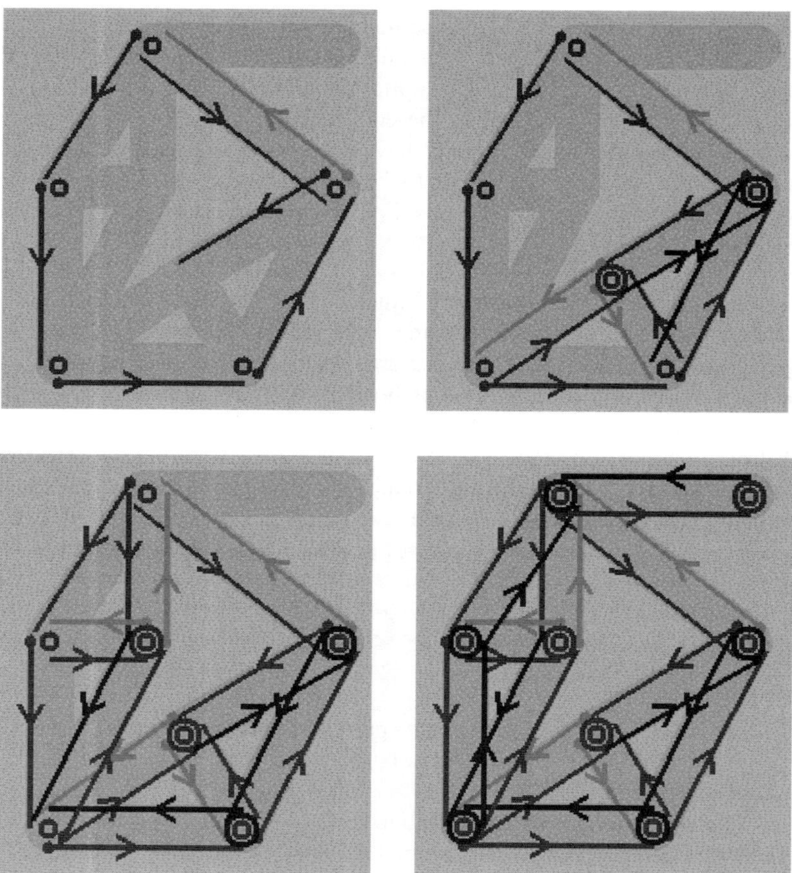

Figure 30.4. *A few stages in the pedestrian's exploration, up to his return to the starting point (the paths to a node that has already been reached are in light gray)*

The method used here looks like the one suggested by Trémaux over a century ago, as described by Lucas in his *Récréations Mathématiques* (*Mathematical Recreations*) [LUC 1891]. It enables us to completely traverse any maze without getting lost, finally returning to the starting point.

This applies to every maze with corridors and crossroads delimited by walls. Let us resume the algorithm: from the entrance point, we move forward down the corridors, passing the crossroads if we have not yet passed them, and for this we ensure we keep the walls on our left (or our right if we prefer). If we get to a dead end, we make a U-turn and return, keeping the walls on our left. If we get to a crossroads we have already passed, there are two cases. First, if we arrive there using a route we took in a single direction, we make a U-turn and return in the other direction, still with the walls on our left. Second, if we get there by a route already traversed in both directions, we go up to the crossroads and take the first route from the left that has not yet been traversed, or else the one that was traversed in a single direction.

Let us take a simple maze example (see Figure 30.5, top). A person enters through the top opening and traverses the maze in a systematic way until he comes back out through the same opening. He follows the walls, keeping them to his left, and crosses the crossroads for the first time, marking them. Hence the route indicated in Figure 30.5 (bottom right) with an intermediate stage (on the left). When he gets to a crossroads he has already passed, he makes a U-turn and he turns back, keeping the walls to his left. This return in the reverse direction when we have already passed in the other direction is indicated with a different color. After a return journey on a path, if the person arrives at a crossroads, he takes the eventual leftmost open route if this route has not already been taken or if it was taken in one single direction. We get the complete route in Figure 30.5 (bottom right).

If we consider the graph of the maze to be directed, with one edge of the graph being replaced by two bidirectional arcs, the journey obtained by the previous algorithm forms a Eulerian cycle, because each graph arc is traversed once and only once.

30.4. Depth-first exploration to determine connected components of the graph

The depth-first exploration program seen at the beginning of this chapter is valid for a directed graph as well as an undirected one. If the graph is undirected and has one single connected component, all the nodes will be reached during the exploration, regardless of the starting point. If the undirected graph has several connected components, as many starting points will be needed to reach all nodes of the graph.

We start at node 0, and the visit function gives all the nodes of the connected component of 0. Next we take the first node that has not been reached (with *alreadyseen*[] = *NO*) and we visit its connected component.

And so on and so forth until all the nodes have been reached. We can modify the program above for it to achieve this. A result is given in Figure 30.6.

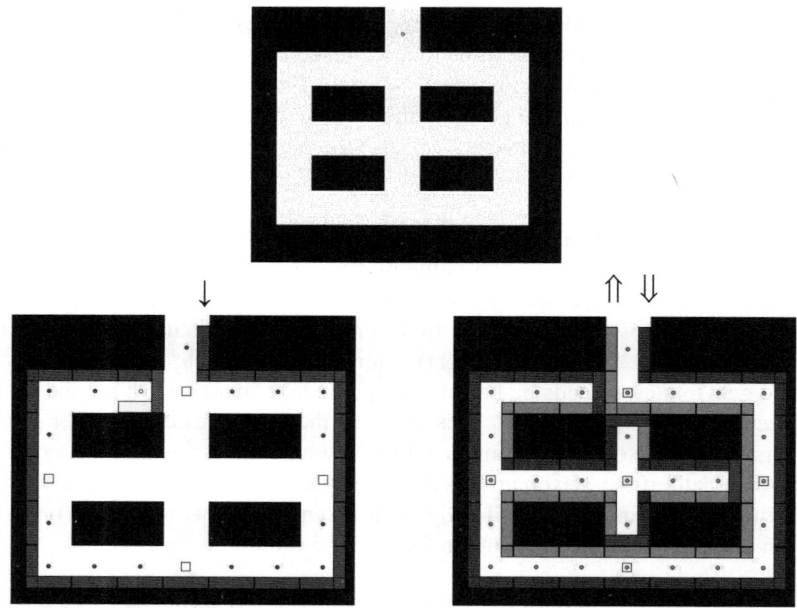

Figure 30.5. *The maze (top); an intermediate step in the traversal (bottom left); and the total traversal up to the exit (bottom right)*

```
ccc=0;                  /* ccc is the connected components counter */
for(i=0; i<N; i++)   { alreadyseen[i]=0; draw a circle on each node }
for(i=0; i<N; i++)   if (alreadyseen[i]==0)    {ccc++; visit(i); }

void visit(int i)   /* visit function */
{
cc[i]=ccc;  /* we give each node the number of its connected component */
alreadyseen[i]=1; draw a bigger circle at the node concerned
for(j=0; j<nbn[i]; j++)
   { neighbor=n[i][j]; if (alreadyseen[neighbor]==0)
                       { line(x[i],y[i],x[neighbor],y[neighbor]); visit(neighbor); }
   }
finished[i]=1; draw an even bigger circle;
}
```

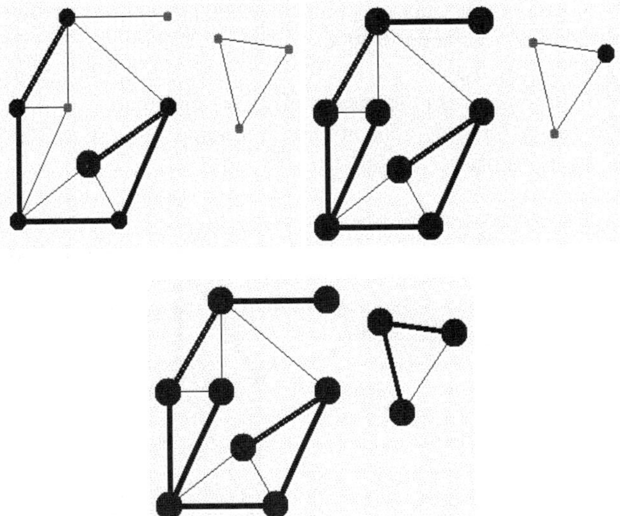

Figure 30.6. *Progressive exploration of the two connected components of this graph*

30.5. Breadth-first traversal

Since depth-first traversal is typically recursive, it can also be carried out by running a stack. It is the above the head of the stack that we expand at each stage, with the list of neighbors of the head node that replaces it, then the new head, etc. In an analogous way, the breadth-first traversal is obtained by running a waiting file: the successors of the head node are placed in a queue and not at the head. They wait for their turn to be expanded. If we consider all the edges to have the same length, i.e. one unit, or even that we put in the same time to traverse them, at stage n the nodes reached are all at a distance less than or equal to n. At certain moments of the process, the nodes that have just been reached for the first time are all at the same distance from the source, hence the analogy with the movement of a fluid. The distance obtained between the source and a node that has just been reached also constitutes the shortest distance from the source to this node.

30.5.1. *Program*

Let us consider the case of the graph in Figure 30.7, starting at vertex 0. We begin by putting 0 in the line. Next we take its neighbors 1257 that we place behind it (while drawing the junctions from 0 to its neighbors), and we drop 0, hence the line 1257.

We now take head 1. Its only neighbor that has not yet been reached is 4, which we place in the queue. We then drop the 1, hence the line 2574. We take head 2, which no longer has any neighbors, and remove it, hence the line 574. We take head 5 and place its neighbors 36 in the queue. Next we eliminate 5, which gives the line 7436. From this point, this line does not stop reducing: 436, then 36, then 6, and we stop when the line is empty.

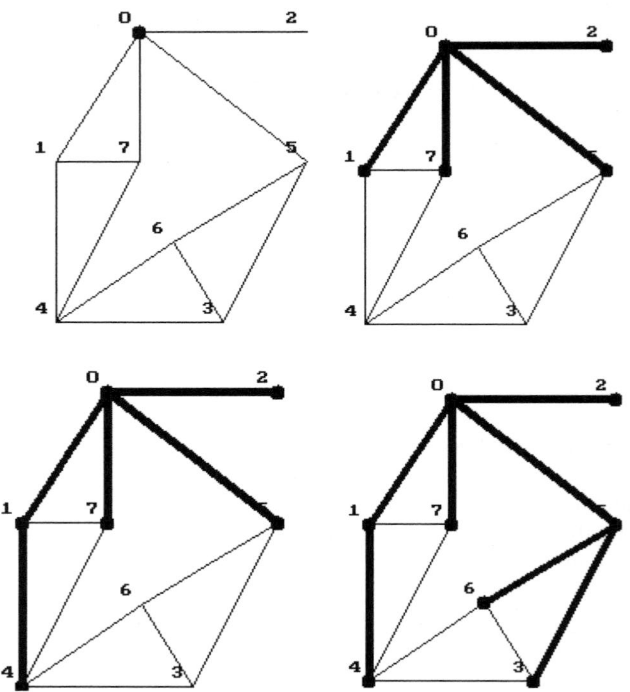

Figure 30.7. *Evolution of breadth-first exploration of a graph*

Here is the corresponding program:

```
startingpt=0;  f[0]=startingpt; alreadyseen[startingpt]=1;  linelength=1;
while(linelength!=0)
  { i=f[0];   /* we take the beginning of the line */

    for(j=0; j<nbn[i]; j++)
      {  neighbor=n[i][j];  if (alreadyseen[neighbor]==0)
          { alreadyseen[neighbor]=1;
            pred[neighbor]=i;
```

```
            line(x[pred[neighbor]],y[pred[neighbor]],x[neighbor],y[neighbor]);
            f[linelength]=neighbor; linelength++;
          }
      }
    for(k=0; k<linelength-1; k++)  f[k]=f[k+1];
    linelength--;
  }
 end=5;  /* a path example, from vertex 0 to vertex 5 */
 k=end;  /*  here the display of the path is done from end to start */
 while(pred[k]!=startingpt) {line(x[k],y[k],x[pred[k]],y[pred[k]]); k=pred[k];}
 line(x[k],y[k],x[pred[k]],y[pred[k]]);
          /*  or recursive display in the correct direction */
           p(end);
}

void  p(int k)
{ if (k!=startingpt) p(pred[k]); line(x[k],y[k],x[pred[k]],y[pred[k]]); }
```

30.5.2. *Example: traversal in a square grid*

In light of the program that follows, the neighbors of a node are placed in a table delimited by an extra buffer box set to 1,000, as for example with 0 that has two neighbors: *neighbor*[0][] = {1, 10, 1,000}. In this case, we use a square grid with 100 points, which facilitates the relation between their number and their coordinates (see Figure 30.8).

During the process, we distinguish the three possible node states: not yet reached by exploration, reached, and finished being explored, with the values 0, 1 and 2 placed in variable *color*[].

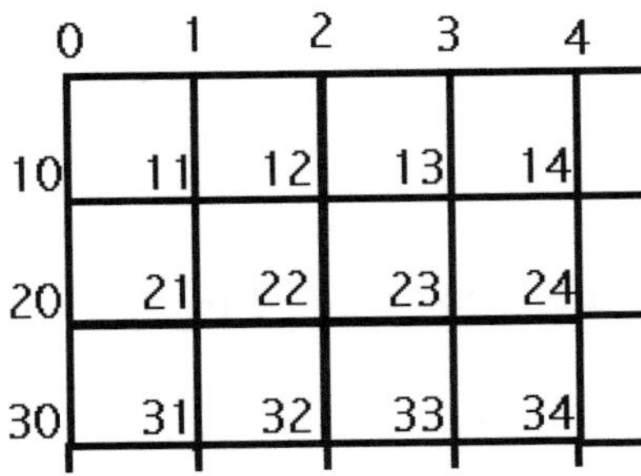

Figure 30.8. *Numbering of nodes of the square grid*

The following program is a slight variation of the previous one. Instead of managing the length of the line, we place an extra buffer (set to 1,000) at the end of the line:

```
main()
{
*/ initial drawing of a square grid with N nodes, with the numbering chosen
easily giving the coordinates of the nodes, then random choice of horizontal,
vertical or diagonal junction edges (see Figure 30.9)*/
start=0;
for(i=0; i<N; i++)  if (i!=start)
   { color[i]=notyetreached; pred[i]=1000; }
color[start]=reached ; distance[start]=0; pred[start]=1000;
circle around the starting point with the color[start]
file[0]=start; file[1]=1000;  /* we put a buffer at 1000 at the end of the line */

while (file[0]!=1000)   /* the large loop, as long as the line is not empty */
    { i = file[0]; j = 0 ;
      while (neighbor[i][j]!=1000)
          { if (color[neighbor[i][j]]== notyetreached)
               {
                color[neighbor[i][j]]=reached;
                distance[neighbor[i][j]]=distance[i]+1;
                pred[neighbor[i][j]]=i;    add(neighbor[i][j]);
                circle around the node neighbor and segment joining the neighbor
                and its predecessor
               }
             j++;
          }
      remove(); color[i]=finished; circle around the node with its color
    }
}

/* function that adds a neighbor u of the first one in the line to the end of the
   line */
void add(int u)
  { int i=0; while (file[i]!=1000) i++;  file[i]=u ; file[i+1]=1000; }

/* function which removes the first one in the line */
void remove(void)
  { int i=0; do { file[i]=file[i+1]; i++ ;} while (file[i]!=1000);}
```

We can also add a function that gives the shortest path from the start to an endpoint, *drawpath (start, end)*.

The results are found in Figures 30.9 and 30.10, with the drawing of a shortest path.

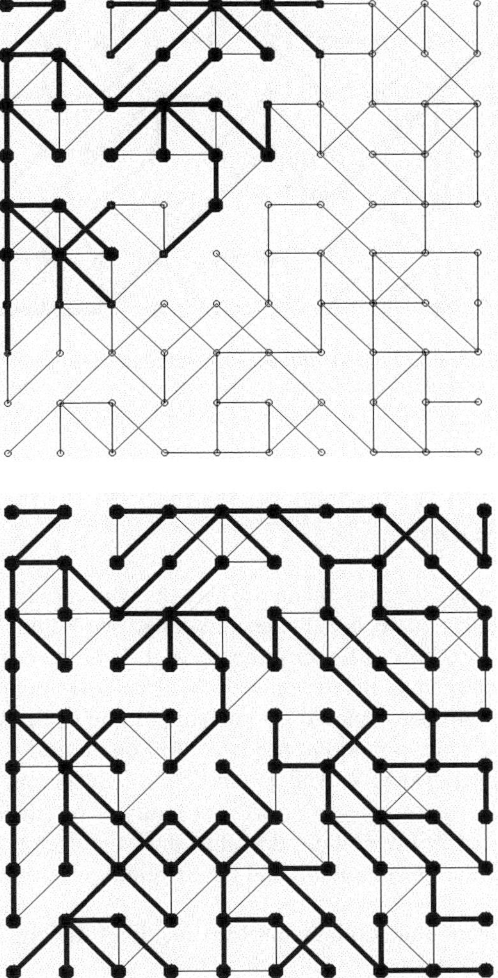

Figure 30.9. *Breadth-first traversal during evolution from the initial node 0, located in the top left, the bottom drawing representing the final exploration tree*

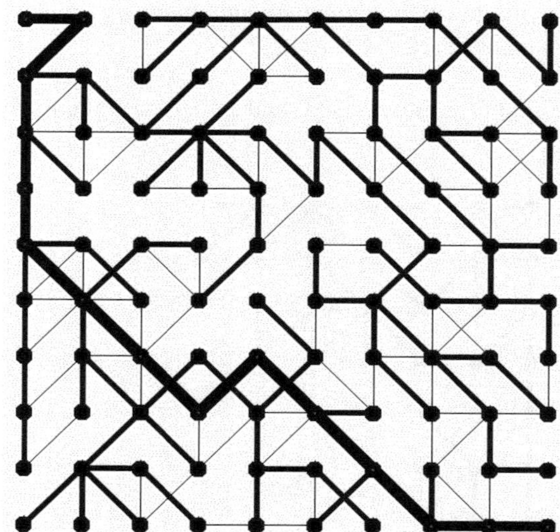

Figure 30.10. *End of exploration and shortest path (in terms of number of nodes traversed) between the two extreme nodes*

30.6. Exercises

30.6.1. *Searching in a maze*

To construct a maze, here is a method where the walls are lines traced in a square grid, with each small square being one unit long. We begin by drawing a large square that serves as a border for this square grid. It is the outer wall (see Figure 30.11, top). Next, the maze of interior walls will be constructed line by line, with each line of unit length being placed on one side of one of the small squares of the grid. To do this, we draw a random vertex of the square grid that will serve as the origin of the line to be drawn, as well as one of the four directions west, south, east or north. This gives a vector, the origin and extremity of which we know. But before tracing the line, we carry out random drawings until the vector's origin is on a wall (initially it is the border of the square) and the extremity is not on a wall.

Then we start again and continue until the inside of the big square is filled with walls, thus constructed line by line, the latter sticking to other lines by their extremities, avoiding closing back on themselves (i.e. avoiding a cycle).

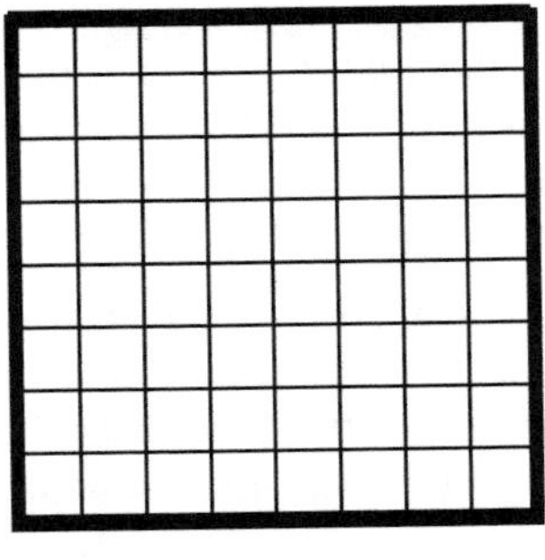

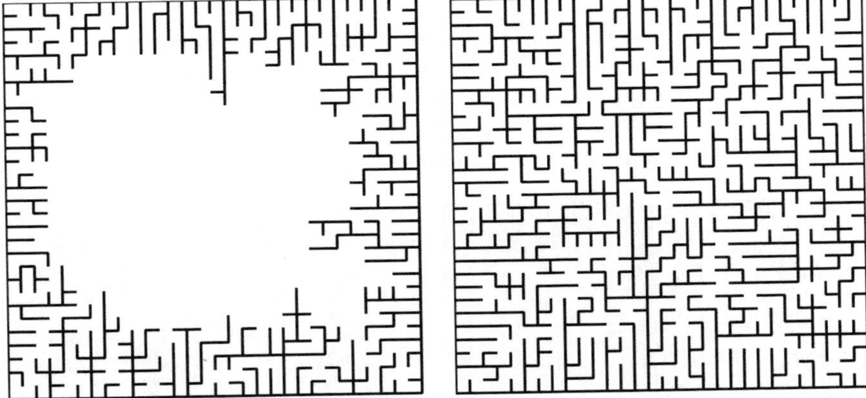

Figure 30.11. *Above the square grid and its outer walls, below the maze in the process of construction delimited by the top of the trees, up to the final stage*

This process constructs trees whose root is found on the border of the square. When every square is filled in this way, we are sure that the trees have a unit distance between them, which forms inserted corridors.

Now let us take the two small squares of unit side located at the opposite sides of the big square. The one on the top left will serve as starting point, and the other is the goal to be reached (we could choose any points located in the corridors if we prefer).

a) Why is there a single path that does not intersect itself again and that joins the two small extreme squares taking the corridors made between the walls?

From the starting point that serves as the root, all of the paths inserted between the walls form a tree, because no cycle can exist. All the points located on the border of the square make up the leaves of this tree (except the starting point, also located on the border). Therefore there is only one path leading from the root to the endpoint. Let us specify that this path creeps in between the tops of the trees that form the walls whose root is always on the border of the big square.

b) How can the path between the start and end points be obtained?

It is sufficient to make a so-called infix traversal of the tree from the capillary paths until we reach the leaf that constitutes the endpoint. At each node of this tree, we choose the edges to take from the right and make a U-turn each time we reach at a dead end, i.e. a terminal node of the tree, located on the border.

c) Describe the program that traces the journey from the starting point to the end.

This program uses the depth-first search that we saw before; this time in a graphic context. Once we have arrived at a point, we do a panoramic test of its neighborhood to the right, then in front, then to the left, and we take the first breach that opens up that is not blocked by a wall, even if it means backtracking if we arrive at a dead end. The results are shown in Figure 30.12.

Figure 30.12. *The maze (left); the drawing making the trees of the walls coming from the border stand out, and the path going from the start to the end by running along the trees that have their root in the borders on the left of and below the square (right)*

d) Resume the construction of the maze without waiting to fill the entire square. Why does the program above always enable us to get a path between the opposite sides of the square?

The program described above (see also section 30.9) gives the path that runs along the top of the trees of the walls whose root is found on the left and bottom borders. It continues to work even in this case where a wall-less zone eventually remains in the center of the square (see Figure 30.13). Choosing to go left during the infix traversal of the path arborescence, we would have a second path also bordering the central hole of the other side.

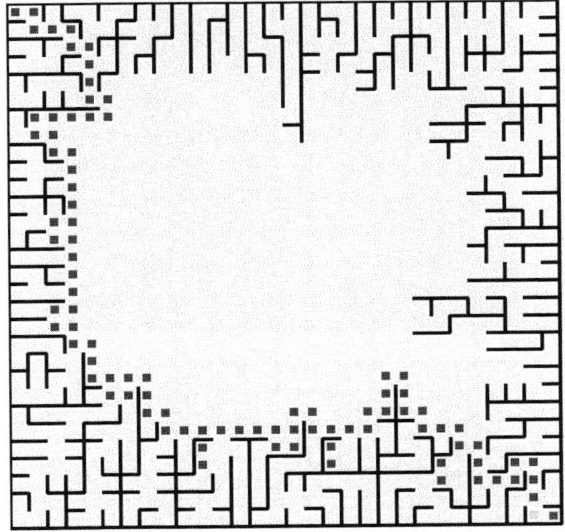

Figure 30.13. *Path running along the top of the trees*

e) Resume the construction of the maze by modifying the initial conditions.

Now, not only can the points on the square border serve as the root for the trees of the walls, but we also add several random anchorage points inside the square, where the trees of the walls will also be able to take root. Then, like before, we complete the filling.

Why are there now several possible paths for joining the opposite sides of this path graph, which is no longer a tree, and why does the program described above still give one of the paths, without the risk of getting lost in the infinite loops?

The capillary path graph is no longer a tree, but as before running along the top of the trees that have their root on the left and bottom borders of the square gives a path (see Figure 30.14).

In section 30.9, you will find the programs enabling construction of the maze in its simplest form, as well as the path leading from the top to the bottom to get out of the maze.

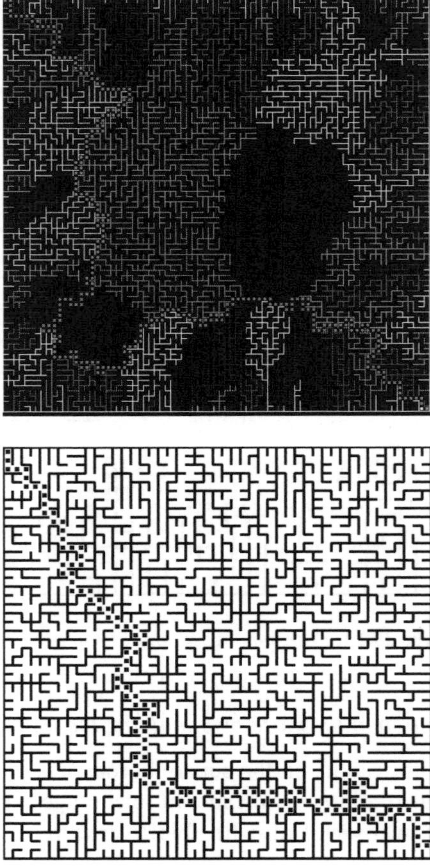

Figure 30.14. *Top: we make the underlying connected components formed by trees coming from the walls stand out, as well as those of the central trees. Bottom: only one path is traced, going from start to end, and still running along the trees that have their root on the left or bottom borders of the square*

30.6.2. *Routes in a square grid, with rising shapes without entangling*

Take a square network with horizontal and vertical lines. From point O serving as the origin, a shape is created from a succession of lines of the square grid, oriented either westwards, eastwards or northwards (but never southwards), all with the same unit length, without any lines passing over each other. Thus the west-east succession is forbidden. $u(n)$ is the number of these rising shapes that are n long. We can see drawings of them in Figure 30.16.

a) Determine u(1) and u(2), drawing the corresponding forms. We will postulate that u(0) = 1.

We find that $u(1) = 3$ and $u(2) = 7$.

b) Show that u(n+1) = 2u(n) + u(n-1).

To do this we separate the $u(n)$ shapes that are n long into three categories:

– $E(n)$ is the number of those ending in an eastward line;

– $W(n)$ in a westward line; and

– $N(n)$ in a northward line.

When we add a line to them to get shapes that are $n + 1$ long, we notice that:

– $W(n + 1) = W(n) + N(n)$, because we can only add back a westward line to a westward or a northward line;

– $E(n + 1) = E(n) + N(n)$ for the same reasons; and

– $N(n + 1) = W(n) + E(n) + N(n)$ because the three directions are possible for adding the extra upward line.

We deduce from this by addition that: $u(n+1) = 2\,u(n) + N(n)$.

Furthermore $N(n + 1) = u(n)$, because we can always add a vertical line to any shape that is n long. From this it results that $N(n) = u(n - 1)$, hence finally:

$$u(n+1) = 2\,u(n) + u(n-1)$$

with the initial conditions $u(0) = 1$ and $u(1) = 3$.

c) Find the explicit form of u(n).

Let $F(x)$ be the generating function associated with $u(n)$. By definition:

$$\begin{aligned}F(x) &= u(0) + u(1)x + u(2)x^2 + u(3)x^3 + \ldots\\ &= 1 + 3x + (2u(1) + u(0))x^2 + (2u(2) + u(1))x^3 + \ldots\\ &= 1 + 3x + 2x\,(F(x) - 1) + x^2 F(x)\end{aligned}$$

$$\begin{aligned}F(x) &= (1 + x) / (1 - 2x - x^2)\\ &= (1 + x) / ((1 - ax)(1 - a'x)), \text{ with } a = 1 + \sqrt{2}\,,\ a' = 1 - \sqrt{2}\\ &= a / (2(1 - ax)) + a' / (2(1 - a'x)).\end{aligned}$$

Developing, this gives: $u(n) = 0.5\,(a^{n+1} + a'^{\,n+1})$.

d) Write a program to find the drawing of all the shapes for a given n.

Information: we start at stage 1 ($n = 1$), with the three numbers 0, 1 and 2 placed in a table *a*[1][] corresponding to the three initial shapes, east, west and north, and making up the first level of an arborescence. Next we exercise the substitution rules $0 \to 02$, $1 \to 12$, $2 \to 012$, which correspond to the level-by-level development of an arborescence that will then have to be read from the bottom up. To do this, we will use a table *b*[*level*][] containing the indices of the predecessors (and not the predecessors). Finally we will write each branch from the top down (see Figure 30.15):

a[1][] 012 (table *b* is useless here)

a[2][] 0212012 *b*[2][]: 0011222

a[3][] 02012120120212012 *b*[3][]: 00111223334455666

Once these tables have been created at each stage (or level) by managing their working length, we will do a traversal (from $i = 0$ to $i = L[level - 1]$), where *L*[] is the length of the tables at each stage, calling the function that will give each one of these forms *pred*().

The program is thus:

```
void pred(int i, int level)
{
 if (level>1)
    { previousindex=b[level][i]]; pred(previousindex,level-1);}
 display a[level][i];
}
```

This is a program that uses the initial theory. We could also create a program analogous to the one in the exercise in Chapter 6 (section 6.6.5). The results are given in Figure 30.16.

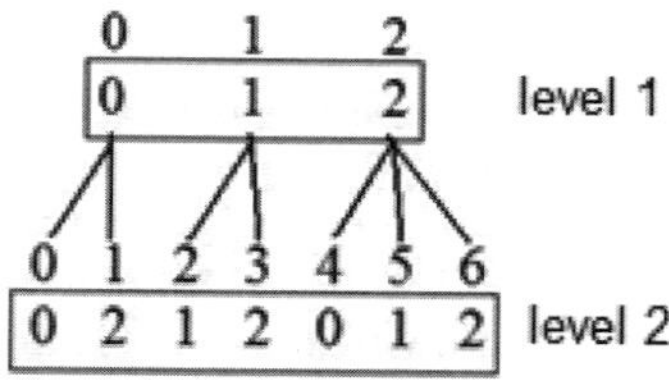

Figure 30.15. *Construction of the tables giving the first two levels of the arborescence*

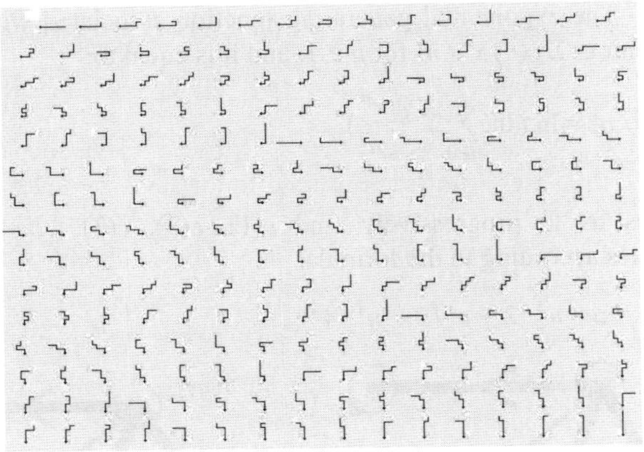

Figure 30.16. *The 239 shapes that are six units long*

30.6.3. *Route of a fluid in a graph*

Let us consider the edges of the (undirected) graph to be pipelines in which fluid flows at a constant rate, taking into consideration the length of the edges. We are led to manage the fluid fronts at each stage in time, blocking them when we arrive at a node where the fluid is already flowing. This is done until the graph is finally filled.

Representing this movement on the computer screen, and registering the moments when a fluid front reaches a node for the first time, we will notably get the shortest paths from the source node to all the other nodes, i.e. what the Dijkstra algorithm makes (see Figure 30.17).

30.6.4. *Connected graphs with n vertices*

We take a set of n points numbered 1, 2, 3, …, n. We are interested in graphs that have these numbered points as vertices (undirected graphs with numbered vertices), as we saw in Chapter 29, section 29.1.2). Out of the $2^{n(n-1)/2}$ graphs, we want to find those that are connected, as well as their number $c(n)$.

For this, it is enough to carry out the exploration of each of these graphs, which gives a tree, and to see whether this tree is a spanning tree (it reaches all the graph vertices), in which case the graph is connected. Experimentally, we find:

$c(1) = 1$, $c(2) = 1$, $c(3) = 4$, $c(4) = 38$, $c(5) = 728$, …

NOTE 30.1.– The exponential generating function associated with the sequence $c(n)$ is, by definition: $\Sigma\, c(n)\, x^n / n!$ for $n \geq 1$, and it is equal to:[1]

$$\Sigma\, c(n)\, x^n / n! = \ln\,(\ln(\sum_{n\geq 0} 2^{C_n^2} \frac{x^n}{n!})$$

This enables us to progressively find $c(1)$, $c(2)$, $c(3)$, …, developing the logarithm in series according to the formula:

$$\ln(1+u) = u - u^2/2 + u^3/3 - u^4/4 + \ldots$$

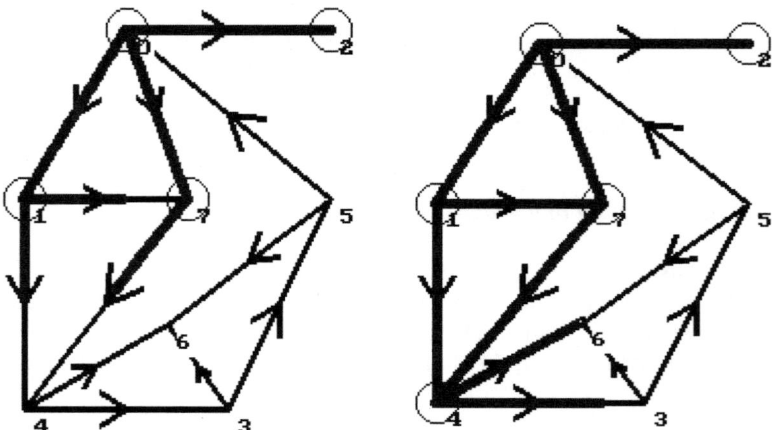

Figure 30.17. *Movement of the fluid at constant speed from node 0*

1. The demonstration of this formula can be found in [STA 01], Volume 2, Chapter 1. We also have the recurrence relation $A_N = 2^{C_N^2} - \frac{1}{N}\sum_{k=1}^{N-1} k C_N^k 2^{C_{N-k}^2} A_k$, where A_N is the number of connected graphs with N nodes (from 1 to N), and $B_N = \frac{1}{N}\sum_{k=1}^{N-1} k C_N^k 2^{C_{N-k}^2} A_k$ is the number of non-connected graphs. To compute B_N we take a favored node, 1 for instance. This node belongs to a connected component with k nodes (k between 1 and $N-1$). We start by choosing the $k-1$ nodes other than 1, hence C_{N-1}^{k-1} cases. At each time, there are A_k ways of building this connected component and $2^{C_{N-k}^2}$ ways of building the rest of the graph. Hence:

$$B_N = \sum_{k=1}^{N-1} C_{N-1}^{k-1} 2^{C_{N-k}^2} A_k = \frac{1}{N}\sum_{k=1}^{N-1} k C_N^k 2^{C_{N-k}^2} A_k\,.$$

30.6.5. *Bipartite graphs*

A graph is said to be bipartite if the set of its vertices can be divided into two parts so that every graph edge joins a vertex that is in one part to a vertex of the other (see Figure 30.18).

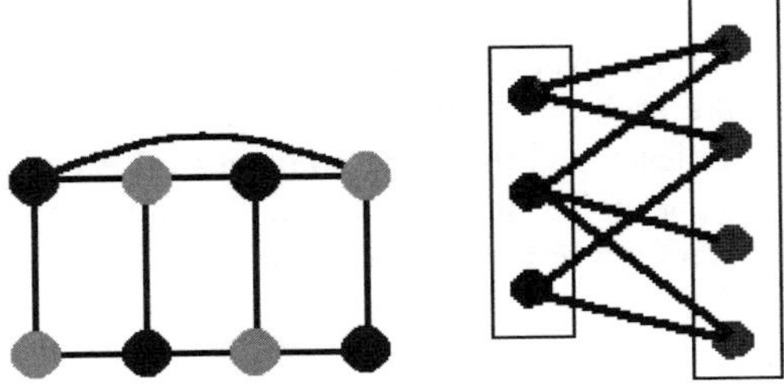

Figure 30.18. *Bipartite graphs: a first example with the vertices in two colors, with each edge joining a vertex in one color to a vertex in the other (left); and another example, with the partition of the set of vertices in two (right)*

This type of graph has the following characteristic property: a graph (supposedly undirected and connected) is bipartite if – and only if – there is no odd length cycle.

Let us show this property. First of all let us assume that the graph is bipartite, with its two collections of vertices – one on the left and the other on the right, as in the drawing in Figure 30.18 (on the right). Let us take a cycle of this graph and start from a vertex on the left to traverse it. At the end of an edge, and more generally with an odd number of edges, we still end up at a vertex on the right. On the other hand, at the end of the traversal of an even number of edges, we always end up on the left-hand side. This forces the cycle to have an even length, in such a way that we can return to the starting point.

Conversely, let us assume that a graph has no cycles of odd length. It can be one of two things. First, it has no cycles, and is a tree that we can color level by level, alternating the color of the vertices. This gives a bipartite graph. Second, it has cycles that are all of even length. Using any exploration algorithm, we know how to construct a spanning tree from a vertex r taken as the root. Let us color the vertices in one of the two colors, depending on whether they are found at an odd or an even level of the tree. The vertices are therefore shared between two sets. If there were an edge of the graph between two vertices a and b of the same set, for example the one that contains root r, there would be a path from r to a of even length, and a path from r to b of even length. We would therefore get a cycle going from r to a, then from a to b, then from b to r, with an odd length, which is contradictory to the hypothesis. An edge can only join one set to the other. We therefore have a bipartite graph.

How do we test whether a graph is bipartite and, if need be, color its vertices in two colors? All we have to do is apply the method we have just seen. We construct a spanning tree, thanks to a depth-first or breadth-first exploration algorithm. Depending on the parity of the level where each vertex is found, we give it one color or the other. Then we take each one of the graph edges that are not in the tree and check whether its extremities are in the same color or not. As soon as an edge has two extremities in the same color, we can affirm that the graph is not bipartite. Conversely, if all the remaining edges have extreme vertices with different colors, the graph is bipartite.

30.7. Returning to a depth-first exploration tree

Let us return to the depth-first exploration program of an undirected (or directed) graph. Instead of using a variable *alreadyseen*(i) to indicate whether a node i is being explored or not, we can take a variable that marks the nodes as soon as they are reached. The nodes are thus numbered in the order they are touched for the first time. This variable goes hand in hand with the variable *finished*(i), which will number the nodes in the order that exploration of them is finished. The exploration program takes the following from:

```
visit (int i)
{  start[i]=++counters;   /* the variable counters is overall defined, where it is
                             set to 0. The variable start starts at 1.
                             Similarly for countere. */
   for(j=0; j < nbneighbors[i]; j+ +)
     { neighbor = n[i][j];  if ( start[neighbor] == 0)
          { line (x[i],y[i],x[neighbor],y[neighbor]);  visit(neighbor); }
     }
   end[i]=++countere;
}
```

The extra information obtained enables us to answer various questions. For example, how can we find the descendants of a node i in the exploration tree? By descendants, we mean all the nodes that are in the sub-tree below i that is its root. For this, all we have to do is to take the j nodes so that $start(j) > start(i)$ and $end(j) < end(i)$.

We will now look at some other problems linked to the exploration of a graph.

30.7.1. *Returning edges in an undirected graph*

During depth-first traversal of an undirected graph, the exploration tree only covers a part of the edges. But what do those that are not in the tree look like?

It can only be edges joining a vertex to one of its ancestors, hence the name *returning edges*, as we notice on the graph in Figure 30.19.[2]

But why are all non-traversed edges returning edges? Let us start by associating the number *start*(i), corresponding to the order of the prefixed traversal of the tree, with each vertex i. If we have two vertices i and j such that *start*(i) < *start*(j), this means that we reach vertex i for the first time before reaching vertex j, and during the traversal, *start*(j) stays at 0 as long as we have not reached this vertex j. When an edge ij is not traversed, this happens on two occasions during exploration: first from j, and then from i. Given that node j was reached after node i, it is the path from j to i that is tried, unsuccessfully, before the path from i to j. This means that we have $0 <$ *start*(i) < *start*(j). In these conditions, the arch from j to i can correspond either to a transversal edge or an edge going back to an ancestor (see Figure 30.20). It cannot be a transversal edge, as if it were we would have finished exploring node i before node j is reached for the first time, and we would have had an edge of the tree from i to j.

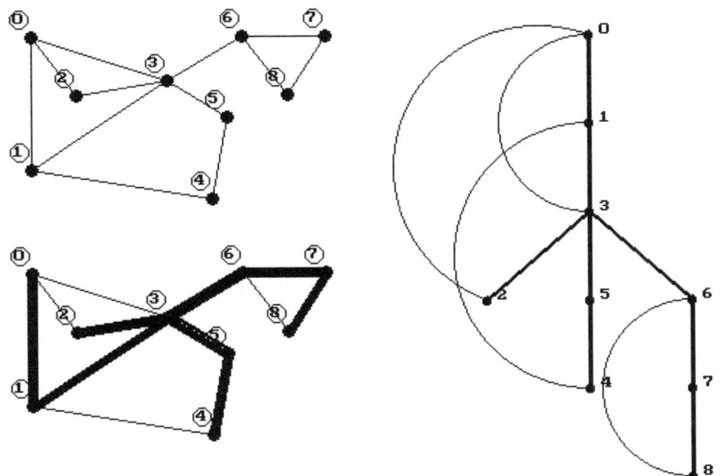

Figure 30.19. *Left: an example of a graph (top), with exploration tree from vertex 0 (bottom); and right: this same tree, with returning edges drawn in the shape of circle arcs, namely edges 20, 30, 41 and 86*

---

2. Conversely, when the graph is oriented, the non-traversed arcs in the exploration tree can be not just returning arcs, but also descending arcs or transverse arcs.

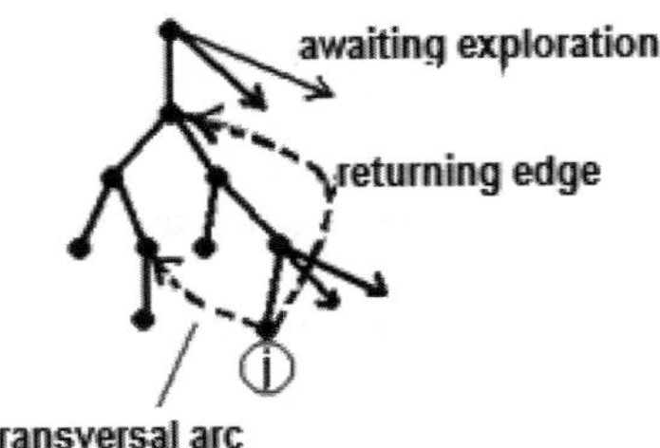

Figure 30.20. *Eventual edges of the graph from vertex j that are not in the exploration tree*

We deduce from this the program that will give the returning edges. The main program simply enters the graph with lists of neighbors at each node, and sets the start of the exploration counter to 0, i.e. *counters*, then it calls the function *explore*(0), from vertex 0. This general function records the edges of the exploration tree, as well as the returning edges. An edge or rather an arc from i to j is given the number $NV*i + j$, and we set the box of table $arce[NV*i + j]$ to 1 when the edge is in the tree, and to 2 when it is a returning edge.

```
void explore(int v)
{ start[v]=++counters;
  for(i=0; i<nbn[v]; i++)
   { neighbor=n[v][i];
     if (start[neighbor]==0)
       { arce[NV*v+neighbor]=1; pred[neighbor]=v;
         trace the line between v and neighbor
         explore(neighbor);
       }
     else if (neighbor!=pred[v] && start[v]>start[neighbor] &&
              start[neighbor]>0)
       { arce[NV*v+neighbor]=2;}    /* neighbor is above v in the tree */
   }
}
```

30.7.2. *Isthmuses in an undirected graph*

Let us take an undirected and connected graph. The latter can present zones of fragility and narrowing, with the presence of edges which, if removed, cause the graph to lose its connectivity.

Such edges look like *isthmuses*, hence their name. We also call them *bridges*, by analogy with a town traversed by a river with a single bridge: destroying the bridge prevents every junction from one bank to the other. The analogy stops there: if there are two bridges, destroying one bridge does not delete the connectivity. The notion of isthmus is therefore better. For example, the graph in Figure 30.21 presents an isthmus between two vertices. The deletion cuts the graph in two.

On the other hand, there is no isthmus if at least two possible paths exist between any two vertices of the graph, which expresses that the two vertices are in a cycle that is inside of the graph. Therefore, an edge is an isthmus if and only if there are no cycles containing this edge in the graph.

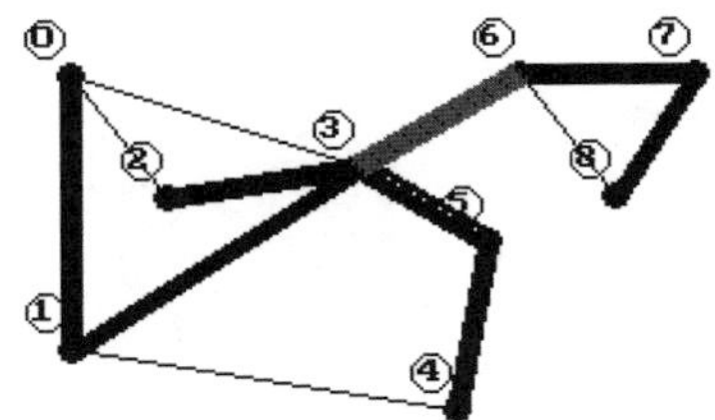

Figure 30.21. *Graph with an isthmus between vertices 3 and 6*

This can be tested thanks to the depth-first exploration of the graph. In the presence of two paths between two vertices, the exploration graph takes only one of them, and the other is made up of a returning edge. When an edge is an isthmus, it is necessarily in the depth-first exploration tree of the graph, in the form (i,j) with $start(i) < start(j)$ and there are no returning edges between a descendant of its bottom extremity j (including j) and an ascendant of its top extremity i (including i). We deduce from this the program enabling us to find the eventual isthmuses. For this we record the edges in the descending direction, when they are present in the exploration tree: an edge (i, j), numbered $NV^*i + j$, is therefore set to 1 in the box of table $arce[NV^*i + j]$. But with each encounter of a returning edge between the bottom vertex l and the vertex k above, all the descending edges between k and l in the exploration tree, which was 1 up until now, are set to 10.

Finally, isthmuses correspond to (descending) edges that have stayed at 1. It is enough to adjust the exploration function in the following way:

```
void explore(int v)
{
int i,j,neighbor,e1,e2;
start[v]=++counters;
for(i=0; i<nbn[v]; i++)
  { neighbor=n[v][i];
    if (start[neighbor]==0)
```

```
        {arce[NV*v+neighbor]=1; pred[neighbor]=v; explore(neighbor); }
    else if (neighbor!=pred[v] && start[v]>start[neighbor] && start[neighbor]>0)
      { e1=pred[v]; e2=v; arce[NV*e1+e2]=10;
       while(e1!= neighbor)  { e2=e1; e1=pred[e2];  arce[NV*e1+e2]=10; }
      }
  }
}
```

In Figure 30.22 we will find another example of a graph, with the exploration tree in thick lines (dark gray) as well as the isthmuses (light gray).

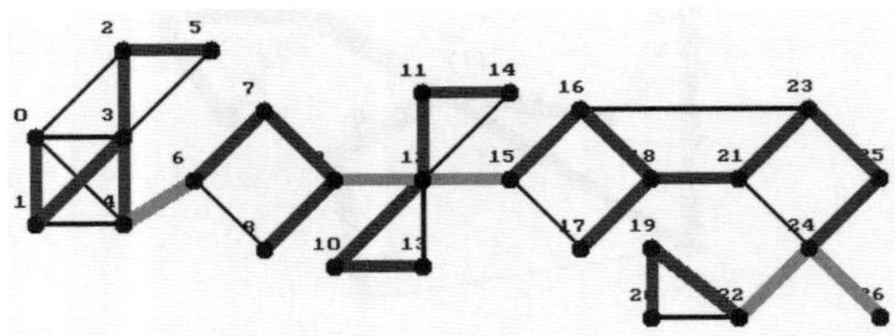

Figure 30.22. *A graph with exploration tree in thick gray lines, and isthmuses in pale gray between 4 and 6, 9 and 12, 2 and 15, 24 and 22, 24 and 26*

30.8. Case of directed graphs

When the graph is directed, a node can be accessible from another without it being the same in the other direction. The notion of connectivity becomes complicated and we introduce the notion of strong connectivity.

30.8.1. *Strongly connected components in a directed graph*

In a directed graph $\vec{G}$, a strongly connected component is made up of all the vertices between which a path always exists. This means that if *i* and *j* are any two vertices in the same strongly connected component, there is not only a path from *i* to *j* but also a path from *j* to *i*.

In this context, a depth-first exploration of graph $\vec{G}$ gives a forest of trees, whose arcs are oriented in the descending direction. These trees only insure us from a path in a single direction between vertices of the same tree, the second vertex being below the first in the tree concerned. They do not constitute the strongly connected components of the graph. What do we do to obtain these? To do this, and this will be explained later, we proceed to two successive depth-first explorations, in the following way:

– do a depth-first exploration of graph $\vec{G}$, and for each vertex i of this graph, associate the number *end*(i) corresponding to the end of the exploration of this vertex;

– construct graph $\vec{G}^{\mathrm{T}}$ called the transpose of $\vec{G}$. This is obtained by reversing the direction of all the arcs of $\vec{G}$, then carrying out a depth-first exploration of $\vec{G}^{\mathrm{T}}$ by starting each tree using vertex i, which has the highest number *end*(i) found before. The forest trees thus obtained will be strongly connected components of $\vec{G}$.

Let us quickly show the validity of this method. We have to prove that the exploration trees of $\vec{G}^{\mathrm{T}}$, in the order they are constructed, are none other than the strongly connected components of $\vec{G}$. First of all, if a path exits from vertex i to vertex j in $\vec{G}$, a path from j to i exists in $\vec{G}^{\mathrm{T}}$, by the very definition of $\vec{G}^{\mathrm{T}}$. Therefore, if i and j are in the same strongly connected component of $\vec{G}$, which means $i \leftrightarrow j$, a path from i to j exists, as well as a path from j to i, and they are also in the same strongly connected component of $\vec{G}^{\mathrm{T}}$, because $j \leftrightarrow i$. This means that $\vec{G}$ and $\vec{G}^{\mathrm{T}}$ have exactly the same strongly connected components.

Let us take a strongly connected component of $\vec{G}$, or of $\vec{G}^{\mathrm{T}}$, and any two vertices i and j that belong to it: $i \leftrightarrow j$. Vertex i is found in one of the exploration trees of $\vec{G}^{\mathrm{T}}$, with a certain root r. Since $i \leftrightarrow j$, j is also in the same tree. We have just shown that a connected component is always included in an exploration tree of $\vec{G}^{\mathrm{T}}$. What remains is to show the reciprocal.

Let us take two vertices i and j that are found in the same tree of the exploration forest of $\vec{G}^{\mathrm{T}}$. This tree has a certain node r as its root. Since we can go down from r to i in this tree, therefore from r to i in graph $\vec{G}^{\mathrm{T}}$, this implies that a path from i to r exists in the initial graph $\vec{G}$. On the other hand, because of the order in which the exploration of $\vec{G}^{\mathrm{T}}$ is done, we know that r has a rank *end*(r) greater than that of i, namely *end*(i). This means that during the exploration of the initial graph $\vec{G}$, vertex i had finished being explored before vertex r. Two possibilities are presented: either i is below r in the same tree, or r is in a tree other than that of i and is constructed after the tree of i. We saw, however, that there is a path from i to r. This condition forbids the second possibility. Therefore i and r are in the same exploration tree of $\vec{G}$, and more specifically i is a descendant of r in this tree, hence the existence of a path from r to i. Finally we get $r \leftrightarrow i$, which means that r and i are in the same strongly connected component of $\vec{G}$ or $\vec{G}^{\mathrm{T}}$. We could show similarly that $r \leftrightarrow j$. Hence $i \leftrightarrow j$: i and j are therefore in the same strongly connected component. We have just shown that an exploration tree of $\vec{G}^{\mathrm{T}}$ is included in a strongly connected component.

Combining the two inclusions obtained, every exploration tree of $\overrightarrow{G}^{\mathrm{T}}$ is a strongly connected component of $\overrightarrow{G}$.

The program that results from this algorithm is given below and a result is shown in Figure 30.23:

Take graph G with its NV vertices written from 0 to NV – 1, and for each vertex i, take table n[i][] of its successors as well as the number nbn[i] of these neighbors. From then on, the program takes care of determining the list of successors nt[k][] of each vertex k in the transpose graph GT, as well as their number nbnt[k], with this table having been set to 0 beforehand;

```
for(i=0; i<NV; i++) for(j=0; j<nbn[i]; j++)
nt[n[i][j]][nbnt[n[i][j]]++] = i;
/* we then launch the exploration procedure of graph G */
for(i=0; i<NV; i++)  explore(i);
/* in table vertex[] we place the names of the vertices following the descending
  order of their end of exploration end[] */
for (i=0; i<NV; i++) {vertex[NV−1−end[i]]=i;}
/* we launch the exploration of GT in order of the vertices placed in vertex[],
after having reset the clocks to 0. The new exploration function exploret() is the
same as the one before except that we use nt[][] and nbnt[] instead of n[][] and
nbn[], and we no longer need end[]. We also add a coloring of each vertex
colour[i]=color, to distinguish the vertices according to the tree in which they
are found.  */
for (i=0; i<NV; i++) s[i]=0;
for(i=0; i<NV; i++) if (s[vertex[i]]==0)
  { exploret(vertex[i]);color++; }
   draw
  }

void explore(int v)
{ int i,j,neighbor;          /* s[] and countere are defined as global variables */
  s[v]=1;
  for(i=0; i<nbn[v]; i++)
    { neighbor=n[v][i];  if (s[neighbor]==0)
            { draw the line between v and neighbor explore(neighbor);}
    }
  end[v]=countere++;
}
```

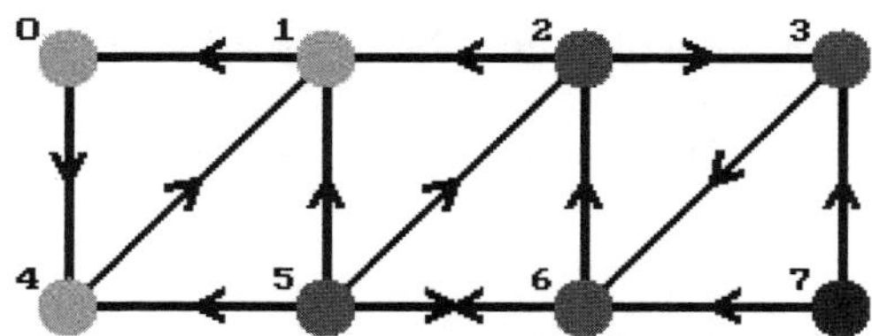

Figure 30.23. *A directed graph and its three strongly connected components, distinguished according to the color of their vertices*

30.8.2. *Transitive closure of a directed graph*

We saw how to look for connected components in the case of an undirected graph. Let us recall that a connected component is the maximum set of vertices accessible from one another. In the forest formed by the depth- (or breadth-)first exploration trees, each tree covers a connected component, and these trees constitute a partition of the graph.

In the case of a directed graph, it is also sufficient to launch a depth-first exploration from a vertex to find all of the accessible vertices. We must repeat the operation for each of the vertices, and the trees obtained have vertices in common – they do not partition the graph. Figure 30.24 gives an example of a directed graph. The exploration trees are traced from each one of the 12 vertices of this graph, which enables us to find out which are the vertices that are accessible from each other.

There is another method that lets us get the same results. With this method, let us introduce the notion of transitive closure of a directed graph G. Transitive closure of G is a graph with the same vertices as G whose arcs link vertex i to vertex j as soon as there is a path from i to j in graph G. Therefore the transitive closure of G contains not only the arcs of G but also other arcs that are the shortcuts of all the paths from one vertex to another in G.

In the graph example of Figure 30.24, its transitive closure will contain arcs from vertex 0 to all the others, from vertex 1 to all the others except 0 and 4, …, from vertex 11 to vertices 5, 8, 9, 10. These results can be read in the accessibility matrix in Figure 30.24, top right, where the entry (i, j) is set to 1 if there is a path from i to j in G (including from i to i) or even an arc from i to j in its transitive closure.

To get this matrix, i.e. the transitive closure of the graph, we use an algorithm attributed to Roy and Warshall, dating from the 1960s, by which Floyd was then inspired to create his shortest paths algorithm (see Chapter 33, section 33.1.2).

To do this, we begin by writing the adjacency matrix of the graph, with a 0 in position (i, j) if there are no arcs from i to j, and 1 if there are – notably, positions (i, i) are set to 1. Then we launch a loop with NV stages, where NV is the number of graph vertices.

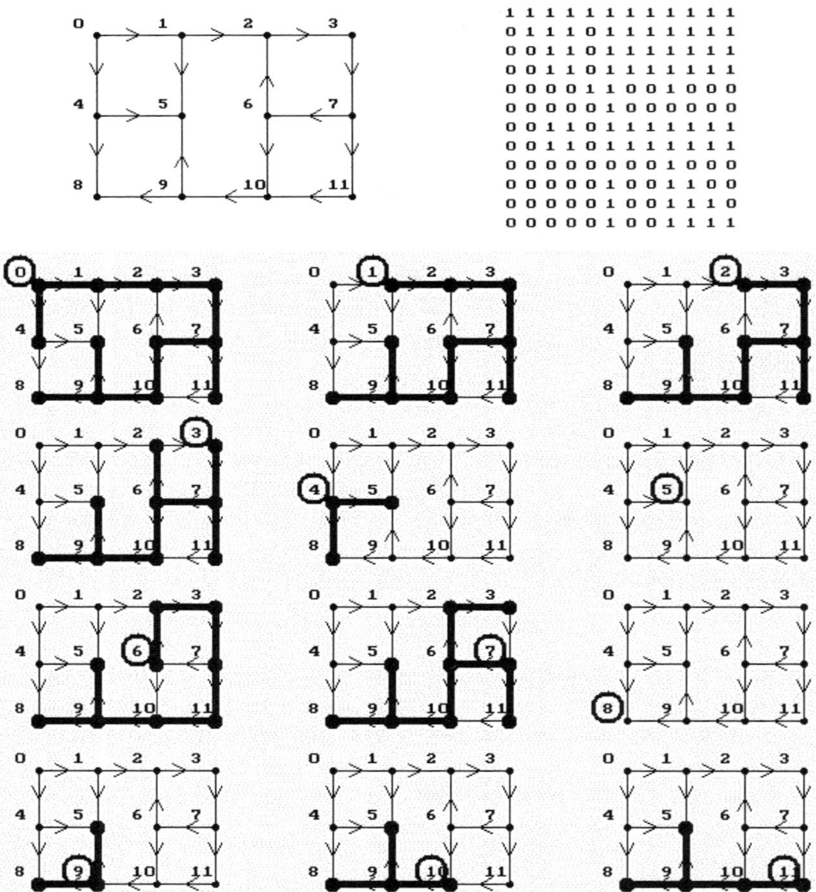

Figure 30.24. *A directed graph, with its accessibility matrix (top); and the 12 exploration trees obtained starting from each of the vertices alternately, which gives all the vertices accessible from the initial vertex (bottom)*

At each new stage, numbered k, every coefficient (i, j) of the matrix, which was 0 up until now, is set to 1 if there is a path from i to j passing through vertex number k. Therefore all the paths from i to j eventually passing though a vertex less than or equal to k are recorded at stage k. After the last stage, with the last vertex as a possible intermediary, we get the transitive closure of the graph.

The program follows:

```
/* Construction of the adjacency matrix s[i][j], in the example of the previous
graph, here with a number of vertices NV=12, and arcs randomly oriented in one
direction or the other */
  for(i=0; i<NV; i++) for(j=0; j<NV; j++) s[i][j]=0;
  for(i=0; i<NV; i+=2) {h=random(2); if (h==0) s[i][i+1]=1; else s[i+1][i]=1;}
  for(i=0; i<NV-4; i++) {h=random(2);if (h==0) s[i][i+4]=1; else s[i+4][i]=1;}
  /* we took random directions for the arcs */
  for(i=0; i<NV; i++) s[i][i]=1;
  s[1][2]=1; s[NV−2][NV−3]=1;
  /* Roy-Warshall algorithm, with the evolution of matrix s[][] */
  for(k=0; k<NV; k++)  for(i=0; i<NV; i++)  for(j=0; j<NV; j++)
  if (s[i][j]==0 && s[i][k]==1 && s[k][j]==1) s[i][j]=1;
```

In the example in Figure 30.25, from a graph with eight vertices we can follow the graph evolution, with the addition of arcs ending up at its transitive closure.

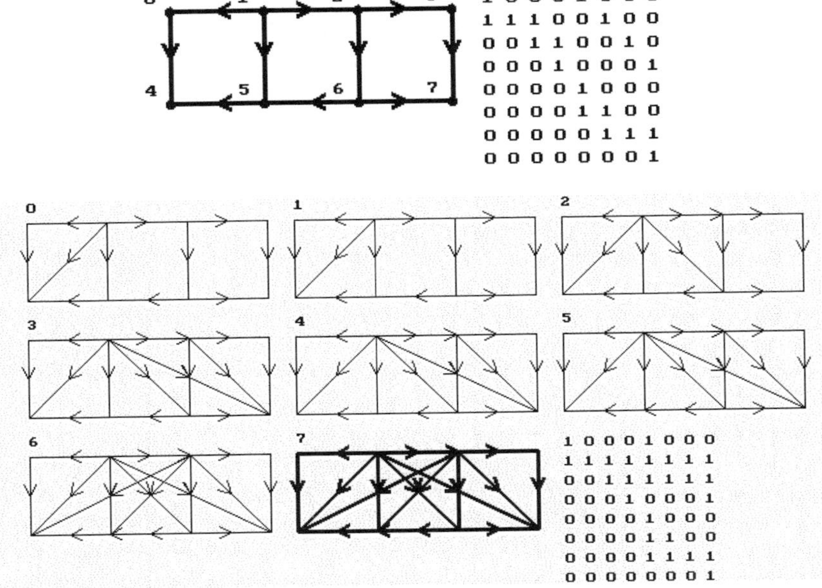

Figure 30.25. *The initial graph, with its adjacency matrix (top); and the graph evolution, from stage 0 to stage 7, corresponding to vertices from 0 to 7. In the end we get the transitive closure of the graph, with the corresponding accessibility matrix (bottom)*

30.8.3. *Orientation of a connected undirected graph to become strongly connected*

Here is the problem: we have an undirected graph G and want to replace each edge ij with an arc, either from i to j or from j to i. Can we obtain a strongly connected graph $\vec{G}$*?*

Two conditions are necessary: the initial undirected graph must be connected, and it must not have an isthmus (see section 30.7.2) because if it has an isthmus *i j*, its orientation in a single direction will enable us to go from *i* to *j* but never from *j* to *i*. We will see that these two conditions are enough, this property being attributed to Robbins [ROB 39].

PROPERTY 30.1.– When an undirected graph is connected and bridgeless, we can always find an orientation of the edges, with each edge being replaced by an arc in such a way as to have a strongly connected directed graph.

Indeed, in a connected undirected bridgeless graph there are always at least two paths between any two vertices. During depth-first exploration of the graph, one of the two paths is taken and we orient the edges traversed during the exploration in the direction of descent in the tree. The other paths correspond to returning edges and we orient them in ascending direction. In this way, any two vertices *i* and *j* are always placed in a directed cycle enabling us to go from *i* to *j* and also from *j* to *i*. Thus we find a strongly connected directed graph. The programming is only a slight variation on previous programs. The application of the algorithm gives the results obtained in Figure 30.26.

30.8.4. *The best orientations on a graph*

Let us return to the graph in the shape of a ladder that N long, with two parallel lines each having $N + 1$ vertices, as well as $N + 1$ traversal lines (see Figure 30.27). Its number of edges is $3N + 1$. Now let us replace each edge with an arc oriented in one of two possible directions. The graphs obtained number 2^{3N+1}. Among them, some are strongly connected, and we can go from any vertex to any other vertex, and others are not strongly connected.

To ensure that there are orientations giving strongly connected graphs, it is enough to ensure that we meet the conditions of Robbins' theorem. The initial, undirected graph is obviously connected and does not have an isthmus. In these conditions, it can be oriented to become strongly connected. Furthermore, we have clear solutions: it is enough to choose contour arcs that are all in the same direction to get a sort of beltway, with the intermediate traversal lines therefore being able to be oriented in any direction.

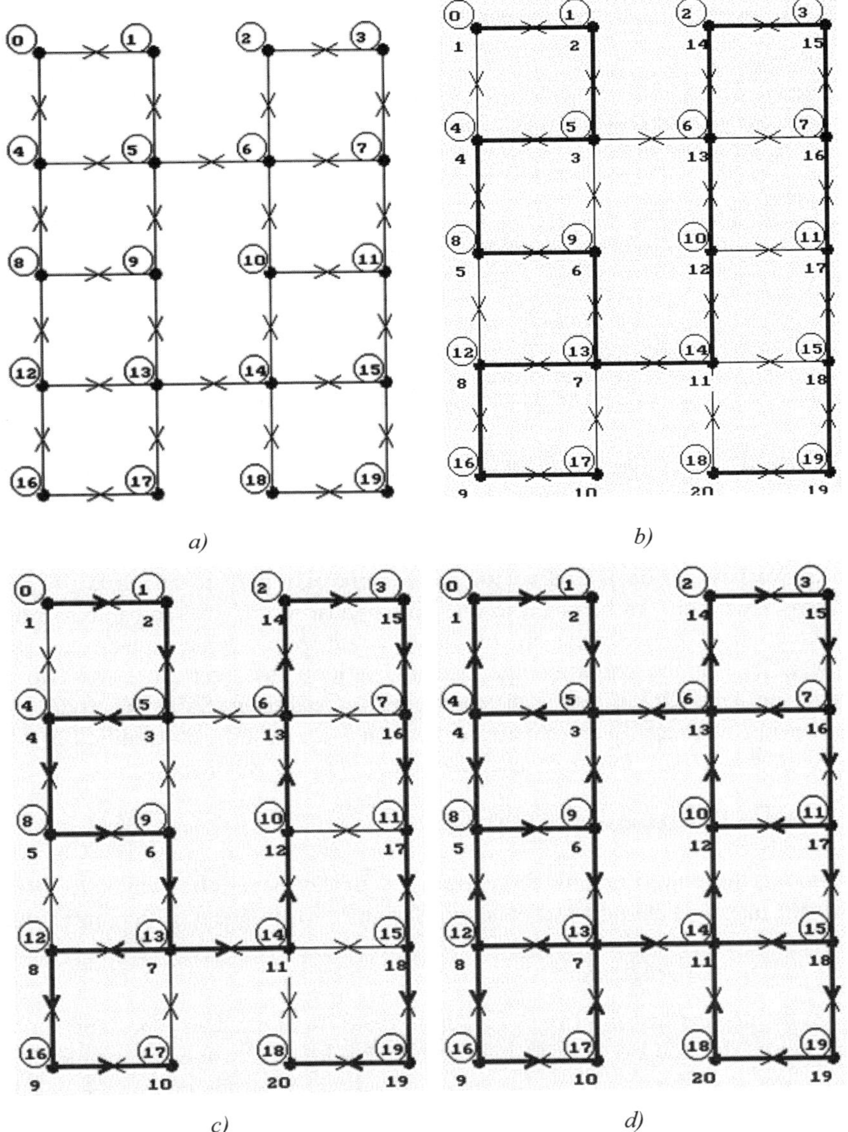

Figure 30.26. *a) The bridgeless, undirected, initial graph; b) exploration tree from a vertex 0 and the numbering of its vertices in the order they are reached; c) orientation of the tree in the direction the vertices were reached; d) additional orientation of returning arcs in ascending direction, and obtaining the directed graph*

30.8.4.1. *Number of oriented graphs*

Let us assume that arc 01 is oriented from 0 to 1, and u(N) is the number of all oriented N-length graphs with this characteristic. This implies that the number of all the directed graphs is double, i.e. 2 u(N), depending on whether we take arc 01 or arc 10 (see Figure 30.27).

We already notice that u(1) = 1. It is the directed square in the trigonometric sense. How do we go from N-length graphs to those N + 1 long?

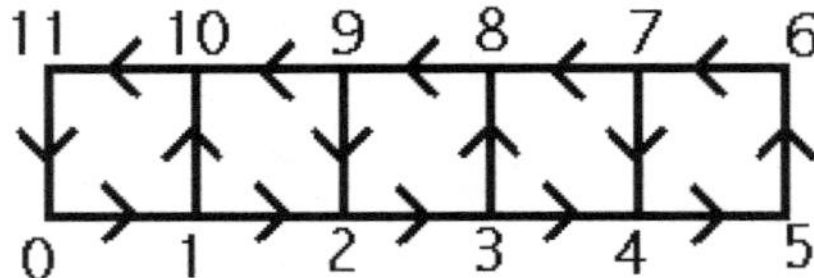

Figure 30.27. *An example of graph orientation in the form of a ladder N = 5 units long, with the presence of a beltway*

All we have to do is add a loop to its right extremity to attach the two new vertices. This loop can be taken in one direction or the other. We can also reverse the direction of the extreme arc of the *N*-length graph, which deletes its strong connectivity, on the condition that we add a loop that reattaches the two new vertices on length $N + 1$ and at the same time re-establishes the connectivity of the two previous vertices. Every other modification is impossible, the addition of a loop not being able to have any more upstream effect. Finally we have:

$$u(N + 1) = 3u(N), \text{ hence } u(N) = 3^{N-1}$$

Among these $u(N)$ graphs, there are 2^{N-1} of that have a beltway since we can orient the intermediate traversal arcs, numbering $N - 1$, in one direction or the other.

30.8.4.2. *The best orientations*

Let us imagine that this type of graph in the form of a ladder represents the plan of a town of the future.[3] In this context, a graph with a beltway is interesting in two ways. First, it enables us to modify at will the direction of the cross streets without losing connectivity, since the beltway is always there to ensure the liaisons. We can therefore ensure a regulation of traffic in real time. On the other hand, a graph presenting a beltway turns out to be better compared to those that do not have a beltway if we want to minimize the distances from one point to the other. This

3. We can consult [ROB 39, ROB 94] on this subject.

seems natural, as if we change the direction of a peripheral arc in relation to the others, we can only provoke additional detours. This is also shown.

What are the criteria that enable us to classify graphs according to their efficiency for going from one point to another?

Simply taking graphs with a beltway, we can begin by looking for the shortest distances $d(u, v)$ from any vertex u to any other vertex v. This can be done by a breadth-first exploration from each vertex, or better by applying Floyd's algorithm, which we will see in Chapter 32. From then on, we can associate the longest distance obtained, i.e. $max\ d(u, v)$, with each of these graphs. Otherwise we can calculate the sum of all the distances obtained, which comes back to adding all the elements of Floyd's matrix. We therefore have a result that is proportional to the average of the shortest distances from one point to another. With the graphs thus classified according to one or the other of these criteria, the best ones are those that give a minimum result. In Figure 30.28, we give the best graphs according to the first criterion, i.e. those that minimize $max\ d(u, v)$. We would think that the most logical solution, namely orienting the $N + 1$ cross streets alternately in one direction then in the other one out of two times, would be the best. This is not the case, in light of the results.

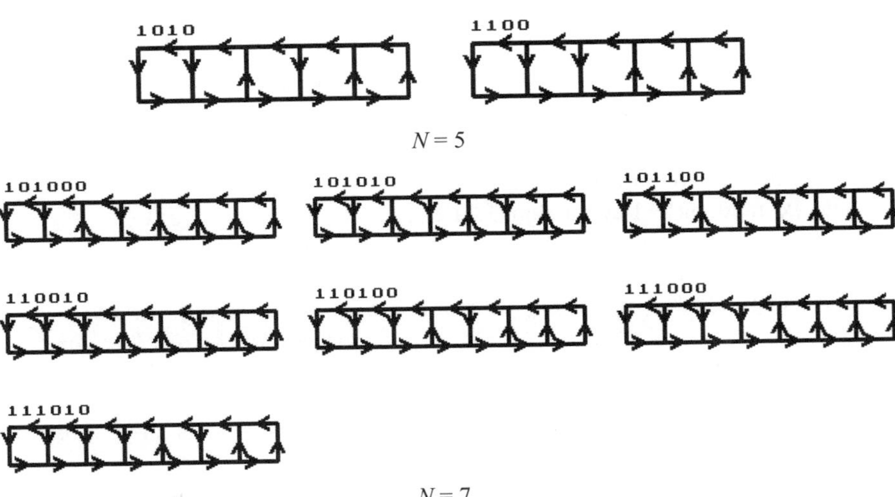

Figure 30.28. *The best graphs for N = 5 with a maximum distance equal to 7 between two vertices (top); and the best graphs for N = 7 with a maximum distance equal to 9 (bottom). The binary numbers located above each graph correspond to the direction of the intermediate cross edges*

30.9. Appendix: constructing the maze (simplified version)

We start with a grid, each square of which has *step* as a side, for example *step* = 10 pixels (see section 30.6.1). This grid itself has a square shape, with vertical lines numbered from 0 to L (for example $L = 47$), and similarly for the horizontal lines. It is on these lines that the walls of the maze will be constructed. We begin by drawing the square that borders the grid, with the color of the walls, i.e.:

rectangle(0,0, step*L, step*L); with color WALLCOLOR,

with the top left corner being at (0, 0) and the bottom right corner being at ($step \times L$, $step \times L$).

Then, as long as the maze has not finished being constructed, we take random points (x, y) on the grid. Each time, we wait for point (x, y) to fall on a wall – initially we wait for the point to fall on the border. In other words, we start over as long as the point falls on the background color of the screen (called BACKGROUNDCOLOR). When we fall on a point attached to the wall, we take its four neighbors and for each neighbor with the background color of the screen, we draw the wall joining point (x, y) to this neighbor. Afterwards we take a new point at random, etc. This gives the following program:[4]

```
for(;;)
{ finished=YES;
  for(x=0;x<=L;x++) for(y=0;y<=L,y++)
  if (getpixel(pas*x,pas*y)!=WALLCOLOR)
    {finished=NO; break;}
 do {x=random(L+1);y=random(L+1);}
 while(getpixel(step*x,step*y)==BACKGROUNDCOLOR);
 for(dir=0;dir<4;dir++)  /* we take the four possible directions */
   { dx=((dir+1)%2)*(1-dir);dy=(dir%2)*(dir-2);  /* variations of x and y
                                                    depending on the direction */
     if (getpixel(step*(x+dx), step*(y+dy)==BACKGROUNDCOLOR)
       line(step*x, step*y, step*(x+dx), step*(y+dy));
   }
  if (finished==YES) break;
}
```

4. This algorithm is simplified, especially when a point (x, y) falls on a wall. Starting with it, we draw walls to all acceptable neighbors, instead of only taking one at random. This at least enables us to speed up the process. On the other hand it has the drawback of accepting the construction of small bits of wall from the border but going to the exterior of the square. Nevertheless this does not perturb the construction of the maze within the border. We can also easily adjust the program to prevent these outgrowths.

Now let us explore this maze, whose corridors have one *step* as their length. We begin at a starting point (*xs*, *ys*) located in the top left, and have the point located in the bottom right as our endpoint.

The path will be drawn with small squares that fit in the corridors, with one side equal to a third of the width *step* of the corridor. The starting square is centered at point (*step* / 2, *step* / 2) and will be colored in light gray. As for the endsquare, we give it a particular color, called ENDCOLOR. For the path that will be drawn, the current point is called (x, y) and is always located in the middle of a corridor surrounded by a square that will be light gray or dark gray during the process, and finally always light gray.

Here is the function *square*() that draws a small square enabling us to visualize the route:

```
void square(int xc, int yc, int color)  /* xc, yc are the coordinates of the center*/
{ int i,j;
  for(i=xc-step/6; i<=xc+step/6; i++)  for(j=yc-step/6;j<=yc+step/6;j++)
    putpixel(i,j,color);
}
```

Then the initial conditions:

```
xs=step/2;ys=step/2;    square(x,y,LIGHTGRAY);
          /* starting point in top left */
square(step*L-step/2,step*L-step/2,ENDCOLOR);
          /* endpoint in bottom right */
x=xs;y=ys; direction=3;  /* (x, y) is the current point, beginning at the start
                  point with a direction towards the bottom */
```

Then we launch a *for* loop that will stop when the current point falls on the endpoint characterized by its color. Each time, the point is oriented according to a certain *direction*, notably we initially chose *direction* = 3, i.e. downwards (direction 0 is to the right, direction 1 is upwards, and direction 2 to the left). We can therefore define three directions in relation to *direction*: to the right, in front or to the left. This gives three potential neighbors. For example, if we choose to go right the variation of x is expressed *dxri*, and that of y is *dyri*. Now we test whether we reach a wall at mid-distance or not (for example at abscissa point $x + step \times dxri\ /\ 2$). Out of the three neighbors, in order of the one on the right, then in front, then on the left relative to *direction*, we choose the first one that is not blocked by a wall at mid-distance and calculate its coordinates (*newx*, *newy*) with the corresponding new direction *newdirection*. We therefore draw the centered square at (*newx*, *newy*) in dark gray, and the front one becomes light gray. This enables us to color the head of the path in a different color to those from before. Then we update: x = *newx*, y = *newy*. Sometimes none of the three neighbors is acceptable, which means that we have arrived at a dead end. In this case we make a U-turn (*newdirection* = (*direction* + 2) % 4) and do not move; since *newx*=x and *newy* = y, the square that was dark gray will move change to light gray.

When we backtrack, there is always an opening at mid-distance, but we arrive on a neighbor that is a light gray square. In this case, we color this point in dark gray and erase the point where we were. We therefore backtrack as long as we do not land on a new opening, and the return journey we carry out is progressively erased. Finally, after erasing all the paths that lead to a dead end, we get (in light gray) the path that ends up at the final point, and the *for* loop stops:

```
for(;;)
  { right=(direction+3)%4;
    dxri=((right+1)%2)*(1-right);dyri=(right%2)*(right-2);
    infront=direction;
    dxin=((infront+1)%2)*(1-infront);dyin=(infront%2)*(infront-2);
    left=(direction+1)%4;
    dxle=((left+1)%2)*(1-left);dyle=(left%2)*(left-2);
    if (getpixel(x+step*dxri/2,y+step*dyri/2)==BACKGROUNDCOLOR)
       { newx=x+step*dxri;newy=y+step*dyri; newdirection=right; }
    else if (getpixel(x+step*dxin/2,y+step*dyin/2)==BACKGROUNDCOLOR)
       { newx=x+step*dxin;newy=y+step*dyin; newdirection=infront; }
    else if (getpixel(x+step/2*dxle,y+step/2*dyle)==BACKGROUNDCOLOR)
      { newx=x+step*dxle;newy=y+step*dyle; newdirection=left;}
    else
      { newx=x;newy=y; newdirection=(direction+2)%4; }

    if (getpixel(newx,newy)==ENDCOLOR)
      {square(x,y,LIGHTGRAY);square(newx,newy,LIGHTGRAY); break;}
           /* end */
    if (getpixel(newx,newy)==LIGHTGRAY)
         { square(newx,newy,DARKGRAY);
           square(x,y,BACKGROUNDCOLOR); }
    else { square(newx,newy,DARKGRAY); square(x,y,LIGHTGRAY); }
     x=newx;y=newy; direction=newdirection;
  }
```

Note that this algorithm is purely graphical. To find out whether we land on a wall or on an opening, depending on the direction tried, the tests are carried out using the management of distinctive colors in the vicinity. In this way we end up with the results presented in Figure 30.12.

Chapter 31

Trees with Numbered Nodes, Cayley's Theorem and Prüfer Code

31.1. Cayley's theorem

Let us consider N points numbered 1, 2, 3, ..., N. We are interested in (free) trees whose nodes are these N points. In this case, this tree consists of N numbered nodes, with linked in such a way that they are all accessible to each other (connected undirected graph) and no cycle is formed (the graph becomes a tree). In Figure 31.1 we will find an example of a tree with nine nodes. Let us specify that such trees have no preferred vertex – they are unrooted and are different from trees whose vertices are undifferentiated (in this case no number would distinguish them). There is a theorem, attributed to Cayley, which gives the number of such trees.

Cayley's theorem: There are N^{N-2} trees with N numbered vertices.

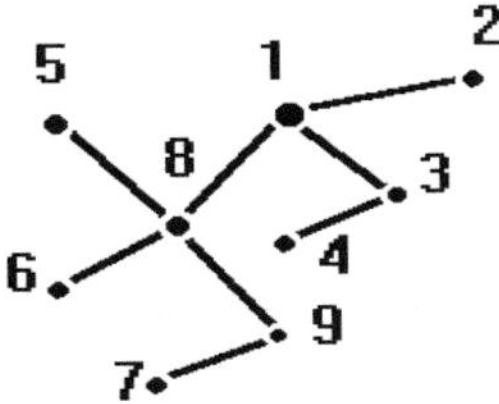

Figure 31.1. *A tree with nine numbered vertices. The Prüfer code of this tree is 1318889*

For example, for $N = 5$ there are 5^3 trees, i.e. 125. In other words, there are as many trees as there are numbers written in base N with $N - 2$ digits.

Here is a first demonstration of Cayley's theorem. Let us consider K_n to be the complete graph with n vertices. Let us recall that a complete graph has each of its vertices linked to all the others by an edge. Every tree with n labeled vertices is none other than a spanning tree of K_n, i.e. a tree whose vertices are all those of K_n, and the edges a part of those of K_n. We therefore use this property, even if it means anticipating what we will see later (in Chapter 33), namely:

PROPERTY 31.1.– The number of spanning trees of a graph is equal to the product of the eigenvalues (except the null value) of the Laplacian matrix divided by the number of vertices. By definition, this Laplacian matrix L is such that each element a_{ii} of its main diagonal is the number of incidence edges at each vertex, i.e. $n - 1$ in this case. Moreover, we set element a_{ij} to -1 or 0 depending on whether or not there is an edge between vertices i and j.

For K_n this gives -1s everywhere, except for the $n - 1$ elements of the diagonal. Therefore $L = nI - J$, where J is the matrix formed exclusively with 1s. We check that the eigenvalues of L are therefore all equal to n except one equal to 0.[1]

Finally, the number of spanning trees of K_n is:

$$(1/n)\, n^{n-1} = n^{n-2}.$$

31.2. Prüfer code

There is another method, constructive and combinatorial, that enables us to find Cayley's theorem. It consists of establishing a bijective link between trees with N numbered vertices and the numbers written in base N with $N - 2$ digits, which number N^{N-2}. Each tree thus ends up being coded by a number, and such a code is attributed to Prüfer (1918). We will now discuss his method.

---

1. Matrix J has rank 1 (all the determinants with dimension 2x2 and more are null). This is translated by the fact that $n - 1$ eigenvalues of J are equal to 0. Actually, when we solve the system of equations $JV = 0$ with V having coordinates $(x_1, x_2, \ldots, x_n)$ in a column, it boils down to a single equation $x_1 + x_2 + \ldots + x_n = 0$. This vector space has dimension $n - 1$ (for example a plane in dimension $n = 3$). It is generated by $n - 1$ linearly independent vectors V. We have just found $n - 1$ eigenvectors associated with eigenvalue 0, since $JV = 0$. We know that the number of linearly independent eigenvectors is less than or equal to the multiplicity order of the associated eigenvalue. As the multiplicity order of eigenvalue 0 is not n, else we would have the null matrix, it is equal to $n - 1$. As an eigenvector is $V(1, 1, \ldots, 1)$, the last eigenvalue is equal to n since $J\,V = nV$.

31.2.1. *Passage from a tree to its Prüfer code*

Let us return to the tree drawn in Figure 31.1 with its nine vertices. Its leaves, or terminal nodes – in this case the nodes with degree 1 of the graph, where only one edge is attached – are 24567 because we write them in ascending order. We will proceed to a progressive pruning of the tree, from which we will remove the edges one after the other in the following way (see Figure 31.2):

– we take the first leaf 2 of the list of leaves, which is linked to vertex 1;

– we keep non-terminal node 1 for the code and we remove edge 21;

– in the pruned tree, the leaves are 4567. We take the first 4 and remove edge 43, keeping 3 for the code, hence the word 13;

– the leaves are now 3567, as 3 became a leaf after this pruning and will not be present in the code word from now on. We remove edge 31, keeping 1 for the code, hence the word 131. The leaves are 1567, with 1 that has now become a leaf (it will no longer be present in the code sequence);

– we remove edge 18, keeping 8 for the code word that becomes 1318. The leaves are 567. We remove edge 58, with the code word becoming 13188;

– the leaves are 67. We remove 68, getting the code word 131888;

– the leaves are reduced to 78. We remove 79 and the code word becomes 1318889;

– only the two leaves 8 and 9 are left, forming edge 89. The process is terminated and we have the code word 1318889, seven characters long.

Let us note that each letter of the code word corresponds to a removed edge, except the last one. As a tree with N nodes has $N - 1$ edges, the code is $N - 2$ characters long, with numbers chosen between 1 and N. More specifically, only the numbers of the nodes that are not leaves are present in the code. During the pruning process, the degree of the extremity nodes of the removed edge are reduced by one, and we always take in the code of the node that is not (yet) a leaf. As each node sooner or later ends up being a leaf, its number is repeated k times in the code, with $k = \textit{node degree} - 1$.

31.2.2. *Reverse process*

Let us start from the code 1318889 that is seven characters long, and step-by-step construct the corresponding tree, which has nine nodes.

The code already enables us to know the degree of each node. For example, node 1 is present twice, and therefore of degree 3. This gives the degree table shown in Table 31.1

1	2	3	4	5	6	7	8	9
3	1	2	1	1	1	1	4	2

Table 31.1.

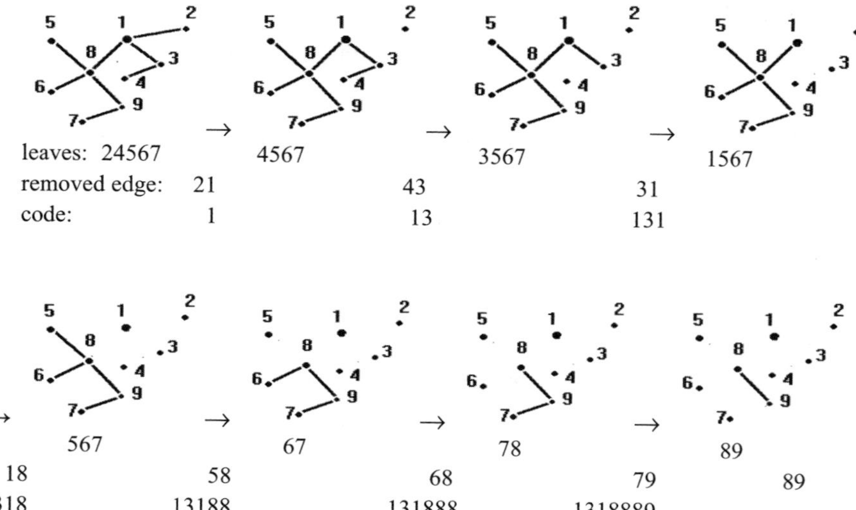

Figure 31.2. *Progressive pruning of the tree with the creation of the code*

The leaves are nodes of degree 1, i.e. the numbers not present in the code word, namely in order 24567. To do as we have before, we take the leaf joining the first leaf to the first number in the code as the edge, i.e. 21. We reduce the degree of 2 and 1 by 1, hence we get the degree table in Table 31.2.

1	2	3	4	5	6	7	8	9
2	0	2	1	1	1	1	4	2

Table 31.2.

For this second stage, the leaves are 4567, and we take the leaf joining the first of the leaves with the second letter of the code as the edge, i.e. 43.

We reduce the degree of 4 and that of 3 by one, hence Table 31.3.

1	2	3	4	5	6	7	8	9
2	0	1	0	1	1	1	4	2

Table 31.3.

For the third stage, the leaves are 3567 and we remove the edge joining the first leaf to the first letter of the code, i.e. 3. The table changes to Table 31.4.

1	2	3	4	5	6	7	8	9
1	0	0	0	1	1	1	4	2

Table 31.4.

For the fourth stage, the leaves are 1567. We take the edge joining the first leaf to the forth letter of the code, i.e. 18. We thus get Table 31.5.

1	2	3	4	5	6	7	8	9
0	0	0	0	1	1	1	3	2

Table 31.5.

We continue in this way, successively taking edges 58, 68 and 79. The last letter of the code has just been taken, and the degree table is reduced to Table 31.6.

1	2	3	4	5	6	7	8	9
0	0	0	0	0	0	0	1	1

Table 31.6.

With the two remaining leaves 8 and 9 we form the last edge 89. Thanks to all the edges obtained, the tree has been reconstituted from its code. There are as many trees with N numbered nodes as there are words $N-2$ characters long in an alphabet of N letters.

31.2.3. *Program*

We take N and begin by creating all the numbers written in base N, with digits 0, 1, 2, …, $N-1$, and that are $N-2$ long. It is sufficient to take all the numbers in decimal from 0 to $N^{N-2}-1$ and convert them into base N. For this, we use the classic method that consists of making successive divisions by N. This is done $N-2$ times, keeping the remainders included between 0 and $N-1$. For the words obtained to be written with digits 1, 2, 3, …, N – as is the case above – it is enough to add 1.

Each word thus obtained is placed in boxes from 1 to $N-2$ of a table $w[N-1]$, and we associate table *degree*$[N+1]$ containing the degrees of each of the nodes from 1 to N with the code word. Next we launch the loop of the stages that give us a tree edge each time. For this, we take all the leaves, i.e. nodes of degree 1 in the degree table and place them in a table *l*[]. The first leaf gives an extremity of the edge, and the other extremity is the letter of the code corresponding to the stage concerned. Lastly, we update the degree table reducing the degree of the extremities of the edge by 1. Note that the use of a table *l*[] for the leaves at each stage is not indispensible, it enables us, however, to distinguish the trees according to the number of their leaves, which we can use afterwards.

```
for(number=0; number<pow(N,N-2.); number++)
{           /* filling of table w[] that contains each code */
 q=number;
 for(i=0; i<N-2; i++)
   { r = q%N; w[N–2–i] = r+1; q = q/N; }
           /*  coordinates of the N points regularly shared on a circle */
 for(i=1; i<=N; i++)
   { x[i]=xorig+radius*cos(2.*M_PI*(i–1)/(float)N);
     y[i]=yorig-radius*sin(2.*M_PI*(i–1)/(float)N);
   }
           /* we create the degree table */
 for(i=1; i<=N; i++) degree[i]=1;
 for(i=1; i<=N–2; i++) degree[w[i]]++;

 for(stage=1; stage<=N–1; stage++)   /* as many stages as edges */
  { k=1;
    for(i=1;i<=N;i++) if (degree[i]==1) l[k++]=i;
    if (stage<=N–2)
      { draw the edge joining l[1] to w[stage]
        degree[w[stage]]--;  degree[l[1]]--;
      }
    else   { draw the last edge, joining l[1] to l[2]    }
  }
}
```

The results obtained are shown in Figure 31.3, as well as in Figure 31.4 where the trees are distinguished according to the number of leaves. Let us recall that, in Chapter 8 on sieve formula, we saw that the number of trees having n vertices, of which k are the leaves, is the number E_k whose generating function is:

$$E(x)=\sum_k E_k x^k=\sum_j C_n^j j^{n-2}(x-1)^{n-j}$$

This can be checked experimentally thanks to the program above. It is the reason for which we used a table *l*[] containing the leaves of each tree, the number of which we can determine. We now give other formulae associated with the number of trees with *n* numbered vertices.

For a tree with n nodes, where d_i is the degree of node i, we get: $\Sigma d_i = 2n - 2$.

We indeed saw that the sum of the degrees of a tree is twice the number of its edges. A tree with *n* vertices has $n - 1$ edges, hence the formula.

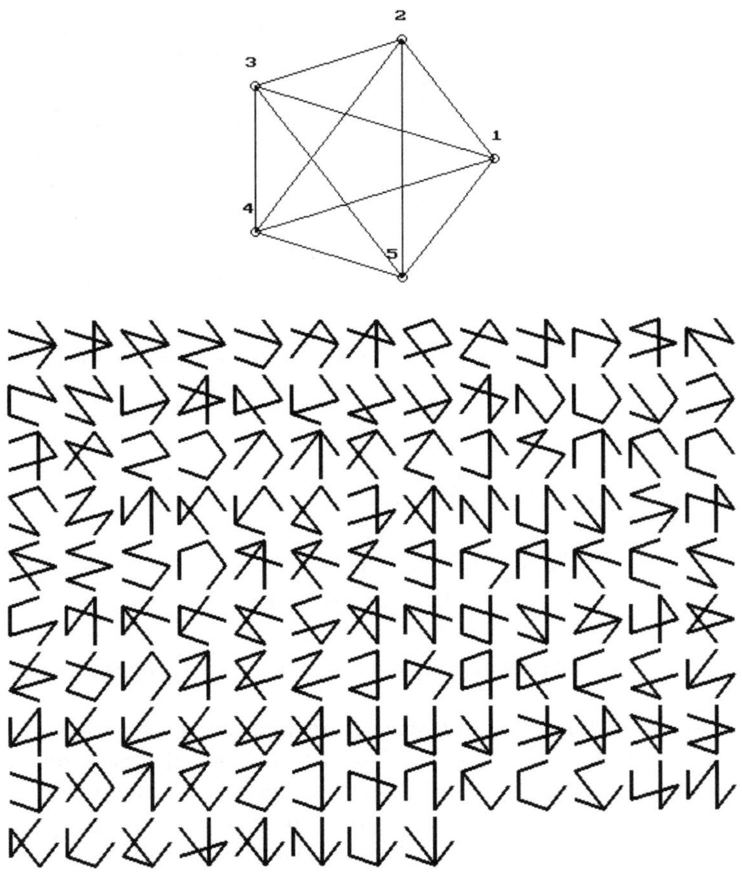

Figure 31.3. *The complete graph K_5, constructed from the regular pentagon with vertices numbered 12345, and its 125 spanning trees (in order of code words 111, 112, 113, 114, 115, 121, 122, etc.)*

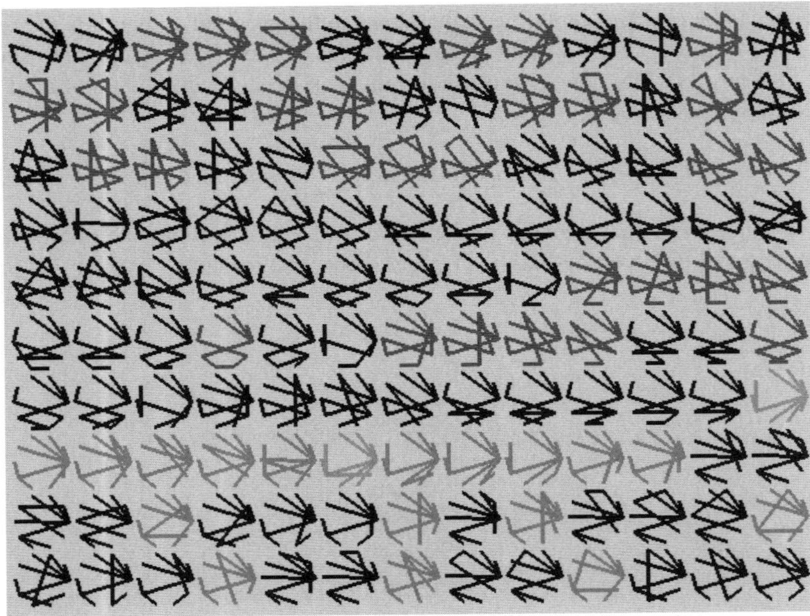

Figure 31.4. *A few trees with 10 vertices, distinguished according to the number of leaves (they can have between two and nine leaves)*

The number of trees with n vertices of degrees d_1, d_2, ..., d_n, all greater than or equal to 1 and whose sum is equal to 2n – 2, is:

$$D_n(d_1, d_2, \ldots, d_n) = \frac{(n-2)!}{(d_1-1)!(d_2-2)!\ldots(d_n-1)!}$$

To verify this formula, let us carry out a demonstration using recurrence.

The formula is true at row 2 since there is a single tree in this case, with $d_1 = d_2 = 1$, and we have $D_2(d_1, d_2) = 1$. Now let us assume that the formula is true at a certain row, $n - 1$, and let us show that it remains true at row n. For this, let us consider a tree with n nodes of $d_1, d_2, \ldots, d_n$ respective degrees with $d_n = 1$, because a tree does not exist without leaves. We can assume, without losing generality that node n is a leaf. Next let us remove this node with the edge that is attached to it and whose other extremity is a certain node j. A tree with $n - 1$ vertices of respective degrees $d_1, d_2, \ldots, d_j - 1, \ldots, d_{n-1}$ is left.

Using a recurrence hypothesis, such trees number:

$$\frac{(n-3)!}{(d_1-1)!(d_2-1)!..(d_j-2)!..(d_{n-1}-1)!}$$

When we take all the trees with n nodes of degrees d_1, d_2, …, d_n with $d_n = 1$ and remove the edge joining leaf n to node j from them, node j can be any one of the nodes other than n. The number of these trees is:

$$D_n(d_1,d_2,...,d_n) = \sum_{j=1}^{n-1} D_{n-1}(d_1,d_2,...,d_j-1,...,d_{n-1})$$

$$= \sum_{j=1}^{n-1} \frac{(n-3)!}{(d_1-1)!(d_2-1)!...(d_j-2)!...(d_{n-1}-1)!} = \frac{(n-3)!}{\prod_{i=1}^{n-1}(d_i-1)!} \sum_{j=1}^{n-1}(d_j-1)$$

with:

$$\sum_{j=1}^{n-1}(d_j-1) = \sum_{j=1}^{n-1} d_j - (n-1) = \sum_{j=1}^{n} d_j - 1 - (n-1) = \sum_{j=1}^{n} d_j - n = 2n-2-n = n-2.$$

We find that:

$$D_n(d_1, d_2, \ldots, d_n) = \frac{(n-2)!}{(d_1-1)!(d_2-2)!...(d_n-1)!}$$

On this occasion, let us recall multinomial formula, which is an extension of binomial formula. This will enable us to have the generating function of $D_n(d_1, d_2, \ldots, d_n)$:

$$(x_1+x_2+...+x_n)^n = \sum_{\substack{k_1+k_2+...+k_n=n \\ k_i \text{ from } 0 \text{ to } n}} \frac{1}{k_1!k_2!...k_n!} x_1^{k_1} x_2^{k_2} ... x_n^{k_n}$$

One way of showing binomial formula is to write $e^{z(x_1+x_2)} = e^{zx_1} e^{zx_2}$ and develop the exponentials in series, which gives:

$$1+(x_1+x_2)z+...+\frac{(x_1+x_2)^n}{n!}z^n+...$$

$$=(1+x_1z+...+\frac{x_1^k}{k!}z^k+...)(1+x_2z+...+\frac{x_2^k}{k!}z^k+...)$$

By making the z^n terms equal, we find binomial formula:

$$\frac{(x_1+x_2)^n}{n!} = \sum_{\substack{k_1+k_2=n \\ k \text{ from } 0 \text{ to } n}}^{n} \frac{x_1^{k_1} x_2^{k_2}}{k_1!k_2!}$$

To get multinomial formula, it is sufficient to do the same with:

$$e^{z(x_1+x_2+x_3+\ldots+x_n)} = e^{zx_1} e^{zx_2} e^{zx_3} \ldots e^{zx_n}$$

For a given n, the generating function of $D_n(d_1, d_2, \ldots, d_n)$ is:

$$F_n(x_1, x_2, \ldots, x_n) = \sum_{\substack{\sum d_i = 2n-2 \\ d_i \geq 1}} D_n(d_1, d_2, \ldots, d_n) x_1^{d_1} x_2^{d_2} \ldots x_n^{d_n}$$

To show this formula, let us use the formula found above:

$$D_n(d_1, d_2, \ldots, d_n) = \frac{(n-2)!}{(d_1-1)!(d_2-2)!\ldots(d_n-1)!}$$

This gives:

$F_n(x_1, x_2, \ldots, x_n)$

$$= x_1 x_2 \ldots x_n \sum_{\substack{\sum d_i = 2n-2 \\ d_i \geq 1}} \frac{(n-2)!}{(d_1-1)!(d_2-2)!\ldots(d_n-1)!} x_1^{d_1-1} x_2^{d_2-1} \ldots x_n^{d_n-1}$$

$$= x_1 x_2 \ldots x_n \sum_{\substack{\sum d'_i = n-2 \\ d'_i \geq 0 \text{ and } d'_i \leq n-2}} \frac{(n-2)!}{d_1'!d_2'!\ldots d_n'!} x_1^{d'_1} x_2^{d'_2} \ldots x_n^{d'_n} \frac{1}{2}$$

postulating $d'_i = d_i - 1$ with i between 1 and n:

$$= x_1 x_2 \ldots x_n (x_1 + x_2 + \ldots + x_n)^{n-2}$$

Note that by setting all the x_i to 1 in the previous formula, we get the number of spanning trees, i.e. n^{n-2}, and again find Cayley's formula.

31.3. Randomly constructed spanning tree

31.3.1. *Wilson's algorithm*

Let us consider a graph with N vertices that we number from 0 to $N-1$. The aim is to construct a spanning tree of this graph, i.e. a tree with N graph vertices as its vertices and some of its edges as edges.

We also want this tree to have 0 as its root. To construct it, we will use what is called Wilson's algorithm [WIL 96]:

– We start at vertex 1 and launch a random walk on the graph, from vertex to neighboring vertex. This is done up until root 0. In this random walk, as soon as a loop is formed we erase it. This random walk is therefore reduced to a sequence of completely distinct vertices, which can only end up at 0, and it gives a branch of the tree in the process of being created. At the same time, we mark the vertices reached.

– We take the first vertex after 1 that is not already marked, and we launch a random walk to distinct vertices in the same way as above, until we reach the first vertex already marked. We also mark the vertices reached on this branch.

– We restart our walk the first vertex that has not yet been marked, which gives a new branch. This is done until the last vertex.

– In the end, we find all the vertices have been reached, and we have a tree with root 0.

Note that, in a tree constructed in this way, we can take any vertex as the root or not take any root at all. It was shown that by this construction method a spanning tree has as many chances of being obtained as any other.

We will program this method in the context of a particular graph. Let us take a graph in the form of a network based on squares inserted in a rectangle $N-1$ long and $M-1$ wide (hence N points on each horizontal, and M on each vertical). The vertices are numbered from left to right and top to bottom (see Figure 31.5). We will begin by making the program that gives the list of neighbors of each vertex.

Each vertex, in general, has four neighbors, except for those of the border. For example, only points i that are not on the upper border have a neighboring vertex to the north, which is expressed by $i-N$ greater than or equal to 0. The number of neighbors is placed in *nbn*[i]. In the perspective of graph design, we also record the coordinates *x*[i], *y*[i] of the vertices.

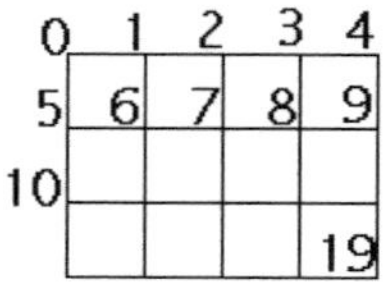

Figure 31.5. *Graph network in a 4×3 rectangle with numbering of the vertices*

```
for(i=0; i<MN; i++)
    {x[i]=xo+step*(i%N); y[i]=yo+step*(i/N); draw the vertices}
for(i=0; i<MN; i++)
  { k=0;
    if (i−N>=0) n[i][k++]=i−N;
    if (i%N!=0) n[i][k++]=i−1;
    if (i+N<MN) n[i][k++]=i+N;
    if ((i+1)%N !=0) n[i][k++]=i+1;
    nbn[i]=k;
  }
draw the edges
```

Now, let us move on to programming Wilson's algorithm by applying it to the previous graph. Throughout the process, we distinguish the vertices that have already been reached (*finished*[*i*] = 1), and the others (*finished*[*i*] = 0). Initially, only root 0 is marked as *finished*. Then from each unfinished vertex *i0*, we launch a branch of distinct successive vertices, which will stop on the first vertex marked as *finished*. The function *branch* chooses a neighboring vertex at random from a vertex, and this is done until the first vertex is *finished*. It erases the loops that can occur. To do this, the successive vertices are placed in a table *a*[], and each time for the neighbor of a vertex we check whether we have not already found it before. For this, we use the function *wherealreadyseen*() which returns either -1 if the neighboring vertex has not yet been found, in which case we move forward one notch in table *a*[], or the position of the vertex if it was already obtained, in which case we return to this position.

```
root=0; finished[root]=1;
for(i0=1; i0<MN; i0++) if (finished[i0]==0)
            /* launching of a branch from vertex i0 */
  { branch(i0);
    for(k=0; k<=counter; k++) finished[a[k]]=1;
            /* the vertices of the branch are finished */
   draw the branch
  }
```

```
void branch(int i)
{ int h,j, neighbor,flag,vertex;
 for(j=0; j<10000; j++) a[j]=0;            /* we set table a[] to 0 */
 vertex=i;counter=0;a[0]=vertex;  /* we put the initial vertex in a[0] */
 for(;;)
   { vertex=a[counter];    /* counter is the index of the boxes in a[]  */
     h=random(nbn[vertex]); neighbor=n[vertex][h];
                                  /* one neighbor of vertex is taken at random */
     if (finished[neighbor]==1) { counter++; a[counter]=neighbor; break;}
                                  /* stop test */
     if (wherealreadyseen(neighbor)== -1)
                    /* if the neighbor has not yet been found, it is recorded in a[] */
          { counter++; a[counter]=neighbor; }
     else {counter=wherealreadyseen(neighbor);}
                                  /* we backtrack to erase the loop */
   }
}

int wherealreadyseen(int n)
  { int j;
    for(j=counter; j>=0; j--)  if (n==a[j]) return j;
    return -1;
  }
```

Figure 31.6 shows a spanning tree thus obtained randomly in a square.

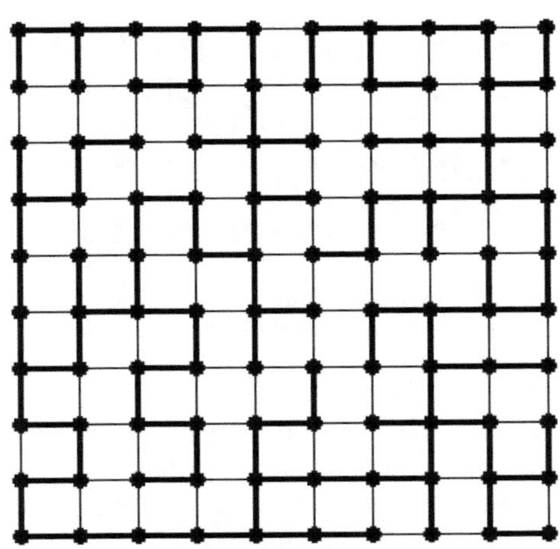

Figure 31.6. *Random spanning tree in a rectangle with N = 10 and M = 10*

31.3.2. *Maze and domino tiling*

We will now use a slight variation of the previous method to construct a maze and deduce from it a way to randomly pave a chessboard with dominos.

We start with a square grid of even length N (see Figure 31.7 with $N = 20$), and first take only the squares of 2 and 2, where both coordinates are even, the origin of the reference point being taken in the bottom left.

The centers of the corresponding squares are indicated in the drawing. We have to construct a forest of trees constructed randomly, the nodes of which are the centers of the squares and the roots of which are located just beyond the eastern and northern border of the square (the points in light gray on the drawing in Figure 31.7).

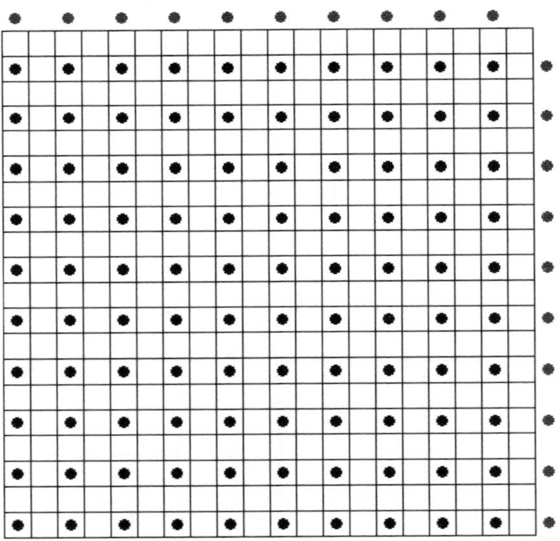

Figure 31.7. *The initial square, with its even squares and points on eastern and northern borders*

To construct a maze we start from a point taken at random in the square and from it we choose one of its neighbors at random, and so on and so forth by successive neighborhoods, pruning any cycle that could be formed during the route that will give a branch of the tree and stopping on an exterior root. Then we start again from another point at random that is not on the branch that has already been constructed, stopping either on an exterior root or on the branch that has already been constructed. We repeat this until all the points of the square are on a branch.

We thus obtain a forest of trees (see Figure 31.8, left), or a single tree if we consider all the points on the exterior borders as making only one (it is sufficient to link them as we see in Figure 31.8, right). Note that the starting points taken to trace the branches constitute the leaves of the trees.

We then take the points of the square where both coordinates are odd, adding an exterior border on the left and below. Then we construct the trees (in light gray in Figure 31.8, right) which fits between the branches of the tree already constructed from the even squares. Only one single possibility exists once the tree of even squares is placed. On the drawing, we also joined the points of the external borders, on one hand those located on the east and north and on the other hand those located on the west and south.

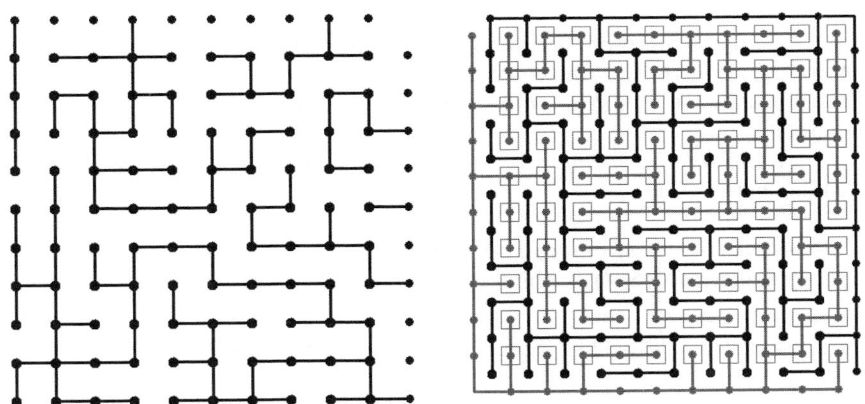

Figure 31.8. *The forest of trees from the even boxes of the square (left); and the two trees obtained by using the even and odd boxes (right)*

We notice that only an opening in the top left and another one in the bottom right survive. If we consider the branches of the two trees (black and gray) to be walls, we get a maze with all its ins and outs enabling us to go from one opening to the other. Note that this corresponds exactly to the traversal of the tree (in black) according to the process seen before in tree exploration. If we start from the top left, this comes back to moving along the walls, always having a black wall on our left and a gray wall on our right.

Lastly, let us traverse the branches of the tree from its leaves, and link each point with its neighbor located one unit from it, surrounding it by a 2×1 rectangle. We therefore get a succession of dominos (see Figure 31.9). When we do this for all the branches of a tree of even squares, then those of odd squares, we get a horizontal or vertical domino tiling of the squares. Here is the program for constructing the tree coming from the even squares, with the rest easily being deduced from it.

We take the length N *of the overall square, and the length of the* step *of each small square.*

/ drawing the centers of the squares where both coordinates are even, these points are numbered from* 0 *to* $N^2 / 4 - 1$*, going from left to right and from bottom to top */*

```
for(i=0; i<N*N/4; i++)
  { x[i]=xo+step*((2*i)%N); y[i]=yo-step*2*(4*i/(2*N));
    draw points x[i], y[i] in black
  }
/* we draw the points of the two eastern and northern borders */
for(i=0; i<N/2; i++) { draw points xo+step*N , yo-step*2*i }
for(i=0; i<N/2; i++) { draw points xo+step*2*i , yo-step*N }
end=NO;
  /* we will stop when end moves to YES: all the points are on the tree */
while (end==NO)
 {
  /* we take a number of a point at random that is not yet on a branch */
 do {r=random(N*N/4); } while (getpixel(x[r],y[r])==BLACK);

 /* we construct the branch originating from this point which will be a leaf of
    the tree */
 branch(r); /* the successive points of the branch are in a table a[] */
 for(k=0; k<= counter; k++){ color the points x[a[k]] , y[a[k]] in BLACK }

/* then we join these points with lines to get a branch of the tree */
 for(k=0; k<counter; k++) line(x[a[k]],y[a[k]],x[a[k+1]],y[a[k+1]]);

/* test to find out if it is finished */
 for(i=0; i<N*N/4; i++) if (getpixel(x[i],y[i])==BLACK) { end=NO; break;}
 if (i==N*N/4) end=YES;
 }

void branch(int leaf)
{
 for(j=0;j<1000;j++) a[j]=0;
   /* the numbers of nodes on the branch will be placed in table a[],
```

```
      which we set to 0 initially */
   a[0]=leaf; counter=0;
   for(;;)
    {vertex=a[counter];
    /* the leaf at the start, then all the nodes that will make up the branch
       are found in vertex */

    /* we look for the coordinates of the four neighbors of vertex */
    xneighbor[0]=x[vertex]+2*step ,yneighbor[0]=y[vertex];
    xneighbor[1]=x[vertex],yneighbor[1]=y[vertex]-2*step;
    xneighbor[2]=x[vertex]-2*step ,yneighbor[2]=y[vertex];
    xneighbor[3]=x[vertex],yneighbor[3]=y[vertex]+2*step;
  /* But a node in fact has two, or three, or four neighbors in the square. Among
the four previous neighbors, we eliminate those that are not colored in BLACK
(they have the background color 0 of the screen) and among the true neighbors, we
take one at random */
    do h=random(4);  while (getpixel(xneighbor[h],yneighbor[h])==0);

  /* If the neighbor obtained is already colored in BLACK (it is already on a
branch or on an exterior border), the branch is finished, and we do a break from the
for loop. As a point on the exterior border does not have a number, we decide to
draw the end of the branch here */
    if (getpixel(xneighbor[h],yneighbor[h])==BLACK)
      {line(x[vertex],y[vertex],xneighbor[h],yneighbor[h]); break;}
    else
     { neighbor[0]=vertex+1;neighbor[1]=vertex+N/2;
              /* numbers of potential neighbors */
       neighbor[2]=vertex-1; neighbor[3]=vertex–N/2;

  /* If the neighbor chosen neighbor[h] is not already in the branch, we take it by
recording it in a[] in position counter (this latter increases by one each time).
Otherwise we proceed to the pruning by putting the counter index in the position
where node neighbor[h] was previously found */
       if (wherealreadyseen(neighbor[h])==-1)
        { counter++; a[counter]=neighbor[h]; }
         else counter=wherealreadyseen(neighbor[h]);
        }
     }
  }

  int wherealreadyseen(int n)
  {  for(j=counter; j>=0; j--)  if (n==a[j]) return 0 ;     return -1; }
```

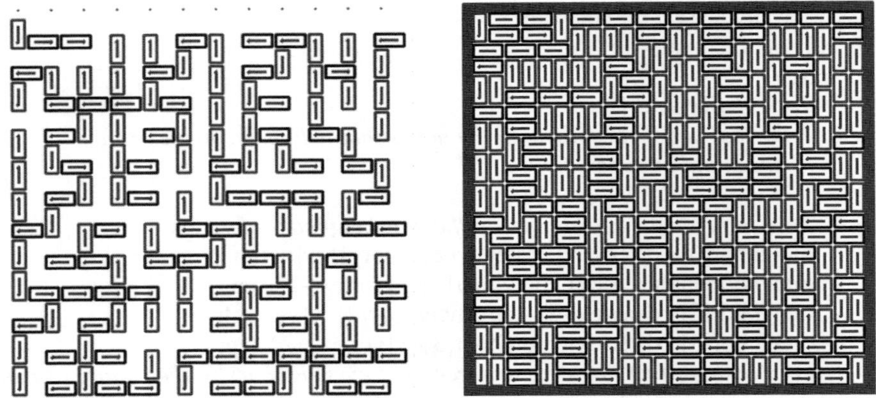

Figure 31.9. *The tree of even squares drawn in the shape of dominos (left); and the complete tiling of the two trees (right)*

Chapter 32

Binary Trees

With the notion of a binary tree, order comes into play, not only vertical as for every tree with its root and its successive levels, but above all horizontal. More specifically, a position on the left or right is attributed to the successors (sons, daughters or children) of each node. By definition, a binary tree is a rooted tree where each of the nodes has no successor, one successor to the left or right, or two successors, as we see in the example in Figure 32.1. We say that the nodes are of degree 0, 1 or 2. A binary tree can also be reduced to an empty tree. To understand the importance of the empty tree, here is how we can give a completely coherent recursive definition of a binary tree: it is either the empty tree or a root node to which one tree is attached on the left and one on the right. If we were to forget the case of the empty tree, the definition would lose all meaning: notably, the tree would not be able to have any leaves, i.e. a node to which two empty trees are attached.

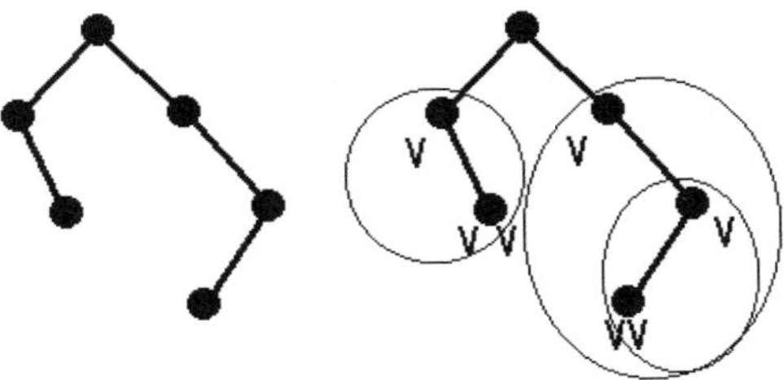

Figure 32.1. *A tree with its sub-trees, notably its empty trees called V*

We also define what is called a complete binary tree. In addition to being an empty tree, it is a rooted tree, such that each node has either no successors or two successors (one on the left and the other on the right), see Figure 32.2. We therefore distinguish two types of nodes: internal nodes, which have two successors, and terminal nodes, without successors. We check that there is always one more terminal node than internal nodes.[1]

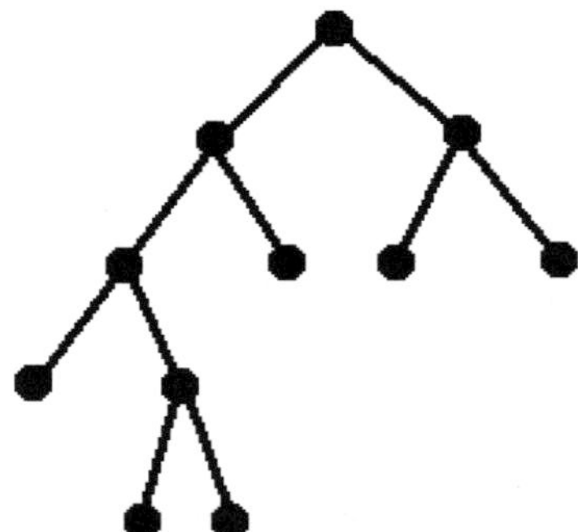

Figure 32.2. *A complete binary tree with 11 nodes, five of which are internal and six of which are terminal*

There is a direct link between a binary tree and a complete binary tree. We can actually associate every binary tree containing n nodes, with a complete binary tree with the same n nodes that now become internal nodes, with $n + 1$ terminal nodes added under them. This process is reversible: it is sufficient to remove the terminal nodes or add them back to move from one type of tree to the other. The computer view of the trees confirms this link between the two ways of drawing a binary tree, filled or not (see Figure 32.3).

In a program, a node is considered as equipped with two hanging branches to which other nodes can be attached. These hanging branches are pointers in the program (see section 32.5, the binary tree sort).

1. Let us show this property. Let n be the number of internal nodes. When the tree is such that $n = 1$, there are two terminal nodes, and the property is true for $n = 1$. Let us assume that the property is true for a certain number n of internal nodes and let us show that it remains so for $n + 1$ nodes, namely that there is one more terminal node. Indeed, the passage from n internal nodes to $n + 1$ internal nodes is done by transforming a terminal node into an internal node with its two terminal nodes, which maintains the difference of 1 between the number of terminal nodes and that of internal nodes.

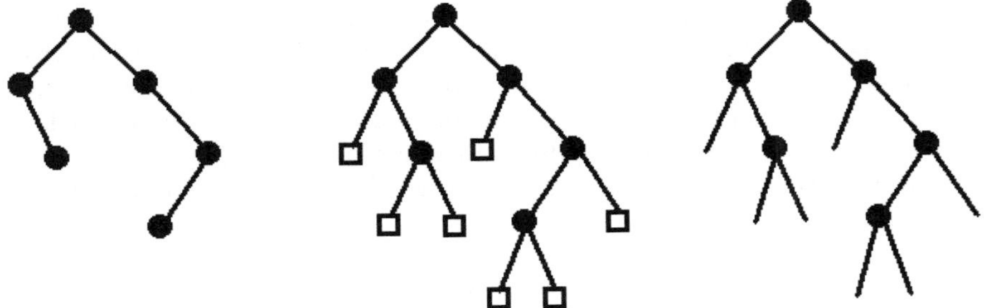

Figure 32.3. *A binary tree (left); the complete corresponding binary tree (center); the same tree as can be programmed on a computer (right)*

32.1. Number of binary trees with n nodes

Let $c(n)$ be the number of binary trees with n nodes (or even with n internal nodes and $n + 1$ terminal nodes, taking the full trees). Due to the empty tree, we get $c(0) = 1$. Let us take $n > 0$. One node is the root. We now need to share the $n - 1$ remaining nodes in the left and right sub-tree in all possible ways. Let us classify the possibilities according to the number of nodes in the left sub-tree. One possibility is that we do not place any nodes on the left (empty sub-tree), which makes $c(0) = 1$ ways, and $n - 1$ nodes in the right sub-tree, with $c(n - 1)$ ways, which makes a total of $c(0)\ c(n - 1)$ cases. The other possibility is that we place a node on the left, and $n - 2$ nodes on the right, which makes $c(1)\ c(n - 2)$ cases. More generally, we place k nodes on the left, hence $c(k)$ left sub-trees, and $n - 1 - k$ nodes on the right, hence $c(n - 1 - k)$ right sub-trees, which makes a total of $c(k)\ c(n - 1 - k)$ trees of that type. This goes for all values of k, from 0 to $n - 1$. Finally the number of trees with n nodes is:

$$c(n) = c(0)\ c(n-1) + c(1)\ c(n-2) + \ldots + c(k)\ c(n-1-k) + \ldots + c(n-1)\ c(0)$$

This recurrence formula, in conjunction with the initial condition $c(0) = 1$, gives Catalan numbers (already encountered in Chapters 9, 10 and 11).

32.2. The language of binary trees

Let us consider the binary magma generated by x, which has a single operation called • as a multiplication, but that is non-associative. In other words, x can be multiplied by itself, as many times as we want, but the product is only made by couples, placed between parentheses.

Actually, with the operation not being associative, the product $(x.x).x$ is not the same as $x.(x.x)$, and the expression $x.x.x$ has no meaning. This binary magma (based on couples) forms a language whose words are based on one letter x and a pair of left and right parentheses. A word in this language, for example, is: $(((x.x).x).((x.x).(x.(x.x))))$, which is also written $(((x\ x)\ x)\ ((x\ x)\ (x\ (x\ x))))$ where the multiplication points are deleted, because they are doing a double job with the pairs of parentheses.

One such word can be represented by a complete binary tree, where the xs are the terminal nodes and the points correspond with the internal nodes, each one of these points being associated with a pair of parentheses, right and left, that surround it (see Figure 32.4). The word formed from x only represents the empty tree.

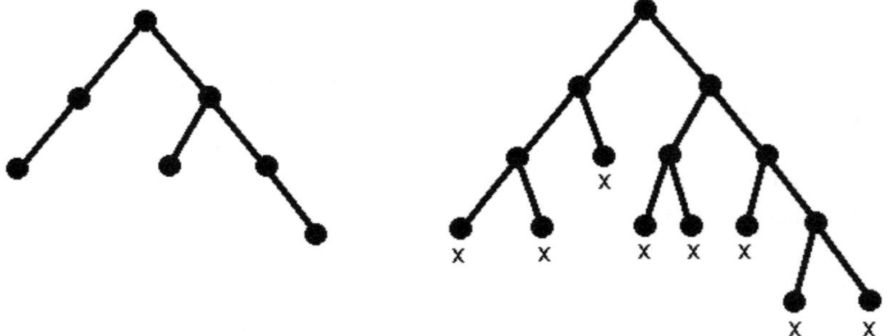

Figure 32.4. *A binary tree with seven nodes (and with eight more hanging branches eventually) (left); and the word (((x x) x) ((x x) (x (x x)))) representing the corresponding complete binary tree with eight terminal nodes and seven internal nodes (right)*

Language A of this binary magma generated by x obeys these two production rules:

– x belongs to language A;

– if words w and w' are in language A, then $(w.w')$ is also in A.

In terms of binary trees, this gives the following definition: the empty tree (called x) is a binary tree, and every couple of binary trees is a binary tree, from which they form the left and the right sub-trees.

This enables us to progressively create the words of the language, from x, by pairing up the words already obtained:

$$x\,,\ (x.x)\,,\ (x.(x.x))\,,\ ((x.x).x)\,,\ ((x.x).(x.x))\,,\ (x.(x.(x.x)))\,,\ \ldots$$

By placing + signs that mean "or", we write the language:

$$A = x + (x.x) + (x.(x.x)) + ((x.x).x) + ((x.x).(x.x)) + (x.(x.(x.x))) + \ldots$$

Using the fact that every element of language A is either x or made up of any pair of elements of A, we also get:

$$A = x + (x + (x.x) + (x.(x.x)) + ((x.x).x) + ((x.x).(x.x)) + (x.(x.(x.x))) + \ldots)$$
$$.(x + (x.x) + (x.(x.x)) + ((x.x).x) + ((x.x).(x.x)) + (x.(x.(x.x))) + \ldots)$$

where we take into consideration the distributivity of the • operation in relation to the + operation. Language A therefore obeys the equation:

$$A = x + (A.A)$$

Now let us make the operation product • associative, which refers to deleting the parentheses. Each word is replaced by a power of x, and we can group words of the form x^k, which enables us to count the number of words with the same number k of letter xs, i.e. with k terminal nodes. Language A is replaced by the generating function:

$$A(x) = c'_0 + c'_1 x + c'_2 x^2 + c'_3 x^3 + \ldots$$

where the coefficient c'_n is the number of complete binary trees having n terminal nodes. Solving the equation: $A(x) = x + A(x)^2$ we find:

$$A(x) = \frac{1-\sqrt{1-4x}}{2}$$

and developing:

$$A(x) = x + x^2 + 2x^3 + 5x^4 + \ldots$$

Now let us consider binary trees in the strict sense, with each node having 0, 1 or 2 successors. Thanks to the bijection seen before, there are as many such trees with

n nodes, i.e. c_n, as complete trees with n nodes and $n + 1$ terminal nodes, i.e. c'_{n+1}. The generating function associated with these trees is therefore:

$$C(x) = A(x) / x,$$

and $C(x)$ verifies:

$$C(x) = 1 + xC^2.$$

Hence:

$$C(x) = \frac{1-\sqrt{1-4x}}{2x} = 1 + x + 2x^2 + 5x^3 + \ldots$$

and we find the generating series of Catalan numbers c_n.

32.3. Algorithm for creation of words from the binary tree language

To have words with N pairs of parentheses, i.e. binary trees with N nodes (or even N internal nodes and $N + 1$ leaves in the case of equivalent complete binary trees), we begin by pairing the $c(0)$ words without parentheses with the $c(N - 1)$ words with $N - 1$ pairs of parentheses. We then pair those with one pair of parentheses with those that have $N - 2$ of them, etc. This implies that in the program, we progressively create words from the shortest ones, keeping them in memory until those with N pairs of parentheses are obtained. The latter are placed in a table $a[n][c][i]$, where n is the number of pairs of parentheses (or internal nodes of the tree), c is the number associated with this word, and i the index of each letter of the word concerned. A word with n internal nodes has $2n$ parentheses and $n + 1$ terminal nodes called x. Its length is $3n + 1$.

```
C[0]=1; a[0][0][0]='x';
      /* in a[][][] the empty word corresponds to n=0, and there is one single
word: C[0]=1 */
for(n=1; n<=N; n++)
      /* we look for words with n nodes, from n=1 up to N */
 { counter=0;
   for(i=0; i<n; i++)
     /* to get words with n nodes, we pair the words with i nodes and those
        with j nodes */
   { j = n–1–i;
     for(k=0; k<C[i]; k++)  for(kk=0; kk<C[j]; kk++)
       { a[n][counter][0]='(';      /* the initial parenthesis */
```

```
        for(nn=0; nn<3*i+1; nn++) a[n][counter][nn+1]=a[i][k][nn];
          /* the first word */
        nn0=3*i+2;
        for(nn=0; nn<3*j+1; nn++) a[n][counter][nn0+nn]=a[j][kk][nn];
          /* the second word */
        a[n][counter][nn0+3*j+1]=')';        /* the end parenthesis */
        counter++;
       }
     C[n]=counter;  /* number of trees with n nodes */
    }
  }
  for(c=0; c<C[N]; c++)
    { for(i=0; i < 3*N+1; i++) printf("%c",a[N][c][i]);  printf("\n"); }
```

Curiously this language of words based on letter *x*s and parentheses will serve to split a polygon into triangles.

32.4. Triangulation of polygons with numbered vertices and binary trees

Let us consider a convex polygon with N vertices labeled 0, 1, 2, .., $N-1$. Let the edges be 0, 1, 2, …, $N-1$, with edge number i joining vertex i and the next vertex. This polygon can be divided into $N-2$ triangles having either the sides of the polygon or the diagonals as its sides, with the entire thing forming a sort of tiling inside the polygon (see Figures 32.5, 32.6, 32.7, for example).

As the drawing in Figure 32.5 indicates, each triangulation is bijectively linked to a rooted binary tree, with $N-2$ nodes. The root is represented as being the center of gravity of the triangle with edge number 0. This triangle separates the polygon into a part triangulated polygon on its left and a part triangulated polygon on its right. The binary tree is constructed by taking the centers of gravity of adjacent triangles, where the leaves correspond to the middles of the edges (except edge number 0). The binary tree has $N-2$ nodes and $N-1$ leaves. The corresponding word has the length: $2(N-2)+N-1=3N-5$.

Knowing the words coding the binary tree will enable us to construct all the triangulations of a polygon, thanks to a simple algorithm. Let us take the example of the word $((x((xx)x))(xx))$ in Figure 32.5, which represents a tree with five internal nodes and six terminal nodes (we omitted the points representing the internal nodes, since the pairs of parentheses play the same role). The tree leaves are associated with the edges of the polygon with seven edges taken in ascending order from 1 to 6, with edge 0 being excluded because it is associated with the root of the tree.

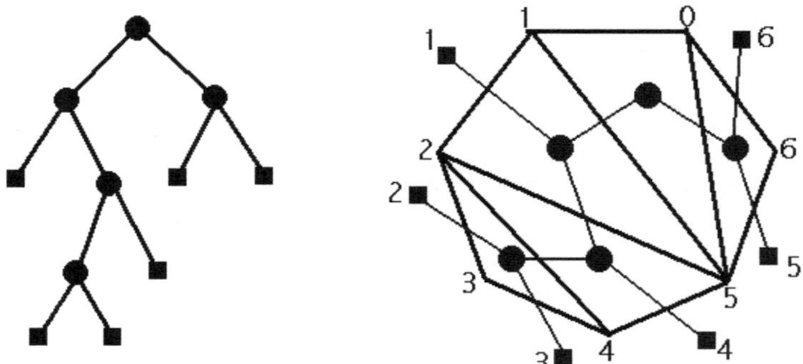

Figure 32.5. *A binary tree associated with the word ((x((xx)x))(xx)) (left); and the same tree corresponding to a triangulation of a polygon with seven sides (heptagon) (right)*

Let us replace the leaves x with these successive whole numbers: ((1((23)4))(56)). We then carry out a traversal of the word, and each time we encounter an internal node with two terminal nodes as successors of the form (a b), we know that this gives a triangle. We replace this node, which has just served its purpose, with a terminal node. We re-do traversals of the word that does not stop shrinking, until only the empty tree remains:

((1 ((2 3) 4)) (5 6)) → ((1(23 4)) (5 6)) → ((1(23 4)) 56) →

((1 234) 56) → (1234 56) → 123456

This method has the advantage of giving us triangles to be constructed. First the triangle (2 3) has edges 2 and 3 as its sides, and 2, 3 and 4 as its vertices. Similarly, triangle (5 6) has 5, 6 and 0 as vertices. Triangle (23 4) has diagonal 23 (joining vertex 2 and vertex 4) and edge 4 as its sides. Its vertices are 2, 4 and 5. And so on and so forth, which gives the triangulation by triangles of 234, 560, 245, 125 and 150 (see Figure 32.6).

To program all possible triangulations of a polygon with N sides (see Figure 32.7 for N = 6), we go back to the previous program in binary trees and code each word by putting -1 for a left parenthesis and -2 for a right one. For example: ((x((x x)x))(x x)) becomes:

((1((2 3) 4))(5 6))

then:

-1 -1 1 -1 -1 2 3 -2 4 -2 -2 -1 5 6 -2 -2

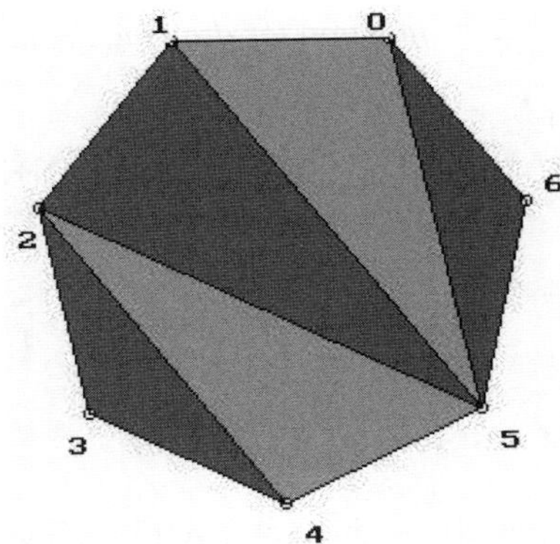

Figure 32.6. *A triangulation of the heptagon corresponding to the word ((x((xx)x))(xx)), obtained by program*

We have the program:

```
for(n=0; n<C[N]; n++)
      /* we take each corresponding word to a binary tree with N nodes */
  { Lo=3*NN−5;
      /* NN is the number of vertices of the polygon with NN=N+2 */
    number=1;
    for(nn=0; nn < Lo; nn++)
      { if (a[N][n][nn]=='(') aa[nn]= -1; if (a[N][n][nn]==')') aa[nn]=-2;
        if (a[N][n][nn]=='x') aa[nn]=number++;
      }
    for(i=1; i<NN; i++) leng[i]=1;
    while(Lo!=1) for(i=0;i<Lo-3;i++)
    if (aa[i]==-1 && aa[i+3]==-2)
      { d=aa[i+1];
        while(d/10!=0) d=d/10;
        e=aa[i+2]; while(e/10!=0) e=e/10;
        f=(aa[i+2]%10+1)%NN;
        drawtriangle(d,e,f);
        aa[i]=aa[i+1]*pow(10.,leng[aa[i+2]])+aa[i+2];
        leng[aa[i]]=leng[aa[i+1]]+leng[aa[i+2]];
        for(j=i+4;j<Lo;j++) aa[j-3]=aa[j];
        Lo-=3;
      }
  }
```

```
void drawing(void)  /* annex function for drawing the points of the polygon */
{ int i;
  for(i=0;i<NNN;i++)
    { xe[i]=xorig+100*cos(M_PI/2.- M_PI/(float)NNN+i*2.*M_PI/(float)NNN);
      ye[i]=yorig-100*sin(M_PI/2.-M_PI/(float)NNN+i*2.*M_PI/(float)NNN);
      draw the point
    }
}

void drawtriangle(long int d, long int e, long int f)
{
 line(xe[d],ye[d],xe[e],ye[e]);     line(xe[e],ye[e],xe[f],ye[f]);
 line(xe[f],ye[f],xe[d],ye[d]);
 xg=(xe[d]+xe[e]+xe[f])/3;yg=(ye[d]+ye[e]+ye[f])/3;
 color the inside of the triangle from its center of gravity (with the function
floodfill)
}
```

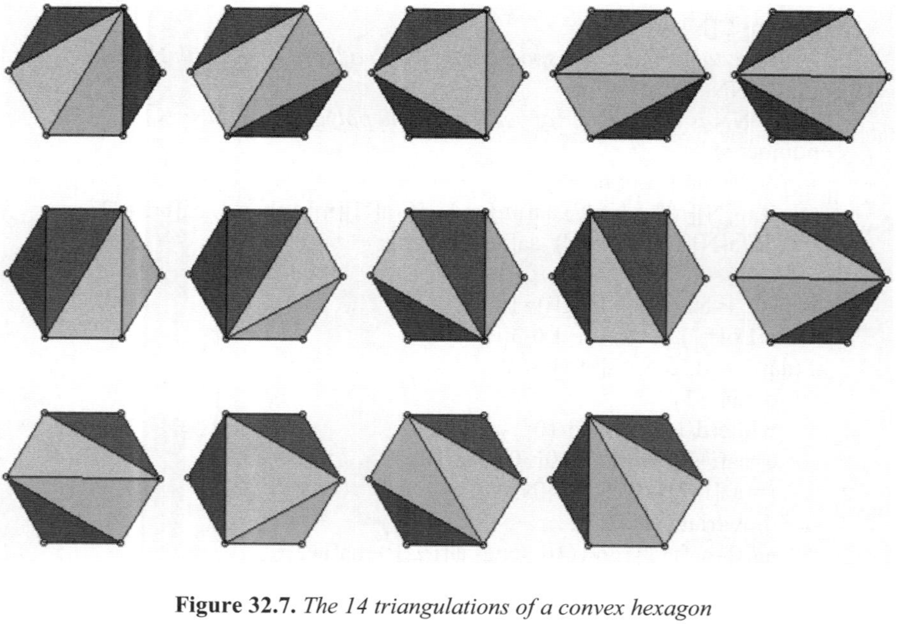

Figure 32.7. *The 14 triangulations of a convex hexagon*

32.5. Binary tree sort or quicksort

This is a (rare) example where the binary tree must be created node after node by the program itself. At the start it is an everyday sorting problem – more specifically the quicksort, also called jeweler's sort.

To sort a pile of diamonds, the jeweler uses a sieve that enables him to separate the pile into two piles. Then he starts again with each of the two piles. The quality of the sort therefore depends on the sieves used at each stage, in such a way that each pile is separated into two almost equal parts. If the holes in the sieves are too big or too small, the sort will be slow.

In computer terms, this is translated in the following way: we start with a list of numbers for sorting. We take the first number, which constitutes the root of the tree we are going to create. Then we take the second number. Depending on whether it is shorter (smaller) or longer (larger) than the first one, we attach it under the root on the left or on the right. We continue in the same way. Each number is brought down in the tree, being attached on left if it is shorter than the node it is passing, and on the right if it is longer. It finally takes the first empty space on which it falls.

For example, the sort for the list of numbers 7935418 produces the binary tree in Figure 32.8. It is the quicksort because the smaller numbers are found on the left of each node of the tree, and the larger numbers on its right, at least if we narrow by half the distance between the two branches under each node at each descent from a level in the tree. By vertical projection onto the ground, we find the sorted list. But how can this be achieved in computer terms?

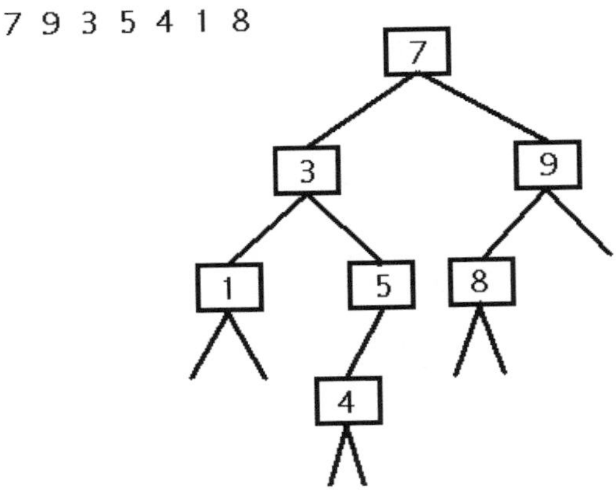

Figure 32.8. *Construction of a binary tree that sorts the numbers from a list of numbers*

The tree is gradually constructed by attaching elementary bricks constructed in this way: n .

This is done in two stages. First we put the root in place. Next we insert the other cells one by one, using a hook that we bring down in the tree, going left or right depending on whether the number to be placed is smaller or larger than the numbers already placed in the cells. When the bottom end of the hook is an empty space, the new cell with its number will be attached. The program, whose principle is indicated in Figure 32.9, results from there.

```
/* the numbers for sorting are supposedly placed in a table a[N] */
/* declaration of the bottom cell */
struct cell { int n; struct cell * l; struct cell * r;};

/* putting the root in place */
root= (struct cell *) malloc (sizeof (struct cell));
root->n=a[0]; root->l=NULL; root->r=NULL;
/* progressive insertion of the numbers in the tree */
for(i=1; i<N; i++)
  { e1= NULL; e2=root;
     /* putting the hook (e1 e2) in place at the top of the tree */
    ptr==(struct cell)malloc (sizeof (struct cell));
    ptr->n= a[i]; ptr->l=NULL; ptr->r=NULL; /* the new cell */
    while (e2!=NULL)    /* we go down the hook in the tree */
              { e1=e2;  if (a[i]<e2->n) e2=e2->l;  else e2=e2->r; }
    if (a[i]<e1->n) e1->l = ptr; else e1->r = ptr;
     /* we permanently attach the cell */
  }
```

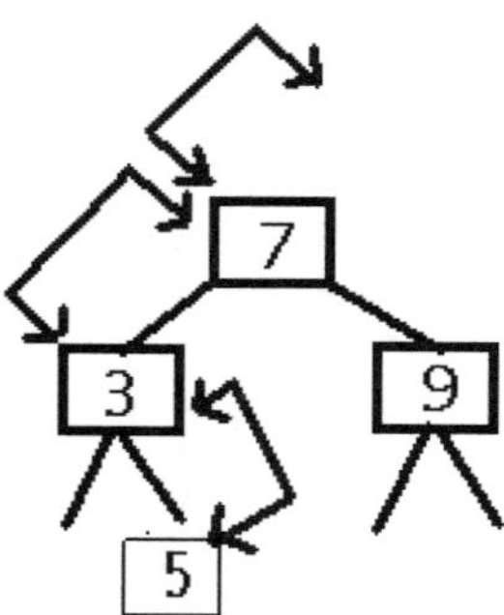

Figure 32.9. *Inserting cell 5 into the tree being constructed*

We are now left to display the result, namely the sorted numbers. For this, we use a function for traversal of the tree, which we launch from the root, i.e. *traversal*(*root*). This function is recalled on each of the nodes of the tree:

```
void traversal(struct cell * r)
{ if (r !=NULL)
      { traversal (r->l);
        printf(“%d”, r->n);
       traversal(r->r);
      }
}
```

The nodes are displayed between the traversals of the left and right trees. It is a so-called infix traversal of the tree, which gives the sorted numbers from the smallest to the largest. We can also display the tree on the screen by generating the coordinates of each cell (see Figure 32.10).

At each stage of tree traversal, the abscissa increases by a constant quantity. With each descent in the tree, the ordinate also increases by a constant quantity. We should also conserve the predecessor of each node in order to be able to draw the junction branches.

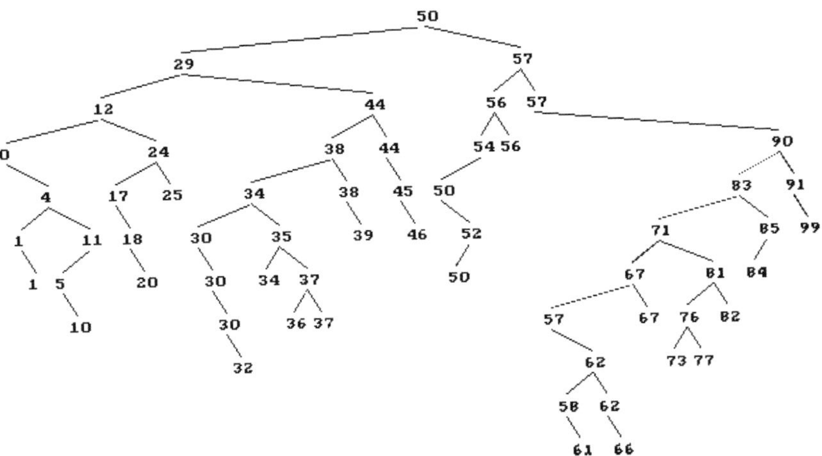

Figure 32.10. *Drawing of the binary tree. Its infix traversal gives the sorted numbers, just as if the tree was being projected on the ground*

Chapter 33

Weighted Graphs: Shortest Paths and Minimum Spanning Tree

With the notion of weighted graphs, new data enters into consideration, namely that a number is associated with each arc or edge of the graph. Such numbers can be positive or negative, but here we will simply take them to be positive. In a problem posed on a graph, searching for a minimum part will correspond to a part of this graph whose sum of numbers associated with the edges will be minimal, out of all the parts of the graph responding to the same conditions. We are essentially concerned with two problems on this subject: searching for the shortest paths between two vertices of a graph, and searching for the minimum spanning tree.

33.1. Shortest paths in a graph

Let us consider a directed graph whose arcs have numbers (supposedly positive) that are associated with them. These numbers can correspond concretely to the length of the arcs, by analogy with the distances on a road network, or even to the flow of traffic.

Let us indicate that the graph can also be undirected. For this, it is sufficient to place bidirectional arrows to get the corresponding directed graph. The problem is finding the shortest path from one vertex to another.

There are several algorithms on this subject, which are divided into two categories:

– algorithms giving the shortest paths from a given vertex to all the others. The main reference in this domain is the so-called Dijkstra algorithm. The most interesting thing is what this algorithm originates from, namely the analogy with the movement of a fluid in lengths of pipe – the edges of the graph – at constant speed from a certain starting point;

– algorithms giving the shortest paths from any vertex to any other one. For this, it is sufficient to repeat an algorithm of the first category for each vertex. There are also specific algorithms, however, like Floyd's algorithm which we will see later.

33.1.1. *Dijkstra's algorithm*

In a weighted directed graph, let us choose a starting point, called 0. The aim is to determine the shortest paths in distances from point 0 to each of the other vertices. For this, we begin by constructing what is called the adjacency matrix. This adjacency matrix is not reduced, like before, to lines and columns from 1 or 0 depending on the presence or absence of arcs between two graph vertices. Now, when an arc joins two points it is their distance that is indicated in the matrix. Notably, the distance from one vertex to itself is set to 0. Where an arc is absent, we consider the distance to be infinite, in other words a very large number. Figure 33.1 is an example of a graph with its weighted adjacency matrix.

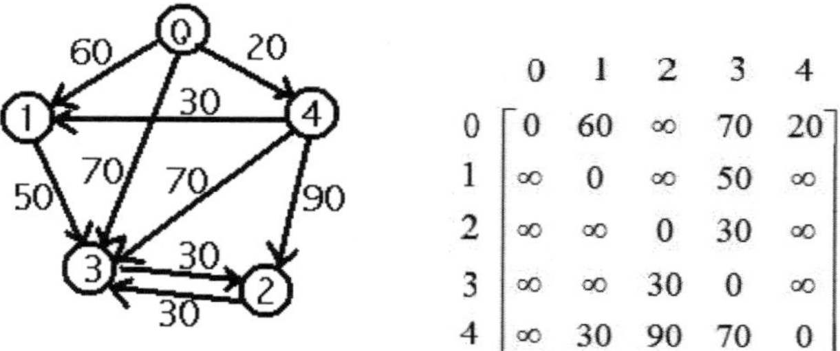

Figure 33.1. *An example of a weighted directed graph, with its adjacency matrix*

Here is how the algorithm is applied to the functions in this example. Initially we place the starting point *0* in a table *S*[], and the other vertices *1*, *2*, *3*, *4*, in a residual table *T*[]. Each time we find the shortest distance from *0* to a certain point in the graph, this point from table *T* will be put in table *S*.

The process of searching for the shortest distances happens in this way: in the *first stage* first expand point *0*, writing its distances to the other points, as indicated in the adjacency matrix directly following the arcs. These distances are placed in a table *d*[*i*], with *i* from 1 to 4 in this case. We notice that the shortest distance obtained, namely 20, is the one from vertex *0* to vertex *4*. We have just found the shortest path from *0* to *4*, as every other path passing through one of the other points can only give a longer distance.

We therefore transfer point *4* from *T* into *S*. Then we expand point *4* in the direction of points of table *T*. If we find a new distance (from *0* passing through *4*) to a certain point shorter than the one we had before, we choose this new distance. For example, the distance from *0* to *1* was 60, but passing through vertex *4* the distance from *0* to *1* becomes 20 + 30 = 50, which is shorter than the one before. In this case, we eliminate the old distance for the new one and at the same time change the predecessor of *1*: it was *0* before, and it now becomes *4*.

Having carried out these eventual modifications, we move on to the *second stage*, re-doing what we did in the first stage: we choose the shortest distance obtained for all the points of *T*, which is in table *d*[]. Here, it is the distance from point *1*, namely 50 (it was equal to 60 but passing through 4 it is equal to 20 + 30 = 50), with the distance from *0* to *2* being 20 + 90 = 110 passing through *4*, and that from *0* to *3* remaining at 70. We are therefore sure that the shortest path from 0 to 1 measures 50 and passes through *4*. Indeed, any other path would need to pass through another point from *T*, and this point is already further. Next we transfer point *1* from *T* into *S*. Table *T* no longer only contains *2* and *3*, the last points to be explored. We continue as above, expanding point *0* to points *2* and *3*, etc. This gives the evolution in Table 33.1, up to the end.

	S	*T*	*d* (1)	*d* (2)	*d* (3)	*d* (4)
	0	1234	60 (0)	∝ (0)	70 (0)	20 (0)
stage 1	04	123	50 (4)	110 (4)	70 (0)	
stage 2	041	23		110 (4)	70 (0)	
stage 3	0413	2		100 (3)		
stage 4	04132	*in d(i) the predecessors are placed between parentheses*				

Table 33.1.

At each stage of the process – four here – we have the minimum distances from point *0* to each other point, through paths that can pass through intermediate points of table *S*.

Taking the smallest distance in table *T* means that point *i* will definitely be at least this far from point *0*, because all the other points of *T* are already at a greater distance and cannot serve as intermediaries for the shortest path to point *i*. We deduce from it the program, the results of which we will see in Figure 33.2.

We begin by filling in the weighted adjacency matrix of the graph, i.e. *edge*[*N*][*N*], where *N* is the number of graph vertices. Then we take the initial conditions for tables *S* and *T*, as well as for table *d*[] of distances to points *1*, *2*, …, *N* – 1, and the table of their predecessors *pred*[], set to 0 at the start. This program assumes that the starting point is node *0*. We note the striking analogy of this program with that of Prim's algorithm, (see section 33.2.1) giving the minimum spanning tree of an undirected graph.

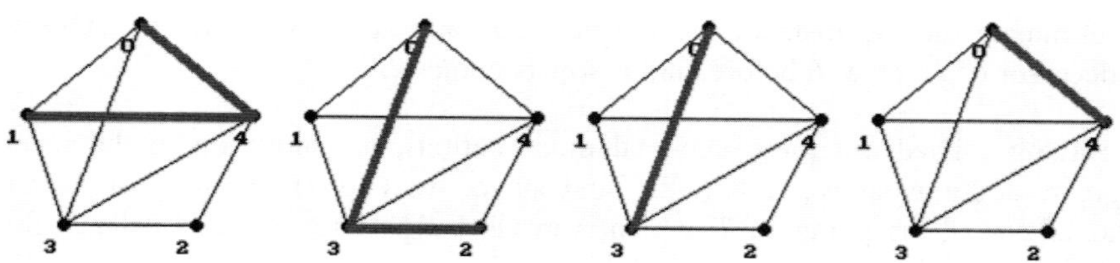

Figure 33.2. *All the shortest paths from vertex 0 for the previously defined graph*

```
S[0]=0;  LS=1 ;  LT=N–1;
for(i=0; i<LT ; i++) T[i]=i+1 ;
for(i=1; i<N; i++)  {  d[i]=edge[0][i];  pred[i]=0; }
/*  stages loop  */
for(stage=1; stage<N; stage++)
  {  mind=30000;
      /* searching for the minimum distance mind, with the
         corresponding point minpoint, and its index mini in T */
     for(i=0; i<LT; i++)
       { point=T[i] ;
         if (d[point]<mind) {mind=d[point]; minpoint=point;  mini=i;}
                /*  we add minpoint to S and we remove it from T */
         LS ++;  S[LS–1]=minpoint;
        for(i=mini;i<LT;i++) T[i]=T[i+1];
        LT --;
      /*  We update the distances table. If we find a path passing through
          minpoint less than the path obtained up until then, we choose this
          new path and set pred[] to minpoint  */
    for(i=0; i<LT; i++)
       {  point=T[i];  newd=mind+edge[minpoint][point];
          if (newd<d[point]) {d[point]=newd;  pred[point]=minpoint; }
       }
  }
      /*   we can display the minimum distances: they are in d[]. Above all
           we want the final display of the shortest paths, thanks to the recursive
```

```
        function path() (see Figure 33.3). Which is how we carry out the display
        of the predecessors in reverse, i.e. paths from 0, is noteworthy */
for(i=1; i<N; i++) { printf("\nShortest route to %d:",i); path(i);

/* the function path() */
void path(int i)
{ if (i==0) printf(" 0 ");
  else { path(pred[i]); printf(" %d ",i); }
}
```

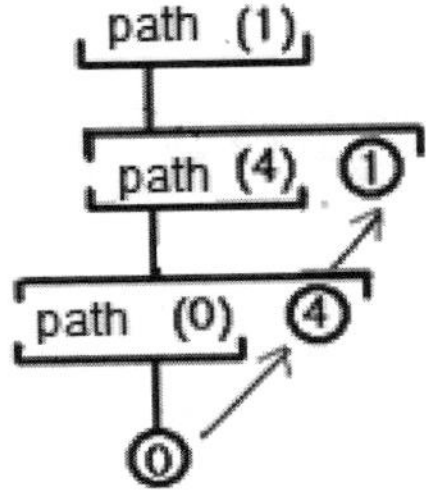

Figure 33.3. *Recursive functioning of the function path()*

33.1.2. *Floyd's algorithm*

Floyd's algorithm, giving the minimum length paths from any vertex to another, has a rare simplicity, which is what makes it so appealing. It consists of a triple loop, with $d[i][j]$ designating what will turn out to be the length of the shortest path from vertex i to vertex j:[1]

```
for(k=1; k<=N; k++) for(i=1; i<=N; i++) for(j=1; j<=N; j++)
if (d[i][k]+d[k][j] < d[i][j] )   d[i]j] = d[i][k] + d[k][j]
```

In initial conditions we take the adjacency matrix, whose elements $d[i][j]$ are the positive numbers associated with the arcs, which we will also consider as distances here. The distances on a succession of arcs are added. By shortest path, we mean the one that gives the shortest distance between two nodes. But how can such an algorithm end up giving all the shortest paths?

1. It is noteworthy that in this case, as a change, we number the vertices from 1 to N. When programming in C language, it is advisable that we use tables declared on a length $N + 1$, where only the boxes indexed from 1 to N, corresponding to the numbers of the vertices, are taken, even if it means leaving box 0, which has no importance, unused.

Let us take the graph in Figure 33.4. We begin by constructing the adjacency matrix, whose elements are the distances $d[i][j]$, where i is the line index and j the column index. At stage 0 of the process, $d[i][j]$ are the numbers associated with arcs ij. When there are no arcs between vertices i and j, we place a large number, called ∞.

Let us also note that $d[i][i]$ elements of the diagonal are set to 0. In other words, we take no account of an eventual loop on a vertex, as is the case in the example for vertex 3, since any traversal of this loop would only lengthen the paths. The shortest distance from a node to itself always remains equal to 0.

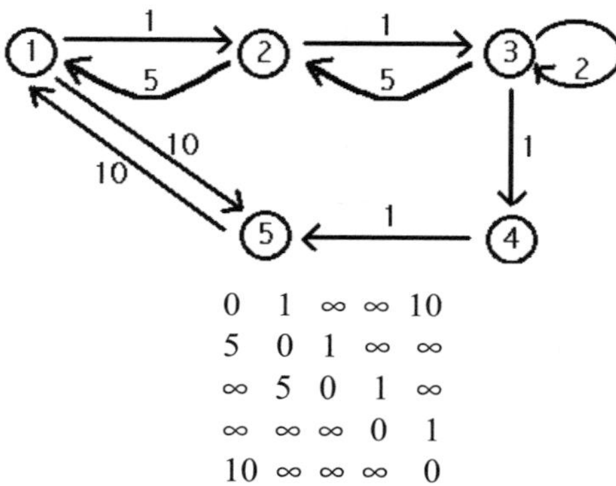

Figure 33.4. *An example of a directed graph, with its adjacency matrix*

We will now proceed to $N = 5$ stages, as many as there are vertices. At stage $k = 1$, we involve vertex 1. We try to find if from i to j, we have a path from i to 1 (with its $d[i][1]$) then from 1 to j (with its $d[1][j]$) which, when we work out the sum of the numbers associated with these arcs, is shorter than the direct traversal ij. If we do have a path, we therefore replace $d[i][j]$ with this number. We do the same for all $d[i][j]$.

In our example this gives:

0 1 ∞ ∞ 10
5 0 1 ∞ **15**
∞ 5 0 1 ∞
∞ ∞ ∞ 0 1
10 **11** ∞ ∞ 0 (the changes are indicated in bold)

Then we move on to stage $k = 2$. If we find a path from i to 2 with its $d[i][2]$ followed by a path from 2 to j with its $d[2][j]$ such that $d[i][2] + d[2][j]$ is less than the current $d[i][j]$, we replace $d[i][j]$ with this new value. Where are we at the end of stage $k = 2$? We have obtained the lengths of the shortest paths from i to j that exclusively accept vertices 1 or 2 as intermediate vertices. We find matrix:

0	1	**2**	∞	10
5	0	1	∞	15
10	5	0	1	**20**
∞	∞	∞	0	1
10	11	**12**	∞	0

and continue in this way until stage $k = 5$. At each k stage we insert node k between nodes i and j when $d[i][k] + d[k][j]$ is less than the current value of $d[i][j]$. This means that we get the shortest distance between i and j in which all nodes from 1 to k can exclusively intervene, and not only node k, because of the stages that came before. In the example, from stage 3 to stage 5 this successively gives:

0	1	2	**3**	10
5	0	1	**2**	15
10	5	0	1	20
∞	∞	∞	0	1
10	11	12	**13**	0

0	1	2	3	**4**
5	0	1	2	**3**
10	5	0	1	**2**
∞	∞	∞	0	1
10	11	12	13	0

0	1	2	3	4
5	0	1	2	3
10	5	0	1	2
11	**12**	**13**	0	1
10	11	12	13	0

At each stage a new matrix is calculated from the old one, but there is no need to use two square tables, with the new one replacing the old one after the sequential traversal. Indeed, at stage k, line k and column k never change, since $d[i][k] = d[i][k] + d[k][k]$ with $d[k][k] = 0$. The eventual changes of $d[i][j]$ only come from this line and this column k, through $d[i][k] + d[k][j]$. The changes can therefore be implemented sequentially on a single table, without the new values obtained interfering with the old ones. This gives the program indicated at the beginning of this section. The last table obtained gives the shortest distance between any two nodes.

What do we do if we also want to find the shortest path from node i to node j, in terms of traversals and not only distances? This is only to be done when the distance $d[i][j]$ is modified. We therefore have to determine the eventual intermediate nodes on the path from i to j. For this, in the program above, we record node k as soon as it becomes an intermediary between i and j, placing it in a table $c[i][j]$, initially set to 0. At each stage of the previous example, this gives:

– for $k = 1$, $c[2][5]=c[5][2]= 1$;

– for $k = 2$ $c[1][3]=c[3][1]=c[5][3]= c[3][5]= 2$;

– for $k = 3$ c[1][4]=c[2][4]=c[5][4]= 3;

– for $k = 4$ c[1][5]=c[2][5]=c[3][5]= 4;

– for $k = 5$ c[4][1]=c[4][2]=c[4][3]= 5.

In the end, the table of intermediaries c[][] is filled, with the boxes remaining at 0, therefore indicating that there are no intermediaries (since the nodes are numbered from 1). Traversal *ij* is thus eventually split in two, with paths from *i* to *k* and then from *k* to *j*. Next all we have to do is start again looking, for the intermediate nodes between *i* and *k*, then between *k* and *j*, which gives a recursive algorithm following an infix traversal, to give the list of intermediate nodes in order. For example, the shortest path from 1 to 5 is obtained as indicated in Figure 33.5.

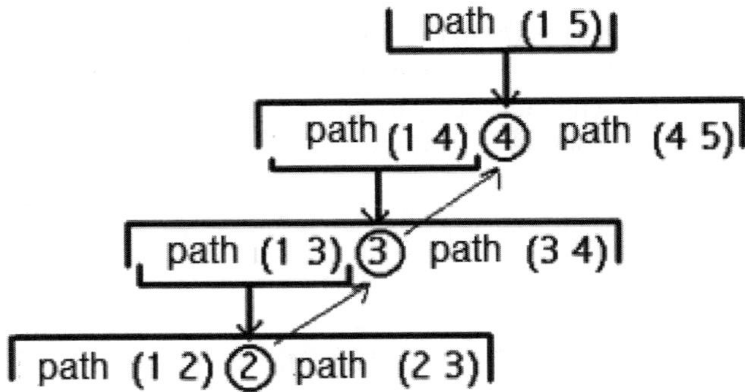

Figure 33.5. *Functioning of the function path() between extreme nodes 1 and 5 with "in order" display of nodes 2, 3 and 4*

Hence the final program:

From the chosen graph, with N *vertices, fill in the adjacency matrix, with* d[i][j]= *distance (or weight) from i to j. Set* d[i][j] *to* ∞ *in the absence of arcs, then set the diagonal to 0:*

```
for(i=1; i<=N; i++) d[i][i]=0;
/* set the matrix of intermediaries to 0 */
for(i=1; i<=N; i++) for(j=1; j<=N; j++)  c[i][j]=0;
for(k=1; k<=N; k++)  for(i=1; i<=N; i++)  for(j=1; j<=N; j++)
    { nd = d[i][k]+d[k][j];   if (nd < d[i][j]) { d[i][j] = nd;   c[i][j] = k; }  }
display the shortest paths
```

To get the shortest path from node i *to node* j*, which corresponds to* d[i][j] *other than* ∞*, call the function* path(i, j) *which displays the intermediate nodes, and add node* i *to the start and node* j *to the end* j.

```
void path (int i, int j)
{ node=c[i][j]) ;
 if (node != 0)
    { path(i, node);
      display node;
      path(node, j);
    }
}
```

As an exercise, let us apply Floyd's algorithm to the graph in Figure 33.6.

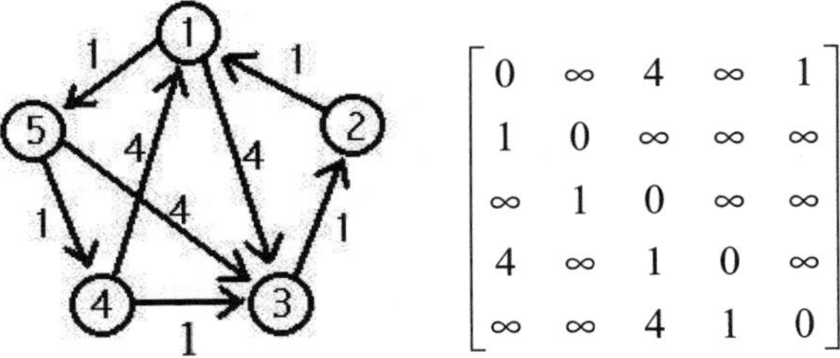

Figure 33.6. *A graph and its weighted adjacency matrix*

We have the following transformations from stage 1 to stage 5:

$$\begin{bmatrix} 0 & \infty & 4 & \infty & 1 \\ 1 & 0 & 5 & \infty & 2 \\ \infty & 1 & 0 & \infty & \infty \\ 4 & \infty & 1 & 0 & 5 \\ \infty & \infty & 4 & 1 & 0 \end{bmatrix} \rightarrow \begin{bmatrix} 0 & \infty & 4 & \infty & 1 \\ 1 & 0 & 5 & \infty & 2 \\ 2 & 1 & 0 & \infty & 3 \\ 4 & \infty & 1 & 0 & 5 \\ \infty & \infty & 4 & 1 & 0 \end{bmatrix} \rightarrow \begin{bmatrix} 0 & 5 & 4 & \infty & 1 \\ 1 & 0 & 5 & \infty & 2 \\ 2 & 1 & 0 & \infty & 3 \\ 3 & 2 & 1 & 0 & 4 \\ 6 & 5 & 4 & 1 & 0 \end{bmatrix} \rightarrow$$

$$\begin{bmatrix} 0 & 5 & 4 & \infty & 1 \\ 1 & 0 & 5 & \infty & 2 \\ 2 & 1 & 0 & \infty & 3 \\ 3 & 2 & 1 & 0 & 4 \\ 4 & 3 & 2 & 1 & 0 \end{bmatrix} \rightarrow \begin{bmatrix} 0 & 4 & 3 & 2 & 1 \\ 1 & 0 & 4 & 3 & 2 \\ 2 & 1 & 0 & 4 & 3 \\ 3 & 2 & 1 & 0 & 4 \\ 4 & 3 & 2 & 1 & 0 \end{bmatrix}$$

The intermediate matrix is: $\begin{bmatrix} 0 & 5 & 5 & 5 & 0 \\ 0 & 3 & 5 & 5 & 1 \\ 2 & 0 & 0 & 5 & 2 \\ 3 & 3 & 0 & 0 & 3 \\ 4 & 4 & 4 & 0 & 0 \end{bmatrix}$

For example, let us apply the function *path* from 2 to 3: with 5 as intermediary, it first gives the path from 2 to 5, which has 1 as its sole intermediary, then the path from 5 to 3, which has 4 as its sole intermediary, hence the shortest path is 21543 of length 4.

33.2. Minimum spanning tree

Let us assume that we have a connected and weighted, undirected graph, i.e. that each edge has a weight, in other words a number that is associated with it. Here again, this number can be the length of the edge or a certain flow of traffic on this edge. Such a graph has spanning trees, which by definition must touch each graph vertex using some of its edges. More specifically, every spanning tree whose vertices are the N graph nodes uses $N-1$ edges from the graph.[2]

Among these spanning trees, one or several, minimum spanning trees are found. The sum of the weight of the edges concerned in these minimum spanning trees is the smallest possible. Our challenge is to find a minimum spanning tree. The algorithms that deal with this problem are linked to a property that is expressed in the following way:

> If we divide the set of graph nodes in two, with one part being S and one part T, then among the graph edges linking a node of S and a node of T, the one which has a minimum weight belongs to a minimum spanning tree.

This property is proven by absurdity. Let us assume that edge AB (joining nodes A and B) of minimum weight does not belong to a minimum spanning tree. Let us take a minimum spanning tree. It has one edge ab, other than AB, joining vertex a from S to vertex b from T, and this edge has a weight greater than that of edge AB, because the latter has the minimum weight. This minimum tree is divided into a sub-tree located at least partially in S and passing through A, as well as a sub-tree located

2. Let us recall that every tree, i.e. an acyclic connected graph, has one edge less than it has vertices, and that every connected graph has spanning trees, this not being the only one obtained during graph exploration from a vertex.

at least partially in *T*, passing through *B*. These two sub-trees are linked by edge *ab* (see Figure 33.7). If we delete edge *ab*, the minimum tree ends up being disconnected and replaced by the two previous sub-trees. If we now add edge *AB*, the two sub-trees are linked and this gives a new spanning tree. This spanning tree, thanks to *AB*, has a lower weight than our minimum spanning tree. We get a contradiction. Our assumption about the minimum tree not having *AB* as an edge was false. The minimum weight edge *AB* joining one part of the graph's nodes to another part must therefore be in a minimum spanning tree.

The so-called Prim's and Kruskal's algorithms result from here. Their names are associated with the search for a minimum spanning tree and the algorithms date from the 1950s.[3]

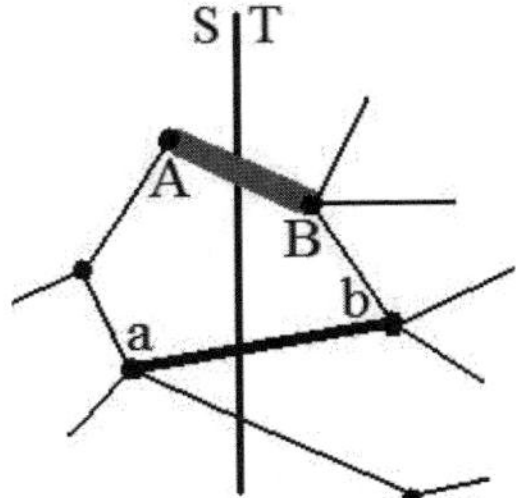

Figure 33.7. *Dividing the graph into two parts, S and T, with the minimum spanning tree containing the cross edge ab, but not the minimum edge AB*

33.2.1. *Prim's algorithm*

From a weighted connected graph, we choose a vertex *A* that will play the role of starting point, or root, for what will gradually become the minimum tree. The set of vertices is therefore separated into two parts, one, *S*, containing the nucleus of the tree – point *A* as it happens – and the other, *T*, containing all the other graph vertices. Thanks to the property above, we know that the minimum tree contains the minimum weight edge *AB* joining a vertex of *S* to a vertex of *T*. We add the new vertex *B* to part *S*, which now contains two vertices of the graph, with part *T* containing all the other vertices. Then we start again, taking the minimum weight edge joining a vertex of *S* and of *T*, which will add a new vertex to part *S*. And so on and so forth, until part *S* contains all the graph's vertices.

3. This style of algorithm already appears in the works of Borukva (1926) and the anthropologist Czekanowski (1909) [GRA 85].

Let us see what this gives in the example in Figure 33.8, where we choose vertex 3 as our starting point. The closest vertex to 3, *via* an edge of the graph, is 5. Then the closest vertex to the set of vertices {3,5} is 2, etc. The junction edges obtained constitute the minimum spanning tree.

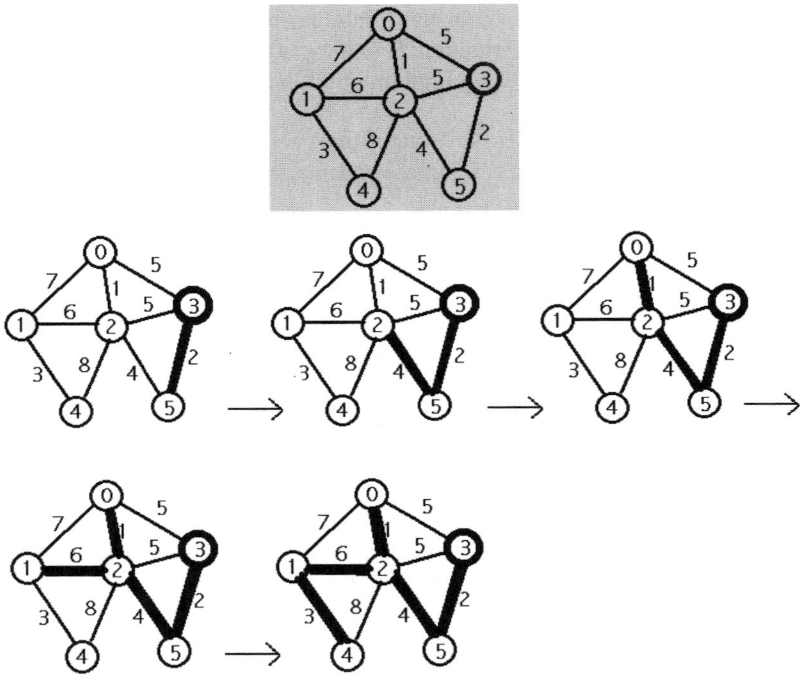

Figure 33.8. *Application of Prim's algorithm starting from vertex 3 on the graph, with its five stages until the minimum spanning tree is obtained*

A program results from this. We begin by entering the graph in the form of its weighted adjacency matrix *P*[*N*][*N*], making *P*[0][1] = 7, *P*[0][2] = 1, *P*[0][3] = 5, *P*[1][0] = 7, etc., and everywhere there is no edge we place a very high weight. Sets *S* and *T* are parts of tables that will evolve over the course of the stages, of which we run the working lengths *LS* and *LT*.

At stage 1 we place the start vertex, called *startingpt*, here 3, in table *S*. The other vertices are placed in table *T*, and thanks to a table *weight*[], we associate with each vertex of *T* the weight of the edge that joins it to vertex *startingpt* of *S*. Thanks to table *pred*[], we also associate the vertex of *S* with them. Then we launch the stages loop, until stage *N* when table *S* contains the *N* graph vertices. At each stage, we look for vertex *K* of *T* with the minimum *weight*[]. Then we add this vertex *K* to table *S*, and remove it from table *T*. Lastly, we must update table *weight*[]. It gives the minimum weight of the junction edges from the vertices of *T* to those of *S*. We must now take into consideration the new vertex *K* that was added to set *S*, hence a new minimum calculation for the *weight*[] of each vertex of *T* and, in case of change, we also place the new vertex of *S* in *pred*[].

At the end of the stages, the minimum graph edges link each vertex of the graph, except the start vertex, to its predecessor in *pred*[]. The program can be found below:

```
S[0]=startingpt;  LS=1;
k=0 ; for(i=0; i<N; i++) if (i !=startingpt) T[k++]=i;   LT=N-1;
for(i=0; i<LT; i++) weight[T[i]]=P[startingpt][T[i}];
for(i=0; i<LT; i++) pred[T[i]]=startingpt;

for(stage=2; stage<=N; stage++)
  { minp=10000;
   for(i=0; i<LT; i++)
   if (weight[T[i]]<minp) {minp=weight[T[i]]; mini=i;}
   K=T[mini];  S[LS]=K;  LS++;
   for(i=mini; i<LT–1; i++) T[i]=T[i+1];
   LT--;
   for(i=0; i<LT; i++)
   if (P[K][T[i]]<weight[T[i]])
      {weight[T[i]]=P[K][T[i]]; pred[T[i]]=K;}
 }
```

33.2.2. *Kruskal's algorithm*

Initially, we take a forest whose trees are each reduced to a vertex of the graph. Then, one after the other, we take the graph edges, which we classified in ascending order beforehand. Thanks to the property previously indicated, the edge thus chosen belongs to the minimum tree, on the condition that it does not create a cycle. Thanks to this progressive addition of edges, the trees of the forest gradually fuse together and grow. In the end, one single tree – the minimum spanning tree – remains. We can see this evolution in our example (see Figure 33.9).

For programming needs, the graph is defined by its *NV* vertices numbered from 0 to *NV* – 1, and by its *NE* edges, the extremities *e*1 and *e*2 of which we specify, where the second has a number greater than the first. In the case of the graph in Figure 33.9, with *NV* = 6 and *NE* = 9, this gives:

edge	0	1	2	3	4	5	6	7	8
extremity *e*1	0	0	0	1	1	2	2	2	3
extremity *e*2	1	2	3	2	4	3	4	5	5

These values are places in tables *e1*[*NE*] and *e2*[*NE*], not forgetting their weight in *w*[*NE*]. Initially they are sorted and placed in ascending order of their weight.

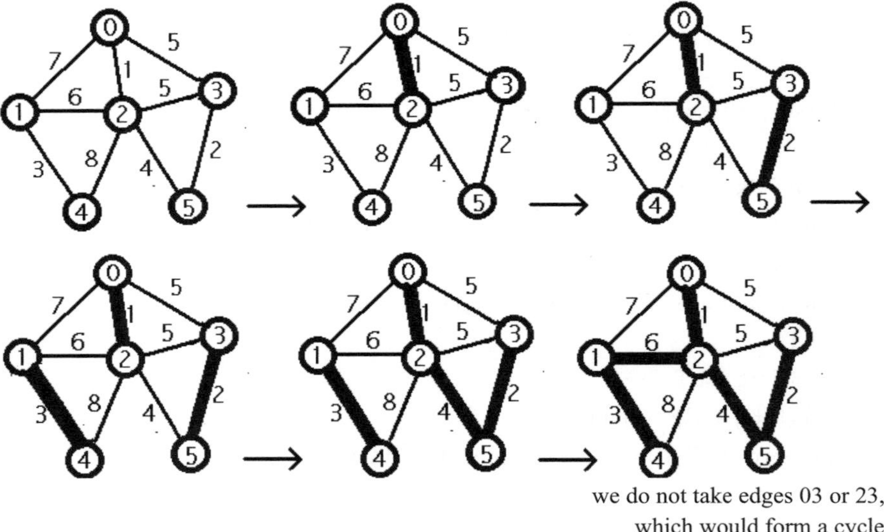

we do not take edges 03 or 23,
which would form a cycle

Figure 33.9. *Functioning of Kruskal's algorithm, from a forest of trees reduced to their root, ending up with the minimum spanning tree*

The trees are each placed in a chained list, with their respective vertices. The forest of *NV* vertices reduced to a point is translated by *NV* chained lists numbered from 0 to *NV* – 1, which each contain one cell, i.e. one vertex. Then during the traversal of the list of edges, certain lists will grow and others will disappear – we will say that they are *out*. When a union of two lists is to be carried out, we attach the first cell of one list to the last cell of the other. We also need a function *searchforwhere(v)* that indicates to us in which list a vertex *v* is found. When we take an edge, we will find out where its extremities are located. If these extremities are not in the same lists, we will make the union of the two lists, in aid of one list, with the other being eliminated. Each list number *i* is accessible via a pointer *first*[*i*], and its last cell carries a pointer *last*[*i*]. The evolution of these chained lists is indicated in Figure 33.10.

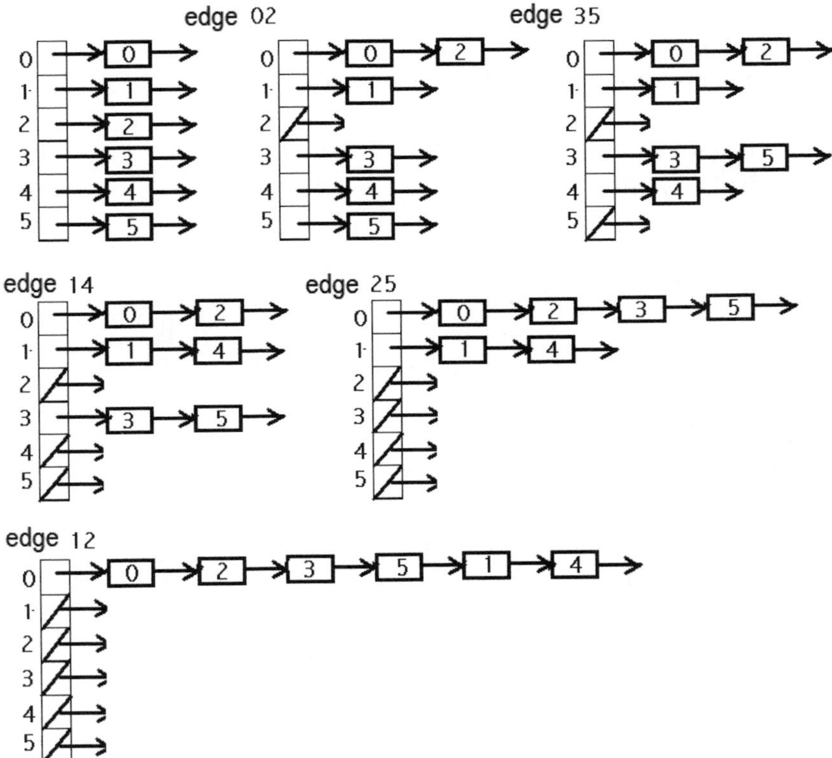

Figure 33.10. *Evolution of the linked lists representing the trees that grow, to end up with the minimum spanning tree*

Here is the corresponding program: we begin by declaring the core cell of the chained lists: *struct cell { int n; struct cell * v;};*. Then we take the number *NV* of graph vertices, the number *NE* of its edges, and enter the numbers of the vertices located at the extremities of each edge, as well as their weight. For example, for edge 0: *e1*[0] = 0, *e2*[0] = 1 and *w*[0] = 6. Then we sort the edges according to their increasing weight. The rest of the program follows:

```
for(i=0; i<NV; i++) out[i]=NO;          /* implementation of the initial forest */
for(i=0; i<NV; i++)
```

```
      { first[i]=(struct cell *) malloc(sizeof(struct cell));
        first[i]->n=i;  first[i]->v=NULL; last[i]=first[i];
      }
   k=0;
   for(i=0; i<NE; i++)
      { a=searchforwhere(e1[i]); b=searchforwhere(e2[i]);
        if (a!=b)
          { last[a]->v=first[b];  out[b]=YES;
            last[a]=last[b];
            edge1[k]=e1[i]; edge2[k]=e2[i];  k++;
          }
        if (finished()==YES) break;
      }
   for(j=0; j<k; j++) printf("(%d %d) ",edge1[j],edge2[j]);
                                    /* the edges of the minimum tree */
   int searchforwhere(int vertex)
   {  for(i=0; i<NS; i++)  if (out[i]==NO)
        { ptr=first[i];
          do  { if (ptr->n==vertex) return i; ptr=ptr->v; }
          while(ptr!=NULL);
        }
   }
   int finished(void)
   {  counter=0;
      for(i=0; i<NS; i++) if (out[i]==NO) counter++;
      if (counter==1) return YES;
      else return NO;
   }
```

Kruskal's algorithm can be generalized to any graph, not necessarily a connected one. It therefore gives a forest of spanning trees associated with each connected component, the total weight of the forest being minimal. In Figure 33.11 we will see a vaster graph than the one before, where the weights of the edges also correspond to their length, with horizontal, vertical or even oblique edges according to the four directions (especially at 45°). We notice that this graph has three connected components, one of which is reduced to three points in the top left, and another reduced to a single point in the top right.

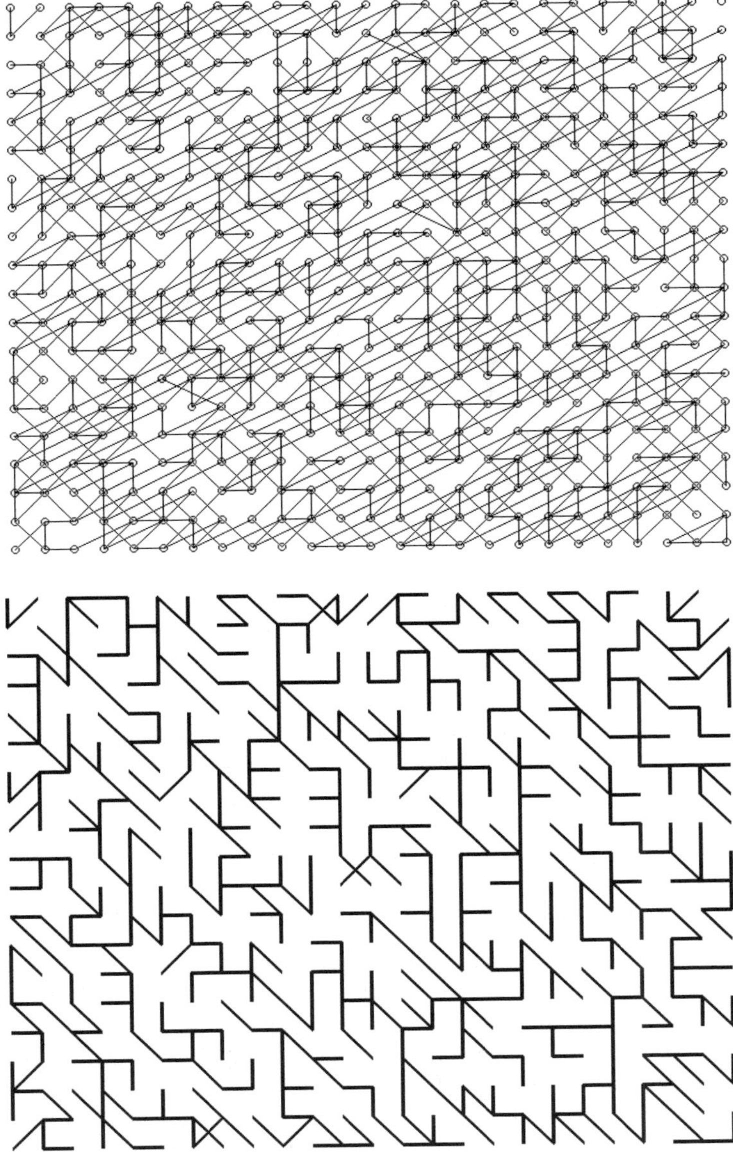

Figure 33.11. *A graph having a main connected component (and two others in the top left and top right), with the minimum forest essentially reduced to the minimum spanning tree of the main connected component*

33.2.3. *Comparison of the two algorithms*

In Figure 33.12 we will find the application of the two algorithms from Kruskal (above) and Prim (below) on the same graph, where the weights are simply Euclidian distances. The two methods are based on the same principle. They are local actions that take place in order to look for a minimum edge, and in the end this ends up being correct overall. By a simple short sighted perspective, the problem is finally resolved in its entirety.

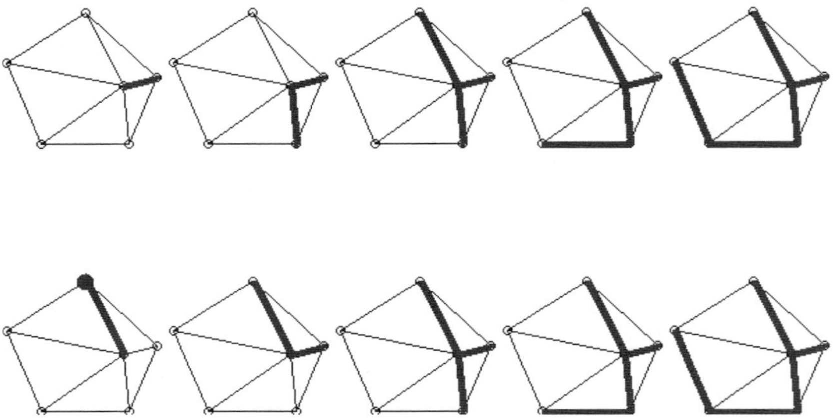

Figure 33.12. *Minimum spanning tree obtained above by Kruskal's algorithm. Below by Prim's algorithm, with the highest vertex as the initial root*

33.2.4. *Exercises*

33.2.4.1. *Connected components of an undirected graph*

We already saw how to find the connected components of an undirected graph during its exploration (see Chapter 30). Here we give another method, curiously very close to Kruskal's algorithm. This is the time to learn to program a problem where sets and unions of sets intervene. Let us recall that in an undirected graph, a connected component is made up of vertices accessible from each other through the use of edges. Each vertex thus ends up being placed in a connected component of the graph with all the vertices that are accessible by it, and the set of connected components forms a partition of the set of vertices.

At the start, the graph is given by its *NV* vertices numbered from 0 to *NV* – 1, and by its *NE* edges numbered from 0 to *NE* – 1, of which we take the two extremities *e1* and *e2*, like in the example in Figure 33.13 with NV = 10: the connected components will be constructed by progressive growths of the trees.

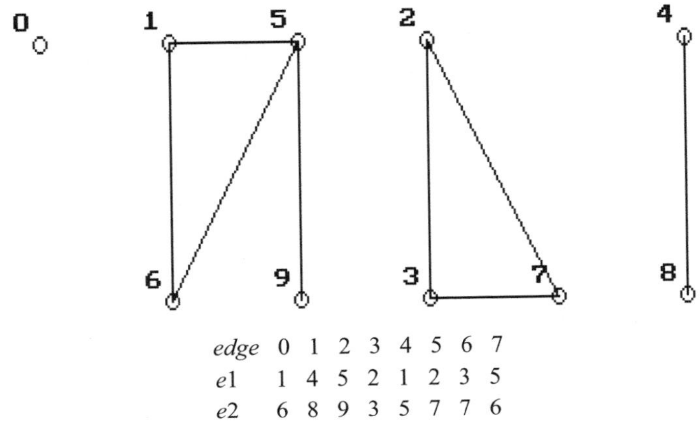

edge	0	1	2	3	4	5	6	7
*e*1	1	4	5	2	1	2	3	5
*e*2	6	8	9	3	5	7	7	6

Figure 33.13. *The initial graph, with its numbered edges, the connected components of which we want to obtain*

At the start, we take the forest made up of trees reduced to a vertex, which makes *NV* components. Then we traverse the set of edges, one after the other. Each time an edge has vertices that are not in the same component as extremities, we group the two components into one single one. The trees grow thanks to this union, and in the end, we find the connected components of the graph. This method applied to the previous example is shown in Figure 33.14.

The program results from it: we run *NV* chained lists numbered from 0 to *NV* – 1, with pointers *first*(*i*) and *last*(*i*) at the extremities. At the start, these lists contain one cell. Then during the traversal of the list of edges, certain lists will get longer, and others will disappear. When a union of two lists is to be done, we attach the first cell of one to the last cell of the other (see Figure 33.15).

We will still need the function *searchforwhere*(*v*) which indicates to us in which list a vertex *v* is found. More or less, this comes back to Kruskal's algorithm.

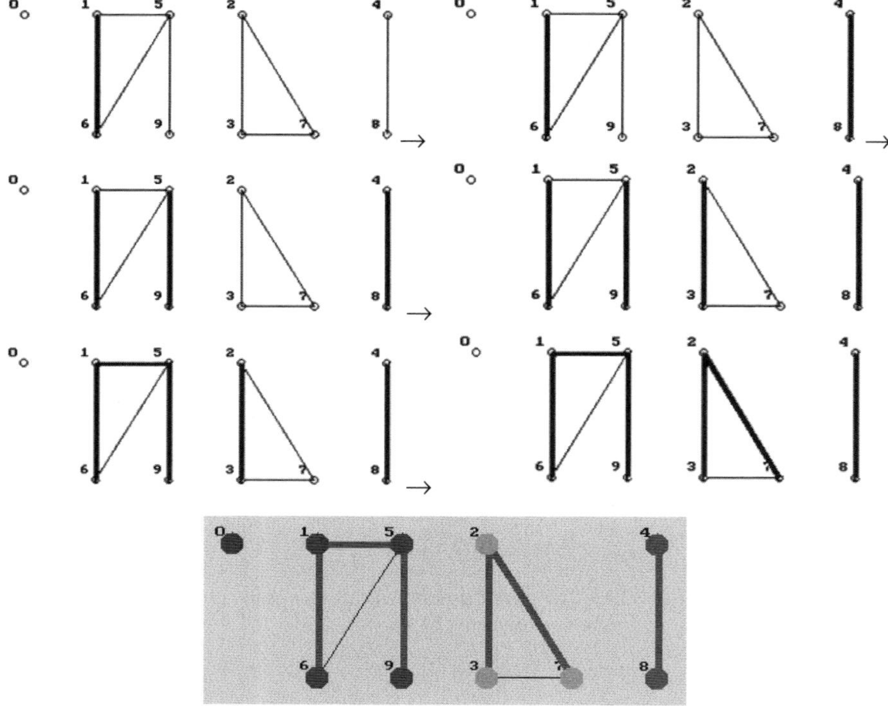

Figure 33.14. *Evolution of the growing trees, to finally find the four connected components of this graph*

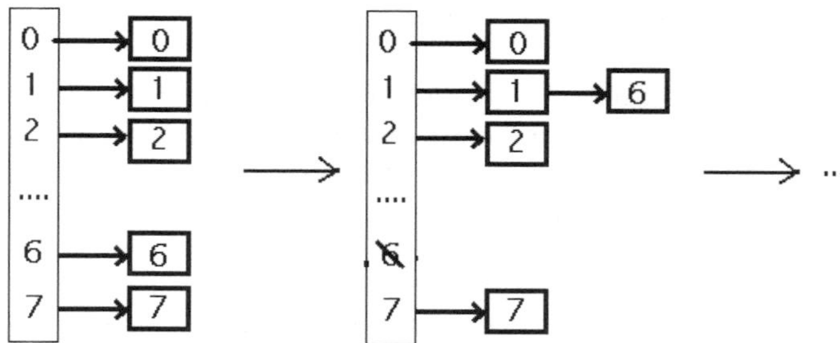

Figure 33.15. *Beginning of the evolution of the chained lists representing growing trees*

Program:

```
struct w { int n; struct w * v;};
main()
{ Enter the NE edges, for example:  e1[0]=1; e2[0]=6;   etc
  for(i=0; i<NV; i++) out[i]=NO;
  for(i=0; i<NV; i++)
    { first[i]=(struct w *) malloc(sizeof(struct w));
      first[i]->n=i;  first[i]->v=NULL;  last[i]=first[i];
    }
  for(i=0; i<NE; i++)
    { a=searchforwhere(e1[i]);   b=searchforwhere(e2[i]);
      if (a!=b)
        { last[a]->v=first[b];  out[b]=YES;  last[a]=last[b];  }
     for (j=0; j<NV; j++) if (out[j]==NO)
      {  ptr=first[j];
        do  {  printf("%d " ,ptr->n); ptr=ptr->v; }  while (ptr!=NULL);
        printf("\n");
      }
    }
}
```

33.2.4.2. *Minimum spanning tree and traveling salesman problem*

A salesman must make a tour by going to *N* cities. We assume that each city is linked to all the others by a route in a straight line. These *N* cities form the vertices of a complete graph, because each vertex is linked to all the others, and the lengths of the edges correspond to Euclidian distances. The mission of the traveling salesman is to make a complete tour by passing through all the cities once and only once, which constitutes what is called a Hamiltonian circuit, but in such a way that his tour is the shortest possible.

For want of obtaining the optimum solution, which on first analysis requires trying all the possible paths, a good method consists of extracting the minimum spanning tree of the complete graph in the first place (see Figure 33.16a). Taking any node of the tree as the root, we then do a depth first traversal of this tree, which gives a succession of vertices reached from the root. We join these vertices in the order thus obtained, then we add a junction edge between the last vertex and the root. Finally we find a closed path passing through all the vertices and which, for lack of being the shortest, is not too far from it. It is finally possible, at least when the graph is not too complex, to delete the crossroads of this path, in order to shorten again, like in Figures 33.16a and 33.16b.

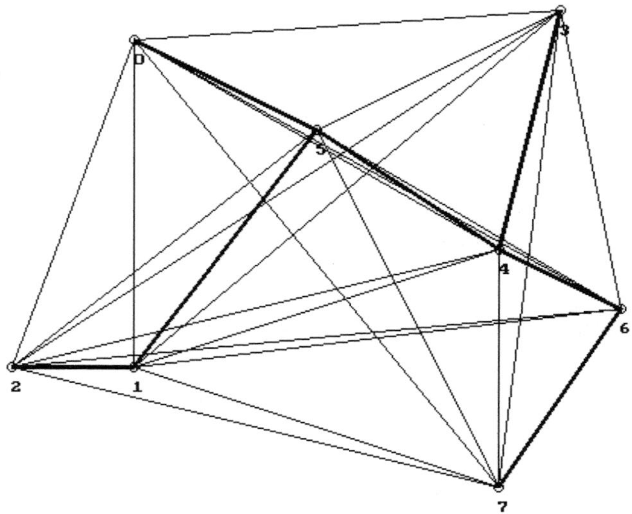

Figure 33.16a. *Complete graph whose vertices number N = 8, with is minimum spanning tree, obtained by Kruskal's algorithm*

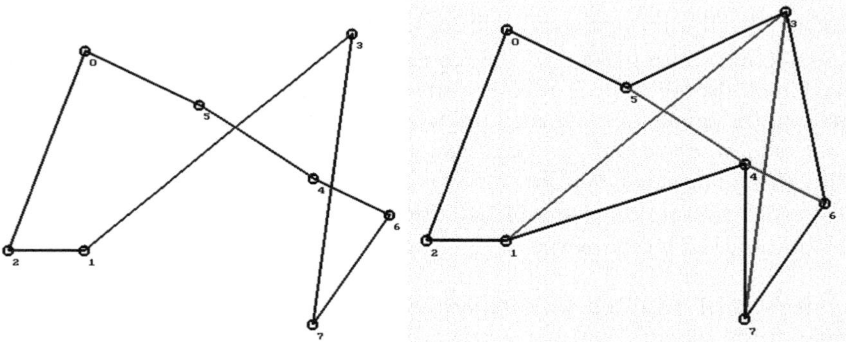

Figure 33.16b. *On the left, the depth first exploration of the minimum spanning tree from the root 0, joining the vertices obtained in order of exploration: 0 5 4 6 7 then 3, then 1 and 2, and final return to 0. Lastly, on the right we delete the crossroads*

Chapter 34

Eulerian Paths and Cycles, Spanning Trees of a Graph

A Eulerian cycle or path on a graph alludes to a route where each arc or edge of the graph is traversed once and only once. A spanning tree refers to a tree with all the vertices of the graph as vertices. We only keep part of the graph edges to constitute this tree. *A priori* these two notions have nothing in common but we will see that a direct link exists between them, at least when the graph is directed. For this, let us begin by widening the strict notion of graph to the more general sense of a multigraph: two vertices can now be joined by several edges or arcs, and we also accept the presence of loops – where a loop is an arc joining a vertex to itself. In what follows, we will continue to speak of graphs and we will need to understand it in its more general sense as being a multigraph.

34.1. Definition of Eulerian cycles and paths

We say that a graph has a *Eulerian cycle* if, upon leaving some vertex of the graph, we end up traversing all the graph edges (or arcs) once and only once, finally ending up at the starting point.

Evidently, if a Eulerian cycle exists, it eventually passes through all the graph vertices, several times. Once such a cycle has been found, any graph vertex can serve as starting (and end) point if we wish, just as we can reverse the direction of the cycle traversal in the case of an undirected graph.

More generally, we say that a graph has a *Eulerian path* (or a *Eulerian chain*), for lack of a Eulerian cycle, if on leaving a starting vertex we end up passing each edge (or arc) of the graph once and only once, with an endpoint that is not the starting point. Here are some examples of graphs eventually presenting Eulerian cycles or paths.

Example 1: we can easily check that a square, considered as an undirected graph, has a Eulerian cycle, but that a cube does not (see Figure 34.1).

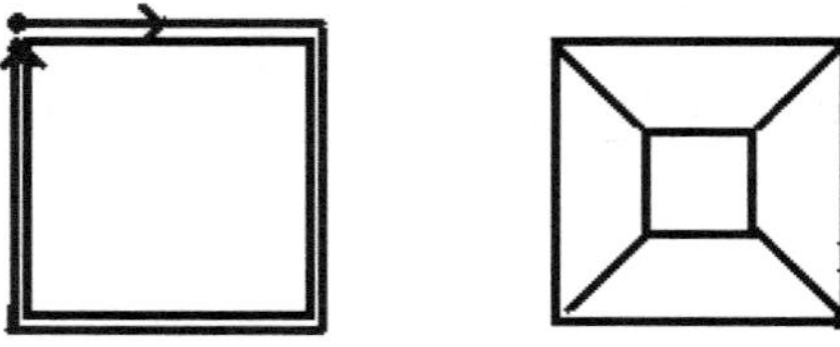

Figure 34.1. *On the left the Eulerian cycle in the square, but on the right, there is none in the cube*

Example 2: consider the three undirected graphs in Figure 34.2. We notice that the first one assumes a Eulerian cycle but no Eulerian paths (with an endpoint other than the starting point), and that the two others do not have a Eulerian cycle but have Eulerian paths.

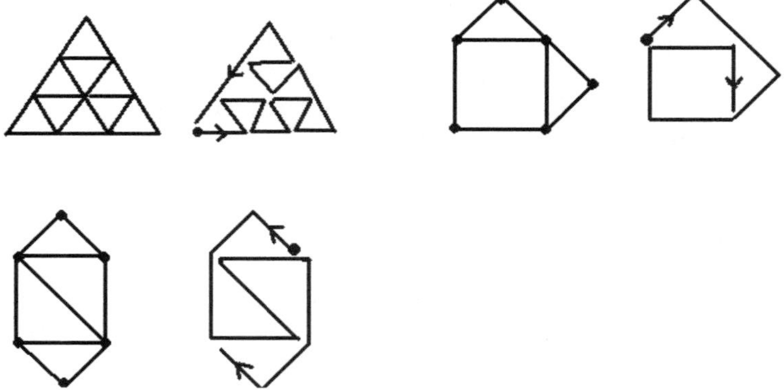

Figure 34.2. *Top left, the presence of a Eulerian cycle. On the right and bottom the presence of a Eulerian path for lack of a cycle*

Example 3: apparently very different problems also appeal to Eulerian cycles or paths. We consider the two graphs, both planar, in Figure 34.3, the first delimiting five regions A, B, C, D and E in the plane, with region E constituting the exterior, and the second having four regions. For each one of these graphs, starting from the exterior and drawing a continuous curve from there without removing the pen, can we cross each graph edge once and only once and return to the exterior? The answer is yes for the first graph and no for the second. Later we will see the link between these problems and Eulerian cycles.

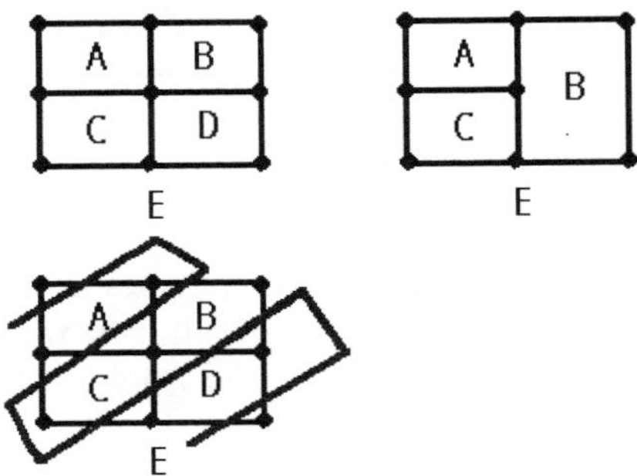

Figure 34.3. *On the left, a continuous line enables us to cross each edge once and only once starting from the exterior and finishing there. On the right it is impossible*

34.2. Euler and Königsberg bridges

The city of Königsberg, now Kaliningrad, is traversed by the river Preger, with the presence of seven bridges shown in the plan in Figure 34.4.

For many years inhabitants asked themselves the following question, trying hard to answer it in practice, i.e. by walking: starting from one's home, is it possible to cross each bridge once and only once, and return home without re-crossing any bridge? Or even this other question: can a pedestrian take a walk crossing each bridge once and only once?

In 1736, it was Leonhard Euler who proved that the answer was no, in both cases. Hence the name Eulerian cycles and paths given to this type of problem. To a certain extent, it was the starting point of graph theory, at least in Europe.

Indeed we show the following properties where the notion of vertex degrees comes in,[1] one related to undirected graphs and the other to directed graphs.

1. Let us recall that the degree of a vertex in an undirected graph is the number of edges that are attached to it. In a directed graph we distinguish the indegree, which is the number of arcs that arrive on the vertex, and the outdegree, which is the number of arcs that start at the vertex.

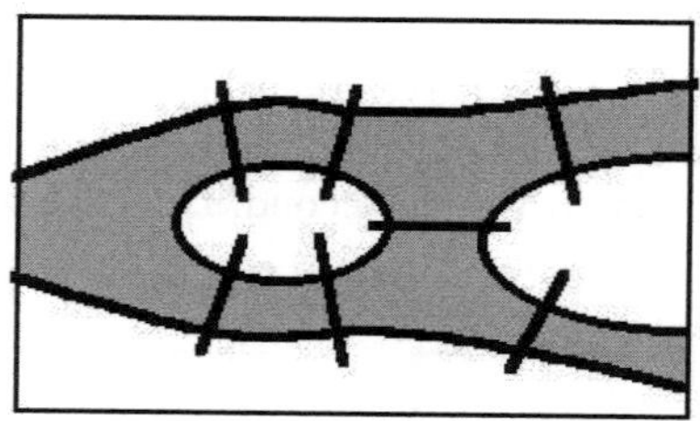

Figure 34.4. *The seven bridges of Königsberg*

PROPERTY 34.1.– An undirected graph assumes a Eulerian cycle iff it is connected (except if it has isolated points) and all its vertices have an even degree. It assumes a Eulerian path if two vertices u and v are of an odd degree and all the others are of an even degree, where the Eulerian paths are therefore between u and v.

PROPERTY 34.2.– A directed graph has a Eulerian cycle iff the subjacent graph (where we delete the orientation) is connected, and the number of arcs arriving at each vertex is equal to the number of arcs coming from this vertex.

Here, we will only carry out the demonstration for the case of the Eulerian cycle in an undirected graph. The two conditions connectivity and vertices of even degree are necessary for a Eulerian cycle. That of connectivity is evident. The degree of a vertex must also be even, as during the traversal of the Eulerian cycle, each time a vertex is crossed, two distinct edges are concerned, one to arrive at the vertex, and the other to leave from it, hence the even number of edges attached to each vertex. It is this that Euler noticed in his time.

These conditions are also sufficient.

Let us start at a vertex. An edge originating from the vertex is used when we continue to move forward traversing the edges. Each time a vertex is crossed, two edges are used. Because of the even number of edges at each vertex, if we end up on a vertex we are sure to be able to start from it again.

We continue to cross vertices in this way, without any blocking, but the number of vertices is finite. We are therefore sure to fall back on the starting vertex, the only one where we took an odd number of edges, namely the starting one. We have just found a cycle on the graph, with part of the edges used once and only once. We now take a remaining edge, if there is one, with its two extreme vertices. If one of these vertices is not in the previous cycle, because of graph connectivity we are sure that there is a path joining it to a vertex of the cycle. Using this path, and pursuing the route, we restart a traversal on edges not yet used, without being blocked because of the even degree of the vertices. Again we obtain a cycle returning to the starting point. This new cycle can then be fused with the previous one to form only one single cycle (see Figure 34.5). If unused edges still remain, we start again in the same way. Each new cycle is fused with the one before it. In the end, all the edges have been used and the progressive fusion of cycles gives a Eulerian cycle. Such a constructive process also constitutes an algorithm that enables us to create a Eulerian cycle.

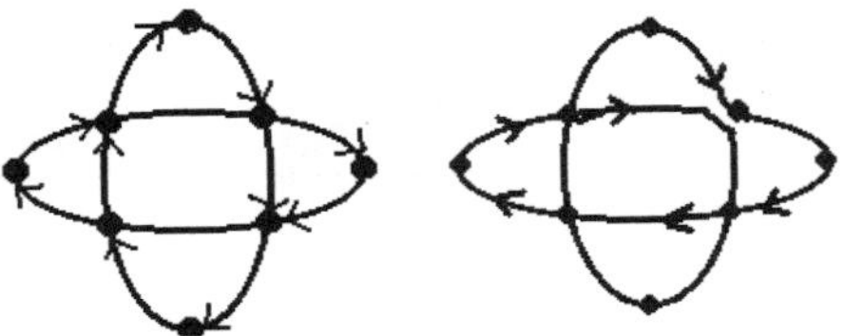

Figure 34.5. *Two cycles and their fusion*

34.2.1. *Returning to Königsberg bridges*

Let us begin by calling the four regions delimited by the river, namely the two islands and the two river banks *A*, *B*, *C* and *D*. Euler had the idea to condense the plan of the city of Königsberg into a graph to answer the problem posed: the regions become the vertices of this graph and the bridges that join them make up the edges (see Figure 34.6).

The property above now enables us to give a theoretical answer to the problem. Island *A* has four bridges to the two banks *C* and *D*, while island *B* has two bridges, one to each bank, with one more between the two islands. We notice that each graph vertex has an odd degree. There are no possible Eulerian cycles or paths.

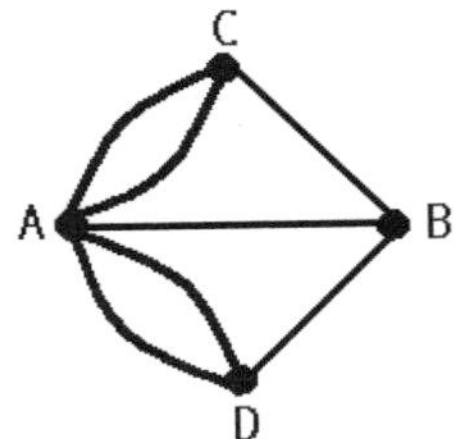

Figure 34.6. *The graph associated with the city of Königsberg*

34.2.2. *Examples*

a) Is it possible to draw the images in Figure 34.7 without lifting the pen or passing along the same line twice?

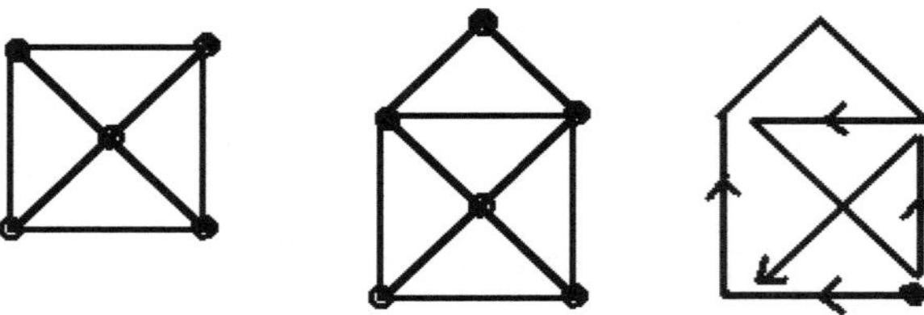

Figure 34.7. *Two graphs, where only the one on the right has a Eulerian path*

In the first case in Figure 34.7, four of the vertices are of an odd degree so there are neither Eulerian cycles nor paths. In the second case, only two vertices are of an odd degree. There are therefore Eulerian paths going from one vertex to the other in describing the entire graph.

b) Returning to example 3 of section 34.1.

Let us take the first graph (see Figure 34.3, left), which is planar with five regions delimited by edges, and replace it with what we call its dual. During this passage, the regions become the vertices of the dual graph, and we place edges between these vertices when the corresponding regions on the initial graph are adjacent, i.e. separated by an edge. We therefore notice the possibility of Eulerian cycles, since all the vertices are of even degree. Therefore, starting from the exterior, we can traverse each edge of the initial graph once and only once, ending up back at the exterior in the end, and all this with one continuous line (see Figure 34.8).

Doing the same for the second graph (see Figure 34.3, right), we would notice the presence of two vertices of odd degree, corresponding to regions *E* and *C*, hence the absence of Eulerian cycles but the possibility of Eulerian paths from *E* to *B*.

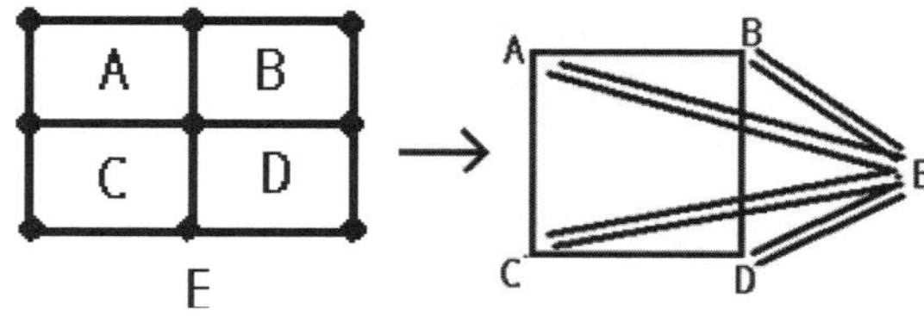

Figure 34.8. *The graph and its dual*

c) Complete undirected graph and Eulerian cycle.

An undirected graph K_n with n vertices is said to be complete if each vertex is linked to all the other vertices by an edge. Thanks to Euler's property, we can affirm that a complete graph K_n has a Eulerian cycle iff n is odd, and it does not have a Eulerian path (or cycle) when n is even and different to 2.

d) Bridges and islands: In the three cases in Figure 34.9, is there a way to traverse each bridge once and only once, finally returning to the starting point?

To answer the question, it is enough to draw the corresponding graphs (see Figure 34.10).

In the first case (*a*), two vertices are of odd degree, and the others of even degree. It is not possible to traverse each bridge once and only once returning to the starting point, but by default there are paths starting at island *A* that end on island *B*.

In the two other cases (*b*) and (*c*), all the vertices are of even degree, and Eulerian cycles exist, enabling us to traverse all the bridges once and only once, returning to the starting point. In the third case, the tree structure of paths enables us to find exactly six Eulerian cycles starting from *D* using edge *DA* first (see Figure 34.11).

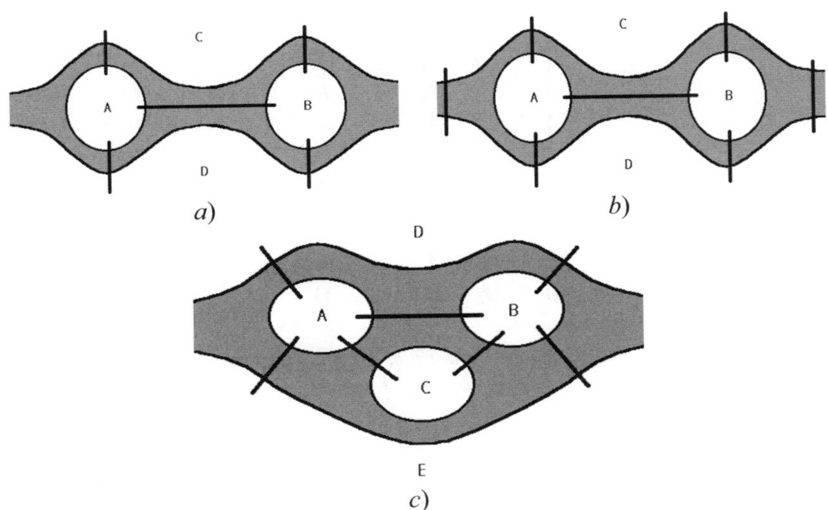

Figure 34.9. *Three drawings of islands and bridges on a river*

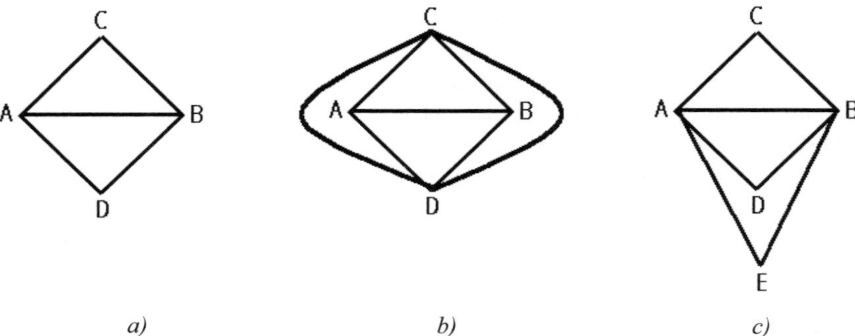

Figure 34.10. *The three graphs corresponding to the diagrams in the previous figure*

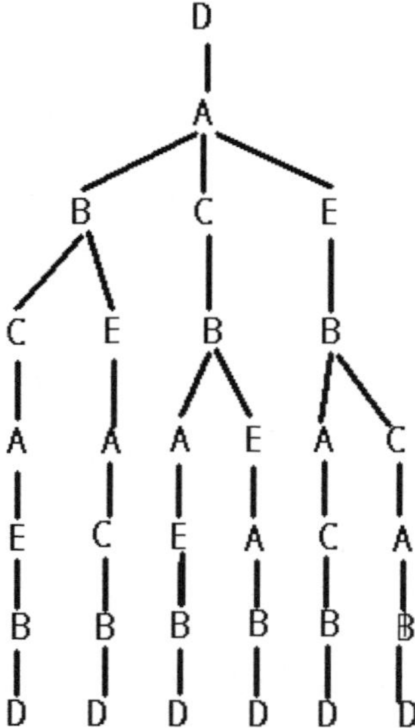

Figure 34.11. *Arborescence of the Eulerian cycles starting from edge DA on the graph in Figure 34.9c*

Let us note that starting from edge *DA*, we are obligated to return through *BD* in the end, since point *D* is of degree 2. We would also have six Eulerian cycles starting from edge *DB*, changing the direction of the traversal in relation to the previous ones. Since the cycles pass through each vertex, the change of the starting point in a cycle does not modify the shape of the cycle either. Therefore there are six shapes of starting point-type cycles in the direction of traversal-types.

34.2.3. *Constructing Eulerian cycles by fusing cycles*

The demonstration above related to Eulerian cycles gives an algorithm that enables us to construct one or more cycles. Let us take for example the directed graph G_4 with eight vertices numbered from 0 to 7, and 16 arcs (see Figure 34.12). This is a so-called de Bruijn graph (see Chapter 37). As we can verify, each vertex has two arcs that start from it, and also two that end at it. It therefore has Eulerian cycles. Let us write the 16 arcs in columns, with their starting vertex on top and their end vertex below:

0 0 1 1 2 2 3 3 4 4 5 5 6 6 7 7
0 1 2 3 4 5 6 7 0 1 2 3 4 5 6 7

The algorithm consists of taking the arcs in succession, in the order of first come, first served according to a method close to the sieve of Eratosthenes, to get Eulerian cycles.

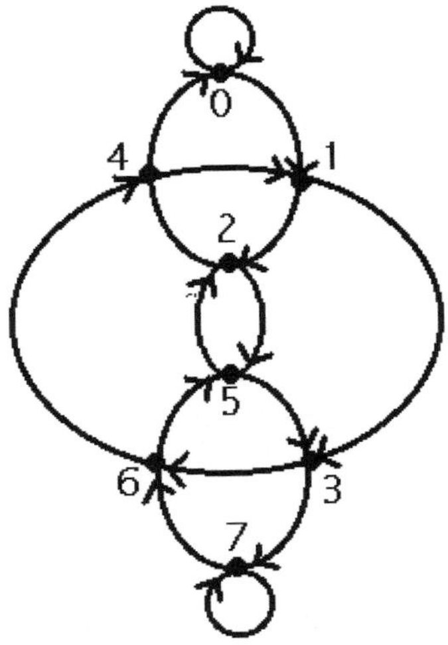

Figure 34.12. *The de Bruijn graph G_4*

We first take arc 00, which gives the first cycle (0). Then taking arcs 01, 12, 24 and 40, we get the second cycle (0 1 2 4). Next from the first remaining arc, 13, we have the third cycle (1 3 6 4). Then we take arc 25 to get the forth cycle (2 5). Then from arc 37 we have the fifth cycle (3 7 6 5). And finally the sixth cycle (7) remains. We now proceed to fuse the cycles. The first one fused with the second gives the cycle (0 0 1 2 4). At this cycle we will fuse the third, which for example makes

(0 0 1 3 6 4 1 2 4). Next we obtain (0 0 1 3 6 4 1 2 5 2 4). Then (0 0 1 3 7 6 5 3 6 4 1 2 5 2 4). And lastly:

(0 0 1 3 7 7 6 5 3 6 4 1 2 5 2 4)

We have just obtained a Eulerian cycle.

Even if several fusions are possible, it is not easy, using this method, to get all of the Eulerian cycles.

34.3. Number of Eulerian cycles in a directed graph, link with directed spanning trees

Let us consider a directed graph G, supposedly connected and balanced, i.e. such that each vertex has as many entering arcs as exiting arcs. Such a graph therefore has Eulerian cycles, enabling us to make a complete tour of the graph using all its arcs once and only once. We therefore say that this graph is Eulerian. In this case, we have a formula linking the number of Eulerian cycles and number of spanning trees of the graph (passing through all the vertices of the graph and made from certain arcs of the graph converging on root r).

PROPERTY 34.3.– Given a connected and balanced directed graph, let us choose an arc e of the graph whose origin is a vertex called r. Let R_r be the number of spanning trees of the graph that has root r, and E_e the number of Eulerian cycles of the graph starting with arc e. We therefore have the relation:

$$E_e = R_r \prod_{vertices\ a} (\text{number of arcs leaving } a\ \text{-1})!$$

where the product is calculated for all the vertices of the graph a.

For the demonstration we will use a constructive method, called the last choice exiting arc that exists in each vertex other than root r.

From a Eulerian cycle starting with an arc e, for each vertex other than the starting point r we take the arc that is used last during the traversal of the Eulerian cycle. This is referred to as the last choice arc and we will show that it forms a unique directed spanning tree (of root r, origin of the initial arc e).

By directed spanning tree of graph G, we mean the sub-graph having all the vertices of G as vertices, and part of the arcs of G as its arcs (for us, the last choice arcs) which form a tree of root r, i.e. a unique path leading from a vertex to the root.

Note that in this case the paths are made in the direction of the rise back up to the root. In Figure 34.13, we see how such a directed tree is presented.

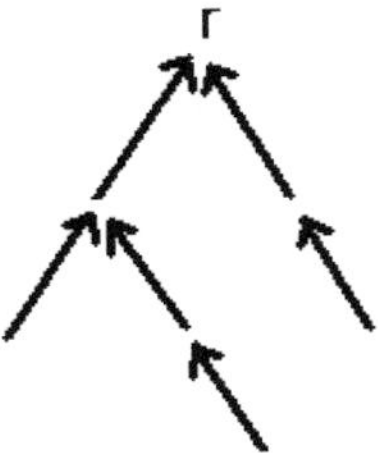

Figure 34.13. *Example of a directed tree, with the arcs rising to the root*

Conversely, from a spanning tree, we will create all the Eulerian cycles that correspond to it from the same method. We will end up with the formula between E_e and R_r.

a) *First let us take a Eulerian cycle* which we traverse from a certain arc e originating from a vertex r. For each graph vertex other than vertex r, let us take the exiting arc that is taken last during the traversal of the Eulerian cycle. At each vertex, except the root, an exiting arc thus ends up attached to it. We have to show that these arcs form a spanning tree of root r. We already notice that there is one arc less than vertices (starting point r being excluded), which is compatible with the notion of tree. We must, however, verify that these arcs are all directed towards the root. For this, let us write the Eulerian cycle based on the succession of vertices and junction arcs:

$$r \rightarrow a \rightarrow b \rightarrow \ldots \rightarrow \underline{a \rightarrow c} \rightarrow \ldots \rightarrow b \rightarrow \underline{c \rightarrow d} \rightarrow e \rightarrow \ldots \rightarrow \underline{e \rightarrow r}$$

In this case, we underline the last choice arc, for example the last arc leaving the vertex called a is $a \rightarrow c$, and never again will vertex a be consequently found in the Eulerian cycle, whereas we will be able to find c again later. The last choice arc leaving c must be found behind the previous one, such as for example $c \rightarrow d$. And so on and so forth until we reach vertex r. Hence the progressive move back up from a vertex a to vertex r. We get a unique path leading from a to r in the graph of the last choice arcs, corresponding to a branch of the tree going back up to the root r. We find a directed spanning tree of root r.

b) *Now let us take a directed spanning tree* and begin a traversal of the graph from an arc e of origin r. Let us see to it that upon arriving at a vertex, first and foremost, we take an exiting arc that is not that of the spanning tree. We only use this arc of the tree in the last extremity, when we no longer have a choice. By doing this, we traverse the vertices without freezing until the final return to vertex r, and we have a cycle. But did we really use all the graph arcs? Let us assume that it is not this way and that an arc of the spanning tree is not in the cycle. Starting from this arc, we are sure to arrive at a vertex of the previous cycle and traverse it, whereas we had already taken the last choice arc at this vertex. We get a contradiction.

c) The breakdown of the number of Eulerian cycles constructed from a spanning tree remains to be done. To construct the Eulerian cycle, we start from root r and, as expected, use arc e, which leads us to vertex v, which follows the root. From v, we choose an arc other than the one of the spanning tree, if this arc exists, which makes *outdegree*(v) – 1 cases. Each time we continue until the next vertex t, hence *outdegree*(t) – 1 arcs other than the tree arc. Each time we choose one of these arcs and we continue in this way. Even if we pass through root r, there are also *outdegree*(r) – 1 exiting arcs available, since arc e was already taken. When we pass back along a vertex a second time, the choice of exit is *outdegree* – 2, and a third time it is *outdegree* – 3. This is done until we run out of arcs, when only the last exiting arc chosen is left, which we take. The number of Eulerian cycles for a spanning tree is:

$$\prod_a (\text{numberofexitingarcsof } a - 1)!$$

The formula we spoke of results from this.

Let us take the example in Figure 34.14. This Eulerian graph can be simplified into another graph with only four vertices, such as indegree = outdegree = 2 for each vertex. From a Eulerian cycle starting with arc AB (see Figure 34.15, top), we construct the spanning tree of root A, following the method of the last exiting arc chosen. Conversely, from a spanning tree we construct a Eulerian cycle (see Figure 34.15, bottom). Because the outdegree is equal to 2 for all the vertices, this Eulerian cycle is unique. It is easy to notice that there are four spanning trees of root A. There are therefore also four Eulerian cycles starting with arc AB.

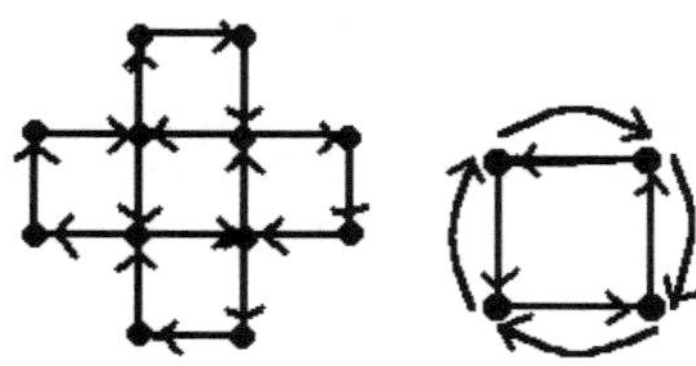

Figure 34.14. *An example of a graph (left); and the simplified graph (right)*

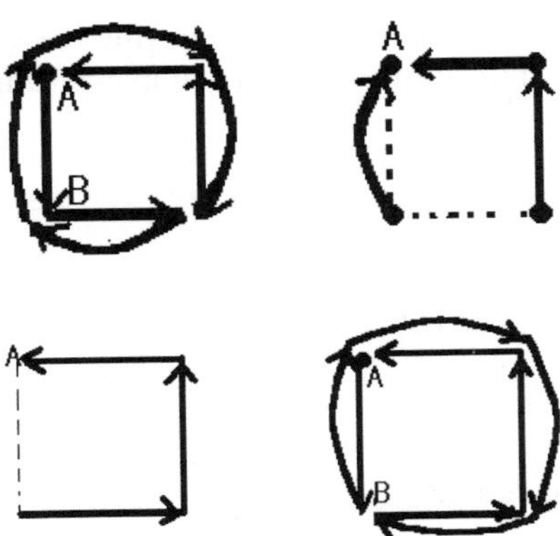

Figure 34.15. *Top: from a Eulerian cycle starting with arc AB (on the left) we construct the spanning tree of root A. Bottom: from a spanning tree, we construct the corresponding Eulerian cycle*

34.3.1. *Number of directed spanning trees*

Counting Eulerian cycles therefore boils down to counting spanning trees. For the latter there is also a formula involving what we call the *Laplacian matrix L* of the graph, linked to the adjacency matrix A whose entries a_{ij} correspond to the number of arcs from vertex i to vertex j. By definition, the Laplacian matrix L of graph G has the entries:

$L_{ij} = -a_{ij}$ if i is different from j

and

L_{ii} = outdegree (vertex i) – a_{ii}

If graph G has loops at some vertices, we can remove them without the Laplacian matrix being modified (L_{ii} does not change).

PROPERTY 34.4.– Let a (loopless) directed graph have p vertices. By definition, its Laplacian matrix L has the coefficients:

L_{ij} = - number of arcs from i to j for $i \neq j$

= outdegree of vertex i when $i = j$

Therefore the number of spanning trees R_k having the vertex numbered k for its root is equal to the determinant of the Laplacian matrix L from which we removed the kth line and k^{th} column:

$$R_k = \det L\text{-}$$

where L- is the Laplacian matrix stripped of its kth line and k^{th} column.

When the graph is Eulerian, the number of spanning trees is independent of the root k that we choose. The determinant of L- is the same no matter what the number k of the removed line and column.

If $\lambda_1, \lambda_2, \lambda_3, \ldots, \lambda_p$ are the eigenvalues of Laplacian matrix L of a Eulerian graph with $\lambda_p = 0$, the number R of spanning trees with (a) given root is:

$$R = \frac{\lambda_1 \lambda_2 \ldots \lambda_{p\text{-}1}}{p}$$

We will not show the formula $R_k = \det L$- here.[2] When the graph is Eulerian, there are as many Eulerian cycles starting with an arc e (of origin r) as with another arc, since this only produces one shift in the cycle. Because of the property in section 34.3, linking the number of Eulerian cycles to those of spanning trees of root r, the number of spanning trees is the same no matter what vertex of the graph we choose as the root of these trees.

Now let us move on to the formula using eigenvalues. The characteristic polynomial of the Laplacian matrix L is the determinant $det(L - xI)$, whose roots are the eigenvalues of L. The constant term in this polynomial is $det\ L$. The characteristic of matrix L is that the sum of the terms of each of the lines and columns are null (with the graph being Eulerian, for each vertex we have indegree = outdegree). If we add all the other columns to the first column, the determinant of L remains unchanged and is nil since the first column became null: $det\ L = 0$. This leads to (at least) one eigenvalue being nil. Now let us take the determinant of $L - xI$. It does not change if we add all the other lines to the last line. Its last line is therefore formed from a succession of $-x$ terms. Factorizing $-x$, this gives:

$$det(L - xI) = -x\ detM(x)$$

2. Readers can refer to [STA 01].

where $M(x)$ is a matrix whose last line only contains 1s, with the rest being identical to what is in matrix $L - xI$. The characteristic polynomial of L is thus written $-x \, detM(x)$. Since the constant term of $detM(x)$ is $detM(0)$, the coefficient of the x term of the first degree in the characteristic polynomial is $-detM(0)$. In turn, the determinant of $M(0)$ does not change when we add all the other columns to the last one. The last column is therefore a succession of 0s, except the last term which is equal to p.

Let us develop $detM(0)$ according to this last column: $detM(0) = p \, det \, L-$, matrix $L-$ being the Laplacian matrix L from which we remove the last line and last column, since the only modifications were made in the last line and last column, and because $L-$ is left. Finally, the coefficient of the x term in the characteristic polynomial is $-p \, det \, L-$. Let $\lambda_1, \lambda_2, \ldots, \lambda_{p-1}$ be the non-null eigenvalues of L, taking $\lambda_p = 0$. When we diagonalize matrix L by changing the base, the characteristic polynomial is expressed:

$$det(L - xI) = (\lambda_1 - x)(\lambda_2 - x)\ldots(\lambda_{p-1} - x)\,(0 - x)$$

The coefficient of the x term is $-\lambda_1 \lambda_2 \ldots \lambda_{p-1}$. We deduce from it that:

$$det(L-) = (1 / p)\, \lambda_1 \lambda_2 \ldots \lambda_{p-1}$$

CONCLUSION.– We have a formula giving the number of Eulerian cycles using a certain initial arc.

Let G be a connected and balanced directed graph with p vertices, and e be a graph arc. The number of Eulerian cycles starting with arc e is:

$$E_e = \det(L-) \prod_{\substack{all\ the \\ graph \\ vertices}} (\text{outdegree of a vertex} - 1)$$

where $L-$ is the Laplacian matrix from which we remove one line and one column of the same index.

If the eigenvalues of L are $\lambda_1, \lambda_2, \ldots, \lambda_{p-1}$ (taking eigenvalue 0 for λ_p) then this number is also:

$$E_e = (1 / p)\, \lambda_1 \lambda_2 \ldots \lambda_{p-1} \prod_{\substack{all\ the \\ graph \\ vertices}} (\text{outdegree of a vertex} - 1)\,!$$

34.3.2. *Examples*

34.3.2.1. *Polygon graph with N vertices, with bidirectional arcs*

Like every directed graph having bidirectional arcs, this graph is Eulerian. If we choose, for example, vertex 0, it is easy to check that a spanning tree occupies all the sides of the polygon except one. The graph presents as many spanning trees of root 0 as it has pairs of successive vertices, i.e. N (see Figure 34.16).

As the graph is regular, with the degree corresponding to the exiting arcs always being 2, there are as many Eulerian cycles starting with 01 as there are trees, i.e. N.

34.3.2.2. *Particular case of a regular graph*

A graph is said to be regular when all the vertices have the same degree. In the case of a Eulerian directed graph, each vertex has the same outdegree d, i.e. the same number of exiting arcs. In this case the Laplacian matrix is very simply linked to the adjacency matrix A of the directed graph, by $L = d\,I - A$. If A has μ_k, with k from 1 to p as eigenvalues, matrix L has $d - \mu_k$ for eigenvalues. We return to calculating the eigenvalues of the adjacency matrix.

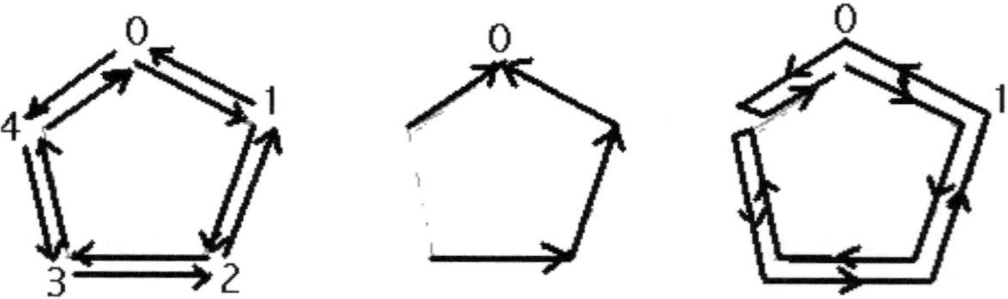

Figure 34.16. *The polygon graph for N = 5 (left); a spanning tree (center); and the corresponding Eulerian cycle starting with 01, according to the last return arcs method (right)*

34.3.2.3. *Postman paths*

Let us consider a directed graph in the form of a square network where each node is linked to its neighbors by two arcs, one in each direction. Let N be the number of nodes on one side length.

For example, for $N = 3$ we have the network indicated in Figure 34.17. This network is supposed to represent the streets that a person, for example a postman, must traverse in one direction and the other, starting from a point 0 located in the top left corner and going first to point 1 located on its right. All arcs must be traversed once and only once. The paths are Eulerian cycles. Actually the graph is Eulerian, being connected and balanced since it has as many arcs arriving on a vertex as arcs leaving from it. The problem is counting and enumerating all possible Eulerian cycles.

In other words, if the postman starts his tour on street 01, how many possibilities does he have to vary his movements?

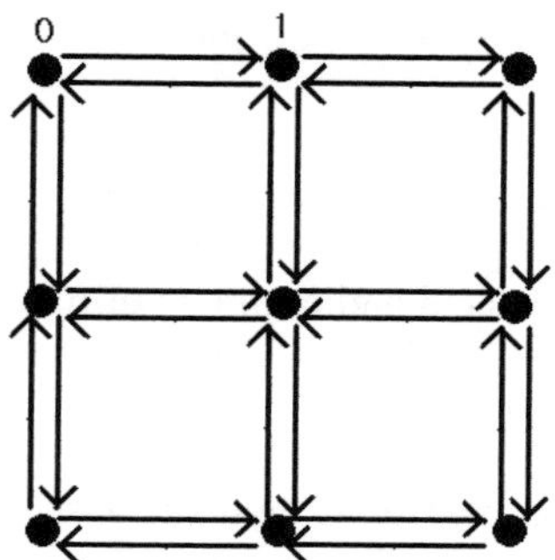

Figure 34.17. *The network of streets the postman must traverse*

The results seem surprising. If for $N = 2$ only four paths (Eulerian cycles) exist, there are 18,432 paths for $N = 3$, and 555,835,392 for $N = 4$. Even for $N = 3$, the postman will have quite a bit of difficulty in using all these different paths during his life. This number would be quite a bit more important if the postman started his tour with an arc that would not necessarily be 01, or if he let himself traverse certain streets twice in the same direction (as we can also have Eulerian graphs in this case).

As we are in the framework of a directed graph, the number of Eulerian cycles E starting from a given arc, here 01, is linked to the number of directed trees T covering the graph, with these graphs having the starting node 0 as their root. We saw the relation that links them $E= R\ \Pi\ (outdegree - 1)!$ with the product being calculated on each of the P graph nodes.

This gives:

– $E = T$ for $N = 2$;

– $E = T\ 2!^4\ 3! = 96\ T$ for $N = 3$ as the central vertex has four for its outdegree, the vertices located in the middle of the sides have three as their degree, and those of the corners have three as their outdegree;

– $E = T\ 2!^8\ 3!^4 = 55{,}296\ T$ for $N = 4$.

We are thus returned to a spanning trees problem. In the next chapter we will see how to simply calculate the number of spanning trees *T*. Already, we can see that a directed graph with bidirectional arcs everywhere has as many spanning trees as the corresponding non-directed graph, where two bidirectional arcs are replaced by only one edge.

34.4. Spanning trees of an undirected graph

Let us consider an undirected graph *G* that is supposedly connected and without loops at any vertex. We can also bijectively associate a directed graph $\underline{G}$ with it, replacing each one of its edges with two arcs in opposite directions (see Figure 34.18). This graph $\underline{G}$ is connected and each one of its vertices has as many entering arcs as exiting arcs: graph $\underline{G}$ is Eulerian. Via this means, we can extend certain properties of directed graphs to undirected graphs.

Notably, every spanning tree of *G* without a specific root can be bijectively associated with a spanning tree of $\underline{G}$ with a specific vertex *A*, on which the branches converge at the root (see Figure 34.19). There are as many spanning trees of *G* as spanning trees of $\underline{G}$ having a vertex *A* as the root.

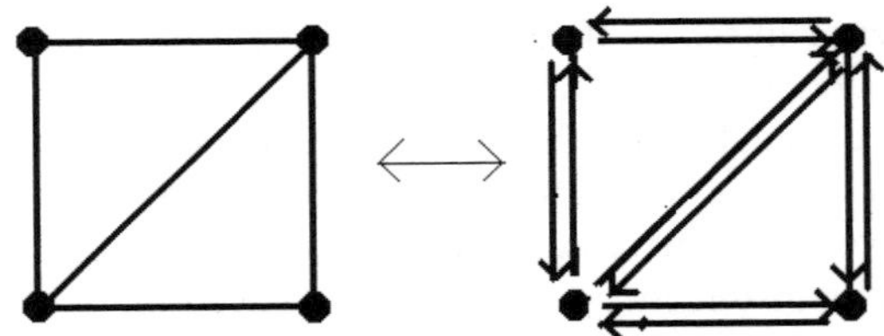

Figure 34.18. *The undirected graph G (left); and the bidirectional directed graph* $\underline{G}$ *that corresponds to it (right)*

We actually know the number of spanning trees of $\underline{G}$ having a certain root *A*. It is the determinant *det* $\underline{L\ -}$, where $\underline{L\ -}$ is the Laplacian matrix of graph $\underline{G}$ from which column and line number *i* were removed.

Now let us define the Laplacian matrix *L* of undirected graph *G*. Its coefficients are:

$$L_{ij} = -m_{ij}$$

where m_{ij} is the number of edges between *i* and *j* vertices: for $i \neq j$, and on diagonal $i = j$, we take the number of edges attached to vertex *i*.

In these conditions, graphs G and $\underline{G}$ have the same Laplacian matrix, $det\ \underline{L\text{-}} = det\ L\text{-}$, and the number of spanning trees of G is: $R_G = det\ L\text{-}$.

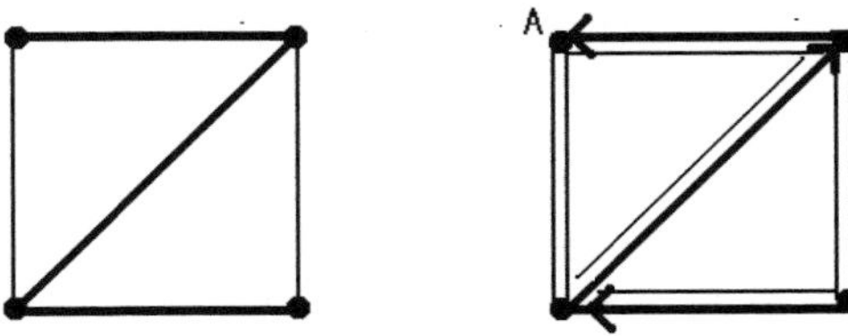

Figure 34.19. *A spanning tree of graph G (without a specific root) (left); and and its corresponding directed graph $\underline{G}$ with its root in A (right)*

We know that $det\ \underline{L\text{-}} = \frac{1}{p}\lambda_1\lambda_2 \dots \lambda_{p-1}$ (with $\lambda_p = 0$) where p is the number of vertices of $\underline{G}$ and λ_i are the eigenvalues of $\underline{L}$. We have just obtained the formula giving the number of spanning trees of undirected graph G.

Let G be a connected, loopless graph with p vertices, whose Laplacian matrix is L. Taking matrix L- obtained by removing any column and line of the same number i from L, the number of spanning trees of G is:

$$R_G = det\ L\text{-} = \frac{1}{p}\lambda_1\lambda_2 \dots \lambda_{p\text{-}1}$$

where the λ_k are the non-null eigenvalues of L.

Nevertheless the analogy between undirected and directed graphs G and $\underline{G}$ stops at spanning trees. For Eulerian cycles, their link with spanning trees exists only for directed graphs. Furthermore, if $\underline{G}$, with its bidirectional arcs, has Eulerian cycles, it is not at all certain that the corresponding undirected graph G has any.

To conclude, let us give two examples of the application of this result.

34.4.1. *Example 1: complete graph with p vertices*

Each vertex is linked to all the others and its degree (number of edges attached to it) is $p - 1$. In this case, where the degree is the same for all vertices, since the graph is regular, the Laplacian matrix L carries $p - 1$ on its diagonal and -1 everywhere else. It is expressed $L = (p - 1)I - A$, where A is the adjacency matrix, or even better $L = pI - J$, where J is the matrix formed uniquely with 1s.

We can easily check that J assumes $\mu_k = p$ as an eigenvalue once and 0 as eigenvalue $p - 1$ times. In turn, matrix L has $p - \mu_k$ as its eigenvalues, i.e. p is repeated $p - 1$ times and 0 once. Hence the number of spanning trees of a complete graph is:

$$R_G = (1 / p)\, p^{p-1} = p^{p-2}$$

We again find Cayley's formula (see Chapter 31).

34.4.2. *Example 2: tetrahedron (see Figure 34.20)*

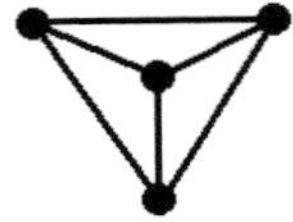

Figure 34.20. *The planar graph associated with a tetrahedron*

The adjacency matrix of the tetrahedron is circulant and its first line is expressed (0 1 1 1). The eigenvalues are:

$$\lambda_k = e^{i\,k\pi/2} + e^{-i\,k\pi/2} + e^{i\,k\pi}, \text{ i.e. } 2\cos(k\pi/2) + (-1)^k$$

i.e. 3 once and -1 three times.

From this, we deduce the eigenvalues of the Laplacian matrix, namely $3 - \lambda_k$, i.e. 0 once and 4 three times. The number of spanning trees is $(1 / 4)\, 4^3 = 16$.

Chapter 35

Enumeration of Spanning Trees of an Undirected Graph

This chapter is devoted to the study of several examples. We will implement the formula giving the number of spanning trees of an undirected graph. In the previous chapter, we saw that this formula boils down to calculating the determinant or eigenvalues of a matrix. This calculation can, however, become very complex. In certain specific cases we will be able to return to the search for a recurrence formula, like in the initial examples that follow. We will also see that moving on to the dual graph sometimes enables us to simplify the calculation. In numerous cases, we will have to restrict ourselves to an experimental study.

35.1. Spanning trees of the fan graph

The fan graph of order n comprises $n + 1$ vertices, where the vertex numbered 0 is linked to all the others, and the other vertices from 1 to n are linked to the next one. It therefore has $2n - 1$ edges, with the shape indicated in Figure 35.1. We have to count the number $u(n)$ of its spanning trees. We already have $u(0) = 1$ and $u(1) = 1$. For n greater than 1, we will choose vertex 1 and distinguish several cases for the spanning trees:

– Vertex 1 is linked to vertex 2 but not to vertex 0, and a tree spans vertices 0, 2, 3, …, n. That gives $u(n - 1)$ possibilities.

– Vertex 1 is linked to vertex 0 but not to vertex 2, and a tree spans vertices 0, 2, 3, …, n. That makes $u(n - 1)$ cases.

– Vertex 1 is linked to vertices 0 and 2. Several possibilities are presented. If the edge between 2 and 3 is not taken, a tree spans graph 0, 3, 4, …, n, and there are $u(n-2)$ cases. If the edge between 2 and 3 is taken but not the one between 3 and 4, a tree spans graph 0, 4, 5, …, n, and this gives $u(n-3)$ cases. Next, if edges 1 to 4 are taken but not the one between 4 and 5, a tree spans graph 0, 5, …, n. We continue in this way until the case where the edges from 1 to $n-1$ are taken but not the one between $n-1$ and n, with a tree spanning vertices 0, n, which makes $u(1) = 1$ cases. Lastly the case where all the edges from 1 to n are taken remains, which gives $u(0) = 1$ cases. Having thus exhausted all the cases, we end up with the formula:

$$u(n) = u(n-1) + u(n-1) + u(n-2) + u(n-3) \ldots + u(1) + u(0) \text{ for } n \geq 2$$

and:

$$u(1) = u(0) = 1$$

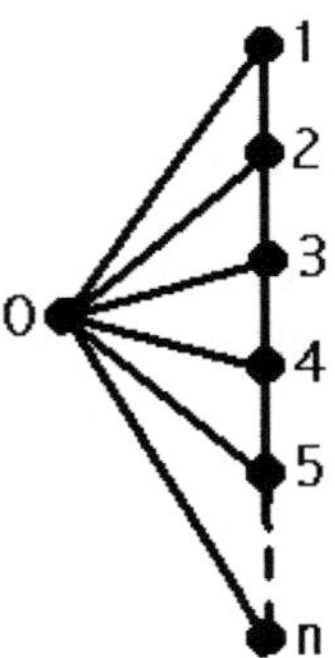

Figure 35.1. *The fan graph of order n*

The generating function associated with the sequence $u(n)$ is $F(X) = \sum_{n \geq 0} u(n)X^n$.

Let us proceed in the following way, making the previous recurrence relation appear in columns:

$$F(X) = u(0) + u(1)X + u(2)X^2 + u(3)X^3 + u(4)X^4 + \ldots$$

$$XF(X) = u(0)X + u(1)X^2 + u(2)X^3 + u(3)X^4 + \ldots$$

$$XF(X) = u(0)X + u(1)X^2 + u(2)X^3 + u(3)X^4 + \ldots$$

$$X^2F(X) = \quad u(0)X^2 + u(1)X^3 + u(2)X^4 + \ldots$$

$$X^3F(X) = \quad u(0)X^3 + u(1)X^4 + \ldots$$

$$X^4F(X) = \quad u(0)X^4 + \ldots$$

Equalizing the coefficient of X^n in $F(X)$, from $n = 2$, with the sum of those of the following lines, we get the F equation:

$$F(X) - u(0) - u(1)X = XF(X) - u(0)X + XF(X) - u(0)X + X^2F(X) + X^3F(X) + \ldots$$

$$= XF(X) - 2X + XF(X) / (1 - X)$$

Hence:

$$F(X)\,(1 - X - XF(X) / (1 - X)) = 1 - X$$

Finally:

$$F(X) = \frac{(1-X)^2}{1-3X+X^2}$$

The development in series of $F(X)$ after $u(0) = 1$ and $u(1) = 1$ gives $u(2) = 3$, $u(3) = 8$, $u(4) = 21$, $u(5) = 55$, $u(6) = 144$, etc. We recognize Fibonacci numbers $f(i)$, here with even i. We know that Fibonacci numbers are defined by the recurrence relation $f(k) = f(k-1) + f(k-2)$, with $f(0) = 0$ and $f(1) = 1$ at the start, and they have $G(Z) = Z / (1 - Z - Z^2)$ as their generating function. We have to check that $u(n) = f(2n)$ for $n \geq 1$, and $u(0) = 1$.

To do this, let us form the series originating from $(G(Z) + G(-Z))/2$, which only contains even powers of $G(Z)$, and more specifically let us take $1 + (G(Z) + G(-Z))/2$, which assumes, for development: $1 + f(2)Z^2 + f(4)Z^4 + f(6)Z^6 +$ etc. Replacing Z^2 with X, we get the series $1 + f(2)X + f(4)X^2 + f(6)X^3 + \ldots$, and must show that we thus find the generating function $F(X)$ of $u(n)$. Indeed:

$$1+\frac{G(Z)+G(-Z)}{2} = 1+\frac{1}{2}\left(\frac{Z}{1-Z-Z^2} - \frac{Z}{1+Z-Z^2}\right)$$

$$= 1+\frac{Z^2}{1-3Z^2+Z^4} = \frac{(1-Z^2)^2}{1-3Z^2+Z^4} = \frac{(1-X)^2}{1-3X+X^2} = F(X)$$

Figure 35.2 shows the results obtained for $n = 3$ and $n = 5$.

35.2. The ladder graph and its spanning trees

This ladder-shaped graph (see Figure 35.3) has n nodes in length, i.e. twice as much altogether.

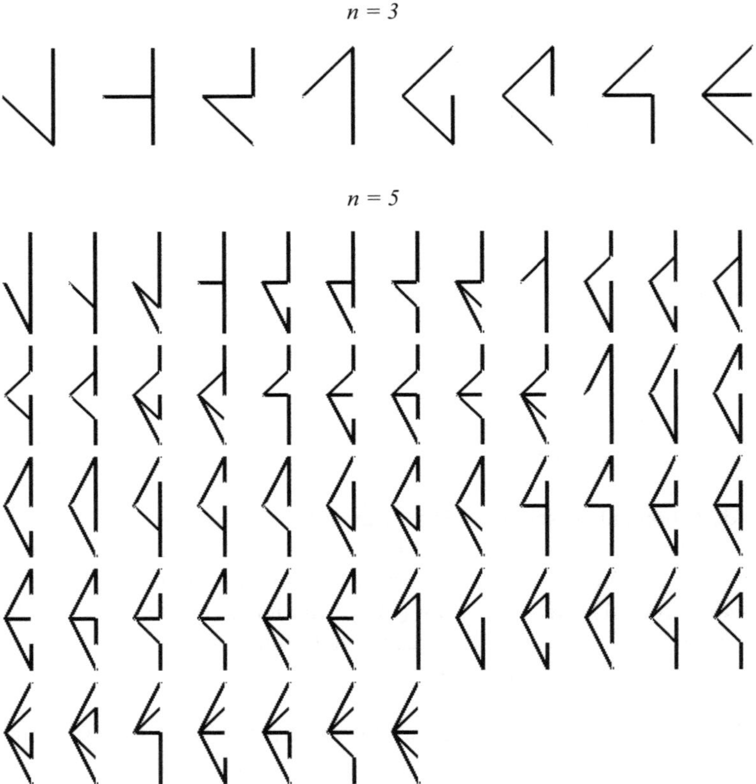

Figure 35.2. *The eight spanning trees of the fan of order 3 (top line); and the 55 spanning trees of the fan of order 5 (below)*

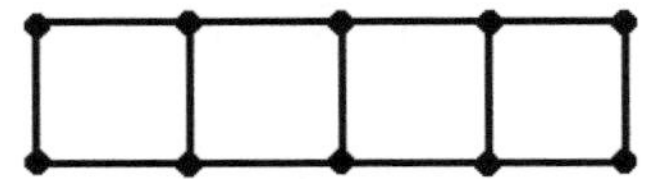

Figure 35.3. *The ladder graph for $n = 5$*

We have to find the number $u(n)$ of its spanning trees. To do this we will classify them according to the shape of their right extremity:

– *the spanning tree ends with two horizontal edges*, which are attached to a tree $n-1$ long, which gives $u(n-1)$ cases;

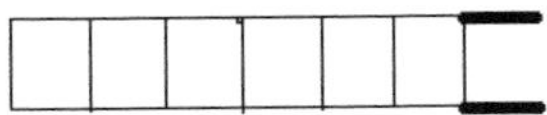

– *the tree ends with a hook one unit long*, with one of the last two edges not taken. This branch is attached to a tree $n-1$ long. That makes $2\,u(n-1)$ cases;

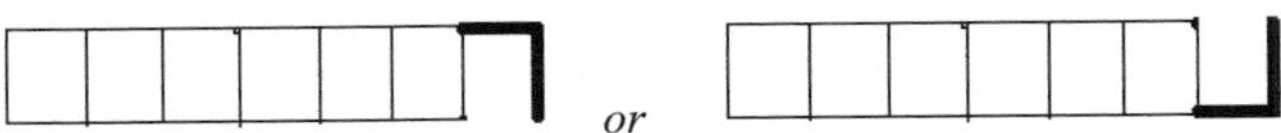

– *the tree ends with a hook two units long*, which is attached to a tree $n-2$ long, hence $2\,u(n-2)$ cases;

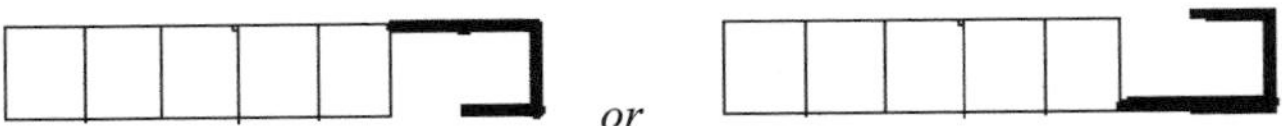

– *step by step we lengthen the type of hook above*. The tree ends with a hook of three units, then four, and so on and so forth until it is $n-1$ long, where this branch is attached to a tree 0 units long, reduced to a vertical line ($n = 1$). That makes:

$$2u(n-3) + 2u(n-4) + \ldots + 2u(1)$$

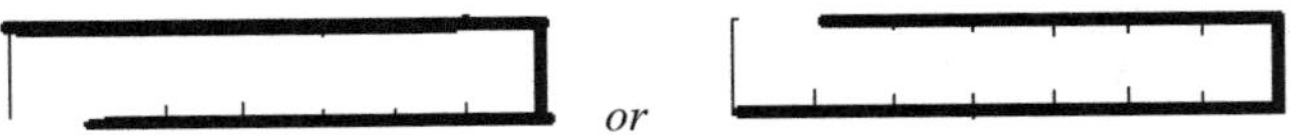

– finally, one last case remains, where the *hook is attached to the ladder 0 units long*, i.e. the unique tree:

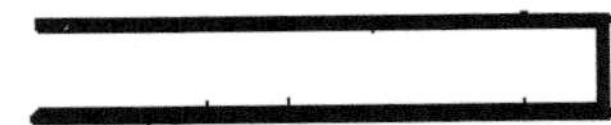

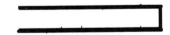

We end up with the formula:

$$u(n) = u(n-1) + 2\,(u(n-1) + u(n-2) + \ldots + u(1)) + u(0)$$

for $n \geq 2$, or even:

$$u(n) = u(n-1) + 2\,(u(n-1) + u(n-2) + \ldots + u(1) + u(0)) - u(0)$$

with $u(0) = u(1) = 1$.

Let us move on to the generating function associated with this sequence, i.e.:

$$F(X) = u(0) + u(1)X + u(2)X^2 + u(3)X^3 + u(4)X^4 + \dots$$

Let us form:

$$XF(X) = u(0)X + u(1)X^2 + u(2)X^3 + u(3)X^4 + \dots$$

$$\begin{aligned} 2XF(X) / (1 - X) = {} & 2u(0)X + 2u(1)X^2 + 2u(2)X^3 + 2u(3)X^4 + \dots \\ & + 2u(0)X^2 + 2u(1)X^3 + 2u(2)X^4 + \dots \\ & + 2u(0)X^3 + 2u(1)X^4 + \dots \\ & + 2u(0)X^4 + \dots \\ & \dots \end{aligned}$$

$$-1 / (1 - X) = -1 - X - X^2 - X^3 - X^4 - \dots$$

By addition, we find that:

$$F(X) - 1 - X = XF(X) - X + 2X F(X) / (1 - X) - 2X - 1/(1 - X) + 1 + X$$

$$F(X)\,(1 - X - 2X / (1 - X)) = 2 - X - 1 / (1 - X)$$

$$F(X) = \frac{1 - 3X + X^2}{1 - 4X + X^2}$$

Developing in series leads to:

$$u(0) = 1,\ u(1) = 1,\ u(2) = 4,\ u(3) = 15,\ u(4) = 56,\ u(5) = 209,\ u(6) = 780,\ \dots$$

35.3. Spanning trees in a square network in the form of a grid

We have already encountered this type of graph in the case of postman paths (see Chapter 34, section 34.3.2.3). It was about a square network in the form of a grid, with bidirectional horizontal and vertical linking arcs, which can be replaced by an undirected square network with unique edges between the nodes when dealing with spanning trees (see Figure 35.4).

We will begin by doing an exhaustive search for spanning trees by computer experimentation, then we will proceed to a theoretical study that will also give us their number.

35.3.1. *Experimental enumeration of spanning trees of the square network*

As a function of the values of N, we find $T(2) = 4$, $T(3) = 192$ and $T(4) = 100,352$ as the number of spanning trees. In Figure 35.5 we will find the 192 trees obtained for $N = 3$, as well as the first trees found for $N = 4$.

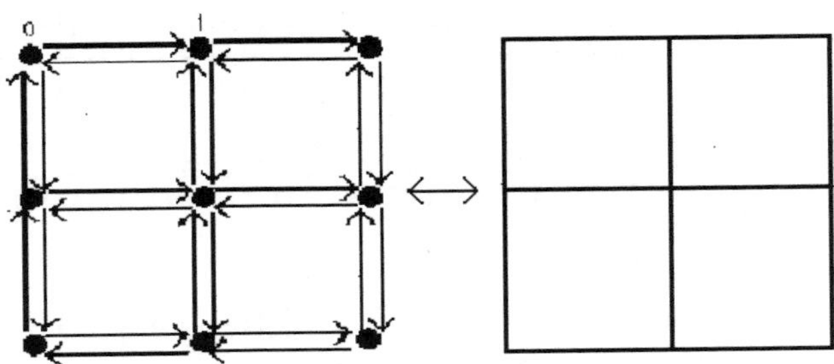

Figure 35.4. *In the search for spanning trees, the directed graph is equivalent to the undirected graph*

Figure 35.5a. *The 192 trees for N = 3*

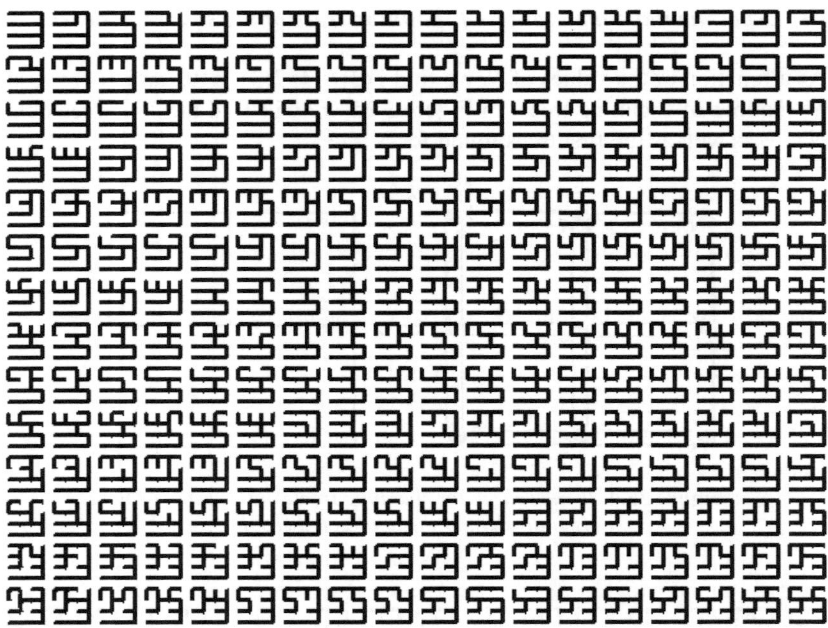

Figure 35.5b. *Some trees obtained for N = 4*

35.3.2. *Spanning trees program in the case of the square network*

Initially we take L number of nodes on one side of the square. The total number of nodes is expressed $NN = L^2$. These nodes are numbered from 0 to $L^2 - 1$ from left to right and top to bottom. The number of arcs is $N = 4L(L - 1)$, and the number of edges is $NE = N / 2$. We begin by determining the neighbors of each node, which we place in a table $n[][]$. $n[i][k]$ is neighbor number k of node i. If node i is not found on the left border, it assumes one neighbor $i - 1$. And similarly in the three other directions. We can also calculate the number of neighbors $nbn[i]$ of each node i:

```
for(i=0; i<NN; i++)
{ k=0;
  if (i%L!=0) n[i][k++]=i–1;
  if (i<NN–L) n[i][k++]=i+L;
  if ((i+1)%L!=0) n[i][k++]=i+1;
  if (i>=L) n[i][k++]=i–L;
  nbn[i]=k;
}
```

Then we determine the edges by joining the nodes to their neighbors, seeing to it that they are taken only once. The number in base *NN* is placed in table *edge*[*q*]: *NN***start*[*q*] + *end*[*q*], where *start*[*q*] and *end*[*q*] are the extreme nodes of edge number *q*. Each time we choose *start* < *end*. For example, for $L = 3$, we find the 12 edges 03, 01, 14, 12, 25, 36, 34, 47, 45, 58, 67 and 78, where we have *start* < *end*:

```
q=0;
for(i=0; i<NN; i++)  for(k=0; k<nbn[i]; k++) if (i<n[i][k])
    {  start[q]=i; end[q]=n[i][k;  edge[q]=NN*i+n[i][k]; q++;  }
```

We now arrive at the important part. A spanning tree by definition touches the $NN = L^2$ nodes. It must therefore include $NN - 1$ edges. To determine them, we will take all the combinations of $NN - 1$ edges taken out of *NE*. For example, for $L = 3$, we have eight edges to be taken from the 12. Among the graphs thus produced, we will proceed to pruning in such a way as to conserve only the spanning trees. To find them, we will make a depth-first exploration of the graph from node 0, and if all the nodes are reached we will have a spanning tree. This method is simple to implement, but it has the disadvantage of creating a large number of objects, a good part of which will finally be eliminated. For $L = 3$, we keep the 192 spanning trees out of the 495 combinations. For $L = 4$, there are 1,307,504 combinations and we only keep 100,352 trees.

The combinations of $NN - 1$ edges out of *NE* are expressed, as usual, in the form of *NE*-length words based on 0 and 1, with $NN - 1$ letter 1s, the remainder being made up of other 0s, indicating that the corresponding edges are not taken.

```
for(i=0; i<NN−1; i++) letter[NE−1−i]=1;
      /* The first combination. For L > 2, this combination never gives a tree. We
do not need to explore it. On the other hand, for L = 2 it gives a spanning tree. We
should amend the program for this case. */

for(;;)  /* passage from one combination to the next */
 {
   i=NE−1; while (letter[i]!=1 || letter[i−1]!=0 && i>0) i--;
   pospivot=i−1;  if (pospivot==-1) break;
   letter[pospivot]=1; letter[pospivot+1]=0;
   l=pospivot+2; r=NE−1;
   while (l<r) { aux=letter[l]; letter[l]=letter[r]; letter[r]=aux; l++; r--; }
   numbernodes=0;
   for(j=0; j<NN; j++) alreadyseen[j]=0;
   explore(0);
   if (numbernodes==NN) numbertrees++;
         /* we can add the drawing of the tree */
```

```
}
printf("%ld: ",numbertrees);

void explore(int i)
 { numbernodes++; alreadyseen[i]=1;
  for(j=0; j<nbn[i]; j++)
   { neighbor=n[i][j];
     if (i<neighbor) a=i*NN+neighbor; else a=neighbor*NN+i;
     for(jj=0; jj<NE; jj++) if (edge[jj]==a) break;
     if (letter[jj]==YES && alreadyseen[neighbor]==NO) explore(neighbor);
   }
 }
```

Let us note that in the exploration function, when we move from one node to a neighbor, the neighbor does not necessarily have a greater number. We should put these nodes in ascending order to find out the corresponding edge and see whether this edge is acceptable in the combination concerned (*letter*[jj]==*YES* in the program). Lastly, this entire program is easily generalized to the search for spanning trees in any graph.

35.3.3. *Passage to the undirected graph, its dual and formula giving the number of spanning trees*

To get the number of spanning directed trees in our square network of bidirectional streets, with their root at 0, we know we need to count the number of spanning trees of the corresponding undirected graph G (see Figure 35.4). This number, as we saw, is *det L-* (see Chapter 34, section 34.4). The Laplacian matrix of G is not particularly simple to calculate, however, especially because the vertices do not all have the same degree (the degrees being 2, 3 or 4). This requires us to use graph G^*, the dual of G, thanks to the following property:

PROPERTY 35.1.– The number of trees spanning an undirected graph G, supposedly connected and based on horizontal and vertical edges, where these edges are formed in the plane of adjacent square regions, is equal to the determinant of matrix $4I - A$, A being the adjacency matrix of graph G^*-, where G^*- is the dual graph G^* from which we removed its exterior vertex.

In other words, if we end up finding out the eigenvalues λ_k of this matrix A, those of matrix $4I - A$ will be $4 - \lambda_k$, and the product of all these eigenvalues will give the number of spanning trees of the initial graph G, for us the square network.

But what is the dual graph G^* of G? Each region delimited by the edges of G becomes a vertex of the dual graph G^*. We link the vertices of G^* by one edge when the link between two vertices traverses an edge of G. For example, for the previous square network this gives the graph in Figure 35.6.

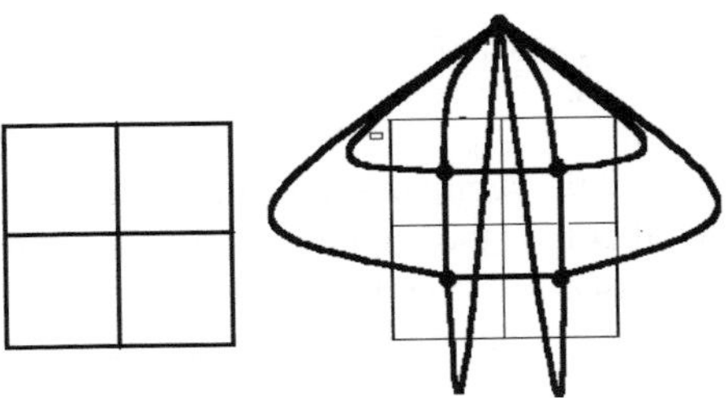

Figure 35.6. *A graph G with nine vertices (left); and its dual G* with its five vertices, one of which is on the exterior, corresponding to the region located outside of the square (right)*

We will assume (this is shown) that graph G and its dual G^* have exactly the same number of spanning trees. It is here that the simplification will occur. When we take the Laplacian matrix L^* of G^* and choose to remove the line and column corresponding to the exterior vertex to get L^*-. One matrix is left, the diagonal of which carries 4s as each remaining vertex of G^* (i.e. the center of a square of G) is of degree 4. Hence, $L^*- = 4I - A$, where A is the adjacency matrix of graph G^*-, i.e. the dual graph G^* stripped of its exterior vertex.

Finally, the number of spanning trees of G is $det(4I - A)$. Now we simply find the eigenvalues of matrix A, itself also the adjacency matrix of a square network, of dimension $N - 1$ in relation to the initial square network G. This invites us to make a detour to specify the notion of the square network and find the eigenvalues of adjacency matrix A of a square network, their product giving us the number of spanning trees in this case.

35.4. The two essential types of (undirected) graphs based on squares

We will begin by defining two ways to compose graphs G and H, having the respective vertices g_i (with i between 1 and N_G) and h_j (with j between 1 and N_H). These graphs are supposedly without double edges or loops. From there we define the sum and product graphs $G + H$ and $G \times H$, which both have the couples of vertices from G and H, i.e. a total of $N_G N_H$ vertices:

– to get $G + H$, we place an edge between the vertex (g_i, h_j) and $(g_{i'}, h_{j'})$ if $i = i'$ and there is an edge between h_j and $h_{j'}$, or if $j = j'$ and there is an edge between g_i and $g_{i'}$;

– for $G \times H$, we place an edge between vertex (g_i, h_j) and $(g_{i'}, h_{j'})$ if there is an edge between g_i and $g_{i'}$ as well as an edge between h_j and $h_{j'}$.

These two graphs have a simple property: the eigenvalues of their adjacency matrix are linked to those of adjacency matrices λ_i of G and μ_i of H. For graph $G + H$, the eigenvalues are $\lambda_i+\mu_j$, and for $G \times H$, we have the eigenvalues $\lambda_i\mu_j$. We will assume these two results.

For example, let us take the segment graph S graded to N vertices for G and also H. Graph $S + S$ is none other than the square network based on horizontal and vertical lines, and graph $S \times S$ is based on squares oriented according to diagonals. The two graphs $S + S$ and $S \times S$ are both inscribed in a large square of the dimensions $N \times N$. We will find the drawings of these two sum and product graphs in Figure 35.7.

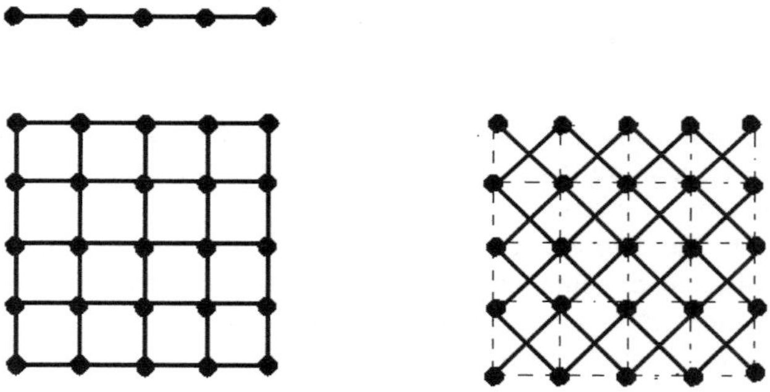

Figure 35.7. *The segment graph S with N = 5 vertices (top); graph S + S (bottom left); and graph S x S (bottom right). Both square graphs are constructed from graph segment S*

We know (see Chapter 13, section 13.4.3) that the graduated segment graph S with N vertices has the eigenvalues $\lambda_i = 2\cos(\pi i / (N + 1))$. We deduce from it the eigenvalues of $S + S$, i.e.: $\lambda_{ij} = 2\cos(\pi i / (N + 1)) + 2\cos(\pi j / (N + 1))$, and those of $S \times S$: $\lambda_{ij} = 4\cos(\pi i / (N + 1))\cos(\pi j / (N + 1))$.

This enables us to return to the problem of the postman circulating in the square network of streets (see Chapter 34, section 34.3.2.3).

Let us begin with graph G_2, which boils down to a simple square. It is not useful to pass through the dual, since each vertex is a degree 2. The eigenvalues of the adjacency matrix of G_2 are $\lambda_{ij} = 2\cos(\pi i / 3) + 2\cos(\pi j / 3)$, i.e. 2, 0, 0 and -2, and those of the Laplacian matrix of G_2 are $2 - \lambda_{ij}$, i.e. 0, 2, 2 and 4. Hence the number of spanning trees, obtained by multiplying the non-null eigenvalues and dividing by the number of vertices, i.e. four spanning trees.

This can also be found by using the dual G_2*- deduced from G_2, namely G_1. Furthermore, the only eigenvalue of the adjacency matrix A of G_1 is 0. That of matrix $4I - A$ is 4, and it is also the number of spanning trees of G_2.

The square graph G_3 with $N = 3$ has G_3^* as its dual. G_3^*- is graph G_2. The eigenvalues of the adjacency matrix of G_2 are, as we saw, 2, 0, 0 and -2. Those of matrix $4I - A$ are 2, 4, 4 and 6, and their product gives the number of spanning trees of G_3, i.e. $2\times4\times4\times6 = 192$.

The square graph G_4 with $N = 4$ has G_4*- as its dual, namely graph G_3, whose eigenvalues are $2\cos(\pi i / 4) + \cos(\pi j / 4)$, i.e. $\pm 2\sqrt{2}$, $\pm\sqrt{2}$ twice, and 0 three times. Those of $4I - A$ are $4 \pm 2\sqrt{2}$, $4 \pm \sqrt{2}$ twice, and 4 three times. Their product is equal to 100,352, and it is the number of spanning trees of G_4.

35.5. The cyclic square graph

Let us start from the undirected (or oriented in two directions) circular graph C_N with N vertices, the adjacency matrix eigenvalues of which we know, i.e.:

$$\lambda_k = 2\cos(2\pi k / N)$$

Now let us form graph $C_N + C_N$. According to the definition of the sum of the two graphs given in the previous example, this graph is the cyclic network, as could be drawn on a torus (see Figure 35.8).

The eigenvalues of its adjacency matrix are:

$$\lambda_{ij} = 2\cos(2\pi i / N) + 2\cos(2\pi j / N)$$

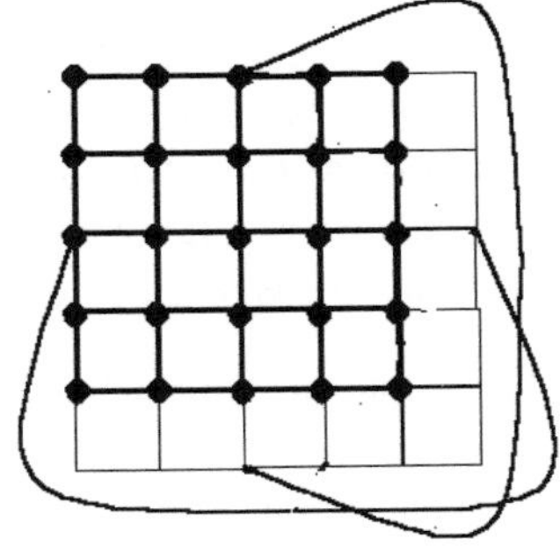

Figure 35.8. *The cyclic square network, where the extreme vertices on the left and right are linked, as well as those above and below*

Unlike the acyclic square network, the Laplacian matrix L of the cyclic network is simpler, because each vertex assumes four neighbors. Hence:

$$L = 4I - A$$

The eigenvalues of the Laplacian matrix are:

$$4 - \lambda_{ij} = 4 - 2\cos(2\pi i / N) - 2\cos(2\pi j / N)$$

We deduce from this that the number of spanning trees of the cyclic square network is equal to $T = (1 / N^2) \Pi \lambda_{ij}$, taking the product of the previous eigenvalues except the null one (for $i = j = 0$). Using the formula $\cos(2\pi i / N) = 1 - 2\sin^2(\pi i / N)$, what remains is:

$$T = \frac{4^{N^2-1}}{N^2} \prod_{\substack{i,j=0 \\ (i,j)\neq(0,0)}}^{N-1} (\sin^2 \frac{\pi i}{N} + \sin^2 \frac{\pi j}{N})$$

35.6. Examples of regular graphs

As we were able to see in several previous examples, the simplest cases to deal with are regular graphs, namely those whose vertices have as many edges attached to them. Here are a few extra cases.

35.6.1. *Example 1*

Let us consider a graph G with an even number N of vertices, with $N = 2K$, and where each vertex has $N - 2$ arcs attached to it.

Next let us take the complementary graph of G (see Figure 35.9). It is made up of K components, each in segment form. The adjacency matrix of a segment K_2 (complete graph with two elements) has the eigenvalues ± 1. For the K components of the complementary $\overline{G}$, which is also regular, with one edge for each vertex, the eigenvalues of the matrix are ± 1, and this is repeated K times.

We know that a regular graph of eigenvalues 1, λ_2, λ_3, …, λ_N, has a complementary graph of eigenvalues $N - 2$, $-\lambda_2 - 1$, $-\lambda_3 - 1$, …, $-\lambda_N - 1$.[1] In this case, the adjacency matrix A of the initial graph G has the eigenvalues $N - 2$, 0 repeated K times, and -2 repeated $K - 1$ times. To find out the number of spanning

1. See [CVE 80].

trees, we take the Laplacian matrix $L = (N-2)I - A$. Its eigenvalues are 0, $N-2$ repeated K times, and N repeated $K-1$ times. We deduce from it that the number of spanning trees is:

$$T = (1/N)(N-2)^{K} N^{K-1} = N^{K-2}(N-2)^{K}$$

$$= 2^{2K-2} K^{K-2} (K-1)^{K}$$

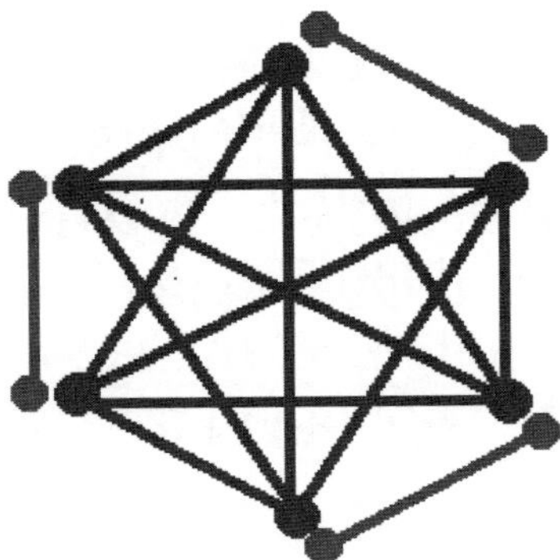

Figure 35.9. *Example of the regular graph for N = 6, with its complementary made up of three segments*

35.6.2. *Example 2: hypercube with* n *dimensions*

Here we will simply give the formula for the number of spanning trees of a hypercube of dimensions n, i.e.:

$$T_{\text{n}} = 2^{2^n - n - 1} \prod_{k=1}^{n} k^{C_n^k}$$

which notably gives:

$T_2 = 4$ and $T_3 = 96$

The spanning trees of the cube are shown in Figure 35.10.

35.6.3. *Example 3: the ladder graph and its variations*

We dealt with this problem at the beginning of this chapter. Now, thanks to the dual graph, we have a new, faster and more flexible method.

Figure 35.10. *The 384 spanning trees of the cube, with 32 trees each having four vertical edges, 128 having three vertical edges, 160 having two vertical edges, and 64 having one vertical edge (the trees with four vertical edges or one single one are in black)*

Let us recall that for a planar graph G, whose edges delimit square regions (or more generally, four-sided polygons), the number of spanning trees is obtained by calculating the product of numbers $4 - \lambda_i$, where λ_i are the eigenvalues of the adjacency matrix of the dual graph G^*- (G^* stripped of its exterior vertex). This could even be generalized to every planar graph whose edges delimit polygonal regions all having k sides, therefore taking the numbers $k - \lambda_i$.

Thus the ladder graph, once the exterior vertex has been removed, has the path graph  as its dual.

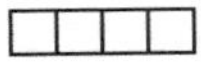

For example, for the ladder graph of order $n = 4$, having eight vertices, the dual graph G^*- is the path graph with three vertices, whose adjacency matrix A assumes the eigenvalues 0, $\pm\sqrt{2}$. Matrix $4I - A$ has the eigenvalues 4, $4-\sqrt{2}$ and $4+\sqrt{2}$, hence the number of spanning trees that is the product of eigenvalues, i.e.: 5×14 = 56.

Here are some extra questions:

a) Show that the ladder graph for $n = 5$: , assumes as many spanning trees as graph .

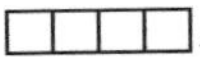

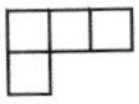

These two graphs have the same dual graph G^*-, namely the path graph with four vertices:  or 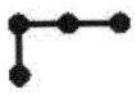 .

We find 209 spanning trees in both cases (see Figure 35.11).

b) Determine the number of spanning trees of the T-shaped graph, i.e. more specifically: .

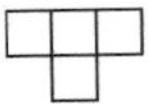

Its dual graph is G 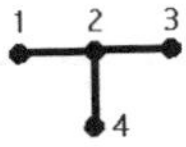 which has the adjacency matrix:

$$A = \begin{pmatrix} 0 & 1 & 0 & 0 \\ 1 & 0 & 1 & 1 \\ 0 & 1 & 0 & 0 \\ 0 & 1 & 0 & 0 \end{pmatrix}$$

The characteristic polynomial is $X^2(X^2 - 3)$, with the eigenvalues being 0 twice and $\pm\sqrt{3}$. We deduce from this that the number of spanning trees is:

$$4.4.(4-\sqrt{3})(4+\sqrt{3}) = 208.$$

These trees are represented in Figure 35.12.

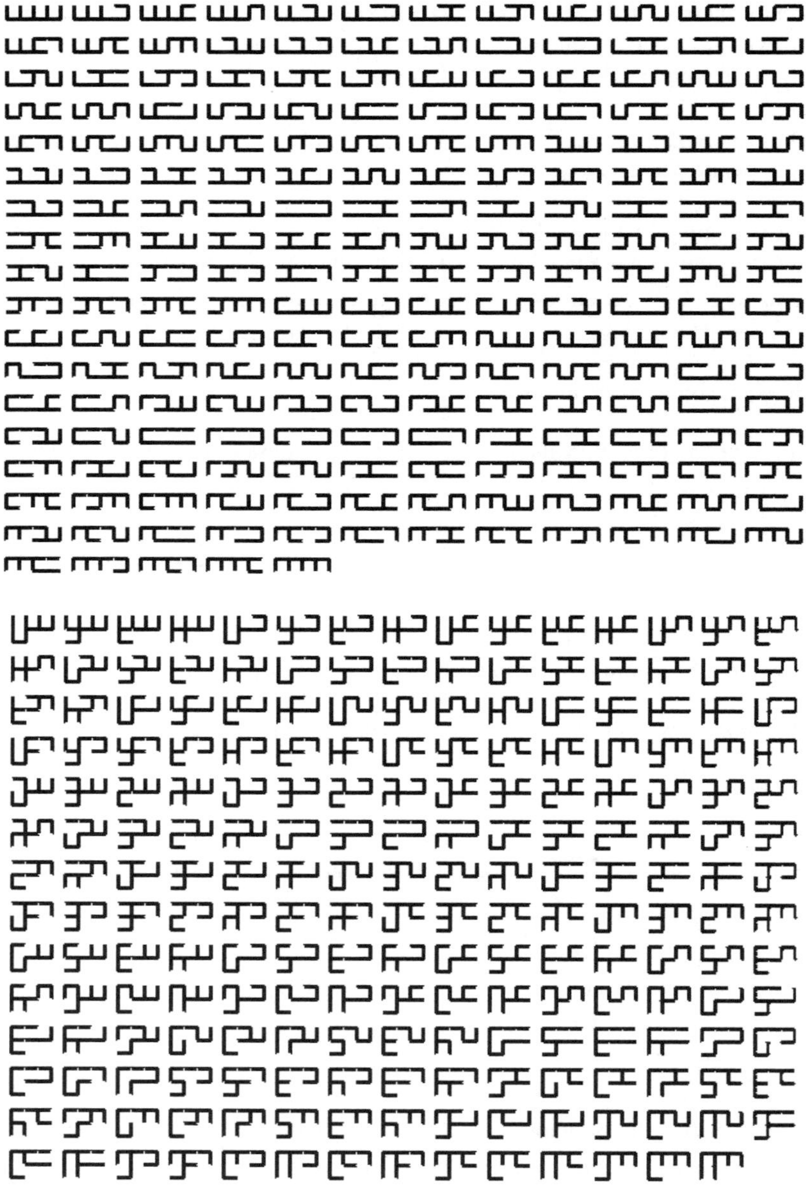

Figure 35.11. *The 209 spanning trees for the two types of graphs* □□□□ *and* (small grid-graph symbol)

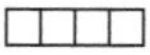

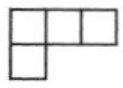

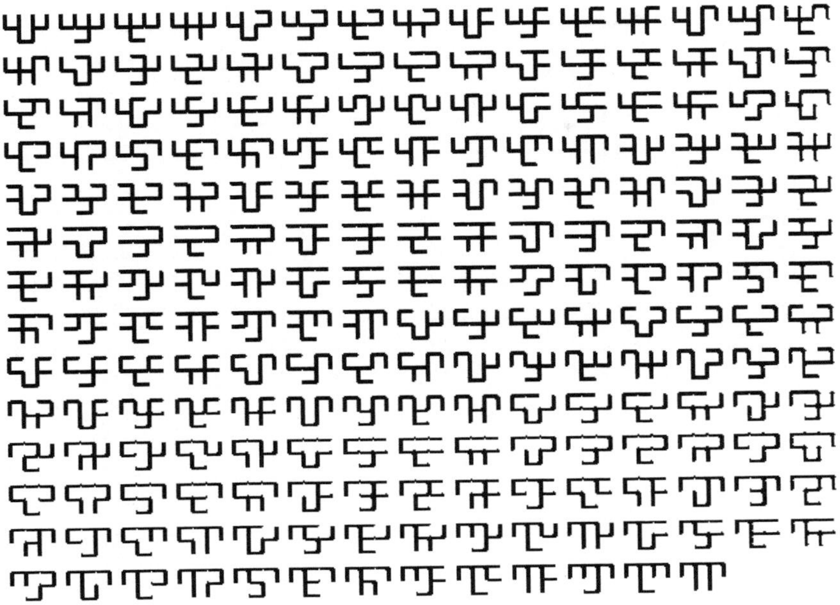

Figure 35.12. *The 208 spanning trees of graph*

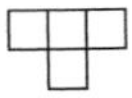

Chapter 36

Enumeration of Eulerian Paths in Undirected Graphs

As we do not have a general formula enabling us to count the number of Eulerian paths on an undirected graph, we are led to theoretically deal with each problem on a case-by-case basis, when this is possible. We will see two examples in what follows. By default, we are satisfied with an experimental study. We will give the style of program that enables us to deal with all the cases that are presented, and we will focus on the example of graphs that came from Africa, particularly rich by their multiplicity and aesthetics.

36.1. Polygon graph with n vertices with double edges

This type of undirected graph is always Eulerian, the degree of each vertex being four. Let us first deal with the case where $N = 3$ (see Figure 36.1).

We take the Eulerian cycles, starting with one of the edges 0 1, where the next vertex can be either 2 or 0. Let us begin with the paths passing through the successive vertices 0 1 2. In this case we find three cycles, i.e. 0 1 2 1 0 2 0, 0 1 2 0 2 1 0 and 0 1 2 0 1 2 0. The case where the cycle begins with 010 remains, and we find a single cycle: 0 1 0 2 1 2 0.

Altogether, the number of cycles is four. Doing this, we have considered the double edges as interchangeable: we can also use one of the two edges 0 1 before the other, and it is also valid for 0 2 or 1 2.

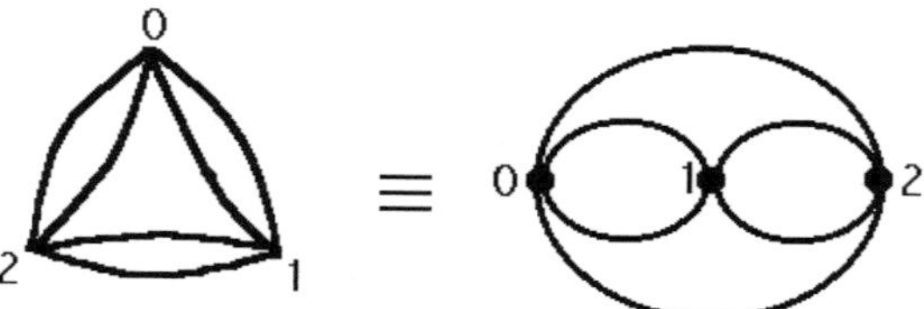

Figure 36.1. *Polygon graph with three vertices and double edges*

Now let us differentiate the three double edges. Having two choices of edges in these three cases, this makes 4 . 8 = 32 cycles starting with one or the other of edges 01. If we now start with edge 02, we also find 32 cycles. Finally, the number of cycles starting at 0 is 64. There would be as many starting from one of the other vertices. This gives 64 starting point-type cycles, and if we are only interested in the shape of these cycles in the sense of traversal-types, there are no more than 32 cycles. This notably applies to the graph in Figure 36.2, with six vertices. It is identical to a triangle with differentiated double edges.

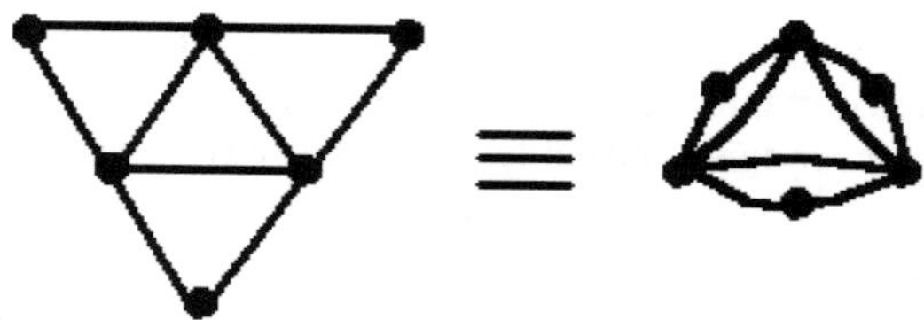

Figure 36.2. *A triangle graph with middle triangles is equivalent to the triangle graph with differentiated double edges*

Now let us take any N and return to the case where we consider the double edges as undifferentiated, starting from one of the two edges 0 1.

If the cycle begins with the succession of all the vertices 0 1 2 3 … (N – 1), the next vertex is either N – 2, which gives a single cycle, or 0 being followed by 1 or N – 1, which produces two cycles. As for N = 3, starting with 0 1 2 3 … (N – 1) always gives three cycles.

The cycle can also begin with the succession 0 1 2 … K (K – 1), where K is included between 1 and N – 2, so each time only one single cycle exists. Hence the total number of cycles starting with one of the edges 0 1: $3 + N - 2 = N + 1$. If we consider the double edges to be different, we get $(N + 1)\, 2^N$ cycles starting with one edge 0 1. There would be as many starting from edge 0 (N – 1).

For example, for $N = 4$ with interchangeable double edges (see Figure 36.3), there are three cycles successively traversing all the vertices (0 1 2 3) and also two cycles, one starting with loop 0 1 0, the other with 0 1 2 1, i.e. five cycles starting from one or the other of edges 0 1. By differentiating the double edges, this gives $5\times16 = 80$ cycles.

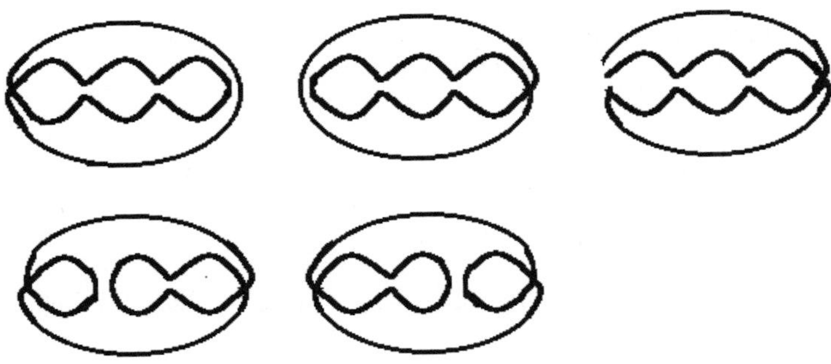

Figure 36.3. *The five core cycles for N = 4. The double edges 0 1, 1 2 and 2 3 are traversed in two directions in four out of five cases*

36.2. Eulerian paths in graph made up of a frieze of triangles

Let us take the graph made up of a strip of identical triangles. The graph of N order has $N + 1$ vertices numbered from 0 to N, alternating above and below (see Figure 36.4 for $N = 7$).

In this type of undirected graph, all the vertices are of even order, except two, and the vertices are called 1 and $N - 1$. Therefore there are Eulerian paths going from vertices 1 to $N - 1$. We have to determine their number $u(N)$. We will show that this sequence obeys the recurrence relation:

$$u(N) = 2\,u(N-1) + 2\,u(N-2)$$

for $N \geq 2$, with $u(0) = 0$ and $u(1) = 1$ initially.

This gives an explicit formula:

$$u(N) = \frac{1}{2\sqrt{3}}((1+\sqrt{3})^N - (1-\sqrt{3})^N)$$

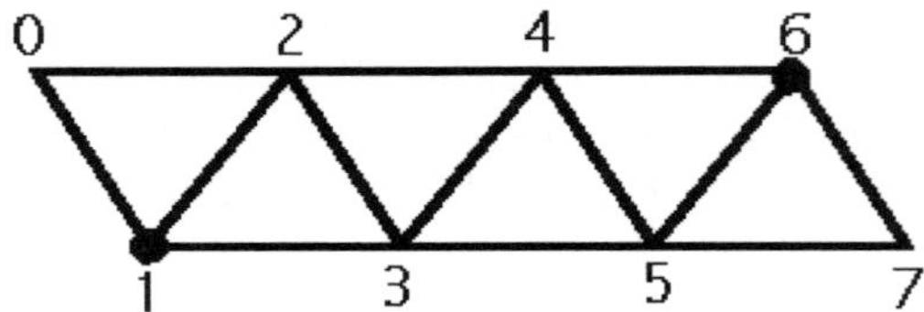

Figure 36.4. *Graph made up of a frieze of triangles, here for $N = 7$, with numbering of the vertices*

Each Eulerian path of the graph of N order is expressed in the form of a word $2N$ characters long based on the $N + 1$ letters from 0 to N, with each letter present twice except for 0 and N, which are present only once.

Let us make an argument using recurrence. Let us start from a Eulerian path on the graph of N order, where vertex N is present once, and vertex $N - 1$ twice, one of which is the last letter of the word. From this Eulerian path of N order, how do we obtain Eulerian paths of $N + 1$ order? The graph of $N + 1$ order contains vertex $N + 1$ and also two edges more, between N and $N + 1$ and between $N - 1$ and $N + 1$. We will obtain the Eulerian paths of $N + 1$ order by attaching the two new edges to vertices N or $N - 1$, the latter being present twice, and the other one single time. We seek to add block $(N + 1, N - 1)$ to vertex N, and we attempt to add block $(N + 1, N)$ to the two vertices $N - 1$.

There are no other choices than the following:

a) We add $(N + 1, N)$ after the last letter $N - 1$ of the path of order N, which always gives a Eulerian path of order $N + 1$.

b) Let us take the other letter $N - 1$ present in the path of N order, i.e. the first one we find in the word, unlike the second one that is always at the end of the word. We distinguish three cases:

- This letter $N - 1$ is preceded by letter N and followed by letter $N - 2$ or $N - 3$. The fact of attaching $N + 1$ and N behind letter $N - 1$, to attempt to move on to the Eulerian path of $N + 1$ order gives the block $N, N - 1, N + 1, N , N - 2$ (or $N - 3$), whereas at the end of the word the block $N - 2, N - 1$ is found, and we will need to add an N in last position to have the path of order $N + 1$. This would make letter N appear three times, i.e. once too many, and there is no possible Eulerian path through this procedure.

- Letter $N - 1$ is followed by N, with the presence of block $N - 1, N$. We therefore replace edge $N - 1, N$ with hook $N - 1, N + 1, N$, then we follow the old path, finally returning to $N - 1$ and adding to it the edge that leads to N.

- Letter $N-1$ is surrounded by letters $N-3$ and $N-2$. In this case, letter N can only be to the right of this letter. If it is found on the left, with its two edges attached, we would have an impossibility. More specifically, letter N can only be linked to $N-1$, and we always have this block N, $N-1$ at the end of the word. In this case, we place hook $N+1$, N behind letter $N-1$, then we add $N-1$ (the one from the end of the word), which enables us to return to what followed letter $N-1$ from the inside, which we resume up to N.

c) Now let letter N be present one single time, and let us add hook $N+1$, $N-1$ to it:

- If we had the succession $N-1, N, N-2$, i.e. a word of the form: $\ldots, N-1, N, N-2, \rightarrow, N-1$, this word becomes: $\ldots N-1, N, N+1, N-1, \leftarrow, N-2, N$, where we reverse the part of the word symbolized by the $\rightarrow$ as well as its extremities $N-2$ and $N-1$, then we add letter N in the last position. This makes a Eulerian path of order $N+1$.

- If in this word we had the succession $N-2, N, N-1$, i.e. the word: $\ldots N-2, N, N-1, \rightarrow, N-1$, we get the new word: $\ldots, N-2, N, N+1, N-1, \rightarrow, N-1, N$.

Here are examples of passage from $N=5$ to $N+1=6$:

$102\underline{45}32134\underline{4}$ gives $102453213\underline{465}$, $102\underline{465}32134\underline{5}$, $1024\underline{56431235}$.

$12013\underline{54}234\underline{4}$ gives $120135423\underline{465}$, $10213\underline{564}234\underline{5}$.

$102\underline{45}31234\underline{4}$ gives $102453123\underline{465}$, $102\underline{465}31234\underline{5}$, $1024\underline{56432135}$.

$13\underline{4}20123\underline{54}$ gives $134201235\underline{465}$, $134\underline{654201235}$, $13420123\underline{5645}$.

This constructive method also enables us to backtrack and move from a Eulerian path of $N+1$ order to the corresponding path of N order.

Let $a(N)$ be the number of Eulerian paths of N order where the first of the two letters $N-1$ is found on the left of the only letter N, and $b(N)$ the one where paths have the block N, $N-1$ inside the word, i.e. somewhere other than at the end of the word. Evidently we have $u(N) = a(N) + b(N)$. On the other hand, the previous construction enables us to affirm that:

$$u(N+1) = 3a(N) + 2b(N)$$

More specifically, from one of the $a(N)$ paths, we always get two paths that are part of the $a(N+1)$ paths, and one that is part of $b(N+1)$, where we form the internal block ($N-1, N+1, N$) with the presence of $N+1, N$. From one of the $b(N)$ paths we always find two of the $a(N+1)$ paths. Hence the recurrence relations:

$$a(N+1) = 2a(N) + 2b(N) \text{ and } b(N+1) = a(N)$$

We deduce from this that $a(N+1) = 2u(N)$ or, if you want, $a(N) = 2\,u(N-1)$.

We also know that:

$$u(N+1) = 3a(N) + 2b(N) = 2a(N) + 2b(N) + a(N) = 2u(N) + a(N)$$

$$= 2u(N) + 2u(N-1)$$

It is sufficient to add the initial conditions to launch the recurrence. The results are given in Table 36.1.

N	0	1	2	3	4	5	6	7
$a(N)$			2	4	12	32	88	240
$b(N)$			0	2	4	12	32	88
$u(N)$	0	1	2	6	16	44	120	328

Table 36.1.

36.3. Algorithm for Eulerian paths and cycles on an undirected graph

For some simple graphs Eulerian paths can be found by a manual search, drawing the arborescence of the paths.

The program that enables us to find all possible Eulerian paths on a computer, including in the case of multigraphs, where two vertices can be joined by several junction edges, results from this.

36.3.1. *The arborescence for the paths*

Let us take the graph formed from two squares placed side by side (see Figure 36.5). The two vertices 1 and 4 are of odd degree and the others of even degree.

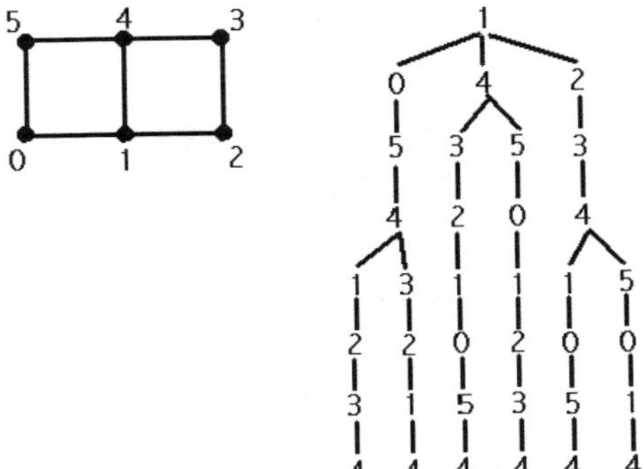

Figure 36.5. *The graph that assumes Eulerian paths from 1 to 4 (left); and the arborescence of Eulerian paths, numbering six (right)*

36.3.2. *Program for enumerating Eulerian cycles*

Let us take the undirected graph in Figure 36.6 as an example, with six vertices numbered from 0 to 5 and 10 edges. Let us first verify that this graph has Eulerian cycles. We notice that the vertices have two or four as their degree. Since the degree of each vertex is even, there are Eulerian cycles.

Now let us move on to the program that will give us all the Eulerian cycles starting at vertex 0 and using edge 0 1 at the start. To construct the tree that will give the Eulerian cycles, we use a recursive function *tree*(*i, level*), with node *i* at a certain level. We therefore take the neighbors of node *i*, first avoiding taking the predecessor of *i* from among them in order to evade traversing the same bidirectional edge twice. We must also refuse to find *edge*(*i, neighbor*) again in the branch that goes back up to the root. To be able to climb back up, we use the predecessors of each level of this branch (see Figure 36.7). From the level numbered *k* which goes from *level* – 1 to 1, we take the edge joining *predecessor*(*k* + 1) to *predecessor*(*k*) and compare it to the one joining neighbor and *i* in one or the other direction. This is what the next function that tests whether the edge between *j* and *jj*, with *j* at the level concerned, is located above (yes or no).

```
int belongstolistofpredecessoredges(int jj, int j, int level)
{ int k;
  for(k=level–1; k>=1; k--)
  if (j==predecessor[k+1] && jj==predecessor[k]
     || jj==predecessor[k+1] && j==predecessor[k])
  return YES;
  return NO;
}
```

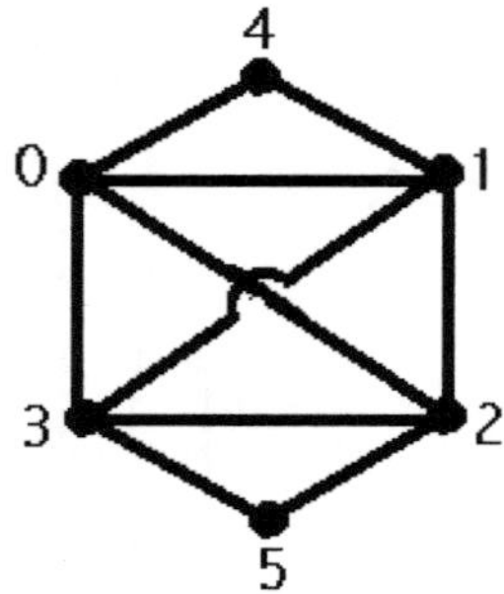

Figure 36.6. *The Eulerian graph taken as an example*

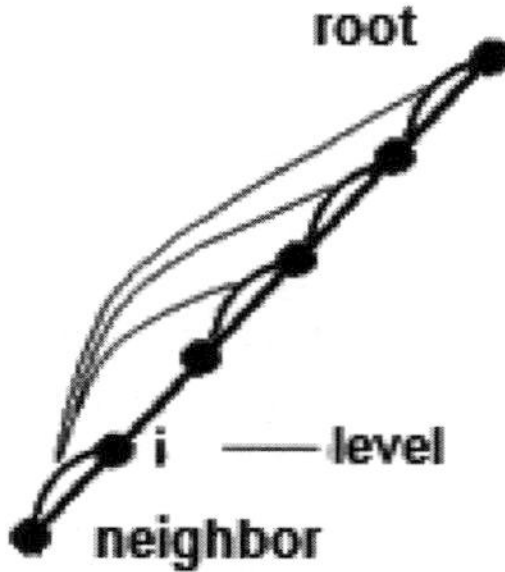

Figure 36.7. *The climb back up in the tree to see whether we find the edge between vertex i and the potential neighbor*

In the main program that follows, we call the function *tree*() from vertex 1, successor of vertex 0, located at level 1.

We obtain 44 Euclidean cycles starting with edge 0 1. We find as many when the first edge traversed is 0 2, and as many from 0 3, as well as with 0 4, i.e. a total of 176 cycles.

With the graph including $NE = 10$ edges, the stop test of function *tree*() is carried out when the $NE - 1^{\text{th}}$ edge is reached during the descent in a branch of the tree. We are therefore sure that the last edge returns to vertex 0, since it is the only vertex where the path passed by an odd number of edges.

Therefore, the arborescence of the paths, starting at level 0, can be stopped at level $NE - 1 = 9$.

The program ensues:

```
main()
{
  /* entry of the graph with the neighbors of each node as well as their number*/
  for(i=0; i<4; i++)
    { k=0;
      for(j=0; j<4; j++) if (i!=j) n[i][k++]=j;}
      for(i=0;i<4;i++) nbn[i]=4;
      n[0][3]=4;n[1][3]=4; n[2][3]=5;n[3][3]=5;
      n[4][0]=0;n[4][1]=1;  n[5][0]=2;n[5][1]=3; nbn[4]=2; nbn[5]=2;
      /* calling the function tree from vertex 1 at level 1 */
     tree(1,1);
      /* we could also do tree(0,0) to get all the solutions */
    }

void tree(int i,int level)
{ if (level==NE-1)
    {  for(k=1; k<=NE−1; k++) printf("%d",predecessor[k]);
       printf("%d",i); }
  else
    { for(j=0; j<nbn[i]; j++)
        { neighbor=n[i][j];
          if (neighbor!=predecessor[level]
              && belongstolistofpredecessoredges(neighbor,i,level)==NO)
            { predecessor[level+1]=i;
              tree(neighbor,level+1);
            }
        }
    }
}
```

Altogether we find 176 Eulerian cycles starting with vertex 0. There are as many starting with each of the four edges coming from vertex 0, i.e. 44 each time.

36.3.3. *Enumeration in the case of multiple edges between vertices*

We will resume an example already seen in a previous chapter, with a square *ACBD* and its two diagonals *AB* and *CD*, one of which – *CD* as it happens – is split into two edges.

This graph, having four vertices and $NE = 7$ edges, has Eulerian paths going from vertices A to B, the only ones of odd degree (see Figure 36.8, left).

A first method consists of adding an artificial vertex on one of the two edges, in such a way as to return to the previous case (see Figure 36.8, right). This gives a graph with five vertices numbered from 1 to 5, and one edge more than before, i.e. $NE + 1 = 8$. The tree for the paths begins at level 0 with vertex 2 as the starting vertex.

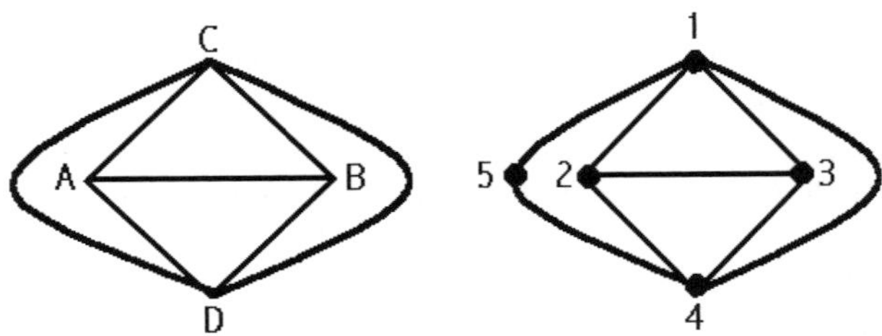

Figure 36.8. *The square graph with its diagonals, one being split (left); and The addition of a vertex to facilitate the search for Eulerian paths (right)*

Hence the main program that gives the adjacency list of the neighbors of each vertex, and calls the function *tree*(2, 0).

```
n[1][0]=2;n[1][1]=3; n[1][2]=4;n[1][3]=5;nbn[1]=4;
n[2][0]=1;n[2][1]=3; n[2][2]=4;nbn[2]=3;
n[3][0]=1;n[3][1]=2; n[3][2]=4;nbn[3]=3;
n[4][0]=1;n[4][1]=2;n[4][2]=3;n[4][3]=5;nbn[4]=4;
n[5][0]=1;n[5][1]=4;nbn[5]=2;
tree(2,0);     printf("\nNumber of cycles: %ld",number);
```

The function *tree*() has the number of vertices *i* and number of the *level* of the tree where it is found as its variables. As for the function *belongstolistofpredecessoredges*(), it is the same as before.

```
void tree(int i, int level)
{ int j,k,neighbor;
  if (level==7)   /* the graph includes NE + 1 = 8 edges */
    { number++; printf("\n%3.ld: ",number);
     for(k=1; k<=7; k++) printf("%d",predecessor[k]);
```

```
        printf("%d",i);
      }
    else
      { for(j=0; j<nbn[i]; j++)
          { neighbor=n[i][j];
            if (neighbor!=predecessor[level] &&
               belongstolistofpredecessoredges(neighbor,i,level)==NO)
               { predecessor[level+1]=i;   tree(neighbor,level+1); }
          }
      }
}
```

This program gives 44 Eulerian paths, of which 16 begin with edge 2 1, 16 beginning with edge 2 4, and 12 starting with edge 2 3, as result.

Another method consists of not differentiating the two edges between 1 and 4. In each Eulerian path this edge will appear twice, which necessitates a modification of the program. First in the adjacency lists of the vertices, the two edges between 1 and 4 are only counted once. Everything happens as if the graph only had six edges instead of $NE = 7$. In the function *tree*(), each path will include seven edges, and we stop at edge 6 after having started at level 0.

It is mainly the function *belongstolistofpredecessoredges*() that has to be modified compared to the previous method.

First we should be able to test the edge between *i* and its predecessor, to compare it to the one between *i* and its potential successor, in the case where it could be 1 4. We can no longer impose *neighbor!=predecessor[level]*. We simply add to the potential *neighbor* a predecessor *predecessor*[*level*+1] in such a way as to test the edges from the level where vertex *i* is found (and no longer from the previous level of that of *i*) and go back up to the root.

On the other hand, we must deal with the case of the double edge 1 4 separately because we accept it is present twice, hence a counter *c*14. If this counter reaches 2, we can no longer accept a new edge 1 4 among the potential neighbors. Hence the following program:

```
main()
{
n[1][0]=2;n[1][1]=3; n[1][2]=4;nbn[1]=3;
n[2][0]=1;n[2][1]=3; n[2][2]=4;nbn[2]=3;
n[3][0]=1;n[3][1]=2; n[3][2]=4;nbn[3]=3;
n[4][0]=1;n[4][1]=2;n[4][2]=3;nbn[4]=3;
```

```
tree(2,0);  printf("\nNumber:%ld",number);
}
void tree(int i,int level)
{ int j,k,neighbor;
  if (level==6)
    { number++;  printf("\n%3.ld: ",number);
      for(k=1; k<=6; k++) printf("%d",predecessor[k]);  printf("%d",i);
    }
  else  for(j=0; j<nbn[i]; j++)
          { neighbor=n[i][j]; predecessor[level+1]= i;
            if (belongstolistofpredecessoredgess(neighbor,i,level)==NO)
              tree(neighbor,level+1);
          }
}

int belongstolistofpredecessorsarcs(int jj,int j, int level)
{ int k,c14=0;
  if ( (j==1 && jj==4)||(j==4 && jj==1) )
   {  for(k=level;  k>=1 k--)
      if (predecessor[k+1]==1 && predecessor[k]==4
         || predecessor[k+1]==4 && predecessor[k]==1) c14++;
      if (c14>1) return YES;
   }
  else for(k=level; k>=1; k--)
     if (j==predecessor[k+1] && jj==predecessor[k]
        || jj==predecessor[k+1] && j==predecessor[k]) return YES;
     return NO;
}
```

This method gives 22 Eulerian paths as a result, half the number of the previous program, which is normal because the two edges 1 4 are not differentiated: we can choose one or the other first in each path.

36.3.4. *Another example: square with double diagonals*

Let us go back to the graph of the complete square with its two diagonals, while splitting two of the opposite sides.

We take four vertices in such a way as not to differentiate the double edges. This graph is in fact an isomorph of the graph made up of the square 0 1 2 3 and its two split diagonals (see Figure 36.9).

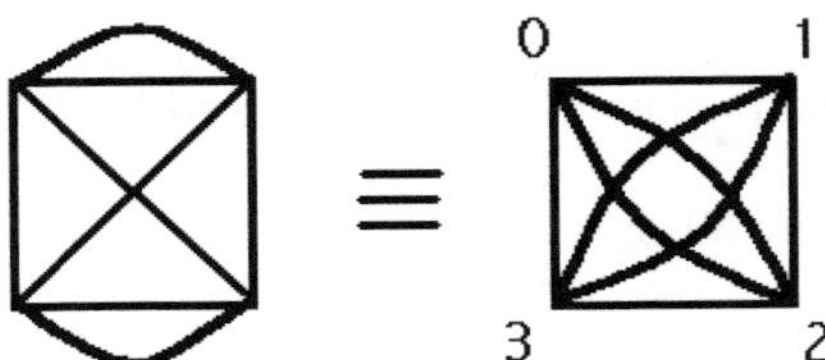

Figure 36.9. *Two representations of the same graph*

Using the previous method, we consider each vertex to have three neighbors and the graph to have eight edges, with edges 0 2 and 1 3 being counted twice but without being differentiated. It is enough for each one to be traversed twice. The main program simply constructs the adjacency lists of each of the four vertices and calls the function *tree*() from vertex 0 and level 0.

```
for(i=0; i<4; i++) { k=0; for(j=0; j<4; j++) if (j!=i) n[i][k++]=j; nbn[i]=3;}
tree(0,0);

void tree(int i,int level)
{ if (level==NE−1)
    { number++;  printf("\n%3.ld: ",number);
      for(k=1; k<=7; k++) printf("%d",predecessor[k]);
      printf("%d",i);
    }
  else  for(j=0; j<nbn[i]; j++)
    { neighbor=n[i][j]; predecessor[level+1]=i;
      if(belongstolistofpredecessoredges(neighbor,i,level)==NO)
       tree (neighbor,level+1);
    }
}

int belongstolistofpredecessoracrs(int jj,int j, int level)
{ int k,c02=0,c13=0;
  if ( (jj==0 && j==2) || (j==0  && jj==2) )
   { for(k=level;k>=1;k--)
     if ((predecessor[k+1]==0 && predecessor[k]==2)
        || (predecessor[k+1]==2 && predecessor[k]==0) )
      c02++;
     if (c02==2)  return YES;
   }
  else if ( (jj==1 && j==3) || (j==1  && jj==3) )
   { for(k=level; k>=1; k--)
```

```
        if ( (predecessor[k+1]==1 && predecessor[k]==3)
            || (predecessor[k+1]==3 && predecessor[k]==1))
          c13++;
        if (c13==2)  return YES;
      }
     else for(k=level; k>=1; k--)
     if (j==predecessor[k+1] && jj==predecessor[k]
         || jj==predecessor[k+1] && j==predecessor[k]) return YES;
   return NO;
   }
```

We find 44 Eulerian cycles starting with vertex 0. If we differentiate the double edges, according to the order in which we take the first then the second, the result must be multiplied by 4, hence 176 cycles. More specifically, if we resume the 44 Eulerian cycles starting with 0, we find 11 of them starting with edge 0 1, as many starting at edge 0 3, and 22 starting at edge 0 2.

It is possible to find this result directly by returning to simple cases. For this, let us separate the circuits according to their start:

– *Cycles starting with edges* 0 1 2. Here we want to find the Eulerian paths from 2 to 0 on the remaining graph, which is drawn in Figure 36.10a. If we consider three edges between 2 and 0 as undifferentiated, there is a single Eulerian path going from 2 to 0, i.e. 2 0 2 0 2 0. But as the edge containing vertices 1 3 is differentiated in this case, we have three paths depending on whether it is taken first, second or third.

– *Cycles starting with edges* 0 1 3. Here we look for the Eulerian paths from 3 to 0 on the remaining graph (see Figure 36.10b). If we do not differentiate the two double edges 0 2 and 2 3, we find four paths from 3 to 0. We must differentiate edge 3 2 passing through vertex 1, however, hence we have eight paths.

We have just found the 11 cycles starting with edge 0 1. There are as many that start with 0 3. Cycles starting at 0 2 remain:

– *Cycles beginning with* 0 2 0. We need to count the Eulerian cycles from 0 to 0 on the remaining graph, with four edges between 3 and 1 (see Figure 36.10c). When we start with vertex 0 on one edge, going towards 1, then three edges are left between 1 and 3, as only one edge containing 2 is differentiated. This gives three cycles returning to 0. We can also start from 0 in the other direction, going towards 3, hence we get three cases again. Finally we find six cycles.

– *Cycles beginning with* 0 2 1. The remaining graph to be traversed is the same as the one with two double edges previously obtained, with one edge to differentiate (see Figure 36.10d). We therefore find eight paths.

As there are also eight cycles starting with 0 2 3, there are 22 cycles where we begin by going from 0 to 2. We have a total of:

$$11 + 11 + 22 = 44 \text{ cycles}$$

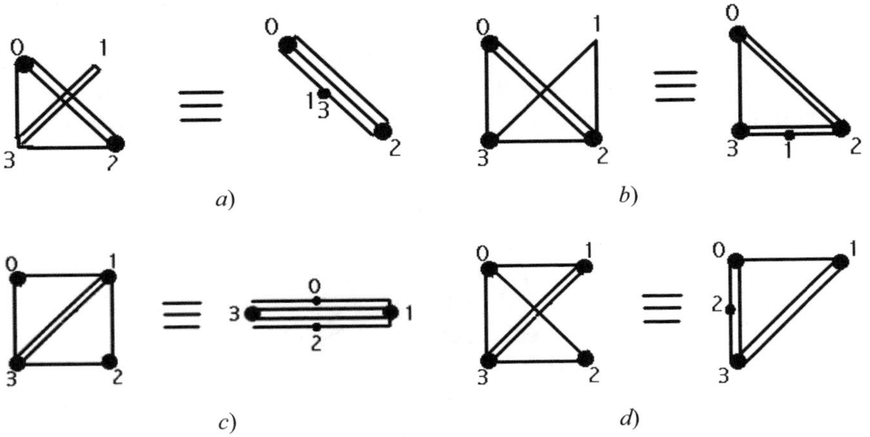

Figure 36.10. *Parts of the remaining graph to traverse in the four cases that are presented, with their simplified equivalents*

36.4. The game of dominos

In this traditional game, a domino carries two numbers between 0 and 6 displayed on each of its two square faces. There are 28 dominos, seven of which have the same numbers on both squares that form them, and $C_7^2 = 7 \,.\, 6 / 2 = 21$ with different numbers. The game consists of aligning them in succession, one after the other, in such a way that two neighboring dominos always have the same number at their junction, for example domino 3-5 followed by domino 5-1. We want to find out how many different layouts are possible, from a first domino followed by all of the others.

36.4.1. *Number of domino chains*

For this, let us construct a graph with seven vertices numbered from 0 to 6, with the edges joining all the vertices two by two, as well as loops at each vertex (see Figure 36.11). It is a complete graph, with the loops in addition.

The 28 edges obtained each correspond to a domino. A valid chain with the 28 dominos aligned constitutes a Eulerian circuit on this graph. As each vertex is of even degree (six if we do not take the loops into consideration), we are assured of the existence of Eulerian cycles. What is left to do is to count them.

Let us start with a simpler problem, with a complete graph with only five vertices. This graph K_5, loopless for the moment, has its vertices numbered from 0 to 4 (see Figure 36.12). Like every complete graph with an odd number of vertices, it has Eulerian cycles because each vertex is of odd degree; four in this case. The number of Eulerian cycles, with the loops in addition on the graph, will give the number of the domino game chains when they have the numbers from 0 to 4.

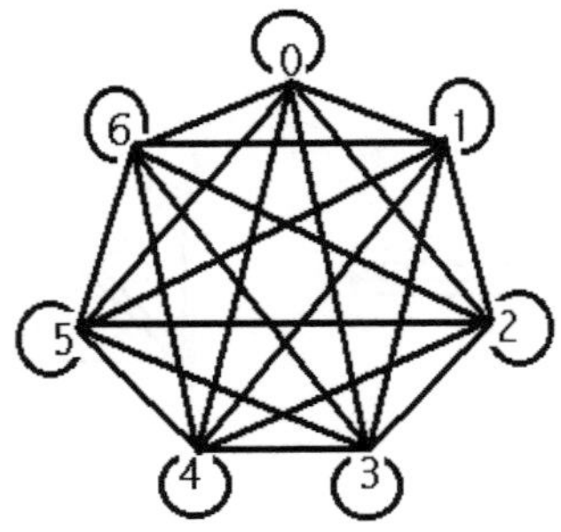

Figure 36.11. *A valid chain of 28 dominos is equal to a Eulerian cycle on this complete graph with seven vertices with loops*

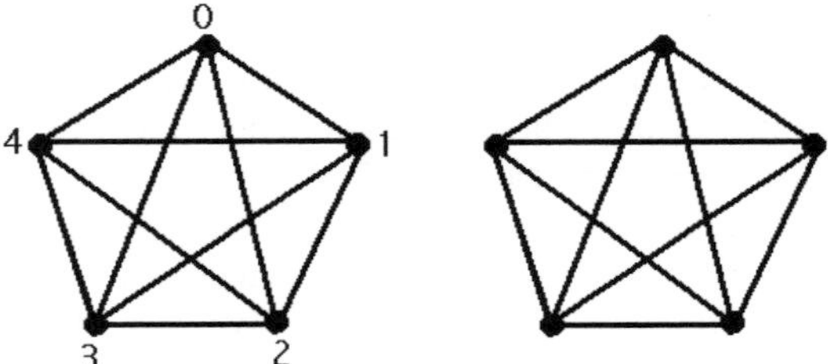

Figure 36.12. *The complete graph K_5 with numbered vertices (left); and its homologue K'_5 without numbering (right)*

To simplify, let us take the complete graph K'_5 where the vertices are no longer numbered. Now the numbering will be done in order of the traversal carried out on this graph.

Let us construct, step-by-step, the Eulerian cycles of K'_5. We start with a vertex, and call it 0. Then we go towards another vertex, also any vertex but it must be different to the one that we have just called 0. We number it 1. Then we go towards a vertex that must be different from those numbered 0 or 1, and we number it 2. To continue, there are two cases: either we return to vertex 0 (we cannot return to 1 or 2) or we go towards a new vertex and we number it 3. We continue in this way: the vertices are numbered in the order where they are reached by the Eulerian cycle. At each stage, either we return to a vertex already reached, on the condition that the corresponding edge has not yet been traversed, or we go towards a new vertex not yet touched. Therefore, either by constructing a search tree or by a program, we find 22 Eulerian cycles on K'_5. This is also proved in the following way, distinguishing two cases:

– *First case*: the cycle begins with 0120. We must then go from 0 to 3 and count the Eulerian paths leading from 3 to 0. The remaining graph is presented as indicated in Figure 36.13a, with three edges to traverse. As these are differentiated, there are three possibilities to choose the first edge, and once this has been chosen, two cases for the second, then a single one for the third, i.e. six paths.

– *Second case*: the cycle begins with 0123. It remains to count the Eulerian paths leading from 3 to 0 on the graph in Figure 36.13b, which we encountered before. We saw that there were four paths from 3 to 0 if we do not differentiate the edges. But here they are differentiated, which makes 4×4 = 16 cycles.

Finally, we find a total of 22 cycles.

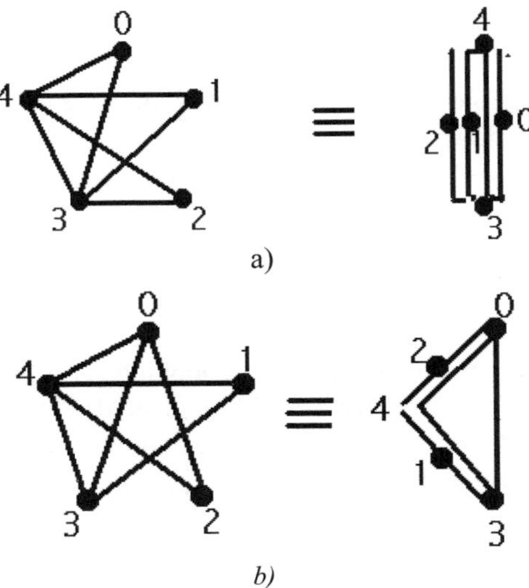

Figure 36.13. *Parts of the graph left to traverse and their simplified equivalents*

Now let us take graph K_5 with numbered vertices, starting from vertex 0. For vertex number 1 of graph K'_5, there are four possible vertices on K_5. Then for vertex number 2 of K'_5, there are three possible vertices on K_5. There are then two for vertex 3 and one for vertex 4. This makes $22\times4\times3\times2 = 528$ cycles starting from 0.

Note that each cycle traverses each vertex twice. Lastly let us add the loops. The loop around 0 can be placed either first, or during the first traversal of vertex 0, or at the end, which gives three cases. As for the loops around the other vertices, they can be placed either during the first traversal of the point, or during the second one, i.e. two cases. This makes $3\times2^4 = 48$ possibilities. Finally, the number of Eulerian cycles on the complete graph with loops is $528\times48 = 25{,}344$ starting at 0. This means that there are 25,344 domino games where we start by placing a domino with a 0 on its left square, the other dominos following on its right. Starting from any number, this result must be multiplied by five.

Let us move on to the case of real dominos with $N = 7$. Placing ourselves on the unnumbered graph K'_7, we find experimentally that the number of Eulerian cycles starting at 0 is 541,568. Starting from the graph numbered K_7, this gives $541568\times6!$ cycles, i.e. 389,928,960 starting from vertex 0. Then adding the loops, we must multiply the previous result by 4×3^6, which gives:

1,137,032,847,360 cycles starting with 0.

To get all the possible domino games, there are seven possible starts, hence a total of 7,959,229,931,520 games.

36.4.2. *Algorithms*

36.4.2.1. *First method*

Let us begin with the exhaustive method, looking for all the Eulerian cycles of the complete graph K_N whose vertices are numbered from 0 to $N - 1$, without placing loops at each vertex. The program that follows gives the way to obtain all the domino games starting with 0 1, and it does not take into consideration the dominos that two numbers that are the same. For $N = 5$, we get 132 games (see Figure 36.14), and for $N = 7$ we get 64,988,160. Then all we have to do is multiply these results by $N - 1$ to get all the games starting with the left square being 0, and we find the previous results.

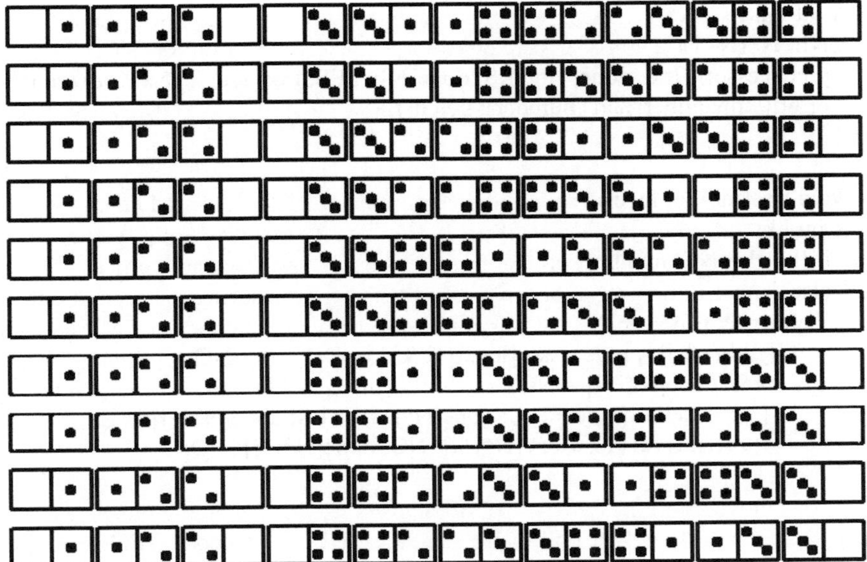

Figure 36.14. *The first 10 of the 132 domino games for N = 5, starting with domino 0-1*

To accelerate the counting, we modified the style of the program slightly. The edges of extremities *i* and *j* (with *i* and *j* between 0 and $N-1$) are numbered with the two numbers $N*i+j$ and $N*j+i$.

We use a table *done*[], the indices of which correspond to the numbers of edges, the content of which is either *YES* or *NO*. At the start this table *NO* is everywhere, then each time an edge is used during the creation of the tree for searching for solutions, its box is set to *YES*.

To avoid this box remaining set to *YES* when a new branch of the tree is explored, where it no longer contains this edge, we reset the box to *NO* using the subtleties of recursivity: *done*[*edge*] = *YES* is in prefixed, *done*[*edge*] = *NO* is in postfixed). Hence the program:

```
#define N 7
#define YES 1
#define NO 0
void tree(int i,int level);
int predecessor[100],NE,done[N*N], number;
main()
```

```
{ int i,j,k;
 NE=N*(N−1)/2;
 predecessor[1]=0; done[1]=YES; done[N]=YES; tree(1,1);  /* we start at 01 */
 printf("\nNumber:%ld",number); getch();
}

void tree(int i,int level)
{ int j,k;
 if (level==NE) number++;
 else
   { for(j=0; j<N; j++)
     if (j!=i && j!=predecessor[level] && done[N*j+i]==NO
        && done[N*i+j]==NO)
        { predecessor[level+1]=i; done[N*j+i]=YES; done[N*i+j]=YES;
          tree(j, level+1);  done[N*j+i]=NO; done[N*i+j]=NO;
        }
   }
}
```

36.4.2.2. *Second method*

Now let us return to the method where the vertices are numbered in the order they are reached, with loopless graph K'_N. For $N = 5$, we get the search tree in Figure 36.15, with its 22 solutions.

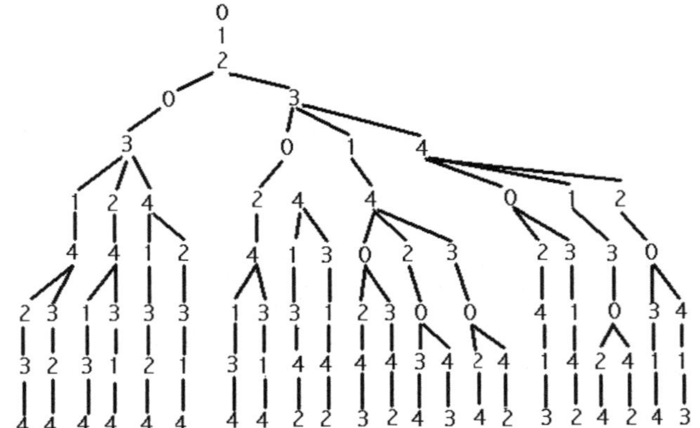

Figure 36.15. *Arborescence of Eulerian paths starting at 0 1 for N = 5, or corresponding domino chains*

For the program, we can start at level 2 by calling the function *tree*(2,2). We must now run a variable *max*[*level*] in such a way that the successor for which we are searching for the level below, is less than or equal to *max*[*level*] + 1, while being different from node *i* at the level we are currently at, and also different from the *predecessor* of the level.

```
#define N 7          /* preliminary declarations */
#define NE (N*(N–1)/2)
#define YES 1
#define NO 0
void tree(int i,int level);
int belongstolistofpredecessoredges(int jj,int j, int level);
int predecessor[NE];int max[NE]; long int number=0;
main()
{ predecessor[1]=0;  predecessor[2]=1; max[2]=2;
  tree(2,2);  printf("%ld",number);
}

void tree(int i,int level)
{ int j,k,neighbor;
  if (level==NE-1)  number++;
  else
   { for(j=0; j<N; j++)
     if (j!=i && j!=predecessor[level] && j<=max[level]+1)
      { neighbor=j;
        if ( belongstolistofpredecessoredges(neighbor,i,level)==NO)
          { predecessor[level+1]=i;
            if (neighbor>max[level]) max[level+1]=neighbor;
            else max[level+1]=max[level];
            tree(neighbor,level+1);
          }
      }
   }
}

int belongstolistofpredecessoredges(int jj,int j, int level)
{ int k;
  for(k=level; k>=2; k--)
  if (j==predecessor[k–1] && jj==predecessor[k]
     || jj==predecessor[k–1] && j==predecessor[k]) return YES;
  return NO;
}
```

Thus we find 22 cycles for $N = 5$, and 541,568 for $N = 7$.

36.4.2.3. *New simplification*

To simplify again, we can group the results above into classes. Let us take the case where $N = 5$, with the first of the 22 Eulerian cycles obtained being: 0 1 2 0 3 1 4 2 3 4. Let us recall that the vertices are numbered according to the order in which they are reached for the first time.

This same cycle can be re-written by moving it one notch, i.e. 1 2 0 3 1 4 2 3 4 0. Now let us renumber the vertices in the order they are taken from 0, which gives the following conversion: 0 1 2 3 0 4 1 3 4 2 (see Figure 36.16). We thus find another of the 22 cycles previously obtained.

Performing 10 cyclic shifts like this on the initial word 10 characters, we get 10 cycles that are equivalent to it. In the example chosen, these 10 cycles are all expressed differently, and they are 10 cycles out of the 22 that we had before.

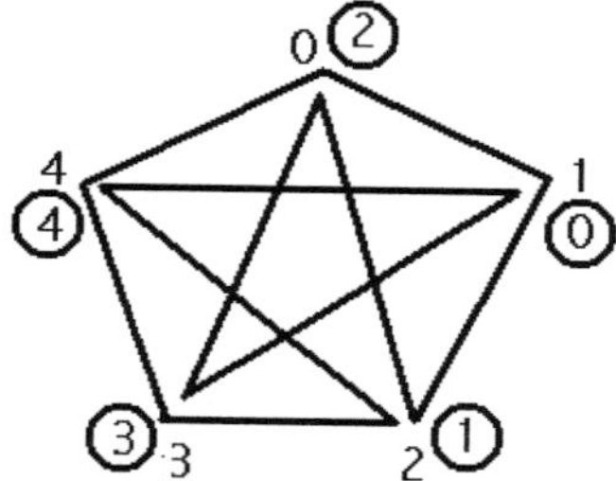

Figure 36.16. *Renumbering of a Eulerian cycle : 1 2 0 3 1 4 2 3 4 0 is transformed into 0 1 2 3 0 4 1 3 4 2*

Next let us take cycle 0 1 2 0 3 1 4 3 2 4, not previously found. Performing 10 cyclic shifts, this again gives 10 different cycles out of the 22. Lastly, let us take one of the two remaining cycles 0 1 2 0 3 2 4 3 1 4. During the 10 shifts, we only find two equivalent cycles.

Finally, thanks to this grouping in classes, we find only three non-equivalent (non-isomorphic) Eulerian cycles given by the words of 10 characters:

0 1 2 0 3 1 4 2 3 4, 0 1 2 0 3 1 4 3 2 4, 0 1 2 0 3 2 4 3 1 4

36.5. Congo graphs

Let us resume the sand drawings as they existed in Africa, especially in the Congo or in Angola (see [GER 95, ZAS 95]). In most cases the graph used starts with a square network of points inscribed in a rectangle. This rectangle has m and n points on its sides, its length therefore being $m - 1$ and its width being $n - 1$. These points are then joined by diagonal edges. Everything happens as if we had a rectangular chessboard on which we would place the movements of the bishop. The graph obtained is then split into two graphs, $P(m, n)$ and $I(m, n)$, with the first one taking points with coordinates of the same parity as vertices, and the second taking points without the same parity, as if we were separating the white squares from the black ones on the chessboard (see Figure 36.17).

It is easy to check that for m and n of different parity, as in the example in Figure 36.17, the two graphs $P(m, n)$ and $I(m, n)$, which are identical (isomorphs), accept Eulerian paths but not cycles. It is the same thing when m and n are both even. But when m and n are both odd, $I(m, n)$ assumes Eulerian cycles, whereas $P(m, n)$ assumes neither cycles nor paths. They are the many configurations allowing Eulerian cycles or paths that produce a multitude of drawings in the sand.

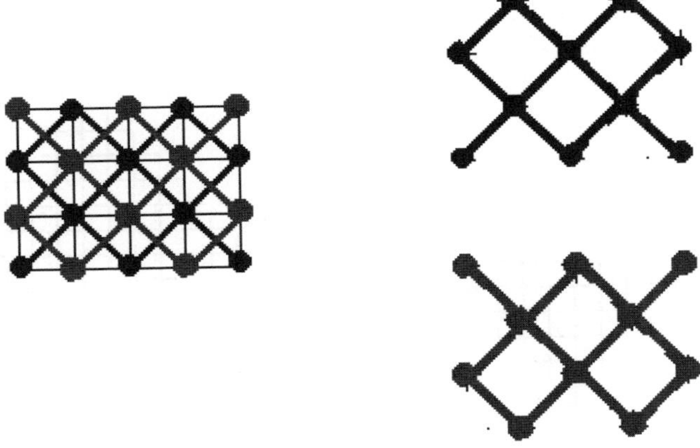

Figure 36.17. *From the bishop's graph on the 4×3 chessboard, graphs P(5, 4) and I(5, 4)*

Two types of drawing essentially stand out from these games (see Figure 36.18). They are Eulerian paths on graphs $P(N + 1, N)$ and $P(2N, N)$. Other drawings, especially on embroidered fabrics dating from the 17th century, make reference to Eulerian cycles on graphs $I(2N + 1, 2N - 1)$ or even $I(2N + 1, 2N + 1)$, the latter being called Aztec diamonds elsewhere.

The Bakuba children of the Congo (see Chapter 1), wanting to preserve the secret of their paths in the sand, drew them so skillfully that in the end it was not known how the drawing had been constructed.

It is the same thing when we observe a drawing programmed on the computer and immediately executed on the screen, like those in Figure 36.18. To understand the progressive creation of such drawings, we have to ask how to make a Eulerian path or cycle visible. On this subject there are two methods, already commonly present in African tradition. One consists of smoothing things over with each change of direction. The other consists of making braids, making a path pass over or under another at each crossroads. A perfect over-under alternation is possible, especially on graphs $I(2N+1, 2N-1)$, and this is found in African embroidered fabrics.

For sand drawings, only one or a few Eulerian paths are chosen. The simplest, and also most aesthetic path, is the one that presents the most symmetries and the fewest changes in direction. Variations that destroy the too perfect symmetries are then introduced. Braiding notably corresponds to a break in symmetry, but in aid of an over-under repetition. Before studying the two types of Congo graphs, let us begin with a simple case.

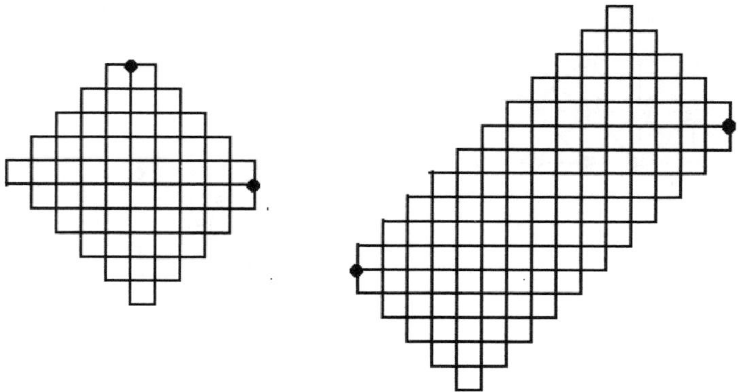

Figure 36.18. *The two types of drawings, the first being P(13, 12) and the second being P(24, 12)*

36.5.1. *A simple case: graphs P(2n, 5)*

These graphs have the shape indicated in Figure 36.19. They have two vertices of odd degree, namely vertex 0 and vertex $4N$.

The aim is to obtain all the Eulerian paths from 0 to $4N$.

Here is the program that enables us to obtain them:

```
main()
{
NV=5*N; NE=4*(2*N-1);  /* number of vertices and number of edges */
for(i=0; i<NV; i++)   /*  neighbors of each node   */
  { k=0;
    if (i<NV–N && i%(2*N)<2*N-1) n[i][k++]=i+N+(i/N)%2;
    if (i/N>0 && i%(2*N)<2*N-1) n[i][k++]=i-N+(i/N)%2;
    if (i<NV–N && i%(2*N)>0) n[i][k++]=i+N+(i/N)%2-1;
    if (i/N>0 && i%(2*N)>0) n[i][k++]=i-N+(i/N)%2-1;
    nbn[i]=k;
  }
for(i=0; i<NV; i++)   /* coordinates of the NV vertices, with the drawing in
                         mind */
      { x[i]=xo+step*(i%N)+step*(i/N)-step*(i/(2*N));
        y[i]=yo+step*(i%N)-step*(i/(2*N));
      }
pred[0]=-1;
tree(0,0);   /*  calling the function creating Eulerian paths  */
}

void tree(int i, int level)
{ if (level==NA–1)
      { number++;
        for(k=1; k<=level; k++) v[k-1]=pred[k];
        v[level]=i; v[level+1]=4*N;
      }

else
     {  for(j=0; j<nbn[i]; j++)
          {neighbor=n[i][j];
           if (neighbor!=pred[level]
              && belongstolistofprededges(neighbor,i,level)==0)
                { pred[level+1]=i; tree(neighbor,level+1); }
          }
     }
}

int belongstolistofprededges(int n, int i, int level)
{ if (level==0) return NO;
   for(k=1; k<=level; k++)
     { if (pred[k]==n  && pred[k–1]==i) return YES;
       if (pred[k]==i  && pred[k–1]==n) return YES;
```

```
    }
  return NO;
  }
```

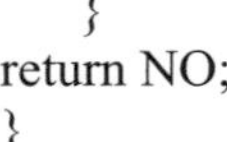

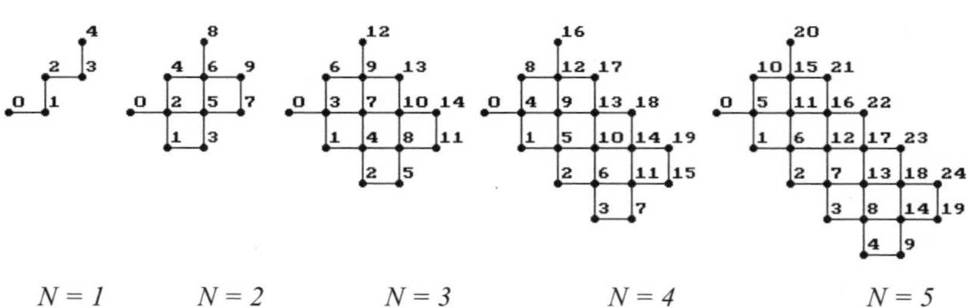

Figure 36.19. *Graphs P(2N, 5)*

We obtain the following results, as well as the drawings in Figure 36.20

N	1	2	3	4	5	6	7
Number of Eulerian paths	1	16	304	5,824	111,616	2,139,136	40,996,864

Table 36.2.

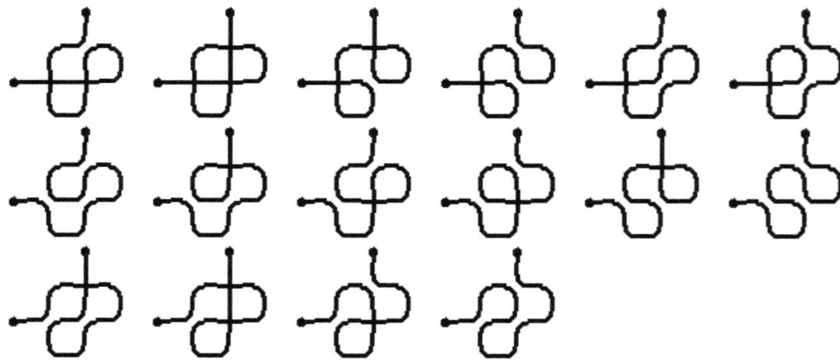

Figure 36.20. *The 16 Eulerian paths for N = 2. It is noteworthy that the second path has three crossroads at right angles, the maximum possible. It is the main path and the one on which Congo drawings are based. It is also this that enables us to create braiding*

Among these paths, those that present a diagonal symmetry axis are particularly interesting (see Figure 36.21). It is easy to check that during the passage from one value of N to the next, their number is multiplied by four each time. The number of these symmetrical graphs is 4^{N-1}.

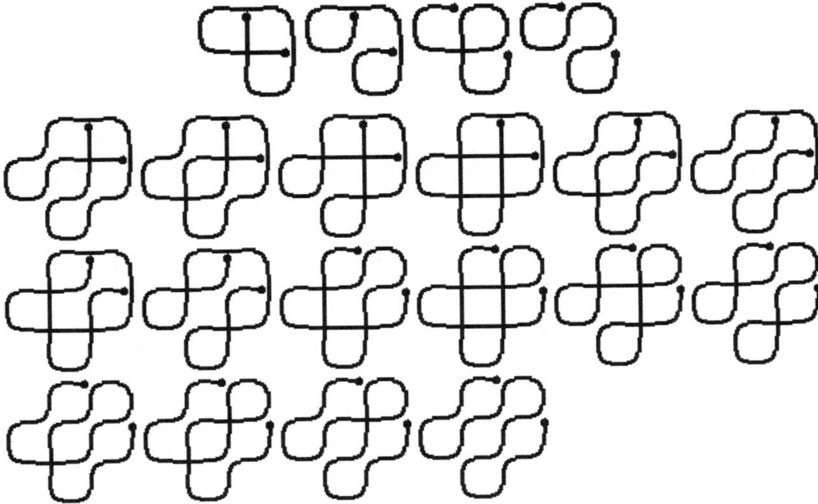

Figure 36.21. *The four symmetrical graphs for N = 2 (first line), and below the 16 that result from them for N = 3 (the fourth being the main Eulerian path)*

On graph $P(2N, 5)$, let us take the sub-graph made up of vertices of degree 4 with its corresponding edges. This sub-graph is graph $P(2N-2, 3)$ which we check is bipartite. This enables us to separate the vertices into two categories. Some are marked // and the others \\, which enables us to create braiding (see [ARF 04]).

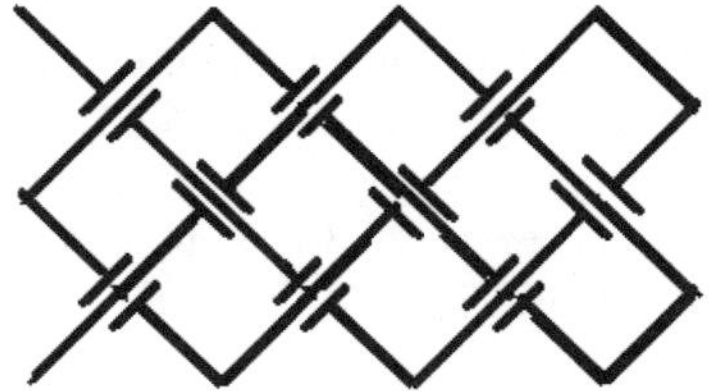

Figure 36.22. *Graph P(8, 5) and bipartite sub-graph P(6, 3) with its vertices // and \\, which enables braiding*

36.5.2. *The first type of Congolese drawings, on P(n + 1, n) graphs, with their Eulerian paths*

The shape of these graphs is given in Figure 36.23 and some drawings are presented in Figure 36.24, in the case where they have a diagonal axis of symmetry. Table 3.3 gives the experimental results of these graphs.

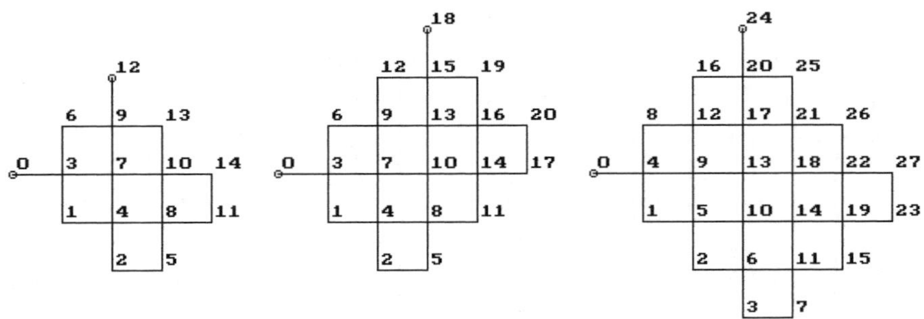

Figure 36.23. *Graphs P(N + 1, N) for N = 5, 6 and 7*

N	4	5	6	7	8
Number of Eulerian paths	16	304	19,856	3,366,208	
Number of symmetrical paths	4	16	176	2,624	46,592

Table 36.3. *Experimental results*

36.5.3. *The second type of Congolese drawings, on P(2N, N) graphs*

These have the characteristic that they assume an axis of symmetry for odd *N*, and a center of symmetry for even *N* (see Figure 36.25).

A few results will be found (see Table 36.4), as well as drawings obtained by the program (see Figures 36.26 and 36.27).

N	2	3	4	5	6
Eulerian paths	1	4	328	111,616	
Symmetrical paths			16		14,336

Table 36.4. *Results of the Congolese drawings*

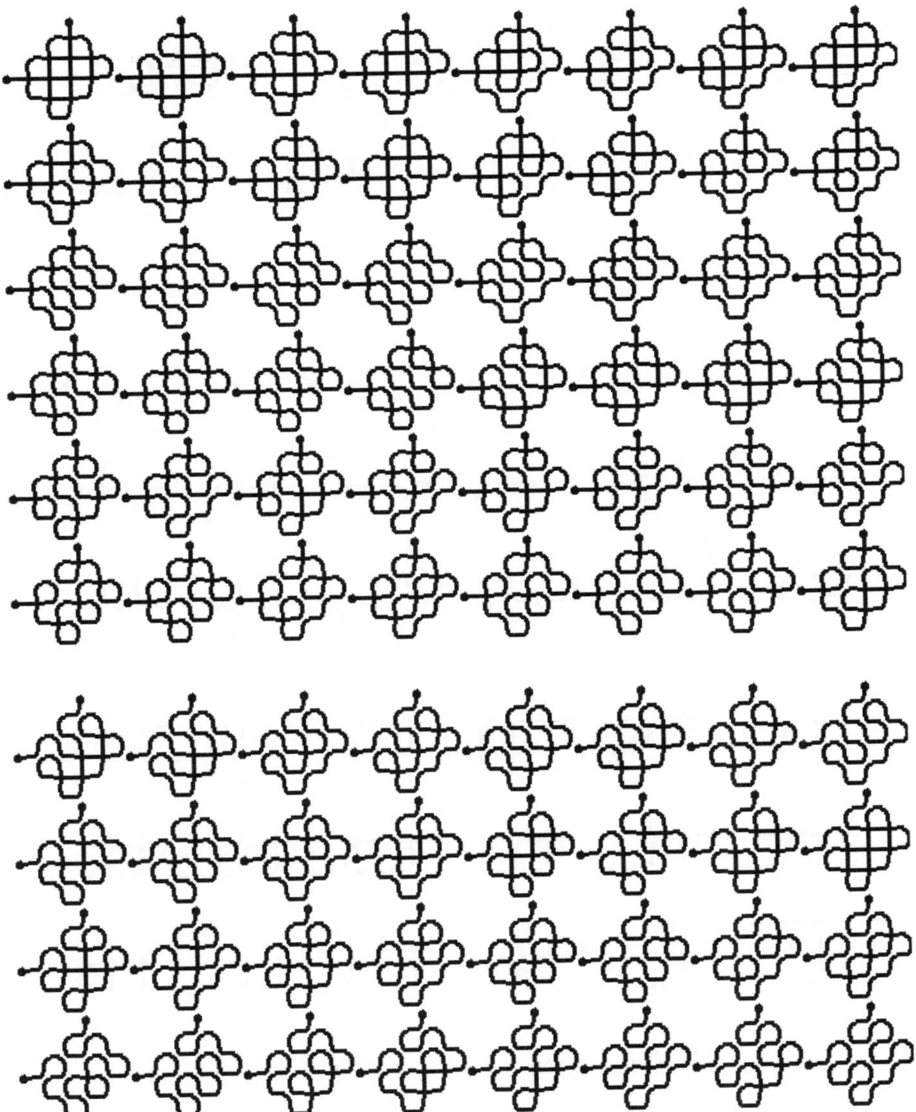

Figure 36.24. *For N = 6 (7×6 rectangle), the first and last of the 176 Eulerian paths assume an axis of symmetry*

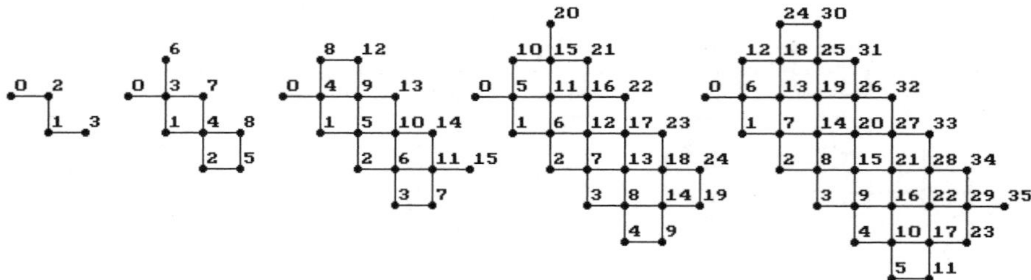

Figure 36.25. *Graphs P(2N, N) for N = 2, 3, 4, 5 and 6*

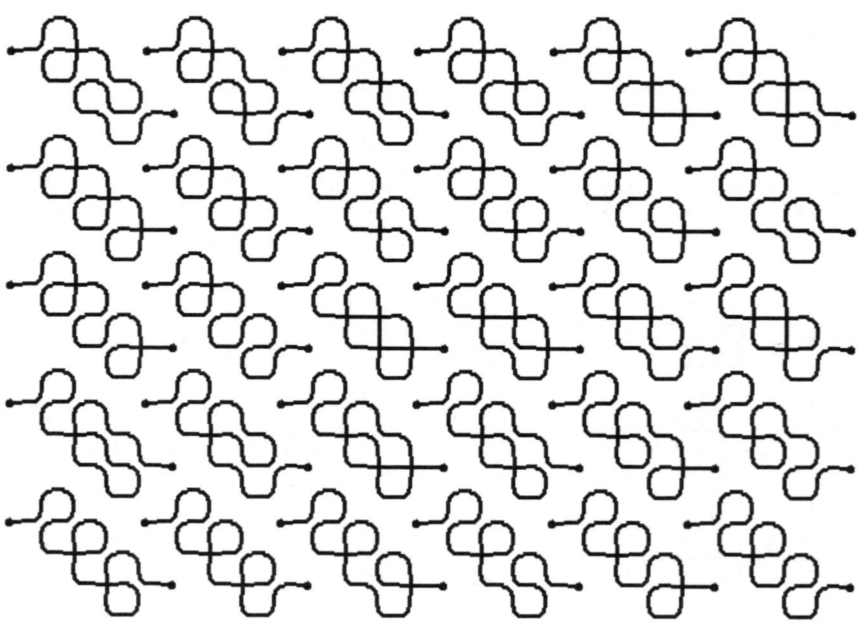

Figure 36.26a. *A few of the Eulerian paths on graphs P(2N, N) for N = 4*

Figure 36.26b. *The 16 symmetrical Eulerian paths through a half-turn for N = 4*

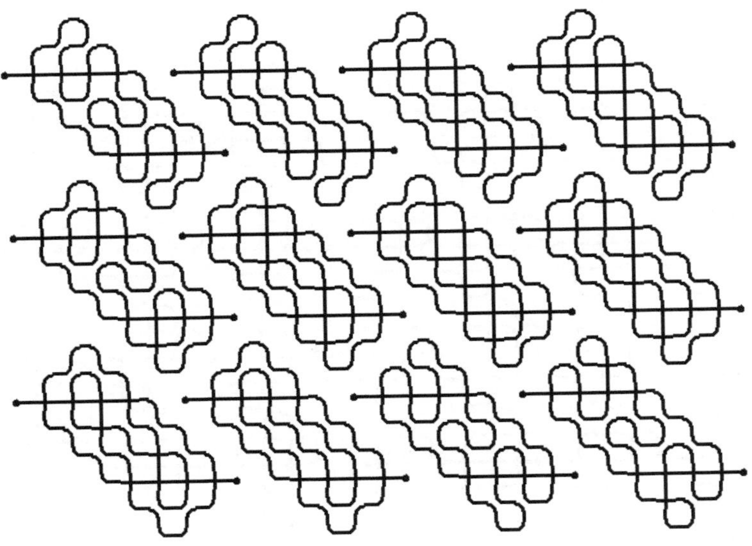

Figure 36.27. *A few of the 14,336 symmetrical paths for N = 6*

36.5.4. *Case of Eulerian cycles on P(2N + 1, 2N – 1) graphs*

We will simply give the shape of these graphs (see Figure 36.28) as well as a few experimental results in the form of drawings (see Figures 36.29 and 36.30) preferring those presenting symmetries.

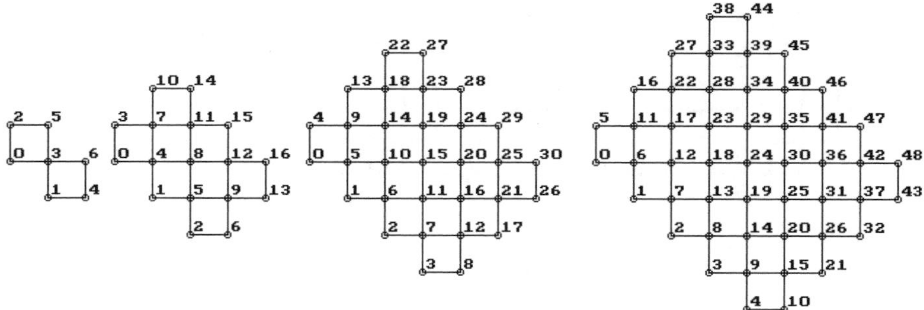

Figure 36.28. *Graphs P(2N + 1, 2N – 1) for N =2, 3, 4 and 5*

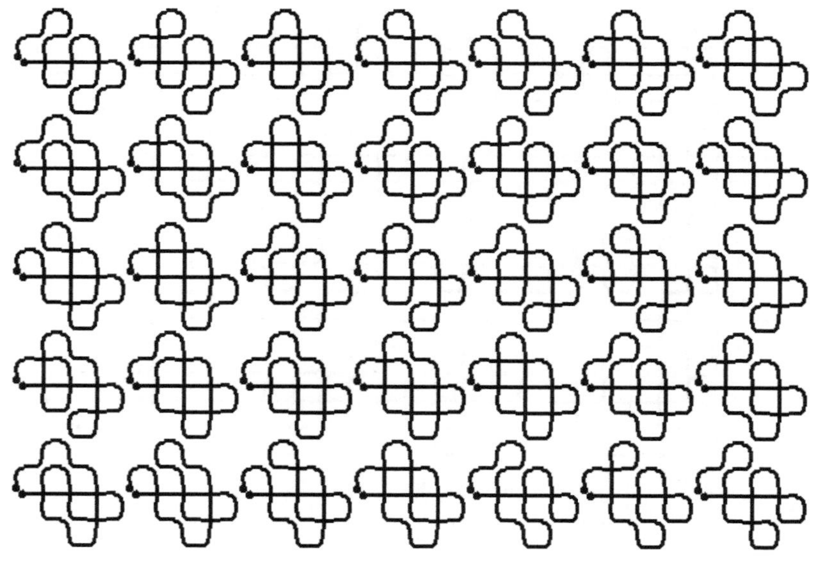

Figure 36.29a. *For N = 3 a few of the 768 Eulerian cycles starting with edge 0 4. There are also 768 cyclic patterns (at the starting point and in the traversal-type direction)*

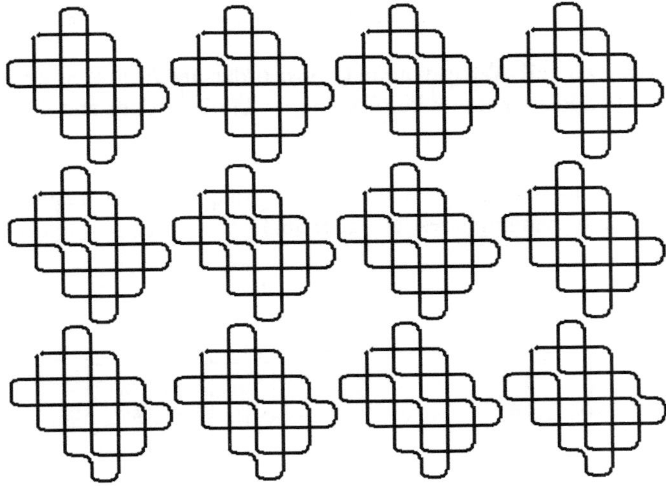

Figure 36.29b. *Still for N = 4, a few of the 7,168 Eulerian cycles with axial symmetry, the first of these patterns being a classic of African embroidery (it also has central symmetry)*

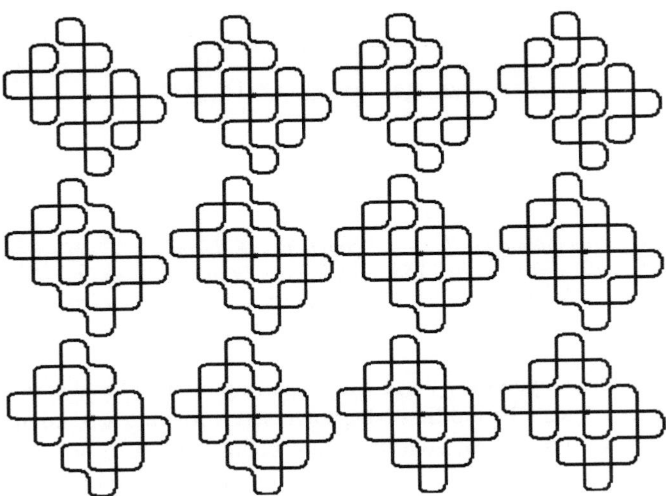

Figure 36.30. *A few of the 2,576 Eulerian cycles with a central symmetry (180° rotation) for N = 4; the second to last is found especially among classic African patterns*

36.5.5. *Case of I(2N + 1, 2N + 1) graphs with their Eulerian cycles*

The patterns we call Aztec diamonds of n order are $I(2n + 1, 2n + 1)$ graphs. They are inscribed in a square, with $((2n + 1)^2 - 1) / 2$ vertices and $4n^2$ edges. They are Eulerian graphs.

For the first values of n, we will see their shape and the results in terms of Eulerian cycles and spanning trees in Figure 36.31.

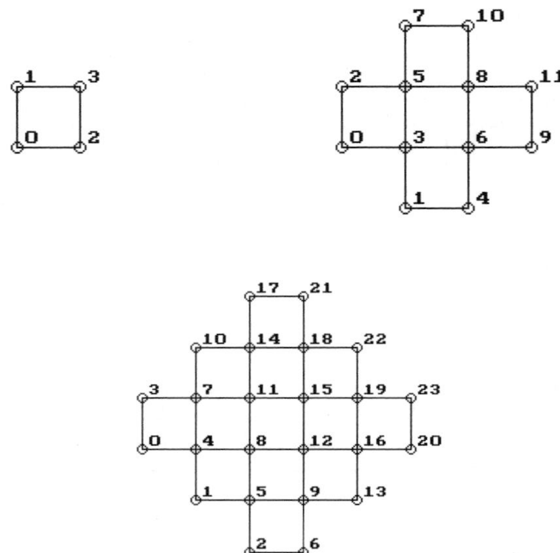

Figure 36.31. *Aztec diamonds, for n = 1 (top left), a Eulerian cycle and 4 spanning trees for n = 2, 40 Eulerian cycles and 768 spanning trees (top right); and for n = 3, 132,160 Eulerian cycles and 18,170,880 spanning trees (bottom)*

Here the Eulerian cycles are those whose starting point is fixed at 0, the vertex of degree 2, of which we take the first edge traversed from vertex 0, i.e. the horizontal edge, with the second vertical edge therefore being the last to be traversed. In the end, they are all Eulerian cycles, at the starting point and in the direction of traversal type (see Figure 36.32, top).

If we were to differentiate the cycles according to their direction of traversal, we would have twice as many cycles (80 for n = 2). If, in addition, we take the symmetries of the square presented by the Aztec diamonds (four rotations and four reflections), the number of cyclic patterns obtained is quite a bit less.

For example, for $n = 2$ on the 40 Eulerian cycles, only eight symmetry-types of the square are left (see Figure 36.32, bottom).

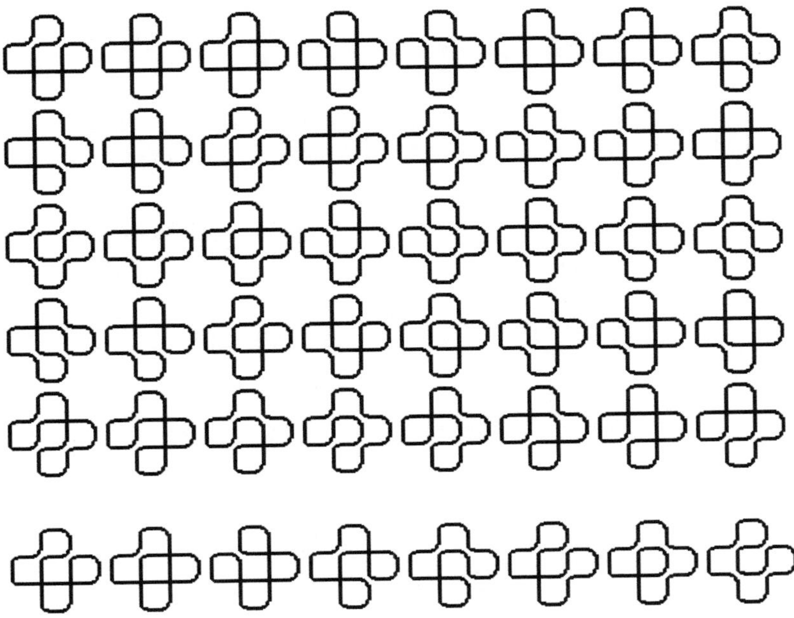

Figure 36.32. *The 40 Eulerian cycles (arbitrary starting point and direction of traversal) for n = 2 (top); and the eight symmetry-type of the square Eulerian patterns (six of them already with an axis of symmetry gives four Eulerian cycles each by rotations, the two remaining give eight cycles by rotations and reflections) (bottom)*

Chapter 37

Hamiltonian Paths and Circuits

We say that a graph assumes a Hamiltonian circuit (or cycle) when, from a starting vertex, following the edges or arcs, passing through each vertex once and only once, we finally end up at the starting point. More widely, we speak of a Hamiltonian path if this path passes once and only once through each vertex, without returning to its starting point. Therefore, while it was edges for Euler, it is vertices for Hamilton. Indeed it is William Hamilton who, throughout the 19th century, between his mathematical theoretical research, commercialized a puzzle based on a graph representing a regular dodecahedron, where a person had to find all the paths passing through each vertex once and returning to the starting point. The 20 vertices were supposed to represent 20 cities, according to the diagram in Figure 37.1.

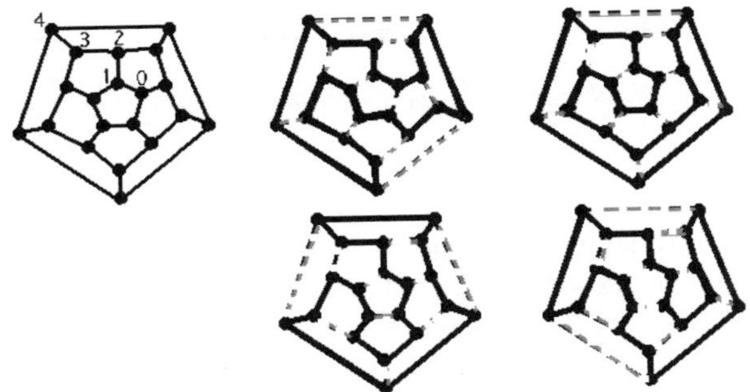

Figure 37.1. *William Hamilton's "Icosian" game, and the four Hamiltonian cycles obtained using the succession of vertices 0 1 2 3 and 4 at the start*

Unlike Eulerian cycles and paths, there is no property enabling us to conclude in general the presence of Hamiltonian cycles or paths. Except in certain specific cases, an exhaustive search is generally imposed. To a certain extent, it is about taking all the permutations of N graph vertices, i.e. $N!$ cases, and seeing the ones among them that can eventually give a Hamiltonian path, depending on the presence or absence of junction edges. Let us note that the more vertices of a high degree a graph has, the greater the chance of obtaining a Hamiltonian circuit or path. It has been shown that if a graph with N vertices, connected, loopless and without multiple edges, is such that each vertex has a degree greater than or equal to $N / 2$, it has a Hamiltonian circuit. But this constraint is not often present. In certain specific cases, we can nevertheless conclude whether Hamiltonian circuits exist or not.

37.1. Presence or absence of Hamiltonian circuits

37.1.1. *First examples*

To show that a graph does not have a Hamiltonian cycle, we consider the cycle, if it existed, as having to traverse the vertices of two degrees, which renders passing along certain edges obligatory, eventually ending up with a contradiction as regards to the presence of a Hamiltonian cycle. Of the four example graphs in Figure 37.2, only the first assumes a Hamiltonian circuit. The three others do not have one as the edges of obligatory passage, marked on the drawings, do not allow the presence of a cycle.

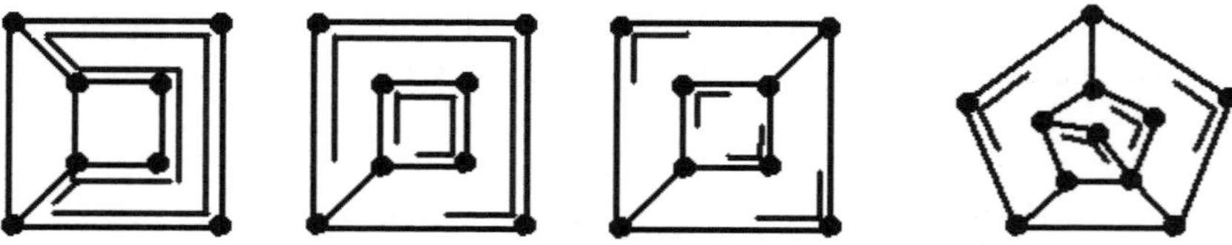

Figure 37.2. *Four graph examples, where only the first has a Hamiltonian circuit*

Another example is called Mr Mu's journey (see [BER 67]). On an 8×8 chessboard, let us consider a particle (or Mr Mu) that can move from one square to a neighboring square in one of the four directions *S*, *N*, *W* or *E*. The separation between white squares and black squares creates a bipartite graph. We want the particle to pass through each square once and only once, and we want it to go from the top left corner of the chessboard to the opposite corner, in the bottom right, which would constitute a Hamiltonian path. Is this possible? The answer is no.

There are 64 squares and the particle should make 63 steps to cover the chessboard, i.e. an odd number of steps. In one step we move from a white square to a black square or *vice versa*. Every other step, we are on the same color. When we go from one corner to the opposite corner, which is necessarily the same color, an even number of steps is necessary. This is a contradiction.

37.1.2. *Hamiltonian circuits on a cube*

Let us take a cube whose vertices are numbered from 0 to 7 (see Figure 37.3). When we start from vertex 0 and use either edge 0 1 or 0 3 or 0 4, we find a total of 12 Hamiltonian circuits, as indicated in Figure 37.3. Let us specify that in this counting, only the shape and direction of the circuit come into play, with the starting point (0 or any other vertex) finally being of little importance.

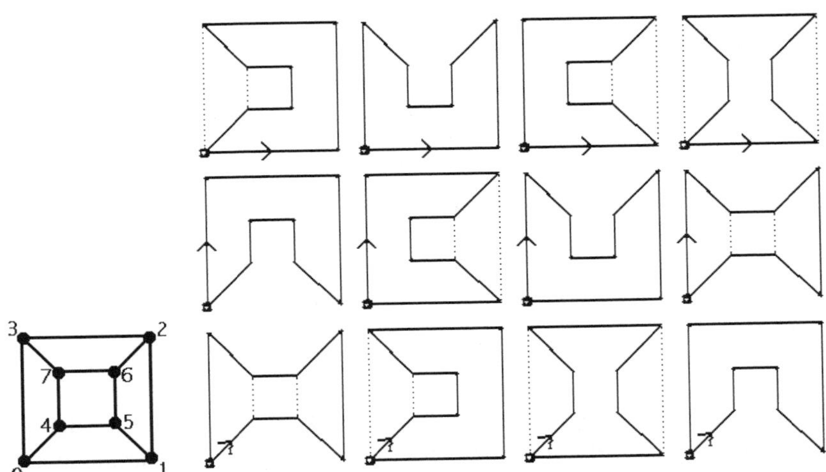

Figure 37.3. *The cube graph (left); and the 12 Hamiltonian circuits (right)*

Let us write the program that enables us to arrive at this result. The arborescence of paths is obtained by starting at vertex 0. Then we take the neighbors of the successive vertices, avoiding having the same vertex a second time on a branch of the tree. This is thanks to the function testing the belonging of an eventual successor to the list of predecessors. We stop when we obtain the eighth vertex, i.e. when the tree level reaches $N - 1 = 7$, where N is the number of graph vertices, provided that the last vertex obtained is a neighbor of vertex 0, i.e. 1, 3 or 4.

```
main()
{ record the three neighbors n[i][j] of each vertex with i from 0 to 7 and j from 0
  to 2, then the coordinates of the 8 vertices for the drawings on the screen
  number=0;
  pred[1]=0;    /* we will call function tree from the three neighbors of
                   vertex 0 */
  for(i=0; i<3; i++) tree(n[0][i],1);
  display number, which is the number of Hamiltonian circuits
}

void tree(int i,int level)
{ if (level==N−1 && (i==1 || i==3 || i==4))  /* we see to it that the last vertex
                                   is one of the three neighboring vertices of 0 */
    { number++;
      display the list of vertices by taking the predecessors of each level
    }
   else for(j=0; j<3; j++)
    { neighbor=n[i][j];
      if (belongstolistofpredecessors(neighbor,level)==NO)
          {pred[level+1]=i; tree(neighbor,level+1); }
    }
}

int belongstolistofpredecessors(int jj, int level)
{ for(k=level; k>=1; k--)  if (jj==pred[k])  return YES;
  return NO;
}
```

If we change the starting point, we always find 12 circuits, which are the same as the previous vertex shift-type ones. There are therefore 12 starting point-type Hamiltonian circuits, with a certain direction of traversal. If we consider the circuits as being able to be used in one direction or the other, only half of them are left. There are therefore six starting point-type and direction of traversal-type Hamiltonian circuits.

More specifically, let us take the four circuits using edge 0 1 at the start. Two of them return to the end through edge 3 0, i.e. in 0: ↓→ , and the two others return through edge 4 0, i.e.: ↙→ at 0. Let us add the two paths obtained by diagonal symmetry of the second case above and starting on edge 0 3: ↑↙. This gives six different circuits, and if we change their direction of traversal we obtain six other ones, which gives all the circuits. Deleting the direction of traversal, we find the six starting point- and direction of traversal-type circuits.

Lastly, if we are only interested in the shape of the symmetry-type of the square circuits, only two circuit shapes remain (see Figure 37.4).

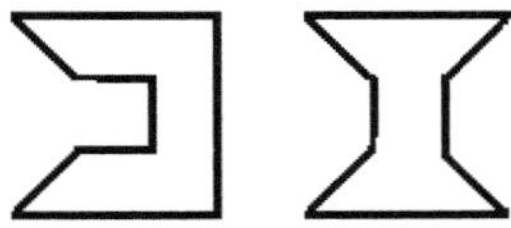

Figure 37.4. *The two shapes of Hamiltonian circuits on the cube*

37.1.3. *Complete graph and Hamiltonian circuits*

Let us take the complete graph K_N with N vertices. Clearly it has $N!$ Hamiltonian circuits, as many as there are permutations of the N vertices. If we consider the starting point does not matter, we can decide to start at a specific vertex and there are only $(N-1)!$ circuits. Lastly, if we assume that the direction of traversal has no importance, only $(N-1)!\,/\,2$ Hamiltonian circuits are left.

To make the program giving these starting point- and at the direction of traversal-type circuits, we decide to start from vertex 0 and construct the arborescence of paths from there. When the tree level reaches $N-1$, we stop and only take the cases where the last vertex has a number greater than that of the following vertex at 0 in the branch of the tree concerned, hence the test *pred*[2] < *i* in the program that follows, one result of which we will see in Figure 37.5:

```
main()
{ number=0; pred[1]=0;
  for(i=1; i<N; i++)  tree(i,1);
  printf("%ld Hamiltonian paths",number);
}

void tree(int i,int level)
{ if (level==N−1 && pred[2]<i)  /* pred[level 2] is at level 1 */
    { number++;printf("\n%3.0d: ",number);
     for(k=1; k<=level; k++) printf("%d ",pred[k]);
     printf("%d ",i);
    }
  else
   { for(j=0; j<N; j++) if (i!=j)
       {neighbor=j;
        if (belongstolistofpredecessors(neighbor,level)==NO)
             {pred[level+1]=i;  tree(neighbor,level+1);}
```

```
        }
      }
  }

  int belongstolistofpredecessors(int jj,int level)
  { int k;
    for(k=level; k>=1; k--) if (jj==pred[k]) return YES;
    return NO;
  }
```

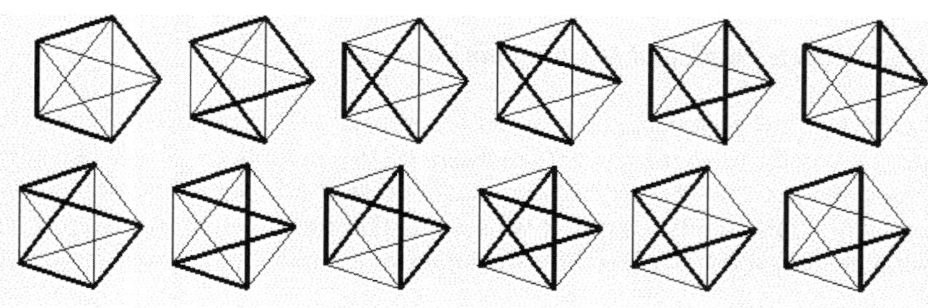

Figure 37.5. *The 12 starting point- and direction of traversal-type Hamiltonian circuits of the complete pentagon K_5*

37.2. Hamiltonian circuits covering a complete graph

We saw that an undirected complete graph K_N, of which each pair of vertices is linked by an edge, has Hamiltonian cycles. There are improvements: when the number of vertices N is odd, it assumes several Hamiltonian cycles having no edge in common. More specifically, it assumes $(N - 1) / 2$ cycles having no edge in common and that completely cover the graph edges. In other words, we get a partition of the graph in $(N - 1) / 2$ Hamiltonian circuits.

37.2.1. *Case where the number of vertices is a prime number other than two*

Let us check that the property above is true when the number of vertices N is an odd prime number. For this, let us number the vertices from 0 to $N - 1$, and recall that here a Hamiltonian cycle is of the starting point-type and the direction of traversal type. To construct one, we can therefore choose a specific starting point, for example the vertex numbered 0, and one of the two possible directions of traversal. The property is verified for the first values of N.

For $N = 3$, we take the cycle joining the successive vertices 0 1 2 of the triangle. For $N = 5$, we get the cycle 0 1 2 3 4 forming the convex pentagon of the vertices, the other cycle being the star pentagon 0 2 4 1 3. For $N = 7$, it is sufficient to take the convex heptagon joining the neighboring vertices between themselves, as well as the two star heptagons joining the vertices in twos and threes (see Figure 37.6).

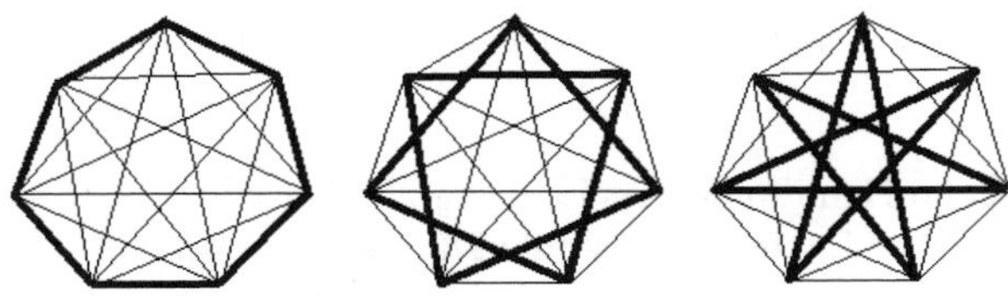

Figure 37.6. *The three Hamiltonian circuits without common edges, covering the entire graph for the seven-sided pentagon*

This is generalized to any odd prime number. Indeed, every arithmetic sequence modulo N, starting at 0, and of common difference r positive and less than N, has N as its smallest period, with the N numbers thus obtained forming a permutation.[1] These $N - 1$ permutations go in pairs when we change the direction of traversal. The $(N - 1) / 2$ permutations give the convex polygon (for $r = 1$) and all possible star polygons. These polygons have no edge in common and finally cover the graph.

We can no longer do the same when the number N is not prime.

37.2.2. *General case*

The general case is about showing that every undirected complete graph K_N, with odd N, has edges that can be covered by $(N - 1) / 2$ disjoint Hamiltonian cycles (not having edges in common).

Let us postulate that $K = (N - 1) / 2$, and number the graph vertices from 0 to $N - 1$. Then let us draw the graph with the vertices 0 to $N - 2$ displayed regularly on a circle, the last vertex $N - 1$ being placed in the center of the circle, as in Figure 37.7.

1. For example, for $N = 7$ we get the sequences modulo 7: 0123456, 0246135, 0362514, with the three other sequences referring to changing the order of traversal. Let us take a sequence; its elements are of the form $q\ r$, with q between 0 and $N - 1$, r being the common difference that is a prime number with N. The N first elements obtained are all distinct in twos: actually if we had $q\ r = q'\ r$ modulo N, with q and q' between 0 and $N - 1$, this would mean that $(q - q')\ r$ would be a multiple of N, and as N is prime with r, N should divide $q - q'$, which leaves $q - q' = 0$ as the only possibility. The N first elements of each sequence are therefore all distinct and form a permutation, the latter then being repeated periodically.

A first Hamiltonian cycle is obtained by starting from the central vertex $N - 1$ and going to vertex 0, placed at the highest point of the circle. Next we go towards vertex 1 located just to the right below 0, then we move horizontally towards vertex $N - 2$ on the left. We then go down on the right towards 2 then horizontally towards $N - 3$ on the left, and so on and so forth until vertex $2K$ at the bottom of the circle, from which we return to the central vertex (see Figure 37.7). This cycle passes through all the vertices and covers N edges of the complete graph, which has $N(N - 1) / 2$ of them.

To get a second Hamiltonian cycle, using N other edges, it is sufficient to start again from vertex $N - 1$ and add 1 modulo $2K$ to the numbers of the vertices (from 0 to $N - 2$) of the previous cycle. This comes back to making a rotation of one notch to move from one cycle to the new one. Then we redo the same thing to move on to a new cycle from the one we just obtained. We therefore find K Hamiltonian cycles with their edges disjoint, all the edges finally being covered by these cycles.[2]

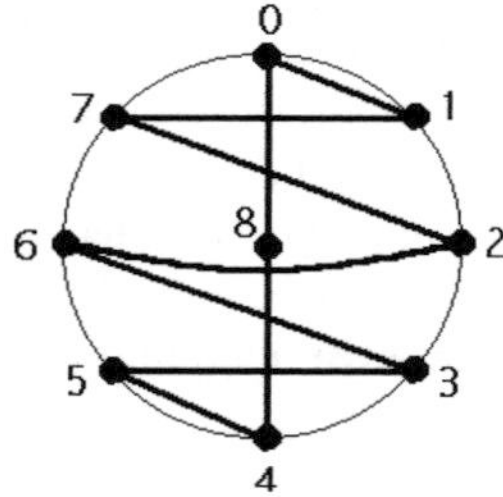

Figure 37.7. *Drawing of the vertices of the complete graph for N = 9 (K = 4), and trace of the first Hamiltonian cycle, the others being deduced by successive rotations of 45°*

In the example of the complete graph K_9, we find the four cycles with disjoint supports:

8 0 1 7 2 6 3 5 4 8

8 1 2 0 3 7 4 6 5 8

8 2 3 1 4 0 5 7 6 8

8 3 4 2 5 1 6 0 7 8

---

2. Each cycle has two edges with vertex $N - 1$ at its extremity. All the edges originating from this vertex are therefore covered by the K cycles, once each. As for the other edges, we can note that the sum of their two vertices is always equal to 0 or 1 modulo $2K$ for the first cycle, 2 or 3 modulo $2K$ for the second, 4 or 5 modulo $2K$ for the third, etc., which proves that we never have the same edge covered by the cycles twice.

The program results from the constructive method above, and we will see one result in Figure 37.8.

```
K=(N−1)/2; modulo=2*K;
for(i=0; i<K; i++)
{ a[0]=N−1; a[1]=i; a[N]=N−1 ;
  q=1+i;  for(j=2; j<N; j+=2)  a[j]=q++;
  q=(K+1+i)%modulo;  for(j=N−2; j>2; j-=2) a[j]=(q++)%modulo;
  display table a[] from box 0 to box N, which gives each of the K cycles
}
```

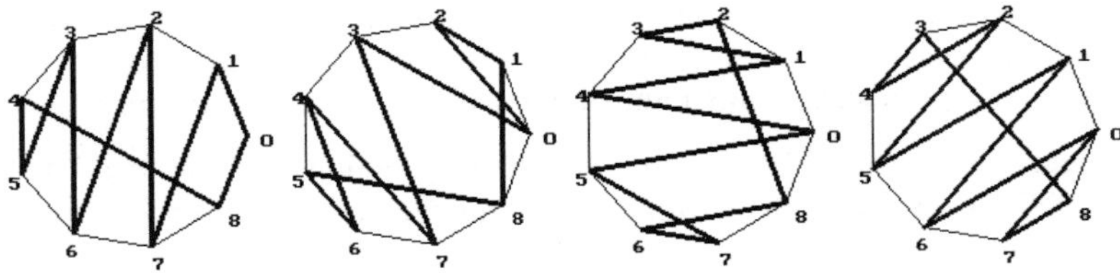

Figure 37.8. *The four Hamiltonian cycles whose union covers all the edges of graph K_9*

37.3. Complete and antisymmetric directed graph

37.3.1. *A few theoretical considerations*

First of all, let us recall a few definitions, all related to completed directed graphs:

– a (loopless) directed complete graph is such that there is at least one arc between two distinct vertices x and y (see Figure 37.9, left);

– a complete 1-graph[3] (directed and loopless) is a graph where between two distinct vertices, whichever they may be, there is either an arc in one direction or two arcs in opposite directions (see Figure 37.9, right). It is antisymmetric if there is a single arc between any two vertices;

– a graph center is a vertex that has minimal eccentricity. By eccentricity of a vertex we mean the maximum distance that separates it from the other vertices starting from it. The eccentricity associated with the center is the radius of the graph;

– a directed graph is strongly connected if there is always a path from one vertex to another, whatever these two vertices may be.

---

3. A p-graph is a graph where each vertex has at most p arcs stemming from it. In a 1-graph, there is at most one arc $a \rightarrow b$ for every vertex couple (a, b).

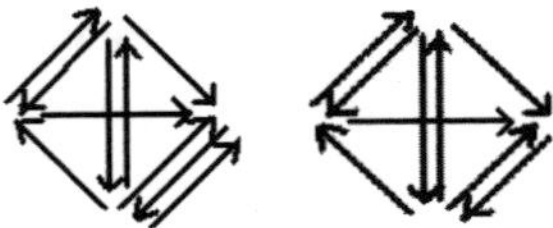

Figure 37.9. *An example of a directed complete graph (left); and an example of a complete 1-graph (right)*

We therefore have the following properties.

PROPERTY 37.1.– In a loopless, directed, complete 1-graph, every vertex x_0 with the greatest exiting degree is a center, and the graph radius is less than or equal to 2.

To show this property, we distinguish two cases:

– There is a vertex where there is a direct junction from it to all the other vertices. This means that this vertex has the number of graph vertices reduced by one as its outdegree (number of arcs leaving it). Its eccentricity is equal to 1, and no vertex can do better. It is therefore a center and the graph radius is equal to 1.

– There is no vertex with an eccentricity equal to 1 as was the case previously. Therefore let us take a vertex x_0 with the maximum outdegree, its eccentricity being greater than or equal to 2.

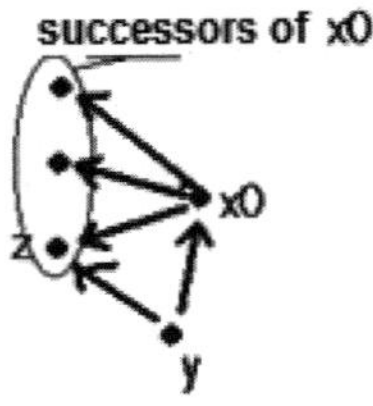

Figure 37.10. *Layout of vertex x_0 of eccentricity greater than 2*

If the eccentricity of x_0 were strictly greater than 2, there would be at least one vertex y located at a distance greater than 2, going from x_0 to y (see Figure 37.10). As the graph is complete, there would therefore be an arc from y to x_0. Now let us take some successor z of x_0. There is no arc going from z to y, otherwise we would have a distance equal to 2 going from x_0 to y. With the graph being complete, there is an arc from y to z. But then all the successors z of x_0 would be successors of y, as well as x_0. For y this would give an outdegree that would be strictly greater than that of x_0. Furthermore, x_0 was supposed to have the biggest outdegree. We get a contradiction. The eccentricity of x_0 cannot be strictly greater than 2. It is therefore equal to 2 and x_0 is a center, with the eccentricity of the other vertices unable to be less.

In Figure 37.11 a few examples of directed complete l-graphs with four vertices *A, B, C* and *D* can be found. The centers of these graphs are circled.

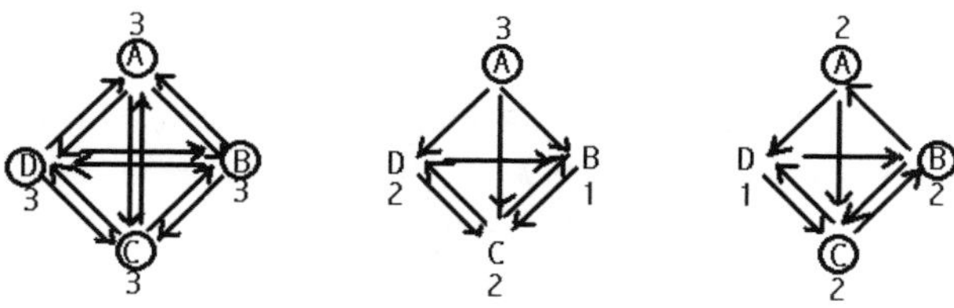

Figure 37.11. *A symmetrical complete l-graph (bidirectional arcs everywhere), every vertex is a center and the radius is 1 (left); a complete l-graph with a single center and the radius is 1 (center); and a complete l-graph with three centers and the radius is 2 (right)*

PROPERTY 37.2.– If a complete l-graph is strongly connected, it has a Hamiltonian cycle.

Let us show this property. Since the graph is strongly connected, there are cycles, and in particular a cycle *Cmax* of maximum length. If its length is equal to the number of graph vertices, the proposition is shown. Else, there is at least one vertex z that is not in this cycle *Cmax*. Due to the complete l-graph, we have three possibilities: a bidirectional junction between a vertex i of cycle *Cmax* and z, or a one-way junction in one direction or the other. The first possibility is to be dismissed, otherwise if we add the derivation $i \rightarrow z \rightarrow i$ to the cycle we could have a new cycle of greater length, which is excluded. Two cases remain:

– either there is an arc $i \rightarrow z$ and in this case the successor s of i on the cycle cannot be a successor of z as, if not, the length of cycle *Cmax* would increase with the derivation $i \rightarrow z \rightarrow s$. As the graph is complete, we therefore have an arc $s \rightarrow z$, and consequently, arcs going from all vertices of cycle *Cmax* to vertex z; or

– there is an arc from z to i, and for the same reasons as before, there are also some from z to the predecessor of i on *Cmax*, and consequently, to all vertices of the cycle.

Now let us take all the vertices z that are not on *Cmax*. Thanks to the above, they are separated into two categories A and B: those with arcs from z to the vertices of the cycle; and those with arcs from the vertices of the cycle to z. Thus we obtain two sets A and B containing all the vertices z outside of the cycle (see Figure 37.12). Neither of these two sets is empty, otherwise we would have a vertex in A or B that would be linked to the vertices of *Cmax* in one direction but never in the other, and we would lose strong connectivity. In these conditions, there is at least one arc from a vertex of B to a vertex of A as otherwise we would again lose strong connectivity. With this arc, preceded by an arc of cycle *Cmax* to B, and followed by an arc of A to cycle *Cmax*, we would find a longer cycle, which is impossible. Therefore the cycle of maximum length can only pass through all the graph vertices, and constitutes a Hamiltonian cycle.

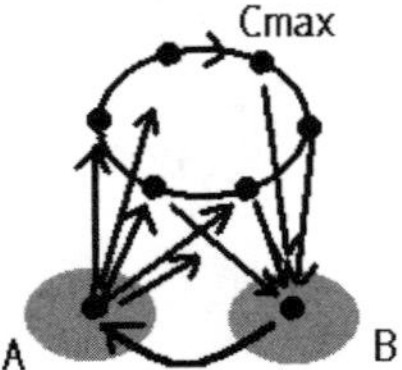

Figure 37.12. *Cycle Cmax and sets A and B*

PROPERTY 37.3.– On a complete l-graph there is at least one Hamiltonian path.

We saw (property 37.1) that a complete l-graph G has a center c, with a finite eccentricity of 1 or 2. From this center we can reach all the vertices of G other than c. Let us add a new vertex z to graph G, with an arc from z to c, and arcs from every vertex of G to z (see Figure 37.13).

The new graph obtained is strongly connected as every derivation through $z \rightarrow c$ allows us to go from one vertex of G to another, and we can go from z to the vertices of G and *vice versa*. The new graph G' is also complete, with all the links being direct. Thanks to property 37.2, graph G' assumes a Hamiltonian cycle. Let us remove vertex z from this cycle. This gives a Hamiltonian path starting at vertex c.

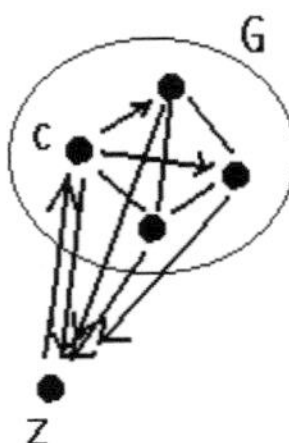

Figure 37.13. *Graph G, its center c, and the new vertex z*

PROPERTY 37.4.– On an antisymmetric and transitive complete l-graph, there is one and only one Hamiltonian path.

Let us show this. There is always a center. In this case this center is a vertex whose outdegree is equal to the number of vertices minus one. Actually, every path leading from c to some other vertex y can be shortened into a direct path from c to y because of graph transitivity: if we have a path $c \to z \to y$, we also have $c \to y$. On the other hand, this center c is unique because if there were a second center c', we would have an arc from c to c' and also an arc from c' to c. As the graph is antisymmetric, this is impossible. We know that there is at least one Hamiltonian path starting from c, thanks to property 37.3.

Now let us remove vertex c and the arcs linked to it. We again get an antisymmetric and transitive complete graph that in turn assumes a unique center c_1, where a Hamiltonian path starts.

Continuing in this way by successive prunings, we find a unique Hamiltonian path. At the same time, we have an algorithm enabling us to construct it. Let us take for example, a complete, antisymmetric and transitive graph with five vertices, like the one in Figure 37.14. Its vertices are numbered by their outdegree, and the Hamiltonian path is 4 3 2 1 0. We can verify that the graph center is vertex 4 of outdegree 4, that it is unique and that we must start at it to have the Hamiltonian path (if we started at another vertex, we would never be able to reach vertex 4).

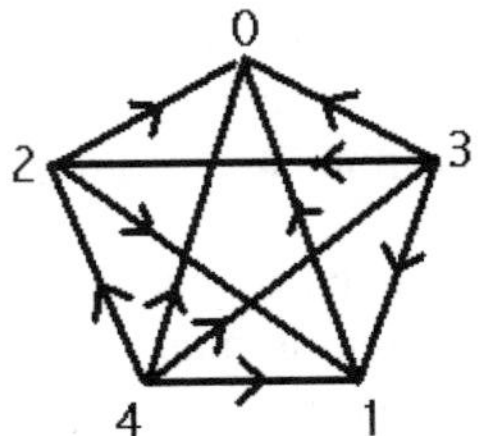

Figure 37.14. *Example of an antisymmetric and transitive complete graph with the unique Hamiltonian path 4 3 2 1 0*

Generalizing, let us take a complete graph with N numbered vertices and make it antisymmetric and transitive, orienting its arcs as a consequence. Let us begin by choosing a vertex of $N-1$ degree and orient all the arcs from it. Note that we can choose this center from the N vertices. Then let us choose a second vertex of $N-2$ degree orienting the arcs, hence $N-1$ vertex choices, etc. Finally, from a complete graph with numbered vertices we can create exactly $N!$ antisymmetric and transitive graphs by orientations of the junction arcs.

PROPERTY 37.5.– On an antisymmetric complete 1-graph, the number of Hamiltonian paths is odd.

By doing orientation reversals of certain arcs, we can always move from an antisymmetric and transitive complete 1-graph to an antisymmetric complete 1-graph.

As we know that an antisymmteric and transitive complete l-graph has a unique Hamiltonian path (property 37.4), all we have to do is prove that the orientation change of some arc on an antisymmetric complete graph does not change the parity of the number of Hamiltonian paths that we know exist (property 37.3).

Let us start from an antisymmetric complete l-graph G with h Hamiltonian paths. On this graph let us choose an arc $a\ b$, from vertex a to vertex b. Then let us take graph G', also complete and antisymmetric, which is deduced from G by changing the orientation of arc $a\ b$, hence arc $b \rightarrow a$. Calling its number of Hamiltonian paths h', we have to show that $h' = h$ [2].

Let us introduce two new graphs:

– *1-graph G_1 being deduced from G by keeping arc $a \rightarrow b$* and adding arc $b \rightarrow a$ to it. It has $h_1(ab)$ Hamiltonian paths using arc $a \rightarrow b$, $h_1(ba)$ Hamiltonian paths using arc $b \rightarrow a$, and $h_1(o)$ Hamiltonian paths using none of the two arcs between a and b. In liaison with graphs G and G', we also have:

$$h = h_1(ab) + h_1(o) \text{ and } h' = h_1(ba) + h_1(o)$$

– *1-graph G_2 being deduced from G by deleting arc $a \rightarrow b$.* This graph is not complete (no arc between vertices a and b), but it remains antisymmetric. The number of its Hamiltonian paths is none other than h_1(o), as we defined it in G_1.

Now let us take graph G'_2 obtained by changing the direction of all the arcs of G_2. This graph G'_2 also has $h(o)$ Hamiltonian paths. On the other hand, the two 1-graphs G_1 and G'_2 are complementary, which means that they have the same vertices and have no arc in common, but their union is such that between two vertices there are two arcs in opposite directions. We therefore have a theorem that indicates to us that the complementary graphs have a number of Hamiltonian paths of the same parity.

Hence $h_1(o) = h_1(ab) + h_1(ba) + h_1(o)$ modulo 2, i.e. $h_1(ab) = h_1(ba)$ [2] and lastly, thanks to the previous relations, $h = h'$ [2].

37.3.2. *Experimental verification and algorithms*

We take a graph with N vertices and a unique arc between each pair of vertices. For example, for $N = 4$ we have graph like the one in Figure 37.15. We can check that this graph has five Hamiltonian paths and a starting point-type Hamiltonian circuit. This Hamiltonian cycle is the extension (return to the starting point in addition) of four Hamiltonian paths.

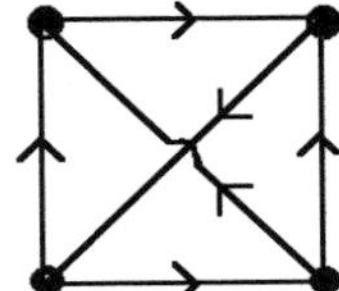

Figure 37.15. *Graph with four vertices and a unique arc between each pair of vertices*

a) For given N, how many such graphs are there?

The number of arcs of a complete graph is $NA = N(N-1) / 2$. As two orientations are possible, the number of graphs is $2^{N(N-1)/2}$. For example for $N = 4$, this gives $2^6 = 64$ graphs, and for $N = 5$ we get $2^{10} = 1{,}024$ graphs.

b) Write the program for creating the graphs.

Let us create the program enabling us to get, for each of the graphs, its arcs numbered from 0 to $NA - 1$, and for each arc i its beginning $e1[i]$ and its end $e2[i]$. We will deduce from it the list of neighbors $n[i][j]$ of each vertex i, as well as their number $nbn[i]$.

To do this, let us begin by numbering the arcs in an arbitrary direction. There are several methods. Here is one. For $N = 6$, for example, with vertices numbered from 0 to 5, we have arcs in the following order: 0 1, 1 2, 2 3, 3 4, 4 5, 5 0, 0 2, 1 3, 2 4, 3 5, 4 0, 5 1, 0 3, 1 4 and 2 5. By doing this, we start by taking the arcs joining the vertices in ones, from 0 1 to 5 0, then those in twos, from 0 2 to 5 1, then those in threes.

```
We take N number of vertices of the complete graph.
NA=N*(N−1)/2;  q=0;
for(k=1; k<=N/2; k++)  for(i=0; i<N; i++)   if (q<NA)
   {e1[q]=i; e2[q]=(i+k)%N; q++; }
```

To get all the possible graphs, we fill a table $a[]$ of length NA with 0s or 1s. Each arc, previously numbered from 0 to $NA - 1$, therefore carries either number 0 or 1 in the table. If it is 0 we keep the extremities $e1$ and $e2$ found previously, and if it is 1 we change the order of the extremities. For example, for $N = 4$ with arcs 0 1, 1 2, 2 3, 3 0, 0 2 and 1 3 numbered from 0 to 5 and table 0 1 0 0 1 1, we take 0 1, 2 1, 2 3, 3 0, 2 0 and 3 1 as arcs.

Filling in the table in all possible ways, which corresponds to NA-length binary numbers, we will have all the graphs with N vertices. This enables us, at the same time, to get the lists of neighbors of each vertex for each of the graphs.

```
for(n=0; n<pow(2,NA); n++)  /* we take each number n from 0 to 2^NA – 1 */
{
 quotient=n;
 for(j=0; j<NA; j++)  { a[j]= quotient%2; quotient=quotient/2; }
 for (i=0; i<N; i++) nbn[i]=0;
 for(i=0; i<NA; i++)  if (a[i]==0) n[e1[i]] [nbn[e1[i]]++] = e2[i];
                       else n[e2[i]][nbn[e2[i]]++] = e1[i];
}
```

c) Write a program to find all of the Hamiltonian paths and circuits.

For each of the graphs obtained above, let us make the search program for all the Hamiltonian paths, and eventually Hamiltonian cycles.

In the previous *for* loop, all we have to do is add a call of function *tree*() from each vertex *i*, at level 0 at the end:

```
number=0; /* number of Hamiltonian paths */
for(i=0; i<N; i++) tree(i,0);

void tree(int i,int level)
{  int j, neighbor;
   if (level==N-1)  number++;
   else
     { for(j=0; j<nbn[i]; j++)
         {neighbor=n[i][j];
          if (belongstolistofpredecessors(neighbor,i,level)==NO)
             { pred[level+1]=i;  tree(neighbour,level+1); }
         }
     }
}

int belongstolistofpredecessors(int jj,int j, int level)
{  int k;
   for(k=level; k>=1; k--)
   if (jj==pred[k])  return YES;
   return NO;
}
```

In Figure 37.16, we will find a few examples of execution of this program.

37.3.3. *Complete treatment of case N = 4*

We will classify the 64 graphs for $N = 4$ according to their number of Hamiltonian paths. As each graph has six arcs, the sum of the exiting degrees of the four vertices is equal to six, the maximum degree being three. The graphs can be classified according to the outdegrees of their four vertices, which gives four cases, with the degrees placed in descending order: 3210, 3111, 2220 and 2211.

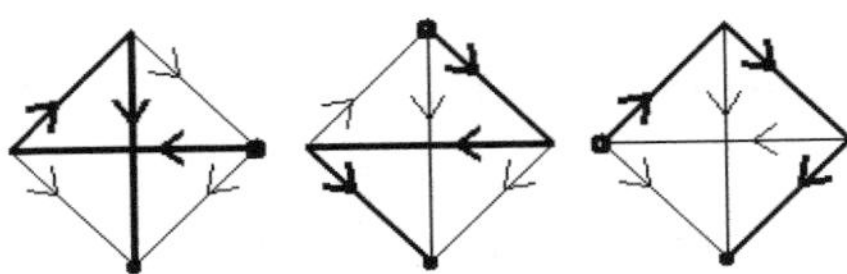

Figure 37.16a. *Among the 64 graphs for N = 4, an example of a directed graph that has three Hamiltonian paths and no cycle*

Figure 37.16b. *Another orientation example with five Hamiltonian paths and one cycle*

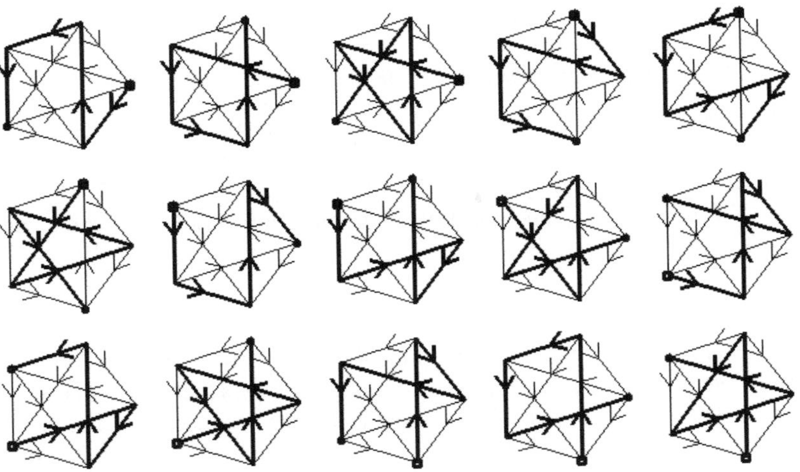

Figure 37.16c. *For N = 5, an example of a directed graph with 15 Hamiltonian paths and three cycles*

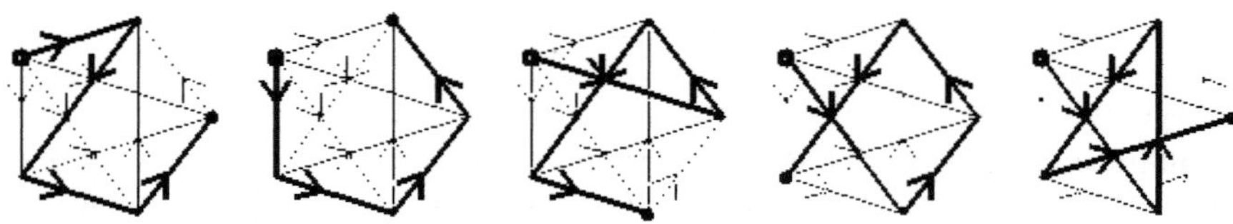

Figure 37.16d. *For N = 5, another example with five Hamiltonian paths and no cycle*

37.3.3.1. The exiting degrees are 3, 2, 1, 0

The graph center is the vertex of degree three, and the l-graph is antisymmetric and transitive: there is a direct path from the center to each of the other vertices. There is a single Hamiltonian path in this case, as we have seen, and it starts at the center, as can be verified in the drawing (see Figure 37.17a). But how many such graphs are there?

For the vertex of degree 3, there are four possibilities. Each time, there are three cases for the vertex of degree two, then two possibilities for the vertex of degree one. Finally we find 24 graphs.

37.3.3.2. *The exiting degrees are 3, 1, 1, 1*

There are four ways to choose the vertex of degree three. Each time, for the opposite vertex of degree one, there are two possibilities. There are no longer other choices. This gives eight graphs. For each of these graphs we find three Hamiltonian paths, all starting with the center of degree three (see Figure 37.17b).

37.3.3.3. *The exiting degrees are 2, 2, 2, 0*

There are four ways to choose the vertex of degree 0, and each time two ways of taking the arcs of the opposite vertex, not leaving any other choice. This makes eight graphs. In each case, we get three Hamiltonian paths, starting from one of the vertices of degree two, and all finishing with the vertex of degree zero (see Figure 37.17c).

37.3.3.4. *The degrees are 2, 2, 1, 1*

There are $A_4^2 = 12$ ways of coupling the two vertices of degree two. If, for example, we had the couple (A, B) the coupling expresses that there is an arc $A \to B$. There are therefore two possibilities for placing the second arc stemming from A, and no choices are left for taking the other arcs. That makes a total of 24 graphs. For each of these graphs, we find five Hamiltonian paths and one Hamiltonian cycle.

The existence of a Hamiltonian cycle is linked to the fact that the graph is complete and strongly connected. This cycle produces four Hamiltonian paths, alternately taking each vertex of the cycle as the starting point and deleting the last arc of the cycle. A fifth Hamiltonian path that is not in the cycle is added (see Figure 37.17d). Finally we find 24 graphs with a single Hamiltonian path, 16 that have three paths, and 24 that have five paths.

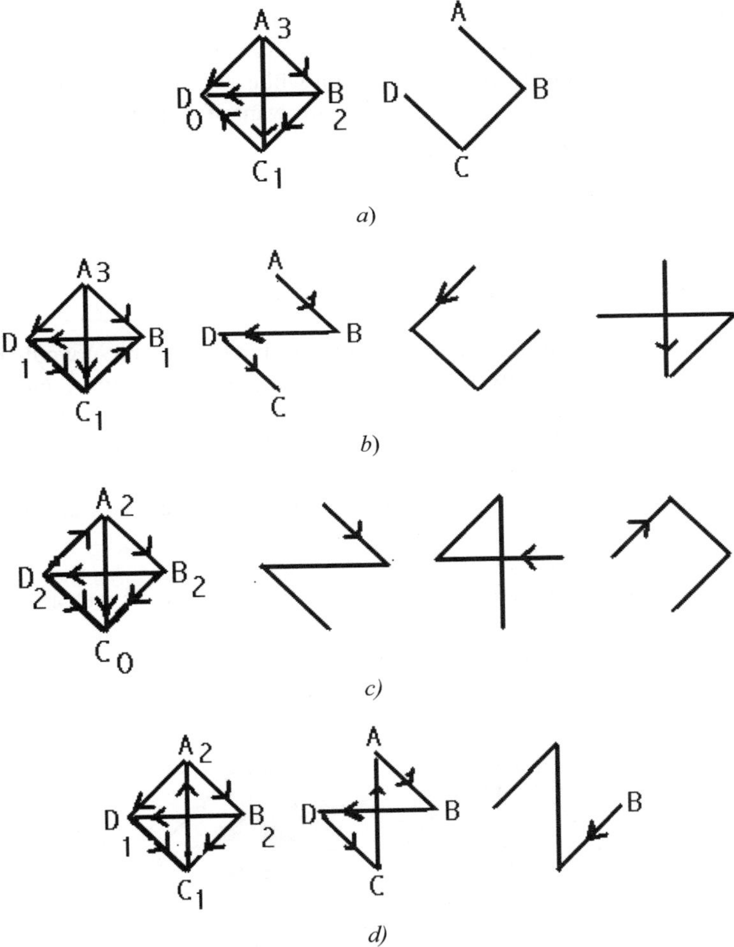

Figure 37.17. *The four cases following the degrees of the vertices*

37.4. Bipartite graph and Hamiltonian paths

An undirected graph is said to be in two parts (or bipartite) when we can separate its vertex set into two parts in such as way that each edge of the graph exclusively joins a vertex of one part and a vertex of the other. One example is that of the chessboard, with its black and white squares. The corresponding graph has the centers of the squares as its vertices, and the horizontal and vertical junctions of the vertices of adjacent squares as edges. Finally this gives a square network, with an alternation of white and black vertices depending on the color of the squares. Such a graph is in two parts, since every edge joins a white vertex and a black vertex. We therefore have the following property, which, for want of assuring us of the presence of Hamiltonian cycles, assures us of their absence.

PROPERTY 37.6.– Let a graph be bipartite where the vertex set can be divided into two parts in such a way that the edges are exclusively junctions between a vertex of one part and a vertex of the other. If the latter has an unequal number of vertices in its two parts, no Hamiltonian cycle exists.

Actually, if there were a Hamiltonian cycle in a bipartite graph, it would be made up of links going by two, forward and back. These links are of even number, i.e. n. Each vertex of one of the two sets is traversed by a cycle in entering and exiting. There are therefore $n / 2$ vertices for the set concerned, and as many for the other. There cannot be an unequal number of vertices in the two sets. Even with an equal number of vertices in the two sets, there is not necessarily a Hamiltonian cycle or path.

Let us take an example, that of the graph in Figure 37.18. As we can see on the drawing on the right, by coloring the vertices with two colors this graph is bipartite, each edge having two vertices of a different color as extremities. According to the property above, it therefore does not have any Hamiltonian cycles.

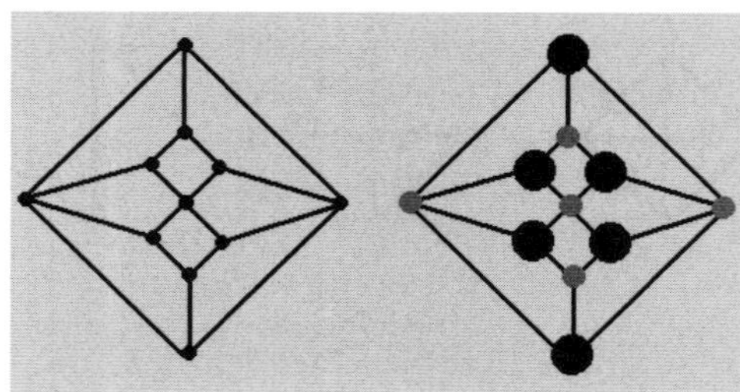

Figure 37.18. *A bipartite graph without Hamiltonian cycles*

37.5. Knights tour graph on the $N \times N$ chessboard

In this type of graph each vertex has eight neighbors, or less if it is close to the boundary of the square, as in the example of the graph in Figure 37.19 in the 4×4 square. We are interested in the Hamiltonian cycles of this graph.

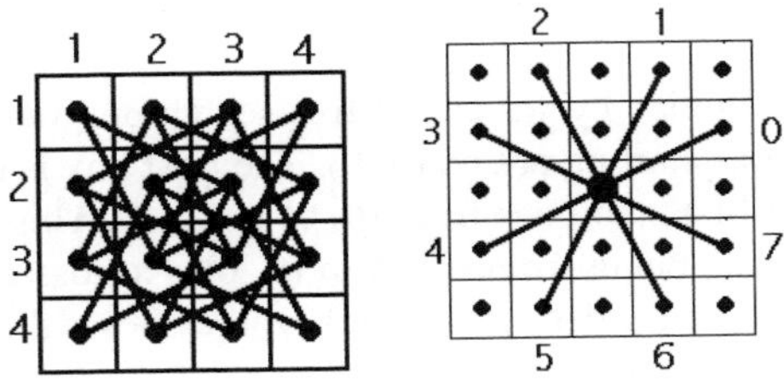

Figure 37.19. *The knight's tour graph on a 4×4 square (left); and the eight neighbors of the vertex (right)*

37.5.1. *Case where N is odd*

Let us show that if N is an odd number there is no Hamiltonian cycle. For this, let us color the boxes of the square in black and white, like a real chessboard. Each of the knight's steps goes from a box of one color to a box of another color. Let us make the knight start from a white box. Each time he makes two steps, he ends up back on a white box.

If there was a Hamiltonian cycle, it would touch the N^2 boxes, and the knight would return to the starting box at the end of N^2 steps. This number is odd, however, and he can only end up on a box with a different color to that of the starting box. This is a contradiction.

37.5.2. *Coordinates of the neighbors of a vertex*

A vertex located at (x, y) has at most eight neighbors. Let us determine their coordinates (xx, yy) as a function of (x, y) and of their direction i (see Figure 37.19, right) in the form:

$$xx = x + dx[\mathrm{i}];\ yy = y + dy[\mathrm{i}]$$

We notice, from the drawing of the neighbors for example, that the neighbor in direction 0 has as coordinates $(x + 2, y - 1)$. We note the same in each direction.

To facilitate the calculations, we pre-calculate the variations of the coordinates in two tables *dx*[8] and *dy*[8], which gives:

dx[8] = {2,1,-1,-2,-2,-1,1,2} and *dy*[8] = {-1,-2,-2,-1,1,2,2,1}

37.5.3. *Hamiltonian cycles program*

To make the Hamiltonian cycles exhaustive search program when N is even, let us consider the knight as starting at box (0, 0). The next box is either (1, 2) or (2, 1). Let us decide that the first step goes from (0, 0) to (1, 2). This leads to the last step of the Hamiltonian cycle being from (2, 1) to (0, 0). No loss of generality follows. The starting point-type and order of traversal-type cycles will finally end up being found. The traversal function that is *knight*(x, y, *level*, *forbidden*) takes the position of the knight x, y as the variable and the direction *forbidden* to prevent the knight returning to the point he has come from. The *level* corresponds to the number of boxes reached, associated with the descent in the arborescence of traversals.

In this case, level 0 corresponds to point (0, 0). We are in fact starting at level 1 corresponding to point (1, 2), the forbidden direction therefore being 2. The stop test takes place when the *level* is equal to $N{*}N - 1$ and the knight has arrived at point (2, 1). To simplify the calculations, each position (x, y) is numbered $Ny + x$, a number in base N that is in bijection with the position. The program follows:

```
main()
{ predecessor[1]=0;
  knight(1,2,1,2);
  printf("%d   END",counter);
}

void knight(int x,int y, int level, int forbidden)
{  int j,number,xx,yy,nextnumber;
   number=y*N+x;
   if (level==N*N−1 && x==2 && y==1)  counter++;
   else { for(j=0; j<8; j++)  if (j!=forbidden)   /* neighbors (xx, yy)  */
          { xx=x+dx[j];  yy = y+dy[j];
            nextnumber=N*yy+xx;
            if (xx>=0 && xx<N && yy>=0 && yy<N &&
               belongstolistofpredecessors (nextnumber, level)==NO)
               {
                predecessor[level+1]=number; knight(xx,yy,level+1,(j+4)%8);
               }
          }
```

```
        }
}

int belongstolistofpredecessors(int j, int level)
{ int k;
  for(k=level−1; k>=1; k--) if (j==predecessor[k]) return YES;
  return NO;
}
```

Solutions only exist for $N = 6$. Already, for $N = 6$ we find 9,862 Hamiltonian cycles: 6,195 of which are in direction 5 from point (1, 2); 636 in direction 6; 620 in direction 7; 636 in direction 0; and 1,775 in direction 1. When N increases, the exhaustive search quickly becomes too long and we are led to develop an algorithm enabling us to have only a few solutions, which is the aim of the next section.

37.5.4. *Another algorithm*

Here is another algorithm that enables us to find only a few Hamiltonian cycles and paths. Each box of the square is taken alternately as the starting box. Each time, we do a traversal in the following way: each box touched is numbered i according to the order of traversal from box 1 of the start. Then we search for all the possible neighbors, namely all those that are in the square and not already numbered. Out of each of these neighbors, we choose the one that, itself, has the fewest possible neighbors. It is this point that is chosen and numbered $i + 1$, and we continue. For some of the starting points, all the boxes end up being touched, which gives a Hamiltonian path or even a Hamiltonian cycle.

In the program below, function $c(x, y)$ is in charge of counting the number of possible neighbors of a position x, y:

```
We take the length N of the side of the square of the chessboard
int dx[8]={2,1,-1,-2,-2,-1,1,2};  int dy[8]={-1,-2,-2,-1,1,2,2,1};
                /* variations of the abscissa and the ordinate for each of the eight
                   neighbors of a point */
main()
{ for(xs=0 ;xs<N; xs++)   /* we take all the starting points xs, ys  */
  for(ys=0; ys<N; ys++)
   { draw the square grid of the chessboard
     for(x=0; x<N; x++) for(y=0;y<N;y++) a[x][y]=0;
            /* we set all the boxes to 0 */
     x=xs; y=ys; a[x][y]=1; counter=1;    /* we number the first square */
     for(;;)
```

```
      /* passage from a point to its best neighbor, draw the junction line */
       { nbnnmini=100; nbn=0;
         for(i=0; i<8; i++)              /* we take all the neighbors of x,y */
           { xx=x+dx[i]; yy=y+dy[i];
                 /* we will take the best neighbor possible */
             if (xx>=0 && xx<N && yy>=0 && yy<N && a[xx][yy]==0)
               {nbn++ ;     /* number of neighbors xx, yy of the vertex x, y */
                nbneighborsoftheneighbor=c(xx,yy);
                if (nbneighborsoftheneighbor <nbnnmini)
                   {imini=i; nbnnmini= nbneighborsoftheneighbor;} }
           }
         if (nbn==0)  break;
                 /* we did not find any neighbor for x,y. Stop test */
         else { oldx=x;oldy=y; x+=dx[imini];y+=dy[imini];
                counter++; a[x][y]=counter;
                join point x,y and point oldx,oldy
              }
       }
      if (counter==N*N)    /* all the boxes were reached */
        { flag=0;
          for(i=0; i<8; i++)  if (xs==x+dx[i] && ys== y+dy[i])
              { flag=1; break;}
          if (flag==1)
              { display "Hamiltonian circuit"; join x,y  to  xs,ys }
          else  display "Hamiltonian path"
        }
      Erase the screen to move on to the next starting point
    }
}

int c(int x, int y)  /* this function returns the number of neighbors of point x, y */
{ int i,cumul,xx,yy;   cumul=0;
  for(i=0; i<8; i++)
    { xx=x+dx[i];yy=y+dy[i];
      if (xx>=0 && xx<N && yy>=0 && yy<N && a[xx][yy]==0)  cumul+=1;
    }
  return cumul;
}
```

One of the very many knight's Hamiltonian traversals with return to the start is shown in Figure 37.20.

Figure 37.20. *One of the Hamiltonian cycles traversed by the knight for N =16*

37.6. de Bruijn sequences

37.6.1. *Preparatory example*

Let us imagine that we completely forgot the access code to open the door of our building. It is a four digit code, and to simplify let us say based on the three numbers 0, 1 and 2, instead of the 10 usual ones. The door must open as soon as the four correct numbers of the code are pressed successively on the three buttons of the digicode. The number of possible codes is $3^4 = 81$. To get them all, we have to press the buttons 4×81= 324 times. Now let us assume that we have the following sequence, 84 digits long (= 81 + 3 because the last three numbers are the same as the starting three) at our disposal:

000010021011120022010221101012122120122220002001202221001102011 22

020212112102111 1000

It is such that each block of four successive numbers gives a code and they are all there. In other words, all we have to do is press 84 buttons in the order previously indicated to get all the codes, a gain ratio compared to the previous method. It is this type of sequence that gives de Bruijn graphs.[4]

---

4. Whereas de Bruijn graphs enable us to obtain all the sequences of this form, some can be found from modular recurrence relations (modulo 3 in the example chosen), we call them M-sequences, and they are dealt with in the framework of the theory of finite fields.

Instead of working on a base of three figures, we will only take two of them, 0 and 1, given that we can generalize what follows in larger bases.

37.6.2. *Definition*

The number sequences that will be concerned are attributed to Nicolaas Govert de Bruijn, who published a study on this subject in 1946. In 1894, the problem was initially posed by De Rivière and solved by Flye Sainte-Marie. The starting idea is the following: we take $\boldsymbol{Z} / 2^n\boldsymbol{Z}$, the set of modular numbers from 0 to $2^n - 1$ (every number that is not in this interval is returned to its interior by adding or subtracting 2^n as many times as necessary). Starting from 0, we carry out the recurrence which makes us move from a choice of x to $2x$ or to $2x + 1$, modulo 2^n, but in such a way that by proceeding in this way the entire set $\boldsymbol{Z} / 2^n\boldsymbol{Z}$ is traversed, with each of its 2^n elements being obtained once and only once. We want to find out if this is possible and, if need be, how many ways.

To answer in the simplest cases, corresponding to the small values of n, we draw a binary tree of root 0. Each node assumes two successors. When the same number returns on the same descending branch, we block the progression of this branch. The problem is to see whether we find descending branches where the 2^n numbers are present once and once alone. The answer is yes in the case where $n = 2$ and $n = 3$, as indicated in Figure 37.21.

Since we are starting from 0 and 1 is the only acceptable successor, the last modular number is necessarily 2^{n-1}, as if this number had appeared before it would have 0 or 1 already present at the start, as successors, which would block the process. Finally, the solutions form a cycle (0 1 .... 2^{n-1}).

An algorithm giving the de Bruijn sequences results from all this. Here is the corresponding program in C language:

```
main()  { predecessor[0]= -1;   tree(0,1); }

void tree(int i,int level)
{ if (level==N)
    { number++; printf("%4.0ld: ",number);
      listeiandpredecessors(i,level);
      for(k=1; k<=N; k++) printf("%d ",s[k]);  printf("\n");
    }
  else
    { for(j=0; j<=1; j++)
        { v=(2*i+j)%N;
```

```
            if (belongstolistofpredecessors(v,i)==NO)
              { predecessor[v]=i; tree(v,level+1); }
        }
    }
}
```

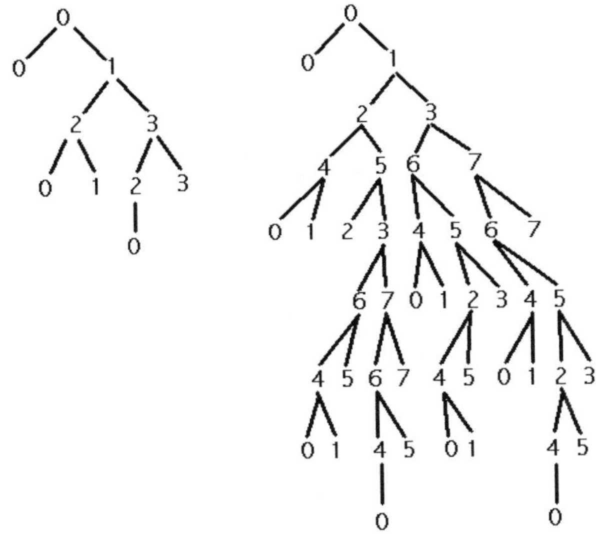

Figure 37.21. *A single solution (0 1 3 2) for n = 2 (left); and two solutions (0 1 2 5 3 7 6 4) and (0 1 3 7 6 5 2 4) for n = 3 (right)*

The use of two functions is noteworthy: the first, *belongstolistiandpredecessors (j,i)*, tests whether or not element j is found in the branch that goes back up from element i in the tree. In other words, this function tests whether j is equal to i or whether j is equal to one of the predecessors or ancestors of i. The second, *listiandpredecessors(i, level)*, records in a table all the elements that go back up from element i located in level *level* to root 0 in the tree. It is i and its ancestors, placed in table *s*[], evidently declared overall, whose boxes are numbered from 1 to N.

```
int belongstolistiandpredecessors (int j, int i)
{  if (j= = i) return YES;
   if (j != i && predecessor[i]== -1) return NO;
           /* we arrived at the root  */
   if (predecessor[i] != -1) belongstolistiandpredecessors(j, predecessor[i]);
```

```
}

void listiandpredecessors(int i,int level)
{ if (i!=-1)  { s[level]=i;    belongstolistiandpredecessor[i],level-1); } }
```

Example of results: the 16 Hamiltonian cycles obtained for $n = 4$ are:

1: 0 1 3 7 15 14 13 11 6 12 9 2 5 10 4 8

2: 0 1 3 7 15 14 13 10 5 11 6 12 9 2 4 8

3: 0 1 3 7 15 14 13 10 4 9 2 5 11 6 12 8

4: 0 1 3 7 15 14 12 9 2 5 11 6 13 10 4 8

5: 0 1 3 6 13 11 7 15 14 12 9 2 5 10 4 8

6: 0 1 3 6 13 10 5 11 7 15 14 12 9 2 4 8

7: 0 1 3 6 13 10 4 9 2 5 11 7 15 14 12 8

8: 0 1 3 6 12 9 2 5 11 7 15 14 13 10 4 8

9: 0 1 2 5 11 7 15 14 13 10 4 9 3 6 12 8

10: 0 1 2 5 11 7 15 14 12 9 3 6 13 10 4 8

11: 0 1 2 5 11 6 13 10 4 9 3 7 15 14 12 8

12: 0 1 2 5 11 6 12 9 3 7 15 14 13 10 4 8

13: 0 1 2 5 10 4 9 3 7 15 14 13 11 6 12 8

14: 0 1 2 5 10 4 9 3 6 13 11 7 15 14 12 8

15: 0 1 2 4 9 3 7 15 14 13 10 5 11 6 12 8

16: 0 1 2 4 9 3 6 13 10 5 11 7 15 14 12 8

The experimental results are not enough. We will now show that this problem always has solutions whatever n may be, and we will even have a formula giving the number of solutions. For this we should prose the problem differently.

37.6.3. *de Bruijn graph*

Let us consider the directed graph whose vertices are numbered from 0 to $2^n - 1$ so that two arcs, reaching vertices $2x$ and $2x + 1$ modulo 2^n, start at each vertex x. The problem above refers to traversing the graph passing through each vertex once and only once, in such a way as to form a cycle. We are led to search for the

Hamiltonian cycles of this graph. In Figure 37.22, we will find the graphs and solutions for $n = 2$ and $n = 3$, as before.

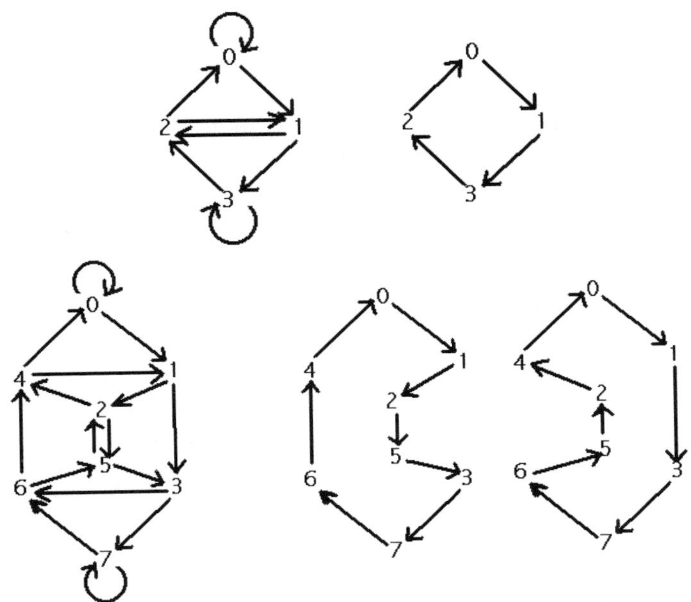

Figure 37.22. *Graph G_2 and its only Hamiltonian cycle for $n = 2$ (above); and graph G_3 and its two Hamiltonian cycles for $n = 3$ (below)*

We know that, in general, there is no formula giving the number of Hamiltonian cycles in a graph. But de Bruijn graphs have an interesting characteristic that links Hamiltonian cycles to Eulerian circuits. Here it is:

FUNDAMENTAL PROPERTY 37.1.– Graph G_n has as many Eulerian cycles as graph G_{n+1} has Hamiltonian cycles.

Let us consider graph G_n. It has 2^n vertices and 2^{n+1} arcs. Expressing the numbers in binary, a vertex of the form xw (x is a number 0 or 1, and w a word based on 0 and 1) has two successors $w0$ and $w1$. If we express it in the form wy (y being the last number), it also has two predecessors, $0w$ and $1w$. The graph is connected, and each node has as many incident arcs as exiting arcs. It therefore has Eulerian circuits. For example, the Eulerian circuits of G_2 are (01213320) and (01332120). The nodes are present twice in each circuit because they are all traversed twice. These circuits can also be expressed in binary in the form

(00101110) and (00111010) where reading is done by blocks of two successive numbers with a one-notch shift each time in a cyclic manner (see Figure 37.23).

Now let us number the arcs in the following way: the arc linking vertex *xw* to the neighboring vertex *wy* is called *xwy*. If we resume the example of G_2, a Eulerian cycle is expressed, as we saw, with an eight-figure word that we read in successive blocks of 2 characters. Now let us read it in blocks of three characters. We therefore obtain the successive arcs of the Eulerian circuit, all different and numbering eight. For example, cycle 00101110 is read by blocks of three figures: 001, 010, 101, 011, 111, 110, 100 and 000. The eight corresponding numbers follow each other by dropping the first number and adding a 0 or 1 to the end, which means a multiplication by two with or without adding 1 modulo 8. This indicates that we circulate on successive vertices of graph G_3 and that all are reached once and only once. In decimal, reading words of G_2 of three characters in binary gives (01253764) and (01376524). They are Hamiltonian cycles of G_3 (see Figure 37.23).

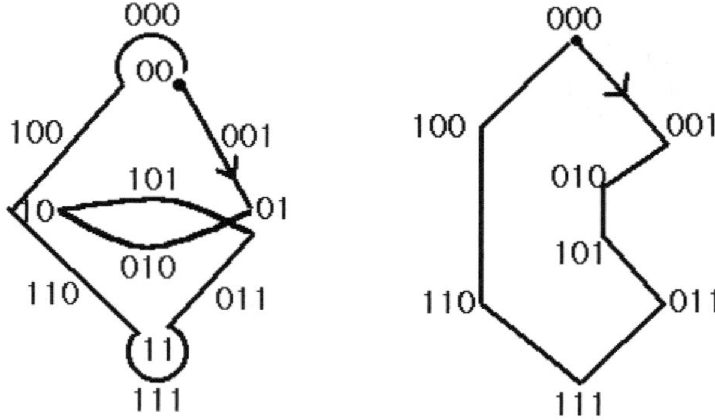

Figure 37.23. *A Eulerian cycle of G_2 and its corresponding Hamiltonian of G_3*

This is generalized. The Eulerian circuits of G_n can be expressed with binary cyclic words that are 2^{n+1} long that we read in blocks of *n* characters.

If we do this reading in blocks of $n + 1$ characters, we come back to reading the successive arcs to the number of 2^n traversed once and once alone. Thanks to the rule of passage by multiplication by two with eventual addition of 1 modulo 2^{n+1}, everything happens as if we were circulating on successive vertices of G_{n+1}. We thus find Hamiltonian cycles of G_{n+1}. Conversely, every Hamiltonian cycle of G_{n+1} expressed in binary gives a Eulerian circuit of G_n by doing the reading in blocks of *n* characters. There are as many Eulerian cycles for G_n as Hamiltonian cycles for G_{n+1}, and these cycles are represented by the same binary cyclic words.

37.6.4. *Number of Eulerian and Hamiltonian cycles of G_n*

We have to count the number of Eulerian circuits of G_n. Since the outdegree of each node is two and the number of Eulerian circuits starting with arc 0 1 is equal to that of directed spanning trees of root 0. Let us introduce the Laplacian matrix L of the graph, which is by definition, in the presence of loops, made up of L_{ij} elements with:

– for $i \neq j$, L_{ij} = - number of arcs from i to j;

– for $i = j$, L_{ii} = number of arcs stemming from i – number of arcs from i to i.

As L_{ii} is the number of arcs stemming from vertex number i other than the loops, the Laplacian matrix does not change if we drop the loops of graph G.

In these conditions, matrix L is linked to the adjacency matrix A by $L = 2I - A$. This implies that if λ_k is an eigenvalue of A, $2 - \lambda_k$ is eigenvalue of L. We know that the number of spanning trees of root 0 is also the product of the non-null eigenvalues of L divided by the number of graph vertices. Let us therefore use an interesting property of graph G_n.

Between one vertex and another, there is one and only one n-length path. Actually, it is sufficient to write the numbers of the two vertices in binary, and to concatenate the two words obtained. Reading the word thus obtained in n-length blocks gives a n-length path and no other path can exist.

Let A be the adjacency matrix of G_n. We know that matrix A^n has $A_{ij}^{(n)}$ as its coefficient, the number of n-length paths between vertices i and j. It results that $A^n = J$, where J is the matrix of which all the coefficients are equal to 1. If λ_k is an eigenvalue of A, λ_k^n is an eigenvalue of A^n. Furthermore, we know that J has 2^n once and 0 $2^n - 1$ times for its eigenvalues. Taking the nth roots, we find that the eigenvalues of A are 2 once and 0 otherwise. We saw that the Laplacian matrix of G_n is $L = 2I - A$, and that if λ_k is an eigenvalue of A, $2 - \lambda_k$ is eigenvalue of L. This gives 0 once and 2 $2^n - 1$ times.

We deduce from this that the number of Eulerian circuits of G_n is:

$$\frac{1}{2^n} 2^{2^n - 1} = 2^{2^n - n - 1}$$

It is also the number of Hamiltonian cycles of G_{n+1}.

The number of Hamiltonian cycles of G_n is therefore $2^{2^{n-1} - n}$.

APPENDICES

Appendix 1

Matrices

Let us recall that a vector, drawn in the form of an arrow, is characterized by its direction, its sense and its length. If we change its origin, conserving its direction, sense and length (here a real number), it is always the same or an equal vector (see Figure A1.1).

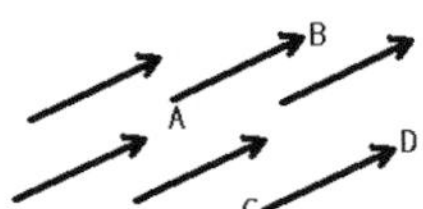

Figure A1.1. *A vector V, drawn in several ways (for example* ***AB***=***CD****)*

Now let us see some transformations making us go from vector $\boldsymbol{V}$ to vector $\boldsymbol{V}'$ following some simple rules. For example, in a plane, every vector $\boldsymbol{V}$ is transformed into $\boldsymbol{V}'$ based on the following rule: $\boldsymbol{V}'$ is deduced from $\boldsymbol{V}$ by rotating it +90°. This is called a vector rotation of angle $\pi/2$, and it is what we call a linear application.

A1.1. Notion of linear application

By definition, a liner application f transforms a vector $\boldsymbol{V}$ into a vector $\boldsymbol{V}'$ by obeying two properties, whatever the vectors concerned:

$$f(\boldsymbol{V}_1+\boldsymbol{V}_2) = f(\boldsymbol{V}_1) + f(\boldsymbol{V}_2)$$
$$f(k\boldsymbol{V}) = k\, f(\boldsymbol{V})$$

k being a real number.

For example, the vector rotation defined above obviously verifies these two properties: it is a linear application.

Now let us take a base, which enables us to give coordinates to the vectors, brought back to this base. In two dimensions, a base is made up of two non-collinear vectors, i.e. non-parallel and non-null, i.e. $\boldsymbol{i}$ and $\boldsymbol{j}$ (see Figure A1.2). In this context, a vector $\boldsymbol{V}$ has the two unique (real) numbers x and y as its coordinates such that:

$$\boldsymbol{V} = x\,\boldsymbol{i} + y\boldsymbol{j}$$

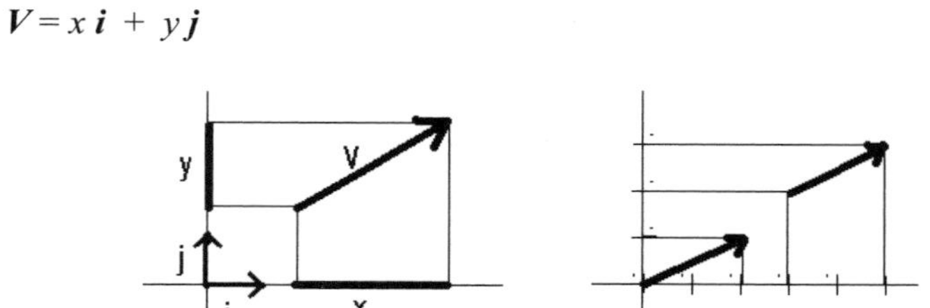

Figure A1.2. *Vector V and its coordinates x and y (left); and two equal vectors (of the same direction, sense and length) have the same coordinates, here 2, 1, i.e.* $\boldsymbol{V} = 2\boldsymbol{i} + \boldsymbol{j}$ *(right)*

Let us remain in two dimensions. How is a linear application f expressed in base $\boldsymbol{i}, \boldsymbol{j}$ when it makes us move from vector $\boldsymbol{V}(x, y)$ to a vector $\boldsymbol{V'}(x', y')$? Thanks to the definition of a linear application, we can write:

$$\boldsymbol{V'} = f(\boldsymbol{V}) = f(x\boldsymbol{i} + y\boldsymbol{j}) = f(x\boldsymbol{i}) + f(y\boldsymbol{j}) = x\,f(\boldsymbol{i}) + y\,f(\boldsymbol{j})$$

Let us consider the images of the base vectors $f(\boldsymbol{i})$ and $f(\boldsymbol{j})$. They have the numbers (a_{11}, a_{21}) and (a_{12}, a_{22}) as respective coordinates. With $\boldsymbol{V'} = x'\boldsymbol{i} + y'\boldsymbol{j}$, we get:

$$\begin{cases} x' = a_{11}x + a_{12}y \\ y' = a_{21}x + a_{22}y \end{cases}$$

The linear application is thus characterized in the base concerned by the four numbers a_{11}, a_{12}, a_{21} and a_{22}. It can be expressed in matrix form:

$$\begin{pmatrix} a_{11} & a_{12} \\ a_{21} & a_{22} \end{pmatrix}$$

It is the matrix A of linear application f in base $\boldsymbol{i}, \boldsymbol{j}$. The expression of the linear application is simplified into:

$\boldsymbol{x}' = A\boldsymbol{x}$, with the column vectors $\boldsymbol{x} = \begin{pmatrix} x \\ y \end{pmatrix}$ $\boldsymbol{x}' = \begin{pmatrix} x' \\ y' \end{pmatrix}$ and:

$$A = \begin{pmatrix} a_{11} & a_{12} \\ a_{21} & a_{22} \end{pmatrix} \qquad \begin{pmatrix} x' \\ y' \end{pmatrix} = \begin{pmatrix} a_{11} & a_{12} \\ a_{21} & a_{22} \end{pmatrix} \begin{pmatrix} x \\ y \end{pmatrix}$$

Therefore to create the column vector $A\boldsymbol{x}$, we have the following rule of development: to get x' we take each term of the first line of A which we multiply by the corresponding term of the column vector $\begin{pmatrix} x \\ y \end{pmatrix}$ proceeding to additions, hence $x' = a_{11}x + a_{12}y$, and similarly for y'. We see what will later become the means of multiplying two matrices appearing.

Let us return to matrix A. We notice that it has the images of the base vectors as its column vectors. For example, the vector rotation above has the matrix $\begin{pmatrix} 0 & -1 \\ 1 & 0 \end{pmatrix}$ on the condition that we choose an orthonormal base ($\boldsymbol{i}$ and $\boldsymbol{j}$) perpendicular and of the same length.

There is another way of looking at this. Instead of simply taking a base and playing on its vectors, we can take a benchmark with an origin O and a base of two vectors, and play on points. This goes back to forcing the vectors to pass through the origin O of the benchmark.

In these conditions, the application $\begin{cases} x' = a_{11}x + a_{12}y \\ y' = a_{21}x + a_{22}y \end{cases}$ transforms a point (x, y) into a point (x', y') in the same way as before, but in this case the origin point O remains fixed, transformed in itself. Therefore, with the same passage relations, the vector rotation defined above becomes a rotation of center O and angle +90°, using points (see Figure A1.3).

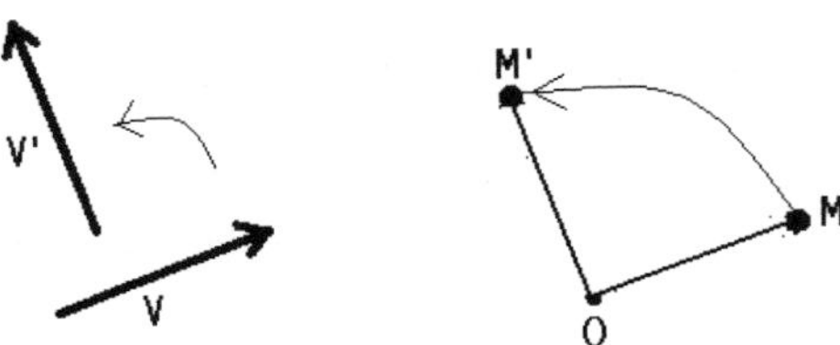

Figure A1.3. *The vector rotation: $V \to V'$, (left); and rotation of center O: $M \to M'$ (right)*

A1.2. Bijective linear application

An application is bijective when every vector ***V'*** of the plane is transformed from a unique vector ***V***, i.e. when every vector ***V'*** assumes a unique antecedent ***V***. We therefore have the following general property.

A linear application is a bijection iff the determinant of its matrix is non-null.

This is easily verified in two dimensions when we know that two vectors are collinear (parallel or one null) iff the determinant[1] made up of the two vectors taken in columns is null, which is written:

$$\begin{vmatrix} a_{11} & a_{12} \\ a_{21} & a_{22} \end{vmatrix} = a_{11}a_{22} - a_{21}a_{12} = 0$$

In other words, in two dimensions the linear application is a bijection iff the images of the two base vectors are non-collinear (non-null and not parallel). Let us take this case with non-collinear $f(\boldsymbol{i})$ and $f(\boldsymbol{j})$, and proceed to a base change, with the old base being ***i*** and ***j***, and the new one $f(\boldsymbol{i})$ and $f(\boldsymbol{j})$. As we have seen, a vector ***V*** of coordinates (x, y) in the old base becomes:

$$\boldsymbol{V}' = xf(\boldsymbol{i}) + yf(\boldsymbol{j})$$

We deduce the following property from this.

PROPERTY A1.1.– Vector ***V'*** image of ***V*** through f has the same coordinates in base $f(\boldsymbol{i}), f(\boldsymbol{j})$ as vector ***V*** in initial base ***i***, ***j***.

So we understand that there is bijection. If we take a vector ***V'*** of coordinates (x', y') in the new base, it assumes a unique antecedent ***V***, a vector having the same coordinates (x', y') in the old base.

Let us take an example, initially with an orthonormal base ***i***, ***j***, as matrix of the application $\begin{pmatrix} 2 & 1 \\ 1 & 2 \end{pmatrix}$ of non-null determinant 4 – 1 = 3. The images of the base vectors are $f(\boldsymbol{i})$ of coordinates (2, 1) and $f(\boldsymbol{j})$ of coordinates (1, 2). A vector $\boldsymbol{V}(x, y)$ in the initial base is transformed into ***V'***, which has the same coordinates (x, y) in the new base $f(\boldsymbol{i}), f(\boldsymbol{j})$.

---

1. For more details on determinants see Appendix 2.

If we take points in place of vectors, fixing the origin O of the benchmark, the square of vertex O and sides $\boldsymbol{i}$ and $\boldsymbol{j}$ is transformed into a parallelogram of which one vertex is O and the sides are $f(\boldsymbol{i})$ and $f(\boldsymbol{j})$ (see Figure A1.4). The corresponding drawing enables us to easily understand how the transformation acts on the points of the plane.

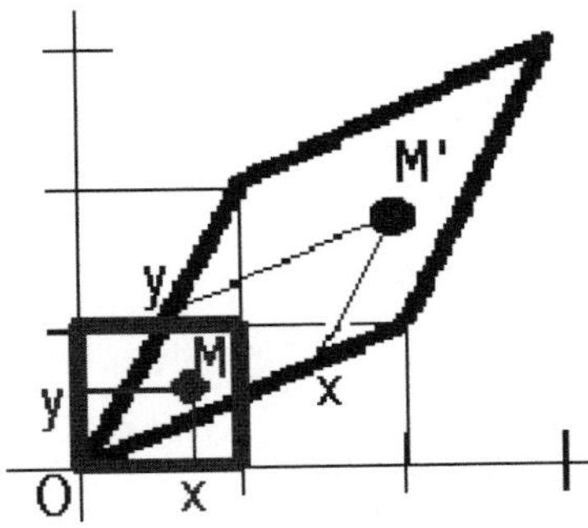

Figure A1.4. *Passage from M to M'*

On the other hand, if the parallelogram formed by $f(\boldsymbol{i})$ and $f(\boldsymbol{j})$ is flattened and reduced to a segment, all the points of the plane are transformed into points aligned on a straight line and there is no longer bijection. Take the application of matrix $\begin{pmatrix} 2 & 4 \\ 1 & 2 \end{pmatrix}$, for example, with its null determinant and the image vectors all having the same direction as vector (2, 1).

A1.3. Base change

We have just dealt with a very particular base change. Now let us move on to the general case. If we change base, the linear application remaining the same, its matrix expression will change since the column vectors of the matrix are now the images of the new base vectors.

Let $\boldsymbol{i}, \boldsymbol{j}$ be the vectors of the initial base and $\boldsymbol{I}$, $\boldsymbol{J}$ those of the new base, with $\boldsymbol{I}$ of coordinates (a, b) in relation to the old base and $\boldsymbol{J}$ (c, d), which is expressed:

$$\boldsymbol{I} = a\boldsymbol{i} + b\boldsymbol{j} \text{ and } \boldsymbol{J} = c\boldsymbol{i} + d\boldsymbol{j}$$

A vector $\boldsymbol{V}$ has as coordinates (x, y) in one, and (X, Y) in the other, with $\boldsymbol{V} = x\boldsymbol{i} + y\boldsymbol{j} = X\boldsymbol{I} + Y\boldsymbol{J}$. There is a link between the old coordinates and the new ones:

$$x\boldsymbol{i} + y\boldsymbol{j} = X(a\boldsymbol{i} + b\boldsymbol{j}) + Y(c\boldsymbol{i} + d\boldsymbol{j}) = (aX + cY)\boldsymbol{i} + (bX + dY)\boldsymbol{j}$$

hence by equalizing the coordinates:

$$\begin{cases} x = aX + cY \\ y = bX + dY \end{cases}$$

this can be expressed in matrix form:

$$x = P\boldsymbol{X}$$

postulating that $\boldsymbol{x} = \begin{pmatrix} x \\ y \end{pmatrix}$ and $\boldsymbol{X} = \begin{pmatrix} X \\ Y \end{pmatrix}$ as column vectors and matrix:

$$P = \begin{pmatrix} a & c \\ b & d \end{pmatrix}$$

The passage matrix P enables us to have the old coordinates in relation to the new ones. We see that its column vectors are the coordinates of the two new base vectors in the old base. As the column vectors of P are none other than non-collinear base vectors, the determinant of P is non-null.

A1.4. Product of two matrices

Let us make two linear applications f and g successively. The first transforms vector $\boldsymbol{V}$ into $\boldsymbol{V'}$, and the second transforms $\boldsymbol{V'}$ into $\boldsymbol{V''}$. This is expressed in a base $\boldsymbol{i}$, $\boldsymbol{j}$, with A and B as matrices representing the linear applications f and g:

$$\boldsymbol{x}' = A\boldsymbol{x} \text{ and } \boldsymbol{x}'' = B\boldsymbol{x}'$$

$$\begin{pmatrix} x' \\ y' \end{pmatrix} = \begin{pmatrix} a_{11} & a_{12} \\ a_{21} & a_{22} \end{pmatrix} \begin{pmatrix} x \\ y \end{pmatrix} \text{ and } \begin{pmatrix} x'' \\ y'' \end{pmatrix} = \begin{pmatrix} b_{11} & b_{12} \\ b_{21} & b_{22} \end{pmatrix} \begin{pmatrix} x' \\ y' \end{pmatrix}$$

Let us do the calculation to move directly from $\boldsymbol{x}$ to $\boldsymbol{x}''$, which corresponds to the product $g \circ f$ of the two applications, i.e. f followed by g, let us recall that:

$\boldsymbol{x}'' = B\boldsymbol{x}' = BA\boldsymbol{x}$, i.e.:

$$\begin{pmatrix} x'' \\ y'' \end{pmatrix} = \begin{pmatrix} b_{11}a_{11} + b_{12}a_{21} & b_{11}a_{12} + b_{12}a_{22} \\ b_{21}a_{11} + b_{22}a_{21} & b_{21}a_{12} + b_{22}a_{22} \end{pmatrix} \begin{pmatrix} x \\ y \end{pmatrix}$$

The product gf of the two linear applications has the product BA of their respective matrices as its matrix. We obtained the multiplication rule of two matrices: to have the term in line i and column j of BA, we take line i of B and column j of A. We multiply each one of their respective terms and then add these products. With $C=BA$, this gives:

$$c_{ij} = \sum_k b_{ik} a_{kj}$$

with k taking values 1 and 2 for 2×2 matrices.

This is generalized to square matrices $n \times n$, where the summation is done for k from 1 to n. We easily verify that the multiplication of two square matrices is associative, but non-commutative.

Now let us take the case where the matrices are said to be regular, i.e. that they are square matrices of $n \times n$ with a non-null determinant. This means that the corresponding linear application is bijective. We saw that by calculating the product gf of two linear applications (f followed by g) of matrices A for f and B for g in a given base, we obtained a linear application of matrix BA. When the two applications are bijective, their determinants $|A|$ and $|B|$ are different to 0. The product of the two bijections also being bijective; the determinant $|BA|$ is different to 0. Moreover, a calculation rule on determinants indicates that $|BA| = |B|\,|A|$. So the product of two regular matrices is a regular matrix. In this context, we can introduce the notion of inverse matrix.

A1.5. Inverse matrix

To simplify this concept, let us remain in two dimensions and consider a bijective linear application f. In a given base $\boldsymbol{i}, \boldsymbol{j}$, its matrix is A, and it is regular. Its determinant $|A|$ is different to 0. This also means that base $\boldsymbol{i}, \boldsymbol{j}$ is transformed by f into two non-collinear vectors $\boldsymbol{I}$ and $\boldsymbol{J}$ (non-null and non-parallel).

With $A = \begin{pmatrix} a_{11} & a_{12} \\ a_{21} & a_{22} \end{pmatrix}$, vectors ***I*** and ***J*** are the column vectors of the matrices:

$$I = \begin{pmatrix} a_{11} \\ a_{21} \end{pmatrix} \text{ and } J = \begin{pmatrix} a_{12} \\ a_{22} \end{pmatrix}$$

As the linear application is bijective, it assumes an inverse f^{-1}, which is also linear. Taking ***I*** and ***J*** as the base, which is valid, the inverse application makes us move from ***I***, ***J*** to ***i***, ***j***. The associated matrix has as the vectors ***i*** and ***j*** plotted in base ***I***, ***J*** as its column vectors. Furthermore, we know that $\begin{cases} I = a_{11}i + a_{21}j \\ J = a_{12}i + a_{22}j \end{cases}$. We now have to find ***i*** and ***j*** as a function of ***I*** and ***J***. Multiplying the first equation by a_{22} and the second by $-a_{21}$, we find $(a_{11}a_{22} - a_{12}a_{21})\boldsymbol{i} = a_{22}\,\boldsymbol{I} - a_{21}\,\boldsymbol{J}$, and similarly for ***j***. Finally, Δ being the non-null determinant of matrix A, this gives:

$$\boldsymbol{i} = \begin{pmatrix} a_{22}/\Delta \\ -a_{21}/\Delta \end{pmatrix} \text{ and } \boldsymbol{j} = \begin{pmatrix} -a_{12}/\Delta \\ a_{11}/\Delta \end{pmatrix}$$

Hence the inverse application matrix A':

$$\frac{1}{\Delta}\begin{pmatrix} a_{22} & -a_{12} \\ -a_{21} & a_{11} \end{pmatrix}$$

As we have $ff^1 = f^1f = Id$, Id being the identity application (nothing moves), we also have $AA' = A'A = I$, I being the identity matrix application made up of a diagonal of 1, the remainder being at 0. Matrix A' is called the inverse of A and it is expressed as A^{-1}. Matrix I is the identity matrix, verifying that $AI = IA = A$ for every matrix A.

In conclusion, regular matrices with the multiplication operation have a structure said to be of non-commutative group: the product of two regular matrices is a regular matrix, the multiplication is associative, it assumes a neutral element I, and every matrix assumes an inverse.

We will note that for 2×2 matrices this inverse matrix A^{-1} is obtained by reversing the main diagonal of A and changing the sign of the other diagonal, with the entire thing being divided by the determinant $\Delta = a_{11}a_{22} - a_{12}a_{21}$.

In the general case of regular $n \times n$ matrices, the inverse matrix A^{-1} of A is obtained by taking the transpose of the co-matrix of A and dividing each term by the determinant of A. Let us specify the terms: the transpose of a matrix is obtained by exchanging its lines and its columns. The co-matrix of A has as an element in line i and column j, the determinant obtained by dropping line i and column j in matrix A, then multiplying this partial determinant by $(-1)^{i+j}$. If you prefer, matrix A^{-1} has as an element in line i and column j, the partial determinant obtained by dropping line j and column i in A, then multiplying it by $(-1)^{i+j}$ and dividing it by $|A|$. For example:

$$A = \begin{pmatrix} 1 & 1 & 0 \\ 0 & 1 & 1 \\ 1 & 0 & 1 \end{pmatrix}.$$

$$|A| = 1 + 1 = 2.$$

$$\text{Co-matrix}A = \begin{pmatrix} 1 & 1 & -1 \\ -1 & 1 & 1 \\ 1 & -1 & 1 \end{pmatrix}$$

$$\text{Transpose of the co-matrix} = \begin{pmatrix} 1 & -1 & 1 \\ 1 & 1 & -1 \\ -1 & 1 & 1 \end{pmatrix}.$$

$$\text{Hence } A^{-1} = \begin{pmatrix} 1/2 & -1/2 & 1/2 \\ 1/2 & 1/2 & -1/2 \\ -1/2 & 1/2 & 1/2 \end{pmatrix}$$

A1.6. Eigenvalues and eigenvectors

Let us consider a $n \times n$ square matrix with real coefficients in a space of dimension n. If we end up finding a non-null vector $\boldsymbol{x}$ with real n (even complex) coordinates such that $A\boldsymbol{x} = \lambda \boldsymbol{x}$ for a certain real (or complex) number λ, we say that λ is an eigenvalue and $\boldsymbol{x}$ an eigenvector associated with eigenvalue λ.

As matrix A represents a certain linear application in one base, an eigenvector is a vector that conserves its direction under the effect of the linear application. Hence the interest in finding out the eigenvalues, when they exist, as then the behavior of the linear application becomes much clearer.

Solving $A\boldsymbol{x} = \lambda \boldsymbol{x}$ refers to solving $(A - \lambda I)\boldsymbol{x} = 0$. It is a system of n equations with n unknowns (the coordinates of $\boldsymbol{x}$) with a parameter λ. This so-called homogeneous system, as its second member is null, assumes the null vector $\boldsymbol{x} = 0$ as a clear solution. The number of solutions to the system depends on the determinant of matrix $A - \lambda I$, which is itself a function of λ. We know that the system assumes a unique solution, here $\boldsymbol{x} = 0$, iff the determinant of $A - \lambda I$ is non-null. In this case, we do not find any eigenvectors. On the other hand, when the determinant of $A - \lambda I$ is null, it assumes infinite solutions, especially of the different vectors of 0. Therefore for the values λ that render the determinant of $A - \lambda I$ null, we find eigenvectors associated with these numbers λ that are eigenvalues.

To get the eigenvalues, we are led to solve the equation:

$$|A - \lambda I| = 0$$

i.e. to searching for the roots of the polynomial $|A - \lambda I|$ of n degree, called the characteristic polynomial of the matrix. Once the eigenvalues have been found, we search for the associated eigenvalues by solving the system $(A - \lambda I)\boldsymbol{x} = 0$. Let us take examples in two dimensions.

– *Example 1*:

$$A = \begin{pmatrix} 2 & 1 \\ 1 & 2 \end{pmatrix}$$

Its characteristic polynomial is:

$$\begin{vmatrix} 2-\lambda & 1 \\ 1 & 2-\lambda \end{vmatrix} = (2-\lambda)^2 - 1 = \lambda^2 - 2\lambda + 3$$

It has 3 and 1 as roots. For $\lambda = 3$, the system is reduced to a single equation $-x + y = 0$, hence an infinite number of eigenvectors that are all multiples of vector $\begin{pmatrix} 1 \\ 1 \end{pmatrix}$. For $\lambda = 1$, the eigenvectors verify $x+y = 0$. They are multiples of vector $\begin{pmatrix} -1 \\ 1 \end{pmatrix}$. Under the effect of the linear application vector (1, 1) becomes (3, 3) and vector (-1, 1) remains invariant. The behavior of the application becomes clearer by using these eigenvectors (see Figure A1.5). A dilation of factor 3 occurs in direction (1, 1), and nothing in the other direction (-1, 1).

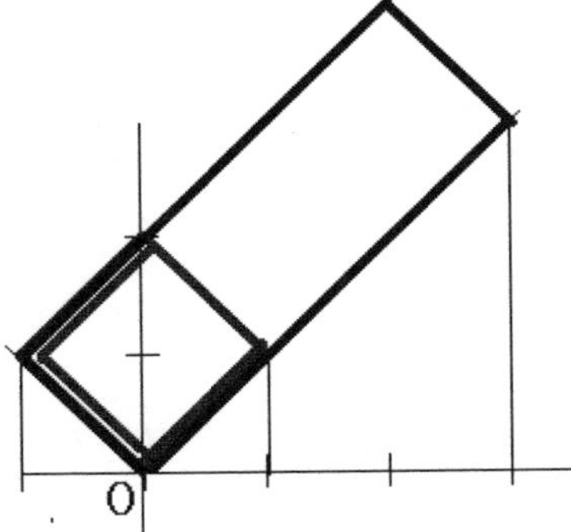

Figure A1.5. *Transformation of example 1 from its eigenvectors*

– *Example 2*:

$$A = \begin{pmatrix} 5/2 & 1/2 \\ -1/2 & 3/2 \end{pmatrix}$$

The characteristic polynomial is:

$$\begin{pmatrix} 5/2-\lambda & 1/2 \\ -1/2 & 3/2-\lambda \end{pmatrix} = \lambda^2 - 4\lambda + 4 = (\lambda - 2)^2$$

The double eigenvalue 2 gives eigenvalues verifying $x + y = 0$. One of them is (1, -1), which is transformed into (2, -2). Let us take this eigenvector as the first base vector and choose for example vector (1, 1) as the second base vector, which is transformed into (3, 1), see Figure A1.6.

Let us indicate that the characteristic polynomial is not only verified by the eigenvalues of a matrix, it also has the property of being verified by the matrix itself, which we call the Cayley-Hamilton equality.

A1.7. Similar matrices

Let us take a linear application of matrix A in one base, transforming a vector $\boldsymbol{x}$ into $\boldsymbol{x}'$, i.e. $\boldsymbol{x}' = A\boldsymbol{x}$. Let us do a base change. Vectors $\boldsymbol{x}$ and $\boldsymbol{x}'$ have their coordinates modified and become $\boldsymbol{X}$ and $\boldsymbol{X}'$. The linear application above takes the form $\boldsymbol{X}' = B\boldsymbol{X}$, where B is the application matrix in the new base.

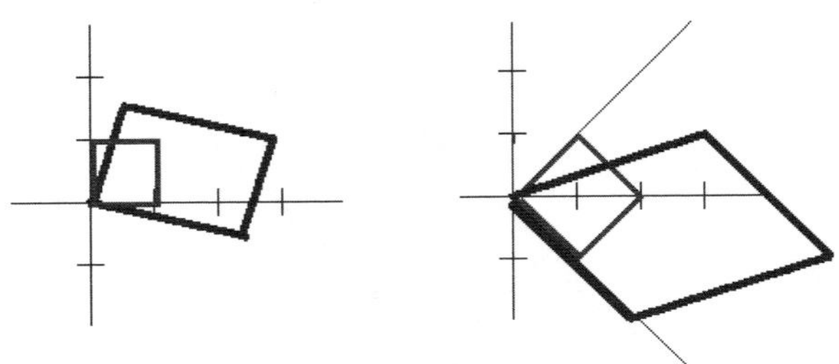

Figure A1.6. *Transformation of example 2 in the initial base (the square becoming the parallelogram) (left); and the same transformation in the new base (right)*

Evidently matrices A and B, which represent the same linear application, are linked to each other. To find this link, let us recall that during a base change the formula of passage from old to new coordinates is $\boldsymbol{x} = P\boldsymbol{X}$, where P is an inversible matrix, hence $\boldsymbol{X} = P^{-1}\boldsymbol{x}$. From $\boldsymbol{x}' = A\boldsymbol{x}$, we have $P\boldsymbol{X}' = AP\boldsymbol{X}$, hence $\boldsymbol{X}' = P^{-1}AP\boldsymbol{X}$, and we find:

$$B = P^{-1}AP$$

We say that matrices A and $P^{-1}AP$ with inversible P are similar, since they represent the same linear application in different bases. Even two matrices A and B are similar if we end up finding an invertible matrix P such that $B = P^{-1}AP$.

Similar matrices have the following properties:

– they have the same characteristic polynomial, therefore the same eigenvalues and eigenvectors. The characteristic polynomial is intrinsic to the underlying linear application;

– they have the same trace, the trace being the sum of the diagonal elements of a matrix;

– they have the same determinant.

In the case where the eigenvectors form a base, like in example 1 above, we get a diagonal matrix D in this base, with each eigenvalue on the diagonal, since the image of the eigenvector (1, 0, 0, …, 0) becomes (λ, 0, 0, …, 0), and similarly for other eigenvectors. We say that matrix A, representing the linear application in a certain base $\boldsymbol{i}\,\boldsymbol{j}$, is diagonalizable, and:

$$D = P^{-1}\,A\,P$$

with P being the passage matrix from base $\boldsymbol{i}\,\boldsymbol{j}$ to the base of the eigenvectors, and D the diagonal matrix.

A1.8. Exercise

Show that all the 2×2 matrices with real coefficients are similar to one of its three matrices, a and b being real numbers:

$$(1)\begin{pmatrix} a & 0 \\ 0 & b \end{pmatrix} \qquad (2)\begin{pmatrix} a & 1 \\ 0 & a \end{pmatrix} \qquad (3)\begin{pmatrix} a & -b \\ b & a \end{pmatrix}$$

The characteristic polynomial of a 2×2 matrix is of second degree. It assumes either two distinct real roots, or a double real root, or two conjugate complex roots. These roots are the eigenvalues. Let us distinguish these three cases.

If the characteristic equation assumes two distinct real roots, the matrix assumes distinct eigenvalues a and b. The corresponding eigenvectors are non-parallel and non-null, matrix A is diagonalizable, and in the base of the eigenvectors it is expressed in the form (1).

Now let us assume that it has a single eigenvalue a. If matrix A is equal to aI, it is of the form (1) with $b = a$. If it is not aI, it has an eigenvector $\boldsymbol{v}$ verifying $A\boldsymbol{v} = a\boldsymbol{v}$. Not all of the non-null vectors of the plane can be eigenvectors, as if it was this way every vector (x, y) would become (ax, ay) and we would have $A = aI$, which we rejected. Therefore a non-null vector $\boldsymbol{X}$ exists such that $A\boldsymbol{X} \neq a\boldsymbol{X}$, hence a non-null vector $\boldsymbol{V}$ such that $\boldsymbol{V} = A\boldsymbol{X} - a\boldsymbol{X}$, i.e. $\boldsymbol{V} = (A - aI)\boldsymbol{X}$. Consequently $(A - aI)\boldsymbol{V} = (A - aI)^2\boldsymbol{X}$. Thanks to the Cayley-Hamilton theorem, we know that $(A - aI)^2 = 0$, hence $(A - aI)\boldsymbol{V} = 0$, $A\boldsymbol{V} = a\boldsymbol{V}$ and $\boldsymbol{V}$ is an eigenvector. On its side, vector $\boldsymbol{X}$ is non-null and non-parallel to $\boldsymbol{V}$, otherwise it would be an eigenvector for eigenvalue a and we would have $A\boldsymbol{X} = a\boldsymbol{X}$. The two vectors $\boldsymbol{V}$ and $\boldsymbol{X}$ form a base, and the similar matrix with A in its new base has the column vectors:

$$A\boldsymbol{X} = \boldsymbol{V} + a\boldsymbol{X} \text{ and } A\boldsymbol{V} = a\boldsymbol{V}$$

It is expressed $\begin{pmatrix} a & 1 \\ 0 & a \end{pmatrix}$, and is of the form (2).

Lastly, let us envisage the case where the two eigenvalues are complex conjugates, i.e. $a \pm ib$ with $b \neq 0$. The Cayley-Hamilton theorem enables us to write:

$$(A - (a + bi)I)\,(A - (a - bi)\,I) = 0, \text{ or even } (A - aI)^2 + b^2I = 0$$

Let us take a non-null vector $\boldsymbol{X}$, and vector $\boldsymbol{V}$ such that $\boldsymbol{V} = \frac{1}{b}(A - aI)\boldsymbol{X}$.

Therefore $(A - aI)\mathbf{V} = -b\mathbf{X}$. Just like $\mathbf{X}$, vector $\mathbf{V}$ is not null, as if this was the case we would have $(A - aI)\mathbf{V} = 0$ hence $-b\mathbf{X}=0$, which is impossible. Vectors $\mathbf{X}$ and $\mathbf{V}$ are not parallel either, as if we had $\mathbf{V} = q\mathbf{X}$ with real q different to 0, the equality:

$$(A - aI)\mathbf{V} = -b\mathbf{X}$$

would become:

$$(A - aI)\mathbf{X} = (-b/q)\mathbf{X}$$

i.e.: $A\mathbf{X} = (a - b / q)\mathbf{X}$

and $\mathbf{X}$ vector with real coordinates would be an eigenvector associated with a real eigenvalue, which is impossible. Vectors $\mathbf{V}$ and $\mathbf{X}$ are non-collinear. We can take them as a new base. We already know that $A\mathbf{V} = a\mathbf{V} - b\mathbf{X}$. On the other hand:

$$(A - aI)^2\mathbf{V} = -b(A - aI)\mathbf{X},$$

i.e.: $-b^2\mathbf{V} = -b(A\mathbf{X} - a\mathbf{X})$,

or: $b\mathbf{V} = A\mathbf{X} - a\mathbf{X}$

or lastly:

$$A\mathbf{X} = b\mathbf{V} + a\mathbf{X}$$

In the new base $\mathbf{V}$, $\mathbf{X}$, the matrix has column vectors $A\mathbf{V}$ and $A\mathbf{X}$, i.e. $\begin{pmatrix} a & b \\ -b & a \end{pmatrix}$, which is form (3).

A1.9. Eigenvalues of circulant matrices and circular graphs

A circulant matrix pxp has the terms $a_0\ a_1\ \ldots\ a_{p-1}$ for line 0, and the following lines are shifted one notch to the right each time, therefore the term in line i and column j is a_{j-i} , $j - i$ eventually being reduced to modulo p. Such a matrix is expressed:

$$A = \begin{pmatrix} a_0 & a_1 & a_2 & a_3 \\ a_3 & a_0 & a_1 & a_2 \\ a_2 & a_3 & a_0 & a_1 \\ a_1 & a_2 & a_3 & a_0 \end{pmatrix} \quad \text{for } p = 4$$

Let ω be the first complex p^{th} root of the unit after 1, i.e.:

$$\omega = \exp(i\, 2\pi / p)$$

The p p^{th} roots of the unit are ω^k with k between 0 and $p - 1$. We therefore verify that the p column vectors of the form $(1, \omega^k, \omega^{2k}, \omega^{3k}, \ldots, \omega^{(p-1)k})$ are eigenvectors, and the p associated eigenvalues are $\lambda_k = \sum_{j=0}^{p-1} a_j\, \omega^{jk}$.

The simplest applications concern the graphs in the shape of a circle.

– *The directed cycle graph* $\underline{C}_n$ is a graph with n vertices, displayed in a circular way, in such a way that each vertex is linked to its successor by a unique arc (see Figure A1.7).

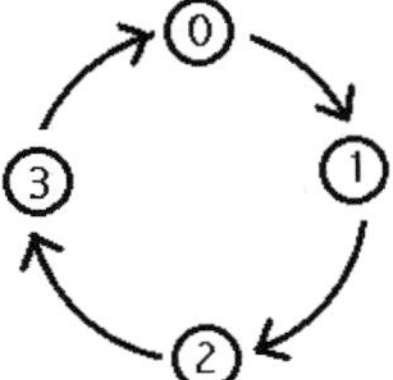

Figure A1.7. *Cycle graph* $\underline{C}_4$

The adjacency matrix is of the form $\begin{pmatrix} 0 & 1 & 0 & 0 \\ 0 & 0 & 1 & 0 \\ 0 & 0 & 0 & 1 \\ 1 & 0 & 0 & 0 \end{pmatrix}$ where $n = 4$, and its eigenvalues are:

$$\lambda_k = e^{i\, 2k\pi/n}$$

with k from 0 to $n - 1$.

– *The bidirectional directed circuit graph* C_n can be seen as the union of two graphs (see Figure A1.8). The first, with its arrows in the upward direction, is the previous graph $\underline{C}_n$, the adjacency matrix A of which we know. The other, with arrows in the opposite direction, corresponds to paths n – 1-length paths, has the adjacency matrix A^{n-1}. The adjacency matrix of C_n is $A + A^{n-1}$, and its eigenvalues are: $e^{i\, 2k\pi/n} + e^{-i\, 2k\pi/n} = 2\cos(2k\pi / n)$.

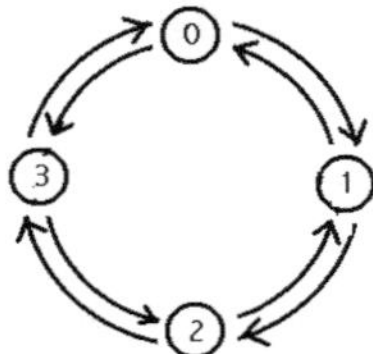

Figure A1.8. *The bidirectional directed graph C_4*

– *The Möbius ladder* is an undirected graph with $2n$ vertices, with a closed circuit for the vertices from 0 to $n-1$, plus diagonal junctions between vertices i and $n+i$ (see Figure A1.9). We can also consider it as a directed graph by replacing each of the edges with two arcs in opposite directions, which does not change anything through the adjacency matrix.

This graph is the union of three graphs, based on graph $\underline{C}_{2n}$, grouping the paths 1 unit long, as well as those that are $2n-1$ units long, and those of n units, with $A + A^{2n-1} + A^{n}$ for its adjacency matrix. The eigenvalues are:

$$\lambda_k = 2\cos(k\pi / n) + (-1)^k$$

with k from 0 to $2n-1$.

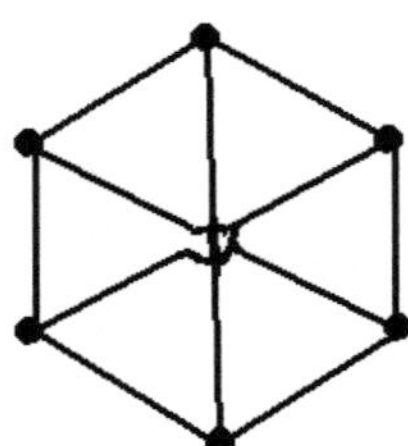

Figure A1.9. *Möbius ladder with six vertices*

The results related to the circulant matrices take all their importance in the counting of trees that cover the graphs (see Chapter 33).

Appendix 2

Determinants and Route Combinatorics

We already encountered determinants in Appendix 1, as the backdrop to linear algebra. They are used particularly in the property that says that a matrix with real or complex coefficients is invertible iff its determinant is not null.[1] In this appendix we will return to the properties of determinants, but apply them to the main object of our work: combinatorics.

A2.1. Recalling determinants

A determinant is expressed in the form of a square $N \times N$ table of numbers, and it is a number obtained by developing this table in the following way.

For example for $N = 3$, we have the determinant of order 3: $\begin{vmatrix} a_{11} & a_{12} & a_{13} \\ a_{21} & a_{22} & a_{23} \\ a_{31} & a_{32} & a_{33} \end{vmatrix}$

where the coefficients are indexed by the line and column where they are found. It is equal to:

$$a_{11}a_{22}a_{33} + a_{12}a_{23}a_{31} + a_{13}a_{21}a_{32} - a_{11}a_{23}a_{32} - a_{12}a_{21}a_{33} - a_{13}a_{22}a_{31}$$

1. Nevertheless let us point out Sheldon Axler's article, *Down with Determinants!* [AXL94], showing that linear algebra, notably matrix diagonalization and the notion of the characteristic polynomial, can be dealt with without ever using determinants. In this context, the notion of determinants would take its true meaning in combinatorics, as we will see in this appendix. The reference on this subject is [GES 85]. See also [AIG 01].

This determinant is the sum of six terms, each of which is the product of three elements of the table of three lines and columns. More specifically, each term contains an element of each line and each column, and is of the form $a_{1p}\, a_{2q}\, a_{3r}$ where pqr is a permutation of 123. It is preceded by a + or – sign, depending on whether this permutation is even or odd. There are as many terms as permutations of the N integers 1, 2, 3, …, N, i.e. $N!$, in this case 3! = 6, with the three even permutations 123, 231, 312 and three odd permutations 132, 213, 321.

We check that a determinant can be developed based on its first line in the following way, for $N = 3$:

$$\begin{vmatrix} a_{11} & a_{12} & a_{13} \\ a_{21} & a_{22} & a_{23} \\ a_{31} & a_{32} & a_{33} \end{vmatrix} = a_{11}\begin{vmatrix} a_{22} & a_{23} \\ a_{32} & a_{33} \end{vmatrix} - a_{12}\begin{vmatrix} a_{21} & a_{23} \\ a_{31} & a_{33} \end{vmatrix} + a_{13}\begin{vmatrix} a_{21} & a_{22} \\ a_{31} & a_{32} \end{vmatrix}$$

Each term a_{1p} of the first line is multiplied by the determinant of $N - 1$ order, here 2, extracted from the one of third order by removing the line and column of the term concerned, and with an alternating + or – sign in the successive terms.

These determinants of $N - 1$ order with their + or – sign are called the cofactors of the terms of the first line. These same determinants without their sign are called the minors. This formula of development according to the first line brings back the calculation of a determinant of N order to that of minors of $N - 1$ order, with the sign problem in addition.

There we have a recursive way of calculating a determinant,[2] by going down to the determinant of second order, obtained by a cross product, as for example:

$$\begin{vmatrix} a_{22} & a_{23} \\ a_{32} & a_{33} \end{vmatrix} = a_{22}a_{33} - a_{23}a_{32}$$

Here are some properties of determinants:

– a determinant can be developed according to its first column, like we did for the first line, or more generally according to any line or column. All we have to do is calculate the sum of the terms of the line or column concerned, each multiplied by their respective cofactors;

– the determinant changes sign if we exchange two lines or columns between themselves;

---

2. Instead of a recursive program, we can program the calculation of a determinant by using the enumeration of permutations. Other methods using modular arithmatics exist.

– the determinant does not change value if we add to one line to another line multiplied by coefficient k. Similarly for columns. In particular, if a determinant has two equal lines or columns, it is null;

– the determinant is a homogeneous linear function of the elements of a line or a column, which is translated by the formulae:

$$\begin{vmatrix} a & b & c+c' \\ d & e & f+f' \\ g & h & i+i' \end{vmatrix} = \begin{vmatrix} a & b & c \\ d & e & f \\ g & h & i \end{vmatrix} + \begin{vmatrix} a & b & c' \\ d & e & f' \\ g & h & i' \end{vmatrix}$$

and:

$$\begin{vmatrix} ka & kb & kc \\ d & e & f \\ g & h & i \end{vmatrix} = k \begin{vmatrix} a & b & c \\ d & e & f \\ g & h & i \end{vmatrix}$$

A2.2. Determinants and tilings

Let us begin by taking a bipartite graph with half the vertices in one color and the other half in another color, with each edge joining a vertex of one color to a vertex of the other color.

If we end up taking a part of the edges, having no extremity in common, but with the extremities of the two sides of each edge giving all the graph vertices, we say that we have a perfect coupling.

For example, for a cube (see Figure A2.1), one of the perfect couplings is obtained with edges 1 1', 2 4', 3 3', 4 2', corresponding to the permutation:

$$\begin{pmatrix} 1 & 2 & 3 & 4 \\ 1' & 4' & 3' & 2' \end{pmatrix}$$

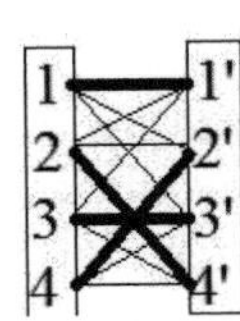

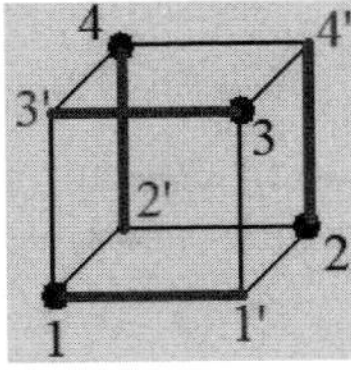

Figure A2.1. *The bipartite graph of the cube and an example of perfect coupling in thick lines (left and right)*

By placing the vertices of one color before those of the other color, i.e. in the order 1 2 3 4 1' 2' 3' 4', the adjacency matrix of the cube graph is presented in the form of blocks:

$$\begin{pmatrix} 0 & A \\ A & 0 \end{pmatrix} \text{ with matrix } A = \begin{bmatrix} 1 & 1 & 1 & 0 \\ 1 & 1 & 0 & 1 \\ 1 & 0 & 1 & 1 \\ 0 & 1 & 1 & 1 \end{bmatrix}$$

Reading the permutations obtained by taking a non-null element in each line and in each column of A, their product therefore being equal to 1, gives the perfect couplings. We proceed as if we were developing the determinant of A, except that we put + signs before each term (which is equal to 1). The sum of the terms gives the number of perfect couplings. It is no longer the determinant but what we call the permanent of A. For example, for the cube we find:

$$perm\ A = 9$$

in particular. If we want the perfect couplings containing edge 1 1', which corresponds to a third of the couplings, it is sufficient to take the permanent:

$$perm \begin{bmatrix} 1 & 0 & 1 \\ 0 & 1 & 1 \\ 1 & 1 & 1 \end{bmatrix} = 1 + 1 + 1 = 3$$

whereas the determinant would be equal to $1 - 1 - 1 = -1$.

Finally we have the property:

$$number\ of\ perfect\ couplings = Perm\ A$$

If a permanent is developed like a determinant, it does not have the determinant's properties, especially the ones that allow us to transform a determinant into a simpler one.

This makes its calculation difficult as soon as the associated matrix has large dimensions. In some particular cases we can nevertheless refer to a calculation of determinants.

Now let us take a graph in the form of a square network, delimited by a border without a hole to the inside, and bipartite with half the vertices in one color and the other half in another. This can be represented by a checkerboard with black and white squares. Its perfect coupling refers to a domino tiling of the checkerboard, such as, for example, the checkerboard in Figure A2.2 and one of the possible tilings.

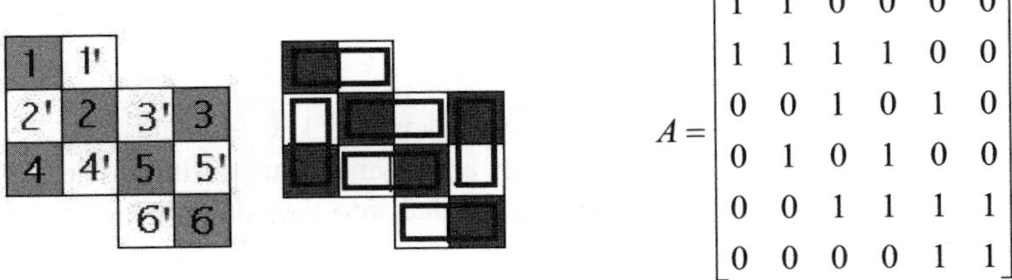

$$A=\begin{bmatrix}1&1&0&0&0&0\\1&1&1&1&0&0\\0&0&1&0&1&0\\0&1&0&1&0&0\\0&0&1&1&1&1\\0&0&0&0&1&1\end{bmatrix}$$

Figure A2.2. *A checkerboard with its numbered squares (left); a domino tiling corresponding to the perfect coupling 1 1', 2 3', 3 5', 4 2', 5 4', 6 6'; and the adjacency matrix where the coefficients of the coupling have number 1s forming a permutation (right)*

The number of tilings is always equal to the permanent of matrix A. Now let us replace the 1s corresponding to vertical lines with is (the complex number such that $i^2 = -1$). It can be shown that the permanent is equal to the modulus of the new determinant thus obtained:

$$\det \bar{A}=\begin{vmatrix}1&i&0&0&0&0\\i&1&1&i&0&0\\0&0&1&0&i&0\\0&i&0&1&0&0\\0&0&i&1&1&i\\0&0&0&0&i&1\end{vmatrix}=1-5i^2+4i^4=10$$

We find 10 tilings, of which one is single if completely horizontal, five have two vertical dominos and four have four vertical ones.

Another checkerboard example is the one given in Figure A2.3.

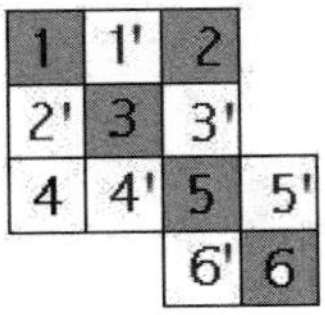

Figure A2.3. *Another checkerboard*

Developing the corresponding determinant gives: $-2i + 4i^3 - 2i^5 = -8i$, i.e. a total of eight possible tilings, more specifically two with a vertical domino, four with three vertical dominos, and two with five vertical ones. For example, a tiling like 1 2', 2 1', 3 3', 4 4', 5 6', 6 5', comes in during the development of the determinant in the form $+i^3$, as it has three vertical dominos, and the + sign because the permutation 2'1'3'4'6'5' is even (two inversions). Note that each tiling contains at least one vertical domino.

Now let us take all the tilings of the 4x4 square. The formula that we saw in Chapter 18 gave 36 tilings. The calculations above enable us to find this result again. Actually, the tilings of the 4x4 square are divided into four categories depending on the positions of the two dominos present in the corners of the square in the bottom left and top right (see Figure A2.4).

We know the number of tilings in all these cases, because what is left is to fill in the two types of checkerboard we studied above. We have a total of 8 + 8 + 10 + 10 = 36 tilings of the 4x4 square.

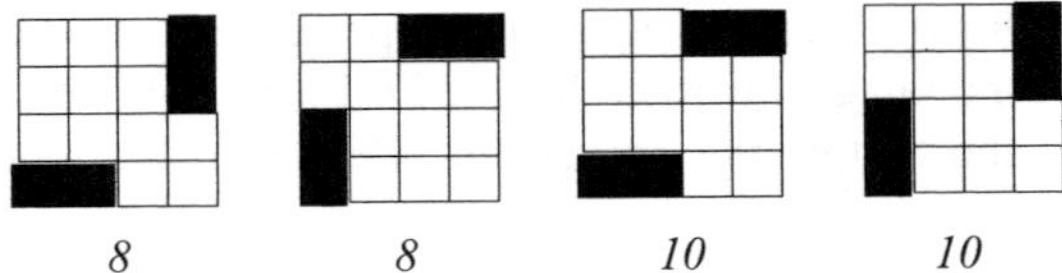

Figure A2.4. *The four layouts of the two dominos in the bottom left and top right on the 4x4 chessboard, with the number of tilings of the checkerboards remaining to be filled*

Finally let us deal with the chessboard with one corner removed, as it happens a square five cubes long and five wide, with one box less in one corner (see Figure A2.5).

The determinant associated with the adjacency matrix is equal, once developed, to:

$$9i^2 - 48i^4 + 78i^6 - 48i^8 + 9i^{10}$$

This means that nine vertical domino tilings exist; 48 with four vertical dominos; 76 with six vertical dominos; 48 with eight vertical dominos; and nine with 10 vertical dominos – i.e. a total of 192 tilings.

This can be found manually, starting by filling in the bottom line (and each time, we fill in the column on the right in all possible ways). Without going into the details, we find:

a) with two horizontal dominos on the bottom line: 95 cases;

b) with one horizontal then two vertical dominos: 25 cases;

c) with one vertical, one horizontal, then one vertical: 16 cases;

d) with two vertical ones then one horizontal: 41 cases; and

e) with four vertical dominos: 15 cases.

These calculations give new results on several shapes of checkerboards. For example, the 41 cases in (*d*) tile the shape 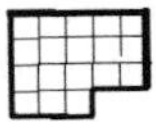 , which corresponds to the tiling of the 5x4 rectangle with a horizontal domino in the bottom right, hence 95 – 41 = 54 tilings for the shape .

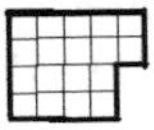

1	1'	2	2'	3
3'	4	4'	5	5'
6	6'	7	7'	8
8'	9	9'	10	10'
11	11'	12	12'	

$$\begin{vmatrix} 1&0&i&0&0&0&0&0&0&0&0&0 \\ 1&1&0&i&0&0&0&0&0&0&0&0 \\ 0&1&0&0&i&0&0&0&0&0&0&0 \\ i&0&1&1&0&i&0&0&0&0&0&0 \\ 0&i&0&1&1&0&i&0&0&0&0&0 \\ 0&0&i&0&0&1&0&i&0&0&0&0 \\ 0&0&0&i&0&1&1&0&i&0&0&0 \\ 0&0&0&0&i&0&1&0&0&i&0&0 \\ 0&0&0&0&0&i&0&1&1&0&i&0 \\ 0&0&0&0&0&0&i&0&1&1&0&i \\ 0&0&0&0&0&0&0&i&0&0&1&0 \\ 0&0&0&0&0&0&0&0&i&0&1&1 \end{vmatrix}$$

Figure A2.5. *A 5×5 chessboard with one corner removed and the associated matrix*

With case (*e*), we find that the number of tilings of the 5x3 rectangle with one corner removed is 15.

For $N = 7$, the same type of calculation[3] gives:

$$-64\, i^3 + 960\, i^5 - 5536\, i^7 + 16288\, i^9 - 27328\, i^{11} + 27328\, i^{13} - 16288\, i^{15} + 5536\, i^{17}$$
$$- 960\, i^{19} + 64\, i^{21}$$
$$= 100352\, i$$, i.e. 100,352 tilings.

3. For these calculations it is advisable to use mathematics software, in the style of Mathematica.

A2.3. Path sets and determinant

The context is the following: on an acyclic directed graph, we take N starting points called 0, 1, 2,…, $N-1$ as well as N endpoints. There is a certain number of paths leading from each starting point to each endpoint 0', 1', 2, …, $N-1$'. We are interested in sets of N paths C_0, C_1, ..., C_{N-1} that have starting points from 0 to $N-1$ and an endpoint taken from N endpoints, where two paths cannot have the same endpoint. Such a set of N paths is characterized by endpoints that constitute a permutation of the N numbers of corresponding points.

For a given permutation, we already find a certain number of path sets, because there is not necessarily a unique path on the graph from i to j'. It is the same for each of the $N!$ permutations of the endpoints. Out of all these path sets, some have paths that intersect or touch each other, and others that have no path that intersects or touches another. We are interested in this last case, and we will see that the number of path sets without intersecting each other is equal to a certain determinant, as we will explain in the following example.

A2.3.1. *First example: paths without intersection in a square network*

Let us take the square network of the quarter plane delimited by the x and the y axes. Let us take the $N = 3$ points of the x axis, of abscissae 0, 1 and 2 as starting points, and the three points of the y axis of ordinates 0, 1 and 2 as endpoints.

A set of three paths is such that they start from points 0, 1 and 2 of the x axis and end up at the three points of the y axis following a certain permutation, for example 1, 0, 2, using either horizontal steps to the left or vertical steps upwards in the square network thus oriented, which gives for example the three paths (0, 1), (1, 0), (2, 2), of the form indicated in Figure A2.6.

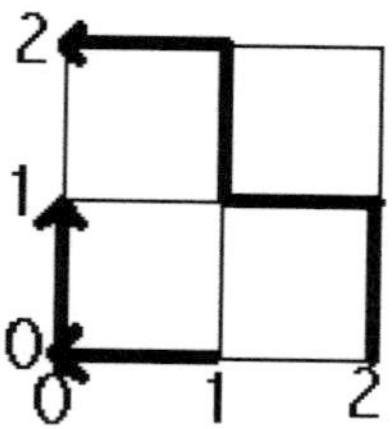

Figure A2.6. *An example of a three-path set*

Coding a horizontal step by 0 and a vertical step by 1, the set of three paths of the drawing is expressed: 0, 1, 1010.

We know that the number of paths c_{ij} from a point of abscissa i of the x axis to a point of ordinate j of the y axis is the number of combinations C_{i+j}^{j}. With this permutation 1 0 2 at the end alone, there are $c_{01}c_{10}c_{22} = C_1^0C_1^0C_4^2 = 1\times1\times6 = 6$ sets of such paths, with these paths being able but not required to intersect each other. We can do the same for each permutation of the endpoints.

Now let us take the determinant:

$$\begin{vmatrix} c_{00} & c_{01} & c_{02} \\ c_{10} & c_{11} & c_{12} \\ c_{20} & c_{21} & c_{22} \end{vmatrix} = \begin{vmatrix} C_0^0 & C_1^1 & C_2^2 \\ C_1^0 & C_2^1 & C_3^2 \\ C_2^0 & C_3^1 & C_4^2 \end{vmatrix} = \begin{vmatrix} 1 & 1 & 1 \\ 1 & 2 & 3 \\ 1 & 3 & 6 \end{vmatrix}$$

$$= 1.2.6 - 1.3.3 - 1.1.6 + 1.1.3 + 1.1.3 - 1.1.2 \text{ by developing the first line}$$

$$= 1$$

The six paths leading to permutation 1 0 2 are found in term 1.1.6 of the development of the determinant, but preceded by the – sign, because permutation 1 0 2 is odd. If we had taken the six terms obtained in the development of the determinant with + signs everywhere, we would have had the total number of sets of three paths leading from 0 1 2 to some permutation of the three endpoints 0 1 2. Such a development with + signs everywhere gives, as we saw, what we call the permanent.

We will now benefit from the presence of + or – signs, depending on whether the end permutation is even or odd. Let us resume our previous example of the three paths 1, 0 and 1010. We notice that they touch each other at one point, the origin O, which is the start of the first path and the end of the second. The part of these two paths after the intersection is 1 for the first and 0 for the second. Let us invert these two path ends: the first path becomes the empty path and the second becomes path 01. We get another set of three paths: empty (from O to O), 01 and 1010 (see Figure A2.7a). The inversion of the two endpoints changes the parity of the end permutation, and in this way we move from the odd permutation 1 0 2 to the even permutation 0 1 2.

Therefore the path set counted with a – sign in the development of the determinant has just been associated with a set of paths with a + sign in this same development. This can be done for each set of paths where there is at least one common point of the paths. During successive tracing of the three paths, we take the first point obtained between two paths and we invert their two ends, i.e. the part of the two paths after this common point (see Figure A2.7b). The inversion of the two endpoints constitutes a transposition that changes the parity of the end permutation.

A set of paths that intersect each other, with an odd end permutation, can always be paired with another set of paths that intersect each other, with an even permutation at the end. In developing the determinant, a path set that can count as 1 with the – sign is associated with a path set that counts as 1 with the + sign, which gives 0 in the calculation each time the path sets have a common point. All the paths with a common point give a null total in the calculation of the determinant.

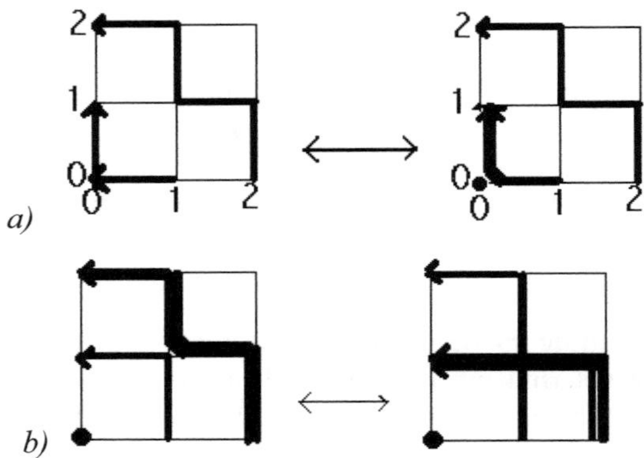

Figure A2.7. *Inversion of the path ends in two examples*

Only the paths having no point of intersection remain. Finally, the determinant gives the number of path sets without intersection.

In the case of our example, only a single path exists, which we easily find. It corresponds to the identity permutation that is even (see Figure A2.8).

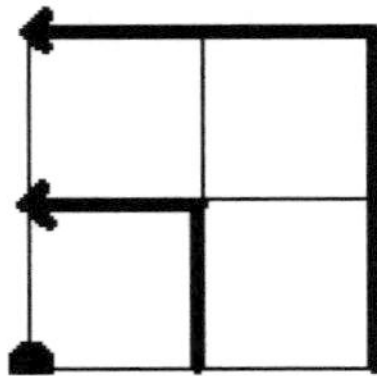

Figure A2.8. *The only path set without intersection*

Hence the determinant is equal to 1. At the same time, we can affirm that between the path sets with even permutation and those with odd permutation, there is one more with an even permutation at the end, and it is exactly this result that gives the determinant.

What has been done for the configurations of $N = 3$ paths can be generalized to any N. Therefore, the determinant including the binomial coefficients c_{ij} in a square table of N lines and columns, which corresponds to a part of Pascal's triangle read diagonally from the top down and from left to right, is always equal to 1. For example:

$$\begin{vmatrix} 1 & 1 & 1 & 1 & 1 \\ 1 & 2 & 3 & 4 & 5 \\ 1 & 3 & 6 & 10 & 15 \\ 1 & 4 & 10 & 20 & 35 \\ 1 & 5 & 15 & 35 & 70 \end{vmatrix} = 1$$

A2.3.2. *Second example: mountain ranges without intersection, based on two diagonal lines*

Now the paths will be mountain ranges based on two types of diagonal lines, upwards or downwards, and always from left to right. The N extreme points are placed on a horizontal axis, with points 0, 1, 2 of abscissae 0, -2, -4 at the start and 0', 1', 2' of abscissae 0, 2, 4 at the end when $N = 3$. The configurations concerned are the sets of three mountain ranges starting from points 0, 1, 2 and ending up at a certain permutation of points 0', 1', 2'. We know that the number of $2i$-length mountain ranges is the Catalan number $c(i)$. Let us take the NxN determinant of which each coefficient $a_{ij'}$ in line i and column j is the number of mountain ranges starting from point i to end up at point j', i.e. the Catalan number $c(j' - i)$.

This determinant is expressed:

$$\begin{vmatrix} c(0) & c(1) & c(2) \\ c(1) & c(2) & c(3) \\ c(2) & c(3) & c(4) \end{vmatrix}$$

The permanent that corresponds to it gives the number of configurations of three mountain ranges. As for the determinant, the presence of + and – signs in its development sets all the configurations that have common points between their three mountain ranges to 0, because they can be grouped in pairs: one with an odd permutation at the end, and the other with an even permutation, like in the example in Figure A2.9.

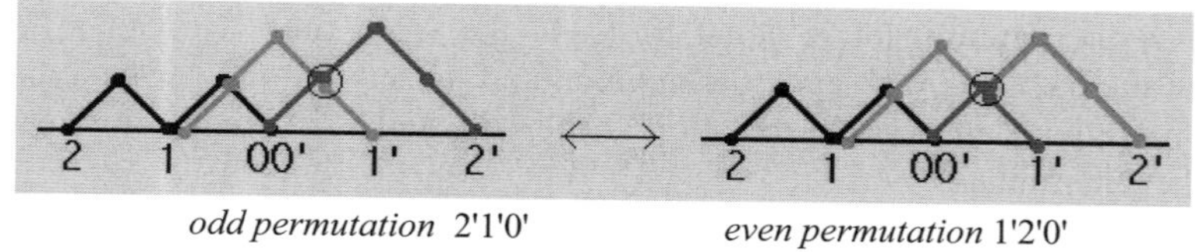

odd permutation 2'1'0' *even permutation* 1'2'0'

Figure A2.9. *Bijective permutation from an odd permutation to an even permutation*

The determinant is therefore equal to the number of configurations without intersection. There is only one single configuration, as is easily seen (see Figure A2.10).

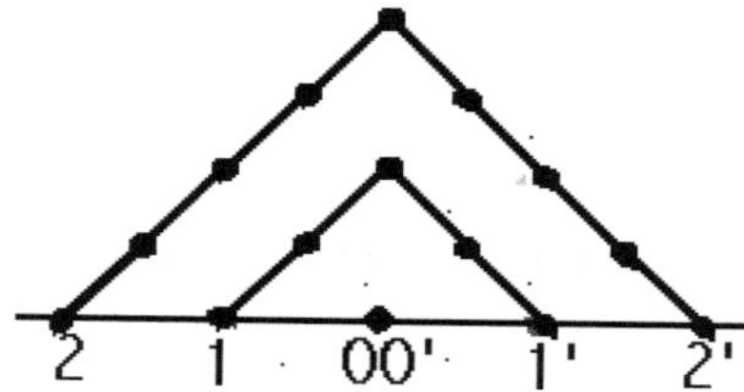

Figure A2.10. *The only configuration of three mountain ranges without intersection*

The determinant formed by Catalan numbers, as we saw for $N = 3$, is equal to 1, and this remains true for any N.

A2.3.3. *Third example: mountain ranges without intersection based on diagonal lines and plateaus. Link with Aztec diamond tilings*

Now let us take mountain chains based on upward diagonal lines (1, 1) and downward ones (1, -1), as well as horizontal plateaus (2, 0) that are 2 units long. Let us recall that the number of such $2i$-length mountain ranges is known. It is the Schröder number $s(i)$, encountered in Chapter 10. We are interested in configurations made up of N of these mountain ranges. On the horizontal axis we take starting points 0, 1, 2 of abscissae -1, -3, -5, and endpoints 0', 1', 2' of abscissae 1, 3, 5, in the case where $N = 3$.

In Figure A2.11, we will see an example of the configuration of three ranges, without intersection, and corresponding to the end permutation 0′, 1′, 2′. As before, the number of such configurations (of three paths here) without intersection is equal to the determinant:

$$\begin{vmatrix} s(1) & s(2) & s(3) \\ s(2) & s(3) & s(4) \\ s(3) & s(4) & s(5) \end{vmatrix} = \begin{vmatrix} 2 & 6 & 22 \\ 6 & 22 & 90 \\ 22 & 90 & 394 \end{vmatrix} = 64$$

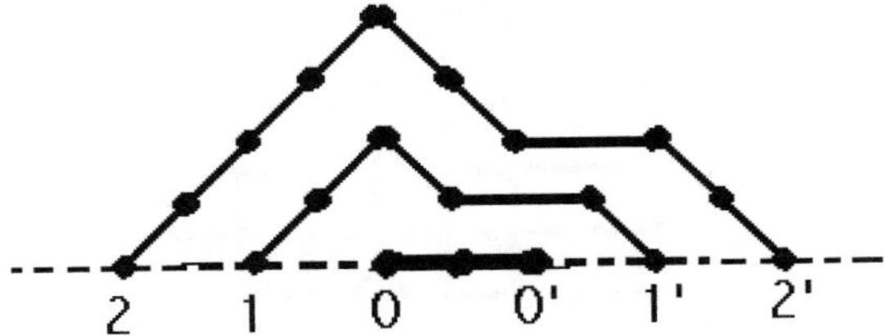

Figure A2.11. *A configuration of three mountain ranges with plateaus without intersection*

The number of these configurations with N ranges without intersection being $T(N)$, we will check that we have: $T(N) = 2^{N(N+1)/2}$.

Let $det_N(s)$ be the determinant above, formed by Schröder numbers. We have just seen that $T(N) = det_N(s)$. Let us introduce $s'(i)$ Schröder numbers of the second kind, which include the number of mountain ranges based on three lines as before, but without a horizontal plateau at level 0.

We saw that: $s'(i) = s(i) / 2$, hence: $det_N(s) = 2^N\ det_N(s')$.

In turn, $det_N(s')$ includes the number of configurations made up of N mountain ranges without horizontal plateaus at level 0, i.e. $T'(N)$. From such a configuration, by removing from it the extreme steps leading to level 1, which becomes level 0, we find a configuration that accepts plateaus at level 0. Thus:

$$T'(N) = T(N-1)$$

Finally, $T(N) = \det_N(s) = 2^N \det_N(s') = 2^N\ T'(N) = 2^N\ T(N-1)$.

With the recurrence relation $T(N) = 2^N\ T(N-1)$, and the initial condition $T(1) = 2$, we deduce the explicit formula: $T(N) = 2^{N(N+1)/2}$.

We saw before, that mountain ranges based on three types of lines are linked to domino tilings of the Aztec diamond. Every tiling of the Aztec diamond of N order is a bijection with a configuration of N mountain ranges with three types of line – (1, 1), (1, -1), (2, 0) – without intersection between, as indicated in Figure A2.12. Note that we had to extend the paths by diagonal lines outside of the Aztec diamond, and that the dominos not traversed by a range are all horizontal. This allows us to affirm that the number of tilings[4] is equal to $2^{N(N+1)/2}$.

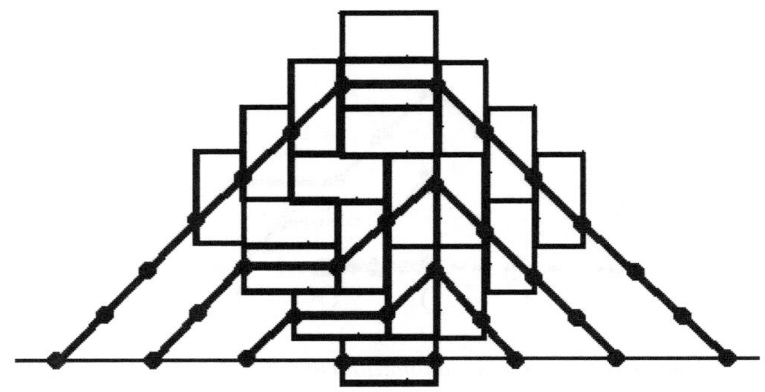

Figure A2.12. *Mountain ranges and domino tiling of the Aztec diamond*

Note that we can re-draw the paths without the lines located outside the Aztec diamond by making them all start at the same altitude (see Figure A2.13). The mountain ranges can therefore touch each other but without crossing each other. From this, we deduce the way to move from any tiling to a completely horizontal tiling. The only admissible moves consist of turning a square block made up of two vertical dominos by making them horizontal, or *vice versa*. Furthermore a vertical block of two dominos corresponds to a peak (in Λ shape) or a valley V.

We want to end up with a configuration where all the mountain ranges are reduced to horizontal plateaus (completely horizontal tiling). To achieve this, we take the ranges one by one starting from the shortest (the lowest on the Aztec diamond), in such a way as to prevent a range from crossing another during the transformations.

For each of the ranges, we begin by transforming each peak into a plateau, then we transform each plateau into a valley, which again gives peaks that we transform into plateaus, etc. In this way we end up leveling out everything, as in Figure A2.14. At the same time, we notice that the number of turns needed is equal to the number of Δ triangles covering the surface between each range and the horizontal axis.

4. The method used here is due to [EU 05], relying on [GES 85]. Other demonstrations of this formula on Aztec diamond tilings are found in [ELK 02, KUO 04]. Notably, a bijection exists between the number of tilings and binary words that are $N(N+1)/2$ long. This constructive method, due to [ELK 02], enables us to create the corresponding tiling from such a number. It was programmed in [FAT 01]: it is sufficient to take a random binary number to have some tiling, with the presence of the phenomenon of the Arctic circle (see Part 3 Introduction).

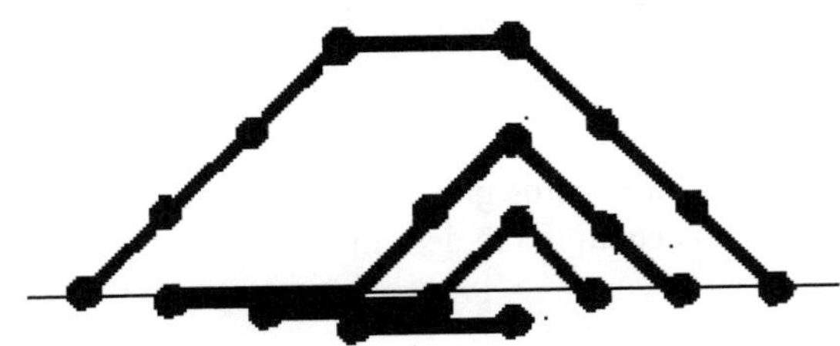

Figure A2.13. *Ranges reduced to the same initial altitude. They can touch but not cross each other*

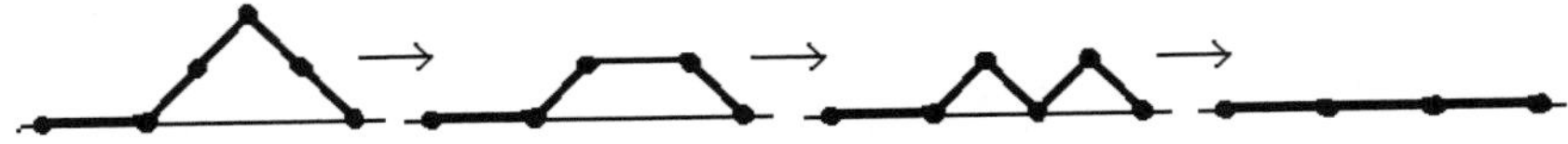

Figure A2.14. *Progressive passage to a completely horizontal range*

A2.3.4. *Diamond tilings*

Let us consider a square network (oriented from left to right), drawn in the form of squares in a diagonal grid inscribed in a rectangle (see Figure A2.15). Here we take three starting points 0, 1 and 2 on the left and three endpoints 0′, 1′ and 2′ on the right, located at a distance of four units on the grid.

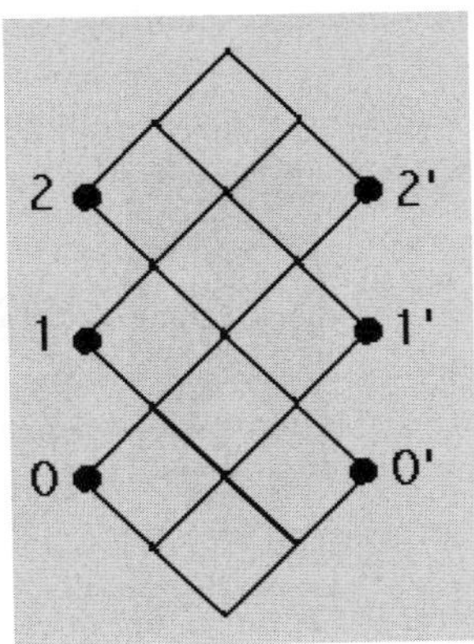

Figure A2.15. *The graph with its three starting and end points*

If $c(i,j)$ is the number of paths from point i to point j, we know that we have:

$$c(0, 0') = C_4^{\,2},\ c(0, 1') = C_4^{\,1},\ c(0, 2') = C_4^{\,0}, \text{ etc.}$$

The number of sets of three paths going from 0 to 0′, 1 to 1′, 2 to 2′, that neither touch or cross each other is equal to the determinant:

$$\begin{vmatrix} c(0,0') & c(0,1') & c(0,2') \\ c(1,0') & c(1,1') & c(1,2') \\ c(2,0') & c(2,1') & c(2,2') \end{vmatrix}$$

In this case, this gives:

$$\begin{vmatrix} 6 & 4 & 1 \\ 4 & 6 & 4 \\ 1 & 4 & 6 \end{vmatrix} = 50$$

Let us take one of these path sets and associate a parallelogram located below each line, as indicated in Figure A2.16.

We have just obtained a hexagonal-shaped tiling (here of sides of successive lengths 2-3-2 from the top) based on parallelograms and squares (see Figure A2.16). A slight deformation of the figure gives a hexagonal-shaped tiling based on identical diamonds, but oriented in three different ways, ◇ ▱ ▱, which gives the experimental results obtained by the corresponding program in Figure A2.17.

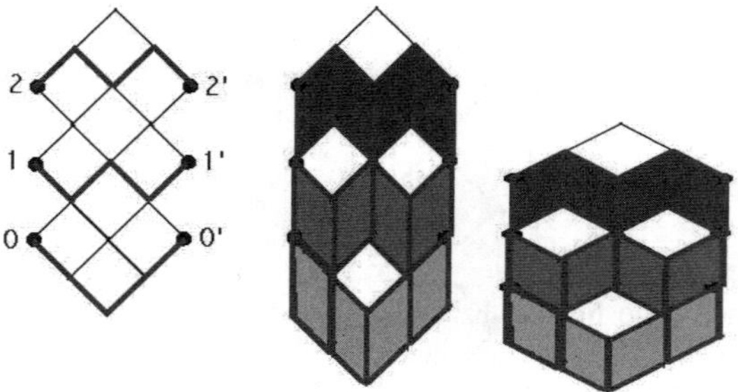

Figure A2.16. *Domino tiling of a 2-3-3 hexagon, from three paths that neither intersect or touch each other on the grid on the left*

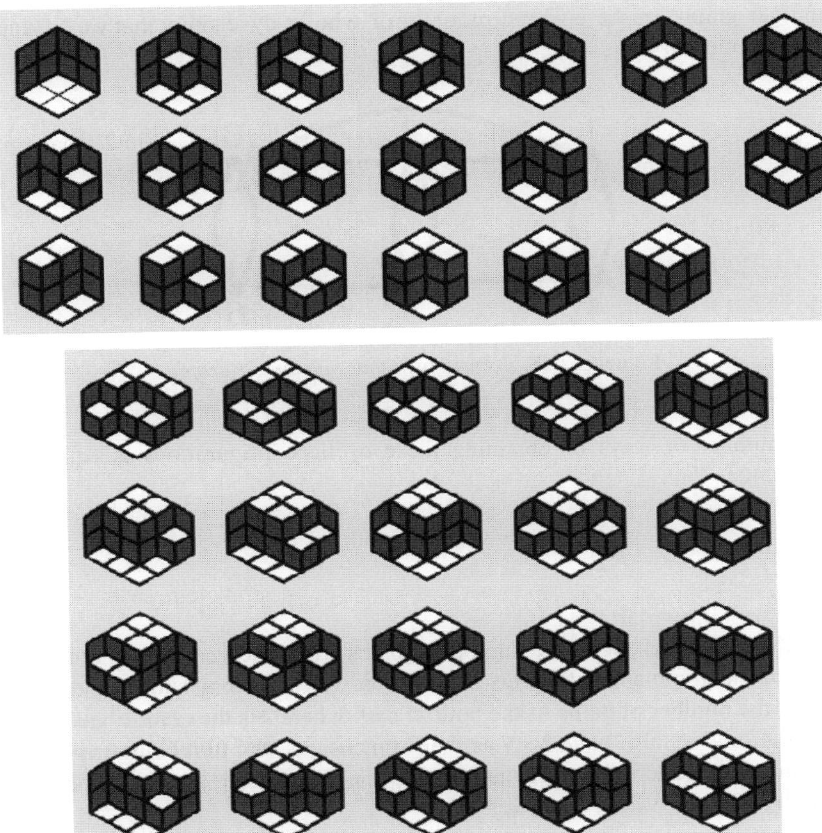

Figure A2.17. *The 20 tilings of a (regular) 2-2-2 hexagon (above); and a part of the 175 tilings of a 3-2-3 hexagon (below)*

A2.4. The hamburger graph: disjoint cycles

The hamburger graph is a directed graph made up of $2N$ vertices displayed on two horizontal lines ,one below the other (see [HAN 06]). The vertices numbered from 1 to N are on the top line and the vertices from $N + 1$ to $2N$ are on the bottom line. For the top vertices, junction arcs are placed at will, but all from left to right. Similarly for the bottom row, with arcs from right to left. Lastly, each vertex at the top is linked to its bottom correspondent by two vertical arcs in opposing directions. More specifically, we are interested in the case where the top and bottom parts of the graph are planar. We therefore say that the hamburger graph is strongly planar. The example of such a graph for $N = 3$ is shown in Figure A2.18. A strongly planar hamburger graph can be covered partially or wholly by disjoint cycles, having no vertex in common.

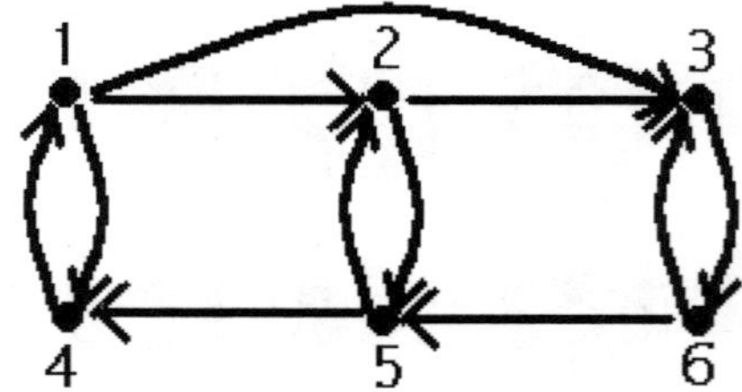

Figure A2.18. *A strongly planar hamburger graph*

The number of ways of obtaining these cyclic configurations is equal to the determinant:

$$\begin{vmatrix} A_1 & I \\ -I & A_2 \end{vmatrix}$$

where A_1 is the matrix with the number of paths from one vertex to another on the top part of the graph as coefficients between the vertices from 1 to N, and A_2 is the matrix of the number of paths of the bottom part, where I is the identity matrix $N \times N$. Matrices A_1 and A_2 also have $N \times N$ as their dimensions, the first being triangular on top because of the left-right orientation, and the other being triangular below. For the graph in Figure A2.18, this gives:

$$\begin{vmatrix} 1 & 1 & 2 & 1 & 0 & 0 \\ 0 & 1 & 1 & 0 & 1 & 0 \\ 0 & 0 & 1 & 0 & 0 & 1 \\ -1 & 0 & 0 & 1 & 0 & 0 \\ 0 & -1 & 0 & 1 & 1 & 0 \\ 0 & 0 & -1 & 1 & 1 & 1 \end{vmatrix} = 14$$

In what follows we will find a few applications of this result.

A2.4.1. *First example: domino tiling of a rectangular checkerboard N long, 2 wide*

Let us consider a rectangular checkerboard N long and 2 units wide with its subjacent graph whose vertices are the centers of the squares and whose edges join each vertex to its neighbors (see Figure A2.19). Note that this graph is bipartite: the vertices can be arranged into two categories, according to their color, and each vertex joins a vertex of one color to a vertex of the other color. When this checkerboard is tiled by dominos, this is equivalent to a perfect coupling of the graph: each vertex of one color is linked once and only once to a vertex of the other color.

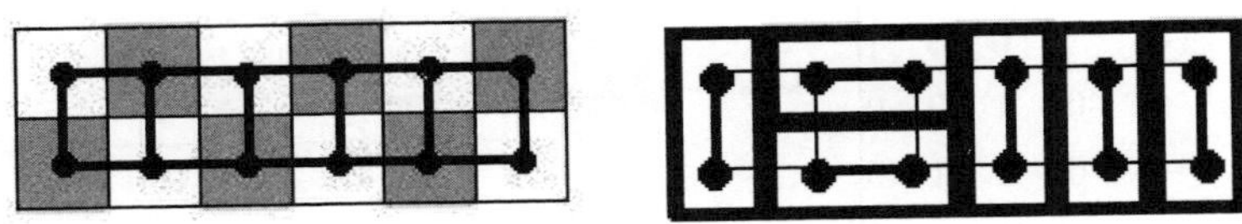

Figure A2.19. *A checkerboard of $N = 6$ long and its subjacent graph (left); and an example of domino tiling of the checkerboard (right)*

The difference between the completely horizontal tiling H and some tiling T gives us a set of C disjoint cycles in the graph. The difference is obtained by conserving the coupling of one tiling that is not in the other, and dropping the common couplings from both tilings (see Figure A2.20).

In this way, we are in a position to associate a collection C of disjoint cycles with every tiling T. Conversely, a set C of disjoint cycles on the graph always gives a tiling T, obtained by the difference with tiling of reference H. There is bijection between the tilings T and the collections C of disjoint cycles in the graph.

In other words, the number of tilings is equal to the number of ways of placing disjoint cycles on the graph.

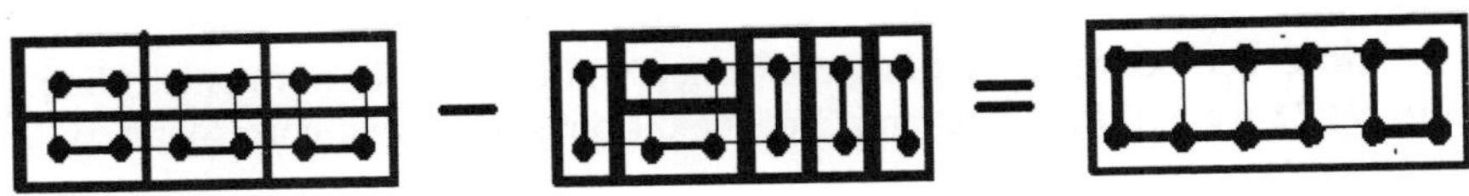

Figure A2.20. *Difference between any tiling and the completely horizontal tiling, leading to a set of cycles*

Now let us transform the graph by replacing each coupling of the horizontal graph H with a single vertex. Let us also orient each remaining horizontal edge in the black-white direction and each vertical edge in the white-black direction, in such a way as to obtain a directed graph (see Figure A2.21).

In the graph thus transformed, the cycles corresponding to the tiling taken as an example are directed cycles. We are now in the conditions of a planar hamburger graph and led to count the number of ways of placing disjoint cycles, since it is also the number of tilings. This comes back to calculating the determinant:

$$\begin{vmatrix} 1 & 1 & 1 & 1 & 0 & 0 \\ 0 & 1 & 1 & 0 & 1 & 0 \\ 0 & 0 & 1 & 0 & 0 & 1 \\ -1 & 0 & 0 & 1 & 0 & 0 \\ 0 & -1 & 0 & 1 & 1 & 0 \\ 0 & 0 & -1 & 1 & 1 & 1 \end{vmatrix} = 13$$

We find again the Fibonacci number F_7.

Figure A2.21. *The transformed checkerboard graph (left); and the cycles corresponding to those of the previous drawing (right)*

A2.4.2. *Second example: domino tilings of the Aztec diamond*

As before, we notice that there are as many ways of tiling the Aztec diamond with dominos as there are configurations of disjoint cycles, the latter being obtained by the difference between the tiling concerned and completely horizontal tiling. In Figure A2.22 we will find an example of the disjoint cycles that correspond to it, in a bijective way.

Now, let us associate a directed graph with the Aztec diamond by condensing it in the following way: we replace each domino of the completely horizontal tiling with a single vertex located at its center and orient the junctions to the right in the top part, and to the left in the bottom part.

For the Aztec diamond of order 3, this gives the condensed directed graph in Figure A2.23 (left). Therefore it is a planar hamburger graph and the cycles found in the example above become disjoint directed cycles (see Figure A2.23, right).

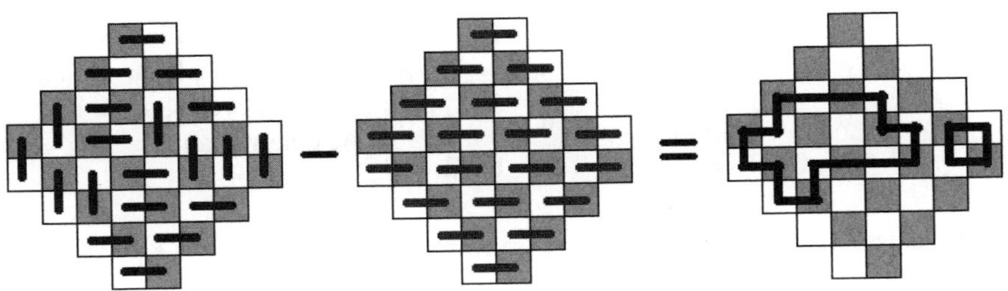

Figure A2.22. *Difference between a tiling of the Aztec diamond of order 4 and the completely horizontal tiling, producing the presence of disjoint cycles*

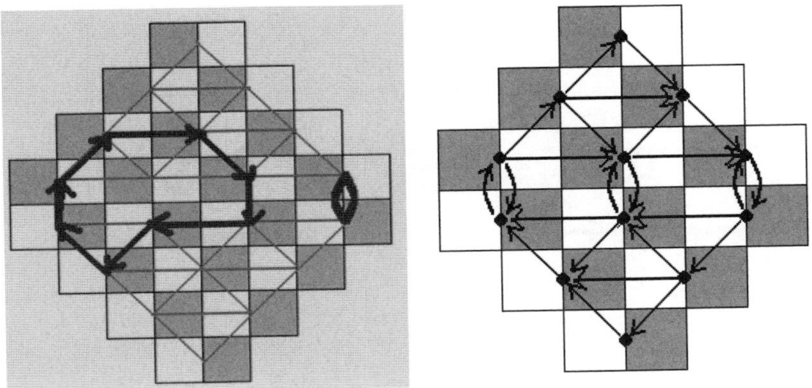

Figure A2.23. *The strongly planar hamburger graph associated with the Aztec diamond of order 3 (left); and the cycles corresponding to the tiling of the previous figure on the diamond of order 4*

We are therefore in a position to apply the theorem associated with the planar hamburger graph. The number of tilings is equal to the number of disjoint cyclic configurations, i.e. to determinant $\begin{vmatrix} A_1 & I \\ -I & A_2 \end{vmatrix}$, where A_1 is the matrix containing the numbers of paths from one vertex to another on the upper part, and A_2 the number of paths on the lower part.

Furthermore, these paths have mountain chains based on two diagonal lines and one horizontal line, corresponding to Schroeder words. These give, for the Aztec diamond of $N = 4$ order, for example:

$$A_1 = \begin{pmatrix} 1 & 2 & 6 & 22 \\ 0 & 1 & 2 & 6 \\ 0 & 0 & 1 & 2 \\ 0 & 0 & 0 & 1 \end{pmatrix}, \quad A_2 = \begin{pmatrix} 1 & 0 & 0 & 0 \\ 2 & 1 & 0 & 0 \\ 6 & 2 & 1 & 0 \\ 22 & 6 & 2 & 1 \end{pmatrix}$$

The calculation of the determinant gives the number of tilings[5] equal to 1,024, corresponding to $2^{N(N+1)/2}$ for $N = 4$.

5. Method from [HAN 06].

Bibliography

[AHO 87] AHO A.V., HOPCROFT J.E., ULLMAN J.D., *Structures de données et algorithmes*, InterEditions, 1987.

[AIG 01] AIGNER M., "Lattice paths and determinants", *Computational Discrete Mathematics*, vol. 2122, Lecture Notes in Comput. Sci, Springer, 2001.

[ARF 04] ARFA H., Cheminements sur des réseaux quadrillés, Thesis, University of Paris 8, 2004.

[ARF 05] ARFA H., Le jeu du permutateur, Thesis, University of Paris 8, 2005.

[AUD 95] AUDIBERT P., Algorithmes et programmation, Thesis, University of Paris 8, 1995.

[AXL 97] AXLER S., *Linear Algebra Done Right*, Springer, 1997.

[BAR 04] BARBIN E., LAMARCHE J.P., (ed.), *Histoire des probabilités et des statistiques*, Ellipses, 2004.

[BEN 05] BENAIM M., EL KAROUI N., *Promenade aléatoire: chaînes de Markov et simulations, martingales et stratégies*, École Polytechnique, 2005.

[BER 67] BERGE C., *Théorie des graphes et ses applications*, Dunod, 1967.

[BER 91] BERSTEL J., PIN J.E., POCCHIOLA M., *Mathématiques et informatique : problèmes résolus*, McGraw-Hill, 1991.

[BER 98] BERNSTEIN P.L., *Against the Gods: The Remarkable Story of Risk,* John Wiley & Sons, 1998.

[BIG 79] BIGGS N.L., "The roots of combinatorics", *Historia Mathematica*, vol. 6, p. 109-136, 1979.

[BOR 38] BOREL E., *Le hasard*, Libraire Félix Alcan, 1938.

[BRU 46] DE BRUIJN N.G., "A combinatorial problem", *Nedl. Akad. Wet., Proc.*, vol. 49, 1946.

[CHU 74] CHUNG K. L., *Elementary Probability Theory with Stochastic Processes*, Springer Verlag, 1974.

[COM 70] COMTET L., *Analyse combinatoire*, Volumes 1 and 2, Presses Universitaires de France, 1970.

[COR 02] CORMEN T.H., LEISERSON C.E., RIVEST R.L., STEIN C., *Introduction à l'algorithmique*, Dunod, 2002.

[COU 08] COURTEBRAS B., DAHAN N., *Mathématiser le hasard: une histoire du calcul des probabilités*, Vuibert, 2008.

[CUC 96] CUCULIERE R., "Les probabilités géométriques", in *Le hasard*, Pour la Science, April 1996.

[CVE 80] CVETKOVIC D.M., DOOB M., SACHS H., *Spectra of Graphs: Theory and Application*, Academic Press, 1980.

[DEM 79] DEMIDOVITCH B., MARON L., *Éléments de calcul numérique*, Mir, 1979.

[DIA 83] DIACONIS P., GRAHAM R.L., KANTOR W.M., *The Mathematics of Perfect Shuffles*, Advances in Applied Math. (4-2), 1983.

[EIS 08] EISERMANN M., *Comment marche Google*, www-fourier.ujf-grenoble.fr/~eiserm/enseignement, 2008.

[ELK 02] ELKIES N., KUPERBERG G., LARSEN M., PROPP J., "Alternating-sign matrices and domino tilings (Parts 1 and 2)", *Journal of Algebraic Combinatorics*, vol. 1, 2002.

[EU 05] EU S.P., FU T.S., "A simple proof of he Aztec diamond theorem", *Electron. J. Combin.*, vol. 12, 2005.

[FAT 01] FATHI A., Pavages du diamant aztèque par des dominos, Thesis, University of Paris 8, 2001.

[FEL 71] FELLER W., *An Introduction to Probability Theory and its Applications*, John Wiley & Sons, 1971.

[FEL 06] FELGENHAUER B., JARVIS F., *Mathematics of Sudoku* 1, available online at: http://www.afjarvis.staff.shef.ac.uk/sudoku/felgenhauer_jarvis_spec1.pdf, 25 January 2006.

[FOA 03] FOATA D., FUCHS A., *Calcul des probabilités : cours, exercices et problèmes corrigés*, Dunod, 2003.

[GER 95] GERDES P., *Les traditions géométriques en Afrique, les dessins sur le sable*, 4 volumes, L'Harmattan, 1995.

[GES 85] GESSEL I., VIENNOT X., "Binomial determinants, paths, and hook length formulae", *Adv. in Math.*, vol. 58, 1985.

[GRA 85] GRAHAM R.L., HELL P., "On the history of the minimum spanning tree problem", *Annals of the History of Computing*, vol. 7, 1985.

[GRA 90] GRAHAM R.L., KNUTH D.E., PATASHNIK O., *Concrete Mathematics, a Foundation for Computer Science*, Addison-Wesley, 1990.

[GRA 94] GRAHAM R., KNUTH D.E., PATASHNIK O., *Concrete Mathematics, a Foundation for Computer Science*, Addison-Wesley, 1994.

[GRA 03a] GRAHAM R.L., KNUTH D.E., PATASHNIK O., *Mathématiques concrètes : fondations pour l'informatique*, Vuibert, 2003.

[GRA 03b] GRASSA N., Cheminements dans les graphes, parcours eulériens et arbres recouvrants, Thesis, University of Paris 8, 2003.

[HAN 06] HANUSA C., "A Gessel-Viennot-type method for cycle systems in a directed graph", *Electron. J. Combin.*, vol. 13, 2006.

[HAR 79] HARARI J., PERSONNAZ D., *Cours de mathématiques, tome 3 Probabilités*, Belin, 1979.

[HAR 95] HARARY F., *Graph Theory*, Perseus Press, 1995.

[JAC 00] JACQUARD A., *Les probabilités*, PUF, 2000.

[JOS 91] JOSEPH G.G., *The Crest of the Peacock, Non-European Roots of Mathematics*, I.B. Tauris & Co Publishers, 1991.

[KNU 73] KNUTH D.E., *The Art of Computer Programming, Fundamental Algorithms*, Volume 1, Addison-Wesley, 1973.

[KRE 76] KREWERAS G., "Aires des chemins surdiagonaux et application à un problème économique", *Cahiers du bulletin universitaire de recherche opérationnelle*, vol. 24, 1976.

[KUO 04] KUO E., "Applications of graphical condensation for enumerating matchings and tilings", *Theoret. Comput. Sci.*, vol. 319, 2004.

[LEN 98a] LENORMAND C., Graphes et cheminements, Thesis, University of Paris 8, 1998.

[LEN 98b] LENORMAND C., Arbres et permutations, Thesis, University of Paris 8, 1998.

[LEV 73] LEVY P., *Œuvres de Paul Lévy*, Gauthier-Villars, 1973-1980.

[LOT 97] LOTHAIRE M. (ed.), *Combinatorics on Words*, Cambridge University Press, 1997.

[LOT 02] LOTHAIRE M., *Algebraic Combinatorics on Words*, Cambridge University Press, 2002.

[MAL 02] MALLET J., MITERNIQUE M., *Probabilités, cours et exercices de mathématiques*, Ellipses, 2002.

[MLO 08] MLODINOW L., *The Drunkard's Walk: How Randomness Rules Our Lives*, Pantheon Books, 2008.

[NAC 05] NACIRI Y., Pavages à base de polyominos, Thesis, University of Paris 8, 2005.

[NAC 06] NACIRI Y., Pavages symétriques à base de dominos, Thesis, University of Paris 8, 2006.

[PEI 04] PEITGEN H.-O., JURGENS H., SAUPE D., *Chaos and Fractals, New Frontiers of Science*, Springer, 2004.

[PIS 70] PISKOUNOV N., *Calcul différentiel et intégral*, Volume 2, Mir, 1970.

[POL 87] POLYA G., READE R.C., *Combinatorial Enumeration of Groups, Graphs, and Chemical Compounds*, Springer-Verlag, 1987.

[RIC 07] RICARD P., *Hasard et probabilités: histoire, théorie et applications des probabilités*, Vuibert, 2007.

[RIF 06] RIFAAI N., Jeux de permutations : jeu de taquin, Thesis, University of Paris 8, 2006.

[ROB 39] ROBBINS H.E., "A theorem on graphs, with applications to a problem of traffic control", *American Math. Monthly*, vol. 46, 1939.

[ROB 94] ROBERTS F.S., YU Y., "On the optimal strongly connected orientations of city street graphs", *Discr. Appl. Math.*, vol. 49, 1994.

[RUS 06] RUSSELL E., JARVIS F., *Mathematics of Sudoku II*, available online at: http://www.afjarvis.staff.shef.ac.uk/sudoku/russell_jarvis_spec2.pdf, 25 January 2006.

[SED 91] SEDGEWICK R., *Algorithmes en C*, Addison-Wesley Europe InterEditions, 1991.

[SLO 95] SLOANE N.J.A., PFOUFFE S., *The Encyclopedia of Integer Sequences*, Academic Press, 1995.

[STA 99] STANLEY R.P., *Enumerative Combinatorics*, Volumes 1 and 2, Cambridge University Press, 1999.

[STA 01] STANLEY R.P., *Enumerative Combinatorics*, Volumes 1 and 2, Cambridge University Press, 2000-2001.

[TAN 05] TANTALO J., *Planarity*, available online at: www.planarity.net., 2005

[TAR 72] TARJAN R.E., "Depth-first search and linear graph algorithms", *SIAM J. Comput.*, vol. 1, 1972.

[TAR 83] TARJAN R.E., *Data Structures and Network Algorithms*, Society for Industrial and Applied Mathematics, 1983.

[TUC 02] TUCKER A., *Applied Combinatorics*, John Wiley & Sons, 2002.

[WIL 90] WILSON R.J., WATKINS J.J., *Graphs, an Introductory Approach*, John Wiley & Sons, 1990.

[WIL 94] WILF H.S., *Generating Functionology*, A.K. Peters, 1994-2006.

[WIL 96] WILSON D.B., "Generating random spanning trees more quickly than the cover time", *Proc. 28th ACM*, 1996.

[YOU 76] YOUSCHKEVITCH A.P., *Les mathématiques arabes (VIIIè-XVè siècles),* Librairie philosophique J. Vrin, 1976.

[ZAS 95] ZASLAVSKY C., *L'Afrique compte*, Choix, 1995.

Index

A

Abu Kamil's problem, 11
adjacency
list, 647
matrix, 414, 497-499, 501, 502, 527, 545, 607, 608, 647, 771, 795, 789-791, 795
alphabetical order, 43, 292, 332
alternate
draws from two boxes, 505
group, 359, 363, 369, 370
anagrams, 120, 135, 202, 242
arrangements, 352
Aztec diamond, 896

B

Bell numbers, 283, 284
Bernoulli's law, 420, 461, 470, 475, 600
bijection, 345
binary numbers, 46, 269, 315
binomial
formula, 25, 283
law, 417, 421-425, 433, 434, 436, 458, 460, 465, 467, 473, 474, 481, 482
birthday paradox, 391, 392, 403
boys and girls, 439
brick walls, 315
Brownian motion, 521, 524
Buffon's needle, 432
Burnside's formula, 227, 231, 232

C

card shuffling, 365
Catalan
mountain, 194
number, 167, 171, 173, 728
triangle, 175-178, 180
Cayley's theorem, 705
central Delaunay numbers, 199
checkered flags, 305
chessboard, 213, 232, 234, 263, 270
Chevalier de Mere problem, 398
chi-squared law, 428, 443-445
circulant matrix, 416, 882
circulation on a cube with any dimensions, 550
closed paths, 262, 263
coloring
of a stick, 239
the vertices of a graph, 150
combinations, 21, 47, 119, 287, 299
with repetitions, 121, 49

complete graph, 150, 254, 349, 711, 765, 814, 816, 839-841
Congo graphs, 820
conjugacy classes, 359
conjugated
  partition, 302
  permutation, 359
connected component, 670
continuous probabilities, 392, 447, 448, 452
cuts in a game of cards, 405
cyclic
  shifts in a rectangle, 371
  words, 266

D

density, 447-449, 451, 452, 454, 456
depth first traversal, 662
derangements, 68, 157, 158
determinant, 263, 269, 342, 415, 498, 500, 528, 545, 546, 607
diagonals of a polygon, 33
Dijkstra algorithm, 683
distribution function, 443, 445, 451-455, 458, 461, 465-468
domino, 79, 200, 204, 271, 273, 331, 336, 337, 339, 340
drawings with replacement, 402, 404, 410
drunken man's walk, 610
dual graph, 788, 789, 795
Dyck paths, 166

E

eigenvalues, 416, 508, 545, 546, 609, 788, 790-792, 795, 878, 884
eigenvectors, 545, 609, 877, 879
elementary
  events, 395-397, 400, 401, 405, 410, 421, 426, 431, 432, 481, 547, 601, 621
  paths, 654
elevator, 597, 598, 600
Euler
  formula, 290
  number, 145
Eulerian
  cycle, 765, 820
  graph, 772
expectation, 417, 418, 421, 432, 433, 435, 437, 438, 453, 461, 462, 469, 473, 480, 482, 488, 490, 493, 494, 512, 539, 551, 565, 567-571, 575, 580-582, 612, 618, 624
explicit form, 95
exponential
  generating function, 101, 284, 352
  law, 454-457

F

Fibonacci sequence, 264, 273, 279, 298
filling
  two boxes, 425
  up of containers, 72
first double heads, 404
flags with vertical stripes, 306
foreign language students, 140

G, H

Galileo's problem, 4, 391, 398
Gambler's ruin problem, 521
game of dominos, 813
Gauss curve, 452
Gauss-Seidel method, 531, 635
generating function, 473
geometric law, 420, 422, 423, 447, 456, 457, 470, 471, 473, 488, 494, 569, 623
golden number, 480
Google, 393, 627, 631
graded segment, 266
Gray code, 60
group of permutations, 366, 375
hamburger graph, 901

heaps, 319
Horner's method, 446
Hypergeometric law, 401, 402, 435-437, 458

I, J

indegree, 770
infix traversal, 678, 735
integer-sided triangles, 132
internal nodes, 726, 728
inversions in a permutation, 354
isthmus, 697

K, L

Königsberg bridges, 761
Kruskal's algorithm, 749
ladder graph, 782, 795
Laplace's equation, 531, 533, 534
Laplacian matrix, 771, 773, 788, 789, 792, 793
last visit to the origin, 515
law of large numbers, 429
left factors, 175, 178

M, N

matches, 601
matrix powers, 255
maze, 676-679, 701
McNugget problem, 411
minimum spanning tree, 750, 751
Mobius ladder, 884
molecular chain, 270
Monte Carlo method, 430
mountain ranges, 168-170, 173, 177, 183, 184, 197, 222, 223
movement
  on a polyhedron, 547
  on a pyramid, 559
multiletter words, 148
Narayana numbers, 186, 207
normal law, 452-454, 458-463

O, P

ordered partitions, 296
outdegree, 771
painting a room, 153
parenthesis words, 165, 215
parity of the number of heads that come out, 481
partitions, 392, 402, 403, 441
  of a set, 275, 285
parts, 139, 147, 275, 281
Pascal's
  law, 487
  triangle, 7
pedestrian's route, 665
permanent, 888, 893
permutation, 45, 51, 155, 156, 249, 341, 346, 347, 349, 350, 355, 356, 358, 360, 361, 363, 366, 367, 371, 375, 380
  cycles, 349, 352-354, 359, 363, 364, 365, 369, 370, 373, 377
pieces on a chessboard, 29
pivot, 45, 50, 53, 208, 209, 290, 296
Poisson distribution, 445, 475
Prim's algorithm, 747
primitive words, 167
probability density, 448
Prüfer
  code, 706
  decoding, 162

Q, R

queens problem, 69
random number, 390, 427-429, 443, 444, 448, 454, 462, 465
recurrence relation, 97, 177, 261, 269, 273, 279, 286, 287, 298, 308, 309, 327, 328, 335, 336, 350, 353
reduced centered normal law, 453, 460
regular graph, 254

repetitive
  drawings, 565, 613
  game of heads or tails, 509
returning edges, 687
robot and the human being, 555
rooks on a chessboard, 28, 155
rooted tree, 650, 651

S

Saint Petersburgh's paradox, 438
sand drawings, 3
Schröder numbers, 198
sect, 620
segment graph, 790
sending post cards, 133
shortest paths, 683, 737
sieve formula, 139, 144, 154, 158
signature of a permutation, 357
smallest number, 403, 404, 409-411
sort by selection-exchange, 40
space of possibles, 413
spanning trees, 706, 714, 768, 772, 785, 788
stack of
  coins, 76
  discs, 322
standard deviation, 407, 418, 432, 433, 452, 559, 461-463
Stirling numbers
  modulo, 286
  of the first kind, 352
strongly connected component, 692
sudoku, 9, 14, 152, 247, 249
surjection, 147

T, U

Taquin game, 368
temperature equilibrium and random walk, 530
throwing balls, 422, 439
tiling, 271, 274, 332-334, 336
  using l-squares, 244
total probability formula, 412, 413, 416, 417, 500, 508, 522, 524, 536, 609, 621, 622, 628, 631
transitive closure, 695
transmitting messages, 413
transpositions, 358, 361-363, 374
travelling salesman, 757
tree, 650, 654, 677-679, 686-688, 720, 722, 723, 734, 735, 787, 806-811, 817-819, 823, 838, 839, 850, 860, 861
tunnel, 602, 603, 607, 610, 612
two people meeting, 450
type of a permutation, 353
uniform law, 448, 449, 451, 452, 454-456, 460, 461

V, W, Y

variance, 418-420, 432, 433, 435, 462, 463, 470, 512, 550, 558, 565, 625
wait for
  an arrangement, 566, 568
  completely different letters, 586
  patterns, 580
  the outcome of a part, 571, 577
  double heads, 500
waiting time for
  double heads, 476
  first success, 407, 456, 494
Wilson's algorithm, 715
winnings sign changes, 517, 520
words without two-sided factors, 589
Yi King, 1